The Facts On File
DICTIONARY OF
THE THEATRE

The Facts On File
DICTIONARY OF THE THEATRE

Edited by
William Packard
David Pickering
Charlotte Savidge

Facts On File
New York • Oxford

The Facts On File Dictionary of the Theatre

Copyright © 1988 by Market House Books Ltd.
Published by arrangement with Sphere Books Ltd.

Facts On File, Inc.
460 Park Avenue South
New York, New York 10016

Library of Congress Cataloging-in-Publication Data

The Facts on File dictionary of theatre.

    1. Theater—Dictionaries.   2. Drama—Bio-bibliography.
I. Packard, William   II. Pickering, David, 1958-
III. Savidge, Charlotte.   IV. Title: Dictionary of
theatre.
PN2035.F27   1988   792'.03   88-28379
ISBN 0-8160-1841-3 (hc)
ISBN 0-8160-1945-2 (pbk)

British CIP data available on request

Facts On File books are available at special discounts when purchased in bulk quantities for businesses, associations, institutions, or sales promotion. Please contact the Special Sales Department at 212/683-2244.
(Dial 1-800-322-8755, except in NY, AK, HI)

Typeset by Market House Books Ltd.
Jacket Design by Linda Kosarin
Printed in the United States of America

10 9 8 7 6 5 4 3 2 1

This book is printed on acid-free paper.

Preface

This dictionary is a comprehensive guide to the theatre; its 5000 articles include entries on actors, actresses, playwrights, directors and producers, plays, venues, genres, technical terms, organizations, and other related topics. In selecting the entries, the editor has taken into account their significance in the history of the theatre, their interest to the general reader, and their usefulness to the theatre student. Thus, such entries as **Sir Henry Irving,** *Much Ado about Nothing,* **Royal National Theatre,** and **unities** will be found interspersed with articles on **fires, ghosts, make-up, taboos, vamp trap**, etc., all in one alphabetical list.

A particular feature of the book is the inclusion of entries for most of the important plays in the history of Western drama. These provide information concerning the author, first performance, alternative titles, brief plot summary, initial reception, and original cast. In addition, the principal dramatic works of major playwrights are listed separately, at the end of their entries.

An effort has been made to include a selection of entries relating to the contemporary stage, especially those performers and writers who may be expected to have a lasting influence. Because the choice of these entries has to be subjective, the editor takes full responsibility for inclusions and omissions.

Finally, I would like to thank our team of contributors for making this such an interesting and entertaining book to edit — and, I hope, to read.

—David Pickering
1988

A Note on Using This Dictionary

Entries are arranged in strict alphabetical order. The extensive use of cross-references has made the book virtually self-indexing. An asterisk (*) preceding a word indicates that further information relevant to the entry being read will be found in the article on the asterisked word. In the case of entries for plays we have generally given the title by which the work is best known in the English-speaking world (usually the English title), followed by alternative titles in parentheses. A date given in parentheses after a play title indicates either the date of its first performance or the date of the performance relevant to the context in which it is being discussed.

This book has been prepared by
Market House Books Ltd., Aylesbury.

Editors:

William Packard
David Pickering
Charlotte Savidge

Contributors:

Deborah Chapman
Hazel Egerton
Rosalind Fergusson
Kurt Ganzl
Ann Hoffmann
Lawrence Holden
Tony Jackson
Richard O'Donoghue
Kate Reddick
Barry Sloan

Introduction

In preparing this dictionary of modern British and American theatre, we were reminded once again that theatre is always made up of individuals—individual actors and directors and playwrights and producers and, yes, individual theatregoers. All these individuals work together in a selfless, headstrong, and heartfelt collaborative effort in order to create the living discipline of an immediate theatrical experience.

But behind any moment-to-moment creation of an onstage reality, no matter what individuals are engaged in the collaboration, there is also an unseen tradition of hundreds of other individuals who have been a part of a world theatre that has been evolving for centuries. And these invisible spirits, the forerunners of our own contemporary theatre, have given us the authentic heritage of today's theatre, whether we are conscious of their real presence or not.

From the earliest Dionysian theatre of the Greeks through the great Renaissance and neoclassic theatres of Europe, Western drama has always served as the clearest mirror for the invisible values of our civilization. When we want to see the highest types of our culture and character, we look to such enduring prototypes as Agamemnon, Oedipus Rex, Medea, Hamlet, Alcestes, and Phèdre. These colossal dramatic figures are gifts that have been given to us by the greatest world dramatists such as Aeschylus, Sophocles, Euripedes, Shakespeare, Molière and Racine. They have been brought to life in our own lifetime by such exemplary actors as Olivier, Gielgud, Richard Burton, Barrault, Bernhardt, Duse, and Papas, under the masterful guidance of strong directors such as Tyrone Guthrie, Michael Cacoyannis, Peter Hall, Dimitrios Rondiris, Paul-Emile Deiber, and Michael St.-Denis.

As we said, all great theatre is always the work of individuals. No matter the nationality or language of origin—from the stark Norwegian world of the modern revolutionary Henrik Ibsen through the unsure Russian world of Anton Chekhov.

And although this present theatre dictionary concentrates on the lives and works of specific practitioners in the British and American theatres, with some mention of the more prominent European dramatists, we have been reminded once again of our enormous debt to all the other great theatres that have had such a singular influence on our modern theatre.

The Facts On File
DICTIONARY OF
THE THEATRE

A

Abba, Marta See Pirandello, Luigi.

Abbey Theatre A theatre founded in Dublin in 1904. Opened by Miss Annie *Horniman, the theatre was the home of the *Irish National Dramatic Society and came into being largely as the creation of W B Yeats and Lady Gregory. It was intended to provide a venue for wholly Irish drama and, as well as Yeats and Lady Gregory themselves, writers who had their work presented there included J M Synge, AE, and Sean O'Casey; amongst the most famous productions in the early years of the theatre was Synge's *The Playboy of the Western World*, which caused riots in 1907. The resident company soon established itself internationally with eventful tours of the US and elsewhere, despite the need for strict economy in production after Miss Horniman withdrew her support in 1910 as the result of a disagreement. Subsequently, under the management of Lennox *Robinson, the theatre was acknowledged as Ireland's national theatre, becoming the first state-subsidized theatre in the English-speaking world in 1924 and the subject of a revival of interest in the 1920s when the plays of Sean O'Casey were first presented there and the company included such celebrated performers as Sara *Allgood, Barry *Fitzgerald, and F J *McCormick. In 1951 the theatre was badly damaged by fire but later restored (1966) and continues to produce a predominantly Irish programme in the main auditorium and experimental drama in the smaller **Peacock Theatre** (first opened in 1925 and reopened in 1967).

Abbot of Misrule See Misrule, Lord of.

Abbots Bromley Horn Dance See Horn Dance.

Abbott, George (1887-) US playwright, who began his career in the theatre as an actor while at Harvard. His first successful play, *The Fall Guy* (1925), was written in collaboration with James Gleason. In 1938 he wrote the successful *The Boys From Syracuse*, a musical based on Shakespeare's *The Comedy of Errors*. His other works include *Love 'em and Leave 'em* (1926), *Broadway* (1926), *Coquette* (1927), *Three Men on a Horse* (1935), *Where's Charley?* (1948), *The Pajama Game* (1954), *Damn Yankees!* (1955), and *Fiorello* (1959). In 1966 the Adelphi Theatre in New York was renamed the George Abbott Theatre in his honour.

Abbott, William (1789–1843) British actor, who appeared at the Haymarket and from 1813 was at Covent Garden. He was the original Appius Claudius in Sheridan Knowles's *Virginius* and played Romeo to Fanny Kemble's Juliet in 1830. Appearances in the US in 1836 were not successful.

abele spelen The earliest vernacular plays of the Netherlands, which evolved in the 13th century alongside the conventional liturgical drama and were based upon chivalric romances. Three 14th-century examples have survived, the most notable of which is the tragedy *Lanseloet van Denemarken*.

Abell, Kjeld (1901–61) Danish playwright and artist, whose plays rejected naturalism in favour of experimentalism. His first work, *Melodien der blev vock* (The Melody that got Lost), was produced in Copenhagen in 1931 and the following year at the Arts Theatre, London. His other plays include *Anna Sophie Hedvig* (1939), often regarded as his finest, *Den blå pekineser* (The Blue Pekingese; 1954), and *Skriget* (The Scream; 1961), which was first performed posthumously.

Abington, Frances (Frances Barton; 1737–1815) British actress, who made her stage debut in 1755 at the Haymarket. In 1756 she moved to Drury Lane, where she remained for three years. Her marriage to the musician James Abington did not last, but as Mrs Abington she was much acclaimed during the next five years in Dublin. Garrick then persuaded her back to Drury Lane, where her leading parts included the first Lady Teazle in *The School for Scandal* (1777). She moved to Covent Garden in 1782 and retired in 1799.

above *See* stage direction.

Absurd, Theatre of the The works of a loosely associated group of dramatists who shared a similar view of the futility of existence. The term itself was derived from an essay by Camus, in which he first described the human condition as "absurd". Beckett, Ionesco, Albee, Adamov, Pinter, and other leading Absurdists allowed the ideas behind a play to dictate its dramatic structure. Despite their dislocated language, illogical plots, and intellectual seriousness, the plays are often comic, reflecting the irrationality of real experience. By the 1960s Albee and Ionesco had turned to a more allegorical form, Pinter to high comedy, and Adamov to the epic theatre of Brecht, while Beckett's works grew steadily shorter and more bizarre.

Accesi An Italian company that presented plays of the *commedia dell'arte* in the early 17th century. Founded in about 1590, the company was led by Pier Maria Cecchini and Tristano Martinelli and twice visited France. Actors with the company included Flamineo Scala and Silvio Fiorillo.

Accidental Death of an Anarchist (*Morte accidentale di un anarchico*) A farce by Dario *Fo. First performance: 1979. A black satire, the play was based upon the investigation following the death of the railway worker Guiseppe Pinelli, who fell from the window of a Milan police station in mysterious circumstances.

Accius, Lucius (170 BC–86 BC) Roman playwright, whose numerous tragedies (of which only fragments and about 40 titles survive) established him as one of the leading writers of his time. Many of his works were translations from earlier Greek plays and tackle subjects from mythology as well as, occasionally, themes taken from Roman history. Some belong to the *praetexta* tradition; all were notable for their forceful rhetoric and violent plots. His critical writings included the *Pragmatica*, an examination of the techniques then open to the dramatist.

Achard, Marcel (Marcel-Auguste Ferréol; 1899–1974) French playwright, who made his reputation in 1923 with *Voulez-vous jouer avec moâ?*, produced by Dullin. Several later plays, including *Marlborough s'en va-t'en guerre* (1924), *Domino* (1931), and *Le Corsaire* (1938), were produced by Louis Jouvet. His plays are sentimental love stories, often derived from the *commedia dell'arte*.

Acharnians, The A comedy by *Aristophanes. First performance: Athens, 425 BC. The earliest surviving comedy by Aristophanes, the play condemns war and revolves around an old farmer, Dicaepolis, who makes his own peace treaty with the Spartans.

Achurch, Janet (Janet Sharp; 1864–1916) British actress, who appeared in the earliest British productions of Ibsen. After appearing at the Adelphi Theatre, she toured with Benson before joining Tree's company. In 1889 she attracted attention as Nora in *A Doll's House* directed by her husband at the Novelty Theatre. She subsequently played two of Shaw's heroines, Candida (which he wrote for her) and Lady Cicely Wayneflete in *Captain Brassbound's Conversion*.

Ackermann, Konrad Ernst (c. 1710–71) German actor-manager, who established the first German National Theatre. He began his acting career as a member of Schönemann's company and toured Europe before marrying Sophie *Schröder and eventually settling in Hamburg in 1765. Here he built a small theatre; quarrels with his stepson, however, severely hampered this enterprise despite the support of Lessing and others.

His daughters, **Dorothea Ackermann** (1752–1821) and **Charlotte Ackermann** (1757–75), both became distinguished actresses at the theatre, appearing in plays by Lessing, Goethe, and Shakespeare until their careers ended with Dorothea's marriage and Charlotte's early death.

Ackland, Joss (Sidney Edmond Jocelyn Ackland; 1928-) British actor, who made his West End debut in *The Hasty Heart* in 1945. Subsequently he spent several years in provincial repertory and touring before joining the Old Vic company in 1958. His parts have ranged from Caliban to Brecht's Galileo at the Mermaid Theatre and Eustace in *The Madras House* (1977) at the National Theatre. Recent successes have included performances as Falstaff at the opening of the Barbican Theatre in 1982 and Captain Hook and Mr Darling in *Peter Pan* (1982). His roles in musicals have included Fredrik in *A Little Night Music* (1975) and Juan Perón in *Evita* (1978).

acoustics The quality of sound transmission in a particular building. In the theatre it is commonly affected by such factors as the design of the auditorium, the carpeting, the distance from the stage to the back row of seats, and the presence of a proscenium arch. Devices designed to improve the acoustical properties of an auditorium have included the *periaktoi of the ancient Greeks, which when correctly angled may have helped to deflect sound towards the audience, the use of a small roof over the stage in the Elizabethan theatre to aim sound downwards, and – to a limited extent – modern electrical amplification equipment.

act A structural division of a play, usually ranging from one to five in number. Division of a tragedy into five acts was introduced in ancient Greece, being first stipulated by Horace in *Ars Poetica*, and became a convention of Elizabethan drama. Shakespeare's tragedies were not originally written in five acts but were so arranged by his editors after Jonson introduced the convention into the English theatre. Comedies of the period frequently favoured a three-act structure, while the 19th century saw a short-lived fashion for division into four acts. Much recent drama has favoured a more flexible structure, often opting for two or three acts and thus limiting intervals to one or two during a performance.

act drop *See* curtain.

acting The performing of a role before an audience. The practice of acting is claimed to have various roots in childhood games and social ritual but first emerged as a disciplined art in Greece in the 5th century BC. *Thespis was the first to perform separately from the chorus and subsequently a second actor was added (by Aeschylus) and then a third (by Sophocles). Euripides in turn emphasized the importance of the actor by reducing the role of the chorus; actors in his day still relied, however, solely upon their voices and static physical presence to achieve their effects.

In the Roman theatre the emphasis was upon a livelier coarser style, incorporating stock characters as well as slapstick and acrobatics; eventually this unfettered form of entertainment offended the church and in the 6th century AD virtually all theatrical activity ceased. The actor was then confined to church ritual and the peripheral traditions of the *jongleurs, *goliards, and *minstrels until medieval times, when members of trade guilds and other amateurs began to present entertainments in their own localities.

ACTING COMPANY

The Renaissance saw the return of the professional actor and a renewal of interest in classical acting techniques; these were absorbed into the highly stylized yet lively and improvizational *commedia dell'arte*, among other new forms. All female roles on the professional stage were played by men, as they had been since Roman times.

Such celebrated companies as the Comédie-Française acquired their own distinctive styles and gradually the actors themselves became the dominant force in the theatre, plays being chosen and even rewritten to suit their particular strengths. Despite the provocative and witty ease of Restoration comedy, acting styles became increasingly artificial and emotionally extravagant during the 17th and 18th centuries, leading ultimately to the rant and shallowness of *melodrama in the 19th-century theatre. Nonetheless, the partial reforms and natural brilliance of such performers as David Garrick, Edmund Kean, the Kembles, and Macready in Britain and Edwin Forrest, the Booths, and the Jeffersons in the US transformed often mediocre material into highly effective theatre.

The foundation of the Duke of Saxe-Meiningen's troupe (in which all the members were considered equal) foreshadowed the decline of the theatre of the stock companies and actor-managers (of whom Sir Henry Irving was one of the best-known) and the emergence of the modern director-controlled drama. *Stanislavsky codified modern acting theory through his work with the Moscow Art Theatre and his ideas have since been developed in many countries, notably in the US by the *Group Theatre and the *Actors' Studio, famous for its *Method acting. The contemporary actor is encouraged to draw upon inner motivations but is also expected to be able to apply to both tragedy and comedy such wide-ranging skills as mime, acrobatics, singing, and dance, whether he is acting under naturalistic or non-naturalistic direction.

More formalized acting techniques continue to be observed, however, in various forms of traditional theatre outside Europe and the US. Notable examples of these survivals include the *Nō* theatre of Japan and some Indian drama, in which a precise range of gestures and movements is rigidly adhered to.

Acting Company *See* City Centre of Music and Drama.

Activism A theatrical philosophy combining elements of both *Expressionism and *Realism. It developed in the 20th century and argued for the realistic presentation of social issues.

actor A male performer in a dramatic entertainment, usually a play. The earliest actors were probably performers in dumb shows and participants in religious ceremonies. The first actor whose name is known to us was Thespis, in whose honour all subsequent performers have often been dubbed Thespians; professional actors, however, did not appear until the 16th century. The Roman actor Quintus Roscius set high standards of acting in the ancient world and similarly lent his name to distinguished actors of subsequent eras, being commemorated by the African Roscius, the Ohio Roscius, the Scottish Roscius, the Young Roscius, and various others. Richard Burbage is generally recognized as the first great English actor, while notable acting dynasties over the years have included the Kembles, the Terrys, and the Redgraves in England and the Barrymores in the US. In ancient Greece actors enjoyed an elevated status; in Rome, however, they were ranked alongside the lowest in society – a position in which they remained until the 19th century when those at the top of their profession became eligible for knighthoods and other forms of public recognition.

actor-manager An actor who also runs the company in which he appears. The great age of the actor-managers was the 19th century, when they included Sir Henry Irving and Sir Herbert Beerbohm Tree.

Actor Prepares, An A treatise on drama theory by *Stanislavsky, published in 1926. The most widely-known of his studies of naturalism, it discusses the psychology of acting and was subsequently used as the basis of the Method theory in the US. His later writings, however, balanced this emphasis upon the actor's importance with his interest in technique and his belief in the need for a production to adopt a particular 'style' to which individual actors may be harnessed.

Actors' Company *See* McKellen, Ian.

Actors' Equity Association *See* American Actors' Equity Association; British Actors' Equity Association; Canadian Actors' Equity Associations.

Actors' Studio A theatre workshop founded in 1947 in New York by Elia Kazan and Lee Strasberg. It exercized enormous influence as a place where professional actors could study and experiment with the *Method acting technique.

Actors' Theatre A production company founded in New York in 1939 for the training of young actors and as a testing ground for new plays. The company, which functioned until 1947, produced notable plays by Ibsen, Shaw, and others at the Provincetown Playhouse in Greenwich Village.

Actors Theatre of Louisville A theatre in Louisville, Kentucky, founded in 1964 and now the State Theatre of Kentucky. It moved into its two permanent homes – the Pamela Brown Auditorium, where classical and modern plays are performed, and the Victor Jory Theatre, where an off-Broadway series is shown – in 1972. The company also makes an annual regional tour.

actress A female performer in a dramatic entertainment, usually a play. The presence of women on the stage was prohibited in early times and only began to become generally acceptable in Europe in the 17th century. Notable early actresses who established strong reputations in defiance of prejudice against their sex included Isabella Andreini in Italy, Carolina Neuber in Germany, and Madeleine Béjart in France; the first woman to grace the stage in England was Margaret Hughes, who first appeared in *The Moor of Venice* in 1660 to enthusiastic applause.

Acts of the Apostles (*Actes des Apôtres*) A mystery play written between 1452 and 1478 by Simon *Gréban, possibly in collaboration with his brother Arnoul Gréban. The play deals with the travels, preaching, and martyrdom of Christ's apostles.

act-tune A piece of music played between the acts of a play. Act-tunes were an accepted feature of the Elizabethan theatre; composers of such music in the Restoration theatre included Purcell.

Adam de la Halle (Adam le Bossu d'Arras; c. 1240 – c. 1288) French poet and musician, traditionally acknowledged as the founder of secular drama in France. Born in Arras, he travelled to Italy in the service of Count Robert II of Artois. His first dramatic work, *Jeu de la feuillée*, performed in Arras in about 1276, is a licentious satirical fantasy; *Jeu de Robin et Marion*, performed in Naples in about 1283, is sometimes regarded as a predecessor of the comic opera.

Adamov, Arthur (1908–70) French playwright, born in Russia. In 1924 he moved to Paris, but he did not begin writing for the theatre until the late 1940s, inspired by the plays of Strindberg. The recurring themes of futility and alienation in such early plays as *Le Professeur Taranne* (1953 Lyons; translated as **Professor Taranne,* 1962) and *Le Ping-Pong* (1955) led to his association with the Theatre of the Absurd. His later plays, including *Paolo Paoli* (1957) and *Le Printemps '71* (1961; translated as **Spring '71*), contain more explicit social and political comment.

Adams, Maude (1872–1953) US actress, born into a theatrical family, who had her first success at the age of five in *Fritz, Our German Cousin*. In the same year, she appeared as Little Eva in *Uncle Tom's Cabin*. She first appeared in New York in 1888 and later played in several works by J M Barrie, the first being *The Little Minister* (1897) as Little Babbie, a part the author enlarged for her. After playing the lead in Rostand's *L'Aiglon*, she toured in *The Merchant of Venice* (1931) and *Twelfth Night* (1934).

ADC *See* Amateur Dramatic Club.

Adding Machine, The An Expressionist drama by Elmer **Rice*. First performance: New York, 1923. The protagonist, a bookkeeper named Mr Zero, represents mankind surviving in a world of extreme mechanization and dehumanization.

Addison, Joseph (1672–1719) English essayist, poet, and playwright, who also served as an under-secretary of state. In 1713 his neoclassical blank verse tragedy *Cato* was successfully staged at Drury Lane, the title role being created by Barton Booth. An attempt to write a moral comedy, *The Drummer*, in 1715 met with failure. His critical writings on the theatre appeared in *The Spectator* and *The Tatler*.

Ade, George (1866–1944) US humorist and playwright, whose career in the theatre began with the New York production of his light opera *The Sultan of Sulu* (1902). This was followed by such comedies as *The County Chairman* (1903) and *The College Widow* (1904), which established his reputation as a leading contemporary playwright.

Adelphi Theatre One of the most popular London theatres in the 19th century, home of the celebrated 'Adelphi dramas'. The present building is the fourth on the site, the theatre having been known in turn as the **Sans Pareil** (1806–19), Adelphi (1819–29), Theatre Royal New Adelphi (1829–67), **Royal Adelphi** (1867–1901), **Century** (1901–02), and Royal Adelphi (1902–40). 'Royal' was dropped from the name in 1940. Well known in the mid-19th century for its burlettas and dramatized versions of Sir Walter Scott's novels, it became (1834) the first theatre in England to have a sinking stage installed. The 'Adelphi dramas', mostly written by J B Buckstone, were produced under the management of Madame Céleste and Ben Webster in the years 1844–53. After being rebuilt in 1858 to resemble the Opéra Comique in Paris, the Adelphi became noted for its romantic melodramas; in 1897 the popular actor William Terriss was shot dead outside the theatre by a madman. Rebuilt again in 1900, it was then used for modern poetic drama and Shakespeare. A period of musical comedy followed from 1908 and then, after further reconstruction in 1930, C B Cochran took over as manager, staging spectacular revues. Marie Tempest made her final stage appearance at the Adelphi in 1940, while Ivor Novello's *The Dancing Years* enjoyed a long run from 1942. After the war Cochran returned to present revues by A P Herbert, including the popular *Bless the Bride* (1947). More recent successes have been *Charlie Girl* (1965), a revival of *My Fair Lady* (1977), and *Me and My Girl* (1985). *See also* George Abbott Theatre.

ad lib To improvise lines not in the script, either on impulse or to cover for some emergency on stage, often inability to remember the original words.

Admirable Crichton, The A comedy by J M *Barrie. First performance: London, 1902. It examines social status in a family who are shipwrecked along with Crichton, their butler; he assumes leadership only to revert to his inferior position when rescue arrives.

Admiral's Men An English company, formed in 1585 and named in honour of its patron, Admiral Lord Howard, that presented original performances of many major plays of the period. In 1590 the company occupied the Theatre, subsequently moving to the Rose Theatre under Henslowe and Edward Alleyn. Members of the company produced several of Marlowe's plays and then transferred to the Fortune Theatre, being renamed **Prince Henry's Men** in 1603. In 1612 they changed their name to **Palsgrave's Men**; they finally disbanded in 1631.

Adolph, Johann Baptist (1657–1708) Austrian playwright, who was a major writer of Jesuit drama. His play *Philemon et Apollonius* was based on a work by Avancini, whose post at the royal court he inherited; other plays were based on the writings of Calderón and Gryphius.

Adrian, Max (Max Bor; 1903–73) British actor, born in Ireland, who first established his reputation playing in *Troilus and Cressida* and *The Doctor's Dilemma* at the Westminster Theatre in 1938. After appearances at the Old Vic and the Haymarket Theatre, he won acclaim as a performer in revue in the 1940s and 1950s and also ventured into musicals and farce. Subsequently he was for several seasons with the Royal Shakespeare Company and contrived one-man shows on Shaw (1966) and on Gilbert and Sullivan (1969).

Advent play *See* liturgical drama.

advertisement curtain *See* curtain.

AE (George William Russell; 1867–1935) Irish poet and playwright. His single play, *Deirdre* (1902), was performed by the Irish National Dramatic Society. He was also one of the founders of the Abbey Theatre, alongside W B Yeats and Lady Gregory.

Aerial Gardens Theatre *See* New Amsterdam Theatre.

Aeschylus (c. 525 BC–456 BC) Greek playwright, born at Eleusis, near Athens, and generally considered to be the earliest important writer of the Western theatrical tradition. Initially a soldier in the Persian Wars, he became the first playwright to achieve official recognition in ancient Greece, establishing himself as a writer, performer, and director and winning three contests, the first in 484 BC. Of his 90 plays only seven survive; they all tackle themes of sin and justice and were written for the Dionysia, usually as parts of connected trilogies.

The only complete extant trilogy – *The *Oresteia*, comprising *Agamemnon*, the *Choephori*, and the *Eumenides*, – was typical of his work, making use of such innovations as a reduced chorus of possibly as few as 12 performers and the introduction of more than one actor. His plays were presented with rudimentary props against painted backcloths and, with his understanding of poetical language, complex structure, and psychological analysis, inspired numerous writers of both classical and modern times, including Sophocles, Euripides, Seneca, Shelley, Voltaire, Eugene O'Neill, and Jean-Paul Sartre.

As well as being a master of tragedy, Aeschylus was also the author of many satyr-plays, of which only fragments are known. According to tradition he died after an eagle mistook his bald head for a rock and dropped a tortoise on it in an attempt to break its shell. His son was the playwright Euphorion.

Principal works:

The *Persians: 472 BC.

*Seven Against Thebes: 469 BC.

*Prometheus Bound: c. 460 BC.

The *Suppliant Women: c. 460 BC.

Agamemnon: 458 BC.

Choephori: 458 BC.

Eumenides: 458 BC.

Aesopus, Claudius (1st century BC) Roman tragic actor, who was admired by both Horace and Cicero. When the latter was exiled Aesopus made appeals on stage for his return. His identification with his roles was so great that he was said to have accidentally killed another actor during a performance.

affective memory An aspect of the *Method theory of acting. The technique involves the invocation of past experiences in an actor's life in order to help him to recreate genuine emotion on stage.

Afinogenov, Alexander Nikolaevich (1904–41) Soviet playwright, whose dramas won popular success and official approval in his own country as well as an audience in the West. He started writing in the 1920s, producing his first play, *Robert Tim*, in 1924; this was followed by (amongst others) *Fear* (1931) and *Distant Point* (1934), which are regarded as two of his finest works. His last play, *On the Eve* (1941), dealing with the German invasion of the USSR, was first performed after his untimely death in an air raid.

Afranius, Lucius (2nd century BC) Roman playwright, considered the leading writer of the *togata* tradition. Of his 44 or more works fragments survive; he was noted for his handling of complex plots and may have been the first to tackle the theme of homosexuality on stage.

African Roscius *See* Aldridge, Ira.

afterpiece A short play, usually a comedy, presented as light relief after a full-length tragedy. Such afterpieces were a common feature of British drama in the 18th century.

After the Fall A psychological drama by Arthur *Miller, alleged to be highly autobiographical. First performance: Washington Square Theatre, New York, 1964. The play takes place in a courtroom where Quintin, the protagonist, reviews his life and examines his relationship to ex-wives Maggie and Louise and to his friend Lou.

Agate, James Evershed (1877–1947) British theatre critic, who was drama critic for *The Sunday Times* from 1923 until his death. He maintained that no actor had achieved greatness since Irving and Bernhardt and was also the author of a nine-part autobiography, *Ego* (1935–47).

His sister was the actress **May Agate** (1892–1960), who studied with Bernhardt and appeared with her in Paris and London. After working with Miss Horniman's company in Manchester, she appeared regularly in the West End. In 1945 she published *Madame Sarah*, a book about her former mentor.

Agathon (d. c. 400 BC) Greek playwright, who developed the function of choral odes, making them musical interludes within a play and thus paving the way for the division of a play into separate acts. He won two dramatic contests (the first in 416 BC) and was mourned after his death by Aristophanes.

agent An intermediary who performs various matters of business connected with the theatre. The first professional literary agents appeared in the 19th century and, also known as author's agents or play agents, commonly assist writers in finding producers for their work; frequently they combine these tasks with those of a talent agent, seeking out unknown actors and actresses and listing themselves under the generic term of theatrical or dramatic agent. Actors' agents negotiate contracts on behalf of actors as well as finding suitable parts for them, while casting agents are employed to find suitable actors for a particular production; many agents combine these two roles. Advance agents handle the business arrangements ahead of touring companies while booking agents organize the tours. Press agents look after all publicity matters connected with a production. Ticket agents buy tickets on behalf of theatre-goers (for a small extra fee), usually acting independently of the theatres themselves.

Aggas, Robert (c. 1619–79) English scene painter and landscape artist. He worked at several major theatres, including the Blackfriars Theatre, the Dorset Garden Theatre, and for Killigrew at Drury Lane. He was the first artist in England to paint movable scenery.

agon An ancient Greek term taken to signify the fundamental conflict essential to classical tragedy. The word may have been derived from that used for gladiatorial contests in which two men fought to the death.

Ainley, Henry (Hinchliffe) (1879–1945) British actor, who achieved immediate success when he was selected by George Alexander to play Paolo in Stephen Phillips's *Paolo and Francesca* at the St James's Theatre in 1902. Subsequently he became highly popular in romantic parts but, after being acclaimed in Shakespearean roles, later developed as a powerful character actor, including *Hassan* (1923), *Macbeth* (1926), and St John Ervine's *The First Mrs Fraser* (1929) among his triumphs.

Aitken, Maria (1945-) British actress, who was the first woman to be elected to the OUDS. Her professional career began with an appearance in *A Streetcar Named Desire* at Coventry in 1967. Subsequently she toured the Far East as Viola in *Twelfth Night* and Hermione in *A Winter's Tale*, played Countess Charlotte Malcolm in the musical *A Little Night Music* (1975), and such stylish roles as Elvira in Coward's *Blithe Spirit* (1976) at the National Theatre and Amanda in *Private Lives* (1980) at the Duchess Theatre. More recent successes include an appearance in Clare Booth Luce's *The Women* (1986).

Akimov, Nikolai Pavlovich (1901–68) Soviet scene designer and director, who became famous for his radical designs for productions at Leningrad's Theatre of Comedy and at the Vakhtangov Theatre in Moscow in the 1920s and 1930s. His most controversial production as a director was his *Hamlet* (1932), in which Hamlet invented his father's ghost and a drunk Ophelia died during an orgy. In 1936 Akimov returned to the Theatre of Comedy, where he staged new Soviet comedies.

Akins, Zoë (1886–1958) US poet and playwright, whose best-known work for the stage was the highly popular *The Greeks Had a Word for It* (1930). Subsequently she won a Pulitzer Prize for her adaptation for the stage of Edith Wharton's novel *The Old Maid* (1935).

Alarcón y Mendoza *See* Ruiz de Alarcón y Mendoza, Juan.

Albanesi, Meggie (Margharita Albanesi; 1899–1923) British actress, whose early death cut short a career of singular promise. After winning the Bancroft Gold Medal at the Royal Academy of Dramatic Art she attracted admiration over the next five years in such roles as Sonia in Heijeerman's *The Rising Sun* (1919), Jill Hillcrest in Galsworthy's *The Skin Game* (1920), Sydney Fairfield in Clemence Dane's *A Bill of Di-*

vorcement (1921), and Daisy in Maugham's *East of Suez* (1922).

Albee, Edward Franklin (1928-) US playwright, who was the adopted grandson of a theatre manager of the same name who ran an early vaudeville circuit and built several theatres during the 1880s. Albee's works deal primarily with the conflict between reality and illusion and the plight of humanity in a decaying world. His first work, the one-act *The Zoo Story*, won him attention, although it was his first success on Broadway, **Who's Afraid of Virginia Woolf?*, for which he received numerous awards, that established his reputation. Albee received a Pulitzer Prize for both *A Delicate Balance* and *Seascape* and has produced and directed a number of his own plays as well as works by other writers. *Lolita* was an adaptation of the novel by Nabokov.
Principal works:
The Zoo Story: 1959.
The Death of Bessie Smith: 1960.
The *American Dream: 1961.
Who's Afraid of Virginia Woolf?: 1962.
The Ballad of the Sad Café: 1963.
Tiny Alice: 1964.
A Delicate Balance: 1966.
All Over: 1970.
Seascape: 1975.
Counting the Ways: 1976.
The Lady from Dubuque: 1980.
Lolita: 1981.
The Man Who Had Three Arms: 1983.

Alberti, Rafael (1902-) Spanish painter, poet, and playwright. He is best known for such popular plays as *El hombre deshabitado* (The Deserted Man; 1930) and *El adefesio* (The Odd One; 1914) and for a collection of Surrealistic poetry entitled *Sobre los Angeles* (Concerning the Angels; 1929).

Albery, James (1838–89) British playwright, whose best known work was *Two Roses* (1870), in which Henry Irving achieved great success as Digby Grant. He was for many years connected with the Criterion Theatre, whose leading lady, Mary Moore (later Lady *Wyndham), he married in 1878.

Their son was the theatre manager **Sir Bronson James Albery** (1881–1971), who took over the Criterion Theatre and subsequently also the New Theatre and Wyndham's Theatre, running them in collaboration with Howard Wyndham. After his death the New Theatre was renamed the Albery in his memory by his son, **Donald Arthur Rolleston** (1914-).

Albery Theatre A theatre in St Martin's Lane, London, formerly the New Theatre. It was opened in 1903 by Charles Wyndham and from 1905 to 1913 saw regular appearances by Fred Terry and Julia Neilson. Other successes included performances by Katharine Cornell and, in 1924, the triumph of Sybil Thorndike in the title role of G B Shaw's *St Joan*. From 1944 to 1950 the theatre was the home of the Old Vic Company, whose own theatre had been bombed; during this period there were many outstanding Shakespeare productions, the players including Edith Evans, John Gielgud, Laurence Olivier, Michael Redgrave, and Ralph Richardson. Subsequently the Lionel Bart musical *Oliver!* (1960–66) ran for a record 2618 performances; it was revived in 1977 for a further three-year run while another departure was the successful rock musical *Joseph and the Amazing Technicolor Dreamcoat* (1973). The theatre was renamed the Albery in 1973 in honour of the former director, Sir Bronson Albery, in order to avoid confusion with the New London Theatre.

Alcano, Cielo d' (13th century) Italian playwright, born in Sicily. He was the author of the first Italian dialect play, written in the **contrasto* tradition.

10

Alchemist, The A satirical comedy by Ben *Jonson. First performance: Globe Theatre, London, 1610. The plot revolves around the machinations of the servant Face, who conspires with the fraudulent alchemist Subtle and Dol Common to dupe a series of gullible visitors to his master's house while the latter is absent during an outbreak of the plague; he eventually placates his outraged master by arranging his marriage to Dame Pliant.

Aldrich, Louis (Louis Lyon: 1843–1901) US actor, who became a celebrated child actor in major Shakespearean roles. Known as the **Ohio Roscius**, he excelled in such parts as Richard III and Home's Young Norval; later in life he appeared regularly opposite Mrs John Drew in Philadelphia and won praise in Bartley Campbell's *My Partner* (1879) and Edward J Swartz's *The Kaffir Diamond* (1888).

Aldridge, Ira (1804–67) British actor, born in the US, who was recognized as the first of the great Black actors. He made his London debut in 1826, playing Othello at the Royalty Theatre and billed as the **African Roscius**. During his subsequent successful career, he played Lear, Macbeth, and other major roles all over Europe. He was particularly popular in Germany and in Russia, where he played Lear with a pale face and black hands.

Aldwych Theatre A theatre in London famous both for its farces and as the headquarters in the capital of the Royal Shakespeare Company. Built as a companion theatre to the Strand, the Aldwych Theatre was opened in 1905 by Seymour Hicks and the US impresario Charles Frohman. It opened with a new version of Hicks's musical play *Blue Bell in Fairyland*, starring Hicks and his wife Ellaline Terriss. Marie Dressler appeared at the theatre in 1909 and in 1911 the first English performance of a Chekhov play, *The Cherry Orchard*, was staged there. During World War I the theatre became a club for Australian soldiers. C B Cochran took over in 1919, introducing among others Sacha Guitry and Yvonne Printemps; later managers included Viola Tree and Donald Calthrop. In 1924 *It Pays to Advertise*, presented by Tom Walls and Leslie Henson, ran for 598 performances. There followed the celebrated series of 'Aldwych farces', written by Ben Travers and performed by a cast headed by Tom Walls and Ralph Lynn; these included *A Cuckoo in the Nest* (1925), *Rookery Nook* (1926), *Thark* (1927), and *A Cup of Kindness* (1929). Subsequent successes included Lillian Hellman's *Watch on the Rhine* (1942); Daphne Du Maurier's *September Tide* (1948), starring Gertrude Lawrence; and Tennessee Williams's *A Streetcar Named Desire* (1949), with Vivien Leigh. In 1960 the theatre became the London home of the Royal Shakespeare Company, until the latter's move to the Barbican in 1982. During the RSC's occupancy such modern plays as Anouilh's *Becket* (1961) and Pinter's *The Homecoming* (1965) were interspersed with Shakespeare, and in 1980 the eight-and-a-half-hour production of *Nicholas Nickleby* was much acclaimed. Now under US ownership, the theatre's recent successes have included the National Theatre production *Brighton Beach Memoirs* and Stoppard's *Hapgood* (1988).

Alecsandri, Vasile (1811–90) Romanian statesman, poet, and playwright, who was the author of a number of successful social comedies. *Iórgu de la Sadagúra* (1844), *The Tyrannic Prince* (1897), and *Ovid* (1885) were all produced at the theatre in Jassy, which Alecsandri had helped to establish in 1840.

Aleichem, Sholom (Solomon Rabinowitz; 1859–1976) Soviet-born Jewish writer, whose sympathetic and humorous accounts of everyday life in Jewish communities of the Ukraine were enormously popular. A

11

number of his novels and stories were adapted for the stage, including the series of comic tales entitled *Tevye the Milkman*, which as the musical *Fiddler on the Roof enjoyed successes on Broadway (1964) and in London (1967).

Aleotti, Giovanni Battista (1546–1636) Italian theatre designer, usually remembered as the architect of the *Teatro Farnese in Parma. Important for its incorporation of a proscenium arch, the theatre originally contained a set of wings probably also designed by Aleotti.

Alexander, Sir George (George Alexander Gibb Samson; 1858–1919) British actor-manager, who was for many years associated with the *St James's Theatre. Having worked as an actor with Irving, Kendal, and Hare, he went into management in 1889 with the aim of building up a prestigious theatre using British plays. Among the authors who had never written for the stage, he put on plays by Thomas Hardy, Arnold Bennett, and John Galsworthy. He was responsible for the production of Oscar Wilde's, *Lady Windermere's Fan* (1892) and *The Importance of Being Earnest* (1893), and for a number of Pinero's works. As an actor he was suited to fashionable drawing-room comedy. His most successful appearances, however, were in Anthony Hope's *The Prisoner of Zenda* (1896), in which he played the dual leading role. He was knighted in 1911.

Alexandra Theatre A theatre in Birmingham, founded in 1901. First known as the Lyceum, it was used for productions of pantomime, melodrama, music hall, and revue before becoming a repertory theatre in 1927. Gradually, however, touring companies took over and since 1976 it has housed touring productions only; it was refurbished in 1979 and now seats 1562.

Several other theatres of the same name have also existed in London – in Highbury Barn (1861–71), Camden (1873–81), and Stoke Newington (1897–1940) – but none now survive.

Alexandre le Grand A tragedy by Jean *Racine. First performance: Paris, 1665, produced by Molière. Two weeks after its opening at the Palais-Royal, Racine transferred the play to the Hôtel de Bourgogne, causing a rift between the two playwrights. The plot concerns the conflict between Alexander the Great and the Indian kings Porus and Taxile, rivals for the love of Axiane.

Alexandrinsky Theatre *See* Pushkin Theatre.

Alexis (c. 375 BC–c. 275 BC) Greek playwright and uncle of Menander, who wrote numerous examples of both Middle and New Comedy. Of the 245 plays attributed to him, only fragments survive.

Alfieri, Vittorio Amedeo, Conte (1749–1803) Italian poet and playwright, who wrote a number of notable verse tragedies, many of which were bitter condemnations of tyranny. Influenced by Voltaire, Rousseau, and Montesquieu, he scored his first success with *Cleopatra* in 1775, after which he wrote a further 20 or so tragedies, of which his masterpiece *Saul* (1782) and *Mirra* (1784) were particularly well received. His other dramatic writings include the comedy *Il Divorzio* (1802).

Alhambra A celebrated music hall in Leicester Square, London, opened in 1854 as an exhibition centre called the **Royal Panopticon of Science and Art**. Seating 3500 people and decorated with a facade in the Moorish style, it became a music hall in 1860 and saw the first appearances in England of the acrobat Léotard (1861), performances of the can-can (which caused the temporary loss of the theatre's licence), drama, ballet, and – after rebuilding in 1883 following a fire – popular revues. Diaghilev's company performed there in 1919 and 1922; subsequent performers, before the building's demolition in 1936, included Gracie Fields. The Odeon cinema now occupies the site.

alienation effect One of the principal theories developed by Brecht in his *epic theatre, sometimes referred to as the **A-effect** or the *Verfremdungseffekt*. The theory stipulates the emotional detachment of both the audience and the actor from the character that is being portrayed in order to emphasize the intellectual significance of what is happening. It suggests the use of various artificial devices, including placards and masks, to help to achieve this effect.

Alizon (fl. 1610–48) French actor, who became famous for his interpretation of female roles. At his best in farce, he appeared at the Faubourg Saint-Germain before transferring to the Hôtel de Bourgogne in 1634.

Allen, Chesney *See* Crazy Gang.

Allen, William (d. 1647) English actor, who joined Lady Elizabeth's Men. His major roles included Grimaldi in Massinger's *The Renegado* and Captain Lanby in Shirley's *The Wedding*. In 1626 he joined the King's Men.

Alleyn, Edward (1566–1626) English actor and manager. After appearances with the Earl of Worcester's company (1583–87), he became a leading actor with the Admiral's Men. Through his marriage to Joan Woodward, stepdaughter of Philip Henslowe, he became closely associated with his father-in-law's theatrical ventures, sharing with him the ownership of the Rose and Fortune theatres. He played leading roles in plays by Marlowe, Greene, Dekker, and Chapman, retiring from the stage around 1604. He then devoted himself to the support of charities and the foundation of Dulwich College.

Alley · Theatre *See* Nina Vance Alley Theatre.

All for Love; or, the World Well Lost A tragedy in blank verse by John *Dryden. First performance: London, 1678. Sharing the same plot as Shakespeare's *Antony and Cleopatra*, the play concentrates on the last hours of the two central characters and, while never achieving the grandeur of the earlier version, focuses on the conflict involved between love and honour.

All God's Chillun Got Wings A controversial play by Eugene *O'Neill. First performance: New York, 1924. The plot depicts the relationship between a Black boy, Jim Harris, and a White girl, Ella Downey, who fall in love, marry, but see their lives gradually disintegrate around them. O'Neill received many angry letters in response to the production, which provoked racist demonstrations.

Allgood, Mollie *See* O'Neill, Maire.

Allgood, Sara (1883–1950) Irish actress, who made her London debut in 1904 as Cathleen in Synge's *Riders to the Sea*. She appeared regularly at the Abbey Theatre, Dublin, in such plays as *The Playboy of the Western World* (1907) and Yeats's *Cathleen ni Houlihan* (1913). She also toured Australia in *Peg o' My Heart* (1916) before returning to the Abbey where she appeared in *Juno and the Paycock* (1924), *The Plough and the Stars* (1926), and other plays.

Allio, René (1921-) French theatre designer, who has done much to encourage the adoption of flexible staging in the modern theatre. His designs advocate the involvement of the technical aspects of a production in the process of collective creation and the use of variable stage shapes. As well as work in France, he has also designed productions for the National Theatre in Britain. Recent successes have included designs for

Marivaux's *Infidelities* (1987) at London's Lyric Theatre, Hammersmith.

All My Sons A play by Arthur *Miller. First performance: New York, 1947. The story revolves around Joe Keller, a factory owner who sells defective engines to the government, resulting in the deaths of many US pilots during World War II and causing his own sons to turn against him.

All-Russian Theatrical Society (VTO) Russian theatre organization founded in 1883 to defend actors' interests. The subsidiary Union of Stage Workers acted on behalf of playwrights and composers. After 1917 the society did much to improve acting standards throughout the USSR and promoted works by contemporary Russian writers; its president from 1916 to 1964 was Alexandra Yablochkina.

All's Well That Ends Well A tragi-comedy by William *Shakespeare, written 1593–1604. First performance: c. 1596. One of the 'problem plays' because of its ambiguous tone, the play focuses upon the unrequited love of the worthy Helena for the arrogant Bertram; the comic subplot centres upon the cowardly Parolles. The play lacks the fantasy of the earlier comedies but is notable for the intensity of Helena's soliloquies and for its study of inner motivation. Virtue, age, and free will are among the themes discussed.

Alma-Tadema, Sir Lawrence (1836–1912) British artist, born in Holland, who designed sets for Irving and Tree. His designs were noted for their scrupulous archaelogical and architectural accuracy. He was knighted in 1899.

Aloni, Nissim (1926-) Israeli playwright and director, who first established his reputation as one of Israel's leading dramatists with the much-acclaimed *Bigdey Ha'melech* (The Emperor's New Clothes; 1961), which

he directed himself. His other works include *Ha'anesiha H'amerikait* (The American Princess), which was performed by the newly-established Theatre of the Seasons (1963), and *Doda Liza* (Aunt Liza; 1969), which marked a departure from his hitherto complex and fantastic style inspired by the Theatre of the Absurd.

alternative theatre *See* collective creation; community theatre; fringe theatre.

Altona A play by Jean-Paul *Sartre, which has also been translated as *Loser Wins* and *The Condemned of Altona*. First performance: Paris, 1959. Set in Germany, the plot centres on the guilt of those involved with the Nazis and depicts the industrialist Von Gerlach and his elder son Frantz, who has lived in isolation since the war.

Altwiener Volkstheater A form of comic play that developed in Vienna during the early 18th century, chiefly under Stranitsky and Prehauser. A variation of the *Haupt-und Staatsaktion*, the tradition – which relied heavily upon comic improvisation and gave free rein to the character Hanswurst – was suppressed by the authorities in the mid-18th century but later re-emerged in the fairy-tale plays and farces that were eventually amalgamated into the operetta.

Alvares, Afonso (16th century) Portuguese playwright, who developed the early Portuguese tradition of the *saint play. His dramas, which were much influenced by the works of Vicente, combined religious sentiments with comic elements; four of them, notably his *Auto de Santo António* (1531), survive.

Álvarez Quintero, Serafín (1871–1938) Spanish playwright, who collaborated with his brother, **Joaquin Álvarez Quintero** (1873–1944), on about 200 light-hearted comedies based largely on life in their native Andalusia. The first, *Esgrima y amor*

(1888), was produced while the brothers were still in their teens. Some of their works, translated by Helen and Harley Granville-Barker, were subsequently performed in London and New York; these included *Fortunato* (1928), and *The Lady from Alfaqueque* (1928).

Alvin Theatre A theatre in New York, situated on West 52nd Street between Broadway and Eighth Avenue. This 1344-seat theatre opened in 1927 with Gershwin's *Funny Face*, the first of a series of successful musicals starring such performers as the Astaires and Ethel Merman. Since 1932 it has also been used for straight drama, notable successes having included works by O'Neill, Sherwood, and Stoppard. Recent productions number amongst them Sondheim's *Company* (1970), *Shenandoah* (1975), and *Annie* (1977).

Amadeus A play by Peter *Shaffer. First performance: 1979. Based on the jealousy of the composer Salieri for his rival Mozart and speculating upon the circumstances surrounding the latter's death, the play provided fine roles for Paul Scofield and Frank Finlay in London and subsequently Ian McKellen and John Wood in New York (1980).

Amateur Dramatic Club (ADC) An amateur theatre group established in Cambridge by F C Burnand in 1855. Drawing upon undergraduates from Cambridge University, the club continues to produce many actors for the professional stage and has won acclaim for productions directed by George Rylands.

amateur theatre Any form of drama in which those involved do not expect payment for their work. Most modern professional theatre has its roots in the amateur tradition; amateur drama is now primarily the province of university groups (*see* university drama departments) and local amateur theatre societies, which present a wide range of productions – occasionally in their own theatres (known as Little Theatres) – and often take part in major drama festivals. Amateur groups are particularly valued for their role in the fringe theatre, as training grounds for future professionals, and in maintaining a theatrical tradition in areas infrequently visited by professional companies. The International Amateur Theatre Association, based at The Hague, was founded in 1952 under E Martin Browne. *See also* National Youth Theatre, theatre in education, British Theatre Association, National Operatic and Dramatic Association.

Ambassadors Theatre A small 20th-century London theatre celebrated for the longest-running production in theatre history, Agatha Christie's *The Mousetrap*. It was designed as one of a pair (with St Martin's Theatre) by W G R Sprague and opened in 1913. Alice Delysia appeared here in revues during World War I, while Ivor Novello made his debut here in 1921 and Vivien Leigh her first West End appearance in *The Mask of Virtue* (1935). During World War II the Ambassadors remained open throughout the blitz with daytime performances by the Ballet Rambert. *The Mousetrap* opened on 25 November 1952 and transferred to St Martin's on 25 March 1974. Successes since then have included the Royal Shakespeare Company's *Les Liaisons Dangereuses* (1987) by Christopher Hampton.

Ambassador Theatre A theatre in New York, situated on West 49th Street between Broadway and Eighth Avenue. This 1121-seat theatre opened in 1921 with the musical *The Rose Girl* under the management of the Shubert brothers. The theatre housed radio and television programmes for a period before returning to straight plays in 1956, since when notable successes have included an adaptation of E M Forster's *A Passage to India* (1962) and plays by Peter Weiss, Robert Anderson, and Molière, as well as the musical *Your Arms Too Short to Box With God* (1980).

Ambigu, Théâtre de l' A theatre on the Boulevard du Temple in Paris, which opened in 1769. For some years it was restricted to performances of puppet shows and children's theatre; after the Revolution, however, it became a popular venue for melodrama. It was then burnt down (1822) and rebuilt in the Boulevard Saint-Martin, where further melodramas – especially those of Dumas *père* and Hugo – were highly successful. It was finally demolished in 1971.

Ameipsas (5th century BC) Greek playwright, who wrote a number of examples of Old Comedy. He is known to have defeated Aristophanes in a contest in 414 BC and to have ridiculed Socrates in another of his plays. Fragments of his work survive.

American Academy of Dramatic Arts A leading US drama school, founded in New York in 1884. Originally called the Lyceum Theatre School of Acting, it offers a Junior and selective Senior Course for promising actors and is now linked to the University of the State of New York.

American Actors' Equity Association A trade union for professional actors founded in 1913. It is affiliated to the American Federation of Labor and has done much to protect performers' interests and secure improvements in pay.

American Company A US theatre company, which was assembled in Charleston under David Douglass in 1763–64 and comprised former members of the elder Hallam's troupe. Successively managed by John Henry and Lewis Hallam (in partnership), Hodgkinson, and lastly – from 1796 – Dunlop, the company was housed at the John Street Theatre and – from 1798 – the Park Theatre. The elder Joseph Jefferson was among its distinguished players between 1795 and 1803. Presenting a wide range of successful productions the group was rivalled only by Wignell's company in Philadelphia and was the first professional US company to stage a play by an American – Thomas Godfrey's *The Prince of Parthia*. It was disbanded in 1805.

American Conservatory Theatre A theatre in Geary Street, San Francisco, which opened in 1910 as the Columbia. In the 1920s it was known as both the Wilkes and the Lurie and, in 1928, was renamed the Geary Theatre. Since 1967 the theatre, which seats 1456, has housed the American Conservatory Theatre Company, which opened with a production of Molière's *Tartuffe*. It is currently the largest and most important regional theatre in the US, producing both classical and modern plays; since 1978 the company has offered a master's degree in acting.

American Dream, The A satirical play by Edward *Albee. First performance: New York, 1961. The play reveals the destructive force of the dishonesty that he perceives beneath the superficial harmony of middle-class US family life.

American Laboratory Theatre A drama school and production company founded in New York in the 1920s by **Richard Boleslavsky** (1889–1937) and **Maria Ouspenskaya** (1876–1949) of the Moscow Art Theatre. The group became the most important channel for the communication of Stanislavsky's ideas in the US and included amongst its pupils Lee Strasberg and Harold Clurman.

American Museum A theatre on Broadway, New York, which was originally opened as a museum by Phineas Taylor Barnum in 1841. It became a theatre in 1849 with its own company and, refurbished in 1850, reopened with Sedley-Smith's melodrama *The Drunkard.* Sold by Barnum in 1855 but under his management again from 1860, it was used to present his shows of extraordinary phenomena until 1865 when it burnt down. Later that year Barnum opened his **New American Museum** also on Broadway in what was formerly the Chinese Rooms, which sometimes staged plays. It burnt down in 1868 during a performance of Harriet Beecher Stowe's *Uncle Tom's Cabin.*

American Music Hall *See* American Theatre.

American National Theatre and Academy (ANTA) A Connecticut-based theatre organization founded in 1935. Organized and conducted entirely by its members, it became the US centre of the International Theatre Institute in 1948 and, two years later, took over the Guild Theatre – renaming it the Anta Theatre – as a venue for experimental drama. It also provided the Washington Square Theatre for Vivian Beaumont's company (1963) and, in 1968, under the National Council on the Arts, became a centre for non-profit-making theatre groups.

American Negro Theatre A theatre organization founded in 1940 in consultation with the writer Abram Hill. The group produced plays on Broadway and in London and Europe, its greatest success being Philip Yordan's *Anna Lucasta* (1944); it ceased operations in the mid-1950s.

American Opera House *See* Chatham Theatre.

American Place Theatre A theatre founded in New York in 1971 for a company set up in 1964 by Wynn Handman and Sidney Lanier, the pastor of St Clement's Church where the company initially performed. In 1971 an experimental theatre group, Sub-Plot, was also established; important productions at the theatre have included Sam Shepard's *Killer's Head* (1975) and *Action* (1975).

American Repertory Theatre *See* Brustein, Robert; Crawford, Cheryl; Le Gallienne, Eva; Webster, Margaret.

American Shakespeare Theatre A theatre in Stratford, Connecticut, which is the home of a celebrated annual summer festival. Originally called the American Shakespeare Festival Theatre, it seats 1534 and opened in 1955 with *Julius Caesar*; its octagonal design echoes that of the Elizabethan theatre. Such stars as Christopher Plummer, Katharine Hepburn, and James Earl Jones have appeared there in plays by Shakespeare, Chekhov, and Tennessee Williams among others; recent triumphs have included Plummer and Jones as Iago and Othello (1981).

American Theatre A theatre on West 42nd Street, New York, that opened in 1893 with Pettit and Augustus Harris's *The Prodigal Daughter*. In 1908 the name was changed to the **American Music Hall** and in 1929 it became a burlesque house. The theatre was demolished after a fire in 1932 but another of the same name was opened two years later on East 55th Street with a production of Sedley-Smith's *The Drunkard*. *See also* Chambers Street Theatre.

American Theatre Association (ATA) A US theatre organization, which was formerly the American Educational Theatre Association. It supports educational and noncommercial theatre in over 2000 drama departments in US colleges and universities.

American Theatrical Commonwealth Company *See* Ludlow, Noah; Smith, Sol.

amphitheatre A circular, semicircular, or elliptical auditorium surrounded by raised seating, which was developed in ancient times originally as a venue for gladitorial contests and similar events, but later for theatrical performances. The Colosseum in Rome, built by 80 AD, could seat 87 000 people.

Amphitruo A comedy by *Plautus. First performance: date unknown. The play is remarkable for its parody of mythological characters and inspired imitations by Molière, Dryden, Giraudoux, and others.

Amphitryon 38 A play by Jean *Giraudoux. First performance: Paris, 1929. It was adapted for the English stage by S N *Behrman and opened in London in 1938. The play is based on the Greek legend of the seduction of Alcmena by Jupiter; Giraudoux claimed his to be the 38th version of the legend – hence the title.

Anatomist, The A play by James *Bridie. First performance: Edinburgh, 1930. Concerning the story of the bodysnatchers Burke and Hare, it established the author as a leading British playwright.

Ancey, Georges (Georges Mathevon de Curnieu; 1860–1917) French playwright, born in Paris. His explicit and bitter comedies (*comédies rosses*) in the style of Henry Becque, including *Les Inséparables* (1889) and *L'Écoles des veufs* (1889), were produced at the Théâtre-Libre by Antoine, but are not now very popular.

Anderson, John Murray (1886–1954) Canadian-born director, author, and lyricist, who contributed to the development of revue and musical comedy in the US. He was involved with the eight editions of the *Greenwich Village Follies*, which began in 1919. He went on to produce and stage musical comedies and revues including Ziegfeld's *Follies*.

Anderson, Dame Judith (Frances Margaret Anderson-Anderson; 1898-) Australian actress, who made her first stage appearance in Sydney in 1915. In 1917 she went to the US, having her first big success in 1924 in Martin Brown's *Cobra*. Subsequently she won acclaim in plays by O'Neill and Pirandello and as Gertrude to Gielgud's Hamlet (1936); other roles included Lady Macbeth opposite Laurence Olivier (1937), Medea (1947), Madame Arkadina in *The Seagull* (1960), and Hamlet (1970).

Anderson, Lindsay (Gordon) (1923-) British director and theatre critic, who first attracted attention while at the Royal Court Theatre, which he joined in 1957. There he designed realistic productions of plays by Arden and other contemporary playwrights, including Keith Waterhouse and David Storey; he has also worked at the National Theatre and the Chichester Festival Theatre as well as having a successful career as a film director. Notable stage productions have included *Serjeant Musgrave's Dance* (1959) and *Home* (1970); more recent successes include Philip Barry's *Holiday* (1987).

Anderson, Maxwell (1888–1959) US playwright whose works, many of which were written partly in verse, reflect his contention that great drama relies upon great poetry. His first play, *White Desert* (1923), was followed by one of Anderson's more successful plays, *What Price Glory?* (1924). Written in collaboration with Lawrence Stalling, the play focused on a soldier in action during World War II. His 'serious comedy' *Saturday's Children* (1927) also met with great success. After *Night Over Taos* (1932) and *Mary Queen of Scots* (1933), he wrote *Both Your Houses* (1933), a play attacking political corruption that won a Pulitzer Prize. Other plays include *Winterset* (1936), *Key Largo* (1939), and *Anne of the Thousand Days* (1948).

Anderson, Miles (1947-) British actor, whose many appearances for the Royal Shakespeare Company have included Poins in *Henry IV Part I*, Orsino in *Twelfth*

Night, and Eilif in Brecht's *Mother Courage*. In 1982 he became the first man to play the part of Peter Pan. At Stratford again in 1988 he played the title role in *Macbeth* and Dorimant in Etherege's *The Man of Mode*.

Anderson, Robert Woodruff (1917-) US playwright, who began his theatrical career while at Harvard. While serving in the US Naval Reserve his play *Come Marching Home* (1945) won critical acclaim. Many of his later plays deal with family relationships; they include *Tea and Sympathy* (1953), *Silent Night, Lonely Night* (1959), *I Never Sang for My Father* (1968), *Solitaire / Double Solitaire* (1971), and *Free and Clear* (1981).

Andreini, Francesco (1548–1624) Italian actor-manager and playwright, who founded and led the Gelosi *commedia dell'arte* company. As an actor he appeared as young lovers with Flamineo Scala's company; later he excelled as Il Capitano. Under him the Gelosi visited France several times between 1571 and 1604.

His wife, **Isabella Andreini** (Isabella Canali; 1562–1604), became the leading actress with the Gelosi company, which she helped to found. Formerly with Scala's company, she was the subject of great adulation both for her acting and for her poetry. Upon her early death, her husband retired from the stage.

Their son, **Giovann Battista Andreini** (c. 1579–1654), also played *commedia dell'arte* roles and was probably one of the cofounders of the Fedeli troupe. Popularly known as **Lelio**, he subsequently toured Italy and visited Paris; he was also the author of several plays, including *L'Adamo* (1613) and *La Centaura* (1622).

Andrews, Harry (Fleetwood) (1911-) British actor, who appeared at the Liverpool Playhouse before coming to London as Tybalt in *Romeo and Juliet* (1935) and accompanying Gielgud to New York in the following year. Subsequently he played numerous classical parts at the Old Vic and at Stratford as well as the title role in Bond's *Lear* at the Royal Court in 1971. His few appearances in other modern plays include Casanova in Tennessee Williams's *Camino Real* (1957), Allenby in Rattigan's *Ross* (1960), and the General in Osborne's *A Patriot for Me* (1983).

Andreyev, Leonid (Nikolaivich) (1871–1919) Russian novelist and playwright, who was a friend of Gorky and enjoyed considerable success with a number of pessimistic dramas before the Revolution of 1917. *Life of Man* (1906) and *He Who Gets Slapped* (1914) won him considerable popularity; after the Revolution, however, he fell from official favour and died in exile.

Androcles and the Lion A play for children by G B *Shaw. First performance: Berlin, 1912. Androcles, a kindly and witty Greek slave, removes a thorn from a lion's paw; subsequently the animal spares him when he is thrown to the lions in the Colosseum.

Andromaque A tragedy by Jean *Racine. First performance: Paris, 1667, with Racine's mistress Mlle Du Parc in the title role. The play is set at the end of the Trojan War: Hector's widow Andromaque, forced to marry Pyrrhus, arouses the jealousy of Hermione, who has Pyrrhus killed and then commits suicide over his body.

Andronicus, Lucius Livius (c. 284 BC–c. 204 BC) Roman playwright, who was the first great writer of Latin drama and poetry. Originally a slave, he produced a translation of a Greek play for the Ludi Romani (*see ludi scaenici*) in 240 BC (the first dramatic performance to be given in Rome), after which he wrote further plays based on Greek originals, usually competing with Naevius. Of his nine tragedies and three comedies only fragments survive.

angel *See* impresario.

Angel, Edward (fl. 1660–73) English actor, who was engaged as a boy by John Rhodes. Later, under Davenant at the Dorset Garden Theatre, he was highly acclaimed as a low comedian. Wycherley describes him as "a good fool" in *The Gentleman Dancing Master* (1671).

Anglin, Margaret (1876–1958) US actress, born in Canada, who began her career under Charles Frohman in 1894. She attracted attention in Rostand's *Cyrano de Bergerac* (1898) and subsequently in plays by Henry Arthur Jones, Shaw, and Dumas *fils*, as well as in numerous classical works and in Shakespearean roles.

animal impersonator An actor or other performer who dresses as an animal, thus following in a tradition that dates from the earliest primitive rituals and the accompanying animal sacrifices. Examples in folk theatre of such impersonation include the *hobby horse of the mummers' play and the Mascarade and the reindeer of the *Horn Dance. In the classical theatre Aristophanes made considerable comic use of animal impersonation, while later instances have included the cats, cows, and horses of English pantomime.

Animation Culturelles, Centres d' *See Décentralisation Dramatique.*

Anna Christie A play by Eugene *O'Neill that was possibly influenced by Theodore Dreiser's *Sister Carrie* (1900). First performance: New York, 1921. The plot follows Anna's descent into prostitution and her eventual return to her father; she then falls in love with an Irish stoker who deserts her when he learns of her past.

Annie Get Your Gun A musical by Herbert and Dorothy Fields that is based on the life of the sharpshooter Annie *Oakley.

First performance: New York, 1946. The music and lyrics by Irving *Berlin include some of his most popular songs, including 'There's No Business Like Show Business' and 'Anything You Can Do I Can Do Better'. Ethel Merman played the title role in the original production.

Annunzio, Gabriele D' *See* D'Annunzio, Gabriele.

Anouilh, Jean(-Marie-Lucien-Pierre) (1910–87) French playwright, born in Bordeaux, who went into the theatre in 1931, becoming secretary to Louis Jouvet. He made his name with *Le Voyageur sans bagage*; after World War II, helped by the success of *Antigone*, his popularity spread to the English-speaking world.

Anouilh's plays are conventionally divided into the light *pièces roses*, the melancholy *pièces noires*, the witty *pièces brillantes*, the bitter *pièces grinçantes*, and the historical *pièces costumées*. Recurring themes include the loss of innocence, the relationship between reality and make-believe, and the inevitability of compromise. His later works became increasingly whimsical in nature.
Principal works:
L'Hermine: 1932; translated as *The Ermine*.
Le Voyageur sans bagage: 1937; translated as *The *Traveller Without Luggage*.
La Sauvage: 1938; translated as *The Restless Heart*.
Le Bal des voleurs: 1938; translated as *Thieves' Carnival*.
Léocadia: 1940; translated as *Time Remembered*.
Le Rendez-vous de Senlis: 1941; translated as *Dinner With the Family*.
Eurydice: 1942; translated as *Point of Departure* (or *Legend of Lovers*).
Antigone: 1944.
L'Invitation au château: 1947; translated as *Ring Round the Moon*.
Ardèle ou la Marguerite: 1948.
La Répétition ou l'Amour puni: 1950; translated as *The Rehearsal*.

La Valse des toréadors: 1952; translated as
The *Waltz of the Toreadors.
Médée: 1953; translated as *Medea*.
L'Alouette: 1953; translated as *The *Lark*.
Pauvre Bitos, ou le Dîner de têtes: 1956;
translated as *Poor Bitos*.
Becket, ou L'Honneur de Dieu: 1959; trans-
lated as **Becket, or the Honour of God*.
Le Nombril: 1981; translated as *The Navel*.

Ansky (Solomon Zainwil Rappoport; 1863–
1920) Jewish ethnologist and man of letters,
born in the USSR. Ansky's writings include
folk and Hasidic tales and poetry, but he is
remembered for the play *The Dybbuk, or between Two Worlds* (1920), which draws its
supernatural theme of possession from
Hasidic doctrine, and provided a major success for the Vilna Troupe and the Habimah
company in Moscow.

Anspacher Theatre *See* Public Theatre.

ANTA *See* American National Theatre and
Academy.

Anta Theatre A theatre on West 52nd
Street, between Broadway and Eighth Avenue in New York, which was built for the
Theatre Guild and opened in 1925 as the
Guild Theatre with a production of Shaw's
Caesar and Cleopatra. In 1950 the theatre
was taken over as a venue for experimental
drama by the American National Theatre
and Academy and renamed the Anta Playhouse. In 1954 the theatre's name was
changed to the Anta Theatre and, three
years later, it began housing commercial
productions. It still houses the ANTA and
the US branch of the International Theatre
Institute.

Anthony Street Theatre A theatre in
Worth Street, New York, which opened as
the Olympic Theatre in 1812 with a Philadelphian company headed by Mrs
Melmoth and Thomas Twaits. The mixed
programme included circus acts as well as

straight drama: the US premiere of M G
Lewis's *Timour the Tartar* took place there
the same year. In 1813, after refurbishment,
the theatre was reopened as the Anthony
Street Theatre with a new company including Mrs Beaumont and Placide. Successive
managements during 1814 renamed the
theatre the **Commonwealth Theatre** and later
the **Pavilion Theatre**. The theatre's popularity peaked in 1820 when Edmund Kean
made his first appearance in New York as
Richard III; after Kean's company left for
the Park Theatre in 1821 the Anthony
Street Theatre was demolished.

Antigone A tragedy by *Sophocles. First
performance: Athens, c. 442 BC. Set against
a background of war, the play concentrates
upon the impact of the central character's
death and inspired imitations by numerous
subsequent writers, including *Anouilh. In
Anouilh's version Antigone is depicted as a
martyr to purity while Creon rejects the
guilt suffered by his counterpart in Sophocles's play.

anti-masque A brief interlude, usually a
dance, performed before or during masques
in the early 17th century. The first such
piece, intended as a contrast to the main
performance, was presented by Jonson in
1609.

Antoine, André (1858–1943) French actor,
director, and theatre manager, who founded
the *Théâtre Libre in Paris in 1887 to promote naturalistic drama. Using mostly amateur actors, he pioneered the naturalistic
movement in France and fostered numerous
innovations in set design and acting, using
real furniture and properties. He presented
French premieres of works by such authors
as Ibsen, Strindberg, Tolstoy, and
Hauptmann. The Théâtre Libre closed in
1894, after which Antoine founded his own
Théâtre Antoine in 1897 then went on to
become director of the Odéon, where he
presented many more influential but finan-

cially unsuccessful dramas between 1903 and 1916. Among those profoundly influenced by him were Jacques Copeau, Otto Brahm, and Grein.

Antonelli, Luigi (1882–1942) Italian playwright, who became a leading exponent of the *teatro del grottesco*. His best-known plays, which express a generally gloomy view of life, include *L'Uomo che incontrò se stesso* (The Man Who Met Himself; 1918), *L'Isola delle scimmie* (The Island of Monkeys; 1922), *La bottega dei sogni* (The Dream Shop; 1927), and *Il maestro* (1933).

Antony and Cleopatra A tragedy by William *Shakespeare, written 1607. First performance: c. 1607. Based upon the writings of Plutarch, the play traces the history of the doomed lovers Antony and Cleopatra and contains some of the most highly-praised love poetry in Shakespeare's dramatic works. Dryden's *All for Love* displaced Shakespeare's play for many years; it was not until 1849 that the latter was revived in its original form.

Anvil Productions *See* Oxford Playhouse.

Anything Goes A musical written by Guy *Bolton, P G *Wodehouse, Howard *Lindsay, and Russel *Crouse. First performance: New York, 1934. A lighthearted story about a series of romances on a steamliner, it scored a major hit with music by Cole *Porter and with Ethel Merman in the leading role.

Anzengruber, Ludwig (1839–89) Austrian playwright and novelist, who became famous for his realistic depictions of life in peasant communities. Most of his plays, in which he made some attempt to represent peasant dialect, were witty comedies – notably *Die Kreuzlschreiber* (1872) and *Der Doppelselbstmord* (1876); others included the antireligious drama *Der Pfarrer von Kirchfeld* (1870), the tragedy *Der Meineidbauer* (1871), and the problem play *Das vierte Gebot* (1877).

Apollodorus of Carystos (3rd century BC) Greek playwright, author of several examples of New Comedy. Of his works, which influenced Terence, only fragments survive.

Apollo Theatre The third oldest theatre in London's Shaftesbury Avenue, opened in 1901. Early successes included *The Girl from Kays* (1902), *Véronique* (1904), and *Tom Jones* (1907), in which Cicely Courtneidge made her London debut. In 1908 the Apollo became the home of the popular *Pélissier Follies*. In 1913 the policy of musical comedy was discontinued and since that date stage play successes have included Ian Hay's *Tilly of Bloomsbury* (1919) and *Housemaster* (1936), a series of plays (including *Hyde Park Corner*, *Espionage*, *The Fugitives*, and *London After Dark*) written by Walter Hackett for his actress wife Marion Lorne in the years 1934–37, and Patrick Hamilton's *Gaslight* (1939). Outstanding wartime productions were Rattigan's *Flare Path* (1942) and Coward's *Private Lives* (1944). In the post-war period, John Dighton's farce *The Happiest Days of Your Life* ran for 605 performances (1948), Hugh Hastings's *Seagulls Over Sorrento* (1950) for 1551 performances, and Marc Camoletti's *Boeing, Boeing* (1962) for 2035 performances. Now under the management of Stoll Moss Theatres, the Apollo's recent productions have included Peter Shaffer's *Lettice and Lovage* (1987), starring Maggie Smith, and Alfred Uhry's *Driving Miss Daisy* (1988).

The **Apollo Theatre** on 42nd Street, between Seventh and Eighth avenues in New York, opened in 1910 as the **Bryant Theatre** and was used for films and vaudeville. In 1920 it became the Apollo Theatre, housing musical comedies until 1924. From 1924 to 1931, George White's *Scandals* were staged there; subsequently, in 1933, it was turned into a cinema once more.

Apollo Victoria Theatre A theatre in Wilton Road, London, which opened in 1980 as a concert hall. Formerly a cinema, it housed a revival of *The Sound of Music* in 1981 and subsequently staged Lloyd Webber's *Starlight Express* (1984).

Appia, Adolphe (1862–1928) Swiss stage designer, who did much to develop staging techniques in the early 20th century. He was particularly noted for his use of lighting to suggest three-dimensional scenery and for his settings for the plays of Shaw and Ibsen, as described in his treatise *Die Musik und die Inscenierung* (1899).

Apple Cart, The A political comedy by G B *Shaw. First performance: Warsaw, 1929. Set in England in the last quarter of the 20th century, the play analyzes the relationship between monarchy and democracy and raises questions about political morality. The more immediate target of the play was allegedly Ramsay MacDonald's socialist government.

apron That part of the stage in front of the proscenium arch, often considerably enlarged in modern theatres. In some theatres the apron, also called the **forestage**, can be extended over the pit.

Aquarium Theatre *See* Imperial Theatre.

aquatic drama A theatrical entertainment, developed in the circuses of Paris, in which much, or all, of the action takes place on water. During the 18th and 19th centuries many major theatres in London were altered to facilitate the performance of such dramas, including Drury Lane, Covent Garden, and Sadler's Wells.

Aquatic Theatre *See* Sadler's Wells Theatre.

Arbuzov, Alexei Nikolayevich (1908–) Soviet playwright, whose works have also been performed in the West. He began writing in the 1920s and achieved his first notable success with *Tanya* (1939). Among his works which have been produced outside the USSR are *It Happened In Irkutsk* (1959), a study of small-town life that was staged in Paris in 1961 and in Sheffield in 1967, and *The Promise* (1965), which was seen in London and New York. *Old World* was premiered in Poland in 1975 and a year later was performed by the Royal Shakespeare Company; it was then produced in Paris and New York.

arc *See* carbon arc spotlight.

Archer, William (1856–1924) British critic and playwright, born in Scotland. In London from 1879 he was dramatic critic successively for *Figaro*, *The World*, *The Tribune*, *The Nation*, and *The Star*. His translation of *Samfundets Støtter* as *The Pillars of Society* was the first version of one of Ibsen's plays to be performed in England (1880); translations of all of Ibsen's other plays followed. His own melodrama *The Green Goddess* had a long run at the St James's Theatre in 1921.

Archetringle A festival of folk theatre that takes place annually on New Year's Eve at Laupen in Switzerland. It culminates in a mock battle between masked performers.

Arch Street Theatre A theatre in Philadelphia, which was opened by William B Wood in 1828. It survived the financial crisis of 1829, brought about by competition from other theatres in the city, and, under Mrs John Drew from 1860 to 1892, became a great success both commercially and artistically.

Arden, John (1930–) British playwright, who emerged as a significant writer for the theatre after becoming associated with the Royal Court Theatre in the 1950s. *Live Like Pigs* (1958) and other early works established his reputation for work much influenced by the theatre of Brecht and culminated in the much-acclaimed drama *Serjeant Musgrave's Dance* (1959), which nonetheless failed in its initial production. Subsequent plays – including *The Happy Haven* (1960), *The Workhouse Donkey* (1963), *Armstrong's Last Goodnight* (1964), and *Left-Handed Liberty* (1965) – aroused less interest. He has also written several plays (notably *The Island of the Mighty* in 1972) in collaboration with his wife, **Margaretta (Ruth) D'Arcy**; since their acrimonious breakup with the Royal Shakespeare Company in 1972 they have concentrated upon producing strongly Marxist drama with amateur groups.

Arden of Faversham Elizabethan prose tragedy, written c. 1592. First performance: c. 1592. Based on a murder case of 1551, its author is unknown, but it has been attributed to Thomas *Kyd and, incorrectly, to Shakespeare.

arena An open acting area in the centre of an auditorium, as used in theatre-in-the-round.

Arena Stage A theatre in Washington DC, which was designed by Harry Weise in 1961 as a theatre-in-the-round. The theatre opened with a production of Brecht's *The Caucasian Chalk Circle*; the resident company has established a strong reputation with both modern and classic drama. Also based there is the community theatre group **Living Stage**.

Arena Theatre A small flexible auditorium attached to the Sherman Theatre in Cardiff, Wales. Opened in 1973 and seating 200, it is used as a venue for both experimental professional companies and amateurs.

Aretino, Pietro (1492–1556) Italian poet, prose writer, and playwright, author of a number of major works in the *commedia erudita* tradition. Although he wrote one good tragedy, *Orazio* (1546), he was better known for his five comedies, of which the most successful was *La Cortigiana* (1526).

Argent, Théâtre de l'Hôtel d' The second oldest theatre in Paris, opened in 1598 under licence from the Confrérie de la Passion, who ran the rival Théâtre de l'Hôtel de Bourgogne. The theatre was run by the father of Marie Venier, who herself appeared there as the leading lady opposite her husband. In 1610 all the Paris theatres were deserted following the assassination of Henry IV; when the actors returned a new company under Lenoir and Montdory took over the Hôtel d'Argent, remaining there until 1634, when the Théâtre du *Marais opened.

Argyll Rooms *See* Trocadero Palace of Varieties.

Arion of Lesbos (c. 625 BC–585 BC) Greek poet and musician, author of the earliest Greek verse drama. His works helped to establish the dithyramb and the satyr-play as serious literary forms. Legend has it that he escaped from pirates by being carried to safety by a dolphin, which was entranced by his singing.

Ariosto, Lodovico (1474–1533) Italian poet and playwright, author of the epic poem *Orlando Furioso*. He was the author of four major comedies of the *commedia erudita* tradition, which were performed under the patronage of the d'Este family in a theatre in Ferrara with scenery designed by Raphael. They included *La Cassaria* (1508) and *I suppositi* (1509), which subsequently influenced Shakespeare's *The Taming of the Shrew*.

Aristophanes (c. 448 BC–380 BC) Greek playwright, author of the only intact surviving examples of *Old Comedy. Of the 11 of his 40 or so plays that are still in existence, the earlier works observe all the conventions of the lively and outspoken satirical drama of the time, while the later ones, notably *Ecclesiazousae* and *Plutus*, are written in the more restrained style of *Middle Comedy. The early plays usually took their titles from the role played by the disguised chorus and were based on little more than a skeleton plot, satirizing such targets as contemporary politicians, fellow-playwrights, and foreigners. The more subdued later works probably reflected the increasingly unsettled political atmosphere in Athens at that time. Largely ignored for many years, many of his plays have been successfully revived in the 20th century.

Principal works:

*The *Acharnians*: 425 BC.

The Knights: 424 BC.

*The *Clouds*: 423 BC.

The Wasps: 422 BC.

*The *Peace*: 421 BC.

*The *Birds*: 414 BC.

**Lysistrata*: 411 BC.

Thesmaphoriazousae: 410 BC.

*The *Frogs*: 405 BC.

Ecclesiazousae: 392 BC.

Plutus: 388 BC.

Aristotle (384 BC–322 BC) Greek philosopher, scientist, and theatre critic, whose theoretical writings represent a detailed analysis of certain types of contemporary drama. Although his writings on comedy are now lost, his theories upon tragedy – laid down in the *Poetics* (c. 330 BC) – countered those of Plato and Socrates and attempted to define the purpose and form of such drama, as exemplified for him in the plays of Sophocles. In order to achieve the ultimate aim of *catharsis*, he approved the use of extreme situations and the manipulation of the audience's emotions; this was usually to be realized through the inevitable downfall of the hero as the consequence of some tragic mistake. In the 17th and 18th centuries, when playwrights began to look to classical

works for guidance as to the function and structure of tragedy, Aristotle's theories were further developed into the concept of the three *unities.

Arlecchino A character of the *commedia dell'arte*, capable of both great stupidity and cunning, who gradually evolved from being one of the *zanni* into the more refined English *Harlequin. He was conventionally dressed in a multi-coloured patched suit and wore a small black mask; in the French tradition he was known as Arlequin. Noted interpreters of the role, which required some skill as an acrobat and dancer, included Tristano Martinelli and Giuseppe Biancolelli.

Arliss, George (Augustus George Andrews; 1868–1946) British actor, who became a popular film actor. His first stage success was in *The Second Mrs Tanqueray* (1901), in which play he went to the US where he remained for 20 years, playing many leading roles. Back in London he spent over a year in Archer's *The Green Goddess* (1921), making his last stage appearance in 1928 as Shylock in New York.

Armin, Robert (c. 1568–c. 1611) British actor and writer, who began as a pupil of Tarleton and probably made his debut as a clown at the Globe. In 1610 he was in the first production of *The Alchemist*; in the 1623 Folio he was also listed as one of the actors in Shakespeare's plays. His own play *The Two Maids of More Clacke* was produced in 1609.

Arms and the Man A play by G B *Shaw. First performance: London, 1894. A mercenary soldier, Bluntschli, breaks into the bedroom of Raina Petkoff and disrupts her idyllic romance with Sergius Saranov. The play mocks the idealism of both love and war. It was later made into a musical by Oscar Straus, as *The Chocolate Soldier*.

Armstrong, William (1882–1952) British actor and director, who first appeared at Stratford-upon-Avon in 1908, then toured widely and worked in several repertory companies before becoming director and producer at the Liverpool Playhouse (1922). When the theatre closed in 1941, he directed several London productions before returning to repertory at Birmingham in 1945 under Barry Jackson.

Arnaud, Yvonne Germaine (1892–1958) French actress, who became one of the leading actresses upon the London stage. After training as a pianist as a child, she made her debut in musical comedy in 1911 at the Adelphi Theatre and won immediate acclaim. Subsequently she triumphed in further musical comedies and farces by Will Evans and Ben Travers among others. Her greatest performances included Mrs Pepys in Fagan's *And So To Bed* (1926) and Mrs Frail in Congreve's *Love for Love* (1943). The Yvonne Arnaud Theatre was opened in 1965 in Guildford, where she lived.

Arne, Susanna Maria (1714–66) British actress and singer. Her career as a tragic actress began in 1736, but was immediately interrupted by a scandal. This was the result of the machinations of her husband Theophilus *Cibber, who had forced her into an affair with her friend William Sloper and then brought an action against him. Eventually she returned to the stage in Dublin, and from then on divided her time between Drury Lane and Covent Garden.

Arnold, Matthew (1822–88) British poet and theatre critic, son of the headmaster of Rugby School. He stressed the cultural importance of theatre and wrote dramatic criticism for the *Pall Mall Gazette*. He also wrote the poetic dramas *Empedocles on Etna* (1852) and *Merope* (1858).

Aronson, Boris (1900–80) Russian-born stage designer, who left Kiev to come to New York in 1923. A year later he designed his first stage production, *Day and Night* (1924), for the Unser Theatre in the Bronx. His innovations included the use of projections in suggesting scenery. Among the shows he designed scenery for were *Fiddler on the Roof* (1964), *Cabaret* (1966), *Company* (1970), *Follies* (1971), and *Pacific Overtures* (1976).

Arrabal, Fernando (1932–) Spanish-born French playwright, who went to Paris in 1955, publishing his first collection of plays in 1958. Associated with the Theatre of the Absurd, Arrabal labelled his works '*Théâtre Panique*'; often blasphemous (*La Cimetière des voitures* parodies the Crucifixion), they depict a fantasy world of horror and betrayal. Childhood memories of the Spanish Civil War dominate the plays: *Et ils passèrent des menottes aux fleurs*, which was banned in 1969, attacks political oppression. His more experimental works include *Orchéstration théâtrale* (1959), which has no dialogue at all.

Principal works:

Pique-nique en campagne: 1959; translated as *Picnic on the Battlefield*.

Fando et Lis: 1961; translated as *Fando and Lis*.

La Cimetière des voitures: 1966; translated as *The Car Cemetery*.

L'Architecte et l'empereur d'Assyrie: 1967; translated as *The Architect and the Emperor of Assyria*.

Et ils passèrent des menottes aux fleurs: 1969; translated as *And They Put Handcuffs on the Flowers*.

Le Jardin des délices: 1969.

La Ballade du train fantôme: 1974.

Baal Babylone: 1980.

Arsenic and Old Lace A comedy-thriller by Joseph Kesselring. First performance: New York, 1941. The plot revolves around two old ladies who invite men to their home in Brooklyn, only to poison them with elderberry wine. The bodies are quietly buried by their brother, who thinks he is Teddy Roosevelt, until a homicidal nephew arrives with his own corpse to conceal. The play was filmed by Frank Capra in 1942.

Art, Théâtre d' A French theatre, founded by Paul Fort in 1891 for the performance of poetic drama. In 1893 it was taken over by Lugné-Poë and renamed the **Théâtre de l'Oeuvre**.

Artaud, Antonin (1896–1948) French actor, director, poet, and playwright, born in Marseilles. Artaud entered the theatre as an actor in the early 1920s and became involved with the Surrealist movement. With the Théâtre Alfred Jarry, which he cofounded with Roger Vitrac, he produced works by Strindberg, Vitrac, and himself. Artaud's own plays made little impact (*Les Cenci* (1935) had only a fortnight's run); his major contribution to the world of drama was his conception of the Theatre of *Cruelty, expounded in the essays collected in *Le Théâtre et son double* (1938; *The Theatre and Its Double*, 1958). Despite the fact that he spent the years between 1937 and 1946 in various psychiatric hospitals, Artaud profoundly influenced many subsequent directors, including Barrault, Blin, and Peter Brook.

Artists of Dionysus Organizations of actors and other members of the theatre in ancient Greece. Dating from the 4th century BC, these guilds ruled on questions relating to performers' wages and acted as governing bodies for the profession as a whole.

Arts Council of Great Britain The major funding body for the arts in Great Britain. Established in 1946 by Royal Charter, it evolved from the earlier **Council for the Encouragement of Music and the Arts** (CEMA) and aims to promote high standards in the arts and increase their accessibility throughout Britain (Northern Ireland has its own separate Arts Council). Receiving its grant directly from government, the council has contributed to the abolition of weekly repertory, the maintenance of relatively low-priced seats, the development of new writing, and investment in new buildings. In recent years most of its responsibility for small scale, community, and young people's theatre has been devolved to regional arts associations.

Arts Laboratory A theatre in Drury Lane, London, opened in 1968. Founded by Charles Marowitz and Jim Haynes, it was much used by a number of theatre companies, including the *Pip Simmons Theatre Group and other fringe theatre organizations before its closure in late 1969.

Arts Theatre A small theatre in Great Newport Street, London, established in 1927 for the staging of unlicensed and avant-garde plays. Seating 337 people, it began as a club theatre with a number of productions that subsequently transferred to major commercial venues before Alec *Clunes took over in 1942. One of its early successes was John Van Druten's *Young Woodley* (1928), a play banned by the Lord Chamberlain. Clunes (and then Campbell Williams) encouraged the performance there of new plays by such playwrights as Christopher Fry, Samuel Beckett, Jean Anouilh, Harold Pinter, and Edward Albee, memorable premieres including *Waiting for Godot* (1955) and *The Caretaker* (1960). The Royal Shakespeare Company took a six-month lease of the theatre for experimental drama (1962), after which (from 1967) the Unicorn Theatre of Caryl Jenner staged entertainments for children. More recent successes by visiting companies have included Stoppard's *Dirty Linen* (1976) and John Godber's *Teechers* (1988).

Asch, Sholom (1880–1957) Jewish novelist and playwright, born in Poland, who made an important contribution to Yiddish literature with such works as *Dos Schottl* (The

Village; 1904), a novel about the life of Jews in rural Poland. His best-known work, *Der Got fun Nikome* (The God of Vengeance; 1907), was a widely-performed play with a religious theme and was first produced by Reinhardt in Berlin.

Asche, Oscar (John Stanger Heiss; 1871–1936) British actor, manager, and playwright, born in Australia of Norwegian descent. He appeared in Benson's company and with Tree before assuming the management of Her Majesty's Theatre in 1902 and presenting numerous Shakespearean productions in which he frequently appeared himself. After creating Hajj in Knoblock's *Kismet* in 1911, he went on to write the popular fantasy **Chu Chin Chow* (1916). His plays *Mecca* (1920) and *Cairo* (1921) were, however, failures.

His wife, **Lily Brayton** (1876–1953), appeared alongside him in many productions.

Ashcroft, Dame Peggy (Edith Margaret Emily Ashcroft; 1907-) British actress, who first appeared at the Birmingham Repertory Theatre in 1926 as Margaret in Barrie's *Dear Brutus* and made her London debut in Feuchtwanger's *Jew Süss* at the Duke of York's Theatre in 1929. She was Desdemona to Paul Robeson's Othello in 1930 and subsequently played a series of Shakespearean heroines at the Old Vic. At the New Theatre she triumphed as Juliet in Gielgud's production in 1935 and as Nina in Komisarjevsky's production of *The Seagull* in 1936. She played leading roles in Gielgud's classical seasons at the Queen's Theatre (1939–40) and at the Haymarket (1944–45) and was a sensation as Hedda Gabler in 1954, which she played in London and Oslo. Her modern roles have included the title role in an adaptation of *The Heiress* (1949) by Henry James, Hester in Rattigan's *The Deep Blue Sea* (1952), and Miss Madrigal in Enid Bagnold's *The Chalk Garden* (1956). She was a founder member of the Royal Shakespeare Company, of which she later became a director, and has frequently appeared with them in Stratford and London, notably as Queen Margaret in *The Wars of the Roses* (1963–64). Her successes since then have included roles in Ibsen's *Ghosts* (1967) and *John Gabriel Borkman* (1975), Beckett's *Happy Days* (1975), Hellman's *Watch on the Rhine* (1980), and *All's Well that Ends Well* (1981).

Ashley, Elizabeth (1939-) US actress, who made her professional debut in 1959 as Louise in *Marcus in the High*. Subsequent celebrated roles have included Mollie Michaelson in *Take Her, She's Mine* (1961), Carrie Bratter in *Barefoot in the Park* (1963), and Margaret in *Cat on a Hot Tin Roof* (1974).

Ashwell, Lena (Lena Pocock; 1872–1957) British actress, who established her reputation in Arthur Jones's *Mrs Dane's Defence* (1900) and took over the Kingsway Theatre in 1907. During World War I she organized overseas companies; afterwards she produced new plays at the Century Theatre (later the Bijou Theatre) in Bayswater, including her own versions of *Crime and Punishment* and *Dr Jekyll and Mr Hyde*.

aside A line or, sometimes, a whole speech addressed by an actor directly to the audience rather than to his fellow-players, who are assumed not to be able to hear him.

ASM *See* stage manager.

Asolo State Theatre A theatre founded in Sarasota, Florida, which became the State Theatre of Florida with a fully professional repertory company in 1966. The resident company, which produces classics, modern plays, and musicals, grew out of the summer festival of 18th and 19th century comedies produced by the Division of Theatre at Florida State University in 1960. In 1973, Florida State University – in conjunction with the Asolo State Theatre – established a Conservatory of Acting which offers courses as part of a master's degree programme.

Asphaleian system An early mechanical system by means of which various parts of the stage floor might be raised or lowered. First developed in 1884 in Austria-Hungary, it was constructed largely of iron, thus reducing the risk of fire.

Assembly Theatre *See* Princess Theatre.

assistant stage manager *See* stage manager.

Association of Community Theatres (ACT) An organization of professional theatrical groups established in New Zealand during the 1970s. It includes the Court Theatre in Christchurch, the Centrepoint Theatre in Palmerston North, and the Fortune Theatre Company in Dunedin.

Astley's Amphitheatre A theatre established by a former cavalry officer, Philip Astley (1742–1814), as a forerunner of the modern circus. A noted rider himself, Astley staged equestrian dramas there as well as various acrobatic entertainments from 1769. The original building (the stage was uncovered until 1784) was based on Roman designs and was subsequently destroyed by fire a number of times before it emerged as the **Royal Amphitheatre of Arts** in 1804. Equestrian dramas, which remained popular under the management of Andrew Ducrow (1793–1848), were then alternated with melodrama until another fire in 1841; regular visitors included Charles Dickens. Rebuilt as Batty's Amphitheatre it was taken over by Dion Boucicault (as the **Theatre Royal, Westminster**) and saw premieres of plays by himself and Sir Walter Scott. Adah Isaacs Menken succeeded Boucicault with the highly successful *Mazeppa* by Lord Byron, after which the theatre was enlarged and reverted to its former use as a circus (renamed **Sanger's Grand National Amphitheatre**). It was demolished in 1895.

Another Astley Amphitheatre was opened in Paris in 1782.

Aston, Anthony (d. 1753) Irish actor, popularly known as **Matt Medley**. He became well known (as Tony Aston) whilst touring the English provinces presenting his *Medley*, a farrago of scenes taken from different plays. Earlier in his career he appeared at Drury Lane and was one of the first professional actors to perform in the US (c. 1703). He was also the author of the pamphlet *Lives of the Late Famous Actors and Actresses by Anthony, vulgo Tony, Aston* and several plays.

Astoria Theatre A theatre in Charing Cross Road, London, built as a cinema in 1927 and popularly known as the 'Jam Factory'. In 1977 it was adapted for the theatre and staged the musical *Elvis*. Under new management since July 1987, it is now a live music venue.

Astor Place Opera House A theatre off Broadway, New York, which opened in 1847. Between opera seasons its actors included Charlotte Cushman, Julia Dean, and George Vandenhoff. Its reputation suffered irrecoverable damage when the anti-British Astor Place riot (in which 22 people died) took place there in May 1849 as a result of the rivalry between Macready (who was appearing there) and the US actor Edwin Forrest. The theatre reopened later that year but its blighted reputation led to its final closure in 1850.

Astor Theatre A theatre on Broadway in New York, which opened in 1906 with *A Midsummer Night's Dream*. In 1913 George M Cohan's dramatization of Earl Bigger's novel *Seven Keys to Baldpate* was seen there. The theatre became a cinema in 1925.

As You Like It A comedy by William *Shakespeare, written c. 1599. First performance: date unknown. The play juxtaposes the two worlds of Frederick's court and the pastoral Arden; the plot revolves around four central couples and includes the enigmatic characters Jaques and Touchstone. Based on Thomas Lodge's *Rosalynde*, the play provided major roles for Macklin, Kitty Clive, Peg Woffington, Charles Kean, and Mrs Siddons among others.

ATA *See* American Theatre Association.

Atelier, Théâtre de l' A theatre close to the Montmartre area of Paris, founded in 1822. As the Théâtre des Élèves, it was originally a venue for melodrama and vaudeville and then a cinema before Charles Dullin took it over in 1922. Subsequently it became a focus of the avant-garde movement, with plays by Achard, Pirandello, and others; it was also recognized as a leading training ground for young actors. From 1940 André Barsacq (and later his son) continued to stage serious drama there.

atellana A form of early Roman *fabula*, named after the town of Atella, near Capua. With its stock of clown characters – Bucco, Dossennus, Maccus, Manducus, and Pappus – it was distinguished by its coarse humour and rustic settings and made extensive use of masks and disguises. Few scripts survive and the emphasis seems to have been upon improvisation; ultimately the *atellana* gave way to mime entertainments.

Athalie A tragedy by Jean *Racine. First performance: Versailles, 1691, by Madame de Maintenon's school for young ladies (for whom the play was written). The plot revolves around the Old Testament story of Athaliah, whose attempt to destroy the house of David is thwarted by the survival of Joash.

Athénée, Théâtre de l' A theatre in Paris, that first became well known (called the Athénée-Comique) as a venue for light entertainment, including melodrama. In 1934 Louis Jouvet transformed its reputation with numerous influential productions of serious drama until his death in 1951, after which it declined.

Athenian drama Greek theatre of the 4th and 5th centuries BC, sometimes referred to as the classical period. This era saw the evolution of both *tragedy and *comedy from choral lyrics and the rituals connected with Dionysus and the emergence through the various drama contests of the great tragic poets, *Aeschylus, *Sophocles, and *Euripides, and the comic poet *Aristophanes. Early tragedy and *Old Comedy tackled such universal issues as justice and suffering but gradually became more interested in character analysis and looser in structure, employing more actors and relying less upon the chorus. Rudimentary scenery and props were in use and towards the end of this period, which also saw the building of the first stone theatres, the rules of drama were codified by Aristotle and *Middle Comedy and *New Comedy developed, ultimately bridging the gap between Athenian and Roman drama. *See also* Hellenistic drama.

Atkins, Eileen (1934-) British actress, who started in repertory at Bangor in Ireland in 1952 before appearing at the Open Air Theatre, Stratford-upon-Avon, and Bristol. Subsequently she played Shakespearean leads with the Old Vic company and was highly acclaimed in Frank Marcus's *The Killing of Sister George* (1965) and as Elizabeth I in Bolt's *Vivat! Vivat Regina!* (1970). Other celebrated performances have included roles in the plays of T S Eliot, Marguerite Duras, G B Shaw, Christopher Fry, and Peter Nichols.

Atkins, Robert (1886–1972) British actor-manager, who first established himself as an excellent Shakespearean actor when engaged by Ben Greet at the Old Vic in 1915. Between 1920 and 1925 he proceeded to stage every Shakespearean play except for *Cymbeline* there. He also directed the first London production of *Peer Gynt*, founded the **Bankside Players,** directed at Stratford, and for over 30 years ran the Open Air Theatre, Regent's Park.

Atkinson, (Justin) Brooks (1894–1984) US theatre critic, who was the drama critic for the *New York Times* from 1926 to 1960. He received a Tony Award for distinguished achievement in the theatre and, upon his retirement, the Mansfield Theatre in New York was renamed the *Brooks Atkinson Theatre in his honour.

Atta, Titus Quintius (d. 77 BC) Roman playwright, author of plays in the *togata* tradition. Very little of his work survives; he was noted in his own time especially for his depiction of women.

Aubignac, François Hédelin, Abbé d' (1604–76) French critic and playwright, born in Paris. His *Pratique du théâtre* (1657; translated as *The Whole Art of the Stage*, 1684), commissioned by Cardinal de Richelieu, emphasizes the strict observance of the three unities. Aubignac also wrote critical commentaries on the works of Corneille and others.

Auckland Theatre Trust *See* Mercury Theatre.

Auden, W(ystan) H(ugh) (1907–73) British poet, who wrote several examples of poetic drama during the 1930s. His verse plays written in collaboration with Christopher Isherwood include *The Dog Beneath the Skin* (1935), *The Ascent of F6* (1936), and *On the Frontier* (1938); other dramatic contributions include opera libretti.

Audiberti, Jacques (1899–1965) French poet, novelist, and playwright, born in Antibes. He moved to Paris in 1925, becoming involved with the Surrealist movement; it was not until the mid-1940s, however, that he made his name as a playwright with such plays as *Quoat-Quoat* (1946), *Le Mal court* (1947), and *La Fourmi dans le corps* (1962). The next two decades saw the performance of almost 30 of his plays, which characteristically depict the conflict between good and evil against a background of the supernatural.

audition A competitive test at which an actor or other performer is invited to demonstrate his aptitude for a particular role, usually in the presence of the director of the planned production. Where the choice of actor is difficult, more than one audition may be held.

auditorium The area of a theatre in which the audience sits, formerly called the **auditory** or **spectatory** (in the 19th century). In the Greek open-air theatre the auditorium was usually cut into a hillside and consisted of a horseshoe of tiered stone or wooden seats rising up from the stage itself; such auditoriums held as many as 17 000 spectators and provided excellent acoustic effects. Roman theatres were based on fundamentally the same design, although the semicircular auditorium (or *cavea*), which was often elaborately decorated and sometimes equipped with an awning to shelter the audience, was usually specially built rather than incorporated into a natural feature. The colossal amphitheatres used for chariot racing and gladiatorial contests usually formed a complete circle.

When the theatrical tradition was revived during medieval times audiences generally stood in front of temporary stages or booths to watch a play, often moving from one small stage to another to follow the action. Such booth stages were also employed in oriental drama and in England eventually developed into the circular Elizabethan playhouse in imitation of the innyards used by travelling players.

The introduction of the proscenium arch in Italy during the Renaissance prompted the revival of the Greek horseshoe design, although elsewhere the conversion of tennis courts into theatres meant that many early auditoriums comprised deep rectangles. Court theatres, however, followed Italian models, with the addition of a Royal Box. In England and France typical auditoriums of the time consisted of tiered **galleries** overlooking a central area known as the **pit**, which was sometimes open to the sky and usually offered the cheapest seats.

During the 17th century features of the English and Italian traditions were combined, typical English auditoriums having rows of **boxes** (traditionally the most expensive seats in the house) along the side only with galleries above them and at the rear of a relatively plain auditorium. Seating for the most ostentatious members of the audience, wishing to be seen as much as to see, was also provided actually on stage, to the detriment of acting standards. Elsewhere in Europe, however, architects created increasingly ornate auditoriums and, by the 19th century, were adding impressive colonnades and porticos to the exterior as well in imitation of the opera houses.

The building of Richard Wagner's Opera House in Bayreuth in 1876 signalled a revolution in theatre design with his rejection of boxes and galleries in favour of a single raked **balcony** of seating facing the stage and austerity in matters of decoration. The orchestra was hidden and the auditorium darkened and a similar spirit of reform and simplicity has characterized auditoriums in the 20th century. This has also been combined, however, with a new experimentation so that the modern auditorium may range from the traditional plan of **orchestra pit** (where the musicians perform), **stalls** (or pit), a small number of boxes on either side, and then an arrangement of balconies or circles (often divided into the **dress circle** and **upper circle**) or galleries (the topmost of which is traditionally called the **gods**) to a single tier of seats or seating on all sides (as in theatre-in-the-round) or some other arrangement made possible by flexible staging.

auditory *See* auditorium.

Audrey, Robert (1908–80) US playwright, whose best-known play was the allegorical drama set in a lighthouse, *Thunder Rock* (1939). Other works included *How To Get Tough About It* (1938) and *Shadow of Heroes* (1958).

Augier, (Guillaume-Victor-)Émile (1820–89) French playwright. Born in Valence, he began with a number of mediocre verse plays, such as *Gabrielle* (1849). His reputation rests on such prose comedies as *Le Gendre de Monsier Poirier* (1854; translated as *Monsieur Poirier's Son-in-law*, 1915), which depict the social life and moral issues of the middle classes, a reaction against the Romantic movement.

Augustan drama English neoclassical drama written during the reign of Queen Anne, in the early 18th century. Named in honour of a distinguished period of Roman writing (27 BC–14 AD), it encompassed much fine tragedy and the plays of Congreve.

Augustus Druriolanus *See* Harris, Sir Augustus.

aulaeum *See* curtain.

Aureng-Zebe An heroic tragedy by John *Dryden. First performance: 1675. Remotely based on contemporary events in India, the play depicts the downfall of an exemplary hero when surrounded by anarchy and vice.

Ausoult, Jeanne (1625–62) French actress, wife of the actor André Baron and mother of Michel Baron. The daughter of strolling players, she excelled in Desjardin's *Manlius* at the Hôtel de Bourgogne, but died before she could act a part Corneille had written for her.

author's night A *benefit performance, traditionally the third night of a production, the proceeds of which – in the 17th and 18th centuries – went to the playwright.

auto sacramental The early *liturgical drama of Spain, the origins of which date back to about 1200. Strongly allegorical, the plays were performed on temporary stages or waggons at major religious festivals (especially during the feast of Corpus Christi), and gradually developed as a powerful tool for Catholic propaganda, notably in the expert hands of Lope de Vega and Calderón. Often seen as the Spanish equivalent of the mystery play in other countries, the genre was eventually prohibited by royal command in 1765.

Avancini, Nikolaus (1611–86) Austrian playwright, who held high posts at the court of Leopold I and was a leading writer of Jesuit drama. His plays, which were noted for their spectacular effects, combined religious sentiment with propaganda in support of the House of Habsburg, as in *Pietas victrix sive Flavius Constantinus Magnus de Maxentio tyranno victor* (1659), in which Leopold I was hailed as a successor to Constantine.

avant-garde A loosely-defined movement in modern drama, a reaction against realism that favoured a more imaginative approach to the theatre and stressed the role of the director as an interpreter of a playwright's ideas. Initiated in France in the 1920s, it developed under Jouvet, Dullin, and others (*see* Cartel) into the experimental drama of post-World War II theatre.

Avignon Festival A major theatre festival founded by Jean Vilar at Avignon in France

in 1947. The festival, held in the open air in July, grew rapidly following the foundation of the Théâtre National Populaire in 1951, significant productions including plays by Shakespeare, Corneille, and Kleist. After Vilar's death in 1971 the festival continued to expand, acquiring a lively fringe tradition, which included performances by the controversial Living Theatre. In recent years the huge numbers of groups attending the festival has led to a loss of identity and of large audiences at all but the most outstanding productions.

Avon Theatre *See* Klaw Theatre; Stratford (Ontario) Festival.

Awake and Sing! A play by Clifford *Odets. First performance: Group Theatre, 1935. The play revolves around a Jewish family, dominated by the mother who has become toughened by poverty and forces her daughter to marry someone she does not love, while breaking up her son's relationship with an orphan girl. The awakening occurs when the daughter defiantly elopes with a racketeer.

Axer, Erwin (1917-) Polish director, who is regarded as one of the leading theatrical figures in contemporary Poland. He is best known for his presentation of numerous modern Polish dramas, including works by Kruczkowski, Mrożek, and Witkiewicz, although he has also directed plays by Brecht, Chekhov, Shakespeare, and others with great success. He founded his own company in Łódź in 1945 and later (1949) established the Contemporary Theatre in Warsaw; subsequently he has also directed plays at the National Theatre in Britain and in several other countries.

Ayala, Adelardo de López *See* López de Ayala, Adelardo.

Ayckbourn, Alan (1939-) British playwright and director, whose many commer-

33

cially successful farces are characterized by his bleak view of the frustration and futility he perceives in British middle-class society. *Relatively Speaking* was his first major London success and set the tone for most of the plays that followed with its suburban setting and underlying bitterness. His plays are notable also for his technical inventiveness: the widely-performed *The Norman Conquests* comprises a trilogy of comedies using the same locale and basic plot, while *Absurd Person Singular* is set in three kitchens on three successive Christmas Eves and *Sisterly Feelings* provides a choice of endings; his more recent works have been distinguished by their increasingly black outlook. In 1975 he had five plays running at once in London's West End. Since 1970 Ayckbourn has been artistic director of the Stephen Joseph Theatre-in-the-Round at Scarborough, where most of his plays have been given their first performance.

Principal works:

Mr Whatnot: 1964.

Relatively Speaking: 1967.

How the Other Half Loves: 1970.

Time and Time Again: 1972.

Absurd Person Singular: 1973.

The Norman Conquests: 1974.

Jeeves: 1975 (with Andrew Lloyd Webber).

Absent Friends: 1975.

Confusions: 1976.

*Bedroom Farce: 1977.

Just Between Ourselves: 1977.

Ten Times Table: 1978.

Joking Apart: 1979.

Sisterly Feelings: 1980.

Taking Steps: 1980.

Season's Greetings: 1980.

Suburban Strains: 1981.

Way Upstream: 1982.

Intimate Exchanges: 1982.

Making Tracks: 1983.

It Could Be Any One of Us: 1983.

A Chorus of Disapproval: 1985.

A Small Family Business: 1987.

Woman in Mind: 1988.

Aylmer, Sir Felix (Sir Felix Edward Aylmer-Jones; 1889–1979) British actor, who began his career with Seymour Hicks at the Coliseum before joining the first Birmingham Repertory Company and appearing in plays by Shakespeare and Shaw. After World War I he resumed his career in both London and New York, becoming identified with roles of dry humour and authority; his most notable parts included Walter Harrowby in Charles Morgan's *The Flashing Stream* (1938) and Sir Joseph Pitts in Bridie's *Daphne Laureola* (1949).

Aymé, Marcel (1902–67) French novelist, short-story writer, and playwright. Aymé's first play, *Lucienne et le boucher*, was produced in 1948; his dramatic works are marked by coarse and sometimes cruel humour and by a blending of fantasy, reality, and the absurd.

Aynesworth, Allan (E Abbot-Anderson; 1865–1959) British actor, director, and manager, whose long career began with Tree's company at the Haymarket in 1887. A handsome gentlemanly actor, he created a number of important roles, including Algernon in *The Importance of Being Earnest* (1895) and Lord Porteous in Maugham's *The Circle* (1921). He was also involved in the management of the New, Garrick, and Criterion theatres.

Ayrenhoff, Cornelius von (1733–1819) Austrian playwright, author of several influential dramas. His plays, written in an attempt to counteract the prevailing light comedies popular in Vienna at the time, were successfully presented at the Burgtheater by Joseph von Sonnenfels.

Ayrer, Jakob (1543–1605) German playwright, who incorporated many of the features of Elizabethan drama in his plays of the *Fastnachtsspiel* tradition. A pupil of Hans Sachs, Ayrer was much influenced by the English Comedians; his 100 or more works include spectacular comedies, tragedies, and histories as well as examples of the *Singspiele* tradition, which he popularized.

B

Babanova, Maria Ivanovna (1900-) Soviet actress, who became the leading actress at the Theatre of the Revolution. She appeared under Komisarjevsky and Meyerhold early in her career and was later directed by Popov and Okhlopkov among others; her most celebrated roles included Juliet and the title role in Arbuzov's *Tanya*.

Bacchae, The A tragedy by *Euripides. First performance: Athens, 406 BC. The most frequently revived of all his works, the play was first produced (by his son) after the author's death and revolves around the contrasting figures of the licentious god Dionysus and the prudish Pentheus.

Bacchus *See* Dionysus.

backcloth A large curtain or painted canvas hung at the back of the stage, usually in conjunction with flats and often with a gauze. In the US it is referred to as a **backdrop**.

backdrop *See* backcloth.

backing flat A flat positioned behind a door or window in order to mask off the backstage area from the audience's view.

backstage That part of a theatre behind the proscenium arch or stage area. It includes the wings, workshops, storerooms, and dressing-rooms.

Back to Methuselah A play by G B *Shaw. First performance: Theatre Guild,

1922. Consisting of five plays in one, it covers the whole of human history and discusses the acquisition of wisdom through longevity; it was considered by Shaw his finest play but is rarely revived. Its first London production was given by Barry Jackson's company, having transferred from the Birmingham Repertory Theatre.

Baddeley, (Madeleine) Angela (Clinton-) (1904–76) British actress, who appeared on stage as a child and made her first adult appearance in *The Beggar's Opera* at the Lyric Theatre, Hammersmith in 1920. Subsequent successes included the title role in Allen Harker's *Marigold* (1927), *The Greeks Had a Word for It* (1934) by Zoë Akins, in which she appeared with her sister, Dodie Smith's *Dear Octopus* (1938), and Rattigan's *The Winslow Boy* (1946). She also appeared in Shakespearean productions and several musicals. She was married to Glen Byam Shaw.

Her sister, **Hermione (Clinton-)Baddeley** (1906–86), began as an actress in such acclaimed revues as *On With the Dance* (1925) and *Still Dancing* (1926) before appearing in straight drama. She then went on to perform in such plays as *When Crummles Played* (1927) by Nigel Playfair, Wycherley's *The Country Wife* (1940), Greene's *Brighton Rock* (1943), and Coward's *Fallen Angels* (1949). Successes in the US included Shelagh Delaney's *A Taste of Honey* (1961) and *The Milk Train Doesn't Stop Here Anymore* (1964) by Tennessee Williams.

Baddeley, Robert (1732–94) British actor, who appeared regularly at Drury Lane. Prior to his stage debut in 1760 he was a gentleman's gentleman, touring the continent and so acquiring a firsthand knowledge of foreign accents. A noted character actor, he created the part of Moses in *The School for Scandal*. The last actor habitually to wear the Royal Livery off the stage, he left a capital sum to provide a cake and wine to be consumed annually on Twelfth Night by the company at Drury Lane. His wife was the actress Sophia *Snow.

Badel, Alan (Firman) (1923–82) British actor, who played numerous classical roles at the Old Vic and at Stratford, including Romeo to Claire Bloom's Juliet (1952), Lovborg in *Hedda Gabler* (1954), and Hamlet (1956). Subsequently he both directed and acted in *The Public Prosecutor* (1957) at the Arts Theatre and *Ulysses in Night-town* (1959). In 1971 he was much admired in Sartre's *Kean*.

Bagnold, Enid (Algerine) (Lady Roderick Jones; 1889–1981) British playwright and novelist, whose best-known work for the stage was *The Chalk Garden* (1955), in which Peggy Ashcroft and Edith Evans both appeared. Other plays included adaptations of her novels *Serena Blandish* (1929), in which Vivien Leigh performed, *Lottie Dundass* (1943), and *National Velvet* (1946), and the three later plays *The Last Joke* (1960), *The Chinese Prime Minister* (1964), and *Call Me Jacky* (1967).

Bahr, Hermann (1863–1934) Austrian writer, whose literary output encompassed a wide range of critical works and essays and almost 80 naturalistic plays. Of these the most notable were *Das Tschaperl* (1898) and the polished urbane farce *Daz Konzert* (1910); he became director at the Deutsches Theater in Berlin in 1906).

Bailey, Pearl (1918–) US actress, who began her career in vaudeville in 1933. She made her Broadway debut 13 years later as Butterfly in *St Louis Woman*; subsequent roles have included Sally Adams in *Call Me Madam* (1966) and Dolly Gallagher in *Hello Dolly!* (1967).

Baird, Dorothea (1875–1933) British actress, who made her first appearance in 1894. She won instant fame in 1895 in the title role of Du Maurier's *Trilby* at the Haymarket; she was married to Henry Brodribb *Irving.

Bajazet A tragedy by Jean *Racine. First performance: Paris, 1672. The play is set in Constantinople in 1638; Bajazet, the sultan's brother, is obliged to marry the powerful Roxane in order to win the throne. When Roxane learns of Bajazet's love for the young princess Atalide, she has him killed.

Baker, George Pierce (1866–1935) US theatre scholar, who did much to promote new writing for the US theatre. His pupils at Harvard, where he also founded the influential '47 Workshop, included Edward Sheldon and Eugene O'Neill; subsequently (from 1925) he continued his important work at Yale.

Baker, Sarah (c. 1736–1816) British actress and manager. After her husband's death in 1769, she developed her own touring circuit in Kent, with her three children – one of whom married the actor William Dowton – all taking part. She presented both comedies and tragedies and built 10 theatres to present them in.

Bakst, Léon (Lev Samoylovich Rosenberg; 1866–1924) Russian artist, who had a profound effect upon both costume and scenery design in the early 20th century. He executed his earliest works for the theatre in 1900 and later won fame for his non-naturalistic designs for Diaghilev's ballets; later he also designed productions of the tragedies of D'Annunzio and plays presented at the Paris Opéra.

balcony *See* auditorium.

Balcony, The (*Le Balcon*) A play by Jean *Genet. First performance: London, 1957. The play is a study of falseness and unreality, in which the roles played by the clients of a brothel are translated to the outside world.

Bald Prima Donna, The (*La Cantatrice chauve*) A play by Eugène *Ionesco. First performance: Paris, 1950. It was staged in London in translation in 1956 and in New York, as *The Bald Soprano*, in 1958. A pioneering work in the Theatre of the Absurd, the play depicts the meaningless existence of two married couples.

Bale, John (1495–1563) English playwright, who became Bishop of Ossory in Ireland. He wrote 21 plays in defence of Protestantism and established a company of travelling actors. He employed the interlude for propaganda purposes and presented moral abstractions alongside specific figures from history in his major work, *Kynge Johan* (c. 1538), which was probably the first historical play in English.

Balieff, Nikita (1877–1936) Russian director, who produced a number of celebrated revues in Paris in the early 20th century. His elaborate shows began with *Le Chauve-Souris* (The Bat) in 1908 and included humorous sketches and songs as well as highly popular appearances by Balieff himself. From 1921 his shows were staged in London by C B Cochran and from 1922 also in New York but closed shortly after Balieff's death.

Ball, William (1931-) US actor and director, who made his stage debut in *Uncle Vanya*, *Candida*, and *Hamlet* (1948). He then toured with Margaret Webster as an actor and later appeared at various Shakespeare Festivals and elsewhere, directing and acting in plays by Molière, Pinero, Arthur Moller, Chekhov, and many others.

ballad opera A form of musical drama, popular in the 18th century, in which spoken dialogue was interspersed with songs set to contemporary tunes. Gay's *The Beggar's Opera* (1728) was the most celebrated example and was typical of the genre in having a distinctly satirical air, originally intended as a parody of Italian opera but also lampooning various political targets. Garrick, Fielding, Colly Cibber, Sheridan, and Thomas Jevon all composed such works, Jevon's *The Devil to Pay* (1731) when performed in Germany inspiring the development of the parallel *Singspiele* tradition there.

Ballard, Sarah *See* Terry, Benjamin.

Balsam, Martin (1919-) US actor, who made his professional debut in *The Play's the Thing* (1941). After World War II, he toured as Norman in *Wedding Breakfast* (1955) and, in 1961, appeared in *The Iceman Cometh*. He also won awards for his performance in *You Know I Can't Hear You When the Water's Running* (1967).

Bałucki, Michał (1837–1901) Polish playwright, author of several bourgeois comedies influenced by Aleksander Fredro. His plays include *Big Shots* (1881) and *The Bachelors' Club* (1890), both of which owed much to Fredro's *Ladies and Hussars* (1825).

Balzac, Honoré de (1799–1850) French novelist and playwright, born in Tours. Balzac is remembered chiefly for his prose works: his plays had little success. *Vautrin* (1840), which was based on his novel *Le Père Goriot*, was banned after its first performance; *Les Ressources de Quinola* (1842) and *Paméla Giraud* (1843) both had relatively short runs. *La Marâtre*, forced to close by the Revolution of 1848, showed more potential, and *Mercadet* (1851), produced after Balzac's death, has received critical acclaim.

Banbury, Frith (1912-) British actor, director, and manager, who made his first appearance in *If I Were You* at the Shaftesbury Theatre in 1933, then appeared in numerous modern comedies and revues, including *Goodness, How Sad!* (1938), *New Faces* (1940), and *Uncle Vanya* (1943). He has since directed productions by Rattigan,

Nichols, and many others in London, New York, and other parts of the world.

Bances Candamo, Francisco Antonio (c. 1662–1704) Spanish playwright, author of the *Teatro de los teatros de los pasados y presentes siglos*, an early account of the Spanish theatre. His plays, notably *Por su Rey y por su dama* (1685), were influenced by Calderón.

Bancroft, Anne (1931–) US actress; who trained at the American Academy of Dramatic Arts and the Actors' Studio before winning awards in *Two for the See-Saw* (1958). In 1959 she was acclaimed in *The Miracle Worker*; she returned to the stage in 1967 to play Regina Giddens in Lillian Hellman's *The Little Foxes*.

Bancroft, Sir Squire (1841–1926) British actor-manager who made his first stage appearance in Birmingham in 1861. After four years touring he went into partnership with **Marie Effie Wilton** (1839–1921), reopening the old Queen's Theatre in 1865 as the Prince of Wales's (*see* Scala Theatre). In 1867 they married and went on to enjoy a long period of success, particularly with the naturalistic plays of T W Robertson. They did much to raise the status of the profession, paying higher salaries and insisting upon improved standards of acting. They retired in 1885 after five years at the Haymarket. Squire Bancroft also became president of the Royal Academy of Dramatic Art, where his name is commemorated by the Bancroft Gold Medal. He was knighted in 1897.

Bandbox Theatre A theatre on East 57th Street, New York, which originally opened as the Adolph Phillip Theatre in 1912 and was renamed the Bandbox Theatre in 1914. It was the New York venue for the Washington Square Players from 1915 until 1917, when it closed.

Bankhead, Tallulah (Brockman) (1902–68) US actress, well known for her eccentric private life as well as for her stage performances. She made her first New York appearance in *The Squab Farm* (1918), then went to London and remained there until 1930. Back in the US she was admired in a wide variety of roles, including Sadie Thompson in *Rain* (1935), Cleopatra in *Antony and Cleopatra* (1937), Regina Giddens in *The Little Foxes* (1939), Sabina in *The Skin of Our Teeth* (1942), Queen in *The Eagle Has Two Heads* (1947), and Blanche du Bois in a revival of *A Streetcar Named Desire*.

Bankrupt, The (*Bankrot*) A play by Alexander *Ostrovsky. First performance: 1849. Written when the author was 25 years old, the play exposed fraudulent practices involving bogus bankruptcies among the traders of Moscow and resulted in Ostrovsky's dismissal from the Civil Service and the banning of the play for 13 years.

Banks, Leslie (James) (1890–1952) British actor, who first appeared with Benson's company in 1911. Later he was at the Birmingham Repertory Theatre and also with the Lena Ashwell Players (1919–20). A versatile actor, his parts ranged from Captain Hook in New York (1924) to Petruchio opposite Edith Evans (1937); he also appeared in Gielgud's classical season at the Haymarket (1944–45) and directed several plays.

Bankside Globe Playhouse *See* Wanamaker, Sam.

Bankside Players *See* Atkins, Sir Robert.

Bannister, Jack (1760–1836) British actor, son of the comedian Charles Bannister (1741–1804). He appeared for the first time at his father's benefit at the Haymarket in 1778. He then moved to Drury Lane, where he became a leading comedy actor. Sir Anthony Absolute and Tony Lumpkin were two of his most celebrated roles. He also collaborated with George Colman the Younger on his one-man show *Bannister's Budget*. In 1783 he married **Elizabeth Harper** (1757–1849), principal singer at the Haymarket until 1793.

Banvard's Museum *See* Daly's Theatre.

Baptiste *See* Deburau, Jean-Gaspard.

Baraka, (Imamu) Amiri (Leroi Jones; 1934-   ) US playwright and poet, who was active in the development of Black theatre. His plays include *Dante* (1962), *Black Mass* (1966), *The Great Goodness of Life (A Coon Show)* (1968), *Sidnee Poet Heroical* (1975), which he also directed, and *The Motion of History* (1977).

Barbican Centre A public entertainments complex in London, named after part of the capital's Roman fortifications. Built on a bombsite from World War II, it was opened in 1982. The Centre includes an art gallery, a concert hall, three cinemas, and two theatres – the **Barbican Theatre**, seating 1166, and a smaller studio theatre, **The Pit**, seating 200. The Barbican is the London home of the Royal Shakespeare Company; productions are given in repertory throughout the year, many of them transferring from Stratford-upon-Avon.

Barbican Nursery *See* nurseries.

Barbieri, Niccolò (1576–1641) Italian actor and playwright, who probably created the character of Scapino in the *commedia dell'arte*. Using the stage name **Beltrame**, he appeared with the Gelosi and the Fideli before finally joining the Confidenti; his play *L'Inavertito* (1629) influenced Molière's *L'Étourdi*.

Bard, Wilkie (William Augustus Smith; 1874–1944) British music hall comedian, who made his London debut at Collins's

Music Hall in 1895. He was famous for his tongue-twisting songs, notably 'She Sells Sea-Shells on the Sea-Shore', and played Pantaloon in pantomime harlequinades.

Barefoot in the Park A comedy by Neil *Simon. First performance: 1963. The play concerns a newlywed couple who rent an apartment in New York but then undergo marital strain as the result of overwork and visits from eccentric neighbours and relations. The play was filmed starring Robert Redford and Jane Fonda in 1967.

barker A person employed by a theatrical company performing at a fair or other similar event to attract an audience to a show. Such barkers were employed in classical times and subsequently became a common feature of fairgrounds throughout Europe and the US.

Barker, Harley Granville- *See* Granville-Barker, Harley.

Barker, Howard (1946-   ) British playwright, who established his reputation as a prominent writer for the fringe theatre while associated with the Royal Court Theatre during the 1970s. *Cheek* and *No One Was Saved* were his first plays to reach the stage (1970); since then his best received works have included *Claw* (1975), *The Love of a Good Man* (1980), which was set on a French battlefield after World War I, *The Poor Man's Friend* (1981), which was written for an enormous cast, *The Castle* (1985), and *The Last Supper* (1988).

Barkworth, Peter (Wynn) (1929-   ) British actor, who made his London debut in Dodie Smith's *Letter from Paris* (1952). Since then his parts have included Captain Mortlock in Coward's *South Sea Bubble* (1956), Edward VIII in Royce Ryton's *Crown Matrimonial* (1972), and Headingly in Michael Frayn's *Donkeys' Years* (1976). In 1987 he had a great success in a solo performance as Siegfried Sassoon, presented in the West End and on a national tour.

Barlach, Ernst (1870–1938) German sculptor and playwright, who was the author of several notable Expressionist dramas. His mystical Gothic plays, which included *Der tote Tag* (The Dead Day; 1919), *Der arme Vetter* (The Poor Cousin; 1919), and *Der Findling* (The Foundling; 1922), tackled such themes as the tension between God and the world and the relationship shared by a father and son.

barn door shutters A pair (or more) of spotlight shutters, used to adjust the size and shape of the beam thrown onto the stage.

Barnes, Clive Alexander (1927–) British theatre and dance critic, who has written for the *New York Post* since 1978. Controversial in recent years for failing to admire commercial Broadway productions as against more experimental drama, he has also written for *Dance and Dancers*, *The Spectator*, and the *New York Times*.

Barnes, Sir Kenneth *See* Royal Academy of Dramatic Art.

Barnes, Peter (1931–) British playwright, who first attracted attention with the eccentric comedy *The Ruling Class* in 1968. Since then he has written several other well-received unconventional comedies, including *Leonardo's Last Supper* (1969), *Noonday Demons* (1969), *The Bewitched* (1973), *Laughter!* (1978), and *Red Noses* (1985) as well as adaptations of Jonson, Feydeau, and others.

Barnes, Thomas (1785–1841) British journalist and theatre critic. Prior to his appointment as editor of *The Times* in 1817, he wrote theatre criticism for the *Examiner*, using the pen-name Criticus; his most important review was that of Kean's Shylock at Drury Lane in 1814.

Barnes Theatre A theatre in the Barnes district of London, opened in 1925. Early productions that attracted comment included Hardy's *Tess of the D'Urbervilles* (1925) and Chekhov's *Uncle Vanya* (1926), which were rapidly followed by a series of Russian dramas in which Gielgud, Laughton, and other leading actors appeared under the direction of Komisarjevsky. After diversifying with two of Drinkwater's plays, the theatre closed in late 1926.

barnstormer A member of a touring troupe of actors who performed in barns and other makeshift theatres during the 19th century. Such groups usually presented entertainments of a coarse and noisy nature, hence the name.

Barnum, Phineus Taylor (1810–91) US showman, founder of the *American Museum in New York. He publicized the midget Charles Stratton, known as General Tom Thumb, while other attractions included a fake mermaid. The popular musical *Barnum* was based on his career.

Baron, André (c. 1601–55) French actor, who appeared at the Théâtre du Marais with Montdory's company before moving in 1641 to the Hôtel de Bourgogne. He excelled in both comedy and tragedy; his death, according to tradition, was caused by a wound from his own prop sword during a performance of Corneille's *Le Cid*.

His son by Jeanne Ausoult, **Michel Baron** (1653–1729), was also an actor, who first appeared on the stage in a boy company with Raisin and Jean de Villiers. Subsequently he was taken on by Molière, until a quarrel with the playwright's wife caused him to leave for a time. After Molière's death, Michel moved to the Hôtel de Bourgogne and appeared in plays by Racine. With his wife, the daughter of La Thorillière, he later joined the Comédie-Française and became the leading actor there. His own plays include *Le Rendez-vous de Tuil-*

leries (1685) and the comedy *L'Homme à bonne fortune* (1686). He was in retirement from 1691 to 1720, but then returned to repeat many of his most celebrated roles.

Barraca, La A Spanish theatre company, founded in 1931 to present classical works to audiences in the provinces. Properly called the Teatro Universitario, the company was led by García Lorca until the Spanish Civil War, after which it was disbanded.

Barrault, Jean-Louis (1910-) French actor, director, and manager, who was first recognized as a leading theatrical figure after World War II. Trained under Charles Dullin and Étienne Decroux, he began his career at the Théâtre de l'Atelier in 1931 and subsequently assisted Antonin Artaud and studied mime, which he employed to good effect in his first independent production – an adaptation with Camus of Faulkner's *As I Lay Dying* – in 1935.

Subsequently he studied Molière and married the actress Madeleine Renaud, whom he met on joining the Comédie-Française under Copeau in 1940. There he appeared in several classic French dramas by Corneille, Racine, and others before founding his own company (the Compagnie Renaud-Barrault) in 1946 and moving into the Théâtre Marigny, where he remained for the next 10 years. As well as such classics as *Hamlet*, the company became famous for productions of plays by Claudel (notably *Christophe Colomb* in 1953), Feydeau, Marivaux, and many others, before eventually moving (1956) to the Théâtre Sarah Bernhardt, the Palais-Royal, and then the Odéon, where further notable productions included plays by Beckett, Genet, and Ionesco.

The student riots of 1968 led to Barrault's return to the independent theatre and immediate success with an extravaganza based on the novels of Rabelais; it was subsequently staged in Britain and the US to equal acclaim. He transferred to a new venue in 1972 and again in 1980, when he moved to his present base (the Théâtre du Rond Point), where he has presented both new plays and revivals of earlier successes. His most famous performance as a mime actor was in the film *Les Enfants du Paradis* (1945), in which he impersonated Deburau.

barrel *See* batten.

Barrett, George Horton (1794–1860) US actor, who first attracted attention as a child on the New York stage in such roles as Home's Young Norval. Subsequently he excelled in the comedies of Sheridan, becoming known as Gentleman George on account of his refined manner.

Barrett, Lawrence (1838–91) US actor and producer, who was much admired in numerous classical roles, both in the US and in Britain, where he managed the Lyceum Theatre for a time. His greatest successes included Sheridan Knowles's *The Hunchback* (1857) and the part of Cassius in *Julius Caesar*.

Barrett, Wilson (1846–1904) British actor-manager, who, after some years in the provinces, established himself in London as a leading actor of melodrama. He became lessee of the Royal Court Theatre in 1879, staging successful productions by Henry Arthur Jones, before taking over the Princess's Theatre, where he remained for five years. His greatest success came in 1882 with the melodrama *The Silver King*. In 1895, he was acclaimed as Marcus Superbus in the pseudo-religious play *The Sign of the Cross*, which he wrote himself while in the US.

Barretts of Wimpole Street, The A play by Rudolf Besier. First performance: 1930. The plot is based on the factual events that occurred in the house of Edward Moulton-Barrett, dominant father of the invalid poet Elizabeth, and culminates in her elopement with Robert Browning.

Barrie, Sir J(ames) M(atthew) (1860–1937) Scottish playwright and novelist, whose earliest theatrical successes were *The Professor's Love Story* (1894) and *The Little Minister* (1897), which was adapted from his own novel. His most famous work, **Peter Pan*(1904), is a whimsical fantasy; a similar note of sentimentality recurs in such plays as *A Kiss for Cinderella* (1916), *Dear Brutus* (1917), and *Mary Rose* (1920). His other works include the social comedies *The *Admirable Crichton* and **What Every Woman Knows*, the period romance **Quality Street*, and the mystery play *Shall We Join the Ladies?* (1922).

Barry, Elizabeth (1658–1713) English actress, who became Betterton's leading lady, appearing at Drury Lane, the Haymarket, and Lincoln's Inn Fields. Her numerous original roles included Belvidera in Otway's *Venice Preserv'd*, Isabella in Southerne's *The Fatal Marriage*, and Lady Brute in *The Provoked Wife*. She was the first English actress to receive a benefit performance and retired in 1710. Although never married, she was the subject of numerous scandals.

Barry, Philip (1896–1949) US playwright, whose first professional production, *You and I*, illustrated a father's attempt to live out his artistic dreams through his son. He followed this with *Cock Robin* and *Holiday* (both 1928), *Hotel Universe* (1930), *The Animal Kingdom* (1932), and *Here Come the Clowns* (1938). His play *The Philadelphia Story* was extremely popular and was successfully adapted for the screen. Later plays included *Liberty Jones* (1941), *Without Love* (1942), and *The Foolish Notion* (1945).

Barry, Spranger (1719–77) Irish actor, who repeated his first success as Othello (at the Smock Alley Theatre, Dublin, 1744) when he came to Drury Lane in 1746. When he and Garrick appeared together they proved a highly popular attraction. In 1750, however, Barry transferred to Covent Garden and the two great actors became rivals, appearing in simultaneous productions of such plays as *Romeo and Juliet* and *King Lear*. A disastrous investment by Barry in a new Dublin theatre in 1758 forced him to move to the Haymarket; in 1766 he was again engaged by Garrick. Two years later he married Ann *Dancer.

Barrymore, Maurice (Herbert Blythe; 1847–1905) British actor, born in India, who made his London debut in 1875. As well as his London appearances, notably at the Haymarket, he worked in the US, later especially in vaudeville, until forced to give up through mental instability. He was also the author of several plays. By his marriage to Georgina *Drew he was the father of the famous Barrymore trio, Lionel, Ethel, and John.

Lionel Barrymore (1878–1954) was the eldest child and made his stage debut at the age of 15. Subsequently he was much admired in New York in plays by George Du Maurier and others although he failed as Macbeth. After 1925 he abandoned the stage for a successful film career.

Lionel's sister, **Ethel Barrymore** (1879–1959), established her reputation as as an excellent US actress with her performance in Clyde Fitch's *Captain Jinks of the Horse Marines* (1901) in New York. This was followed by the lead in *Cousin Kate* (1903) by H H Davies and the role of Nora in *A Doll's House*, in which her brother also appeared. Her Shakespearean roles included Juliet, Ophelia, and Portia, while beauty and intelligence also ensured her success in plays by Pinero, Dumas *fils*, and many others. In 1928 the *Ethel Barrymore Theatre opened with a performance by her in Martínez Sierra's *The Kingdom of God*; roles late in life included Gran in *Whiteoaks* (1938) by Mazo de la Roche and Miss Moffat in Emlyn Williams's *The Corn Is Green* (1940).

Lionel's younger brother, **John Barrymore** (1882–1942), first appeared as an as actor in 1903 as Max in *Magda*. After success in

J M Barrie's *Pantaloon* (1905) and W S Gilbert's *The Fortune Hunter* (1909) he became highly popular, although it was not until 1916, when he played Falder in Galsworthy's *Justice*, that he was recognized as a serious actor. Subsequent major roles included the lead in George Du Maurier's *Peter Ibbetson* (1917), Fedor in *The Living Corpse* (1918), Giannetto Malespini in *The Jest* (1919), and, from 1922, Hamlet, which was considered his finest part and provided him with a record-breaking run of 101 performances. Later in life he appeared in films but suffered from alcoholism.

Barrymore, Richard Barry, Earl of (1760–93) British theatre enthusiast, who owned a small puppet theatre in Savile Row, London. He built the first indoor private theatre in England at his house in Wargrave, Berkshire but the upkeep ruined him financially and the theatre was demolished in 1792.

Barrymore, William (1759–1830) British actor and author of several melodramas. His *Trial by Battle; or, Heaven Defend the Right* was the first play presented at the Old Vic (then the Royal Coburg) in 1818.

Barsacq, André (1909–73) French director and manager, born in the Crimea, who began his career under Dullin at the Théâtre de l'Atelier. After attracting attention with such productions as Jonson's *Volpone* (1928), he founded (1937) a travelling company, the Compagnie des Quatre Saisons, with Jean Dasté and went on to produce almost all the works of Jean Anouilh by 1953. After World War II he succeeded Dullin at the Atelier, where he presented numerous works by new playwrights as well as many Russian classics.

Bart, Lionel (Lionel Begleiter; 1930–) British composer and lyricist, whose first musical, *Wally Pone* (1958), was written for the Unity Theatre. The following year he wrote the lyrics for the musical *Lock Up Your Daughters* and the songs for *Fings Ain't Wot They Used t'Be* before achieving international success with *Oliver!*, which was based on Dickens. After further success with *Blitz!* (1962) and *Maggie May* (1964), his career foundered with the failure of *Twang!!* (1965) and *La Strada* (1969).

Barter Theatre A theatre in Abingdon, Virginia, which was founded during the Depression, opening in 1933. The name came from the theatre's practice of trading tickets for services and meals for the actors. Seating 380, it became the official state theatre of Virginia in 1946. A second theatre, the Barter Playhouse, was built in 1971 to house both classical and contemporary plays.

Bartholomew Fair A prose comedy by Ben *Jonson, written to be acted at court on St Bartholomew's Day. First performance: 1614. A kaleidoscope of brief scenes, the play presents numerous characters in the crowd at the Smithfield Fair and satirizes the extravagant behaviour of traders, showmen, gamblers and the hypocritical Puritan Zeal-of-the-land Busy.

Barton, John Bernard Adie (1928-) British director, who became famous for his interpretations of Shakespeare's historical dramas at Stratford-upon-Avon in the 1960s. Previously a director with the Marlowe Society and the Amateur Dramatic Club at Cambridge, he won great acclaim for such productions as *The Taming of the Shrew* (1964), *The Wars of the Roses* cycle (1963), and *Henry IV* as *When Thou Art King* (1969). More recent productions have included Marlowe's *Dr Faustus* (1974), *The Greeks* cycle (1979) from the plays of Euripides and others, and Sheridan's *The School for Scandal* (1983). He also directed *The Vikings at Helgeland* at Den Nationale Scene in Berlin in 1983.

Bassermann, August (1848–1931) German actor and manager, who excelled in the tragedies of Schiller and others. He became manager of the Manheim Theatre in 1886 and later ran a theatre in Karlsruhe and visited New York to further acclaim.

His nephew, **Albert Bassermann** (1867–1952), was also an actor and became one of the leading interpreters of naturalistic drama. He made his debut at Mannheim and later appeared under Max Reinhardt and Otto Brahm in Berlin, where he excelled in the plays of Ibsen. He was also highly successful in works by Goethe, Schiller, and Shakespeare, notably as Lear and Shylock. He emigrated to the US in the 1930s, appearing in films before returning to Europe in 1945.

Batalov, Nikolai Petrovich (1899–1937) Soviet actor, who established his reputation in comic roles with the Moscow Art Theatre, which he joined in 1916. Subsequently he also showed a talent for satire, his most successful parts including Beaumarchais's Figaro and roles in the plays of Ivanov, notably Vasska Okorka in *Armoured Train 14–69*.

Bateman, Hezekiah Linthicum (1812–75) US impresario, who was the head of a notable theatrical family. Having married the daughter of Joseph Cowell, he did much to further the careers of his daughters and, while lessee of the Lyceum Theatre in London, presented Henry Irving in *The Bells* with enormous success.

His eldest daughter, **Kate Josephine Bateman** (Mrs George Crowe; 1842–1917), first acted as a child under her father in 1847. Subsequently she toured the US and Britain in many Shakespearean parts and plays by other authors, most notably in Daly's *Leah the Forsaken* (1863) in which she appeared opposite Henry Irving. Successes at the Lyceum included *Othello*, *Richard III*, and Tennyson's *Queen Mary*.

Hezekiah Bateman's second daughter, **Virginia Frances Bateman** (1843–1940), made her adult debut as an actress at the Haymarket in 1868. Later she also appeared at the Lyceum, married (1882) Edward *Compton, and helped to run the Compton Comedy Company.

Hezekiah's third daughter, **Isabel Emilie Bateman** (1854–1934), first appeared on stage as an adult under her father at the Lyceum Theatre in 1871. She was much admired in such intense roles as Ophelia and Desdemona, both opposite Henry Irving, despite her dislike for theatre in general. Subsequently she ran the Sadler's Wells Theatre for a time before eventually retiring in 1898 to become a nun.

Bates, Alan (Arthur) (1934–) British actor, who established his reputation in 1956 as Cliff Lewis in *Look Back in Anger* at the Royal Court. Subsequently he appeared in plays by O'Neill, Pinter (notably as Mick in *The Caretaker* in 1960), and Storey and acted in films and on television. More recent successes have included various Shakespearean roles and performances in *Butley* (1971), *Otherwise Engaged* (1975), *Stage Struck* (1979), and *Melon* (1987) – all by Simon Gray.

Bathyllus (1st century BC) A celebrated writer and *pantomimus* of ancient Rome. Together with Pylades he contributed greatly (as a performer of comic roles) to the popularity of the mime dance tradition.

batten A length of wood or metal used to strengthen a flat or to hang lighting or scenery from. A metal batten may also be referred to as a **barrel** or **spot bar** in Britain and as a **pipe** (**pipe batten**) in the US. Light battens, when comprising a number of lights mounted in a row of compartments, are known as **compartment battens** or **magazine battens** in Britain and as **strip lights** or **border lights** in the US. Positioned immediately behind the proscenium arch, they are used primarily for colour mixing.

Baty,   (Jean-Baptiste-Marie-)Gaston (1885–1952) French director and playwright, who established his reputation with a series of plays in which great emphasis was placed upon the pictorial aspects of the production. Having opened a theatre in his own name in 1930, he staged a combination of both new plays and classics, of which the most notable included Dostoevsky's *Crime and Punishment* (1938) and plays by Jean-Jacques Bernard. He joined the Comédie-Française in 1936; of his own plays the most successful was *Dulcinée* (1938), which was loosely based on *Don Quixote* by Cervantes.

Bauer, Wolfang (1941–) Austrian playwright, noted for his popular comedies of modern manners. One of a number of young Graz-based writers in local dialect to emerge in the late 1960s, he won attention with such plays as *Sylvester oder das Massaker im Hotel Sacher* (Sylvester or the Massacre in Hotel Sacher; 1971) and *Film und Frau* (1971), which was performed in London in 1972 as *Shakespeare the Sadist*.

Bäuerle, Adolf (1786–1859) Austrian playwright, who introduced the character *Staberl to the Viennese stage in the play *Die Bürger in Wien* (1813). Inspired by the popularity of Staberl when played by Ignaz Schuster, Bäuerle went on to write a further four plays around him as well as numerous other plays based on fairy tales.

Bauernfeld, Eduard von (1802–90) Austrian playwright, whose numerous light comedies depicting Viennese society dominated the Vienna Burgtheater for many years. A friend of Grillparzer and Schubert, he discussed social and political issues in such successful plays as *Das Liebes-Protokoll* (1834) and *Aus der Gesellschaft* (1867).

Baxter, Anne (1923–) US actress, who made her New York debut in 1936. Later she toured the US with Raymond Massey in *John Brown's Body* (1953) and in 1957 appeared on Broadway in *The Square Root of Wonderful*.

Baylis, Lilian Mary (1874–1937) British theatre manageress, who founded the Old Vic and new Sadler's Wells theatres and became famous for her devotion to the London stage between the wars. She first appeared on stage as a child and later toured in South Africa; in 1912 she established the Old Vic (originally a temperance music hall run by her aunt, Emma Cons) as a leading venue for Shakespearean productions, subsequently presenting the whole canon between 1914 and 1923, including uncut versions of *Hamlet*. Her productions of Shakespeare were acclaimed for their simplicity and, especially in later years, for the high standard of acting; other playwrights whose work was performed there included Ibsen. In 1931 she reopened the old Sadler's Wells Theatre as a venue for ballet, the companies under her charge eventually becoming the Royal Ballet and the English National Opera.

Bayreuth A town in Bavaria, Germany, in which Richard Wagner established his famous Festspielhaus in 1876. Based on designs by the architect **Gottfried Semper** (1803–79), the starkly simple layout of the auditorium had a profound effect upon subsequent theatre building.

Bear Gardens Museum A theatre museum in Bankside, London, founded close to the site of the Globe Theatre by Sam Wanamaker in 1972. The museum specializes in the drama of Shakespeare and his contemporaries.

Beaton, Sir Cecil Walter Hardy (1904–80) British stage designer and photographer, who was knighted in 1972. Having produced designs for a number of ballets and revues, he designed the costumes and scenery for numerous London productions, including Gielgud's production of *Lady Windermere's Fan* (1945) and Coward's *Quadrille* (1952). After 1954 he worked chiefly for the New York stage, achieving his greatest success with his designs for the musical *My Fair Lady* (1956), which also appeared in the film version.

Beaubour, Pierre Tronchon de (1662–1725) French actor, who succeeded Baron as a member of the Comédie-Française in 1691. He was criticized for his inclination to rant in tragedy and, according to contemporary sources, would probably have been more successful as a comic actor.

Beauchâteau (François Chastelet; d. c. 1665) French actor, who acted at the Hôtel de Bourgogne until 1634 and then appeared at the Théâtre de Marais before returning to the Bourgogne in 1642. He and his wife, **Madeleine de Pouget** (1615–83), were later satirized by Molière in *L'Impromptu de Versailles* (1664) and criticized by others for their sentimental performances.

Beaumarchais, Pierre-Augustin Caron de (1732–99) French playwright, born in Paris. The son of André-Charles Caron, a clockmaker, Beaumarchais acquired his new surname and a position at the court of Louis XV through his first marriage. Having served for a time as music teacher to the king's daughters, he was able to buy himself into higher office as a result of successful financial speculations, which ultimately led to litigation and scandal. He subsequently undertook secret diplomatic missions for the king, sold arms to American revolutionaries, published the first complete edition of Voltaire's works, and faced exile and imprisonment during the Revolution.

His earliest dramatic works, a series of *parades* (sketches), were followed by the un-

remarkable *Eugénie* and *Les Deux Amis*. His comedies of intrigue, *The Barber of Seville* and *The *Marriage of Figaro*, were extremely successful, however, and were used as bases for libretti by Rossini and Mozart, respectively.

Principal works:

Eugénie: 1767.

Les Deux Amis ou le Négociant de Lyon: 1770.

Le Barbier de Séville: 1775; translated as *The Barber of Seville*.

Le Mariage de Figaro ou la Folle Journée: 1874; translated as *The Marriage of Figaro*.

La Mère coupable: 1792.

Beauménard, Rose-Petronelle le Roy (1730–99) French actress, wife of the actor Bellecour. She excelled in plays by Molière while with the Comédie-Française from 1749 and became highly popular; she also appeared in plays by Marivaux, Favart, and Beaumarchais with varying success. An attempted comeback after she was ruined financially by the Revolution was a failure.

Beaumont, Sir Francis (1584–1616) English playwright, who is usually remembered for his successful collaboration on several plays with John Fletcher. Before meeting Fletcher in 1605, he had already achieved success with *The Woman Hater* (1606), repeating it with the satirical *The *Knight of the Burning Pestle*. With Fletcher he wrote at least half a dozen plays, including *Philaster; or, Love Lies Bleeding* (1609), *The Maid's Tragedy* (1610), and *A King and No King* (1611). Beaumont retired as a playwright on his marriage in 1613.

Beauval (Jean Pitel; c. 1635–1709) French actor, who appeared with Molière's company in such plays as *Le Malade Imaginaire*. Never regarded as a particularly gifted actor himself, his wife – the daughter of Filandre – was nevertheless a popular comic actress. When Molière died husband and wife moved to the Hôtel de Bourgogne and later became part of the Comédie-Française.

Beaux' Stratagem, The A comedy by George *Farquhar. First performance: 1707. The plot revolves around two young gentlemen, Archer and Aimwell, who pretend to be master and servant in the hope of furthering their fortunes in love and money.

Beazley, Samuel (1786–1851) British architect and playwright. He was responsible for the Lyceum Theatre, St James's Theatre, the Adelphi frontage, and the colonnade of Drury Lane. He was also author of several farces and short comedies.

Beccari, Agostino (d. 1598) Italian playwright, noted for his pastoral *Il Sacrifizio* (c. 1544). Performed before the royal court at Ferrara, it may have had a strong influence upon the subsequent works of Tasso.

Beck, Heinrich (1760–1803) German actor, who made early appearances in Ekhof's company before transferring to Mannheim in 1778. There he performed in plays by Schiller and ventured into theatre management with Iffland.

Beck, Julian *See* Living Theatre.

Becket, or the Honour of God (*Becket ou l'Honneur de Dieu*) A *pièce costumée* by Jean *Anouilh. First performance: Paris, 1959. The play is based on Thomas à Becket's relationship with Henry II, culminating in Becket's martyrdom and Henry's penitence.

Beckett, Samuel (1906–) Irish playwright, who in 1927 moved to Paris where he worked for James Joyce. Here he began writing novels, remaining an inhabitant of Paris for most of the rest of his life – indeed some of his best-known works were written in French. In his first published play, *Waiting for Godot, and such later

works as *Endgame, he turned against conventional British and US theatre, allying himself with such pioneering writers as Joyce and such directors as Blin; he also attempted to explore a genuinely new territory for the theatre, abandoning such basic elements as plot, action, and character in his examination of the human predicament.

Regarded as a leading writer for the Theatre of the Absurd, he has become widely-known for his unique combination of nihilism and humour, his characters being torn between the pointlessness of their lives and their seemingly inexhaustible instinct to keep going. The later works (including several radio plays) show a progression towards a far more private and more confined world in which the characters are barely capable of communication. *Not I*, *Footfalls*, and *Rockaby* are all monologues for women. Beckett was awarded a Nobel Prize in 1969. Principal dramatic works:

En attendant Godot: 1953; translated as *Waiting for Godot.*
Fin de partie: 1957; translated as *Endgame.*
*Krapp's Last Tape: 1958.
*Happy Days: 1961.
Play: 1963.
Breath: 1969.
Not I: 1971.
That Time: 1976.
Footfalls: 1976.
Ghost Trio: 1976.
. . . But the Clouds . . . : 1977.
A Piece of Monologue: 1980.
Rockaby: 1980.
Ohio Impromptu: 1981.
Quad: 1982.
Catastrophe: 1982.
Nacht und Traüme: 1983.
What Where: 1983.

Becque, Henry François (1837–99) French playwright, associated with naturalism. Becque's plays, produced at André Antoine's Théâtre Libre, were not fully appreciated by their first audiences. *Les Corbeaux* (1882; translated as *The Vultures*, 1913) is a powerful drama of greed and opportunism, while the comedy *La Parisienne* (1885; translated as *The Woman of Paris*, 1955) centres on the amorality of the heroine.

Bedford Music Hall A theatre in Camden, London, that was opened in 1861 and enjoyed a long career as a venue for music hall entertainments. Seating 1168, it saw appearances by George Leybourne and Marie Lloyd among many others; it was later used for revivals of popular plays for a time before being demolished in 1969.

bedroom farce A broad comedy in which much of the action centres about one or more bedrooms. Such farces commonly exploit mistaken identity, lost clothing, and sexual innuendo for comic effect and have proved an important part of the staple diet of the commercial theatre in the 20th century.

Bedroom Farce A farce by Alan *Ayckbourn. First performance: National Theatre, London, 1977. A bleak suburban comedy, the action revolves around three married couples and takes place in their respective bedrooms, which are presented simultaneously on the stage.

Beekman Street Theatre *See* Chapel Street Theatre.

Beerbohm, Sir (Henry) Max(imilian) (1872–1956) British playwright and theatre critic, who succeeded G B Shaw as drama critic for the *Saturday Review* in 1898. He wrote vividly about a wide range of dramatic productions and was the author of several successful plays, notably *The Happy Hypocrite* (1900), a novel, and short stories. His drama criticism was collected in *Around Theatre* (1953) and *More Theatres* (1968). In 1908 he married the actress Florence Kahn; Herbert Tree was his half-brother.

Beeston, Christopher (c. 1570–1638) English actor and manager, who was a member of Strange's Men at the outset of his career and, possibly, also appeared with the Chamberlain's Men. He was at the Rose Theatre in 1602, but gave up acting when he became manager of the Cockpit in 1616. He remained there until the company, known as Queen Henrietta's Men from 1625, disbanded in 1636. He then formed a company of young players called Beeston's Boys.

Following his death his son, **William Beeston** (c. 1606–82), took over, but was imprisoned for staging an unlicensed play. After the closure of the theatres during the Commonwealth he re-established the young training company at Salisbury Court, but was forced by the army to close in 1649. He reopened the theatre in 1660, thus providing a link between Elizabethan drama and that of the Restoration.

Beggar's Opera, The A ballad opera by John *Gay. First performance: 1728. The light-hearted plot follows the rivalry between Polly Peachum and Lucy Lockit over the philandering highwayman Macheath. Highly successful in its own time, it was adapted in the 20th century by Benjamin Britten and inspired *The *Threepenny Opera*.

Behan, Brendan (Francis) (1923–64) Irish playwright, whose experiences as a member of the IRA were reflected in his richly ironic and inventive plays. He was imprisoned twice and eventually died an alcoholic, his tumultuous life story providing the material for the autobiography *Borstal Boy* (1958). *The *Quare Fellow* established his reputation in the theatre when presented by Joan Littlewood in 1958, while the tragicomedy *The *Hostage* was seen in New York and London as well as Dublin and reflected the influence of Brecht. Behan's third play, *Richard's Cork Leg*, was unfinished as his death but was later adapted for performance (1972) at the Abbey Theatre;

his only other dramatic work was *The Big House* (1957), a television play.

Behn, Mrs Aphra (1640–89) English playwright and novelist, who was employed as a spy in the Netherlands and was imprisoned for debt – being released according to tradition on the intervention of Killigrew – before becoming the first professional female writer in England in the 1670s. She wrote more than a dozen lively and often coarse plays, of which the most famous was *The *Rover*; others included the comedies *The Lucky Chance* (1686) and *The Emperor of the Moon* (1687), which was inspired by the *commedia dell'arte* and influenced the early development of the English pantomime. A friend of Dryden, Etherege, Otway, and other leading literary figures, she recalled her early years in Surinam in her novel *Oroonoko, or the History of the Royal Slave*, adapted for the stage by Southerne in 1695.

Behrman, S(amuel) N(athaniel) (1893–1973) US playwright, who was the author of many popular sophisticated light comedies as well as several less successful tragedies and serious dramas. He established his reputation with the comedy of manners *The Second Man* (1927); many of his subsequent works were adaptations of plays by other authors, of which the best known included *Amphitryon '38* (1938), based on Giraudoux, *The Pirate* (1942), from a play by Ludwig Fulda, and *I Know My Love* (1949), based on Achard's *Auprès de ma blonde* – all starring the Lunts. His other original works numbered amongst them *No Time for Comedy* (1939), and *The Cold Wind and the Warm* (1958), which both had a strong autobiographical element.

Beil, Johann David (1754–94) German actor, who was a member of Ekhof's company in Gotha and later transferred to Mannheim where he appeared in comedy and in plays by Schiller. He also performed in works by his friend Iffland; after his early death Iffland inherited several of his roles.

Béjart, Joseph (1616–59) French actor, the eldest member of a theatrical family closely associated with Molière. He was with Molière in the Illustre-Théâtre company and subsequently created parts in the celebrated playwright's *L'Étourdi* and *Dépit amoureux*.

His sister, **Madeleine Béjart** (1618–72), was an actress and had a profound influence upon the young Molière. She was a cofounder with him of the Illustre-Théâtre and eventually accompanied him to Paris in 1658. She excelled in classical tragedy and in the soubrette roles that Molière wrote for her in such plays as *Les Précieuses ridicules* and *Tartuffe*.

Her sister, **Geneviève Béjart** (1624–75), was also an actress with Molière's company, appearing chiefly in tragedy under her mother's maiden name, as Mlle Hervé.

Another sister, **Armande-Grésinde-Claire-Élisabeth Béjart** (1641–1700), became the target of malicious gossip upon her marriage to Molière in 1662, through the suggestion that she was in fact the playwright's daughter by Madeleine. The scandal was eventually defused by Louis XIV, who acted as godfather to their first child. The marriage was less than happy, despite the fact that Armande, who was trained as an actress by her husband, went on to create several major roles in Molière's plays, including Célimène in *Le Misanthrope* and Elmire in *Tartuffe*. When Molière died, she oversaw the troupe's amalgamation with the company from the Théâtre du Marais and subsequently the formation of the Comédie-Française.

Belasco, David (David Valasco; 1859–1931) US actor-manager and playwright, of Portuguese-Jewish parentage, who was a dominant figure in US theatre in the early 20th century. Popularly known as the 'Bishop of Broadway' and famous for his flamboyant personality, he successfully linked the sentimentalism of Victorian drama with the new naturalism of modern European writers, directing or producing over 300 plays on Broadway alone.

He began his career in San Francisco, subsequently working briefly with Boucicault and then moving to New York, where he eventually became stage manager under Daniel Frohman at the Madison Square Theatre (1882). He was soon recognized as a prolific playwright and adaptor of old plays and novels in both New York and London, his most successful works including *The Heart of Maryland* (1895), *Madame Butterfly* (1900), and *The Girl of the Golden West* (1905), of which the latter two have survived in operatic versions by Puccini.

In 1902 he acquired the Republic Theatre and renamed it the Belasco Theatre, subsequently staging many of his own plays there with such performers as David Warfield and George Arliss. Later he also built and opened the Stuyvesant Theatre (again renamed the Belasco Theatre in 1910), which remained his base until his death.

Belasco Theatre A theatre on West 42nd Street, New York, which was opened as the **Stuyvesant Theatre** in 1907. The name was changed three years later in honour of its manager, David Belasco, and the theatre reopened with Belasco's *The Lily*. From 1935 to 1941 it housed the Group Theatre, whose production of *Trio* (1944) by Dorothy and Howard Baker aroused controversy with its discussion of lesbianism and led to the theatre's closure. For a period of four years from 1949 to 1953 it was used for broadcasting but subsequently reverted to live drama; the theatre is now owned by the Shubert Organization. Recent productions seen there include *The Rocky Horror Picture Show* (1975) and *Ain't Misbehavin'* (1981).

Belcari, Feo (1410–84) Italian playwright, author of several early *sacra rappresentazione*. A native of Florence, he collaborated

with Antonio Meglio upon an influential play depicting the Last Judgement.

Belfast Civic Arts Theatre A theatre in Belfast, Northern Ireland, opened in 1944 as the **Mask Theatre** in a converted loft. Early plays included performances of major European dramas; as the Belfast Arts Theatre it then added plays by leading US writers before moving in 1961 to Botanic Avenue. Civil unrest caused the theatre's closure from 1971 to 1976, when it prospered once more (seating 500) with a wide variety of productions, from work by native writers to musicals and plays for children.

Bel Geddes, Norman (1893–1958) US scene designer, who paved the way for *theatre-in-the-round in 1915 when he initiated the idea of a theatre without a proscenium. His designs for Volmöller's *The Miracle* in 1923 earned him recognition and, in 1935, he employed *composite setting for a production of Kingsley's *Dead End*.

His daughter, **Barbara Bel Geddes** (1922-), made her stage debut in 1940. After her New York debut in *Out of the Frying Pan* (1941), she enjoyed success in 1945 in d'Usseau and Gow's *Deep Are the Roots*. Later roles included Margaret in *Cat on a Hot Tin Roof* (1955) and Katherine Johnson in *Silent Night, Lonely Night* (1959); more recently she became even more widely known for her portrayal of Miss Ellie in the *Dallas* television series.

Belgrade Theatre A theatre in Coventry, opened in 1958 and named in recognition of a gift of timber for its erection sent from Belgrade in Yugoslavia. The first of the *civic theatres, the building includes accommodation for the resident company (which also presents the annual Coventry mystery play cycle) and space for exhibitions. Major productions that have been staged there include plays by Wesker and Bond and numerous acclaimed plays for children. Under the successive managers Brian Bailey and

Warren Jenkins the company has maintained an extremely varied programme, while experimental drama has also flourished in a smaller studio theatre, the Belgrade Venue. The main auditorium seats 900 people.

Belgravia Theatre *See* Royal Court Theatre.

Bell, John (1745–1831) British publisher and journalist. He brought out an acting edition of Shakespeare, based on the prompt books of the patent theatres and edited by Francis Gentleman, in 1773. *Bell's British Theatre* is a valuable selection of plays and prefaces.

Bell, John Joy (1871–1934) Scottish playwright, who specialized in writing in the Scottish vernacular. His one-act comic plays include *Courtin' Christina*, *The Pie in the Oven*, and *Wee MacGregor's Party*, while his most famous work is a tense thriller, *Thread o'Scarlet* (1923).

Bell, Marie (Marie-Jeanne Belon; 1900–85) French actress and manager, who became a leading performer in tragedy at the Comédie-Française, which he joined in 1921. She excelled in dramas by Racine as well as in modern works by Claudel, Félicien Marceau, and Jean Genet; she was manager of the Théâtre du Gymnase from 1959.

Bellamy, George Anne (c. 1727–88) British actress, who acquired her Christian names by mistake; she should have been christened Georgiana. The illegitimate daughter of Lord Tyrawley, she was engaged by Christopher Rich at Covent Garden, where she played opposite James Quin. Garrick subsequently engaged her at Drury Lane, casting her as Juliet to his Romeo. She was never a great actress and was involved in numerous scandals. She retired in 1785, publishing an unreliable six-volume autobiography.

Bellecour (Jean-Claude-Gilles Colson; 1725–78) French actor and playwright, who was one of the best-known comic actors of the Comédie-Française. He began as an artist but excelled in comedy after joining the Comédie-Française in 1750 at the urging of Richelieu, soon relinquishing his tragic roles to Lekain. His wife was the actress Rose-Petronelle le Roy Beauménard.

Belleroche (Raymond Poisson; c. 1630–90) French actor, who was much admired in comic roles at the Hôtel de Bourgogne, despite his slight stutter. He was particularly identified with the role of *Crispin, who appeared in several of his own comedies. His son was the actor Paul *Poisson.

Bellerose (Pierre le Messier; c. 1592–1670) French actor-manager, who became leader of Valleran-Lecomte's company on the latter's death and subsequently took over the combined troupe at the Hôtel de Bourgogne in 1634. He was popular in both comedy and tragedy and excelled as the central character in Corneille's *Le Menteur*, amongst other roles.

Belleville *See* Turlupin.

Bell Inn An inn in Gracechurch Street in London, where plays were staged in the late 16th century. Companies that performed there included the Queen's Men.

Belloy, Pierre Laurent Buirette de (1727–75) French playwright. De Belloy's reputation rests on the patriotic tragedy *Le Siège de Calais*, first performed in Paris in 1765, which appealed to the rising spirit of nationalism in France at the time; his other plays are of little worth.

Bells, The An adaptation by Leopold *Lewis of *Le Juif Polonais* by *Erckmann-Chatrian. First performance: Lyceum Theatre, 1871. Sir Henry *Irving's performance as the burgomaster, haunted by his guilt for an undiscovered murder that he has committed, established him as the leading actor of his day and restored the theatre's fortunes.

Bellwood, Bessie (Elizabeth Ann Katherine Mahoney; 1857–96) British music hall performer, formerly a rabbit-skinner in Bermondsey. She developed a notorious line in suggestive songs and was idolized by her audiences; she was also successful in New York.

Belmont Theatre A theatre on West 48th Street, New York, which was opened as the Norworth Theatre in 1918. Later that year the name was changed to the Belmont; plays staged there included the Pulitzer Prize-winning *Miss Lulu Bett* (1920) by Zona Gale and Philip Barry's *You and I* (1923). The theatre was turned into a cinema in 1936 and was finally demolished in 1951.

below *See* stage direction.

Beltrame *See* Barbieri, Niccolò.

Benavente y Martínez, Jacinto (1866–1954) Spanish playwright and critic, noted for his many satirical comedies. These include *La noche del sabado* (1903), *Los intereses creados* (1907), which as *The Bonds of Interest* was the first play performed by the Theatre Guild in New York in 1919, and *La Malquerida* (The Passion Flower; 1913), which was presented in New York in 1920 and in London in 1926. His enormous output included over 150 original plays, as well as translations of Molière and Shakespeare. He was awarded a Nobel Prize in 1922.

benefit A special performance of a play, the proceeds of which go to a specified member or members of the cast (customarily on their retirement) or to a particular worthy cause.

Benelli, Sem (1875–1949) Italian playwright, noted for his historical dramas written in blank verse. Most renowned of these was *La cena della beffe* (1909), which as *The Jest* was produced in New York in 1919. His other works include *Tignola* (The Bookworm; 1908), *L'amore dei tre rei* (The Love of the Three Kings; 1910), and his last major work, *Orfeo e Proserpina* (1928).

Benfield, Robert (d. 1649) English actor, who appeared with Lady Elizabeth's Men in plays by Beaumont and Fletcher and later with the King's Men, appearing as Antonio in *The Duchess of Malfi* (1619) and in major roles in plays by Massinger. He is in the 1623 Folio list of actors in Shakespeare's plays and was a shareholder in the Globe and Blackfriars theatres.

Benger, Sir William (d. 1572) English court official, who was appointed Master of the Revels in 1559. His period in office saw the reduction of the role to that of censorship only.

Bennett, Alan (1934–) British actor and playwright, who first attracted attention as a member of the celebrated *Beyond the Fringe* revue in 1960. His first play, the satirical *Forty Years On* (1968), established his reputation as a playwright with a particularly acute ear for ordinary language and the pathos and ironies of everyday life when performed in London with a cast including John Gielgud and subsequently Emlyn Williams; successes since then have included *Getting On* (1971), the farce *Habeas Corpus* (1973), in which Bennett himself appeared, *The Old Country* (1977), dealing with the state of mind of an exiled spy, *Enjoy* (1980), *Kafka's Dick* (1986), and several highly-acclaimed one-act plays and monologues for television.

Bennett, (Enoch) Arnold (1867–1931) British novelist and playwright, who had some success with such plays as *Milestones*

(1912) – which was written in collaboration with Edward Knoblock and inspired Coward's *Cavalcade* – and *The Great Adventure* (1913), which was based on one of his novels. His later dramatic works, which were less successful, include *London Life* (1924) and *Mr Prohack* (1927).

Bennett, Hywel (1944-) British actor, born in Wales, who first appeared in London as Ophelia in a youth production of *Hamlet* (1959). He then trained at RADA and worked in the provinces before performing at the Mermaid Theatre as Prince Hal in *Henry VI Parts I and II* (1970) and Antony in *Julius Caesar* (1972) at the Young Vic. Subsequently he played Simon in Simon Gray's *Otherwise Engaged* (1977), Andreas Capodistriou and Inspector Bowden in Anthony Shaffer's *The Oily Levantine* (1979), and won praise in Chekhov's *Three Sisters* (1987). He has also worked as a guest director at leading repertory theatres and made numerous television appearances.

Bennett, Jill (1931-) British actress, who began her career at Stratford in 1949. Subsequently she participated in Olivier's season at the St James's Theatre in 1951, appearing in *Antony and Cleopatra* and *Caesar and Cleopatra*, and excelled as Isabelle in Anouilh's *Dinner with the Family* (1957). She has also appeared in several plays by John Osborne (to whom she was married 1968–77), including his version of *Hedda Gabler* (1976); she played Gertrude in the Royal Court production of *Hamlet* (1980). Stage successes since then have included *The Little Foxes* (1981) and *Dance of Death* (1983).

Bennett, Richard (1872–1944) US actor, who became highly popular in romantic leading roles. His many successes, achieved in spite of his own unpredictable nature and occasional criticisms of the audience delivered from the stage, included plays by Barrie, Brieux, O'Neill, and Shaw as well as Maxwell Anderson's *Winterset* (1935).

Benserade, Isaac de (1613–91) French poet and playwright. His literary output consisted chiefly of poetry and libretti for the royal ballets, on which he collaborated with Molière. *Cléopâtre* (1636) is generally considered to be the best of his mediocre dramatic works.

Benson, Sir Frank Robert (1858–1939) British actor-manager, who first appeared on the professional stage (at the Lyceum) in 1882. A year later he led his own company on tour in the provinces, presenting plays by Shakespeare – notably the first production of *Hamlet* in its entirety (1899) – at Stratford-upon-Avon at an annual summer festival from 1886 to 1916. He was knighted in 1916 by George V at Drury Lane, becoming the only actor to be thus honoured actually inside a theatre.

His wife was the actress **Constance Featherstonhaugh** (1860–1946), who was a leading lady with his celebrated company for many years.

Benthall, Michael (1919–74) British theatre director, who was a prominent member of the Oxford University Dramatic Society and subsequently codirector with Tyrone Guthrie of *Hamlet* at the Old Vic in 1944. He was noted for his Shakespearean and classical productions and was director of the Old Vic from 1953 to 1959.

Bentley, Eric Russell (1916-) British theatre critic, director, and playwright, who did much to popularize the plays of Brecht. In 1950 he was coproducer with Brecht of *Mother Courage* in Munich; he has also directed plays by O'Neill, Lorca, and cummings. His own plays include *Are You Now Or Have You Ever Been...?* (1972), *The Recantation of Galileo Galilei* (1973), and *Expletive Deleted* (1974).

Beolco, Angelo (c. 1502–42) Italian actor and playwright, who had an early influence upon the development of the *commedia dell'arte*. He became popularly known as **Il Ruzzante**, after the talkative character he created, and was the author of several plays (written in his native Paduan dialect) that have enjoyed revivals in the 20th century.

Bérain, Jean (1637–1711) French theatrical designer, who executed elaborate stage designs for plays by Molière. He succeeded Vigarani at the Salle des Machines and worked at the Paris Opéra, subsequently designing influential exotic costumes and decorations for performances at the royal court.

Bérard, Christian (1903–49) French artist and designer, who became famous for his romantic and historical designs for both ballets and plays in the 1930s and 1940s. He was particularly noted for his work on productions of Molière and Marivaux under Jouvet and Barrault as well as for his collaborations with Jean Cocteau in both the theatre and the cinema; their works together included *La Machine infernale* (1934) and *L'Aigle à deux têtes* (1946).

Bergbom, Kaarlo (1842–1906) Finnish theatre manager, who established the Finnish National Theatre in 1872. Members of his company presented many of Ibsen's plays, including the first performance of *John Gabriel Borkman* (1897).

Bergerac, Cyrano de *See* Cyrano de Bergerac, Savinien.

Berghof, Herbert (1909–) Austrian-born actor, director, and teacher who came to New York in 1939 to direct *From Vienna* at the Music Box Theatre. He made his New York stage debut in *Reunion*, which he also codirected. In 1964 he founded the Herbert Berghof Studio in New York, where he teaches acting.

Bergman, Hjalmar Frederik Elgerus (1883–1931) Swedish novelist, playwright, and short-story writer, who is regarded as one of Sweden's most important writers after Strindberg. His earliest stage successes were the one-act plays, *Dödens Arlekin* and *Herr Sleeman Kommen* (both 1917); later works included the comedy *Swedenhjelms* (1925), *Petrasket* (The Baron's Will; 1928), and adaptations of two of his own novels – *Hans Nåds Testamente* and *Makurells i Wadköping* (God's Orchid; 1919) – which were both produced in 1930.

Bergman, (Ernst) Ingmar (1918–) Swedish director, who has become recognized as one of the foremost 20th-century directors for the cinema but has also won acclaim for his work in the theatre. He led an amateur theatre group while still at university and later took over theatres in Halsingborg (1944–46) and Gothenburg (1946–49); his early stage successes included his own play *Kaspers död* (Kasper's Death; 1942) and Camus's *Caligula* (1946). Subsequently he worked at Malmo (1952–60) and at the Kungliga Dramatiska Teatern (1963–66), specializing in intense psychological dramas by Strindberg, Chekhov, Brecht, Ibsen, and others. In 1977 he transferred to Munich after an argument with the Swedish tax authorities. In 1987 his production of *Hamlet* with the Stockholm Royal Dramatic Theatre was seen at the National Theatre.

Bergner, Elisabeth (1900–) Austrian actress, who became a leading performer in Berlin in the 1920s and later in London (from 1933). She established her reputation under Reinhardt as Shaw's St Joan in 1924 and subsequently excelled in Shakespeare in such roles as Portia and Juliet. Other celebrated successes included plays by Strindberg, O'Neill, and Giraudoux; in London and New York she appeared in plays by Barrie, Webster, Rattigan, and others, as well as repeating her interpretation of St Joan.

Bergopzoomer, Johann Baptist (1742–1804) Austrian actor, who was a friend of Friedrich Schröder. He began his career in Vienna, appearing in conventional Viennese comedies but later was much admired for his performances in tragedy in both Vienna and in Germany with Kurz's company.

Bergstrøm, Hjalmar (1868–1914) Danish playwright, whose dramas often tackled the social and political problems of his day. The class struggle was discussed in *Lynggaard and Co* (1905) and the emancipation of women in *Karen Bornemann* (1907).

Berkoff, Steven (1937–) British playwright and actor, who founded the London Theatre Group, which has presented several of his plays. His works include *Metamorphosis* (1969), from Kafka; *The Fall of the House of Usher* (1974), from Edgar Allan Poe; *East* (1975), which applied the language of high tragedy to life in London's East End; *Greek* (1979), based on the Oedipus story; *West* (1983), an adaptation of the Beowulf legends; *Sink the Belgrano!* (1987), which was a parody of *Henry V*; and *Decadence* (1987).

Berlin, Irving (Israel Baline; 1888–) Russian-born US songwriter, who also wrote several major Broadway musicals. His first full Broadway score was *Watch Your Step* (1914); subsequent successes included several editions of both Ziegfeld's *Follies* and *The Music Box Revue* (staged at his own *Music Box Theatre), *As Thousands Cheer* (1933), **Annie Get Your Gun*, and **Call Me Madam*.

Berliner Ensemble A German theatre company, founded by Bertolt *Brecht and Helene *Weigel in 1949. Based in East Berlin, it moved from the Deutsches Theater to the Theater am Schiffbauerdamm in 1954 and established a strong reputation for its productions of Brecht's works. After his death it was led by Weigel for many years

and subsequently (since 1977) by Manfred Wekwerth. In recent years it has diversified with plays by Shaw and Wedekind among others.

Bernadon A comic character of the Viennese theatrical tradition, developed by Joseph Kurz from *Hanswurst. In the course of his adventures he frequently finds himself embroiled in struggles against the supernatural.

Bernard, Tristan (Paul Bernard; 1866–1947) French playwright. His light comedies, in which good use is made of such devices as disguise, intrigue, and mistaken identity, include *L'Anglais tel qu'on le parle* (1899), *Triplepatte* (1905; translated as *Toddles*, 1907), and *Le Petit Café* (1911).

His son, **Jean-Jacques Bernard** (1888–1972), was also a playwright. His dramas of the Theatre of *Silence include *Le Feu qui reprend mal* (1921, translated as *The Sulky Fire*, 1926), *Martine* (1922; translated 1927), and *Le Printemps des autres* (1924; translated as *The Springtime of Others*, 1934).

Bernhardt,   Sarah(-Marie-Henriette) (1844–1923) French actress, acknowledged as one of the most admired performers ever to appear on the French stage. Noted for her distinctive voice and romantic looks, she began her career at the Comédie-Française in 1862 and subsequently established an international reputation as a fine as well as eccentric and tempestuous actress in tragedy. In 1880 she also ventured into theatre management. Her greatest performances included the title roles in Shakespeare's *Hamlet*, Racine's *Phèdre*, and Scribe's *Adrienne Lecouvreur*, Doña Sol in Hugo's *Hernani*, Marguerite Gautier in *La Dame aux camélias* by Dumas *fils*, the King of Rome in Rostand's *L'Aiglon*, and various characters in the melodramas of Sardou. After her right leg was amputated in 1915 she continued to appear to undiminished acclaim in parts written specially for her until her death.

Bernini, Giovanni Lorenzo (1598–1680) Italian sculptor, architect, and artist, noted for his development of stage effects for use in the theatres of Rome. His spectacular scenery and stage machinery, including storm effects and transformation scenes, influenced many later designers, notably Inigo Jones.

Bernstein, Aline (Aline Frankau; 1881–1955) US scene designer, whose first work was for the Indian play *The Little Clay Cart* (1924). She also worked on productions of Moeller's *Caprice* (1928), Chekhov's *The Seagull* (1929), *Romeo and Juliet* (1930), Molnár's *Liliom* (1932), Barry's *The Animal Kingdom* (1932), Elmer Rice's *Judgement Day* (1934), Hellman's *The Children's Hour* (1934) and *The Little Foxes* (1939), and Cocteau's *The Eagle Has Two Heads* (1949).

Bernstein,   Henry(-Léon-Gustave-Charles) (1876–1953) French playwright, born in Paris. Bernstein's early successes were powerful melodramas; he subsequently turned to psychological themes, notably in *Le Secret* (1913) and *La Galérie des glaces* (1924). The son of a Jewish banker, he attacked anti-Semitism in *Samson* (1907) and *Israël* (1908) and Nazism in *Elvire* (1940).

Bernstein, Leonard (1918-) US composer, conductor, and pianist, who has written numerous celebrated musical scores for stage shows. He composed the scores for *On the Town* (1944), *Wonderful Town* (1953), *Candide* (1956), and *West Side Story* (1957). He also composed incidental music for Barrie's *Peter Pan* (1950).

Bersenev, Ivan Nikolaievich (Ivan Nikolaievich Pavlishchev; 1889–1951) Soviet actor and director, who was the leading figure at the Lenkom Theatre from 1938. He began his career in Kiev under Mardzhanov,

and appeared at the Moscow Art Theatre from 1928 to 1938; his most successful productions included Simonov's *And So It Will Be* (1944) and other contemporary Soviet plays.

Bertinazzi, Carlo (1713–83) Italian actor of the *commedia dell'arte*, who specialized in the role of Arlequin. Popularly known as **Carlin**, he was one of the few Italian actors still performing with the Comédie-Italienne in the early 18th century, having succeeded Tommaso Vicentini at the Hôtel de Bourgogne in 1741.

Bertolazzi, Carlo (1870–1916) Italian playwright, author of several notable plays written in the Milanese dialect. *El nost' Milan* (Our Milan; 1893) was revived by Strehler in 1955; other plays include *L'egoista* (1900) and *Lulù* (1903).

bespeak performance A special performance given during the 19th century at which a single patron, or group of patrons, bought all the tickets and chose the play to be performed. The proceeds from the evening were shared amongst the cast.

Bessenyi, György (c. 1746–1811) Hungarian playwright, regarded as the most influential writer for the early Hungarian theatre. His plays include the comedy *The Philosopher* (1777) and a number of historical tragedies.

Besson, Benno (1922-) Swiss director and actor, who became a leading member of Brecht's Berliner Ensemble. He began his career under Serreau in Paris and with Brecht worked on several notable adaptations of Molière, Farquhar, and others. Subsequently he has produced dramas at the Deutsches Theater (1961–69), where his successes included works by Aristophanes and Offenbach, at the Volksbühne (1969–79), where his productions included *Spectacles I and II* and Müller's *Die Schlacht*, and at the Théâtre de la Comédie in Geneva (1979-). He has also been praised for contributions to the Avignon Festival.

Betterton, Thomas (c. 1635–1710) English actor, son of a cook in Charles I's household. He began acting for John Rhodes at the Cockpit, then joined Davenant at Lincoln's Inn Fields. When Davenant died in 1671, Betterton took over his company, moving to Dorset Garden. When his company amalgamated with Killigrew's in 1682, he became the leading actor at Drury Lane, confirming his reputation in plays by Shakespeare and contemporary playwrights. Unable to put up with Christopher *Rich's management, he returned to Lincoln's Inn Fields in 1695, opening with the first performance of *Love for Love*. 10 years later he moved to the Haymarket, where he made his final appearance in 1710. The foremost figure of the Restoration stage, he was buried in Westminster Abbey. His wife was the actress Mary *Saunderson.

Betti, Ugo (1892–1953) Italian playwright, poet, and short-story writer, often regarded as Italy's most outstanding dramatist since Pirandello. A judge by profession, Betti wrote over 20 plays, many of which have a courtroom setting or are in the form of a legal investigation, including *Delitto all'isola delle capre* (Crime on Goat Island; 1948) and *Corruzione al Palazzo di Giustizia* (Corruption in the Palace of Justice; 1949), which number among his most important plays. His other works include *I nostri sogni* (Our Dreams; 1937), a charming light comedy, *Frano allo scala Nord* (Landslide; 1936), *Ispezione* (The Inquiry; 1947), and *L'aiuola bruciata* (The Burnt Flowerbed; 1952).

Betty, William Henry West (1791–1874) British boy actor brought up in Ireland. Hailed initially as the Minor Roscius, he was publicized by his father, hoping for long-term exploitation, as the **Young Roscius**. This publicity led to engagements at Covent Garden and Drury Lane in the 1804–05 season. Playing the great Shakespearean tragedies, he evoked near hysteria with his performances. Two years later, however, he was hissed off the stage while playing Richard III. He retired at the age of 17.

Beverley, William Roxby (c. 1811–89) British scene painter, who studied with Clarkson Stanfield. He worked first as an actor and scene painter for his father, who managed the Theatre Royal, Manchester. In 1853 he was appointed scenic director at Covent Garden; a year later he moved to Drury Lane, where he remained for 30 years. He was famous, in particular, for his pantomime designs and sets for Charles Kean's Shakespearean productions.

Beyond the Horizon A play by Eugene *O'Neill. First performance: Broadway, 1920. Set in New England, it revolves around the Mayo brothers, Robert and Andrew, a farmer and a seaman; Robert proves to be the real adventurer though he fails as a farmer. The play reaches a climax when Ruth, who married Robert, confesses her love for Andrew. The play won a Pulitzer Prize.

Bharata (fl. 500 AD) Indian sage, who established the basic rules for early Indian drama in his treatise *Natyashastra*. He defined theatre as a means of achieving spiritual peace and laid down the various gestures and eye movements available to the actor, as well as giving guidance on dance, playwriting, and theatre architecture.

Bhāsa (2nd century AD) Indian playwright, author of the earliest known Sanskrit drama. His 13 surviving plays, notably *Svapnavasavadatta*, were heroic romances based on prose epics and had a profound influence upon the writings of Kālidāsa and on the popular anonymous play *The Little Clay Cart*.

Biancolelli, Giuseppe Domenico (c. 1637–88) French actor, born in Italy, who became famous for his interpretation of Arlequin, the French version of Arlecchino in the *commedia dell'arte*. Popularly known as **Dominique**, he played an important part in persuading Louis XIV to allow him and his fellow-players to perform in French rather than Italian. One of his daughters married the son of Françoise La Thorillière.

His youngest son, **Pietro Francesco Biancolelli** (1680–1734), was also an actor. Known as Dominique le Jeune, he appeared as Arlequin, Pierrot, and subsequently in straight plays with Riccoboni's company.

Bibiena, Ferdinando (1657–1743) Italian theatrical designer, who – with his brother **Francesco Bibiena** (1659–1739) – established the Bibiena family (originally called **Galli**) as leading architects of baroque theatres throughout Europe. Ferdinando contributed towards the building of the Teatro Farnese in Parma and subsequently moved to Vienna, where he collaborated upon further theatrical designs with Francisco and his own sons.

Ferdinando's eldest son **Alessandro Bibiena** (1686–1748) became an architect, while his other sons **Giuseppe Bibiena** (1695–1756), **Antonio Bibiena** (1697–c. 1774), and **Giovanni Maria Bibiena** (1700–74) all worked on theatre design.

Giuseppe's son **Carlo Bibiena** (1721–87) contributed to the design of the Bayreuth opera-house and, together with other members of the family, helped to develop the use of the perspective scene.

Bible-history *See* mystery play.

Bickerstaffe, Isaac (1735–1812) British playwright, born in Ireland, who wrote or collaborated on numerous comedies and ballad operas. *Thomas and Sally; or, the Sailor's Return* was staged at Covent Garden in 1760 and was followed by such pieces as *Love in a Village* (1762), *The Maid of the Mill* (1765), and *Lionel and Clarissa* (1768). In 1772 he was suspected of a capital offence and fled to the Continent, where he died in penury.

Biddles, Adelaide Helen (1837–1921) British actress, who first appeared as a child in Charles Kean's company. In 1856 she married the actor-manager Charles Calvert (1828–79). She played leading parts in his company and, after his death, toured extensively. Her son was the actor Louis *Calvert.

Bidermann, Jakob (1578–1639) German playwright and priest, an important writer of Jesuit drama. His best known play, *Cenodoxus* (1602), depicts the founding of the Carthusian order and was revived in Munich in 1958.

Bijou Theatre A theatre in Bayswater, London, which was a regular venue for performances presented in order to protect an author's copyright. Plays by Shaw and Wilde were among those produced there in the late 19th century; in 1925 Lena Ashwell renamed the theatre the **Twentieth Century Theatre** and appeared there in numerous plays by Masefield, Dostoevsky, and others. After 1933 the building was only sporadically used as a theatre and finally became a warehouse.

An earlier **Bijou Theatre** opened in the Haymarket in 1862, staging both plays and concerts; it was burnt down in 1876.

Another **Bijou Theatre** opened on Broadway, New York, in 1878 as the **Brighton Theatre**. Later renamed the **Broadway Opera House**, it became the Bijou in 1880 and prospered with appearances by Lillian Russell. Rebuilt in 1883, it saw the adult debut of Julia Marlowe and many musicals before demolition in 1915.

The **Bijou Theatre** on West 45th Street, New York, opened in 1917. Plays staged there included works by Barrie, Ibsen, and Benn Levy; it then became a cinema (1931–

45). Russel Crouse and Howard Lindsay's *Life With Father* was staged there from 1945 to 1947, while subsequent successes have included O'Neill's *A Moon for the Misbegotten* (1957), Greene's *The Potting Shed* (1957), and – after another period as a cinema (1962–72) – the pantomime *Mummenschanz* (1977).

A smaller **Bijou Theatre** opened on West 48th Street, New York, in 1970 as part of the Playhouse Theatre.

Bill-Belotserkovsky, Vladimir Naumovich (1884–1970) Soviet playwright, who worked in the US from 1911 to 1917, acquiring there the nickname Bill, which he tacked on to his surname. His first play, *Echo* (1924), was set in the US although his best-known play, *Hurricane* (1925), was set in Russia during the Civil War, being first staged at the Mossoviet Theatre and since being performed in many other East European countries.

Billetdoux, François (1927–) French playwright, born in Paris. A student of Charles Dullin, Billetdoux made his name in 1959 with the tragi-comedy *Tchin-Tchin*. Noted for their unconventional plots, his plays include *Le Comportement des époux Bredburry* (1960) and *Va donc chez Törpe* (1961), in which a series of suicides takes place at the same inn.

Billinger, Richard (1890–1965) Austrian novelist, playwright, and poet, whose first play, *Das Perchtenspiel*, was produced by Max Reinhardt in 1928. Others include *Die Hexe von Passau* (The Witch of Passau; 1935), which was used by Ottmar Gerster as the basis for an opera (1941), *Das nachte Leben* (1953), and *Menschen nennen es Schicksal* (1962).

Bill of Divorcement, A A play by Clemence *Dane. First performance: 1921. Written in the style of Pinero, it argued that insanity is sufficient grounds for divorce and caused considerable controversy.

Billy Liar A comedy by Willis *Hall and Keith *Waterhouse, based on the latter's novel. First performance: London, 1960. The play revolves around Billy, who relieves the boredom of life in his family in northern England with a series of fantasies, which inevitably lead to trouble.

Billy Rose Theatre *See* Nederlander Theatre.

Biltmore Theatre A theatre on West 47th Street, between Broadway and Eighth Avenue, New York, which opened in 1925. Seating 994, the theatre attracted attention early on with Mae West's notorious *Pleasure Man* (1928), which was banned by the authorities, and appearances by the Federal Theatre Project (1936). Later in 1936 it was taken over by Warner Brothers and, from 1952 to 1962, it was used as a broadcasting studio. In 1963 it reopened for live drama with Neil Simon's *Barefoot in the Park*. Productions since then have included *Hair* (1968) and William Douglas Home's *The Kingfisher* (1978).

Bio-Mechanics An approach to the direction and training of actors developed by Meyerhold as a reaction against Stanislavsky's ideas. The theory called for the suppression of all emotion and character and the complete domination of a production by the director. In order to achieve this stark detachment it stipulated attention to movement and gesture and the removal of almost all items of scenery; the theory failed to have any lasting influence.

Bird, Robert Montgomery (1806–54) US novelist, playwright, and poet, whose popular dramas used classical settings to explore topical issues. *The Gladiator* (1831), which had over 1000 performances, focuses upon slavery and the fight for liberty. Other works included *Ordalloossa* (1832) and *The Broker of Bogota* (1934); all of his plays were produced by the actor Edwin Forrest.

Bird, Theophilus (1608–64) English actor, whose father, **William Bird** (d. 1624) was one of the Admiral's Men. Theophilus joined Queen Henrietta's Men at the Cockpit as a player of female roles, appearing in plays by Massinger, Heywood, and Thomas Nabbes. Subsequently he married Christopher Beeston's daughter, Anne, and served as his father-in-law's agent in the purchase of Salisbury Court. Later he also appeared under Killigrew at Drury Lane.

Birds, The A comedy by *Aristophanes. First performance: Athens, 414 BC. The play revolves around the attempt of two Athenians to create a fantasy utopia between heaven and earth.

Birman, Serafima Germanovna (1890–1976) Soviet actress and director, who began her career at the Moscow Art Theatre and later became one of the leading figures at the Lenkom Theatre, which she joined in 1938. There she directed notable versions of plays by Rostand, Simonov, and Tolstoy as well as making numerous successful personal appearances.

Birmingham Repertory Theatre A theatre in Birmingham, opened in 1913 at the instigation of Barry *Jackson, who also provided much of the necessary finance. After the first production, *Twelfth Night*, the theatre presented a number of plays by John Drinkwater and Shaw until the theatre was forced to close temporarily in 1924. After its reopening a series of commercial successes – notably Jackson's innovative modern-dress *Hamlet* (1925) and *Macbeth* (1928) – secured the theatre's future and it became respected for its staging of foreign works and for its training of young actors, including Olivier, Paul Scofield, and Albert Finney. Numerous productions transferred to London and New York and in 1971 the company moved into a new theatre, seating 900, in the centre of Birmingham. Since then the theatre has been used for largely commercial productions, although experimental drama is still performed in the smaller studio theatre, seating 160.

Bíró, Lajos (1880–1948) Hungarian playwright, best known for the satirical play *The Family Circle* (1909), which exposes hypocrisy in bourgeois society. Other works, which were seen throughout Europe and the US, included *The Yellow Lily* (1910), *Patricia's Seven Houses* (1946), which was loosely based on Shaw's *Widowers' Houses*, and *Our Katie* (1946).

Birthday Party, The Harold *Pinter's first full-length play. First performance: Arts Theatre, Cambridge, 1958. Peter Wood directed and Richard Pearson played Stanley, the central figure whose self-delusions and fears are played upon by the sinister visitors who, under the pretext of celebrating his birthday, proceed to destroy his identity.

Bjørnson, Bjørnstjerne (1832–1910) Norwegian poet, playwright, and novelist, who became Ibsen's successor at the Bergen Theatre in 1857 and went on to establish an international reputation as a writer and public figure, winning a Nobel Prize in 1903. The son of a pastor, he was a fervent patriot and in his early dramatic works (1857–64) drew heavily upon Norwegian folklore and history. Later, however, he adopted Socialist ideals and became widely-known for the social dramas *En fallit* and *Redaktøren*; other plays discussed religious intolerance and contemporary social evolution. The most highly regarded of these later works is *Over Ævne I*, in which he examines the position of the individual in society. From 1865 to 1867 he was artistic director of the Kristiana Theater, where his son – **Bjørn Bjørnson** (1859–1942) – was director from 1885 to 1893 before taking over the Nationaltheatret in 1899.

Principal dramatic works:

Mellen Slagene: 1857; translated as *Between the Battles*.

Halte-Hulde: 1858; translated as *Lame Hulda*.

Kong Sverre: 1861; translated as *King Sverre*.

Sigurd Slembe: 1862.

Maria Stuart i Skotland: 1864.

De Nygifte: 1865; translated as *The Newly-Marrieds*.

Sigurd Jorsalfar: 1872.

Kong Eystejn: 1872.

Redaktøren: 1874; translated as *The Editor*.

En fallit: 1875; translated as *The Bankrupt*.

Kongen: 1877; translated as *The King*.

Det ny system: 1879; translated as *The New System*.

En Handske: 1883; translated as *A Gauntlet*.

Geografiog Kjælighed: 1885; translated as *Love and Geography*.

Over Ævne I: 1883; translated as *Pastor Sang*.

Paul Lange og Tora Parsberg: 1893.

Over Ævne II: 1895; translated as *Beyond Human Power*.

Laboremus: 1901.

Daglannet: 1904.

Når den ny vin blomstrer: 1909; translated as *When the New Wine Blooms*.

Black, George (1890–1943) British impresario, who presented a series of revues in London during and after World War II, with his sons George and Alfred. Their successes included *Apple Sauce* (1940), *Piccadilly Hayride* (1946), and *Take It From Us* (1950).

Black-Ey'd Susan A nautical drama by Douglas *Jerrold. First performance: 1829. The lovely Susan remains faithful to William, her absent sailor-husband; William, however, catches his own captain attempting to seduce her, strikes him, and is sentenced to death. Sentiment and excitement mount until a last-minute reprieve.

Blackfriars Theatre A theatre erected in the grounds of an old monastery in London. It was first adapted as a private theatrical venue by Richard Farrant, master of the choirboys at Windsor, in 1576. After his death in 1581 a combined boy company appeared there briefly until 1584. In 1596 James Burbage attempted to revive another part of the monastery as a theatre but met with official opposition and it was not until 1600, when his son Richard Burbage leased the theatre to the Children of the Chapel Royal, that performances were again undertaken there. From 1608 to 1642 the King's Men were the resident company, presenting plays by Shakespeare, Jonson, and others and the venue became highly popular with the English nobility; productions there were notable for their use of scenery and music. The theatre was demolished in 1655.

blackout The extinguishing of all stage lighting, either suddenly (a **snap blackout**) or gradually, to allow for a scene change, suggest a break in the action, or achieve some other stage effect.

Blacks, The (*Les Nègres*) A play by Jean *Genet. First performance: Paris, 1959. It explores the theme of racial conflict through a troupe of black actors who perform a play within a play, in which a white woman is ritually murdered.

Blagrove, Thomas (d. 1603) English court official, who was appointed clerk to the *Master of the Revels in 1560. He was in charge of censorship in English drama for many years, subject to the Lord Chamberlain, but never became Master himself.

Blakely, Colin (George Edward) (1930–87) British actor, born in Ireland, who first attracted attention in O'Casey's *Cock-a-Doodle-Dandy* at the Royal Court in 1959. Subsequently he appeared with the Royal Shakespeare Company, the National Theatre, and in films. His finest roles included Pizarro in Shaffer's *The Royal Hunt of the Sun*, Kite in *The Recruiting Officer*, and Joe Keller in Miller's *All My Sons*.

Blanchar, Pierre (1896–1963) French actor, who began his career at the Odéon in 1919. He excelled in numerous plays by contemporary authors, including Achard, Salacrou, Montherlant, and Camus; he also enjoyed a successful career in films. He appeared at the Comédie-Française from 1939 to 1946.

Blanchard, Kitty *See* Rankin, Arthur McKee.

Blanchard, William (1769–1835) British actor, born at York. His early attempts to run several northern theatres failed; in 1800 he arrived at Covent Garden as Bob Acres in *The Rivals* and stayed there for 34 years, except for a brief visit to the US in 1832. He was particularly noted for comedy character parts.

Blanchard's Amphitheatre *See* Chatham Theatre.

Bleasdale, Alan (1946-) British playwright, best-known for his television play series *The Boys From the Blackstuff* (1983), set in Liverpool. His works for the stage include *Having a Ball* (1981) and *Are You Lonesome Tonight?* (1985), a musical about the life of Elvis Presley.

Blin, Roger (1907–84) French actor and director, who became famous primarily as a director of notable works of the Theatre of the Absurd. Having previously worked with Artaud and Barrault, he won praise in the 1950s for his direction of such plays as *En attendant Godot* (1953), in which he played Pozzo, and other works by Beckett, as well as for plays by Adamov and Genet.

Blithe Spirit A comedy by Noël *Coward. First performance: London, 1941. It centres on the activities of Madame Arcati, a medium, and Elvira, a troublesome ghost who returns to haunt her late and recently remarried husband Charles; it enjoyed lengthy runs in both London and New York.

Bliziński, Józef (1827–93) Polish playwright, author of several comedies much influenced by the plays of Aleksander Fredro. His other dramatic works include such problem plays as *The Wrecks* (1877), which tackle various moral issues.

blocking The process of deciding at rehearsal the basic movement of the actors on the set, usually written down for later reference.

Blok, Alexandr Alexandrovich (1880–1921) Russian poet and playwright, who was a major figure of the Russian Symbolist movement. Such poetic dramas as *The Puppet Show* (1906) and *The Rose and the Cross* (eventually staged in Britain in 1941) reflect the mixture of romance and despair that characterized his poetry.

Blondel *See* minstrel.

Blondin, Charles (Jean-François Gravelet; 1824–97) French tightrope walker, who became a popular star of British music hall. Best-known for his tightrope crossings of the Niagara Falls, he was much admired for his high wire act at the Crystal Palace in London from 1861 and made his last appearance in 1896.

blood tub *See* gaff.

Blood Wedding (*Bodas de sangre*) A tragedy by *García Lorca. First performance: Madrid, 1933. The first part of a famous trilogy of folk tragedies, being followed by *Yerma* (1934) and The *House of Bernarda Alba* (1945), the play was based on an actual news item and concerns the rivalry and eventual deaths of two rivals for a bride's hand; at the heart of the play is the conflict between passion and honour. It has also been translated as *Marriage of Blood*.

Bloom, Claire (1931-) British actress, who established her reputation in 1949, when she appeared in London in Fry's *The Lady's Not for Burning*. Subsequently she appeared at the Old Vic alongside Gielgud and others in various Shakespearean productions and began a successful film career. More recent successes have included Ibsen's *Hedda Gabler* (1971), Bolt's *Vivat! Vivat Regina!* (1972), *A Streetcar Named Desire* (1974) by Tennessee Williams, *Rosmersholm* (1977) by Ibsen, Chekhov's *The Cherry Orchard* (1981), and *These are Women* (1981-82), a study of several Shakespearean heroines.

blue *See* border.

boards The constituent parts of a stage floor, variously supported by vertical posts, tie-bars, or bracing. Hence the phrase "tread the boards", meaning acting in general.

Boar's Head Inn An inn in the Whitechapel district of London, where plays were staged in the 16th century. In 1595 the stage and galleries were roofed over and improved; the inn remained in use as a theatrical venue as late as 1616.

boat truck A movable platform, upon which a component part of the set can be wheeled onto the stage or, alternatively, raised up to it from below.

Bobèche (Antoine Mandelot; 1791-c. 1840) French actor, who specialized in farce, making many appearances in parades with **Galimafré** (Auguste Guérin; 1790-1870) at the Boulevard du Temple. Jokes at Napoleon's expense, however, obliged Bobèche to go into exile for a time before making a

shortlived comeback, while Galimafré retired as a performer in 1814.

Bobo A comic character of the early Spanish theatre. A rustic clown, he appeared in the plays of Lope de Rueda and others. The *gracioso* figure may have inherited some of his traits.

Bocage (Pierre-François Tousez; 1797-1863) French actor, who appeared for many years at the Odéon after failing to be accepted at the Comédie-Française. He became especially popular in melodrama and was eventually invited to join the Comédie-Française but quickly returned to the Odéon, becoming its director in 1845.

Bodel, Jean (c. 1165-c. 1210) French poet and playwright, whose *Jeu de Saint Nicolas*, first performed at Arras in 1200, was the first French miracle play. The plot concerns a Saracen king's conversion to Christianity after the restoration of his stolen treasure by Saint Nicholas. Bodel's poetic works include a *chanson de geste* and a moving farewell to his friends.

Boeck, Johann Michael (1743-93) German actor, who appeared with his wife as a member of the troupe at Mannheim. His greatest success was as Karl Moor, a part which he was the first to create, in Schiller's *Die Räuber* in 1782.

Bogdanov, Michael (1938-) British director, who became an associate director for the National Theatre in 1980. Earlier in his career he attracted attention working with Peter Brook, Barrault, and other leading figures on plays by Shakespeare and Molière with the Royal Shakespeare Company, the Young Vic, and other groups. His productions for the National Theatre have included Brenton's *The Romans in Britain* (1980), Molière's *The Hypochondriac* (1981), and Chekhov's *Uncle Vanya* (1982); for the Royal Shakespeare Company he also directed the massive cycle of seven plays *The Wars of the Roses*. In 1986 he cofounded the English Shakespeare Company with the actor Michael Pennington.

Bogusławski, Wojciech (1757–1829) Polish actor, director, and playwright, often regarded as the father of Polish theatre. He wrote more than 80 plays, of which the most important was the comic opera *Cracovians and Highlanders* (1794). As an actor, he was the first Polish Hamlet, appearing in his own version of Shakespeare's play; from 1783 to 1814 he was the director of the Polish National Theatre in Warsaw.

Boileau-Despréaux, Nicolas (1636–1711) French critic, a friend of Racine, La Fontaine, and Molière. In his influential critical writings he argued for the observance of classical standards in both drama and poetry.

Boisrobert, François le Métel, Seigneur de (1592–1662) French playwright. He found favour with Cardinal de Richelieu and exploited his position to assist other writers. A founder member of the Académie Française, he wrote several plays, of which the comedy *La Belle Plaideuse* (1654) is the only one of any lasting merit.

Boleslavsky, Richard *See* American Laboratory Theatre.

Bolt, Robert (Oxon) (1924–) British playwright, who had his first West End success with *Flowering Cherry* in 1957, a Chekhovian study with Ralph Richardson in the leading role. *A *Man for All Seasons* was an enormous success in 1960 with Paul Scofield and Leo McKern and was acclaimed for its use of Brechtian devices; another historical drama, *Vivat! Vivat Regina!*, depicting the relationship of Elizabeth I and Mary Queen of Scots, was similarly successful in 1970. Other works have included *The Tiger and the Horse* (1960), starring Michael and Vanessa Redgrave, *Gentle Jack* (1963), starring Edith Evans, the children's play *The Thwarting of Baron Bolligrew* (1965), and *State of Revolution* (1977), as well as several screenplays.

Bonarelli della Rovere, Guidobaldo (1563–1608) Italian playwright, whose pastoral *Filli di Sciro* (1607) was the most successful of the 17th century. English translations were also executed and presented before the royal court at London.

Bond, Edward (1934–) British playwright, whose first play, *The Pope's Wedding*, was presented at the Royal Court Theatre in 1962. Bond's later plays have been premiered by not only the Royal Court but the National Theatre, the Royal Shakespeare Company, and various politically active minority groups. Bond has maintained an uncompromising commitment to socialism. His earlier plays use parable-like forms, emphasizing the unjust nature of capitalist societies through violent and often stunning stage imagery (notably the stoning of a baby in **Saved*; later plays, however, have taken a more didactic and rational stand.
Principal works:
The Pope's Wedding: 1962.
Saved: 1965.
Early Morning: 1968.
Narrow Road to the Deep North: 1968.
Lear: 1971.
The Sea: 1973.
Bingo: 1973.
The Fool: 1975.
A-A-America!: 1976.
The Woman: 1978.
The Bundle: 1978.
The Worlds: 1979.
Restoration: 1981.
Summer: 1982.
Restoration: 1988.

Bonfils Theatre A theatre in Denver, Colorado, which was founded as the University

Civic Theatre in 1929. The current building, opened by Helen Bonfils, provides a place for amateur actors to work with professional theatre staff and produces both large- and small-scale productions, some aimed primarily at young audiences. In 1972 the Denver Centre for the Performing Arts was created to coordinate the various activities being undertaken, encompassing both the Bonfils Theatre and the **Helen Bonfils Theatre Complex**, built in 1980.

Bonstelle, Jessie (Laura Justine Bonesteel; 1872–1932) US actress and manager, who was a pioneer of civic theatre in the US. Known as the 'Maker of Stars', she worked with Augustin Daly for some years before taking up management and eventually establishing an important civic theatre in Detroit in 1928; performers who benefited from her support included Katharine Cornell.

Bontempelli, Massimo (1978–1960) Italian writer, who had a very active and varied literary career as playwright, poet, novelist, short-story writer, and critic. He is remembered chiefly for such novels as *Il figlio di due madri* (The Son of Two Mothers; 1930) and such plays as *La guardia della luna* (1920), *Nostra Dea* (1925) and *Minnie la candida* (1929).

Bon Ton Theatre *See* Koster and Bial's Music Hall.

book An alternative term for the script of a play – used chiefly of musicals, in which case it contains the dialogue but not the music or the lyrics for the show. The term **libretto** is the equivalent term for opera.

book ceiling A hinged ceiling made from a pair of flats, formerly an integral part of a box set.

book flat A hinged flat, capable of standing without any other means of support. In the US such a flat is usually called a **twofold**.

book-holder An Elizabethan term for the *prompter. Traditionally the book-holder was also in charge of all the props.

book-keeper A member of the Elizabethan acting company, who served as its librarian, copying play scripts and being responsible for them when they were not in use. In the Restoration theatre he was also sometimes employed as a prompter.

book wing An arrangement of attached wings, usually four in number, capable of being revolved so as to present a different scene, turning like the pages of a book.

boom A vertical batten in the wings or a horizontal batten suspended across the stage upon which lighting equipment is mounted; the lights themselves thus mounted may also be referred to as booms.

booth A temporary theatre, consisting of a sturdy platform and sometimes equipped with rudimentary items of scenery and props, in which travelling acting troupes formerly presented theatrical performances at fairs throughout Europe. The more elaborate booths consisted of a large tent (in which the stage and auditorium were housed) and had a smaller platform at the entrance that was used to attract an audience from (*see* parade). Flourishing until the 19th century, such booths provided venues for a wide variety of entertainments, from popular comedies and tragedies to melodramas and, in a reduced form, Punch and Judy shows.

Booth, Barton (1681–1733) British actor, who worked in Dublin before joining Betterton at the Lincoln's Inn Fields Theatre in 1700. His performance in *The Distressed Mother* (1712) brought fame, and in 1713 his interpretation of Cato in Addison's play confirmed him as the leading tragedian of the day. He was renowned for his habit of striking and holding dramatic attitudes during a play. For a time he also partnered Cibber and Wilks in the management of Drury Lane.

Booth, Junius Brutus (1796–1852) US actor, born in England, who was the head of a famous US theatrical family. He appeared regularly at Covent Garden and, from 1820, Drury Lane in leading Shakespearean roles and became a rival of Edmund Kean. In 1821, however, he left his wife and emigrated to the US with a flower-seller, Mary Ann Holmes, whom he married in 1851 and by whom he had 10 children. He was particularly admired as Richard III and Shylock, to which his grand style of acting was well suited, but suffered increasingly from melancholia and eventually madness.

His son **Junius Brutus Booth** (1821–83) began his acting career in 1835 on tour with his father and, in 1852, played Iago to his father's Othello. A member of the Bowery Theatre stock company, his best part was Dan Lowrie in *The Lass o' Lowrie's* (1878) by Frances Hodgson Burnett. His younger son, **Sydney Barton Booth** (1873–1937), was also an actor and star in vaudeville.

Edwin Thomas Booth (1833–93), another son of Junius Brutus Booth senior, was the first US actor to establish a major reputation as a tragedian in European theatrical circles. He first appeared in one of his father's productions and, at the age of 18, played the title role in *Richard III*. His most acclaimed tragic roles included Shylock in *The Merchant of Venice*, Hamlet, and the title role in Bulwer-Lytton's *Richelieu*. He also built Booth's Theatre in New York, opening it in 1869 playing Romeo to his second wife Mary McVicker's Juliet. After bankruptcy in 1873 he toured internationally and appeared alongside Irving in London. In 1888 he became associated with

the Players' Club, although his later years were marred by melancholia.

Edwin's younger brother **John Wilkes Booth** (1839–64) was also an actor but is usually remembered as the assassin of President Lincoln, whom he shot at Ford's Theatre on 14 April, 1865 during a production of *Our American Cousin*. It has been suggested that he was jealous of Edwin Booth's success and hoped the crime would make him equally famous.

Booth, Shirley (Thelma Booth Ford; 1907–) US actress, who made her first stage appearance in *The Cat and the Canary* (1919). Six years later she made her New York debut, going on to appear in such plays as *The Philadelphia Story* (1939) and *My Sister Eileen* (1940). She received awards as Grace Woods in Fay Kanin's *Goodbye, My Fancy* (1948) and as Lola in William Inge's *Come Back, Little Sheba* (1950). She has also appeared in musicals and on television.

Booth's Theatre A large theatre built for Edwin Booth on 23rd Street, New York. Its features included a hydraulic lift system for lowering three-dimensional scenery to the cellar and a stage with no rake. It opened in 1869 with *Romeo and Juliet* starring Booth and Mary McVicker. Booth gave many of his best performances here in subsequent seasons, supported by such players as Lawrence Barrett and Charlotte Cushman. It was also the venue for the first New York appearance of Adelaide Neilson and the last appearances of Kate Bateman, the younger James Wallack, and Charles Thorne. Other famous performers to appear included Joseph Jefferson III, Janauschek, and Minnie Maddern (later Mrs Fiske).

By 1874, following Booth's bankruptcy in 1873 and his elder brother Junius Brutus Booth's failure as manager, the theatre had passed out of the family's control. Subsequent successes included *Henry V* and Byron's *Sardanapalus*, both directed by Louis

Calvert. Boucicault took over the theatre in 1879 but the building was demolished after *Romeo and Juliet*, with Modjeska and Maurice Barrymore, was staged in 1883.

Booth Theatre A theatre on West 45th Street, New York, which opened in 1918 with Arnold Bennett's *The Great Adventure*. Productions staged there have included Kaufman and Hart's *You Can't Take It With You* (1936), which ran for two years, William Saroyan's *The Time of Your Life* (1934), Inge's *Come Back, Little Sheba* (1950), and Bernard Pomerance's *The Elephant Man* (1979). The theatre seats 766.

Borchert, Wolfgang (1921–47) German playwright, short-story writer, and poet, whose single drama, *Draussen vor der Tür* (1947), reflected his experiences as a soldier and prisoner during World War II and its aftermath. The play expressed the despair he felt at the desolation of Germany in the immediate post-war years.

border A narrow strip of curtain or other material hung across the stage behind the proscenium arch. Formerly called a **top drop**, it is used to conceal lighting and other equipment from the audience's view. If painted as foliage it is usually referred to as a **tree border**; if painted as sky it is called a **sky border** or **blue**.

border lights *See* batten.

Borisova, Yulia Konstantinovna (1925-) Soviet actress, who became famous in plays by contemporary Soviet authors at the Vakhtangov Theatre, where she first appeared in 1949. She was highly acclaimed in works by Arbuzov and in Dostoevsky's *The Idiot* (1958).

Bottomley, Gordon (1874–1948) British poet and playwright, whose poetic dramas *King Lear's Wife* (1915), *Britain's Daughters* (1922), *Gruach* (1923), and *Laodice and Da-*

nae (1930) reflect the influence both of Shakespeare and of Japanese *Nō* plays. His other works include *The Acts of St Peter* (1933), written for the Exeter Cathedral Festival.

Boucicault, Dion(-ysius) Lardner (c. 1822–90) Irish playwright, actor, and director, born in Dublin, who was the author of roughly 250 popular plays, including adaptations of other plays, melodramas, and musical extravaganzas. After beginning as an actor, under the name Lee Morton, he established his reputation with **London Assurance* – one of the most popular plays of the century – and subsequently worked with Ben Webster at the Adelphi Theatre. Later he joined Charles Kean at the Princess's Theatre, where his most notable success was his adaptation of *The *Corsican Brothers*. *The Poor of New York* (later retitled after whichever city the play was being performed in) made his name in the US, while *The Octoroon*, in which – as in several other of his plays – his lover Agnes Robertson (by whom he had four children) appeared, broke new ground in seriously examining the lot of the US negro.

His other works include a series of Irish plays, of which *The Colleen Bawn* – about the murder of an Irish girl by a British officer – was the most successful, melodramas based on horse-racing, and dramatizations of stories by Dickens and Washington Irving. He also ran a school for young actors, pressed for copyright protection (despite his own transgressions), and pioneered the matinée performance and use of the box set.

Principal works:

London Assurance: 1841.

The Corsican Brothers: 1852.

The Poor of New York: 1857.

Jessie Brown; or, the Relief of Lucknow: 1858.

The Octoroon; or, Life in Louisiana: 1859.

Dot: 1859.

The Colleen Bawn; or, the Brides of Garryowen: 1860.

BOUCICAULT, DOT

Arrah-na-Pogue; or, The Wicklow Wedding: 1864.

Hunted Down: 1866.

The Flying Scud; or, Four-Legged Fortune: 1866.

Babil and Bijou; or, the Lost Regalia: 1872.

The Shaughraun: 1874.

Boucicault, Dot (Darley George Boucicault; 1859–1929) British actor-manager and playwright, son of Dion Boucicault, who appeared in his father's company before becoming director at the Duke of York's Theatre in London (1901–15). His finest roles included Sir William Gower in Pinero's *Trelawney of the 'Wells'*; his wife was the actress Irene *Vanbrugh.

Boucicault, Nina (1867–1950) British actress, daughter of Dion Boucicault. She began her career in her father's company, appearing in *The Colleen Bawn* in 1885. Later successes included *Charley's Aunt* by Brandon Thomas and *The Light that Failed*, based on Kipling's story; she was best-known, however, as the first to play the title role in Barrie's *Peter Pan* (1904).

Bouffes du Nord, Théâtre des *See* International Centre of Theatre Research.

Boulevard du Temple A fairground in Paris, where a number of notable *booths formerly existed. Of these small theatrical venues, the most significant included the permanent stages of the *Ambigu, the *Funambules, and the *Gaîté; authors for these theatres included Dumas *père* and Pixérécourt. The site was destroyed when Paris was extensively redesigned in 1862.

Boulevard plays A form of popular French drama of the late 19th and 20th centuries, equivalent to that presented in the West End in London and Broadway in New York. Traditionally encompassing farce and domestic drama, the genre developed from the plays performed in the fairground booths of Paris and reached its peak before World War I; it has since declined. Successful playwrights of *Boulevard* plays have included Feydeau, Labiche, and Achard.

Bourchier, Arthur (1863–1927) British actor-manager. A founder-member of the Oxford University Dramatic Society, he left Oxford to join Lillie Langtry's company in 1889. He was manager of the Garrick Theatre from 1900 to 1906 and appeared frequently with his wife, Violet *Vanbrugh. In 1910 he transferred to Her Majesty's Theatre, where he appeared with Tree.

Bourdet, Édouard (1887–1945) French playwright and administrator of the Comédie-Française (1936–40). His plays are social satires, characterized by sharp psychological insight. *La Prisonnière* (1926) deals with lesbianism and *La Fleur des pois* (1932) with homosexuality; *Vient de paraître* (1927) attacks the commercial world of publishing and literature.

Bourgogne, Théâtre de l'Hôtel de The first permanent theatre to be built in Paris, erected in the ruins of the palace of the dukes of Burgundy by the *Confrérie de la Passion in 1548. Long and narrow in shape, with a small stage, the theatre was hired out to travelling companies until about 1610, when the King's Players, run by Valleran-Lecomte, were installed there. The Hôtel de Bourgogne then remained the most important venue in the city until the opening of the Théâtre du Marais in 1634 and the emergence of Molière; in 1680 the resident company was absorbed into the Comédie-Française. Subsequently the theatre was used for performances of the Comédie-Italienne until 1783.

Boursault, Edmé (1638–1701) French playwright, chiefly remembered for *Le Portrait du peintre* (1663), an attack on Molière prompted by the latter's *Critique de l'École des Femmes*; the two men were later reconciled. Boursault's finest plays were written during the last two decades of his life: *Le Mercure galant* (1683) satirized a periodical of that name, whose editor's objections led to the adoption of the play's alternative title *La Comédie sans titre*.

Bouschet, Jan *See* Sackville, Thomas.

Bouwmeester, Louis (1841–1925) Dutch actor, who became a leading figure of the first Dutch national theatre. He appeared, often alongside his sister **Theo Bouwmeester** (1850–1939), in plays by Dumas *fils*, Sardou, and others and was much admired as Shakespeare's Shylock.

Bowery Theatre A theatre in New York, which opened in 1826 as the New York Theatre, Bowery and enjoyed early success with appearances by Edwin Forrest. In 1828 the theatre was burned down but reopened later the same year and had further success under the management of Hamblin before being burned down again in 1836. It re-opened in 1837, burned down in 1838, re-opened in 1839, burned down in 1845, and reopened again four months later. Edward Eddy made his first appearance there in 1851 and became a great favourite, briefly working as manager there. In 1858 it became a home of pantomime and, as the **Old Bowery Theatre**, melodrama and burlesque. The theatre closed in 1878 and reopened a year later as the **Thalia Theatre**, housing German-language plays. After further fires in 1923 and 1929, it was closed and not rebuilt.

Another **Bowery Theatre**, later called the **Stadt Theatre**, opened as a venue for circus acts in 1835 and subsequently staged both plays and German opera.

A **New Bowery Theatre** was opened by the managers of the Bowery Theatre in 1859. Run by George L Fox, it staged a variety of shows until being destroyed by fire in 1866.

box *See* auditorium.

box office The area, customarily in the foyer of a theatre, where tickets may be purchased for current or future performances. It is usually run by the box office manager and his assistants.

box set A naturalistic set, in which the three walls (and sometimes the ceiling) of a room are constructed from flats in order to increase the illusion of reality. The box set was introduced to Britain by Madame Vestris in 1832 but has been less widely used in modern drama.

Boy Bishop A boy chosen to oversee the merrymaking at an annual festival observed at various choir schools and other religious establishments throughout Europe in medieval times. Nominally a religious occasion, the festival provided an opportunity for the performance of plays in Latin until the practice was ended during the Reformation. The tradition was often amalgamated with the festivities associated with the Feast of Fools.

boy companies (*or* children's companies) Theatrical companies first organized in the 16th century from the choirboys at the Chapels Royal in London and Windsor and from those at St Paul's cathedral. Under such Masters as Richard Farrant, William Cornish, Sebastian Westcott, Nathaniel Giles, and Philip Rosseter, the companies acquired a fine reputation for their performances of masques and disguisings at Court before being introduced to the professional theatre. Regularly on stage at the Blackfriars Theatre from 1576 and later at the Whitefriars Theatre and elsewhere, members of the companies acted in first performances of major plays by Lyly, Jonson, Chapman, and many others and several of them, including Ezekiel Fenn, Nathan Field, William Ostler, John Rice, and Richard Robinson, went on to become popular adult actors. The fashion for child actors, which attracted the scorn of Shakespeare and other writers of serious drama, died out, however, by 1615.

Boyfriend, The A musical written and composed by Sandy *Wilson. First performance: Players' Theatre, London, 1953. Evoking memories of the musical comedies of the 1920s, the show ultimately transferred to Wyndham's Theatre for a run of more than five years and provided the basis of a successful film.

Boyle, Roger *See* Orrery, Lord.

Boyle, William (1853–1923) Irish playwright, whose works were performed in the Abbey Theatre, Dublin. *The Building Fund* (1905) is a comic exploration of avarice, while *The Eloquent Dempsey* (1906) satirizes political duplicity and *Family Failing* (1912) deals with indolence. *The Mineral Workers* (1906) and *Nic* (1916) both examine the impact of modern values on traditional Irish life.

bozze An early form of stage lighting, first developed in Italy in the 17th century. It consisted of a glass globe fitted with handles and a wick and could be used to achieve colour effects when placed behind bottles of coloured liquid.

Bracco, Roberto (1862–1943) Italian playwright and progenitor of the Theatre of *Silence. A versatile dramatist, Bracco wrote such comedies as *Il frutto acerbo* (Bitter Fruit; 1904), dramas in the vein of Ibsen, notably *Fantasmi* (Ghosts; 1906), and naturalistic studies of Neapolitan life, including *Don Pietro Caruso* (1895). His most important play was *Il piccolo santo* (The Little Saint; 1909). Because he actively opposed Fascism, Bracco's work suffered a long period of neglect and only in recent years has there been a renewed interest in his once popular plays.

brace A length of wood used to support a flat, usually held in place by a weight and attached to the flat by means of a hook and eye.

Bracegirdle, Anne (c. 1663–1748) British actress, who began her stage career under Betterton. Despite the murder of William *Mountfort in a quarrel over her favours, she enjoyed a chaste reputation, although she was the mistress of Congreve for several years. She is credited with creating Congreve's Angelica in *Love for Love* (1695) and Millamant in *The Way of the World* (1700). She is also thought to have been the first woman to play Portia in *The Merchant of Venice*.

Brady, William Aloysius (1863–1950) US actor, producer, and manager, who produced many successful plays in the Manhattan, 48th Street, and Playhouse theatres of New York. These included Du Maurier's *Trilby* and Harriet Beecher Stowe's *Uncle Tom's Cabin*. He made his acting debut in 1882 and by 1888 had formed his own touring company; he was also manager to Helen Hayes, Douglas Fairbanks, Grace George (his wife), and Alice Brady (his daughter).

Brahm, Otto (Otto Abrahamsohn; 1856–1912) German director and critic, who did much to encourage the development of Realism in the early 20th century. Under the influence of André Antoine, he founded the *Freie Buhne in Berlin in 1889, where he presented plays by Ibsen and Tolstoy. Subsequently he directed the Deutsche Theater in Berlin and trained actors in the naturalistic style of Stanislavsky. Later he took over the Lessing Theater in Berlin.

Braithwaite, Dame (Florence) Lilian (1873–1948) British actress, who first appeared as a professional in South Africa and subsequently with Benson's company, finally joining Alexander's company at the St James's Theatre in 1901. Acclaimed as a performer of long-suffering heroines, she also triumphed as the mother in Coward's *The Vortex* in 1924 and later appeared in light comedies, notably *Arsenic and Old Lace* (1942).

Branagh, Kenneth (1961-) British actor and director, born in Ireland. After winning the Bancroft Gold Medal at RADA he made an outstanding London debut as Judd in Julian Mitchell's *Another Country* (1982). With the Royal Shakespeare Company at Stratford-upon-Avon in 1984 his roles included Henry V. In 1986 he founded the **Renaissance Theatre Company**, starred in his own play *Public Enemy*, and directed *Twelfth Night*. His company went on to present a season of Shakespeare in Birmingham in 1988 and revived the tradition of the actor-manager with productions directed by Judi Dench and other leading performers.

Brand A verse tragedy by Henrik *Ibsen, published in 1866. First performance: Stockholm, 1885. Initially composed as a narrative poem but later rewritten in Italy, the play – in which the hero faces a series of exacting choices – is an ironic and symbolic exploration of the complacency and bleakness Ibsen perceived in the Norwegian character. It was an immediate success and secured the playwright's reputation in Europe.

Brandane, John (John MacIntyre; 1869-1947) Scottish playwright and doctor, who wrote for the Scottish National Players and later became one of their directors. His humorous and carefully observed plays, notably *The Glen is Mine*, employ Highland settings. He was also influential in encouraging James Bridie to become a dramatist.

Brandão, Raul (1867–1930) Portuguese novelist and playwright, who was the author of a number of naturalistic plays tackling the issues of poverty and oppression. *Jesus Cristo em Lisboa* is typical, depicting the arrival of Christ in the slums of Lisbon.

Brandes, Georg (Morris Cohen) (1842–1927) Danish theatre critic and scholar, who did much to reform Scandinavian literature in the late 19th century. Encouraged by Ibsen, he argued for the increased use of naturalistic styles in his many lectures, collected as *Hovedstrømninger* (Main Currents in Nineteenth-Century Literature; 1872–90). He also supported such notable playwrights as Bjørnson, Kielland, and Strindberg and was a champion of Nietzsche; his writings include biographies of Shakespeare, Goethe, and Voltaire.

Brandes, Johann Christian (1735–99) German actor and playwright, who became popular as a writer of monodramas during the 1770s. He had little success as an actor, appearing with the companies of Schönemann, Schuch, and subsequently Iffland.

His wife was the actress **Esther Charlotte Henrietta Koch** (1746–84), who was much acclaimed in tragedy; his daughter **Minna Brandes** (1765–88) also appeared on the stage.

Brando, Marlon (1924-) US actor, born in Nebraska. After being expelled for indiscipline from acting school in New York, Brando attended the Actors' Studio, where he studied with Elia Kazan. He first appeared on Broadway in *I Remember Mama* (1944). Subsequent theatre performances included *Truckline Cafe* (1946), *Candida* (1946), and *The Eagle Has Two Heads* (1946). *A Streetcar Named Desire* (1947) made Brando's reputation on Broadway and four years later in the cinema. Thereafter he largely confined himself to the cinema, as a leading exponent of *Method acting.

Branner, Hans Christian (1903–66) Danish novelist, short-story writer, and playwright, who first achieved success in the theatre with a dramatization of his novel *Rytteren* (1949). This was followed by the comedy *Søskende* (1951), *Thermopyloe* (1957), which was set during the Occupation, and several radio plays.

Brasseur, Pierre (Pierre Espinasse; 1905–72) French actor, who first appeared on stage as a child and later became one of the leading actors in Paris, following initial success in *Le Sexe faible* (1929). He was praised in strong romantic roles in plays by Claudel, Sartre, Anouilh, Montherlant, and Shaw, being particularly admired as Edmund Kean in Sartre's adaptation of Dumas *père's Kean*. His film roles included a celebrated impersonation of Frédérick Lemaître in Carné-Prevert's *Les Enfants du paradis* (1944).

Brayton, Lily *See* Asche, Oscar.

Bread and Puppet Theatre A US theatre company, which was founded by Peter Schumann in 1961 to present large-scale popular theatre on socialist principles. Typical productions involve the use of massive puppets; noted successes have included *The Cry of the People for Meat* (1969). The company has been based in Vermont since 1974.

Brecht, (Eugen) Bertolt (Friedrich) (1898–1956) German playwright, director, and poet, who is recognized as one of the most important figures in 20th century drama. Brecht wrote his first works for the theatre – much influenced by Expressionism – while studying medicine in Munich after World War I; these ultimately led to appointments at the Munich Kammerspiele (1921) and then as assistant to Reinhardt at the Deutsches Theater in Berlin in 1924.

Mann ist Mann marked the beginnings of his theory of *epic theatre and the introduction of the controversial *Verfremdungseffekt* style of acting, theories defined in his treatise *Kleines Organon für das Theater* (1949). After marrying his second wife, He-lene *Weigel (who appeared in many of his plays), in 1928, Brecht collaborated with Kurt *Weill on a series of celebrated didactic musical dramas, many of which featured Weill's wife Lotte *Lenya. Other influences at that time included that of oriental drama, notably through the translations of Arthur Waley.

In 1933 Brecht and his wife fled Nazi Germany, finally arriving in the US in 1941. During this unsettled time he wrote most of his best-known plays, in which he studies the human condition with great sensitivity while encouraging his audience to maintain a coolly intellectual detachment from the events being portrayed, often in highly poetic terms. A fervent critic of capitalism and totalitarianism, his Marxist leanings led eventually to his examination (1947) by the notorious Committee for Un-American Activities, before which he defended himself with great skill.

In 1949 he and his wife returned to East Germany, founding the *Berliner Ensemble at the Theater am Schiffbauerdamm to present many of Brecht's early works as well as his adaptations of plays by Shakespeare and others. All his dramas after 1928 were distinguished by an increasingly overt Marxist element. This has contributed greatly to the controversy that his plays have continued to arouse in the years since his death, despite a general acceptance of his brilliance as a writer and theorist for the stage.

Principal works:

Baal: 1923 (written 1918).

Trommeln in der Nacht: 1922; translated as *Drums in the Night*.

Im Dickicht der Städte: 1923; translated as *In the Jungle of the Cities*.

Edward II: 1924.

Mann ist Mann: 1926; translated as *A Man's a Man*.

Die Dreigroschenoper: 1928; translated as *The *Threepenny Opera*.

Aufstieg und Fall der Stadt Mahagonny: 1927; translated as *The Rise and Fall of the City of Mahagonny*.

Happy End: 1929.

Der Jasager und der Neinsager: 1929–30.

Die sieben Todsünden: 1933; translated as *The Seven Deadly Sins*.

Die heilige Johanna der Schlacthöfe: 1959 (written 1930s); translated as *St Joan of the Stockyards*.

Mutter Courage und ihre Kinder: 1941; translated as **Mother Courage and Her Children*.

Leben des Galilei: 1943; translated as **Galileo*.

Der gute Mensch von Sezuan: 1943; translated as *The *Good Woman of Setzuan*.

Schweik in the Second World War: 1943.

Der kaukasische Kreidekreis: 1954 (written 1945); translated as *The *Caucasian Chalk Circle*.

Herr Puntila und sein Knecht Matti: 1948; translated as *Herr Puntila and his servant Matti*.

Die Tage der Kommune: 1949; translated as *The Days of the Commune*.

Die Gesichte der Simone Machard: 1957; translated as *The Vision of Simone Machard*.

Der aufthaltsame Aufstieg des Arturo Ui: 1958; translated as *The Resistible Rise of Arturo Ui*.

Brécourt, Guillaume Marcoureau, Sieur de (1638–85) French actor and playwright. Brécourt performed with the Théâtre du Marais and with Molière's company before joining the Hôtel de Bourgogne in 1664. Forced into exile for a time after he killed a coachman in a quarrel, he ended his career with the Comédie-Française. He excelled both in comic roles and in the tragedies of Racine; as a playwright he was less successful.

Bredero, Gerbrand Adriaansz (1585–1618) Dutch poet and playwright, born in Amsterdam, who was the author of three celebrated late medieval farces, notably the *Farce of the Cow* (1612). Together with his comedies set against a background of cosmopolitan Dutch life, the best of which was *The Spanish Brabanter* (1617), these effectively established the Dutch comic tradition. His work was characterized by the realism with which he contrasted the conflicting worlds of the gentry and the common people.

breeches part A role in which an actress plays a male character, a common feature of English comedies of the early 18th century. Noted performers of such parts included Peg Woffington, Mrs Bracegirdle, and Mrs Mountfort. Subsequently the tradition was maintained on the Victorian stage by such distinguished actresses as Madame Vestris and Sarah Bernhardt (who was famous for her Hamlet) and by various music hall performers; in the 20th century it has survived primarily in cabaret and pantomime, in which the *principal boy is conventionally played by an actress. *Compare* female impersonator.

Brenton, Howard (1942–) British playwright best known for the controversial play *The *Romans in Britain*. His early plays were performed in the late 1960s at the Royal Court's Theatre Upstairs and subsequently he became resident dramatist at the Royal Court (1972–73). His most significant plays have included *Brassneck* (with David Hare, 1973), *The Churchill Play* (1974) and *Epsom Downs* (1977). Most of his plays present vivid, often disturbing, images, ranging from homosexual violence to urban terrorism. His most recent plays have included a translation of Brecht's *Galileo* (1980), *A Short, Sharp Shock* (1980), *Pravda* (1985), and *Greenland* (1988); in 1988 the National Theatre staged a season of his work.

Bresselau, Menahem Mendel (1760–1827) Jewish playwright, whose plays were heavily influenced by Moses Luzzato. His play *Yaldut Ubahrut* (1786) was written for a bar mitzvah.

Bretón de los Herredos, Manuel (1796–1873) Spanish poet and playwright, who was the author of over 180 original plays and adaptations of Spanish, French, and German dramas. He established his reputation with his first play, *A la vejez, viruelas* (1824), and went on to write numerous gently satirical bourgeois comedies, including the well-known *Marcela, o ¿cual de los tres?* (1831).

Brice, Fanny (Fannie Borach; 1891–1951) US actress and singer, married to Billy Rose, who began her long career with Ziegfeld's *Follies* in 1910. In 1931 she appeared in the play *Crazy Quilt*, written by her husband. Her life was dramatized in Styne's *Funny Girl*.

bridge An extension of the flies, capable of being raised and lowered in order to facilitate work on lighting and scenery. In the US it is often referred to as an **elevator**. *See also* catwalk.

Bridges, Dr John *See* Stevenson, William.

Bridges-Adams, William (1889–1965) British director, who worked at various provincial repertory theatres before being appointed director of the theatre in Stratford-upon-Avon as successor to Frank Benson. He directed 29 of Shakespeare's plays there before the fire of 1926 and subsequently oversaw the opening of the new theatre in 1932; in 1934 he left to work for the British Council.

Bridie, James (Osborne Henry Mavor; 1888–1951) Scottish doctor, playwright, and founder of the Glasgow Citizens' Theatre. His success with The **Anatomist* launched him upon a prolific writing career. His plays are somewhat loosely constructed, but the dialogue is engaging and vital. Many explore Scottish themes, especially the conflict between puritanism and worldliness; others range from comedies and biblical plays to historical dramas and ballad operas. His greatest success came in 1949 when Edith Evans was much acclaimed in the leading role of *Daphne Laureola*.
Principal works:
The Anatomist: 1930.
Tobias and the Angel: 1930.
Jonah and the Whale: 1932.
A *Sleeping Clergyman: 1933.
Susannah and the Elders: 1937.
What Say They?: 1939.
Mr Bolfry: 1943.
It Depends What You Mean: 1944.
Doctor Angelus: 1947.
Daphne Laureola: 1949.
Mr Gillie: 1950.
The Queen's Comedy: 1950.

Briers, Richard (1934–) British actor, who began his career with the Liverpool Playhouse company and made his West End debut in 1959. Acclaimed as a comedy and farce actor, well-known for his television appearances, he has also been praised for stage performances in such plays as Stoppard's *The Real Inspector Hound* (1968), Ayckbourn's *Absurd Person Singular* (1973), *Richard III* (1972), Ibsen's *The Wild Duck* (1980), and as Malvolio (1987).

Brieux, Eugène (1858–1932) French playwright, born in Paris. His plays deal with social evils – the unethical behaviour of a magistrate in *La Robe rouge* (1900), venereal disease in *Les Avariés* (1902; translated as *Damaged Goods*, 1911) – and were praised by G B Shaw. Other plays include *Le Trois Filles de M Dupont* (1897).

Brigadoon A musical fantasy by Alan Jay **Lerner and Frederick *Loewe. First performance: Broadway, 1947. This story of the accidental intrusion of two modern Americans into a bewitched Scottish village reached London in 1949 and was successfully filmed in 1954.

Brighella A character of the *commedia dell'arte*, one of the *zanni*. Formerly depicted as a thieving rogue, he gradually diminished into a scheming but sentimental servant.

Brighouse, Harold (1882–1958) British novelist and playwright, who became associated with the 'Manchester School' of playwrights (*see* New Drama). He wrote over 50 one-act and 16 full-length plays, many for the newly-established repertory theatres before World War I. His plays, which were frequently set in his native Lancashire, included *Dealing in Futures* (1909), *The Northerners* (1914), *Zack* (1916), *Garside's Career* (1914) and the still-performed **Hobson's Choice*.

Brighton Theatre *See* Bijou Theatre.

bristle trap A trap by means of which an actor appears through overlapping bristles or foliage.

Bristol Hippodrome A theatre in Bristol, opened in 1912 as a home of variety. Seating 1975, the original theatre contained a large water tank and was used for circuses and musical as well as dramatic productions. In 1948 a fire destroyed the building; it was subsequently rebuilt as a venue for leading touring companies, including the National Theatre.

Bristol Old Vic A theatre in Bristol, reconstructed (1941–43) from the old **Theatre Royal**. The oldest working theatre in England (founded in 1766), it reopened under its present name with *She Stoops to Conquer* by Oliver Goldsmith and later acquired its own respected resident company (founded by Hugh *Hunt in 1946). Successful productions since then have included the musical *Salad Days* (1954), *Love's Labour's Lost* (1964), and *Born in the Gardens* (1979) by Peter Nichols. The theatre was extensively altered and enlarged in the 1970s and now seats 647; it also includes a smaller studio theatre, the New Vic, seating 150, and a theatre school.

Britannia Music Hall *See* Rotunda.

Britannia Theatre A theatre in Hoxton, London, which opened in 1841 as the Britannia Saloon, providing free entertainment for diners. After a period as a music hall it became a venue for plays under Sam *Lane – who ran it until 1871 – in 1843, being considerably enlarged in 1850. Sam Lane's wife Sara took over the management on her husband's death and the theatre prospered, its pantomimes being particularly successful. Closed for a time in 1903, the theatre later reverted to its use as a music hall and then became a cinema; it was destroyed by bombs during World War II.

British Actors' Equity Association A trade union for professional actors in Britain, established in 1929 to oversee matters relating to actors' salaries, conditions of employment, etc. Equity was originally set up under the guidance of Ben Webster and replaced earlier models, including H B Irving's and Seymour Hicks's Actors Union. It now regulates radio, film, and television drama as well as stage performances and defends the rights of its members against actors from outside the association; it also helps to subsidize ailing professional companies. The rival **Variety Artists Federation**, founded in 1906, merged with Equity in 1968.

British Council A British organization dedicated to the promotion of British culture abroad. It established a specialist drama department in 1939, amalgamating it with dance in 1980, and helps to organize overseas tours by British companies as well as offering publicity and advice and arranging visits to Britain by distinguished theatrical figures from other countries.

British Drama League *See* British Theatre Association.

British Theatre Association (BTA) A British theatre organization, which helps to coordinate amateur drama throughout Britain. Originally called the **British Drama League**, it was founded in 1919 by Geoffrey Whitworth (1883–1951) and fosters contact between amateur groups (as well as some professional companies), runs a library service, and stages a national drama festival annually. Parallel organizations elsewhere in Britain include the Scottish Community Drama Association, founded in 1926, the Amateur Drama Association in Wales, founded in 1965, and the Amateur Drama Council in Ireland, founded in 1952. The **International Amateur Theatre Association**, based in The Hague, was established by E Martin Browne in 1952.

British Theatre Museum Association *See* Theatre Museum.

Britton, Nellie *See* Lang, Matheson.

Brizard, Jean-Baptiste (1721–91) French actor, who became noted as a player of elderly characters after joining the Comédie-Française in 1756. His roles included Henry of Navarre in Colle's *La partie de chasse d'Henri IV* (1774) and the first French King Lear (1782).

Broadhurst, George Howells (1866–1952) US playwright, born in England, who wrote such comedies as *What Happened to Jones* (1897) before winning acclaim with such dramas as *The Man of the Hour* (1906) and *Bought and Paid For* (1911). From 1917 he presented plays at his own Broadhurst Theatre.

Broadhurst Theatre A theatre on West 44th Street, New York, which was opened in 1917 by George Broadhurst with the New York premiere of G B Shaw's *Misalli-*

ance. Since then a number of musicals and straight plays have been staged there, including *Broadway* (1926), *Men In White* (1933), *Pal Joey* (1952), *Cabaret* (1966), *More Stately Mansions* (1967), and *Amadeus* (1980). The theatre seats 1185.

Broadway The street in New York City that runs through the theatre district in Manhattan; the street itself, the district around it, and the commercial theatre in New York are all referred to as Broadway. Broadway became the centre of the New York theatre in the 1850s; by the 1890s, thanks to its brilliant lighting, it was known as The Great White Way. It reached its peak in the 1920s, when it boasted 80 theatres. Since then it has suffered a gradual decline due to escalating costs; serious drama is now confined to *off-Broadway or *off-off-Broadway theatres, leaving Broadway to specialize chiefly in lavish musicals and light comedies employing a small cast.

Broadway Music Hall *See* Wallack's Lyceum.

Broadway Opera House *See* Bijou Theatre.

Broadway Theatre A theatre on Broadway, New York, which opened in 1847 with Sheridan's *The School for Scandal*, starring Henry Wallack. Based on London's Haymarket Theatre, it became the home of the former Park Theatre company in 1848; performers who appeared there included Edwin Forrest, Charlotte Cushman, and the Bateman family. It collapsed in 1855, was rebuilt, but closed for good in 1859.

A second **Broadway Theatre** was opened on Broadway, New York, in 1880 as the **Metropolitan Casino** with Fanny Davenport in Sardou's *Tosca*. Subsequent successes included *Ben Hur* (1899), pantomime, and Frances Hodgson Burnett's *Little Lord Fauntleroy* (1907). It was turned into a cinema in 1913 and demolished in 1929.

The **Broadway Theatre** on Broadway and 53rd Street, New York, was opened as a cinema in 1924. It has been used for live productions since 1930. From 1930 to 1935 it housed Earl Carroll's *Varieties* and other vaudeville shows; it was then used as a cinema until 1943, when Moss Hart's *Lady in the Dark* was staged there. Other productions seen there have included *Gypsy* (1959), *Cabaret* (1968), *Candide* (1974), *The Wiz* (1977), and *Evita* (1979).

A fourth **Broadway Theatre** was opened on Broadway in 1837, its name being changed from the **Euterpean Hall**.

Brockmann, Johann Franz Hieronymus

(1745–1812) German actor, who was a leading member of Schröder's company at Hamburg. His roles there included Hamlet (1776); subsequently he was equally acclaimed at the Burgtheater in Vienna.

Bródy, Sándor (1863–1924) Hungarian novelist and playwright, who wrote a number of influential naturalistic dramas. Best known for his prose works, he had his biggest stage success with a dramatization of his novel *Snow White* (1901).

Brody Singers Performers of Yiddish entertainments in Russia during the 19th century. Named after the town of Brody (then in Poland), these performers specialized in comic and sentimental music, sketches, and dance and provided the basis for the early Yiddish theatre in Russia.

Broken Jug, The (*Der zerbrochene Krug*) A one-act comedy by Heinrich von *Kleist. First performance: Weimar, 1808. The plot revolves around a village magistrate who finds himself presiding at the trial of an innocent man accused of a crime he himself has committed; the play failed when first produced by Goethe but was later recognized as a comic masterpiece.

Brome, Richard (c. 1590–1653) English playwright, who is thought to have been a servant of Ben Jonson and established his reputation as a writer of comedy with *The Lovesick Court*, a parody of heroic tragedy. Subsequent successes included *The Northern Lass* (1629) and *A Jovial Crew, or, the Merry Beggars* (1641), which was performed by Christopher Beeston's company shortly before the closing of the theatres. Other plays – of which 15 survive – provided material for works by Aphra Behn and Dryden among others.

Bronnen, Arnolt (1895–1959) German playwright and theatre critic, who wrote a number of radical plays in the Expressionist tradition. He established his reputation with *Vatermord* (1922), which dealt with incest and patricide; subsequent works, including *Die Geburt der Jugend* (1922) and *Reparationen* (1926) reflected his sympathy for the Nazi cause. His few works after World War II included *Die jungste Nacht* (1958).

Brook, Peter Stephen Paul (1925-) British director and stage designer, who is widely recognized as one of the most innovative directors upon the contemporary British stage. He produced his first play, Marlowe's *Dr Faustus*, in 1943 at the Torch Theatre in London at the age of 18, and attracted immediate attention with his eye for the essentials of a production and his challenging approach.

After further successes he produced *Love's Labour's Lost* (1946) at Stratford-upon-Avon for Sir Barry Jackson and then won great acclaim with such plays as Anouilh's *Ring Round the Moon* (1950) and Otway's *Venice Preserv'd* (1953), in both of which he directed Paul Scofield to great effect. In 1955 his *Hamlet* was staged as far away as the USSR and in 1962 he was appointed codirector of the newly-formed Royal Shakespeare Company. Celebrated productions with the RSC since then have included *King Lear* (1962), Weiss's *Marat/Sade* (1964), Seneca's *Oedipus*

(1968), an enormously admired *A Midsummer Night's Dream* (1970) – famous for its acrobatics and white set, and *Antony and Cleopatra* (1978). In recent years he has also worked extensively in Africa and in Paris, where he founded the International Centre of Theatre Research in 1970. Works there have included a stage adaptation of the Hindu *Mahabharatu*, which lasted 10 hours. In 1988 he directed a revival of Chekhov's *The Cherry Orchard* in New York.

Brooke, Gustavus Vaughan (1818–66) British actor, born in Dublin and known as the **Dublin Roscius** or **Hibernian Roscius**. After touring the provinces, he appeared at the Olympic Theatre in 1848, and was acclaimed as Othello, Hamlet, Richard III, and in other roles associated with Edmund Kean. He was drowned when his ship foundered in the Bay of Biscay whilst returning from an Australian tour.

Brooklyn Theatre A small theatre in New York, opened in 1871 and run by the family of F B Conway until 1875 when under Palmer it had a short, but successful season. Burnt down during a performance of Oxenford's *The Two Orphans* in 1876, it was never rebuilt.

Brooks Atkinson Theatre A theatre on West 47th Street, between Broadway and Eighth Avenue, New York, which opened as the **Mansfield Theatre** in 1926. Seating 1088, it was used for broadcasting before reopening as the Brooks Atkinson in 1960. Productions housed in the theatre have included Ansky's *The Dybbuk* (1926), Connelly's *Green Pastures* (1930), Neil Simon's *Come Blow Your Horn* (1961), Tennessee Williams's *The Milk Train Doesn't Stop Here Anymore* (1964), Joseph A Walker's *The River Niger* (1973), Bernard Slade's *Same Time, Next Year* (1975), and Lanford Wilson's *Talley's Folly* (1980).

Brooks Theatre *See* Cleveland Play House.

Brough, Lionel (1836–1900) British actor, born in Pontypool. He began as an actor in a play by his brother **William Brough** (1826–70), produced at Covent Garden in 1854; later he developed his own one-man show. In 1864 Lionel was engaged at Liverpool; subsequently he established himself as a fine comedian, especially in the plays of Sheridan and Goldsmith.

His daughter was the actress **Mary Brough** (1863–1934), who made her stage debut in 1881 in Brighton and later appeared alongside Lillie Langtry in London. She was particularly successful as a comic actress in the farces of Ben Travers at the Aldwych Theatre.

Mary's cousin was the actress **Fanny Whiteside Brough** (1854–1914), who first appeared on stage in 1869 in pantomime. She too excelled in comic roles, being the first to play such parts as Mary Melrose in H J Byron's *Our Boys* (1875) and frequently appearing at Drury Lane.

Brown, Pamela (1917–75) British actress, who first attracted attention in Shakespearean parts at Stratford-upon-Avon. Subsequent roles included Nina in *The Seagull*, Gwendolen in *The Importance of Being Earnest*, and – with Gielgud's company – Millamant in Congreve's *The Way of the World* and Aquilina in Otway's *Venice Preserv'd*. In Shakespeare, she was particularly admired as Juliet, Ophelia, and Goneril; she also appeared in plays by Aldous Huxley, Christopher Fry, Wycherley, and Shaw.

Browne, Coral (Edith) (Mrs Vincent Price; 1913–) Australian actress, who came to London in 1934 after appearances in Australia and made her British debut in Philip Johnson's *Lover's Leap*. She soon emerged as a leading actress in such plays as Maugham's *Lady Frederick* (1946) and later won acclaim with the Old Vic company as Lady Macbeth (1956) and Gertrude in *Hamlet* (1958). Her many other roles have included Mrs Warren in Shaw's *Mrs Warren's Profession* (1970) at the National Theatre.

Browne, E(lliot) Martin (1900–80) British actor and director, who was associated with the revival of poetic and religious drama in England. He directed all of T S Eliot's plays, including the first production of *Murder in the Cathedral*, and directed the **Pilgrim Players** from 1939 to 1948. In 1951 he produced the York Cycle of mystery plays, which had not been acted since 1572. *See also* British Theatre Association.

Browne, Maurice (1881–1955) British actor, playwright, and theatre manager, who established his reputation in the US and effectively founded the Little Theatre movement when he opened the Chicago Little Theatre in 1912. After directing on Broadway, he moved to London, taking over the Savoy Theatre in 1929 and subsequently acquiring control over the Globe and Queen's theatres. His London productions included *Othello* (1929), with Paul Robeson, Peggy Ashcroft, and himself in the main roles, *Hamlet* (1930), with Gielgud, and plays by Fagan and others.

Browne, Robert (fl. 1583–1620) English actor, who belonged to Worcester's Men before becoming a well-known comedian on the Continent, where he spent a lot of time between 1590 and 1620. He and his companies toured Holland and Germany with a selection of plays, jigs, and biblical pieces; in 1595 they were appointed players and musicians to the Landgrave of Hesse-Cassel, proceeding thence to Heidelberg, Frankfurt, and Strasbourg.

Browne, W Grahame *See* Tempest, Dame Marie.

Browning, Robert (1812–89) British poet and playwright, author of three verse dramas. *Strafford* (1837) was produced by Macready at Covent Garden with scant success; *A Blot on the 'Scutcheon* (1843) was staged at Drury Lane with Phelps in the lead, while *Colombe's Birthday* was performed at the Haymarket in 1844. Of his other plays *Pippa Passes* is occasionally revived.

Browning Version, The A one-act play by Terence *Rattigan. First performance: London, 1948. It is an intense study of an unpopular classics master, Crocker Harris, and his relationships with his unfaithful wife, one of her lovers, and an unexpectedly sympathetic schoolboy.

Bruckner, Ferdinand (Theodor Tagger; 1891–1958) Austrian playwright, who established his reputation with the controversial *Krankheit der Jugend* (Malady of Youth; 1926). Subsequent successes included *Die Verbrecher* (The Criminals; 1928) and *Elizabeth von England* (1930), which both tackled contemporary themes of justice in an historical context, and a reinterpretation of Shakespeare's *Timon of Athens* (1933) as a criticism of Nazi Germany. Working in the US from 1936 to 1951, he also wrote modern equivalents of classical tragedy and adapted an old Indian play as *Das irdine Wägelchen* (The Little Clay Cart; 1957).

Brückner, Johannes (1730–86) German actor, who was a pupil of both Lessing and Ekhof and became a much-admired member of Koch's company. He excelled in tragedy; his most famous role was the central character of Goethe's *Götz von Berlichingen*.

Brueys, David-Augustin de (1640–1723) French playwright. Brueys wrote several plays for the Comédie-Française in collaboration with Jean *Palaprat; his own works, with the exception of *L'Avocat Pathelin* (1706), were less successful.

Brun, (Johan) Nordahl (1745–1816) Norwegian playwright, poet, bishop, and statesman, who was the author of the stirring patriotic tragedy *Zarine* (1772). Based in Copenhagen, he also wrote the first Norwegian national anthem, hymns, and a further tragedy, *Einer Tanbeskielver* (1772).

Brunelleschi, Filippo *See paradiso.*

Bruno, Giordano (1548–1600) Italian philosopher, scientist, and playwright, who was burnt at the stake as a heretic by the Inquisition in Rome. A friend of Sir Philip Sidney, he was the author of a single play, *Il Candelaio* (The Candlemaker; c. 1582), which attacked corruption but was banned; it was revived in 1965. *The Heretic* (1970), by Morris West, was based upon his life.

Brunton, Anne *See Merry, Anne.*

Brunton, Elizabeth *See Yates, Frederick Henry.*

Bruscambille (Jean Deslauriers; fl. 1610–34) French actor, who established his reputation in the Paris fairs. Subsequently he accompanied Jean Farine to the Hôtel de Bourgogne where he demonstrated his facility in farce and his control over unruly audiences.

Brustein, Robert (1927–) US actor, director, and critic, who founded the Yale Repertory Theatre, where he also worked as a director, in 1966. Subsequently he moved (1980) to Harvard, where he directed the professional **American Repertory Theatre** company in performances of Shakespeare, Brecht, and many others.

Bryan, Dora (Dora Broadbent; 1924–) British actress, who appeared as a child in pantomime at Manchester in 1935. She came to London in Coward's *Peace in Our Time* (1947), had a two-year run as Eva in Arthur Macrae's *Traveller's Joy* (1948), and subsequently established herself as an engaging comedienne in numerous revues and musicals.

Bryant, Michael (1928–) British actor, whose first appearance was in Tennessee Williams's *A Streetcar Named Desire* at Brighton (1951). He went on to establish his reputation in Peter Shaffer's *Five Finger Exercise* (1958) at the Comedy Theatre and in Rattigan's *Ross* (1961) at the Haymarket. He was acclaimed as Teddy in Pinter's *The Homecoming* (1965) while with the Royal Shakespeare Company and later joined the National Theatre (1977), appearing in numerous roles, from Sir Paul Plyant in Congreve's *The Double Dealer* (1978) to Enobarbus in *Antony and Cleopatra* (1987).

Bryant's Opera House *See Koster and Bial's Music Hall.*

Bryant Theatre *See Apollo Theatre.*

Bryden, Bill Campbell Rough (1942–) Scottish director and playwright, who became one of the directors associated with the National Theatre in 1975. Previously with the Belgrade Theatre in Coventry, the Royal Court Theatre, and Edinburgh's Lyceum Theatre, he won praise at the National Theatre for such productions as Synge's *The Playboy of the Western World* (1975) and in 1978 took over the Cottesloe Theatre, where he has staged several influential promenade productions ranging from mystery plays to a series of works by Eugene O'Neill and Arthur Miller's *The Crucible*.

BTA *See British Theatre Association.*

Bucco A character of the Roman *atellana*, probably a fat clown. He was the main character in two plays by Pomponius.

Buchanan, Jack (Walter John) (1890–1957) Scottish actor-manager and director, who made his first London appearance in a comic opera, *The Grass Widow*, in 1912, and went on to become a star of revue and musical comedy. Outstanding in *A to Z* at the Prince of Wales's Theatre in 1921, he subsequently appeared in a memorable series of musical shows, including *Sunny* (1926), *Wake Up and Dream* (1929), and *This'll Make You Whistle* (1936). His work in straight comedy included Lonsdale's *Canaries Sometimes Sing* (1947) and Alan Melville's *Castle in the Air* (1949).

Büchner, Georg (1813–37) German playwright and doctor, who was the author of three plays anticipating the Expressionist movement of the 20th century. Büchner was a political radical and his works betray his inner pessimism and sympathy for the oppressed. His first play, *Danton's Death*, was a gloomy assessment of the French Revolution and was not acted until 1903; *Leonce und Lena* – not acted until 1895 – criticized Romanticism, while *Woyzeck* has been much praised in recent years despite being unfinished at the time of Büchner's early death from typhoid fever.

Buck, Sir George (d. 1623) English historian and poet, who succeeded his uncle, Sir Edmund Tilney, as *Master of the Revels in 1610 but was removed from office in 1622 due to his mental infirmity. Unfortunately, his records concerning the Elizabethan theatre were destroyed by fire.

Buckingham, George Villiers, Second Duke of (1628–87) English playwright and statesman, best known for his burlesque of heroic drama *The *Rehearsal* (1671), which lampooned Dryden and provided the basis for Sheridan's *The Critic*. A leading political force during the Restoration, he was also the author of an adaptation of Fletcher's *The Chances* (1623).

Buckley's Olympic *See* Olympic Theatre.

Buckstone, John Baldwin (1802–79) British actor, playwright, and manager, who ran the Haymarket Theatre from 1853 until his death. As a comic actor he was encouraged by Edmund Kean, appearing as the original Gnatbrain in *Black-Ey'd Susan* (1829). His many farces and melodramas include *Luke the Labourer* (1826), *The Green Bushes* (1845), *The Flowers of the Forest* (1847), and *Leap Year* (1850). *See also* ghosts.

Buero Vallejo, Antonio (1916-) Spanish dramatist, best-known for his sociohistorical plays, which include *Un soñador para un pueblo* (1958) and *Las meniñas* (1960). His play *Historia de una escalera* (1949) was written while he was a political prisoner and represented a Spanish expression of Socialist Realism.

Buffalo Bill *See* Cody, William Frederick.

Bugaku A form of early Japanese musical dance, which had a strong influence upon the *Nō* drama. Usually based upon Chinese religious texts, such pieces were performed by dancers wearing masks both at Court and before audiences at religious festivals from the 7th century AD onwards.

built stuff Any piece of three-dimensional scenery specially constructed for use on stage, including rostra, items of furniture, and landscape features.

Bulandra, Lucia Sturdza- *See* Sturdza-Bulandra, Lucia.

Bulgakov, Mikhail Afanaseyev (1891–1940) Soviet playwright and novelist, who established his reputation with a dramatization of his novel *The White Guard* as *The Days of the Turbins* in 1926. Presented by Stanislavsky at the Moscow Art Theatre, it later fell foul of the Bolsheviks; other works for the Moscow Art Theatre included *The Flight*, *The Cabal of Saintly Hypocrites*

(1936), which depicted Molière's struggle with the censors, and a version (1941) of *Don Quixote* by Cervantes. He also adapted Gogol's *Dead Souls* for the stage with great success in 1930; several of his works have been revived since his death.

Bull, Ole (1810–80) Norwegian violinist, who oversaw the establishment of the first Norwegian national theatre. Det Norske Teatret (*see* Nationale Scene), which opened in Bergen in 1850, employed a Norwegian rather than a Danish staff, including Ibsen and Bjørnson among its members.

Bull Inn An inn at Bishopsgate in London, where a number of plays were staged between 1576 and c. 1600. Companies that appeared there included the Queen's Men, who visited it in 1583.

Bullins, Ed (1935-) Black US playwright, who became a leading figure in the Black theatre of San Francisco and Harlem. Author of such plays as *Clara's Ole Man* (1965), *The Duplex* (1970), and *The Fabulous Miss Marie* (1971), he has had works regularly produced at the New Lafayette and American Place theatres.

Bulwer-Lytton, Edward George Earle, Lord (1803–73) British novelist, playwright, and statesman, who took to writing to augment his income and achieved success with a number of novels and three highly acclaimed plays. *The Lady of Lyons; or, Love and Pride* (1838), *Richelieu; or, the Conspiracy* (1839), and *Money* (1840) provided Macready, Irving, and others with good parts and were all revived several times.

Bunn Hill Nursery *See* nurseries.

Bunraku The best known form of Japanese puppet theatre, in which almost lifesize dolls act out a dramatic narrative set to music (*see* Jōruri). Until the 18th century the three operators needed for each puppet remained hidden behind a screen; since then, however, they have appeared behind the puppets themselves, the assistants being dressed entirely in black and wearing black hoods. The tradition had its roots in the Asian puppet theatre imported in the 11th century and reached its peak in the 18th century after which the genre declined until only one *Bunraku* theatre remained, at Osaka.

Buontalenti, Bernardo (c. 1536–1608) Italian stage designer and theatre architect, known as *delle Girandole* after his firework displays. Employed by the Medici family in Florence, he organized numerous entertainments incorporating lavish stage effects and elaborate costumes.

Burbage, James (c. 1530–97) English actor and manager, who began as a joiner and actor with Leicester's Men. He lived in Shoreditch and in 1576 acquired a 21 year lease of nearby land, on which he erected the *Theatre. Later he converted part of a former monastery into the Blackfriars Theatre, but died before it opened.

His elder son, **Cuthbert Burbage** (c. 1566–1636), was also an actor in his earlier years and jointly inherited the theatres with his brother, becoming involved in disputes over the land at Shoreditch. The Burbages eventually dismantled the Theatre and reconstructed it as the *Globe Theatre on Bankside, forming a syndicate with Shakespeare and others.

Cuthbert's brother, **Richard Burbage** (c. 1567–1619), who made his acting debut as a boy at the Theatre, became the leading player at both the Globe and Blackfriars theatres. The first great English actor, he created the parts of Hamlet, Lear, Othello, Richard III, and other Shakespearean characters; he also appeared in plays by Webster, Jonson, and Beaumont and Fletcher.

Bürgerliches Trauerspiel A theatre movement in Germany, which had its origins in the domestic dramas of Lessing. The genre was notable chiefly for making middle-class characters the central figures in tragedy for the first time; writers connected with the movement included Schiller and Hebbel.

Burgoyne, John (1722–92) British general and playwright, author of the popular comedy *The Heiress*, which was staged at Drury Lane by Sheridan in 1786. Remembered for his defeat at Saratoga in the US War of Independence, he was later depicted by G B Shaw in *The *Devil's Disciple*.

Burgtheater A theatre in the Imperial Palace in Vienna, built in 1741. Originally used by French and German companies it came to the fore in 1776, when Emperor Josef II decreed that it was to become the home of serious drama in Austria in opposition to the tradition of the *Altwiener Volkstheater*. Under the management of Sonnenfels and Schreyvogel the theatre soon acquired a considerable reputation, actors there – including Schröder – appearing in both established classics and plays by contemporary European writers. Subsequently Heinrich Laube (1806–84) brought a new impetus to the Burgtheater and staged popular performances of well-made plays from France as well as installing early examples of the box set. In 1888 the resident company moved to a new theatre, where Anton *Wildgans staged significant Expressionist productions after World War I; this theatre was later rebuilt in 1955 after suffering severe damage during World War II. Reopened by Berthold *Viertel, the company – although now presenting little experimental drama – established a high reputation for spectacle and high standards of performance in classical plays.

Burk, John Daly (c. 1775–1808) Irishborn playwright, who emigrated to the US in 1796. His patriotic play *Bunker Hill; or, the Death of General Warren* (1797) was a favourite with US audiences for many years.

He died in a duel with a Frenchman, who had challenged him for insulting Napoleon.

Burke, Billie *See* Ziegfeld, Florenz.

burla A comic scene interpolated into *commedia dell'arte* performances. Not usually a part of the plot itself, the *burla* provided minor characters with an opportunity to indulge in slapstick humour. The word *burla* later gave rise to the terms *burletta and *burlesque.

burlesque A genre in English drama that first developed in the late 17th century. Essentially comic satires of more serious forms of drama, such plays included Buckingham's *The Rehearsal* (1671), which lampooned heroic drama, and Sheridan's *The Critic* (1779), which parodied sentimental plays. Gay's *The Beggar's Opera* (1728) similarly ridiculed the conventions of opera, although subsequently burlesque lost its satirical edge in the 19th century, when H J Byron's parodies of popular melodrama became popular. Manifestations of the tradition in 20th century British theatre have been confined largely to *revue.

The **burlesque** tradition in the US theatre is broadly unrelated to the British form and was first devised by Michael Leavitt (1843–1935) in the 1860s. Performances consisted of three parts – the first comprising songs and comic sketches, the second (known as the 'olio') variety acts, and the third more singing and sketches as well as parodies and political satire. The distinguishing feature of these shows was the emphasis upon their erotic content, notably with the **strip-tease**, which was first incorporated in the 1920s and quickly became the prime event starring such performers as Gypsy Rose Lee (1914–70). The tradition came to an end with the introduction of prohibition in the 1930s.

burletta Originally a farce with music and subsequently a form of production developed as a means of evading the restrictions on drama outside the patent theatres during the 19th century. In the latter context, many straight dramas, including those of Shakespeare, were embellished with songs and dances in order to be regarded outside the scope of the licensing laws.

Burnaby, Davy *See* pierrot troupes.

Burnand, Sir Francis Cowley (1836–1917) British playwright and founder of the *Amateur Dramatic Club at Cambridge. He wrote numerous burlesques and adaptations from the French.

burnt-cork minstrels *See* minstrel show.

Burton, Richard (Walter) (Richard Walter Jenkins; 1925–84) British actor, son of a Welsh miner, who made his stage debut in 1943 in *The Druid's Rest* by Emlyn Williams. After service with the RAF he appeared in several plays by Christopher Fry, including *The Lady's Not For Burning* (1949); in the 1950s he played numerous Shakespearean roles at Stratford and the Old Vic before concentrating upon his film career. Occasional stage appearances after that included the musical *Camelot* (1960) and *Hamlet* (1964), directed by John Gielgud. He also appeared on Broadway in Shaffer's *Equus* (1976) and in *Private Lives* (1983) with Elizabeth Taylor.

Burton, William Evans (1804–60) British actor and manager, who was engaged in 1831 as an actor at the Haymarket, where he appeared with Edmund Kean. Subsequently he moved to the US, acting under his own management in Philadelphia and, in 1848, opening his own theatre, Burton's (*see* Chambers Street Theatre), in New York. There he appeared in a variety of comic parts, including Dickensian and Shakespearean characters. His move to the Metropolitan Theatre in 1856, however, brought little success at a time of financial crisis, and he was forced to close.

Bury, John (1925–) Welsh stage designer, who has been head of design at the National Theatre since 1973. Previously with Joan Littlewood's Theatre Workshop and then in charge of design with the Royal Shakespeare Company (1964–71), he has become well-known for his use of texture and three-dimensional sets for plays by such authors as Ibsen, Behan, Dürrenmatt, Shakespeare, and Pinter. His recent successes have included designs for *Hamlet* (1975), Marlowe's *Tamburlaine the Great* (1976), and Peter Shaffer's *Amadeus* (1979).

Busch, Ernst (1900–80) German actor, who began his career in cabaret in Germany in the 1920s and appeared at the Deutsches Theater in Berlin after World War II. He became a leading member of Brecht's company in 1950, appearing in such celebrated works as *Mutter Courage und ihre Kinder* (1954).

busker A street performer, typically a musician, juggler, or other entertainer who performs to passers-by or theatre-goers as they queue to enter the theatre. Derived from the word *buskin* (*see* cothurnus), the term is also sometimes used for performers of Punch and Judy.

Butti, Enrico Annibale (1868–1912) Italian playwright, whose social dramas depict the futility of the struggle of the individual against society. Influenced by Ibsen, his plays include *Il vortice* (The Vortex; 1892), *L'Utopia* (1894), *La corsa al piacere* (The Pursuit of Pleasure; 1900), and *La tempesta* (1901).

Byam Shaw, Glen Alexander (1904–81) British actor and director, who appeared in London, Oxford, and New York during the 1920s before joining Gielgud's company at the Queen's Theatre (1937–38). After World War II he concentrated on direction, beginning with Rattigan's *The Winslow Boy* in 1946. Subsequently he worked at both the

Old Vic and the Young Vic before becoming codirector with Anthony Quayle at the Shakespeare Memorial Theatre in 1953; he was sole director there from 1956 to 1959. Later successes included Rattigan's *Ross* (1959); he took over the Sadler's Wells Opera company in 1962.

Byron, George Gordon, Lord (1788–1824) British poet and author of a number of poetic dramas. In 1815 he became a member of the committee at Drury Lane, where his *Marino Faliero* was produced in 1821. After his death, Macready appeared in *Werner* (1830), *Sardanapalus* (1834), and *The Two Foscari* (1838); his choral tragedy *Manfred* was staged at Covent Garden in 1834.

Byron, Henry James (1834–84) British playwright and actor, noted for his many burlesques and extravaganzas. His comedies *War to the Knife* (1865) and *A Hundred Thousand Pounds* (1866) were amongst those produced at the Prince of Wales Theatre (later the Scala Theatre) where he was associated with the Bancrofts in management. The most successful of all his works was, however, *Our Boys*, which began a record-breaking run at the Vaudeville Theatre in 1875.

C

cabaret A form of entertainment combining music and various forms of theatre at a club or other venue with an intimate atmosphere. Having its origins in music hall, cabaret includes at one extreme solo acts presented in small bars and at the other spectacular revues staged at famous restaurants and even theatres. During the 1930s, cabaret became one of the liveliest areas of German theatre, attracting such major figures as Brecht and acquiring a strong po-

litical identity; subsequently it flourished in Britain and the US during the 1950s and 1960s.

Cabaret *See I am a Camera.*

Caecilius Statius (c. 219 BC–c. 166 BC) Roman playwright, who translated many Greek works for the Latin stage. Originally a slave, he adapted about 40 comedies, many by Menander; only titles and fragments survive.

Caen, Compagnie de *See Décentralisation Dramatique.*

Caesar and Cleopatra A history play by G B *Shaw. First performance: Berlin, 1906. In Shaw's comedy, Caesar's greatness is emphasized, whereas Cleopatra is depicted as little more than an animal. Unlike Shakespeare's Cleopatra, Shaw's queen is a 16-year-old temptress, while the character of Caesar is used to represent Shaw's concept of the Life Force that stimulates man's progress.

Café La Mama *See La Mama Experimental Theatre Club.*

Caffé Cino A theatre and coffee house on Cornelia Street, New York, which opened in 1958 and became the first venue for plays of the off-off-Broadway theatre movement. Plays were produced here from 1961 to 1967 and included many new US works.

Calderón, Maria (17th century) Spanish actress, popularly known as La Calderona. She performed in *autos sacramentales* and *comedias* before retiring to enter a convent; she was also the mistress of Philip IV of Spain.

Calderón de la Barca, Pedro (1600–81) Spanish playwright, regarded as the most important successor to Lope de Vega. Born in Madrid, he was the author of approximately 120 well-constructed religious and secular plays, including tragedies, comedies, histories, and philosophical dramas. Of his secular plays, *La vida es sueño* – a depiction of the state of mind of a prince who is released after having been locked up all his life in prison – is regarded as the best; other notable works of the type include *La alcade de Zalamea*, a study of revenge and seduction. His most celebrated plays on religious themes include *La cena de Baltasar, El gran teatro del mundo*, and *El mágico prodigioso*, which was set in the time of Diocletian. In 1651 he was ordained as a priest, becoming chaplain of honour to the king in 1663; from this date he concentrated upon the writing of numerous *autos sacramentales* noted for their poetic power and masterly theatricality. His works inspired many later writers to execute adaptations and translations of his plays, notably Killigrew and Wycherley in the English tradition, Tuke in the French, and Schlegel and Tieck in the German.

Principal works:

El segreto a voces: 1626.

Casa con dos puertos mal es de guarda: 1629; translated as *It is Difficult to Guard a House with Two Doors*.

El príncipe constante: 1629.

La dama duende: c. 1629; adapted as *The Parson's Wedding*.

La devocion de la cruz: c. 1633.

El mayor monstruo, los celos: c. 1634; translated as *No Monster Like Jealousy*.

La cena de Baltasar: c. 1634; translated as *Belshazzar's Feast*.

A secreto agravio, secreta venganza: 1635; translated as *Secret Vengeance for Secret Insult*.

El medico de su honra: 1635; translated as *The Surgeon of His Honour*.

El mágico prodigioso: 1637; translated as *The Wonder-Working Magician*.

El pintor de su deshonra: 1637; translated as *The Painter of His Dishonour*.

La vida es sueño: c. 1638; translated as *Life's a Dream*.

El alcalde de Zalamea: c. 1640; translated as *The Mayor of Zalamea*.

El gran teatro del mundo: c. 1645; translated as *The Great World Theatre*.

La hija del aire: 1653.

Caldwell, Zoë (1934–) Australian actress, who was one of the original members of the Union Theatre Repertory Company in Melbourne. She appeared with the Shakespeare Memorial Theatre Company at Stratford-on-Avon in 1958 and later performed at the Royal Court Theatre, the Stratford (Ontario) Festival, the Tyrone Guthrie Theatre, and elsewhere in numerous acclaimed parts; her roles have included Millamant in Congreve's *The Way of the World* (1965), Cleopatra (1967), Jean Brodie in Muriel Spark's *The Prime of Miss Jean Brodie* (1968), and Mary Tyrone in O'Neill's *Long Day's Journey Into Night* (1976).

California Suite A series of short comedies by Neil *Simon. First performance: 1976. The plot concerns the guests at a Beverly Hills hotel and their various adventures. The play was filmed in 1978 starring Alan Alda, Jane Fonda, Walter Matthau, Maggie Smith, Michael Caine, and Elaine May.

call board A noticeboard situated in the backstage area, upon which messages for the cast and stage crew are displayed.

call boy A former member of the stage crew, who was responsible for making sure that actors were ready to take their cue to go on stage.

call doors *See* proscenium doors.

Call Me Madam A musical by Howard *Lindsay, and Russel *Crouse, with music and lyrics by Irving *Berlin. First performance: New York, 1950. A Washington hostess, Sally Adams, is appointed ambassador to Lichtenberg and falls in love with the foreign minister. The play was filmed in

1953 with Ethel Merman, who starred in the original production.

Callow, Simon (1949-) British actor, who first appeared in London with the Edinburgh Traverse Theatre in 1974. Subsequent parts have included several with the Joint Stock Company, Mozart in Peter Shaffer's *Amadeus* at the National Theatre, and Tony Perrelli in Edgar Wallace's *On the Spot* (1984) at the Albery. In 1988 he directed Willy Russell's *Shirley Valentine* at the Vaudeville Theatre and starred in a revival of Goethe's *Faust*.

Calmo, Andrea (1509–71) Italian playwright, actor, and gondolier, who appeared in early *commedia dell'arte* productions. As an actor he specialized in playing elderly men.

Calvert, Louis (1859–1923) British actor, son of the provincial actor-manager **Charles Calvert** (1828–79). Louis Calvert worked with Irving at the Lyceum and in the companies of Ben Greet and Frank Benson before becoming a leading actor for the Vedrenne-Barker management at the Royal Court Theatre, where he was the original Broadbent in Shaw's *John Bull's Other Island* (1904) and William in a revival of *You Never Can Tell* (1905). A forceful actor, whose range encompassed Sir Peter Teazle and Andrew Undershaft in Shaw's *Major Barbara*, he was a respected manager and ran his own touring company.

Calvo-Sotelo, Joaquín (1905-) Spanish playwright, who was the author of the immensely popular drama dealing with religious conflict *La muralla* (The Impasse; 1954). His other plays include his first success, *Cuando Llego la noche* (When Night Falls; 1943), and *Milagro en la Plaza del Progreso* (Miracle in Progress Square; 1953).

Câmara, João da (1852–1908) Portuguese playwright, author of several notable histori-

cal dramas and comedies. He also encompassed realism in *Os Velhos* (The Old Ones; 1893) and symbolism in *Meia Noite* (Midnight; 1900).

Cambridge Festival Theatre A theatre in Cambridge, which became a focus of development in stage design under the management of Terence *Gray (1926–33). Formerly known as the Barnwell Theatre, it was totally reorganized by Gray, who removed the proscenium arch and explored the possibilities of a flexible split-level acting area as well as experimenting with innovative lighting arrangements. After 1933 the theatre was run on a less adventurous commercial basis and was finally taken over by the Cambridge Arts Theatre as a workshop and store.

Cambridge Theatre A theatre in the Seven Dials district of London, opened in 1930. The opening production was *Charlot's Masquerade*, starring Beatrice Lillie. Seasons of plays, ballets, and films were presented for some years, and later Sunday concerts; in 1934 the theatre played host to the Comédie-Française. For two years from 1946 the Cambridge was the headquarters of the newly founded New London Opera Company. Since 1952 a policy of plays and musicals has been maintained, the most successful including William Douglas Home's *The Reluctante Debutante* (1955), Keith Waterhouse's *Billy Liar* (1960–62), Tommy Steele in *Half a Sixpence* (1963–64), Ingmar Bergman's version of Ibsen's *Hedda Gabler* (1970) with Maggie Smith, Jonathan Miller's production of Chekhov's *Three Sisters* (1976), and the US musical *Chicago* (1979). Recent productions include Kander and Ebb's musical *The Rink* (1988). Also in 1988 it became the home of the newly reconstituted D'Oyly Carte opera company.

Cameri Theatre A theatre company established in Palestine in 1944 in reaction to the formalized realism favoured by other contemporary theatre groups. Presenting plays by such authors as Goldoni, the Čapek brothers, and García Lorca, the company established a strong reputation; after the founding of Israel in 1948 it also staged naturalistic works by leading contemporary writers in Hebrew as well as continuing to present plays by Brecht, Pinter, and other foreign playwrights. In 1961 it moved to Tel-Aviv, becoming the city's official resident theatre company in 1970.

Cameron, Beatrice See Mansfield, Richard.

Caminelli, Antonio (1436–1502) Italian playwright, also known as **Il Pistoia**. His play *Filostrato e Panfile* (1499) was influenced by the tragedies of Seneca and by the tradition of the *sacra rappresentazione*.

Camões, Luís Vaz de (c. 1524–80) Portuguese poet and playwright, usually remembered for the epic poem *Os Lusíadas*. He spent much of his life in the Portuguese colonies and was the author of three plays based on classical themes. *Os Anfitriões*, *El-Rei Seleuro*, and *Filodemo* (his best play) were all influenced by the works of Vicente.

Campbell, Herbert (1846–1904) British music hall comedian. He started in minstrel shows and even appeared as an actor at Drury Lane in 1882. From 1891, by which time he weighed 19 stone, he partnered the diminutive Dan Leno in 14 consecutive Drury Lane pantomimes.

Campbell, Ken (1941–) British director, who took over the Everyman Theatre, Liverpool, in 1980 after previously establishing a strong reputation with his leadership of the **Science Fiction Theatre of Liverpool**. Successes with the earlier group included the *Illuminatus* (1976) cycle of five plays, cowritten with Chris Langham, and Neil Oram's *The Warp* (1979); at the Everyman Theatre Campbell has presented a series of experi-

mental dramas, many aimed at young audiences. Recent works include *The Hitchhiker's Guide to the Galaxy* (1979) and *War With the Newts* (1981).

Campbell, Mrs Patrick (Beatrice Rose Stella Tanner; 1865–1940) British actress, who became one of the most famous actresses of her day on account of her exceptional stage presence and biting wit. She made her debut in Liverpool in 1888 and subsequently appeared in melodrama at the Adelphi Theatre in London before being selected to create Paula in *The Second Mrs Tanqueray* (1893), in which part she established her reputation. Later she triumphed in the title role of Pinero's *The Notorious Mrs Ebbsmith* (1895), in numerous Shakespearean parts whilst joint-manager of the Lyceum, and alongside Bernhardt in Maeterlinck's *Pelléas et Mélisande* (1904). She also excelled in the plays of Ibsen and Shaw, who wrote *Pygmalion* for her and with whom she entered into a long and celebrated correspondence.

Campen, Jacob van (1595–1657) Dutch architect, who designed the first theatre to be built in Amsterdam (c. 1638). The **Schouwburg** shared many features with Palladio's Teatro Olimpico; a proscenium arch was subsequently added by Jan Vos. The theatre was destroyed by fire in 1772.

Campion, Thomas (1567–1629) English poet, musician, and doctor, who wrote a number of masques for the court of James I. He may also have contributed pieces for the public stage through his friend Philip Rosseter.

Campistron, Jean Galbert de (1656–1723) French playwright, born in Toulouse. Sent to Paris by his father in 1673, he found a friend in the actor Jean-Baptiste Raisin and later entered the service of Louis XIV. Campistron's dramatic output consisted largely of tragedies in the style of Racine and Corneille, notably *Andronic* (1685), *Alcibiade* (1685), and *Tiridate* (1691).

Camus, Albert (1913–60) French novelist, playwright, and essayist, born in Algeria. Better known for his novels, Camus nevertheless made a significant contribution to the Theatre of the *Absurd. He also produced successful stage adaptations of novels by William Faulkner and Dostoevsky. His own works include *Le Malentendu* (1944), *Caligula* (1945), *L'État de siège* (1948; translated as *State of Siege*, 1958), and *Les Justes* (1949; translated as *The Just Assassins*, 1958). He died in a car crash.

Canadian Actors' Equity Association A trade union for professional actors in Canada, established in 1955 as a branch of the American Actors' Equity Association and becoming independent in 1976. Based in Toronto, it maintains close links with its US counterpart; it also has an office in Vancouver.

Candida A play by G B *Shaw, influenced by the plays of Ibsen. First performance: South Shields, 1895. Arguably Shaw's best constructed play, it presents the conflict between commonsense and poetry, as personified by the relationship between Candida and the poet Marchbanks. In the end Candida, torn between Marchbanks and her conventional Christian Socialist husband, chooses the latter and Marchbanks renounces their way of life.

Candler Theatre *See* Sam H Harris Theatre.

Cane, Andrew (fl. 1620–44) English actor, originally a goldsmith, often referred to as **Cane the Clown**. He was with Lady Elizabeth's Men in 1622, then with Princes Charles's Men at the Fortune Theatre. After the closure of the theatres in 1642 he continued to appear at the Red Bull Theatre; during the Civil War, however, he resumed his former trade.

Cañizares, José de (1676–1750) Spanish playwright. Several of his plays were largely derived from the works of Lope de Vega.

Cankar, Ivan (1876–1918) Czechoslovakian playwright, who emerged as the most important figure in Czechoslovakian theatre in the early 20th century. Much influenced by Ibsen and subsequently by Symbolism, he was the author of six plays – the first being *Jakob Ruda* (1900) – notable for their poetic intensity.

Canterbury Music Hall A theatre in Lambeth, London, opened as a music hall in 1852 by Charles *Morton close to his Canterbury Tavern. The venue was so successful that Morton soon rebuilt it as the larger New Canterbury Music Hall, seating 1500 people. After Morton gave up his interest in the theatre, it was redesigned in three tiers, remaining one of the most popular of all music halls – with several royal patrons – until the genre died out in the 20th century. It was destroyed by bombs in World War II.

Cantor, Eddie (Isidore Itzkowitz; 1892–1964) US singer and actor, who first attracted attention as a jumpy pop-eyed, often blackfaced, music hall act. He then turned to musical comedy and revue and was associated for many years with Ziegfeld's *Follies*. He later became a Hollywood star but made a final Broadway appearance in *Banjo Eyes* (1941).

capa y espada, comedia de *See comedia.*

Čapek, Karel (1890–1938) Czech playwright, novelist, and travel-writer, whose early plays, notably *RUR (1921), and *Ze života hymzu* (The *Insect Play; 1921), deal with the underlying discord between man and his universe. The latter play, written with his brother **Josef Čapek** (1887–1945), who died in Belsen, was followed by such works as *Bílá nemoc* (The White Scourge; 1937) and *Matka* (The Mother; 1938), which expressed his concern about the rise of Fascism in Europe, as well as *Adam the Creator* (1927), which was a sequel to *The Insect Play*.

Capitano, Il A character of the *commedia dell'arte*, a pretentious but cowardly soldier. He probably inherited much of his character from that of Plautus's *Miles Gloriosus.

Capon, William (1757–1827) British architect and painter, born at Norwich, the son of an artist. In 1794 John Philip Kemble engaged him as scenic director at Drury Lane, where he produced painstakingly accurate historical sets. After Drury Lane burnt down in 1808, he accompanied Kemble to Covent Garden where his magnificent Shakespearean settings were universally acclaimed.

Captain Brassbound's Conversion A play by G B *Shaw. First performance: London, 1900. Originally written for Ellen Terry, the play – one of *Three Plays for Puritans* – suffers from its reliance upon contrived situations. The plot revolves around the shrewd Lady Cicely Waynflete, who successfully 'tames' the vengeful pirate Brassbound.

Capuana, Luigi (1839–1915) Italian Realist novelist, playwright, and critic, who wrote several notable dramas in the *verismo* tradition. Generally considered the first Italian writer to adopt the ideals of naturalism, he wrote several plays in the Sicilian dialect, of which *Malia* (1895) and *Lu Cavalieri Pidagna* were the most successful.

Caragiale, Ion Luca (1852–1912) Romanian playwright and short-story writer, who is generally considered Romania's greatest writer for the theatre. His satirical comedies, notably *O noapte furtunoasă* (A Stormy Night; 1879) and *O scrisoare pierdută* (The Lost Letter; 1884), mocked political and social pretensions and were all staged at the National Theatre in Bucharest, of which he was briefly director-general (1888–89).

carbon arc spotlight A spotlight with two carbon electrodes, formerly widely used for its brilliant, though flickering, beam before the introduction of the electric incandescent bulb. It was informally referred to as an **arc**.

Caretaker, The A play by Harold *Pinter. First performance: Arts Theatre Club, 1960, with Alan Bates, Peter Woodthorpe, and Donald Pleasence in the cast. The play's action is a struggle for power between two brothers and the tramp, Davies, who tries to ingratiate his way into their house.

Carey, Joyce (1898–) British actress, daughter of Gerald *Lawrence and Lilian *Braithwaite. She is chiefly associated with comedies, particularly those of Coward; she has also excelled in such roles as Lady Markby in Wilde's *An Ideal Husband* (1966) and as Agatha Christie's Miss Marple. Under the name Jay Mallory she wrote the successful play *Sweet Aloes* (1934).

Carl, Karl (Karl Andreas von Bernbrunn; 1789–1854) Austrian actor, playwright, and director, who managed theatres in Munich and Vienna with great success. Noted himself as an actor in romantic parts, he popularized *Staberl in Germany and later wrote numerous farces in collaboration with Nestroy for the Viennese stage. He also oversaw the building of a new Leopoldstädter Theater in 1847.

Carlin *See* Bertinazzi, Carlo.

Carmontelle (Louis Carrogis; 1717–1806) French artist and playwright. He wrote light comedies, published in the collections

Proverbes dramatiques (1768–81) and *Théâtre de campagne* (1775); the former created a genre that was subsequently developed by Alfred de Musset.

Carney, Kate (1868–1950) British music hall singer. She began her career singing Irish ballads, but later established herself as the 'Cockney Queen', performing songs of East London life.

Carnival play *See Fastnachtsspiel.*

Carnovsky, Morris (1897–) US actor, who made his New York debut in 1922 in *The God of Vengeance* by Sholom Asch. He then appeared with the Theatre Guild (1923–30) and subsequently with the Group Theatre, starring in Paul Green's *The House of Connelly* (1931) and *Awake and Sing!* (1935) and *Golden Boy* (1937) by Clifford Odets. His performances with other companies have included Ibsen's *An Enemy of the People* (1950). Since 1956 he has made regular appearances at the American Shakespeare Festival in Stratford, Connecticut, notably as King Lear.

Caroline drama English drama of the reign of Charles I (1625–42). The period saw many elaborate masques and pastorals, notably those of Milton, Jonson, and Inigo Jones, and the domestic intrigues of James Shirley and Richard Brome, while John Ford was the foremost writer of tragedy. The theatre outside London languished during Charles I's reign, which culminated in the closure of all theatres by Parliament upon the outbreak of the Civil War (*see* Interregnum).

Carousel A musical by Rodgers and *Hammerstein. First performance: New York, 1945. Based on Ferenc Molnár's play *Liliom*, the plot revolves around a fairground barker who is killed during an attempted robbery but is given a last chance to make amends on earth.

carpenter's scene A scene that takes place at the front of the stage before the curtain, thus enabling the stage crew to change the set unnoticed by the audience and without a break in the action. It remains a common device in pantomime and musical comedy.

carpet cut A slot in the stage in which a carpet or other stage cloth is secured by means of hinged flaps.

Carretto, Galleotto del (d. c. 1530) Italian playwright. His plays *Timon* (1497) and *Sofonisba* (1502) were heavily influenced by the tragedies of Seneca and by the tradition of the *sacra rappresentazione.*

carriage-and-frame system A method of effecting a rapid change of scenery, developed in Italy in the 17th century. Also called the **chariot-and-pole system**, it consisted of pairs of flats mounted on wheeled platforms, which were drawn beneath the stage by ropes on a network of rails so that as one flat disappeared into the wings another automatically took its place.

Carroll, Earl (1893–1948) US impresario, who built and ran the *Earl Carroll Theatre. In 1923 he staged the first of a series of his own revues, *Earl Carroll's Vanities*. Among the straight plays be produced was Leon Gordon's *White Cargo* (1923).

Carroll, Paul Vincent (1900–68) Irish playwright. From 1945 he lived in England, where he wrote film and television scenarios as well as plays on Irish themes. Heavily influenced by Ibsen, he won an Abbey Theatre prize for *Things That Are Caesar's* in 1932. His most successful play was *Shadow and Substance* (1934), which won a New York Drama Critics Circle Award, a success which he repeated with *The White Steed* (1939). Other works include two lively satirical comedies.

Cartel A loosely-defined association of four leading French actor-managers in the 1920s, which aimed to create a new theatrical impetus. The combined efforts of the various members of the Cartel – Baty, Dullin, Jouvet, and Pitoëff, who in 1936 shared the directorship of the Comédie-Française – triggered the *avant-garde movement.

Carton, Richard Claude (Richard Claude Critchett; 1856–1928) British playwright and actor, whose career as a writer blossomed with the success of *Liberty Hall* in 1892. He then embarked upon a series of farcical comedies, which often starred his wife, Katherine Mackenzie *Compton, the best-known being *Lord and Lady Algy* (1898).

Cartoucherie de Vincennes *See* Soleil, Théâtre du.

Cartwright, William (c. 1606–c. 1687) English actor, presumed to be the son of **William Cartwright** (fl. 1590–1622), who at one time leased, in partnership, the Fortune Theatre. The younger Cartwright was a member of Prince Charles's Men at Salisbury Court and joined Killigrew at Drury Lane after the Restoration. His most notable roles included Corbaccio in Jonson's *Volpone* (1663).

Casarés, Maria (1922-) French actress, born in Spain, who moved to France during the Spanish Civil War. She established her reputation in Synge's *Deidre of the Sorrows* (1942) and in existentialist dramas by Camus, Sartre, and Anouilh; her classic roles have included Racine's Phèdre at the Comédie-Française (1952–54) and Lady Macbeth at the Avignon Festival (1954). She joined the Théâtre National Populaire in 1955, subsequently appearing in intense modern dramas by such authors as Genet, Brecht, and Bond.

Casino Theatre A theatre on Broadway, New York, which opened in 1883 and became the leading musical-comedy theatre in New York. The theatre closed after the production of *The Desert Song* (1926) and was demolished in 1930.

Casona, Alejandro (Rodríguez Álvarez; 1900–65) Spanish playwright, who wrote humorous plays for performance by a travelling theatre, El Teatro del Pueblo. His most successful plays include *La sirena varada* (1934) and *Prohibido suicidarse en primavera* (1937).

Casson, Sir Lewis (Thomas) (1875–1969) British actor and director, who began with the Vedrenne-Barker management and then the Horniman company in Manchester. The husband of Sybil Thorndike, he acted with her and directed her in many plays, touring widely with her at home and abroad. He also directed and appeared in classical productions at the Old Vic and other theatres; contemporary roles included Gertler in *I Have Been Here Before* (1937) and the Professor in *The Linden Tree* (1947) by J B Priestley. He was knighted in 1945.

Caste A play by T W *Robertson. First performance: 1867. The play, a dramatic exposition of class prejudice, centres upon Esther Eccles, a girl from the ballet who marries into the aristocracy. Her husband, falsely reported killed in battle, returns to rescue her from the effects of social snobbery.

CAS Theatre *See* Community Arts Service.

Castro y Bellvís, Guillén de (1569–1631) Spanish playwright, author of *La mocedades del Cid* (c. 1599), a play in two parts upon which Corneille based *Le Cid* in 1637. A friend of Lope de Vega, he was also the author of several comedies and stage adaptations of *Don Quixote* by Cervantes.

catharsis A theoretical concept, formulated by Aristotle in his *Poetics*. It denotes the emotional purification of the audience ideally achieved at the end of a tragedy.

Cathleen Ni Houlihan A verse play by W B *Yeats and Lady *Gregory. First performance: Dublin, 1902, by the Irish National Dramatic Society. Based on a well-known ballad, the play was warmly welcomed by Irish nationalists. It depicts the adventures of Michael Gillane, who joins in the struggle for Irish independence in 1798 at the bidding of an old woman, later revealed as the mystical Queen of Ireland.

Cat on a Hot Tin Roof A drama by Tennessee *Williams. First performance: New York, 1955. The plot concerns Brick, an alcoholic, and Maggie, the 'cat', who wants a child but cannot have one by Brick as he is impotent. Brick's father, moreover, desperately wants a grandson as he is dissatisfied with his two sons. The play won a Pulitzer Prize.

Cats A musical by Andrew *Lloyd Webber. First performance: New London Theatre, London, 1981. Based on settings of poems from T S Eliot's *Old Possum's Book of Practical Cats*, the show centres on a series of dances and was first directed by Trevor Nunn.

catwalk A narrow bridge above the stage from which scenery and lighting equipment can be manhandled.

Caucasian Chalk Circle, The (*Der Kaukasische Kreidekreis*) A play by Bertolt *Brecht, written in 1943–45. First performance: Minnesota, 1948. First performed in German by the Berliner Ensemble in 1954, it revolves around a woman's attempts to retain custody of a small child against its biological mother and her final appeal for justice at the court of a bogus judge.

cauldron trap A square trap positioned upstage; so-called from its use in the witches scene in *Macbeth*.

Cavalcade A play by Noël *Coward. First performance: Drury Lane, 1931. The play presents a patriotic and panoramic view of British life from 1899 to 1930 through the history of the Marryot family and employs a huge cast. Subsequently it was successfully turned into a film.

Cave, Joe (Joseph Arnold Cave; 1823–1912) British music hall comedian, who was the first performer to work a black-faced comedy act. Later he became manager of the Marylebone Music Hall.

Cawarden, Sir Thomas (d. 1559) English court official, appointed *Master of the Revels in 1545. During his time the involvement of this office in censorship became more profound; Cawarden did, however, live just long enough to supervise the revels for the coronation of Queen Elizabeth I.

Cecchi, Giovanni Maria (1518–87) Italian playwright, author of numerous comedies, notably *Assiulo* (1550), and religious plays. His use of various additional comic characters in biblical stories was a significant development in the foundation of an Italian secular theatrical tradition.

Cecchini, Pier Maria (1575–1645) Italian actor and playwright of the *commedia dell'arte*, who was known on stage as **Fritellino**. He became leader of the Accesi troupe in 1600 and often appeared with his wife Orsola, who was known as **Flaminea** and later moved with him to join the Fedeli company.

ceiling-cloth A cloth used to provide the ceiling of a box set as an alternative to a rigid book ceiling.

Céleste, Céline (1814–82) French actress, noted for her expressive performances in both dance and pantomime. After visiting New York she played in London in 1830 and later appeared at Drury Lane and elsewhere in speaking parts in such plays as *A Tale of Two Cities* (1860) by Dickens. She also managed the Adelphi Theatre with Ben Webster for a time.

Celestina, La A dialogue novel by Fernando de *Rojas, regarded as the most important piece of Spanish dramatic writing of the 15th century. A popular and frequently humorous study of tragic love, it was also highly successful in English, Italian, and French adaptations, including that of John *Rastell.

cellar The area directly beneath the stage, used for storage, the operation of stage equipment, and for access to the stage through traps.

Celle castle A castle in the town of Celle in Germany, which is also the home of one of the oldest theatres in Europe. Completed by 1674, it was designed in the baroque style and seated 330 people; numerous balls and dramatic entertainments were staged there in front of the Hanoverian Court. Many years later Schröder appeared there, although the theatre fell into disuse for long periods. It was restored in 1935 and the resident company was revived in 1950.

Celtis, Conradus (Conrad Pickel; 1459–1508) German scholar, who did much to promote the study of classical drama in Cologne, Heidelberg, and as a professor at the university of Vienna. He published the plays of Hroswitha in 1501 and was himself the author of two dramatic works, the masques *Ludus Dianae* (1501) and *Rhapsodia, laudes et victoria Maximiliani de Boemannis* (1504).

CEMA *See* Arts Council.

Cenci, The A verse tragedy by Percy Bysshe *Shelley, published in 1819. First performance: 1886. It recounts the murder of a rich Italian nobleman, Count Cenci, who has turned against his family but has developed an incestuous passion for his daughter.

censorship *See* Lord Chamberlain.

Centlivre, Susannah (1667–1723) English playwright and actress, who established herself as a successor to Aphra Behn with her play *The Gamester* in 1705. As an actress she appeared predominantly in male roles; of her many comedies of intrigue the most celebrated were *The Busie Body* (1709), *The Wonder: a Woman Keeps a Secret* (1714), and *A Bold Stroke for a Wife* (1718). Some of David Garrick's most popular roles were in Mrs Centlivre's plays.

Central School of Speech and Drama A drama school in London, founded in 1906 by the actress **Elsie Fogerty** (1866–1945). Initially concerned chiefly with the performance of poetic drama, it was based in the Albert Hall before moving to the Embassy Theatre.

Central Theatre of the Soviet Army *See* Red Army Theatre.

Centre 42 *See* Round House.

Centres Dramatiques *See Décentralisation Dramatique.*

centrestage *See* stage direction.

Century Grove *See* Century Theatre.

Century Theatre A theatre on 62nd Street, New York, which opened in 1909 as the **New Theatre**. It reopened as the Century in 1911, housing musicals and some acclaimed Shakespearean productions. Other successes were Vollmöller's *The Miracle*

(1924) and Reinhardt's version of *A Midsummer Night's Dream* (1927). The theatre closed in 1929 and was demolished, together with the **Cocoanut Grove** or **Century Grove** theatre on its roof, in 1930.

Another **Century Theatre** opened on Seventh Avenue, New York, as the **Jolson Theatre** in 1921. The theatre was named the Century in 1944 and housed visiting companies from Britain, France, and the USSR, including Stanislavsky's Moscow Art Theatre in 1923. Known as the **Venice Theatre** from 1934 to 1937, it housed several other companies (including the Federal Theatre Project and the Old Vic company) before demolition in 1961.

See also Adelphi Theatre; Bijou Theatre.

Cervantes Saavedra, Miguel de (1547–1616) Spanish novelist and playwright, who turned to literature after service in the army, having lost the use of his left hand as the result of a wound received at the battle of Lepanto (1571) and having been imprisoned for five years after his capture by pirates. His romance *Don Quixote de la Mancha* has provided numerous subsequent writers with material for their own plays, including an adaptation by W G Wills in which Irving appeared. Of his works written specifically for the stage 16 survive; the best include the *comedia Pedro de Urdemalas*, the full-length play *El cerco de Numancia*, and *El trato de Argel*.

Césaire, Aimé (1913-) West Indian poet and playwright, whose plays reject European influences and make extensive use of African rhythms and history. His best-known works, written in French, include *La Tragédie du roi Christophe* (1963) and *Une saison au Congo* (1967), both of which discuss the problems faced by newly-independent African states, and a version of *The Tempest* (1969) highlighting racial themes.

Český Krumlov A castle in Czechoslovakia, site of one of the oldest existing theatres in Europe. Built in 1766 in the baroque style, it contains 10 unique sets of scenery (by Viennese artists) notable for their use of perspective effects and much original stage machinery. The theatre is still occasionally used for dramatic presentations.

Chaikin, Joseph (1935-) US actor, director, and producer, who made his New York debut in *Dark of the Moon* (1958), then joined the Living Theatre. In 1964 he founded the *Open Theatre, which he ran on the principles set down in his book *The Presence of the Actor* (1972).

Chaillot, Palais de A theatrical venue in Paris, close to the Eiffel Tower, which contains several stage areas and exhibition spaces. The original building was the home of Gémier's Théâtre National Populaire from 1920 to 1934; after rebuilding in 1937 it became the base of a second Théâtre National Populaire led by Vilar and Wilson before extensive reorganization in the 1970s (*see Décentralisation Dramatique*).

chairman The master of ceremonies in a music hall. The post had been largely dropped by the 1890s.

Chairs, The (*Les Chaises*) A play by Eugène *Ionesco. First performance: Paris, 1952. The chairs of the title, assembled to seat the invisible guests of an elderly married couple, dominate the stage: the two old people finally commit suicide.

Chamberlain's Men An English theatrical company founded in 1594. Including Shakespeare amongst its members, the company, for which Shakespeare wrote the majority of his plays, performed at the Theatre until 1599 and then at the Globe Theatre, led by Richard Burbage. They also appeared at the court of Elizabeth I and were ultimately renamed the *King's Men after the accession of James I in 1603. Apart from Shakespeare, other playwrights who had their work performed by the company included Jonson, Dekker, and Beaumont and Fletcher.

Chambers of Rhetoric Associations of rhetoricians, first organized in both northern France and the Low Countries (where they were known as **Rederykers**) in the 12th and 13th centuries. These groups of writers staged drama festivals and developed various Continental equivalents of the mystery, miracle, and morality plays, notably the allegorical *spel van sinne*. Their reputation eventually declined and the last such chambers were disbanded in the early 17th century.

Chambers Street Theatre A theatre in Chambers Street, New York, which opened as Palmo's Opera House in 1844. From 1848 to 1856 it was known as Burton's Chambers Street Theatre under the management of William E Burton, who successfully staged Shakespeare as well as plays based upon novels by Dickens. Subsequently Edward Eddy presented a popular season of farce and melodrama. Renamed the **American Theatre** under E L Davenport in 1857 it was closed within a month.

Champagne Charlie *See* Leybourne, George.

Champion, Harry (1866–1942) British music hall comedian, who abandoned his early negro act to become a cockney comic. He had a long career singing, sometimes at tremendous speed, such songs as 'Any Old Iron', 'Boiled Beef and Carrots', and 'I'm Henry the Eighth I am, I am'.

Champmeslé, Charles Chevillet (1642–1701) French actor and playwright, who performed in the provinces before appearing at the Théâtre du Marais, the Hôtel de Bourgogne, and, ultimately, the Comédie-Française. He excelled in tragedy, notably in Racine's *Bérénice* (1670). His own plays

include the comedy *Crispin Chevalier* (1673), *Le Florentin* (1685), and *La Coupe enchantée* (1688).

His wife was the celebrated actress **Mlle Champmeslé** (Marie Desmares; 1643–98), who eventually became the leading tragic actress with the Comédie-Française. She established her reputation while at the Théâtre du Marais and inspired Racine, who became her lover, to write such parts as Bérénice, Roxane, and Phèdre for her. She became famous for her musical intonation and subsequently attracted large audiences to the Hôtel de Bourgogne, where she was from 1670, and the Comédie-Française, where she remained from 1680 until her death, often playing opposite Michel Baron.

Champs-Élysées, Comédie des *See* Comédie des Champs-Élysées.

Chancerel, Léon (1886–1965) French playwright and director, noted for his production of plays for young audiences. He founded Le Théâtre de L'Oncle Sebastien for this purpose in Paris in 1935 and served as head of both the Société d'Histoire du Théâtre and the Centre Dramatique. A prize in his name is awarded biannually for outstanding plays for children.

Changeling, The A tragedy by Thomas *Middleton and William *Rowley. First performance: London, 1622. The play concentrates on the relationship and ultimate downfall of the ugly but determined De Flores and the headstrong Beatrice.

Chanin's 46th Street Theatre *See* 46th Street Theatre.

Channing, Carol (1921-) US actress and singer, who first appeared in New York in 1941. Her most successful roles in musical comedy have included Lorelei Lee in *Gentlemen Prefer Blondes*, Eliza Doolittle in *Pygmalion*, and Dolly Gallagher Levi in *Hello Dolly!*.

Chantilly, Mlle (Marie-Justine-Benoiste Duronceray; 1727–72) French actress, who was married to the playwright Charles Simon *Favart. She became an important member of the Comédie-Italienne and was responsible for introducing more realistic costumes in productions there.

Chapel Street Theatre A small theatre in Chapel Street, New York, which was also later known as the **Beekman Street Theatre.** Opened by David Douglass in 1761, it staged the first New York performance of *Hamlet*, with the younger Hallam as Hamlet. Douglass's company left in 1762, after which amateurs and members of the British garrison used the building until 1766, when a mob burst in during a performance and damaged the building; it was never used again.

Chapman, George (1560–1634) English poet, playwright, and translator of the works of Homer. After spending some years elsewhere in Europe (1585–91) he returned to London to write for Philip Henslowe. He is best known for the comedy *Eastward Ho!* (1605), for which he was imprisoned with his collaborators Marston and Jonson, the tragedy *Bussy d'Ambois* (1604), and its sequel *The Revenge of Bussy d'Ambois* (c. 1610).

Chappuzeau, Samuel (1625–1701) French writer. His *Le Théâtre français* (1674), containing information about contemporary drama, is a valuable work of reference on 17th-century French theatre. He also wrote a number of comedies, collected in *La Muse enjouée ou le Théâtre comique.*

Charing Cross Music Hall See Gatti's.

Charing Cross Theatre A theatre in King William Street, London, which was initially known as the Polygraphic Hall. It became a notable venue in 1872 when Mrs *Stirling appeared with great success as Mrs Mala-

prop in *The Rivals* for the first time; subsequent productions included numerous burlesques as well as a few plays and early comedies by Pinero. It closed in 1895 and was demolished to make way for the rebuilding of Charing Cross Hospital.

chariot-and-pole system See carriage-and-frame system.

Charke, Charlotte (c. 1710–60) British actress, daughter of Colley *Cibber. Noted for her eccentricities, she appeared at the Haymarket, Drury Lane, and Lincoln's Inn Fields. She also worked as a puppeteer and a conjuror's assistant. Her autobiography appeared in 1755.

Charles Hopkins Theatre See Punch and Judy Theatre.

Charleson, Ian (1949–) British actor, born in Edinburgh, where he made his debut with the Young Vic company at the 1972 Festival. Subsequently he played Hamlet (1975) with the Cambridge Theatre Company and important parts with the Royal Shakespeare Company; among his leading roles at the National Theatre have been Sky Masterson in *Guys and Dolls* (1982) and Brick in Tennessee Williams's *Cat on a Hot Tin Roof* (1988).

Charley's Aunt A farce by Brandon *Thomas. First performance: London, 1892. It ran for four years at the Royalty Theatre with W S Penley as the leading character, who finds his use of his aunt in Brazil as an unknowing tool in his own plans leads to complications; it has subsequently been made into a highly successful musical, *Where's Charley?*, with songs by Frank Loesser.

Charlot, André (1882–1956) British impresario, who organized numerous celebrated musical entertainments in London during the 1920s and 1930s. Before World War I he presented revues at the Alhambra featuring such stars as Jack Buchanan; after the war *Charlot's Revue* (seen in both London and New York in two editions, 1924 and 1925) established Noël Coward in such shows and also featured Gertrude Lawrence and Beatrice Lillie.

Charon, Jacques (1920–75) French actor and director, who became a leading director of farce and vaudeville at the Comédie-Française. Previously he worked with Gaston Baty before winning praise for such productions as Feydeau's *Un Fil à la patte* (1964), which was also seen in London.

Chatham Theatre A theatre between Duane and Pearl streets, New York, which was opened in 1823, as the **Pavilion Theatre**, by Barrière – a pastry cook who held a licence to provide entertainments at Chatham Gardens nearby. Seating 1300 persons, it was the first theatre in New York to be lit by gas and housed a talented company that included Joseph Jefferson I (who made his final New York appearance there in 1825), Joseph Jefferson II, Henry Wallack, and James Hackett. Upon Barrière's death in 1826 Wallack and Hackett took over the theatre with limited success, renaming it the **American Opera House** in 1829. From 1830 Blanchard presented a mixed bill of straight and equestrian drama until, under Hamblin, the theatre (known as **Blanchard's Amphitheatre**) was closed down in 1832.

Another **Chatham Theatre** was opened on Chatham Street, New York, in 1839. Seating 2200, it was managed for a time by Charles Thorne and then (as the **New National Theatre**) by Frank Chanfrau. Under Purdy's management Edwin Booth made his first New York appearance there in 1850, large crowds came to see Beecher Stowe's *Uncle Tom's Cabin* (1853), and Adah Isaacs Menken made her New York debut (1859). After a fire in 1860 it became the **Union Theatre**, the **National Concert Hall**, and finally the

National Music Hall before being demolished in 1862.

Chauve-Souris A revue produced by the Russian theatre director Nikita *Balieff. First performance: Chauve-Souris Club, Paris, 1908. The highly successful *Chauve-Souris* consisted of sketches, burlesques, songs, and pantomime and was first seen in London in 1921 and in New York in 1922.

Chayefsky, Paddy (1923-) US playwright, best known for the play *The Tenth Man* (1959). Other works include *Middle of the Night, Gideon, The Latent Heterosexual,* and *The Passion of Josef* (which he also directed).

Cheeseman, Peter (1932-) British director who, after managing Stephen Joseph's Studio Theatre Company, became (1962) director of Joseph's *Victoria Theatre in Stoke-on-Trent. Since then he has staged there a series of local documentary plays and has overseen (1986) the company's move to the larger New Victoria Theatre.

Chekhov, Anton (Pavlovich) (*or* Tchehov, Tchekhov; 1860–1904) Russian playwright and short-story writer, whose enormously influential plays are regarded as classics of the modern theatre. Of a humble background, Chekhov made his first attempts at dramatic writing – the successful one-act comedies *The Bear, The Proposal,* and *The Wedding* – after studying medicine in Moscow. After the success of *Ivanov, however, he experienced failure with the full-length play *The Wood Demon*; when *The *Seagull also failed in 1896 Chekhov nearly abandoned the theatre. Nemirovich-Danchenko and Stanislavsky, however, revived the play at the Moscow Art Theatre in 1898 with great success and Chekhov, who married Olga *Knipper – an actress with the company – in 1901, went on to follow it with a series of increasingly accomplished works that only ended with his early death.

His plays, of which *The *Cherry Orchard* is usually considered his masterpiece, place great emphasis on ensemble playing and express his awareness of both the comic and tragic aspects of daily life; although not tightly plotted, they are now accepted as brilliant atmospheric portrayals of the tensions inherent in prerevolutionary Russia.

Suffering from tuberculosis, Chekhov lived in the country at Melikhovo from 1892 to 1898 and spent the last years of his life at Yalta in the Crimea. The first English translations of his plays were performed within five years of his death.

Principal dramatic works:

The Bear: 1888.
The Proposal: 1889.
Ivanov: 1889.
The Wedding: 1890.
The Seagull: 1896.
*Uncle Vanya: 1899.
*Three Sisters: 1901.
The Cherry Orchard: 1904.

Chelidonius, Benedictus (16th century) Austrian humanist and churchman, abbot of the Schottenkloster in Vienna. He was the author of the religious drama *Voluptatis cum virtute disceptatio* (1515), which discusses the nature of virtue and vice.

Chelsea Theatre *See* Royal Court Theatre.

Chelsea Theatre Centre A US off-off-Broadway company, which was founded in 1965 in order to stage new plays and rarely-performed classics. It was named after its original home in Chelsea, New York, but three years later moved to the Brooklyn Academy of Music. Among the works produced before the company closed in 1981 were Imamu Barak's *Slaveship* (1969), Gay's *The Beggar's Opera* (1972), Allen Ginsberg's *Kaddish* (1972), Voltaire's *Candide* (1973), and Kleist's *The Prince of Homburg* (1976).

Chénier, Marie-Joseph(-Blaise) de (1764–1811) French playwright and politi-

cian, born in Constantinople. Brother of the poet André de Chénier and a member of the Convention, he wrote patriotic songs and historical tragedies, which provided excellent parts for Talma and others. Fired by the spirit of the Revolution, such plays as *Charles IX* (1789) and *Caius Gracchus* (1792) were very popular in their time.

Cherkassov, Nikolai Konstantinovich (1903–66) Soviet actor, who established his reputation in comedy acts in music hall but later won acclaim in classical roles. He made his debut at the Leningrad Theatre of Young Spectators in 1926, subsequently appearing at the Puskhin Theatre in Leningrad from 1933 in both modern and classic roles as well as starring in films by Eisenstein.

Cherry Lane Theatre A theatre on Commerce Street, New York, which opened in 1924. In 1927 it was taken over for a year by the New Playwrights Theatre, who reopened it with Paul Sifton's *The Belt*. Since then it has been used by a number of companies, notably On-Stage Productions, Theatre 1960, and Theatre 1967. Successful productions have included plays by Albee, Beckett, Ionesco, and Pinter.

Cherry Orchard, The The last play of Anton **Chekhov. First performance: Moscow Art Theatre, 1904. Regarded by many as Chekhov's masterpiece, the play revolves around a country family's debate as to the future of their orchard and constitutes a sensitive portrayal of the landowning class in prerevolutionary Russia. Stanislavsky's production of the play as an essentially melancholic tale contradicted Chekhov's more optimistic outlook.

Chess A musical written by Tim **Rice, with music by Bjorn Ulvaeus and Benny Andersson. First performance: Prince Edward Theatre, London, 1986. The plot revolves around the romantic entanglement of a Soviet chess champion with the former lover of his US opponent.

Chestnut Street Theatre A theatre in Philadelphia, Pennsylvania, built in 1793 for an English company hired by Thomas Wignell and later known as 'Old Drury'. It was the first US theatre to be built in the English proscenium style, being a direct copy of the Theatre Royal at Bath. Seating 2000, it was subsequently (from 1803) managed by William Wood and the elder William Warren, who successfully maintained the theatre's virtual monopoly of acting in Philadelphia until the Walnut Street Theatre opened in 1811. A stock company took over until 1820 when, damaged by fire, it was closed until 1822. It was again destroyed in 1855 and not rebuilt until 1863; it closed finally in 1910.

Chettle, Henry (1560–1607) English playwright and printer, of whose many plays only the revenge tragedy *Hoffmann* (1603) survives. As a printer he was responsible for the publication of *A Groatsworth of Wit* by Robert Greene.

Chevalier, Albert (1861–1923) British music hall performer, who became immensely popular as a singer of cockney songs. Before beginning his music hall career he appeared as an actor in comedy, burlesque, and melodrama; as a music hall artist he first performed at the London Pavilion in 1891. His songs included 'Knocked 'Em in the Old Kent Road' and 'My Old Dutch'.

Chevalier, Maurice (1888–1972) French singer, who became a leading performer of revues and musical comedies both on stage and in films. He became highly popular as Mistinguett's partner in Paris before World War I, sporting a straw hat and cane and adopting an exaggerated French accent.

Chiado, António Ribeiro (d. 1591) Portuguese playwright. His loosely-plotted plays, set in Lisbon, are notable for their realistic characterization and naturalistic dialogue.

Chiarelli, Luigi (1884–1947) Italian playwright, whose plays are characterized by the grotesque humour and violent realism of the *teatro del *grottesco*. His most successful play, a farcical comedy entitled *La maschera e il volta* (The Mask and the Face; 1916), satirizes modern society and has been widely translated and performed throughout Europe. His other plays include the comedy *Una più due* (One Plus Two; 1935) and *Il cerchio magico* (The Magic Circle; 1937).

Chicano Theatre A group of Mexican-American theatre companies, which perform in both Spanish and English throughout the US. Their productions rely heavily upon improvisation and focus on such social problems as unemployment, housing, education, drug abuse, racism, and low wages. The first Chicano group was the **Teatro Campesino** (Fieldworkers' Theatre), which was formed in 1965 in California from striking vineyard workers. Later groups – most of which are concentrated in the SW US – were made up of college and university students; the most important companies have included the **Teatro de los Barrios** in Texas (founded in 1969), the **Teatro del Piojo** (founded in Seattle in 1970), the **Teatro de la Gente** (founded in San José in 1970), and the **Teatro de la Esperanza** (founded in Santa Barbara in 1971). Their activities include annual festivals and conferences.

Chichester Festival Theatre A theatre in Chichester, built in 1962 as the site for an annual summer drama festival on the lines of that presented at the Stratford (Ontario) Festival in Canada. Seating 1394 in its hexagonal auditorium, it was directed by Laurence Olivier from 1962 to 1966 and saw the early development of the company that later became the *National Theatre. Plays presented at the festival have included those of Chekhov, Arden, Shaffer, Brecht, Bolt, and Ibsen. John Clements succeeded Olivier as director in 1966 and was himself replaced by Keith Michell in 1974. Peter Dews staged notable revivals during his stay (1978–80) before Patrick Garland became director in his stead.

Chicken Soup with Barley The first play in a trilogy by Arnold *Wesker. First performance: Belgrade Theatre, Coventry, 1958. The three acts follow the lives of Sarah Kahn and her family as their socialist ideals are tested out and post-war disillusion sets in, although Sarah's passionate beliefs remain unextinguished.

Chikamatsu Monzaemon (Sugimori Nobumori; 1653–1724) Japanese playwright, who is widely regarded as the greatest writer for the theatre that Japan has produced. He began his career writing for the puppet theatre alongside Takemoto Gidayū in Osaka, establishing the distinctive 'Gidayū music' style of the *Jōruri* tradition. Subsequently he spent 15 years writing *Kabuki* drama, before returning to the puppet theatre in 1703, after which he wrote many of his finest plays. These included such domestic tragedies as *Sonezaki Shinjū* (The Love Suicides at Sonezaki; 1703) and such historical romances as *Kokusenya kassen* (The Battles of Coxinga; 1715).

children's companies *See* boy companies.

Children's House, The Lillian *Hellman's first play. First performance: New York, 1934. The plot concerns two teachers accused of lesbianism and culminates in the closure of the school and suicide. The underlying theme is prejudice and its destructive power.

children's theatre Theatrical productions presented specifically for a young audience. A feature predominantly of 20th-century drama, children's theatre has flourished in various Communist states, often with propa-

gandist aims in mind, as well as in several European countries. Important organizations founded to cater for children's theatre have included Chancerel's Théâtre de l'Oncle Sebastien (1935–39) in France and the National Youth Theatre in Britain. *See also* amateur theatre, boy companies, Jesuit drama, school drama, Westminster Play, Young Vic Theatre.

Chionides (5th century BC) Greek poet. In 486 BC he became the winner of the first competition for comedy in the City Dionysia.

Chips with Everything A play by Arnold *Wesker. First performance: Royal Court Theatre, London, 1962, directed by John Dexter. The play dramatizes the training undergone by Royal Air Force recruits and highlights the damage that class divisions and heirarchical institutions can do to individuals.

Chirgwin, George H (1854–1922) British music hall performer, who first appeared on stage as a child in 1861. Later he became famous for his solo minstrel performances as 'The White-eyed Kaffir' (so-called because of his bizarre eye make-up).

Chocolate-Coloured Coon *See* Elliott, G H.

Chodorov, Jerome *See* Fields, Joseph.

Choerilus (6th century BC) Greek playwright, who succeeded Thespis as the earliest major figure in classical drama. He is thought to have been the author of about 160 plays, the first of which was presented in approximately 520 BC.

choregus A patron of theatrical productions in ancient Greece. Responsible for managing and paying the *chorus, the *choregi* were chosen in rotation from among the wealthiest citizens and competed against each other. In return for their involvement, the *choregi* were excused payment of taxes during that year.

choreography The planning and execution of stage dances, usually directed by a specialist choreographer.

chorus A group of actors who support those who undertake the main roles (the principals) in a production. The concept of the chorus was developed in ancient Greek drama, when its members – who danced and sang dithyrambs – numbered 50. Later, however, the size of the chorus was reduced and it was redeveloped as a passive commentator upon the main action, often delivering the prologue; in Elizabethan times the role was frequently undertaken by a single actor. In modern musical shows the chorus is employed chiefly for crowd scenes and song-and-dance routines.

Chorus Line, A A musical by Marvin *Hamlisch. First performance: New York, 1975. This acclaimed musical based upon gruelling auditions for a Broadway show won a Pulitzer Prize and was later turned into a successful film by Sir Richard Attenborough.

Christiania Theatre *See* Kristiania Theater.

Christie, Dame Agatha Mary Clarissa (1890–1976) British novelist and playwright, whose play The *Mousetrap* became the longest running production in commercial theatre. She adapted several of her crime novels for stage, among them *Ten Little Niggers* (1943), *Murder on the Nile* (1946), and *The Hollow* (1951); her other plays include *Witness for the Prosecution* (1953), *The Spider's Web* (1954), and *The Unexpected Guest* (1958). Some of her novels have also been adapted by other writers, notably *Murder at the Vicarage* (1950) by Moie Charles

and Barbara Toy and *A Murder is Announced* (1977) by Leslie Darben.

Chronegk, Ludwig (1837–91) German actor-manager and director, who became the director of the Meininger company in 1871. He began as an actor in comedy in Berlin but later appeared successfully in Shakespearean parts. He became manager of the company in 1877 and subsequently superintendent of the Court theatres (1884) under the Duke of Saxe-Meiningen himself.

Chu Chin Chow A musical comedy by Oscar *Asche, with music by Frederic Norton. First performance: His Majesty's Theatre, London, 1916. A retelling of *Ali Baba and the Forty Thieves*, it was staged with Asche himself playing the robber chief and enjoyed a record-breaking run of nearly five years.

Churchill, Caryl (1938-) British playwright, who first attracted attention as a writer associated with the Joint Stock Theatre Company with the historical play *Light Shining in Buckinghamshire* (1976). Her plays since then have included *Cloud Nine* (1978), which discusses sexual identity, *Top Girls* (1982), *Fen* (1982), *A Mouthful of Birds* (1986), and *Serious Money* (1987).

Churchill, Frank *See* Lewes, George Henry.

Cibber, Colley (1671–1757) British actor-manager and dramatist. The son of a sculptor, he joined Betterton's company in 1690. As an actor he excelled as Sir Novelty Fashion in his own play *Love's Last Shift* (1696), which was later acknowledged as the first sentimental comedy, and as Lord Foppington in *The Relapse*. Amongst his subsequent successes as a writer were *She Would and She Would Not; or, the Kind Imposter* (1702) and *The Careless Husband* (1704), as well as adaptations of Molière and Fielding.

His adaptation of *Richard III* held the stage for more than a century.

In 1711 he became part of the celebrated triumvirate management of Drury Lane in which role, despite his innate tactlessness, he contributed much to the theatre's prosperity. In 1730 he was appointed poet laureate; he was also author of the autobiography *Apology for the Life of Mr Colley Cibber, Comedian* (1740).

His son, **Theophilus Cibber** (1703–58) was also an actor at Drury Lane, where he became notorious for his dissolute behaviour. Continually at odds with Quin and Macklin, he eventually fled abroad to escape his creditors. Cleared by his second wife, Susanna Arne, he brought two scandalous actions against her friend, William Sloper, and his popularity declined. He was living in penury when invited to Dublin in 1758 and lost his life in a shipwreck after setting sail from Holyhead. *See also* Charke, Charlotte.

Cicognini, Giacinto Andrea (1606–60) Italian playwright, author of over 40 plays. His writing was heavily influenced by the works of Lope de Vega and Calderón, which were performed by various Spanish touring companies in Naples, where he lived. He was the author of the earliest Italian version of the Don Juan story.

Cid, Le A tragedy by Pierre *Corneille. First performance: Paris, 1636 or early 1637. Based on *Las mocedades del Cid* by Guíllen de *Castro y Bellvís, the plot centres on the conflicts of love, honour, and duty. The play's success was resented by Corneille's rivals; the acrimonious battle of pamphlets that ensued is known as the *querelle du Cid*.

cieco d'Adria, Il *See* Groto, Luigi.

Cincinnati Playhouse in the Park A theatre, housing two auditoriums, which opened in Cincinatti, Ohio, in 1959. It became the professional playhouse for the Ohio River Valley area, producing both classical and modern plays as well as many world premieres. The theatre's two auditoriums are the **Thompson Shelterhouse** and the **Robert S Marx Theatre**.

Cinquevalli, Paul (Paul Kestner; 1859–1918) British music hall performer, born in Poland. After a trapeze accident he took up juggling as a therapy and developed it to a standard never surpassed. Billed as 'The Human Billiard Table', he was a star of the halls for over 20 years.

Cinthio, Il *See* Giraldi, Giovanni Battista.

Circa Theatre A theatre in Wellington, New Zealand, opened in 1976 and run independently of the state subsidized theatre system. Run on a co-operative basis, it was founded by members of the Downstage Theatre company and has enjoyed commercial success with a number of comedies.

circle *See* auditorium.

Circle, The A comedy by W Somerset *Maugham. First performance: London, 1921. Often considered Maugham's finest play, *The Circle* revolves around a young married woman's decision to elope with her lover, a rubber planter from Malaya, in defiance of the advice she receives against this.

Circle-in-the-Square A theatre-in-the-round in Sheridan Square, New York, which opened in 1951 as the home of José Quintero's Loft Players. In 1954 the theatre was closed as a fire hazard but reopened in 1956 with O'Neill's *The Iceman Cometh* and became a popular off-off-Broadway venue. The theatre was demolished in 1960 and the company moved to the New Stages Theatre (now the Circle-in-the-Square Downtown), opening there in 1960 with Wilder's *Our Town*. The company then moved to the new Joseph E Levine Theatre (1972), where it presents four plays each year. Recent productions have included the musical *I'm Getting My Act Together and Taking It on the Road* (1978) and *As Is*, one of the first plays to deal with AIDS.

Circle Repertory Company An off-off-Broadway company founded in 1969 to produce new US plays. In 1974 it moved into a new permanent home, the Circle Repertory Company Theatre in Sheridan Square, New York (formerly the **Sheridan Square Playhouse**). It has won particular acclaim for productions directed by **Marshall W Mason** (1940-), its greatest successes including Mark Medoff's *When You Comin' Back, Red Ryder?* (1973) and several plays by Lanford Wilson (1937-).

circuit A group of theatres in the same geographical area that are visited on a regular basis by the same touring companies. The circuit system was developed in the 18th century and played a crucial role in the training of young actors. Some of the most important British circuits were those named after Aberdeen, Exeter, Kent, Manchester, Newcastle, Norfolk and Suffolk, Norwich, Winchester, and York.

circus A public entertainment, distantly related to the theatre proper, featuring animals, clowns, acrobats, and the like. Descended from the gladiatorial shows and festivals of ancient Rome, the circus has remained linked to the central dramatic tradition, most clearly in the melodramas, dog dramas, equestrian dramas, and music hall of the 19th century.

City Centre of Music and Drama A theatre on West 55th Street, New York, which opened in 1943 with the New York Philharmonic Orchestra. Seating 2935, it served as the home of the New York City Ballet and the New York City Opera until 1960, when they both moved to the Lincoln Centre. Today the City Centre hosts dance companies and foreign troupes; it was also the home of the **Acting Company**, which was formed in 1972 by graduates of the Julliard School, until 1975.

City Dionysia *See* Dionysia.

City of London Theatre A theatre in Norton Folgate, London, designed by Samuel *Beazley and opened in 1837. It enjoyed early success with dramatizations of the works of Charles Dickens and then prospered (1848–68) under the experienced managers Nelson Lee and Johnson with productions featuring leading performers. Subsequently the theatre's reputation declined and it became a home of melodrama; it was destroyed by fire in 1871.

City Pantheon *See* City Theatre.

City Theatre A theatre in Grub Street (later Milton Street), London, opened in 1829. Formerly a chapel, it was run first by the comic actor John Bedford (who renamed it the **City Pantheon**) and then by John Kemble Chapman (1830–31), who attracted leading performers of the day, including Edmund Kean and Ellen Tree, to the theatre. From 1831 to 1836 the theatre shared companies with the Royal Coburg (*see* Old Vic), after which the building was used as a warehouse.

The first **City Theatre** in New York opened on Warren Street in 1822 as an amateur venue. It closed a year later during a yellow fever epidemic.

Another **City Theatre** in New York opened as part of the City Saloon on Broadway in 1837. It enjoyed considerable success with appearances by Joe Cowell before closing later the same year.

A third **City Theatre** in New York opened on East 14th Street in 1910. It soon became a home of vaudeville and housed the Yiddish Art Theatre for a time before becoming a cinema in 1929 and being demolished in 1952.

Ciulei, Liviu (1923-) Romanian director and actor, who succeeded Lucia Sturdza-Bulandra as artistic director of the Municipal Theatre in 1961. He appeared there under his own direction in a number of acclaimed productions, including Dürrenmatt's *Play Strindberg* (1972) before moving to the Guthrie Theatre in Minneapolis in 1980 (again as artistic director), where his successes have included several of Shakespeare's plays and premieres of new US dramas.

Civic Repertory Company *See* Le Gallienne, Eva.

civic theatre (*or* **municipal theatre**) A system by which certain theatres in Britain are funded by local government on the principle that there should be active civic support for the cultural life of the community. The first such theatres were often erected by a city council and then leased to an independent theatre trust, as was the case with the first in the field, the Belgrade Theatre, Coventry (1958). Alternatively, they were sometimes funded by a partnership between local government, the Arts Council, and other organizations (as with the Nottingham Playhouse) or even (uniquely in the case of Manchester's Library and Forum Theatres) wholly owned and operated as fully-fledged repertory theatres by a city council. More recently civic authorities have purchased and refurbished some of the old touring theatres as prestigious regional centres for the arts, thus contributing to the revival of large-scale touring by national companies; notable examples include Bradford's Alhambra Theatre and Nottingham's Theatre Royal. *See also* Repertory Theatre Movement.

Clairon, Mlle (Claire-Josèphe-Hippolyte Léris de la Tude; 1723–1803) French actress, who became a leading member of the Comédie-Française. Earlier in her career she performed in minor parts at the Comédie-Italienne, attracting the praise of Garrick before appearing in such major tragic roles as Racine's Phèdre (1743). Under the guidance of Marmontel and Diderot she successfully tempered her declamatory style and encouraged the introduction of more historically-accurate costume. In 1765, however, she was imprisoned over a dispute involving another actor; upon her release she found shelter with Voltaire, in whose plays she had acted, and confined her activities to writing her *Mémoires* (1779) and to private theatricals, dying in poverty after the Revolution.

Clandestine Marriage, The A comedy by George *Colman the Elder and David *Garrick. First performance: 1766. Fanny Sterling and Lovewell have secretly married, while her father makes plans for her to marry Lord Ogleby; the play was enormously popular but led to a dispute between the two authors after Garrick refused to appear in it.

Clark, John Pepper (1935-) Nigerian poet and playwright, who is the author of a number of plays based on African myth. A trilogy, consisting of *Song of a Goat* (1962), *The Masquerade* (1964), and *The Raft* (1964), evoked Greek tragedy and established his reputation; later works include *Ozidi* (1966).

Clarke, Austin (1896–1974) Irish poet, playwright, and novelist, born in Dublin. His reputation rests primarily on his poetry but in his youth he was inspired by W B Yeats and the work of the Abbey Theatre and turned to poetic drama. This is reflected in his own verse plays, the first of which was *The Son of Learning* (1927), and in his work with the Dublin Verse-Speaking Society and the Lyric Players.

Claudel, Paul(-Louis-Charles-Marie) (1868–1955) French poet, playwright, and diplomat. Claudel's conversion to Catholicism in 1886 had a profound effect on his literary work: his plays present the conflict of good and evil, the quest for salvation, and other Christian themes. Despite recognition in Germany and elsewhere in the 1920s, it was not until 1943, with Jean-Louis Barrault's production of *Le Soulier de satin*, that Claudel's plays began to receive attention in France.

Principal works:

Tête d'or: 1919 (published 1890).

La Ville: 1955 (published 1893); translated as *The City*.

Partage de midi: 1948 (published 1906); translated as *Break of Noon*.

L'Annonce faite à Marie: 1912; translated as *The *Tidings Brought to Mary*.

L'Échange: 1914; translated as *The Exchange*.

L'Ôtage: 1914; translated as *The Hostage*.

Le Pain dur: 1949 (published 1918).

Le Soulier de satin: 1943 (published 1929); translated as *The *Satin Slipper*.

Claus, Hugo (1929-   ) Belgian poet, novelist, and playwright, who has dominated Belgian theatre since World War II. Influenced by Artaud while in Paris and writing in Dutch, he has won acclaim for such plays as *A Bride in the Morning* (1953), *Sugar* (1958), *Friday* (1969), and *Leopold II* (1970), several of which are set against a Flemish background but treat themes ranging from family relationships to colonialism. Later works include *Orestes* (1976), which was derived from Euripides.

Clements, Sir John (Selby) (1910–88) British actor-manager, who became well-known for his revivals of classic plays. He founded his own repertory company at the Intimate Theatre in north London in 1935 and subsequently directed 42 plays, playing leads in 36 of them. In a revival of *Private Lives* in 1944 he played opposite **Kay Hammond** (Dorothy Katharine Standing; 1909–80), whom he married and with whom he enjoyed a long stage partnership. As actor-

manager his triumphs included seasons at the St James's and Saville theatres and a record-breaking run of *The Beaux' Stratagem* at the Phoenix Theatre (1949). In 1964 he succeeded Olivier as director of the Chichester Festival Theatre, stepping down in 1973; he virtually retired after his wife's death.

Cleveland Play House A theatre in Cleveland, Ohio, which was founded in 1915 and became the home of the first resident professional theatre company in the US. The company has staged many US and world premieres in the theatre's two auditoriums (the **Drury** and the **Brooks** theatres), including Paul Zindel's *The Effect of Gamma Rays on Man-in-the-Moon Marigolds* (1969), Arbuzov's *Confessions at Night* (1975), and Gorky's *The Romantics* (1978). A third auditorium, the **Euclid-77th Street Theatre**, was added nearby in 1949.

Clifton, Harry (1832–72) British music hall singer, who sang such sentimental moralistic songs as 'Paddle Your Own Canoe' and 'Pretty Polly Perkins of Paddington Green'.

Clive, Kitty (Catherine Raftor; 1711–85) British actress, who was engaged by Colley Cibber to sing at Drury Lane. Her merit as an actress was discovered when she played Nell in the farce *The Devil to Pay*, by Coffey. Throughout her career, spent mostly at Drury Lane, she hankered to play tragedy, although her real strength lay in high comedy and farce. In consequence, she and Garrick quarrelled constantly although they admired each other's work. She retired in 1769 to a house at Twickenham given to her by Horace Walpole.

cloak-and-sword play *See comedia.*

Close Studio Theatre *See* Glasgow Citizens' Theatre.

closet drama A play written for reading as opposed to actual performance. Works of this type include the plays of Seneca and much Victorian poetic drama.

cloth A length of canvas or other material suspended from the flies and used for scenic purposes. It was formerly called a **drop** in Britain and is still referred to by that name in the US. When coloured blue to represent the sky it is called a **sky cloth**.

clouding A border, sometimes movable, painted to resemble a cloudy sky. Such borders were in common use in masques.

Clouds, The A comedy by *Aristophanes. First performance: Athens, 423 BC. The play, in which Socrates and the Sophists became the butt of the author's satire, seeks to ridicule contemporary education and morality.

clown A comic character of both the theatre and the circus, distinguished by his outlandish appearance and boisterous comedy. The modern clown is directly descended from the clowns of Shakespeare, many of which were first created by Richard Tarleton and were largely derived from the medieval Fool or Jester. Subsequently the attributes of such early clowns were combined with features from the characters of the *commedia dell'arte* until the familiar clown of the pantomime and modern circus had evolved. Joseph *Grimaldi is universally recognized as one of the greatest exponents of the role.

Clunes, Alec (Sheriff de Moro) (1912–70) British actor, director, and manager, who ran the Arts Theatre in London from 1942 to 1950, presenting acclaimed productions of such plays as *Awake and Sing!* by Clifford Odets and *The Lady's Not For Burning* by Christopher Fry. He also appeared many times at Stratford and elsewhere in plays by Shakespeare, Shaw, and others.

Clurman, Harold Edgar (1901–80) US director, manager, author, and theatre critic. After studying under Boleslavsky he appeared in 1924 at the Greenwich Village Playhouse. In 1925 he joined the Theatre Guild; subsequently, in 1931, he founded the Group Theatre with Lee Strasberg and Cheryl Crawford. There he produced plays by Odets before the group broke up in 1940, after which he went on to direct works by such writers as Inge, Anouilh, O'Neill, Arthur Miller, Lillian Hellman, Giraudoux, and Chekhov.

Coal Hole *See* song-and-supper rooms.

Coates, Robert (1772–1848) British amateur actor, born in Antigua, who hired theatres at Bath, Brighton, and Richmond to promote himself as Romeo. Dubbed Romeo Coates, he ignored public ridicule and performed at the Haymarket to universal scorn, after which he retired into obscurity.

Cobb, Lee J (Leo Jacoby; 1911–76) US actor, who began his career at Pasadena Playhouse in 1929, made his New York debut in *Crime and Punishment* (1935), and later joined the Group Theatre. His roles included Mr Carp in Clifford Odets's *Golden Boy* (1937) and Lammanawitz in Irwin Shaw's *The Gentle People* (1933). His most famous part was Willy Loman in Arthur Miller's *Death of a Salesman* (1949).

Coborn, Charles (Colin Whitton McCallum; 1852–1945) British music hall performer, who introduced Albert Chevalier to the halls. Of his own songs the most popular were 'Two Lovely Black Eyes' and 'The Man Who Broke the Bank at Monte Carlo'.

Coburg Theatre *See* Old Vic Theatre.

Coburn, Charles (Douville) (1877–1961) US actor-manager, who – with his wife Ivah Wills (1882–1937) – founded the Coburn Shakespearean Players. Although he also played such well-established roles as Hamlet, Othello, and Shylock, his greatest success was as Old Bill in Bruce Bairnsfather and Arthur Eliot's *The Better 'Ole* (1918). After his wife died he embarked on a long film career, but returned to the stage as Falstaff in *The Merry Wives of Windsor* (1946) and won acclaim as Grandpa Vandenhoff in Kaufman and Hart's *You Can't Take It with You*.

Coburn Theatre *See* Daly's 63rd Street Theatre.

Cochran, Sir Charles Blake (1872–1951) British impresario, noted for his production of revues, comedies, and musicals. After experience as an actor and agent, he produced Ibsen's *John Gabriel Borkman* in New York in 1897. Subsequent productions included Reinhardt's *The Miracle* (1911), celebrated series of revues at the Ambassadors and then the London Pavilion (featuring a chorus of 'Young Ladies'), and several plays by Noël Coward. He also imported to Britain plays by O'Casey, O'Neill, and many others and arranged Sacha Guitry's first appearance in London (1920). After World War II he scored his greatest commercial success with the musical comedy *Bless the Bride* (1947).

Cockpit A theatre in Drury Lane, London, originally opened as a venue for cockfighting in 1609. Adapted by Christopher Beeston in 1616, it was destroyed in a riot in 1617 and rebuilt as the Phoenix, which housed a number of companies in succession. Floridor's company opened there in 1635 and Beeston's Boys were installed in 1637. Davenant then took over, staging illegal performances after the closure of the theatres in 1642; in 1660 the theatre was reopened by John Rhodes, who was himself succeeded by George Jolly. The theatre was closed in 1665 after audiences defected to Drury Lane.

Another theatre of the same name was opened in Gateforth Street, London, in 1970 for use by schools and youth theatre groups.

Cockpit-in-Court A theatre in Whitehall, London, which was converted from a cockpit around 1604. Performances were given there before the Court and subsequently the public by the King's Men and other companies intermittently until 1664.

Cocktail Party, The A poetic drama by T S *Eliot. First performance: Edinburgh Festival, 1949. Based on *Alcestis* by Euripides, the play revolves around the godlike psychoanalyst Harcourt-Reilly, who penetrates the illusions surrounding the true identities of the four main characters.

Cocoanut Grove *See* Century Theatre.

Cocteau, Jean (Maurice) (1889–1963) French poet, novelist, playwright, film director, and critic; one of the most versatile artists of the *avant-garde movement. Challenged by Diaghilev at the Ballets Russes, he began writing ballets and plays in his early twenties. His dramatic works range from classical tragedy to romantic melodrama. After World War II, Cocteau devoted himself to the cinema and it is in this role that he is usually remembered.
Principal dramatic works:
Antigone: 1922.
Orphée: 1926; translated as *Orpheus*.
La Voix humaine: 1930; translated as *The Human Voice*.
La Machine infernale: 1934; translated as *The Infernal Machine*.
Les Chevaliers de la Table Ronde: 1937.
Les Monstres sacrés: 1940; translated as *The Holy Terrors*.
La Machine à écrire: 1941.
L'Aigle à deux têtes: 1946; translated as *The Eagle Has Two Heads*.

Cody, William Frederick (1846–1917) US showman, known as **Buffalo Bill**, who was a rider for the Pony Express and a scout in the US Civil War. In 1872 he began appearing in plays written for him and, in 1883, went on to create his own Wild West Show featuring sharpshooter **Annie Oakley** (1860–1926). The pair became famous worldwide and were depicted in Irving Berlin's *Annie Get Your Gun* (1946).

Coffey, Charles (d. 1745) British playwright, noted for his ballad operas. Such pieces as *The Beggar's Wedding* (1729) and *The Devil to Pay* (1731), adapted from a play by Thomas Jevon, greatly influenced the development of the *Singspiele* form of ballad opera in Germany.

Coghill, Neville (Henry Kendal Aylmer) (1899–1980) British theatre scholar, who founded the Friends of the OUDS group in Oxford in 1940. The organization presented much-admired productions of plays by such authors as Ibsen, often touring widely; its last production was in 1946. Previously, in 1936, Coghill had founded the Oxford University Experimental Theatre Club to present new and little-performed – and often experimental – works by both British and foreign writers with casts and crews consisting solely of undergraduates.

Coghlan, Rose (1850–1932) US actress, born in Britain, who spent most of her career on the New York stage. She was highly acclaimed at Wallack's Theatre and elsewhere in such roles as Lady Teazle in Sheridan's *The School for Scandal* and in a variety of modern parts as well as in Shakespeare. Other successes included her starring appearance in the premiere of Wilde's *A Woman of No Importance* (1893).

Cohan, George M(ichael) (1878–1942) US actor, playwright, and manager, who first appeared on stage with his parents in *The Four Cohans*. He wrote for the vaudeville stage and made his New York debut in his own play, *The Governor's Son*, in 1901. After playing in *Little Johnny Jones* (1904) and *George Washington, Jr* (1906) he opened (1911) the *George M Cohan Theatre, where he continued to appear in his own plays as well as in O'Neill's *Ah, Wilderness* (1933) and works by other authors.

Cohan and Harris Theatre *See* Sam H Harris Theatre.

Cohen, Gustave (1879–1958) French theatre historian, who devoted his career to the study and revival of ancient liturgical drama. His *Histoire de la mise en scène dans le théâtre religieux français du moyen age* (1906) was an authoritative account of the medieval tradition of religious drama. Cohen also formed his own amateur group at the Sorbonne – Les Théophiliens – to present various examples of the genre, including Adam de la Halle's *Jeu de Robin et de Marion* and other works.

Coleridge, Samuel Taylor (1772–1834) British poet and critic, whose blank verse tragedy *Remorse* was successfully produced at Drury Lane in 1813. He wrote two other plays, neither of which was acted, *The Fall of Robespierre* (1794) and *Zapolya* (1817), and translated Schiller's *Wallenstein*. He also lectured on Shakespeare, whose plays he edited.

Coliseum *See* London Coliseum.

Collé, Charles (1709–83) French playwright and songwriter. He wrote *parades* (sketches) for fairground theatres and several comedies. *La Partie de chasse de Henri IV* (1774) was banned by Louis XV for depicting the king in informal conversation with his subjects, which was regarded as disrespectful; it was later performed under Louis XVI.

collective creation The development of a theatrical production through the collaboration of several persons, who work on the project from beginning to end. Drawing heavily upon such techniques as improvisation, the process became popular in alternative theatre during the 1960s, although it is thought that the much earlier *commedia dell'arte* troupes and Elizabethan companies may have operated in a similar way. Notable exponents of the system in modern times have included the Living Theatre, the Open Theatre, the San Francisco Mime Troupe, and the Performance Group in the US and the People Show, Welfare State International, and the Pip Simmons Theatre Group in Britain.

Collier, Constance (1878–1955) British actress, who began her career on stage as a child before becoming a Gaiety Girl. Subsequently she played leading roles with Tree's company from 1901 to 1908 – notably in Shakespeare – and appeared in the US. She played Gertrude to John Barrymore's Hamlet in 1925 and, with Ivor Novello, wrote the play *The Rat*, which ran for a year. Other successful roles included Nancy in *Oliver Twist*, and Anastasia in *The Matriarch* by G B Stern.

Collier, Jeremy (1650–1726) British pamphleteer, best known for his *Short View of the Immorality of the English Stage* (1698), in which he castigated the plays of Dryden, Congreve, Vanbrugh, and others, and protested against the ridiculing of clergymen on the stage. The pamphlet provoked a number of retaliatory essays.

Collier, John Payne (1789–1883) British literary critic, who falsified documents from various sources and published an edition of Shakespeare's plays based on his forgeries. In 1852 he claimed to have bought a copy of the second Folio extensively annotated in a 17th-century hand. His forgeries were exposed some years later.

Collin d'Harleville, Jean-François *See* Harleville, Jean-François Collin d'.

Collins, Lottie (1866–1910) British music hall performer. She first appeared as a skipping-rope dancer, then worked with her two sisters and became a solo act in 1881. In 1891 she became an overnight success with the song 'Ta-Ra-Ra-Boom-De-Ay'.

Collins, Sam (1827–65) British music hall performer and manager, formerly a chimney-sweep. Although born in London, he usually appeared as a genial Irishman. He was one of the first stars of the Canterbury Music Hall; in 1863 he opened the famous *Collins's Music Hall in Islington.

Collins, (William) Wilkie (1824–89) English novelist and playwright, author of dramatizations of both of his famous detective novels, *The Woman in White* and *The Moonstone*, which were produced at the Olympic Theatre in 1871 and 1877 respectively. He also collaborated with Charles Dickens on various plays, notably *No Thoroughfare*, which was staged at the Adelphi Theatre in 1867.

Collins's Music Hall A theatre on Islington Green, London, opened in 1851 as part of the Lansdowne Arms public house. A purpose-built theatre was erected there in 1863, seating 600, by Sam *Collins and became extremely popular as a music hall. Enlarged in 1897, it later staged repertory before declining as a venue for striptease and comedy. It was demolished after a fire in 1958.

Colman, George (1732–94) British playwright and theatre manager, usually called the Elder to distinguish him from his son. He was encouraged to write for the theatre by Garrick, who produced his first play, *Polly Honeycombe*, at Drury Lane in 1760. After the success of *The Jealous Wife* in 1761, he collaborated with Garrick in writing *The *Clandestine Marriage* and took over Covent Garden; seven years later he succeeded Foote at the Haymarket. In all, he wrote or adapted some 30 plays, as well as editing the works of Beaumont and Fletcher, and executing translations of Terence and Horace.

His son, **George Colman** (1762–1836), was known as the Younger and made his name as a playwright with *Inkle and Yarico* (1787), eventually succeeding his father as manager of the Haymarket. His many plays included, at the Haymarket, *The Battle of Hexham* (1789), *Sylvester Daggerwood* (1795), and *The Heir-at-Law* (1797); at Drury Lane, the tragedy *The Iron Chest* (1796); and, at Covent Garden, *John Bull; or, the Englishman's Fireside* (1803). Despite his reputation for recklessness, he was appointed Examiner of Plays in 1824, in which capacity he proved unexpectedly censorious.

Colon, Jenny (1808–42) French actress, who began at the Opéra-Comique and later appeared elsewhere in Paris and in Britain. She was highly popular for her lively, good-humoured performances until her career was ended by her early death.

Colonial Theatre *See* Hampden, Walter.

Colosseum A theatre in Regent's Park, London, opened in the 1830s. Plays were staged there under Braham and Frederick Yates until about 1840.

Colosseum Theatre *See* Herald Square Theatre.

colour wheel A metal disc fitted with small circles of coloured gel, which when rotated in front of a spotlight produces a succession of differently coloured beams.

Colum, Padraic (1881–1972) Irish playwright, poet, and novelist. His most important contribution to drama belongs to the early part of his career when he became a member of the Irish National Dramatic Society, a signatory of the original Abbey Theatre charter, and the author of three of the company's earliest plays. *Broken Soil* (1903) and *The Land* (1905) explore the preoccupation of small farmers with the land they work; *Thomas Muskerry* (1910) examines small-town society. After 1914 he lived mostly in the US, where he worked on a series of *Nō* plays.

Columbine One of the central figures of the harlequinade. The daughter of Pantalone and the lover of Harlequin, she originally began as one of the *zanni* of the *commedia dell'arte*, a servant girl named Columbina.

Columbus Circle Theatre *See* Majestic Theatre.

comedia A genre of Spanish drama of the 17th century, usually subdivided into the *machine play and the *comedy of intrigue. The latter category included the popular *comedia de capa y espada* (or **cloak-and-sword play**), which – written by such writers as Torres Naharro, Lope de Vega, and Tirso de Molina – dealt with the various romantic adventures of young courtiers and exercised a strong influence upon playwrights of the 19th century.

comedia a fantasía *See* Torres Naharro, Bartolomé de.

comedia a noticia *See* Torres Naharro, Bartolomé de.

Comedians A play by Trevor *Griffiths. First performance: Nottingham Playhouse, 1975. The play follows a group of budding stand-up comedians who have to put their newly-learnt craft to the test at a local bingo hall. In the process Griffiths presents a disturbing and theatrically rivetting debate about the politics of change.

comédie-ballet A form of musical play popular at the court of Louis XIV during the 17th century. Combining elements of dance, music, and dialogue and involving the participation of the courtiers themselves, the *comédie-ballet* was transformed by *Molière, who placed the emphasis upon the dialogue in such pieces as *Le Bourgeois gentilhomme* (1671). Ultimately the genre gave way to opera and operetta.

Comédie-Canadienne, Théâtre de la See Gélinas, Gratien.

Comédie des Champs-Élysées A theatre in the Avenue Montaigne, Paris, opened in 1912. Productions there by Gémier during the 1920s made the theatre a focus of the avant-garde movement; subsequent directors included the Pitoëffs, Jouvet, and Giraudoux. Anouilh took the theatre over in the 1950s, staging *boulevard* plays as well as his own works.

Comédie-Française The French national theatre, also called the **Théâtre-Français** and **La Maison de Molière**, which was formed in 1680 by the combination of the companies from the Théâtre du Marais (with which Molière's troupe had already merged) and the Théâtre de l'Hôtel de *Bourgogne. After appearing at various venues with a virtual monopoly of the theatre in Paris, the company split during the Revolution, the more reactionary actors remaining where they were under Molé (as the **Théâtre de la Nation**) and the others being installed by Talma (as the **Théâtre de la République**) in what was to become the permanent home of the Comédie-Française, now in the Place de Théâtre-Française in the Rue de Richelieu. In 1803 the two halves reunited and in 1812 Napoleon set down the rules by which the company would be run. These established the holding of shares in the company, following a probationary period, by the actors themselves (as *pensionnaires* or the more senior *sociétaires*) and the granting of pensions to long-serving members. The Comédie-Française underwent some reorganization in 1945 and 1959; actors and actresses with the company in the 20th century have included Sarah Bernhardt and Jean-Louis Barrault.

Comédie-Italienne The name by which the companies presenting the Italian *commedia dell'arte* in France were known after 1680, in order to distinguish them from the indigenous *Comédie-Française. Italian companies first appeared in France in the 16th century and gradually absorbed many native French elements; important venues in Paris associated with the Comédie-Italienne included the Salle du Petit-Bourbon and the Palais-Royal, both of which were shared with Molière until 1680, when the Comédie-Italienne moved to the Hôtel de Bourgogne. In 1697, however, the Comédie-Italienne companies were banished from France, allegedly for offending Madame de Maintenon; after their return in 1716 they became increasingly distant from their Italian origins and gradually turned to comic opera; the remaining group (known as the **Théâtre Favart**) amalgamated with a rival troupe (the **Théâtre Feydeau**) to form the new **Opéra-Comique** in 1801. Leading figures of the Comédie-Italienne included Fiorillo, Biancolelli, Costantini, Riccoboni, and Bertinazzi; writers linked to the tradition included Dufresny, Regnard, Palaprat, and Marivaux.

comédie larmoyante A form of sentimental comedy that became popular in France during the 18th century. Leading practitioners of plays of the genre, which usually carried a strong moral message, included La Chaussée; the style is generally considered as prefiguring the plays of the more realistic *drame.

comédie rosse See Ancey, Georges.

comedy A form of drama distinguished by its humorous content and happy ending. Derived from the Greek words for 'revel-song', comedy has its roots in the ritual celebrations from which the lively satires of Aristophanes and his successors (notably Menander) emerged; it was traditionally written in simple language and identified with plays dealing with the lower classes and with affairs of the day. During the Roman era comedy typically revolved around the obstacles faced by young lovers and was frequently boisterous and coarse in nature, a tradition that was eventually revived in the *commedia dell'arte* following the disappearance of comedy as a form in itself during the Middle Ages. Subsequently it was elevated by Shakespeare, Jonson, Molière, and many others, who drew their realistic characters from all levels of society and successfully married the form with highly elegant and sophisticated language capable of conveying significant comments upon human nature.

Subdivisions of the form include the *comédie larmoyante*, the *comedy of humours, the *comedy of intrigue, the *comedy of manners, the *comedy of morals, *romantic comedy, and *sentimental comedy. Following the apotheosis of sophisticated wit in the comedies of Oscar Wilde and Noël Coward, the 20th century has seen a return to the earlier bawdy and less subtle tradition in the revival of *farce and the frequent combination of both comedy and tragedy. *See also* satire.

Comedy of Errors, The An early comedy by William *Shakespeare. First performance: London, 1594. Revolving around a series of mistaken identities involving two sets of identical twins, the plot is derived from *Menaechmi* by Plautus, which was itself based on an earlier Greek model. The complex plot and addition of a second set of twins demonstrates Shakespeare's early understanding of structure and inventiveness.

comedy of humours A form of comedy in which the focus is placed upon a particular trait of personality of one or more of the characters. The genre – which was named after the medieval concept of the body holding four liquids (or humours), the balance of which decided a person's character – found full expression in the plays of such English writers as *Fletcher and *Jonson.

comedy of intrigue A form of comedy in which the action revolves around various complicated and highly farcical situations. Ultimately deriving from a Roman tradition, the comedy of intrigue was later developed in Spain and subsequently taken up by writers of the 17th and 18th centuries, examples being written by Shakespeare (notably *The Comedy of Errors*) and Molière among others.

comedy of manners A form of witty and often daring comedy in which various social shortcomings are satirized by being made to appear ridiculous. Descended from the *New Comedy of Menander, the comedy of manners was revived by Molière in such plays as *Les Précieuses ridicules* (1658) and *Le Médecin malgré lui* (1666) and later developed by such writers as Jonson, Etherege, Vanbrugh, Wycherley, Congreve, Farquhar, Goldsmith, and Sheridan. In more recent times the tradition, distinguished by the elegance and sophistication of its humour, has been continued by Wilde, Coward, and other critics of the affectations of society. *See also* Restoration drama.

comedy of morals A form of comedy in which the playwright condemns socially unacceptable behaviour. The supreme example of the genre, which was an extreme version of the comedy of manners, is Molière's *Tartuffe*.

Comedy Theatre A theatre in London's West End that has a long-standing reputation for both drama and comedy. Intended originally as the home of comic opera, it was built in Panton Street, off the Haymarket, and opened in 1881 with Audran's *The Mascotte*. Violet Melnotte, on becoming lessee in 1885, introduced dramas to the theatre. In 1887 Beerbohm Tree produced *The Red Lamp* by W Outram Tristam, while under Charles Hawtrey's management (1888–92 and 1896–99) straight comedy was alternated with farce. The first real success of the early 1900s, Lonsdale and Messager's *Monsieur Beaucaire*, ran for over 400 performances. Marie Tempest appeared in several plays in 1907–09, Gerald Du Maurier in 1910, and Marie Löhr the following year. John Hartley Manners's *Peg o' My Heart* (1914) ran for 710 performances, and in later years, under various managements, a mixed policy of plays, revues, and musicals was adopted. From 1956 to 1959 the Comedy became the headquarters of the New Watergate Theatre Club, which presented such plays as Tennessee Williams's *Cat on a Hot Tin Roof* (1958) and Peter Shaffer's *Five Finger Exercise* (1959), both refused a licence by the Lord Chamberlain. More recent successes have included the Alan Ayckbourn comedy *Time and Time Again* (1972) and transfers from other theatres.

Another **Comedy Theatre** was built by the Shuberts on West 41st Street, New York, and opened in 1909 with Zangwill's *The Melting Pot*. In 1937 it was renamed the **Mercury Theatre** and housed numerous productions directed by Orson Welles, including Shaw's *Heartbreak House* and Buchner's *Danton's Death*. In 1938 it was also the focus of national alarm when Welles's company broadcast H G Wells's *The War of the Worlds* from it, convincing many that an actual Martian invasion was taking place. The building was demolished in 1942.

The **Comedy Theatre** in Leningrad was founded in 1929. It is famous chiefly for the productions of Nikolai *Akimov staged from the 1920s onwards. He became Art Director of the theatre in 1936.

Comella y Villamitjana, Luciano Francisco (1751–1812) Spanish playwright, who was the author of more than 100 plays. He was highly popular in his own day but was ridiculed in the plays of Fernández de Moratín.

command performance A performance of a play or other entertainment given in response to a request by a member of a royal family or national leader. In Britain such performances are held annually and usually have a charitable purpose.

commedia dell'arte An Italian comic theatrical tradition that evolved during the 16th century and later exerted a profound influence upon drama throughout Europe. Improvised about basic three-act skeleton plots, the *commedia dell'arte* (also known as the *commedia a soggetto*) featured a variety of stock characters, including *Pantalone, Il *Capitano, Il *Dottore, and the *zanni, all of whom had their own distinctive costumes and masks.

The genre was derived ultimately from Greek theatre, via the Roman *atellana*, and incorporated numerous theatrical disciplines, including acrobatics, mime, and comic slapstick routines. Leading Italian companies of the *commedia dell'arte*, which performed at various courts or travelled with their own portable stage, included the *Gelosi, the *Desiosi, the *Confidenti, the *Uniti, the *Accesi, and the *Fedeli. These companies subsequently toured Europe, inspiring the foundation of *commedia dell'arte* troupes elsewhere, notably in France where the *Comédie-Italienne flourished. Fiorillo played an important role in bringing the *commedia dell'arte* to London in the late 17th century, where elements of the Italian tradition were readily absorbed into the English theatre, most lastingly in the *harlequinade and, subsequently, the *pantomime. By the end of the 18th century the tradition had largely fallen from fashion, although the

20th century has seen a widespread revival of interest in the form. *See also burla, lazzo.*

commedia erudita An Italian theatrical form of the 16th century, a more scholarly counterpart to the *commedia dell'arte*. Unlike the *commedia dell'arte*, the *commedia erudita* was based upon written scripts (derived largely from the comedies of Plautus and Terence) and was intended for performance before educated audiences. Among those who wrote for the *commedia erudita* were Aretino, Ariosto, Della Porta, and Machiavelli.

Commonwealth Theatre *See* Anthony Street Theatre.

Community Arts Service (CAS) A theatre company in Auckland, New Zealand, which toured productions throughout North Island from 1947 to 1962. Connected to Auckland University, it presented numerous classics as well as the first production in New Zealand of Beckett's *Waiting for Godot* (1958).

community theatre Theatre that has as its primary aim the performance of plays for and within specific communities – as opposed to the theatre-for-all approach of most commercial and repertory theatres. Whereas in the US such theatre is synonymous with amateur theatre, in Britain there are numerous professional companies set up with the express purpose of reaching communities that rarely if ever go to the theatre, either because of the distance involved or because there is no tradition of conventional theatre-going. The plays performed by such groups usually focus upon issues of immediate concern (sometimes adopting a high political profile) or upon the community's own history (often researched with the help of local people) and are toured to community centres, church and school halls, and labour clubs. Many companies combine community work with *theatre-in-education;

others target their work at specific groups, typically communities that are in some way underprivileged. The best-known community theatre groups in Britain are Ed Berman's Inter-Action, founded in London in 1968, and those initiated by writer Ann Jellicoe in rural Devon and Dorset since the 1970s.

Compagnia Dei Giovani An Italian theatre company, founded in 1954 by Romolo Valli and Giorgio de Lullo. Subsequently renamed I Giovani del Teatro Elisio, it toured internationally with plays by Fabbri and Pirandello.

Compagnia Reale Sarda An Italian theatre company, founded in Turin in 1821. It established its reputation with old-fashioned dramas by Goldoni and his contemporaries but later diversified with productions of well-made plays; actors with the company included Salvini and Ristori. It was disbanded in 1855 when its official grant was withdrawn.

Compagnie des Quinze A French theatre company, founded by actors from Copeau's company in 1929. Led by Michel Saint-Denis, it excelled with productions of the plays of André Obey before breaking up in 1934.

compartment batten *See* batten.

composite setting A stage setting, formerly called a **multiple setting** and first developed in medieval drama, in which three or more different locations are presented simultaneously upon the stage. In the US it is called a **simultaneous-scene setting**.

Compton, Henry (Charles Mackenzie; 1805–77) British actor, born in Huntingdon. After 11 years in the provinces, he reached Drury Lane in 1837, where he became a noted character actor and exponent of Shakespeare's clowns. He transferred to the Haymarket in 1853.

His daughter, **Katherine Mackenzie Compton** (1853–1928), became an actress and excelled in the comedies of her husband, Richard *Carton.

His son, **Edward Compton** (1854–1918), acted in the provinces and was the author of two plays. In 1881 he organized the Compton Comedy Company, which toured successfully for over 30 years.

He married Virginia Frances *Bateman in 1882 and became the father of the actress **Fay Compton** (Virginia Lillian Emmeline Compton; 1894–1978), who established her reputation in the plays of J M Barrie and Somerset Maugham. Subsequently Fay was acclaimed in plays by Dodie Smith, Noël Coward, and Ibsen as well as in numerous Shakespearean roles, notably as Ophelia to the Hamlets of John Barrymore (1925) and John Gielgud (1939). Later performances included Lady Bracknell in *The Importance of Being Earnest* and appearances in pantomime.

concert party A summer show comprising songs, dances, and sketches, of the type popular at British seaside resorts in the early 20th century.

Concert Theatre *See* John Golden Theatre.

Condell, Henry (d. 1627) English actor, who was recorded as a member of the Chamberlain's Men in 1598. He remained with the company until his death, although he gave up acting in about 1616. He appeared in several of Jonson's plays and probably in supporting Shakespearean roles. He was a shareholder in the Globe and Blackfriars theatres and, with Heminge, edited the First Folio of Shakespeare's plays.

Confidenti An Italian *commedia dell'arte* company, founded in 1574. Led by Pellesini, the company toured Europe for many years until, under the patronage of Giovanni de' Medici, it returned to Italy led by Flamineo

Scala. When it was disbanded in 1621 some of its members joined the Fedeli.

Confidential Clerk, The A poetic drama by T S *Eliot. First performance: Edinburgh Festival, 1953. Based on *Ion* by Euripides, it is a farcical comedy about a financier's search for the illegitimate son who is to be his heir.

Confrérie de la Passion An amateur theatre company founded in Paris in 1402. Drawing its actors from the merchants and craftsmen of the city, the company became highly respected for its performances of mystery plays and in 1518 was given a monopoly of theatre in Paris. Subsequently, however, the Church took exception to the company's increasingly liberal attitudes and in 1548, as the company was moving into its new home at the building that later became the Théâtre de l'Hôtel de Bourgogne, it was prohibited from presenting religious works. In the years that followed the Confrérie de la Passion ceased to present its own productions and leased the theatre to other companies, retaining its restrictive control over all theatrical activity in Paris until 1595; the company was finally disbanded in 1676.

Congreve, William (1670–1729) English playwright, regarded as the foremost writer of the English comedy of manners during the Restoration. He achieved sufficient success in 1692 with his comedy *The *Old Bachelor* at Drury Lane, with Betterton and Mrs Bracegirdle in the cast, to persuade the management to produce his satire *The Double Dealer* the following year. *Love for Love,* with which Betterton opened the new Lincoln's Inn Fields Theatre in 1695, confirmed his reputation and won him a share in the theatre. His tragedy *The Mourning Bride* was publicly, if not critically, acclaimed in 1697 although *The *Way of the World*, coldly received at that time, is considered his most brilliant work. His comedies have been frequently revived in the 20th century.

Principal works:

The Old Bachelor: 1692.

The Double Dealer: 1694.

Love for Love: 1695.

The Mourning Bride: 1697.

The Way of the World: 1700.

Connection, The A play by Jack *Gelber. First performance: Living Theatre, 1959. The plot concerns a group of drug addicts who are waiting for someone to arrive with a fresh supply of narcotics. It caused considerable controversy and virtually created the off-Broadway theatre.

Connelly, Marc(us) Cook (1890–1980) US playwright, who also directed and acted in a number of productions. He began his career as a theatrical journalist and collaborated as a writer with George Kaufman before winning a Pulitzer Prize in 1930 with his play *The Green Pastures*, which he also directed with a Black cast. His other plays include *The Farmer Takes a Wife* (1934), *Everywhere I Roam* (1938), and *The Flowers of Virtue* (1942).

Conquest, George Augustus (1837–1901) British actor, playwright, and theatre manager, son of the actor-manager **Benjamin Conquest** (Benjamin Oliver; 1805–72). Educated in France, he translated and adapted several French plays, which were produced under his father's management, and wrote numerous successful pantomimes and melodramas. He managed the Grecian Theatre with his father, and, in 1881, took over the Surrey Theatre. His three sons also appeared regularly in pantomime.

Conservatoire National d'Art Dramatique A drama school in Paris, founded in 1786 and closely linked to the Comédie Française. Opened as the École de Déclamation, it has produced such leading performers as Talma, Mlle Rachel, Sarah Bernhardt, and Constant Coquelin. It underwent some reorganization in 1968.

Constant Wife, The A comedy by W Somerset *Maugham. First performance: New York, 1926. The play revolves around a long-suffering wife's achievement of independence from her profligate husband and eventual triumphant elopement to Italy with her lover.

Constructivism *See* Meyerhold, Vsevolod Emilievich.

Contact Theatre Company A theatre company based in Manchester, founded in 1973 at Manchester University. It was established by Hugh Hunt and aims to bring drama into the surrounding community.

Contat, Louise (1760–1813) French actress, who excelled as a comic actress at the Comédie-Française, which she joined in 1776. A pupil of Préville, she was particularly admired in the plays of Beaumarchais and Marivaux.

Contemporary Theatre, A *See* Seattle Repertory Theatre.

Conti, Italia (1874–1946) British actress, who – at the instigation of Charles Hawtrey – founded the Italia Conti School for dancers, singers, and actors. From 1929 to 1938 she herself appeared annually as Mrs Carey in *Where the Rainbow Ends* at the Holborn Empire. Pupils at her school included Gertrude Lawrence.

Contrast, The A comedy by Royall *Tyler. First performance: John Street Theatre, 1787. The first indigenous play to be produced in the US, it contrasts the duplicity of Dimple, who abandons his fiancée in favour of a wealthy coquette, with the honesty of Dimple's brother.

contrasto A form of early Italian theatrical entertainment, related to the **lauda*. Dating from the 13th century, it usually revolved about a central dispute, usually with a religious or domestic theme.

Conway, William Augustus (1789–1828) British actor, born in Ireland, who made his London debut in 1813 at Covent Garden, where he played classic leads for two years. Upset by adverse criticism after appearances at the Haymarket, he then went to New York, opening as Hamlet. He subsequently appeared alongside Thomas Cooper and with Macready (1826–27). Suffering a mental breakdown, he finally drowned himself in Charleston harbour.

His son, **Frederick Bartlett Conway** (1819–74), became a leading figure on the New York stage in the 1860s, opening the first theatre in Brooklyn in 1863. Subsequently he opened the Brooklyn Theatre also and assembled an admired stock company there.

Cook, Peter (1937-) British comedy actor and writer, who wrote the revues *Pieces of Eight* (1959) and *One Over the Eight* (1960) while still at Cambridge University. He was co-author of the celebrated satirical revue *Beyond the Fringe*, in which he appeared at the Edinburgh Festival and elsewhere in 1960, and subsequently toured widely with Dudley *Moore in *Behind the Fridge*.

Cooke, George Frederick (1756–1812) British actor, greatly admired by Edmund Kean. He arrived at Covent Garden in 1800 after many years in the provinces. He made his successful London debut as Richard III and went on to play Shylock and Iago with equal acclaim, despite his dependence upon alcohol. He was also one of the first British actors to tour the US; his alcoholism, however, gradually alienated his audience and probably contributed to his death later in the tour.

Cooke, Thomas Potter (1786–1864) British actor, popularly known as Tippy. He became known as an actor of engaging nautical characters but achieved particular fame as William in *Black-Ey'd Susan* at the Surrey Theatre in 1829.

Cooper, Dame Gladys (Constance) (1888–1971) British actress, who made her London debut in *The Belle of Mayfair* (1906) and subsequently established herself as an outstanding actress in both comedy and straight drama. She was much admired in plays by such authors as Maugham, Pinero, and Shaw, often appearing under her own joint-management with Frank Curzon at the Playhouse. In 1934 she made her New York debut in Keith Winter's *The Shining Hour* and from then on appeared regularly on both sides of the Atlantic. Later roles included performances in plays by Shakespeare, Bagnold, and Coward, as well as numerous film appearances.

Cooper, Thomas Abthorpe (1776–1849) US actor, born in Britain, who was one of the first British actors to transfer permanently to the US. Having won acclaim on the London stage in Shakespearean and other major roles, he went to the US in 1796 to appear at the Chestnut Street Theatre; later he joined the American Company and toured the eastern states in such roles as Macbeth.

Co-Optimists *See* pierrot troupes.

Copeau, Jacques (1879–1949) French actor, director, and critic, who was a prominent figure in the reaction against Realism in the early 20th century. Advocating attention to the play itself rather than to sets and costume, he took over the Théâtre du Vieux-Colombier in 1913, staging influential productions of classic plays by Molière, Shakespeare, and Claudel among others. The theatre itself echoed the Elizabethan stage with no proscenium arch or wings and little scenery, the emphasis being thrown instead upon lighting and the acting of the company (which included Charles Dullin and Louis Jouvet).

In 1924 Copeau founded a company of young actors – known as *'les Copiaus'* – in Burgundy, training them in his techniques (which included the extensive use of mime); many of these actors subsequently appeared in the innovative Compagnie des Quinze of Copeau's nephew and assistant Michel Saint-Denis. In 1936 Copeau was recognized as a major reformer of French stage practice when he was made a director of the Comédie-Française.

Coppin, George Selth (1819–1906) Australian theatre manager and actor, born in Britain, often called the 'father' of Australian theatre. He sailed to Australia in 1843 and in due course he formed his own company and built six theatres, to which he lured leading performers from Britain and the US.

copyright The legal entitlement of the owner of a dramatic work to claim a fee (known as a **royalty**) in exchange for his permission for its performance or publication. Developed during the 19th century through the efforts of Planché, Bulwer-Lytton, and others, copyright as it related to the theatre began as a highly ambiguous legal concept and it became customary for many playwrights – including G B Shaw – to stage special 'copyright performances' of their plays prior to publication in order to feel certain that their rights were legally protected. The Berne Conventions of 1886 and later years did much to bring the various copyright laws of different countries into line and to extend protection into the fields of film, radio, and television; other international agreements on the subject include the Universal Copyright Convention of 1952. Copyright in most countries is generally recognized as lasting for 50 years following the author's death. Any infringement of copyright amounts to a civil offence and can give rise to actions for damages and injunctions. Prior to the development of modern copright law, playwrights either sold their plays outright or relied upon proceeds from publication or special benefit performances (*see* author's night); more fortunate writers drew on other sources of income or survived on the generosity of their patrons.

Coquelin, Constant-Benoît (1841–1909) French actor, known as Coquelin *aîné*, who is usually remembered as the first actor to create Rostand's Cyrano de Bergerac (1897). He was, with his brother, **Ernest-Alexandre-Honoré Coquelin** (1848–1909) or Coquelin *cadet*, a leading member of the Comédie-Française and later toured with Sarah Bernhardt throughout Europe and the US, being particularly admired in the plays of Molière. Coquelin *cadet* died insane shortly after his brother's sudden death.

Coriolanus A tragedy by William *Shakespeare, probably his last. First performance: date unknown. Successful in battle, the hero Caius Marcus Coriolanus subsequently reveals his contempt for the common masses and after being banished changes sides. The play tackles military and political themes and culminates in Coriolanus's own death when, at the entreaties of his mother Volumnia and his wife Virgilia, he spares Rome and is murdered by his new Volscian allies.

Corneille, Pierre (1606–84) French playwright, born in Rouen; one of the most important figures in the history of French drama. After studying with the Jesuits, Corneille followed his father and grandfather into the legal profession and held office in Rouen for some 20 years. He began writing for the theatre in the late 1620s; encouraged by the success of *Mélite*, he produced four more comedies and a tragicomedy (*Clitandre*) before turning to tragedy, the genre in which he made his greatest contribution to French literature. His classical tragedies (including Le *Cid and *Horace), in which the portrayal of the moral conflicts and emotional sufferings of the central characters takes precedence over the representation of action, heralded a new era in French drama.

He also produced Psyché, a comédie-ballet, written in collaboration with Molière and Philippe Quinault, while the tragedy Andromède pioneered the 17th-century tradition of the *machine play. After 1650 Corneille's popularity began to decline and in the 1660s he was gradually eclipsed by Racine; the plays of his latter years enjoyed limited success but proved to be of no lasting merit.

He also encouraged his younger brother, **Thomas Corneille** (1625–1709), who produced some 40 plays – largely comedies in the Spanish style and romantic tragedies, notably Timocrate (1656), before abandoning the theatre in favour of lexicography.
Principal works:
Mélite: 1629.
Clitandre: 1631.
La Veuve: 1631–32.
La Galerie du palais: 1632.
La Suivante: 1633.
La Place royale: 1633–34.
Médée: 1635.
L'Illusion comique: 1635–36.
Le Cid: 1636–37.
Horace: 1640.
Cinna: 1641.
Polyeucte: 1641–42.
La Mort de Pompée: 1642–43.
Le Menteur: 1643.
Rodogune, princesse de Parthes: 1645.
Héraclius: 1646–47.
Don Sanche d'Aragon: 1649.
Andromède: 1650.
Nicomède: 1651.
Oedipe: 1659.
La Toison d'or: 1660.
Sertorius: 1662.
Psyché: 1671.

Cornell, Katharine (1893–1974) US actress, who made her London debut with great success in Louisa Alcott's Little Women (1919) and her New York debut as Sydney in Clemence Dane's A Bill of Divorcement in 1921. She went on to become the leading actress of her day, playing such parts as Shaw's Candida (1924) and Elizabeth in Rudolf Besier's The Barretts of Wimpole Street (1934). She was usually directed by her husband, Guthrie McClintic; her later appearances included the Countess in Fry's The Dark Is Light Enough (1955) and Mrs Patrick Campbell in Jerome Kilty's Dear Liar (1960).

corner trap A small square trap positioned downstage, through which actors may make entrances.

Corn is Green, The A comedy by Emlyn *Williams. First performance: London, 1938. The play revolves around Miss Moffat, an indomitable schoolteacher in the Welsh valleys; in the original production Williams himself played the miner Morgan Evans and Sybil Thorndike played Miss Moffat.

Cornish, William (fl. 1509–23) English Gentleman of the Chapel Royal, who organized the choirboys of the Chapel Royal into a boy company. The company entertained regularly at court, often in elaborate disguisings.

Cornish Rounds Ancient open-air theatres in Cornwall, once used for performances of mystery plays. In use until the 17th century, these were usually cut into a slope and were circular in shape; other features included a trench from which actors could make sudden entrances.

Coronet Theatre See Eugene O'Neill Theatre.

Corpus Christi play See mystery play.

Corrie, Joe (1894–1968) Scottish playwright and actor, who was the author of a number of celebrated one-act plays on Scottish themes. Such pieces as *The Shillin'-a-Week Man* were performed in music halls throughout Scotland and northern England in the late 1920s; longer plays included *In Time o'Strife* (1930) and *Master of Men* (1944).

Corsican Brothers, The A melodrama by Dion *Boucicault. First performance: 1852. An adaptation of an earlier French play, this tale of duelling and revenge was immensely successful in a production by Charles Kean and was subsequently revived many times.

Corsican trap *See* ghost glide.

Cort Theatre A theatre on West 48th Street, between Sixth and Seventh avenues, New York, which opened in 1912 with John Hartley Manners's *Peg o' My Heart*. Early productions seen at the theatre included Chekhov's *Uncle Vanya* (1930), Anouilh's *Antigone* (1946), Joseph Kramm's *The Shrike* (1952), and Goodrich and Hackett's *The Diary of Anne Frank* (1955). The theatre was used for television productions between 1969 and 1972, when it reopened for live productions with *All the Girls Come Out to Play*; recent successes have included Samm-Art Williams's *Home* (1980).

Cosmopolitan Theatre *See* Majestic Theatre.

Cossa, Pietro (1830–81) Italian playwright, author of a number of verse tragedies based on classical models. His more successful plays include *Nerone* (1872), a version of the life of Nero, and the antireligious *Cola di Rienzo* (1874) but all his works were marred by the poor quality of his poetry and by his interest in Realism, which did not combine well with the demands of classical tragedy. Other plays include *Pushkin* (1870) and *Messalina* (1876).

Costa, Francisco da (1533–91) Portuguese playwright, who wrote a number of poems and seven plays during his long imprisonment in Morocco, where he died. Some of his plays on biblical subjects were first performed by his fellow-prisoners.

Costantini, Angelo (c. 1655–1729) Italian actor of the *commedia dell'arte*, who appeared chiefly as Messetino with the Comédie-Italienne in Paris. In 1697, when the company was exiled, he moved to Brunswick where he was imprisoned for 20 years after becoming involved in a love triangle with the Duke there. He was also the author of a biography (1695) of Tiberio Fiorillo.

Coster, Samuel (1579–1665) Dutch physician and playwright, who was a friend of many of the leading playwrights in the Netherlands at that time. In 1617 he opened the first Dutch Academy in Amsterdam in order to promote study of the theatre and learning in general.

costume The clothing worn on stage by an actor or other performer. Pioneered by the ancient Greeks, who developed specific costumes for each character in both tragedy and comedy, the art of costume revived in medieval times and culminated in the fabulous costumes of the masques, as well as in the more formalized outfits of the *commedia dell'arte*. During the 17th century most actors appeared in contemporary dress, although there was a gradual movement towards more elaborate clothing in the early 18th century that eventually led to a reversion to contemporary styles by Garrick and others. The 19th century saw the first authentically costumed versions of Shakespeare and, with the advent of realism, a demand for historical accuracy. The 20th century has seen increasingly imaginative designs ranging from the completely naturalistic to the highly symbolic as well as the linking of costume with lighting and other aspects of theatrical design so that it is no longer considered in isolation. *See also* wardrobe.

cothurnus A thick-soled shoe worn by the tragic actor in the classical Greek and Roman theatre. Also known as a *buskin*, it was adopted in order to differentiate the principals from the chorus, who wore low shoes. *See also soccus.*

Cottesloe Theatre One of the three theatres comprising the *National Theatre in London, opened in 1977. Seating 400, it was named after the chairman of the South Bank Theatre Board and has been used for a wide variety of serious dramas, notably US works and *promenade productions. Successful plays there, which have featured many leading performers, have included *Lark Rise* (1978), *The Iceman Cometh* (1980), and *The Crucible* (1980).

Couldock, Charles Walter (1815–98) US actor, born in Britain, who appeared regularly in the US and Canada from 1849. Closely associated with most of the leading players of his day, he was particularly successful in Kotzebue's *The Stranger* (1849), Tom Taylor's *Our American Cousin* (1858), and Steele Mackaye's *Hazel Kirke* (1880).

Council for the Encouragement of Music and the Arts *See* Arts Council.

Counsell, John (1905-) British actor, who established a repertory company at the **Theatre Royal**, Windsor, in 1938 and made the theatre there an important provincial venue. Although there is no company now resident at Windsor, the theatre continues to present both new works and revivals.

counterweight system An arrangement of lines and weights that enables the raising and lowering of heavy pieces of scenery. A theatre equipped with such a system is occasionally described as a counterweight house. *See also* hand-worked house.

Country Girl, The A play by Clifford *Odets. First performance: New York, 1950. The plot concerns a woman who blossoms, despite her alcoholic husband, when she becomes a singer. It was seen in Britain as *Winter Journey* in 1952. The play was filmed in 1954 with Bing Crosby and Grace Kelly.

Country Wife, The A comedy by Sir William *Wycherley. First performance: 1674. The play concerns a jealous husband's attempts to keep his young wife away from temptation whilst staying in London; it was later successfully adapted by Garrick as *The Country Girl* (1766).

Courteline, Georges (Georges-Victor-Marcel Moineaux; 1858–1929) French playwright, short-story writer, and journalist, born in Tours. His comedies are lively farces satirizing military life, as in *Les Gaîtes de l'escadron* (1896), the legal profession, and a variety of other contemporary targets.

Courtenay, Tom (Daniel) (1937-) British actor, who made his professional debut as Konstantin in *The Seagull* in Edinburgh in 1960 and then transferred to the Old Vic. Subsequently he was acclaimed in the title role of *Billy Liar* (1961), played Andrei in Frisch's *Andorra* (1964) with the National Theatre company, and appeared in major Shakespearean roles with the 69 Theatre Company, Manchester. Other successes have included Lord Fancourt Babberley in *Charley's Aunt* (1971), Norman in Ayckbourn's *The Norman Conquests* (1974), the title part of *The Dresser* by Ronald Harwood (1980), and Ben Travers's *Rookery Nook* (1986).

Court Fool A performer, also known as the **King's Jester**, who was retained by a royal court in the late medieval period to amuse members of the court with stories, music, and his wit. Dressed in a parti-coloured suit after the fashion of the *Fool of folk drama, from which tradition that of the Court Fool was quite distinct, he enjoyed special licence in satirizing the follies of noble society. It was from this tradition that Shakespeare's Fools were derived.

Courtneidge, Dame Cicely (Esmeralda)

(1893–1980) British actress, who played Peaseblossom in *A Midsummer Night's Dream* as a child and later appeared in her actor-manager father's shows. In one of these she met her future husband, the actor **Jack Hulbert** (1892–1978), thus beginning a famous stage partnership in revues and musical comedies, from *By the Way* at the Apollo (1925) to *Under Your Hat* at the Palace (1938). In later years she appeared in straight comedy roles in such plays as Ronald Millar's *The Bride and the Bachelor* (1956) and Cooney and Chapman's *Move Over, Mrs Markham* (1971). Jack Hulbert's brother, **Claude Hulbert** (1900–64), also appeared in revue.

Court Street Theatre *See* Milwaukee Repertory Theatre.

Court Theatre *See* Royal Court Theatre.

Covent Garden (Royal Opera House)

England's national opera house, home of the Royal Opera and the Royal Ballet. The present building, currently the subject of a controversial extension scheme, is the third theatre on the site. The first, known as the **Theatre Royal, Covent Garden**, was designed for the pantomimist John Rich and opened in 1732, in rivalry to the Theatre Royal, Drury Lane; David Garrick acted at both theatres and Peg Woffington made her debut at Covent Garden in 1740.

At first plays alternated with opera, George Frederick Handel composing several operas and oratorios specially for the thea-

tre; the piano was played for the first time in public here in 1767. Subsequent milestones included the first performances of Oliver Goldsmith's *She Stoops to Conquer* (1773) and Sheridan's *The Rivals* (1775). John Kemble bought a share in the management in 1803 but in 1808 the theatre was destroyed by fire.

A new theatre, modelled on the Temple of Minerva at Athens, opened in 1809 but an increase in the price of seats brought about the infamous **Old Price Riots**, which lasted for 61 days. Mrs Siddons made her farewell appearance at Covent Garden in 1812 and Macready his debut there in 1816. The following year John Kemble was succeeded in management by his brother Charles, who in 1823 staged an innovatory revival of *King John* with costumes designed by Planché.

Carl Maria von Weber was musical director from 1824 to 1826, but the theatre went into decline and was only revived by the popularity of Fanny Kemble, who first appeared there in 1829. Edmund Kean made his final appearance at Covent Garden in 1833, while in 1837 Macready inaugurated the use of limelight in the theatre.

In 1847 the theatre was reopened as The Royal Italian Opera House but was again burned down in 1856. Rebuilt with a portico featuring the Flaxman reliefs salvaged from the previous building, Covent Garden reopened in 1858 and prospered with appearances by Adelina Patti and the burning down of Her Majesty's Theatre in 1867. Augustus Harris's management (1888–96) marked one of the theatre's most successful periods, with the installation of electric light and performances by all the leading singers of the day. Sir Thomas Beecham was musical director in 1919–20 and artistic director from 1933 until the outbreak of World War II.

Used as a dance hall during the war, the theatre was reopened in 1946 as the national opera house, home of the Royal Opera Company and from 1956, the Sadler's Wells

Ballet Company (later the Royal Ballet). Since then virtually all the world's greatest singers, dancers, and conductors have performed at Covent Garden, which is celebrated for its lavish presentations.

Coward, Sir Noël (Pierce) (1899–1973) British actor, playwright, and composer, who is considered the foremost writer of the English comedy of manners since Wilde. He made his stage debut at the age of 10 in a Christmas play at the Crystal Palace and, by 1920, was playing juvenile leads in West End comedies and writing songs, sketches, and plays. He sang and danced through the revue *London Calling* (1923), having contributed to the book and score, and, in 1924, caused a sensation as actor and author with his play *The *Vortex*. Subsequently he exhibited wit, glamour, and impeccable comedy acting in a succession of revues, plays, and romantic musicals opposite such stars as Gertrude Lawrence and the Lunts. During World War II he wrote the song 'London Pride', and scripted, directed, and starred in the film *In Which We Serve*. His post-war plays never repeated his earlier success but he triumphed as a cabaret star in London and the US and was acclaimed as King Magnus in Shaw's *The Apple Cart* (1953) at the Haymarket. His farewell appearance was in his triple bill, *Suite in Three Keys*.
Principal works:
The Vortex: 1924.
*Fallen Angels: 1925.
*Hay Fever: 1925.
On With the Dance: 1925.
This Year of Grace: 1928.
Bitter Sweet: 1929.
*Private Lives: 1930.
*Cavalcade: 1931.
*Design for Living: 1933.
Tonight at 8.30: 1936.
*Blithe Spirit: 1941.
*Present Laughter: 1943.
*This Happy Breed: 1943.
Relative Values: 1951.

Nude With Violin: 1956.
*Look After Lulu: 1959.
Waiting in the Wings: 1960.
Suite in Three Keys: 1966.

Cowell, Joseph Leathley (1792–1863) British actor, born in Devon. He appeared at Drury Lane and toured the Lincoln circuit in an entertainment called *Cowell Alone; or A Trip to London* before making his US debut as a comic actor in 1821. He was most successful as Crack in Knight's *The Turnpike Gate*.

His son, **Samuel Houghton Cowell** (1820–64), also played Crack successfully and toured the US, where he was popularly known as the **Young American Roscius**. Subsequently, in London, he made such a hit singing at the Grecian Theatre that he took to the music halls, in which he became a popular performer.

Cowl, Jane (1884–1950) US actress and playwright, who began her career under Belasco in 1903. Subsequently she won particular acclaim in such Shakespearean roles as Juliet and Viola and in the plays of Coward, Dumas *fils*, Shaw, Robert Sherwood, and Thornton Wilder. Her own plays included *Hervey House*, directed in London by Tyrone Guthrie in 1935.

Cowley, Abraham (1618–67) English playwright, whose most successful play was the comedy *The Guardian* (1642), presented at Lincoln's Inn Fields as *Cutter of Coleman Street* in 1661. A precocious writer who had his first works published at the age of 15, Cowley's other dramatic pieces include the Latin play *Naufragium Jaculare* (1638) and the pastoral drama *Love's Riddle* (1638). A Royalist, he was imprisoned during the Civil War.

Cowley, Hannah (1743–1809) British playwright, whose first play, *The Runaway*, was successfully produced by Garrick in 1776. She followed it with twelve others, including *Who's the Dupe?* (1779), *The Belle's Stratagem* (1780), which was her most popular work and has been frequently revived, *A Bold Stroke for a Husband* (1783), and *The Town before You* (1794).

Cowley, Richard (d. 1619) English actor, who appeared with Strange's Men before joining the Chamberlain's Men in about 1594. He is in the 1623 Folio list of actors in Shakespeare's plays and is known to have appeared as Verges to the Dogberry of Kempe.

Cox, Robert (d. 1655) English comic actor, who developed the *droll during the suppression of the theatre in the 1640s. He combined scenes from Shakespeare and others with original pieces by himself and such varied entertainments as rope-dancing and juggling. In 1653, whilst performing at the Red Bull Theatre, he was arrested and imprisoned.

Crabtree, Charlotte (1847–1924) US actress, who began her career as a child and became a leading performer of burlesque and extravaganza. Popularly known as **Lotta**, she toured mining camps before first appearing in New York in 1865.

Craig, Edith Geraldine Ailsa (1869–1947) British actress and stage director, daughter of Ellen Terry and E W Godwin. After stage appearances with both her mother and Sir Henry Irving and stage management for Ellen Terry's 1907 tour of the US, Edith Craig left the theatre and studied music in London and Berlin. On returning to London she directed the Pioneer Players in some 150 plays between 1911 and 1921.

Her brother, **(Edward Henry) Gordon Craig** (1872–1966), worked as a stage director, designer, and theorist and had an immense influence on the theatre both in Europe and the US. After a time as an actor, he directed several plays – including *The Vikings at Helgeland* and *Much Ado About Nothing*, which both had his mother in the cast – between 1901 and 1903 before concentrating upon stage design and dramatic theory. Although he contributed designs for *Venice Preserv'd* (1904), *Rosmersholm* (1906), *Hamlet* (1911), and *The Pretenders* (1926), he was most influential for his many ideas about nonrepresentational settings and atmospheric effects, as detailed in his book *On the Art of the Theatre* (1911).

Craig Theatre *See* George Abbott Theatre.

Crane, Ralph (c. 1550–c. 1632) English public official, who executed copies of several contemporary plays for actors, prompters, and authors. He was employed as scrivener to the King's Men from time to time between 1615 and 1625 and is known to have taken down plays by Fletcher, Massinger, and Middleton.

Crates (fl. 450 BC–470 BC) Greek actor and playwright, author of some of the earliest examples of Old Comedy. As an actor he appeared in plays by Cratinus; as a playwright he won his first contest in 450 BC and was highly praised by Aristophanes and Aristotle. Fragments of his works survive.

Cratinus (c. 520 BC–c. 423 BC) Greek playwright, author of several major examples of Old Comedy. Lampooned as a drunkard by Aristophanes in *The Knights*, he defeated Aristophanes in a contest a year later (424 BC) with his play *The Bottle*, which also took his drunkenness as its subject. Fragments of his plays survive.

Craven, Lady Elizabeth (Margravine of Anspach; 1750–1828) British playwright and amateur actress. She married Lord Craven in 1767 and presented her plays in a privately built theatre at their house at Newbury. After Craven's death in 1791 she married the Margrave of Anspach and continued to stage her plays at the private theatre that they built at Brandenburgh House, Hammersmith.

Craven, Hawes (Henry Hawes Craven Green; 1837–1910) British scene painter, who studied stage design at the Britannia Theatre. He attracted attention at the Olympic, then worked at Covent Garden, Drury Lane, and the Theatre Royal, Dublin, before going to the Lyceum. There he painted scenery for nearly all of Henry Irving's productions, beginning with *The Bells* in 1871.

Crawford, Cheryl (1902–) US actress, director, and producer, who began her career in 1923 with the Theatre Guild. Subsequently she was one of the three founders of the Group Theatre (1930), cofounded a summer theatre in Maplewood, New Jersey (1941), and joined with Eva Le Gallienne and Margaret Webster to found the **American Repertory Theatre** (1946). Having helped to establish the Actors' Studio in 1947, she became Joint-General Director of the Anta play series produced by the American National Theatre and Academy (1950), presenting plays by Tennessee Williams, Brecht, Arbuzov, and many others.

Crawford, Michael (Michael Dumbell Smith; 1942–) British actor, who began his stage career in Coventry at the age of 16. His talent for comedy was revealed in Neil Simon's *Come Blow Your Horn* (1962) and subsequently he became well-known as a television performer. In 1971 he returned to the stage in Anthony Marriott and Alastair Foot's *No Sex Please, We're British* (1971) and went to enjoy outstanding success in the musicals *Billy, Barnum,* and, in 1987, Andrew Lloyd Webber's *The Phantom of the Opera,* in which he triumphed in New York the following year.

Crazy Gang A group of seven British comedians, immensely popular on the London stage (especially at the Palladium and the Victoria Palace) from the 1930s to the 1960s. Specializing in revues featuring their own distinctive style of boisterous farcical humour, the Gang consisted of **Bud Flanagan** (Robert Winthrop; 1896–1968) and **Chesney Allen** (William Allen; 1894–1982); **Jimmie Nervo** (James Holloway; 1897– 1975) and **Teddy Knox** (Albert Edward Cromwell-Knox; 1896–1974); **Charlie Naughton** (1887–1976) and **Jimmy Gold** (James McConigal; 1886–1967); and 'Monsewer' **Eddie Gray** (1897–1969).

Crébillon, Prosper Jolyot de (1674– 1762) French playwright, born in Dijon. Crébillon was highly acclaimed in the 18th century – his admirers compared him with Racine – but his plays, which include *Idomenée* (1705) and *Rhadamiste et Zénobie* (1711), are generally considered to be too crudely melodramatic to rank among the great tragedies of French theatre. Elected to the Académie Française in 1731, he became court censor in 1735, a position that provoked the enmity of his rival Voltaire.

Creditors, The (*Fordringsägare*) A play by August *Strindberg. First performance: 1890. Written in the same year as *Miss Julie,* the play again tackles sexual relationships, this time through the writer Tekla, who draws her own strength from the men around her, destroying them in the process.

crepidata See *palliata.*

Crepuscolari, I A theatrical movement in Italy during the early 20th century. Distinguished by its subdued, melancholic tone, it found its best expression in the plays of Martini and Lodovici, among others.

cresset A knot of tarred rope, usually enclosed in a small iron cage, that when burning produced rudimentary stage lighting in the Elizabethan theatre.

Crispin A character of traditional French comedy, derived from *Scaramuccia and Il *Capitano from the *commedia dell'arte*. A cunning valet, he was a prominent figure in the plays of Scarron, Lesage, and Regnard.

Criterion Theatre A theatre in London's West End, which was originally built entirely underground. Situated in Regent (now Piccadilly) Circus on the site of an old inn, it opened in 1874 with the comedy *An American Lady* by the theatre's first manager H J Byron. Charles Wyndham was manager from 1875 to 1899 and lessee from 1879 until his death in 1919. His leading lady and wife from 1916, Mary Moore (Mrs James Albery), inherited the Criterion on her husband's death; in 1931 it passed to her son, Sir Bronson Albery. In 1883 the theatre was closed for reconstruction, which included the installation of electricity; it was further remodelled in 1902. Early productions ranged from light comedy and farce to more serious plays by Henry Arthur Jones. During World War I the Walter Ellis farce *A Little Bit of Fluff* (1915) ran for 1241 performances. Marie Tempest appeared in several plays in 1926–29. Outstanding productions of the 1930s were Ivor Novello's comedy *Fresh Fields* (1933) and Terence Rattigan's immensely popular *French Without Tears* (1936), which ran for 1039 performances. The theatre was used as a studio by the BBC during World War II. Samuel Beckett's *Waiting for Godot* was transferred from the Arts Theatre in 1955, while in recent years the Criterion has staged successful plays by such writers as Alan Ayckbourn, Simon Gray, David Mercer, and Tom Stoppard. Ray Cooney's *Run for your Wife!*, with Ernie Wise, passed its 2000th performance in 1988.

The **Criterion Theatre** on Broadway, New York, opened in 1895 (as the Lyric Theatre) as part of the Oscar Hammerstein Olympia complex. The theatre was renamed the Criterion in 1899 and saw appearances by Julia Marlowe, John Hare, Irene Vanbrugh, and Lionel Barrymore before being converted into a cinema. It was demolished in 1935.

critic One who is paid to write reviews and similar articles on the theatre. The earliest influential commentator upon the theatre was Aristotle; of his successors the most distinguished have included Sir Richard Steele (who was the first to outline the role of the modern critic), William Hazlitt (who was noted for his reviews of Edmund Kean), Leigh Hunt, G B Shaw, Max Beerbohm, James Agate, and Kenneth Tynan in Britain, Victor Hugo in France, and James Huneker (remembered as a champion of Ibsen and Shaw) and George Nathan in the US. Some of the most famous criticisms over the years have included Shaw's notorious "there is no eminent writer ... whom I despise as entirely as I despise Shakespeare", the anonymous review of *Oklahoma!* "no legs, no jokes, no chance", and Penelope Gilliatt's memory of *Waiting for Godot*, which she said "arrived in London ... like a sword burying itself in an overupholstered sofa".

Critic, The A farce by *Sheridan. First performance: 1779. Dangle, an amateur critic, Sneer, a malicious wit, and Sir Fretful Plagiary, attend a rehearsal of a tragedy by Puff; their comments provide a scathing satire upon the contemporary theatre and literary criticism.

Critique de l'École des Femmes, La A comedy by *Molière, written in response to criticism of *L'École des Femmes* (*see* School for Wives, The). First performance: Paris, 1663. It consists of a conversation in which the central characters discuss the original play. *See also Impromptu de Versailles, L'.*

Croft, Michael *See* National Youth Theatre.

Crommelynck, Fernand (1888–1970) Belgian playwright, writing in French, who established his reputation in 1920 with Lugné-Poë's production in Paris of the savage tragi-comedy *Le Cocu magnifique*. His early works were influenced by Maeterlinck but never met with the success of his masterpiece upon the theme of marital infidelity, which was subsequently seen in London and Moscow with great acclaim; later works, chiefly imitations of his most famous play, included *Tripes d'or* (1925) and *Une Femme qui a le couer trop petit* (1934).

Cronyn, Hume (1911-) Canadian actor, who made his debut in 1931 with the National Theatre Stock Company. After success on Broadway in such plays as *She Stoops to Conquer* (1935) and Chekhov's *Three Sisters* (1937), he married Jessica Tandy, with whom he appeared in Jan de Hartog's *The Fourposter* (1951) and other plays. Subsequent roles have included Jimmie Luton in *Big Fish, Little Fish* (1961), Polonius in Gielgud's *Hamlet* (1964), and the title roles in Peter Luke's *Hadrian VII* (1969) and Beckett's *Krapp's Last Tape* (1972).

Crooked Mirror, Theatre of the A theatre in Leningrad (then St Petersburg), founded in 1908. It soon established itself as a centre of satirical drama with works by Evreinov, Andreyev, and Gogol, whose play *The Government Inspector* was one of its greatest successes. Closed from 1918 to 1922, it continued without attracting great attention until 1931.

Cross Keys Inn An inn in Gracechurch Street in London, where plays were staged by such companies as Strange's Men during the late 16th century. It ceased to operate as a theatrical venue in about 1596.

Crothers, Rachel (1878–1958) US playwright and theatre scholar, who wrote and produced her own plays very successfully from 1906, when her first play *The Three of Us* appeared on Broadway, until 1937. Her subjects ranged from the frustrated position of women in contemporary US society, as in *A Man's World* (1909), to the problems of the younger generation, as in *Nice People* (1921). Her most important play was *Susan and God* (1937), in which a woman becomes absorbed in a religious cult.

Crouse, Russel *See* Lindsay, Howard.

Crowder's Music Hall *See* Greenwich Theatre.

Crowe, Mrs George *See* Bateman, Hezekiah Linthicum.

Crowne, John (c. 1640–c. 1703) English playwright, who wrote a masque and a number of plays for performance at the court of Charles II. The most memorable character in his first comedy, *The Country Wit* (1675), was later developed into the central figure of his play *Sir Courtly Nice* (1685). His other dramatic works include 11 tragedies and the heroic drama *The Destruction of Jerusalem by Titus Vespasian* (1676–77).

Crow Street Theatre A theatre in Dublin, opened in 1758 by Spranger Barry and Henry Woodward in competition with the Smock Alley Theatre. With a companion theatre of the same name in Cork, the Crow Street Theatre finally closed in 1820.

Crucible, The A drama by Arthur *Miller. First performance: New York, 1953. Ostensibly a play about the Salem witch trials that took place in 1693, resulting in the deaths of 20 people, it was intended as a veiled criticism of the anti-communist purge instituted in the US by Senator McCarthy.

Crucible Theatre A theatre in Sheffield, opened in 1971 and inheriting the repertory company of the Sheffield Playhouse, which it replaced. Seating 1000 people, the theatre includes a studio theatre as well as the main auditorium and has built a reputation for performances of contemporary plays and local documentaries as well as for taking drama out into the surrounding communities. Recent years have seen successes with US musicals as well as the staging of numerous major snooker tournaments.

Cruelty, Theatre of A theatrical genre of the 20th century, based on the ideas of Antonin *Artaud, as expressed in his treatise *Le Théâtre et son double* (1938). It advocated the use of the primitive, ritualistic, and shocking in attracting the audience's interest; writers of the genre included Genet, Arrabal, Orton, and Weiss.

Cruger's Wharf Theatre A theatre in New York, otherwise known as the **Wharf Theatre**, built in 1758 by David Douglass. It opened with Rowe's *The Tragedy of Jane Shore* and closed a few months later with *Richard III*. Its talented company included the widow of Lewis Hallam and her three children.

Cruz Cano y Olmedilla, Ramón Francisco de la (1731–94) Spanish playwright, who wrote a number of distinctive *sainetes*, sketches, and libretti. His realistic depiction of the lower classes of Madrid foreshadowed much Spanish drama of the 19th century.

Csiky, Gergely (1843–91) Hungarian playwright, who introduced Realism into the Hungarian theatre. His satirical bourgeois dramas include *The Parasites* (1880), *Glittering Misery* (1881), *The Stomfay Family* (1883), and *The Grandmother* (1891).

Csokor, Franz Theodor (1885–1969) Austrian playwright, whose early works reflected the influence of Büchner and Expressionism. His most admired plays included *Die rote Strasse* (1918), *Gesellschaft der Menschenrechte* (1929), and *Dritter November 1918* (1937), which depicted the defeated Austro-Hungarian army at the close of

World War I. His later works included two trilogies on religious themes – of which the most notable single play was *Cäsars Witwe* (1952) – and *Das Zeichen an der Wand* (1962).

Cuckoo in the Nest, A A farce by Ben *Travers. First performance: Aldwych Theatre, London, 1925. The first of the Aldwych farces, the play established the author's reputation. It was filmed in 1933.

cue A signal, commonly the closing words of an actor's speech, which notifies another actor or a member of the stage crew that the time for him to deliver a line or perform some other prearranged action is imminent.

Cueva, Juan de la (c. 1543–1610) Spanish playwright and poet, an important predecessor of Lope de Vega. Much influenced by Seneca, he wrote plays based upon Spanish history and the tragedy *Los Siete infantes de Lara* (The Seven Princes of Lara), as well as such comedies of manners as *Comedia del viejo enamorado* (Comedy of the Infatuated Old Man) and *El Infamador* (The Backbiter).

Cumberland, Richard (1732–1811) British playwright, whose numerous pieces for the stage exemplified the prevailing style of sentimental comedy. His most successful play was *The West Indian*, produced by Garrick in 1771; others include *The Brothers* (1769), *The Fashionable Lover* (1772), and *The Jew* (1794). He was caricatured by Sheridan as Sir Fretful Plagiary in *The Critic*. His *Memoirs* (1806–07) are a useful source of information on 18th-century theatre.

Cummings, Constance (1910–) British actress, born in the US, who has spent most of her career on the London stage. She appeared in various works by her husband, **Benn Wolfe Levy** (1900–73), while her most celebrated classic roles have included Shakespeare's Juliet and Shaw's St Joan. Other successes have included plays by Albee and Robert Sherwood and, with the National Theatre, Chekhov and O'Neill; her more recent performances have numbered amongst them parts in Arthur Kopit's *Wings* (1978) and Shaw's *Mrs Warren's Profession* (1982).

cup-and-saucer drama A drawing-room drama in which issues of contemporary social relevance are treated in a sober, realistic way, albeit via sometimes artificial plots. The term was first used to describe the plays of T W Robertson.

curtain The heavy cloth used to screen the stage from the audience's view before, after, and sometimes at points during a performance. Curtains were first used, as the *aulaeum* and *siparium*, by the Romans and were reintroduced in the 16th and 17th centuries; Irving was the first to lower a curtain during scene changes. Also known as the **act drop, tabs**, or house curtain, it is usually augmented by a safety curtain and, formerly, by an **advertisement curtain** bearing details of the theatre's sponsors.

curtain call The reappearance on stage of members of the cast to take a bow at the end of a performance in response to the audience's applause. *See also* proscenium doors.

curtain-music Music played while the curtain is closed, usually before a performance begins. Formerly, music was also often played between acts.

curtain-raiser A one-act play or other brief entertainment presented before the main drama. Curtain-raisers, usually short farces, were a common feature of theatre in the 19th century.

curtain set An arrangement of curtains, including borders and backcloth, which comprises the entire setting, usually without the use of flats. It is known in the US as a **drapery setting**.

Curtain Theatre A theatre in Shoreditch, London, opened in 1577 close to the Theatre. Little is known of the construction of the building, which housed the Chamberlain's Men and several other companies over the years. *Romeo and Juliet* and *Henry V* may have had their first performances there and Jonson's *Every Man in His Humour* was given its premiere at the Curtain in 1598. The building itself was still standing possibly as late as 1666.

The **Curtain Theatre** in Glasgow was a small company that presented productions from 1932 in a Victorian terraced house in the city, eventually moving into the Lyric Theatre in 1935. The group presented works by Scottish writers until 1940, when it closed (although similar productions continued until the opening of the Pitlochry Festival Theatre in 1949).

Cusack, Cyril (1910-) Irish actor, who joined the Abbey Theatre company in 1932 and gave his first London performance as Richard in O'Neill's *Ah, Wilderness!* in 1936. He established a fine reputation in plays by such Irish writers as Shaw, Synge, and O'Casey, while his classical roles have included Romeo (1945) and Hamlet (1957) at the Gaiety Theatre, Dublin, which he managed for a time after leaving the Abbey in 1945. He was also highly acclaimed in France in *Krapp's Last Tape* by Samuel Beckett (1960). Parts with the Royal Shakespeare Company have included Cassius in *Julius Caesar* (1963); subsequently he joined The National Theatre, excelling as Antonio in *The Tempest* (1974) and Fluther Good in O'Casey's *The Plough and the Stars* (1977).

His daughter, **Sinéad Cusack** (1948-), made her stage debut at the age of 12 at the Olympia Theatre, Dublin and later played juvenile leads at the Abbey. In 1972 she played Juliet at the Shaw Theatre in London and subsequently took over as

Grace Harkaway in Boucicault's *London Assurance*. She joined the Royal Shakespeare Company in 1979 and has been admired in plays by O'Keeffe, Beaumont and Fletcher, and Aphra Behn among others. She is married to the actor Jeremy *Irons.

Cushman, Charlotte (Saunders) (1816–76) US actress, who intended to be an opera singer but turned to acting and made her debut in New York as Lady Macbeth in 1836. She went on to win acclaim in such roles as Meg Merrilies in Scott's *Guy Mannering* and Lady Gay Spanker in Boucicault's *London Assurance*, as well as playing Shakespearean heroes and heroines in both the US and the UK. Among her controversial male portrayals were Romeo, Cardinal Wolsey, and Claude Melnotte in Bulwer-Lytton's *The Lady of Lyons*.

cut-cloth A cloth cut so that scenery behind it is partially revealed. Such a cloth is usually termed a cut-out drop in the US.

Cwmni Theatre Cymru *See* Theatr Gwynedd.

cyclorama A curved curtain or other barrier positioned so as to screen both the rear of the stage and part of the wings from the audience's view and to create an impression of space. Some theatres have permanent domed cycloramas made of cement. In Germany, where the cyclorama was first developed, it is known as a *Rundhorizont*.

Cyder Cellars *See* song-and-supper rooms.

Cymbeline A romance by William *Shakespeare. First performance: Globe Theatre, London, 1611. One of Shakespeare's last dramatic works, the play combines elements of folklore and British and Roman history in telling the story of the restoration of Imogen to her father, Cymbeline. Shakespeare's plot was derived from Boccaccio's *Decamer-*

on and culminates in a series of revelations in the final scene.

Cyrano de Bergerac An heroic comedy by Edmond *Rostand. First performance: Paris, 1897. The eponymous hero, embarrassed by his long nose, nobly refrains from declaring his love for Roxane and encourages her romance with his rival Christian; the play enjoyed lasting success, not only in France but also in Britain and the US.

Cyrano de Bergerac, Savinien (1619–55) French writer, born in Paris. In 1641 he abandoned his military career in favour of philosophy, literature, and science. He produced just two plays, the tragedy *La Mort d'Agrippine* (1653) and the comedy *Le Pedant joué* (1654), and is better known for his stories. Thanks to Edmond Rostand's play *Cyrano de Bergerac* and other semihistorical accounts, he is also remembered for his extremely large nose.

D

Dada A movement in art and literature that had a marked effect upon drama in the early 20th century. In reaction to conventional rational theatre it adopted a nihilistic tone and challenged the complacency of contemporary audiences. It began simultaneously in New York and Zurich in 1916 and flourished in Paris and elsewhere during the 1920s.

Dadié, Bernard Binlin (1916-) African novelist, playwright, poet, and statesman, who became Minister of Culture for the Ivory Coast and and has built up a strong reputation in French-speaking African theatre. His early plays included *Les Villes* (1933) and the historical play *Assémien Déhylé, roi du Sanwi* (1936), while later more satirical works associated with the

Theatre of the Absurd number amongst them *Monsieur Thôgô-gnini* (1969) and *Les Voix dans le vent*.

Dagerman, Stig (1923–54) Swedish playwright, novelist, and short-story writer, whose Expressionist plays treat such themes as fear, anxiety, death, and destruction. His best plays, *Den Dödsdömde* (The Condemned; 1947), in which a condemned man faces the terror of death, and *Skuggan av Mart* (The Shadow of Mart; 1948), are dominated by a sense of overwhelming evil and foreshadowed Dagerman's eventual suicide.

Dagmarteatret A theatre in Copenhagen, founded in 1883. Under Bjørn Bjørnson the theatre enjoyed a strong reputation during the 1890s and challenged the Kongelige Teater as the chief theatrical venue in the capital. It closed in 1937 and was demolished.

Dalberg, Wolfgang Heribert, Baron von (1750–1806) German theatre manager, who ran the National Theatre at Mannheim from 1778. His achievements there included the first German translation of Shakespeare's *Julius Caesar* and the production of Schiller's *Die Räuber* in 1782.

Dalin, Olof von (1708–63) Swedish poet, playwright, and essayist, who played a crucial role in introducing Swedish writers and audiences to the classical French plays of Molière and others. He was editor of the influential *Savanska Argus* weekly newspaper and the author of several plays.

Dallas Theatre Centre A theatre, designed by the architect Frank Lloyd Wright, which opened in Dallas, Texas, in 1959. The centre has two auditoriums: the large **Kalita Humphreys Theatre**, which shows classical plays as well as contemporary works, and the smaller Down Centre Stage Theatre, which is used for new plays. The centre also has an academic programme for a graduate degree in theatre arts.

Daly, (John) Augustin (1839–99) US theatre manager and playwright, who presided over the emergence of a new independent US theatre in the late 19th century. As manager of the Fifth Avenue Theatre and then of his own *Daly's Theatre in New York, he led a distinguished company (including John Drew and Ada Rehan) and presented many plays either written or adapted (sometimes needlessly) by himself. He also opened Daly's Theatre in London, where his productions were equally well received.

Daly's 63rd Street Theatre A theatre on West 63rd Street in New York, which was originally a children's cinema (called the **Davenport Theatre**). It opened as Daly's in 1922 and was later renamed the **Coburn Theatre** (1928), the **Recital Theatre** (1932), the **Park Lane Theatre** (1932), and **Gilmore's Theatre** (1934). In 1936 the Federal Theatre Project took it over (as the **Experimental Theatre**) for the New York premiere of Shaw's *On the Rocks*. The theatre was demolished in 1957.

Daly's Theatre A theatre on Broadway, New York, which opened as **Banvard's Museum** (later renamed **Wood's Museum**) in 1867. The majority of the productions seen here were burlesque and variety shows with the occasional straight play after 1872; the theatre was remodelled in 1879 and, under the management of Augustin Daly, became one of the most successful playhouses in New York, featuring such stars as Ada Rehan. The theatre was a cinema from 1915 to 1920, when it was demolished.

Daly opened another **Daly's Theatre** off Leicester Square, London, in 1893 in conjunction with George *Edwardes. The theatre quickly established itself as an important venue for musicals as well as the plays of Shakespeare, Dumas *père*, and others featuring such leading performers as Violet Vanbrugh and Eleonora Duse. Subsequent successes included *The Merry Widow* (1907) and the musical *The Maid of the Mountains* (1917) before a series of failures led to a decline and the theatre's closure in 1937; the Warner Cinema now stands on the site.

dame A comic female character of the English pantomime, traditionally played by a man. Celebrated exponents of such roles as Widow Twankey, Mother Goose, Dame Trot, and the two Ugly Sisters have included Dan Leno and George Robey.

D'Amico, Silvio (1887–1955) Italian theatre scholar and theatre critic, who was the author of numerous authoritative accounts of the history of the stage. He is best known for his massive *Enciclopedia dello Spettacolo* and for the academy of dramatic art founded by him in 1935 and now named in his honour; other writings included numerous theatrical reviews.

Dancer, Ann (Ann Street; 1734–1801) British actress, born at Bath. After nine years at the Crow Street Theatre in Dublin, she accompanied Spranger Barry to the Haymarket in 1766. A year later she played Juliet to his Romeo there, after which they transferred to Drury Lane. In 1762 they were married; on Barry's death in 1778, she married again, appearing as Mrs Crawford. She excelled in both high comedy and tragedy.

Danchenko, Vladimir Nemirovich- *See* Nemirovich-Danchenko, Vladimir.

Dancourt, Florent Carton (1661–1725) French actor and playwright. Dancourt abandoned his legal studies for a career on the stage after marrying into a theatrical family. He acted with the Comédie-Française for some 33 years and wrote many witty comedies of manners depicting contemporary society and village life, notably

Le Chevalier à la mode (1687) and *La Maison de campagne* (1688).

His daughters, **Marie-Anne-Armande Dancourt** (1684–1745) and **Marie-Anne-Michelle Dancourt** (1685–1780), made many successful stage appearances as Manon and Mimi respectively. As children they performed in plays by their father; subsequently they joined the Comédie-Française, Manon retiring a year later (1702).

Dandy Dick A farce by *Pinero. First performance: 1887. The plot centres on the fortunes of the Reverend Augustin Jedd and his family, each of whom is relying on the eponymous racehorse to achieve particular ends.

Dane, Clemence (Winifred Ashton; 1888–1965) British novelist and playwright, whose drama *A *Bill of Divorcement* (1921) established her reputation. Her other plays include *Will Shakespeare* (1921), *Naboth's Vineyard* and *Granite* (both 1926), *Wild Decembers* (1932), which is about the Brontë family, and *Eighty in the Shade* (1958), which was written for Sybil Thorndike and Lewis Casson.

Dangerous Corner A play by J B *Priestley. First performance: London, 1932. One of the so-called time plays, it traces a series of events resulting from a chance remark at a dinner party and culminates in a suicide.

Dangeville, Mlle (Marie-Anne Botot; 1714–96) French actress, who was much admired in comic roles with the Comédie-Française, which she joined in 1730. She excelled in the plays of Marivaux, in which she appeared with Préville, and was highly popular with her fellow-players; Collé's banned play *La Partie de chasse d'Henri IV* was given its first performance in her garden.

Daniel, Samuel (1563–1619) English poet and playwright, who wrote a number of works for the court of James I. His tragedy *Philotas* (1604) led some to believe that its author sympathized with the rebellion of the Earl of Essex in 1600 and caused a decline in his popularity. His other plays include the tragedy *Cleopatra* (1594), pastorals, and masques.

D'Annunzio, Gabriele (Gabriele Rapagnetta; 1863–1938) Italian poet, playwright, and novelist, whose writing for the stage is distinguished by intense passion and highly poetic language. His plays, which enjoyed the enthusiastic support of Eleonora Duse, include the tragedies *La Città morta* (1898) and *La Gioconda* (1899) and the French mystery play *Le Martyre de Saint Sébastien* (1911). His most outstanding play is generally considered to be *La figlia di Jorio* (1904), a poetic expression of his delight in the natural world; other important works for the stage included *Francescala Rimini* (1902). In 1919 D'Annunzio became a national hero for his capture of the port of Fiume for Italy; subsequently, however, his reputation has suffered from the identification of his turbulent idealism with Fascist philosophy.

Danske Skueplads, Den A theatre in Copenhagen, opened in 1722. Over the next five years it was used for the presentation of 28 comedies specially written by Ludvig Holberg, effectively laying the foundation of the Danish theatrical tradition. In 1748 the resident company transferred under royal patronage to a new theatre, which was named the *Kongelige Teater in 1770.

Danton's Death (*Dantons Tod*) A play by Georg *Büchner, written in 1835. First performance: Berlin, 1903. A pessimistic account of the conflict between Robespierre and Danton during the French Revolution, the play was influenced by Büchner's disenchantment with contemporary politics.

D'Arcy, Margaretta (Ruth) *See* Arden, John.

Darlington, W(illiam) A(ubrey) (1890–1979) British theatre critic and playwright, who was drama critic for *The Daily Telegraph* from 1920 to 1968. Also a writer for *The New York Times* from 1936 to 1960, he was the author of the play *Alf's Button* (1924), based on one of his own novels, and biographies of Sheridan (1932) and J M Barrie (1938).

Dasté, Jean (1904–) French actor and director, who began his career with Copeau's company in Burgundy. Later he joined Saint-Denis's Compagnie des Quinze and assisted Barsacq with the newly-established Compagnie des Quatre Saisons before moving to Grenoble and then to St Étienne (1947) to take over the local dramatic centre founded under the *décentralisation dramatique* policy. This centre became famous for his productions of both classics and new plays, including works by Brecht, until his resignation in 1970.

Daubeny, Sir Peter Lauderdale (1921–75) British impresario and manager, whose achievements included visits to Britain by many leading foreign companies and the management of the annual World Theatre Season from 1964 to 1973. Early in his career he worked at the Liverpool Playhouse and presented acclaimed productions in London; later successes included Henry James's *The Aspern Papers* (1959) and the controversial play *The Connection* (1961) by Jack Gelber.

Dauvilliers (Nicolas Dorné; c. 1646–90) French actor, who was regarded as a brilliant performer of the great tragic roles. With his wife, the daughter of Raymond Poisson, he appeared with Molière's company until the playwright's death; subsequently he was briefly with the troupe led by Molière's widow before joining the

Comédie-Française in 1680. According to legend his genius in tragedy eventually caused him to go mad during one of his performances and to attempt to kill himself with a property sword; he died in an asylum.

Davenant, Sir William (1606–68) English playwright, alleged to be the illegitimate son or godchild of William Shakespeare. His early work for the theatre included masques for the court of Charles I and his comic masterpiece *The Wits* (1633). In 1656 he evaded the Puritans' restrictions on drama by presenting *The Siege of Rhodes*, a play with music that is generally regarded as the earliest English opera. After the Restoration he obtained a royal patent to open the Lincoln's Inn Fields Theatre; subsequently he built the theatre at Dorset Garden. He became poet laureate in 1638 and executed several adaptations of Shakespeare's plays.

Davenport, Edward Loomis (1815–77) US actor, who was a popular performer of leading Shakespearean and other roles in both Britain and the US. He became a member of Mrs John Drew's troupe in 1843 and subsequently won acclaim on both sides of the Atlantic in such parts as Hamlet, Othello, and Richard III and in Boucicault's *The Corsican Brothers*, working for some years with Mrs Mowatt. Back in the US he formed his own company and toured widely, several other members of his family also appearing with his troupe.

His daughter, **Fanny Lily Gipsy Davenport** (1850–98), played her first adult role in 1865 and subsequently appeared with Augustin Daly's company in New York. Later she led her own touring company, continuing to appear in a wide variety of Shakespearean and other roles, notably in the plays of Sardou.

Davenport, Jean *See* Lander, Jean Margaret.

Davenport, Lizzie *See* Mathews, Charles.

Davenport Theatre *See* Daly's 63rd Street Theatre.

Davidson, Gordon *See* Mark Taper Forum.

Davies, Hubert Henry (1869–1917) British playwright, whose plays include *Cousin Kate* (1903), in which Ethel Barrymore played the leading role, *Mrs Gorringe's Necklace* (1903), and *The Mollusc* (1907). His most commercially successful work was his last play *Outcast* (1914), which explored double standards of morality.

Davies, Robertson (1913-) Canadian playwright and novelist, who was the author of a number of plays written in collaboration with Tyrone Guthrie for the Stratford (Ontario) Festival and of several books on Shakespeare. Other works for the theatre have included *Fortune My Foe* (1949), *A Masque of Aesop* (1952), *Love and Libel* (1960), which was an adaptation of one of his own novels, and such comedies as the satirical *Question Time* (1975).

Davis, Fay *See* Lawrence, Gerald.

Davis, Hallie Flanagan *See* Flanagan, Hallie.

Davis, John (1822–75) British-born playwright, actor, and manager, who worked in the British theatre before emigrating to the US in 1855. He successfully ran a theatre in New Orleans until the city's capture during the Civil War; his plays included *The Roll of the Drum* (1861), which was performed throughout the Confederate South.

Day, John (c. 1574–c. 1640) English playwright, who collaborated on numerous plays with Dekker, Rowley, Chettle, and many others. His own plays include the allegorical *The Parliament of Bees* (c. 1607) and the *Isle* *of Gulls* (1606), which caused considerable controversy on account of its satirical view of Anglo-Scottish relations.

Dean, Basil Herbert (1888–1978) British actor, playwright, and director, who became a leading director on the London stage. He began his career with Miss Horniman's company in Manchester and later worked at the Liverpool Playhouse before reaching London in 1919. Significant productions under his direction included Clemence Dane's *A Bill of Divorcement* (1921), James Elroy Flecker's *Hassan* (1923), and J B Priestley's *Johnson Over Jordan* (1939). Having presented entertainment for the troops in World War I, he controlled the many productions organized by ENSA during World War II. Later productions included Priestley's *An Inspector Calls* (1946).

Death of a Salesman A play by Arthur *Miller. First performance: New York, 1949. The play concerns Willy Loman, a salesman, who is obsessed with materialistic success and the desire to be personally popular; his disappointment in his two sons, Biff and Happy, finally leads him to kill himself. The play won a Pulitzer Prize.

Deathwatch (*Haute Surveillance*) A play by Jean *Genet. First performance: Paris, 1949. Lefranc and Maurice, minor criminals, aspire to the glory of their cellmate Yeux-Verts, a murderer: Lefranc finally kills Maurice in a futile attempt to gain Yeux-Verts's prestige.

De Brie, Mlle (Catherine Leclerc de Rozet; c. 1630–1706) French actress, who played many major roles in the plays of Molière. She joined Molière's company in 1650 and was highly popular in such roles as Agnès in *L'École des femmes*; subsequently she was one of the founder-members of the Comédie-Française.

Deburau, Jean-Gaspard (Jan Kašpar Dvořák; 1796–1846) French pantomimist, born in Bohemia, who – under the stagename **Baptiste** – redeveloped the character of *Pierrot. Around 1811 he became involved with the Théâtre des Funambules on the Boulevard du Temple, where he inherited the role of Pierrot and transformed him into the melancholy but hopeful lover who became one of the most popular figures of the harlequinade.

His son, **Charles Deburau** (1829–73), eventually succeeded him in the role before going on to open the first Théâtre Marigny in 1858.

De Camp, Maria Theresa (1773–1838) British actress, wife of Charles *Kemble. She was engaged at the Haymarket in 1786 and achieved fame as Macheath six years later. She accompanied the Kembles to Covent Garden in 1806 and in 1808 was successful in her own play *The Day After the Wedding*.

Décentralisation Dramatique The development in France of a new theatrical tradition with government backing following World War II. The policy of encouraging the foundation of theatre companies outside Paris after 1945 had a fundamental effect upon the French theatre with numerous groups receiving a state subsidy outside the capital. Regional organizations, or **Centres Dramatiques**, cover each area of France; of these the most significant have included André Calvé's group and Jean Dasté's **Comédie de Saint-Étienne** in eastern France, the **Grenier de Toulouse** in the south-west, the **Comédie de l'Ouest** based in Rennes, the **Centre Dramatique de Sud-Est** in the southeast (later renamed Action Culturelle du Sud-Est), the Théâtre de la Commune d'Aubervilliers, the Théâtre des Amandiers based at Nanterre, and the **Compagnie de Caen**, founded in 1968. As well as the Centres Dramatiques, which organize regular theatrical productions and tours, other institutions established under the policy include the **Maisons de la Culture**, which foster the development in the provinces of the arts in general, the **Centres d'Animation Culturelle**, and the **Troupes Permanentes**, comprising touring companies based on their own theatre. In addition to all these organizations, the state also subsidizes the **Théâtres Nationaux**, which include the Comédie-Française and other leading national theatre companies.

Deep Blue Sea, The A drama by Terence *Rattigan. First performance: London, 1952. The play is a moving portrayal of the plight of a judge's wife whose affair with a dissolute ex-fighter pilot leads to her attempted suicide. It has provided a fine role for such leading actresses as Peggy Ashcroft, Celia Johnson, Googie Withers, and Penelope Keith. The film version starred Kenneth More and Vivien Leigh.

Deevy, Teresa (1894–1963) Irish playwright, born in Waterford. Her portrayals of ambition and Irish rural life include *Temporal Powers* (1931), which won an Abbey Theatre prize. Her best-known play was *Katie Rooke* (1936); her later contributions were primarily for the radio.

de Filippo, Eduardo (1900–84) Italian actor-manger and playwright, who wrote a number of plays strongly influenced by the *commedia dell'arte* tradition. He and other members of his family earned a high reputation for their presentation of his plays at their own theatre in Naples. The most successful included the comedy *Filumena Marturano* (1946) – later filmed as *Marriage Italian Style*, *Grande magia* (Grand Magic; 1948), *Le voci di dentro* (Voices from Within; 1948), seen at London's National Theatre in 1983, and *Il figlio di Pulcinella* (The Son of Pulcinella; 1959). *Saturday, Sunday, Monday* (1959) was also well received in a National Theatre production starring Laurence Olivier and Joan Plowright.

Defresne *See* Dufresne.

Deirdre of the Sorrows A tragedy by J M *Synge. First performance: Abbey Theatre, Dublin, 1910. Unfinished at the time of Synge's death, the play is based on the legendary tale of Deirdre and Naisi's fatal relationship and is notable for its poetic intensity.

Déjazet, Pauline-Virginie (1798–1875) French actress, who became highly popular for her performances in male roles. She began her career in vaudeville, moving to the Palais-Royal in 1831 and establishing herself as a major actress of both male and female characters. Subsequently she appeared at the Variétés and the Gaîté before taking over the Folies-Nouvelles (as the Théâtre Déjazet) in 1859. Her most famous roles included Voltaire, Napoleon, and one of the men in Sardou's *Monsieur Garat*.

Dejmek, Kazimierz (1924-) Polish director, who succeeded Leon Schiller as head of the theatre in Łódź in 1949. He established his reputation with productions of contemporary plays, moving to the National Theatre in Warsaw in 1960 and then working abroad and back in Łódź. His most celebrated successes have included plays by Fredro, Mickiewicz, and Mrożek.

Dekker, Thomas (c. 1570–c. 1632) English playwright, who wrote or collaborated on at least 40 plays. Among the most celebrated of his collaborations were *Satiro mastix* (1601), written with Marston, *The Honest Whore* (1604) and *The Roaring Girl* (1610), written with Middleton, *The Virgin Martyr* (1620), written with Massinger, and *The Witch of Edmonton* (1621), written with both Rowley and Middleton. Of his own plays the most important was *The *Shoemaker's Holiday*.

Delacorte Theatre An open-air theatre in Central Park, New York, which was opened by Joseph Papp in 1962 for the purpose of housing the New York Shakespeare Festival. The theatre seats 1936 people, who pay no admission charge for the summertime performances of Shakespeare.

de la Motte, Houdar *See* Houdar de la Motte, Antoine.

Delane, Dennis (d. 1750) British actor, born into an Irish family. After appearances at the Smock Alley Theatre, he transferred (1734) to the Goodman's Fields Theatre, where he played Shakespearean leads for four years. Later he also appeared at Covent Garden and Drury Lane.

Delaney, Shelagh (1939-) British playwright, who established her reputation at the age of 17 with *A *Taste of Honey* (1958). A calculated counter to the sophisticated theatre of Terence Rattigan and others, it was highly acclaimed for its uncomprising realism on its premiere by Joan Littlewood's Theatre Workshop. A second play, *The Lion in Love*, about a failing marriage, was first presented in 1960; since then she has concentrated upon the television and cinema. Her only other work for the stage has been *The House That Jack Built* (1978).

de la Tour, Frances (1944-) British actress, who first appeared with the Royal Shakespeare Company in 1965 as a beggar in *Timon of Athens* and remained until 1971, when she played Helena in Peter Brook's *A Midsummer Night's Dream*. She played the title role in *Hamlet* in 1979, won three prestigious awards for her performance in Tom Kempinski's *Duet for One* in 1980, and was a memorable St Joan (1984) in the National Theatre revival of Shaw's play. More recent successes have included William Luce's *Lillian* (1986).

Delaunay, Louis-Arsène (1826–1903) French actor, who had a long career as a performer of young lovers. He began at the Odéon before transferring to the Comédie-Française in 1848; many of his finest parts were in plays by de Musset, Hugo, Marivaux, and Regnard.

Delavigne, Casimir (1793–1843) French playwright and poet, born in Le Havre. His tragedies, influenced in style both by neoclassicism and by Romanticism, treat historical subjects rather than classical legend, as in *Les Vêpres siciliennes* (1819). Delavigne also wrote comedies, notably *L'École des vieillards* (1823).

Della Porta, Giambattista (1538–1615) Italian scientist, philosopher, and playwright, author of a number of major plays of the *commedia erudita* tradition. His comedies, most of which drew on works by Plautus and other earlier writers, included *Il due fratelli rivali*, which influenced Shakespeare's *Much Ado About Nothing*, *La fantesca*, and *La trappolaria*.

de Loutherbourg, Philip James *See* Loutherbourg, Philip James de.

Delysia, Alice (Alice Lapize; 1889–1979) French actress and singer, who was highly popular in revue, notably under C B Cochran. She began her career in 1903 at the Moulin Rouge in Paris as a chorus girl, subsequently attracting attention with Yvonne Printemps at the Folies-Bergère and elsewhere. She joined Cochran in London in 1914 and appeared in many of his revues, including *Odds and Ends* (1914) and *On With the Dance* (1925). She also performed in several light comedies in the 1930s and toured during World War II.

Dench, Dame Judi (Olivia) (1934-) British actress, who made her professional debut as Ophelia with the Old Vic company in 1957. After excelling there as Juliet in 1960, she worked with the Royal Shakespeare Company, at the Oxford Playhouse, and at

Nottingham and made her musical debut in *Cabaret* at the Palace Theatre in 1968. Subsequent successes with the Royal Shakespeare Company have ranged from Grace Harkaway in Boucicault's *London Assurance* (1970) to Imogen in *Cymbeline* (1979) and Brecht's *Mother Courage* at the Barbican (1984). At the National Theatre she also played Wilde's Lady Bracknell (1982) and Shakespeare's Cleopatra (1987), in which role she completed a record 100 performances. In 1988 she directed *Much Ado About Nothing* for Kenneth Branagh's Renaissance Theatre Company. She is married to the actor Michael Williams (1935-).

Denison, (John) Michael (Terence Wellesley) (1915-) British actor, who first appeared in *Charley's Aunt* at Frinton in 1938, then took part in the London Mask Theatre season at the Westminster Theatre, where his roles included Paris in *Troilus and Cressida* (1938) and Lexy in *Candida* (1939). After World War II he featured in West End comedies and thrillers and toured South Africa with his wife, Dulcie *Gray, with whom he has often appeared. His finest roles since then have included performances in the plays of Shakespeare, Ibsen, Wilde, and Barrie.

Dennis, John (1657–1734) English theatre critic and playwright, who wrote nine moderately successful plays, the best known being the tragedy *Rinaldo and Armida* (1699), *Liberty Asserted* (1704), and *Appius and Virginia* (1709), which was ridiculed by Pope in his *Essay on Criticism*. He also produced adaptations of plays by Shakespeare, a number of pamphlets defending the theatre, as well as a considerable amount of neoclassical literary criticism.

Derwent, Clarence (1884–1959) British actor, who went to the US in 1915, made his first New York appearance as Undershaft in Shaw's *Major Barbara*, and remained to play important supporting roles

for the next 31 years. In 1945 he established the annual Clarence Derwent Awards in New York and London for the best supporting performances.

Desclée,   Aimée-Olympe   (1836–74) French actress, who excelled as heroines in the plays of Dumas *fils*, who did much to encourage her. Early appearances at the Gymnase were not successful but after Dumas saw her with a touring company he arranged her return to Paris, where she triumphed in several of his plays before her sudden death.

Deseine, Mlle *See* Dufresne.

designer One who undertakes the design of the costumes, scenery, lighting, and other technical aspects of a particular production, usually working in close collaboration with the director. The earliest designers included Giacomo Torelli and Philippe James de Loutherbourg.

Design for Living A comedy by Noël *Coward. First performance: New York, 1933. The plot revolves around a *ménage à trois*, whose members reject conventional values. Coward himself appeared with the Lunts in the original production.

Desiosi An Italian *commedia dell'arte* company, possibly founded by Diana da *Ponti in about 1581. Actors with the Desiosi included Tristano Martinelli, who appeared as Arlecchino; when the company disbanded after several years many of its members joined the Accesi.

Desire Under the Elms A drama by Eugene *O'Neill. First performance: New York, 1924. The play examines the relationship between the New England farmer Ephraim Cabot and his wife, Abbey Putnam, who becomes involved with Ebon, the son of Ephraim's first marriage. The tragic

139

consequences reflect the troubles of contemporary US society.

Desjardins, Marie-Catherine-Hortense (Mme de Villedieu; 1632–83) French writer, originally a member of Molière's company. After an adventurous youth she produced many fashionable short novels and a number of plays, of which the best-known is the tragedy *Manlius Torquatus* (1662).

Desmares, Nicolas (c. 1645–1714) French actor and playwright, brother of Mlle Champmeslé. After appearing with a French troupe at Copenhagen and in the provinces, he joined the Comédie-Française where he was praised in peasant roles.

His daughter was the actress **Charlotte Desmares** (1682–1753), who was trained by Mlle Champmeslé and, with Mlle Duclos, inherited many of her roles at the Comédie-Française. Her greatest successes included Voltaire's *Oedipe*.

Desmarets de Saint-Sorlin, Jean (1595–1676) French poet and playwright. A protégé of Cardinal de Richelieu and a founder member of the Académie Française, he wrote plays of varying quality: the witty comedy *Les Visionnaires* (1637), which satirized polite society and anticipated Molière, was an immense success. His only other work of note was *Mirame* (1641).

Desœillets, Mlle (Alix Faviot; 1621–70) French actress, who was much admired in tragedy at the Hôtel de Bourgogne despite her lack of striking looks. She first appeared in Paris after many years in the provinces and excelled in plays by Corneille and Racine; she retired immediately, however, upon seeing Mlle Champmeslé act in one of her roles for the first time.

Destouches (Philippe Néricault; 1680–1754) French playwright, born in Tours. A member of a troupe of strolling players in his youth, he worked for several years at the French embassy in London, returning in 1723. His most successful comedies, *Le Philosophe marié* (The Married Philosopher; 1727) and *Le Glorieux* (The School for Arrogance; 1732), were influenced both by Molière and by English Restoration drama.

detail scenery Small items of scenery, generally *built stuff, that are introduced during a performance on a formal stage or other stage setting.

deus ex machina A literary convention by means of which the central dilemma in a play is unexpectedly resolved by the appearance of a new character, traditionally a god, who immediately settles all disputes. The concept was originally developed in ancient Greek tragedy.

deuteragonist *See* protagonist.

Deutsch, Ernst (1890–1969) German actor, born in Prague, who became a leading performer of Expressionist drama. He established his reputation in Hasenclever's *Der Sohn* (1916) and subsequently appeared under Reinhardt with great success until moving to the US (1933); after his return to Germany in 1947 he won further praise in plays by Hauptmann, Lessing, Schnitzler, and others.

Deutsches Theater A theatre group founded in Berlin in 1883 to promote the performance of new works. Led by Adolf L'Arronge, Josef Kainz, and Agnes Sorma, the group first performed popular historical dramas. It subsequently won new fame under Max Reinhardt and, after World War I, Heinz Hilpert. It became the National Theatre of East Berlin in 1946 and was run by Besson from 1961 to 1969.

de Villiers, Claude Deschamps *See* Villiers, Claude Deschamps de.

Devils, The An historical drama by John *Whiting. First performance: London, 1961. Based on Aldous Huxley's novel *The Devils of Loudon*, it was first presented by the Royal Shakespeare Company. The play concerns the alleged possession by demons of some French nuns and bears the influence of Brecht.

Devil's Disciple, The A comedy by G B *Shaw. First performance: New York, 1897. Set during the American War of Independence, the play follows the adventures of the villainous but romantic Dick Dudgeon and satirizes the conventions of melodrama. Despite his reputation as a disgrace to his family, Dick cannot help himself from taking the place of a condemned clergyman on the gallows, driven by his own innate virtue.

Devine, George (Alexander Cassady) (1910–66) British actor and theatre director, who was president of OUDS before appearing in Gielgud's London seasons. He became director and manager of Saint-Denis's London Theatre Studio (1936–39), taught at the Old Vic school, played Tesman to Peggy Ashcroft's Hedda Gabler (1954), and directed Gielgud in a curious Japanese-designed *King Lear* (1955). In 1956 he founded the English Stage Company at the Royal Court Theatre in London, where he presented the work of such innovative playwrights as Osborne, Pinter, and Bond.

Devrient, Ludwig (1784–1832) German actor, who was judged the greatest performer of tragedy of the Romantic era in Germany. Appearing with Iffland's company from 1814, he caused a sensation in such passionate roles as King Lear and Franz Moor in Schiller's *Die Räuber*. Later in his career he was confined to comedy roles only and, frustrated as a serious actor, he abandoned himself to alcohol.

His eldest nephew, **Karl August Devrient** (1797–1872), was also an actor, who played many leading roles at the Court Theatre in Dresden. His greatest successes included major parts in plays by Schiller, Goethe, and Shakespeare.

Another nephew, **(Philipp) Eduard Devrient** (1801–77), began as an opera singer but later worked at the Court Theatre in Dresden and the Court Theatre at Karlsruhe as an actor and director. He also published the first history of the German stage (1848–74) and translations of Shakespeare (1873–76).

A third nephew, **(Gustav) Emil Devrient** (1803–72), was also a much-acclaimed actor at the Court Theatre in Dresden and elsewhere. He was particularly admired in the tragedies of Goethe, Schiller, and Shakespeare.

Eduard's son, **Otto Devrient** (1838–94), was active as an actor, playwright, and director and was the author of three tragedies. He worked at the Karlshruhe Court Theatre and later at Weimar, where his production of Geothe's *Faust* (1876) in the style of a mystery play was much discussed.

Karl's son, **Max Devrient** (1857–1929), made his acting debut in Dresden in 1878 and later appeared throughout Germany and in Vienna in plays by Goethe, Schiller, and Shakespeare. Although admired chiefly as a tragedian, he was also highly successful in comic roles.

Dewhurst, Colleen (1926–) Canadian actress, who made her professional debut in the Anta revival of *Desire Under the Elms* (1952). She performed in the New York Shakespeare Festival from 1956 to 1959, playing Tamora in *Titus Andronicus*, Katherine in *The Taming of the Shrew*, Lady Macbeth in *Macbeth*, and Cleopatra in *Antony and Cleopatra*. Other successes have included Albee's *Who's Afraid of Virginia Woolf?* (1965), Brecht's *The Good Woman of Setzuan* (1970), and *Hamlet* (1972).

Dexter, John (1925–) British actor and director, who first attracted attention with his productions for the English Stage Company at the Royal Court Theatre in the 1950s. Following success with a trilogy of Wesker's plays, he scored further successes with plays by Lillian Hellman, G B Shaw, and Shakespeare among others, several of which were presented by the National Theatre (1963–66). Actors who have appeared under his direction have included Laurence Olivier, who played Othello with the National Theatre, and Alec Guinness; his most recent productions have included a number of operas at New York's Metropolitan Opera House and Brecht's *Life of Galileo* (1980).

Dias, Baltasar (16th century) Portuguese playwright, who lived in Madeira. Despite his blindness, he wrote a number of popular though inconsequential plays influenced by the works of Vicente.

Dibdin, Charles (1745–1814) British actor, playwright, and songwriter, noted for his ballad operas. He established his reputation as an actor in Bickerstaffe's *The Padlock* in 1768, after which he appeared in a series of one-man shows (1788–93).

His illegitimate children by the actress Harriet Pitt included Charles *Pitt and **Thomas John Dibdin** (1771–1841), who was also an actor, playwright, and songwriter. He first appeared on stage (at the age of four) at Drury Lane as Cupid to the Venus of Mrs Siddons. After experience in the provinces he achieved fame as the author of such stirring naval dramas as *The Mouth of the Nile* (1798), *Naval Pillar* (1799), and *Nelson's Glory* (1805). His pantomimes, notably *Mother Goose* (1806), were also highly acclaimed. He speculated disastrously with the Surrey Theatre and briefly managed the Haymarket.

Dickens, Charles (John Huffam) (1812–70) British novelist, who was an enthusiastic amateur actor and, with his friends, gave performances in his private theatre at *Tavistock House, his home in London. As an actor he was praised for his portrayal of comic roles and for his many solo dramatic readings of his works both in Britain and the US. Early in his career he wrote several pieces for performance at the St James's Theatre, chiefly operatic burlettas and farces; later he collaborated with Wilkie Collins on *No Thoroughfare*, which was produced by Ben Webster in 1867. More influential, however, have been the numerous stage adaptations of his prose works, including versions of *The Cricket on the Hearth*, *The Old Curiosity Shop*, *Great Expectations*, *The Pickwick Papers*, and *A Tale of Two Cities*. Highly successful musical adaptations in recent years have included Bart's *Oliver!*, the Royal Shakespeare Company's *Nicholas Nickleby*, and *The Mystery of Edwin Drood*.

didascalia A teacher of drama in ancient Greece, or a production itself. The term was also used of various catalogues relating to dramatic entertainments, of which fragments survive.

Diderot, Denis (1713–84) French philosopher, encyclopedist, novelist, essayist, playwright, and critic. The son of a cutler, he led a bohemian existence in the company of Rousseau and others before devoting himself seriously to writing. The *Encyclopédie* (1751–72) is Diderot's major work: his plays, such sentimental bourgeois dramas as *Le Fils naturel* (published 1757; performed 1771 Paris), *Le Père de famille* (published 1758; performed 1761 Paris), and *Est-il bon? Est-il méchant?* (written 1781), form only a small part of his literary output. His dramatic theories, however, contained in such works as *Le Paradoxe sur le comédien* (published 1830; written in the 1770s), strongly influenced European theatre over the next 100 years.

Digges, Dudley (1879–1947) US actor, born in Ireland, who remained in the US after a visit with the Abbey Theatre company in 1904. He joined the newly formed Theatre Guild in 1919, working with them both as actor and director for 11 years. His parts ranged from Mr Zero in Elmer Rice's *The Adding Machine* (1932) to Andrew Undershaft in Shaw's *Major Barbara* (1928). His final performance was as Harry Hope in O'Neill's *The Iceman Cometh* (1946).

Digges, Dudley West (1720–86) British actor. The first actor to play Young Norval in Home's *Douglas* (1756), he was highly acclaimed at the Haymarket as Cato, Wolsey, and in other classic roles.

Dikie, Alexei Denisovich (1889–1955) Soviet actor and director, who studied under Stanislavsky at the Moscow Art Theatre. Later he worked at various theatres, attracting attention for his direction of plays by Faiko, Ostrovsky, Sofronov, and others as well as for his acting in such works as Korneichuk's *Front* (1942) at the Vakhtangov Theatre.

Dillingham, Charles Bancroft (1868–1934) US theatre manager, who became a noted associate of Charles Frohman in New York. As well as fostering the US careers of many leading performers, he presented the first US production of Shaw's *Man and Superman* (1905), opened the Globe Theatre (later the Lunt-Fontanne Theatre), and managed vaudeville at the Hippodrome Theatre.

dimmer An electrical or mechanical means of dimming stage lighting, controlled in the modern theatre from a central computerized dimmer board.

Dionysia The religious festivals held annually in ancient Greece in honour of the god of wine, *Dionysus. Initially the festivals involved simple rites and processions; subsequently, however, a tradition of dramatic presentations developed, most notably at the **City Dionysia** or **Great Dionysia** (held in late March and early April), where the daily entertainment included three tragedies and a satyr-play all by the same author. Such festivals usually concluded in contests for dithyrambs. Key figures in the development of the early Greek festivals included Thespis and Pisistratus. *See also* Lenaea, Rural Dionysia.

Dionysus (*or* Bacchus) The Greek god of nature and wine, whose worship led ultimately to the development of the earliest Greek drama (*see* Dionysia). The rites associated with Dionysus included the wearing of the symbolic phallus, a custom which passed directly into the comic tradition. The supernatural servants of Dionysus, half man and half animal, also had a fundamental influence upon the *satyr-play. *See also* dithyramb.

diorama A type of *panorama, which makes use of special lighting, cut-out scenery, and transparencies to create three-dimensional effects and an impression of movement.

Diphilus of Sinope (d. 290 BC) Greek playwright, author of several important examples of New Comedy. Only titles and fragments of his plays, which influenced Terence and Plautus, survive.

director The person in overall charge of a production, in Britain called the producer until 1956, when it was officially agreed that the British theatre would adopt the US usage. The director co-ordinates all aspects of a show and is responsible for deciding how a particular script is to be interpreted. Until the 20th century the role was variously undertaken by the author, the stage manager, the prompter, or the leading actor. Madame Vestris and David Belasco were among the first to fulfil the role; their successors have included such notable figures as Stanislavsky, Granville-Barker, Copeau, Jouvet, Baty, Dullin, Pitoëff, Piscator, Jessner, Taïrov,

DISGUISING

Okhlopkhov, Vakhtangov, Saint-Denis, Eva Le Gallienne, Strasberg, Kazan, Clurman, Basil Dean, Peter Brook, Peter Hall, and Joan Littlewood.

disguising A form of dramatic entertainment presented at the English Court during the 15th and 16th centuries. Participants in disguisings, which often included music, dancing, and the exchanging of gifts, included the nobility themselves; by the mid-16th century such entertainments were generally referred to as **masks**.

dithyramb A hymn sung in honour of *Dionysus during festivals or banquets in ancient Greece. Performed by a chorus of 50 actors dressed as satyrs and led by the *protagonist, the earliest dithyrambs, which were improvised, were presented in the 7th century BC; the form acquired literary status later through the efforts of Arion of Lesbos and became a part of the Dionysia, during which poets would compete against each other in the form. Lasus of Hermione was the most celebrated composer of dithyrambs; fragments by other writers survive. Ultimately the form was supplanted by tragedy.

Dmitrevsky, Ivan Afanasyevich (1733–1821) Russian actor and administrator, who dominated the St Petersburg theatre. He began as an amateur with Volkov and later performed with Sumarokov's company before visiting Paris to study the French theatre. He excelled in plays by Molière, Sumarokov, and Fonvizin.

Dmitriev, Vladimir Vladimirovich (1900–48) Soviet stage designer, who established a strong reputation for his work at the Moscow Art Theatre and the Vakhtangov Theatre before his early death. He was particularly acclaimed for his settings for plays by Ostrovsky and Gorky and for Virta's *Our Daily Bread* (1947).

Dmitri of Rostov (Daniel Tuptalo; 1651–1709) Russian churchman and playwright, who became a bishop and was canonized in 1757. He was the author of six verse plays on religious themes, notably *The Nativity Play*, *The Penitent Sinner*, and *The Resurrection of Christ*.

Döbbelin, Karl Theophil (1727–93) German actor-manager, who began as a strolling player and later led his own troupe in Berlin. His company, established after encouragement from Gottsched, was noted for its production of plays by Lessing, including a much-acclaimed *Minna von Barnhelm* (1768) and a less successful *Nathan der Weise* (1783), in which Döbbelin played the leading role in his customary ranting style.

Dockstader, Lew (George Alfred Clapp; 1856–1924) US minstrel and vaudeville performer, who appeared with amateur blackface troupes in Hartford, Connecticut before turning professional and eventually teaming up with the Dockstader Brothers Minstrels in 1876. 10 years later his attempt to run his own theatre in New York failed, but he continued in partnership with George Primrose (1952–1919), working the vaudeville circuit and revitalizing the act by introducing topical satire.

Dock Street Theatre A theatre in Dock Street, Charleston, South Carolina, which opened in 1736 with Farquhar's *The Recruiting Officer*, but closed only a year later.

A second **Dock Street Theatre** opened in 1937 on the site with the same opening bill, produced by the resident **Footlight Players**. Together with the Carolina Art Association, the Players maintained control of the theatre until 1941, when the Players moved to another building and the Art Association formed its own company for Dock Street. The Players returned to the theatre in 1952 and since 1958 have had sole control of the venue.

Docteur amoureux, Le A partly improvised farce by *Molière, in the Italian style. The play had already been seen by provincial audiences when it was staged before Louis XIV in 1658, following a performance of Pierre Corneille's *Nicomède* by Molière's troupe: its success earned the company the patronage of the king.

Doctor's Dilemma, The A tragi-comedy by G B *Shaw. First performance: Royal Court Theatre, 1906. Sir Colenzo Ridgeon has the choice of treating either a dissolute artist or a fellow general practitioner; his indecision is used to attack contemporary medical ethics.

documentary theatre A form of theatre, also known as **Theatre of Fact**, in which productions are closely based upon historical truth. Although the genre has its roots in the classical theatre, it only developed as a recognizable theatrical form in the 1950s and 1960s, notably in Germany with the drama of Hochhuth and Weiss among others. Subsequently it has become a major feature of contemporary drama, often concentrating upon local history. *See also* Living Newspaper.

Dodd, James (1734–96) British actor, who served a long provincial apprenticeship before Garrick engaged him at Drury Lane in 1765. He established himself as the natural successor to Colley Cibber in playing foppish roles, creating the role of Sir Benjamin Backbite in *The School for Scandal* and being acclaimed as Aguecheek in *Twelfth Night*.

Dodsley, Robert (1703–64) English playwright and bookseller. In 1735, through Pope's influence, his play *The Toy Shop* was staged at Covent Garden with great success, after which he set up as a publisher. He continued to write plays, including *The King and the Miller of Mansfield* (1737), *The Blind Beggar of Bethnal Green* (1741), and

the tragedy *Cleone*, which was well received in 1758. As a publisher his list contained works by Dr Johnson, Goldsmith, and others.

dog drama A form of drama popular in the 19th century, in which live dogs appeared on stage as part of the cast. In Britain dog drama was a huge success when presented at Drury Lane; plays written specially to include canine performers included Pixérécourt's celebrated *Le Chien de Montargis, ou la Fôret de Bondy* (1814).

Doggett, Thomas (c. 1670–1721) British actor, who was the most original comedian of his day. Ben in *Love for Love* (1695) and Fondlewife in *The Old Bachelor* (1693) were both written for him by Congreve. In 1710 he joined Colley Cibber and Wilks as managers of Drury Lane, but resigned in protest on the admission of Barton Booth as fourth shareholder. His name is familiar in Doggett's Coat and Badge, a sculling prize he founded on the accession of George I; it is still competed for by Thames watermen on 1 August.

Doherty, Brian *See* Shaw Festival.

Dolce, Lodovico (1508–68) Italian playwright, noted for the violence of his plays. His notoriously bloody tragedies, most of which were derived from classical subjects, include *Giocasta*; other more sophisticated works include *Marianna* (1565).

Doll's House, A (*Et Dukkehjem*) A tragedy by Henrik *Ibsen. First performance: Copenhagen, 1879. The central character in the play, which caused a sensation, is Nora Helmer, who is torn between her own feelings and her trust in authority; she ultimately leaves her husband in an attempt to establish her own independence.

Dominion Drama Festival A major theatre festival founded in Canada in 1933. Presented at different locations each year, the festival did much to stimulate the native Canadian theatre before finally coming to an end in 1978.

Dominique *See* Biancolelli, Giuseppe Domenico.

Don Carlos, Infant von Spanien A romantic tragedy by Friedrich von *Schiller. First performance: 1789. Set in the time of Philip II of Spain, *Don Carlos* was Schiller's first historical drama and also his first written in blank verse.

Don Juan A stock character of the Spanish theatrical tradition, the subject of numerous amorous adventures. Descended from various legendary figures, Don Juan, who is usually depicted as an arrogant self-indulgent lover, was first introduced to the stage in Tirso de Molina's *El Burlador de Sevilla y Convidado de Piedra* (1630). In this piece Don Juan is punished for his wrongdoing by a statue that accepts his mocking invitation to share supper with him. Don Juan has subsequently appeared in the theatrical traditions of many different countries, inspiring works by Molière, Goldoni, Rostand, Shaw, Tennessee Williams, and other playwrights, as well as Mozart's opera *Don Giovanni.*

Donmar Warehouse Theatre A small theatre in Earlham Street, Covent Garden, London, originally the vat room of a large brewery, and later a banana warehouse. It was converted by Donald Albery, who named it after himself and the actress Margaret Fontaine. In 1977 the Donmar became the studio theatre in London of The Royal Shakespeare Company until their move to the Barbican in 1982. Recent productions have included Mustapha Matura's *Trinidad Sisters* (1988), based on Chekhov. It has an open stage and seats 244 people.

Doone, Rupert *See* Group Theatre.

Dorset Garden Theatre A theatre on the bank of the Thames, off Fleet Street in London, opened in 1671 by Henry Harris and Thomas Betterton. Originally an idea of Sir William Davenant, the theatre (initially called the **Duke of York's House**) may have been the work of Sir Christopher Wren but was somewhat flawed by its peculiarly narrow auditorium. Early productions there included the plays of Dryden and Davenant's version of *Macbeth* (1673), which established the theatre as a venue for opera. Betterton triumphed in several works by Shadwell and Mrs Barry was acclaimed in plays by Otway, notably *Venice Preserv'd* (1681); other writers connected with the theatre included Aphra Behn, Sir George Etherege, and Sir William Wycherley. Financial considerations, however, led to the amalgamation of the resident company with that at Drury Lane in 1682 and the virtual end of productions at Dorset Garden. Renamed the Queen's Theatre in 1687, it was later used for circus-type entertainments before demolition in 1709.

Dorst, Tankred (1925-) German playwright, who began his career in puppet theatre but later developed as a leading writer of the Theatre of the Absurd and of Expressionist drama. *Grosse Schmährede an der Stadtmauer* (Great Vituperation at the City Wall; 1961) was acclaimed for its echoes of Brecht's plays, while *Toller* (1968) was based on events in the life of Ernst Toller. *Eiszeit* (Ice Age; 1973) drew on the experiences of Knut Hamsun.

Dorval, Marie-Thomase-Amélie (1798 – 1849) French actress, who first appeared on stage as a child and later achieved fame when she appeared as Amélie in *Trente Ans, ou la Vie d'un joueur* (1827) alongside Frédérick. In 1835 she arrived at the Comédie-Française in *Chatterton* by Vigny, who was her lover; shortly after, however, she she left the company, partly due to the hostility of Mlle Mars. In 1847 she had a further success in Racine's *Phèdre* at the Odéon but subsequently died in poverty.

Dossenus A stock character of the Roman *atellana*. He was probably a hunchback and shared some of the traits of character of *Manducus.

Dostoevsky, Fyodor Mikhailovich (1821–81) Russian novelist, whose celebrated novels dealing with both moral and political themes have also had some success in stage adaptations. Of these the most notable have included *The Idiot* (acclaimed at the Old Vic in 1970 in a version by Simon Gray), *The Brothers Karamazov*, and *Crime and Punishment*.

Dotrice, Roy (1925-) British actor, born in Guernsey, who spent 10 years in provincial repertory companies before joining the Stratford-upon-Avon company in 1958. He remained for seven years, during which he also appeared at the Aldwych Theatre in roles ranging from Caliban to John of Gaunt. He has since given numerous solo performances in many countries, most notably as Aubrey in *Brief Lives*.

Dottore, Il A character of the *commedia dell'arte*, often appearing as a counterpart to *Pantalone. Conventionally portrayed as a verbose physician or lawyer called **Graziano**, Il Dottore could be played with or without a mask and usually appeared dressed in black with a white ruff. The character did not pass into the English harlequinade but was further developed in the French theatre in the plays of Molière.

double masque *See* masque.

Douglass, David (d. 1786) US actor-manager, who founded the celebrated *American Company in New York. He installed the troupe successively in Cruger's Wharf, the Chapel Street Theatre, and in John Street before erecting for them the first permanent theatre in the US – the Southwark Theatre in Philadelphia. His productions included Thomas Godfrey's *The Prince of Parthia* (1967), the first native US tragedy; his actors included John Henry.

Downes, John (fl. 1662–1710) British stage prompter and writer. When the Lincoln's Inn Fields Theatre opened in 1661, Downes was engaged as prompter. In 1708 he published *Roscius Anglicanus or an Historical Review of the Stage*, a valuable source of information about early Restoration drama.

downstage *See* stage direction.

Downstage Theatre A theatrical company based in Wellington, New Zealand. Founded in 1964 by a group of playwrights and actors, it presented works by local writers as a café-theatre before moving into the **Hannah Playhouse** in 1970. Designers with the company have contributed greatly to the development of stage design in New Zealand.

Dowton, William (1764–1851) British actor, who abandoned his apprenticeship as an architect to become a strolling player. After several years spent touring, he made his debut at Drury Lane as Sheva in *The Jew* by Richard Cumberland. He soon became a respected character-actor, playing parts like Hardcastle in *She Stoops to Conquer* and Sir Hugh Evans in *The Merry Wives of Windsor*. He was also critically acclaimed for performances as Falstaff.

D'Oyly Carte, Richard (1844–1901) British impresario. As a concert agent he produced Gilbert and Sullivan's *Trial by Jury* at the Royal Theatre in 1875; the success of this and other Gilbert and Sullivan works enabled him to build the *Savoy Theatre and to become involved in the management of several provincial theatres. He also built the Royal English Opera House (now the Palace Theatre).

Drachmann, Holger Henrik Herholdt (1846–1908) Danish poet, novelist, and playwright, who is usually remembered for his passionate lyrical poetry, which was initially influenced by Georg Brandes but later extolled patriotism and romanticism. Of his dramatic works the most significant is the fantasy *Der var en Gang* (Once Upon a Time; 1885), for which Peter Lange-Muller wrote the music; others include several melodramas and the plays *Brav Karl* (1888) and *Der gronne Haab* (Green Hope; 1903).

drag artist *See* female impersonator.

Drake, Alfred (Alfred Caparro; 1914-) US actor, who became a noted star of musical comedy. In 1943 he was acclaimed as Curly in *Oklahoma!*; other roles have included Macheath in *Beggar's Holiday* (1946), the king in *The King and I* (1953), and Shakespearean parts.

Drama and Comedy, Theatre of *See* Taganka Theatre.

drama school An institution at which persons intending to pursue a career in the theatre receive training. Formerly, all training in the theatre was acquired through actual experience, the first specialist schools only being founded in the late 18th century. The *Conservatoire National d'Art Dramatique, established in Paris in 1786, was among the first great schools; leading establishments of the same kind founded since then include the *Lunacharsky State Institute of Theatre Art in the USSR, the *London Academy of Music and Dramatic Art, the *Royal Academy of Dramatic Art, and the *Central School of Speech and Drama in Britain, and the *American Academy of Dramatic Arts in the US. Alternatively, aspiring actors and directors can receive an education in drama at various *university drama departments.

dramatis personae The members of the cast in a particular production, or – more commonly – the characters they portray.

drame A form of French drama in which elements of comedy and tragedy were combined in the dramatization of middle-class issues and concerns. First defined by Diderot, the *drame* was descended from the *comédie larmoyante* and *tragédie-Bougeoise* of Voltaire; other writers of the genre included Sedaine and Mercier.

Draper, Ruth (1884–1956) US actress, who was acclaimed in her own dramatic monologues. She toured widely in such monologues as 'Opening a Bazaar', 'Showing the Garden', 'Three Generations', 'Mr Clifford and Three Women', and 'An English House Party'.

drapery setting *See* curtain set.

drawing-room drama A play that takes place largely in a genteel domestic setting, typically examining middle-class values.

Dream Play, A (*Ett drömspel*) A play by August *Strindberg, written in 1902. First performance: 1907. Written during the course of his third marriage, the play, which is highly poetic, is a passionate debate upon the unreality of existence and is often quoted for its conclusion "Mankind's to be pitied".

dress circle *See* auditorium.

dressing-room One or more rooms situated in the backstage area of a theatre where actors may put on their costumes and make-up; they also rest in their dressing rooms between appearances and after performances.

Dressler, Marie (Leila Koeber; 1871–1934) US star of vaudeville, best remembered for the song 'Heaven Will Protect the Working Girl' from the musical *Tilly's Nightmare* (1894). In 1914 she left the theatre to work in films.

dress rehearsal A rehearsal at which members of the cast appear in full costume and make-up as though for an actual performance; it is usually the final rehearsal before the opening night.

Drew, Mrs John (Louisa Lane; 1820–97) US actress and manager, born in London into an acting family, who was taken to the US by her mother and made her debut as the Duke of York in *Richard III* at the Walnut Street Theatre, Philadelphia, in 1827. Subsequently she appeared throughout the US alongside such notable actors as the elder Edwin Booth, Joseph Jefferson, and Edwin Forrest in such roles as Lady Macbeth. Her most celebrated role was Mrs Malaprop in Sheridan's *The Rivals* in which part she frequently toured, but her chief claim to fame was her forceful management of Philadelphia's Arch Street Theatre from 1869 to 1892, during which time she produced a consistently high standard of classic and contemporary drama.

Her son, **John Drew** (1853–1927), took to the stage, somewhat reluctantly, at his mother's theatre in Philadelphia in 1873. Invited to New York by Augustin Daly, he made his debut in 1875 and subsequently became well-known as a comedian and was referred to as 'the first gentleman of the stage'. He appeared several times in London and was much admired as Petruchio in *The Taming of the Shrew*. Later he worked for Charles Frohman, his parts including the title role in Maugham's *Jack Straw* (1908) and Major Arthur Pendennis in a version of Thackeray's novel (1916).

Mrs John Drew's daughter, **Georgiana (Emma) Drew** (1856–92), made her debut at her mother's Arch Street Theatre in 1872.

She later joined Daly's company in New York, opening as Mary Standish in his play *Pique*. In 1876 she married fellow-actor Maurice *Barrymore and became the mother of the three famous Barrymores – Ethel, John, and Lionel. She continued to act in Modjeska's and Charles Frohman's companies until her premature death.

Dr Faustus, The Tragical History of A tragedy in blank verse by Christopher *Marlowe. First performance: London, c. 1588. Based upon the German Faust legend, the play focuses on the aspiration and subsequent downfall of Dr Faustus, who sells his soul to the Devil in exchange for magical powers.

Drinkwater, John (1882–1937) British poet, playwright, actor, and manager, a founder member of the Birmingham Repertory Theatre. His early poetic dramas, of which the most successful was *X=O; a Night of the Trojan War* (1917), were followed by such acclaimed plays as *Abraham Lincoln* (1919) and the comedy *Bird in Hand* (1927) as well as several historical dramas.

droll A short comic entertainment that developed in England during the Commonwealth, when more elaborate drama was difficult to present without attracting the hostile attention of the Puritan authorities. It often consisted of an extract from a longer play and usually included a dance; the most famous performer of drolls was Robert *Cox.

drop *See* cloth.

Drottningholm Theatre A theatre, also run as a museum, in a royal palace near Stockholm, built in 1766. Originally used by a French company, it enjoyed a considerable reputation under Gustaf III from 1772 to 1792, when productions there were designed by Louis-Jean Desprey. It was little used in the 19th century and restored in

1921, since when it has been an occasional venue for opera. It contains well-preserved items of stage machinery and scenery.

drum-and-shaft system An arrangement of lines attached to a central drum above the stage, enabling several heavy pieces of scenery to be moved at the same time. Widely used in the Renaissance and Baroque theatre, the system was gradually superseded by machinery capable of moving items of scenery simultaneously but independently of each other.

Druriolanus, Augustus See Harris, Sir Augustus.

Drury Lane (Theatre Royal) The oldest and most famous of London's theatres. Opened in 1663, the theatre is (with Covent Garden) one of Britain's two *patent theatres, having been granted its charter by Charles II in 1662. The original theatre was built by Thomas Killigrew and saw the first stage appearance of Nell Gwynn in 1665 before being burnt down seven years later. Rebuilt to a design by Sir Christopher Wren in 1674 and with John Dryden as resident playwright, the theatre was plagued by rifts in the management (notably during the tenure of Christopher Rich) but achieved stability in 1711 under the celebrated management of Colley Cibber, Thomas Doggett, and Robert Wilkes. David Garrick first appeared there in 1742 and took over in 1746. During the following 30 years he presided over many notable productions; in 1776 Sheridan succeeded him, beginning his term by staging the first production of The School for Scandal. Sarah Siddons became a firm favourite at Drury Lane, as did John Kemble, who first appeared there in Hamlet in 1789.

Rebuilt in 1791–94, burnt down in 1809, and again reopened in 1812, the theatre staged increasingly varied productions, from classic plays and melodrama to pantomime and concerts. Despite successful seasons by

Edmund Kean (1814–20) and William Macready (1841–43), the theatre's fortunes declined until 1880 when the impresario Augustus Harris and his successor Arthur Collins revived interest with large-scale productions of opera and ballet and spectacular melodramas. In recent years the theatre has been the venue for a number of successful musicals, notably Ivor Novello's Glamorous Night (1935) and The Dancing Years (1939), Oklahoma! (1947–51), South Pacific (1951–53), The King and I (1953–58), My Fair Lady (1958–63), A Chorus Line (1976–79), and 42nd Street (1984–). See also ghosts.

Druten, John Van See Van Druten, John.

Dryden, John (1631–1700) English poet, critic, and playwright, who wrote the most important examples of the genre of English heroic drama. The author of nearly 30 plays in a variety of styles, he is now usually remembered for the tragedy *All for Love and for such elegant comedies as *Marriage à la Mode, as well as for his critical writing. His heroic drama Almanzor and Almahide was satirized by Buckingham in The Rehearsal. Several of his works have been successfully revived in the 20th century.

Principal dramatic works:

The Wild Gallant: 1663.

The Rival Ladies: 1664.

The Indian Queen: 1664 (with Sir Robert Howard).

The Indian Emperor: 1665.

Secret Love; or, the Maiden Queen: 1667.

Sir Martin Mar-All; or, the Feign'd Innocence: 1667.

An Evening's Love; or, the Mock Astrologer: 1668.

Tyrannic Love; or, the Royal Martyr: 1669.

Almanzor and Almahide; or, the Conquest of Granada: 1670–71.

Marriage à la Mode: 1671.

The Assignation; or, Love in a Nunnery: 1672.

Amboyna; or, the Cruelties of the Dutch to the English Merchants: 1673.

Aureng-Zebe: 1675.
All for Love; or, the World Well Lost: 1677.
Amphitryon: 1690.

Držić, Marin (1508–67) Yugoslavian playwright, author of several pastorals and comedies written in the vernacular. Such comedies as *Uncle Maroje* (1550) were produced at Dubrovnik and have been revived in the 20th century.

Dubé, Marcel (1930-) French-Canadian playwright, whose most successful works include adaptations in French of major contemporary US dramas, notably the plays of Arthur Miller. His own plays range from *Le Bal triste* (1950), and *Zone* (1953), which were both influenced by socially-aware US drama, to the poetic *Florence* (1961), the musical comedy *Il est une saison* (1965), and the tragedy *Au Retour des oies blanches* (The White Geese; 1966), which is regarded as his finest work. He was closely associated for some years with the Théâtre du Nouveau Monde.

Dublin Roscius *See* Brooke, Gustavus Vaughan.

Dublin Theatre Festival A major theatre festival founded in Dublin in 1957. Taking place in October each year, the festival involves all of Dublin's theatres and includes a healthy fringe; notable productions have included plays by O'Casey, Synge, Wilde, Tennessee Williams, and Yeats. The festival of 1958 was cancelled due to the controversy over plans to present O'Casey's *The Drums of Father Ned*; in recent years the emphasis has been upon new Irish drama.

Duchess of Malfi, The A tragedy in blank verse by John *Webster. First performance: London, c. 1619. The play explores the predicament of the widowed Duchess, who secretly marries her steward in defiance of her two brothers and is then hounded to her death by the malcontent Bosola.

Duchess Theatre A Tudor Gothic style theatre in Catherine Street, off the Strand in London. It opened in 1929 under the joint management of Jack de Leon and his sister Delia; a year later theatre history was made here when the curtain was rung down before the close of the first performance of *The Intimate Revue* – the shortest run of any London production. J B Priestley became associated with the theatre in the 1930s with the presentation of such plays as *Eden End* (1934) and *Time and the Conways* (1937). In 1935 Emlyn Williams appeared in his own play *Night Must Fall*, which ran for over a year, while T S Eliot's *Murder in the Cathedral* received its first West End production at the Duchess in 1936. The outbreak of World War II interrupted the run of Emlyn Williams's *The Corn is Green*; the major success of the war years was Noël Coward's *Blithe Spirit* (1942), first produced at the Piccadilly Theatre. Post-war successes have included plays by Rattigan, Agatha Christie, and William Douglas Home. In 1974 the nude revue *Oh, Calcutta!* transferred from the Royalty Theatre and ran until 1980. In 1987 the theatre played temporary host to the Players' Theatre.

Ducis, Jean-François (1733–1816) French playwright, remembered for his adaptations of Shakespeare. Working from inferior translations, he restyled such plays as *Hamlet* (1769) and *Othello* (1792) to conform with the rules of classical tragedy and the tastes of his audience. Ducis's own tragedies, which include *Oedipe chez Admète* (1778) and *Abufar* (1795), are of little worth.

Duclos, Mlle (Marie-Anne de Châteauneuf; 1668–1748) French actress, who inherited many of the great tragic roles formerly played by Mlle Champmeslé at the Comédie-Française. Renowned for her tempestuous character, she made many enemies amongst the troupe, especially over her vindictive treatment of Adrienne Lecouvreur.

Du Croisy (Philibert Gassot; c. 1625–95) French actor, who began his career in the provinces before joining Molière's company at the Petit-Bourbon in 1659. A large man, he appeared in several of Molière's plays, notably as the first Tartuffe (originally called Panulph) in 1667.

Ducrow, Andrew (1793–1842) British equestrian performer, who was chief equestrian and rope dancer at *Astley's Amphitheatre. In 1823 he played in Planché's *Cortez* at Covent Garden; the following year he appeared at Drury Lane. He became joint owner of Astley's in 1825 and never recovered from its destruction in 1841.

Duel of Angels (*Pour Lucrèce*) Jean *Giraudoux's last play, written in 1944. First performance: Paris, 1953. Translated by Christopher Fry, the play was produced in London in 1958 with Vivien Leigh as Paola, who tricks the virtuous Lucille into believing that she has committed adultery, driving her ultimately to suicide.

Duenna, The A comedy interspersed with songs by *Sheridan. First performance: Covent Garden, 1775. With music by Sheridan's father-in-law, Thomas Linley, the play revolves around the intrigues of Donna Louisa as she escapes a marriage she does not wish.

Duff, Mrs (Mary Ann Dyke; 1794–1857) US actress, born in London, who began her career as a dancer in Dublin. In 1810, with her second husband – John Duff (1787–1831) – she went to Boston where they opened as Romeo and Juliet. In 1812 they went to Philadelphia where she also achieved some distinction, but never attracted the same popularity in New York when she made her debut there as Hermione in Philips's *The Distressed Mother* in 1823. She toured extensively after her husband's death, remarried twice, and appeared in New Orleans in 1836 in the title role of Rowe's *The Tragedy of Jane Shore* and as Portia in *The Merchant of Venice*.

Dufresne (Abraham-Alexis Quinault; 1693–1767) French actor, sometimes called **Defresne**, who was the most important member of a family of actors who appeared at the Comédie-Française. Dufresne joined the company in 1712 and excelled in heroic roles, eventually succeeding Beaubour in such roles in 1718. His most celebrated parts included the title role in *Oedipe* (1718) by Voltaire and the central character in *Le Glorieux* (1732) by Destouches.

His wife, **Mlle Deseine** (1705–67), was also a popular actress but retired in 1736 due to ill health.

Dufresne, Charles (c. 1611–c. 1684) French actor-manager, whose company – regarded as one of the best in France – combined with the Illustre-Théâtre of Molière in about 1644. Dufresne subsequently handed over the leadership of the amalgamated troupe to Molière but continued to appear as an actor until 1659.

Dufresny, Charles Rivière (1648–1724) French playwright, a great-grandson of Henri IV. Dufresny's first plays were produced by the Comédie-Italienne; his best comedies, however, were those written for the Comédie-Française in the early 18th century, notably *L'Esprit de contradiction* (1700), *Le Double Veuvage* (1702), and *La Coquette du village* (1715).

Dugazon (Jean-Baptiste-Henri Gourgaud; 1746–1509) French actor, who excelled in comic roles at the Comédie-Française, which he joined in 1771. One of the first members of the acting school that became the Conservatoire in 1793, he was particularly successful in the plays of Scarron.

Duke of York's House See Dorset Garden Theatre.

Duke of York's Theatre The first theatre to be built in St Martin's Lane, London. It opened in 1892 as the **Trafalgar Square Theatre**, the name being changed to the Duke of York's in 1895. From 1897 it came under the management of Charles Froham; Marie Tempest, Gerald Du Maurier, and Irene Vanbrugh all appeared here in the early 1900s. Frohman also presented several plays by J M Barrie, notably *The Admirable Crichton* (1902) and *Peter Pan*, which was staged every Christmas from 1904 to 1914. He was less successful in his attempt to introduce the repertory system to London in 1910; among the plays he staged that year were G B Shaw's *Misalliance*, John Galsworthy's *Justice*, Granville Barker's *The Madras House*, and a revival of Pinero's *Trelawny of the 'Wells'*. In 1916 Jean Webster's *Daddy Long-Legs* ran for 514 performances. Under Violet Melnotte's management (1923–28) there followed the successful revue (written mainly by Noël Coward) *London Calling*. Roland Pertwee's *Is Your Honeymoon Really Necessary?* (1944) provided the theatre with the longest run; later productions have included Frank Marcus's *The Killing of Sister George* (1965), Arthur Miller's *The Price* (1969), and Alan Ayckbourn's *How the Other Half Loves* (1988). The Duke of York's was purchased by Capital Radio in 1978 and reopened as a theatre in 1980.

Dukes, Ashley (1885–1959) British playwright, theatre critic, and manager, who founded the Mercury Theatre in Notting Hill Gate, London, where he presented many important new British and foreign plays. He adapted many foreign works himself, notably Fernando de Rojas's *La Celestina* as *The Matchmaker's Arms* (1930), Sternheim's *Die Marquise von Arcis* as *The Mask of Virtue* (1935), and Machiavelli's *Mandragola* (1939); of his own plays the most successful was *The Man With a Load of Mischief* (1924). His wife was the ballet dancer Marie Rambert.

Duke's Theatre *See* Holborn Theatre.

Dullin, Charles (1885–1949) French actor and producer, who founded a famous experimental company in 1919 and subsequently installed it at his own Théâtre de l'Atelier in Paris. He began his career under Copeau at the Vieux-Colombier and later won acclaim for his productions of both French classics and experimental dramas by such authors as Pirandello and Cocteau. He became a director at the Comédie-Française in 1936 and his pupils included Jean-Louis Barrault; as an actor he triumphed over his own physical deformity in such roles as Harpagon in Molière's *L'Avare*.

Dumas, Alexandre (Dumas *père*; 1802–70) French novelist and playwright, son of a Napoleonic general. Dumas made his name with *Henri III et sa cour* (1829), the first of a series of spectacular melodramas on historical and romantic themes, which included *Antony* (1831), *La Tour de Nesle* (1832), and *Kean, ou Désordre et génie* (1836). In retrospect, however, Dumas *père* is more widely admired for his novels, notably *Les Trois Mousquetaires* (The Three Musketeers; 1844) and *Le Comte de Monte Cristo* (The Count of Monte Cristo; 1844–45), both of which were adapted for the theatre.

His illegitimate son, **Alexandre Dumas** (Dumas *fils*; 1824–95) was also a playwright and novelist, best known for the play *La Dame aux camélias* (1852; translated as *The *Lady of the Camellias* or *Camille*). His subsequent plays were moralizing social dramas in which he preached against such evils as the destruction of marriage and family life by illicit liaisons and prostitution. *Le Fils naturel* (1858) and *Un père prodigue* (1859) are exposés of the shame and misery caused by the stigma of illegitimacy and give some insight into Dumas's attitude to his father.

Du Maurier, Sir Gerald (Hubert Edward) (1873–1934) British actor-manager, son of the artist and writer George Du Maurier and father of the novelist Daphne du Maurier. After appearances with Tree's company he first came to public attention in 1902 in *The Admirable Crichton* at the Duke of York's Theatre and went on to appear in many of Barrie's other plays. He achieved lasting fame as Raffles, the gentleman cracksman, in 1906; in 1910 went into management with Frank Curzon at Wyndham's Theatre, specializing in light comedy. Subsequently he moved to the St James's Theatre where he played in *The Last of Mrs Cheyney* (1925).

dumb show *See* mime.

Dumb Waiter, The A one-act play by Harold *Pinter. First performance: Hampstead Theatre Club, 1960. About two hired gangsters waiting for their orders to kill an as yet unknown victim, the play is a simple yet powerful study of a relationship under pressure, genuinely a comedy of menace.

Dumesnil, Mlle (Marie-Françoise Marchand; 1713–1803) French actress, who was highly regarded for her passionate performances in the tragedies of Corneille, Racine, and Voltaire. She joined the Comédie-Française in 1737; her greatest successes there included the title role in Voltaire's *Mérope* (1743). Late in life she published her memoirs in reply to criticisms by Mlle Clairon.

Dunlap, William (1766–1839) US playwright and manager, who was one of the first dominant figures to emerge in the early development of US theatre. He studied art in London and wrote his first play (in New York) in 1787; his second, *The Father; or, American Shandyism* (1789) established his reputation while the tragedy *Leicester* (1794) indicated his versatility. He became a manager of the American Company in 1796 and opened the Park Theatre – with Hodgkinson – in 1798, productions there including his *André*, which was the first US tragedy on strictly native themes. Disruption caused by yellow fever epidemics and financial pressures led to his bankruptcy in 1805, but he remained assistant manager at the Park Theatre until 1812; subsequently he organized a US tour by George Fredericke Cooke and wrote a *History of the American Theatre* (1832).

Dunlop, Frank (1927-) British director, who founded the Young Vic in 1970 and remained as its director and guiding light until 1974 when the company became wholly independent of the National Theatre. He continued to direct there and elsewhere until, in 1984, he was appointed director of the Edinburgh Festival. Productions for which he won particular acclaim at the Young Vic included Molière's *Scapino*, *Comedy of Errors*, and *Joseph and his Amazing Technicolour Dreamcoat*. He has also worked at the Nottingham Playhouse (1963–64), the National Theatre, and with the Royal Shakespeare Company.

Dunnock, Mildred (1900-) US actress, who studied with Lee Strasberg and Elia Kazan and mader her New York debut in 1932. She had her first big success in 1949 as Linda Loman in *Death of a Salesman*; subsequent roles included Gina in *The Wild Duck* (1951) and Big Mama in *Cat on a Hot Tin Roof* (1955), as well as parts in *The Milk Train Doesn't Stop Here Anymore* (1962) and *The Glass Menagerie* (1966).

Dunsany, Edward John Moreton Drax Plunkett, Lord (1878–1957) Irish playwright. His first play, *The Glittering Gate* (1907), was written for the Abbey Theatre at the request of W B Yeats; several of his later plays were also staged there. His many other plays include *The Gods of the Mountain* (1911) and *If* (1921).

Dunville, Thomas Edward (1870–1924) British music hall comedian, who, after his London debut at Gatti's in 1890, became famous as an eccentric comedian. Sporting ludicrous clothes and clownish make-up, he sang such equally ludicrous songs as 'Dinky Doo'. Successful in variety and pantomime for 30 years, he drowned himself in a fit of depression after his popularity had waned.

duologue A short theatrical presentation or single scene in which only two actors deliver lines (although they may be supported by other silent performers). The form became popular in Germany during the late 18th century as part of triple bills and remains a common feature of modern drama.

Du Parc, Mlle (Marquise-Thérèse de Gorla; 1633–68) French actress, who appeared with Molière's troupe before transferring to the Hôtel de Bourgogne. There she excelled in the tragedies of Racine, notably as Andromaque (1667). She joined Molière's company in 1653 after marrying the comic actor René Berthelot (c. 1630–64), who – known as **Gros-René** due to his bulk – had been with Molière since 1648. She died in childbirth; scurrilous rumours had it that she was in fact poisoned by Racine, her lover.

Durang, Christopher (1949-) US playwright, who has established a strong reputation for his satirical plays. His best-known works include *I Don't Generally Like Poetry But Have You Read 'Trees'* (1972), *The Vietnamization of New Jersey* (1977), *Sister Mary Ignatius Explains It All For You* (1979), in which four former students exact their revenge upon the nun who taught them, and *Laughing Wild* (1987).

Durante, Jimmy (James Francis Durante; 1893–1980) US actor and singer, familiarly known as 'Schnozzle', who started as a honky-tonk pianist in 1910, eventually forming a crazy musical trio that appeared in musicals up to 1931. He continued on his own in such shows as *Strike Me Pink* (1933) and became increasingly famous in films and cabarets.

Duras, Marguerite (1914-) French novelist, playwright, and screenwriter, who made her name with the film script for *Hiroshima mon amour* (1959). Born in Indochina, she moved to Paris in 1932. Her plays explore a variety of themes – solitude, futility, lack of communication, crime – and are generally associated with the Theatre of the Absurd. *Savannah Bay*, in which an ageing actress reflects upon her daughter's death by drowning, was written for Madeleine Renaud.

Principal dramatic works:
Le Square: 1956.
Les Viaducs de la Seine-et-Oise: 1960; translated as *The Viaduct*.
Les Eaux et les forêts: 1965.
Des Journées entières dans les arbres: 1965; translated as *Days in the Trees*.
L'Amante anglaise: 1968; translated as *A Place Without Doors*(or *The Lovers of Viorne*).
India Song: never performed (written 1973).
L'Eden Cinéma: 1977.
Savannah Bay: 1984.

D'Urfey, Thomas (1653–1723) English playwright, who wrote numerous songs, satires, melodramas, and farces; many of his dramatic works were adaptations of earlier pieces. He was prosecuted for profanity in 1698.

Dürrenmatt, Friedrich (1921-) Swiss playwright and novelist, who is regarded, together with Max Frisch, as one of the two most important post-war German-language dramatists. His satirical and often experimental black comedies, noted for their grotesque humour and rapid changes of mood, ridicule hypocrisy, greed, and the inhumanity of post-war bourgeois society. The deliberate formlessness of several of his absurdist dramas, which he justifies in his essay *Theaterprobleme* (1955) reflects his concern with the breakdown of moral values and failure of social responsibility. His most successful plays include *The Visit* (1956), a black comedy that deals with an old woman's revenge against the money-worshipping villagers of her native town, and *The Physicists* (1962) – a bitter tragi-comedy which tackles the theme of the abuse of power. He has also written numerous radio plays, published in the collection *Gesammelte Hörspiele* in 1961, and adapted plays by Strindberg and Shakespeare.

Principal works:

Es steht geschrieben : 1946.

Der Blinde: 1948.

Romulus der Grosse: 1949.

Die Ehe des Herrn Mississippi: 1952; translated as *Mr Mississippi's Marriage*.

Ein Engel kommt nach Babylon: 1953.

Der Besuch der alten Dame: 1956; translated as *The Visit*.

Die Oper einer Privatbank: 1960.

Die Physiker: 1962; translated as *The Physicists*.

Der Meteor: 1966; translated as *The Meteor*.

Du Ryer, Pierre (c. 1605–58) French playwright, born in Paris. Du Ryer's early dramatic works consisted largely of tragicomedies and comedies, notably *Les Vendanges de Suresne* (1633); he subsequently wrote tragedies on biblical and classical themes, influenced by Pierre Corneille. *Scévole* (1644), set in ancient Rome, is generally considered to be his masterpiece.

Duse, Eleonora (1859–1924) Italian actress, who was regarded by G B Shaw and others as superior even to Sarah Bernhardt as a performer of tragedy. Unlike her rival, Duse was capable of great subtlety in her acting, and was ideal as the intense and enigmatic heroines of Ibsen, notably Ellida in *The Lady from the Sea*, Rebecca West in *Rosmersholm*, and Hedda Gabler. She established her reputation in Italy in 1878 with her interpretation of Zola's *Thérèse Raquin* and later toured France and South America and subsequently the world with her own company. In 1894 she fell in love with the poet Gabriele D'Annunzio, who wrote several plays for her, including *La Gioconda* (1898), *La Città morta* (1898), and *Francesca da Rimini* (1902). Other major successes included passionate performances in the plays of Sardou and Dumas *fils*. Internationally acclaimed, she died after coming out of retirement to tour the US.

Dust Hole *See* Scala Theatre.

Dutch Courtesan, The A comedy by John *Marston. First performance: London, c. 1605. In analysing the relationship of the earnest Freewell and the cynical Malheureux, Marston examines the conflict between reason and desire typical of the Renaissance man.

Dybwad, Johanne (1867–1960) Norwegian actress, who became famous for her interpretation of roles in the plays of Ibsen. The leading actress with the Nationaltheatret from 1899, she toured widely in such parts as Nora in *A Doll's House* and Rebecca West in *Rosmersholm*.

E

Eagle Theatre *See* Standard Theatre.

Earl Carroll Theatre A theatre on 50th Street and Seventh Avenue, New York, which was the home of Earl Carroll's *Vanities* in the 1920s. Another theatre of the same name opened on the site in 1931. Seating 3000, it closed due to financial difficulties during the Depression and reopened briefly in 1932 as the Casino and in 1938 as the Casa Mañana.

Earth Spirit (*Erdgeist*) A play by Frank *Wedekind, written in 1893. First performance: 1902. Taking as its main theme the consequences of repressed sexuality, the play introduces the beautiful and sensual Lulu, who eventually turns to prostitution; her story was continued in *Pandora's Box.

Easmon, Raymond Sarif (c. 1930-) African playwright, who has become a dominant figure in the theatre of Sierra Leone. Such satires directed at colonialism and politics as *Dear Parent and Ogre* (1964) have enjoyed enormous popularity throughout Africa.

East, John Marlborough (1860–1924) British actor, manager, and director. After working as an actor he became manager of the Lyric Theatre in Hammersmith in 1892. His productions there of pantomime and melodrama, in which he often appeared himself, established a strong local following; he later worked on productions at the Britannia in Hoxton and at Crystal Palace.

East London Theatre See Royalty Theatre.

East 74th Street Theatre See Phoenix Theatre.

Eastside Playhouse See Phoenix Theatre.

Eberle, Oskar (1902–56) Swiss director, who became famous for his revivals of liturgical drama and other theatrical works of the 16th century. His greatest successes included Calderón's *El gran teatro del mundo* in Einsiedeln and the Lausanne Passion Play as well as his close involvement with various leading drama festivals.

ecclesiastical drama See liturgical drama.

Echegaray, José (1832–1916) Spanish playwright, who received a Nobel Prize in 1905. Such plays as *El locos dios* (The Divine Madman; 1900) and *El gran Galeoto* (1881) employ verse forms to great effect and treat such controversial themes as social tensions and inherited disease.

Eckenberg, Johann Carl (1685–1748) German actor, who was also a talented acrobat and juggler. He was the leader of a company of actors with similar skills and presented entertainments of the most varied kind throughout Europe, offering a popular alternative to the classical repertory of Caroline Neuber and others.

Eddington, Paul (Clark) (1927-) British actor, who made his London debut in *The Tenth Man* (1961) at the Comedy Theatre. He was associated for many years with the Bristol Old Vic company as actor and director, his numerous roles including Palmer Anderson in Iris Murdoch and J B Priestley's *A Severed Head*, which he also played in London and New York. In addition to television work, he has continued to appear regularly in the West End in such plays as Frayn's *Noises Off* (1982) and Rattigan's *The Browning Version* (1988).

Eden Theatre See Phoenix Theatre.

Edgar, David (1948-) British playwright, who began with such topical works as *Dick Deterred* (1973), based on the career of Richard Nixon. His later works include such political and socialist plays as *Destiny* (1976), *Wreckers* (1977), *Maydays* (1983), *Entertaining Strangers* (1985), which is set in Victorian Dorset during a cholera epidemic, and *That Summer* (1987). He also adapted (1980) *Nicholas Nickleby* for the Royal Shakespeare Company.

Edinburgh Civic Theatre Company See Lyceum Theatre.

Edinburgh Festival A leading international festival of music and drama that takes place annually in Edinburgh, for three weeks during August. Founded in 1947, the festival includes, in addition to music, a wide variety of productions by British and foreign companies, including the Royal Shakespeare Company. T S Eliot's *The Cocktail Party* and *The Confidential Clerk*, Thornton Wilder's *The Matchmaker*, and Ray Lawler's *The Unshaven Cheek* all had their first performances at the Edinburgh Festival. In recent years the unofficial Fringe · has developed, featuring miscellaneous and often bizarre theatrical works by both professional and amateur groups.

Edison Theatre A theatre on West 47th Street, New York, which opened in 1970 with the musical *Show Me Where the Good Times Are*. The theatre has also housed such contemporary productions as Kurt Vonnegut's *Happy Birthday, Wanda June* (1970), and the revue *Oh, Calcutta!* (1976).

Edouin, Willie (William Frederick Bryer; 1846–1909) British actor, who began as a child-actor in pantomime. As an adult, his greatest success was in burlesque, in which he appeared in both Britain and the US. He was also manager of the Strand Theatre for some time.

Edward II A history play by Christopher *Marlowe. First performance: London, 1593. The play explores the relationship between the weak king and his favourite, Gaveston, and culminates in the former's violent death; it was a major influence upon Shakespeare's *Richard II*.

Edwardes, George (1852–1915) British theatre manager, of Irish parentage, who worked at the Gaiety Theatre, Dublin, before transferring to the Savoy Theatre in 1881. Having gone into partnership with Hollingshead at the old *Gaiety Theatre in London in 1885, he became sole manager a year later and began a series of musical comedies featuring a handpicked chorus of 'Gaiety Girls'. He opened Daly's Theatre in 1893 and a new Gaiety Theatre in 1903.

Edwards, Hilton (1903–82) British actor and director, noted for his performances in the plays of Shakespeare. After numerous appearances at the Old Vic, he founded the Gate Theatre in Dublin with Micheál MacLiammóir in 1927, directing many plays there and at the Gaiety Theatre himself. He presented *Hamlet* at Elsinore in 1937 and subsequently toured widely with the Gate Theatre company.

Edwards, Richard (c. 1523–66) English playwright and poet. His tragi-comedy of devoted friendship, *Damon and Pithias*, was performed before Elizabeth I by the Children of the Chapel Royal, of which he was Master, probably at Christmas 1565. His other plays include *Palamon and Arcite* (1566).

Edwin, John (1749–90) British actor, who succeeded to the comedy parts formerly played by Ned Shuter at Covent Garden and excelled in the comic light operas and burlesques of O'Keeffe. Although a heavy drinker, he was also acclaimed in a number of Shakespearean character roles.

His son, **John Edwin** (1768–1803), was also an actor, who appeared with his father at the Haymarket and later organized productions for the Earl of Barrymore's private theatre. His wife was the actress **Elizabeth Rebecca Richards** (c. 1771–1854), who appeared at Drury Lane.

eidophusikon A model theatre of the type first developed by Philip James de Louterbourg in London in 1781. With a stage just six feet wide, it was used for the demonstration of various atmospheric lighting effects, chiefly those produced by transparencies, and foreshadowed the interest of designers in lighting during the 19th century.

Eisenhower Theatre A theatre in Washington DC, which opened in 1971 with a revival of Ibsen's *A Doll's House*. Seating 1142, it is a major part of the **John F Kennedy Centre for the Performing Arts**; it has no repertory company but stages touring shows. Productions there have included the world premieres of the musical *Annie* (1977) and Kopit's *Wings* (1978).

Ek, Anders (1916–79) Swedish actor, noted for his strong performances in both classical and modern works. He began his career in Gothenburg after World War II and later appeared with the Kungliga Dramatiska Teatern and in Stockholm, excelling in plays by authors as diverse as Shakespeare, Strindberg, and O'Neill. He was often directed both on stage and on the screen by Ingmar Bergman.

Ekhof, Konrad (1720–78) German actor and director, who played a crucial role in the foundation of a German theatrical tradition. In 1739 he joined Schönemann's company and over the next 17 years evolved a new naturalistic style of acting, appearing in leading roles in German adaptations of French plays. In 1753 he established an Academy of Acting; after it closed he remained with Schönemann's troupe for a time before spending five years with Ackermann's company and then touring with Abel Seyler and becoming a friend of Goethe at Weimar. Subsequently he took over the theatre at Gotha, inviting Iffland to join his company and making his final appearance as the Ghost in *Hamlet*. His greatest acting successes included roles in the domestic dramas of Lillo, Lessing, Diderot, and Edward Moore.

ekklykema An item of stage machinery used in the ancient Greek theatre. It consisted of some type of wheeled platform, upon which actors could be brought on stage.

Ekman, Gösta (1890–1938) Swedish actor, director, and manager, who was noted for his idiosyncratic interpretation of major tragic roles in the plays of Ibsen, Shakespeare, and Shaw. He ran the Svenska Teater in Stockholm from 1913 until it was burnt down in 1925, after which he moved to the Oscarsteater and the Vasateater with equal success.

Elder Statesman, The A poetic drama by T S *Eliot. First performance: Edinburgh Festival, 1958. Based on *Oedipus at Colonus* by Sophocles, it deals with a former prime minister who, faced by the irresponsible actions of his youth, comes to terms with himself.

Electra A tragedy by *Sophocles. First performance: Athens, 409 BC. The play details the events surrounding the death of Orestes and the subsequent anguish of Electra. Another tragedy of the same name was written by *Euripides and was first performed in Athens in 413 BC. It was a highly influential study of the subjects of death and madness.

Elen, Gus (Ernest Augustus Elen; 1862–1940) British music hall singer, who achieved fame as a cockney comedian at the Middlesex Music Hall in 1891. His popular sentimental songs included 'If It Wasn't For the 'Ouses In Between' and 'It's A Great Big Shame'.

Elephant and Castle Theatre A theatre built on the site of the *Newington Butts Theatre in Newington, London in 1872. It was used primarily for pantomime and melodrama before eventually becoming a cinema.

elevator *See* bridge.

Eliot, T(homas) S(tearns) (1888–1965) Anglo-American poet, playwright, and critic, who wrote several successful poetic dramas.

His first major play, often considered his best, was *Murder in the Cathedral*, which reveals the influence of the medieval *Everyman* as well as that of Greek tragedy and church ritual. In his subsequent plays he moved closer to the language and settings of contemporary drama, *The *Cocktail Party* in particular being commercially successful. He won a Nobel Prize in 1948.

Principal dramatic works:

Murder in the Cathedral: 1935.

*The *Family Reunion*: 1939.

The Cocktail Party: 1949.

*The *Confidential Clerk*: 1953.

*The *Elder Statesman*: 1958.

Elizabethan drama English drama covering the period of the reign of Elizabeth I (1558–1603). The Elizabethan age saw a great flowering in the English theatre, culminating in the works of William *Shakespeare. As the effects of the Renaissance made themselves felt, English playwrights were attracted to the drama of Ancient Greece and Rome; the plays of Seneca (translated between 1559 and 1581) and others had a profound influence on such major writers as John Lyly, Christopher Marlowe, Robert Greene, Thomas Kyd, and George Peele, although all of them – especially Shakespeare – were prepared to reject their classical models for the sake of theatricality.

The first classically-based English comedy, *Ralph Roister Doister*, was written in 1552 and the first true English tragedy, *Gorbuduc*, in 1562; other forms of drama that developed significantly during the period included *revenge tragedy. In the early years of Elizabeth's reign, during which the mystery play and other types of religious theatre were curtailed, drama was largely confined to the royal court (*see* masque) and private venues, including inn courtyards. In 1576, however, James Burbage opened the Theatre, which was the first permanent public theatre in England; it was soon followed by the Curtain Theatre (1577), the Rose Theatre (1587), the Swan Theatre (1594), and, ultimately, the Globe Theatre (1599), where so many of Shakespeare's plays were first performed.

With the support of influential patrons, the number of acting companies also increased dramatically during this period in answer to the new wider popularity of the theatre; among them such celebrated groups as the rival Chamberlain's Men and Admiral's Men and various *boy companies. As well as the Burbages, actors with these companies (who also undertook all female roles and often acquired a personal financial interest in the theatres in which they appeared) included Edward Alleyn, William Kempe, and the young Ben Jonson, who was destined to become the dominant figure of *Jacobean drama. *See also* Renaissance drama.

Elizabethan Stage Society A British theatre organization established by William Poel in 1894 to specialize in production of plays from the Elizabethan period. The group revived the techniques and scenery of the theatre of Shakespeare's day: its productions of such works as *Twelfth Night* (1895), *Everyman*, and *Romeo and Juliet* (1905) – although not profitable – proved highly influential.

Elizabethan Theatre Trust, Australian A theatre organization founded in Australia in 1955 and named in honour of a visit by Elizabeth II in 1954. Based in the Majestic Theatre in Melbourne under Hugh Hunt, it promoted national tours by professional companies and encouraged new Australian writing as well as running a successful company, which included such stars as Judith Anderson. The company was eventually disbanded and the trust's work taken over by the Australian Council.

Elliott, Denholm (Mitchell) (1922-) British actor, who made his West End debut in Chetham-Strode's *The Guinea Pig* (1945) and then won an award for his performance in Fry's *Venus Observed* (1950). The same year he appeared on Broadway in Anouilh's *Ring Round the Moon*, after which he featured in a number of successful London productions and seasons at Stratford-upon-Avon as well as in the US. In 1949 he began a highly successful film career.

Elliott, G(eorge) H(enry) (1884–1962) British music hall singer, billed as 'The Chocolate Coloured Coon'. Originally a minstrel singer, he became the leading singer of 'coon' songs in the style of Eugene Stratton, reviving many of his successes.

Elliott, Maxine (Jessie Dermot; 1868–) US actress, noted for her looks and stage presence, who first appeared in H A Jones's *The Middleman* in New York in 1890. She teamed up with the comedian Nat Goodwin, whom she later married, in 1895, and appeared with him in such parts as Lydia Languish in Sheridan's *The Rivals* (1897) and Mrs Weston in Clyde Fitch's *The Cowboy and the Lady* (1899). After divorce she opened her own theatre in 1908, retiring in 1911 but making a successful comeback in the 1920s.

Her sister, **Gertrude Elliott** (1874–1950), also attracted praise in the plays of Clyde Fitch and later worked under Forbes-Robertson, marrying him in 1900. Their daughter was the actress Jean *Forbes-Robertson.

Elliott, Michael (1931–84) British director, who began his professional career with an acclaimed production of *Brand* for the 59 Theatre Company at the Lyric Theatre, Hammersmith, in 1959. Seasons followed at Nottingham, Glasgow, Stratford, the Old Vic, and the National Theatre before, in 1968, he founded the 69 Theatre Company in Manchester, which in 1976 became the *Royal Exchange Theatre Company. His sensitive productions of Ibsen and Shakespeare gained him an international reputation.

Elliston, Robert William (1774–1831) British actor-manager, who made his London debut in 1796 under George Colman the Younger. Widely admired in the great tragic roles, he also appeared in works by Sheridan, O'Keeffe, and others. In 1819, having held the lease of the Surrey Theatre for several years, he took over Drury Lane. There, known as The Great Lessee, he engaged such popular actors as Kean, Vestris, and Macready. Within seven years, however, he was bankrupt and had to return to the Surrey Theatre.

Elsinore Shakespeare Festival A festival of Shakespearean drama, devoted exclusively to productions of *Hamlet*, that takes place annually at Kronberg Castle, Elsinore, in Denmark. The traditional location for the story of Hamlet, Elsinore has seen visits by many leading foreign companies, including the Old Vic company at the first festival in 1937 and the Prospect Theatre company in 1978.

Eltinge, Julian (William Dalton; 1883–1941) US actor, who became famous for his impersonation of glamorous young women. After his debut in such a role in the musical *Mr Wix of Wickham* (1905), he toured with a minstrel show for two years, and then, for the next four years, played Hal Brooke, a character who disguises as a woman, in the musical comedy *The Fascinating Widow* (1911). He went on to appear in the musicals *The Crinoline Girl* (1914) and *Cousin Lucy* (1915) and to star in vaudeville throughout the 1920s.

Eltinge Theatre A theatre on West 42nd Street, New York, which was named after Julian *Eltinge. It opened in 1912 with Jane Cowl in the melodrama *Within the Law*, her first starring role. Several successful productions followed and by 1930 it had become a celebrated venue for burlesque. It closed in 1942 and was converted into a cinema.

Embassy Theatre A theatre in Hampstead, London, opened in 1928. Several new plays, including *The Dominant Sex* (1934) by Michael Egan, transferred successfully from here to the West End. It survived damage in World War II and was run for a time by Anthony Hawtrey before being taken over by the Central School of Speech and Drama in 1957.

Emery, John (1777–1822) British actor, born into a theatrical family in Sunderland. He established his reputation at an early age and in 1798 joined the company at Covent Garden. He excelled in the portrayal of comic rustics in Shakespeare, although Tyke in Thomas Morton's *School of Reform* was his most famous role.

His son, **Samuel Anderson Emery** (1817–81), was also an actor. After provincial tours, he won much acclaim for his portrayals of Dickensian characters at the Lyceum. He continued to play in London for upwards of 30 years, performing numerous parts associated with his father.

Sam's daughter, **(Isabel) Winifred Maud Emery** (1862–1924), began her acting career at the age of eight and made her adult debut in London at the Imperial Theatre in 1879. She later went with Henry Irving to the US and established herself in a number of Shakespearean roles. In 1888 she married Cyril *Maude and appeared under his management at the Haymarket in a variety of parts.

Emmet, Alfred *See* Questors Theatre.

Emney, Fred (1900–80) British comedian, son of the music hall star **Fred Emney** (1865–1917). He first appeared on stage in Edward Sheldon's *Romance* (1915), then toured the US in vaudeville for more than 10 years, returning to England to become a major personality in revues and musical comedies. He also appeared in such legitimate comedies as Pinero's *The Schoolmis-*

tress (1950) and Priestley's *When We Are Married* (1970).

Emperor Jones, The An early play by Eugene *O'Neill. First performance: 1920. The play depicts a Black emperor regressing to his aboriginal roots after he sees how he has oppressed and exploited his own people. Paul Robeson won great acclaim in the title role.

Empire A theatre in Leicester Square, London, opened in 1884. After being used as a venue for various light satirical entertainments, it became a popular music hall in 1887 under George Edwardes and Augustus Harris. Audiences flocked to the Empire both for its magnificent ballets and its promenade, which was a haunt of prostitutes. After World War I it became a home of revues and musical comedies, of which those by George Gershwin were the most significant. In 1927 the building was demolished; a cinema now occupies the site. *See also* Grand Theatre.

Empire Theatre A theatre in Liverpool, opened in 1866 as the New Prince of Wales (later renamed the Alexandra). With its large auditorium, seating 2312, it has been a venue for all types of theatrical entertainment; it was much altered in 1979 when it was taken over by the local council.

The **Empire Theatre** on Broadway and 40th Street in New York opened in 1893 with Belasco's *The Girl I Left Behind Me*. Subsequently it was used by the companies of Charles Frohman, John Drew, and Maude Adams. Among the theatre's many successes were Barrie's *Peter Pan* (1905), Kester's *When Knighthood was in Flower* (1901), and Shaw's *Captain Brassbound's Conversion*, starring Ellen Terry. Julia Marlowe, Ethel Barrymore, and Jane Cowl all won acclaim at the theatre before the controversy caused by Bourdet's *La Prisonnière* resulted in temporary closure in 1926. Katharine Cornell appeared there in 1928, 1931, and 1937, while Gielgud played Hamlet there in 1936. Crouse and Lindsay's *Life With Father* ran from 1939 to 1945; the theatre finally closed and was demolished in 1953.

Encina, Juan del (1469 – c. 1539) Spanish playwright, poet, and composer, who was the author of several influential pastorals, set to his own music. A priest, he worked as a dramatist at the court of the Duke of Alba from 1492, writing early examples of Spanish secular drama. Subsequently he travelled to Italy, where his play *Égloga de Plácida y Vitoriano* is known to have been performed in 1513.

Endgame (*Actes sans paroles*) A one-act play by Samuel *Beckett, written in French, 1954 – 56. First performance: Royal Court Theatre, London, 1957. The play is a bleak drama in which the two main characters – the blind Hamm and his servant Clov – eke out their remaining days in a deteriorating world, with Hamm's legless parents dying in nearby dustbins. The play's pervasive ironic humour gives it much of its humanity.

Enemy of the People, An (*En folkefiende*) A play by Henrik *Ibsen. First performance: Oslo, 1882. The play, written in the wake of the hostility aroused by *Ghosts* and possibly reflecting Ibsen's own feelings about the public's response to his work, presents the dilemma faced by a man of truth who finds himself at odds with a corrupt society.

English Aristophanes *See* Foote, Samuel.

English Comedians Troupes of English actors who toured the German states during the late 16th and early 17th centuries, when the native drama was comparatively undeveloped. The first of these companies, all of which relied upon visual comedy or the services of an interpreter to communicate with

their audiences, appeared in Holland and Denmark in the 1580s. The most famous of the early troupes was that led by Robert Browne, who began with Worcester's Men but left to produce plays in Leiden in 1591 and subsequently toured widely until 1619. Numerous other groups, presenting jigs, short comedies, and versions of works by Shakespeare, Kyd, and other contemporaries, followed – some establishing permanent bases in German theatres.

The most popular actors included Thomas Sackville, who led a company at Wolfenbüttel and was the creator of the comic character Jan Bouschet, and Robert Reynolds, upon whose character Pickelhering the German clowns Hanswurst and Thaddädl were later modelled. By 1630 the troupes were presenting an ever-increasing number of native German works and ultimately the tradition was absorbed into the indigenous theatre (*see Haupt- und Staatsaktionen*). The last reference to a troupe of English Comedians still touring was in 1659.

English Stage Company A British theatre company founded by George Devine in 1955 to promote new and experimental drama. The company eventually made its permanent home at the Royal Court Theatre, becoming highly influential with premieres of works by Arden, Osborne (notably *Look Back in Anger* in 1956), Wesker, and others from the 1950s onwards.

Ennius, Quintus (239 BC – 169 BC) Roman poet and playwright, who became the leading tragic writer after Andronicus and Naevius. Many of his 20 or so tragedies (of which only titles and fragments survive) were based on Euripides and were notable for their sympathy with the characters and their poetic language. Despite the fact that his highly rhetorical style was lampooned by Plautus and that he failed in his attempts to write comedy, he remained much admired after his death, his poetry creating for him a lasting reputation as the father of Roman literature.

ENSA *See* Entertainments National Service Association.

enter *See* stage direction.

Entertainer, The A play by John *Osborne. First performance: Royal Court Theatre, 1957, with Laurence Olivier as Archie Rice. The decline of the music hall and the comic Archie Rice is presented as a metaphor for the decline of a society; the action moves constantly between music hall and family scenes.

Entertaining Mr Sloane A comedy by Joe *Orton. First performance: London, 1964. Based on a plot featuring murder, blackmail, and various sexual perversions, the play is distinguished by Orton's humorous use of bland, even elegant, language to express his anarchic subject matter and effectively established his reputation. At the centre of the play is a young murderer who attempts to blackmail a woman and her brother but then finds himself under their control.

Entertainments National Service Association (ENSA) A British theatre organization established just before World War II to provide a variety of entertainments for troops and other war workers serving both at home and overseas. It was managed by Basil Dean from Drury Lane and operated on all the war fronts.

Enthoven, Gabrielle (1868–1950) British theatre historian, who donated her own huge collection of theatrical artefacts to the Victoria and Albert Museum in London in 1924. Herself an amateur actress and playwright, she administered the collection for many years and became the first president of the Society for Theatre Research.

entremé A brief entertainment presented during the course of a banquet in Spain. Originally a feature of Corpus Christi processions in Catalonia, it was later adapted for use during lengthy plays and often concluded in a dance. Writers of such pieces included Quiñones de Benavente, Lope de Vega, and Cervantes.

Epicharmos (c. 530 BC–c. 440 BC) Greek poet and playwright, who wrote important early examples of Old Comedy. Only titles and fragments of his comic plays, which tackled mythological themes and influenced Plautus, survive.

epic theatre A form of theatre based on an appeal to the intellect rather than to the emotions, as developed in Germany during the 1920s. Developed by Brecht and Piscator among others, the theory of epic theatre was derived from Aristotle; it advocated disregard for the unity of time and other theatrical conventions but emphasized the need for political relevance. *See also* alienation effect.

Epidaurus The earliest surviving example of an ancient Greek theatre, built during the 4th century BC. Designed by the architect Polycleitus, it seated 14 000 spectators and included a circular orchestra, a raised stage, and an elaborate *skene* building; the theatre, which has been much restored, is still in use.

epilogue A brief scene or speech given at the end of a performance, often encapsulating the underlying significance of what has preceded it.

Epiphany play *See* liturgical drama.

equestrian drama A form of theatre, popular in London in the early 18th century, in which spectacular displays of horsemanship were an integral feature of a production. The most important venues included

Astley's Amphitheatre, Covent Garden, and Drury Lane; plays presented included equestrian versions of Shakespeare and *Mazeppa* (1823), which was based on a poem by Lord Byron. Leading performers of equestrian drama included Edward Alexander Gomersal and Andrew Ducrow.

Equity *See* American Actors' Equity Association; British Actors' Equity Association; Canadian Actors' Equity Association.

Equus A play by Peter *Shaffer. First performance: 1973. Revolving around a psychiatrist's exploration of the mental state of a stable-boy who has blinded a number of horses, the play was highly praised as a reflection upon the conflict between rationality and instinct. It was subsequently filmed with Richard Burton, Peter Firth, and Jenny Agutter.

Erckmann-Chatrian (Émile Erckmann; 1822–99 *and* Alexandre Chatrian; 1826–90) French writers, who collaborated on several popular novels and plays, set in Alsace, notably *Le Juif polonais* (1869; adapted as *The *Bells*, 1871). Their association ended in litigation in 1889.

Erlanger's Theatre *See* St James Theatre.

Ernst, Paul (1866–1933) German playwright, critic, and prosewriter, best-known for his historical hero-tragedies modelled on Aristotelian ideals. His writing for the stage developed from such early naturalistic dramas as *Lumpenbagasch* (1898) to neoclassical tragedies, notably *Demetrios* (1905) and *Canossa* (1908), in which he extols a heroic conception of life. Other major works include *Manfred und Beatrice* (1912), *Preussengeist* (1914), and the comedy *Der heilige Crispin* (1910).

Ervine, St John Greer (1883–1971) Irish playwright, born in Belfast. As a young man he became acquainted with G B Shaw, whose biography he wrote (1956). In 1915 he was appointed manager at the Abbey Theatre for one disastrous season. His early plays, notably *Jane Clegg* (1913), discussed various social problems; later he wrote drawing-room comedies for the London stage.

Escamilla, Antonio de (Antonio de Vazquez; d. 1695) Spanish actor and manager, who led his own company and excelled in *Gracioso* parts. He specialized in the presentation of *zarzuelas* and in the plays of Calderón.

Esmond, Henry Vernon (Henry Vernon Jack; 1869–1922) British actor-manager and playwright. He began writing plays when he was in Alexander's company at the St James's Theatre, where he was admired in *The Second Mrs Tanqueray* (1893). With his wife, **Eva Moore** (1870–1955), he toured in many of his own plays, which included the sentimental comedy *Eliza Comes to Stay* (1913).

Espert I Romero, Núria (1936–) Spanish actress, who has appeared in many major Spanish works as well as other modern European plays at the head of her own company, which she founded in 1959. Her most celebrated roles include Claire in Genet's *Les Bonnes* (1969) and the title role in García Lorca's *Yerma* (1971), under the direction of Victor García. In 1986 she won acclaim for her direction of García Lorca's *The House of Bernarda Alba* in London.

Espy, L' *See* L'Espy.

Esslair, Ferdinand (1772–1840) German actor and manager, who took over the Court Theatre in Munich in 1820. He began his career in the provinces and later excelled in passionate roles in the plays of Schiller.

Estcourt, Richard (1668–1712) English actor, who began as a strolling player at

Worcester. He reached Drury Lane in 1704 where Christopher Rich engaged him to play comedy roles. He was an incorrigible mimic and the friend of Addison, Steele, and other distinguished contemporaries.

Estébanez, Joaquín See Tamayo y Baus, Manuel.

Est Parisien, Théâtre de l' A theatre in Paris, formerly a cinema, which opened in 1963. It was founded as the home of the La Guilde company of Guy Rétoré, which established its reputation with a mixed programme during the 1950s and acquired a wide popular following. The theatre was given a state subsidy in 1964.

Ethel Barrymore Theatre A large theatre on West 47th Street, New York, which was opened by Lee Shubert in 1928 with Ethel Barrymore (after whom it was named) in *The Kingdom of God* by Martínez Sierra. Notable productions that followed included Coward's *Design for Living* (1933), Elsie Schauffler's *Parnell* (1935), Emlyn Williams in his own play *Night Must Fall* (1936), and Clare Boothe's *The Women* (1936). Among its distinguished players have been Marlon Brando and Jessica Tandy in the prizewinning *A Streetcar Named Desire* by Tennessee Williams (1947), John Wood in Stoppard's *Travesties* (1975), and Alec McCowen in Christopher Hampton's *The Philanthropist* (1971). Other modern productions have included Peter Shaffer's double-bill *Black Comedy* and *White Lies* (1967), David Mamet's *American Buffalo* (1977), and Bernard Slade's *Romantic Comedy* (1979).

Etherege, Sir George (1634–91) English playwright, who wrote the first of the English comedies of manners. His first play, the verse drama *The Comical Revenge; or, Love in a Tub* (1664), contained a comic element that he went on to develop in the highly successful comedies *She Would if She Could* and *The *Man of Mode*, his finest play.

Ethiopian opera A feature of the *minstrel show, in which parodies of Shakespeare and opera were performed by actors in blackface make-up. Many of these burlesques were based on works by T D Rice.

Euclid-77th Street Theatre See Cleveland Play House.

Eugene O'Neill Theatre A theatre on West 49th Street, New York, which opened as the **Forrest Theatre** in 1925. Called the **Coronet Theatre** from 1945, it was renamed after Eugene O'Neill in 1959, when his play *The Great God Brown* was seen there. Recent productions staged there have included a number of plays by its owner, Neil Simon, among them *The Prisoner of Second Avenue* (1971), *California Suite* (1976), *Chapter Two* (1979), and *I Ought To Be In Pictures* (1980). The theatre seats 1075.

Eugene O'Neill Theatre Centre See O'Neill, Eugene.

Euphorion (5th century BC) Greek playwright, the son of Aeschylus. Although none of his work survives, he is known to have defeated both Euripides and Sophocles in drama contests.

Eupolis (c. 446 BC–411 BC) Greek playwright, regarded as one of the masters of Old Comedy. His 18 plays, the first of which was produced in 424 BC, won several contests and were notorious for their frankness and satirical content. Many fragments, notably of *The Demes*, survive.

Euripides (484 BC–406 BC) Greek playwright, probably born at Salamis, who became the third major tragic writer of the ancient Greek theatre, alongside Aeschylus and Sophocles. The author of possibly as many as 92 plays (of which 17 tragedies and one satyr-play survive), he suffered in his own lifetime from unpopularity with the audience in Athens – he was even lampooned by his admirer Aristophanes – and won only five contests at the Dionysia. This was probably on account of his individualistic stance on several topics, notably on women (the central characters in several of his plays) and against war at a time when Athens was in conflict with Sparta, and may have contributed to his departure from Athens as an old man.

The characters in his plays, which deal almost exclusively with mythological subjects, are depicted with greater realism than was attempted by his contemporaries and foreshadowed later, more psychologically subtle drama, especially the tragedies of Seneca and the New Comedy of Menander. Using straightforward language, he tackled such themes as incest, revenge, madness, and repression. He was also responsible for such innovations as the *prologue and the *deus ex machina and did much to expand the conventional Greek tragedy, adding elements of sentimentalism, romance, and even comedy (notably in Alcestis, Ion, *Iphigenia in Tauris, and Helen). The *Bacchaehas been revived many times in the 20th century on account of its psychological intensity and in 1980 the Royal Shakespeare Company staged seven of his plays as part of a highly-acclaimed cycle of Greek plays.

Principal works:

Alcestis: 438 BC.

Medea: 431 BC.

Hippolytus: 428 BC.

Children of Heracles: c. 428 BC.

Hecuba: c. 426 BC.

*The *Trojan Women*: 415 BC.

Iphigenia in Tauris: c. 414 BC.

**Electra*: 413 BC.

Helen: 412 BC.

Phoenician Women: 411 BC.

Orestes: 408 BC.

The Bacchae: date unknown.

Ion: date unknown.

Iphigenia in Aulis: date unknown.

Madness of Heracles: date unknown.

*The *Suppliant Women*: date unknown.

Euston Palace *See* Regent Theatre.

Euterpean Hall *See* Broadway Theatre.

Evans, Dame Edith (Mary) (1888–1976) British actress, who began her career as Shakespeare's Cressida directed by William Poel for the Elizabethan Stage Society in 1912. Particularly admired in comedy, she became one of the most distinguished actresses of her time, playing many of the great Elizabethan and Restoration roles, including Millamant in Congreve's *The Way of the World* (1924 and 1927), Shakespeare's Cleopatra, Rosalind, and the Nurse (1926), and Mrs Sullen in Farquhar's *The Beaux' Stratagem* (1930). She also excelled in portrayals of such Shavian characters as Lady Utterword in *Heartbreak House* (1921) and Orinthia in *The Apple Cart* (1929).

At the New Theatre in 1935 she was again the Nurse in Gielgud's *Romeo and Juliet* and, in 1937, Rosalind in *As You Like It*. In 1939, again with Gielgud, she appeared in her most famous role, Lady Bracknell in *The Importance of Being Earnest*. In addition to classical parts, she starred in many modern plays by such authors as James Bridie, N C Hunter, and Enid Bagnold. In the 1959 Stratford-upon-Avon season she was acclaimed as the Countess of Roussillon in *All's Well That Ends Well* and as Volumnia in *Coriolanus*. After being directed by Coward in his own play *Hay Fever* for the National Theatre Company in 1964, she tended to work more in films and television, but returned to the stage for a final appearance in *Edith Evans ... and Friends* in 1974.

Evans, Maurice Hubert (1901-) US actor and manager, born in Britain, who began his career in Cambridge and then joined the Old Vic company, playing Shakespearean roles. He made his New York debut as Romeo in 1935 and toured widely in Shakespeare in World War II. His other roles included John Tanner in his own production of *Man and Superman* (1947), Crocker-Harris in *The Browning Version* (1949), Hjalman Ekdal in *The Wild Duck* (1951), and King Magnus in *The Apple Cart* (1956). Among his subsequent successes have been *Holiday* (1980) and *On Golden Pond* (1981) as well as several films.

Evans, Will (1875–1931) British music hall comedian, who made his stage debut at Drury Lane while still a child. He appeared in clown make-up and presented slapstick sketches and monologues, performing in every Drury Lane pantomime from 1911 to 1919. He was also part author of *Tons of Money*, the first of the famous Aldwych farces.

Evans's A *song-and-supper room in Covent Garden, London, established in the cellar of a hotel around 1820. It became famous under the management of the comic actor W C Evans, who presented such leading performers as Charles Sloman and Sam Cowell as well as early minstrel shows in the 1840s. In 1856 the building was enlarged and Evans's became a popular music hall before finally closing in 1880 as a result of the rivalry of other venues. The *Players' Club took over the building in 1934.

Everyman An English morality play by an unknown author, probably based upon a Dutch original, *Elckerlyc* (c. 1495). First performance: c. 1500. The play depicts the desertion of the hero by all the virtues except Good Deeds when he dies. It was revived in 1901 by William Poel; Hugo von Hofmannsthal wrote a German version, *Jedermann*, in 1920.

Every Man in his Humour A comedy by Ben *Jonson. First performance: London, 1598. First performed by the Chamberlain's Men, with Shakespeare in the cast, the play tackles the conflict between the young and the old through Knowell and his son Edward and is notable for such creations as Kitely, who suspects his wife of adultery, and the vainglorious Bobadil.

Everyman Theatre A theatre in Liverpool, opened by Terry *Hands and others in 1964. It quickly established a reputation as an important venue for the performance of new works, including plays by Bond and Pinter, as well as for entertainments with a local flavour, notably the musical *John, Paul, Ringo... and Bert* (1974) and other plays by Willy Russell, and dramas by Alan Bleasdale and John McGrath. The theatre was rebuilt in the 1970s and was taken over by Ken *Campbell in 1980, being used subsequently for influential experimental drama.

Another theatre of the same name opened in Hampstead, London, in 1920 and over the next six years prospered under Norman *Macdermott. Plays by Shaw were regularly performed there; other successes included works by Bjørnson, Coward, Ibsen, and Pirandello. After 1926 Raymond Massey managed the theatre for a time; it was converted into a cinema in 1947.

Evita A musical by Tim *Rice and Andrew *Lloyd Webber. First performance: London, 1978. Based on the career of Eva Perón, who rose to become the wife of the leader of Argentina before her early death, it reinforced the West End's gathering reputation as a focus of the musical stage to rival Broadway.

Evreinov, Nikolai Nikolaivich (1879–1953) Russian playwright, who became a leading writer of Symbolist drama. He expressed his opposition to the naturalistic theories of Stanislavsky in the comic satires *Revisor* (1912) and *The Fourth Wall* (1915); other notable works written before his eclipse with the emergence of Socialist Realism included the monodrama *The Theatre of the Soul* (1912), in which he defined his own understanding of the theatre, and *The Chief Thing* (1921).

Ewald, Johannes (1743–81) Danish poet and playwright, whose historical drama *Rolf Krage* (1770), which was inspired by his reading of Shakespeare and Ossian, was the first true Danish tragedy. Of his other dramatic writings the operetta *Fiskerne* (The Fishermen; 1780) is the best known.

exit *See* stage direction.

Experimental Theatre *See* Daly's 63rd Street Theatre.

Expressionism A philosophical movement in the theatre and arts in general that developed in Germany around 1910. Its exponents, who included Georg Kaiser and Ernst Toller, sought – often in intensely poetic language – to probe their central character's innermost feelings and usually depicted him in conflict against external realities that threaten to repress his individuality. Forerunners of the movement included Strindberg and Wedekind. After World War I the movement was enlivened by the support of the Dadaists, who emphasized the symbolic element in Expressionist drama as well as adopting a more extreme approach to philosophical issues. Eventually, during the 1920s, the movement succumbed to its own obsession with itself, although its influence remained strong upon such writers as Brecht and O'Neill.

extravaganza A lavish theatrical entertainment popular in England in the 19th century. Combining music, satire, and elaborate costumes and sets, most extravaganzas were based on myths or folk-stories and resembled pantomime; leading writers of the genre included J R Planché and H J Byron.

Eyre, Richard (1943–) British director, who succeeded Sir Peter Hall as director of the National Theatre (now the Royal National Theatre) in 1988. Noted especially for his productions of contemporary drama and, more recently, of musicals, Eyre first achieved national recognition while artistic director of the Nottingham Playhouse (1973–78). His recent productions include Alan Bennett's *Kafka's Dick* (1986) and Cole Porter's *High Society* (1987).

Eysoldt, Gertrud (1870–1955) German actress, who was much admired in the plays of Ibsen, Maeterlinck, Wedekind, and other modern authors. She began her career with the Meninger company in 1890; subsequently she acted under Reinhardt and performed in the controversial first production of Schnitzler's *Reigen* in Berlin (1921).

F

Fabbri, Diego (1911–80) Italian playwright, whose Roman Catholic upbringing is reflected in all his plays. *The Knot* (1935), his most famous play, incurred the disapproval of the Fascist authorities and was rewritten as *The Swamp* (1942). After World War II, however, Fabbri emerged as the leading Italian writer of poetic drama with such plays as *Inquisizione* (Inquisition; 1950), *Processo di famiglia* (Family Trial; 1955), and *Processo a Gesù* (The Trial of Jesus; 1955).

Fabre d'Églantine (Philippe-François-Nazaire Fabre; 1750–94) French playwright, actor, and poet, who played an important role in the French Revolution and died on the guillotine. He wrote satirical comedies inspired by contemporary politics, notably *Le Philinte de Molière ou la Suite du Misanthrope* (1790).

fabula The Latin term for a play. It was used of works of various different types, including those of the *atellana, *palliata, *praetexta, *rhinthonica, *riciniata, *saltica, *togata, and *trabeata.

Fact, Theatre of See documentary theatre.

Fagan, James Bernard (1873–1933) Irish-born playwright, director, and actor, who began his stage career in Frank Benson's company in 1895. Later he became manager of the Royal Court Theatre and in 1923 the Oxford Playhouse. The productions staged there employed several young actors and actresses destined to become leading performers of their generation. He became director of the Festival Theatre in Cambridge in 1929. His own plays include *The Wheel* (1922), *And So to Bed* (1926), and *The Improper Duchess* (1931).

Faiko, Alexei Mikhailovich (1893–) Soviet playwright, whose best-known play was *The Man with the Portfolio* (1928), which depicted the spiritual dilemma of a university professor who disapproves of the new government but keeps his opposition to himself. Other works included *Lake Lyul* (1923), which was produced by Meyerhold, and the comedy *Don't Set Yourself up as God!* (1957).

fair A public festivity, originally asociated with market trading, held at regular intervals in towns and villages throughout Europe since medieval times. The early fairs provided ample opportunities for the presentation of theatrical entertainments, which varied from solo performances by jugglers and acrobats to full-scale plays presented in a temporary theatre (*see* booth). Eventually some of these sites became the homes of permanent theatrical enterprises, notably in the case of the **Saint-Germain** and **Saint-Laurent fairgrounds** in Paris, and witnessed the emergence of many significant theatrical figures in the 17th and 18th centuries despite opposition from other established theatrical companies. In England such fairs as those held at Saint Bartholomew and South-wark in London included puppet shows, drolls, and performances of complete plays, while those held in Germany and elsewhere on the Continent provided venues for troupes of travelling English players (*see* English Comedians). Similar gatherings in Italy and Spain in particular also contributed to the development of the *commedia dell'arte*.

Fairbrother, Sydney (Sydney Parselle; 1872–1941) British actress, who made both her first (1889) and her last (1938) appearances at the Haymarket. She excelled as Wally in *Two Little Vagabonds* (1896) by G R Sims and Arthur Shirley, Proserpine in Shaw's *Candida* (1904), partnered the elder Fred Emney in a music hall sketch (1912–14), and played Mahbubah in Asche's *Chu Chin Chow* (1916–20). Latterly, she played numerous character parts.

Falckenberg, Otto (1873–1947) German director, who became famous for his work in contemporary drama at the Munich Kammerspiele (1915–44). Having first attracted attention with Strindberg's *Spöksonaten* in 1915, he subsequently won acclaim for his evocative production of plays by Barlach, Brecht, and Shakespeare among others.

Fallen Angels A comedy by Noël *Coward. First performance: London, 1925. It deals with two married women nervously awaiting the reappearance of their former lover in their lives, drinking heavily as they do so.

falling flap A hinged flat, formerly much used to execute rapid changes of scene. When the hinged section is released the flat presents an entirely different view.

false proscenium An arrangement of flats or cloths by means of which the opening of the proscenium arch is reduced in size. In the US the false proscenium is usually referred to as a **portal opening**.

Family Reunion, The A poetic drama by T S *Eliot. First performance: 1939. It draws upon *The *Oresteia* of Aeschylus in its exploration of the guilt of Harry Monchensey over the mysterious death of his wife but suffers from the uneasy combination of classical convention and contemporary subject matter.

fan effect *See* transformation scene.

Fanny's First Play A play by G B *Shaw; his first commercial success. First performance: London, 1911. The plot centres around the son and daughter of two respectable families who, after serving a term in jail, marry totally unconventional spouses. As well as satirizing middle-class values the play also lampoons several contemporary drama critics.

farce A form of drama characterized by its broad humour and complicated plot. Farce relies heavily upon stereotypes and slapstick comedy and is in its modern form descended from the plays of such writers as Labiche, Feydeau, and Pinero, written in the 19th and early 20th centuries. In its ancient form it had its roots in satyr-plays and ritual celebrations and played an important role in the plays of Plautus, Terence, and others. It was also a characteristic feature of much medieval and religious drama and, through the *commedia dell'arte*, had an influence upon the plays of Molière and his contemporaries. Short farces were often performed during the 18th and 19th centuries in both Britain and the US as part of an evening's entertainment alongside full-length tragedies. *See also* bedroom farce.

Farine, Jean (fl. 1600–35) French actor, who appeared at Paris fairgrounds before moving to the Hôtel de Bourgogne. Thought to have begun as a quack doctor, he was popular in improvised farces, appearing with Bruscambille.

Farjeon, Herbert (1887–1945) British critic, author, and revue librettist, whose *Nine Sheep* (1938) and *The Little Revue* (1939) were highly successful. He also collaborated with his sister Eleanor on such musical plays as *The Glass Slipper* (1944).

Farquhar, George (1678–1707) English playwright and actor, born in Ireland. Through his friendship with Robert Wilks his first play, *Love and a Bottle*, was successfully produced at Drury Lane in 1698; the following year, *The Constant Couple; or, a Trip to the Jubilee*, met with a brilliant reception, the hero (played by Wilks) later becoming a famous breeches part for Peg Woffington. After its sequel, *Sir Harry Wildair* (1701), and several less successful works he went on to write *The *Recruiting Officer* and *The *Beaux' Stratagem*, which are considered among the finest of all Restoration comedies.

Principal works:

Love and a Bottle: 1698.

The Constant Couple; or, a Trip to the Jubilee: 1699.

Sir Harry Wildair: 1701.

The Inconstant; or, the Way to Win Him: 1702.

The Twin Rivals: 1703.

The Stage Coach: 1704.

The Recruiting Officer: 1706.

The Beaux' Stratagem: 1707.

Farr, Florence (Mrs Edward Emery; 1860–1917) British actress and director, who popularized the plays of Ibsen, Yeats, and Shaw on the London stage. She acted in *Widower's Houses* (1892), the first of Shaw's plays to be staged in London, and produced *The Land of Heart's Desire,* the first of Yeats's plays to be given in the capital. Subsequently she collaborated with Granville-Barker on revivals of plays by Euripides before emigrating to Ceylon as a teacher.

Farren, Elizabeth (1759–1829) British actress, the daughter of strolling players. She played at Wakefield and Liverpool before her Haymarket debut as Kate Hardcastle in *She Stoops to Conquer* in 1777. She also appeared at Covent Garden and Drury Lane, becoming the natural successor to Mrs Abington. She married the Earl of Derby in 1797 and retired from the stage.

Farren, William (1725–95) British actor, who played important parts at Drury Lane and Covent Garden. He was the original Careless in *The School for Scandal* (1777) and Leicester in *The Critic* (1779). In 1784 he transferred to Covent Garden.

His son, **William Farren** (1786–1861), made his Covent Garden debut as Sir Peter Teazle in *The School for Scandal* in 1818 and was subsequently acclaimed in numerous Shakespearean parts. He suffered a stroke in 1843 but continued to act, becoming for a time manager of the Strand and Olympic theatres.

His grand-daughter, **Ellen Farren** (1848–1904), known as as Nellie, first appeared at the Olympic in 1864. For 30 years she was a leading star at the Gaiety Theatre, where she first appeared in 1868.

Fastnachtsspiel (*or* Carnival play) A form of German medieval drama that developed separately from the liturgical theatrical tradition during the 15th century. The plays, generally episodic ribald farces, were usually performed in the open air by amateur companies and combined elements of both the morality play and liturgical drama with some satirical comment. Writers of such Carnival plays included Hans Rosenplüt and Hans Sachs; the central comic character was that of the *Narr.

fate drama *See Schicksaltragödie.*

Father, The (*Fadren*) A play by August *Strindberg. First performance: 1887. The first of Strindberg's famous analyses of sexual conflict, the play depicts the descent of an army captain into madness at the hands of his merciless wife, Laura.

Faucit, Helen (1817–98) British actress, daughter of theatrical parents, who made her debut at Covent Garden in 1836 in *The Hunchback* by Sheridan Knowles. She remained at the theatre when Macready took over, then went with him to the Haymarket and Drury Lane. In 1838 she created Pauline in Bulwer-Lytton's *The Lady of Lyons*; she also excelled in Shakespeare.

Faust A play by *Goethe, written in two parts (1770–1808) and generally considered to be his masterpiece. First performance (of complete work): Weimar, 1876. Drawing heavily upon Marlowe's celebrated version (*see Dr Faustus, The Tragical History of*), it was inspired by a puppet-play that Goethe saw as a young man and provided an excellent vehicle for the expression of his ideals concerning human aspiration.

Faust, Johann (c. 1480–1540) German conjuror, who became the central character of numerous plays and other theatrical entertainments following the publication of his biography in 1587. Marlowe's *The Tragical History of *Dr Faustus* (c. 1589–92) combined Faust's life with the medieval legend of a man who sold his soul to the devil; subsequent dramatic versions of Faust's life included a puppet play and dramas by Lessing, Goethe, Grabbe, and Stephen Phillips.

Favart, Charles Simon (1710–92) French playwright, librettist, and director of the Opéra-Comique, Paris. He wrote comic operas and sentimental or pastoral comedies, sometimes in collaboration with his wife, the actress Mlle *Chantilly.

Favart, Théâtre *See* Comédie-Italienne.

Faversham, William (1868–1940) US actor, born in London, where he first appeared in John Oxenford's *Retained for the Defence* (1885). Stranded in New York after the failure of *Pen and Ink* (1887), he went on to enjoy a successful career, spending many years in Charles Frohman's company in parts ranging from Romeo to Algernon in Wilde's *The Importance of Being Earnest*. In management on his own he won particular acclaim in Stephen Phillips's *Herod* (1909), as Mark Antony in *Julius Caesar* (1912), and as Iago in *Othello* (1914).

Fay, Frank J (1870–1931) Irish actor, who – with his brother **William George Fay** (1872–1947) – worked tirelessly for the Irish National Theatre movement and assisted in the creation of the Abbey Theatre company in 1904. They were in most of the Abbey productions, including *The Playboy of the Western World* (in which William played Christy Mahon), until 1908, when they went to the US to stage a repertory of Irish plays. On returning, Frank became a speech teacher in Dublin, while William went on to direct plays at Nottingham (1920–21) and Birmingham (1925–27) and appeared in many London productions.

Feast of Fools A New Year's festivity common to many European churches and other religious establishments during medieval times. Possibly descended from ancient Roman traditions, the Feast of Fools emerged in France during the 12th century and conventionally included the performance of a dramatic entertainment. The festivity, which provided ample opportunity for feasting and merriment, was nominally under the control of an elected temporary king, or *Boy Bishop, chosen from the lower ranks of the clergy; the post eventually evolved into that of the Abbot of *Misrule. Due to the scandalous nature of the custom, it had generally died out in England by 1500 and in France by 1700.

Featherstonhaugh, Constance *See* Benson, Frank Robert.

Fechter, Charles Albert (1824–79) French actor, who became popular throughout Europe and the US as a performer of tragic and melodramatic roles, which he could deliver in both English and French. He first appeared at the Comédie-Française in 1840 but later toured extensively in works by Dumas *fils*, Hugo, and others. His passionate character made him a great success with audiences but caused offence with many fellow-actors. Later in his career he managed the Lyceum in London for a time and opened a theatre in his own name.

Fedeli An Italian *commedia dell'arte* company, founded by Giovanni Andreini c. 1601. After acquiring actors from the Gelosi and Accesi, the company toured extensively before disbanding around 1650. Actors with the Fedeli included Tristano Martinelli.

Federal Theatre Project A nationwide theatre scheme, initiated in the US in 1935 as part of President Roosevelt's New Deal programme. Its main purpose was to provide employment for out of work actors, directors, designers, stage hands, vaudeville artists, circus entertainers, and puppeteers and to boost national morale. Under Hallie Flanagan, it quickly established itself as a pioneer of socially-concerned theatre. Among its most controversial productions were the *Living Newspapers, but of equal interest were the plays for children, new dramas, revivals of the classics, large-scale pageants, tours, vaudeville entertainments, and special programmes for ethnic communities. Tickets were either free or very low-priced. The Project was abruptly closed down in 1939 following alleged communist infiltration.

Fehling, Jürgen (1885–1968) German director, who became a leading figure of the Realist tradition in the theatre of Berlin.

Trained initially under Reinhardt, he later advocated a more Expressionist approach, presenting notable dramas by Brecht and Barlach among others at the Staadstheater (1922–32), before ultimately reviving the use of the box set and favouring sparse scenic detail. His most famous productions included several plays by Shakespeare featuring such actors as Kortner, Krauss, and Gründgens.

female impersonator A male actor who performs female roles, in modern times usually for comic effect. The tradition has its roots in the Greek and Elizabethan theatre, in which boys or men performed all female roles, as was also the case in the Chinese and Japanese theatre. In the modern theatre female impersonators (or **drag artists**) conventionally appear as *dames in pantomime and in their own speciality acts; leading contemporary exponents of such roles include Danny La Rue and Barry Humphries. *Compare* breeches part.

Fenn, Ezekiel (b. 1620) English actor, noted as a boy player of female characters. His roles included Sophonisba in Nabbes's *Hannibal and Scipio* at the Cockpit in 1635 and Winnifred in Dekker and Rowley's *The Witch of Edmonton*. Subsequently he played male parts with Beeston's company.

Fennell, James (1766–1816) British actor, who began by playing Othello at Edinburgh, subsequently repeating the part at Covent Garden. In 1791 he acted in his own play *Linda and Clara, or the British Officer*. Between 1797 and 1806 he acted in the US under Wignell.

Fenton, Lavinia (1708–60) British actress, who made her debut at the Haymarket in 1726 in Otway's *The Orphan*, subsequently playing Cherry in *The Beaux' Stratagem*. In 1728, at the Lincoln's Inn Fields Theatre, she created Polly Peachum in *The Beggar's Opera*. In 1751 she married the Duke of Bolton.

Ferber, Edna *See* Kaufman, George S.

Fernández, Lucas (c. 1474–1542) Spanish playwright and musician, who wrote six plays notable for their simple comedy and use of music. Much influenced by the plays of his rival Encina, his works comprise three religious dramas, notably the *Auto de la Passión*, and three secular comedies, which anticipated the development of the *zarzuela*.

Fernández de Moratín, Nicolás *See* Moratín, Nicolás Fernández de.

Ferrari, Paolo (1822–89) Italian playwright, who established his reputation with *Goldoni e le sue sedici commedie* (1853), which took Goldoni as its subject. His later works, in which he adopted conservative views on a number of social issues, included *Il duello* (1868), *Il suicido* (1875), and *La satira e Parini* (1865), based on the life of the poet Giuseppe Parini.

Ferreira, António (1528–69) Portuguese playwright and poet, author of the celebrated *Tragédia de Dona Inêz de Castro* (c. 1558), which inspired numerous imitations. His other works include the two comedies *O Gioso* and *Bristo*.

Ferrer, José Vicente (1912–) US actor, who made his debut in 1934 on a showboat on the Long Island Sound. He then joined Joshua Logan's Stock Company and made his New York debut (1935). After success in Maxwell Anderson's *Key Largo* (1939) and Brandon Thomas's *Charley's Aunt* (1940), he played Iago to Paul Robeson's Othello (1943) to great acclaim; othe roles have included Cyrano de Bergerac, Volpone, and Richard III.

Festival Theatre *See* Cambridge Festival Theatre.

Feuchtwanger, Lion (1884–1958) German novelist and playwright, who is usually remembered for *Jew Süss* (1925), an historical drama derived from his own novel. A Jewish intellectual hated by the Nazis, he became associated with Expressionist circles and wrote several dramas in collaboration with Brecht, notably *Eduard II* (1924), *Kalkutta* (1927), and *Die Gesichte der Simone Machard* (1942). Other important dramatic works include *Drei Angelsächsische Stücke* (Three Anglo-Saxon Plays; 1927).

Feuillère, Edwige (1907–) French actress, who established her reputation at the Comédie-Française in the 1930s. Trained at the Conservatoire, she appeared initially both on stage and in films in lightweight romantic roles, but was recognized as a leading tragic actress in 1937 with her performance in Becque's *La Parisienne* and subsequently Dumas *fils's La Dame aux camélias* (1940 and 1952). She went on to play in the premieres of Giraudoux's *Sodome et Gomorrhe* (1943), Cocteau's *L'Aigle à deux têtes* (1946), and Claudel's *Partage de midi* (1948), among other important works. More recent successes have included Arbuzov's *Old World* (1977).

Feydeau,   Georges(-Léon-Jules-Marie) (1862–1921) French playwright, who began writing for the theatre in the 1880s and produced some 40 farces during his career. The plays owe their success to well-structured plots, witty dialogue, improbable situations, and the skilful manipulation of traditional comic devices. His reputation has grown stronger since his death, partly through revivals at the Comédie-Française.

Principal works:

Tailleur pour dames: 1887.

Un Fil à la patte: 1894; adapted as *Cat among the Pigeons*.

L'Hôtel du Libre Échange: 1894; translated as *Hotel Paradiso*.

Le Dindon: 1896.

La Dame de chez Maxim: 1899; translated as *The Girl from Maxim's*.

La Puce à l'oreille: 1907; adapted as *A Flea in Her Ear*.

Occupe-toi d'Amélie: 1908; translated as *Keep an Eye on Amélie*; adapted as *Look After Lulu*.

On purge bébé: 1910.

Feydeau, Théâtre See Comédie-Italienne.

Ffrangcon-Davies, Gwen (1891–) British actress, who had her first London success as Etain in Rutland Boughton's *The Immortal Hour* (1920). During her long career she played many important roles, including Eve in Shaw's *Back to Methuselah* (1923), Elizabeth Moulton-Barrett in Rudolf Besier's *The Barretts of Wimpole Street* (1930), and Lady Macbeth, opposite John Gielgud (1942). She appeared in South Africa for several years from 1943 but was at Stratford-upon-Avon in 1950 to play Queen Katherine in *Henry VIII* and Regan among other parts. Later interesting performances included Miss Madrigal in Enid Bagnold's *The Chalk Garden* (1957), Amanda in Tennessee Williams's *The Glass Menagerie* (1965), and Madame Voynitsky in *Uncle Vanya* (1970).

fiabe A form of drama developed in Italy in the 18th century by Carlo *Gozzi. A derivative form of the *commedia dell'arte*, the *fiabe* retained the traditional elements of comic improvisation and stock characters while adding a new strain of fantasy; most examples of the genre took mythological subjects as their theme.

Fiddler on the Roof A musical by Jerry Bock, based on Sholom Aleichem's *Tevye the Milkman*. First performance: New York, 1964. Starring Zero Mostel as Tevye, who struggles to get his many daughters married, it enjoyed a run of eight years on Broadway, establishing a record for any musical.

The London production of 1967 starred Topol, as did the celebrated film version.

Field, Nathan (1587–c. 1620) English actor and playwright, who began as a boy actor with the Children of the Chapel Royal, appearing in plays by Jonson at the Blackfriars Theatre. In 1604 he was particularly acclaimed in Chapman's *Bussy d'Ambois*. He wrote the plays *A Woman is a Weathercock* (1609) and *Amends for Ladies* (1611) and collaborated on others with Massinger and Fletcher.

Field, Sid (1904–50) British performer in music hall, who was popular as the comic character Slasher Green. He appeared in the provinces before reaching London in 1943 and appearing in revues; he retired from the stage in 1949.

Fielding, Henry (1707–54) British novelist and playwright, author of a number of comedies and burlesques. His first real success was *The Author's Farce* (1730), which ridiculed contemporary fashions, as did **Tom Thumb the Great*, which was a resounding triumph. In 1731 he daringly depicted royalty on the stage in *The Welsh Opera; or, The Grey Mare the Better Horse*, after which he satirized the government in *Quixote in England* (1734), *Pasquin* (1736), and *The Historical Register for the Year 1736* (1737), which he produced when he became manager of the Haymarket. The Licensing Act of the same year was in part a response to his satirical writing and effectively ended his association with the theatre.

Fields, Gracie (Grace Stansfield; 1898–1979) British actress and singer, born in Rochdale, where she first appeared at the Hippodrome in 1910. She topped the bills at all the major music halls and was much loved for her lively delivery of such songs as 'The Biggest Aspidistra in the World'.

Fields, Joseph (1895–1966) British playwright, who collaborated with **Jerome Chodorov** (1911–) on such plays as *My Sister Eileen* (1940), *Wonderful Town* (1953), and *Anniversay Waltz* (1954). He also assisted Anita Loos in the stage adaptation of her novel *Gentlemen Prefer Blondes* (1949) and worked with Oscar Hammerstein.

Fields, Lew *See* Weber and Fields.

Fields, W C (William Claude Dukenfield; 1879–1946) US actor, originally a comic juggler, who became a celebrated comedian and appeared in many editions of Ziegfeld's *Follies*. Throughout the 1920s he played haughty gravel-voiced misanthropic characters in musicals, including Eustace McGargle in *Poppy* (1923) and Q Q Quayle in *Ballyhoo* (1930), and appeared in vaudeville throughout the US and Europe. He then embarked on an immensely successful career in films.

Fierstein, Harvey (1954–) US playwright, who has established a reputation for his plays on homosexual themes. *Torch Song Trilogy* (1982) was highly successful off-off-Broadway while the musical *La Cage aux folles* (1983) was acclaimed in New York and London.

Fifth Avenue Theatre A theatre on Broadway, New York, which opened in 1867 and specialized in minstrel shows, but was shut down after a brawl in the auditorium in which a man was killed. In 1869 it reopened with John Brougham starring in one of his own plays. Daly became manager later that year; his own version of *Frou-Frou* by Meilhac and Halévy was a great success as was Bronson Howard's *Saratoga* in 1870. Refurbished in 1872, it was destroyed by fire in 1873.

A second **Fifth Avenue Theatre** was opened by Daly in 1874 with a loss-making production of *Love's Labour Lost*. Daly's own play *The Big Bonanza* (1875) restored the theatre's finances and saw the first New York appearance of John Drew. Subsequently Georgiana Drew make her New York debut there in H J Byron's *Our Boys*. In 1878, under Stephen Fiske, Mary Anderson and Helen Modjeska also played their first New York roles there. The theatre was eventually demolished in 1908 after several changes of name.

58th Street Theatre *See* John Golden Theatre.

51st Street Theatre *See* Mark Hellinger Theatre.

54th Street Theatre *See* George Abbott Theatre.

Filandre (Jean-Baptiste Monchaingre; 1616–91) French actor-manager, also known under the names Jean Mathée and Paphetin. He spent most of his acting career in the provinces and the Low Countries, although he did appear at the Théâtre du Marais as Floridor's successor from 1647 to 1648.

Filippo, Eduardo de *See* de Filippo, Eduardo.

Finlay, Frank (1926-) British actor. He first attracted attention in controversial new plays at the Royal Court Theatre, playing such roles as Harry Kahn in Wesker's *Chicken Soup with Barley* (1958) and Private Attercliffe in Arden's *Serjeant Musgrave's Dance* (1960). With the National Theatre company in 1964 his impressive Iago to Olivier's Othello set the seal on his reputation. Subsequently he played Jesus Christ in Dennis Potter's *Son of Man* at the Round House (1969), while other important parts with the National have included Peppino in de Filippo's *Saturday, Sunday, Monday* (1973–74) and Salieri in *Amadeus* (1981). In 1985 he appeared as Captain Bligh in the musical *Mutiny* at the Piccadilly Theatre.

Finney, Albert (1936-) British actor. After starting his career at the Birmingham Repertory Theatre he appeared in London in Jane Arden's *The Party* (1958) and at Stratford-upon-Avon. He triumphed in the title roles of *Billy Liar* (1960) and Osborne's *Luther* (1961) and went on to demonstrate his range with the National Theatre, playing roles as diverse as Jean in Strindberg's *Miss Julie* to Poche in the Feydeau farce, *A Flea in Her Ear*. He was an associate artistic director at the Royal Court from 1972 to 1975 and, when the National company moved onto the new Lyttelton and Olivier stages, excelled as Hamlet (1975) and in the title role in Marlowe's *Tamburlaine the Great* (1976). In 1983 he was back at the Old Vic directing and starring in a revival of Arden's *Armstrong's Last Goodnight*. In 1986 he won awards in Lyle Kessler's *Orphans*.

Fiorillo, Silvio (d. c. 1633) Italian actor of the *commedia dell'arte*, who was famous for his interpretation of Il Capitano and was probably the first to play Pulcinella. He ran his own company in Naples and visited France with the Accesi; he was also the author of several plays and scenarios.

He is thought to have been the father of **Tiberio Fiorillo** (1608–94), who was born in Naples and eventually appeared with *commedia dell'arte* companies in Paris. Appearing at the Petit-Bourbon and the Palais-Royal, he excelled as Scaramuccia, in which role he appeared without a mask. He also made successful appearances in London and wrote an autobiography; he continued acting into his old age.

Another of Silvio's sons, **Battista Fiorillo** (fl. 1614–51), also appeared as Scaramuccia.

Fire-Raisers, The (*Biedermann und die Brandstifter*) A black comedy by Max *Frisch, regarded as a major example of the Theatre of the Absurd. First performance: Zürich, 1958. Written originally as a radio play in 1953, it condemns the passive attitude of complacent citizens to fire-raisers and reflects Frisch's lack of faith in human responsibility.

fires Although stringent safety precautions have reduced the risk of fire in the modern theatre, a great many theatres have been destroyed in this way over the years. Casualties in the days of candles and gas lighting included such celebrated venues as Shakespeare's Globe Theatre (1613), Drury Lane (1672 and 1809), and Covent Garden (1782 and 1808). The worst fire in British theatre history was however, in 1887 at the Theatre Royal in Exeter, when 186 people died. In the US, a fire at the Brooklyn Theatre in 1876 cost 300 lives, whilst a fire at the Iroquois Theatre in Chicago in 1903 caused 600 deaths, despite the fact that the building was allegedly fireproofed. Elsewhere, even worse disasters occurred at Karlsruhe in 1847, when 631 people died, and at St Petersburg in 1836, when fire killed 800. The most tragic theatre fire of all time, however, happened in China in 1845 when 1670 people lost their lives. The introduction of electricity has done much to improve safety standards and has thankfully put an end to the many tales of actors' costumes being ignited by dangerous stage lighting.

Fisher, Clara (1811–98) British actress, who made a sensational debut at Drury Lane at the age of six, appearing in Garrick's *Gulliver* and impersonating Richard III. She moved with her family to the US in 1827, where she played light comedy roles.

Fiske, Minnie Maddern (Marie Augusta Davey; 1865–1932) US actress, of theatrical parentage, who began on stage at the age of three under her mother's name, Maddern. By the time she was five she had made her New York debut and within 10 years was a star. She retired on her marriage to Harrison Grey Fiske (1861–1942), but soon reappeared in her husband's *Hester Crewe* (1893) and as Nora in Ibsen's *A Doll's House* (1894), the first of a number of modern socially provocative roles; among others were parts in Hardy's *Tess of the D'Urbevilles* and Ibsen's *Hedda Gabler* and *Rosmersholm*. For a time she and her husband also managed the Manhattan Theatre (1901–07), where she directed a series of distinguished plays in opposition to the Theatrical Syndicate. She was seen subsequently in many light comedies, notably as Mrs Malaprop in Sheridan's *The Rivals*.

Fitch, (William) Clyde (1865–1909) US playwright, whose prolific output began with *Beau Brummell* (1890), which was written for Richard Mansfield. Subsequently he enjoyed considerable success with such plays as *Nathan Hale* (1898), *Barbara Frietchie* (1899), and *Captain Jinks of the Horse Marines* (1901), in which Ethel Barrymore appeared. Other works, which did much to make Broadway the focus of US commercial drama, included melodramas, *The Girl with Green Eyes* (1902) – on the theme of jealousy, and *The Truth* (1907), which is regarded as one of his finest plays. His last play, *The City* (1909), was an impassioned protest against urban values.

Fitzball, Edward (1792–1873) British playwright, whose vast output of melodramas, adaptations, and nautical dramas were performed at the minor London theatres. They included *The Pilot; or, a Tale of the Sea* (1825), a spectacular version of *The Flying Dutchman* (1827), *The Red Rover; or, the Mutiny on the Dolphin* (1829), *Jonathan Bradford; or, the Murder at the Wayside Inn* (1833), which was based on a true murder case, and *Paul Clifford* (1835).

Fitzgerald, Barry (William Joseph Shields; 1888–1961) Irish actor, who was for many years at the Abbey Theatre, Dublin and established his reputation as Captain Boyle, a part written for him by O'Casey in *Juno and the Paycock* (1924). He came to London in the same author's *The Silver Tassie*

(1929) and thereafter appeared regularly in both cities and also in films.

Fitzmaurice, George (1877–1963) Irish playwright, who spent most of his life in Dublin. His first play, *The Country Dressmaker* (1907), was a conventional peasant comedy, but later he created such bizarre and fanciful tragi-comedies as *The Dandy Dolls* (1908) and *The Magic Glasses* (1913). His early work was extremely popular at the Abbey Theatre, but from 1923 until his death none of his plays was staged there.

Fitzroy Theatre *See* Scala Theatre.

Five Finger Exercise A play by Peter *Shaffer. First performance: London, 1958. This examination of the tensions underlying the relationships between members of a middle-class family was enormously successful in its first production, directed by John Gielgud, and established the author's reputation.

Flaminia *See* Cecchini, Pier Maria.

Flanagan, Bud *See* Crazy Gang.

Flanagan, Hallie (Mrs Philip H Davis; 1890–1969) US theatre scholar and director, who controlled the Federal Theatre Project from 1935 to 1939. A pioneer of experimental drama and the Living Newspaper technique, she presided over more than 1000 productions under the project and published several authoritative accounts dealing with contemporary US theatre.

Flanders, Michael (1922–75) British actor and lyric writer, who first appeared in Shaw's *You Never Can Tell* at Oxford in 1941. Later, crippled by poliomyelitis, he collaborated with Donald *Swann, contributing to many notable revues, including *At the Drop of a Hat* (1956).

Flare Path A play by Terence *Rattigan. First performance: London, 1942. Drawing on Rattigan's own experiences in the RAF, it depicted the strain suffered by both pilots and their families during the Battle of Britain and attracted enormous wartime audiences in both Britain and the US.

flat A rectangular wooden frame, covered in canvas or some other material, painted, and used as a constituent part of a box set. Usually supported by weights and braces, flats were first introduced in the 17th century and are still used in a variety of adaptations.

Flavio *See* Scala, Flamineo.

Fleck, Johann Friedrich Ferdinand (1757–1801) German actor, who was much admired in plays of the *Sturm und Drang* movement. At the National Theatre in Berlin he distinguished himself with passionate – though unpredictable – performances in the plays of Schiller and Shakespeare and his early death was much regretted.

Flecker, (Herman) James Elroy (1884–1915) British poet and playwright, whose two poetic dramas were staged posthumously. *Hassan, an oriental melodrama, was acclaimed for its combination of extravagant spectacle, impressive poetry, and incidental music by Delius; his other play, *Don Juan* (1926), however, suffered from weak characterization.

Fleetwood, Charles (d. 1745) British theatre manager, who – having bought the Drury Lane patent – went into partnership there with Theophilus Cibber and then Macklin. A notorious gambler and spendthrift, he was disgraced and forced to give up in 1744. His tenure was notable for the first engagement of Garrick at Drury Lane, Macklin's sensational Shylock, and a walkout by the company.

Fleschelles *See* Gaultier-Garguille.

Fletcher, John (1579–1625) English playwright, who met Francis Beaumont in 1605 and subsequently worked with him on several plays before Beaumont's retirement in 1613. He then became playwright for the King's Men, working on his own and collaborating with Shakespeare, Massinger, and others. Fletcher's own plays include *The Faithful Shepherdess* (1608), the tragedy *Bonduca* (1613), and the comedies *Wit Without Money* (1614), *The Wild Goose Chase* (1621), and *The Chances* (1625). His plays with Beaumont include *Philaster; or, Love Lies Bleeding* (1609), *The Maid's Tragedy* (1610), and *The Scornful Lady* (1613). With Shakespeare he probably worked on *The Two Noble Kinsmen*, *Henry VIII*, and a lost play.

Fleury (Abraham-Joseph Bénard; 1750–1822) French actor, who was highly popular as a comic actor with the Comédie-Française. A protégé of Voltaire, he joined the company in 1778 and was its leader until 1818, surviving imprisonment during the Revolution and being much admired in the plays of Molière, especially as Alceste in *Le Misanthrope*.

flexible staging Any system of staging that can be readily adapted to provide a variety of acting areas. Most modern theatres have favoured such systems rather than conventional proscenium arch designs.

flies The area above the stage, from which scenery, lighting, and other equipment can be suspended.

flipper A small extension to a flat, usually attached by a hinge at right angles in order to give added support.

float *See* footlight.

floodlight A lighting unit capable of illuminating a large area of the stage with a diffuse beam, sometimes referred to simply as a flood.

Florence, William Jermyn (or **James**) (Bernard Conlin; 1831–91) US actor, who made his New York debut in 1850 as Hallagan in John Brome's *Home*. For 12 years he played mostly Irish parts, often acting with his wife, **Malvina Pray** (1831–1906), and also appeared at London's Drury Lane in the farce *The Yankee Housekeeper* (1856). Subsequently he was highly successful in such parts as Bob in Tom Taylor's *The Ticket-of-Leave Man*, George D'Alroy in T W Robertson's *Caste* (produced in New York without permission), and as Bardwell Slote in Woolf's *The Mighty Dollar* (1876). In his last years he also played Sir Lucius O'Trigger in Sheridan's *The Rivals* and Zekiel Homespun in Colman the Younger's *The Heir-at-Law* for Joseph Jefferson.

Floridor (Josias de Soulas, Sieur de Primefosse; c. 1608–71) French actor, who became leader of the company at the Hôtel de Bourgogne. Much admired in the plays of Corneille and Racine, he led a strolling company in the provinces before joining the Théâtre du Marais in 1638 and then moving to the Hôtel de Bourgogne in 1647. He was noted for his restrained acting style.

Flower Drum Song A musical by Richard *Rodgers and Oscar *Hammerstein II. First performance: New York, 1958. The plot depicts the immigrants of San Francisco's Chinatown and the romantic problems they encounter. The musical was made into a film in 1961.

fly gallery An elevated platform in the flies, running parallel to the side of the stage, where ropes used to hang scenery and stage equipment can be secured.

flying effect The practice, first developed in the ancient Greek theatre, of lowering scenery or actors to the stage by means of ropes or wires (to which a performer is attached by a harness) in order to create the illusion of flight.

Fo, Dario (1926-) Italian playwright and actor-manager, who has attracted considerable attention with his controversial revues and plays on political themes. A skilled mime artist, he and his wife Franca Rama established a popular cabaret act in the 1950s and subsequently attacked such targets as Fascism and Communism in such plays as *Gli arcangeli non giocano al flipper* (Archangels Don't Play the Pin-Tables; 1959) and *Settimo; ruba un po'meno* (Seventh: Thou Shalt Steal a Little Less; 1964). *Morte accidentale di un anarchico* (*Accidental Death of an Anarchist; 1970) was written for the La Commune company and enjoyed long runs in London; more recent successes have included *We Won't Pay! We Won't Pay!* (1974), seen in London as *Can't Pay? Won't Pay!*, and *Trumpets and Raspberries* (1984).

focus lamp A unit of lighting, also called a **lens spot**, the beam of which is adjusted by a lens. Generally replaced by the Fresnel spot, it is still used in Germany, where it is known as a *Linsenscheinwerfer*.

Foersom, Peter (d. 1817) Danish actor, noted for his early translations into Danish of the plays of Shakespeare. His translations included *Hamlet* (1813), in which he played the title role.

Fogerty, Elsie *See* Central School of Speech and Drama.

Folies-Bergère A music hall in Paris, opened in 1869 as a venue for pantomime and opera. Popular for its long and fashionable promenade, it became widely known under the management of Paul Derval from 1919 to 1966 for its shows featuring large numbers of scantily clad beautiful young women. Mistinguett and Maurice Chevalier also appeared here.

Folies Dramatiques, Théâtre des A theatre on the Boulevard du Temple in Paris, opened in 1831 on the site of the Théâtre de l'Ambigu. It was a home of melodrama and saw the early success of Frédérick in one of his own plays. Demolished in 1867, a new theatre of the same name was erected in the rue de Bondy. *See also* Kingsway Theatre.

Folies-Marigny *See* Marigny, Théâtre.

Folies-Nouvelles, Théâtre des A theatre in Paris, opened in 1852 as a venue for pantomime and opera. Subsequently it staged various unsophisticated dramas before being renamed the Théâtre Déjazet in 1859 in honour of the actress Pauline-Virginie *Déjazet, who appeared there over several years.

folk theatre A form of early rural drama, usually linked to specific festivals in the agricultural calendar. Common to most European countries with a strong agricultural tradition, folk theatre includes various ritual dances, notably the *Horn Dance and *Morris Dance in Britain, as well as entertainments with a stronger dramatic element. Well-known examples of folk theatre elsewhere include the *Archetringle of Switzerland, the antics of the Bavarian Wild Men, and the *Mascarade of France. Ultimately such forms of theatre evolved into the mummers' play and contributed to the development of liturgical drama. *See also* Plough Monday, Robin Hood play.

follow spot A spotlight that can be directed by hand so that its powerful beam can be kept trained upon an actor or other mobile object on the stage.

Folz, Hans (c. 1435–1513) German poet, playwright, and publisher, who was the author of early examples of the *Fastnachtsspiel*. Based in Nuremberg from about 1459, he also influenced the development of the *meistersänger* tradition.

Fontanne, Lynn *See* Lunt, Alfred.

Fonvizin, Denis Ivanovich (1744–92) Russian playwright, noted for his plays satirizing the pretensions of the upper classes. His successful comedy, *Brigadir* (The Brigadier-General; 1766–69), lampooned those members of the nobility who sought to imitate French manners; it was followed by his masterpiece, *Nedorosl* (The Minor; 1782), in which he took up wholly Russian themes concerning land ownership and serfdom. In 1783, however, Fonvizin fell from favour with Catherine the Great on account of his interest in social issues and his plays were banned.

Fool A clown who appeared in the medieval *Feast of Fools and in various festivities associated with folk theatre. He wore a brightly-coloured suit (called motley) with a hood to which bells, horns, or ass's ears were attached and played an important comic role in both the morris dance and the mummers' play. He was armed with a *marotte* or bauble, comprising a miniature Fool's head mounted on a short stick, or a wooden sword. *See also* Court Fool.

Fools, Feast of *See* Feast of Fools.

Foote, Samuel (1720–77) British actor-manager and playwright, who became an actor in 1744 and was often called the **English Aristophanes**. Taking over the Haymarket Theatre in 1747, he exhibited a talent for biting caricature in a series of plays that he wrote and performed. The Haymarket having no play licence, Foote evaded the law by claiming to hold lectures or tea parties at which any entertainment was free. His first successful play, *The Englishman in Paris*, was produced at Drury Lane in 1753; his most celebrated play, *The Minor*, ridiculed the Methodist movement and was staged at the Crow Street Theatre, Dublin, then at the Haymarket in 1760. In 1766 he obtained a limited patent through the Duke of York's influence as compensation for the loss of a leg through a practical joke in which the duke had been involved.

footlight A lighting unit positioned at floor level at the front of the stage, usually one of a strip of such lights, in order to illuminate the stage area from a low angle. In Britain such lights are sometimes referred to as **floats**.

Footlight Players *See* Dock Street Theatre.

Footlights Club A theatre group in Cambridge, founded in 1883. Comprising members of Cambridge University, it presents an annual revue, which tours nationally and has brought to light a long line of comic talents. Women have been admitted since 1957.

footlights trap A long narrow opening across the front of the stage of older theatres, into which the footlights sank when a dimming of the stage lighting was desired.

fops' alley An area of the pit or forestage in the Restoration theatre. Visible from the rest of the auditorium, the area was popular with dandies of the day as a place to show off their dress and broadcast opinions of the play being presented.

Forbes-Robertson, Sir Johnston (1853–1937) British actor-manager who was a pupil of Samuel Phelps. Having made his debut in 1874, he became a member of Irving's company at the Lyceum in 1882. After touring the US with Mary Anderson he returned to the Lyceum under his own management to play Romeo to the Juliet of Mrs Patrick Campbell. In the same season he appeared as Hamlet, an outstanding performance. He also excelled in works by Pinero and Henry Arthur Jones, and was especially successful in an adaptation of Jerome K Jerome's *The Passing of the Third Floor Back* (1908).

He married Gertrude *Elliott; their daughter, **Jean Forbes-Robertson** (1905–62), came to prominence as an actress as Sonia in Komisarjevsky's production of *Uncle Vanya* in 1926. She followed it with equally acclaimed performances as Juliet, Peter Pan (which she played for eight consecutive seasons), and numerous classical roles. Her modern parts included Tessa in Margaret Kennedy's *The Constant Nymph* (1928) and Kay in Priestley's *Time and the Conways* (1937); more unusually, she also appeared as Oberon, Everyman, and Jim Hawkins in *Treasure Island*.

Ford, John (1586–1639) English playwright, who wrote his first plays in 1628, after training as a lawyer. Of the plays he wrote alone the most significant was *'Tis Pity She's a Whore*; the others include *Love's Sacrifice* (1627), *The Lover's Melancholy* (1628), and *The Broken Heart* (1629), all of which tackle various self-destructive obsessions. He probably collaborated with William Rowley and Dekker on *The Witch of Edmonton* (1621) and with Dekker on *The Sun's Darling* (1624).

Forde, Florrie (Florence Flanagan; 1876–1940) Australian-born music hall singer, whose career began in Sydney in 1894. She came to London in 1897 and became famous for leading the audience in such rousing songs as 'Hold Your Hand Out, Naughty Boy' and 'Down at the Old Bull and Bush'.

Ford's Theatre A theatre in Washington DC, which opened in 1862 as Ford's Atheneum in a former church. The theatre was later rebuilt, opening in 1863 as Ford's Theatre. It closed, however, after President Lincoln's assassination there by John Wilkes Booth on 14 April, 1865, during a performance of Tom Taylor's *Our American Cousin*. In 1932 it became a museum. It was remodelled on the original auditorium and reopened in 1968, since when productions have included the musicals *Don't Bother Me, I Can't Cope* and *Your Arms Too Short to Box With God*.

forestage *See* apron.

Formalism A theatre movement in the USSR following the Revolution of 1917. Championed by such directors as Meyerhold and Akimov, it advocated the subjection of an actor's individuality to the intentions of the director alone; it soon lost favour with audiences and had to be abandoned.

formal stage A stage setting in which a simple arrangement of scenic features remains basically unchanged throughout a performance, apart from alterations to the *detail scenery.

Formby, George (George Hoy Booth; 1904–61) British music hall singer, who became popular with comic songs delivered in a Lancashire accent to high-speed banjulele accompaniment. Famous for such songs as 'Mr Wu' and 'When I'm Cleaning Windows', he starred in numerous film comedies.

Forrest, Edwin (1806–72) US actor, who made his first appearance at the age of 10 in an amateur production. In 1820 he appeared as Young Norval in Home's *Douglas*, after which he gradually built up a reputation as the finest player of tragic roles in the US, noted for his resonant voice and grand style. He played many Shakespearean roles, including King Lear, Hamlet, Macbeth, Othello, and Mark Antony. He also excelled as Spartacus in Bird's *The Gladiator*

(1831), a part which was written for him, and the title role in Stone's *Metamora* (1829). He appeared with success in London but became involved in public rivalry with Macready, which culminated in the famous riot (1849) at the Astor Place Opera House. In 1872 he made his last performance, in Bulwer-Lytton's *Richelieu*.

Forrest Theatre *See* Eugene O'Neill Theatre.

Fort, Paul (1872–1960) French poet, director, and manager, who founded the Théâtre d'Art in 1890 as a centre of the French Symbolist movement. Previously he ran the Théâtre Mixte, where he developed his theories of abstract theatre; he abandoned drama altogether in 1892 after failing to reconcile the physical reality of the actors with his abstract ideals and was succeeded by Lugné-Poë.

Fortune Theatre A theatre in Cripplegate, London, which opened in 1600 as the home of the *Admiral's Men. Some details of its construction are known and its two round wooden galleries could probably hold 1000 people; a statue of the Goddess of Fortune stood over the entrance. It established a strong reputation as a popular venue before being burnt down in 1621; it was rebuilt in 1623 in brick but was less successful. Subsequently it was partially dismantled by the Puritans, being totally demolished in 1661.

Another theatre of the same name opened in 1924 in Russell Street, Covent Garden, London. The first theatre to be built in the capital after World War I, it began with plays by such authors as Galsworthy, Lonsdale, and O'Casey – many staged by J B Fagan. After World War II it became better known as a home of revue with performances by Kenneth Horne, Joyce Grenfell, and Flanders and Swann, among others; *Beyond the Fringe* was a major success in 1961. Since then several plays – notably *Sleuth* (1973) by Anthony Shaffer, *Murder at the Vicarage* (1976) by Agatha Christie, and *The Brothers Karamazov* (1981) – have been successfully presented. In 1981 attempts to stage runs of plays from the provinces and fringe theatres caused a financial crisis.

Fortuny, Mariano *See Kuppelhorizont.*

48th Street Theatre A theatre on West 48th Street, New York, which opened in 1912. Known as the **Windsor Theatre** from 1937 to 1943, it housed mostly opera and musical comedy but a few straight plays were also seen there, including *Harvey* (1944) and *Stalag 17* (1951). It was demolished in 1955.

44th Street Theatre A theatre on West 44th Street, New York, which opened as the New Weber and Fields Music Hall. Seating 1463, it housed musicals and light opera with a few classical plays having been produced in 1915. The Marx Brothers had a successful run there in 1928, while subsequent successes included plays by J B Priestley, Paul Green, and Moss Hart. A smaller theatre on the roof, known as the **Nora Bayes Theatre**, was occupied for a time by the Federal Theatre Project. Both theatres were demolished in 1945.

49th Street Theatre A theatre on West 49th Street, New York, which opened in 1921. The theatre housed both new plays and revivals of classics, notably works by Ibsen and Strindberg and productions by the Federal Theatre Project. Mei Lanfang appeared there in 1930. In 1938 it became a cinema and was later demolished.

46th Street Theatre A theatre on West 46th Street, New York, which originally opened as **Chanin's 46th Street Theatre** in 1925. Seating 1338, it was renamed in 1932 and had major successes with such musicals as *Hellzapoppin* (1938), *Finian's Rainbow* (1947), and *Guys and Dolls* (1950). Recent productions have included *I Do! I Do!* (1966), *No, No, Nanette* (1971), and *The Best Little Whorehouse in Texas* (1978).

Forum Theatre *See* Library Theatre; Vivian Beaumont Theatre.

Foss, Wenche (1917-) Norwegian actress, who established her reputation in light comedy at the Oslo Nye Teater but later went on to play many serious parts also. She won acclaim in Ibsen's plays at the Nationaltheatret, where she first appeared in 1952, as well as in the comedies of Molière and others; more recent successes have included Arbuzov's *Old World* (1978) and William Douglas Home's *The Kingfisher* (1980).

14th Street Theatre A theatre on West 14th Street, New York, which originally opened as the **Théâtre Français**, staging plays in French until 1871. It was then known as the Lyceum Theatre for a period and became the 14th Street Theatre in 1886. In 1932 the theatre was taken over by Eva Le Gallienne as a home for her Civic Repertory Company until 1932. The theatre was demolished in 1938.

Fox, G(eorge Washington) L(afayette) 1825–77) US actor, who first appeared on stage at the age of seven in Boston. His New York debut came in 1850 when he joined the National Theatre under the name Lafayette Fox, remaining for several seasons and playing numerous parts. Later, moving to the Bowery Theatre, he became a celebrated pantomime performer, a reputation he maintained at the Olympic where his successes included *Humpty Dumpty* (1868), burlesques of *Hamlet* and *Macbeth* (1870), and *Wee Willie Winkie* (1870).

fox wedge A wooden wedge placed under a flat in order to compensate for any rake in the stage.

Foy, Eddie (Edwin Fitzgerald Foy; 1856–1928) US actor and entertainer. He began in vaudeville in 1869, then settled in Chicago (1888), where for six years he clowned his way through such extravanganzas as *Bluebeard Jr* (1890) and *Little Robinson Crusoe* (1893). Subsequently he starred in such musical comedies as *Up and Down Broadway* (1910) before returning to vaudeville and bringing his seven children into his act.

foyer The area of the theatre between the auditorium and the entrance; refreshments may often be purchased here. *See also* box office.

Fragson, Harry (Harry Potts; 1869–1913) Anglo-French entertainer at the piano, who became a popular café concert singer in Paris and subsequently achieved a high reputation in music hall. Famous for such songs as 'Hullo, hullo, Who's Your Lady Friend?', he was fatally shot by his father in a fit of insanity.

France, Théâtre de *See* Odéon, Théâtre National de l'.

Frank, Bruno (1887–1946) German playwright, who was the author of several popular sophisticated comedies. *Sturm im Wasserglass* (1930) was successful in Britain in an adaptation by James Bridie, while other plays include the historical drama *Zwölftausend* (Twelve Thousand; 1927).

Franklin Theatre A small theatre in Chatham Street, New York, which opened in 1835 with a season of classic comedy headed by Thomas Morton's *The School of Reform*. Although Junius Brutus Booth acted in several tragedies there (1836–37), it became well-known as a venue for melodrama and farce. In 1837 Joseph Jefferson III made his New York debut there, aged eight. The theatre did not prosper financially until 1841, when the company of the Park Theatre appeared there and *Fifteen Years of a*

New York Fireman's Life had its first performance. After 1842 it was used for pantomime. The authorities closed the theatre in 1854 after a scandal involving *tableaux vivants*.

Franz, Ellen (1839–1923) German actress, who was the wife of George II, Duke of Saxe-Meiningen. Her influence was largely responsible for the Duke's interest in the theatre and his support for the famous Meininger company.

Fraser, Claude Lovat (1890–1921) British artist and stage designer, who executed designs for the Lyric Theatre in Hammersmith. His designs for *As You Like It* and *The Beggar's Opera* there in 1920, derived from the romantic styles of the 18th century, inspired a whole new school of stage design.

Frayn, Michael (1933–) British playwright and novelist, who established his reputation in the theatre with *The Two of Us* (1970). Subsequently he enjoyed success with such bitter comedies as *Alphabetical Order* (1975), *Donkeys' Years* (1976), and *Clouds* (1976); more recent works have included *Make and Break* (1980), *Noises Off* (1982) – which parodies farce and includes scenes depicting events behind the set itself – and translations of Chekhov and Tolstoy.

Frazee Theatre *See* Wallack's Theatre.

Frédérick (Antoine-Louis-Prosper Lemaître; 1800–76) French actor, who was a major exponent of Romantic drama in the popular theatres of the Boulevard du Temple. He established his reputation in a parody of the role of Robert Macaire in the melodrama *L'Auberge des Adrets* in 1823, the part becoming identified with him from that time on. The sequel, *Robert Macaire* (1834), was equally successful, as were subsequent performances in such plays as *Trente Ans, ou la Vie d'un joueur*, *Othello*,

Hamlet, and *Kean, ou Désordre et génie*, which was written for him by Dumas *père*. His forceful style of acting also suited him to the plays of Victor Hugo, notably *Ruy Blas*, in which he appeared at the opening of the Théâtre de la Renaissance in 1838. Towards the end of his life, however, tastes changed and he died in poverty.

Fredro, Aleksander (1793–1876) Polish poet and playwright, who fought in the Napoleonic Wars and subsequently became famous for his well-constructed comedies in the style of Molière and Goldoni. His finest works were written early in his career as a playwright and include the comedies *Mąż i żona* (Husband and Wife; 1822), *Śluby panieńskie* (Maidens' Vows; 1833), and *Zemsta* (Vengeance; 1834), which is generally regarded as his masterpiece. After criticism by the Romantics, he ceased to write for 19 years before producing several more, less distinguished, works.

Freear, Louie (1873–1939) British comic actress, whose career encompassed Shakespeare, musical comedy, and variety. She was acclaimed in London in the musical comedy *The Gay Parisienne* (1896) and made a great hit as Fifi in *A Chinese Honeymoon* at the Strand Theatre (1901).

Freedley, George Reynolds (1904–67) US theatre historian, who founded the Theatre Collection of the New York Public Library. Having studied under George Baker at Yale, he worked with the Theatre Guild and in 1939 cofounded the Theatre Library Association; he was also connected with the management of the American National Theatre and Academy.

Freie Bühne A theatre club in Berlin, founded in 1889 by Otto Brahm. A home of naturalistic drama, it presented plays by Bjørnson, Holz, Ibsen, Hauptmann, Strindberg, Tolstoy, Zola, and others at several theatres as well as running its own literary paper; actors with the club included Agnes Sorma. In 1894 it was linked up with the Deutsches Theatre, where it continued to promote experimental drama.

Freie Volksbühne *See* Volksbühne.

French Without Tears A farce by Terence *Rattigan. First performance: London, 1936. Rattigan's first great success in the theatre, this play ran for 1049 performances and has been revived many times. It revolves around a French language course arranged for candidates to the civil service at a French resort.

Fresnay, Pierre (Pierre Laudenbach; 1897–1975) French actor, who established his reputation at the Comédie-Française during the 1920s. After 1927 he appeared many times in London, succeeding Coward himself in *Conversation Piece* (opposite his wife Yvonne *Printemps) in 1934. From 1937 he and his wife appeared together under their own management at the Théâtre de la Michodière in a series of popular comedies.

Fresnel spot A spotlight capable of producing a bright but soft-edged beam, frequently used in combination with other similar lighting units. It was named after the French scientist Augustin Jean Fresnel (1788–1827), who invented the type of lens on which it is based.

Freytag, Gustav (1816–95) German novelist and playwright, who was the author of several plays in the well-made play tradition. His most successful play was *Die Journalisten* (1852); his critical writings include *Technik des Dramas*, which discusses the nature of the well-made play.

Fridolin *See* Gélinas, Gratien.

Friel, Brian (1929–) British playwright, born in Northern Ireland, who is the author

of several acclaimed plays on Irish themes. His first play, *This Doubtful Paradise* (1959), was followed by such successful dramas as *Philadelphia, Here I Come!* (1964), *Lovers* (1967), *The Freedom of the City* (1973), and *Faith Healer* (1979), in which Helen Mirren was highly praised. *Translations* (1980), similarly set against a background of political tension in Northern Ireland, is regarded as his finest play to date; other works include a translation of Chekhov's *Three Sisters* (1981) and *Aristocrats* (1988).

Friml, Rudolph (1881–1972) US composer, born in Czechoslovakia, whose successful comedies and operettas included *Rose-Marie* (1924). Other works for the theatre in a similar romantic vein were *The Firefly* (1912) and *The Vagabond King* (1975).

fringe theatre Experimental theatre in Britain that takes its name from the 'alternative' drama that developed around the official *Edinburgh Festival in the 1950s and has now become as important a feature of the festival as the main programme. Fringe theatre groups range from professional small-scale theatre companies to student and amateur drama societies performing both new and classic works; the first fringe theatre group in Britain was the Traverse Theatre, through which C P Taylor and Tom Stoppard first emerged. Fringe drama has since become an important feature of the artistic life of London and the major metropolitan centres (equivalent to New York's off-off-Broadway) and at other arts festivals too. The best known fringe venues at present in London include the Hampstead Theatre Club, the Almeida, the Half Moon Theatre, the Donmar Warehouse, The Pit (at the Barbican), and the National Theatre's Cottesloe Theatre. Leading fringe groups include the Hull Truck theatre company, the 7:84 touring company, and the Pip Simmons theatre group; writers connected with such troupes include Howard Brenton and David Hare.

Frisch, Max (Rudolf) (1911-) Swiss playwright and novelist, who is now (with Dürrenmatt) regarded as the most significant post-war German-language dramatist. His socially challenging dramas, characterized by ironic dialogue and experimental farce, include *Nun singen sie wieder* (Now They Sing Again; 1945), *Die chinesische Mauer* (The Great Wall of China; 1946), *Als der Krieg zu Ende war* (When the War was Over; 1949), and – more recently – *Triptychon* (1980). His most outstanding works are the radio play *Biedermann und die Brandstifter* (The *Fire Raisers; 1953), a bitter satire on bourgeois complacency, and *Andorra* (1961), a controversial tragedy about anti-semitism.

Fritellino *See* Cecchini, Pier Maria.

Frogs, The A comedy by *Aristophanes. First performance: Athens, 405 BC. One of Aristophanes's milder late works, the play satirizes tragedies of the day, comparing Euripides and Aeschylus, and anticipates his development of Middle Comedy.

Frohman, Daniel (1851–1940) US manager, who – together with his brother **Gustave Frohman** (1855–1930) – managed the Lyceum Theatre in New York with great success from 1885. Previously business manager of the Madison Square Theatre, Daniel Frohman assembled a renowned stock company at the Lyceum, presenting many acclaimed productions of plays by such authors as Pinero and H A Jones among others. Daniel was also manager of Daly's Theatre from 1899 to 1903.

Another brother, **Charles Frohman** (1860–1915), established his reputation as a successful manager with Bronson Howard's *Shenandoah* (1888) and subsequently presided over an excellent stock company at the Empire Theatre from 1893. His successful productions for the London stage included Klein's *A Night Out* (1896) and plays by J M Barrie – including *Peter Pan* (1904) –

and George Edwardes; at one point he controlled five London theatres simultaneously. He was drowned when the *Lusitania* sank in 1915.

front of house Those parts of a theatre in front of the stage. These include the auditorium, foyer, bars, and offices.

Fry, Christopher (Christopher Harris, 1907-) British playwright, who established his reputation as a leading writer of poetic drama in the 1940s with such mystical plays as *The Boy with a Cart* and *The Firstborn*. In 1940 he became director of the Oxford Playhouse and he subsequently enjoyed great commercial success with his lively and eloquent comedies, starting with *A Phoenix Too Frequent*. The *Lady's Not For Burning* provided John Gielgud with a West End success, while Olivier was admired in the tragicomedy *Venus Observed*. *The Dark Is Light Enough* was less successful despite the performance of Edith Evans and by the late 1950s Fry's elevated style had been eclipsed by the new aggressive realism of Osborne and the other Royal Court playwrights. Later works have included translations of Anouilh, Giraudoux, and Ibsen, and several screenplays.
Principal works:
The Boy with a Cart: 1937.
The Tower: 1939.
A Phoenix Too Frequent: 1946.
The Firstborn: 1948.
Thor, With Angels: 1948.
The Lady's Not For Burning: 1948.
Venus Observed: 1950.
A Sleep of Prisoners: 1951.
The Dark Is Light Enough: 1954.
Curtmantle: 1961.
A Yard of Sun: 1970.

Fugard, Athol (1932-) South African playwright, director, and actor, whose plays frequently tackle issues raised by racialism and repression. He began his career in Cape Town, founding an experimental company there, and acted in *No Good Friday*, his first play, in 1959. He also appeared on stage in such later works as the acclaimed *Blood Knot* and established another theatre group – the Serpent Players – in Port Elizabeth in 1963, where he directed works by authors ranging from Brecht to Sophocles. He has also experimented with the techniques of improvisation and collective creation in such pieces as *Sizwe Bansi Is Dead* and several of his later plays have been seen in Britain and the US, often featuring the actor James Earl Jones. His *Notebooks 1960–1977* (1984) detail his experiences in the South African theatre.

Principal works:
No Good Friday: 1959.
Ngogo: 1960.
The Blood Knot: 1961.
Hello and Goodbye: 1965.
Boesman and Lena: 1969.
The Coat: 1971.
Sizwe Bansi Is Dead : 1972.
The Island: 1973.
Statements after an Arrest under the Immorality Act: 1972.
Dimetos: 1975.
A Lesson from Aloes: 1978.
Master Harold and the Boys: 1982.
The Road to Mecca: 1985.

Fulham Theatre *See* Grand Theatre.

Fuller, Isaac (1606–72) English scene painter, who worked in London after the Restoration, having studied in Paris. In 1669 he successfully sued the Drury Lane management in respect of his fee for painting a scene in Dryden's *Tyrannic Love*.

Fuller, Rosalinde (1892–1982) British actress, who started in the chorus of the Folies-Bergère in 1918. Subsequently she performed in revue in New York, where she appeared in her first straight part in 1921 and, the following year, played Ophelia to John Barrymore's Hamlet. She made her London debut in 1927 and went on to appear with Wolfit's Shakespearean company and in the plays of Shaw and Chekhov as well as in her own solo programmes, in which she toured the world.

Fulton Theatre *See* Helen Hayes Theatre.

Funambules, Théâtre des A theatre on the Boulevard du Temple in Paris, which opened in 1816 on the site of a former booth. Early productions were predominantly circus-type entertainments and harlequinades; later, however, Deburau appeared there as Pierrot and the theatre became known for its pantomimes, which were notable for their elaborate technical effects. The theatre was demolished in the rebuilding of Paris in 1862.

Futurism A movement in the theatre and the arts in general that developed in the early 20th century in response to a new optimism about the future and rejection of the past. Developed initially by Marinetti, who coined the term Futurism in a manifesto in 1909, the movement called for a new faith in technology and dynamic action but ultimately fell from favour after being identified with Nazi philosophy. It did, however, stimulate a new interest in fragmented language and plot and challenged accepted practices in staging and lighting.

Fuzelier, Louis (1672–1752) French playwright and editor of the literary periodical *Mercure de France* (1744–52). He collaborated with Lesage, Piron, and others on numerous plays for fairground theatres and also wrote for the Opéra-Comique, the Comédie-Italienne, and the Comédie-Française.

Fyffe, Will (1885–1947) Scottish comic performer in the music hall, who began in melodrama and revue. He became immensely popular in sketches and as the singer of such songs as 'I Belong ta Glasgae'.

G

Gabrielli, Francesco (1588 – c. 1636) Italian actor of the *commedia dell'arte*, who played a major role in the development of the character Scapino. He appeared with the Accesi and later became a prominent member of the Confidenti and is known to have appeared in Paris in 1624 with the Fedeli.

gaff A building temporarily converted for use as a theatre (especially in the 19th century), usually for the presentation of cheap productions of music hall and melodrama, in which case it was called a **blood tub**. In Scotland the equivalent term was **geggie**.

Gaiety Theatre A theatre in the Strand, London, opened in 1864 as the **Strand Musick Hall**. Closed in 1866, it was rebuilt and, seating 2000 people, reopened in 1868 as a venue under John *Hollingshead and subsequently became famous for its burlesques, in which Nellie Farren, E W Royce, Edward Terry, and Kate Vaughan were highly acclaimed together from 1876 onwards. George Edwardes took over in 1885 with a similar programme until, in 1892, he staged *In Town*, one of the earliest examples of musical comedy and the first of many such productions at the theatre, usually featuring a famous chorus of 'Gaiety Girls'. When the Strand was widened the theatre was closed in 1903 and a new Gaiety opened close to the Aldwych, holding 1338 people. Musical comedy continued there after Edwardes died but with less success and, after diverting into straight drama in the 1920s and 1930s, the theatre closed in 1939, being demolished in 1957.

Another theatre of the same name opened in Dublin in 1871 and was used at first by touring companies from England. Later it became a venue for Irish works under the auspices of the *Irish Literary Theatre (1900 – 01) but subsequently reverted to a largely English programme. The Gate Theatre company performed regularly at the Gaiety during World War II, after which the theatre staged both Irish and English drama. After alteration in 1955, the theatre was saved from demolition by the television presenter Eamonn Andrews and now stages a wide variety of entertainments.

A third Gaiety was opened in Manchester in 1908, in what had been a music hall, by Miss Annie *Horniman as a home for the first repertory company in England. The first production, *Reaping the Whirlwind* by Allan Monkhouse, effectively founded a tradition of serious drama in Manchester; subsequent writers for the theatre included Harold Brighouse, Stanley Houghton, and St John Ervine. Lewis *Casson later took the theatre over but financial troubles led to the end of the company in 1917. The theatre became a cinema in 1921.

The **Gaiety Theatre** on Broadway, New York, opened in 1908. It housed live drama until 1932, when it became a cinema and burlesque house. Leading performers who appeared there included John Barrymore and Frank Bacon, who enjoyed great success in his own play *Lightnin'* (1918). Among other plays staged there were Lonsdale's *Aren't We All?* (1923) and Somerset Maugham's *Rain* (1926). The theatre was renamed the **Victoria Theatre** in 1943.

Gaîté, Théâtre de la A theatre on the Boulevard du Temple in Paris, which opened in 1764 as a venue for puppet shows. After diversifying with mime and circus-type entertainments, it was rebuilt in 1805 as a home of melodrama, especially the plays of Pixérécourt (who managed it from 1823 to 1834), and was again reconstituted (in 1862) on a new site as the Théâtre de la Musique.

galanty show *See* shadow play.

Galdós, Benito Pérez *See* Pérez Galdós, Benito.

Galileo (*Leben des Galilei*) An historical play by Bertolt *Brecht, written 1937–39. First performance: Zürich, 1943. The play draws upon Galileo's life story to highlight the conflict between weakness and integrity and provided Charles Laughton with an acclaimed part on its first English-language production in Los Angeles in 1947.

Galimafré *See* Bobèche.

gallery *See* auditorium.

Galli *See* Bibiena, Ferdinando.

Gallienne, Eva Le *See* Le Gallienne, Eva.

Gallina, Giacinto (1852–97) Italian playwright, author of several plays in the Venetian dialect. Such early plays as *Le Barufe in famegia* (Family Quarrels; 1872) were influenced by Goldoni; later, however, he satirized contemporary society in several plays and ventured into tragedy with *La famegia del santolo* (The Godfather's Family; 1892), which is considered his masterpiece.

Gallo Theatre *See* New Yorker Theatre.

Galsworthy, John (1867–1933) British novelist and playwright, whose first play – The *Silver Box* (1906) – was an immediate success. His interest in justice and moral issues reappears in such works as *Strife* (1909), *Justice* (1910), *The Eldest Son* (1912), *The *Skin Game* (1920), and *Loyalties* (1922). His plays belong to the well-made play tradition and are rooted in the social issues of his time. He won a Nobel Prize in 1932.

Gambon, Michael (1940-) British actor, born in Dublin, who made his debut in *Othello* in 1962. He has worked frequently with the Royal Shakespeare and National Theatre companies, interspersed with appearances in Ayckbourn's *The Norman Conquests* (1974) and Simon Gray's *Otherwise Engaged* (1976). He played the title role in *King Lear* and Antony in *Antony and Cleopatra* at Stratford-upon-Avon and the Barbican, and won the Olivier Best Actor Award in Arthur Miller's *A View from the Bridge* (1987). In 1988 he appeared in the title role in Chekhov's *Uncle Vanya* at the Vaudeville. His performance in Dennis Potter's television series *The Singing Detective* has been widely praised.

Game of Love and Chance, The (*Le Jeu de l'amour et du hasard*) A comedy by Pierre *Marivaux. First performance: Comédie-Italienne, Paris, 1730. The plot concerns the courtship of Dorante (disguised as his valet Arlequin) and Silvia (disguised as her maid Lisette).

Gammer Gurton's Needle An early English farce, probably by William *Stevenson. First performance: Christ's College, Cambridge, c. 1560. The mischievous beggar Diccon generates confusion following the loss of Gammer Gurton's needle while repairing her servant Hodge's trousers.

Ganassa, Zan (Alberto Naseli; d. c. 1583) Italian actor-manager of the *commedia dell'arte*, who led one of the first Italian companies to tour in other countries. He presented productions in Paris in 1571 and at the marriage of the King of Navarre (subsequently Henry IV) a year later; tours of Spain in the 1570s had a profound influence upon the early Spanish theatrical tradition.

Garção, Pedro António Correia (1724–72) Portuguese poet, playwright, and critic, who did much to reform Portuguese drama along classical lines. His verse comedies, *Teatro Novo* (New Theatre) and *Assembléia ou Partida* (Meeting or Parting), satirized life in contemporary Lisbon and contained much of his finest poetry.

Garcia, Victor (1934-) Argentinian director, who moved to France in 1961 and established a reputation for his innovative productions of plays by such authors as Arrabal and Genet. His controversial production of García Lorca's *Yerma* (1971) involved the use of a huge trampoline.

Garcia de la Huerta, Vicente (1734–87) Spanish playwright, poet, and critic, who is best known as the author of the celebrated tragedy *Raquel* (1778). His critical writings were less influential, with several major writers being omitted from his 16-volume *Teatro español* (1785–86).

García Gutiérrez, Antonio (1813–84) Spanish playwright, usually remembered for the popular drama *El trovador* (The Troubadour; 1836), upon which Verdi's opera *Il trovatore* was later based. His other works include the plays *Venganza catalana* (Catalan Vengeance; 1864) and *Juan Lorenzo* (1865) and a number of *zarzuelas*.

García Lorca, Federico (1898–1936) Spanish poet and playwright, who is considered the most significant figure in modern Spanish literature. His early lyrical and experimental plays, written in a spirit of revolt against the contemporary fashion for Realism, were chiefly written for performance by the travelling theatre La Barraca, of which he was both founder and director. He is best remembered for his evocative portrayals of Andalusian peasant life and for his intense poetic tragedies treating such themes as frustrated womanhood and the conflict between love and honour. His most famous work is the trilogy *Bodas de sangre*, **Yerma*, and *La Casa de Bernarda Alba*. He was executed by Nationalist partisans in 1936, shortly after the outbreak of the Spanish Civil War.

Principal works:

El maleficio de la mariposa: 1920; translated as *The Butterfly's Curse*.

Mariana Pineda: 1927.

La zapatera prodigiosa: 1930; translated as *The Shoemaker's Amazing Wife*.

Bodas de sangre: 1933; translated as **Blood Wedding*.

Yerma: 1934.

La Casa de Bernarda Alba: 1945; translated as *The *House of Bernarda Alba*.

Garden Theatre A theatre in Madison Avenue, New York, which opened in 1890. Among its distinguished players were Sarah Bernhardt in Sardou's *La Tosca* (1891) and Ben Greet and his company in a season of Shakespeare (1910). Other productions included Gilbert's *The Mountebanks* (1893) and Hauptmann's *The Weavers* (1915). The theatre became the **Jewish Art Theatre** in 1919 and was demolished in 1925.

Gardin, Vladimir (1877–1965) Russian actor, who established his reputation in modern drama in St Petersburg under Vera Komisarjevskaya but later moved (1907) to Finland to present plays banned in Russia and toured Europe. As well as parts in the plays of Hauptmann and Andreyev, he excelled as Potrassov in Tolstoy's *The Living Corpse*, in which role he appeared in Moscow in 1912. Subsequently he appeared solely in films.

Garnier, Robert (1544–90) French playwright and lawyer, a major figure in French Renaissance drama. His plays, lyrical vehicles for his patriotic, moral, and religious ideals, consist of six tragedies on classical themes; the first French tragi-comedy, *Bradamante* (published 1582), based on Ariosto's *Orlando Furioso*; and the biblical tragedy *Les Juives* (published 1583), which is generally considered to be his masterpiece.

Garrett, João Batista de Almeida (1799–1854) Portuguese poet, novelist, and playwright, who wrote the first Portuguese works influenced by the Romantic movement. He established his reputation as a playwright early in his career with such politically liberal plays as *Lucrécia* (1819) and *Catão* (1821), which led to his exile in England. Appointed Inspector-General of Theatres in 1836, his masterpiece was the tragedy *Frei Luís de Sousa* (1843).

Garrick, David (1717–79) British actor, manager, and playwright, whose new approach to acting revolutionized the theatre of his day. He was born at Hereford and educated at Lichfield, where he organized a production of *The Recruiting Officer*. In 1737 he came to London with Dr Johnson, under whom he had studied classics in Lichfield, and read for the Bar before joining his uncle's wine business. After becoming involved in the amateur theatre, he went with Giffard, manager of Goodman's Fields Theatre, to Ipswich, where he worked professionally under the name Lyddal; he made his first appearance in *Oronooko*, adapted from a novel by Aphra Behn, in about 1741. Despite his short stature he proved a revelation as Richard III and was engaged by Fleetwood at Drury Lane for the rest of the season; in the summer he went to Dublin, where he embarked on a lengthy affair with Peg *Woffington.

In the long successful career that followed, Garrick played at both Covent Garden and Drury Lane, settling at the latter when he became joint patentee in 1747. His style of acting was in marked contrast to that of James Quin, who said of him: "If the young fellow is right, I and the rest of the players have been all wrong". Among his most famous roles were Hamlet, Lear, Abel Drugger, Archer in *The Beaux' Stratagem*, Bayes in *The Rehearsal*, and Sir John Brute in *The Provoked Wife*. Garrick wrote more than 40 plays, of which *Miss in her Teens* (1747) and *Bon Ton; or High Life Above Stairs* (1775) had some success; he also collaborated with George Colman the Elder on *The *Clandestine Marriage*.

His management led to at least two instances of controversy – his employment of

French dancers in 1755 at a time when Britain and France were on the verge of war and his abolition of the third act admission concession in 1762 caused serious rioting and a brief retirement abroad. Summoned back by royal command, he restored his popularity with revivals of his most celebrated roles. He also imported a number of major reforms from abroad, including the removal of members of the audience from the stage itself, the concealment of lighting, and the adoption of naturalistic backdrops.

A somewhat vain man, Garrick's pageant (1769) for the Shakespeare jubilee celebrations at Stratford-upon-Avon drew some malicious ribaldry when he offered pieces of his own and apparently excluded anything by Shakespeare. He and his wife, the actress **Eva Maria Veigel** (1724–1822), who often appeared as **Mlle Violetta**, finally retired in 1776 to his sumptuous mansion at Hampton Court. He was buried in Westminster Abbey.

Garrick Club A London club in Garrick Street, founded in 1831 and named after the actor David Garrick. It was established as a club for actors and educated men and included Charles Kemble, Macready, and Charles Mathews among its first members; subsequent members have included Henry Irving, Beerbohm Tree, Forbes-Robertson, and many other leading performers and writers for the theatre. It houses a fine collection of theatrical portraits.

Garrick Theatre A theatre in Whitechapel, London, which opened in 1831 under Benjamin Conquest. Destroyed by fire in 1846, it reopened in 1854, staging popular plays at a modest standard; Beerbohm Tree made his professional debut there in 1879. The theatre closed in 1881.

A second **Garrick Theatre** was opened in Charing Cross Road, London, by W S Gilbert for the actor-manager John Hare. It was constructed partially below ground, the dress circle being on street level; a copy of

Gainsborough's portrait of David Garrick was hung in the foyer. The theatre opened in 1889 with a production of Pinero's *The Profligate*. Under Hare's management both Sir Johnston Forbes-Robertson and Mrs Patrick Campbell played here, the latter being much acclaimed in *The Notorious Mrs Ebbsmith* (1895). Arthur Bourchier was manager from 1900 to 1915 and C B Cochran the lessee from 1918 to 1924. In 1935 Walter Greenwood's *Love on the Dole*, in which Wendy Hiller made her name, was staged there. A series of farces presented by Brian Rix from 1967 were also immensely popular, as was Ira Levin's thriller, *Death Trap* (1978–81). Recent productions have included Coward's *Easy Virtue* (1988).

The **Garrick Theatre** on West 35th Street, New York, was opened as **Harrigan's Theatre** in 1890. The theatre was later run by Richard Mansfield – who presented William Gillette, Ethel Barrymore, and others there in plays by Shaw and Clyde Fitch – and renamed the **Vieux-Colombier**. In 1919 it reopened as the Garrick with a production of Benavente's *The Bonds of Interest* by the Guild Theatre, which remained until 1925. It was demolished in 1932.

Gascoigne, George (c. 1542–77) English playwright and poet. His adaptation from the *I suppositi* of Ariosto, *The Supposes* (1566), was the first native comedy entirely in prose; Shakespeare based the subplot of *The Taming of the Shrew* directly on it. Gascoigne also translated Lodovico Dolce's *Giocasta*.

Gascon, Jean (1921–88) French-Canadian actor and director, who established his reputation with notable productions of classic plays by many European playwrights. He trained at the Vieux-Colombier in Paris before returning to Montreal and founding (1951) the Théâtre du Nouveau Monde, where he remained as artistic director until 1966. He won particular praise for his productions of Molière and Strindberg as well

as for his contributions to the Stratford (Ontario) Festival (1967–74). He became director-general of the National Theatre School of Canada in 1960.

Gaskill, William (1930–) British director, who became director of the Joint Stock Company in 1973. He established his reputation as a director with the English Stage Company (1957–59 and 1965–72), later working at the National Theatre (1963–65 and 1979) and with the Royal Shakespeare Company (1961–62). His most succesful productions have included plays by John Osborne at the Royal Court and a series of works by N F Simpson and Edward Bond as well as classic plays by Brecht and Farquhar; among his more recent works have been Middleton and Rowley's *A Fair Quarrel* (1979).

Gaspar, Enrique (1842–1902) Spanish playwright, whose plays satirizing contemporary bourgeois society helped to establish the concept of Realism in the Spanish theatre. His most successful plays include *Las personas decentes* (1890) and *La eterna cuestión* (1895).

Gassman, Vittorio (1922–) Italian actor-manager, who has won acclaim in many productions presented by his own company, the **Teatro Popolare Italiano**, since the 1950s. He made his debut in 1943 and has enjoyed success in both comic and tragic roles in plays ranging from Alfieri's *Oreste* to Sartre's *Kean*; other major successes have included performances as Sophocles's Oedipus, Ibsen's Peer Gynt, and Shakespeare's Iago, Orlando, and Othello as well as numerous film roles.

Gassner, John Waldhorn (1903–67) US theatre critic, scholar, and playwright, born in Hungary, who established his reputation with adaptations of many major foreign works for the Theatre Guild in the 1930s. As well as translations of plays ranging from works by Sophocles to modern plays by Stefan Zweig, he also published notable studies of the theatre and collections of plays.

Gate Theatre The first London club theatre, which opened in 1925 in a converted warehouse in Floral Street, Covent Garden. In 1927 it moved to Villiers Street, near Charing Cross, where it was under the management of Norman Marshall from 1934 to 1940. In addition to plays by such authors as Lillian Hellman, Afinogenov, Cocteau, and Steinbeck, the theatre became known for its annual Gate Revue. The building was destroyed by bombs in 1941.

The **Gate Theatre** in Dublin opened in 1930 in the Rotunda Buildings as a home for a company founded by Hilton *Edwardes and Micheál *MacLiammóir in 1928. After early performances at the Peacock Theatre (*see* Abbey Theatre), the company presented plays by Shaw, Aeschylus, Goethe, and others at the Court Theatre until 1936, when a rival company under the Earl of *Longford took a share in the theatre, presenting its own separate programme until 1961. After World War II Lady Longford continued to run the theatre, which was closed periodically before acquiring state support in 1969 and was subsequently used by both its own resident company and other troupes. Successful productions have included numerous revivals of plays by both Irish writers and playwrights from other countries.

A third **Gate Theatre** opened in a public house in Notting Hill Gate, London, in 1979 as a venue for fringe theatre. Since then it has attracted much interest and briefly spawned an offshoot in Battersea (1982–84).

Gateway Theatre A theatre in Edinburgh, which opened in 1946 under the management of the Church of Scotland. Productions staged there included plays by a resident company as well as successful offerings by visiting troupes and a company run by Robert *Kemp despite controversy between the church authorities and the theatre management. The company was closed in 1965 when the *Lyceum Theatre was opened.

gatherer An official in the Elizabethan theatre who collected entrance money from the audience as they came into the auditorium. The money that was collected then passed either to the *housekeepers, who had a claim to receipts from the particular area of the theatre in which the spectactor was sitting or to the owners of the building itself. *Compare* sharer.

Gatti, Armand (1924–) French playwright and film director, born in Monaco. Gatti produced dramas of social and political protest, inspired by such events as the execution of Sacco and Vanzetti, two Italian immigrants, in the US in 1927 (*Chant publique devant deux chaises électriques*, 1966). *La Deuxième Existence du camp de Tatenberg* (1962) is based on Gatti's experiences in a Nazi concentration camp. Works since then include *La passion du Général Franco* (The Passion of General Franco), which was banned until 1976, and films made in collaboration with John Arden.

Gatti's A music hall in the Westminster Bridge Road, London, opened by the brothers Carlo and Giovanni Gatti in 1865. Originally a restaurant, it was known as Gatti's-Over-the-Arches to distinguish it from another musical hall opened by the Gatti brothers in 1866, known as Gatti's-Under-the-Arches. Gatti's-Over-the-Arches seated 1183 people and saw the first London appearance of Harry Lauder, eventually closing in 1924. Gatti's-Under-the-Arches became the **Hungerford Music Hall** in 1887 and then the **Charing Cross Music Hall** before being turned into a cinema in 1910.

Gaultier-Garguille (Hugues Guéru; c. 1573–1633) French actor, who excelled in farce and also appeared, as **Fleschelles**, in serious drama. He probably performed at the Paris fairs before appearing at the Hôtel de Bourgogne alongside Turlupin and Gros-Guillaume.

Gaussin, Jeanne-Cathérine (1711–67) French actress, who was much admired for her evocation of pathos in performances at the Comédie-Française, which she joined in 1731. She excelled in the plays of Racine, Voltaire, and especially in the comedies of La Chaussée.

Gautier, Théophile (1811–72) French poet, novelist, theatre critic, and journalist, who was a leading figure of the French Romantic movement. He defended the works of Victor Hugo and was himself the author of several melodramas and libretti for a number of ballets.

gauze An expanse of loosely woven fabric, which can be made to appear opaque when lit from behind. In the US it is referred to as a **scrim**. *See also* transparency.

Gay, John (1685–1732) English playwright and poet, whose first play, *What d'ye Call it*, was produced in 1715. He achieved his greatest success with *The *Beggar's Opera*, staged at Lincoln's Inn Fields in 1728. Its sequel, *Polly*, was refused a licence and was not performed until 1777. Gay also wrote several comedies, a tragedy, and the book for Handel's *Acis and Galatea* (1732).

geggie *See* gaff.

gel A colour filter, which when placed in front of a light colours the beam. Gels were formerly made of gelatin but are now made of plastic.

Gelber, Jack (1932-) US playwright, whose first play, *The *Connection* (1959), won several awards. After this study of drug addiction, he wrote such plays as *The Apple* (1961), *The Cuban Thing* (1968), *Sleep* (1972), and *Barbary Shore* (1974). He is resident playwright at the American Place in New York and has also directed Wesker's *The Kitchen* (1966), Kopit's *Indians* (1968), and *Jack Gelber's New Play: Rehearsal* (1976) among other works.

Gélinas, Gratien (1909-) French-Canadian actor, playwright, and director, who founded the famous **Théâtre de la Comédie Canadienne** in Montreal in 1958. Known as **Fridolin**, after a character in his own revues, he presented major plays by Anouilh, Marcel Dubé, and others as well as his own works, of which *'Tit-Coq* (Lil' Rooster; 1948) broke the record for the longest-running Canadian play. He was also a leading performer at the Stratford (Ontario) Festival; since 1970 he has devoted himself to films.

Gelosi An early Italian *commedia dell'arte* company, founded by Flamineo Scala in Milan c. 1568. Members of the company appeared before the French Court of Henry III in 1577 and subsequently toured many European countries. Leading actors with the Gelosi included Giovann and Isabella *Andreini; after Isabella's death in 1604 the company was disbanded.

Gémier, Firmin (Firmin Tonnerre; 1869–1933) French actor, director, and manager, who became a leading performer on the Paris stage during the 1920s. Trained under Antoine, he had his first major success in 1896, as Ubu in Lugné-Poë's production of Jarry's *Ubu Roi*, after which he appeared in numerous roles, sometimes under his own direction. He managed the Théâtre Antoine from 1906 and founded the Théâtre Ambulant – a group travelling by rail – in 1911; during World War I he presented Shakespeare in Paris and staged extravaganzas with Gaston Baty at the Cirque d'Hiver. Subsequently he managed the Théâtre National Populaire, the Comédie des Champs-

Elysées, and the Odéon, producing notable versions of plays by many foreign and contemporary playwrights and ultimately inspiring the revived TNP of Jean Vilar.

General Utility *See* stock company.

género chico *See zarzuela.*

Genet, Jean (1910–86) French novelist, playwright, and poet, born in Paris. An abandoned illegitimate child, he spent much of his youth in institutions and prisons in various European cities. He produced five plays, which attacked society and its prejudices; they all attracted considerable attention, both for their ritualistic violence and their poetic language. Influenced by Sartre, Genet explored the themes of illusion and unreality through such topics as politics and sexual perversion.

Principal works:

Les Bonnes: 1947; translated as *The *Maids*.

Haute Surveillance: 1949; translated as **Deathwatch*.

Le Balcon: 1960 (published 1956); translated as *The *Balcony*.

Les Nègres: 1959; translated as *The *Blacks*.

Les Paravents: 1961; translated as *The Screens*.

Geneva A play by G B *Shaw. First performance: Malvern Festival, 1938. The play is based upon the concept of dictators being brought before a court of human justice to answer charges brought against them and satirizes the helplessness of the League of Nations against Nazi Germany.

Gengenbach, Pamphilus (c. 1480–1525) German playwright, noted for his virulent attacks on the Roman Catholic church. His play *Totenfresser* (1521) was unsparing in its criticism of the Pope; his other writings include the morality play *Das Spiel von den zehn Altern* (1515).

genteel comedy A form of polite comedy popular in the early 18th century. It had much in common with both Restoration comedy, which preceded it, and sentimental comedy of the later 18th century.

Gentleman, Francis (1728–84) British actor, critic, and playwright, born in Dublin. He began as an actor in the English provinces, sometimes appearing in his own plays; subsequently he was engaged by Foote at the Haymarket. In 1770 he published *The Dramatic Censor*, a collection of judicious notices of contemporary plays.

Gentleman Dancing Master, The A comedy by Sir William *Wycherley. First performance: London, c. 1671. Gerrard pretends he is Hippolita's dancing master in order to win her hand before she is married to her affected cousin.

George, Mlle (Marguerite-Josephine Weymer; 1787–1867) French actress, who was highly regarded in her day for her performances in the great tragic roles. Noted for her tempestuous manner, she first appeared at the Comédie-Française in 1802 and subsequently established her reputation in such parts as Lady Macbeth and Jocasta as well as in the historical plays of Dumas and de Vigny. Rumour had it that her many lovers included Napoleon, Talleyrand, and Metternich.

George Abbott Theatre A theatre on West 54th Street, between Seventh and Eighth avenues, New York, which opened as the **Craig Theatre** in 1928. Seating 1401, it was renamed the **Adelphi Theatre** in 1934. The theatre was later taken over (1936) by the Federal Theatre Project for a period and then used for broadcasting. In 1958 it reopened for live drama as the **54th Street Theatre**; it was renamed after the playwright George Abbott in 1966. The theatre was demolished in 1970.

George Dandin; ou, le Mari confondu A comedy by *Molière. First performance: Versailles, 1668. George Dandin is a rich peasant who has married the daughter of a gentleman; treated with contempt by his wife and humiliated by her parents, he blames himself for his misfortunes.

George M Cohan Theatre A theatre on Broadway, New York, which was opened by Cohan himself in 1911. Successes there included Klein and Glass's *Potash and Perlmutter* (1913), several farces, and Clemence Dane's *A Bill of Divorcement* (1921), starring Katharine Cornell. The theatre was converted into a cinema in 1933 and was demolished in 1938.

Georgian Theatre A theatre in Richmond, Yorkshire, which is one of the oldest working theatres in England. Seating 400, it opened in 1788, being renamed the Theatre Royal from 1811 to 1848, when it closed. A restored 238-seat theatre was reopened in 1963, becoming a home for amateurs and musical productions as well as a museum (from 1979).

Germanova, Maria Nikolaevna (1884–1940) Russian actress, who was much admired in intense Expressionist dramas under Nemirovich-Danchenko. She began her career at the Moscow Art Theatre in 1904 in Shakespeare; subsequently she excelled in plays by Ibsen, Maeterlinck, and Dostoevsky as well as in Andreyev's *Katerina Ivanovna* (1912), which was written for her.

Gershwin, George (1898–1937) US composer of musical comedies, who – often working in collaboration with his brother **Ira Gershwin** (Israel Gershwin; 1896–1983) as his lyricist – created a long series of highly successful Broadway musicals in the 1920s and 1930s. Early successes included the song 'Swanee' and contributions to George White's *Scandals* (1920–24); subsequent full-scale productions included the jazz-orientated *Lady, Be Good!* (1924), *Oh, Kay!* (1926), *Funny Face* (1927), *Strike up the Band* (1930), *Girl Crazy* (1930), and the Pulitzer Prize-winning *Of Thee I Sing* (1931). *Porgy and Bess* (1935), his only opera, is still widely performed.

Ghelderode, Michel de (1898–1962) Belgian playwright, who was the author of several plays notable for their combination of the comic and the grotesque. Written mostly in French, his 50 or so works – generally farcical tragedies – began with *Les Vieillards* (1919) and include amongst them *Escurial* (1927), *Barabbas* (1928), *Pantagleize* (1929), *Hop! Signor* (1935), and *Mademoiselle Jaïre* (1934). *Fastes d'enfer* (1929) provoked a riot when revived by Barrault in Paris in 1949.

Ghéon, Henri (Henri Léon Vangeon; 1875–1944) French playwright and poet, who revived medieval religious drama in the 1920s and 1930s. Many of his plays, based on biblical stories and the lives of the saints, were written for Ghéon's amateur troupe; they include *Le Pauvre sous l'escalier* (1921) and *Le Noël sur la place* (Christmas in the Market Place; 1935).

Gherardi, Evaristo (1663–1700) Italian actor of the *commedia dell'arte*, who appeared with the Comédie-Italienne in Paris. He was much admired as Arlecchino and published many of the scenarios used by the company.

ghost glide A type of trap by means of which an actor standing on a wheeled platform appears to glide across the stage as he is raised up to it through a long narrow stage cut. A variation of the ghost glide is known as the **Corsican trap** after its introduction in Boucicault's *The Corsican Brothers* (1852).

ghosts There are numerous traditions concerning haunted venues around the world, although the best known are concentrated in the British theatre. The most famous instances include the reputed haunting of the Haymarket by John *Buckstone and the reported appearances during matinées at Drury Lane of a man in grey – believed by some to be the ghost of a man killed in a fight in the 18th century. Sightings of both ghosts are regarded as good omens for the play currently in production. Other British venues with similar traditions include the Adelphi Theatre, where the murdered actor William *Terris is said to appear, the Bristol Old Vic, where Mrs *Siddons is reported to have been sighted, and York's Theatre Royal, which lays claim to the ubiquitous unidentified shadowy figure seen during rehearsals.

Ghosts (*Gengangere*) A play by Henrik *Ibsen, the most controversial of all his works. First performance: Chicago, 1882. The play adopts the theme of venereal disease as a symbol of inherited guilt and repressed individuality in conventional society; it was widely condemned when it first appeared but is now recognized as having had a formative influence upon 20th-century Realist drama.

Ghost Sonata, The (*Spöksonaten*) A play by August *Strindberg. First performance: Intima Teatern, Stockholm, 1908. The most deeply symbolic of Strindberg's later works, the play imitates the discontinuity of a dream and anticipated much 20th century drama.

Giacometti, Paolo (1816–82) Italian playwright, best remembered for *La morte civile* (The Outlaw; 1861), which depicts the plight of an escaped criminal who kills himself rather than disgrace his family and which remained popular in Italy for many years. His other plays include the historical drama *Elisabetta regina d'Inghilterra* (1853).

Giacosa, Giuseppe (1847–1906) Italian playwright, who wrote influential dramas in the Italian *verismo* tradition. He enjoyed considerable success with such comedies as *Una partita a scacchi* (A Game of Chess; 1871) and *La zampa del gatto* (The Cat's Paw; 1883) as well as with the historical drama *Signora di Challant* (1891), in which Bernhardt and Duse both excelled, but later turned to social dramas influenced by Ibsen. *Diritti dell'anima* (The Rights of the Soul; 1894) and other plays of the same type suffered from a lack of psychological penetration but are interesting as depictions of contemporary bourgeois society in Italy.

Gibbons' Tennis Court *See* Vere Street Theatre.

Gibbs, Mrs *See* Logan, Maria.

Gibson, William (1914-) US playwright, who is best known for the play *The Miracle Worker* (1959), based on the education of the blind and deaf Helen Keller. His other works include *Two for the Seesaw* (1958) and *Twelve Carols in a Pear Tree* (1975).

Gide, André (1869–1951) French novelist, critic, and playwright. Gide is remembered chiefly for his semi-autobiographical stories and novels; his contribution to the theatre is of comparatively minor importance. His own plays include *Le Roi Candaule* (1901), *Saül* (1903), and *Oedipe* (1931); he also produced translations of Shakespeare, notably *Hamlet* (1946).

Giehse, Therese (1898–1975) German actress, who became a leading performer in both Munich and Zurich, appearing in premieres of many important modern dramas. Much admired for her technical virtuosity, she starred in the first productions of Ibsen's *Mutter Courage und ihre Kinder* (1941) and his adaptation of Gorky's *The Mother* (1949) as well as in plays by such authors as Dürrenmatt, Hauptmann, and O'Casey.

Gielgud, Sir (Arthur) John (1904-) British actor, a great nephew of Ellen Terry, who trained for the stage at the Royal Academy of Dramatic Art and made his debut as the Herald in *Henry V* at the Old Vic in 1921. He then worked in Fagan's Oxford Repertory Company and in London took over from Noël Coward as Nicky in *The Vortex* (1925). When he joined the Old Vic company in 1929 he began the series of great Shakespearean roles, including Hamlet, Prospero, Romeo, and Macbeth, for which he is famous. In 1932 he triumphed as Joseph Schindler in Ronald Mackenzie's *Musical Chairs*, following it with another popular success in the title role of Gordon Daviot's *Richard of Bordeaux* in the West End.

In his own season at the Queen's Theatre (1937–38) his parts included Shylock and Richard II, while in 1939 he revived the most famous of all his comedy parts, John Worthing in *The Importance of Being Earnest*, having played it previously at the Lyric, Hammersmith, in 1930. He first appeared at Stratford-upon-Avon in the 1950 season, playing such roles as Benedick, Lear, Cassius, and Angelo. During the years 1956–64 he was seen worldwide in his solo Shakespearean performance *The Ages of Man*, after which he reappeared in London in such contemporary plays as David Storey's *Home* (1970) and Pinter's *No Man's Land* (1975), in both of which he acted alongside Ralph Richardson. Other successes have included performances in the plays of Chekhov, Congreve, Fry, Jonson, Seneca, and Sheridan. Throughout his career he has also won praise as a director of both classical and modern plays; he has appeared frequently in films and on television. A fine speaker of verse and a widely admired tragedian, as well as being shrewd and subtle in comedy, he has been a leading member of the profession for more than half a century. He was knighted in 1953.

Giffard, Henry (c. 1695–1772) British actor and manager, who ran the Goodman's Fields Theatre from 1733 until 1737, when the Licensing Act was passed. Giffard was himself involved in the passing of the strict licensing laws, having been rewarded by Walpole for drawing his attention to the controversial play *The Golden Rump*, which provided the government with the excuse it needed to impose tighter regulation of the theatre. After 1737, Giffard continued to run the Goodman's Fields Theatre, introducing Garrick to the professional stage and subsequently moving with him to Drury Lane for a time.

Gigaku A processional dance drama, imported to Japan from Korea in 612 AD. Consisting of a series of both comic and serious scenes performed by masked actors, the tradition was entirely replaced by the *Bugaku* tradition by the 12th century.

Gilbert, Gabriel (1620–80) French playwright and poet, who was secretary to Queen Christina of Sweden. Gilbert's dramatic output consists largely of mediocre tragedies and tragi-comedies; *Hippolyte* (1646) may have been used by his contemporary Jean Racine as a source for the latter's masterpiece *Phèdre*.

Gilbert, Mrs George H(enry) (Ann Hartley; 1821–1904) US actress and dancer, born in Britain, who settled with her husband in the US and made her New York debut in 1864 as Baroness Freitenhorsen in *Finesse*. Subsequently she specialized in playing comic elderly ladies, making a particular success as the Marquise de St Maur in T W Robertson's *Caste* (1867). She joined Daly's company and remained, on and off, for 30 years before going to Charles Frohman's company, her last appearance being as Granny Thompson in *Granny* (1904).

Gilbert, John (John Gibbs; 1810–89) US actor, who made his first appearance in

Boston in 1828. He toured the Mississippi area until 1834 and was most admired for his performances in Boston, New York, and elsewhere as Sir Anthony Absolute in *The Rivals* and Sir Peter Teazle in *The School for Scandal*. He toured with Lester Wallack's company from 1861 until 1888.

Gilbert, Sir William Schwenk (1836–1911) British playwright and lyricist, remembered for his long collaboration with the composer **Sir Arthur Sullivan** (1842–1900) on the 'Savoy' operas. Prior to meeting Sullivan, he wrote comic verses, short plays, operettas, and burlesques. His play *The Palace of Truth* was presented at the Haymarket by Buckstone in 1870, whilst other serious dramas, including *Pygmalion and Galatea* (1871), were also well received. His first significant collaboration with Sullivan produced *Trial by Jury*, which prompted Richard D'Oyly Carte to commission further work from them. *HMS Pinafore* established their joint reputation; of their many subsequent works written for the Opera Comique and the Savoy Theatre many are regularly revived.
Principal works (with Sullivan):
Thespis; or, the Gods Grown Old: 1871.
Trial by Jury: 1875.
The Sorcerer: 1877.
HMS Pinafore: 1878.
The Pirates of Penzance: 1880.
Patience: 1881.
Iolanthe: 1882.
Princess Ida: 1884.
The Mikado: 1885.
Ruddigore: 1887.
The Yeoman of the Guard: 1888.
The Gondoliers: 1889.
Utopia (Limited): 1893.
The Grand Duke: 1896.

Gilchrist, Connie (Constance Macdonald Gilchrist; 1865–1946) British actress, who appeared in pantomime and as a skipping-rope dancer before becoming famous in B E

Woolf's play *The Mighty Dollar* in 1880. She continued with a brief career in musical comedy that ended on her marriage to the Earl of Orkney in 1889.

Gilder, (Janet) Rosamund de Kay (1891-) US theatre critic and administrator, who helped to found and run the Federal Theatre Project, the American National Theatre and Academy, the Institute for Advanced Studies in Theatre Arts, and the International Theatre Institute (1948). From 1948 to 1954 she was the Anta representative to UNESCO.

Giles, Nathaniel (fl. 1595–1634) English theatre manager, Master of the Children of the Chapel Royal from 1597 to 1634. He was responsible for the celebrated series of plays performed by the company at the Blackfriars Theatre until 1608.

Gill, Claes (1910–73) Norwegian actor, director, and author, who was admired in roles ranging from parts in the plays of Ibsen to those of Brecht, T S Eliot, and Pirandello. He was artistic adviser to the Riksteatret, the State Travelling Theatre, from 1968.

Gill, Peter (1939-) Welsh director, actor, and playwright, who began his career at the Royal Court Theatre in the 1960s, attracting attention with plays by authors ranging from D H Lawrence to Webster. In 1977 he became the first director of the Riverside Studios, where his successes included Chekhov's *The Cherry Orchard* (1978) and Middleton and Rowley's *The Changeling* (1978); in 1980 he joined Peter Hall as a director of the National Theatre, where he has directed plays by Turgenev and Shaw among others. His own plays include *Kick for Touch* (1983) and *Mean Tears* (1987).

Gilmore's Theatre *See* Daly's 63rd Street Theatre.

Gingold, Hermione (1897–1987) British actress, who appeared first as a child in 1908 and subsequently became a star of intimate revue. Revues in which she appeared included *Sweet and Low* and its sequels; other triumphs numbered amongst them plays by Coward and Stephen Sondheim's *A Little Night Music*.

Giraldi, Giovanni Battista (1504–73) Italian novelist, poet, and playwright, popularly known as **Il Cinthio**. A native of Ferrara, Giraldi was the author of *Orbecche* (1541), the earliest modern Italian tragedy to be constructed on classical lines; his other tragedies include *L'Altile* (1543), *Cleopatra* (1543), and *Epizia* (1547), which were largely based upon stories that he subsequently collected in the *Hecatommithi* (1565). His preference for a happy ending effectively created *tragi-comedy, while his use of romantic and chivalric material inspired such subsequent writers as Greene, Shirley, and Shakespeare.

Giraud, Giovanni (1776–1834) Italian playwright, who was the only significant writer of comedy in Italy in the period following Goldoni. His *L'aio dell'imbarazzo* (1807) was subsequently made into a comic opera by Donizetti.

Giraudoux, (Hippolyte) Jean (1882–1944) French novelist, playwright, and essayist, born in Bellac. A diplomat, he began writing for the theatre in 1928, having already published several successful novels: his first play, *Siegfried*, marked the beginning of a long collaboration with Louis *Jouvet. Giraudoux's dramatic works, many of which are based on biblical stories, fairy tales, and classical mythology, are characterized by the blending of fantasy with reality, humour with tragedy, and the supernatural with the mortal.

Principal dramatic works:

Siegfried: 1928.

Amphitryon 38: 1929.

Judith: 1931.

Intermezzo: 1933; translated as *The Enchanted*.

La Guerre de Troie n'aura pas lieu: 1935; translated as *Tiger at the Gates*.

Électre: 1937; translated as *Electra*.

Ondine: 1939.

La Folle de Chaillot: 1945; translated as *The *Madwoman of Chaillot*.

Pour Lucrèce: 1953; translated as *Duel of Angels*.

Gitana, Gertie (1888–1957) British music hall singer, who became a favourite performer at the age of 16. A chance engagement at London's Holborn Empire set her off on a bill-topping career of 30 years, singing such sentimental songs as 'Nellie Dean'.

GITIS *See* Lunacharsky State Institute of Theatre Art.

Gjoka, Pjeter (1913–) Albanian actor, who began his career in Tirana in 1947. He established his reputation as a leading performer in such roles as Bubnov in Gorky's *The Lower Depths* and King Lear; he has also appeared in several plays by the Albanian writer Kol Jakova.

Glasgow Citizens' Theatre A flourishing repertory company in Glasgow, founded in 1943 and based in the **Royal Princess's Theatre**, which was built in 1878. James *Bridie oversaw the early years of the company, encouraging the performance of native Scottish drama; since 1969, however, the company – known for maintaining low admission prices – has presented flamboyant revivals of classic plays and built up an international reputation. Successes in recent years have included plays by Bridie himself, *A Day in the Death of Joe Egg* (1967) by Peter Nichols, and *The Milk Train Doesn't Stop Here Anymore* (1969) by Tennessee Williams; productions under **Giles Havergal** (1938–), who took over in 1969, have numbered amongst them *Antony and Cleopatra* (1972). Important experimental productions were also staged at the **Close Studio Theatre**, attached to the main theatre, between 1965 and 1973, when it was destroyed by fire.

Glasgow Repertory Theatre A theatre company established in Glasgow in 1909. It built up a strong reputation with performances at the Royalty Theatre, Glasgow, of plays by Shaw, Chekhov, and others as well as a few native Scottish playwrights. It closed after the outbreak of World War I.

glass crash A sound effect simulating the breaking of a sheet of glass, usually produced live by pouring broken glass and china from one bucket into another.

Glass Menagerie, The A drama by Tennessee *Williams. First performance: New York, 1945. The play concerns the unhappy family life of a Southern belle and focuses on Laura, the shy daughter with a limp, and Amanda Wingfield, the mother, who cannot deal with life effectively. The role of Amanda Wingfield provided Laurette Taylor with her last major role.

Gleich, Joseph Alois (1772–1841) Austrian playwright, whose many moral comedies transformed the Viennese theatre. Writing for the Leopoldstädter and Josefstädter theatres, he wrote over 200 such plays, of which *Der Eheteufel auf Reisen* (1822) is one of the best known.

Globe Playhouse *See* Wanamaker, Sam.

Globe Theatre A round wooden theatre built in 1598–99 south of the river Thames at Bankside in Southwark by Cuthbert Burbage with timber from the *Theatre at Shoreditch. It was used solely in the summer months, since only the stage and galleries were roofed. William Shakespeare was both a shareholder and an actor at the

Globe, where many of his plays were staged by the Chamberlain's Men. In 1613 the theatre caught fire during a performance of *Henry VIII* and was destroyed. Rebuilt the following year with the help of public subscriptions and a royal grant, it was closed by the Puritans in 1642 and demolished two years later. A reconstruction of the Globe Theatre on the South Bank is scheduled to open in 1991 (*see* Wanamaker, Sam).

The **Globe Theatre** in Newcastle Street, London, known together with the Opera Comique as one of the Rickety Twins on account of its somewhat ramshackle structure, was opened in 1868 on the site now occupied by Bush House. It was designed, built, and managed by Sefton Parry and had an audience capacity of 1800. Popular successes included *The Private Secretary* (1884) and *Charley's Aunt* (1893), which ran there for 1466 performances. The theatre was closed in 1902 as part of the Strand improvement scheme.

The **Globe Theatre** in Shaftesbury Avenue, London, was originally named the Hicks Theatre, after Sir Seymour Hicks, and was designed as a twin to the Queen's Theatre. The theatre was opened under Frohman in 1906; its first big hit was *Brewster's Millions* (1907), with Gerald Du Maurier in the leading role. Renamed the Globe in 1909, the theatre was managed by Marie Löhr and her husband Anthony Prinsep from 1918 to 1927. Subsequently, under the management of H M Tennent and currently of Stoll Moss Theatres, its notable successes in comedy and light musicals have included Dodie Smith's *Call it a Day* (1935–36), Terence Rattigan's *While the Sun Shines* (1943–46), Christopher Fry's *The Lady's Not For Burning* (1949) with John Gielgud and Pamela Brown, Robert Bolt's *A Man for All Seasons* (1960), starring Paul Scofield, several plays by Alan Ayckbourn, the award-winning comedy *Daisy Pulls It Off* (1983–86), and Peter Shaffer's *Lettice and Lovage* (1987) with Maggie Smith.

See also Lunt-Fontanne Theatre; New York Theatre.

Glory A tableau, popular in Renaissance drama, in which an actor playing a god descended to the stage in a blaze of light. He was lowered on one of a series of platforms (painted to represent clouds and sky) operated by a drum-and-shaft system.

glove-puppet See puppet theatre.

gobo An item of lighting equipment, used to alter the shape or pattern of a light beam. It consists of a cut-out masking device and is commonly used to achieve atmospheric lighting effects.

Godfrey, Charles (Paul Lacey; 1851–1900) British music hall performer, who became famous as a singer of songs combining drama and pathos, exemplified by 'On Guard', the story of a Balaclava veteran. For 10 years he topped the bills performing similar pieces, interspersed with lighter songs.

gods See auditorium.

Godwin, Edward William (1833–86) British architect and stage designer, who lived with Ellen *Terry from 1862 and became the father of Edith and Edward Gordon *Craig. An expert in classical architecture and costumes, his career as a theatrical designer blossomed with the Bancrofts' *The Merchant of Venice*, in which Ellen Terry returned to the stage in 1875. He published the results of his research in *The Architecture and Costume of Shakespeare's Plays*.

Goering, Reinhardt (1887–1936) German playwright, who became a leading figure in the early development of Expressionism. The highly stylized *Seeschlacht*, which is set on board a battleship during the battle of Jutland, was immensely influential through its production by Reinhardt in Berlin in 1918. Later works included an account of the death of Captain Scott.

Goethe, Johann Wolfgang von (1749–1832) German playwright, poet, novelist, scholar, and statesman, whose work in the theatre had an enormous influence upon the course of drama throughout Europe. Goethe became interested in the theatre at an early age after seeing performances of French plays in Frankfurt, where he was born; his career as a playwright is usually dated, however, from his discovery of the plays of Shakespeare, which he first read while training as a lawyer in Strasbourg. This reading inspired his first great drama, *Götz von Berlichingen*, which constituted a major contribution to the *Sturm und Drang* movement and which, together with the novel *Die Leiden des jungen Werthers* (The Sorrows of Young Werther; 1774), established him as the leader of the Romantics in Germany.

In 1775 he moved to the court at Weimar, where he became prime minister and director of the state theatre; here he wrote plays on contemporary subjects. In 1786 he began a two-year visit to Italy, as a result of which he rejected Romantic ideals in favour of Classicism. This was reflected in his rewriting of his prose drama *Iphigenie auf Tauris* along classical lines and in his subsequent plays. Having acted as an amateur in some of his plays himself, he became director (1791–1817) of a professional company at the Court Theatre in Weimar, where Schiller also worked with him; members of the company, which became famous throughout Europe, included Iffland. After describing the life of Schröder in the novel *Wilhelm Meisters theatrealische Sendung* in 1795, he went on to write his masterpiece for the stage, the poetic drama *Faust*, which encapsulates the author's philosophy of unceasing aspiration in all fields of human enterprise. Due to its great length it is often staged in its less complex original draft, known as the *Ur-Faust*.

Principal dramatic works:
Götz von Berlichingen: 1773.
Stella: 1776.
Clavigo: 1779.
Iphigenie auf Tauris: 1779.
Egmont: 1787.
Torquato Tasso: 1807.
Faust: Part I, 1829; Part II, 1854.

Gogol, Nikolai Vasilievich (1809–52) Russian novelist and playwright, author of the first Russian plays in the Realist tradition. He is best known for the novel *Dead Souls* (1842; first successfully dramatized by Stanislavsky in 1928) but his career as a poet and actor started earlier, under the influence of his friendship with the actor Shchepkin. His masterpiece, the satirical comedy *The *Government Inspector* (first seen in London in 1920), resulted in his exile in Rome (1842–48); subsequent dramas included farces and comedies. During his last years he succumbed to religious mania and depression.
Principal dramatic works:
Revizor: 1836; translated as *The Government Inspector*.
Marriage: 1842.
Gamblers: 1842.
On Leaving the Theatre After a Performance of a New Comedy: 1842.

Gold, Jimmy *See* Crazy Gang.

Golden, John *See* John Golden Theatre; Royal Theatre.

Golden Boy A play by Clifford *Odets. First performance: Group Theatre, New York, 1937. The plot revolves around a boxer, who – in his attempts to gain material wealth and superficial success – becomes warped, relying on his life as a professional boxer to achieve his goals. A musical version was first staged in 1964 in New York.

Golden Theatre *See* John Golden Theatre; Royale Theatre.

Goldfaden,   Abraham   (Abraham Goldenfoden;   1840–1908) Yiddish playwright and poet, who effectively founded the Yiddish theatrical tradition. He was born in Russia, acting in Ettinger's *Serkele* in 1825, but later emigrated to Poland in 1875 and then Romania, where he established the first Yiddish theatre at Jassy in 1876.   Subsequently   he   toured   Russia, Romania, and elsewhere before finally settling in New York in 1903. He was the author of almost 400 plays, including *The Recruits* (1877), *Shulamit* (1880), and *David at War* (1904).

Goldoni, Carlo (1707–93) Italian playwright, born in Venice, who played a key role in the development of the modern Italian theatrical tradition by reforming many aspects of the *commedia dell'arte*. The author of nearly 300 plays in Italian or French, he provided written parts where the actors had formerly relied upon improvisation and added a new note of realism in his characterization, provoking opposition from many actors of the *commedia dell'arte* and his rival Carlo Gozzi. After writing numerous plays for the theatres in Venice, he moved to Paris to direct the Comédie-Italienne and produced French versions of his own works; he retired in 1764 and died in poverty following the French Revolution. His most celebrated comedies include *I pettegolezzi delle donne, La locandiera*, in which Duse excelled, *I rusteghi*, and *Il ventaglio*.
Principal works:
Belisario: 1734.
Il servitore di due padroni: 1743; translated as *The Servant of Two Masters*.
La vedova scaltra: 1748; translated as *The Wily Widow*.
La putta onorata: 1749.
La Pamela: 1750.
I pettegolezzi delle donne: 1750.
Il bugiardo: 1750; translated as *The Liar*.
La bottega del caffè: 1750; translated as *The Coffee House*.
Il vero amico: 1750.

GOLDSMITH, OLIVER

La locandiera: 1753.

Il malcontenti: 1755.

Un Curioso accidente: 1757.

I rusteghi: 1760; translated as *The Boors*.

L'impresario delle Smirne: 1760; translated as *The Impresario of Smyrna*.

Le baruffe chiozzote: 1762; translated as *Squabbles in Chioggia*.

Il ventaglio: 1764; translated as *The Fan*.

Le Bourru bienfaisant: 1773; translated as *The Kindly Curmudgeon*.

Goldsmith, Oliver (1730–74) British poet, playwright, and novelist, who became one of Dr Johnson's circle. His comedy *The *Good-Natured Man*, rejected by Garrick, was produced by the elder Colman at Covent Garden in 1768 with some success, but it was the instantaneous triumph of **She Stoops to Conquer* in 1773 that made his reputation as a dramatist. Many years after his death his novel *The Vicar of Wakefield* was also successfully adapted for the stage.

goliard A member of a troupe of wandering theatrical performers, chiefly clerics and students, common throughout Europe in medieval times. Notorious for their licentious and riotous behaviour, the goliards – who declared allegiance to the legendary Bishop Golias – presented satirical pieces that frequently criticized the Church until the authorities forbade clerics from participating in such entertainments (1227); in the later Middle Ages the term goliard consequently became virtually synonomous with *jongleur and *minstrel. Works performed by such groups included short plays (one example being the *Commedia Bile*) and poems in praise of wine and women (collected as the *Carmina Burana* in the 19th century).

Gombrowicz, Witold (1904–69) Polish playwright and novelist, who spent most of his life in exile in Argentina, Germany, and France. He was the author of three notable dramas anticipating the development of the Theatre of the Absurd, *Iowna, Princess of Burgundy* (1957), *Marriage* (1963), and *Operetta* (1967), which have since been revived in several countries.

Gomersal, Edward Alexander (1788–1862) British actor, who became a leading performer at *Astley's Amphitheatre. He also made successful appearances in melodrama at most major provincial theatres.

Goncourt, Edmond(-Louis-Antoine Huot) de (1822–96) French writer who collaborated with his brother **Jules(-Alfred Huot) de Goncourt** (1830–70) on novels, plays, works of social history and criticism, and the famous *Journal des Goncourt*, begun in 1851. Their plays, which include *Henriette Maréchal* (1865) and dramatizations of their novels, form the least significant part of their literary output.

Gonzaga, Pietro Gottardo (Pyotr Fyodorovich; 1751–1831) Italian artist, who did much notable work for a number of Italian and Russian theatres. He moved to Russia in 1792, where he worked at theatres in Moscow and St Petersburg, designing scenery chiefly for opera and ballet. In 1817 he was asked to design a theatre at Arkhangelskoye; subsequently he went on to execute 12 influential sets of scenery in the neoclassical style for this theatre.

Goodman Memorial Theatre A theatre in Chicago, which was built in memory of the playwright Kenneth Sawyer Goodman to house both an acting school and a resident professional company. It opened in 1925, seating 683, but the Depression forced the company to disband. In the 1950s visiting professional players performed with students, while during the 1960s a professional company took over the theatre and student performances were presented in the adjacent Goodman Theatre Studio. The theatre's connection with the school ended in 1977 when the theatre was incorporated into the Chicago Theatre Group Inc. It now offers a mixed programme of classic revivals and new works.

Goodman's Fields Theatre A theatre in Whitechapel, London, opened (as **Odell's Theatre**) by Thomas Odell in 1727. After the first performance, *The Recruiting Officer* by Farquhar, it was used for presentations of plays by Fielding and later taken over by Henry Giffard. Following a series of circus-type entertainments and use as a warehouse, it was destroyed by fire in 1802.

Another theatre of the same name opened early in 1732 under Giffard, who installed a distinguished company, thrived until 1737, when it lost its licence. Goodman's Fields reopened in 1740 and, later the same year, saw the professional debut of Garrick, as Richard III. It closed finally, however, in 1742 under pressure from the *patent theatres.

Good-Natured Man, The A comedy by Oliver *Goldsmith. First performance: Covent Garden, 1768. In an attempt to cure the good nature of the gullible central character, his father has him arrested for debt so that he can discover who his real friends are.

Goodwin, Nat(haniel Carl) (1857–1919) US actor, who made his debut in Joseph Bradford's *Law in New York* (1874) in Boston. He enjoyed great success as a mimic in New York, then formed his own farce-comedy troupe, the Froliques. In the 1890s he adopted a more serious polished style, most notably in the title role of Clyde Fitch's *Nathan Hale* (1899) and in other parts opposite his wife, Maxine Elliott; his attempts at Shakespeare, however, were failures.

Good Woman of Setzuan, The (*Der gute Mensch von Sezuan*) A play by Bertolt *Brecht, written in 1938–41. First performance: Zürich, 1942. One of Brecht's most acclaimed plays, it explores the dilemma faced by a good person in a greedy society and focuses on a woman who invents a male companion (impersonating him herself) as a defence against those around her.

Gorboduc; or, Ferrex and Porrex The first English tragedy in blank verse, written by Thomas *Norton and Thomas *Sackville in 1561. It was influenced by Seneca and narrates the disasters that befell Britain when Gorboduc divided the kingdom between his sons.

Gorchakov, Nicolai Mikhailovich (1899–1958) Russian producer, who became a senior administrator of the Moscow stage after experience as Stanislavsky's assistant at the Moscow Art Theatre in the 1920s. His productions of plays by Sheridan and Russian playwrights were highly praised; he later became director of the Moscow Theatre of Drama (1933–38) and of the Theatre of Satire (1941–43). He was also appointed to the Lunacharsky State Institute of Theatre Art. His many writings on the theatre provide valuable insights on Stanislavsky's methods.

Gordin, Jacob (1853–1909) Jewish playwright, born in the Ukraine, who became a prominent figure in the Yiddish theatre of New York. His many plays include Jewish adaptations of many foreign masterpieces, among them *The Jewish King Lear* (1892) and *God, Man and Devil* (1900), which was derived from Goethe's *Faust*.

Gordon-Lennox, Cosmo *See* Tempest, Marie.

Goring, Marius (1912-) British actor, who made several youthful appearances before moving into adult roles at the Old Vic, where his parts included Hamlet (1935) and Ariel (1940). Fluent in French and German, he has often played leading classical roles in those languages on the Continent. He was Richard II and Petruchio at Stratford-upon-Avon in 1953 and Angelo in *Measure for Measure* for the Royal Shakespeare Company in 1962. He took over as Andrew Wyke in Peter Shaffer's *Sleuth* in 1971. More recent appearances have been in *Zaîde* at the Old Vic (1982) and in Jeffrey Archer's *Beyond Reasonable Doubt* (1987).

Gorky, Maxim (Alexei Maximovich Pyeshkov; 1868–1936) Russian novelist, playwright, and short-story writer, whose plays reflect his sympathy for society's outcasts. His most successful drama, *The *Lower Depths*, portrays life in Moscow's underworld. Regarded as a political activist by the authorities, he was arrested for revolutionary activity in 1905 and spent the next few years as an exile in the US. Of his major dramas, which have been criticized by some for their technical shortcomings, *Somov and Others* and *Yegor Bulychov and Others* form part of an unfinished cycle of plays intended to cover Russian history from 1917 to the 1930s. He returned to Russia in 1931; his novel *The Mother* was successfully dramatized by other hands.
Principal dramatic works:
Meshchane: 1902; translated as *Scenes in the House of Bersemenov*.
Na dne: 1902; translated as *The Lower Depths*.
Dashniki: 1904; translated as *Summer Residents*.
Vragi: 1906; translated as *The Enemies*.
Vassa Zheleznova: 1906; translated as *Mother Zheleznova*.
Zykovy: 1913; translated as *The Zykovs*.
Yegor Bulychov i drugiye: 1932; translated as *Yegor Bulychov and Others*.
Dostigayev i drugiye: 1933; translated as *Dostigayev and Others*.
Yakov Bogolomov: 1941.
Somov i drugiye: unfinished; translated as *Somov and Others*.

Gorky Theatre, Grand A theatre in Leningrad, which opened in 1919 under Alexander *Blok. Named in honour of Maxim Gorky, it began with a mixed programme of Russian and foreign works before presenting various Expressionist dramas by Shaw and O'Neill amongst others. After damage in World War II, it became a venue for productions of Shakespeare, which were later repeated by the resident company in London (1966). Other successes included plays by Dostoevsky and Griboyedov, as well as Chekhov and Gogol.

Goset *See* Moscow State Jewish Theatre.

Gôt, Edmond-François-Jules (1822–1901) French actor, who joined the Comédie-Française in 1850 and later became its leader. He was highly regarded both in comedy, notably in the plays of Molière, and in classical roles.

Gottsched, Johann Christoph (1700–66) German playwright and literary critic, who did much to promote the observance of the rules of classical drama in the German theatre. With Carolina Neuber, he published the *Deutsche Schaubühne* (1740–45), a suggested repertory for the national theatre that included some adaptations by himself of French plays. Of his own dramatic works the most successful was *Der sterbende Cato* (1732), adapted from Addison's *Cato* (1713); after quarrelling with Neuber, however, he had little more to do with the theatre.

Götz von Berlichingen A play by *Goethe, his first major drama. First performance: Berlin, 1773. Inspired by his reading of Shakespeare, the play presents an idealized depiction of a robber-baron and, with its disjointed action and historical focus, had a profound influence upon the development of the *Sturm und Drang* movement.

Gough, Michael (1917-) British actor, who began by playing small parts at the Old Vic in 1936 and, after World War II, appeared in roles ranging from Laertes in *Hamlet* (1951) to Joe in Jack Ronder's *This Year, Next Year* (1960). Among many parts for the National Theatre he played Glen in

John Osborne's *Watch It Come Down* (1976) and Ernest in Ayckbourn's *Bedroom Farce* (1977). In 1986 he was Dillwyn Knox in Hugh Whitemore's *Breaking the Code*.

Gough, Robert (d. 1625) English actor, first recorded as playing a female role in Tarleton's *The Seven Deadly Sins*, with Strange's Men in about 1590. Later he was with the King's Men and was included in the 1623 Folio list of actors in Shakespeare's plays. It is thought that he may have been the original Juliet, as well as the first Portia in *The Merchant of Venice*.

Gourgaud, Françoise *See* Vestris, Françoise.

Government Inspector, The (*Revizor*) A satirical comedy by Nikolai *Gogol. First performance: St Petersburg, 1836. The play depicts the corruption inherent in small town bureaucracy through a confusion of identity that results in a petty clerk being mistaken for a government inspector; in its initial production it survived the censor only through the support of Tsar Nicholas I.

Gow, Ronald (1897–) British playwright, who collaborated with Walter Greenwood on an adaptation of the latter's novel *Love on the Dole*, which provided a great success for Wendy Hiller in 1935. She later married him and in 1946 played the lead in his adaptation of Hardy's *Tess of the D'Urbervilles*.

Goward, Mary Ann *See* Keeley, Robert.

Gozzi, Carlo (1720–1806) Italian playwright and poet, who resisted the attempts of Goldoni to reform the *commedia dell'arte*. He lampooned Goldoni in *L'amore delle tre melarance* (The Love of Three Oranges; 1761), which was highly popular at the time and was later made into an opera by Prokofiev; his own attempts to reform the *commedia dell'arte* were confined to the de-

velopment of the **fiabe*, in which improvisation remained a key element. Such fantasy plays as *Il corvo* (The Raven; 1761), *Il re cervo* (King Stag; 1761), and *Turandot* (1765), which was later made into an opera by Puccini, had a particularly strong influence upon writers in Germany, including Goethe and Schiller.

Grabbe, Christian Dietrich (1801–36) German poet and playwright, whose plays anticipated the Expressionist movement of the 20th century. He first became involved with the theatre in Berlin and wrote his first significant play, the satirical *Scherz, Satire, Ironie und tiefere Bedeutung*, in 1822; the more important of his later works include the tragedy *Don Juan und Faust* (1829), the experimental *Napoleon oder die Hundert Tage* (1831), and *Herzog Theodor von Gothland* (1827). He led an unhappy life and died early from alcoholism and tuberculosis.

Gracioso A comic servant character of the Spanish theatrical tradition, who was a common figure in plays of the Golden Age. Derived from *Bobo, the clown of Lope de Rueda's interludes, the *Gracioso* character can in fact be traced back to ultimately Roman origins. Used for purposes of both satire and intrigue, he appeared in plays by Gil Vicente, Torres Naharro, Calderón, and Augustín de Moreto, among others.

Graham, Mary Ann (1728–87) British actress, the second wife of Richard *Yates. She was at Drury Lane until 1767, then went to Covent Garden, where she was successful in a wide range of tragic parts.

Gramatica, Irma (1873–1962) Italian actress, who made her debut as a child. She won acclaim as lively young heroines in the plays of Halévy, Meilhac, and Sardou as well as for appearances in contemporary Italian plays by such authors as Giacosa and Verga; she also triumphed in Shakespearean roles, including Lady Macbeth (1938).

Her younger sister, **Emma Gramatica** (1875–1965), also began her career as an actress while still a child and gradually built up a reputation for her interpretation of roles in the realistic dramas of Ibsen, Pirandello, and Shaw, often playing in German and Spanish and touring widely. Other successes included works by D'Annunzio, Rosso di San Secondo, and Rostand.

grande See zarzuela.

Grand Guignol A theatrical genre that developed in France in the 19th century, featuring short plays based upon various sensational events, including murder, rape, and hauntings. Popular in the Montmartre area of Paris at the end of the 19th century, the Grand Guignol was also successfully presented in London in the early 20th century.

grand master control A device attached to a dimmer board, allowing simultaneous changes of lighting over all or part of a set. In recent years such control has been greatly facilitated by the introduction of increasingly sophisticated computerized lighting systems.

Grand Opera House A theatre on Eighth Avenue and 23rd Street, New York, which opened as **Pike's Opera House** in 1868. It was renamed in 1869 and was used for light opera, melodrama, and the occasional classic play as well as by touring companies. It became a cinema in 1938 and was demolished in 1961.

Grand Theatre A theatre in Islington, London, which opened in 1870 as the Philharmonic Music-Hall. It staged various entertainments before being destroyed by fire in 1883. Reopened the same year, it suffered further fires in 1887 and 1900 and – renamed the **Islington Empire** in 1908 – became a venue for touring companies, panto-mime, and variety until 1932, when it became a cinema.

Another theatre of the same name opened in London in 1897 and saw performances of musical comedies and shows starring Gertie Millar. It was renamed the **Fulham Theatre** in 1906 and subsequently the **Shilling Theatre** but was ultimately demolished in 1958.

Grandval, François-Charles Racot de (1710–84) French actor, who joined the Comédie-Française in 1729 and inherited the tragic roles of Dufresne. Much admired for the passion of his acting, he retired at the age of 52; his subsequent successful return to the stage ended when members of the audience, probably hired by some jealous fellow-performers, jeered him in Voltaire's *Alzire*.

Granovsky, Alexander (Abraham Ozark; 1890–1937) Jewish actor and director, who was a leading figure in the Yiddish theatre tradition in Russia in the early 20th century. He founded the Jewish Theatre Studio in Leningrad in 1919 (later the Moscow State Jewish Theatre) and staged works by Maeterlinck and Aleichem among others; other notable successes included his adaptation of Isaac Peretz's poem *Night in the Old Market* (1925). Subsequently he directed plays for the Habimah company.

Granville-Barker, Harley (1877–1946) British actor, director, playwright, and theatre scholar, whose productions of the plays of Shaw and Shakespeare had a profound effect upon the course of 20th-century drama. He began his career as an actor, appearing with Ben Greet, Mrs Patrick Campbell, and William Poel among others, and first became associated with G B Shaw when he was chosen to play Marchbanks in the London premiere (1900) of *Candida* by the Stage Society. More Shaw premieres followed and in 1904 Granville-Barker and J E Vedrenne took over the Royal Court Theatre, where they staged a celebrated series of

Shavian dramas and other new works over the next three years. As well as plays by Galsworthy, Ibsen, and Yeats the Royal Court also presented Granville-Barker's own play *The Voysey Inheritance* (1905) and attempted, until it was banned by the Lord Chamberlain, to stage his *Waste* also. Granville-Barker's other best-known play, *The Madras House*, was seen at the Duke of York's Theatre in 1910. Granville-Barker established a strong reputation as a director for his faithfulness to the text and won particular praise for his lively productions of such Shakespearean plays as *Twelfth Night* and *A Midsummer Night's Dream*, which were presented at the Savoy Theatre during 1912–14; he virtually retired from the stage, however, in 1918 after marrying a wealthy divorcée. His first wife was the actress Lillah McCarthy.

Grassi, Paolo *See* Piccolo Teatro della città di Milano.

Grau, Jacinto (1877–1958) Spanish playwright, who made his name in the theatre with stylized dramas written under the influence of Pirandello. His most important works include *El hijo pródigo* (The Prodigal Son; 1918), *El señor de Pigmalión* (1923), and the satirical drama *El burlador que no se burla* (1930).

grave trap A rectangular trap in the centre of the stage, named after its use in the gravediggers scene in *Hamlet*.

Gray, Dulcie (Winifred Catherine Gray; 1919-) British actress, whose career has been closely associated with that of her husband, Michael *Denison. After her debut, in Noël Coward's *Hay Fever* in 1939, she appeared at the Open Air Theatre, Regent's Park, and toured South Africa in a variety of productions. She also performed in her own play, *Love Affair,* at the Lyric, Hammersmith in 1955, while appearances with her husband have included the title role in

Shaw's *Candida* (1960) and Gina Ekdal in Ibsen's *The Wild Duck* (1970). More recently she has played Lady Sneerwell in *The School for Scandal* (1983) and Teresa Browne in Graham Greene's *The Living Room* (1987).

Gray, 'Monsewer' Eddie *See* Crazy Gang.

Gray, Simon James Holliday (1936-) British playwright and novelist, who established his reputation with his play about a university professor facing a personal crisis, *Butley* (1971). Alan Bates was highly praised in the central role and has since appeared in Gray's *Otherwise Engaged* (1975), the comedy thriller *Stage Struck* (1979), and *Quatermaine's Terms* (1981). Gray's other successes have included his first play, *Wise Child* (1967), in which Alec Guinness appeared, *Molly* (1977), starring Billie Whitelaw, *Close of Play* (1979), which featured Michael Redgrave, and *The Common Pursuit* (1988). He also adapted Dostoevsky's *The Idiot* for the National Theatre in 1970.

Gray, Terence (1895-) British theatre manager, who cofounded the Festival Theatre, Cambridge, in 1926. His reforms of staging techniques there, which included the removal of the proscenium arch and footlights and the use of multilevel staging, had enormous influence upon European theatre. His most celebrated productions included Aeschylus's *Oresteia* and various other classics; his associates at the theatre, until he retired in 1933, included Maurice Evans and Flora Robson.

Graziano *See* Dottore, Il.

Great Dionysia *See* Dionysia.

Great Queen Street Theatre *See* Kingsway Theatre.

Great Vance, The *See* Vance, Alfred.

Gréban, Arnoul (c. 1420–71) French playwright and organist, author of the Passion play *Mystère de la Passion*. Written in the early 1450s, it depicts the creation and fall of Adam and the life of Christ. Arnoul Gréban is believed to have collaborated with his brother Simon in the mystery play *Actes de Apôtres* (*Acts of the Apostles).

Grecian Theatre A theatre in Shoreditch, London, opened around 1830 as a concert hall. After a slow start, it became a venue for performances of Shakespeare and was enlarged in 1858 to hold 3400 people. Subsequently it diversified into pantomime and ballet under the *Conquest family, being rebuilt in 1876 and eventually sold to the Salvation Army in 1881.

Greco-Roman drama Theatre within the Greek and Roman sphere of influence between the great age of Athenian drama and the Roman drama of the 1st century AD. Overlapping with Greek New Comedy, as exemplified in the plays of Menander, this era saw the emergence of a new generation of writers, notably Plautus and Terence, who worked from older Greek models, as well as the development of the Roman semicircular auditorium and the increasing secularization of the theatre.

Greek drama *See* Athenian drama; Greco-Roman drama; Hellenistic drama.

Green, John (fl. 1606–27) English actor, who led a company of English Comedians on the Continent in succession to Robert Browne. His name figures intermittently in annals of German theatre up to 1627.

Green, Julian (Hartridge) (1900–) French writer, best known for his novels. Born in Paris of US parents, he is the author of the plays *Sud* (1953), *L'Ennemi* (1954), *L'Ombre* (1956), *Demain n'existe pas* (1979), and *L'Automate* (1980), which echo the sombre themes of his novels.

Green, Paul Eliot (1894–1981) US playwright, whose many plays depict rural life in North Carolina, his native state. *In Abraham's Bosom* (1926) won him a Pulitzer Prize for its condemnation of the South's decadence, while *The House of Connelly* became the inaugural production of the Group Theatre in 1931. *Tread the Green Grass* was well received in 1932 and Kurt Weill provided the music for the pacifist play *Johnny Johnson*, which was produced by Orson Welles in 1936. *The Last Colony* (1937) was the first of a series of 15 **symphonic dramas** based on episodes in US history; these were all performed outdoors and combined both amateur and professional performers.

green baize A green stage carpet, traditionally used in sets of the 18th and 19th centuries when a tragedy was to be performed.

greencoat A member of the stage-crew of the Restoration theatre. Usually dressed in green livery, the greencoats were responsible for bringing on and taking off items of furniture and detail scenery between scenes.

Greene, (Henry) Graham (1904–) British novelist and playwright, whose association with the theatre began with the stage adaptation of his novel *Brighton Rock* (1943). Subsequently he adapted his novel *The Heart of the Matter* (1950) himself (with Basil Dean), writing his first play – *The Living Room* – in 1953. Plays that followed this study of suicide have included *The Potting Shed* (1957), on religious themes, the comedy *The Complaisant Lover* (1959), the farcical tragedy *Carving a Statue* (1964), *The Return of A J Raffles* (1975), and *The Great Jowett* (1981).

Greene, Robert (c. 1560–92) English playwright, who is usually remembered for his attack on Shakespeare in *A Groatsworth of Wit Bought with a Million of Repentance*. His play *Friar Bacon and Friar Bungay*

(1589) was an early example of romantic comedy; he may also have collaborated with Kyd and other leading contemporaries. His other plays include *Alphonsus, King of Aragon* (1587), *James IV* (1590), *A Looking Glass for London and England* (1590), and *Orlando Furioso* (1591).

green man A mythological character who often appeared dressed in green and adorned with leaves in early English folk theatre. Associated with Spring and the accompanying fertility rites, he also appeared in the Morris Dance and may have provided a model for the central figure of the Robin Hood play.

green room A room in the backstage area of a theatre, set aside for the use of the cast and stage crew. It was formerly used for the reception of visitors before and after a performance.

Green Room Club A social club in Adam Street, London, founded in 1866. Established by members from the Junior Garrick Club, it traditionally includes a majority of actors and actresses in its membership.

Greenwich Theatre A theatre in Crooms Hill, London, opened as a concert hall in 1855. After a period as **Crowder's Musical Hall** from 1871, it became the Greenwich Hippodrome in 1911 and subsequently underwent a number of changes, including use as a cinema and warehouse. In 1969 it was reopened under its original name, seating 426 and incorporating a restaurant, art gallery, and jazz club; it has since enjoyed success with plays by Alan Ayckbourn, Coward, and Peter Nichols among others; directors there have included Jonathan Miller.

Greet, Sir Ben (Philip Barling; 1857–1936) British actor-manager, remembered for his performances of Shakespeare's plays for schools and in the open air. One of the

cofounders of the Old Vic, where he staged 24 Shakespearean productions, he undertook several tours of the UK and the US with his own company. He was knighted in 1929.

Gregory, (Isabella) Augusta, Lady (1852–1932) Irish playwright, who was one of the founders of the *Abbey Theatre. In 1896 she met W B Yeats and set about reorganizing Irish theatre. Her best plays, written in Irish dialect, included such comedies as *Spreading the News* (1904), the tragi-comic *The Gaol Gate* (1906), and the tragedy *Dervorgilla* (1907). She provided dialect versions of Molière's plays and assisted Yeats with various works, including *The Pot of Broth* (1902) and *Cathleen Ni Houlihan*. She also championed J M Synge and G B Shaw and brought Sean O'Casey to public notice.

Gregory, Johann Gottfried (1631–75) German Lutheran pastor, who presented various theatrical productions at the royal court in Moscow, where he was appointed in 1658. Such entertainments as *The Play of Artaxerxes* (1672) and *The Comedy of Young Tobias* (1673) were performed in a theatre at the summer palace at Preobrazhen by Russian actors trained by Gregory himself.

Grein, Jack Thomas (Jacob Thomas Grein; 1862–1935) British playwright, theatre critic, and manager, born in Holland, who did much to popularize the 'theatre of ideas' of Ibsen, Shaw, and others. His **Independent Theatre Club** presented important early productions of such plays as *Ghosts* and *Widower's Houses* despite much adverse criticism.

Grenfell, Joyce (Joyce Irene Phipps; 1910–79) British actress and writer, whose success in Farjeon's *The Little Revue* (1939) secured her appearances in several other intimate revues, notably *Sigh No More* (1945), *Tuppence Coloured* (1947), and *Penny Plain* (1951). She performed satirical monologues and songs and, after appearing in *Joyce Grenfell Requests the Pleasure* in 1954, toured the world in solo entertainments. She became a personality on radio and television and appeared in several films.

Grenier de Toulouse *See Décentralisation Dramatique.*

Grenier-Hussenot, Les A French theatre company founded in 1946 by the actors Jean-Pierre Grenier and Olivier Hussenot, former members of Chancerel's touring troupe. The group performed in cabarets in Paris, presenting a wide range of entertainments, from music and acrobatics to mime and satire. The company was broken up in 1957.

Gresset, Jean-Baptiste-Louis (1709–77) French poet and playwright, born in Amiens. A Jesuit teacher, Gresset was forced to leave the order as a result of his satirical poem *Vert-Vert* (1734) and other comic verses. He subsequently turned to the theatre, producing the tragedy *Édouard III* (1740) and several comedies, of which *Le Méchant* (1747), a witty study of fashionable society, was the most successful.

Grévin, Jacques (1538–70) French playwright, poet, and doctor; author of the early French tragedy, *La Mort de César* (1561), modelled on the works of Seneca. Grévin's other plays are lively satirical comedies.

Gribov, Alexei Nikolayevich (1902–77) Soviet actor, who became one of the most popular performers with the Moscow Art Theatre, which he joined in 1924. He was particularly acclaimed for his impersonation of peasant characters, although he also appeared as Lenin (1942) and in several classical parts.

Griboyedov, Alexander Sergeivich (1795–1829) Russian playwright and diplomat, author of the celebrated comedy *Gore ot uma* (Woe from Wit; 1822–24), which

was not performed until 1831 due to its satirical comments upon contemporary Moscow society. Chatski, the hero, became a stock character of the Russian theatre and a favourite role of many actors, while several of the aphorisms in the play became popular proverbs. Having fought in the army against Napoleon, Griboyedov became Russian minister in Tehran in 1828, dying there at the hands of a mob. He also translated Molière and other French writers.

grid A framework of metal or wood over the stage area, used for the hanging of lighting equipment and scenery; it is more formally known as a **gridiron**.

Grieg, Nordahl (1902–43) Norwegian poet, novelist, and playwright, whose early experimental dramas, notably *Barrabas* (1927), treat such themes as violence and freedom. His principal works include the anti-war play *Vår ære og vår makt* (Our Honour and our Power; 1935) and *Nederlaget* (Defeat; 1937), which deals with the Paris Commune of 1871. He died in an air raid in World War II.

Grieve, William (1800–44) British scene painter, who worked as a boy at Covent Garden but became well known for his achievements at Drury Lane. Especially famed for his moonlight scenes, he once had the distinction of being called in front of the curtain after a performance in 1832. His elder brother, **Thomas Grieve** (1799–1882), was also respected as a scene painter.

Griffiths, Trevor (1935-) British playwright, whose plays reflect his Marxist commitment and belief in the need for social change. Such plays as *Occupations* (1970), *The Party* (1973) and *Comedians have been performed by groups as diverse as the Royal Shakespeare Company and the 7:84 Theatre Company. After the success of *Comedians* (1975), Griffiths turned for a while to television; later stage plays have included

Oi! for England (1982) and *Real Dreams* (1986).

Grillparzer, Franz (1791–1872) Austrian playwright, who was a leading figure of the Romantic movement. The pessimism of many of his 12 tragedies was a reflection of his own troubled life, in which he suffered from the early death of his father, his mother's suicide, and various unhappy love affairs. His early tragedies were modelled on classical lines, although the historical drama *König Ottokars Glück und Ende*, which was highly praised after initial opposition from the censors, drew heavily upon Schiller; *Der Traum ein Leben* was based on Calderón. After the failure of his one comedy, *Weh' dem, der lügt*, in 1838 he released no more plays for production in the theatre.
Principal works:
Die Ahnfrau: 1817; translated as *The Ancestress*.
Sappho: 1819.
Das goldene Vliess: 1820.
König Ottokars Glück und Ende: 1825.
Des Meeres und der Liebe Wellen: 1831.
Der Traum ein Leben: 1834; translated as *Life Is a Dream*.
Die Jüdin von Toledo: 1888.
Libussa: 1874.

Grimaldi, Joseph (1778–1837) British clown, commonly called **Joey**, who was born in London, the illegitimate son of the ballet master at Drury Lane. He appeared as a child at Sadler's Wells so successfully that he was taken into pantomime at Drury Lane and continued to appear at both theatres. In 1806 he was engaged at Covent Garden, where he remained for the next 17 years, transforming the English pantomime. Noted for his mastery of acrobatics and mime, he retired in 1823; all clowns are now named Joey in his honour.

Gringore, Pierre (c. 1475–1538) French actor and playwright, who wrote antipapal pieces on behalf of Louis XII. The chief Fool with a company in Paris, he was the author of several satirical *soties*, in which he appeared himself, and the plays *Le Jeux du prince du Sots* (1511) and *Mystère de Saint-Louis*.

Gripsholm Theatre A theatre in Sweden, constructed inside a fortress built in 1535 during the time of Gustavus Vasa. Opened in 1782, the theatre survives intact, complete with various items of stage machinery and scenery.

Grock (Charles Adrien Wettach; 1880–1959) British music hall clown, born in Switzerland, who performed acrobatics at the age of 12, touring with his family group of Tyrolean singers. Subsequently he went into partnership with a clown named Brick, but after 1911 appeared as a solo act almost continuously at the London Coliseum until 1924, when he returned to the Continent. He presented an hour-long act of virtuoso musical numbers in which everything invariably went wrong.

groove A narrow channel made of wood, along which a flat could be slid on and off the stage; the groove system was eventually replaced by the carriage-and-frame system in the 19th century.

Gropius, Walter *See* Totaltheater.

Gros-Guillaume (Robert Guérin; fl. 1598–1634) French actor, who became a popular player in farce alongside Turlupin and Gaultier-Garguille at the Hôtel de Bourgogne, after appearing in the Paris fairs. A fat man, he also appeared in tragedy under the stagename **La Fleur**. Several other members of his family were also on the stage, including his son-in-law François Juvenon (c. 1623–74), who also appeared as La Fleur and inherited the tragic roles of Montfleury, and his grandson, who appeared as *La Tuillerie.

Gros-René *See* Du Parc.

Grosses Schauspielhaus A theatre in Berlin, converted from a circus by Hans *Poelzig and opened in 1919. The theatre, built for Max Reinhardt, was remarkable for its rejection of the conventional proscenium arch in favour of flexible staging and a cyclorama, with the audience of 3000 seated on three sides of the acting area. It was subsequently altered and renamed the Friedrichsstadt-Palest.

Grossman, Jan (1925-) Czech director, who established his reputation while with the company of the Theatre on the Balustrade in Prague, notably with the plays of Václav Havel. He took over the company in 1962 and won acclaim in London as part of the World Theatre Seasons of 1967 and 1968, presenting Kafka's *Der Prozess* and his own *King Ubu*, adapted from Jarry. He then worked in exile until 1974, when he became director of the City Theatre in Cheb.

Grossmith, George (1847–1912) British actor, who became famous for his solo entertainments at the piano; subsequently he played principal parts in several Gilbert and Sullivan operas. Thereafter, he devoted himself mainly to performing his own sketches and songs, and wrote *Diary of a Nobody* (1892) with his brother **Weedon Grossmith** (1852–1919), who was also an actor. George's sons, **George Grossmith** (1874–1935) and **Lawrence Grossmith** (1877–1944), had distinguished acting careers, the former being associated with a number of successful revues.

Groto, Luigi (1541–85) Italian playwright and poet, often known as **Il cieco d'Adria** ('The blind man of Adria'). *Adriana* (1578) was an early version of the story that eventually provided the material for Shakespeare's *Romeo and Juliet*; other works included pastorals and comedies as well as the bloodthirsty tragedy *La Dalida* (1572).

Grotowski, Jerzy (1933-) Polish director, who has established an international reputation as a leading figure in contemporary experimental drama. He was trained at the Cracow Theatre School and became well-known for his great interest in the role of the actor while director of the Polish Theatre Laboratory in Wrocław during the 1960s. With this company he advocated audience participation and manipulation of the audience's emotions, emphasizing innovative use of movement and voices and sparse settings; noted productions included plays by Calderón and Wyspiański (chief of which was *Akropolis* in 1966) as well as Shakespeare. His influence has been strong upon directors throughout Europe and the US, notably upon the work of Peter Brook in Britain and the Living Theatre and other groups in the US, although much of his more recent work upon the theatre has been carried out in private, especially since he disbanded the Theatre Laboratory company in 1976. Some of his avant-garde ideas were, however, laid out in *Towards a Poor Theatre* (1968).

Grottesco, Teatro A theatre movement that developed in Italy during World War I in reaction to the heroic dramas of D'Annunzio. The movement derived its name from the subtitle of Chiarelli's *La maschera e il volto* (The Mask and the Face; 1916) and explored such issues as hypocrisy and the conflict between appearances and reality; writers of the genre included Bontempelli and Rosso di San Secondo.

groundrow A long low piece of scenery, basically a small flat, which is often painted to suggest an horizon. The upper edge can be shaped to represent mountains, waves (a **sea row** or **water row**), or other features.

Group Theatre A theatre organization founded in New York in 1931 by Harold Clurman, Cheryl Crawford, and Lee Strasberg to present serious drama outside the commercial theatre. The successor to the Theatre Guild, it established a strong reputation with plays by Paul Green, Sidney Kingsley, William Saroyan, and – above all – Clifford Odets, producing *Awake and Sing!* (1935) and *Waiting for Lefty* (1935) among other important works. The group also did much to disseminate the theories of Stanislavsky in the US before disbanding in 1941, short of money and internally split.

In 1933 another **Group Theatre** was founded in London at the Westminster Theatre to produce experimental and non-commercial drama. Under the direction of **Rupert Doone** (1904–66), it presented notable works by T S Eliot, W H Auden, and Stephen Spender, among others, often in collaboration with the composer Benjamin Britten. It closed during World War II and was briefly revived in the early 1950s.

Grove Theatre A shortlived theatre in Bedlow Street (later Madison Street), New York, which opened in 1804, with a company of then untried actors. The theatre only opened on nights when the Park Theatre was closed; it was renamed the Covent Garden Theatre after a successful pantomime presented by Signor Bologna of London's Covent Garden.

Gründgens, Gustav (1899–1963) German actor and director, who established his reputation in strong romantic parts in Berlin in the 1930s. He was particularly praised in the plays of Shaw and as Shakespeare's Hamlet (1938); subsequent successes included Mephistopheles in Goethe's *Faust* (1957–58), in which role he toured widely. After World War II he worked chiefly in Düsseldorf and Hamburg as well as in films; as a director he presented notable productions of Osborne's *The Entertainer* (1957) and plays by Brecht. His early life was the basis of

Klaus Mann's controversial novel *Mephisto* (1936); he apparently committed suicide in Manila.

Grundy, Sydney (1848–1914) British playwright, who wrote numerous adaptations of French pieces, beginning with *A Little Change* at the Haymarket Theatre in 1872. *A Pair of Spectacles* (1890), from *Les Petits Oiseaux* by Labiche and Delacour, was the most successful; others include *The Silver Shield* (1885), *The New Woman* (1894), and *A Fearful Joy* (1908).

Gryphius, Andreas (1616–64) German poet and playwright, author of five tragedies remarkable for their bloodletting and horror. Typical of these was *Murdered Majesty; or, Charles Stuart, King of Great Britain* (1649), in which he depicted the recent trial and execution of Charles I; others included *Catharina von Georgien* (1647) and *Papinianus* (1659), both studies of Christian martyrs. Gryphius also wrote the early domestic drama *Cardenio und Celinde* (1647) and several comedies, of which *Horribilicribifax* (1663) is regarded as the best.

Gual, Adriá (1872–1943) Spanish playwright and director, who founded the celebrated but shortlived **Teatro Intim** in Barcelona in 1903. The company presented productions of many classic plays, ranging from works by Aeschylus to Spanish dramas, achieving high standards of acting and staging, which ultimately contributed to the revival of Spanish drama during the 1920s and 1930s. Gual's own plays included *Misteri de Dolor*.

Guare, John (1938–) US playwright, who established his reputation with *A Day for Surprises* (1965) and *The Loveliest Afternoon of the Year* (1966). Other plays have included *Muzeeka* (1967), *The House of Blue Leaves* (1970), and a musical version of *The Two Gentleman of Verona* (1973); later works include *Rich and Famous* (1976) and *Bosoms and Neglect* (1979).

Guarini, Giovanni Battista (1538–1612) Italian poet, playwright, and diplomat, who ranks alongside Torquato Tasso (whose post as court poet at Ferrara he inherited in 1579 as a result of Tasso's mental illness) as the creator of the Italian pastoral. His tragicomedy *Il pastor fido* (The Faithful Shepherd; 1598) was revived many times in Italy, England, and France and inspired numerous imitations. His other writings include the treatise *Compendio della poesia tragicomica* and the comedy *L'idropica*.

Guérin d'Étriché, Isaac François (c. 1636–1728) French actor, who married Armande Béjart after the death of her first husband, Molière. He was initially at the Théâtre du Marais before joining the Comédie-Française and subsequently becoming its leader. His finest roles included Harpagon in Molière's *L'Avare*.

Guerrero, María (1868–1928) Spanish actress, who became the leading national theatrical performer in Spain in the late 19th century. Acclaimed in both classical Spanish plays and in contemporary works by such authors as Benavente, Pérez Galdós, and the Álvarez Quintero brothers, she also managed her own theatre, now renamed the Teatro Nacional María Guerrero in her honour.

Guignol A character of the French puppet theatre. Probably first introduced in Lyons during the late 18th century, he was derived from the character of *Polichinelle from the *commedia dell'arte*. He eventually lent his name to the *Grand Guignol.

Guilbert, Yvette (Emma Laure Esther Guilbert; 1865–1944) French singer, who became a leading performer in French music hall. Known as '*la diseuse fin-de-siècle*',

she first appeared in 1887 and soon became popular for her apparently unknowing delivery of highly *risqué* songs. Extremely thin and heavily made up, she habitually appeared in yellow with long black gloves, in which costume she was depicted in famous posters by Toulouse-Lautrec. Later in her career she sang traditional *chansons* in Europe and the US as well as appearing in many plays.

Guild Theatre See Anta Theatre.

Guillot-Gorju (Bertrand Hardouin de St Jacques; 1600–48) French actor, who began his career as a barker at the Paris fairs before appearing in farce at the Hôtel de Bourgogne. He was much encouraged by Bellerose, whose daughter he married, but later retired to become a doctor.

Guimerà, Àngel (1849–1924) Spanish poet and playwright, born in Tenerife, who is generally regarded as the most significant Catalan dramatist. Inspired by the French Romantics, his early poetic historical tragedies include *Gala Placidia* (1879), and *L'ànima morta* (The Dead Soul; 1892). His later naturalist plays, of which the rural drama *Terra Baixa* (1896) is the most outstanding, portray contemporary peasant life.

Guinness, Sir Alec (1914–) British actor, who first attracted attention with the Old Vic company in the 1936–37 season, playing supporting parts in plays by Shakespeare and Chekhov. He then took part in Gielgud's season at the Queen's Theatre before returning (1938) to the Old Vic to appear as Hamlet in modern dress and as Bob Acres in Sheridan's *The Rivals*. After World War II, he appeared in his own adaptation of Dostoevsky's *The Brothers Karamazov* (1946) and, during the Old Vic season from 1946–48, was highly praised in such roles as Richard II, the Fool in *King Lear*, and Abel Drugger in Jonson's *The Alchemist*. Since then he has played successfully in T S Eliot's *The Cocktail Party* (1949), Terence Rattigan's *Ross* (1960), and Alan Bennett's *Habeas Corpus* (1973). In 1984 he appeared as Shylock at the Chichester Festival Theatre. His many screen successes include *The Bridge on the River Kwai*, *Kind Hearts and Coronets*, and television appearances as John Le Carré's George Smiley.

Guitry, Lucien-Germain (1860–1925) French actor and playwright, who made his stage debut in 1878. Later he undertook lengthy tours of Europe and appeared with Sarah Bernhardt, as well as managing the Théâtre de la Renaissance.

His son was the actor and playwright **Sacha Guitry** (Alexandre-Pierre-George Guitry; 1885–1957), who was born in St Petersburg. He wrote over 100 plays, mainly light comedies in the style of *Boulevard* theatre. He also produced such serious biographical dramas as *Pasteur* (1919), in which his father played the principal role, and wrote and directed several films. The third of his five wives was Yvonne *Printemps.

Gundersen, Laura (1832–98) Norwegian actress, regarded as the first significant actress of the theatre in Norway. She first appeared at the Kristiana Theater in 1850 and excelled in the plays of Bjørnson, Ibsen, and Shakespeare.

Gunnell, Richard (d. 1634) English actor, manager, and playwright. An actor with Palsgrave's Men he took a share in the Fortune Theatre in 1618 and subsequently became manager there. In 1629, with William Blagrove, he built and then managed the Salisbury Court Theatre. His two plays are now lost.

Gustav III (1746–92) King of Sweden (1771–92), who did much to foster the development of the Swedish theatre. He founded the Kungliga Dramatiska Teatern

in 1788 and was himself the author of *Gustav Adolphs ädelmod* (Gustav Adolph's Magnanimity; 1783) and other plays.

Guthrie, Tyrone (1900–71) British actor and director, great-grandson of the actor Tyrone Power. After appearing under J B Fagan at Oxford, he worked as a director in Cambridge before presenting his first London play, *The *Anatomist*, at the Westminster Theatre in 1931. Subsequently he became famous for his productions of Shakespeare at the Old Vic, which included *Measure for Measure* (1933), with Charles Laughton and later Emlyn Williams, *Hamlet*, with Laurence Olivier (1937) and with Alec Guinness in modern dress the following year, *A Midsummer Night's Dream* (1937–38), with Robert Helpmann. He was also largely responsible for the foundation of the *Stratford (Ontario) Festival, where he continued to advocate the use of the open stage, and directed major revivals of Jonson and Chekhov. The theatre in Minneapolis was named after him in 1971 (*see* Guthrie Theatre). Other important productions included Molière's *Tartuffe* (1967) with Gielgud at the Old Vic.

Guthrie Theatre A theatre in Minneapolis, Minnesota, which opened as the Minneapolis Theatre in 1963. In 1971 the theatre, which seats 1441 and contains a seven-sided thrust stage, was renamed in honour of its designer, Tyrone Guthrie. Among the productions presented there have been plays by Shakespeare, Chekhov, Arthur Miller, Molière, Rostand, and Wilder. Michael Langham succeeded Guthrie as director in 1971; subsequent directors have included Liviu Ciulei.

Gutzkow, Karl Ferdinand (1811–78) German playwright and novelist, who was the author of the celebrated Jewish play in defence of intellectual freedom, *Uriel Acosta*, written in 1847. His other writings for the stage include the satirical comedy *Das Urbild des Tartüffe* (The Model for Tartuffe; 1844).

Guys and Dolls A musical by Jo Swerling and Abe Burrows with songs by Frank Loesser. First performance: New York, 1950. A romantic tale set in the world of the New York gangsters, it was based on the stories of Damon Runyon; it was filmed in 1955 with Frank Sinatra, Marlon Brandon, and Gene Simmons.

Gwynn, Nell (1650–87) English actress, initially an orange-girl at Drury Lane. Charles Hart trained her for the stage and she made her debut in 1665 as Cydaria in Dryden's *The Indian Emperor*. Despite her limitations as an actress, she was popular in comedy and was especially acclaimed as Florimel in Dryden's *Secret Love*. She became mistress of Charles II in about 1669 and retired from the stage a year later.

Gyllenborg, Carl (1679–1746) Swedish playwright, author of some of the earliest Swedish comedy. His play *Den Swenska sprätthöken* (The Swedish Dandy; 1740) was the first native Swedish play to be presented at the Svenska Dramatiska Teatern.

Gymnase, Théâtre du A theatre in the Boulevard Bonne-Nouvelle, Paris, which opened in 1820 as a drama school. In 1830 the theatre's fortunes improved with successful productions of the plays of Eugène Scribe; later the plays of Sardou and Dumas *fils* were among notable premieres given there and the theatre established its reputation as one of the capital's most important venues for comedy and melodrama. Leading performers there have included Bernhardt and Lucien Guitry; the theatre now presents a mixed programme of drama under Marie *Bell.

H

Habimah Theatre A Jewish theatre company, established in Moscow in 1917. Performing plays in Hebrew, the group began under the direction of Stanislavsky's pupil Vakhtangov; they presented his celebrated production of Ansky's *The Dybbuk* for the first time in 1922. Linked to the *Moscow Art Theatre, the company toured the world during the 1920s with *The Dybbuk* and plays by Calderón, Chekhov, Shakespeare, and other major playwrights. Eventually the company settled in Palestine in 1931, ultimately becoming Israel's national theatre in 1958, based in Tel-Aviv. The company was reorganized in 1970 and moved into a fully-equipped National Theatre.

Hackett, J(ames) H(enry) (1800–71) US actor, who first appeared professionally in 1826 as Justice Woodcock in *Love in a Village*. He soon became celebrated for his Yankee characterizations, notably as Solomon Swop in *Jonathan in England* (1828). He also achieved a reputation for his portrayals of Falstaff and other comic Shakespearean characters, in which he appeared in both London and New York, where he was also manager of the Astor Place Opera House.

His son was the actor **James K(eteltas) Hackett** (1869–1926), who was with Daly's company in 1892, numbering Jaques in *As You Like It* among his parts. With Daniel Frohman from 1895 to 1899 he was acclaimed in romantic comedy and drama, especially as Rudolf in Hope's *The Prisoner of Zenda*; subsequent attempts at Shakespeare – his last appearance was as Macbeth in 1924 – were less successful. Having opened a theatre (later Wallack's Theatre) in New York, he staged an influential *Othello* in 1914.

Hackett, Walter (1876–1944) US playwright and manager, who became a popular producer of light comedy on the London stage, most of his productions featuring his wife, Marion Lorne. He opened the Whitehall Theatre in 1930 and later worked at the Apollo, his successes including such plays as *He Didn't Want To Do It* (1915), *The Way to Treat a Woman* (1930), and *London After Dark* (1937).

Hafner, Philipp (1731–64) Austrian playwright, whose plays effectively established the Viennese comedy of manners, the *Volksstück*. His plays, notably *Megära die förchterliche Hexe* (1755), *Der geplagte Odoardo* (1762), and *Der Furchtsame* (1764) combined literary merit with strong theatricality.

Hagen, Uta Thyra (1919–) US actress, born in Germany, who made her stage debut in Coward's *Hay Fever* (1935). In 1937 she appeared with Eva Le Gallienne's Civic Repertory Company as Ophelia, making her New York debut a year later as Nina in Chekhov's *The Seagull*. She acted with her first husband, José Ferrer, in Maxwell Anderson's *Key Largo* (1939); roles since then have included Desdemona (1942–45), Blanche in *A Streetcar Named Desire* (1948), Joan in *Saint Joan* (1951), Martha in *Who's Afraid of Virginia Woolf?* (1962), and Ranevskaya in *The Cherry Orchard* (1968). Her second husband was Herbert Berghof.

Haigh, Kenneth (1931–) British actor, who made his name as the original Jimmy Porter in John Osborne's *Look Back in Anger* (1956) in both London and New York. With the Royal Shakespeare Company his parts have included James in Harold Pinter's *The Collection* (1962) and numerous Shakespearean roles; in 1982 he played the title role in *Othello* at the Young Vic.

Haines, John Thomas (1797–1843) British playwright and actor, who was the author of numerous melodramas and nautical dramas. His dramatization of Scott's *Quentin Durward* was staged at the Coburg Theatre (later the Old Vic Theatre) in 1813; subsequently he appeared in Manchester in several of his own dramas, including *Hulme Hall; or, Manchester in Olden Times* (1828) and *The Factory Boy; or, The Love Sacrifice* (1840). Back in London he produced further nautical and domestic pieces, of which *My Poll and My Partner Joe* (1835) enjoyed the greatest success.

Haines, Joseph (d. 1701) English actor, who ran a booth at Bartholomew Fair before joining the company at Drury Lane. Noted for his practical jokes, he was a fine low comedian, singer, and dancer and became one of the first English Harlequins when he appeared in an adaptation of Molière's *Les Fourberies de Scapin*.

Hair A rock musical by Galt MacDermot, Gerome Ragni, and James Rado. First performance: New York, 1967. The plot involves a young man from Oklahoma, who on his way to enlist in the Vietnam War, becomes captivated by Flower Children. The musical caused a stir with a scene in which the entire cast appeared naked on stage.

Hale, Binnie (Beatrice Hale Monro; 1900–84) British actress, who made her name in the highly successful musical *No, No, Nanette* (1925) and went on to appear in many musical comedies with Jack Buchanan, Bobby Howes, and others. In 1947 she took over the Duke of York's Theatre, where she appeared in the revues *One, Two, Three* and its successor *Four, Five, Six*.

Her brother **Sonnie Hale** (Robert Hale Monro; 1902–59) was a light comedian who appeared in many musicals of the 1930s, sometimes with his wife Jessie Matthews.

Hale, Louise (Louise Closser; 1872–1933) US actress, who began her career in Detroit in 1894, toured in Augustus Thomas's *Arizona*, and was acclaimed as Prossy in Shaw's *Candida* on her New York debut in 1903. Later notable parts, before she went over to films, included Fairy Berylune in Maeterlinck's *The Blue Bird* (1910) and Mrs Atkins in O'Neill's *Beyond the Horizon* (1920).

Halévy, Ludovic *See* Meilhac, Henri.

Halevy, Mosche *See* Ohel Theatre.

Hall, Sir Peter (Reginald Frederick) (1930-) British director and manager, who was closely linked with the Royal Shakespeare Company before becoming head of the National Theatre (1973–88). He began his career while still at Cambridge University and then worked at the Theatre Royal, Windsor, before moving to the Arts Theatre in London, where he successfully produced plays by such authors as Anouilh and Beckett. He formed his own company in 1957 and established himself as a director at Stratford-upon-Avon with his version of *Love's Labour's Lost* (1956). After further successes with Shakespearean works he was appointed managing director of the newly-created RSC in 1960 and oversaw its occupation of London's Aldwych Theatre. There followed such influential and highly-praised productions as *The Wars of the Roses* cycle (1963) before his resignation as managing director in 1968. Subsequently he presided over the foundation of the National Theatre (now the Royal National Theatre) and its transfer (1976) from the Old Vic; his successes with the National Theatre ranged from Pinter's *No Man's Land* (1975) to *Hamlet* (1975), Marlowe's *Tamburlaine the Great* (1976), Chekhov's *The Cherry Orchard* (1978), Shaffer's *Amadeus* (1979), and Wilde's *The Importance of Being Earnest* (1982). From 1980 he shared control of the Olivier and Cottesloe theatres with Peter Gill. On leaving the National Theatre he embarked upon plans to establish a transatlantic production company.

Hall, Willis (1929-) British playwright, whose long collaboration with the novelist and playwright **Keith (Spencer) Waterhouse** (1929-) has resulted in a number of highly praised works for the theatre. The most significant of Hall's early (solo) works was *The Long and the Short and the Tall* (1959), a brutal portrayal of a British patrol lost in Malaya during World War II; others included the double bill *Last Day in Dreamland* and *A Glimpse of the Sea* (1959). **Billy Liar* was the first play written by Hall and Waterhouse together; among the many successful plays that have followed has been *England, Our England* (1962), the comedy *All Things Bright and Beautiful* (1962), the farce *Say Who You Are* (1965), and two adaptations of plays by Eduardo de Filippo – *Saturday, Sunday, Monday* (1973) and *Filumena* (1980). Hall's other solo works include the children's play *Kidnapped at Christmas* (1975), while in 1986 Waterhouse had a solo success with *Mr and Mrs Nobody*.

Hallam, Lewis (1714–56) US actor, born in Britain, who emigrated with his family to the US in 1752 and installed a notable company at the Nassau Street Theatre in New York in 1753. Subsequently he toured a wide range of plays to Philadelphia, Charleston, and Jamaica.

His children included the British actress Mrs *Mattocks and the US actor **Lewis Hallam** (c. 1740–1808), who became leading man with Douglass's American Company in 1758, was the earliest known US Hamlet, and won acclaim as Arsaces in the first professionally produced American play, Godfrey's *The Prince of Parthia* (1767). He took over the company in 1786 and was later associated with Hodgkinson and Dunlap in reopening the Southwark Theatre, Philadelphia, and the John Street Theatre, New York.

hall keeper *See* stage door-keeper.

halls *See* music hall.

Hallström, Per (1866–1960) Swedish playwright, poet, novelist, and critic, who was particularly noted for his translations of Shakespeare in the 1920s. His own plays included the tragedy *Bianco Capello* (1900), the comedy *Erotikon* (1908), the saga *Tusen och en natt* (A Thousand and One Nights; 1910), and several historical dramas.

ham An actor who habitually overacts, commonly from reasons of vanity, inexperience, or lack of genuine talent. The term was particularly relevant in the 19th century, when many actors favoured a ranting style of delivery.

Hamblin, Thomas Sowerby (1800–53) British actor and manager, who performed at Sadler's Wells and Drury Lane before making his US debut in 1825 at the Park Theatre, New York. In 1830 he took over the Bowery Theatre, which was burnt down three times during his tenure. In 1848 he moved to the Park Theatre, only to have this destroyed by fire the same year.

Hamlet, Prince of Denmark A revenge tragedy by William *Shakespeare, written c. 1600. First performance: c. 1600. Often described as Shakespeare's greatest dramatic work, the play revolves about Hamlet's desire for vengeance following his father's murder and culminates in the death of virtually all the central characters. The text contains some of Shakespeare's finest soliloquies and provides some of the most celebrated roles in the theatre. Hamlet's "To be or not to be" soliloquy is arguably the best-known passage in the theatre; other celebrated scenes include the play within a play before which Hamlet himself instructs the players about the nature of acting.

Hamlisch, Marvin (1944–) US composer, who is best known for the score of *A *Chorus Line* (1975), which received a Pulit-zer Prize. His more recent work includes the music for *They're Playing Our Song* (1979).

Hammerstein II, Oscar (1895–1960) US lyricist, whose first contribution to a musical was the book and lyrics for *Always You* (1920). Subsequently he worked on *The Desert Song*, *The New Moon*, *Show Boat,* and *Music in the Air* and collaborated with the composer **Richard Rodgers** (1902–79) on a series of highly popular shows. These included *Oklahoma!*, *Carousel*, *South Pacific*, *The *King and I*, *Flower Drum Song*, and *The *Sound of Music*. Earlier Rodgers also enjoyed success in collaboration with Lorenz *Hart on such musicals as *The Girlfriend* (1926), *On Your Toes* (1936), *The Boys from Syracuse* (1938), and *Pal Joey* (1940). After Hammerstein's death, Rodgers worked on several musicals with Stephen *Sondheim.

Hammerstein's Theatre *See* Manhattan Theatre.

Hammerton, Stephen (d. c. 1648) English actor, who joined the King's Men after beginning as a boy actor at the Salisbury Court Theatre. Having played Oriana in Fletcher's *Wild Goose Chase* in 1631, he became greatly admired in female roles.

Hammond, Kay *See* Clements, John Selby.

Hampden, Walter (Walter Hampden Dougherty; 1879–1955) US actor, who began his career with Frank Benson's company and at the Adelphi Theatre in London. He returned to the US in 1907 and won acclaim in Kennedy's *The Servant in the House* (1908) and *Cyrano de Bergerac* (1923). His Shakespearean roles included Caliban, Hamlet, Macbeth, Oberon, Othello, Romeo, and Shylock. In 1925 he took over the **Colonial Theatre** and renamed it Hampden's; his productions there included *Henry V*, Benavente's *The Bonds of Interest*, and Bulwer-Lytton's *Richelieu*.

Hampshire, Susan (1942-) British actress, who established a strong reputation for her television work but has also played many classic parts on the stage. Her roles have included Kate Hardcastle in Goldsmith's *She Stoops to Conquer* (1966), Nora in Ibsen's *A Doll's House* (1972), Katherina in *The Taming of the Shrew* (1954), and Ann Whitefield in Shaw's *Man and Superman* (1978).

Hampstead Theatre Club A theatre organization founded in Hampstead, London, in 1959, which presented the London premieres of plays by Harold Pinter and Ionesco between 1959 and 1962. The club then moved to Swiss Cottage, where it presented several successful plays, including Laurie Lee's *Cider with Rosie* (1963) and Aubrey's *Brief Lives* (1967), which transferred to the West End. Rehoused nearby in 1970, the club has since had further success with productions of plays by Michael Frayn, Brian Friel, and Tennessee Williams among others.

Hampton, Christopher James (1946-) British playwright, who established his reputation with his first play, *When Did You Last See My Mother?* (1966), which was presented at the Royal Court Theatre before moving to the West End. As resident playwright at the Royal Court (1968–70), he enjoyed further success with *Total Eclipse* (1968) and *The Philanthropist* (1970) while the unconventional *Savages* (1973), concerning the kidnapping of a British diplomat in South America, provided Paul Scofield with a fine role. *Treats* (1976), *After Mercer* (1980), and *Tales from Hollywood* (1982) were among the plays that followed (several of which were performed by the National Theatre) – as well as translations of Chekhov, Ibsen, and Molière. *Les Liaisons Dangereuses* (1986), following the adventures of a notorious seducer in prerevolutionary France, provided him with his greatest suc-cess to date in a production by the Royal Shakespeare Company.

Hampton Court Palace Theatre The oldest surviving Elizabethan theatre in England, part of the royal palace of Hampton Court in London. Plays were presented in the Great Hall of the palace from 1572 and were famed for their lavish production. Several monarchs saw plays over the Christmas period there, among them the works of Shakespeare. In 1718 George I allowed members of the public in to see productions by the company of Colley Cibber, including *Hamlet* and *Henry VIII*, although no further performances are recorded after 1731.

Hamsun, Knut (1859–1952) Norwegian novelist, poet, and playwright, who won a Nobel Prize in 1920. The comedy *Livet ivold* (In the Grip of Life; 1910) was first produced by the Moscow Art Theatre and subsequently by Reinhardt; other plays included the trilogy *Aftenrøde* (Afterglow; 1898), based on the hero Ivar Karenko, and the historical drama *Dronningen Tamara* (Queen Tamara; 1903).

Hancock, Sheila (1933-) British actress, who made her first West End appearance in Peter Coke's *Breath of Spring* (1958). She established her reputation in Charles Dyer's *Rattle of a Simple Man* (1962) and went on to combine straight and musical theatre, starring in the musicals *Annie* (1978) and *Sweeney Todd* (1980); she has also worked with the National and Royal Shakespeare companies as director and actress. Her parts have included Julia in Albee's *A Delicate Balance* (1969) and Paulina in *The Winter's Tale* (1981).

Handke, Peter (1942-) Austrian playwright and novelist, who acquired a controversial reputation with his *Publikumsbeschimpfung* (Offending the Audience; 1966), in which he renounced conventional modes of communication. *Kaspar* (1968) reflected the influence of Wittgenstein, while *Der Ritt über den Bodensee* (1971) developed his exploration of alternative means of expression by using only clichéd language and movement. Other plays include *Die Unvernünftigen sterben aus* (The Foolish Ones Die Out; 1974) and the monologue *A Sorrow Beyond Dreams* (1977).

Handl, Irene (1901–87) British actress, whose remarkable impact as Beer in Gerald Savory's *George and Margaret* in 1937 launched her as a comedy-character actress. Her other stage appearances included Mrs Puffin in Arthur Lovegrove's *Goodnight, Mrs Puffin* (1961), Thirza Tapper in the Chichester Festival Theatre revival of Eden Phillpotts's *The Farmer's Wife* (1967), and May in Peter Nichols's *The Freeway* (1974) at the National Theatre.

hand-prop *See* prop.

Hands, Terry David (1941-) British director, who became joint artistic director of the Royal Shakespeare Company with Trevor Nunn in 1978 and chief executive in 1986. Earlier in his career he helped to found the Everyman Theatre in Liverpool, where his productions included Osborne's *Look Back in Anger* and Arrabal's *Fando and Lis*. He then became artistic director of the RSC's Theatregoround Company (1966) and subsequently artistic director of the RSC, directing all of Shakespeare's history plays by 1980. Productions by other authors have included Arbuzov's *Old World* (1976), T S Eliot's *Murder in the Cathedral* (1972), Gorky's *The Children of the Sun* (1979), and Genet's *The Balcony* (1987). He has also directed several productions for the Comédie-Française (1975–77).

hand-worked house A theatre in which the ropes used to suspend scenery are adjusted manually rather than by means of a counterweight system. Such a theatre was formerly also referred to as a **hemp house** or **rope house**.

Hankin, Edward Charles St John (1869–1909) British playwright, author of several plays on social issues. Of his markedly cynical works, only *The Return of the Prodigal* (1905) was revived, in 1948.

Hanlon-Lees A British theatre company, comprising the six Hanlon brothers, who became famous in several countries as acrobats during the 1870s. Their spectacular displays of trickwork and mime included *Le Voyage en Suisse*, presented in Paris in 1879 and London in 1880, as well as acclaimed drunk scenes and mock disasters; the group finally disbanded during the 1890s.

Hannah Playhouse *See* Downstage Theatre.

Hannen, Nicholas (James) (1881–1972) British actor, who scored his first London success as Nelson in Hardy's *The Dynasts* (1914). His subsequent career encompassed a wide range of parts, from comedies by Pinero and Milne to Greek tragedy and the plays of Shakespeare, Shaw, and Chekhov; he often appeared with his wife, Athene *Seyler.

Hansberry, Lorraine (1930–65) US Black playwright, who established her reputation before her early death with *A Raisin in the Sun* (1959), a study of a Black family facing disaster. Her only other play to be performed in her lifetime was *The Sign in Sidney Brustein's Window* (1964), which is set in the Jewish community of New York.

Hansen, Christiern (16th century) Danish playwright, a major figure in the early Danish theatrical tradition. He was the author of several examples of school drama, notably *Den utro hustra* (The Unfaithful Wife) and *Dorothiae Komedie*.

Hanswurst A stock character in Viennese comedy of the 18th century. Descended from legendary German figures, he took on some of the coarser characteristics of the *zanni* of the *commedia dell'arte* and was heavily influenced by the clown Pickelhering, developed by Robert Reynolds and the English Comedians. When played by Stranitsky and Prehauser he became increasingly cunning and sophisticated and was dressed in a red jacket and blue smock decorated with a green heart. Ultimately the disruption caused by his presence in all types of plays attracted adverse criticism from Gottsched and Caroline Neuber; the character was subsequently transformed by Kurz into that of *Bernadon.

happening A form of theatrical event that became popular during the 1960s. An extension of the techniques used in improvisation, happenings were designed to appear spontaneous and included preplanned interruptions from the audience in the middle of a play and unannounced displays of street theatre, all designed to take spectators by surprise. The fashion had largely died out by the end of the decade.

Happy Days (*Oh! Les beaux jours*) A play by Samuel *Beckett. First performance: New York, 1961. This one-woman play, in which the central character slowly sinks into the ground until only her head can be seen was interpreted by Madeleine Renaud with great success in 1965; other actresses in the role have included Peggy Ashcroft.

Hardwicke, Sir Cedric (Webster) (1893–1964) British actor and director, who first appeared at the Lyceum in 1912 before going on to the Birmingham Repertory Theatre, where he was acclaimed as Churdles Ash in Phillpotts's *The Farmer's Wife* in 1924. Appearances at the Malvern Festival Theatre and elsewhere won him a reputation as a Shavian actor; subsequent performances included Edward Moulton-Barrett in *The Barretts of Wimpole Street* (1930) and Dr Haggett in Emlyn Williams's *The Late Christopher Bean* (1933) as well as roles in films in the US. In 1948 he joined the Old Vic company and excelled in the plays of Shakespeare, Marlowe, and Chekhov before finally moving to New York.

Hardy, Alexandre (c. 1570–c. 1632) French playwright, who is believed to have produced more than 600 plays during the first three decades of the 17th century. Hardy wrote for several troupes of actors and was probably the first professional playwright in France. His influential plays – tragedies (notably *Marianne*, published 1625), tragi-comedies, and pastorals – were written to cater for popular tastes, ignoring many of the rules and conventions of the contemporary theatre.

Hardy, (Timothy Sydney) Robert (1925-) British actor, whose career began at the Shakespeare Memorial Theatre in 1949. Subsequently he appeared in classic plays at the Old Vic and again at Stratford-upon-Avon as well as in the US, where he played the title roles in *Henry V* and *Hamlet* in 1964. Apart from his numerous television and film roles, his stage appearances have included Shaw in Jerome Kilty's *Dear Liar* (1982) at the Mermaid, and, in 1988, Winston Churchill in the musical *Winnie* at the Victoria Palace.

Hardy, Thomas (1840–1928) British novelist, poet, and playwright, whose epic Napoleonic drama *The Dynasts* (1903–08) was adapted by Harley Granville-Barker in 1914. His only other play was *The Tragedy of the Queen of Cornwall* (1923), based on the Tristan and Iseult story. *Tess of the D'Urbervilles* was one of his novels successfully adapted for the stage by other hands.

Hare, David (1947-) British playwright and director, who cofounded the Portable Theatre (1968–71). He became literary manager and resident dramatist first at the Royal Court Theatre (1969–71) and then at the Nottingham Playhouse (1973). His plays usually have a sharp political edge and include *Slag* (1970), *Knuckle* (1974), *Teeth 'n' Smiles* (1975), and *Plenty* (1978). Other successes have been *Fanshen* (1975), about the struggle of a Chinese village to come to terms with the Revolution, and *A Map of the World* (1982), about British attitudes to the 'third world'. He has also collaborated with Howard *Brenton, both as director of several of his plays and as writer, notably in *Brassneck* (1973) and *Pravda* (1985). More recent works are *The Bay at Nice* (1986) and *Wrecked Eggs* (1986). He directed his first Shakespearean play, *King Lear*, at the National Theatre in 1986.

Hare, Sir John (1844–1921) British actor-manager. He made his first stage appearance at Liverpool; subsequently he made his London debut under the Bancrofts at the Prince of Wales' Theatre (later the Scala Theatre) in 1865. After several more successful appearances, he took over the Royal Court Theatre before entering into partnership with the Kendals at the St James's Theatre. In 1889 he took over the Garrick Theatre, where his greatest success was as Goldfinch in Grundy's *A Pair of Spectacles*. He was knighted in 1907.

Hare, J(ohn) Robertson (1891–1979) British actor, who became one of the team that performed the famous series of farces at the Aldwych Theatre between 1924 and 1933. He featured in 12 consecutive productions, creating such characters as Sloley-Jones in *A Cuckoo in the Nest* (1925) and Harold Twine in *Rookery Nook* (1926), both by Ben Travers. He went on to create similar characters in numerous subsequent farces and appeared in the musical *A Funny Thing Happened on the Way to the Forum* (1963); late in life he visited South Africa in John Chapman's *Oh, Clarence!* (1968).

Harlequin A central character of the *harlequinade, the lover of Columbine, who was derived from the character *Arlecchino of the Italian *commedia dell'arte*. In the English tradition the emphasis was placed upon his magical powers, especially his ability to disguise himself as a different character; he was eventually absorbed into the character of the principal boy.

harlequinade An English theatrical tradition derived ultimately from the Italian *commedia dell'arte*. Incorporating elements of music, mime, trickwork, and disguise, it revolved around the central figures of the lovers *Harlequin and *Columbine and the clown Pantaloon (*see* Pantalone). The genre first developed out of Weaver's *Italian night scenes in the early 18th century; gradually, however, the fairytale element and the comic scenes featuring Pantaloon took precedence over the romantic content and led to the evolution of the *pantomime. The harlequinade itself was reduced to a brief epilogue and finally disappeared completely in the mid-20th century.

Harleville, Jean-François Collin d' (1755–1806) French playwright, whose moralizing comedies raised the spirits of Parisian theatregoers during the Revolution. His most successful plays included *L'Inconstant* (1786), *L'Optimiste* (1788), *Les Châteaux en Espagne* (1789), and *Le Vieux Célibataire* (1792).

Harper, Elizabeth *See* Bannister, Jack.

Harrigan, Ned (1845–1911) US actor, manager, and playwright, who formed a highly successful partnership with the female impersonator **Tony Hart** (Antony Cannon; 1855–91). They appeared in New York in a series of plays, one of the earliest being *The Mulligan Guards*. They parted company in 1885, but Harrigan continued to revive his plays and opened a theatre in his own name (later the Garrick Theatre) in 1890.

Harrigan's Park Theatre *See* Herald Square Theatre.

Harrigan's Theatre *See* Garrick Theatre.

Harris, Sir Augustus Henry Glossop (1852–96) British theatre manager, son of the theatre manager **Augustus Glossop Harris** (1825–73). The younger Harris acquired control of *Drury Lane in 1879, reopening it with *Henry V* and launching a spectacular series of annual pantomimes, in which he engaged the great stars of the music halls. He was a complete man of the theatre and was affectionately nicknamed **Augustus Druriolanus.**

Harris, Henry (c. 1634–1704) English actor, who appeared with Davenant's company after the Restoration. He became joint manager, with Betterton, of Lincoln's Inn Fields in 1668 and subsequently a shareholder in the Dorset Garden Theatre. Among his Shakespearean roles were Aguecheek, Romeo, and Wolsey; he retired in 1681.

Harris, Julie Ann (1925–) US actress, who joined the New York-based Old Vic company in 1946 and appeared in *Henry IV, Part II* and *Oedipus* (1946). She won acclaim in Carson McCullers's *The Member of the Wedding* (1950) and consolidated her reputation by playing Sally Bowles in *I Am a Camera* (1951). Her roles since then have included Joan of Arc in Anouilh's *The Lark* (1955), Margery Pinchwife in Wycherley's *The Country Wife* (1957), Juliet (1960), Ophelia (1964), Ann Stanley in Jay Allen's *Forty Carats* (1968), and Emily Dickinson in William Luce's *The Belle of Amherst* (1976).

Harris, Robert (1900–) British actor, who first appeared in 1923 in J M Barrie's *The Will.* Among his important parts in a long career have been Hamlet (1931) at the Old Vic, Marchbanks in Shaw's *Candida* (1937) in New York, and, in the Stratford-upon-Avon season of 1946–47, Prospero and the title role in Marlowe's *Doctor Faustus.* He toured the US in 1963–64 as Sir Thomas More in Robert Bolt's *A Man for All Seasons* and later triumphed as the headmaster in Alan Bennett's *Forty Years On* (1970).

Harris, Rosemary (1930–) British actress, who made her first London appearance in *The Seven Year Itch* (1953). She played leading parts with the Bristol Old Vic company and went with the London Old Vic company to the US (1956) as Cressida in *Troilus and Cressida.* Subsequent successes in Britain have included appearances at the Chichester Festival Theatre (1962), in the National Theatre's inaugural *Hamlet* (1963) as Ophelia, in Neil Simon's *Plaza Suite* (1969), and in Shaw's *Heartbreak House* (1983). In the US she excelled in such roles as Eleanor in James Goldman's *The Lion in Winter* (1966) and as Blanche Dubois in Tennessee Williams's *A Streetcar Named Desire* (1973).

Harrison, Rex (Carey) (1908–) British actor, who worked in repertory at the Liverpool Playhouse before making his London debut at the Everyman Theatre in 1930. After various West End appearances he enjoyed outstanding success in 1936, first in New York in *Sweet Aloes,* then in London in *French Without Tears.* He has since become a star of stage and screen on both sides of the Atlantic, specializing in refined English characters in comedies by such authors as Coward, Van Druten, and Behrman. His greatest triumph came in 1956 as Professor Higgins in the musical *My Fair Lady,* which he played for two years on Broadway before transferring to Drury Lane. Among his later appearances in London and New York have been *Heartbreak House* (1983), Lonsdale's *Aren't We All?* (1984), and Barrie's *The Admirable Crichton* (1988).

His second wife was the German actress **Lilli Palmer** (Lilli Peiser; 1914-), whose stage successes alongside him included *The Love of Four Colonels*.

His fourth wife was **Rachel Roberts** (1927–80), who appeared with him in *Platonov* and other plays; her other successes included the title role in the musical *Maggie May* (1964).

Harrison, Richard Berry (1864–1935) US Black actor, whose parents escaped from slavery to Canada, where he was brought up. Returning to Detroit, he became a teacher of elocution and drama and toured giving solo Shakespearean and other recitals. As an actor he was known for a single role, 'De Lawd' in March Connolly's *The Green Pastures* (1930), which he played nearly 2000 times.

Harris Theatre *See* Sam H Harris Theatre; Wallack's Theatre.

Hart, Charles (d. 1683) English actor, who was a boy player of female roles with the King's Men, prior to serving as a soldier during the Commonwealth. After the Restoration he became a principal heroic actor at and shareholder in Drury Lane and trained Nell Gwynn for the stage.

Hart, Lorenz (1895–1943) US lyricist, who collaborated with Richard *Rodgers on such musicals as *No! No! Nanette* (1925), *On Your Toes* (1936), and *The Boys from Syracuse* (1937), which was based on *The Comedy of Errors*. Other successes included *Pal Joey* (1940), *Lady in the Dark* (1941), and *By Jupiter* (1942).

Hart, Moss (1904–61) US playwright, whose first major success came with his play *Once in a Lifetime* (1930), upon which he collaborated with George *Kaufman. Other collaborations with Kaufman included *Merrily We Roll Along* (1934), *You Can't Take It With You* (1936), which won a Pul-

itzer Prize, and *The Man Who Came to Dinner* (1939). Solo works included *Winged Victory* (1943), *Christopher Blake* (1946), *Light Up the Sky* (1948), and *The Climate of Eden* (1952). He also contributed to the musicals *As Thousands Cheer* (1933), *The Great Waltz* (1934), and *I'd Rather Be Right* (1937) and directed *Dear Ruth* (1944), *Anniversary Waltz* (1954), *My Fair Lady* (1956), and *Camelot* (1960) among other shows.

Hart, Tony *See* Harrigan, Ned.

Hart House Theatre A theatre founded by Raymond and Vincent Massey in 1919 in Toronto, Canada as an experimental venue for the University of Toronto. Seating 500, it was used for premieres of several significant new Canadian works before closing in 1939 and being reopened in 1947 as part of the university. It gradually acquired a respected resident company and in 1966 a University Graduate Centre for the Study of Drama was founded there. The theatre and the centre have been run by several notable professional directors, including Robert Gill and Ronald Bryden.

Hartley, Elizabeth (Elizabeth White; 1751–1824) British actress, who appeared briefly at the Haymarket in 1769 and toured the provinces before her Covent Garden debut in 1772. She combined outstanding beauty with an arresting personality – Sir Joshua Reynolds painted her several times – and she remained at Covent Garden throughout her career. In 1780 she created Lady Touchwood in Mrs Cowley's *The Belle's Stratagem*.

Hartzenbusch, Juan Eugenio (1806–80) Spanish playwright, of German extraction, whose reputation was founded on the highly popular romantic tragedy *Los amantes de Teruel* (1837). Subsequently he enjoyed some success with a number of comedies and adaptations of Spanish dramas of the Golden

Age and edited the plays of Tirso de Molina, Calderón, Lope de Vega, and others.

Harvard Dramatic Club A theatre club at Harvard University, founded in 1908 to produce plays written by Harvard and Radcliffe students and graduates as well as foreign plays. Since 1960 it has staged productions at the Loeb Drama Centre, in Cambridge, Massachusetts.

Harvey, John Martin- *See* Martin-Harvey, John.

Harwood, Harold Marsh (1874–1959) British playwright and manager, who achieved success with his first play, *Honour Thy Father* (1912), and consolidated it with *The Grain of Mustard Seed* (1920). Among his other works are *The Man in Possession* (1930), *The Mask* (1913), and *Billeted* (1917) – the last two written in collaboration with his wife, **Fryniwyd Tennyson Jesse** (1889–1958).

Harwood, John Edmund (1771–1809) US actor, who began his career at Philadelphia's Southwark Theatre, where his parts included Plagiary in Sheridan's *The Critic* and Stephano in *The Tempest*. In 1803 he had enormous success as Dennis Brulgruddery in Colman the Younger's *John Bull* and, in 1806, was again highly acclaimed as Falstaff. Latterly he played several high comedy roles.

Hasenclever, Walter (1890–1940) German playwright, poet, and novelist, whose early Expressionist dramas dealt with the themes of tyranny and revolt. His most outstanding play, *Der Sohn* (1916), which explores the relationship between a father and his son, was followed by an adaptation of *Antigone* (1917) by Sophocles and the antiwar play *Der Retter* (1919). Subsequently he turned to more conventional comedies, including *Ein besserer Herr* (A Man of Distinction; 1926), and *Ehen werden in Himmel*

geschlossen (Marriages are Made in Heaven; 1928). He committed suicide in a French internment camp in 1940.

Hasenhut, Anton (1766–1841) Austrian actor, who developed the stock character *Thaddädl. He was praised by Grillparzer for his acting but fell from popularity by the 1820s, audiences having tired of conventional comedy.

Hassan A poetic drama by James Elroy *Flecker. First performance: London, 1922. This spectacular oriental drama enjoyed enormous success on its first production, complete with music by Delius and extravagant costumes and scenery, under Basil Dean at Her Majesty's Theatre. The distinguished cast was headed by Henry Ainley.

Hasse, Otto Eduard (1903–78) German actor, who trained under Reinhardt and went on to become one of Germany's leading performers, appearing first in Munich then, after World War II, in Berlin. Plays in which he triumphed ranged from Goethe's *Faust* (1945) to Jerome Kilty's *Dear Liar* (1959) and the premiere of Hochhuth's controversial *Soldaten* (1967).

Hatton Garden Nursery *See* nurseries.

Hauch, Johannes Carsten (1790–1872) Danish poet, novelist, and playwright, who became a leading member of the Romantic movement in Denmark. His melancholic tragedies based on Danish historical figures include *Svend Grathe* (1841) and *Marsk Stig* (1850); others include *Søstrene paa Kinnekullen* (The Sisters of Kinnekullen; 1849).

Hauptmann, Gerhart (1862–1946) German playwright, novelist, and poet, who established his reputation in the theatre with his first play *Vor Sonnenaufgang*, which was hailed as a landmark in German naturalistic drama. Subsequently he wrote several notable dramas dealing with such themes as heredity, psychiatry, suicide, and determinism and characterized by stark realism and strong social comment. His deep compassion for the poor and exploited was expressed in *Die Weber*, a historical drama written in his native Silesian dialect which portrays the despair of a group of weavers during a futile rebellion in 1844. His later work, in which he blended realism and fantasy, led to his association with Symbolism and the Romantic movement. Both his dream play *Hanneles Himmerlefahrt* and the fairy drama *Und Pippa tanzt* were successfully performed throughout Europe. Other notable works include the satirical comedy *Der Biberpelz* and *Die Atriden*, a dramatic cycle in four parts, which bitterly condemns Nazi brutality. He was awarded a Nobel Prize in 1912.

Principal works:

Vor Sonnenaufgang: 1889; translated as *Before Dawn*.

Das Friedensfest: 1890; translated as *The Coming of Peace*.

Einsame Menschen: 1891; translated as *Lonely People*.

Die Weber: 1892; translated as *The Weavers*.

Der Biberpelz: 1893; translated as *The Beaver Coat*.

Hanneles Himmelfahrt: 1893; translated as *The Assumption of Hannele*.

Florian Geyer: 1896.

Die versunkene Glocke: 1896; translated as *The Sunken Bell*.

Führman Henschel: 1898.

Der Rote Hahn: 1901; translated as *The Red Rooster*.

Rose Bernd: 1903.

Und Pippa tanzt: 1906.

Die Ratten: 1911.

Der Atriden: 1941.

Haupt- und Staatsaktionen Plays of the early native German theatrical tradition, directly descended from those presented by the English Comedians. The plays (several of which, written for performance in Vienna, survive) drew on various European sources and showed a preference for the more sensational aspects of drama, with much high rhetoric interspersed with comic scenes featuring such clowns as Pickelhering and Hanswurst. *See also Altwiener Volkstheater.*

Hauteroche, Noël-Jacques le Breton de (c. 1616–1707) French actor and playwright, who appeared at both the Théâtre du Marais and the Hôtel de Bourgogne before becoming a founder-member of the Comédie-Française in 1680. He was satirized in Molière's *L'Impromptu de Versailles* (1663) but was himself the author of several comedies in the style of Molière.

Havergal, Giles *See* Glasgow Citizens' Theatre.

Hawtrey, Sir Charles (Henry) (1858–1923) British actor-manager, who made his debut at the Prince of Wales's Theatre in 1881. He soon went into management on his own, achieving success in 1833 with his adaptation of Von Moser's comedy *The Private Secretary*. Subsequently he acquired a fine reputation as a light comedian, whose most successful parts included Lord Goring in Wilde's *An Ideal Husband* (1895) and William in Somerset Maugham's *Home and Beauty* (1919). From 1911 he produced the annual Christmas play *Where the Rainbow Ends* with a cast of 50 child actors, one of whom was Noël Coward.

Háy, Gyula (1900–75) Hungarian playwright, who first attracted attention with *Gott, Kaiser, Bauer* (1932), which was produced by Reinhardt in Berlin. He lived in exile from Hungary for many years and was imprisoned for a time for his involvement in the 1956 rebellion. His early plays included the tragedy *Tiszazug* (1945), which was variously revived as *The Midwife*, *Haben*, and *To Have and To Hold*; later works numbered amongst them *Das Pferd* (1964), which depicted Caligula, and the anticommunist *Gaspar Varros Recht* (1965).

Hay, Ian (John Hay Beith; 1876–1952) British playwright and novelist, whose early plays *Tilly of Bloomsbury* (1919) and *A Safety Match* (1921) were adaptations of his own humorous novels. He also collaborated on various light comedies with Seymour Hicks, P G Wodehouse, Stephen King-Hall, and Anthony Armstrong.

Hayduk theatre A form of Bulgarian theatre based upon stories surrounding the *hayduks*, Bulgarian outlaws who resisted domination by Turkey until liberation in 1878. The best examples of the tradition were influenced by Byron and Schiller and included works by such authors as Iordanov, Karavelov, Velichkov, and Ivanov. Throughout the 20th century the *hayduk* themes of nationalism and patriotism have ensured frequent revivals of the genre, despite restrictions imposed by the state.

Haye, Helen (1874–1957) British actress, who had a long and highly-respected career that began at the Pier Theatre, Hastings, in 1898. After a London debut as Gertrude in *Hamlet* at His Majesty's Theatre in 1910, she appeared regularly in the West End in such parts as Mrs Pritchard in Maugham's *Caesar's Wife* (1920), Lady Sneerwell in Sheridan's *The School for Scandal* (1935), and Mrs Higgins in *Pygmalion* (1939). Her work as a teacher at the Royal Academy of Dramatic Art and elsewhere was well known.

Hayes, Helen (Helen Brown; 1900–) US actress, who made her debut as a child in 1905. In 1907 she played the lead in Frances Hodgson Burnett's *Little Lord Fauntleroy*, making her adult debut in Kaufman and Connelly's *To the Ladies* (1922). Her roles since then have included Cleopatra in Shaw's *Caesar and Cleopatra* (1925), Mary Queen of Scots in Maxwell Anderson's *Mary of Scotland* (1933), Queen Victoria in Housman's *Victoria Regina* (1937), Amanda in Tennessee Williams's *The Glass Menagerie* (1941), Norma Melody in O'Neill's *A Touch of the Poet* (1958), and Mrs Antrobus in Wilder's *The Skin of Our Teeth* (1961). In 1964 she founded the Helen Hayes Repertory Company, which presented Shakespeare readings.

Hay Fever A comedy by Noël *Coward. First performance: London, 1925. The four members of the unconventional Bliss family each invite a weekend house guest unbeknown to the others; the action develops from the problems which arise from their arrangements and the gradual disintegration of the party in the face of the family's eccentric behaviour.

Haymarket (Theatre Royal) One of London's best-loved theatres, dating from 1720. Initially called the **Little Theatre in the Hay**, it was built on a site of an old inn but was confined at first to amateur performances. Henry Fielding became manager in 1735; in defiance of the Patent Theatres legislation then in force he staged a number of his own satires, with the result that censorship was introduced in 1737 and the theatre closed.

In 1747 Samuel Foote tried to get round the law by charging only for refreshments; after he had lost a leg in an accident brought about by a jest, the Duke of York compensated Foote by obtaining a royal patent allowing the theatre to open during the summer months. An annual licence was granted in 1777. George Colman the Elder took over the theatre in 1776, passing control to his son in 1794; when one of Foote's satires, *The Tailors*, was revived in 1805, hundreds of London tailors rioted and had to be dispersed by soldiers.

The theatre was remodelled by John Nash in 1921 with an elegant Corinthian portico on a site slightly to the south of the original building. In 1825 Madame Vestris sang

'Cherry Ripe' in John Poole's comedy *Paul Pry* and in 1833 Julia Glover caused a sensation as Falstaff in Shakespeare's *The Merry Wives of Windsor*. Benjamin Webster took over the management in 1837, producing and acting in many of his own plays; J B Buckstone was manager from 1853 to 1878, a period of outstanding success – his ghost is said still to haunt the theatre.

From 1855 it became known as the Theatre Royal; under the management of Squire and Marie Bancroft in the early 1880s, the theatre was largely rebuilt, housing the first 'picture frame' stage. Herbert Beerbohm Tree was manager from 1887 to 1896, during which time Oscar Wilde's *A Woman of No Importance* (1893) and *An Ideal Husband* (1895) were staged. Tree made sufficient profits from his productions of *Trilby* (1895), based on George Du Maurier's novel, to enable him to build Her Majesty's, a new theatre on the opposite side of the road.

In 1904 the Haymarket was again remodelled and further alterations were made in 1939–41, following which Gielgud staged a celebrated season (1944–45). Subsequent successes have included plays by Rattigan, N C Hunter, Enid Bagnold, and John Mortimer.

The **Haymarket Theatre** in Leicester opened in 1973. Seating 710, it established its reputation almost immediately with the musicals *Cabaret* and *Joseph and the Amazing Technicolour Dreamcoat*. Productions since then have included pantomimes, revivals of classic plays, further musicals – notably *Oliver!*, *My Fair Lady*, and *Oklahoma!* – and plays by such contemporary authors as Ayckbourn, Pinter, and David Storey.

Hazlitt, William (1778–1830) British theatre critic and essayist, who wrote numerous theatrical reviews for various periodicals, becoming parliamentary and dramatic critic for the *Morning Chronicle*. In 1817 he published *Characters of Shakespeare's Plays*,

and, in the following year, some of his criticisms in *A View of the English Stage*.

Heartbreak House A comedy by G B *Shaw. First performance: New York, 1920. The young Ellie Burn rejects wealthy Boss Mangan and prepares to marry Captain Shotover; the play analyses attitudes to wealth and was intended as a warning to contemporary society. Set during World War I, it was inspired in part by Chekhov's *The Cherry Orchard*.

Heavy Father *See* stock company.

Heavy Woman *See* stock company.

Hebbel, Friedrich (1813–63) German playwright, author of several pessimistic tragedies notable for their psychological insight. Hebbel, who was much influenced by Hegel's theories of history, excelled in the portrayal of oppressed women and established his reputation with *Judith* (1840) and *Maria Magdalena* (1844), both of which had women as their central characters. Later plays included the tragedies *Herodes und Mariamne* (1849) and *Agnes Bernauer* (1852), the *Die Nibelungen* trilogy (1861), and *Gyges und sein Ring* (1869), which was based on the legend of King Cambyses.

Hébertot, Jacques (1886–1970) French director, manager, and critic, who did much to further the performance of foreign works on the Paris stage. He acquired control of the Comédie des Champs-Élysées and the Théâtre des Champs-Élysées in 1919 and installed Jouvet as director of both before subsequently working with Baty. He concentrated on his role as a critic from 1926 to 1940 and then took over the Théâtre des Arts, renaming it the Théâtre Hébertot and presenting many major foreign dramas there.

Hedberg, Tor (1862–1931) Swedish playwright, son of a minor writer for the theatre, who wrote several plays depicting working-class life in Stockholm. His best-known works include *En Tvekamp* (A Duel; 1892), the comedy *Nattrocken* (The Dressing Gown; 1893), the tragedy *John Ulfsjerna* (1907), and *Perseus och vidundret* (Perseus and the Monster; 1917). He was director of the Kungliga Dramatiska Teatern from 1910.

Hedda Gabler A play by Henrik *Ibsen, probably the most frequently performed of all his works. First performance: 1890. The play revolves around Hedda Gabler Tesman, who is bored with life and isolated from those around her, and ends with her suicide, which she sees as the only solution to her problems.

Hedgerow Theatre A theatre founded in 1923 in Moylan, Pennsylvania, which is the second oldest surviving repertory company in the US. It presents a mixture of modern and classical plays, while the Hedgerow Theatre School offers a three-year course in acting.

Hedqvist, Ivan (1880–1935) Swedish actor, who was highly acclaimed in naturalistic drama. Appearing at the Svenska Teatern in Stockholm (1906–09 and 1922–25) and then with the Kungliga Dramatiska Teatern (1909–19 and 1927–32), he was much admired in Shakespearean roles and as Sophocles's Oedipus.

Heiberg, Gunnar Edvard Rode (1857–1929) Norwegian playwright, who is generally regarded as the most significant Norwegian dramatist since Ibsen. He is best remembered for his witty moralistic plays, notably *Tante Ulrikke* (1884) and *Folkeraadet* (1897), which treat contemporary and social issues. His most successful plays, *Balkonen* (The Balcony; 1894) and *Kjærlighedens Tragedie* (The Tragedy of Love; 1904) attempt to explore erotic rela-

tionships. Other works of note include *Kunstnere* (The Artists; 1893) and *Gerts Have* (Gert's Garden; 1894).

Heiberg, Johan Ludvig (1791–1860) Danish playwright and poet, who became a leading intellectual figure in Copenhagen and was the author of theoretical writing upon the Danish theatre. He was director of the Kongelige Teater for a time and created a type of popular satirical folk musical known as Danish vaudeville; his plays include *Julespøg og Nytaarsløjer* (Christmas and New Year Fun and Games; 1816), *Elverhøj* (Elfin Hill; 1828), and his masterpiece *En Sjæl efter Døden* (A Soul After Death; 1841).

His wife was the actress and playwright **Johanne Luise Heiberg** (Johanne Luise Pätges; 1812–90), who first appeared at the Kongelige Teater in 1826 and subsequently played in both tragedy and vaudeville, establishing herself as the leading Danish actress of her day. She was also herself the author of several vaudevilles.

Heijermans, Herman (1864–1924) Dutch playwright and novelist, best remembered for his socially challenging dramas treating such diverse themes as free love and anti-Semitism. His strong socialist ideals and contempt for bourgeois hypocrisy are reflected in such plays as *Op Hoop van Zegen* (The Good Hope; 1900), in which he champions the cause of exploited fisherman, and *Glück Auf* (1911), in which he expresses his concern about the working conditions of miners.

Heinrich Julius, Duke of Brunswick (1564–1613) German scholar and patron of the arts, who maintained Thomas Sackville's troupe of English Comedians at Wolfenbüttel for many years. The company often appeared in plays written by the duke himself, which combined features of the *commedia dell'arte* with the English tradition.

Heiress, The A play by Ruth and Augustus Goetz, based on the book *Washington Square* by Henry *James. First performance: New York, 1947. The plot revolves around a young woman's revenge on her money-hungry mother; the play was filmed in 1949 with Olivia De Havilland, Montgomery Clift, and Miriam Hopkins.

Held, Anna *See* Ziegfeld, Florenz.

Helen Bonfils Theatre Complex *See* Bonfils Theatre.

Helen Hayes Theatre A theatre on West 46th Street, New York, which opened as a full-time theatre in 1911. In 1955 the **Fulton Theatre**, as it was originally known, was renamed the Helen Hayes after the acclaimed actress. She appeared there herself in 1958 as Nora in *A Touch of the Poet* by Eugene O'Neill; other successes included plays by Lonsdale, d'Usseau and Gow, and Kaufman and Ferber. The theatre was demolished in 1982.

Hellenistic drama Greek theatre of the 3rd and 4th centuries BC, specifically that outside Athens itself but within the Athenian sphere of influence. Also known as Colonial drama, it encompassed *New Comedy, mime, and some tragedy as well as the critical writings and collections of theatrical scholars in Alexandria. Its greatest exponents included Menander. *See also phlyax.*

Hellinger, Mark *See* Mark Hellinger Theatre.

Hellman, Lillian (1905–84) US playwright, whose first play, The *Children's Hour* (1934) established her reputation. Subsequent successes included *Days to Come* (1936), *The *Little Foxes* (1939) chronicling events surrounding an avaricious Southern family, *The *Watch on the Rhine* (1941), *The Searching Wind* (1944), *Another Part of the Forest* (1946), which she also staged, *The

Autumn Garden (1951), and *Toys in the Attic* (1960). She also adapted several novels for the stage, including Voltaire's *Candide* (1956).

Hello Dolly! *See Matchmaker, The.*

Helpmann, Sir Robert (Murray) (1909–86) Australian ballet dancer, choreographer, actor, and director, who appeared in many Shakespearean and other major roles. He made his debut as a dancer in musical comedy in Sydney in 1923 and subsequently toured Australia before joining the Vic-Wells Ballet in London in 1933. In 1937 he attracted attention as an actor playing Oberon in *A Midsummer Night's Dream* at the Old Vic; subsequently he played Hamlet (1944) and Flamineo in Webster's *The White Devil* (1947) among other important roles and, in 1948, joined the company at Stratford-upon-Avon. His successful roles there included Shylock, Hamlet, and King John, while back in London (and later New York) he acted with Olivier and Vivien Leigh in *Antony and Cleopatra* (1951). As a director he presented T S Eliot's *Murder in the Cathedral* in 1953, Giraudoux's *Duel of Angels* (1960), and the musical *Camelot* (1964) among other works.

Heminge, John (1556–1630) English actor, possibly born at Shottery, near Stratford-upon-Avon. He was in Burbage's company at the Theatre and is credited with playing the original Falstaff. He was probably the business manager for the company and was a shareholder in the Globe and Blackfriars theatres. He is known to have appeared in several of Jonson's plays and, with Condell, was responsible for collecting the First Folio of Shakespeare's plays.

hemp house *See* hand-worked house.

Henderson, John (1747–85) British actor, born in London. He first came to attention playing Hamlet at Bath in 1772, after which he appeared as Macbeth, Richard III, Hotspur, Lear, and in other great roles. In 1777 George Colman the Elder engaged him at the Haymarket, where he made a sensational debut as Shylock. Later he transferred to Drury Lane at Sheridan's request and then to Covent Garden. In 1785 he gave readings of William Cowper's *John Gilpin*, turning it into a bestseller.

Henry, John (1738–94) US actor, born in Ireland, who made his New York debut as Aimwell in Farquhar's *The Beaux' Stratagem* (1767). He was for many years a leading actor with the American Company and was the first professional to play Sir Peter Teazle in the US. He eventually became co-manager of the company, but was supplanted by John Hodgkinson in 1792.

Henry VIII, The Famous History of the Life of King A history play by William *Shakespeare, written c. 1613. First performance: Globe Theatre, London, 1613. Possibly written in collaboration with John Fletcher, the play traces the relationship of Henry VIII with Anne Boleyn and the consequent political machinations of Wolsey and Cranmer. At the play's first performance the Globe Theatre was accidentally destroyed by fire.

Henry V, The Life of King A history play by William *Shakespeare, the last part of a trilogy on the king's life, written 1599. First performance: c. 1599. A patriotic celebration of Henry V's successful reign, the play describes Henry's changed character since the days of his wild youth. The play takes on heroic proportions with its recounting of a glorious period in English history, most memorably with the king's 'St Crispin's Day' speech and the great victory over the French at Agincourt. Henry's prowess in battle is further underlined by his feelings for the common soldier and wooing of the French princess Katherine.

Henry IV A history play in two parts by William *Shakespeare, written c. 1597. First performance: c. 1597. With *Henry V* the play forms a trilogy on the life of Henry V, who is celebrated as the ideal monarch; the folly of mankind that Prince Hal rejects is personified in the character of Falstaff. The two plays vividly depict events in the taverns of London and at the royal court and the consequences of Hotspur's rebellion. Hotspur is killed by Hal in Part I; when Hal is crowned at the end of Part II Falstaff is banished.

Henry Miller's Theatre A theatre on 43rd Street, New York, which opened in 1918 with *The Fountain of Youth* by the Álvarez Quintero brothers. The majority of the plays produced there were straight dramas, the most notable including Coward's *The Vortex* (1925). Sherriff's *Journey's End* (1929), Wilder's *Our Town* (1938), and Eliot's *The Cocktail Party* (1950). In 1969 it was converted into a cinema.

Henry VI A history play by William *Shakespeare, written in three parts 1591–92. First performance: c. 1592. Possibly a collaboration with Greene or Nash, the tetralogy depicts the disintegration of England under Henry's weak command and culminates in Henry's own murder at the end of the Wars of the Roses. Events portrayed include the deaths of Joan of Arc, Talbot, and the Duke of Gloucester, the marriage of Henry to Margaret of Anjou, the coronation and murder of Edward VI, and the rise of the future Richard III. The most admired scenes include York's speech after his capture and Henry's thoughts upon civil war.

Hensel, Sophie Friederike (Sophie Friederike Sparmann; 1738–89) German actress, who distinguished herself as a performer of tragic heroines as a member of Ackermann's company in Hamburg. Her vicious temper won her many enemies and severely hampered the career of her second husband, Abel Seyler.

Henshaw, James Ene (1924-) African playwright, who trained as a doctor and became the first internationally-recognized Nigerian writer for the theatre. His plays, which typically depict people in authority facing moral dilemmas concerning bribery and corruption, include *This Is Our Chance* (1956), *A Man of Character* (1960), *Medicine for Love* (1964), and *Dinner for Promotion* (1967).

Hensler, Karl Friedrich (1761–1825) Austrian playwright, author of notable examples of the *ritterdrama*. In the operatic *Das Donau eibchen* (1797) he combined the approach of the German Romantics with Austrian folklore with great success.

Henslowe, Philip (d. 1616) English theatre owner, whose notes and diaries are a valuable source of information about the theatre of the time. He built the Rose Theatre in 1587, the Fortune – in partnership with Edward Alleyn (who married his stepdaughter) – in 1600, and the Hope in 1613, becoming the most consistently successful of all Elizabethan impresarios.

Henson, Leslie (Lincoln) (1891–1957) British actor, who scored his first success in 1915 in *Tonight's the Night*. After service in the Royal Flying Corps he appeared in *Kissing Time* (1919), the first of several long-running musicals in which he played at the Winter Garden Theatre. He also entered management with Tom Walls, presenting several of the Aldwych farces, and subsequently leased the Gaiety Theatre (1935–39), starring in several successful musicals. After World War II he excelled as Pepys in *And So to Bed* (1951) and Pooter in *The Diary of a Nobody* (1955).

Hepburn, Katharine Houghton (1909-) US actress, who is best known for her many film roles. She made her stage debut in 1928, early roles including Katia in *A Month in the Country* (1930). She returned to Broadway in 1939 in Philip Barry's *The Philadelphia Story*; subsequently she played Rosalind in *As You Like It* (1950) and toured Australia (1955) with the Old Vic company. In 1957 she appeared at the Shakespeare Festival in Stratford, Connecticut. In 1969 she played the title role in the musical *Coco*; stage appearances since then have included parts in *A Matter of Gravity* (1976) and *The West Side Waltz* (1981).

Herald Square Theatre A theatre on Broadway, New York, which opened as the **Colosseum Theatre** in 1874. It was successively renamed the Criterion (1882), **Harrigan's Park Theatre** (1885), the **Park Theatre** (1889), and finally the Herald Square Theatre (1894). The opening play in 1894 was Shaw's *Arms and the Man* starring Richard Mansfield. For several years the Herald opposed the Theatrical Syndicate but eventually (1900) it became a venue for vaudeville, after the Shubert family had assumed the management. The building was demolished in 1915.

Herbert, Sir Henry (1596–1673) English public official, appointed *Master of the Revels in 1623. Brother of the poet George Herbert, he held office until the closure of theatres in 1642 but failed to reassert his powers after the Restoration in opposition to Killigrew and Davenant. His office records provide valuable information about the 17th-century theatre.

Heřczeg, Ferenc (1863–1954) Hungarian playwright and novelist, whose dramatic output consists of comedies and historical plays, notably *Pogányok* (1902), *Bizánc* (1904), and *A hid* (1925). His most successful play, *Az ezü st róka* (1921), has been performed throughout Europe.

Herlie, Eileen (1920-) British actress, born in Scotland, who established her reputation as the Queen in Cocteau's *The Eagle Has Two Heads* (1947) at the Haymarket. After further successes as Euripides's Medea (1948) and as Pinero's Mrs Tanqueray (1950) she made her New York debut as Mrs Molloy in Thornton Wilder's *The Matchmaker* (1955), subsequently remaining in the US, where her roles have included Gertrude in Gielgud's *Hamlet* (1964) and Martha in Albee's *Who's Afraid of Virginia Woolf?* (1971).

Her Majesty's Theatre A theatre in the Haymarket, London, which is the fourth built on the same site. The original theatre, called the **Queen's Theatre** (1705–14) and then the **King's Theatre** (1714–1837), opened in 1705 under the management of Vanbrugh and Congreve and became known primarily as a venue for opera. Destroyed by fire in 1789 and rebuilt in 1790–91, it became the largest opera house in England. The auditorium was subsequently remodelled (1816–18) by Nash and Repton, who also added three exterior colonnades and the Royal Opera Arcade. During its heyday as an opera house (1830–50) the theatre, which was renamed Her Majesty's in 1837, enjoyed a reputation as a highly fashionable venue but closed in 1852 after most of its patrons had defected to Covent Garden. Reopened in 1856 after Covent Garden had been burned down, Her Majesty's was itself destroyed by fire in 1867 and, when rebuilt, remained empty until it was sold in 1874. After another change of ownership in 1877 more opera was staged; there were also plays, minstrel shows, pantomimes, and even boxing. Sarah Bernhardt acted at the theatre in 1886 and 1890 but after the Christmas pantomime of 1890 Her Majesty's was again closed; when the building was demolished in 1891 only the Royal Opera Arcade was left standing. The present theatre was financed by Beerbohm Tree; it was opened in 1897 and continued (as **His Maj-**esty's Theatre from 1902) under Tree's acclaimed management until his death in 1917. The musical *Chu Chin Chow* (1916) ran for a record 2238 performances. There were also two seasons of Diaghilev's Ballets Russes (1926 and 1928); other successes included Coward's *Bitter Sweet* (1929), Priestley's *The Good Companions* (1931), and Barrie's *The Boy David* (1936). Among notable post-war productions at the theatre, which reverted to the name Her Majesty's in 1952, were Robert Morley's *Edward My Son* (1947) and the musicals *Brigadoon*, *West Side Story*, and *Fiddler on the Roof*. Andrew Lloyd Webber's musical *The Phantom of the Opera* opened in 1986.

Hermann, David *See* Vilna Troupe.

Hernani A verse drama by Victor *Hugo. First performance: Comédie-Française, Paris, 1830. On its opening night the play provoked a riot between rival supporters of Romanticism and Classicism. The plot concerns the love of the outlaw Hernani for Doña Sol, which is brought to a tragic end by Doña Sol's guardian.

Hero-Combat play *See* mummers' play.

Herodas (c. 300 BC–250 BC) Greek playwright, one of the foremost writers of Hellenistic drama. Nine of his mime plays, which were probably intended for solo performers, survive.

heroic drama A form of theatre popular in England during the Restoration. Much influenced by French classical tragedy, heroic drama obeyed the three unities and was written in rhymed couplets. Its preoccupation, however, with such noble themes as the conflict between love and honour (as expressed most eloquently in works by John Dryden) made it vulnerable to parody and, following Buckingham's satire *The Rehearsal* (1671), it was no longer found acceptable on the English stage.

Heron, Matilda (Agnes) (1830–77) US actress, born in Ireland, who first appeared at Philadelphia's Walnut Street Theatre in 1851 and made her New York debut as Lady Macbeth at the Bowery Theatre in 1852. Following a visit to Paris, she adapted *La Dame aux Camélias* by Dumas *fils* as *Camille* and played it with tremendous success throughout the US.

Hertz, Henrik (1798–1870) Danish poet and playwright, who wrote numerous comedies and dramas for production at the Kongeliche Teater under J L Heiberg. Of his 50 plays, only *Sparekassen* (The Savings Bank; 1836), *Sven Dyrings Hus* (The House of Sven Dyring; 1837), and *Kong Renes Datter* (King René's Daughter; 1843) have been revived.

Hevesi, Sándor (1873–1939) Hungarian director, who did much to reform the Hungarian stage after founding the Thália Society in 1904. Presenting works by contemporary Hungarian authors, the group was run on principles similar to those of Stanislavsky and Gordon Craig; subsequently Hevesi directed influential productions at the National Theatre in Budapest.

Heywood, John (1497–1578) English playwright, best known for the interlude *The Four PP* (c. 1520), which has been described as an important bridge between medieval and Elizabethan drama. Several of his other plays, which include *The Pardoner and the Friar* (1519), *Johan Johan* (c. 1520), *The Play of the Wether* (1533), and *The Play of Love* (1533), exploit the possibilities of audience involvement with characters addressing them directly.

Heywood, Thomas (c. 1570–1641) English playwright and actor, possibly a relation of John Heywood. A member of both the Admiral's Men and Queen Anne's Men, he eventually succeeded Dekker as the writer of mayoral pageants for the City of London (1631–39). He claimed to have been involved in the writing of about 220 plays, of which only 35 have survived. His dramatic works ranged from studies of mythology, including a series of four plays ending with *The Iron Age* (c. 1611–c. 1613), to the masterly domestic tragedy *A *Woman Killed with Kindness*. Others include *The Wise Woman of Hogsdon* (1604), *If You Know Not Me, You Know Nobody* (1604–05), *The Rape of Lucrece* (1607), *The Fair Maid of the West* (1610 and 1631), and the lost comedy *Love's Masterpiece*. His other writing includes an *Apology for Actors* (1612).

Hibernian Roscius *See* Brooke, Gustavus Vaughan.

Hicks, Sir (Edward) Seymour (1871–1949) British actor-manager and playwright, who made his debut at the Grand Theatre, Islington in 1887. He subsequently appeared in parts as diverse as Scrooge (1901) and Valentine Brown in Barrie's *Quality Street* (1902) as well as in musical comedy, farce, and music hall; his revue *Under the Clock* (1893) was the first such entertainment seen in London. He wrote several successful plays including *Bluebell in Fairyland* (1901), which was revived annually at Christmas for many years. He also built and managed the *Aldwych and the Hicks (now the *Globe) theatres, and managed *Daly's. He often appeared with his wife, the actress Ellaline *Terriss.

Hicks Theatre *See* Globe Theatre.

Hilar, Karel Hugo (Karel Hugo Bakule; 1885–1935) Czech director, who became a leading figure of the Realist movement. Influenced by the theories of Stanislavsky and Gordon Craig, he worked first at the Municipal Theatre in Prague and then at the National Theatre; his greatest successes included premieres of plays by the Čapek brothers.

Hill, Aaron (1685–1750) British play-wright, who was ridiculed for his *Elfrid, or the Fair Inconstant* (performed at Drury Lane in 1710) and satirized by Pope. He was briefly lessee of the Haymarket and wrote the book for Handel's opera *Rinaldo*, which he produced in 1711. His plays include *The Fatal Vision* (1716), *Athelwold* (1732), and translations from Voltaire.

Hill, Jenny (Elizabeth Pasta; 1851–96) British music hall performer, who struggled her way onto the halls through singing in East End pubs. Billed as The Vital Spark, she excelled at such melodramatic songs as 'The Little Stowaway'.

Hillberg, (Carl Wilhelm) Emil (1852–1929) Swedish actor, who made his debut in Stockholm in 1873 as Benvolio in *Romeo and Juliet*. He formed his own shortlived experimental theatre group in 1901 and was a pioneer of naturalistic acting in the Swedish theatre. He excelled in the plays of Strindberg and Ibsen, including *The Father* and *Brand*, while other roles included Macbeth, Shylock, and Doolittle in Shaw's *Pygmalion*.

Hiller, Dame Wendy (1912–) British actress, who came to prominence after five years in repertory at Manchester as Sally in Walter Greenwood's *Love on the Dole* (1935), adapted by Ronald *Gow, whom she later married. She played important roles in seasons at the Bristol Old Vic (1946), at the Old Vic in London (1955–56), and was acclaimed in New York as Isobel in Robert Bolt's *Flowering Cherry* (1959); she also appeared as Miss Tina in Michael Redgrave's adaptation of *The Aspern Papers* (1962) by Henry James. For the National Theatre she played Gunhild Borkman in Ibsen's *John Gabriel Borkman* (1975–76). In 1987 she gave a memorable performance as Lady Bracknell in Wilde's *The Importance of Being Earnest* at the Royalty. In 1988 she appeared in Alfred Uhry's Pulitzer Prize-winning *Driving Miss Daisy*.

Hilpert, Heinze (1890–1967) German director, who became a noted figure in the German Realist movement. He first attracted attention with Brückner's *Der Verbrecher* (1928) and later managed the Deutsches Theater (1939–45); other successes included several works by Zuckmayer.

Hindle Wakes A play by Stanley *Houghton. First performance: Manchester, 1912. The heroine refuses to marry her lover, a millowner's son, because she does not love him and cannot see why she should be condemned for having indulged in temporary pleasure.

Hippodrome A theatre in Leicester Square, London, which opened in 1900. Originally a circus and a venue for aquatic drama, it was briefly a music hall before becoming a home of ballet and revue in the 1920s. Musical comedy then followed, successes including works by Ivor Novello, until, in 1958 it was reorganized as a restaurant and cabaret called the **Talk of the Town**, which closed in 1982.

Hippodrome Theatre A theatre on Sixth Avenue, between 43rd and 44th streets, New York, which opened in 1905 with *A Yankee Circus on Mars*. The largest theatre in the US, it became a vaudeville house in 1923 and, in 1928, a cinema. The theatre closed in 1936 after an unsuccessful production of *Jumbo* under the owner, Billy Rose. Three years later it was demolished.

Hirsch, John Stephen (1930–) Canadian director, born in Hungary, who has won acclaim for his work at a number of venues both in Canada and elsewhere. His many ventures have included a company founded to present musical comedy, the foundation of the Theatre 77 group, direction at the Manitoba Theatre Centre, and participation (with Jean Gascon) in the Stratford (Ontario) Festival. His most celebrated works have included plays by Ansky, Brecht, Chekhov, Frisch, James Reaney, and Shakespeare. He has also directed plays for the New York stage and in Israel.

Hirsch, Robert Paul (1925-) French actor, who established his reputation in comic roles at the Comédie-Française, where he appeared regularly from 1948 to 1974. Noted for his idiosyncratic and highly original interpretation of such roles as Arlequin, Scapin, Tartuffe, and Bouzin in Feydeau's *Un fil à la patte* (1964), he has also appeared in serious roles in such works as Dostoevsky's *Crime and Punishment* (1963).

Hirschbein, Peretz (1880–1949) Jewish actor and playwright, who founded his own Yiddish company in Odessa in 1908. The troupe performed several plays translated by Hirschbein himself as well as his celebrated studies of Jewish rural life, *The Blacksmith's Daughters* (1915) and *Green Fields* (1919).

Hirschfeld, Kurt (1902–64) German theatre manager, critic, and director, who established his reputation after moving to Zurich in 1933. There he presented influential premieres of plays by Brecht and Frisch among other important productions and did much to foster the emergence of new playwrights, including Dürrenmatt.

His Majesty's Theatre *See* Her Majesty's Theatre.

Hoadly, Benjamin (1706–57) English physician and playwright, who with his brother **John Hoadly** (1711–76) wrote *The Contrast*, produced at Lincoln's Inn Fields in 1731, and subsequently won acclaim for the comedy *The Suspicious Husband* (1747). The success of the latter was due largely to the acting of Garrick as Ranger.

hobby horse An animal character of early folk theatre throughout Europe, usually played by an actor disguised by a wickerwork frame in the shape of a horse. A fea-

ture of the Morris Dance, mummers' play, and other ancient folk theatre traditions in England, the hobby horse probably had its origins in primitive animal worship; later in its evolution it was reduced to a pole with a carved horse's head on top of it, a popular children's toy. *See also Mascarade.*

Hobson, Sir Harold (1904-) British theatre critic, who has done much to defend avant-garde theatre since writing his first critical pieces in 1931. As critic for the *Sunday Times* since 1944, he has also paid particular attention to developments in contemporary French theatre.

Hobson's Choice A comedy by Harold *Brighouse. First performance: 1915. Set in Salford in 1880, it celebrates the overthrow of Hobson, an oldfashioned, tyrannical father, and his narrow middle-class attitudes by his daughter Maggie, who defies him by marrying the hapless Willie Mossop and eventually taking over her father's shoe shop. It was filmed in 1954 with Charles Laughton and John Mills.

Hochhuth, Rolf (1931-) Swiss playwright, writing in German, who is the author of several controversial left-wing documentary dramas. He first achieved success in the theatre with *Der Stellvertreter* (The *Representative; 1963), which questions the attitude of the Roman Catholic Church towards the Nazi persecution of the Jews during World War II. His second play, *Soldaten; Nekrolog auf Genf* (Soldiers; 1967), accused Winston Churchill of complicity in the death of the Polish general Sikorski and the bombing of Dresden in 1945. Other plays, which have proved less successful, include *Guerillas* (1970) and *Lysistrate und Nato* (1974).

Hochwälder, Fritz (1911-) Austrian playwright, whose early historical dramas reflect his preoccupation with the concepts of social and divine justice and interest in the unities. In *Das heilige Experiment* (The Strong Are Lonely; 1945), he examines the conflict between politics and religion in 18th-century Spanish America under the Jesuit rule. Other works that deal with the themes of persecution and retribution include *Der Flüchtling* (The Fugitive; 1945) and *Der öffentliche Ankläger* (The Public Prosecutor; 1948), which is set during the French Revolution.

His later dramas, which show the influence of Grillparzer, are modern recreations of the mystery and morality plays; they include *Donadieu* (1953), the comedy *Der Unschuldige* (The Innocent Man; 1958), and *Der Befehl* (The Command; 1968).

Hock-Tuesday play An example of early English folk theatre, also called a Hocktide play or Hock play, which is presented annually in Coventry on the third Tuesday after Easter. The tradition was revived in 1575 and performances depicted the conquest of Danish invaders by the English (mounted on hobby horses) and their subsequent imprisonment by English women. Its origins probably lay in an earlier custom by virtue of which women could demand a forfeit from any man they 'hocked' (caught), the men having their turn the next day.

Hodgkinson, John (John Meadowcroft; 1767–1805) British actor, who began in the provinces before moving to the US at the instigation of John Henry. Among his early roles were Macheath, Macbeth, Jaffier, and Bob Acres. He was in management with Dunlap at the Park Theatre, New York, and achieved distinction in Dunlap's *André*. He died during a yellow fever epidemic.

Hodson, Henrietta (1841–1910) British actress and manager. Her first stage appearances were in Scotland and she became a popular burlesque actress in the provinces before coming to London in 1866. Her second husband acquired control of the Queen's Theatre, where she subsequently appeared alongside Henry Irving. In 1871 she took over the Royalty Theatre, which she ran for seven years, presenting numerous burlesques.

Hofmannsthal, Hugo von (1784–1929) Austrian playwright and poet, who rejected naturalism in his early plays in favour of more poetic theatre. His early lyrical verse plays, notably *Der Tor und der Tod* (Death and the Fool) established his reputation as a perfect stylist and colourful romantic. He also adapted and modernized several classical dramas, including Euripides's *Elektra*, which deals with the theme of sexual repression, and Sophocles's *Ödipus und die Sphinx* (Oedipus and the Sphinx), a study of incest.

His most famous work, *Jedermann* (Everyman) a modernized version of an old morality play, marked the beginning of a series of dramas with social and religious implications, which finally ended with his last play, *Der Turm* (The Tower). He also achieved recognition as the librettist for Richard Strauss's operas, notably *Elektra* (1909), *Der Rosenkavalier* (1911), and *Ariadne auf Naxos* (1912), and as cofounder of the Salzburg Festival in 1920.

Principal works:

Der Tor und der Tod: 1898; translated as *Death and the Fool*.

Der Abenteurer und die Sängerin: 1898; translated as *The Adventurer and the Singer*.

Elektra: 1903.

Ödipus und die Sphinx: 1905; translated as *Oedipus and the Sphinx*.

König Ödipus: 1907; translated as *King Oedipus*.

Alkestis: 1909.

Jedermann: 1911; translated as *Everyman*.

Der Schwierige: 1921; translated as *The Difficult Man*.

Der Turm: 1925; translated as *The Tower*.

hoist *See* slote.

Holberg, Ludvig, Baron (1684–1754) Norwegian playwright, historian, and philosopher, who played a major role in the development of the theatre in Denmark and is often referred to as the 'Molière of the North'. According to tradition, he visited many European cultural centres as a young man, travelling on foot, and acquired a particular taste for the works of Plautus and Molière. On his return to Denmark he produced a series of satirical comedies, many of which he wrote and directed himself, at the first Danish-language theatre (the Danske Skueplads in Copenhagen), effectively founding the Danish theatrical comic tradition. Apart from a further six plays written after the reopening of the theatre in 1747 he retired as a playwright in 1731.

Principal works:

Den politiske Kandestøber: 1722; translated as *The Political Tinker*.

Jeppe paa Bjerget, eller den forvandlede Bonde: 1722; translated as *Jeppe of the Mountains*.

Jean de France: 1722.

Mester Gert Westphaler: 1722; translated as *The Babbling Barber*.

Den Vægelsindede: 1723; translated as *The Weathercock*.

Barselstuen: 1723; translated as *The Lying-in Room*.

Jacob von Tyboe: 1724.

Henrik og Pernille: 1724.

Den Stundesløse: 1726; translated as *The Fussy Man*.

Erasmus Montanus: 1742.

Holborn Empire A theatre in High Holborn, London, which opened in 1857 as **Weston's Music Hall**. Highly popular, it was enlarged in 1887 to hold 2500 people and renamed the **Royal Holborn**, witnessing the first appearances of Bessie Bellwood and J H Stead, among others. After a decline it was rebuilt in 1905 and reopened as the Holborn Empire. Performers who subsequently triumphed there included Albert Chevalier, Dan Leno, and Sybil Thorndike, who acted in plays by Shaw and Euripides. From 1922 to 1939 Italia *Conti presented

an acclaimed annual Christmas show for children there; the building was damaged by bombs in 1940 and demolished in 1960.

Holborn Theatre Royal A theatre in High Holborn, London, opened in 1866. After initial success with *The Flying Scud* by Dion Boucicault, the theatre foundered until 1875, when – renamed the **Mirror Theatre** – a dramatization of *A Tale of Two Cities* was a success. The theatre continued (as the **Duke's Theatre**) with burlesques and other types of drama under a series of managers until destruction by fire in 1880.

Holcroft, Thomas (1745–1809) British playwright, who recounted his experiences as a strolling player in his novel *Alwyn, or the Gentleman Comedian*. The reception of his first play, *Duplicity*, at Drury Lane in 1881 encouraged him to write a succession of comedies. Having visited Paris, he presented *The Marriage of Figaro* by Beaumarchais at Covent Garden in 1784. His best known piece, *The Road to Ruin*, appeared in 1792 and has been frequently revived. *A Tale of Mystery* (1802), adapted from Pixérécourt, was probably the first melodrama to appear on the London stage.

Holland, George (1791–1870) British actor, who was already an experienced comedian when he went to the US and became an instant success at the Bowery Theatre, New York. He acted often in New Orleans and the South and spent six years in William Mitchell's burlesques in New York. He later joined Wallack's company, playing character parts until shortly before his death.

Hollingshead, John (1827–1904) British theatre manager, who opened the *Gaiety Theatre in 1868. There he inaugurated the matinée system and pioneered the use of electric light. For 18 years he presented burlesques, interspersed with serious new plays. In 1880 he became the first manager to stage Ibsen in London with *The Pillars of Society*.

Holloway, Joseph (1861–1944) Irish architect, theatre critic, and diarist, born in Dublin. He was employed by Miss Horniman to renovate the building that became the original *Abbey Theatre. Despite the conservatism of his views, he was regarded by many playwrights as a valuable guide to popular taste. Throughout his adult life he kept a copious diary, which is a valuable source of information about the Dublin theatre.

Holm, Ian (Ian Holm Cuthbert; 1931–) British actor, who made his debut as a spear-carrier at Stratford-upon-Avon in 1954, eventually becoming a prominent member of the Royal Shakespeare Company. His parts with the company included Troilus (1962), Henry V (1964), Lenny in Pinter's *The Homecoming* (1965), and Romeo (1967); among later roles have been Nelson in Rattigan's *A Bequest to the Nation* (1970) and Hatch in Edward Bond's *The Sea* (1973) as well as numerous film and television parts.

Holt, Bland (1853–1942) British actor-manager, who emigrated with his family to Australia at an early age. He made his stage debut in Sydney in 1876; subsequently he excelled as a comedian and in melodrama and was particularly noted for his spectacular productions.

Holt, Helen Maud *See* Tree, Sir Herbert (Draper) Beerbohm.

Holz, Arno (1863–1929) German novelist and playwright, who collaborated with Johannes Schlaf on the gloomy and brutal *Die Familie Selicke* (1890), which was highly influential upon the early development of naturalism. It was one of the earliest productions of the Freie Bühne and inspired numerous imitations by such authors as Gerhart Hauptmann.

Home, John (1722–1808) Scottish minister, who resigned his living after the sensational success of his tragedy *Douglas* at Edinburgh in 1756. The following year the play was produced at Covent Garden; none of his later works, however, won equal acclaim. The character of Young Norval became a favourite role of Dudley Digges, Spranger Barry, William Betty, and John Howard Payne, while Mrs Siddons excelled as Lady Randolph.

Home, William Douglas (1912–) British playwright and actor, whose plays consist largely of sophisticated light comedies. *The Chiltern Hundreds* (1947), starring A E Matthews, established his reputation; of the many comedies that followed the most successful included a sequel, *The Manor of Northstead* (1954), and *The Reluctant Debutante* (1955). More serious was the drama on prison life *Now Barabbas . . .* (1947); more recent successes have numbered amongst them *The Reluctant Peer* (1964), starring Sybil Thorndike, *The Secretary Bird* (1968), *The Jockey Club Stakes* (1970), with Alastair Sim, *Lloyd George Knew My Father* (1972), with Ralph Richardson and Peggy Ashcroft, *The Kingfisher* (1977), and *After the Ball is Over* (1985).

Home and Beauty A farce by W Somerset *Maugham. First performance: London, 1919. Performed in the US as *Too Many Husbands*, the play deals with a woman who rejects two war heroes in preference for a civilian involved in black-market trading.

Homecoming, The A drama by Harold *Pinter. First performance: Royal Shakespeare Company, Aldwych Theatre, 1965. The play is a savagely funny depiction of a family of men, each of whom makes a bid to possess the woman their successful brother Teddy has brought to visit them.

Hooft, Pieter Corneliszoon (1581-1647) Dutch poet and playwright, who was the author of a number of notable histories on classical themes. As well as such historical works as *Geeraedt van Velsen* (1613) and *Baeto* (1617) he wrote the pastoral *Grandida* (1605) and the comedy *Warenar* (1616).

Hope Theatre A theatre in Southwark, London, which was opened in 1613 by Philip *Henslowe after the destruction of the rival Globe Theatre. Also used for bear and bull baiting, it was similar in design to the Swan Theatre, with a roofed stage. Early productions included Jonson's *Bartholomew Fair* (1614), although no records survive of plays being acted there after 1616. The resident company was *Lady Elizabeth's Men (later Prince Charles's Men). The building was demolished c. 1687.

Hopgood, Alan (1934-) Australian actor and playwright, who established a strong reputation with *And The Big Men Fly*, first presented by the Union Theatre Repertory Company in 1963. Subsequent successes have included *Private Yuk Object* (1966), set during the Vietnam War, and *Terribly, Terribly* (1968).

Hopkins, Anthony (1937-) British actor, born in Wales, whose stage career began at the Library Theatre, Manchester, when he appeared in Brendan Behan's *The Quare Fellow* in 1960. He then spent seven years with the National Theatre Company at the Old Vic, after which many of his stage appearances were in the US, where he took over from Richard Burton in Peter Shaffer's *Equus* in 1974. Later he returned to the National Theatre, where he appeared as Lambert le Roux in Brenton and Hare's *Pravda* (1985), as King Lear (1987), which he played 100 times, and as Antony in *Antony and Cleopatra* (1987).

Hopkins, Priscilla *See* Kemble, John Philip.

Horace A tragedy by Pierre *Corneille. First performance: Paris, 1640. The play is based on Livy's account of the battle between the Horatii and the Cuiratii. Patriotism and honour take precedence over the ties of love between the two families.

Hordern, Sir Michael (Murray) (1911-) British actor, who made his first professional appearance in *Othello* in London in 1937. After World War II, he established his reputation at Stratford-upon-Avon during the 1952 season, playing such roles as Caliban and Jaques, before going on to the Old Vic (1953-54), where he excelled as Malvolio. Subsequently he was much admired in eccentric character parts in plays by John Mortimer, Ibsen, and – with the Royal Shakespeare company once more (1962) – Pinter and Dürrenmatt. More recent successes have included Stoppard's *Jumpers* (1972), Waugh's *The Ordeal of Gilbert Pinfold* (1977), *The Tempest* (1978), *The Rivals* (1983), in which he played Sir Anthony Absolute at the National Theatre, and Shaw's *You Never Can Tell* (1987). He has also built up a strong reputation for his many screen and television appearances.

Horn Dance An early English folk entertainment performed annually at Abbot's Bromley in Staffordshire on the first Monday after 4 September. The male dancers wear ancient reindeer antlers and the tradition is regarded as an illustration of how primitive ritual evolved into a recognizable theatrical form.

Horniman, Annie Elizabeth Fredericka (1860-1937) English-born lady of independent means who used her wealth to support various theatrical ventures, most notably financing the purchase and equipping of the *Abbey Theatre in Dublin (1904). She had a high regard for W B Yeats, but her relationship with Lady Gregory was difficult and her attitude towards the members of the company was condescending and even hostile at times. She withdrew her backing in 1910, when the theatre remained open on the day of King Edward VII's funeral. In 1907 she invested in the *Gaiety Theatre, Manchester, and until 1921 she promoted the production there of new plays by local authors.

Horowitz, Israel (1939-) US playwright, whose first play to be produced was *The Comeback* (1957). His successes since then have included *This Play is About Me* (1961), *Hop, Skip, and Jump* (1964), *The Indian Wants the Bronx* (1966) – a brutal one-act play about the knifing of an immigrant by two street hoodlums, *Rats* (1968), *The Wakefield Plays* (1973–76), and *The Reason We Eat* (1976). He was playwright-in-residence for the Royal Shakespeare Company (1965) and a Rockefeller Foundation Fellow in Playwriting (1967–70).

Hostage, The A tragi-comedy by Brendan *Behan. First performance: Dublin, 1957. Seen originally in a Gaelic version, the play was successfully performed by Joan Littlewood's Theatre Workshop in 1959; the hostage of the title is an English soldier who is held prisoner in a broken-down Irish brothel and is eventually murdered. It includes songs and dances and speeches addressed directly to the audience; in London it became famous for Behan's speeches from the stage.

Hôtel d'Argent, Théâtre de l' *See* Argent, Théâtre de l'Hôtel de.

Hôtel de Bourgogne, Théâtre de l' *See* Bourgogne, Théâtre de l'Hôtel de.

Hotel Paradiso (*L'Hôtel du libre échange*) A farce by Georges *Feydeau. First performance: Paris, 1894. The play opened in London in 1956, with Alec Guinness as Boniface, whose adulterous assignation with Marcelle is interrupted by unforeseen circumstances.

Houdar de La Motte, Antoine (1672–1731) French playwright, poet, librettist, and critic, born in Paris. His tragedy *Inès de Castro* (1723) was immensely successful; he also wrote comedies, the first of which (*Les Originaux*, 1693) had such an unfavourable reception that he was discouraged from writing for the theatre for several years afterwards. In his critical works he attacked the rules of classical drama.

Houghton, (William) Stanley (1881–1913) British playwright, who was one of the 'Manchester School' of authors. Much influenced by Ibsen, he became famous for his realistic dramas, most of which were presented by Miss Horniman's company at the Gaiety Theatre in Manchester. The most successful of his works was the controversial *Hindle Wakes* (1912), in which a poor girl unexpectedly refuses to marry her rich seducer. His other plays include *The Dear Departed* (1906) and *The Younger Generation* (1910).

housekeeper The owner of all or part of an Elizabethan theatre, who was entitled to an agreed percentage of the admission receipts in return for maintaining and paying rent for the building itself. Shakespeare was a housekeeper at the Globe Theatre but, like all other housekeepers, had no claim to playscripts or the wardrobe, unlike *sharers.

houselights The lighting used to illuminate the auditorium, as distinct from the exit lights and those directed towards the stage.

Houseman, John *See* Welles, Orson.

House of Bernarda Alba, The (*La Casa de Bernarda Alba*) A tragedy by *García Lorca, written in 1936. First performance: Madrid, 1945. The last part of his famous trilogy of folk tragedies, the other parts being *Blood Wedding* (1933) and *Yerma* (1934), the play revolves around the tensions and frustrations of four daughters, who are confined to their house in mourning by their mother.

House of Ostrovsky See Maly Theatre.

Housman, Laurence (1865–1959) British playwright, brother of the poet A E Housman. The series of plays collected as *Victoria Regina* (1935) was immensely successful in New York with Helen Hayes as the queen, but was banned (until 1937) in Britain from the public stage for its presentation of royalty. Other works included the full-length play *Prunella* (1904), which drew on the *commedia dell'arte* tradition, and the one-act series *The Little Plays of St Francis*.

Howard, Alan (Mackenzie) (1937-) British actor, who began his career at the Belgrade Theatre, Coventry, before appearing at the Royal Court Theatre in 1959 in Arnold Wesker's *Roots*. He was in the Chichester Festival season of 1962 and came to prominence for his performance as Simon in Julian Mitchell's adaptation of Ivy Compton-Burnett's *A Heritage and Its History* at the Phoenix Theatre in 1965. Since then he has excelled in many roles with the Royal Shakespeare Company, playing such parts as Hamlet (1970), Coriolanus (1977), Richard II (1980), and Nikolai Pesiakoff in Stephen Poliakoff's *Breaking the Silence* (1984).

Howard, Sidney Coe (1891–1939) US playwright, who established his reputation with the comedy-drama *They Knew What They Wanted* (1924), which won a Pulitzer Prize and was later made into the musical *The Most Happy Fella*. He wrote his earliest pieces while with George Pierce Baker's Workshop '47 at Harvard and was later a cofounder of the Theatre Guild and a member of the Playwrights' Company. Other works included *Lucky Sam Carver* (1925),

which concerned the love affair of a nightclub owner and a society lady, *The Silver Cord* (1926), about an obsessive relationship between a mother and her sons, and *The Ghost of Yankee Doodle* (1937), as well as the screenplay for the film *Gone With the Wind* (1939). He died in a farming accident.

Hoyt's Theatre See Madison Square Theatre.

Hroswitha (c. 932–83 AD) Benedictine nun from Gandersheim in Saxony, who was the author of several early Christian dramas. Her six prose plays, *Paphnutius*, *Dulcitius*, *Gallicanus*, *Callimachus*, *Abraham*, and *Sapienta*, were modelled on the style of Terence and were not originally intended for production, although they have been successfully staged in the 20th century. The plays form an important link between the classical tradition and mystery plays and morality plays.

Hubert, André (c. 1634–1700) French actor, who created numerous roles in Molière's plays as a member of Molière's company, to which he transferred from the Théâtre du Marais in 1664. His roles included several elderly women and character parts; he later took charge of the company's finances and management together with La Grange.

hubris The concept of pride and its consequences as depicted in ancient Greek tragedy. Heroes guilty of such presumption were portrayed as having offended the gods and thus deserving of their own inevitable downfall.

Hudson Theatre A theatre on West 44th Street, between Broadway and Sixth Avenue, New York, which opened in 1903 with *Cousin Kate* by H H Davies. Important productions there included the New York premieres of Shaw's *Man and Superman* (1905) and plays by Maugham, Henry Arthur Jones, Booth Tarkington, and Sean O'Casey. Ethel Barrymore appeared there in Mazo de la Roche's *Whiteoaks* in 1938 while further success came in 1945 with *The State of the Union* by Lindsay and Crouse. From 1934 to 1937 and again from 1949 to 1960 it was used for broadcasting. In 1968, after productions by the Actors' Studio, it was converted into a cinema and, 10 years later, was renovated to become the 1000-seat cabaret Savoy.

Hughes, Margaret (1643–1719) English actress, believed to be the first woman to have appeared professionally on the London stage. After her debut, as Desdemona in *The Moor of Venice* (Killigrew's version of *Othello*) at the Vere Street Theatre on 8 December 1660, she transferred to Drury Lane and then to the Dorset Garden Theatre.

Hugo, Victor(-Marie) (1802–85) French poet, novelist, and playwright, who was a prominent figure of the Romantic movement. He made his first significant contribution to the theatre with the preface to *Cromwell*, in which he championed the ideals of Romantic drama. The best of Hugo's lyrical melodramas were produced between 1830 and 1843, when the failure of *Les Burgraves* caused him to concentrate on such prose works as the immensely successful novel *Les Misérables* (1862), adapted as a musical in 1986.
Principal dramatic works:
Cromwell: date unknown (published 1827).
*Hernani: 1830.
Marion de Lorme: 1831.
Le Roi s'amuse: 1832.
Lucrèce Borgia: 1833.
Marie Tudor: 1833.
Angelo, tyran de Padoue: 1835.
*Ruy Blas: 1838.
Les Burgraves: 1843.

Huis-Clos A play by Jean-Paul *Sartre, which has also been variously translated as *Vicious Circle*, *In Camera*, and *No Exit*.

First performance: Paris, 1944. The three principal characters find themselves in hell and discover that each is condemned to be tormented by the others for evermore.

Hulbert, Jack *See* Courtneidge, Dame Cicely.

Humphries, Barry (1934–) Australian actor, who came to the UK in 1959 and first appeared in London in *The Demon Barber* at the Lyric, Hammersmith. He was the original Mr Sowerberry in the musical *Oliver!* (1960), later playing Fagin in the revival (1968). He is, however, best known for his creation Dame Edna Everage, in which role he has given numerous one-man performances, including *Housewife! Superstar!* at the Apollo Theatre (1976) and *Back with a Vengeance* (1987) at the Strand.

Huneker, James Gibbons (1860–1921) US theatre critic, who did much to popularize European drama in the US. Among the notable playwrights championed by Huneker in the *Sun* and *New York Times* were Ibsen and Shaw.

Hungerford Music Hall *See* Gatti's.

Hunt, Hugh Sydney (1911–) British director and playwright, who became artistic director at the Abbey Theatre, Dublin in 1935 and subsequently became the first director of the Bristol Old Vic company (1945–48) and then director of the London Old Vic (1949–53), during which time he was responsible for many memorable productions, notably *Love's Labour's Lost*, *Hamlet*, *Twelfth Night*, and *Romeo and Juliet*. In 1955 he was appointed director of the Elizabethan Theatre Trust in Sydney, while on his return to the UK he became the first professor of drama at Manchester University (1961–73) and, once again, artistic director of the Abbey Theatre (1969–71). He has also written several books on the theatre.

Hunt, (James Henry) Leigh (1784–1859) British writer and critic, whose *Critical Essays on the Performers of the London Theatre* (1808) was a collection of his reviews printed in the *News* between 1805 and 1807. He also wrote theatre criticism for the *Examiner*, which he ran with his brother until 1813, when he was imprisoned for attacking the Prince Regent. His own plays included *A Legend of Florence* (1840) and *Lovers' Amazements* (1858).

Hunter, N(orman) C(harles) (1908–71) British playwright, who established his reputation with the Chekhovian *Waters of the Moon* (1951), which provided fine roles for Edith Evans and Sybil Thorndike. Notable amongst the plays that followed were *A Day by the Sea* (1953), again starring Sybil Thorndike, *A Touch of the Sun* (1958), which featured Michael and Vanessa Redgrave, and *The Tulip Tree* (1963).

Hurry, Leslie (1909–78) British stage designer, who began his career in ballet but later produced sombre atmospheric designs for the theatre much influenced by Surrealism. His most well-known designs included those for Marlowe's *Tamburlaine the Great* (1951), Otway's *Venice Preserv'd* (1953), and Tennessee Williams's *Cat on a Hot Tin Roof* (1958).

Hutt, William (1920–) Canadian actor and director, who began his career at the Hart House Theatre in Toronto and later became a leading performer and director at the Stratford (Ontario) Festival, where he first appeared in 1953. He has won acclaim all over the world for roles in the plays of Shakespeare, Molière, Marlowe, and other classical playwrights as well as in modern plays by Albee, Coward, and O'Neill. Other successes have included Caesar in Shaw's *Caesar and Cleopatra* (1969), Falstaff (1978), and the title role in Chekhov's *Uncle Vanya* (1978).

Hyde, Douglas (1860–1949) Irish playwright, scholar, poet, and first president of Eire. His main objective was the restoration of the Irish language. As a playwright and actor, he contributed to the early work of the *Irish Literary Theatre; Casadh an tSugain* (1901) was the first play in Irish ever performed on the professional stage. Several other plays in Irish followed between 1902 and 1904, often using scenarios provided by W B Yeats and Lady Gregory.

I

I am a Camera A play by John *Van Druten, based on the novel *Goodbye to Berlin* by Christopher Isherwood. First performance: New York, 1951. The play depicts the decadent cabaret of Berlin in the 1930s at the time when Hitler was coming to power. The plot is concerned with Sally Bowles, a singer, and Isherwood himself, the homosexual Englishman who admires her from afar and becomes, for her, a camera. In 1967 it was turned into the musical *Cabaret* by Fred Ebb, John Kander, and Joe Masteroff and provided a major film role for Liza Minelli.

Ibsen, Henrik (Johan) (1828–1906) Norwegian playwright, who is regarded as the father of 20th-century drama. The son of a merchant who went bankrupt when the playwright was eight years old, he first worked for a chemist in Grimstad. He was studying medicine when he began his long association with the theatre, attempting his first plays and subsequently working in the theatres at Bergen and Christiania (now Oslo).

The romantic drama *Catilina* bore the influence of both Scribe and Schiller and was followed by a series of plays on subjects drawn from Scandinavian history, of which the first to be performed was *The Burial*

Mound; one of the most highly praised was *The Vikings at Helgeland*. In 1863 he won a scholarship for *The Pretenders*, although it was the lengthy poetic drama **Brand* that finally established his reputation. In 1864 he left Norway and lived in Italy and Germany, visiting his native land only briefly in 1874 and 1885 before returning permanently in 1891.

Brand and **Peer Gynt* soon became internationally recognized for their technical mastery, psychological insight, and bleakness of vision. In 1877, Ibsen embarked upon the group of 12 prose dramas exploring the themes of morality and reality in modern society that constitutes the largest body of his work. The first was *Pillars of Society*, while *A *Doll's House* remains his most widely performed play and **Ghosts* – with its use of venereal disease as a metaphor for the sense of guilt inherent in corrupt society – was his most controversial. *An *Enemy of the People* further developed the characteristic theme of an individual's resistance in a morally impoverished society, while *The *Wild Duck, Rosmersholm, The Lady from the Sea*, and **Hedda Gabler* highlighted Ibsen's preoccupation with isolation and obsession.

The last four plays, *The *Master Builder, Little Eyolf, John Gabriel Borkman*, and **When We Dead Awaken*, witnessed a return to the symbolic drama of his early years, together with a stronger element of autobiography with their focus upon the psychology of the artist.

Principal works:

Catilina: 1850.

Norma, eller en politikers kjærlighed: 1851.

Sankthansnatten: 1853; translated as *St John's Night*.

Kjæmpehøjen: 1854; translated as *The Burial Mound*.

Fru Inger til Osteraad: 1855.

Gildet paa Solhoug: 1856; translated as *The Feast at Solhoug*.

Olaf Liljekrans: 1857.

Hæmændene paa Helgeland: 1857; translated as *The Vikings at Helgeland*.

Kjælighedens Komedie: 1873 (published 1872); translated as *Love's Comedy*.

Kongsemnerne: 1863; translated as *The Pretenders*.

Brand: 1885 (published 1866).

Peer Gynt: 1876 (published 1867).

De Unges Forbund: 1869; translated as *The League of Youth*.

Kejser og Galilæer: 1896 (published 1873); translated as *Emperor and Galilean*.

Samfundets Støtter: 1877; translated as *Pillars of Society*.

Et Dukkehjem: 1879; translated as *A Doll's House*.

Gengangere: 1882; translated as *Ghosts*.

En folkefiende: 1882; translated as *An Enemy of the People*.

Vildanden: 1886 (published 1884); translated as *The Wild Duck*.

Rosmersholm: 1886.

Fruen fra Havet: 1888; translated as *The Lady From the Sea*.

Hedda Gabler: 1890.

Bygmester Solness: 1892; translated as *The Master Builder*.

Lille Eyolf: 1894.

John Gabriel Borkman: 1896.

Naar vi Døde Vaagner: 1900; translated as *When We Dead Awaken*.

Ibsen, Lillebil (1899-) Norwegian dancer and actress, who married Ibsen's grandson, the film director Tancred Ibsen (1893–1978), in 1919. Having established her reputation as a dancer, she joined the Oslo Nye Teater in 1928 and attracted praise for her interpretation of comic roles, although she was also admired in Ibsen's *A Doll's House* and *Ghosts*. Later in her career she appeared at the Nationaltheatret in modern works.

Iceman Cometh, The A drama by Eugene **O'Neill. First performance: New York, 1946. The play depicts a group of disillusioned drinkers, who discuss their dreams in a nihilistic fashion; the coming of death is represented by the anticipated arrival of the man who delivers the ice to the saloon in which they are drinking.

Ideal Husband, An A comedy by Oscar *Wilde. First performance: 1895. Mrs Cheveley, a dazzling adventuress, attempts to blackmail a politician with an incriminating letter; the threat fails when his wife recognizes her as a fellow schoolgirl who was expelled for theft.

Iden, Rosalind *See* Wolfit, Sir Donald.

Iffland, August Wilhelm (1759–1814) German actor and playwright, who was the dominant figure at the German National Theatre at Mannheim during its most successful period. He began his career under Ekhof at Gotha in 1780 and saw his first plays produced at Mannheim a year later; subsequently he established himself as a distinguished – if superficial and conservative – performer of refined comedy throughout Germany, appearing at Hamburg with Schröder and meeting Goethe in Weimar during his travels. He created Franz Moor in Schiller's *Die Räuber* in 1779 and became manager of the Berlin National Theatre in 1798, being promoted to director-general of the royal theatres in Prussia in 1811.

I Have Been Here Before A play by J B *Priestley. First performance: London, 1937. One of the so-called time plays, it speculates upon the metaphysical possibility of escaping from time that recurs into time that spirals.

Illustre-Théâtre A French theatrical company founded in 1643, whose members included the Béjart family and Molière, who made his first stage appearance with the company. Presenting plays by Corneille, Du Ryer, and Tristan L'Hermite in the provinces, the company had been disbanded by 1645; its constitution provided the basis for that of the Comédie-Française.

Ilyinsky, Igor Vladimirovich (1901-) Soviet actor and director, who made his debut in 1918 in Petrograd and subsequently became a leading performer under Meyerhold (1920–35) and then at the Maly Theatre. He has been particularly admired in the plays of Crommelynck and Ostrovsky, while other successes have included plays by Mayakovsky, Korneichuk, and Vishnevsky; he was also acclaimed as Lenin in an adaptation (1967) of John Reed's *Ten Days That Shook the World* and as the director of Sofronov's *Honesty* (1962).

Immermann, Karl (1796–1840) German director, who hoped to emulate the success of Goethe at Weimar at the theatre in Düsseldorf, of which he was director from 1834 to 1837. His attempts to improve artistic standards failed, however, to meet with public approval.

Imperial Theatre A theatre in Westminster, London, which opened in 1876 as part of the Royal Aquarium complex. Originally known as the **Royal Aquarium Theatre**, it saw the last appearance of Samuel Phelps. It changed hands in 1878, enjoying success with revivals of classic plays. Lillie Langtry became closely associated with the theatre, briefly managing it in 1882 and later rebuilding the interior (1900). The theatre failed to prosper, however, and Langtry withdrew in 1903; until 1906 it was run successfully by Lewis Waller. The interior of the theatre was later incorporated into a cinema in Canning Town and was destroyed by fire in 1931.

The **Imperial Theatre** on West 45th Street between Broadway and Eighth Avenue in New York opened in 1923 as a venue for musicals. Among the many musicals seen there have been *Annie Get Your Gun* (1946), *Fiddler on the Roof* (1964), *They're Playing Our Song* (1979), and *Chess* (1988).

Importance of Being Earnest, The A comedy by Oscar *Wilde, regarded as his finest play. First performance: 1895. Jack Worthing's fictitious younger brother Earnest becomes an embarrassment when his friend Algernon assumes Earnest's identity to court Jack's ward; Algernon's aunt, Lady Bracknell, furthermore refuses consent to Jack's marriage to her daughter on account of his uncertain lineage. Lady Bracknell provided Edith Evans with her most famous role.

impresario A presenter of theatrical entertainments, usually of those with a strong musical element. Impresarios may include the major financial backers (or **angels**) of a production as well as those persons more immediately involved in arranging the presentation of a particular show or in managing a theatre or company. *See also choregus.*

Impromptu de Versailles, L' A comedy by *Molière. First performance: Paris, 1663. Edmé *Boursault, slighted by an apparent caricature of himself in *La *Critique de l'École des Femmes*, had attacked Molière in a play of his own: Molière responded in this play by ridiculing Boursault and the actors of the Hôtel de Bourgogne.

improvisation A theatrical production given without the use of a script, relying upon an actor's ability to create his role as he performs it. An integral feature of the medieval mystery play, improvisation was reintroduced as a tool in serious drama by Stanislavsky in the 20th century, both as an aid in rehearsal and as a basis for actual performances (*see* happening).

Inadmissible Evidence A play by John *Osborne. First performance: Royal Court Theatre, 1964. In the original production Nicol Williamson brilliantly played the failing lawyer, whose monologues – expressing his feelings of disconnection from both the world at large and the individuals closest to him – form the core of the play.

Inchbald, Elizabeth (1753–1821) British playwright and actress. She married an actor, Joseph Inchbald, in 1772 and appeared with him in Bristol and elsewhere. After his death in 1779 she appeared at Covent Garden and began writing plays. George Colman the Elder produced her *A Mogul Tale, or Descent of the Balloon* at the Haymarket in 1784 and *I'll Tell You What* in 1785.

incidental music Any music written specifically for use in a theatrical production, without being an integral part of the plot itself. The most celebrated examples include numerous songs and dances for the plays of Shakespeare, instrumental tunes to accompany melodrama, and electronic music used to create atmosphere in many modern productions. Leading composers who have written such music for the stage include Beethoven, Mendelssohn, Bizet, Grieg, Sibelius, Debussy, Tchaikovsky, Vaughan Williams, Elgar, Delius, and Britten.

Incorporated Stage Society *See* Stage Society.

Independent Theatre Club *See* Grein, Jack Thomas.

Indipendenti, Teatro sperimentale degli An Italian theatre company, established in 1922 in a room in the old Roman baths of Virgilio Marchi. The group established a reputation for experimental productions of plays by Jarry, Wedekind, and others as well as for performances of Futurist drama.

Inge, William (1913–73) US playwright, who began as a theatre critic in 1943. His first successful play was *Come Back, Little Sheba* (1950), a study of a lonely, desolate, wife. His next play, *Picnic*, received a Pulitzer Prize in 1953; *Bus Stop* (1955) and *The Dark At the Top of the Stairs* (1957) also won acclaim. His less successful later works included *A Loss of Roses* (1959), *Natural Af-*

fection (1962), *Where's Daddy?* (1966), and *Summer Brave* (1962).

Ingegneri, Angelo (c. 1550–c. 1613) Italian writer on stage techniques, noted for his treatise *Della poesia rappresentativa e del modo di rappresentare le favole sceniche* (1598). In this work he places particular stress upon the correct use of stage lighting, suggesting – among other things – that the auditorium should remain in complete darkness.

In Good King Charles's Golden Days The last complete play by G B *Shaw. First performance: Malvern Festival, 1939. Based on dialogue rather than dramatic action, the play presents such historical figures at Charles II, Isaac Newton, and Nell Gwynn in conversation.

inner stage An alcove at the back of the stage, concealed by a curtain, where a member of the cast can be 'discovered'. It was a common feature of the Elizabethan stage, although argument continues over its exact description.

Insect Play, The (*Ze zivota hymzu*) A play by Karel and Josef *Čapek. First performance: Prague, 1921. This allegorical fantasy in which a tramp finds himself shrunk to the size of insects, who regard him with scorn while going about their largely materialistic business, attracted much attention outside Czechoslovakia. It has been variously seen as *And So Ad Infinitum* and *The World We Live In*.

inset A small piece of scenery placed within a larger piece in order to facilitate a rapid change of set.

Inspector Calls, An A play by J B *Priestley. First performance: London, 1946. The play revolves around the figure of a mysterious police inspector, who interrupts an evening at the household of the prosperous Birling family in order to explore their various connections with a tragic suicide.

Institute for Advanced Studies in the Theatre Arts (IASTA) A US theatre organization founded in New York in 1958 by Dr and Mrs John Mitchell. It provides professional theatre workers with the opportunity to work with foreign directors and to learn foreign techniques; productions there have ranged from the plays of Sophocles to those of Molière and *Nō* plays.

interlude A brief dramatic piece – often comical in nature – that was presented in the 15th century as part of an evening's entertainment during a banquet. Such sketches were first performed in England during the reign of Henry VII, who employed a small group of professional actors for the purpose; John Heywood later developed the interlude as a distinct theatrical form but it disappeared altogether during the reign of Elizabeth I. *See also entremé; intermezzo.*

intermezzo A brief, usually comic, passage presented at banquets or between the acts of lengthy serious works in Italy during the 15th and 16th centuries. They were commonly based upon subjects taken from mythology or classical history. *See also entremé; interlude.*

International Amateur Theatre Association *See* British Theatre Association.

International Centre of Theatre Research A theatre organization founded in 1970 by Peter Brook to provide a point of contact between actors from different nations. As well as discussing drama theory, the company has presented highly original works in Africa, the US, and elsewhere, often relying upon improvisation. In 1974 it moved to the old **Théâtre des Bouffes du Nord** in Paris, where it continues to stage a range of experimental works, as well as touring widely.

International Federation for Theatre Research A theatre organization established in London in 1955 under the aegis of the British Society for Theatre Research. Dedicated to recording and studying the theatrical tradition of its numerous member countries, it publishes a journal and coordinates research by national theatre research organizations as well as staging major conferences. It also runs its own institute at the Casa Goldoni in Venice.

International Theatre *See* Majestic Theatre.

International Theatre Institute (ITI) A theatre organization founded in Prague under the aegis of UNESCO in 1948 to promote international theatrical contacts. Based in Paris, it publishes its own journal and stages conferences; its national centres offer studying facilities and information.

Interregnum The period between the closure of the English theatre by the Puritans in 1642 and its reopening on the coronation of Charles II in 1660. The closure of the theatres upon the fall of the monachy had become inevitable as the majority of those connected with the theatre had sided with the Royalists and had made London's theatres centres of intrigue against the parliamentarian cause. The performance of all plays was prohibited as offending against religious, political, and moral sensibilities and most actors and playwrights were forced to retire or return to their previous trades.

Cromwell and many of his followers, however, had no wish to outlaw the theatre as such and allowed the performance of drama in schools and some private productions; Davenant, for example, was one of the few professionals who found ways to continue to present theatre performances, albeit of a somewhat uncontroversial nature. Some illicit productions were staged at such venues as the Cockpit and the Red Bull,

but in general the theatre lay dormant for 18 years, creating a damaging gap in a hitherto unbroken national tradition.

Intima Teatern A theatre in Stockholm, founded in 1907 as a venue for the plays of Strindberg. Over the next three years many of Strindberg's later works were performed there before the theatre (renamed the Lilla Teatern) closed in 1913.

Another theatre of the same name was opened in Engebreksplan, Stockholm, in 1911 and was eventually (1921) absorbed into the *Kungliga Dramatiska Teatern as the Mindre Dramatiska Teatern, later the Komediteatern, and ultimately a cinema.

Intimate Theatre A theatre founded by John *Clements in Palmers Green, London, in 1935. The theatre provided a mixed programme of drama on a weekly repertory basis and was the first London theatre to reopen after the outbreak of World War II.

Ionesco, Eugène (1912-) French playwright, born in Romania, who was a pioneer of the Theatre of the *Absurd. In his first play, *The Bald Prima Donna*, Ionesco revealed his preoccupation with the failure of language as a tool for communication; subsequent plays examined the absurdity of existence, the dominant presence of inanimate objects, the alienation and impotence of man, and the sterility of social relationships. Ionesco also published a collection of essays on the theatre, *Notes et contre-notes* (1962; translated as *Notes and Counternotes*, 1964).

Principal works:

La Cantatrice chauve: 1950; translated as *The *Bald Prima Donna*.

La Leçon: 1951; translated as *The *Lesson*.

Les Chaises: 1952; translated as *The *Chairs*.

Amédée ou Comment s'en débarrasser: 1954; translated as *Amédée, or How to Get Rid of It*.

Le Nouveau Locataire: 1955; translated as *The New Tenant*.

Tueur sans gages: 1959; translated as *The Killer*.

Rhinocéros: 1960; translated as **Rhinoceros*.

Le Roi se meurt: 1962; translated as *Exit the King*.

Le Piéton de l'air: 1963; translated as *A Stroll in the Air*.

Le Mire: 1972.

Ion of Chios (5th century BC) Greek playwright, who was the author of several elegant tragedies. His other writings included his memoirs, the first such work recorded.

Iphigenia in Tauris A tragedy by **Euripides. First performance: Athens, c. 414 BC. Unlike most of his earlier works, this play has a happy ending and reveals the author as a master of romantic drama. Iphigenia is to be sacrificed to Artemis but is carried off by him to Tauris where she subsequently saves the life of her brother Orestes and escapes with him. The story also inspired later versions by Goethe and Racine and an opera by Gluck.

Iphigenie auf Tauris A play by **Goethe, first written in a prose version in 1779 and later in verse (1786–88). First performance: (first version) Weimar, 1779; (second version) 1802. Based on the story by Euripides, the play in its later version brilliantly combined the classical plot with contemporary thought concerning human redemption.

Ipsen, Bodil Louise Jensen (1889–1964) Danish actress, who became a leading interpreter of Ibsen's heroines. She made her debut at the Kongelige Teater in 1909 and later won acclaim in such roles as Nora in *A Doll's House* and Strindberg's Miss Julie.

Ireland, Kenneth *See* Pitlochry Festival Theatre.

Ireland, William Henry (1777–1835) British writer, whose Shakespearean forgeries deceived both scholars and his own father, an antiquarian book dealer, who was responsible for their publication. *Vortigern and Rowena*, which Ireland claimed to have discovered with other lost plays of Shakespeare, was produced by Sheridan at Drury Lane in 1796 before the fraud was finally exposed.

iris An adjustable diaphragm of overlapping metal leaves, by means of which the size of the area illuminated by a spotlight may be altered.

Irish Literary Theatre An Irish theatre organization founded in 1899 by Lady Gregory and W B Yeats to promote native Irish drama. Presenting plays by its founders among others, it moved into the Gaiety Theatre in 1900, subsequently staging the first Gaelic play, Douglas Hyde's *Casadh an tSugáin*, before being taken over by the **Irish National Dramatic Society.

Irish National Dramatic Society An Irish theatre company founded in 1902 by Frank and W G Fay as successor to the **Irish Literary Theatre. Presenting plays by W B Yeats and Lady Gregory as well as such authors as Synge and Padraic Colum, the company later appeared in London (1903) and inspired the foundation of the Abbey Theatre. A sister company in Ulster, formed in 1904, became part of the Ulster Group Theatre in 1939.

Irish Theatre *See* Provincetown Players.

iron *See* safety curtain.

Irons, Jeremy (1948-) British actor, who began his career with the Bristol Old Vic company before establishing himself as a popular leading man on both stage and screen. After a long run in the musical *Godspell* (1971–73), he appeared at the Round

House as Petruchio (1975) and as Harry Thunder in O'Keeffe's *Wild Oats* (1977). In New York he appeared in Tom Stoppard's *The Real Thing* (1983) and played Hamlet at the Globe Theatre, Utah. In 1986 he starred in Aphra Behn's *The Rover* and in major Shakespearean roles both at Stratford-upon-Avon and at the Mermaid Theatre. He is married to the actress Sinead *Cusack.

Irving, Sir Henry (John Henry Brodribb; 1838–1905) British actor-manager, who dominated the late Victorian stage. He was born at Keinton Mandeville, Somerset, but from the age of 10 lived in London. After seeing Samuel Phelps at Sadler's Wells he joined the Lyceum Theatre, Sunderland in 1856. Moving to Edinburgh, he probably played more than 350 parts in 30 months.

He spent the next seven years touring, joining the company at the St James's Theatre, where he made his debut in Mrs Cowley's comedy *The Belle's Stratagem* in 1866. He then moved to the Queen's Theatre and for the first time acted with Ellen Terry. In 1870 he appeared as Digby Grant in James Albery's *The Two Roses* at the Vaudeville Theatre; in the following year he so impressed Hezekiah Bateman, the manager of the Lyceum, that he offered Irving a three year contract. With Irving's sensational success in *The *Bells*, which was ideally suited to his intense and mesmeric style of acting, Bateman's ailing theatre recovered; in 1878 the Bateman management assigned the lease of the theatre to Irving, who celebrated this event with a revival of *Hamlet*, in which he defied convention by playing the central character as a victim of his own tenderness. At the same time he also secured as his leading lady Ellen Terry, with whom he was to appear in such plays as *The Merchant of Venice* (1879), *The Corsican Brothers* (1880), *Romeo and Juliet* (1882), *King Lear* (1892), and Tennyson's *Becket* (1893). From 1883 he and his company also undertook regular

visits to the US and Canada, and in 1895 he was made the first theatrical knight.

Ill health and financial worries, exacerbated by a fire at his Southwark store, undermined his last years. After giving up the Lyceum he made a final US tour in 1904; during a subsequent short provincial tour he collapsed and died in the Midland Hotel, Bradford, after a performance of *Becket*. He was buried in Westminster Abbey.

His eldest son, **Henry Brodribb Irving** (1870–1919), was an actor-manager, who made his debut in Robertson's *School* in 1891. After further engagements with the companies of Ben Greet and George Alexander, he was acclaimed in 1902 in the title role of Barrie's *The Admirable Crichton* and subsequently as Hamlet in 1905. He then formed his own company and toured the world in many of his father's parts. At different times he managed the Shaftesbury, Queen's, and Savoy theatres; he was married to the actress Dorothea *Baird.

Henry Irving's younger son, **Laurence Sidney Brodribb Irving** (1871–1914), was also an actor and playwright, who began his career under Frank Benson. As well as *Peter the Great* (1898), which he wrote for his father, and *The Unwritten Law* (1910), he was the author of several adaptations of plays by Sardou. As an actor he was highly praised in Ibsen's *The Pretenders* in 1913; he and his wife were drowned in a shipwreck in the St Lawrence.

Henry Brodribb Irving's son, **Laurence Henry Forster Irving** (1897-), became a stage designer and the author of a noted biography of his grandfather, *Henry Irving: the Actor and his World* (1951). As a designer he was praised for Eliot's *Murder in the Cathedral* (1935) and Priestley's *I Have Been Here Before* (1937).

Irving, Washington (1783–1859) US author, who wrote several accounts of the US stage. *The Letters of Jonathan Old Style* included a series of observations on the theatre, as did *Salmagundi* (1807). In 1826 two plays by Irving were seen, *Charles II* and *Richelieu*, both written in collaboration with John Payne. His short story 'Rip Van Winkle' was also adapted for the stage.

Irwin, May (Georgia Campbell; 1862– 1928) US singer and actress, born in Canada, who began as a musical act with her sister in 1875 and subsequently became a successful burlesque artiste. She then played important supporting roles on the legitimate stage in Daly's company for some years, but returned to vaudeville in 1892 and made a spectacular hit in John J McNally's *The Widow Jones* (1895). Similar farces and musicals followed; her last major appearance was in *The 49ers* (1922).

Isaacs, Edith Juliet (1878–1956) US theatre critic, who championed the plays of such authors as G B Shaw and Robert Sherwood in her magazine *Theatre Arts* (1919–45). She also helped to found the Federal Theatre Project, the American National Theatre and Academy, and other influential theatrical ventures.

Isle of Dogs, The A play by Thomas *Nashe and Ben *Jonson. First performance: Swan Theatre, 1597. Now lost, the play was first presented by Pembroke's Men and led to a temporary closure of the London theatres and the imprisonment of the two authors on charges of sedition.

Islington Empire *See* Grand Theatre.

Italian night scenes An English dumb show, introduced from France in 1702 by John *Weaver. The genre was derived from the *commedia dell'arte* and featured characters from the Italian tradition in an English setting; it incorporated dancing and trickwork and gradually evolved into the *harlequinade.

Italian Straw Hat, An (*Un chapeau de paille d'Italie*) A comedy by Eugène

*Labiche. First performance: Paris, 1851. An English adaptation by W S Gilbert is frequently revived. The straw hat of the title is eaten by a young man's horse on the morning of his wedding; he then seeks to replace it.

ITI *See* International Theatre Institute.

Ivanov The first full-length play by Anton *Chekhov. First performance: Alexandrinsky Theatre, St Petersburg, 1889. The play, a pessimistic drama culminating in the suicide of the central character, was a popular success despite the inability of the conventional troupe at the Alexandrinsky Theatre to understand the innovative naturalistic style of Chekhov's writing.

Ivanov, Vsevold Vyacheslavovich (1895– 1963) Soviet novelist and playwright, who began his career in Leningrad as a protégé of Gorky. His Civil War plays include Moscow Art Theatre's first Soviet play *Bronepoyezd No 14–69* (Armoured Train 14–69; 1927) – a true story related by the crew of an armoured train, *Blokada* (1929), and *Golubi Mira* (1937). Other works included *Lomonosov* (1953), about a celebrated scientist.

J

Jack-in-the-Green *See* Robin Hood play.

jack-knife stage A method of staging in which one or more rostra are pivoted on castor wheels at one corner, thus enabling them to be swung quickly into and out of the stage area.

Jackson, Sir Barry Vincent (1879–1961) British director, manager, and playwright, whose amateur company, the **Pilgrim Players**, became professional in 1913 when he built and opened the *Birmingham Repertory Theatre. Jackson managed the theatre for over 20 years, presenting a wide variety of plays, including modern-dress productions of Shakespeare, masterpieces by foreign authors, and much new drama, some of which was written by Jackson himself. In 1929 he founded the *Malvern Festival as a vehicle for Shaw's plays; from 1945 to 1948 he served as a director of the Shakespeare Memorial Theatre. He was knighted in 1925.

Jackson, Glenda (1936-) British actress, who spent several years in provincial repertory companies after graduating from RADA; she made her West End debut in Bill Naughton's *Alfie* (1963). She joined the Royal Shakespeare Company in 1964 and was highly acclaimed in such leading roles as Ophelia, the Princess of France in *Love's Labours Lost*, and Charlotte Corday in Peter Weiss's *Marat/Sade*. Since then she has combined international status as a film star with stage appearances ranging from Masha in Chekhov's *Three Sisters* (1967), Ibsen's Hedda Gabler (1975), and Shakespeare's Cleopatra (1978), to powerful performances in O'Neill's *Strange Interlude* (1985) and Lorca's *The House of Bernarda Alba* (1986).

Jacobean drama English drama covering the period of the reign of James I (1603–25). Although Shakespeare was still writing plays until about 1611, the dominant figure writing for the Jacobean stage was Ben *Jonson, whose bitter *comedy of humours echoed a new realism in the theatre in the face of increasing opposition from the Puritans. In collaboration with Inigo Jones, he was a major force in the creation of extravagant courtly masques that adopted a high scholarly tone and the inspiration for such admirers as Beaumont, Chapman, and Fletcher. The harshness underlying Jonson's satires was also a feature of Jacobean tragedy, which became obsessed with the idea of evil; through the plays of Middleton and Rowley, Tourneur, and Webster, it moved

increasingly towards unsparing displays of excess and horror.

In terms of organization, James I himself imposed strict controls upon the theatre of the day, placing all theatre companies under direct royal command; leading actors under this regime included Edward Alleyn and Richard Burbage. The period also saw the demise of the boy company, the growing influence of neoclassical theories from the Continent, and the gradual decline of audiences foreshadowing the closure of the theatres in 1642 when *Caroline drama came to an abrupt end.

Jacobi, Derek (George) (1938-) British actor, who appeared with the National Youth Theatre and at Cambridge before making his professional debut at Birmingham in N F Simpson's *One Way Pendulum* in 1960. In 1963 he joined the National Theatre company, where he acted in plays by Shakespeare, Chekhov, Webster, Coward, and others; in 1972 he toured with the Prospect company, winning further acclaim in such roles as Oedipus, Ivanov, Hamlet, and Pericles. More recent successes have included appearances with the Royal Shakespeare Company in New York (1983), Rostand's *Cyrano de Bergerac* (1986), and the part of Alan Turing in Hugh Whitemore's *Breaking the Code* (1986). In 1988 he ventured into direction with Kenneth Branagh's Renaissance Theatre Company.

Jacopone da Todi (c. 1230–1306) Italian poet and playwright, who is the only writer of *lauda known by name. He wrote nearly 90 such pieces, most of which revolved around a central *contrasto* or argument; many of them were written during his imprisonment by Pope Boniface VIII for supporting criticism of the papal elections.

Jahnn, Hans Henny (1894–1959) German playwright, novelist, and poet, whose controversial Expressionist dramas explore the ambivalent, often violent, nature of human sexuality. His major plays, in which he merges dreams with reality, include *Pastor Ephraim Magnus* (1919), *Die Krönung Richards III* (1921), *Medea* (1926), *Armut, Reichtum, Mensch und Tier* (Poverty, Wealth, Man and Beast; 1948), and *Thomas Chatterton* (1956).

Jakobsson, Jökull (1933–78) Icelandic novelist and playwright, whose realistic dramas depict life in impoverished northern communities. His plays set in Iceland include *Hart i bak* (Hard Aport; 1962) and *Songur skóarans og dóttir bakarans* (Song of the Shoemaker and the Baker's Daughter; 1978), which revolves around a small fishing village.

Jakova, Kol (1917–) Albanian playwright, actor, and director, who founded the People's Theatre in Tirana in 1945. His plays include two notable modern revenge tragedies – *Halili e Hajrija* (1955) and *Toka Jonë* (Our Soil; 1955) – and plays depicting Albania's struggle for independence.

James, David (1839–93) British actor, who began his career in Charles Kean's company at the Princess's Theatre in 1857. Subsequently he was notable in burlesque at the Strand Theatre before assuming joint management of the Vaudeville Theatre, which he built, in 1870. Here he was particularly successful in Albery's *Two Roses* (1870) and in H J Byron's *Our Boys* (1875), which ran for 1362 performances.

James, Henry (1843–1916) US novelist, a British subject from 1915, whose first produced play was *Guy Domville* (1895). His other plays were *The High Bid* (1909), *The Outcry* (1917), and *The Other House* (1969). Among the successful plays taken from his books were *Berkeley Square* (1928) from *The Sense of the Past*, *The Heiress* (1947) from *Washington Square*, *The Innocents* (1950) from *The Turn of the Screw*, *A Boston Story* (1908) from *Watch and Ward*, and *The*

Spoils (1968) from *The Spoils of Poynton* (1968).

Janauschek, Francesca Romana Maddalena (1830–1904) Czech actress, who established an international reputation as a performer of the great tragic roles. After early appearances in Prague, she spent 10 years in Frankfurt before being acclaimed in such roles as Lady Macbeth, Medea, and Mary Queen of Scots throughout Europe and in the US, where she played (in German and later in English) opposite Edwin Booth and other leading actors.

Jarry, Alfred (1873–1907) French playwright, novelist, and poet, whose farce *Ubu roi* was to have a profound influence on the Surrealist movement and the Theatre of the Absurd. Jarry's subsequent plays, sequels to *Ubu roi*, lacked the spirit of the original; he also wrote poems, stories, and novels and developed his theory of the absurd through 'Pataphysics, the science of imaginary solutions. His premature death was caused by alcoholism.

Principal dramatic works:
Ubu roi: 1896.
Ubu enchaîné: 1900.
Ubu sur la butte: 1901.

Jarvis, Martin (1941–) British actor, who played the title role in *Henry V* for the National Youth Theatre while still at RADA. His professional career began in 1962 at Manchester and he made his London debut in Anouilh's *Poor Bitos*. Subsequent parts have included Octavius in Shaw's *Man and Superman* (1966), Hamlet (1973), Arnold Champion-Cheney in Maugham's *The Circle* (1976), and Gerald in Ayckbourn's *Woman in Mind* (1986).

Jeans, Isabel (1891–1985) British actress, who was highly successful in the Phoenix Society productions of 16th and 17th century plays during the 1920s, playing such parts as Cloe in Fletcher's *The Faithful*

Shepherdess (1923) and Laetitia Fondlewife in Congreve's *The Old Bachelor* (1924). Her unique gift for sophisticated high comedy was brilliantly illustrated in such parts as Victoria in Maugham's *Home and Beauty* (1942) and Lady Bracknell in *The Importance of Being Earnest* (1968). She also made successful appearances in plays by Novello, Constance Collier, Sherwood, Lonsdale, Shaw, Chekhov, Anouilh, and T S Eliot.

Jefferson, Joseph (1774–1832) US actor, born in Britain, the son of a minor Drury Lane actor, he appeared in Boston in 1795 and made his New York debut as Squire Richard in Vanbrugh's *The Provok'd Husband* the following year. For upwards of 30 years he was leading actor at the Chestnut Street Theatre, Philadelphia, excelling in such comedy parts as Farmer Ashfield in Morton's *Speed the Plough*.

By his son, also **Joseph Jefferson** (1804–42), an actor and scene painter of modest ability, he was the grandfather of the third and best-known **Joseph Jefferson** (1829–1905), who made his stage debut at the age of four, performing alongside the comedy singer T D Rice. After his father died he toured with his mother and was soon playing important roles alongside such actors as John Brutus Booth. He subsequently joined Laura Keene's company and achieved great success in such parts as Pangloss in Colman the Younger's *The Heir-at-Law* and Asa Trenchard in Tom Taylor's *Our American Cousin*. With Dion Boucicault in New York he went on to play Caleb Plummer in a version of Dickens's *The Cricket on the Heath* (1859) and Salem Scudder in Boucicault's *The Octoroon* to equal acclaim before visiting Australia and then London in 1865, and attracting lasting fame in the title role of Boucicault's adaptation of Washington Irving's *Rip Van Winkle* (1865), which he continued to play throughout his career.

Jefford, Barbara (Mary) (1930-) British actress, who made her debut in Brighton in 1949. Later she appeared in several seasons at Stratford-upon-Avon and made her London and New York debuts as Andromache in Giraudoux's *Tiger at the Gates* (1955). She established her reputation as a classical actress while with the Old Vic company (1956–62) and has also met with similar success in such plays as Shaw's *Saint Joan* (1960), O'Neill's *Mourning Becomes Electra* (1961), and Pirandello's *Six Characters in Search of an Author* (1963), which she revived at the National Theatre in 1987.

Jellicoe, (Patricia) Ann (Mrs Roger Mayne; 1927-) British playwright and director, who established her reputation with *The Sport of My Mad Mother* (1958) four years after founding an open stage theatre club, The Cockpit Theatre. This brutal reflection of contemporary urban society was successfully produced at the Royal Court Theatre and was followed by the comedy *The Knack* (1961). In 1979 she founded the Colway Theatre Trust to produce large-scale community plays in Lyme Regis and other towns in the area; these have included *The Tide* (1979) and *The Reckoning* (1980).

Jerome, Jerome K(lapka) (1859–1927) British humorist, novelist, and playwright, who is best known for the comic novel *Three Men in a Boat*. As well as humorous commentaries upon contemporary theatre, he was also the author of several plays, of which the most successful was *The Passing of the Third Floor Back* (1908), in which Christ – played by Forbes-Robertson to great acclaim – reappears in a boarding-house in London.

Jerrold, Douglas William (1803–57) English actor and playwright, whose early successes included the farce *Paul Pry* (1827) and the melodrama *Fifteen Years of a Drunkard's Life* (1828). Engaged by Elliston to write for the Surrey Theatre, he achieved his biggest success with *Black-Ey'd Susan*. He went on to become manager of the Strand Theatre in 1836.

His son **William Blanchard Jerrold** (1826–84) wrote the farce *Cool as a Cucumber* (1851), performed by Charles Mathews the Younger at the Lyceum Theatre.

Jesse, Fryniwyd Tennyson *See* Harwood, Harold Marsh.

Jessner, Leopold (1878–1945) German director, who became a leading figure of the Expressionist movement in Berlin. His work – much influenced by Reinhardt – was particularly important for his development of the *Spieltreppe*, a form of multilevel staging that avoided the use of representational scenery which he introduced while director of the Berlin State Theatre (1919–30). His most famous production was Wedekind's *Der Marquis von Keith* (1920).

Jester *See* Court Fool.

Jesuit drama Plays written and performed by pupils of the various Jesuit colleges throughout Europe between the 16th and 18th centuries. The Jesuit Order, founded in 1534, realized the potential of drama in spreading religious propaganda at an early stage and rapidly transformed it from a tool in the education of Jesuit students into a regular feature of the Jesuit calendar, comprising spectacular performances in which music, scenery, costume, and other elements were all combined. By 1750 dramatic performances were being presented at frequent intervals at nearly 300 Jesuit colleges.

The plays themselves, the subjects of which were generally taken from classical or holy writings, were initially given in Latin and adopted a high moral tone; later, however, female characters were introduced and writers drew on more varied sources for their plays, which were increasingly performed in the vernacular. By the 17th century Jesuit drama encompassed elements of

opera and ballet and had acquired a reputation for sumptuousness with huge casts, large orchestras, and elaborate stage effects; eventually this extravagance contributed to the imposition of certain limitations upon such productions and ultimately the suppression of the order as a whole in 1773. Famous authors in the tradition included Scammacca and Tuccio in Italy, Avancini and Adolph in Austria, and Bidermann in Germany; pupils influenced by the form numbered amongst them Calderón, Corneille, Molière, and Voltaire.

Jesus Christ Superstar A musical by Tim *Rice and Andrew *Lloyd Webber. First performance: New York, 1970. Based upon the life of Christ and featuring extensive use of rock music, it broke all records for a musical, its British run at the Palace Theatre lasting from 1972 to 1980.

Jevon, Thomas (1652–88) English actor and playwright, who excelled in low comedy. As one of the earliest English Harlequins, he appeared in Aphra Behn's *The Emperor of the Moon* in 1687 at the Dorset Garden Theatre, where he also performed in his own play *The Devil of a Wife*.

Jewish Art Theatre *See* Garden Theatre.

Jewish Drama Ensemble *See* Moscow State Jewish Theatre.

Jew of Malta, The A drama in blank verse by Christopher *Marlowe. First performance: London, c. 1590. The action, which is melodramatic and violent, focuses upon the villainous but complex Barabas and constitutes a scathing comment upon contemporary religious attitudes.

jig A short comic *afterpiece, which was performed in the smaller Elizabethan theatres. It consisted of rhymed verses often dealing with affairs of the day, which were sung and danced by a group of three or four actors, including a clown. A common feature of the repertory of the English Comedians, the tradition had died out by the Restoration; celebrated performers of jigs included Kempe and Tarleton.

Jim Crow *See* Rice, Thomas Dartmouth.

Jirásek, Alois (1851–1930) Czech playwright, who was the author of several plays notable for their realistic exploration of contemporary society. These included *Father* (1894); other works numbered amongst them the historical trilogy *Jan Žižka* (1903), *Jan Hus* (1911), and *Jan Roháč* (1918) and the Symbolist play *The Lantern* (1905).

Jodelet (Julian Bedeau; c. 1590–1660) French actor, brother of L'Espy, who was noted for his performances in comedy. After appearing with Montdory's company at the Théâtre du Marais, he moved to the Hôtel de Bourgogne for a time before returning to the Marais to appear in a celebrated series of farces written for him by Thomas Corneille, Scarron, and others. He always performed with his face whitened with flour; eventually he was persuaded into joining Molière's company in 1658 and appeared as the Vicomte de Jodelet in *Les Précieuses Ridicules* (1659).

Jodelle, Étienne (1532–73) French playwright and poet, who was a member of the group of seven Renaissance poets known as La Pléiade. Jodelle's *Cléopâtre captive*, one of the earliest French tragedies, and the comedy *Eugène* were first performed at the court of Henri II in 1552 or 1553; the plays were seminal works in the development of classical drama.

Jodrell Theatre *See* Kingsway Theatre.

Joey *See* Grimaldi, Joseph.

John Bull's Other Island A play by G B *Shaw. First performance: Royal Court Theatre, 1904. The play discusses the conflict between the English and Irish through the two central characters and argues for Irish independence. The preface, written in 1906, is one of Shaw's most provocative political essays.

John F Kennedy Center for the Performing Arts *See* Eisenhower Theatre.

John Golden Theatre A theatre on West 58th Street, New York, which was opened in 1926 and named after the actor and director **John Golden** (1874–1955). The Theatre Guild occupied the theatre for a time, producing plays by Sidney Howard and O'Neill, but in 1935 (after a brief period as the **58th Street Theatre**) it was converted into a cinema. It was later used for revue (as the **Concert Theatre**) and as a television studio.

The **John Golden Theatre** on West 45th Street, New York, opened as the **Theatre Masque** in 1927. John Golden took over the theatre in 1937, opening it with *And Now Goodbye*. Since 1959 the theatre has been used for revues, which have included *At the Drop of a Hat* (1959) and *Beyond the Fringe* (1962). Other productions have been plays by Stoppard and Robert Anderson.

Johnny Jacks Play *See* mummers' play.

Johnson, Dame Celia (1908–82) British actress, who, on leaving RADA, scored early London successes in Merton Hodge's *The Wind and the Rain* (1933) and as Elizabeth Bennet in Helen Jerome's dramatization of *Pride and Prejudice* (1938). After a successful appearance in Daphne Du Maurier's *Rebecca* (1940) she made several films with Noël Coward, including the celebrated *Brief Encounter*. She returned to the stage in 1947 as Shaw's Saint Joan, subsequently starring in such modern comedies as Ayckbourn's *Relatively Speaking* (1967) and William Douglas Home's *The Dame of Sark* (1974). She also appeared for the National Theatre as Mrs Solness in Ibsen's *The Master Builder* (1964); at the Chichester Festival Theatre she played in Chekhov's *The Cherry Orchard* (1966) and was highly praised as Gertrude to the Hamlet of Alan Bates in 1971.

Johnson, Elizabeth (fl. 1790–1810) US actress, who was with the American Company in Boston and New York. At the Park Theatre, managed for a time by her husband, she played such leading Shakespearean roles as Rosalind and Imogen and became celebrated for her portrayal of elegant ladies in high comedy. She was also known for her serious portrayal of male roles, notably as Young Norval in Home's *Douglas* (1804).

Johnson, Dr Samuel (1709–84) British lexicographer, critic, and essayist. His pamphlet *A Compleat Vindication of the Licensers of the Stage* (1739) was an ironical attack on the censors, while his single tragedy *Irene* was produced by Garrick without success in 1749. His edition of Shakespeare's plays with notes and emendations was published in 1765.

Johnson Over Jordan A play by J B *Priestley. First performance: London, 1939. The play revolves around the character of a recently deceased businessman who reflects upon aspects of his career, his pursuit of pleasure, and his happiest memories.

Johnston, (William) Denis (1901–84) Irish playwright and lawyer, born in Dublin. His theatrical debut, the innovative *The Old Lady Says "No!"* (1929) was first produced at the Gate Theatre in Dublin. He consolidated his reputation with a succession of plays including *The *Moon In The Yellow River* (1931) and *Strange Occurrence on Ireland's Eye* (1956), which revealed his understanding of contemporary Ireland. He was a director of the Gate Theatre, and also produced plays for the Abbey Theatre.

Johnston, Henry Erskine (1777–1845) British actor, who was extravagantly hailed as the **Scottish Roscius** when he played Hamlet at the Theatre Royal, Edinburgh in 1794. Playing Young Norval in Home's *Douglas* in full Highland costume, he caught the public imagination; in 1797 he began a five-year engagement at Covent Garden, after which he retired to obscurity.

John Street Theatre A theatre in John Street, New York, which was built of wood and painted red; under David Douglass it opened in 1767 as the first permanent New York theatre. The first production was Farquhar's *The Beaux' Stratagem*. Until the War of Independence the American Company staged many plays there, including the New York premieres of *Macbeth*, *The Merchant of Venice*, Jonson's *Every Man in His Humour*, and Dryden's *All For Love*.

Renamed the **Theatre Royal** during the British occupation, it was used by British officers, among them the gifted scenery painter Major John André. In 1785 the American Company returned to present regular seasons, managed by the younger Hallam and John Henry. Productions included Royall Tyler's *The Contrast* (1787), Dunlap's *The Father; or, American Shandyism* (1789), John O'Keeffe's *The Poor Soldier*, Garrick's *Hamlet*, and works by Sheridan and Colman the Elder as well as Shakespeare. Among the distinguished players of the company were Thomas Wignell, Mrs Owen Morris, Joseph Jefferson I (who made his New York debut there in 1796), and the English actor John Hodgkinson. Hodgkinson became more popular than either John Henry or Hallam, who left, in 1794 and 1797 respectively. An unsuccessful season by a visiting company in 1797 prompted the American Company to return. The theatre was closed in 1798 and later sold by Hallam.

Joint Stock Company A British theatre company founded in 1974 by David Hare and William Gaskill. Employing a policy of involving the playwright closely with the process of production, the group has successfully staged such plays as Hare's *Fanshen* (1975), Brenton's *Epsom Downs* (1977), Stephen Lowe's *The Ragged Trousered Philanthropists* (1978), and Caryl Churchill's *A Mouthful of Birds* (1986).

Jolly, George (fl. 1640–73) English actor, who was the last notable member of the English Comedians. He returned to London after the Restoration and managed the Cockpit from 1661 to 1665, when his licence was withdrawn. Subsequently he ran the nursery attached to the patent theatres.

Jolly Boys' Play *See* mummers' play.

Jolson, Al (Asa Yoelson; 1883–1950) US actor and singer, best known for his work in blackface revue and musical comedy. Among the productions he appeared in were *La Belle Paree* (1911), *Whirl of Society* (1912), *Dancing Around* (1914), and *Sinbad* (1918), in which he sang 'My Mammy' and 'Swanee', his two most famous songs.

Jolson Theatre *See* Century Theatre.

Jones, Freddie (1927-) British actor, who joined the Royal Shakespeare Company and first attracted attention in Peter Weiss's *Marat/Sade* (1964). He acted in the premiere of David Mercer's *Flint* (1970) at Oxford and later appeared as Mathias in a revival of Leopold Lewis's *The Bells* (1976). In 1980 he was highly praised as Sir in Ronald Harwood's *The Dresser* and subsequently played Arthur Langley in the same author's *Tramway Road* (1984).

Jones, Henry Arthur (1851–1929) British playwright, who built up a controversial reputation with his comedies and serious plays on such themes as religious hypocrisy. Regarded in his day as a major exponent of socially relevant theatre, he is now largely forgotten because of his tendency towards the melodramatic. *The Silver King* (1882) – cowritten with Henry Herman – was his first big success, while subsequent works that were praised by Shaw and others included *The Dancing Girl* (1891), which starred Julia Neilson, *Michael and His Lost Angel* (1896), concerning a guilt-ridden priest, and *Mrs Dane's Defence* (1900).

Jones, Inigo (1573–1652) English architect and stage designer, who studied in Italy and was influenced by the work of Parigi and Palladio. A major exponent of baroque theatre design, he was attached to Prince Henry's household in 1604 and took over production of the Court *masques. His long association with Jonson began in 1605 but gradually developed into a feud over the relative importance of the spoken word and visual splendour. After *Chloridia* in 1631, Jones engineered Jonson's dismissal. During the Civil War, however, he fell from favour, was twice fined, and died in straitened circumstances.

Jones, James Earl (1931-) US Black actor, who made his stage debut in 1949 in Arnand d'Usseau's *Deep Are the Roots*. He had a long-running association with Joseph Papp's New York Shakespeare Festival, performing as Oberon (1961), Caliban (1962), Othello (1964), Macbeth (1966), Claudius in *Hamlet* (1972), and Lear (1973). Other successes have included Genet's *The Blacks* (1961), Fugard's *The Blood Knot* (1964), Büchner's *Danton's Death* (1965), Chekhov's *The Cherry Orchard* (1973), O'Neill's *The Iceman Cometh* (1973), and Steinbeck's *Of Mice and Men* (1974).

Jones, Margo (1913–55) US producer and director, whose early productions included Tennessee Williams's *You Touched Me* (1943). In 1945 she founded an experimental theatre in Dallas, Texas to present works by contemporary playwrights and avant-garde productions of older works. She directed *The Glass Menagerie* on Broadway in 1945;

other presentations included Williams's *Summer and Smoke* and Maxwell Anderson's *Joan of Lorraine*.

Jones, Richard (fl. 1583–1615) English actor, who was a leading member of the English Comedians. Formerly with the Admiral's Men, he joined Robert Browne and his company in 1610 and became very popular on the Continent.

Jones, Robert Edmond (1887–1954) US stage designer and director, whose designs for Anatole France's *The Man Who Married a Dumb Wife* (1915) signalled a major reform of US stage design in general. Of his other atmospheric designs, influenced by Craig, Appia, and Copeau, the most important included those for O'Neill's *The Great God Brown* (1926) and several Shakespearean productions, notably *Hamlet* (1922).

jongleur A travelling entertainer of a type common throughout Europe during the Dark Ages. The jongleurs included both men and women who, embracing such diverse theatrical skills as acrobatics, juggling, and singing, sometimes performed only their own material (in which case they were also called *trouvéres*); such entertainers usually worked as solo performers. *See also* minstrel.

Jonson, Ben (1572–1637) English playwright, regarded as second only to Shakespeare among the playwrights of his time. After training as a bricklayer and distinguishing himself in the war in Flanders, he joined Henslowe's company in 1597; shortly afterwards he narrowly escaped death for killing a fellow-actor in a duel and was imprisoned for his part in The **Isle of Dogs*. Unsuccessful as an actor, he established his reputation with **Every Man in his Humour* and was subsequently acclaimed as the greatest playwright of his day for his numerous tragedies, comedies, and masques. None of his plays written after a temporary

exile (1616) from the theatre, however, have remained on the stage; earlier works that have enjoyed frequent successful revivals include **Volpone; or, The Fox*, The **Alchemist*, and **Bartholomew Fair*. Of his various collaborations, the most important were those with Marston and Chapman on *Eastward Ho!* (1605), which resulted in another period in prison, and the many sumptuous masques he produced with Inigo Jones. His greatest plays are memorable for their lively invocation of contemporary London and for their condemnation of human greed and materialism.

Principal works:

The Isle of Dogs: 1597 (with Nashe).
Every Man in his Humour: 1598.
Every Man out of his Humour: 1599.
Cynthia's Revels: 1600.
The Poetaster: 1601.
Eastward Ho!: 1605 (with Chapman and Marston).
Sejanus: 1603.
Volpone; or, The Fox: 1612.
Epicoene; or, the Silent Woman: 1609.
The Alchemist: 1610.
Bartholomew Fair: 1614.
Catiline: 1611.
The Devil is an Ass: 1616.

Jordan, Dorothy (1762–1816) British actress, who was born in Ireland, the illegitimate daughter of an actress. After five years as Miss Francis at the Crow Street Theatre in Dublin under Daly, by whom she was seduced, she joined Tate Wilkinson's company at York. As she was then pregnant, at his suggestion she adopted the name of Mrs Jordan. In 1785 Sheridan engaged her at Drury Lane as an understudy to the tragic actress Mrs Siddons, but she went on to establish her reputation playing the comic heroines of Shakespeare and breeches parts. Subsequently she excelled in the comedies of Farquhar, Congreve, and Sheridan himself. She was the mother of 15 illegitimate children, of which William IV, when Duke of Clarence, fathered 10.

jornada A Spanish term for a division within a play, equivalent to an act.

Jōruri A dramatic narrative, chanted during a performance of the *Bunraku* puppet theatre. Named after a 15th-century ballad about a certain Princess Jōruri, these stories tended to be subordinated to the accompaniment of the three-stringed *shamisen* until the emergence of the two greatest writers of the *Jōruri*, Takemoto Gidayu (1651–1741) and Chikamatsu Monzaemon, in the 17th century. Their collaboration, resulting in a style known as 'Gidayu music', marked the most celebrated period of the Japanese puppet theatre; subsequently Japanese playwrights opted to write instead for the real actors of the *Kabuki* tradition.

Joseph, Stephen (1927–67) British director and actor, who was a tireless advocate of theatre-in-the-round. After studying in the US, he formed the Studio Theatre Company in Scarborough in 1955, touring the north of England and testing the viability of his staging ideas. In 1962 he created the country's first permanent theatre-in-the-round, the *Victoria Theatre, in a small converted cinema in Stoke-on-Trent.

Journey's End A play by R C *Sherriff. First performance: London, 1928. Set in a World War I dug-out, it concentrates on the relationship between the youthful Lieutenant Raleigh and Captain Stanhope. The action takes place offstage, but the reactions of the characters are realistically presented.

Jouvet, Louis (1887–1951) French actor and director, whose work had a profound effect upon French theatre production after World War I. He made his Paris debut in 1910 in *The Brothers Karamazov* and then joined Copeau at the Vieux-Colombier, where he excelled in plays by Shakespeare. In 1922 he became director of the Comédie des Champs-Élysées, scoring a major success with Romain's *Knock, ou le Triomphe de la médecine* in 1923. Later he became closely associated with the plays of Giraudoux and Molière. His innovations included reform of stage lighting and the use of highly evocative settings.

Joyce, James (Augustine Aloysius) (1882–1941) Irish novelist, poet, and playwright, born in Dublin. Joyce was an outspoken champion of Ibsen; at the age of 18 his essay 'Ibsen's New Drama' was published in *The Fortnightly Review* and attracted considerable comment. His single play, *Exiles* (1919), deals with the freedoms and constraints of marriage and anticipates the complexities of his fiction.

Juell-Reimers, Johanne (1847–82) Norwegian actress, who was highly acclaimed in the plays of Ibsen and Bjørnson. Her early death cut short her promising career; her daughter was Johanne *Dybwad.

Julian Eltinge Theatre See Eltinge Theatre.

Julius Caesar A history play by William *Shakespeare, written c. 1599. First performance: c. 1599. The play traces the events surrounding the assassination of Julius Caesar and anticipates Shakespeare's major tragedies in its concentration upon the conscience-stricken Brutus and his fellow conspirators after Caesar's death. Caesar himself dies relatively early in the play but he remains the central figure, reappearing as a corpse during Mark Antony's famous speech to the Roman mob and as a ghost before the deaths of Cassius and Brutus.

Jumpers A comedy by Tom *Stoppard. First performance: 1972. The play revolves around George Moore, a professor of moral philosophy, whose lengthy moral arguments combine with the antics of a team of acrobats (jumpers) to parody academic philosophy.

Juno and the Paycock The second play by Sean *O'Casey. First performance: Abbey Theatre, Dublin, 1924. Set in the slums of Dublin during the civil strife of 1922, the play traces the disintegration of the Boyle family as a result of the war.

Justice A play by John *Galsworthy. First performance: Savoy Theatre, 1910. The play deals with the imprisonment, persecution, and suicide of a clerk who commits forgery to rescue a woman mistreated by her husband; it allegedy inspired reform of the law relating to solitary confinement.

Juvarra, Filippo (1678–1736) Italian architect and stage designer, who designed a theatre in Rome in the Palazzo della Cancellaria for Cardinal Ottoboni. He also executed a number of designs for scenery for this theatre and worked for the queen of Poland and for Joseph I of Austria.

juvenile drama *See* toy theatre.

Juvenile Lead *See* stock company.

K

Kabuki A form of Japanese drama, which evolved from the traditional *Nō* theatre in about 1600. Combining drama, music, mime, and other disparate theatrical elements, the *Kabuki* drew on plots from the *Jōruri* tradition but emphasized the dominance of the actors over the musicians and playwrights. The genre encompasses various types of plays, ranging from histories to domestic dramas and it was formerly customary for a number of scenes from different pieces to be combined to make up a complete programme, which could last for a whole day. In the past, spectators at a *Kabuki* production could indulge in conversation and eating as the performance con-

tinued; such practices have, however, had to be curtailed to meet the expectations of audiences in the 20th century. Variations in this century have included the *Shimpa and the *Shingeki, which reflected European influences.

Kachalov, Vasili Ivanovich (Vasili Ivanovich Shverubovich; 1875–1948) Soviet actor, who became a leading performer at the Moscow Art Theatre. Having trained in the provinces, he was much admired in the plays of Ibsen, Shakespeare, Dostoevsky, and Leo Tolstoy (notably as the Reader in *Resurrection*) as well as in the premieres of Griboyedev's *Woe from Wit* (1906) and Ivanov's *Armoured Train 14–69* (1927).

Kagura An early form of Japanese dance drama. Based on mythological themes, the tradition was imported from China in about 540 AD.

Kahn, Florence (1877–1951) US actress, who first became known for her appearances opposite Richard *Mansfield and later through her interpretations of Ibsen's women, whom she played throughout the US. In 1908, while playing Rebecca West in *Rosmersholm* in London, she married Max Beerbohm and virtually retired from the stage.

Kainz, Josef (1858–1910) German actor, who was noted for his distinctive voice. He first appeared with the Meininger company and later acted in Vienna, Munich, and Berlin as well as touring the US in such roles as Hamlet, Tartuffe, and Cyrano de Bergerac.

Kaiser, Georg (1878–1945) German playwright, who became a leading Expressionist writer. His major works, distinguished by their lack of plot development, stark language, and nameless characters representing general types, deal with the theme of man's regeneration through misfortune. His most successful dramas include the satirical comedy *Die Bürger von Calais* (1917), *Von Morgensbis Mitternachts* (1917), and the trilogy *Die Koralle* (1917), *Gas I* (1918), and *Gas II* (1920). His condemnation of the brutality of dictatorship led to his works being banned in 1933.

Kālidāsa (d. 373 AD–415 AD) Indian playwright, who was the most celebrated author of early Sanskrit drama. His play *Shakūntalā* provided the basis for Wagner's *Der Ring des Nibelungen* and influenced Goethe.

Kalita Humphreys Theatre *See* Dallas Theatre Centre.

Kameri Theatre *See* Cameri Theatre.

Kamerny Theatre A theatre in Moscow, founded in 1914 by Alexander *Taîrov. Intended for the performance of experimental dramas in contrast to the naturalistic productions of the Moscow Art Theatre, it presented numerous foreign works until Taîrov died in 1950, when the company's influence declined.

Kamińska, Ida (1899–1980) Polish-Jewish actress, who ran the **Polish State Jewish Theatre**, founded by her mother Ester Rachel Kaminska (1868–1925) in Warsaw, from 1921 to 1939. Acclaimed as an actress in the plays of Ibsen and Brecht, she reformed the theatre after World War II, renaming it after her mother and leading it on a tour of Polish cities and then through Europe before finally closing it in 1968 and moving to the US.

Kantor, Tadeusz (1915-) Polish director and set designer, who has established an international reputation for his work at the Stary Theatre in Cracow (1945–55) and subsequently at his own experimental Cricot 2 theatre. His most celebrated productions have included plays by Witkiewicz and his own *Dead Class* (1975) and *Wielopole, Wielopole* (1979), several of which have also been seen in other countries.

Karatygin, Vasily Andreyevich (1802–53) Russian actor, who was noted for his attention to historical accuracy in his roles. He did much background research for his performances and excelled in classical tragedy, despite his tendency towards artificiality in his acting style.

Kasperl A character of the Austrian *Altwiener Volkstheater*, derived from that of the clown *Hanswurst. First played in 1764 by Laroche, he was also presented as a puppet character in the *Kasperltheater*, the Austrian equivalent of Punch and Judy.

Katayev, Valentin Petrovich (1897-) Soviet novelist and playwright, whose dramatic output consists chiefly of socially-challenging dramas criticizing the morality of the NEP (New Economic Policy) period after the Rusian civil war. His best-known plays include *Kvadratura Kruga* (Squaring the Circle; 1928), which is a comedy about cramped living conditions, and *The Primrose Path* (1934). More recent works number amongst them dramatizations of his own novels and *Violet* (1974).

Katona, József (1791–1830) Hungarian playwright, regarded as the father of the Hungarian theatrical tradition. His celebrated five-act tragedy *Bánk Bán* (1814) depicts the dilemma faced by the regent, Bán Bánk, when the queen's brother seduces his wife and concludes in the queen's murder; it was later made into an opera by Ferenc Erkel. No other plays by Katona are known.

Kaufman, George S (1889–1961) US playwright, who wrote his first plays in collaboration with Marc Connelly. After cowriting *Merton of the Movies* (1922) and *Beggar on Horseback* (1924), he wrote *The Butter and Egg Man* (1925) and *The*

Cocoanuts (1925) on his own; collaborations with **Edna Ferber** included *Dinner at Eight* (1932) and *Stage Door* (1936). He also wrote several light comedies in collaboration with Moss Hart, including *Once in a Lifetime* (1930), *Merrily We Roll Along* (1934), *You Can't Take It With You* (1936), and *The Man Who Came to Dinner* (1939). He also wrote and directed several musicals.

Kazan, Elia (1909-) US actor and director, who made his first appearance with the Group Theatre in 1935. Subsequent roles included Eddie Fuseli in Odets's *Golden Boy* (1937) and Ficzur in Molnár's *Liliom* (1940). He is best known as a director, his productions including Wilder's *The Skin of Our Teeth* (1942), Tennessee Williams's *A Streetcar Named Desire* (1947) and *Cat on a Hot Tin Roof* (1955), and Arthur Miller's *Death of a Salesman* (1949). In 1947 he cofounded the Actors' Studio. He published his autobiography in 1988.

Kean, Edmund (c. 1789–1833) British actor, who was the son of a strolling player, Ann (Nance) Carey, and a minor actor, Edmund Kean (1770–92). By the age of eight he had already played small parts at Drury Lane and acquired an extravagant notion of his own importance; subsequently he toured as a strolling player, marrying an actress in 1808. In 1814 his sensational debut as Shylock at Drury Lane established an immediate reputation; his Richard III a fortnight later consolidated it. Hamlet, Othello, and Iago followed and, in 1815, he was particularly successful as Sir Giles Overreach in *A New Way to Pay Old Debts*.

Now an accepted member of society, Kean became acutely aware of his lack of culture, which he attempted to disguise by indulging in an orgy of excesses. After a disappointing Lear at Drury Lane he visited the US in 1820, where again he impressed audiences with both his passionate acting and his wild behaviour. Temperamentally he was ideally suited for such roles as Macbeth, Othello, and Shylock, all of which he played with murderous intensity. In 1825 his affair with Charlotte Cox, wife of a City alderman, ended in scandal and a blackening of his public image. Kean's habitual drunkenness also resulted in several non-appearances, a gradual decline in his health, and quarrels with managers. In 1832 he played Othello to Macready's Iago, thrilling the audience but reducing himself to utter exhaustion. His final performance was again as Othello with his son, **Charles (John) Kean** (1811–68), as Iago; he died at Richmond six weeks later. His son subsequently took over the Princess's Theatre where, with his wife, the actress **Ellen Tree** (1805–80), he produced a series of historical plays, which were acclaimed for their authenticity.

Kean, Thomas (fl. 1749–50) US actormanager, who (in partnership with Walter Murray) produced Shakespearean, Restoration, and contemporary plays – among them Gay's *The Beggar's Opera* and Congreve's *Love for Love* – in Philadelphia and New York (1749–50). He then took a touring troupe – the **Virginia Company of Comedians** – to Virginia, but no subsequent records exist of his activities. This was possibly the first professional US theatre company.

Keane, Doris *See* Sheldon, Edward Brewster.

Keane, John Brendan (1928-) Irish playwright, who has established a controversial reputation with a long series of plays distinguished by strong characters and emotional situations. His works include *Sive* (1959), his first play for the stage, the trilogy *Values* (1973), and *The Chastitute* (1980).

Kedrov, Mikhail Nikolayevich (1893–1972) Russian actor and director, who spent most of his career at the Moscow Art Theatre. Having trained under Stanislavsky, he won particular acclaim for his production of

Chekhov's *Uncle Vanya* (1958) and *The Winter's Tale*.

Keeley, Robert (1793–1869) British actor, who, after experience in the provinces, was acclaimed at the Adelphi Theatre in 1819 as Jemmy Green in Pierce Egan's *Tom and Jerry*. A natural comedian, he excelled as Sairey Gamp in *Martin Chuzzlewit* by Dickens and Dogberry in *Much Ado About Nothing*.

In 1844 he took over the management of the Lyceum, in company with his wife, the actress **Mary Ann Keeley** (Mary Ann Goward; 1806–99). She made her professional debut at the Lyceum (then the English Opera House) in 1825. Later she appeared at Covent Garden, the Adelphi, and under Madame Vestris at the Olympic Theatre, usually alongside her husband. At the Adelphi she had her greatest success as Jack Sheppard in Buckstone's play of that name. She also spent two seasons at Drury Lane with Macready.

Keene, Laura (Mary Moss; c. 1826–73) British actress and manager, who began as an actress with Madame Vestris. She was seen in New York in 1851, went to Australia, and then returned to the US. She was a member of Wallack's company in New York and enjoyed success as a comedy star. In 1856 she opened her own theatre, thus becoming the first woman theatre manager, and achieved a major hit with *Our American Cousin* (1858). During the US Civil War she went on tour; it was at one of her company's performances of *Our American Cousin* at Ford's Theatre in Washington that President Lincoln was assassinated in 1865.

Kelly, Fanny (Maria) (1790–1882) British actress, who made her adult acting debut in Glasgow in 1807 and was then at the Haymarket. Subsequently she played at Drury Lane for upwards of 30 years, where her parts included Ophelia to Kean's Hamlet. In 1840 she opened a theatre in Soho, later called the Royalty, where she unsuccessfully attempted to run a school for actresses.

Kelly, Hugh (1739–77) British playwright and theatre critic, whose comedy *False Delicacy* (1768) was produced at Drury Lane by Garrick in a successful effort to overshadow Goldsmith's *The Good-Natured Man* at Covent Garden. His other works include the comedy *A School for Wives* (1773).

Kemble, John Philip (1757–1823) British actor and manager, who spent his childhood acting in the touring company of his parents, Roger Kemble (1722–1802) and Sarah Ward (d. 1807). As an actor in the provinces he built a fine reputation especially in northern England, often appearing alongside his three brothers and four sisters, the eldest of whom became famous as Sarah *Siddons. Following two seasons at Dublin's Smock Alley Theatre, during which he fell in love with Elizabeth *Inchbald, he made his Drury Lane debut as Hamlet in 1783. His subtle performance was well received and he became identified with such great tragic roles as Coriolanus, Cato, and Alexander. He succeeded Sheridan as manager of Drury Lane and remained there until 1802, when he bought a one-sixth share in *Covent Garden and became the manager and leading tragedian there. In 1808 his imposition of price increases triggered the infamous OP riots. He married the actress **Priscilla Hopkins** (1755–1845) in 1787.

John's younger brother, **Stephen Kemble** (1758–1822), was also an actor and manager. His first major role was Shylock, in Dublin, but the success of his appearances on stage was often limited on account of his enormous bulk. He played Othello and even Hamlet, but is remembered as the only actor able to play Falstaff without padding. He became a prominent manager, running theatres in Edinburgh, Newcastle, and other northern towns, and was briefly manager of Drury Lane (1818).

John's youngest brother, **Charles Kemble** (1775–1854), was also an actor. He made his first stage appearance in *Macbeth*, alongside John and Sarah Siddons at the opening of Drury Lane. Initially he specialized in such parts as Richmond, Laertes, Edgar, and Mercutio but later moved on to play romantic leads. He inherited the management of Covent Garden in 1817 but only survived financially through the success of his daughter. Subsequently he toured the US. He retired in 1832 and was appointed Examiner of Plays. His wife was Maria Theresa *De Camp.

Charles's daughter, **Fanny Kemble** (Frances Anne Kemble; 1809–93), became an actress in 1829 when she was persuaded onto the stage at Covent Garden as Juliet by her father in an effort to avert bankruptcy. For three years she filled the theatre and made several profitable tours. She also toured the US, marrying an American, Pierce Butler, in 1834. In 1848 she divorced Butler and returned to England, partnering Macready in *Macbeth*, *Othello*, and other plays. Subsequently she embarked upon a series of successful dramatic readings.

Kemp, Robert (1908–67) Scottish playwright, who wrote in both Scots and English. His varied works include such pageants as *The Saxon Saint* (1949) and *The King of Scots* (1951), history plays, which include *John Knox* (1960), and light plays, notably *The Penny Wedding* (1957). He also adapted Lyndsay's *The Thrie Estaitis* for Guthrie in 1948; his finest play was *The Other Dear Charmer* (1951), which discussed Robert Burns's affair with Mrs MacLehose.

Kempe, William (fl. 1579–1600) English comic actor, who appeared in many of Shakespeare's early plays. Noted as a clown, he toured Holland and Denmark, eventually joining the Chamberlain's Men in 1594 and creating such roles as Dogberry in *Much Ado About Nothing* and Peter in *Romeo and Juliet*. He did not stay long at the Globe,

leaving to join Worcester's Men and to perform on the Continent. His nine days' morris dance from London to Norwich in 1600, undertaken for a bet, has passed into legend.

Kempson, Rachel *See* Redgrave, Sir Michael.

Kendal, Felicity (1946-) British actress, who grew up in India, where she toured from an early age in her parents' Shakespearean company. She made her London debut in 1967 and subsequently appeared in Ayckbourn's *The Norman Conquests* (1974) and in Frayn's *Clouds* (1978), before playing leading parts at the National Theatre, including Constanze in Peter Shaffer's *Amadeus* (1979) and Desdemona in *Othello* (1980). In 1988 she starred in Tom Stoppard's *Hapgood*.

Kendal, W H (William Hunter Grimston; 1843–1917) British actor-manager, who began in repertory in Glasgow before coming to the Haymarket in 1866, where he met the actress **Madge Sholto Robertson** (1848–1935), whom he married in 1869. Thereafter they always acted together, going into partnership at the St James's Theatre with John Hare in 1879. Always a reliable actor, he was admired in such parts as Andrew Quick in Ernest Hendrie and Metcalfe Wood's *The Elder Miss Blossom* (1898) and Frank Maitland in Godfrey's *The Queen's Shilling* (1879). Madge Kendal was even more popular, excelling in comic roles alongside her husband, although other parts included Ophelia (1865). W H Kendal was an excellent manager, toured several times in the US and the provinces, and played through two more London seasons at the St James's in 1901 and 1905.

Kenna, Peter (1930-) Australian actor, director, and playwright, who established his reputation with *The Slaughter of St Teresa's Day* (1959). Subsequent successs have included *Talk to the Moon* (1963), *Muriel's Virtues* (1966) – which he directed, the comedy *Listen Closely* (1972), and the trilogy *A Hard God* (1973), *Furtive Love* (1978), and *An Eager Hope* (1978).

Kenny, Sean (1932–73) British stage designer, architect, and director, born in Ireland, who made a reputation for his innovative approach to stage mechanics, especially working with Joan Littlewood and Lindsay Anderson on such plays as Behan's *The Hostage* (1958). He ultimately became Art Director at the Mermaid Theatre and a prominent figure with the National Theatre. His most celebrated productions included Lionel Bart's musicals *Oliver!* and *Blitz*, in which the moving sets were controlled by a minimum number of stage crew. He was also closely associated with the Chichester Festival Theatre and designed the New London Theatre.

Kern, Jerome (1885–1945) US composer, whose best-known musical was *Show Boat* (1927). Other successes included *Music in the Air* (1932), which – like *Show Boat* – was created in collaboration with Oscar Hammerstein II.

Kerr, Alfred (Alfred Kempner; 1867–1948) German theatre critic, who became one of the foremost advocates of naturalism in Germany. His writings, published in 1917 as *Die Welt in Drama*, supported the theories of Ibsen and Shaw among others, while later works refuted the Expressionists.

Khmelev, Nikolai Pavlovich (1901–45) Soviet actor and director, who eventually succeeded Nemirovich-Danchenko at the Moscow Art Theatre (1943). Earlier in his career he won acclaim in plays by Bulgakov, Chekhov, Ivanov, Maeterlinck, Pogodin, and Tolstoy at the Moscow Art Theatre, which he joined in 1919, and as director from 1937 of the Yermolova Theatre.

Kielland, Alexander (1849–1907) Norwegian novelist and playwright, whose masterpiece was the novel *Garman og Worse* (Garman and Worse; 1880), which he also adapted for the stage in 1883. Other dramatic pieces include *Tre Par* (Three Couples; 1886) and *Professoren* (The Professor; 1888).

Killigrew, Thomas (1612–83) English playwright and manager, who founded the Drury Lane Theatre in 1662. Noted for his wit, Killigrew was the author of several tragi-comedies, of which the licentious drama *The Parson's Wedding* (1641), modelled on a play by Calderón, was the most successful. During the Restoration he was – with Davenant – the dominant figure in serious drama, leading a company that included Mohun, Hart, and Nell Gwynn. In 1673 he succeeded Sir Henry Herbert as Master of the Revels.

Kimberley, Mrs Charlotte (1877–1939) British theatre manageress and playwright, who ran a circuit of provincial theatres from her base at the Grand Theatre in Wolverhampton. She wrote more than 40 popular melodramas, including *Tatters* (1919) and *Kiddie o' Mine* (1921).

Kinck, Hans (1865–1926) Norwegian novelist, short-story writer, and playwright, whose works concentrate upon social problems and highlight his love of nature and rural life. The poetic drama *Driftekaren* (The Drover; 1908) is his best-known play; others include its sequel, *Paa Rindalslægret* (At Rindal Camp; 1925)

King, Dennis (Dennis Pratt; 1897–1971) British actor and singer, who began his career in repertory at Birmingham but achieved fame in New York in 1924, when he played Jim Kenyon in *Rose Marie*. Thereafter he worked chiefly in the US; among his few London appearances were D'Artagnan in a musical version of *The*

Three Musketeers (1930) and Dinsmore in Mark Reed's farcical comedy *Petticoat Fever* (1936). In New York his range of parts included Jason in Euripides's *Medea* (1947), General Burgoyne in Shaw's *The Devil's Disciple* (1950), and Bruno Mahler in Kern's *Music in the Air* (1951) as well as leading roles in the plays of Chekhov, Ibsen, and Lillian Hellmann.

King, Hetty (1883–1972) British music hall performer, who topped the bills worldwide as a male impersonator. Her most famous song was 'All the Nice Girls Love a Sailor'.

King, Tom (1730–1804) British actor, who came to Drury Lane in 1748 in *A New Way to Pay Old Debts*. After a time in the provinces he returned to Drury Lane in 1759, appearing in numerous comedy roles. In 1766 he was acclaimed as Lord Ogleby in *The Clandestine Marriage*, and in 1777 he created Sir Peter Teazle in *The School for Scandal*.

King and I, The A musical, based on Margaret Langdon's *Anna and the King of Siam*, created by Richard Rodgers and Oscar *Hammerstein II. First performance: New York, 1951. The plot concerns an English governess who arrives in Siam to teach the king's 67 children and falls in love with him herself. The king was played by Yul Brynner opposite Gertrude Lawrence in the original production; while Brynner played opposite Deborah Kerr in the film version of 1956.

King John, The Life and Death of A history play by William *Shakespeare, written c. 1596. First performance: date unknown. A political study of the struggle between King John and the French, the play is notable chiefly for the witty character of Philip Falconbridge, who offers numerous comments upon contemporary politics and morality. The play also explores the conflict

of conscience involved when John's nobles are forced by their horror at his behaviour into siding with their country's enemies against their own king.

King Lear A tragedy by William *Shakespeare, written c. 1605. First performance: London, 1606. Lear's decision to divide his country between his three daughters according to the extent of their love for him precipitates the disintegration of his whole world and his own descent into madness and death. The play is widely regarded as one of Shakespeare's finest and is notable for its psychological complexity and great eloquence. The central role of the father, who is made wise by his own tragedy when it is already too late is considered one of the finest and most demanding parts for the older actor in the theatre.

King of Misrule *See* Misrule, Lord of.

King's Concert Rooms *See* Scala Theatre.

King's Jester *See* Court Fool.

Kingsley, Ben (1943-) British actor, who joined the Royal Shakespeare Company in 1970, his roles there including Squeers in *Nicholas Nickleby* (1980) and the title role in *Othello* (1985). In 1983 he starred in the one-man play *Edmund Kean* by Raymund FitzSimons at the Haymarket. For the National Theatre he has played Mosca in Jonson's *Volpone* and Sparkish in Wycherley's *The Country Wife* among other parts. He also won an Oscar for his portrayal of Gandhi in the film of that name.

Kingsley, Sidney (1906-) US playwright, whose first play, *Men in White* (1933), won a Pulitzer Prize. Subsequent plays have included *Dead End* (1935), *Ten Million Ghosts* (1936), *The World We Make* (1939), *The Patriots* (1943), *Detective Story* (1949), a dramatization of Arthur Koestler's

Darkness at Noon (1951), the farce *Lunatics and Lovers* (1954), and *Nightlife* (1962).

King's Men An English theatre company, which began as the (Chamberlain's Men. Renamed in 1603 on the accession of James I, the company was resident at the Globe (and later the Blackfriars Theatre) and included Shakespeare among its members. It performed many of Shakespeare's greatest plays, usually with Richard Burbage at the head of the cast, the company's business being managed first by Heminge and Condell and later by Taylor and Lowin. The King's Men also presented plays by such authors as Beaumont and Fletcher, Jonson, Webster, Middleton, and, later, Massinger and Shirley. After the death of James I, the company appeared under the patronage of Charles I at the Cockpit-in-Court and elsewhere; it disbanded in 1642 when the theatres were closed.

King's Theatre A theatre in the Hammersmith Road, London, which opened in 1902. Touring companies, including that of Sir Donald Wolfit, used the theatre until it adopted a repertory system and ultimately became a BBC venue; it was demolished in 1963. *See also* Her Majesty's Theatre.

Kingston, Gertrude (Gertrude Konstam; 1866–1937) British actress and manager, who enjoyed a long and successful acting career before building and opening the *Little Theatre in 1910 to house a repertory company. The theatre did not prosper, despite her own appearances on stage, but did much to nurture the repertory theatre system in Britain. In 1913 she acted in Shaw's *Great Catherine*, which was written for her.

Kingsway Theatre A theatre in Holborn, London, which opened in 1882 as a venue for comedy, called the **Novelty Theatre**. Renamed the **Folies-Dramatiques**, the **Jodrell Theatre**, and then the Novelty once more, it saw its first significant production in 1889 with the English premiere of Ibsen's *A Doll's House*, featuring Janet Achurch. After further changes of name (and the accidental stabbing to death of an actor in the drama *Sins of the Night*) the theatre was rebuilt by W S Penley as the **Great Queen Street Theatre**; performances during his tenure included Synge's *The Playboy of the Western World* (1907) by the Abbey Theatre company. Lena Ashwell ran the theatre for a time under its present name and was succeeded by Granville-Barker and Lillah McCarthy, who staged important works by Shaw and Arnold Bennett. In 1925 Barry Jackson brought his celebrated modern-dress *Hamlet* to the Kingsway, while in 1940 Sir Donald Wolfit staged a season of Shakespearean plays. It was bombed in World War II and demolished in 1956.

Kipphardt, Heinar (1922–82) German playwright, who became a leading writer of documentary drama. His best-known works, most of which explore the effects of political action upon helpless minorities, include *In der Sache J Robert Oppenheimer* (In the Matter of J Robert Oppenheimer; 1964), about McCarthyism in the US, and *Joel Brand* (1965); later works included the black comedy *Die Nacht, in der Chef geschlachtet wurde* (The Night the Boss was Slaughtered; 1967).

Kirchmayer, Thomas (1511–63) German playwright and humanist, who attacked the Roman Catholic church in several plays. Using the name **Naogeorg**, he was the author of *Pammachius* (1538), which was also performed in England in an adaptation by John Bale.

Kisfaludy, Károly (1788–1830) Hungarian poet and playwright, author of the first notable Hungarian comedies. His plays, which brought common rural characters onto the Hungarian stage for the first time, include *A Tatárok Magyarországon* (1819), *Kérök* (1819), and *Csalódások* (1828).

Kitchen, Michael (1948-) British actor, who was with the National Youth Theatre and at the Belgrade Theatre, Coventry, before attending RADA. An actor of considerable versatility, he has often appeared with the National Theatre Company in such plays as Ayckbourn's *Bedroom Farce* (1977) and Stoppard's *Rough Crossing* (1984). With the Royal Shakespeare Company he played Mercutio in *Romeo and Juliet* and Bolingbroke in *Richard II* during 1986–87, as well as Hogarth in Nick Dear's *The Art of Success*.

kitchen-sink drama A genre of British theatre that attracted much attention in the 1950s. Originally intended as a derogatory epithet, the phrase invoked the working-class settings of such innovative plays as John Osborne's *Look Back in Anger* (1956) and works by Arnold Wesker, in contrast to the middle-class world of the West End theatre at that time.

Kivi, Alexsis (Alexsis Stenvall; 1834–72) Finnish novelist and playwright, regarded as the father of the modern Finnish theatre. His tragedy *Kullervo* (1860) established his reputation; subsequent works for the stage include his acclaimed rural comedy *Nummisuutarit* (The Village Cobblers), *Kihlaus* (The Betrothed), the biblical play *Lea*, and *Karkurit* (The Refugees).

Kjer, Bodil (1917-) Danish actress, who became one of the leading performers at the Kongelige Teater in Copenhagen. Making her debut in 1937, she was subsequently praised in plays ranging from Greek tragedy to Molière and Strindberg as well as in contemporary Danish works.

Klaw Theatre A theatre on 45th Street, between Broadway and Eighth Avenue, New York, which opened in 1921 with *Nice People* by Rachel Crothers. The Theatre Guild occupied it in 1925–26 and presented notable plays by G B Shaw; it was later renamed the **Avon Theatre** and, in the late 1930s, became a broadcasting studio. It was demolished in 1954.

Kleist, (Bernd Wilhelm) Heinrich von (1777–1811) German playwright, whose powerful dramas had a strong influence on the Romantic movement. After resigning from the Prussian army, he produced several dramas on pathological themes; subsequently, whilst he was in a French prison as a suspected spy, he adapted Molière's *Amphitryon* before embarking upon his intense poetic play *Penthesilea*, now regarded as one of his finest works. *The *Broken Jug* was realized as a German comic classic only after Kleist's death, while *Prinz Friedrich von Homburg* was also later praised as a penetrating psychological drama. Depressed by lack of recognition by Goethe and others, Kleist killed himself in a suicide pact with a terminally ill woman at the age of 34.
Principal works:
Die Familie Schroffenstein: 1804.
Robert Guiskard: 1808.
Penthesilea: 1808.
Der Zerbrochene Krug: 1808; translated as *The Broken Jug* (or *The Chippit Chantie*).
Die Hermannsschlacht: 1871 (written 1808).
Käthchen von Heilbronn: 1810.
Prinz Friedrich von Homburg: 1821; translated as *The Prince of Homburg*.

Klinger, Friedrich Maximilian (1752–1831) German playwright and novelist, whose play *Der Wirrwarr oder Sturm und Drang* (1777) inaugurated the *Sturm und Drang* movement. Klinger's early plays, which included *Die Zwillinge* (The Twins; 1776), were impassioned rebellions against rationalism and owed much to the works of Shakespeare; later, however, he wrote comedies and historical tragedies of a more conventional type.

Klopstock, Friedrich Gottlob (1724–1803) German poet, who was also the author of six plays on religious and historical themes. These comprise a trilogy on German history that takes the warrior Arminius as its central character and the religious works *Der Tod Adams* (1757), *Salomo* (1769), and *David* (1772), which were influenced by Milton's *Paradise Lost*.

Knepp, Mary (d. 1677) English actress, who was trained by Killigrew and appeared in his first company at Drury Lane. She often performed in the comedies of Sir Charles Sedley, whose mistress she became, and was much admired by Samuel Pepys.

Knickerbocker Theatre A theatre on 38th Street and Broadway, New York, which opened as Abbey's Theatre in 1893 and enjoyed early success with appearances by Irving and Ellen Terry. In 1896 the theatre was taken over by Al Hayman and renamed the Knickerbocker. A number of celebrated actors and actresses appeared there, including Lillian Russell, Sarah Bernhardt, Maude Adams, and Otis Skinner. The theatre was demolished in 1930.

Knight of the Burning Pestle, The A comedy by Sir Francis *Beaumont. First performance: c. 1607. Written for the boy company at the Blackfriars Theatre, the play was a highly successful satire of the romantic histories currently popular.

Knipper-Chekhova, Olga (Leonardovna) (1870–1959) Russian actress, who married Chekhov in 1901. She was highly acclaimed as her husband's heroines – notably as Masha in *Three Sisters* – in performances at the Moscow Art Theatre, of which she was a founding member. She stayed with the company after the Revolution, making her last appearance in 1946, in Oscar Wilde's *An Ideal Husband*. Other Chekhovian roles she created included Madame Ranevskaya in *The Cherry Orchard* (1904).

Knoblock, Edward (Edward Knoblauch; 1874–1945) US playwright, later a British citizen, who became famous for his many adaptations of foreign works and novels for the stage. His most popular plays included *The Good Companions* (1931) – a version of J B Priestley's novel, and an adaptation of Vicki Blaum's *Grand Hotel* (1931) as well as his immensely successful fantasy *Kismet* (1911), which was based on a French original, and *Marie-Odile* (1915). Other works numbered amongst them *Milestones* (1912), upon which he collaborated with Arnold Bennett.

Knowles, (James) Sheridan (1784–1862) British actor and playwright, who was born in Ireland. His first work to be produced was *Caius Gracchus* (1815); later his tragedy *Virginius; or, the Liberation of Rome* was successfully produced by Macready at Covent Garden in 1820. Among his other plays were *The Hunchback* (1832) and *The Love Chase* (1837).

Knox, Teddy *See* Crazy Gang.

Knudsen, Erik (1922-) Danish poet and playwright, whose dramas satirize such subjects as advertising and the pop culture of the 1960s. His best-known works include such plays as *Friedleben* (1954), the musical *Frihed det bedste Guld* (Freedom the Best Gold; 1961), and the political farce *Laen Dem ikke ud* (1966).

Koch, Esther *See* Brandes, Johann Christian.

Koch, Frederick Henry (1877–1944) US theatre scholar, who did much to promote drama education in the US university system. He was particularly noted for his influential work at the University of North Carolina and for his training of Paul Green and other significant US playwrights.

Koch, Heinrich Gottfried (1703–75) German actor-manager, who was a prominent member of Carolina Neuber's company before eventually taking over Schönemann's troupe. His finest roles were in classical comedy, although he also appeared in tragedy and was active as a scene-painter; he was acclaimed as a manager and ultimately settled his company in Leipzig.

Koltai, Ralph (1924-) German stage designer, who has spent most of his career in the British theatre. He established his reputation with his designs for the Royal Shakespeare Company, which he became associated with in 1962, for plays by Brecht and Marlowe and others as well as Shakespeare. Subsequently he has also been acclaimed for designs for the National Theatre, where his successes have included Ibsen's *Brand* (1978) and Brecht's *Baal* (1979). Recent designs include those for Horace McCoy's *They Shoot Horses, Don't They?* (1987) at the Mermaid Theatre.

Komisarjevskaya, Vera Fedorovna (1846–1910) Russian actress and manager, who established her reputation at the Alexandrinsky Theatre, which he joined in 1896. Sister of the director Theodore *Komisarjevsky, she appeared in the unsuccessful first production of Chekhov's *The Seagull* and subsequently founded her own theatre (in her own name), where she presented major dramas by Chekhov, Gorky, and Ibsen among others from 1905. Later she presented a number of Symbolist dramas, working briefly with Meyerhold, and visited the US. Her finest roles included Ibsen's Nora and Hedda Gabler.

Komisarjevskaya Theatre A theatre in Leningrad, which was opened in 1904 by Vera *Komisarjevskaya. Staging works by major Russian authors, it was directed by Meyerhold from 1906 to 1907 and saw several influential Surrealist productions. Subsequently Nikolai Evreinov and Theodore Komisarjevsky worked at the theatre until the company broke up in 1908. The theatre was reopened in 1959.

Komisarjevsky, Theodore (1882–1954) Russian director and designer, who did much to popularize the theories of Stanislavsky in Britain after emigrating from Russia in 1919. The brother of the actress Vera *Komisarjevskaya, he established his reputation in Britain at the Barnes Theatre in the 1920s with his lively productions of plays by Chekhov and other Russian authors. Later he attracted further attention at the Shakespeare Memorial Theatre with such plays as *Macbeth* (1933), which featured aluminium scenery, *King Lear* (1936), and *The Taming of the Shrew* (1939). His wife, Peggy Ashcroft, appeared in many of his productions.

Komissarov, Aleksandr Mikhailovich (1904–79) Russian actor, who became a leading performer at the Moscow Art Theatre, which he joined in 1924. He was particularly admired in comic roles in the works of Beaumarchais, Sheridan, and Tolstoy but also appeared in Chekhov and Gogol. Later roles included Alyosha in Gorky's *The Lower Depths* and Bobchinsk in *The Government Inspector*.

Kongelige Teater A theatre in Copenhagen, which was first opened in 1748. In 1770 it came under royal patronage and was enlarged; rebuilt in 1874, it became famous for its productions of Ibsen's plays. A second stage (the Stærekassen) was opened in 1931.

Koonen, Alisa Georgievna (1889–1974) Soviet actress, who was married to Alexander Taîrov, with whom she founded the *Kamerny Theatre in 1914. Having begun with the Moscow Art Theatre, she then worked under Mardzhanov before meeting Taîrov and working closely with him until 1950. Notable performances under her husband's direction included Scribe's Adrienne Lecouvreur (1919) and roles in Racine, Shakespeare, and Shaw.

Kopit, Arthur (1937-) US playwright, whose early plays included *On the Runway of Life You Never Know What's Coming Off Next* (1957), *Across the River and Into the Jungle* (1958), *Sing To Me Through Open Windows* (1959), and the celebrated farce *Oh Dad, Poor Dad, Mamma's Hung You In the Closet and I'm Feelin' So Sad* (1960). His other works include *The Day the Whores Came Out to Play Tennis* (1965), *Indians* (1968), *Wings* (1979), the musical *Nine* (1980), and *End of the World (with Symposium to Follow)* (1984).

Korneichuk, Alexander Evdokimovich (1905–72) Soviet playwright, whose plays observe all the conventions of Socialist Realism. His works range from *The Wreck of the Squadron* (1934), which depicts events from the civil war, and *Front* (1942), which was set against the German invasion of the Ukraine, to the satirical comedy *Mr Perkins's Mission to the Land of the Bolsheviks* (1944) and *Makar Dobrava* (1948).

Korsh Theatre A theatre in Moscow, which opened in 1882. Between 1885 and 1912 it became famous for a variety of Russian and foreign productions presented by its accomplished company, which included Leonidov, Moskvin, and Orlenev. It was finally closed in 1932.

Kortner, Fritz (1892–1970) Austrian actor and director, who became a leading performer of Expressionist drama under the direction of Jessner. Early in his career he became famous for his passionate style of delivery in such roles as Richard III and Gessler in Schiller's *Wilhelm Tell* but he later adopted a more thoughtful approach in performances of plays by Shakespeare, Ibsen, and Sophocles among others. He also appeared in films in the US and after World War II directed authoritative versions of Shakespeare and Molière as well as many German classics.

Koster and Bial's Music Hall A theatre on West 23rd Street, New York, which was previously called **Bryant's Opera House**. Koster and Bial enlarged and reopened it in 1879 for musical shows and by 1881 it had a good reputation for light entertainment featuring famous vaudeville stars from abroad. Koster and Bial left in 1893 and it closed. Subsequently it reopened briefly as the **Bon Ton Theatre** but was demolished in 1924.

Kott, Jan (1914-) Polish critic and theatre scholar, who has attracted much attention for his controversial views of the plays of Shakespeare. His critical writings have examined such aspects as sexual psychology and the influence of changing society upon the plays; they have had some impact upon the productions of Peter Brook.

Kotzebue, August (Friedrich Ferdinand) von (1761–1819) German playwright, who was a prolific author of popular sentimental melodrama loosely derived from the *Sturm und Drang* movement. His many well-constructed plays include lurid historical dramas, comedies, and studies of German bourgeois society; among the most successful were the melodrama *Menschenhass und Reue* (1789) and *Die Spanier in Peru* (1796), which was adapted by Sheridan as *Pizarro*. He divided his time between Germany and Russia and was director of the German theatre in St Petersburg.

Koun, Karolos (1908-) Greek director, who established his reputation with a series of productions of classical plays in Athens in the 1930s. Subsequently he has won acclaim for plays by such modern writers as Ibsen, Tennessee Williams, and Pirandello and has presented successful productions by the Greek National Theatre company in Paris and London and elsewhere. He has also worked with the Royal Shakespeare Company, producing *Romeo and Juliet* in 1967.

Krannert Centre for the Performing Arts An arts centre in Urbana, Illinois, which opened in 1969. With four indoor theatres and an outdoor amphitheatre seating 560, it is one of the largest university performance centres in the US. The Great Hall is used for concerts, the Festival Theatre for opera, ballet, and modern dance, the Playhouse for drama, and the Studio Theatre for experimental theatre and music.

Krapp's Last Tape (*La Dernière Bande*) A one-act play by Samuel *Beckett, written in 1957. First performance: Royal Court Theatre, 1958. In this monologue an old man listens to the tape he recorded 30 years before, trying to recapture a fleeting love affair he had as a man in his prime: reconciling the past with the present proves both painful and comic.

Krasiński, Zygmunt (1812–59) Polish playwright and poet, author of several Romantic dramas reflecting revolutionary ideals. His plays, which were published anonymously, include *Nieboska komedia* (The Undivine Comedy; 1835), which was influenced by Goethe's *Faust* and anticipated the political upheavals of the early 20th century, and *Irydon* (not performed until 1908), which has a classical setting. Leon Schiller was among his many modern admirers.

Krasnya Presnya Theatre See Realistic Theatre.

Krauss, Werner (1884–1959) Austrian actor, who was widely praised in the plays of Shakespeare and in other classical roles. Seen chiefly in Berlin and Vienna, he established his reputation in a series of plays by Wedekind and later excelled in such intense parts as Macbeth and Lear, although he also won acclaim in modern dramas by Shaw and others. His committed performance in Feuchtwanger's *Jew Süss* under the Nazis led to his trial after the war.

Krejča, Otomar (1921–) Czech director, who established an international reputation with productions for the *Theatre Behind the Gate, which he founded in 1965. He began his career at the Vinohrady Theatre and then worked with the National Theatre, where his successes included *Hamlet* and plays by Chekhov and Josef Topol. After the Theatre Behind the Gate disbanded in 1972 Krejča eventually moved (1976) to Germany.

Kristiania Theater A theatre in Oslo (formerly Kristiania or Christiania), which was founded in 1827. The first theatre was destroyed by fire in 1835 and reopened in 1837, staging an almost entirely Danish programme. The first native Norwegian works were presented after 1850, notably the plays of Bjornson and Ibsen (who were both closely associated with the management of the theatre), and it became the focus of the national drama. In 1852 the theatre amalgamated with the rival Det Norske Teatret and ultimately, in 1899, the company transferred to the new *Nationaltheatret under Bjornson.

Krleža, Miroslav (1893–1981) Yugoslavian playwright, novelist, essayist, and poet, who was the author of several influential cycles of plays. *Legende* (1933), based upon the stories of Christ, Michelangelo, and Columbus, depicts the futile struggle to find meaning in existence; later social dramas – notably the trilogies *Golgota* (1920–23) and *The Gemblays* (1928–30) – reflect his strong nationalist and socialist views.

Krog, Helge (1889–1962) Norwegian playwright, essayist, and theatre critic, whose first play, *Det store Vi* (The Great We; 1917), criticized exploitation by the press. His later plays show the influence of Gunnar, Heiberg and Ibsen, the most successful including *Konkylien* (Happily Ever After; 1929) and *Oppbrudd* (Break-Up; 1936).

Krones, Therese (1801–30) Austrian actress, who established herself as a major actress of exceptional promise before her early death ended her career. She made her first appearance in Vienna in 1821 and attracted attention for her forceful acting and skill at improvisation, excelling in the comedies of Gleich, Meisl, Bauerle, and Raimund, especially as Youth in *Der Bauer als Millionar* (1826).

Kruczkowski, Leon (1900–62) Polish novelist and playwright, who established his reputation in the theatre with a stage adaptation of his novel *Kordian i cham* (1935), which was produced by Leon Schiller. Other works included *A Hero of Our Time* (1935), the first of several plays attacking the Nazis, and *Julius and Ethel* (1954), which defended the alleged spies, the Rosenbergs.

Kummerfeld, Karoline (1745–1815) German actress, who began her career with Ackermann's company in 1758. After falling foul of Sophie Hensel on account of her popularity she transferred to Leipzig and subsequently Gotha and Mannheim, winning the praise of Goethe, Ekhof, and Dalberg.

Kungliga Dramatiska Teatern A theatre in Stockholm, which was established in 1737. Under various names and based in a succession of buildings, the original company eventually combined with the Swedish Royal Opera in 1792 and moved into its own Kungliga Mindre Teatern in 1794. After a fire in 1825, the company transferred to the Opera House until 1863 when it acquired a new home. The present theatre opened in 1908 with a performance of one of Strindberg's plays, a studio being added in 1936 and the whole complex being renovated in 1957–60.

Kuppelhorizont An early form of cyclorama invented by **Mariano Fortuny** (1871–1949) in 1902; it consisted of a dome of reflective coloured silk.

Kurbas, Alexander Stephanovich (1887–1942) Soviet actor and director, who became a leading figure in the development of the theatre in the Ukraine in the 1920s and 1930s. He was particularly active in the theatre at Kharkov, where he emphasized the influence of the director over all aspects of a production; the quality of the company he formed there was highly praised.

Kurz, Joseph Felix von (1715–84) Austrian actor, who was a leading figure in Viennese comedy of the 18th century. He was responsible for creating the stock character *Bernadon, but outlived the popularity of the conventional improvised comedy in which he excelled.

Kvapil, Jaroslav (1868–1953) Czech playwright and director, who was the author of several popular plays based on folktales. As a director he presented 21 plays by Shakespeare at Prague's National Theatre between 1900 and 1918.

Kyd, Thomas (1558–94) English playwright and friend of Christopher Marlowe who, like him, was arrested on charges of atheism. None of his early work survives and he remains best known for The *Spanish Tragedy*, which initiated the genre of the revenge tragedy. Kyd is also thought to have written a pre-Shakespearean version of *Hamlet*, now lost, and possibly to have contributed to *Titus Andronicus* and *Arden of Faversham*.

Kynaston, Ned (Edward Kynaston; c. 1640–1706) English actor, one of the last boy actors to play female roles. He was highly acclaimed playing women at the Cockpit under Rhodes and at the Vere Street Theatre under Killigrew. He went on to play important male roles at Drury Lane, excelling as Shakespeare's Henry IV.

Kyōgen A form of Japanese farce, which was traditionally presented after or between *Nō* plays. Usually performed by the minor actors in the *Nō* production, the *Kyōgen* is customarily acted out without the use of musical accompaniment or masks and with highly stylized movements.

L

Laberius, Decimus (106 BC–42 BC) Roman nobleman, who was the author of the earliest written mime dramas. Having provoked Julius Caesar, he was forced to appear in one of his own mimes in about 45 BC in open rivalry with Publilius Syrus. Parts of 42 of his mimes have survived.

Labiche, Eugène (1815–88) French playwright, who was the author or coauthor of more than 170 light comedies and farces in the vaudeville tradition. After his first play in 1838 he wrote prolifically for some 40 years; his most successful plays included *Un chapeau de paille d'Italie* (An *Italian Straw Hat; 1851), *Le Voyage de M Perrichon* (1860), *La Poudre aux yeux* (1861), and *La Cagnotte* (1864).

Labor Stage *See* Princess Theatre.

La Calprenède, Gautier de Costes de (c. 1610–63) French novelist and playwright. His plays, tragedies and tragi-comedies in the classical tradition, include *La Mort de Mithridate* (1635), *Bradamante* (1637), and *Le Comte d'Essex* (1638).

Lacey, Catherine (1904–79) British actress, whose first big success was as Leonora Yale in Mordaunt Shairp's *The Green Bay Tree* (1933). Noted for her powerful emotional acting, she went on to play Shakespearean parts at Stratford-upon-Avon and the Old Vic, Clytemnestra in both Sopho-cles's *Electra* (1951) and Aeschylus's *Oresteia* (1961), and Elizabeth I in Schiller's *Mary Stuart* (1958). Her Agatha in Eliot's *The Family Reunion* (1939 and 1946) was also highly praised.

La Chapelle, Jean de (1655–1723) French playwright and novelist. A nobleman in the service of the Prince de Conti, he wrote four tragedies, notably *Cléopâtre* (1681), and the comedy *Les Carrosses d'Orléans*.

La Chaussée, Pierre Claude Nivelle de (1692–1754) French playwright, who was the creator of the *comédie larmoyante*, a genre of popular sentimental comedy. La Chaussée was over 40 when he began writing plays; such moralizing comedies as *La Fausse Antipathie* (1733), *Le Préjugé à la mode* (1735), and *Mélanide* (1741), which blend pathos with humour, gave rise to the bourgeois drama of Diderot and others.

Lackaye, Wilton (1862–1932) US actor, who first appeared professionally in New York in Boker's *Francesca da Rimini* in 1883. After numerous appearances alongside Fanny Davenport he went on to win acclaim in many Shakespearean and contemporary roles, including Svengali in Du Maurier's *Trilby* (1895); in 1904 he produced and played in Ibsen's *The Pillars of Society*. A highly respected actor, he was seldom absent from the stage until his retirement in 1927 and was a cofounder of the American Actors' Equity Association.

Lacy, John (d. 1681) English actor, who was a member of the first Drury Lane company. He was much admired as Falstaff and created Bayes in Buckingham's *The Rehearsal*. He wrote several plays, *The Old Troop or Monsieur Raggou* being based on his experiences during the Civil War.

Lady Elizabeth's Men An English theatre company that was formed under the patronage of James I's daughter in 1611. Members of the company appeared at Court and at the Hope under Henslowe until disbanding in 1614, then (reformed in 1622) at the Cockpit under Christoper Beeston; leading actors with the company included Nathan Field. The reformed company presented several plays by such major authors as Middleton and Rowley, Massinger, and Heywood before breaking up in 1625 because of plague.

Lady of the Camellias, The (*La Dame aux camélias*) A play by Alexandre *Dumas *fils*, also known in English as *Camille*. First performance: Paris, 1852. Adapted from Dumas's novel of the same name, the play provided the basis of Verdi's opera *La Traviata* (1853). The plot centres on the courtesan Marguerite Gautier and culminates in her death from tuberculosis in the arms of her lover.

Lady's Not For Burning, The A poetic comedy by Christopher *Fry. First performance: Arts Theatre, London, 1948. Set in the Middle Ages, this romantic comedy in which the heroine is accused of witchcraft was widely praised for its eloquent use of language. The role of Thomas Mendip provided a fine role for Alec Clunes at the Arts Theatre and subsequently for John Gielgud at the Globe.

Lady Windermere's Fan A comedy by Oscar *Wilde. First performance: 1892. Lady Windermere, believing her husband is involved with Mrs Erlynne, decides to elope with Lord Darlington. When Lord Windermere discovers his wife's fan in Lord Darlington's apartments, Mrs Erlynne claims that she took it by mistake, suggesting that she herself had an assignation with Darlington.

La Fleur *See* Gros-Guillaume.

La Fosse, Antoine d'Aubigny de (1653–1708) French playwright, who was born in Paris. *Manlius Capitolinus* (1698), which is generally regarded as the best of La Fosse's tragedies, was inspired by Thomas Otway's *Venice Preserv'd*.

Lagerkrist, Pär (1891–1974) Swedish poet, novelist, and playwright, who won a Nobel Prize in 1951. His Expressionist plays *Den svåra stunden* (The Difficult Hour; 1918) and *Himlens hemlighet* (The Secret of Heaven; 1921) were profoundly influenced by the writings of Strindberg and concern the anxiety of life without meaning and hope; of his later more optimistic works the most important include *De vises sten* (The Philosopher's Stone; 1948), *Låt människan leva* (Let Man Live; 1951), and *Barabbas* (1953).

La Grange (Charles Varlet; 1639–92) French actor, who was a prominent member of Molière's company at the Palais-Royal. He played young lovers in several plays by Molière and Racine and kept invaluable records of all the company's activities. After Molière's death he helped to run the troupe and edited an edition of Molière's plays, published in 1682.

His wife, **Marie La Grange** (1639–1727), appeared under the stagename Marotte in plays by Molière and Rostand and eventually joined the Comédie-Française.

Lagrange-Chancel, François-Joseph de (1677–1758) French playwright and author of satirical pamphlets attacking the Duc d'Orléans. His dramatic works consist of mediocre tragedies on classical themes, notably *Ino et Mélicerte* (1713).

La Harpe, Jean-François de (1739–1803) French playwright and critic, who was the embittered author of several undistinguished tragedies. *Le Comte de Warwick* (1763) and *Mélanie* (1778) were among the best of these; far better, however, was his critical work *Cours de littérature ancienne et* *moderne* (1799–1805), in which he excelled in his discussion of drama of the 17th century.

Lahr, Bert (Irving Lahrheim; 1895–1967) US actor, who became a star of vaudeville and burlesque. He was very successful as the prizefighter in the musical *Hold Everything* (1928) and went on to appear in the revues *Life Begins at 8.40* (1934), *George White's Scandals of 1936* (1935), and *The Show is On* (1938). He also played in the musical *Du Barry Was a Lady* (1939), *Waiting for Godot* (1956), *Hotel Paradiso* (1957), and *A Midsummer Night's Dream* (1960). He is best remembered as the Cowardly Lion in the film *The Wizard of Oz* (1939).

La Mama Experimental Theatre Club An avant-garde theatre group founded as the **Café La Mama** in New York in 1961 by Ellen Stewart. Among the group's first productions was the musical *Hair* (1967); subsequent shows included several utilizing rock music in a similar way. Groups modelled after La Mama have been formed in the UK, Australia, Canada, South America, and throughout Europe; the **Mabou Mines** group in Nova Scotia, founded in 1970, was among the most successful.

Lamb, Charles (1775–1834) British essayist and writer. As well as writing poetry and contributing articles on drama to periodicals he wrote several plays, of which *Mr H* was unsuccessfully produced at Drury Lane in 1806. The following year his *Tales from Shakespeare*, written jointly with his sister **Mary Lamb** (1764–1847), was well received.

Lambs A supper club founded in London during the 1860s. Its members – never more than 24 in number – included such distinguished theatrical figures as Squire Bancroft and Henry Irving. Disbanded in the 1890s, it spawned a US counterpart – which still exists – in New York in 1875.

LAMDA *See* London Academy of Music and Dramatic Art.

La Motte-Houdar *See* Houdar de La Motte, Antoine.

Lanchester, Elsa *See* Laughton, Charles.

Landen, Dinsdale (James) (1932–) British actor, who toured Australia with the Old Vic company before appearing in London in Rodney Ackland's *Dead Secret* (1957). Subsequently he played Shakespearean roles at Stratford-upon-Avon and at the Open Air Theatre, Regent's Park, and was John in Michael Frayn's *Alphabetical Order* (1975). For the National Theatre he has appeared in such plays as Ben Travers's *Plunder* (1976 and 1978), Shaw's *The Philanderer* (1978), and Chekhov's *Uncle Vanya* (1982).

Lander, Mrs (Jean Margaret Davenport; 1829–1903) US actress, who was the daughter of a British actor-manager with whom she appeared in New York in 1838, playing Young Norval in Home's *Douglas* and even, during her adolescence, Shylock and Sir Peter Teazle. As an adult she developed a substantial range of parts, including Marguerite in *La Dame aux camélias* by Dumas *fils* and Peg Woffington in Reade's *Masks and Faces*. She continued after her husband, General Lander, was killed in the US Civil War, until her final appearance in 1877 as Hester Prynne in her own version of Hawthorne's *The Scarlet Letter*.

Land of Heart's Desire, The A poetic drama by W B *Yeats. First performance: 1894. Based on an old Irish legend, it tells how a fairy disguised as a child appears in the home of an elderly farmer and lures his wife away.

Lane, Louisa *See* Drew, Mrs John.

Lane, Lupino (Henry George Lupino; 1892–1959) British actor, who made his

London debut as a comedian in 1903. He went on to star in musical comedies in London and New York and also to appear in films, while in 1935 he created the character Bill Snibson in *Twenty to One*; he played the same character again with great success two years later in another musical, *Me and My Girl*, which he also produced and directed.

Lane, Sam (1804–71) British theatre manager, who managed the *Britannia Theatre following the change in the licensing law in 1843. He staged both full-blooded dramas and comedies; after he died, his widow **Sara Lane** (1823–99) continued to manage the theatre, appearing annually in its famous pantomime.

Lang, (Alexander) Matheson (1879–1948) British actor-manager and playwright, born in Canada, who first appeared on stage in 1897 in Wolverhampton. Subsequently he moved to London, toured the West Indies, and then returned in 1900 to work under Vedrenne and Granville-Barker at the Royal Court in plays by Ibsen and Shaw. After scoring his first great success in Hall Caine's *The Christian* (1907), he founded his own company, and toured the world, presenting Shakespeare's plays and modern romantic drama. Subsequently he was acclaimed in the title role of *Mr Wu* (1913), a melodrama by Harry Vernon and Harold Owen, and in the Shakespearean productions of Lilian Baylis at the Old Vic Theatre.

His wife, **Nellie Britton** (Hutin Britton; 1876–1965), was the leading actress with her husband's company.

Langendijk, Pieter (1683–1756) Dutch playwright, author of several notable comedies much influenced by the works of Molière. His plays include *The Mutual Marriage Hoax* (1714), which is regarded as the finest Dutch comedy of manners of the time.

Langer, František (1888–1965) Czech playwright, whose best-known play was the comedy *The Camel Through the Needle's Eye* (1923), which was brought to Broadway by the Theatre Guild in 1929. Other works included the serious Expressionist dramas *Periphery* (1925) and *The Angel in Our Midst* (1931).

Langham, Michael (1919–) British director, who won praise for his work with the Stratford (Ontario) Festival (1956–67) and at the Guthrie Theatre (1971–78) in Minneapolis, at both of which he was successor to Guthrie himself. He presided over a fine company at Stratford (Ontario), productions ranging from Shakespeare to Marlowe, Gilbert and Sullivan, and Molière; his successes at the Guthrie Theatre included Rostand's *Cyrano de Bergerac* (1971) and Wilder's *The Matchmaker* (1976).

Langner, Lawrence (1890–1962) US patent agent and director, born in Wales, who was a cofounder of the Washington Square Players (1914) and of the Theatre Guild. He directed over 200 plays for the Theatre Guild and also founded the American Shakespeare Theatre at Stratford, Connecticut and the New York Repertory Company (1931) as well as writing several plays himself.

Langtry, Lillie (Emilie Charlotte Le Breton; 1853–1929) British actress, daughter of the Dean of Jersey. Known as The Jersey Lily, her fame as a beauty and as mistress of the future King Edward VII ensured a sensational response when she took to the stage. She began with small parts but eventually graduated to play Rosalind, Cleopatra, and other leading roles in England and the US with her own company.

La Noue, Jean Sauve de (1701–c. 1761) French actor and playwright, whose play *Mahomet II* (1739) provided Voltaire with the raw material for his *Mahomet, ou le* *fanatisme* (1742). Voltaire took steps to ensure La Noue was allowed to give the first performance of his play and subsequently arranged for him to play the title role himself at the Comédie-Française in 1742.

Lansbury, Angela (1925-) US actress, born in Britain, who made her New York debut in 1957 in *Hotel Paradiso*. She went on to appear in such works as Sondheim's *Anyone Can Whistle* (1964), *Gypsy* (1974), and *Sweeney Todd* (1979) as well as making many television appearances.

Lantern Theatre A theatre in Dublin, which opened in a cellar in 1957. In 1963 it was reopened in new premises and became well known for productions of poetic drama, Shakespeare, and works by native Irish authors, including Yeats, Padraic Colum, and O'Casey. The theatre closed in 1972 due to insurance problems stemming from the close proximity of the British Embassy.

Laplace, Pierre Antoine de (1707–93) French scholar, who translated numerous English plays into French. His *Théâtre Anglais* (1745–48) introduced many of Shakespeare's plays to French audiences for the first time.

Laporte *See* Venier, Marie.

Lapotaire, Jane (1944-) British actress, who, after working at the Bristol Old Vic, played Jessica in *The Merchant of Venice* (1970) and other parts with the National Theatre company and then joined the Royal Shakespeare Company in 1974. She had outstanding success in 1978 in the title role of Pam Gems's *Piaf* in London and, later, New York; other successes at the National Theatre have included Otway's *Venice Preserv'd* (1983) and *Antigone* (1984). In 1988 she acted in a French version of Jean-Claude Carrière's *L'Aide-Mémoire* in Paris.

Larivey, Pierre de (c. 1540–1619) French playwright, who was noted for his spirited adaptations in French of Italian comedies, collected as *Comédies facétieuses* (1579, 1611). His nine plays, of which *Les Ésprits* was the most widely known, had a strong influence upon Molière; other works include *Le Laquais, La Veuve,* and *Les Jaloux.*

Lark, The (*L'Alouette*) A *pièce costumée* by Jean *Anouilh. First performance: Paris, 1953. It was translated into English by Christopher Fry and also adapted by Lillian Hellman. This is Anouilh's interpretation of Joan of Arc's trial for heresy. Its production in London in 1955 with Dorothy Tutin was highly successful.

Laroche, Johann (1745–1806) Austrian actor, who created the character *Kasperl in 1764 in Graz. Subsequently he appeared in Vienna under Marinelli, where he became one of the leading comedians of his day.

Laroque (Pierre Regnault Petit-Jean; c. 1595–1676) French actor, who succeeded to the leadership of Montdory's company at the Théâtre du Marais. Despite his abilities as a manager the Marais eventually had to resort to staging elaborate machine plays as a result of the rivalry with the Molière and the Hôtel de Bourgogne. Players with the company during his time included Mlle Champmeslé.

Larra y Sanchez de Castro, Mariano José de (1809–37) Spanish playwright and journalist, noted for his satires on contemporary society. As well as writing theatre criticism and adapting French plays for the Spanish theatre, he wrote the play *Macías* (1834), in which he expressed his Romantic ideals. He committed suicide on being rejected by his mistress.

L'Arronge, Adolf (1838–1908) German playwright and director, who founded the Deutsches Theater in Berlin in 1883. He was responsible for assembling a fine company, later inherited by Otto Brahm, and helped reform contemporary acting styles; his plays include *Mein Leopold* (1873), *Hasemanns Töchter* (1877), and *Doktor Klaus* (1878).

La Rue, Danny (Daniel Patrick Carroll; 1928-) British female impersonator, born in Ireland, who played in the chorus of drag shows, pantomimes, and revues before achieving fame in cabaret and on television. Subsequently, he has been immensely successful in spectacular pantomimes and such revues as *Danny La Rue at the Palace* (1970).

lashline *See* throwline.

Lashwood, George (1864–1942) British music hall performer, who made his London debut at the Middlesex Music Hall in 1889. Billed as 'The Beau Brummel of the Halls' because of his elegant attire, he performed such popular songs as 'The Death and Glory Boys' and 'After the Ball'.

La Taille, Jean de (c. 1540–c. 1608) French poet, playwright, and author of the treatise *De l'art de la tragédie* (1572), in which he formulated some of the basic rules of classical tragedy, notably that of the *unities. His plays include the comedy *Les Corriveaux* (1574).

Laterna Magica *See* Svoboda, Josef.

La Thorillière, Françoise Lenoir de (1626–80) French actor, who performed in the provinces before first appearing at the Théâtre du Marais in 1659. Subsequently he transferred to the Palais Royal to act under Molière; after Molière's death he moved to the Hôtel de Bourgogne where he effectively delayed the formation of the Comédie-Française. He was married to Laroque's niece; his son married Biancolelli's daughter, while one daughter became the wife of Michel Baron and another married Florent Dancourt.

La Tuillerie (Jean-François Juvenon; 1650–88) French actor and playwright, grandson of Gros-Guillaume. He was best suited to tragedy and appeared at the Hôtel de Bourgogne from 1672, occasionally also playing in minor comic roles. His plays included several tragedies and farces.

lauda A form of early Italian devotional drama. The *lauda* had its roots in the hymns of praise of the 12th and 13th centuries, which eventually evolved into religious celebrations incorporating songs and dialogue that in turn developed into *sacra rappresentazione. During the Renaissance the *lauda* became a part of the secular theatre and led ultimately to the development of the oratorio.

Lauder, Sir Harry (Hugh Mackennan; 1870–1950) Scottish music hall singer and comedian. Originally a coal miner, he made his first English appearance, as an Irish comic, in 1896. He had an overnight success at Gatti's in 1900 and subsequently – dressed in a kilt and carrying a crooked walking stick – consolidated his reputation with such songs as 'Roamin' in the Gloamin'' and 'Keep Right on to the End of the Road'.

Laughton, Charles (1899–1962) US actor, born in Britain (he became a US citizen in 1940). Laughton made his professional stage debut in Gogol's *The Government Inspector* (1926) and soon gained recognition as a highly individual character actor on both sides of the Atlantic. In 1933 he appeared under Guthrie at the Old Vic, where he consolidated his reputation in such roles as Lopakhin in Chekhov's *The Cherry Orchard*, Prospero in *The Tempest*, and Angelo in *Measure for Measure*; in 1937 he became the first British actor to star at the Comédie Française, playing Sganarelle in Molière's

Le Médecin malgré lui. Subsequently he concentrated upon his film career, although he returned to the stage in 1947, collaborating with the author upon Brecht's *Galileo* in New York. He also directed several other productions in New York (including Shaw's *Major Barbara* with himself playing Undershaft) and in Britain appeared as Richard Brough in Jane Arden's *The Party* (1958) and as Bottom and King Lear at Stratford-upon-Avon (1959).

In 1961 he directed his wife, **Elsa Lanchester** (1902–87), who had appeared with him in various productions, in her one-woman show *Elsa Lanchester – Herself.*

Lavedan, Henri (1859–1940) French playwright and novelist. His dramatic output consists largely of successful comedies of manners and moralizing comedies concerned with social problems, notably *Le Prince d'Aurec* (1894) and its sequel, *Les Deux Noblesses* (1897).

Lavinia *See* Ponti, Diana da.

Lawler, Ray (1921–) Australian playwright and actor, who became internationally known with his drama about old age, *Summer of the Seventeenth Doll* (1955), in which he played the leading role himself. Subsequent plays have included *The Unshaven Cheek* (1963), *A Breach in the Wall* (1970), and *Kid Stakes* (1976), but have failed to arouse equal interest.

Lawrence, D(avid) H(erbert) (1885–1930) British novelist, poet, and playwright, whose dramas are set against much the same background as his highly influential novels. He wrote eight plays, of which the most successful included *The Widowing of Mrs Holroyd* (1926), written in 1914, *A Collier's Friday Night* (1965), which was written in 1906, and *The Daughter-in-Law*, first produced in 1967 at the Royal Court.

Lawrence, Gerald (1873–1957) British actor, who began his career in Benson's Shakespearean company and later worked with Irving, playing Henry II to Irving's Becket on the night of the great actor's death. After working in the US, he directed a Shakespeare season at the Royal Court Theatre, appeared in Tree's company, and in 1912 enjoyed great success in Shaw's *Captain Brassbound's Conversion.* After World War I his appearances included the title role in Booth Tarkington's *Monsieur Beaucaire* (1923) and Juggins in Shaw's *Fanny's First Play* (1931). He was married to Lilian *Braithwaite (by whom he was the father of Joyce Carey) and subsequently to the US actress **Fay Davis** (1872–1945), who was much admired in Hope's *The Prisoner of Zenda* in 1895.

Lawrence, Gertrude (Gertrud Klasen; 1898–1952) British actress, who attracted attention in revues and musicals before playing her first dramatic role in 1928. Many memorable performances followed, especially as Amanda in Noël Coward's *Private Lives* (1930), which was written for her. Other Coward successes included *Tonight at 8.30* (1935–36) and *Blithe Spirit* (1945). She was also highly successful as Liza Elliot in Moss Hart's Broadway musical *Lady in the Dark* (1941) and, in her final appearance, as the English governess in *The King and I* (1951). Her autobiography, *A Star Danced*, was published in 1945.

Lawrence, Slingsby *See* Lewes, George Henry.

Lawson, Wilfrid (Wilfrid Worsnop; 1900–66) British actor, who first appeared in London in 1928 in *Sweeney Todd* at the Elephant and Castle Theatre. He was subsequently in a number of revivals of Shaw's plays with both Charles Macdona's and Barry Jackson's companies and, in 1933, made a strong impression in *Gallows Glorious* by Ronald Gow at the Shaftesbury

Theatre. In 1937 he gave an outstanding performance in Priestley's *I Have Been Here Before* and was highly praised for his Doolittle in the film *Pygmalion*. Despite his notorious drinking, he later appeared successfully in Bridget Boland's *The Prisoner* (1954) and Ibsen's *Peer Gynt* (1962) among many other plays.

Laxness, Halldór Kiljan (1902-) Icelandic novelist and playwright, whose satirical play *Silfurtunglið* (The Silver Moon; 1954); criticized US influence upon post-war Icelandic society. The most important of his other works is *Dufnaveizlan* (The Pigeon Banquet; 1966); he was awarded a Nobel Prize in 1955.

Laye, Evelyn (1900-) British actress, who began her stage career in Harold Owen and H M Vernon's *Mr Wu* at Brighton in 1915 and made her first appearance in London at the Gaiety Theatre in *The Beauty Spot* in 1918. She became a leading star in musical comedy, variety, pantomime, and revue between the wars, successes including *The Merry Widow* (1923), *Blue Eyes* (1927), *Bitter Sweet* (1929), and *Lights Up* (1940). She later played in such comedies as Anthony Kimmins's *The Amorous Prawn* (1959) and Marriott and Foot's *No Sex Please – We're British* (1971).

lazzo A verbal aside or comic gesture with which actors of the *commedia dell'arte* might embellish the main dialogue and action. An essential feature of the whole *commedia dell'arte* tradition, the success of such interpolations as the eating of an imaginary fly or a comment upon some topical matter were a measure of a performer's ability and were used to enliven the action when it flagged. *Compare burla*.

Leal, José da Silva Mendes (1818–86) Portuguese playwright and statesman, who was the author of several melodramas and plays tackling social issues. Such works as *Os Dois Renegados* (1839) and *Pobreza Envergonhada* (1858) were much influenced by the plays of Dumas *père* and Dumas *fils*.

Leblanc, Georgette (1867–1941) French actress and singer, who was particularly associated with the plays of Maeterlinck. She created most of Maeterlinck's heroines between 1896 and 1910, among them Aglavaine in *Aglavaine and Selysette*, which was written for her.

Lecouvreur, Adrienne (1692–1730) French actress, who became enormously popular for both her talent and her beauty after her first appearance at the Comédie-Française, in Crébillon's *Électre*, in 1717. Despite the hostility of other leading actresses, she triumphed in plays by Racine and Molière, employing a new naturalistic style. Her brief but eventful life later provided the basis for the play *Adrienne Lecouvreur* (1849) by Scribe and Legouvé, in which both Rachel and Bernhardt had great success.

Lederer Theatre Complex *See* Trinity Square Repertory Company.

Lee, Canada (Leonard Lionel Cornelius Canegata; 1907–52) US Black actor, who worked in several Black companies before coming to prominence as Bigger in Paul Green's adaptation of Richard Wright's novel *Native Son* (1941). Later roles included Caliban in *The Tempest* (1945) and Bosola, played in whiteface make-up, in Webster's *The Duchess of Malfi* (1946).

Lee, Gypsy Rose (Rose Louise Hovick; 1914–70) US actress, who appeared as a striptease artist in burlesque on Broadway and with Ziegfeld's *Follies* (1936). The musical comedy *Gypsy* (1959) was based on her life.

Lee, Nathaniel (c. 1653–92) English playwright, remembered for his historical tragedies. Chief of these were *The Rival Queens; or, the Death of Alexander the Great* (1677), in the first performances of which Betterton and Mrs Barry appeared, and *The Duke of Guise* (1682), on which he collaborated with Dryden. He died insane in Bedlam.

leg A cloth or a narrow flat, also referred to as a **tail**, which is used as part of a set of borders, usually to mask the wings.

Le Gallienne, Eva (1899-) US actress, director, and producer, born in Britain, whose first success, as Julie in Molnár's *Liliom* (1921), led to five years of Broadway roles. In 1926 she founded the **Civic Repertory Company**, which performed major foreign works by such playwrights as Shakespeare, Molière, Goldoni, Rostand, Tolstoy, Giraudoux, and Ibsen. She herself toured in Ibsen's *A Doll's House*, *The Master Builder*, and *Hedda Gabler* from 1934 to 1935. In 1946 she cofounded the **American Repertory Theatre** with Cheryl Crawford and Margaret Webster. During the 1960s she appeared with the National Repertory Theatre in Maxwell Anderson's *Elizabeth the Queen* and Euripides's *Trojan Women*, while in 1968 she appeared in Ionesco's *Exit the King* and directed Chekhov's *The Cherry Orchard*.

legitimate drama Any dramatic production presented at the patent theatres rather than at an unlicensed venue during the 18th century. Because this meant in practice plays that did not need to include musical or other interpolations in order to evade the theatre laws, the term eventually came to be used of any straight drama (especially those of literary merit) as opposed to a musical comedy, vaudeville show, or similar entertainment.

Legrand, Marc-Antoine (1673–1728) French actor and playwright, who was a member of the Comédie-Française. A popular performer, he specialized in comic roles and wrote a number of successful plays for the company, notably *Le Roie de Cocagne* (1718) and *Cartouche* (1721).

leg show Any theatrical entertainment in which the principal feature is the appearance of scantily-clad chorus girls. Examples include many performances of burlesque and revue.

Lehmann, Beatrix (1903–79) British actress, who first appeared at the Lyric, Hammersmith in 1924, and established her reputation in a series of performances at the Gate Theatre Club in 1929. Subsequently she was acclaimed in such roles as Winifred in Rowley's *The Witch of Edmonton* (1936) and as Lavinia in O'Neill's *Mourning Becomes Electra* (1937). She appeared at Stratford-upon-Avon in 1947, notably as Portia in *The Merchant of Venice* and Isabella in *Measure for Measure*, while later successes included performances in plays by Ustinov, Anouilh, Pinter, and T S Eliot as well as Michael Redgrave's adaptation of *The Aspern Papers* (1959).

Leicester's Men An English theatre company formed from the household of the Earl of Leicester in 1559. One of the earliest acting companies, its members included James Burbage and William Kempe; after the death of the Earl of Leicester in 1588 the company was merged with Strange's Men.

Leigh, Mike (1943-) British playwright, who emerged as an unconventional exponent of the technique of collective creation while at the Midlands Art Centre in Birmingham. His plays, which are arrived at almost entirely by rehearsal through improvisation, include *Bleak Moments* (1970), *Wholesome Glory* (1973), *Babies Grow Old* (1974), the celebrated black comedy *Abigail's Party* (1977), and *Goose-Pimples* (1981).

Leigh, Vivien (Vivien Mary Hartley; 1913–67) British actress, who made her stage debut in 1935 in *The Masque of Virtue* by Ashley Dukes in London. Subsequently she married Laurence Olivier, having played Ophelia to his Hamlet in 1937, and secured the role of Scarlett O'Hara in the celebrated film *Gone with the Wind*. She went on to appear with Olivier in many classical and other roles, including both Shakespeare's and Shaw's Cleopatra in 1951. An actress of great beauty and strength of character, she excelled under Olivier's direction as Blanche Dubois in Tennessee Williams's *A Streetcar Named Desire* (1949) and was later admired as Viola, Lady Macbeth, and Lavinia in *Titus Andronicus* at Stratford-upon-Avon (1955). After an Australian tour in 1962, she made her debut in a musical, *Tovarich*, in New York, after which she suffered increasingly from ill health.

Leighton, Margaret (1922–76) British actress, who began her career at the Birmingham Repertory Theatre. She achieved a high reputation as a stylish actress with the Old Vic company (1944–47), playing such roles as Raina in Shaw's *Arms and the Man* and Regan to Olivier's Lear. Subsequently she was Celia in Eliot's *The Cocktail Party* (1950), Rosalind, Ariel, and Lady Macbeth in the 1952 Stratford-upon-Avon season, and partnered Coward in Shaw's *The Apple Cart* (1953). She also appeared in Rattigan's *Separate Tables* for nearly four years in London and New York and was then acclaimed as Beatrice to Gielgud's Benedick on Broadway (1959). She returned to England in 1967 and continued to be successful in plays by Shakespeare, Sheridan, and Ivy Compton-Burnett.

Leisewitz, Johann Anton (1752–1806) German playwright, who is best known for the fratricidal tragedy *Julius von Tarent* (1776), an example of the *Sturm und Drang* movement, which had a profound influence upon Schiller's *Die Räuber* (The Robbers; 1781). His other works include the short plays *Die Pfädung* (The Distraint; 1775) and *Der Besuch um Mitternacht* (The Midnight Visit; 1775).

Leivick, Halper (1888–1962) Jewish poet and playwright, who escaped life imprisonment in the USSR and eventually settled in the US, where he became famous for his play *The Golem* (1925), which was first produced in Moscow by the Habimah company. He published 20 prose dramas in addition to his poetry, which drew heavily upon his Soviet experiences.

Lekain, Henri-Louis (Henri-Louis Cain; 1729–78) French actor, who was praised by Voltaire as the finest player of tragedy in his day. He began as an amateur in 1748 and eventually won the support of Voltaire, who provided him with a theatre and assisted in his training. In 1750 Lekain appeared for the first time at the Comédie-Française, in Voltaire's *Brutus*, and soon established himself as a great favourite despite his short stature and harsh voice. He went on to triumph in several of Voltaire's plays, including *L'Orphelin de la Chine* and *Tancrède*, and made a number of significant reforms, banishing spectators from the stage, encouraging historical accuracy in costumes and scenery, and adopting a more natural style of delivery. He died from a chill caught after appearing as Vendôme in Voltaire's *Adélaide du Guesclin*.

Leko *See* profile spot.

Lelio *See* Andreini, Francesco; Riccoboni, Luigi.

Lemaître, Antoine-Louis-Prosper *See* Frédérick.

Lenaea A religious festival held annually (in January and February) in ancient Greece in honour of *Dionysus. The emphasis of the various drama contests held during the festival was upon comedy, although tragedy was later added after comedy was also permitted in the City Dionysia in the 5th century BC.

Lenkom Theatre A theatre in Moscow, established as an amateur venue in 1927. The theatre later acquired professional status and became highly respected under such leading directors as Simonov, Bersenev, and Birman; in recent years it has specialized in plays for younger audiences.

Leno, Dan (George Galvin; 1860–1904) British music hall performer, who made his first London appearance as the contortionist Little George at the age of four. He subsequently developed as a dancer and singer, and, in 1880, won the clog-dancing championship of the world at Leeds. In 1883, London saw him for the first time as Dan Leno and, from 1888 until his death, he appeared annually in the Drury Lane pantomime. He specialized in comic songs and was for a time partnered by Herbert Campbell; his best pantomime roles included Widow Twankey and Mother Goose. He died insane.

Lenoble, Eustache (1643–1711) French lawyer and writer. In 1697 the Comédie-Italienne was expelled from France for performing Lenoble's mediocre play *La Fausse Prude*, which was seen to be an attack on Louis XIV's wife, Mme de *Maintenon.

Lenoir, Charles (fl. 1610–37) French actor-manager, who led a company in the provinces before coming to Paris under the patronage of the Prince of Orange. In 1630 he and Montdory produced Pierre Corneille's first play, *Mélite*, in Paris; four years later they moved into the Théâtre du Marais but were subsequently deprived of many of their actors by Louis XIII, who ordered their transfer to the Hôtel de Bourgogne.

Lenormand, Henri-René (1882–1951) French playwright, whose pessimistic dramas were inspired by Freudian psychology. In *Les Ratés* (The Failures, 1924) the lives of a failed writer and actress end in degradation, murder, and suicide; in *Le Simoun* (1920) the incestuous passion aroused by a daughter in her father is resolved only by her untimely death.

Lensky, Alexander Pavlovich (1847–1908) Russian actor, who championed performance of the plays of Ibsen in Russia. As director of the Maly Theatre in Moscow he did much to reform current acting practices and fostered interest in the classical repertory as well as in more natural styles of delivery.

lens spot *See* focus lamp.

Lenya, Lotte (1900–81) German actress and singer, who was closely associated with the works of Brecht and her husband Kurt Weill. Among the premieres in which she created major roles were *Mahagonny* (1927) and *The Threepenny Opera* (1928). She left Germany for the US during the Nazi period, later appearing in various films (including a James Bond movie) and stage shows, among them *Cabaret* (1966). She was famous for her distinctive atonal singing voice.

Lenz, Jakob Michael Reinhold (1751–92) German poet, playwright, and friend of Goethe, who played an important role in the development of the *Sturm und Drang* movement. He formulated the rules of Romantic drama in his treatise *Anmerkungen über Theater* (1774) and *Die Soldaten* (written 1774–75), which influenced Büchner's *Woyzeck*.

Leonard, Hugh (John Keyes Byrne; 1926–) Irish playwright and critic, who has written several dramas based on Irish themes that have won wide praise for their technical virtuosity. *The Big Birthday* (1956) attracted attention when seen at the Abbey Theatre and was followed by the equally successful *A Leap in the Dark* (1957); subsequent works have included *The Passion of Peter Ginty* (1961), which was derived from Ibsen's *Peer Gynt*, and *Stephen D* (1962), which drew on the writings of James Joyce. The theme of betrayal is frequently involved; others include the British-Irish relationship, as in *The Au Pair Man* (1968), and terminal illness, as in *A Life* (1978). Other plays include *Da* (1973), *Moving Days* (1981), and *Scorpions* (1983).

Leonidov, Leonid Mironovich (1873– 1941) Russian actor and director, who became a leading performer of tragic roles at the Moscow Art Theatre. Having begun his career at the Korsch Theatre in Moscow in 1901, he won great acclaim as Dmitri Karamazov in Dostoevsky's *The Brothers Karamazov* as well as in the plays of Ibsen, Chekhov, and Gogol among others.

Leonov, Leonid (Maximovich) (1899-) Soviet novelist and playwright, whose work is distinguished by intricate plot structure and detailed characterization. He has written 12 plays, 11 of which were produced in Moscow theatres between 1936 and 1946. His best-known play is *Nashestviye* (Invasion; 1942), a story of Nazi oppression which has also been adapted for film and opera. His later dramas, which include the acclaimed *Obyknovennyy chelovek* (1940) and *Zolotaya Kareta* (1946), reveal his growing interest in moral issues.

Leopoldstädter Theater A theatre in Vienna, which was opened in 1781 by Karl *Marinelli as a venue for conventional Viennese burlesque and folk theatre. Noted performers who appeared there included Laroche and Anton Hasenhut. It was demolished in 1945.

Léotard, Jules (1830–70) French acrobat, who became an enormously popular performer in music hall. He made his first London appearance at the Alhambra in 1861 and his skill was later commemorated in the song 'The Daring Young Man on the Flying Trapeze'. The conventional practice costume of dancers and acrobats is called a leotard in his honour.

Lermontov, Mikhail Yurevich (1814–41) Russian poet, novelist, and playwright, who was the foremost Russian writer associated with the Romantic movement. Much influenced by Byron, he spent some time in exile in the Caucasus and, after military service, was eventually killed in a duel. His writing for the theatre comprises three plays, of which the first was *The Spaniards* (written in 1830), which criticized the Tsar and was banned. This was followed by *Menschen und Leidenschafter*, which was influenced by the *Sturm und Drang* movement, and *Masquerade* (written in 1835 and performed in 1852), which reflected his interest in Shakespeare and Byron and is regarded as his finest dramatic work.

Lerner, Alan Jay (1918–86) US lyricist, whose first works to be produced were the book and lyrics for *The Life of the Party* (1942). Subsequently he wrote the book and lyrics for such shows as *Brigadoon* (1947), *Paint Your Wagon* (1951), *My Fair Lady* (1956), *Camelot* (1960), and *Gigi* (1973, filmed in 1959), on all of which he collaborated with the composer **Frederick Loewe** (1904–88).

Lernet-Holenia, Alexander (1897-) Austrian poet and playwright, who revived the tradition of the *Haupt-und Staatsaktionen* with his historical plays. He was also the author of several comedies, notably *Österreichische Komödie* (1926) and the sexual fantasy *Ollapotrida* (1926).

Lesage, Alain René (1668–1747) French novelist and playwright, best known for the novel *Gil Blas de Santillane* (1715–35). During the early years of the 18th century he wrote a number of plays for the Comédie-Française; the satirical comedy *Turcaret*, his greatest success, caused considerable offence to its victims in the world of finance. Lesage subsequently became associated with the Parisian fairs, for which he produced around 100 works – vaudevilles, sketches, farces, and comic-opera libretti – often in collaboration with other writers, including Fuzelier and Piron.
Principal works:
Crispin rival de son maître: 1707; translated as *Crispin, Rival of His Master*.
Turcaret ou le Financier: 1709.

Lescarbot, Marc (c. 1570–1642) French playwright, whose masque *Le Théâtre de Neptune en la Nouvelle France* (1606) was the first play to be performed in Canada. A lawyer by training, he directed the masque himself at Port Royal (now Annapolis Royal in Nova Scotia).

L'Espy (François Bedeau; d. 1663) French actor, brother of Jodelet, who was popularly known as Gorgibus after the character he created in two of Molière's plays. Like his brother he appeared at the Théâtre du Marais and at the Hôtel de Bourgogne before ultimately joining Molière's company in 1659. Subsequently he oversaw the rebuilding of the Palais-Royal in 1660.

Lesser, Anton (1952–) British actor, who since 1977 has done much notable work with the Royal Shakespeare Company. His Shakespearean performances have included Romeo (1980), Hamlet (1982), and Troilus (1985); other successes have been Edward Bond's *The Fool* (1981) and Richard Nelson's *Principia Scriptoriae* (1986).

Lessing, Gotthold Ephraim (1729–81) German playwright and theatre critic, whose writing had a lasting influence upon the German theatrical tradition. An admirer of Shakespeare, he argued in his capacity as a critic for a freer approach to drama in such critical essays as the *Hamburgische Dramaturgie* (1767–68); as a playwright he expressed his preference for a theatre released from the conventions of the French tradition in such passionate and realistic dramas as the tragedy *Miss Sara Simpson*, his first major success. *Emilia Galotti* consolidated his reputation as an innovator in tragedy, while in **Minna von Barnhelm* he applied his ideas to comedy; his last play, *Nathan der Weise*, was a poetic drama.
Principal works:
Miss Sara Simpson: 1755.
Minna von Barnhelm: 1767.
Emilia Galotti: 1772.
Nathan der Weise: 1783; translated as *Nathan the Wise.

Lesson, The (*La Leçon*) A one-act play by Eugène *Ionesco. First performance: Paris, 1951. The manic power of the professor gradually increases during the course of the 'lesson': he finally loses control of himself and kills his student.

Letourneur, Pierre (1736–88) French scholar, who is remembered for his prose versions of Shakespeare's plays. Published in 20 volumes (1776–83), Letourneur's collection was more comprehensive and his translation more accurate than previous French versions.

Levey, Barnett (1798–1837) Australian theatre manager, born in London, who went to Sydney in 1825 and in 1832 staged the first professional theatre production in Australia, when he presented *Black-Ey'd Susan* at the Royal Hotel. Subsequently he staged comedies, melodramas, and even some Shakespeare.

Levin, Hanoch (1943–) Israeli playwright and director, who has established a controversial reputation with such moving but humorous plays as *The Adventures of Solomon Grip* (1969). Other works, which lampoon such targets as bourgeois society and sexual stereotyping, include *Hefetz* (1972) and *Jacoby and Leidentahl – Temporary Title* (1973).

Levy, Benn W *See* Cummings, Constance.

Lewes, George Henry (1817–78) British writer and critic, lover of the novelist George Eliot. He was the grandson of an actor and was himself an actor for a short time; first, professionally, in Manchester, then in Charles Dickens's amateur theatricals. He wrote or adapted many plays under the names **Slingsby Lawrence** and **Frank Churchill**. He also wrote theatre criticism for the *Leader* and contributed long articles on the stage to the *Pall Mall Gazette*, which were subsequently published as *On Actors and the Art of Acting* (1875).

Lew Fields Theatre *See* Wallack's Theatre.

Lewis, Leopold David (1828–90) British playwright, whose adaptation of Erckmann-Chatrian's *Le Juif Polonais* as *The *Bells* provided Irving with his most celebrated role (1871). His other plays include *The Wandering Jew* (1873) and *The Foundlings* (1881).

Lewis, Mabel Gwynedd Terry- *See* Terry-Lewis, Mabel Gwynedd.

Lewis, Matthew Gregory (1775–1818) British playwright, author of the popular novel *Ambrosio; or, The Monk* (1795). He wrote numerous melodramas, including *The Castle Spectre* (1797), staged at Drury Lane, *The East Indian* (1799), and *Timour the Tartar* (1811), which was performed at Covent Garden. He died of yellow fever while returning from a visit to Jamaica.

Leybourne, George (Joe Saunders; 1842–84) British music hall performer, who became famous as a singer and *lion comique*. The success of his rendering of 'Champagne Charlie', which he sang in London for the first time at the Canterbury Music Hall, set the seal on his career. In the 1880s his popularity declined and he managed and chaired a number of minor halls, occasionally working a double act with his daughter, Florrie.

Liberty Theatre A theatre on West 42nd Street, between Seventh and Eighth avenues, New York, which opened in 1904 with *The Rogers Brothers in Paris*, which starred the musical comedy team for which the theatre was built. Subsequent successes included the Black musical *Blackbirds of 1928*. In 1933 the theatre became a cinema.

Library Theatre A theatre in Manchester, which opened in the basement of the public library in 1946. A resident company was founded in 1952 and a companion theatre, the **Forum Theatre**, was added a few miles away at Wythenshawe in 1971. In recent years the Library Theatre has been used for the presentation of contemporary drama, while the Forum is used for musicals and more commercial theatre.

licence An authorization allowing a theatre to present public performances or permitting the production of a particular work or type of entertainment. Conditions that have to be met before a venue in Britain can be licensed were stipulated in the 1843 Theatres Act, which also modified the absolute licensing powers of the *Lord Chamberlain (acquired under the **Licensing Act** of 1737), and later repeated in that of 1968, which ended the Lord Chamberlain's monopoly and confirmed local authorities as the chief licensing bodies.

Licensing Acts *See* licence.

lighting The illumination of the stage by artificial light. Early methods of lighting, which was first recognized as an important feature of theatrical production when indoor performances were first given during the Renaissance, included the use of candles, cressets, and *bozzi*. Crucial innovations during the early history of lighting technology by such figures as Sebastiano Serlio and Nicola Sabbattini included the introduction of footlights, the use of reflectors to increase the intensity of light beams, and – after much resistance from those who came to the theatre to be seen as much as they did to see – the dimming of the lights in the auditorium (customary since 1876). The development of gas lighting in the early 19th century represented a major advance despite the risks involved (*see* fires). The Chestnut Street Theatre in Philadelphia was the first to have gas installed (1816); the first British stage to be thus lit was that at the Lyceum Theatre (1817). At much the same time the first *limelights were developed, anticipating the introduction of the modern spotlight. In 1881 the Savoy Theatre became the first public building in London to be lit throughout by electricity, the use of which had already been pioneered at the California Theatre in San Francisco in 1879. The introduction of electricity revolutionized stage lighting throughout the world by providing lighting of great power and flexibility by virtue of irises, gobos, colour wheels, and numerous other mechanical devices. Those who championed its use included Sir Henry Irving, André Antoine, David Belasco, and Adolphe Appia. Lighting is controlled in the modern theatre by highly sophisticated computerized dimmer boards, which can coordinate the illumination of an entire set; other recent innovations have included experiments with ultraviolet light, lasers, and holography.

Lillie, Beatrice (Gladys) (Constance Sylvia Munston, Lady Peel; 1898-) British actress and singer, born in Canada, who became one of the foremost stars of British revue and cabaret. Having started in 1914 in London as a ballad singer, she established her reputation for sophisticated comedy in André Charlot's revues during World War I, making her first US appearance in 1924. She sported a distinctive short hairstyle and specialized in Surrealistic sketches and humorous songs; among her successes were her solo show *An Evening with Beatrice Lillie* (1954) and the role of Madame Arcati in a musical version of Coward's *Blithe Spirit* (1964).

Lillo, George (1693–1739) British playwright, whose first successful play, *The London Merchant; or, the History of George Barnwell*, which was based on an old ballad, was produced at Drury Lane in 1731 and repeatedly revived over the next 100 years in several countries. His later plays include *Guilt Its Own Punishment; or, Fatal Curiosity*, which was produced at the Haymarket in 1736, and a version of *Arden of Faversham*, which was published posthumously. His plays had an early influence on the development of domestic drama.

limelight A form of lighting, widely used in the 19th century, by means of which a brilliant beam could be thrown onto the stage. First developed in 1816, the beam, which could be adjusted manually in order to follow an actor or other moving object on the stage, was produced by heating a piece of lime until it became incandescent.

Lincoln Centre for the Performing Arts *See* Vivian Beaumont Theatre.

Lincoln's Inn Fields Theatre A theatre in Portugal Street, London, which opened as a tennis-court in 1656 (as **Lisle's Tennis-Court**). In 1661 Sir William Davenant reopened it as a home for the Duke's Company, installing the first proscenium arch to be seen in a theatre in London. It was also equipped with movable scenery and saw many appearances by Thomas Betterton in *Hamlet* and other classic plays by Calderón, Dryden, and others. When the Dorset Garden Theatre opened in 1671 the company left Lincoln's Inn Fields and Killigrew took it over for a time. Reverting to a tennis-court in 1675, it was refitted by Congreve, Betterton, Mrs Bracegirdle, and Mrs Barry in 1695, and reopened with *Love for Love*. The new company moved out in 1705 after many successes and in 1714 Christopher Rich and subsequently his son John Rich restored it, presenting the first English pantomime there in 1716. Seating over 1400 people, it saw major productions of Farquhar and the first performance of Gay's *The Beggar's Opera* (1728). In 1732 Rich transferred to his new theatre in Covent Garden and Lincoln's Inn was used for various musical entertainments, as well as for a few plays produced under Giffard. After closing in 1744, the building became a barracks, an auction room, and a china warehouse, being finally demolished in 1848.

Lincoln's Men An English theatre company, formed from the household of the first Earl of Lincoln, which performed at Court during the 1570s. Disbanded in the late 1570s, a later company of the same name flourished from 1599 to 1610.

Lindberg, August (1846–1916) Swedish actor, who was closely associated with early performances of the plays of Ibsen. He created Oswald in *Ghosts* in 1883 and toured Scandinavia in many other leading roles in both Ibsen and Shakespeare, eventually joining the company at the Kungliga Dramatiska Teatern in Stockholm.

Linden Tree, The A play by J B *Priestley. First performance: London, 1947. The play revolves around a family reunion at which the differences in values between the two generations become painfully clear; Lewis Casson and Sybil Thorndike appeared in the original production.

Lindsay, Howard (1889–1968) US actor, director, and playwright, whose greatest success came in 1939 with his adaptation – in collaboration with **Russel Crouse** (1893–1966) – of Clarence Day's *Life With Father*, in which Lindsay played Father. Subsequently he and Crouse shared a Pulitzer Prize for *State of the Union* (1945); other works together included *Life With Mother* (1948).

Lindsay, Robert (1949–) British actor, who worked in repertory at Manchester before taking over in the rock musical *Godspell*. As well as comic roles both on stage and on television, he has played the title role in the Manchester Royal Exchange Theatre's *Hamlet* (1984) and Bill Snibson in the musical *Me and My Girl* (1985) in both London and New York.

Lindstrom, Erik (1906–74) Swedish actor, who became a leading interpreter of tragic roles at the Swedish National Theatre, where he was trained. He began his career in comedies by Sheridan, Shaw, and others but later won acclaim in such parts as Peer Gynt, Faust, Hamlet, Macbeth, and Strindberg's Gustav III.

Linsenscheinwerfer *See* focus lamp.

lion comique A popular figure of the music hall tradition in Britain, who first appeared around 1865. The *lions comiques* assumed the character of aristocratic, handsome, young men who sang such comic songs in praise of wine as 'Champagne Charlie'; leading interpreters of the role included George Leybourne and Alfred Vance.

Lipman, Maureen (1946–) British actress, who spent two years in repertory at Manchester before joining the National Theatre at the Old Vic, where her roles included Molly Molloy in Ben Hecht and Charles MacArthur's *The Front Page*. She established a reputation as a unique comedy actress in such plays as Richard Harris's *Outside Edge* (1979) and Philip King's *See How They Run* (1986). In 1987 she starred in Bernstein's *Wonderful Town*, while in 1988 she opened in a one-woman show about Joyce Grenfell, *Re-Joyce*.

Lisle's Tennis-Court *See* Lincoln's Inn Fields Theatre.

Liston, John (1776–1846) British actor, who was born in Soho, London. Initially a strolling player, he attempted tragic roles without success until he was persuaded by Stephen Kemble to play old men and comic rustics, as which he received immediate acclaim. In 1805 George Colman the Younger presented him at the Haymarket, establishing him as a leading comedian and – whilst at the Olympic Theatre with Madame Vestris – the first to be paid more than a tragedian.

Little Drury Lane Theatre *See* Olympic Theatre.

Little Foxes, The A play by Lillian *Hellman. First performance: New York, 1939. This acclaimed study of a family of ruthless industrialists during the US Civil War provided a Broadway triumph for Elizabeth Taylor as Regina on its revival in the 1980s; the film version of 1941 starred Bette Davis and Herbert Marshall.

Little Theatre A theatre in Adelphi, London, which was opened in 1910 by the actress Gertrude *Kingston. Seating 250, it was converted from part of a bank and, in 1911, saw the stage debut of Noël Coward in *The Goldfish*. Subsequent successes included Shaw's *Fanny's First Play* (1911) and G K Chesterton's *Magic* (1913) before it was closed due to damage from bombs in 1917. Reopened in 1920, it became a venue for revues featuring such leading performers as Cicely Courtneidge and Jack Hulbert,

while plays presented there during the 1930s included *Whiteoaks* (1936) by Mazo de la Roche. It was bombed in 1941 and demolished in 1949.

The **Little Theatre** on West 44th Street, between Broadway and Eighth Avenue, in New York was opened by Winthrop Ames in 1912. The theatre was subsequently enlarged and redecorated when the Shuberts took it over but later became a broadcasting studio and lecture hall. It reopened as a theatre in 1963 with a production of *Tambourines to Glory* by Langston Hughes. In 1964 the theatre's name was changed to the **Winthrop Ames Theatre** after its founder; it was then used once more for television before reopening as a theatre in 1974 with a production of Ray Aranha's *My Sister, My Sister*. Albert Innaurato's *Gemini* began a long run in 1977.

The **Little Theatre** repertory company in Bristol was founded in 1923 by the actor Rupert Harvey (1887–1954) and rapidly built a strong reputation with productions of plays by Barrie, Shaw, and local authors. Financial pressures forced the company to disband in 1934, after which their base in the Lesser Colston Hall was acquired by the **Rapier Players** (1935–61) and then handed over to the Bristol Old Vic. A new company was installed there in 1980.

Little Theatre Guild of Great Britain A British theatre organization, which was founded in 1946 to coordinate the activities of *Little Theatres throughout the country. It produces publications related to the amateur theatre as well as arranging conferences and other contacts.

Little Theatre in the Hay *See* Haymarket Theatre.

Little Theatre of the Deaf (LTD) *See* O'Neill, Eugene.

Little Theatres Small independent theatres run on an amateur basis. Such enterprises, which often attain high artistic standards, include the famous *Maddermarket Theatre in Britain, while the oldest British example is reputably the Stockport Garrick Society, founded in 1901. The phenomenon also played a major role in the development of drama in Canada, where during the 1920s the Little Theatre Movement resulted in the opening of numerous tiny venues, of which the most influential included the *Hart House Theatre in Toronto and the French Compagnons de Saint-Laurent. Notable US examples include the *Neighborhood Playhouse and the venues of the *Washington Square Players and the *Provincetown Players.

Little Tich (Harry Relph; 1868–1928) British music hall comedian, who became famous not only for his small stature (he was only four feet in height) but also for his singing and eccentric dancing in oversized boots. He appeared in the annual Drury Lane pantomime from 1891 to 1894, in the farce *Lord Tom Noddy* at the Garrick Theatre (1896), and in numerous burlesques in England and the US.

Littlewood, (Maudie) Joan (1914-) British director, who won renown for her direction of the *Theatre Workshop company in Stratford, East London, in the 1950s and early 1960s. In 1934 she began her close collaboration with the folksinger Ewan McColl in Manchester, setting up the experimental Theatre of Action, which was later reformed as the **Theatre Union** and again after World War II as the Theatre Workshop. The company moved into the Theatre Royal, Stratford, in 1953, where Littlewood presented a programme of popular theatre for working-class audiences ranging from *Volpone, Mother Courage*, and *The Quare Fellow*, to *A Taste of Honey, Fings Ain't Wot They Used T'Be*, and *Oh, What a Lovely War!*. She emphasized the importance of training and rehearsal as well as improvisation around the text and ensemble

acting, and was one of the first British directors to understand Brecht's ideas. Projects since 1964 have included the establishment of a theatre school in Tunisia and much work in France (from 1975).

liturgical drama (*or* ecclesiastical drama) The various forms of medieval religious drama that preceded the secular tradition in Europe. Written in Latin and incorporating chanted dialogue and music, the earliest religious drama developed during the 10th century from such *tropes as the famous *Quem Quaeritis?*, performed at Easter as part of the Mass and, later, of Matins. Subsequently such episodes were expanded to cover various stories from the scriptures and were increasingly performed outside the church itself. Those illustrating the Christmas story became known as **Nativity plays**, while those given at Easter were referred to as **Advent plays**; other performances linked to specific religious festivals included the **Epiphany play**. Ultimately, the plays became separated from the church completely and were written in the vernacular; they also came to include a strong comic element, gradually evolving into the more sophisticated *mystery play. *See also auto sacramental*; miracle play; Passion play; *sacra rappresentazione*; saint play.

liturgy An obligation placed upon prominent citizens of ancient Greece, requiring selected noblemen to undertake, among other tasks, the duties of a *choregus*.

Livanov, Boris Nikolayevich (1904–72) Soviet actor and director, who spent most of his career at the Moscow Art Theatre, which he joined in 1924. As an actor, his appearances ranged from Beaumarchais to Chekhov and Gogol, whose *Dead Souls* (adapted by Bulgakov) provided him with enormous success in the role of Nozdryov. As a director he was particularly praised for his revival of Dostoevsky's *The Brothers Ka-*

ramazov in 1960 and for Chekhov's *The Seagull* in 1970.

Liverpool Playhouse The oldest surviving repertory theatre in Britain, which opened in 1911 and known as the Liverpool Repertory Theatre until 1916. Inspired by Miss Horniman's company in Manchester, the theatre was reconstructed from the old Star Theatre, where melodrama had been staged since 1866. The theatre presents a wide variety of entertainment and, in recent years, has become famous for its productions of plays by contemporary writers, including Bennett, Pinter, and Stoppard. Actors who have trained with the repertory company there have included Michael Redgrave, Rex Harrison, and Ian McKellen. The main auditorium seats 762 while a smaller studio theatre – the Playhouse Upstairs – seats 120.

Living Newspaper A form of documentary theatre that developed in a number of countries in the early 20th century and became a major feature of the *Federal Theatre Project during the 1930s. Directed initially by Elmer Rice and later by Joseph Losey and others, these productions – three of which were written by Arthur Arent – dealt with matters of immediate public concern (the invasion of Ethiopia, the plight of the farmers, the trade union movement, poverty, and the threat of syphilis) and relied upon a strong mixture of carefully documented historical fact, domestic realism, political satire, and a campaigning editorial voice.

Livings, Henry (1929-) British actor and playwright, who established his reputation while with the Theatre Workshop. His plays, chiefly comedies and farces, include *Big Soft Nellie* (1961), *Nil Carborundum* (1962), which has an RAF setting, *Eh?* (1964), *Jonah* (1974), *Jug* (1975), *Pennine Tales* (1983), and *This is My Dream* (1987).

Living Stage *See* Arena Stage.

Living Theatre An off-Broadway theatre group in New York, which was founded in 1951 by Julian Beck and **Judith Malina**. Among the group's many influential avant-garde and experimental productions were Jack Gelber's *The Connection* (1959), which relied to an extent on improvisation, Jackson MacLow's *The Marrying Maiden* (1960), the outcome of which was decided by cards and dice, and a version of *Antigone* (1967) set during the Vietnam War. From 1964 to 1968 the Living Theatre toured Europe, finally disbanding in 1970.

Lloyd, Marie (Matilda Alice Victoria Wood; 1870–1922) British music hall singer, who began her career on the halls in 1885. By 1891 she was starring with Dan Leno and Little Tich in her first Drury Lane pantomime and had built up a huge popular following for her warmheartedness and her suggestive rendering of such songs as 'The Boy I Love is Up in the Gallery' and 'A Little of What You Fancy Does You Good'. She died three days after collapsing on stage at the Edmonton Empire.

Lloyd Webber, Andrew (1948-) British composer, who established his reputation in the theatre by collaborating with Tim Rice on such popular musicals as *Joseph and the Amazing Technicolour Dreamcoat* (1968), *Jesus Christ Superstar (1970), and *Evita (1976). His other successes include *Cats (1981), based on T S Eliot's poems, Starlight Express (1984), in which the cast wore roller-skates, and The *Phantom of the Opera (1987). His company, the Really Useful Company, is based at London's Palace Theatre and includes Prince Edward among its members.

loa A form of prologue common to Spanish drama up to the 17th century. Such introductory passages varied from brief speeches to complete short plays related to the main drama; by the 17th century they were used only before performances of *autos sacramentales* or new plays.

Lobanov, Andrei Mikhailovich (1900–59) Soviet director, who established his reputation working under Reuben Simonov in the 1930s. His greatest successes included plays by Chekhov and Ostrovsky as well as productions of contemporary works; from 1945 to 1956 he worked at the Yermolova Theatre.

Lobsterscope A slotted metal disc, which produces a flickering lighting effect suggesting slow motion when rotated in front of a spotlight.

Locatelli, Basileo (d. 1650) Italian collector of *commedia dell'arte* plays. His collection, preserved in the Biblioteca Casanatense in Rome, comprises more than 100 such scenarios in two separate volumes.

Locatelli, Domenico (1613–71) Italian actor of the *commedia dell'arte*, who – under the stage name **Trivellino** – became famous in the role of Arlecchino. He spent much of his acting career in Paris.

Lodovico, Cesare Vico (1885–1968) Italian playwright, who became well-known for his works for the theatre in the *crepusolari* tradition. Such plays as *L'idiota* (1915), derived from Dostoevsky, *La donna di nessuno* (Nobody's Woman; 1919), and *L'incrinatura, o Isa, dove vai?* (The Flaw, or Isa, Where are You Going?; 1937) reflect the influence of Chekhov and explore the theme of failure of communication; he was also a noted translator of Shakespeare.

Loeb Drama Centre A theatre built in 1960 for Harvard University. Seating 556, it is used by the Harvard-Radcliffe Dramatic Club and the American Repertory Theatre, a professional company in residence at Harvard since 1980. An additional experimental theatre seats 120.

Loewe, Frederick *See* Lerner, Alan Jay.

Logan, Joshua (1908–) US author, director, and producer, who studied under Stanislavsky and went on to stage such productions as *South Pacific* (1949), *Wish You Were Here* (1951), and *The World of Suzie Wong* (1958). Other successes included *Annie Get Your Gun* (1946), and *Mister Roberts* (1948).

Logan, Maria (1770–1844) British actress. She was a godchild of John *Palmer and made her debut at the Haymarket in 1783. In 1787 she appeared at the Goodman's Fields Theatre, as Mrs Gibbs, under which name she continued to act after her second marriage, to George *Colman the Younger. She also played as Drury Lane and Covent Garden, returning to the Haymarket when her husband succeeded his father as manager.

Lohenstein, Daniel Caspar von (1635–83) German playwright, who was the author of a number of violent melodramas, which were highly popular as closet drama. His plays include *Ibrahim Bassa* (1650), *Cleopatra* (1661), *Epicharis* (1665), and *Ibrahim Sultan* (1673).

Löhr, Marie (1890–1975) British actress and manager, born in Australia, who began her career in the theatre in the company of her godparents, the Kendals. Subsequently she appeared with Tree at His Majesty's, notably as Lady Teazle, and with her husband, Anthony Prinsep, went into management at the Globe Theatre (1918). They were not very successful, although Lonsdale's *Aren't We All?* (1923), in which she played Margot Tatham, was an exception. Other popular roles included Mrs Darling in Barrie's *Peter Pan* (1927), Muriel Weston in Dodie Smith's *Call It a Day* (1935), and Mary Jarrow in Esther McCracken's *Quiet Wedding* (1938).

London Academy of Music and Dramatic Art (LAMDA) A drama school in London, which was founded in 1861 by T H Yorke-Trotter. Now situated in Cromwell Road, it has its own theatre, where Peter Brook and Charles Marowitz staged their famous Theatre of Cruelty season in 1964.

London Assurance A comedy by Dion *Boucicault. First performance: 1841. Written under the pseudonym Lee Morton, it anticipated modern social drama and established Boucicault's reputation, being highly acclaimed in its first production – which featured the first use of a box set – with Madame Vestris and Charles James Mathews and revived throughout the late 19th century. The plot hinges on a courtship involving an impoverished young man and a beautiful but worldly young woman.

London Casino See Prince Edward Theatre.

London Coliseum A theatre in St Martin's Lane, London, which was opened by Sir Oswald Stoll as a music hall in 1904, being called simply the **Coliseum** from 1931 before reverting to its original name in recent times. Equipped with the first revolving stage in London and with an auditorium larger than either Drury Lane or Covent Garden, it failed to prosper at first. Forced to close temporarily in 1906, its fortunes revived with productions featuring such leading actresses as Ellen Terry and Sarah Bernhardt. Diaghilev's Ballets Russes appeared there for three seasons before the theatre switched to musical comedy in 1932; successful shows after World War II included *Guys and Dolls* (1953) and *The Pajama Game* (1955). The theatre then became a cinema (1961–68) before being reopened as the home of the Sadler's Wells Opera Company (now the English National Opera); it seats 2358. It was also the scene of the first stage demonstration of television (1930).

London Hippodrome See Hippodrome.

London Palladium A variety theatre in Argyll Street in London's West End, often the chosen venue for the Royal Variety Show. It was designed by Frank Matcham and opened in 1910 as the Palladium, with a luxurious palm court at the back of the stalls and the largest seating capacity (2306) of any London theatre. Spectacular revues were staged throughout the 1920s and Barrie's *Peter Pan* was performed annually from 1930 to 1938. The name London Palladium was used from 1934, soon after the theatre had become the home of the Crazy Gang shows, which ended in 1938 with *These Foolish Things*. Today variety, spectacular revue, and an annual pantomime maintain the Palladium tradition and feature artistes of international renown. The longest-running show in the theatre's history to date has been *Barnum* (1981), starring Michael Crawford. *Ziegfeld* opened there in 1988.

London Pavilion A music hall in the Haymarket, London, which originally opened as a *song-and-supper room before being adapted as a music hall in 1861. Seating 2000 people, it saw appearances by many leading performers before demolition in 1885. It was rebuilt in the same year and continued with a typical music hall programme until 1918, when C B *Cochran converted it for the presentation of such revues as *Blackbirds* (1926), *On With the Dance* (1925), and *One Dam Thing After Another* (1927). Variety was staged there from 1931 until 1934 when the building became a cinema, closing in 1981.

London Theatre Studio See Saint-Denis, Michel Jacques.

Longacre Theatre A theatre on West 48th Street, between Broadway and Eighth Avenue, New York, which opened in 1913. The theatre was originally used for musical comedies but, by 1925, straight plays were also being produced there. Between 1944 and 1953 the theatre was used for broadcasting but was then reopened with *Ladies of the Corridor* (1953). A number of contemporary plays have since been seen there, including Ionesco's *Rhinoceros* (1961), Anderson's *I Never Sang for My Father* (1968), *Ain't Misbehavin'* (1978), and Medoff's *Children of a Lesser God* (1980).

Long Day's Journey Into Night A drama by Eugene *O'Neill, written in 1941. First performance: Stockholm, 1956. The play is set in 1912 and concerns James Tyrone, an actor, his wife Mary, a drug addict, and their sons Jamie, an alcoholic, and Edmund, who represents O'Neill. The plot reaches a climax when Mary, who has been away to cure her drug problem, returns home uncured.

Longepierre, Hilaire-Bernard de Roqueleyne (1659–1721) French playwright and classical scholar, born in Dijon. In his *Parallèle de Corneille et de Racine* (1686) Longepierre praised Racine, on whose great tragedies he modelled his own moderately successful plays, notably *Médée* (1694).

Longford, Sixth Earl of (Edward Arthur Henry Pakenham; 1902–61) Irish playwright and director, who became closely associated with the *Gate Theatre in Dublin in 1931. In 1936 he formed an independent company, Longford Productions, which specialized in staging classic plays at the Gate Theatre. His own plays included translations with his wife from Irish, Greek, Spanish, and French literature.

Long Wharf Theatre A theatre in New Haven, Connecticut, which opened in 1965. It houses one of the most influential companies in the US, which has successfully transferred to Broadway several times in plays by David Storey and Lillian Hellman, among others.

Lonsdale, (Leonard) Frederick (1881–1954) British playwright and librettist, who was the author of numerous examples of the comedy of manners, similar to those of Somerset Maugham. Among his most successful plays were *Aren't We All?* (1923), *The Last of Mrs Cheyney* (1925), and *On Approval* (1926), all of which are notable for their elegance and wit. His libretti for musical comedies include *The Maid of the Mountains* (1917), *Madame Beaucaire* (1919), and *Madame Pompadour* (1923).

Look After Lulu An adaptation by Noël *Coward of Georges *Feydeau's farce *Occupe-toi d'Amélie*. First performance: London, 1959, with Anthony Quayle and Vivien Leigh in the leading roles. The original French version opened in Paris in 1908.

Look Back in Anger John *Osborne's first and immensely successful play, written with encouragement from George Devine. First performance: Royal Court Theatre, 1956. Directed by Tony Richardson with Kenneth Haigh as Jimmy Porter, the articulate working-class anti-hero, who lives with Alison (Mary Ure) his middle-class girlfriend, the play voiced post-war feelings of frustration, class-consciousness, and disillusionment among the young. It inspired several other new writers (including Arnold Wesker) to write for the stage.

Loot A farce by Joe *Orton. First performance: Cambridge Arts Theatre, 1965. Much revised for its first London production in 1966, the play caused a considerable stir with its theme of police corruption and its use of a dead corpse as a comic device in the tradition of knockabout comedy.

Lope de Rueda *See* Rueda, Lope de.

Lope de Vega *See* Vega Carpio, Lope de.

López de Ayala, Adelardo (1829–79) Spanish playwright and statesman, who began as a writer of Romantic drama but later contributed to the development of the Realist tradition in Spain. His early works include the historical plays *Un hombre de estado* (1851) and *Rioja* (1851); plays critical of contemporary society include *El tanto por ciento* (1861).

Loraine, Robert (1876–1935) British actor-manager, who became a prominent member of Ben Greet's company before achieving popularity in such dashing roles as D'Artagnan in *The Three Musketeers* (1899). Later he won acclaim in New York as John Tanner in Shaw's *Man and Superman* (1905) and flew for the RFC during World War I, returning triumphantly to the stage as Rostand's Cyrano de Bergerac in 1919. Other successful performances included Mirabell to Edith Evans's Millamant in Congreve's *The Way of the World* (1924) and the title role in Strindberg's *The Father* (1927).

Lorca, Federico García *See* García Lorca, Federico.

Lord Chamberlain A British public official, who formerly exercised complete control over the licensing and **censorship** of dramatic works. The influence of the Lord Chamberlain's office, dating from Tudor times, was laid down by statute in 1737; prior to that date the *Master of the Revels – who was ultimately responsible to the Lord Chamberlain – took charge of all such matters. A wave of public reaction against the liberality of the Restoration theatre had led to a demand for moral supervision of the stage and, under the 1737 act, the Lord Chamberlain was granted powers to intervene directly – without giving reasons – to curb any excess he judged to contravene prevailing moral standards; it also made him the sole licensing authority. An Examiner of Plays worked under him, inspecting copies of new dramatic works; by 1968 three English readers and one Welsh

one undertook these duties in the Lord Chamberlain's office, checking for examples of indecency, profanity, impropriety, sedition, and libel. Notable Examiners over the years included George Colman the Younger and Charles Kemble.

Resistance to the Lord Chamberlain's unfettered power eventually led to its limitation in 1843. It was finally abolished in the **Theatres Act** of 1968 in the wake of the *Lady Chatterley* trial of 1960. In other countries centrally directed censorship has been abandoned in all but Communist and more orthodox religious states; notable victims of censorship over the years have included Jonson's *Eastward Ho!*, Shaw's *Mrs Warren's Profession*, and Tennessee Williams's *The Rose Tattoo*.

Lord of Misrule *See* Misrule, Lord of.

Lorne, Marion (1888–1968) US actress, who became highly popular in London in a long-running series of comedies written by her husband, Walter Hackett, and George H Broadhurst. After her first appearance in London in 1915 (following 10 years on Broadway in light drama) she had successes regularly until returning to the US in 1938, notably at the Whitehall Theatre, which Hackett opened in 1931.

Losey, Joseph (1909–84) US film director, whose stage production of Brecht's *Galileo* in 1947 and work with the Living Newspaper proved highly influential. Initially working as a stage manager, he was inspired by Okhlopov's experiments in the USSR to dispense with proscenium settings when he worked on the Living Newspaper project in 1936 until clashes with Hallie Flanagan forced his resignation. *Galileo*, with Charles Laughton and the author himself participating, was later turned into a film.

Lotta *See* Crabtree, Charlotte.

Loutherbourg, Philip James de (1740–1812) German artist and stage designer, who became resident scenic director at Drury Lane under Garrick (and subsequently Sheridan) in 1773. He made important innovations in the use of scenery and lighting, placing a new emphasis upon naturalistic detail, and devised machines for producing various sound effects; he also employed his skill as an artist in painting backcloths depicting romantic landscapes and experimented with the effects of perspective. He made further advances in transparencies and encouraged the use of built stuff; after his retirement from the theatre he went on to develop the *eidophusikon.

Love for Love A comedy by William *Congreve. First performance: 1695. Valentine, in return for settlement of his debts, agrees with his father to sign away his inheritance; however, Angelica (with whom he is in love) beguiles Sir Sampson and gets possession of the bond.

Love in a Village A comic opera by Isaac *Bickerstaffe, with music by Thomas Arne and others. First performance: 1762. A rustic idyll based on *The Village Opera* (1728) by Charles Johnson, it had a profound influence upon the course of English light musical drama.

Love of Four Colonels, The A comedy by Peter *Ustinov. First performance: London, 1951. The plot revolves around a Sleeping Beauty in a German castle who is courted by four colonels from the British, French, Soviet, and US occupying armies; Ustinov himself acted the main role in the first production.

Love's Labour's Lost A comedy by William *Shakespeare, written c. 1594–95. First performance: c. 1594–95. The play satirizes the futile attempts of the young King of Navarre and three courtiers to follow a life of celibacy for three years and contains many topical allusions. Largely ignored until the 20th century, it is now admired for its comic devices and sense of humanity.

Low Comedian See stock company.

Lower Depths, The (*Na dne*) A play by Maxim *Gorky, generally considered to be his finest. First performance: Moscow Art Theatre, 1902. Set in a derelict doss-house in Moscow, the play depicts the miserable lives led by the inhabitants with uncompromising realism and was internationally acclaimed.

Lowin, John (1576–1653) English actor, who became an important member of the King's Men and was included in the First Folio list of Shakespearean actors. He succeeded Heminge as Falstaff and may have received advice for playing Henry VIII from Shakespeare himself. He appeared in *Sejanus* (1603) and *The Malcontent* (1604) and possibly created the roles of Bosola in *The Duchess of Malfi* and Volpone. With Taylor, he became business manager for the company and acquired a small shareholding in the Blackfriars Theatre.

Lucille La Verne Theatre See Princess Theatre.

Lucy Rushton's Theatre See New Yorker Theatre.

Ludi Romani See *ludi scaenici.*

ludi scaenici The various dramatic entertainments presented at public games in ancient Rome. Theatrical productions were first undertaken at the **Ludi Romani** (held annually in September in honour of Jupiter), for which Livius Andronicus presented the first Latin tragedy and comedy in 240 BC. In subsequent years the type of play given at such festivals was varied to include farces and mime.

Ludlow, Noah Miller (1795–1886) US actor-manager, who founded one of the first US companies in 1815. He toured widely and ran the Chatham Theatre in New York for a time. From 1835 to 1853 he comanaged the **American Theatrical Commonwealth Company** with Sol Smith as well as running several other theatres.

Ludwig, Otto (1813–65) German playwright and novelist, who established his reputation in the theatre with a psychological drama depicting provincial life, *Die Erbförster* (The Hereditary Forester; 1850). Other dramatic writings include the drama *Die Makkabäer* (1852) and studies of Shakespeare.

Lugné-Poë, Aurélien-François (1869–1940) French actor-manager and director, who succeeded Paul Fort as head of the influential Théâtre d'Art (renamed the **Théâtre de l'Oeuvre**) in 1893. A leading figure in the reaction against Realism, he presented important productions of plays by Maeterlinck, Ibsen, and Strindberg among others; other celebrated productions included Wilde's *Salome* (1895), the premiere of Jarry's controversial *Ubu-roi* (1896), Claudel's *L'Annonce faite à Marie* (1912), and Anouilh's *L'Hermine* (1932).

Lun See Rich, John; Woodward, Harry.

Lunacharsky, Anatoli Vasilevich (1875–1933) Soviet playwright and politician, who did much to reorganize the national theatre after the Revolution of 1917. As the first Commissar for Education he encouraged the performance of new plays and evolved the theory of *Socialist Realism as well as ensuring the continued survival of such noted venues as the Moscow Art Theatre. His own plays included *Oliver Cromwell* and *Thomas Campanella*.

Lunacharsky State Institute of Theatre Art (GITIS) A drama school in the USSR,

which was founded in 1878 and given its modern name in 1934 in honour of Anatoli *Lunacharsky. The oldest such establishment in the USSR, it numbered Nemirovich-Danchenko among its staff; its pupils have included many future members of the Moscow Art Theatre.

Lundequist, Gerda (1871–1959) Swedish actress, who won acclaim in leading tragic roles at the Kungliga Dramatiska Teatern (1889–91) and 1906–11) and the Svenska Teatern (1891–1906). Her most successful parts included Sophocles's Antigone and Lady Macbeth.

Lunt, Alfred (1892–1977) US actor, who formed a famous acting partnership with his British wife **Lynn Fontanne** (1887–1983). Married in 1922, the Lunts appeared together regularly in sophisticated comedies by such writers as S N Behrman and Noël Coward. Notable successes included Shaw's *Arms and the Man*, Molnár's *The Guardsman*, Coward's *Design for Living*, and Dürrenmatt's *The Visit*. Before their marriage, Alfred Lunt made his reputation in Booth Tarkington's *Clarence* (1919).

Lunt-Fontanne Theatre A theatre on West 46th Street, New York, which opened in 1910 as the **Globe Theatre**. Originally used for musicals, it housed a number of revues in the 1920s, including Ziegfeld's *Follies* and George White's *Scandals*. It was used as a cinema from 1931 to 1958, when it was renovated and converted into the 1714-seat Lunt-Fontanne Theatre. It opened with the Lunts's production of Dürrenmatt's *The Visit*. Since that time it has housed numerous musicals.

Lupino, Barry (1882–1962) British actor and dancer, who was resident comedian at the Britannia Theatre, Hoxton, for some years before establishing his reputation in musicals and pantomimes, which he often wrote himself. His West End appearances included Charlie Bang in *The Millionaire Kid* (1932) and Sir John in *Me and My Girl* (1941).

His brother, **Stanley Lupino** (1894–1942), started as a variety artist but became a highly successful revue and musical comedy actor and writer. He was in several shows at the London Hippodrome and was very popular in such shows as *Love Lies* (1929) at the Gaiety and *Over She Goes* (1936) at the Saville.

Luscius Lanuvinus (2nd century BC) Roman playwright, chiefly remembered as a rival of Terence. He attacked Terence on a number of grounds, including plagiarism, provoking replies in several of Terence's prologues; of his own plays and translations of Menander nothing survives.

Lutèce, Théâtre de A theatre in the rue de Jussieu, Paris, which is used for the presentation of largely experimental dramas. It was a noted venue for the Theatre of the Absurd, with productions of plays by Genet, Obaldia, and others.

Luther A play by John *Osborne. First performance: Theatre Royal, Nottingham, 1961. Another of Osborne's powerful studies of individual rebels, the play is most convincing when it portrays Luther's psychological and physiological rather than his religious struggles; in the original production Luther was played by Albert Finney.

Luzan y Claramont, Ignacio (1702–54) Spanish scholar, who was a leading figure of the Spanish neoclassical theatre. In such theoretical writings as *Poética* (1737) he attempted to translate Italian ideas into the Spanish drama and argued for rigid observance of the unities. In his later years, however, he conceded that the playwright need not follow such rules so exactly.

Luzzato, Moses Hayim (1707–47) Jewish playwright, who was born in Italy and lived in Amsterdam and was the author of plays in both Hebrew and Italian. His early plays include *Migdal Oz* (Tower of Victory); his works written after he became interested in cabbalism include the play *Tehilla Layesharim* (Praise for Uprightness) and some theatre criticism.

Lyceum Theatre A theatre in Wellington Street, London, which opened in 1771 as a venue for concerts and exhibitions. It was converted into a theatre in 1794 and eventually became the home of the Drury Lane company (1809–12) after the Theatre Royal was damaged by fire. In 1815 it was renamed the Theatre Royal English Opera House and saw appearances by Fanny Kelly and the elder Charles Mathews before destruction by fire in 1830. Re-erected close to the old site in 1834 as the Royal Lyceum and English Opera House, it was run with considerable success by Robert Keeley and then Madame Vestris and the younger Charles Mathews, notably through spectacular productions of Planché. The Convent Garden Theatre company was there from 1856 to 1859, after which Hezekiah Bateman took over. Henry Irving's performance in *The Bells* (1871) transformed the theatre's reputation overnight; subsequently Irving became the manager, triumphing in numerous performances opposite Ellen Terry, from 1878 his celebrated leading lady. This great period came to an end in 1902, when Irving made his last appearance; the theatre was then used for music hall, melodrama, and pantomime. In 1939 John Gielgud staged performances of *Hamlet* there and the theatre subsequently (1945) became a dance hall. In the 1980s a campaign gathered strength to turn the deteriorating theatre into a new home for British ballet companies.

Another theatre of the same name opened in Edinburgh in 1883 as a venue for touring companies, notably that of Henry Irving. Eventually, in 1964, it acquired its own resident company – the **Edinburgh Civic Theatre Company** – and was used for presentations of both classic and modern plays, with an emphasis on work by Scottish authors (notably under Bill *Bryden). A young Lyceum company was founded in 1975 in a studio theatre nearby but became the subject of controversy over funding.

The **Lyceum Theatre** on 4th Avenue, New York, was opened in 1885 by Steele Mackaye but foundered until it was taken over by Daniel Frohman, who staged numerous successes there. It was demolished in 1902.

The **Lyceum Theatre** on 45th Street and Broadway, New York, opened in 1903 with *The Proud Prince*. Barrie's *The Admirable Crichton* had its premiere there, while other significant productions included visits by Charles Wyndham's company and plays directed by Belasco. David Warfield and Ethel Barrymore appeared there to great acclaim after World War I, while later successes included Kaufman and Hart's *George Washington Slept Here* (1940), Clifford Odets's *The Country Girl* (1950), Osborne's *Look Back in Anger* (1957), and Pinter's *The Caretaker* (1961). More recent productions have been the musical *Your Arms Too Short to Box with God* (1976) and Kopit's *Wings* (1979).

Lycophron (b. c. 324 BC) Greek poet and playwright, who lived in Alexandria and is usually remembered for the surviving poem *Alexandra*. He was also the author of comedies and many tragedies, of which nothing remains.

lycopodium An explosive powder formerly employed to produce realistic flame effects. Derived from a type of moss, it was usually ignited in a special holder, known as a lycopodium flask.

Lyly, John (c. 1554–1606) English novelist and playwright, whose plays were performed by boy companies at Court. The most important of his elaborately written plays discussing courtly love was *Endymion, the Man in the Moon* (1588), a love story in which the title figure represented the Earl of Leicester and Cynthia Elizabeth I. Other plays included *Alexander and Campaspe* (1584), *Sappho and Phaon* (1584), *Midas* (1589), and the witty *Mother Bombie* (1589). His most influential work, however, was his prose fiction *Euphues* (1578) and its sequel, *Euphues and his England* (1580).

Lyndsay, Sir David (1486–1554) Scottish poet and playwright, whose *An Pleasant Satyre of the Three Estates* (1552) follows a similar plot to John Skelton's *Magnyfycence*. The play criticizes the clergy and comments on aspects of Scottish politics.

Lynn, Ralph (1882–1962) British actor, famous for his performances as the affable but fatuous aristocratic heroes of numerous farces. After success in *Tons of Money* at the Shaftesbury Theatre in 1922, he consolidated his reputation in the celebrated Aldwych farces (1922–33). When the series ended he turned to films, returning to the stage in 1944 in *Is Your Honeymoon Really Necessary?*. He also starred in further farces by Ben Travers alongside his old companion Robertson Hare.

lyric The text of a song in a stage show. *See also* book.

Lyric Hall *See* Lyric Theatre.

Lyric Opera House *See* Lyceum Theatre.

Lyric Players An Irish theatre company founded in 1944 by Austin Clarke for the performance of poetic drama. Appearing at the Abbey Theatre in Dublin, the group produced many plays by Clarke himself, including *The Viscount of Blarney* (1944) and *The Plot Succeeds* (1950).

The **Lyric Players** of Belfast were founded as an amateur company in 1951 and were run on similar lines to Clarke's group, presenting Irish poetic drama by Yeats and others. The company moved into its own theatre in 1952 where notable productions included Greek tragedies, Chekhov's *The Seagull* (1956), and modern works. In 1968 the group, which includes members from Northern Ireland, Eire, and England, acquired a new theatre and received a state subsidy.

Lyric Theatre A theatre in Hammersmith, London, which was opened in 1888 as the **Lyric Hall**, then redesigned in 1890 and reopened as the **Lyric Opera House**. Rebuilt five years later to a design by Frank Matcham, Lily Langtry spoke the prologue on the opening night in 1895 but thereafter the theatre's reputation declined and it became known locally as 'the Blood and Flea Pit'. In 1918 Nigel Playfair renamed it the Lyric Theatre, launching a successful phase with A A Milne's *Make Believe*; John Gay's *The Beggar's Opera* ran for three and a half years from 1920 and a revival of Congreve's *The Way of the World* (1924) with Edith Evans was highly acclaimed. Ellen Terry made her final stage appearance there in Walter De La Mare's *Crossings* in 1925. After Playfair's departure in 1933, the theatre's fortunes again fluctuated; it remained closed for some time prior to 1944, when Baxter Somerville gave it a new lease of life, many of his productions – by such authors as John Mortimer and Pinter – transferring to the West End. After Somerville's death in 1963, however, the Lyric's fortunes again ebbed, and in 1966 it was closed. A new Lyric Theatre, seating 537, opened in King Street in 1979 with a production of Shaw's *You Never Can Tell*. It maintains a reputation for serious theatre and is complemented by the smaller Lyric Studio Theatre in the same building.

The **Lyric Theatre** in Shaftesbury Avenue is the oldest surviving theatre in the Avenue. It opened in 1888 with the comic opera *Dorothy* starring Marie Tempest. For some years the theatre specialized in comic operas, while Eleonora Duse made her London debut there in *La Dame aux Camélias*

(1892) by Dumas *fils*. Sir Johnston Forbes-Robertson became manager in 1902 and appeared alongside his wife Gertrude Elliot. In 1906 Lewis Waller took over and staged successful revivals as well as the musical *The Chocolate Soldier* (based on Shaw's *Arms and the Man*). During the 1920s and 1930s Leslie Howard, Tallulah Bankhead, Sir Alfred Lunt, and Lynn Fontanne were among those who featured in popular musicals and plays. Yvonne Arnaud appeared in *The Nutmeg Tree* in 1941, and the Lunts returned to the Lyric during World War II in a celebrated series of Rattigan plays. In 1950 *The Little Hut* with Robert Morley ran for 1261 performances. The tradition of serious theatre and popular musicals has since been maintained with such productions as *Grab Me a Gondola* (1956), Alan Bennett's *Habeas Corpus* with Alec Guinness (1973), and the National Theatre production of Ayckbourn's *A Chorus of Disapproval* (1986). The theatre is now under the management of Stoll Moss Theatres.

The **Lyric Theatre** on West 42nd Street, New York, opened in 1913 with Richard Mansfield in *Old Heidelberg*. In its earlier years several of Ibsen's plays were produced there; later productions included many of Florenz Ziegfeld's musical comedies. The theatre was then converted into a cinema.

Lysistrata A comedy by *Aristophanes. First performance: Athens, 411 BC. In an attempt to end the war between Athens and Sparta the women of Athens refuse to sleep with their men until peace is declared; the play has been seen as a satire upon the recent defeat against Sicily.

Lyttelton Theatre One of the three theatres comprising the *National Theatre in London, opened in 1976. Named after the first chairman of the National Theatre Board, it seats 890 and opened with *Hamlet*, starring Albert Finney. Subsequent productions on its adjustable proscenium stage have included predominantly new works, including plays by Ayckbourn, Pinter, Arthur Miller, and Terence Rattigan.

Lytton, Edward George Earle Bulwer-
See Bulwer-Lytton, Edward George Earle, Lord.

Lyubimov, Yuri Petrovich (1917-) Soviet director, who established his reputation with his production of Brecht's *The Good Woman of Setzuan* at the Vakhtangov Theatre after World War II. Subsequently he transferred to the Taganka Theatre and presented notable avant-garde works depending upon the techniques of collective creation.

Lyubimov-Lanskoy, Yevsei Osipovich (1883–1943) Soviet actor and director, who played an important role in adapting the old Russian stage to the new demands created by the Revolution of 1917. His productions of Bill-Belotserkovsky's *Storm* at the Trades Union Theatre in 1926 was highly influential; from 1941 he worked at the Maly Theatre.

M

Mabou Mines *See* La Mama Experimental Theatre Club.

McAnally, Ray(mond) (1926-) Irish actor, who played many classic Irish parts at the Abbey Theatre, Dublin, between 1947 and 1963. He made his first London appearance in 1962 in Edna O'Brien's *A Cheap Bunch of Nice Flowers*, later taking over as George in Edward Albee's *Who's Afraid of Virginia Woolf?* (1964) and appearing as Macduff in *Macbeth* and Lopakhin in *The Cherry Orchard* at Chichester in 1966. In 1988 he was highly praised for his performance as G B Shaw in Hugh Whitemore's *The Best of Friends*.

Macbeth A tragedy by William *Shakespeare, written c. 1605. First performance: c. 1610. One of the most celebrated plays in the English language, *Macbeth* depicts the central character's disintegration as he wins power abetted by his ambitious wife and then, struggling with his own conscience against the forces of destiny, gradually loses it through his own use of violence. The play contains much of Shakespeare's best-known poetry and has provided many actors and actresses with their most acclaimed roles. It is believed that Shakespeare's choice of subject – the murder of a rightful Scottish king – was inspired by the recent accession of James I, whose patronage Shakespeare's company sought. The Gunpowder Plot of 1605 may also have been relevant. *See also* taboos.

McCallum, John (1914-) Australian actor, who has divided his career between Britain and Australia. Trained at RADA, he made his debut in 1934 in Brisbane, appeared with the Old Vic company from 1937 to 1940, and, after World War II, won acclaim in such varied plays as Barrie's *Peter Pan* (1956) and Lesley Storm's *Roar Like a Dove* (1957). He married Googie *Withers in 1948, touring widely with her in many plays, including Maugham's *The Constant Wife* (1957) and William Douglas Home's *The Kingfisher* (1978). He has continued to play a key role in the development of the Australian theatre, encouraging the production of new plays, some of which he has directed himself.

McCarthy, Lillah (1875–1960) British actress, who is usually remembered for her performances of such Shavian characters as Nora in *John Bull's Other Island* (1905), Margaret Knox in *Fanny's First Play* (1911), and Lavinia in *Androcles and the Lion* (1913), performed under the direction of Granville Barker, whom she married in 1906. She also appeared in Greek tragedy, Shakespeare, and Shaw in the US, which she visited with her husband in 1914, and ran the *Little Theatre for a time. Other successes included performances in the plays of Barrie and Somerset Maugham as well as appearances opposite Matheson Lang (1920–21); she virtually retired on her second marriage.

McClintic, Guthrie (1893–1961) US actor, director, and producer, who directed many notable productions starring his wife, the actress Katharine Cornell. Previously associated with the companies of Jessie Bonstelle and Winthrop Ames, he attracted attention with his production of Michael Arlen's *The Green Hat* in 1925; other successes included plays by Rudolf Besier, G B Shaw, and Shakespeare, notably *Hamlet* (1936) with John Gielgud.

McCormick, F J (Peter Judge; 1891–1947) Irish actor, who spent most of his career with the Abbey Theatre company, which he joined in 1918. He appeared in over 500 plays and created many of O'Casey's characters, including Joxer Daly in *Juno and the Paycock* (1924) and Jack Clitheroe in *The Plough and the Stars* (1926).

McCowen, Alec (Duncan) (1925–) British actor, who began in repertory and made his London debut at the Arts Theatre as Maxim in *Ivanov* (1950). Subsequently he worked with the Old Vic and Royal Shakespeare companies, playing such roles as Richard II, Touchstone, Malvolio, and the Fool in *King Lear*. As a member of the National Theatre company he starred in Molière's *The Misanthrope* (1973) and Shaffer's *Equus* (1973), while his successes in London and New York have included the title role in Peter Luke's *Hadrian VII* (1968) and Christopher Hampton's *The Philanthropist* (1971). His remarkable one-man performances of *St Mark's Gospel* (1978), *Kipling* (1984), and *Modern Love* (1982) have also been highly praised.

Maccus A character of the Roman *atellana*, whose popular appeal lay in his innate stupidity. He was the central figure of a number of plays by such authors as Novius and Pomponius, in the titles of which his name appeared; he was probably usually presented as a greedy peasant.

Macdermott, The Great (Gilbert Hastings Farrell; 1845–1901) British music hall singer and actor. His success in burlesque led to his career on the halls, where his biggest hit was 'We Don't Want To Fight but By Jingo! if we do'.

McEwan, Geraldine (Mrs Hugh Cruttwell; 1932–) British actress, who made her stage debut in 1949 at the Theatre Royal, Windsor, and subsequently established her reputation in light comedy. As well as appearances at the Royal Court Theatre and other notable London venues, she also acted at Stratford-upon-Avon from 1958, her roles there including Ophelia and Beatrice in *Much Ado About Nothing*. In 1962 she won great praise as Lady Teazle in Sheridan's *The School for Scandal*; of her roles since then the most successful have included parts in plays by Peter Shaffer and, with the National Theatre Company, John Arden, Congreve, Feydeau, Giraudoux, Maugham, and Strindberg. More recent successes have been Rattigan's *The Browning Version* and *A Harlequinade* in 1980 and Sheridan's *The Rivals* (1983). In 1988 she worked as a director in collaboration with Kenneth Branagh's Renaissance Theatre company.

MacGowran, Jack (1918–73) Irish actor, who trained with the Abbey and Gate Theatres in Dublin, and appeared at both for a period of six years (1944–50). He was first seen in London as Young Covey in O'Casey's *The Plough and the Stars* (1954). His subsequent career was much associated with the plays of Samuel Beckett; he played Clov in *Endgame* (1958), Lucky in *Waiting*

for Godot (1964), and devised his own solo programmes on Beckett, giving the final one in New York in 1970.

McGrath, John (1935-) British playwright, director, and founder of the *7:84 Theatre Company. He founded the company in 1971 to bring socialist theatre to the working classes, writing and directing most if its productions himself and touring various 'fringe' venues. He formed a second company in 1973 to tour Scotland. Notable productions have included *The Cheviot, the Stag, and the Black, Black Oil* (1973), *Blood Red Roses* (1980), *The Baby and the Bathwater* (1984), and *Mhàri Mhór* (1987).

Machado, Simão (16th century) Portuguese playwright, author of two notable plays in the style of Vicente. *O Cerco de Diu* was a historical drama, while *Comedia da Pastora Alfea* was a pastoral comedy.

Machiavelli, Niccolò di Bernardo dei (1469–1527) Italian playwright and political theorist, usually remembered for the treatise *The Prince* (1513). He was the author of several comedies of the *commedia erudita* tradition, of which *La Mandragola* (1513–20) is considered a masterpiece. *La Mandragola*, which depicts the betrayal of the heroine, has been revived several times in recent years; other plays include *Clizia* (1525), which drew on works by Plautus.

machine play A form of spectacular dramatic entertainment presented in France during the 17th century and involving extensive use of elaborate stage machinery. Mostly presented at the Théâtre du Marais, plays written for the genre included Corneille's *Andromède* (1650) and Molière's *Amphitryon* (1668).

Mackay, Charles (c. 1785–1857) Scottish actor, who joined the Theatre Royal, Edinburgh in 1818. In 1819 his astonishing success as Bailie Nicol Jarvis in Isaac Pocock's adaptation of Scott's *Rob Roy* established him as a player of Scottish character parts.

McKellen, Ian (Murray) (1939-) British actor, who – after acting in the provinces – made his London debut as Godfrey in *A Scent of Flowers* by James Saunders in 1964. Four years later he confirmed his status as a major actor when he played the title roles in *Richard II* and Marlowe's *Edward II* with the Prospect Theatre Company. In 1972 he became a founder member of the **Actors' Company** (which was controlled by the actors themselves) and, with the Royal Shakespeare Company, went on to play Faustus (1974), Romeo (1976), and Macbeth (1977). He performed his own one-man show *Acting Shakespeare* (which he later took to the US) in Edinburgh in 1977 and later was much admired as Salieri in Shaffer's *Amadeus* (1980). As a member of the National Theatre he has been acclaimed in Chekhov's *Wild Honey* and as Coriolanus.

McKenna, Siobhán (1922–86) Irish actress, whose career began with the Gaelic Repertory Theatre in Galway in 1940. After working at the Abbey Theatre, Dublin, she made her London debut as Nora Fintry in Carroll's *The White Steed* (1947). She subsequently became well known in London, New York, and Dublin for her interpretations of the great Irish heroines in the plays of O'Casey, Synge, and others. She also appeared in the plays of Shaw, Chekhov, and Brecht, being particularly admired as Shaw's St Joan (1954), Chekhov's Madame Ranevskaya (1968), and in her own one-woman entertainment, *Here Are Ladies* (1970).

McKenna, Virginia (1931-) British actress, who began in repertory at Dundee and made her West End debut in *A Penny for a Song* in 1951. Her Shakespearean work included Perdita (1951) and Rosalind (1954); other roles have been Sister Jeanne in John Whiting's *The Devils* (1961) for the

Royal Shakespeare Company and parts in films and musicals, notably in *A Little Night Music* (1976), *The King and I* (1979), and *Winnie* (1988).

McKenzie, Julia (Kathleen) (1941-) British actress, who came to prominence in such musical shows as *Company* (1972), *Cole* (1974), and *Side by Side by Sondheim* (1976). At the National Theatre she triumphed as Miss Adelaide in *Guys and Dolls* (1982); appearances in straight plays have included several comedies by Alan Ayckbourn, including Susan in *Woman in Mind* (1986). In 1987 she starred as Sally Plummer in the musical *Follies*.

McKern, Leo (Reginald) (1920-) Australian actor, who came to Britain in 1946 and has since enjoyed numerous successes on the stage and in films. With the Old Vic company he played several of the great clown parts before joining the Shakespeare Memorial Theatre company in 1952. Subsequent parts in the West End have included Big Daddy in Tennessee Williams's *Cat on a Hot Tin Roof* (1958) and the Common Man in Robert Bolt's *A Man for All Seasons* (1960). He has also played the title role in Ibsen's *Peer Gynt* and Iago in *Othello* at the Old Vic, worked on television as John Mortimer's Rumpole, and played Leon in Michel Frayn's adaptation of Anouilh's comedy *Number One* in 1984.

Mackinley, Jean Sterling *See* Williams, Harcourt.

Macklin, Charles (Charles McLaughlin; c. 1697–1797) British actor, born in Northern Ireland, who began his career as a strolling player. After being engaged by Christopher Rich at the Lincoln's Inn Fields Theatre in 1725, he subsequently appeared at Drury Lane as Captain Brazen in *The Recruiting Officer*. However, it was his startling interpretation of Shylock in 1741 that established him as a leading tragedian, who

was later to excel in such roles as Iago and Macbeth. He also became known for his volatile nature: in 1735 he killed an actor during a quarrel over a wig and was tried for murder but conducted his own defence and managed to get the charge reduced to manslaughter. He also wrote a number of plays, of which *Love à la Mode* (1759) and *The Man of the World* (1781) were frequently revived.

McLellan, Robert (1907-) Scottish playwright, who established his reputation with plays written for the Curtain Theatre in Glasgow in the 1930s. His plays, many of which are written in Scottish dialect, include *King Jamie the Saxt* (1937), *The Flouers o' Edinburgh* (1948), *Young Auchinleck* (1962), and *The Hypocrite* (1967).

MacLiammóir, Micheál (1899–1978) Irish actor, playwright, and designer, who acted as a boy in Tree's company and later, with Hilton Edwards, founded a Gaelic theatre in Galway and the *Gate Theatre, Dublin. At the Gate he designed some 300 productions and appeared as Romeo, Hamlet, and Othello among others. His London appearances included, as actor and author, Lee in *Ill Met by Moonlight* and Martin in *Where Stars Walk*, while in 1960 he had great success in his one-man celebration of Oscar Wilde, *The Importance of Being Oscar*, with which he later toured the world. He also devised two other solo performances, *I Must Be Talking to My Friends* (1963) and *Talking about Yeats* (1970).

McMahon, Gregan (1874–1941) Australian actor and director, who helped to found the influential Melbourne Repertory Company in 1911. Under his direction the company presented the first Australian productions of plays by Shaw and other notable contemporary European playwrights.

McMaster, Anew (1894–1962) Irish actor-manager, who first attracted attention in

The Scarlet Pimpernel (1911) with Fred Terry's company. He went on to act in repertory, in the West End, and in Ireland, and in 1925 formed his own Shakespearean touring company. He was much acclaimed in many of the great leading roles, including Shylock, Hamlet, and Coriolanus.

MacNamara, Brinsley (John Weldon; 1890–1963) Irish playwright, novelist, and short story writer, who joined the Abbey Theatre as an actor in 1910. His reputation and notoriety rest primarily upon his early fiction, but he also achieved success as a playwright, most notably with the grim drama *Margaret Gillan* (1933). He also wrote a number of successful comedies.

Macowan, Michael (1906–80) British actor and director, who gave up acting in preference for directing in 1931 and presented numerous memorable productions of contemporary plays at the Old Vic Theatre, the Shakespeare Memorial Theatre, and the Westminster Theatre (1936–39). He was also connected with the Old Vic Theatre School and was head of the London Academy of Music and Dramatic Art (1954–66).

Macrae, (John) Duncan (1905–67) Scottish actor, whose successes ranged from the title role in Robert McLellan's *Jamie the Saxt* (1937) to Widow Twankey. He was frequently seen at the Edinburgh Festival, where he played in Lyndsay's *Ane Pleasant Satyre of the Thrie Estaitis* in 1948. Appearances in London included the leading part in Bridie's *Mr Bolfry* (1943), John in Ionesco's *Rhinoceros* (1960), and Harpagon in Molière's *The Miser* (1966).

Macready, William Charles (1793–1873) British actor-manager, of Anglo-Irish parentage, who became one of the most celebrated players of his day, despite his unmanageable temper and dislike of the theatre in general. When his father, an actor-manager, found himself in financial trouble, Macready reluc-

tantly abandoned his education and became an actor, making his debut in 1810 at Birmingham, playing Romeo. In 1816 he began a five year contract at Covent Garden; subsequent appearances over the next 16 years, as Rob Roy, Hamlet, Lear, and Macbeth, established him as a distinguished tragedian second only to Kean. Other successes included Bulwer-Lytton's *The Lady of Lyons* (1838) and *Richelieu* (1839). He took over the management of Covent Garden in 1837, greatly improving the general standard of drama there and then repeated his reforms at Drury Lane. He also toured the provinces and the US, where his last visit, in 1849, culminated in the famous riot at the *Astor Place Opera House, triggered by the ill-feeling between himself and Edwin Forrest. He retired in 1851.

MacSwiney, Owen *See* Swiney, Owen.

Madách, Imre (1823–64) Hungarian playwright, poet, and philosopher, usually remembered for the tragic drama *Az ember tragédiája* (The Tragedy of Man; 1883). Taking its central characters from the story of the biblical Creation, the play became one of the most popular works in the Hungarian theatre and was much translated; other works include *The Last Days of Csák* (1886) and *Moses* (1888).

Madame Sans-Gêne A comedy by Victorien *Sardou, written in collaboration with Émile Moreau. First performance: Paris, 1893. Madame Sans-Gêne is the nickname of the heroine of the play, the laundress whose husband becomes one of Napoleon's marshals; the title role was created by Réjane.

Maddermarket Theatre A repertory theatre in Norwich, which opened in 1921. Constructed in the style of the Elizabethan playhouse, it was soon recognized as a leading venue for amateur drama, holding 300 people, under the directorship of Walter Nugent Monck (1877–1958). Actors in productions, which change every month, are traditionally never named in programmes.

Maddern, Minnie *See* Fiske, Minnie Maddern.

Maddox, Michael *See* Meddoks, Mikhail Egrovich.

Madison Square Theatre A theatre on 24th Street, New York, which was opened by Steele Mackaye in 1879 for his company of students to use as a repertory theatre. This failed but the theatre was successfully reopened under Daniel Frohman in 1880 with Mackaye's *Hazel Kirke*. In 1882 it was also the venue for Viola Allen's New York debut in Hugo's *The Hunchback of Notre Dame*. From 1885 Albert M Palmer took over, staging many new works, including the first simple translation of Ibsen's *A Doll's House* with Beatrice Cameron and Richard Mansfield (in the 1889–90 season). Palmer was succeeded by Hoyt in 1891, who remained there until 1900. Renamed **Hoyt's Theatre** in 1905, it continued to prosper with such plays as Heijerman's *A Case of Arson* (1906). The theatre was demolished in 1908.

Madras House, The A comedy by Harley *Granville-Barker. First performance: Duke of York's Theatre, 1910. Dealing with the topic of female repression through the premarital adventures of the six Huxtable girls, it is distinguished by its natural and eloquent dialogue.

Madwoman of Chaillot, The (*La Folle de Chaillot*) A play by Jean *Giraudoux. First performance: Paris, 1945. It depicts the defeat of materialism, in the form of an oil prospector and his greedy associates, by the humanitarian madwoman, Countess Aurélie.

Maeterlinck, Maurice (1862–1949) Belgian poet and playwright, who became a leading writer of Symbolist drama. Such early poetic dramas as *La Princesse Maleine* (1899), *L'Intruse* (The Intruder; 1890), and *Les Aveugles* (The Sightless; 1891) all contain elements of legend and allegory and create an oppressive sense of mystic awareness. *Pelléas et Mélisande* (1892) was his greatest success and was later used as the libretto for Debussy's opera of the same name. Other notable works included a marionette play, *La Mort de Tintagîle* (1894), *Joyzelle* (1903), *L'Oiseau Bleu* (The Blue Bird; 1909), *Mary Magdalene* (1910), *Les Fiançailles* (The Betrothal; 1918), and *Le Bourgmestre de Stilmonde* (1918). He was awarded a Nobel Prize in 1911.

Maffei, Francesco Scipione (1675–1755) Italian playwright, author of the influential verse tragedy *Merope* (1713). Educated by the Jesuits, Maffei made use of classical and French models in his highly successful work, which had a great effect upon such playwrights as Alfieri, Lessing, and Voltaire. He also executed translations of several classical plays, collected in *Teatro italiano* (1723).

magazine batten *See* batten.

maggio A form of early Italian theatrical entertainment, which traditionally took place in May. It is known to have involved the spectacular representation of battles and other similarly sensational events but no scripts of the genre have survived.

Magistrate, The A farce by *Pinero. First performance: Royal Court Theatre, 1885. A bumbling magistrate manages to evade the police in a raid on an inn one evening, but other members of his family are brought before him in his official capacity in the morning.

Magnes (5th century BC) Greek playwright, author of early examples of Old Comedy. He is known to have won a contest in 472 BC; few fragments of his work survive.

Magnon, Jean (1620–62) French playwright and friend of Molière. Magnon wrote for the short-lived Illustre-Théâtre in the mid-1640s: his first play, *Artaxerce*, was staged by that company in 1644. He subsequently produced several other plays of mediocre quality and an encyclopedic work.

Mahelot, Laurent (fl. 1633) French stage designer, who executed designs for numerous productions at the Théâtre de l'Hôtel de Bourgogne. Notes on his settings are preserved in his *Mémoire*, which gives details of plays presented in 1633 and 1634; it is now kept in the Bibliothèque Nationale in Paris.

Maids, The (*Les Bonnes*) A play by Jean *Genet. First performance: Paris, 1947, directed by Louis Jouvet. The maids, sisters Solange and Claire, take turns at impersonating their mistress in a ritual game that culminates in symbolic murder.

Maintenon, Madame de (Françoise d'Aubigné; 1635–1719) French noblewoman, who was the second wife of Louis XIV. The widow of the playwright Paul Scarron, she exercized considerable influence over the king and caused the banishment of the Comédie-Italienne in 1697 after one of their plays had given her offence. She did, however, enjoy private theatricals and encouraged Racine to write plays for performance at her school for poor girls at Saint-Cyr; she also wrote a number of brief pieces for the same purpose herself.

Maíquez, Isidoro (1768–1820) Spanish actor, regarded as the first notable player of tragedy in Spain. Trained under Talma, he appeared as Othello in 1802 but was later caught up in political intrigues and exiled from Madrid.

Mairet, Jean (1604–86) French playwright, who was born in Besançon. Mairet's early plays were pastoral tragi-comedies,

which were followed by the comedy *Les Galanteries du duc d'Osonne* (1632) and his masterpiece, the Roman tragedy *Sophonisbe* (1634). This was the first French tragedy to observe the rules of classical drama, notably the theory of the unities, which Mairet had discussed in the preface to *Silvanire* (1630). One of Pierre Corneille's opponents in the *querelle du *Cid*, he abandoned the theatre in 1640.

Maison de Molière, La *See* Comédie-Française.

Maisons de la Culture *See* *Décentralisation Dramatique*.

Majestic Theatre A theatre in Columbus Circle, New York, which opened as the **Cosmopolitan Theatre** in 1903 with a series of musicals. Renamed the **Park Theatre** in 1911, it saw appearances by Mrs Patrick Campbell and Herbert Tree among others before being turned into a cinema in 1923. Known as the **International Theatre** from 1944, then the **Columbus Circle Theatre** from 1945 to 1946, then the International once more, it eventually became a television studio and was demolished in 1954.

The **Majestic Theatre** on West 55th Street, between Broadway and Eighth Avenue, New York, opened in 1927. It was used for musical comedy until 1935, when the Moscow Art Players took it over to produce a series of Russian plays. After 1945, when the musical *Carousel* was produced there, the theatre was again used for musicals, including *The Music Man* (1957), *Fiddler on the Roof* (1967), *The Wiz* (1975), and *42nd Street* (1981).

Major Barbara A play by G B *Shaw. First performance: Royal Court Theatre, 1905. Major Barbara, a member of the Salvation Army, is faced with having to accept money from a whisky distiller and an arms manufacturer if her work is to continue; her moral dilemma leads ultimately to her resignation.

make-up The use of cosmetics in altering an actor's physical appearance in order to suit him for a certain role or to compensate for the blanching effects of stage lighting. Dating from the earliest forms of ritual drama, the art of make-up was revolutionized by the introduction of gas and electric lighting and has now developed into a highly technical practice. The invention of greasepaint by the opera singer Ludwig Leichner (b. 1836) did much to improve standards of make-up throughout the theatre and helped to banish the harmful effects of earlier paints containing white lead; more recent innovations have included the introduction of water-based cosmetics and fluorescent colour.

Malade imaginaire, Le The last of Molière's comedies. First performance: Palais-Royal, 1673. The play revolves around Argan, who is convinced that he is seriously ill and is determined that his daughter shall marry a doctor but eventually becomes a doctor himself. After the fourth performance of the play Molière, who had appeared in the title role, collapsed and died. Recent English translations include *The Hypochondriac* (1981) by Alan Drury.

Malcontent, The A tragi-comedy by John *Marston, often considered his best work. First performance: 1604. The plot resembles that of *Measure for Measure*, although Marston's study of corruption, lust, and greed through the Duke (disguised as Malevole) is more harshly satiric in tone.

Malina, Judith *See* Living Theatre.

Malleson, (William) Miles (1888–1969) British actor, director, and playwright, who became famous as a somewhat eccentric comedy actor in such roles as Gobbo in *The Merchant of Venice* (1919) and Scrub in

Farquhar's *The Beaux' Stratagem* (1927). Of his several original plays only *The Fanatics* (1927) had a long run, although his adaptations from Molière, including *The Miser* (in which he played the title role at the New Theatre in 1949), were more successful. Other parts included Merlyn in the musical *Camelot* (1964).

Malone, Edmond (1741–1812) British literary critic, born in Dublin, who became noted for his studies of Shakespeare. He published his *Attempt to ascertain the Order in which the Plays of Shakespeare were written* in 1778 and his own edition of Shakespeare's plays in 1790. In 1796 he was the first to denounce the forgeries of William Ireland.

Malvern Festival A major theatre festival founded at Malvern, Hereford and Worcester, in 1929 by Barry Jackson. The festival became internationally known for its close association with the plays of G B Shaw, productions including the English premieres of *The Apple Cart* (1929), *In Good King Charles's Golden Days* (1939), and *Too True to Be Good* (1932) among others. Other successes included plays by Bridie, Drinkwater, and Priestley. The festival came to a halt during World War II, being revived briefly in 1949 and – as a festival of Elgar and Shaw – again in 1977.

Maly Theatre A theatre in Moscow, which opened in 1824 as the home of a company originally founded in 1806. The Maly (meaning small) is the oldest surviving theatre in the capital and began with productions of Shakespeare and the classics as well as of plays by such contemporary Russian playwrights as Gogol and Griboyedov. Between 1854 and 1885 many plays by Ostrovsky were performed there, meeting with such success that the theatre became popularly known as the **House of Ostrovsky**. Since the Revolution the theatre has continued to present contemporary Russian works, as well as revivals of the classics.

Mamet, David (1947-) US playwright, who founded the St Nicholas Theatre Company in Chicago. Among his plays presented by the company have been *Duck Variations* (1974) and *Sexual Perversity in Chicago* (1974). Other works include the comedy *American Buffalo* (1975), *A Life in the Theatre* (1977), *Glengarry Glen Ross* (1983), and *Speed-the-Plow* (1988), which reached Broadway.

manager *See* producer.

Man and Superman A play by G B *Shaw, written 1901–03. First performance: Royal Court Theatre, 1905. Through the relationship of Tanner and Ann, the play argues the dominance of women over men and the need for man to dedicate himself to the creation of something greater than himself; at its heart is a full analysis of love and marriage. The act 'Don Juan in Hell' is sometimes performed separately.

Manducus A stock character of the Roman *atellana*. He was essentially a clown with a large mouth and a hooked nose and may have represented greed or gluttony. *See also* Dossenus.

manet *See* stage direction.

Man for all Seasons, A An historical play by Robert *Bolt. First performance: London, 1960. A highly acclaimed treatment of the life of Sir Thomas More and his conflict with Henry VIII, the play examines moral dilemmas and makes effective use of the doubling of roles by a Brechtian commentator called the Common Man.

Manhattan Theatre A theatre on Broadway, between 53rd and 54th streets, New York, which opened as **Hammerstein's Theatre** in 1927. It was renamed the Manhattan

in 1931 and continued to be used primarily for musicals. In 1934 it became a music hall and, two years later, was taken over by the Federal Theatre Project, opening with *American Holiday* (1936). The theatre was thereafter used for broadcasting and renamed the Ed Sullivan Theatre in 1967.

Manoel Theatre A theatre in Malta, which was founded in 1731. It was a popular venue for a mixed programme of opera and drama for over a century, being renamed the Royal Theatre while under British occupation. It was restored in 1957 and reopened in 1960 as the National Theatre of Malta.

Man of Mode, The The last comedy by Sir George *Etherege. First performance: 1676. The plot revolves around Dorimant (modelled on the Earl of Rochester), who throws over two mistresses in order to pursue the heiress Harriet, and Young Bellair, who is ordered by his father to marry Harriet but loves another.

Manrique, Gómez (c. 1415–90) Spanish poet, soldier, diplomat, and playwright, who is the earliest writer for the Spanish theatrical tradition known by name. His dramas include the Nativity play *La representación del Nacimiento de Nuestro Señor* (c. 1475) and secular pieces.

Mansfield, Richard (1854–1907) US actor, born in Berlin, who began his career in the operas of Gilbert and Sullivan before establishing his reputation in New York, where he first appeared in 1882. He became one of the most popular US stars in leading roles in such plays as *Dr Jekyll and Mr Hyde* (1887), Clyde Fitch's *Beau Brummell* (1890), and Rostand's *Cyrano de Bergerac* (1898). His most admired Shakespearean parts included Richard III and Henry V; he also presented the first US productions of Shaw's *Arms and the Man* (1894) and *The Devil's Disciple* (1897) and the first English language version of Ibsen's *Peer Gynt* (1906).

His wife, **Beatrice Cameron** (1868–1940), often appeared alongside him, her most successful roles including Nora in Ibsen's *A Doll's House* (1889).

Mansfield Theatre *See* Brooks Atkinson Theatre.

Mantell, Robert Bruce (1854–1928) US actor, born in Scotland, who became a popular star of melodrama and later attracted praise for his interpretation of Shakespearean roles. He spent some time in the US with Modjeska early in his career; later he formed his own touring company in the US and excelled in plays by such authors as Boucicault and Bulwer-Lytton.

Mantle, Robert Burns (1873–1948) US theatre critic and editor, who edited a long series of US play anthologies from 1920 until his death. He also wrote drama criticism for several leading US newspapers.

Manuel, Niklaus (1484–1530) Swiss artist, playwright, soldier, and statesman, who expressed many of the ideals of the Reformation in his writings. A native of Berne, he criticized the extravagance of the Roman Catholic church, notably in *Der Ablasskramer* (1526), in which a corrupt cleric falls victim to those he has duped.

Man Who Came to Dinner, The A play by George S *Kaufman and Moss *Hart. First performance: New York, 1939. The play revolves around a quick-tongued radio announcer, based on Alexander *Woollcott, who breaks his hip on tour and is forced to stay with a family in the suburbs for several weeks, during which he terrorizes the family.

Manzoni, Alessandro (Francesco Tomaso Antonio; 1785–1873) Italian novelist and playwright, who was the author of the two romantic tragedies *Il conte di carmognola*

and *Adelchi*. The plays are notable chiefly for their lyrical choruses and historical accuracy; he is usually remembered, however, for the novel *I promessi sposi* (The Betrothed).

Marais, Théâtre du A theatre in Paris, one of the earliest public theatres in France, which was opened in a converted tennis court in the Rue Vieille-du-Temple in 1634. Notable early productions there by Montdory's company included some of Corneille's comedies, his tragedy *Le Cid* (1637), and *La Mariane* by Tristan L'Hermite. Subsequently many of the actors moved to the Hôtel de Bourgogne and the Théâtre du Marais declined until Jodelet appeared there in a series of new farces. In 1644 a fire gutted the building; after the theatre was rebuilt productions continued until 1680, when the resident company (which amalgamated with Molière's troupe on his death in 1673) became part of the new Comédie-Française.

Marat/Sade, The (*Die Ermordung des Jean-Paul Marat, dargestellt von der Truppe des Marquis de Sade im Irrenhaus von Charenton*) A drama by Peter *Weiss, the full title of which is *The Persecution and Assassination of Marat as Performed by the Inmates of the Charenton Asylum under the Direction of the Marquis de Sade*. First performance: Berlin, 1964. Depicting Marat and the Marquis de Sade together in discussion of their respective philosophies in the bath-house of an asylum, the play ends with Marat's death and a re-enactment of the French Revolution by the asylum's inmates.

Marble, Danforth (1810–49) US actor, who began as a silversmith before establishing himself as an actor in Yankee character roles. He was particularly successful as Sam Patch in a series of three plays based on the character and possibly written by Marble himself. He was also admired in similar roles in London and elsewhere before his early death.

Marcadé, Eustache (d. 1440) French theologian and poet, author of a lengthy early Passion play, *La Passion d'Arras*. 25 000 lines long and unremarkable in style and content, the play is nonetheless of importance as a pioneering work in this genre.

Marceau, Fèlicieu (Louis Carette; 1913-) French novelist, essayist, and playwright, whose plays are characterized by his wry humour and idiosyncratic style. His plays, which are all comedies, include *L'Oeuf* (The Egg; 1956), *La Bonne soupe* (1959), *L'étouffe-chrétien* (1961), and *Les cailloux* (1962).

Marceau, Marcel (1923-) French mime actor, who is regarded as the foremost performer of mime in modern times. His most famous mime character is Bip, a whitefaced clown dressed in a white costume with a tall black hat with a flower in it, who is descended from the traditional Pierrot figure and first appeared in 1946, after Marceau had trained with Dullin and Barrault. Other performances have included a celebrated mime drama based on Gogol's *The Overcoat*, another on the story of David and Goliath, and numerous brief sketches. He founded his own École de mimodrame de Paris at the Théâtre de la Porte-Saint-Martin in 1978.

Marcel, Gabriel (1889–1973) French philosopher and playwright, who was an early exponent of Existentialism. Converted to Roman Catholicism in 1929, Marcel examines man's alienation and frustration in such plays as *Le Coeur des autres* (1921) and *Le Chemin de Crète* (1936).

Marching Song A drama by John *Whiting. First performance: London, 1954. Regarded by some as Whiting's finest work, this play depicts the dilemma faced by a general who, having lost in war, is forced to choose between public trial or suicide.

Mardzhanov, Konstantin Alexandrovich (1872–1933) Soviet director, who became famous for his work in the theatre in Georgia. Having worked with the Moscow Art Theatre from 1910 to 1913, he founded the Free Theatre, which included such influential figures as Taïrov, and then returned to Georgia, where he produced innovative productions of Shakespeare and plays by Georgian writers. In 1928 he founded a theatre in Kutaisi; this was moved to Tbilisi in 1930 and later renamed in his honour.

Maréchal, Marcel Louis-Noël (1937-) French actor and director, who has established a strong reputation as one of the leading figures in French provincial theatre. His innovative productions of both Shakespeare and contemporary works by such authors as Audiberti and Brecht have attracted much attention; his other successes have included *Capitaine Fracasse* (1972), based on a novel by Gautier. Since 1975 he has been based in Marseilles.

Maria Stuart An historical play by Friedrich von *Schiller. First performance: 1800. The play depicts the last three days in the life of Mary, Queen of Scots (complete with a fictional meeting with Elizabeth I) and portrays her redeeming acceptance of her fate.

Marigny, Théâtre A theatre in the Champs-Élysées, which was founded in 1850. It was run for a time by Deburau's son and later renamed the Théâtre des Champs-Élysées and the Folies-Marigny, being used for performances of vaudeville. Demolished in 1881, it was rebuilt as a music hall in 1896 and acquired its present name in 1901. It was sumptuously refurbished in 1925 and became an occasional venue for the Comédie-Française as well as the company of Jean-Louis Barrault and Madeleine Renaud (1946–56).

Marinelli, Karl (1744–1803) Austrian actor, playwright, and impresario, who was a leading figure in the tradition of Viennese folk comedy. Author of such plays as *Der Ungar in Wien* (The Hungarian in Vienna; 1773) and *Dom Juan, oder der steinerne Gast* (1783), he installed a burlesque company at the Leopoldstädter Theater in 1781 and encouraged such influential figures as Johann Laroche and Anton Hasenhut.

Marinetti, Filippo Tommaso (1876–1944) Italian actor, novelist, poet, and playwright, who wrote in Italian and French and was effectively the founder of *Futurism. His play *Le Roi Bombance* (1909) aroused much controversy with its use of the digestive system as an allegory of the corruption of mankind; other writings included theatrical pieces advocating Futurism and Fascist ideals.

marionette *See* puppet theatre.

Marivaux, Pierre Carlet de Chamblain de (1688–1763) French playwright, journalist, and novelist. The majority of Marivaux's plays were first produced by the Comédie-Italienne, who proved initially to be better interpreters of his style than the Comédie-Française. Characterized by perceptive psychological insight and by a subtlety of language (*marivaudage*) that causes problems for his translators, Marivaux's sophisticated romantic comedies were not fully appreciated in their time but are now admired for their handling of female characters and had a strong influence upon Alfred de Musset among others.

Principal works:

Arlequin poli par l'amour: 1720.

La Surprise de l'amour: 1722.

La Double Inconstance: 1723.

Le Jeu de l'amour et du hasard: 1730; translated as The *Game of Love and Chance*.

Les Fausses Confidences: 1737.

L'Épreuve: 1740.

Mark Hellinger Theatre A theatre on West 51st Street, between Broadway and Eighth Avenue, New York, which opened as a cinema in 1930. It became the **51st Street Theatre** in 1936 with George Abbott's *Sweet River* and again in 1940 with *Romeo and Juliet*. In 1949 it was given its modern name in honour of the critic and playwright **Mark Hellinger** (1903–47), who wrote the first newspaper column on Broadway. From 1956 to 1962 it was used for musicals; more recent productions have included *On a Clear Day You Can See Forever* (1965), *Jesus Christ Superstar* (1971), and *Sugar Babies* (1979).

Mark Taper Forum A theatre in Los Angeles, which was built in 1967. It houses the Centre Theatre Group, a non-profit-making organization created by the University of California Extension. The Forum has a pentagonal thrust stage and a semicircular auditorium seating 750; significant premieres there have included Mark Medoff's *Children of a Lesser God* (1980). Its director since 1965 has been **Gordon Davidson** (1933-).

Marlowe, Christopher (1564–93) English playwright and poet, who was born in Canterbury and educated at Cambridge. Little is known of Marlowe's adult life, but he may have been a government spy, was arrested and charged with atheism, and died in a tavern brawl. In his brief writing career, he did much to liberate English drama from the constraints of the medieval and Tudor tradition. His accomplished use of blank verse, first fully apparent in *Tamburlaine the Great*, inspired numerous contemporaries, including Shakespeare. *The Tragical History of *Dr Faustus* made the soliloquy a means of analyzing character, whilst his last play, *Edward II*, broke new ground in its treatment of historical subject-matter and was the first of his works to develop a range of characters. *The *Jew of Malta* may have been a model for Shakespeare's *The Merchant of Venice*. Despite the fact that his plays survive only in much-revised forms, Marlowe's works have been revived many times in the 20th century and have been much praised for their lyrical and theatrical qualities.

Principal works:

Tamburlaine the Great: Part I, 1587; Part II, 1588.

The Tragical History of Dr Faustus: c. 1589–92 (published 1604).

The Jew of Malta: c. 1590 (published 1633).

Edward II: c. 1591–92.

Marlowe, Julia (Sarah Frances Frost; 1866–1950) US actress, born in Britain, who established her reputation as an adult actress in New York in Mrs Lovell's *Ingomar* (1887). Subsequently she excelled in leading roles in Shakespeare (including Juliet and Lady Macbeth) and Sheridan among others and married the actor E H Sothern.

Marlowe Society A theatre group based at Cambridge University, which was founded in 1908 and dedicated to the performance of plays from the Elizabethan and Jacobean periods. The society originated in a production of Marlowe's *Dr Faustus* in 1907; notable figures connected with the group have included the poet Rupert Brooke, George Rylands, Peter Hall, and John Barton. Women have played in the society since 1934.

Marmontel, Jean-François (1723–99) French writer, who was a friend and protégé of Voltaire. Marmontel's dramatic works are the least important part of his output; his plays include the tragedies *Denys le Tyran* (1748) and *Aristomène* (1749), several comedies, and opera libretti.

Marowitz, Charles (1934-) US director, who ran his own **Open Space Theatre** company in London from 1968 to 1981. He arrived in Britain in 1956 and later worked with Peter Brook, notably upon the celebrated Theatre of Cruelty season in 1964;

subsequently he worked with the Traverse Theatre Club in Edinburgh before establishing the Open Space Theatre in London, presenting there plays by US writers, Shakespeare, and many contemporary authors. Since 1982 he has been artistic director of the Open Space Theatre in Los Angeles.

Marriage à la Mode A comedy by John *Dryden. First performance: London, 1672. One of Dryden's most elegant and popular comedies, the play contrasts romantic and aristocratic ideas about love and includes some of the author's finest songs. The plot derives from the decision of Rhodophil and Doralice to embark on new love affairs after two years of marriage.

Marriage of Figaro, The (*Le Mariage de Figaro ou la Folle Journée*) A comedy by Pierre de *Beaumarchais. First performance: Comédie-Française, Paris, 1784. A sequel to *The Barber of Seville* (1775), the play continues the story of Figaro and the intrigues of Count Almaviva. Figaro's complaints about social injustice led to the play being banned for three years by Louis XVI. Mozart's opera *Le nozze di Figaro* (1786) is based on this work.

Mars, Mlle (Anne-Françoise-Hippolyte Boutet; 1779–1847) French actress, who began her acting career as a child under Mlle Montansier. Noted for her beauty, she made her debut at the Comédie-Française in 1795 after being encouraged by Mlle Contat and subsequently excelled in the plays of Molière as well as in tragedy.

Marshall, Norman (1901–80) British director and manager, born in India, who became in 1926 one of the directors under Terence Gray at the Cambridge Festival Theatre. On taking over the Gate Theatre in London in 1934 he presented many challenging new plays, including works by Housman and Steinbeck. After World War II he continued to direct in London and for television and also formed his own touring company, as well as advising on the foundation of the National Theatre.

Marshall Theatre *See* Richmond Theatre.

Marston, John (c. 1575–1634) English playwright, who wrote several plays of his own as well as collaborating on others. His own plays include the tragedies *Antonio and Mellida* and *Antonio's Revenge* (both 1599), the comedy *What you Will* (1601), and his two finest works *The *Malcontent* and *The *Dutch Courtesan*. He collaborated with Jonson and Chapman on *Eastward Ho!* (1605), narrowly escaping imprisonment for it, and with Shakespeare on *Troilus and Cressida*. After another tragedy, *The Insatiate Countess* (1610), he was imprisoned for offending James I and took holy orders, writing no more for the theatre.

Martin, Mary (1913-) US actress, who made her first appearance in 1938. She went to Hollywood in 1939 but returned to the stage in 1943 in the musical *One Touch of Venus*; subsequent roles included Tchao-Ou-Niang in *Lute Song* (1945–46), Annie Oakley in *Annie Get Your Gun* (1947), and Ensign Nellie Forbush in *South Pacific* (1949). In 1959 she appeared as Maria Rainer in *Sound of Music*, while in 1965 she toured in *Hello, Dolly!*. More recent successes include Arbuzov's *Do You Turn Somersaults?* (1978).

Martin Beck Theatre A theatre on West 45th Street, between Eighth and Ninth avenues, New York, which opened in 1924 with *Madame Pompadour* and was later occupied by the Theatre Guild and then the Group Theatre. Productions staged there included the US premiere of Shaw's *The Apple Cart* (1930), Hellman's *Watch on the Rhine* (1941), O'Neill's *The Iceman Cometh* (1946), Voltaire's *Candide* (1956), and Albee's *The Ballad of the Sad Café* (1963), *A Delicate Balance* (1966), and *All Over* (1971). A revi-

val of Hellman's *The Little Foxes* with Elizabeth Taylor in 1981 was also enormously successful.

Martinelli, Drusiano (d. c. 1607) Italian actor, who was a member of the first *commedia dell'arte* company to visit England (1577). With his wife Angelica he ran the Uniti company for some time.

His brother, **Tristano Martinelli** (c. 1557–1630), was probably the first actor to play Arlecchino. He appeared with the Confidenti, the Desiosi, the Accesi, and other companies in Paris and elsewhere.

Martínez de la Rosa, Francisco (1787–1862) Spanish playwright and statesman, who was twice prime minister of Spain. After writing several insignificant neoclassical dramas he had more success with a series of comedies influenced by Moratín and then played a major role in the development of the Romantic tradition in Spain with such plays as the historical drama *Aben-Humeya* (1830) and *La conjuración de Venecia* (1830), which were modelled on the works of Victor Hugo and other French writers. Other plays include *Doña Isabel de Solís*, which was influenced by the writing of Sir Walter Scott.

Martínez Sierra, Gregorio (1881–1947) Spanish playwright and director, who was director of the influential **Teatre Eslava** in Madrid from 1917 to 1925. His own plays include *Canción da cuna* (The Cradle Song; 1910), his best known work, *El Reino de Dios* (The Kingdom of God; 1916), *Sueño de una noche de agosto* (The Romantic Young Lady; 1918), and *Triángulo* (Take Two From One; 1930). As a director he was influential for his adoption of the ideas of Adrià Gual and encouragement of García Lorca, whose first play, *La maleficio de la mariposa* (The Butterfly's Curse; 1920), he produced.

Martin-Harvey, Sir John (1863–1944) British actor-manager, who spent 14 years with Irving at the Lyceum before forming his own management there in 1899 and having an immediate success as Sydney Carton in *The Only Way,* Freeman Wills's adaptation of Dickens's *A Tale of Two Cities.* He revived the play many times during his career in response to public demand, although other acclaimed parts included Count Skariatine in Charles Hannan's *A Cigarette Maker's Romance* (1901), Hamlet (1904), the title role of *Oedipus Rex* (1912), and characters in the plays of G B Shaw. Towards the end of his career he toured in many of his old Lyceum successes.

Martini, Fausto Maria (1886–1931) Italian playwright, who became a leading writer in the *crepuscolari* tradition. Such plays as *Il giglio nero* (The Black Lily; 1913) and the acclaimed *Ridi, pagliaccio!* (Laugh, Clown, Laugh!; 1919) satirize bourgeois attitudes, while *L'altra Nanetta* (The Other Nanette; 1923) reflected the influence of Pirandello. Later plays were close in style to those of the Theatre of Silence.

Martinson Hall *See* Public Theatre.

Martoglio, Nino (1870–1921) Italian playwright, who was the author of several notable plays written in Sicilian dialect. His most successful work was the comedy *L'aria del continente* (1915), in which attempts to impose modern standards on an island community meet with failure; he also collaborated on a number of plays with Pirandello.

Martyn, Edward (1859–1923) Irish playwright and cofounder of the *Irish Literary Theatre. His plays were influenced by Ibsen and his own Catholicism. *The Heather Field* (1899) typifies his interest in the conflict between an idealistic man and a ruthless woman. In 1914 he founded the the short-lived Irish Theatre in Dublin.

Martynov, Aleksandr Evstafevich (1816–60) Russian actor, who began as a vaude-ville performer before establishing his reputation as a straight actor in the plays of Gogol, Ostrovsky, and Turgenev. He was trained by Karatygin and later became one of the first actors to favour a naturalistic style of delivery.

Marylebone Music Hall A music hall in Marylebone High Street, London, which was opened in 1858 by Sam *Collins. It was one of the most popular venues of its kind for many years but was finally closed in 1894 having fallen into disrepair.

Marylebone Theatre *See* West London Theatre.

Mascarade An early form of folk theatre that developed in the Soule region of southern France. It had several features in common with the mummers' play, including the appearance of a hobby horse.

Masefield, John (1878–1967) British poet, playwright, and novelist, whose poetic dramas were much influenced by Greek tragedy and Japanese *Nō* theatre but are not altogether satisfactory as performance pieces. They include *The Campden Wonder* (1907), based on an unsolved murder case, *The Tragedy of Nan* (1908), and *The Tragedy of Pompey the Great* (1919), as well as plays on biblical themes. He became poet laureate in 1930.

mask A covering used to conceal an actor's face or head, in order to achieve some ritualistic or symbolic effect on stage. Masks were extensively used in Greek and Roman drama (partly to accentuate facial expression), in Tudor masques (when they were called **visors**), and, covering the upper part of the face, in the *commedia dell'arte*. In the modern theatre they remain an integral feature of Japanese and Chinese drama and are occasionally used elsewhere in training or for a specific stage effect as well as in mime and pantomime. *See also* disguising.

masking piece A flat or other item of scenery used to screen the backstage area or a portion of the stage from the audience's view.

Mask Theatre *See* Belfast Civic Arts Theatre.

Mason, Marshall W *See* Circle Repertory Company.

masque A form of lavish amateur theatrical entertainment, which reached its height as an elaborate dramatic spectacle in royal courts during the early 17th century. The tradition evolved from the *disguisings and processions of masked figures in performances of mummers' plays in medieval times and probably began its development into its later form in Italy during the 16th century. It typically involved the arrival at festive gatherings of masked revellers, who danced with the guests and sometimes presented allegorical or mythological poetic dramas, such productions becoming increasingly spectacular in terms of costume, scenery, and machinery. The masque soon spread to France, where it inspired the development of the *Mascarade, and was ultimately revived in England (where it was also called **mask**) and became a part of many royal celebrations, often staged as a compliment to the monarch or a visiting dignitary.

In 1605 Ben Jonson and Inigo Jones collaborated on the first of a series of fabulous court masques, in which their innovations included the opening *anti-masque and the **double masque**, in which performers played more than one role. Gradually, however, the literary merits of their collaborations were sacrificed to spectacle, leading to Jonson's eventual withdrawal from the partnership on acrimonious terms and the abandonment of the form to technical virtuosity alone. Charles I and his queen took part in the dances themselves and, when the theatres were closed in 1642 by the Puritans, the masque had become too closely associated with the monarchy to survive its fall, subsequent works described as masques – notably Milton's *Comus* (1634) – having little in common with the original form. The tradition did, nonetheless, leave at least one practical legacy – the proscenium arch designed by Inigo Jones – and had some influence upon the development of opera.

Massey, Charles (d. 1635) English actor, who joined the Admiral's Men in 1597. His plays *Malcolm, King of Scots* (1602) and *The Siege of Dunkirk* (1603) were performed by the company but are now lost. He was named as one of the lessees of the Fortune Theatre in 1618 and again in 1622.

Massey, Raymond Hart (1896–1984) US actor and director, born in Canada, who was the senior member of a famous theatrical family. He made his first appearance at the Hart House Theatre in Ibsen's *Rosmersholm* (1922) and soon attracted attention with his powerful acting, distinctive voice, and striking looks. Subsequent successes included performances in plays by O'Neill, Shaw, and Robert Emmet Sherwood, notably as Abraham Lincoln in Sherwood's *Abe Lincoln in Illinois* (1938) – his most celebrated role. He was also acclaimed in such Shakespearean parts as Brutus, Hamlet, and Prospero and was manager of the Everyman Theatre for a time; he spent the later part of his career solely in the US and enjoyed further popularity for his appearances in the television series *Dr Kildare*.

His son, **Daniel (Raymond) Massey** (1933–), made his London debut in 1958. Among his many West End appearances have been Jack Absolute in *The Rivals* (1966) and John Worthing in *The Importance of Being Earnest* (1968); for the National Theatre, Robert in Harold Pinter's *Betrayal* (1978) and Jack Tanner in Shaw's *Man and Superman* (1981); and, for the Royal Shakespeare Company, Aguecheek in *Twelfth Night* (1983) and Henry Trebell in Granville Barker's *Waste* (1985). In 1987 he played Ben Stone in Stephen Sondheim's musical *Follies*.

Raymond Massey's daughter, **Anna Massey** (1937-), has also become well-known on the British stage. She established her reputation in *The Reluctant Débutante* (1955); roles since then have included Lady Teazle (1962) and parts in the plays of Shaw, Tennessee Williams, and Simon Gray.

Massinger, Philip (1583–1640) English playwright, who wrote about 40 plays, of which half survive. A frequent collaborator of such notable contemporaries as Tourneur, Dekker, and Fletcher, he became chief dramatist of the King's Men in 1625. Best known for *A *New Way to Pay Old Debts*, he was also the author of such plays as *The Duke of Milan* (1620), *The Roman Actor* (1626), *The Great Duke of Florence* (1627), and the comedies *The City Madam* (1632) and *The Guardian* (1633).

Master Builder, The (*Bygmester Solness*) A play by Henrik *Ibsen. First performance: Berlin, 1893. The play revolves around a leading architect, who is disturbed when a young woman challenges his view of life; she also acts as a catalyst for the guilt he feels towards his own wife and for his concern that he is losing both his idealism and artistic integrity.

Master of Santiago, The (*Le Maître de Santiago*) A play by Henri de *Montherlant. First performance: Paris, 1948. The hero, Don Álvaro, is reluctant to compromise his ideals in order to restore his fortunes; his daughter Mariana ultimately supports him.

Master of the Revels An English court official, who was in charge of theatrical productions at Court from the reign of Henry VII until 1737. Working under the Lord Chamberlain, he began as the organizer of various court revels until, in 1558, the current holder – Sir Thomas Cawarden – was also given powers to exercize the role of censor in the English theatre. As sole issuer of theatrical licences the Revels Office wielded great influence until its eventual abolition in 1737, when its powers passed to the Lord Chamberlain. Noted members of the Revels Office included Sir Thomas Benger, Thomas Blagrove, Sir Edmund Tilney, and Sir Henry Herbert.

mastersingers *See meistersänger.*

Matchmaker, The A play by Thorton *Wilder, based on his earlier play *The Merchant of Yonkers* (1938), which was adapted from a play by Nestroy. First performance: Edinburgh Festival, 1954. The play concerns a grain merchant who goes to a matchmaker in search of a wife only to have her fall in love with him. As *Hello Dolly!* it was also highly successful as a musical, providing exciting roles for a number of actresses, ranging from Carol Channing and Betty Grable to Pearl Bailey and, on film, Barbra Streisand.

Mathews, Charles (1776–1835) British actor, who became famous for his portrayal of eccentrics. Interested in following a stage career from an early age, Mathews first attracted attention when he and another youth paid 15 guineas to be allowed to present *Richard III* at the Richmond Theatre, in which they fought an exceptionally long duel, each refusing to be killed. After engagements at Dublin, Swansea, and elsewhere, he was taken on by George Colman the Younger at the Haymarket in 1803 and rapidly made a reputation as a comedian. Seasons at Drury Lane and Covent Garden followed, during which he appeared in such roles as Falstaff and Sir Peter Teazle. He then evolved his own one-man shows, called *Mr Mathews At Home*, in which he toured successfully for 20 years, even after being crippled in a carriage accident in 1814.

His son was the actor **Charles James Mathews** (1803–78), who with Frederick Yates replaced his father as manager of the Adelphi Theatre in 1835. He then joined Madame *Vestris at the Olympic in his own comedy *The Humpbacked Lover* (1835). Three years later he married her and together they went into management at Covent Garden. By 1842 he was bankrupt in spite of producing over 100 plays, including *London Assurance*. He and his wife subsequently appeared at Drury Lane and the Haymarket before taking over the Lyceum in 1847. When his wife died he married the actress **Lizzie Davenport** (d. 1899) and later made a world tour.

Mathurins, Théâtre des A theatre in the rue des Mathurins, Paris, which was opened in 1906 by Sacha *Guitry. It became a popular venue for *boulevard* plays before being taken over by the Pitoëffs in 1934, subsequently being used for the presentation of plays by Ibsen, Pirandello, and Shaw amongst others. In 1939 the management changed hands again and the theatre's programme came to include numerous revivals of classic plays by such authors as Molière.

matinée A performance given during the afternoon (or, rarely, the morning), as opposed to those given in the evening. The first recorded matinée performance was given at the Olympic Theatre in New York in 1843. Many theatres offer matinées once or twice a week; they tend to attract audiences consisting of children and organized outings.

Matthews, A(lfred) E(dward) (1869–1960) British actor, who began as a call boy, stage manager, understudy, and touring actor before achieving success in innumerable West End roles in the plays of Pinero, Barrie, Galsworthy, and others. In 1910 he made his New York debut as Algernon in Wilde's *The Importance of Being Earnest*. Later in his career he was acclaimed in William Douglas Home's comedy *The Chiltern Hundreds* (1949). He repeated his success in New York, in the subsequent film, and in a sequel, *The Manor of Northstead* (1954).

Matthews, (James) Brander (1852–1929) US playwright and theatre historian, who spent his career at Columbia University. His books on the theatre greatly influenced professional critics and the general theatre-going public in the US.

Matthews, Jessie (Margaret Matthews; 1907–81) British actress, who began as a dancer in pantomime and revue and later became a popular star of musical comedy. In 1927 she triumphed in the revue *One Dam Thing After Another*, while a year later she starred in Coward's *This Year of Grace*; in 1930, she reached perhaps the height of her fame in *Ever Green*. Songs with which she became identified included 'A Room With a View' and 'My Heart Stood Still'. Subsequently she was equally successful in films and as Mrs Dale in the long-running radio serial *Mrs Dale's Diary*.

Maude, Cyril (1861–1951) British actor-manager, whose successful career began in the US in 1884. He was comanager, with Frederick Harrison, of the Haymarket from 1896 to 1905, where, with his wife Winifred *Emery as leading lady, he staged a series of distinguished productions. In 1905 he moved to the Playhouse, which he ran for 10 years. He also served as president of the Royal Academy of Dramatic Art.

Maugham, W(illiam) Somerset (1874–1965) British novelist, playwright, and short-story writer, whose works are characterized by his clear simple style and masterly perception of human nature. He wrote his first play in 1904 and by 1908 had four plays, including the marital comedy *Lady Frederick*, running simultaneously in London. Subsequent dramas (mostly comedies of manners) included *Our Betters* (1917), a satire on social-climbers in the US, *Home and Beauty* (1919), The *Circle* (1921), *East of Suez* (1922), which brilliantly recreated the atmosphere of an eastern city's streets, The *Constant Wife* (1926), and *The*

Sacred Flame (1928). He also wrote the antiwar play *For Services Rendered* (1932).

Maurstad, Alfred (1896–1967) Norwegian actor, who became a leading performer at the Nationaltheatret in Oslo, which he joined in 1931. He was particularly admired in plays by Bjørnson, Holberg, and Ibsen.

His wife, **Tordis Maurstad** (1901-), has been acclaimed as an actress of strong classical roles with the Norske Teatret. Her greatest successes have included performances in works by Euripides, Sophocles, Ibsen, Strindberg, and O'Neill.

Alfred's son, **Toralv Maurstad** (1926-), has won equal acclaim in both classical works by Shakespeare and others and contemporary plays. He has appeared many times at the Oslo Nye Teater, becoming manager there in 1967, and at the Nationaltheatret, of which he became manager in 1978.

Max, (Alexandre) Édouard de (1869–1925) French actor, who was regarded as one of the finest actors of his day in both comedy and tragedy. Trained at the Paris Conservatoire under Worms, he was particularly admired in the tragedies of Racine and first appeared at the Comédie-Française in 1915.

Maxine Elliott's Theatre A theatre on 39th Street, between Broadway and Sixth Avenue, New York, which was built for the actress after whom it was named and opened in 1908. Early productions included Jerome K Jerome's *The Passing of the Third Floor Back* (1909) and Synge's *The Playboy of the Western World* (1911), which provoked a riot. After 1934 the theatre was taken over by the Federal Theatre Project, which produced such plays as *Horse Eats Hat* and *Dr Faustus* directed by Orson Welles. Subsequently used for broadcasting, it was demolished in 1959.

Mayakovsky, Vladimir Vladimirovich (1893–1930) Soviet poet and playwright, who became one of the leading figures of the Futurist movement. A committed supporter of the Revolution, he had his first success in the theatre with the play *Vladimir Mayakovsky – A Tragedy*, which he wrote, directed, and performed in 1913. This was followed by *Misteriya-buff* (Mystery-Bouffe; 1918), in which he parodied aspects of Christianity and revealed his sympathies with the October Revolution. Of his other works the most important include the two satirical dramas *Klop* (The Bedbug), an allegory about the emergence of the new Soviet regime, and *Banya* (The Bath House), both of which were first produced by Meyerhold. He shot himself in his Moscow flat after a failed love affair.

Mayakovsky Theatre A theatre in Moscow, which opened in 1922 as the **Theatre of the Revolution**. It was used initially for propagandist drama but was later transformed under Popov as a venue for leading contemporary Russian plays by Pogodin and others. Popov was succeeded in 1943 by Okhlopkov, who produced numerous acclaimed productions, including works by Shakespeare and Brecht. The theatre continues to present a wide range of both Soviet and foreign drama.

Mayfair Theatre The smallest commercial theatre in London, seating 310, which was originally the ballroom of the Mayfair Hotel. Designed by George Beech, it opened in 1963 with a revival of Pirandello's *Six Characters in Search of an Author*, with Sir Ralph Richardson and Barbara Jefford. Its longest running productions have included the popular revue *Beyond the Fringe* (1964–66) and Christopher Hampton's *The Philanthropist* (1970–73).

Mayne, Rutherford (Samuel Waddell; 1878–1967) Irish playwright and actor, born in Japan, who became a crucial figure in the

*Ulster Group Theatre. His early works are set in rural Ulster. His plays for the Abbey Theatre included *Peter* (1930) and *Bridgehead* (1934).

mazarine floor *See* mezzanine floor.

Meadow Players *See* Oxford Playhouse.

Measure for Measure A comedy by William *Shakespeare, written c. 1604. First performance: c. 1604. One of the 'problem plays', this dark comedy examines the inevitable compromise of romantic love through the hypocritical behaviour of the powerful Angelo towards Isabella, who seeks to save the life of her brother by her wits. The intellectual preoccupation of the author with such themes as power, temptation, and religion meant that the play was only rarely performed until the 20th century.

mechane An item of stage machinery used in the ancient Greek theatre. It consisted of a large crane from which actors could be suspended in mid-air, as if in flight.

Meddoks, Mikhail Egrovich (Michael Maddox; 1747–1825) Russian theatre manager, born in Britain, who enjoyed a monopoly of the theatre in Moscow from 1780 to 1795, when the theatre he built there (on the site of the present Bolshoi Theatre) was finally destroyed by fire. He arrived in Russia in 1767 and inherited his monopoly from Prince Ourusov; his company consisted of actors transferred from various notable private theatres.

Medea A tragedy by *Euripides. First performance: Athens, 431 BC. The play revolves around the powerful character of the enchantress Medea; the author's depiction of her as treacherous and murderous – she kills all those around her – led to accusations of mysogeny against him.

Medici, Lorenzo de' (1449–92) Italian poet and patron of the arts, who was virtual ruler of Florence as a member of the Medici family. Known as 'Lorenzo the Magnificent', he was the author of an example of the *sacra rappresentazione*, performed in Florence in 1499.

medieval drama European theatre of the Middle Ages, loosely covering the period from the 10th to the 16th centuries. Following the decline of classical drama the theatre in Europe was reduced to the activities of *minstrels, *jongleurs, and other itinerant performers; it only began to reawaken in the 10th century, when various religious houses started to employ theatrical techniques as part of the liturgy (*see* liturgical drama). At the same time the native *folk theatre was beginning to gather impetus.

The earliest manifestations of medieval religious drama were the *neume and *trope, from which a tradition of Easter plays grew (*see Quem Quaeritis?*). The earliest surviving play to treat a nonliturgical theme was the vernacular *Jeu d'Adam*, performed in France in 1170; subsequently (in 1311), the Feast of Corpus Christi was made a fixed date for theatrical performances, stimulating the development of the *miracle play and *mystery play in England and France, the *sacra rappresentazione* in Italy, the *auto sacramental* in Spain, and the *Geistliche Spiele* in Germany, where there was also the less well-known tradition of the *saint play.

Responsibility for the production of dramatic works (usually performed on open-air stages or on carts – *see* pageant) was taken up by town guilds in the late 14th century, by which time the drama of the secular tradition (including the *Robin Hood play and *mummers' play in England) was already well-developed. The allegorical and humorous *play, borrowed from both secular and liturgical traditions, began the movement of the theatre away from the Church and foreshadowed the development of farce. Various royal courts, with their weakness for *pageants and *disguising, fostered the development of a more rarified theatrical genre that ultimately became the *masque.

The foundation of the *Confrérie de la Passion in France in 1402, meanwhile, constituted the establishment of the first company to occupy a permanent playhouse, while the first professional actors in England were appointed by Henry VII in 1493 to perform *interludes at Court in the winter and to tour the country with plays in the summer. By the 16th century the basic rules of tragedy, comedy, and farce – as well as the use of scenery – had been established, which enabled the fully mature theatre to emerge in the Renaissance. *See also* Elizabethan drama; Feast of fools; Renaissance drama.

Medley, Matt *See* Aston, Anthony.

Medoff, Mark (1940-) US playwright, whose first play was *The Kramer* (1972). Subsequent successes were *The Wager* (1972), *When You Comin' Back, Red Ryder?* (1973), *The Conversion of Aaron Weiss* (1977), and *Children of a Lesser God* (1980), a play about deafness which reached Broadway and won a Tony Award. More recent works include *The Heart Outright* (1986) and *The Homage That Follows* (1987).

Medwall, Henry (c. 1475–1514) English playwright, whose interlude *Fulgens and Lucrece* (c. 1500) was the first native comedy to show Italian influences. The play includes song contests, wrestling, and jousting as diversions from the main plot. He was also the author of the traditional allegorical play *Nature* (c. 1490–1501).

Meggs, Mary (d. 1691) English orange-seller popularly known as **Orange Moll**. A widow, Mrs Meggs was awarded the concession to sell oranges and other refreshments at Drury Lane when it opened in 1663. Pepys, to whom she retailed scandals concerning Nell Gwynn, refers to her several

times in his *Diary*. After she fell into arrears she was replaced in 1682 and a legal dispute ensued that only ended when she died.

Mei Lanfang (1894–1961) Chinese actor, singer, and dancer, who is generally regarded to have been the greatest performer of the Chinese theatrical tradition. Having made his first professional appearance at the age of 14, he later became (from 1919 to 1935) the best-known performer of Peking Opera in the West, usually playing female (*dan*) roles and transforming them into central characters for the first time. His acting influenced Nemirovich-Danchenko, Stanislavsky, Brecht, and many others.

Meilhac, Henri (1831–97) French playwright, born in Paris. In collaboration with the writer **Ludovic Halévy** (1834–1908) he produced such successful comedies as *Froufrou* (1869) and libretti for Jacques Offenbach's operettas, notably *La Belle Hélène* (1864), *La Vie parisienne* (1866), and *La Grand-Duchesse de Gérolstein* (1867).

Meininger Company A theatre company founded in 1874 by George II, Duke of Saxe-Meiningen. Run by the duke and his wife themselves with the help of the actor Ludwig Chronegk, the troupe made significant innovations in emphasizing the role of the director and the importance of good ensemble playing, particularly in crowd scenes. It was also influential in its use of historically accurate costume and scenery and experimental stage lighting, its ideas being spread throughout Europe during its many tours of Shakespearean and other classic works to London and other European centres. Admirers of the group who saw it before it ceased to tour in 1890 included Stanislavsky and Antoine; actors under the duke numbered amongst them Bassermann, Eysoldt, and Kainz.

Meisl, Karl (1775–1853) Austrian playwright, who was a leading writer for the Viennese theatre in the early 19th century. His many popular plays, which rely heavily on visual effects, include the satirical *Der lustige Fritz* (1818).

meistersänger (*or* mastersinger) A travelling poet and musician of medieval Germany. The *meistersängers* – who according to tradition were descended from 12 poets of ancient times – were trained in school groups, which were organized in the same way as craft guilds and competed regularly against each other; members passed through several grades before attaining the rank of master. Hans Sachs did much to revitalize the tradition in the 16th century, although the material, usually expressing a strong moralistic or religious sentiment, remained fairly restricted in terms of metre, melody, and subject matter. The tradition, which virtually disappeared after 1600, was especially strong in southern Germany, where the most important centre was Nürnberg.

Melbourne Theatre Company An Australian theatre company, which was founded at the University of Melbourne in 1953. It established its reputation with an early production of Ray Lawler's *Summer of the Seventeenth Doll* in 1955 and subsequently concentrated on works by leading contemporary Australian playwrights, including Alan Hopgood and Patrick White. It became the resident company at the **Russell Street Theatre** in 1966, being directed by Tyrone Guthrie in 1970, and in 1973 moved into St Martin's Theatre and then the Athenaeum Theatre in 1977, where productions have included several experimental dramas.

Mélite A comedy by Pierre *Corneille. First performance: Paris, 1629. Marking Corneille's debut as a playwright, *Mélite* concerns the love affairs and intrigues of the five central characters: Mélite and Tircis, Chloris and Philandre, and Éraste, whose unrequited love for Mélite drives him to revenge.

Mellon, Mrs Alfred (Sarah Jane Woolgar; 1824–1909) British actress, who made her London debut at the Adelphi Theatre in 1843. Her first successes were in burlesque, but later she was associated with Ben Webster's management in a series of domestic dramas. In 1860 she created the part of Anne Chute in Boucicault's *The Colleen Bawn*.

Mellon, Harriot (1777–1837) British actress, who was engaged by Sheridan at Drury Lane in 1795. She remained there, successfully playing comic parts, until her marriage to the banker Thomas Coutts in 1815. Five years later she married the Duke of St Albans.

Melmoth, Mrs Charlotte (1749–1823) US actress, born in Britain, who became highly popular in leading tragic roles at the Park Theatre in New York from 1793. Previously she had appeared at both Covent Garden and Drury Lane before moving to the US to join the American Company; later in her career she had further success at the Chestnut Street Theatre in Philadelphia.

Melo, Francisco Manuel de (1608–66) Portuguese statesman and playwright, who was the author of *Auto do fidalgo aprendiz* (The Apprentice Nobleman; c. 1646), which was highly regarded in a time when little of value was being written for the Portuguese stage. It was modelled on the style of Vicente and itself had some influence upon Molière.

melodrama A form of drama, popular in the 19th century, in which emphasis is placed upon the more sensational aspects of the plot rather than upon characterization or underlying philosophical significance. The term itself was derived from German opera of the 18th century, in which it meant a piece of music in which a character's emotions are expressed by the orchestra rather than by the dialogue; translated into the straight theatre melodrama signified the use of dramatic lighting and atmospheric effects, exaggerated heroes and villains, and improbable plots to achieve a desired emotional impact.

The plays of Pixérécourt – who was himself influenced by Goethe and Schiller – were among the first to be classed as melodramas and were enormously popular in both France and England, music playing a major role in their production. Later, however, the musical content became less important and by Victorian times melodrama had become a variety of straight drama, which could range from the overtly sensationalist productions of the penny gaff theatres to such dramatically poignant works as Leopold Lewis's *The Bells*, in which Irving had his first great success, *The Corsican Brothers* by Dion Boucicault, and *Uncle Tom's Cabin* by Harriet Beecher Stowe.

The genre, which at its height stimulated some of the most spectacular and involved productions ever staged at Drury Lane and elsewhere, lost favour towards the end of the century as audiences tired of its naivity, implausibility, and conventionally happy endings, although some have argued that the form has enjoyed an unnoticed renaissance in the second half of the 20th century through cinema and television. *See also* monodrama.

melodramma A form of musical play that was popular in Italy in the 18th century. Derived from the pastoral, it provided the basic material for numerous operas.

Melpomene *See* Muses.

Melucha Theatre *See* Moscow State Jewish Theatre.

Melville, Walter (1875–1937) British manager and playwright, who – with his brother **Frederick Melville** (1879–1938) – managed the Lyceum Theatre for 25 years. The brothers staged numerous spectacular

pantomimes there, as well as their own vivid and highly successful melodramas, which included *The Worst Woman in London* (1899) and *The Ugliest Woman on Earth* (1904).

Menaechmi A comedy by *Plautus. First performance: date unknown. The plot, which revolves around the confusion of identities between a pair of twins, provided the inspiration for plays by Hans Sachs and Carlo Goldoni and for Shakespeare's *The Comedy of Errors*.

Menander (c. 343 BC–292 BC) Greek playwright, who is now recognized as the leading exponent of Greek *New Comedy and consequently the father of the modern comic tradition. Menander was largely ignored by theatre historians until a number of his plays were discovered during the 20th century, the first in 1905. In contrast to such predecessors as Aristophanes he placed a new emphasis upon the romantic content of his plays and reduced the role of the chorus as well as relying heavily upon masked stereotypes as the main characters. His sophisticated and realistic social comedies exerted a strong influence upon such subsequent Roman writers as Plautus and Terence and, ultimately, upon the comedy of manners of Molière, Wilde, Coward, and others.

Reconstructions of his plays have included Gilbert Murray's *The Rape of the Locks* (1941), based on the *Perikeiromene*, and *The Arbitration* (1945), based on the *Epitrepontes*, as well as Vellacott's *The Misanthrope*, based on the *Dyskolos*. Highly acclaimed in his own time, Menander declined invitations to visit royal courts in both Egypt and Macedonia, preferring to remain in Athens; he is believed by popular tradition to have drowned whilst swimming in the harbour there.

Principal works (dates unknown):
Aspis.
Dyskolos.
Epitrepontes.
Heros.

Misoumenes.

Orge.

Perikeiromene.

Samia.

Menken, Adah Isaacs (Dolores Adios Fuertes; 1835–68) US actress, who became famous in the title role of a stage adaptation of Bryon's *Mazeppa*, which she first played in London in 1861. In a scanty costume and riding a horse, she later repeated the role with equal success in New York and then at Astley's Amphitheatre.

Men's Dramatic Ceremony *See* mummers' play.

Men Without Shadows A play by Jean-Paul *Sartre, which has also been translated as *The Victors*. First performance: Paris, 1946. The plot concerns the internal conflicts of a group of captured Resistance fighters, who ultimately choose to confess in the face of torture.

Mercer, David (1928–80) British playwright, whose dramas explore the themes of Marxism, social alienation, and class and generation conflict. He began with a series of plays for television, writing *Ride a Cock Horse* – his first full-length work for the stage – in 1965. Subsequent plays included *After Haggerty* (1970), about a drama critic, *Flint* (1970), about a roguish Irish priest, *Cousin Vladimir* (1978), depicting a Soviet emigré's arrival in Britain, and *No Limits to Love* (1980).

Merchant, Vivien (Vivien Thomson; 1929–82) British actress, who became well-known in the plays of her then husband, Harold Pinter, playing such roles as Sarah in *The Lover* (1963), Ruth in *The Homecoming* (1965), and Anna in *Old Times* (1971). Other roles included Lady Macbeth (1967) for the Royal Shakespeare Company and Bertha in Joyce's *Exiles* (1970).

Merchant of Venice, The A comedy by William *Shakespeare, written c. 1596. First performance: date unknown. Drawing on numerous sources, the play depicts the outwitting of the Jewish usurer Shylock by the disguised Portia after he has demanded a pound of the merchant Antonio's flesh in settlement of a bond. Themes of the play include justice, religious discrimination, and the logic of the law.

Mercier, Louis-Sébastien (1740–1814) French playwright, remembered for his bourgeois dramas in the style of Denis Diderot. These include *La Brouette du vinaigrier* (1755) and *Le Déserteur* (1782). He also produced plays on historical themes, adaptations of Shakespeare, and a *Traité du théâtre ou Nouvel Essai sur l'art dramatique* (1773), in which he developed Diderot's dramatic theories.

Mercury Theatre A theatre in Notting Hill Gate, London, which was opened in 1933 by Ashley *Dukes. Seating 150, it concentrated on performances of ballet and new drama, notably T S Eliot's *Murder in the Cathedral* (1935), Auden and Isherwood's *The Ascent of F6* (1937), and O'Neill's *Days Without End* (1943). Subsequent productions included much poetic drama and children's plays. The Ballet Rambert used the theatre exclusively for some time up to 1966, since when plays have been staged there by the International Theatre Club and touring companies.

Another theatre of the same name opened in Auckland, New Zealand, in 1910 as a cinema. After several changes of name, it acquired a resident company in 1968 (run by the **Auckland Theatre Trust**) and was reconstructed to provide two auditoriums. Recent years have seen an emphasis upon productions by native playwrights from New Zealand.

See also Comedy Theatre.

Mermaid Society A theatre group established in London in the 1900s to present Elizabethan and Jacobean works. Notable productions included Milton's *Comus* (1903) and Jonson's *A Hue and Cry After Cupid* (1908).

Mermaid Theatre A theatre in Puddle Dock, Blackfriars, London, that was opened in 1959 under Bernard *Miles. It began as a private theatre in the garden of Miles's house in 1951, while its Elizabethan stage was first constructed in 1953 at the Royal Exchange. The new theatre of 1959, seating 500, was converted from a bombed Victorian warehouse and became an important venue for revivals of Jacobean and Elizabethan drama as well as contemporary works; notable productions in recent years have included the musical shows *Cowardy Custard* (1972), *Cole* (1974), and *Side by Side by Sondheim* (1976). In 1981 the theatre was reopened – including the Molecule Club studio theatre for children – as part of a controversial office complex and then experienced a financial crisis after a series of failures. After a year's occupation by the Royal Shakespeare Company (1987–88), the theatre launched a new programme of commercial drama.

Merman, Ethel (Ethel Zimmermann; 1909–84) US actress, who began her career in 1928 in cabaret. She appeared in vaudeville in 1929 and made her Broadway debut a year later in the musical *Girl Crazy*. Her performance in *Anything Goes* (1934) made her a star and she went on to play such roles as Annie Oakley in *Annie Get Your Gun* (1946), Rose in *Gypsy* (1959), Sally Adams in *Call Me Madam* (1965), and the lead in *Hello, Dolly!* (1970).

Merry, Ann (Anne Brunton; 1768–1808) British actress, daughter of a provincial theatre manager. After appearances at Bath, she was engaged at Covent Garden in 1795.

Having married the dramatist Robert Merry, she was invited by *Wignell, who became her second husband, to the US in 1796, where she became a leading tragic actress before marrying William *Warren and dying in childbirth.

Merry Wives of Windsor, The A comedy by William *Shakespeare, written c. 1598. First performance: c. 1600. Probably written for performance before Elizabeth I, the play presents the image of Falstaff in love and his subsequent downfall at the hands of the two women he pursues. It differs from Shakespeare's other comedies of the same period by being set in England, rather than a fictitious country, but retains similar elements of fantasy, chiefly through the mythological figure of Herne.

Merson, Billy (William Henry Thompson; 1881–1947) British comedian and clown, who became popular for such songs as 'The Spaniard That Blighted my Life'. Later he appeared in revue and musical comedy and had a long run in *Rose Marie* at Drury Lane (1925).

mescidato A form of secular drama that developed in Italy from the religious *sacra rappresentazione*. Based on nonliturgical themes, but employing the structure of the religious drama, the *mescidato* led ultimately to the development of the pastoral towards the end of the 16th century.

Messel, Oliver Hilary Sambourne (1905–78) British stage designer, who established his reputation with his costumes and masks for Cochran's revues in the late 1920s. His early sets, which included that for Novello's *Glamorous Night* (1935), were noted for their sophistication; subsequently he developed a more romantic style. Among others, he designed sets for the plays of Wycherley, Shakespeare, Sheridan, Fry, and Anouilh.

Messenius, Johannes (1579–1636) Swedish playwright, who wrote a number of plays based on Swedish history. Six of his plays, the earliest of which is *Disa* (1611), survive.

Method The US interpretation of the theories of Stanislavsky concerning the psychology of acting. Stanislavsky's ideas were imported to the US by Richard Boleslavsky and were first explored by his Laboratory Theatre in New York during the 1920s. One of his pupils, Lee Strasberg, subsequently developed the system with the Group Theatre and, in 1947, combined with Elia Kazan and others in founding the Actors' Studio; this became the principal training centre in the Method technique. Actors trained in the approach relied to a large extent upon their inner motivations to bring stage characters to life. For this reason the Method has provoked considerable hostility. Its critics point to an inevitable tendency towards introspective mumbled speeches. It has, however, been used to good effect in many contemporary plays and even more significantly in the cinema, by such noted exponents as Marlon Brando.

Metropolitan Casino *See* Broadway Theatre.

Metropolitan Music Hall A music hall in the Edgware Road, London, which began as a concert room in an inn but was rebuilt in 1862 to seat 4000 people (named **Turnham's Grand Concert Hall**). It became the Metropolitan in 1864 and thrived until 1897, when it was again reconstructed; subsequently it declined into a venue for touring companies, wrestling, and television, being demolished in 1963.

Metropolitan Theatre A theatre on Broadway, New York, which opened in 1854 with limited success. Successively managed by Laura Keene, Burton, Boucicault (who renamed it the Winter Garden in 1859), and Edwin Booth, its distinguished players included Rachel, John Sleeper Clarke, Charlotte Cushman, Sothern, and the Florences. Edwin Booth made a record 100 appearances as Hamlet here in the 1864–65 season. Among other productions were dramatizations of Dickens by Boucicault, Joseph Jefferson's *Rip Van Winkle*, and works by Shakespeare and Racine. In 1867 the theatre was destroyed by fire.

Meyerhold, Vsevolod Emilievich (1874–1942) Soviet actor and director, who first emerged as a leading exponent of experimental drama at the Moscow Art Theatre, which he joined in 1898. A pupil of Nemirovich-Danchenko, he soon established himself as an important theorist of the avant-garde theatre, forming his own company in 1902 and becoming assistant to Stanislavsky for a time. His development of the theory of *Bio-Mechanics led to conflict, however, with both Stanislavsky and subsequently (1908) with Vera Komisarjevskaya, after which he led his own company in St Petersburg and consolidated such concepts as the invisible 'fourth wall', through which the audience sees the play, and **Constructivism**, which called for the use of abstract multilevel settings.

Following the Revolution of 1917 Meyerhold was the first director to stage new Soviet drama by such authors as Mayakovsky but later fell into official disfavour on resisting the policy of Socialist Realism. In 1938 he was arrested and subsequently both he and his wife died in mysterious circumstances.

mezzanine floor (*or* mazarine floor) An area below the stage, part of the cellar, used for the manipulation of traps. In the US the term is also applied to the dress circle.

Mezzetino A character of the *commedia dell'arte*, one of the *zanni*. Costantini excelled in the role, usually dressed in red and white; in the French tradition the character was known as Mezzetin and provided one of Préville's most celebrated parts.

Michell, Keith (1928-) Australian actor and singer, who has divided his career between Australia and Britain. He made his debut in 1947 in Adelaide, then appeared at the Old Vic and the Young Vic before joining the Royal Shakespeare Company and touring Australia. He has been praised in several Shakespearean roles, among them Antony in *Antony and Cleopatra* (1956), as well as in such musicals as *Robert and Elizabeth* (1964) and *Man of La Mancha* (1968). Other successes have included Ronald Miller's *Abelard and Heloise* (1970), Rostand's *Cyrano de Bergerac*, and Shaw's *The Apple Cart*, in which he appeared while artistic director (1974–77) of the Chichester Festival. Plays since then have numbered amongst them *On the Rocks* (1982).

Mickiewicz, Adam (1798–1855) Polish poet and playwright, who inaugurated the Romantic movement in Poland. A native of Vilna, he was deported to Russia in 1823 and subsequently lived in Italy, Germany, and France. His most celebrated play, *Dziady* (Forefather's Eve), was written in four parts and not performed until 1901, since when it has been regularly presented; its combination of patriotism and mysticism represent a unique interpretation of Romantic drama.

Middle Comedy A style of ancient Greek comedy that developed from *Old Comedy, specifically in the last two plays of Aristophanes. Less exuberant and more strongly plotted than earlier works, the plays of this period showed a preoccupation with social rather than political issues and prepared the way for the *New Comedy that succeeded it.

Middlesex Music Hall A music hall in Drury Lane, London, which was popularly known as **Old Mo**. Originally called the

Mogul Saloon, it became a venue for music hall entertainments in 1847 and was renamed in 1851. Leading performers who appeared there for the first time included Dan Leno. It was rebuilt in 1872, 1891, and 1911, when it became the New Middlesex Theatre of Varieties seating 3000 (*see* Winter Garden Theatre).

Middleton, Thomas (c. 1570–1627) English playwright, who often worked in collaboration with leading contemporary writers. With William Rowley he wrote such plays as *The *Changeling*, while with Dekker he wrote *The Honest Whore* (1604–05) and *The Roaring Girl* (1610). His own plays range from comedies about London society, including *A Trick to Catch the Old One* (1605) and *A Chaste Maid in Cheapside* (1911), to such romantic comedies as *Anything for a Quiet Life* and the satirical *Women Beware Women*. His political satire *A Game of Chess* (1624) was immensely popular both on stage and, after it was banned, in print.

Midsummer's Night's Dream, A A comedy by William *Shakespeare, written c. 1595. First performance: date unknown. Regarded as one of Shakespeare's finest works, the play combines reality with fantasy and interweaves the parallel relationships of the fairies, ruled by Oberon and Titania, with the human lovers and a group of amateur actors through whom Shakespeare employs the device of a play within a play. In the 20th century the play has inspired notable productions by Max Reinhardt and Peter Brook among others.

Mielzner, Jo (1901–76) US scene designer, born in Paris, whose first designs were for the Lunts's production of Molnár's *The Guardsman* (1924). Subsequent designs included *Romeo and Juliet* (1934), *Hamlet* (1936), Maxwell Anderson's *Winterset* (1935) and *High Tor* (1937), Tennessee Williams's *The Glass Menagerie* (1945), *A Streetcar Named Desire* (1947), and *Cat on a Hot Tin*

Roof (1955), *Finian's Rainbow* (1947), *Guys and Dolls* (1950), and *The King and I* (1951).

Mikhoels, Salomon Mikhailovich (Salomon Michailovich Vosky; 1890–1948) Jewish actor, who became a leading performer at the Moscow State Jewish Theatre, which he managed from 1927. He began his career in 1919 in Leningrad under Granovsky; his successes included Sholom Aleichem's *Agents* (1921) and *King Lear* (1935).

Miles, Bernard (James), Baron (1907-) British actor and director, who made his debut in a minor role in *Richard III* at the New Theatre in 1930. Subsequently he was acclaimed with the Old Vic company in such roles as Iago (1942) and Face in *The Alchemist* (1947). He also created his own solo act as a West Country rustic and, in 1951, founded the *Mermaid Theatre, where his roles included Caliban and Macbeth. He opened the new Mermaid Theatre in 1959 with *Lock Up Your Daughters*, his own adaptation of Fielding's *Rape upon Rape*; since then he has directed and played in many productions, ranging from Brecht to Shakespeare. He was knighted in 1969 and made a baron in 1979.

Miles Gloriosus A stock character of the New Comedy of ancient Greece. A boastful but cowardly soldier, he also featured in plays by the Roman writer Plautus and subsequently in the *commedia dell'arte* as Il *Capitano. He was also the model for Shakespeare's Pistol and Falstaff.

Miles's Musick House *See* Sadler's Wells Theatre.

Millar, Gertie (1879–1952) British musical comedy actress, who became one of the 'Gaiety Girls' of George *Edwardes in 1901, playing Cora Bellamy in *The Toreador*. She remained with Edwardes for a number of years, went to New York in *The Girls of*

Gottenburg (1908), and returned to the Gaiety Theatre in *Our Miss Gibbs* (1909). Among her other shows were *The Quaker Girl* (1910), *Gipsy Love* (1912), and *Flora* (1918). After the death of her first husband, the composer Lionel Monckton, she married the Earl of Dudley.

Millar, Sir Ronald (Graeme) (1919-) British actor and playwright, whose first great success was the farce *The Bride and the Bachelor* (1956), which was followed by the sequel *The Bride Comes Back* (1960). Earlier plays included *Murder From Memory* (1942), *The Other Side* (1946), *Frieda* (1946), *Champagne for Delilah* (1949), and *Waiting for Gillian* (1954), based upon a novel by Nigel Balchin. After his commercial success of the late 1950s he dramatized three C P Snow novels, *The Affair* (1961), *The New Man* (1962), and *The Masters* (1963), before writing the musical *Robert and Elizabeth* (1964) about the Brownings. Subsequent plays were *Number Ten* (1967), the comedy *They Don't Grow on Trees* (1968), *Abelard and Heloise* (1970), and two more adaptions of Snow's novels: *The Case in Question* (1975) and *A Coat of Varnish* (1982).

Miller, Arthur (1915-) US playwright, who established his reputation with *All My Sons* (1947). Subsequently *Death of a Salesman* (1948) won Miller a Pulitzer Prize and recognition as a leading US playwright. His plays – most of which depict US family life – tackle such themes as illusion and reality, hypocrisy, reconciliation, and self-discovery, while *The *Crucible* was interpreted as a scathing attack on McCarthyism. It has been alleged that his unhappy marriage to the film star Marilyn Monroe influenced *After the Fall*; more recent works have failed, however, to excite equal attention.

Principal works:

All My Sons: 1947.

Death of a Salesman: 1949.

The Crucible: 1953.

A *View From the Bridge: 1955.
After the Fall: 1964.
Incident at Vichy: 1964.
The Price: 1968.
Danger: Memory!: 1987.

Miller, Henry (1860–1926) US actor, born in Britain, who made his debut in Toronto in 1878. As leading man with the Empire Theatre Stock Company he played Sydney Carton in *The Only Way* and produced and played in Vaughan Moody's *The Great Divide* (1906). His other successes included Charles Kennedy's *The Servant in the House* (1908) and Moody's *The Faith Healer* (1910). In 1916 he opened *Henry Miller's Theatre in New York.

Miller, Jonathan Wolfe (1934–) British director, who first attracted attention as a member of the Cambridge Footlights revue *Beyond the Fringe* in 1960. A qualified doctor of medicine, Miller first ventured into direction in 1962, when he directed Osborne's *Under Plain Cover* at the Royal Court Theatre; subsequently he directed plays in both London and New York, ranging from Sheridan's *The School for Scandal* (1968), *King Lear* (1969) with Michael Hordern, and *The Merchant of Venice* (1970) with Olivier, to Chekhov's *The Seagull* (1973). As an associated director of the National Theatre from 1973 to 1975 he continued with productions of Beaumarchais, Shakespeare, and Peter Nichols, among others, while works elsewhere have included further plays by Chekhov (notably *Three Sisters* in 1976), Ibsen, and Wilde. In recent years he has also directed a series of operas. He took over at the Old Vic Theatre in 1986; since then his productions have included Racine's *Andromache* (1988) with Janet Suzman.

Miller, Marilyn (Mary Ellen Reynolds; 1898–1936) US actress, who became a major star of musical comedy. Her greatest successes included *Sally* (1921), *Sunny*

(1926), *As Thousands Cheer* (1933), and *Crazy Quilt*.

Millo, Mattei (1814–96) Romanian actor and playwright, who was the first artistic director of the Romanian National Theatre in Bucharest. His plays were largely satirical comedies lampooning contemporary society; as a director he did much to improve standards of performance.

Mills, Florence (1895–1927) US Black singer, whose vaudeville act won her a place in the New York revue *Shuffle Along* in 1922. She was brought to London by C B Cochran in his revue *Dover Street to Dixie* and later starred in *Blackbirds* (1926) both on Broadway and in London, being especially remembered for her song 'Bye Bye Blackbird'.

Mills, Sir John (Lewis Ernest Watts; 1908–) British actor, who made his stage debut at the London Hippodrome in 1929 and the following year played Lord Fancourt Babberley in Brandon Thomas's *Charley's Aunt* at the New Theatre. During the 1930s he played leading parts in several musicals, including Coward's *Cavalcade* (1931) and, in 1939, joined the Old Vic company as Puck in *A Midsummer Night's Dream* and Young Marlow in Goldsmith's *She Stoops to Conquer*. He made his New York debut in 1961 in the title role of Rattigan's *Ross*. Well-known for numerous films, he has continued to appear in the theatre in plays as varied as Priestley's *The Good Companions* (1974) and Brian Clark's *The Petition* (1987). His daughters **Hayley Mills** (1946–) and **Juliet Mills** (1941–) are both actresses.

Milne, A(lan) A(lexander) (1882–1956) British novelist and playwright, best known for his Winnie-the-Pooh stories. He also wrote several light comedies, including *Mr Pim Passes By* (1919), *The Dover Road* (1923), and *The Truth about Blayds* (1923) as well as *Toad of Toad Hall* (1929), a highly successful stage adaptation of Kenneth Grahame's *The Wind in the Willows*.

Milton, Ernest (1890–1974) British actor, born in the US, who enjoyed a strong reputation in leading roles in the West End following his first London appearance in 1914. He became a member of the Old Vic company in 1918 and won acclaim for his individual interpretation of major Shakespearean and other classic parts, including Shylock and Macbeth. Other successes included Pirandello's *Henry IV* (1925), Ansky's *The Dybbuk* (1927), Patrick Hamilton's *Rope* (1929), Laurence Housman's *Prunella* (1930), Massinger's *A New Way To Pay Old Debts* (1944), and Hochwälder's *The Strong Are Lonely* (1955). He also appeared in two plays of his own, *Paganini* and *Timon of Athens* and joined the Royal Shakespeare Company in 1962, appearing in plays by Middleton and Camus among others.

Milton, John (1608–74) English poet and author of the closet drama *Samson Agonistes* (1671; performed 1900). He also wrote two masques: *Comus*, on the subject of maiden purity, was first performed at Ludlow Castle in 1634 while *Arcades* (1633) deals with family affection. Both were probably written at the request of the musician Henry Lawes.

Milwaukee Repertory Theatre A theatre in Milwaukee, Wisconsin, which was founded as the Fred Miller Theatre in 1954. Its resident company moved to the 504-seat **Wehr Theatre** in 1969 and has produced a wide variety of plays, including Tennessee Williams's *A Streetcar Named Desire* (1967), Ibsen's *A Doll's House* (1971), David Rabe's *Sticks and Bones* (1973), Sam Shepard's *La Turista* (1974), and Peter Nichols's *A Day in the Death of Joe Egg* (1975). In 1973 the company also founded an experimental venue, the **Court Street Theatre**.

mime (*or* dumb show) A form of theatrical performance in which no words are spoken and meaning is conveyed through movement and gesture alone. In ancient Greek and Roman drama the term had a somewhat different meaning; it was used both of comic entertainment that contained dialogue in which the emphasis was upon physical action (including real executions and nudity on stage) and of certain literary pieces intended for reading rather than for actual performance. The former mimes were presented by small casts who wore distinctive costumes but no masks and acted out simple, largely improvised, plots; they influenced the comedy of Plautus and others to such an extent that they eventually overshadowed all other contemporary drama. In the 5th century AD the overt vulgarity of these productions led to the excommunication of all mime performers by the Church. Writers of the latter form, which was eventually absorbed by the *atellana*, included Laberius and Publilius Syrus.

The modern silent mime show is descended from the *commedia dell'arte*, which itself borrowed from the Roman *pantomime tradition. In the early 19th century Deburau established France as the leading centre for the genre; celebrated French performers in the 20th century have included Jean-Louis Barrault and Marcel Marceau. Elsewhere mime is important primarily as a tool in the training of actors.

Minack Theatre An open-air theatre in Porthcurno, Cornwall, which was founded in 1933 by Miss Rowena Cade. Amateur companies presented plays at the theatre, which was carved out of a cliff, until 1939, when World War II forced its closure; it reopened in 1949 and flourished after 1959, when the Minack Theatre Society was formed. A wide variety of plays are presented there before an audience of up to 600 throughout the summer by companies from all over Britain.

Minna von Barnhelm A comedy by Gotthold *Lessing. First performance: 1767. The play depicts the effect the unfair dismissal of an army officer after the Seven Years' War has upon his relationship with his fiancée and is notable for its spirited dialogue and excellent characterization.

Minotis, Alexis (1900-) Greek actor and director, who has been closely associated with the performance of many classical Greek works as well as with the tragedies of Shakespeare and contemporary plays. He made his debut in 1925 and, after appearances in the US, joined the Greek National Theatre, for whom he directed (1939–67 and 1974–80) many plays, often acting in them himself. He has also produced many productions at Epidauros and has visited London in such roles as Hamlet and Oedipus. He ran his own company from 1967 to 1974, presenting mostly modern dramas.

Minskoff Theatre A theatre on Broadway, between 44th and 45th streets, New York, which opened in 1973 with the musical *Irene*. Productions staged there since then have included *Hello, Dolly!* (1973) and a revival of *West Side Story* (1980).

minstrel A musician or other entertainer commonly seen at courts throughout medieval Europe. Initially the term was used solely of those performers in the service of a particular nobleman; later, however, it was also used of the travelling entertainers formerly known as *jongleurs. The earliest minstrels emerged during the 12th century, inheriting the ancient traditions preserved by the *goliards, and were usually attached to a court on a fairly permanent basis, as in the case of Richard I's **Blondel**. In the 14th and 15th centuries minstrel guilds were formed in many European towns, organizing the training of these performers and protecting their interests against their itinerant counterparts. Little of their music, which was largely improvised until the 15th century, has survived; the tradition eventually died out during the 16th century.

minstrel show A musical entertainment that was derived from the blackface act of T D Rice in the mid-19th century. Originally a US tradition, it incorporated Negro songs and was aimed at family audiences; eventually the White performers (called **Burnt-cork Minstrels**) were replaced by Black singers and musicians. Features of these shows included witty patter between the characters Interlocutor and Bones. The minstrel show ultimately declined, its performers moving into the music hall or touring seaside resorts; revivals in the 20th century have included Britain's Black-and-White Minstrel Show, which was popular on television and at the Victoria Palace in the 1960s.

miracle play In the French liturgical drama tradition, a *saint play dealing with events from the life of the Virgin Mary or one of the saints. *See also* mystery play.

Mira de Amescua, Antonio (c. 1574–1644) Spanish playwright, who wrote several influential comedies and plays on religious and historical themes. His best-known work was *El esclavo del demonio* (The Devil's Slave; 1612) in which he explores the concept of damnation.

Miranda, Francisco de Sá de (1485–1558) Portuguese playwright, who was the author of the earliest examples of Portuguese neoclassical drama. His two comedies *Estrangeiros* and *Vilhalpandos* were both based upon the rules of the classical drama of Italy, which he visited in the 1520s. Fragments of his tragedy *Cleopatra* survive.

Mirbeau, Octave (1848–1917) French novelist, playwright, and critic. His plays, naturalistic dramas influenced by Henry Becque, include *Les Mauvais Bergers* (1897) and the satirical *Les Affaires sont les affaires* (Business is Business; 1903).

Mirren, Helen (1946-) British actress, who began her career with the National Youth Theatre. She began her long association with the Royal Shakespeare Company in 1968 and has been highly acclaimed in such roles as Ophelia (1970), Lady Macbeth (1974), and Moll Cutpurse in Middleton and Dekker's *The Roaring Girl* (1983). Her contemporary parts have included Maggie in David Hare's *Teeth 'n' Smiles* (1975) at the Royal Court and appearances in *The Bed Before Yesterday* by Ben Travers at the Lyric Theatre (1975). She was also much admired in the title role of *The Duchess of Malfi* at the Royal Exchange Theatre in 1980.

Mirror Theatre *See* Holborn Theatre Royal.

Misalliance A play by G B *Shaw. First performance: Duke of York's Theatre, 1910. The play, which was greeted with puzzlement at first, debates the relationship between parents and children and focuses on the desire of a young woman for change.

Misanthrope, Le A comedy by *Molière. First performance: Paris, 1666. The central character, Alceste, can see no good in his fellow man but remains blind to his own shortcomings. Exasperated by polite society, he resolves to spend the rest of his life in solitary exile.

Miser, The (*L'Avare*) A comedy by *Molière, inspired by Plautus's *Aulularia*. First performance: Paris, 1668. Harpagon's avarice has alienated the affection of his family: he chooses for his daughter an old husband and plans to marry his son's sweetheart himself. He is ultimately forced to bow to his children's wishes.

Misrule, Lord of An official commonly appointed at Court and at noble houses and colleges throughout England in the late 15th and early 16th centuries to preside over the Christmas festivities. Also called the **Abbot of Misrule** or **King of Misrule** (or **Abbot of Unreason** in Scotland), he reigned for a period from twelve days to three months, coordinating all the entertainment and ruling over his own mock court, in much the same way as the *Boy Bishop presided at choir schools. His function at the royal court was eventually taken over by the Master of the Revels. *See also* Feast of Fools.

Miss Julie (*Fröken Julie*) A play by August *Strindberg, written in 1888. First performance: 1889. Revolving around the meeting and subsequent sexual relationship between a footman and the sensual Miss Julie, a member of a decaying aristocracy, the play comprises Strindberg's most savage dismissal of human nature through the enmity of the sexes.

Mistinguett (Jeanne-Marie Bourgeois; 1875–1956) French actress and singer, who became a leading star of music hall, comedy, and revue in Paris between the wars. Famous for her beautiful legs and lively manner, she became the most popular performer at the Moulin Rouge and the Folies-Bergère, where she was partnered by Maurice Chevalier and appeared in increasingly fabulous costumes, performing both songs and comic sketches.

Mitchell, Maggie Julia (1832–1918) US actress, who was much loved in the role of Fanchon in a stage adaptation of George Sand's novel *La Petite Fadette*, in which part she appeared for many years from 1861. She first attracted attention as a child at the Bowery Theatre; other adult successes included Charlotte Brontë's *Jane Eyre* and Bulwer-Lytton's *The Lady of Lyons*.

Mitchell, Warren (1926-) British actor, who made his first professional appearance at the Finsbury Park Open Air Theatre in 1950, and came to the West End in the Musical *Can-Can* (1954). Well-established in television as a comedy character actor, he appeared in Johnny Speight's one-man show *The Thoughts of Chairman Alf* at the Theatre Royal, Stratford, in 1976, and subsequently in many other theatres in the UK and Australia. Other successes have included *King Lear* (1978), Arthur Miller's *Death of a Salesman* (1979), and *Ducking Out* (1983).

Mitchell, William (1798–1856) British actor, who, after 15 years of experience as an actor and stage manager, emigrated to the US in 1836. He established himself as the leading producer and performer in burlesque when he took over the tiny Olympic Theatre in New York.

Mitchell's Olympic *See* Olympic Theatre.

Mitzi E Newhouse Theatre *See* Vivian Beaumont Theatre.

Moberg, (Carl Artur) Vilhelm (1898–1973) Swedish novelist and playwright, who based much of his work upon his rural upbringing. His early plays were rustic farces but his later works included *Vär ofödde son* (Our Unborn Son; 1945), which depicts the tragic consequences of an illegal abortion.

Mochalov, Pavel Stepanovich (1800–45) Russian actor, who was highly regarded as a player of tragedy despite his resistance to the reforms of Shchepkin and others. Relying on inspiration rather than technique, he was admired as the great tragic heroes of Shakespeare and Schiller but later suffered from alcoholism and changes in public taste away from his romantic style of acting.

Modena, Gustavo (1803–61) Italian actor, son of a comic actor, who first appeared in a touring company before leading his own

troupe throughout Italy and later appearing elsewhere in Europe with great success in all types of drama. Political unrest brought him to London in the 1830s; subsequently he formed a company in Milan and, among other important innovations, introduced Shakespeare to the Italian stage.

Modjeska, Helena (Helena Opid; 1840–1909) Polish actress, who became internationally famous as an actress of great emotional power after emigrating to the US in 1876. She also acted in London (1880–82 and 1890), where her roles included Juliet to the Romeo of Forbes-Robertson and was acknowledged as ranking with Bernhardt and Duse – particularly in the role of Lady Macbeth.

Mogul Saloon *See* Middlesex Music Hall.

Mohun, Michael (c. 1620–84) English actor, who, with Charles Hart, was the foremost actor in the first company at Drury Lane. Formerly a boy actor under Beeston, he was particularly acclaimed as Volpone, Iago, and in the plays of Nathaniel Lee.

Moiseiwitsch, Tanya (1914-) British stage designer, who began her career with designs for the Abbey Theatre in Dublin (1935–39). Subsequently she worked at the Oxford Playhouse (1941–44), the Old Vic (1944–49), the Guthrie Theatre, Minneapolis, the National Theatre, and both Stratford-upon-Avon and Stratford, Ontario. Her numerous designs have included many for the plays of Shakespeare, Molière, Chekhov, Jonson, Congreve, Rattigan, Brecht, John Mortimer, and Gogol as well as those for several operas.

Moissi, Alexander (1880–1935) German actor, born in Albania of Italian parents, who began his career in 1902 in Prague but first attracted attention in Berlin. He was much admired in such Shakespearean roles as Romeo and Oberon under Reinhardt at the Deutsches Theater, while other successes included plays by Goethe, Ibsen, Shaw, and Schiller as well as the classical works of Sophocles and Aeschylus; in 1930 he played Hamlet in German in London at the same time as Gielgud played it in English at the neighbouring Queen's Theatre.

Molander, Olof (1892–1966) Swedish director and manager, who had a profound influence upon the national theatre while head of the Kungliga Dramatiska Teatern during the 1920s. His most important productions included both classic works and the plays of Strindberg.

Molé, François-René (1734–1802) French actor, who became highly popular in comic roles at the Comédie-Française. Despite his reputation for comedy, he also had the distinction in 1769 of being the first French Hamlet, in a version of Shakespeare's play by Ducis. A supporter of the Revolution he was not, unlike most of his contemporaries, imprisoned during the events of 1789 but continued to appear, under the management of Mlle Montansier.

Molière (Jean-Baptiste Poquelin; 1622–73) French playwright and actor, born in Paris; he was a master of comedy whose contribution to the theatre in this genre is unsurpassed. The son of Jean Poquelin, upholsterer and *valet de chambre* to the king, Molière was educated by the Jesuits at the Collège de Clermont and subsequently studied law. Expected to take over his father's position at court, he became involved in the early 1640s with a family of actors (the *Béjarts) and opted instead for a theatrical career.

In 1643, encouraged by Madeleine Béjart, he cofounded the *Illustre-Théâtre, an unsuccessful venture that culminated in his imprisonment for debt. From 1645 to 1658 he toured the provinces with a troupe of actors, performing farces inspired by the Italian *commedia dell'arte*, one of which – *Le *Docteur amoureux* – was to earn the company Louis XIV's favour and a place at the Petit-Bourbon Theatre in Paris. *Les Précieuses ridicules* (1659) was Molière's first major success; it was followed by a series of comedies that revolutionized the genre, delighting his audiences, scandalizing his critics, and exasperating his rivals.

In 1661 the company moved to the Palais-Royal; the following year saw Molière's unfortunate marriage to Armande Béjart, the flirtatious young sister (or the playwright's own daughter, according to contemporary gossip) of Madeleine. Having weathered the storm aroused by *L'École des Femmes* (see *Critique de l'École des Femmes, La*), largely through the king's support, Molière faced an even greater outcry after the first performance of *Tartuffe* at Versailles in 1664: it was five years before the final version could be staged in Paris. Meanwhile, he continued to write, act, and direct, producing four new plays in 1666 and two or three each year between 1667 and 1671. He died in February 1673, after collapsing on stage during a performance of *Le *Malade imaginaire*.

Molière's plays have entertained theatregoers in Paris and elsewhere for more than 300 years. Their lasting appeal may be attributed to the playwright's innate sense of comedy and to the wide range of his satirical attacks. In his hands such characters as the cuckold, the miser, the hypocrite, the social climber, the hypochondriac, and the misanthropist have provided numerous actors and actresses with their most celebrated roles.

Principal works:

L'Étourdi ou les Contretemps: 1655; translated as *The Blunderer*.

De Dépit amoureaux: 1656; translated as *The Amorous Quarrel*.

Le Docteur amoureux: 1658.

Les Précieuses ridicules: 1659; translated as *The Affected Young Ladies*.

Sganarelle ou le Cocu imaginaire: 1660.

L'École des Femmes: 1662; translated as *The *School for Wives*.

La Critique de l'École des Femmes: 1663.
*L'*Impromptu de Versailles*: 1663.
Tartuffe ou l'Imposteur: 1664.
Don Juan ou le Festin de pierre: 1665.
*Le *Misanthrope*: 1666.
Le Médecin malgré lui: 1666; translated as *The Doctor in Spite of Himself*.
Amphitryon: 1668.
**George Dandin; ou, le Mari confondu*: 1668.
L'Avare: 1668 Paris; translated as *The *Miser*.
Le Bourgeois gentilhomme: 1670; translated as *The Prodigious Snob*.
Psyché: 1671 (with Pierre Corneille and Philippe Quinault).
Les Fourberies de Scapin: 1671; translated as *The Cheats of Scapin*.
Les Femmes savantes: 1672; translated as *The Blue-Stockings* (or *The Learned Ladies*).
Le Malade imaginaire: 1673; translated as *The Imaginary Invalid* (or *The Hypochondriac*).

Molina, Tirso de *See* Tirso de Molina.

Molnár, Ferenč (Ferenč Neumann; 1878–1952) Hungarian novelist and playwright, who established an international reputation with his farces and fantasies. His works include *Az Ördög* (The Devil; 1907), *A hattyú* (The Swan; 1920), and *A vörös malom* (The Red Mill; 1923). The film and musical comedy *Carousel* (1945) was based upon his mystery play *Liliom* (1909), while *The Guardsman* (1910) provided a successful vehicle for the Lunts; other successes included *The Glass Slipper* (1924), which was based upon the story of Cinderella. Molnár became a US citizen in 1940.

Momus The god of clowns, derived from the mythological Greek god of ridicule. Used occasionally as an alternative name for a clown, Momus also appeared as a character in masques and harlequinades.

Monakhov, Nikolai Federovich (1875–1936) Russian actor, who served a long apprenticeship in café theatre in St Petersburg before joining Mardzhanov's Free Theatre in 1913 and attracting much attention. Subsequently he won acclaim in operetta with the Moscow Art Theatre, achieving his greatest success as Philip II in Schiller's *Don Carlos*.

Moncrieff, Gladys (1893–1976) Australian actress, who was particularly successful in operetta and musical comedy. Known as 'Our Glad', she became highly popular in shows by Gilbert and Sullivan as well as in native Australian productions and revivals of popular musicals.

Moncrieff, William (George) Thomas (1794–1857) British playwright and manager, who wrote a number of melodramas and burlesques for performance in minor theatres. He also adapted several novels, especially those of Dickens. At various times he managed the Regency Theatre (later the Scala Theatre), Coburg Theatre (later the Old Vic Theatre), Vauxhall Gardens, and Astley's Amphitheatre.

Monkhouse, Allan Noble (1858–1936) British theatre critic and playwright, who was especially supportive of Miss Horniman's Gaiety Theatre. His works for the company included *Reaping the Whirlwind* (1908), *Mary Broome* (1911), and the satirical *Nothing Like Leather* (1913). His finest play, *The Conquering Hero* (1924), deals ironically with the theme of war.

monodrama A short theatrical presentation in which only one actor speaks (occasionally also known as a melodrama). Such productions – often extracts from longer works – enjoyed a brief vogue in Germany in the late 18th century, performed by Johann Christian Brandes. In the modern theatre such pieces are normally referred to as **monologues**.

monologue *See* monodrama.

Montague, Henry James (Henry James Mann; 1844–78) US actor, who opened the Vaudeville Theatre in New York in 1870. Returning to New York in 1874 he appeared with Lester Wallack in a series of successful comedies by such authors as Clement Scott, T W Robertson, and Tom Taylor. He also founded the Lambs theatre club in 1875.

Montaland, Céline (1843–91) French actress, who established her reputation playing children at the Comédie-Française. Later in life she transferred (1860) to adult roles, the best of which included the mother in Daudet's *Jack* at the Gymnase.

Montansier, Mlle (Marguerite Brunet; 1730–1820) French actress, who became manageress of several important French theatres. After managing a theatre at Rouen she was made responsible for the theatre at Versailles, which she rebuilt in 1777. After the Revolution she moved to Paris and established a fashionable salon; she narrowly escaped the guillotine after being accused of Royalist sympathies by Fabre d'Églantine. Subsequently she managed the Palais Royal until 1806.

Montchrétien, Antoine de (c. 1575–1621) French playwright and economist. In 1605 he fled to England after killing an adversary in a duel; he returned to France six years later but was killed during a Protestant insurrection in 1621. Montchrétien's lyrical tragedies, influenced by Garnier, include *Sophonisbe* (1596), *L'Écossaise* (1601), *David* (1601), and *Aman* (1601).

Montdory (Guillaume des Gilberts; 1594–1651) French actor-manager, who was acknowledged as the first great French actor for his performances of Corneille. After training with Valleran-Lecomte and Lenoir, he scored his first major success in Paris in 1630, in *Mélite*. Subsequently he opened the Théâtre du Marais and appeared as Ro-drigue in the first production of *Le Cid*, his most celebrated tragic role. He was also acclaimed as Herod in Tristan l'Hermite's *La Mariane*, in which role he was appearing before Richelieu when he was struck down by paralysis of the tongue and had to retire.

Montfleury (Zacherie Jacob; c. 1600–67) French actor, who became a prominent figure at the Hôtel de Bourgogne. An extremely fat man, he excelled in tragedy, although he was the subject of satirical comment in *L'Impromptu de Versailles* (1663) by Molière, with whom Montfleury continued an acrimonious relationship, accusing the playwright of marrying his own daughter.

His son was the playwright **Antoine (Jacob) Montfleury** (1639–85), who was also involved in the rivalry with Molière. His plays, most of which were presented at the Hôtel de Bourgogne, include *L'Impromptu de l'Hôtel de Condé* (1663), which was written in reply to Molière's *L'Impromptu de Versailles*.

Montherlant, Henri(-Marie-Joseph-Millon) de (1896–1972) French novelist and playwright, born in Paris. He became actively involved in bullfighting and other sports in his youth and extolled in his early writings physical strength, courage, and heroism. Having made his name as a novelist, he began writing for the theatre during World War II. His plays, notably *La Reine Morte* (1942), *Le maître de Santiago* (The *Master of Santiago; 1948), and *La Ville dont le prince est un enfant* (1951), were influenced by Pierre Corneille and Racine.

Month in the Country, A A play by Ivan *Turgenev, written in 1850 and regarded as his finest work for the theatre. First performance: 1872. Originally entitled *The Student*, the play has no single hero but depicts various lovers and other characters and concentrates on their inner motivations.

Montparnasse, Théâtre *See* Baty, Gaston.

Moody, William Vaughn (1869–1910) US playwright, whose first success was *The Great Divide* (1906). This and *The Faith Healer* (1909) greatly stimulated the development of US drama away from the more sentimental and melodramatic productions that had previously characterized it.

Mooney, Ria (1904–73) Irish actress, who was invited to join the Abbey Theatre company after success as an amateur in Chekhov's *The Proposal.* O'Casey chose her to play Rosie Redmond in *The Plough and the Stars* (1926), after which she toured England and the US, staying in New York for some years as assistant director with the Civic Repertory Theatre. Later, after some time with the Gate Theatre company, she returned to the Abbey as its first woman producer.

Moon in the Yellow River, The A play by Denis *Johnston. First production: Abbey Theatre, Dublin, 1931. It explores the state of contemporary Ireland through the eyes of a German engineer. The play has been successfully presented in several languages.

Moore, Dudley (1935–) British actor and songwriter, who was one of the quartet who appeared in the satirical revue *Beyond the Fringe* (1960) in Edinburgh, London, and New York. After starring in *Play It Again, Sam* at the Globe Theatre in 1969, he joined Peter *Cook to tour in their own revue, *Behind the Fridge.* Subsequently he has become well-known for his screen appearances.

Moore, Edward (1712–57) British playwright, author of the sentimental dramas *The Foundling* (1747) and *The Gamester* (1753). The latter was the result of a collaboration with David Garrick, who played the role of Beverley in it with great success at Drury Lane.

Moore, Eva *See* Esmond, Henry Vernon.

Moore, George (Augustus) (1852–1933) Irish novelist, poet, and playwright. His particular contribution to drama came in the 1890s when he helped to establish the *Irish Literary Theatre. He also collaborated with W B Yeats on the rewriting of Edward Martyn's *The Tale of a Town* as *The Bending of the Bough* (1900); his other plays include *The Strike at Arlingford* (1893) and, also with Yeats, *Diarmuid and Grania* (1901).

Moore, Maggie (Margaret Sullivan; 1851–1926) US actress, who spent much of her career in Australia with her husband J C Williamson, notably in the much-revived comedy *Struck Oil; or, the Pennsylvanian Dutchman.* She excelled in comic roles and operetta and also appeared on tour in Britain from 1903 to 1908.

Moore, Mary *See* Wyndham, Sir Charles.

moral interlude A short dramatic entertainment that developed during the 16th century from the morality play. Although it retained the humour and educating purpose of the earlier form, it was notable especially for its development of the purely allegorical figures into more realistic characters.

morality play A medieval allegorical drama, usually depicting the contest between various personified virtues for the soul of a man, which gradually supplanted the mystery play during the 15th century. The earliest major example of the genre, which was probably encouraged by the church for its propaganda value, was *The Castle of Perseverance* (c. 1405); this work was also notable for the comic character Backbiter, who was introduced for purely theatrical reasons, specifically to keep the action going. The form developed the coarse humour and grotesque detail of the mystery play and ultimately evolved into the *moral interlude of the Tudor stage; it also played a key role in the establishment of the first troupes of professional actors. The more well-known morality plays include *Everyman* and *Magynfycence*, by John Skelton. *See also* Vice.

Moratín, Nicolás, Fernández de (1737–80) Spanish poet and playwright, author of a number of plays influenced by French neoclassical tragedy. Noted primarily as a poet, he wrote the three tragedies *Lucrecia* (1763), *Hormesinda* (1770), and *Guzmánel Bueno* (1777).

His son was **Leandro Fernández de Moratín** (1760–1828), who was the leading Spanish neoclassical playwright of his time. He was much influenced by French dramatists, especially Molière, and wrote a number of successful plays satirizing theatre criticism – including *La comedia nueva* (The New Comedy; 1792) – and marriages of convenience – as in his most celebrated work for the stage, *El sí de las niñas* (When a Girl Says Yes; 1806).

Mordvinov, Nikolai Dmitrievich (1901–66) Soviet actor, who became a leading performer of tragic roles at the Mossoviet Theatre in Moscow, where he first appeared in 1940. He began his career at the Gorky State Theatre in Rostov in 1936 and later won acclaim in plays by such diverse authors as Shakespeare, Lermontov, Korneichuk, and Goldoni.

Moreto y Cabaña, Agustín (1618–69) Spanish playwright, who was the author of over 100 dramas, including several notable comedias influenced by Lope de Vega and Tirso de Molina. Trained as a lawyer, he was highly popular in his own time with such comedies as *El desdén con el desdén* (Scorn for Scorn; 1654) and *El lindo Don Diego* (1662), which was his most celebrated play.

Morgan, Charles Langbridge (1894–1958) British novelist, essayist, playwright, and theatre critic of *The Times* (1926–39)

in succession to A B Walkley. He was also the author of the carefully crafted plays *The Flashing Stream* (1938), *The River Line* (1952), and *The Burning Glass* (1954).

Morley, Robert (1908–) British actor, who first appeared professionally (as an elderly pirate) in *Treasure Island* (1928). After many years in the provinces, during which he ran his own summer repertory company in Cornwall, he came to prominence in London at the Gate Theatre Club in 1936, playing the title role in *Oscar Wilde* by Leslie and Sewell Stokes. He repeated the role on Broadway in 1938. Thereafter, he appeared in numerous successes, ranging from Kaufman and Hart's *The Man Who Came to Dinner* (1941) to Alan Ayckbourn's *How the Other Half Loves* (1970). He has also performed his own solo entertainments and appeared frequently on film and television; his own plays include *Goodness, How Sad!* (1938) and *Edward My Son* (1947). His son **Sheridan Morley** (1941–) is a theatre critic.

Morosco Theatre A theatre on 45th Street, New York, which opened in 1917 with *Canary Cottage* by Elmer Harris and Oliver Morosco, after whom the theatre was named. Successful productions staged there since then have included O'Neill's *Beyond the Horizon* (1920), George Kelly's *Craig's Wife* (1925), Coward's *Blithe Spirit* (1941), Miller's *Death of a Salesman* (1949), Tennessee Williams's *Cat on a Hot Tin Roof* (1955), and several successful transfers from the London stage, among them plays by David Storey, Simon Gray, Rattigan, and Ayckbourn. The theatre was demolished in 1982.

Morris, Clara (Clara Morrison; 1846–1925) US actress, born in Canada, who became highly popular for her spirited performances in melodrama. After extensive experience in various parts of the northern US she joined Daly's company in New York and won acclaim in Wilkie Collins's *Man and Wife* and *Article 42* (1872). Subsequently she appeared in many varied roles, attracting large audiences to such plays as *The Lady of the Camellias* by Dumas *fils*, Sardou's *Odette* (1892), and her own adaptation *Claire* (1894). Her classic parts included Lady Macbeth, while later in her career she also ventured into vaudeville.

Morris Dance A rural folk dance performed in England. One of the entertainments bridging the gap between ancient ritual and recognizable folk theatre, the Morris Dance probably sprang from Moorish origins, having similar counterparts throughout Europe as well as on other continents, and has strong associations with folk myth and superstition (dances being regularly performed at May Day celebrations and other notable events in the agricultural calendar). Dancers (traditionally male although female troupes now flourish) sometimes blacken their faces and conventionally dress in white, attaching bells to the legs or body and often carrying sticks or handkerchiefs; they may also be accompanied by a Fool and hobby horse and figures linked to the tradition of the Robin Hood play. *Compare* Horn Dance.

Morselli, Ercole Luigi (1882–1921) Italian playwright, who became a leading writer in the *crepuscolari* tradition. He won acclaim for his modern treatment of mythical subjects in *Orione* (1910), *Glauco* (1919), and *Belfagor* (1930).

Mortimer, John Clifford (1923-) British novelist and playwright, who has written many plays, of which several have been based upon his experiences as a barrister. The need for communication and the plight of the lonely and unsuccessful are recurrent themes. His first play, the one-act *The Dock Brief*, won the Italia Prize in 1957; other plays have included another one-act, *Lunch Hour* (1961), *The Wrong Side of the Park*

(1960), *Two Stars for Comfort* (1962), *The Judge* (1967), and *Cat Among the Pigeons* (1969), which was an adaptation of a play by Feydeau. *A Voyage Round My Father* (1970) was an autobiographical play focusing upon his relationship with his blind father. More recent plays include *The Lady from Maxim's* (1977) and *A Little Hotel on the Side* (1984), both based on Feydeau. He is best-known for his television series *Rumpole of the Bailey*.

Morton, Charles (1819–1904) British music hall manager, often referred to as the 'father of the halls'. Born in Hackney, he became landlord of the Canterbury Tavern in Lambeth. Here he decided to build the *Canterbury Music Hall, opening it with Sam Cowell as the first star attraction. He opened the Oxford Music Hall in 1861 and went on to run several other successful halls.

Morton, Thomas (c. 1764–1838) British playwright, who was the author of a number of successful plays, including *Speed the Plough* (1798), which was famous for the character of the censorious Mrs Grundy, who never appears but is frequently referred to. Among his other comedies were *The Way to Get Married* (1796), *A Cure for the Heart-Ache* (1797), *Secrets Worth Knowing* (1798), and *The School of Reform; or, How to Rule a Husband* (1805), which enjoyed several revivals.

His son, **John Maddison Morton** (1811–91), was the author of numerous farces, many adapted from the French, the most successful being *Lend Me Five Shillings* (1846) and *Box and Cox* (1847).

Moscow Art Theatre A theatre in Moscow, which was founded in 1898 by *Nemirovich-Danchenko and *Stanislavsky. Their company soon established a controversial reputation with their naturalistic production of Chekhov's *The Seagull*, which had already proved a failure at the more conventional Alexandrinsky Theatre. Subsequently the company presented the premieres of *Uncle Vanya* (1899), *Three Sisters* (1901), and *The Cherry Orchard* (1904), as well as the first production of Gorky's *The Lower Depths* (1902). After the Revolution the company toured Europe and the US (1922–23), returning to present new Soviet dramas by such playwrights as Bulgakov and Ivanov. Stanislavsky's influence on the theatre was profound; the first actors to be trained there in his style of acting included Kachalov, Olga-Knipper, and Moskvin. The company continued to tour internationally and acquired an extra new building on the Tverskoy Boulevard in 1973, in addition to an acting school.

Moscow State Jewish Theatre A theatre founded in Leningrad by Alexander *Granovsky in 1919, known in Yiddish as the **Melucha Theatre** and in Russian as the **Goset**. Two years later it transferred to Moscow, presenting Yiddish plays by Sholom Aleichem and acquiring a new venue seating 766. Under Salomon *Mikhoels, the theatre continued to stage a mixture of Yiddish and classic plays, including works by Shakespeare; when Mikhoels died in 1948 the company broke up until 1962, when it was resurrected as the **Jewish Drama Ensemble**.

Moskvin, Ivan Mikhailovich (1874–1946) Russian actor, who was a founding member of the Moscow Art Theatre. He played leading roles in many of the company's early productions, winning particular praise in plays by Tolstoy, Chekhov, Gorky, Gogol, Ostrovsky, and Pogodin.

Mossop, Henry (1729–74) British actor, born in Ireland. At Drury Lane he played many leading tragic parts successfully, but failed in his ill-advised attempts to play young lovers. He was resentful of Garrick and eventually returned to Dublin, where his efforts to manage the Smock Alley Theatre were disastrous; subsequently he starved to death in London.

Mossoviet Theatre A theatre in Moscow, which opened in 1923 as a venue for politically-orientated drama. The earliest productions staged there included plays by Bill-Belotserkovsky; later productions under such leading directors as Lyubimov-Lanskoy and Zavadsky have included plays by Lermontov, Shakespeare, and Shaw.

Mostel, Zero (1915–77) US actor, who began his career in cabaret and made his Broadway debut in vaudeville. Subsequent stage roles included Argan in Molière's *The Imaginary Invalid* (1952), Shu Fu in Brecht's *The Good Woman of Setzuan* (1956), Leopold Bloom in *Ulysses in Night-town* (1958), John in Ionesco's *Rhinoceros* (1961), Prologus in the musical *A Funny Thing Happened on the Way to the Forum* (1962), and Tevye in the musical *Fiddler on the Roof* (1964).

Mota, Anrique da (16th century) Portuguese poet and playwright, author of several plays and collaborations with Vicente. It is not known whether any of his satirical works, which include *Farsa do Alfaiate*, were staged.

Mother Courage and her Children (*Mutter Courage und ihre Kinder*) A play by Bertolt *Brecht, written 1938–39. First performance: Zürich, 1941. Set during the Thirty Years' War, the play discusses the responsibilities shared by an entire population in time of war and the link between the most innocuous contribution to the war effort and the worst atrocities.

motion The *puppet theatre presented by travelling puppeteers during the 16th and 17th centuries. At this time most puppet shows were based on biblical stories, although sources became increasingly varied as the tradition developed.

Moulin Rouge A dance hall in Paris, which opened in 1899. It became well known as a home of dancing, music hall, and cabaret, acquiring some notoriety for early performances of the can-can. Noted managers of the Moulin-Rouge have included Mistinguett, while posters for the dance hall by Toulouse-Lautrec were much admired and imitated elsewhere. *See also* New York Theatre.

Mounet-Sully (Jean Sully Mounet; 1841–1916) French actor, who excelled as a player of the great tragic roles. He first appeared at the Comédie-Française in 1872 in Racine's *Andromaque*; subsequently he was consistently successful, his many triumphs including the plays of Victor Hugo.

Mountfort, William (1664–92) English actor and playwright, who appeared at the second Theatre Royal, Drury Lane. The author of such plays as *Greenwich Park* (1691) and a farcical version of *Dr Faustus* (1697) he was highly regarded as an actor of gentlemen in plays by Wycherley and others. He was murdered at the orders of one Captain Hill over the favours of Anne Bracegirdle. His wife was the actress Susanna *Percival.

Mountview Theatre School A drama school in Crouch Hill, London, which was founded in 1947 as an amateur company. Acquiring its own small theatre, which was rebuilt after a fire in 1963, it gradually built up a strong reputation for productions of both classics and modern plays, touring widely. The drama school itself was opened in 1969 and presents regular free performances by its students in the Mountview Theatre and Judi Dench studio theatre, opened in 1971.

Mourning Becomes Electra A three-part trilogy by Eugene *O'Neill. First performance: New York, 1931. The trilogy, based on Aeschylus's *Oresteia*, depicts the incestuous relationships between Ezra Mannon, his wife Christine, Adam Brant, Orin, and Lavinia and is set in Puritan New England.

Mousetrap, The A play by Agatha *Christie. First performance: Ambassador's Theatre, London, 1952. Originally written for radio, this thriller ran for 21 years before transferring to St Martin's Theatre in 1974 to continue its record-breaking unbroken run. The original cast included Richard Attenborough and his wife Sheila Sim.

Mowatt, Anna Cora (1819–70) US playwright and actress, who was best known for *Fashion* (1845), a satirical drama that mocked the trend for affected European manners in contemporary US society. Her other plays include *Gulzara* (1841) and *Armand* (1847); as an actress she was particularly successful as Pauline in Bulwer-Lytton's *The Lady of Lyons* (1845) and later led her own company.

Mrożek, Sławomir (1930-) Polish playwright and short story writer, who was the author of several satirical plays associated with the Theatre of the Absurd. His best-known work is the political satire *Tango* (1965); his other plays include *Policja* (The Police; 1958), *The Turkey Cock* (1961), *Na pełnym morzu* (Out at Sea; 1961), *Karol* (Charlie; 1962), *Striptease* (1962), *The Hunchback* (1976), and *A Summer's Day* (1983).

Mrs Warren's Profession A play by G B *Shaw, written in 1893. First performance: New Haven, 1902. The play's subject, prostitution, and its onslaught upon the social conditions that make prostitution possible caused a scandal and opposition from the censor. Acclaimed for its straightforward approach to a usually romanticized subject, it is generally considered one of Shaw's finest plays.

Much Ado About Nothing A comedy by William *Shakespeare, written c. 1598. First performance: c. 1598. A comedy of deception and disguise revolving around a masked ball, the play is especially notable for the lively relationship of Beatrice and Benedick and for the comic pomposity of the constable, Dogberry. The central story of Claudio and Hero dated back to a Greek romance; most of the other characters are thought to have been Shakespeare's inventions.

Müller, Heiner (1929-) East German playwright, whose critically acclaimed works range from the strongly socialist *Der Lohndrücker* (The Scab; 1950) and *Die Korrektur* (The Correction; 1958) to adaptations of the classics. *Philoktet* (1968) is regarded as his best classically-based play although he has also written popular versions of *Macbeth* and Schwartz's *The Dragon*.

multiple setting *See* composite setting.

mummers' play A form of early English folk theatre, which had its roots in primitive ritual. Also known as the **Men's Dramatic Ceremony** and having a central theme of death and resurrection, the mummers' play usually depicts the killing of a hero in battle and his subsequent revival at the hands of a doctor, the hero being **St George** and his opponent the **Turkish Knight** in most versions of the tradition. Other characters who appear in the piece can include a Fool, a man dressed as a woman (all parts being traditionally played by men), Father Christmas, and the doctor's assistant Johnny Jacks (hence the alternative name of **Johnny Jack's Play**). The play usually concludes with the **Quête**, a procession of characters who deliver some verse and collect money from the audience.

The earliest mummers (the name possibly being taken from the German word for mask) were street performers, who danced and enacted dumb shows at festivals throughout Europe from the 13th to the 16th centuries. The mummers' play then grew more elaborate, becoming intertwined with the early development of the masque in Italy; by the 18th century, when the first surviving contemporary accounts were written, it had numerous local variations throughout England, usually classed into three groups.

Features of the **Hero-Combat Play** include the dressing of the cast in rags or torn paper (hence the **Paper Boys' Play** of Marshfield in Avon) and the blacking of their faces, while the **Sword Play** of NE England depicts the hero's death in battle against a group of dancers. The third type, the now moribund **Wooing Ceremony** of the E Midlands was remarkable in having two women (played by men) – the Lady and Dame Jane – as central roles. Some of the more unusual extant variations include the **Pace-Egg Play** of Yorkshire, which involves a search for hidden Easter eggs, and the **Soul-Cakers Play** of Cheshire, for which special cakes are baked. The mumming tradition survives in various villages throughout the country; other alternative names by which it is known include the **Jolly Boys' Play** and the **Tipteerers' Play**.

Munday, Anthony (1560–1633) English playwright, who began as a child actor with Oxford's Men. Also active as a translator, pamphleteer, and writer of ballads and pageants, he collaborated with Chettle and probably with Shakespeare on *Sir Thomas More* (1593–95). Other plays attributed to him include *Two Italian Gentlemen; or, Fedele and Fortunio* (1584) and *John a Kent and John a Cumber* (c. 1594).

Munden, Joseph (1758–1832) British actor, who – after a long time in the provinces – moved to Covent Garden in 1790, where he succeeded John Edwin the Elder. Over the next 30 years he played a range of comic parts before transferring to Drury

Lane, where he appeared with Edmund Kean.

Muni, Paul (Muni Weisenfreund; 1895–1967) US actor, who became a leading performer with the New York Jewish Art Theatre, which he joined in 1926. His greatest successes included the role of Willie Loman in Arthur Miller's *Death of a Salesman* (1949).

municipal theatre *See* civic theatre.

Munk, Kaj Harald Leininger (1889–1944) Danish playwright, priest, and poet, who was murdered by the Gestapo for his resistance to the German occupation of Denmark. His best known religious dramas include *En Idealist* (Herod the King; 1928), which was heavily criticized when first performed (1928) but was later praised by the critics, and *Ordet* (The Word; 1932), a miracle play. He expressed his opposition to the German occupation in such plays as *Han sidder ved Smeltediglen* (He Sits at the Melting Pot; 1938), which focuses upon the persecution of the Jews, and *Niels Ebbesen* (1942).

Murder in the Cathedral A poetic drama by T S *Eliot. First performance: Canterbury Cathedral, 1935. It concerns the martyrdom of Thomas à Becket in the Cathedral in 1170. Admired features of the play include the prose speeches by Becket's murderers. It promoted considerable interest in verse plays and has been revived many times.

Murdoch, James Edward (1811–93) US actor, who was highly successful in classic comedies by such authors as Aphra Behn, Sheridan, and Shakespeare. His most admired roles included Charles Surface in *The School for Scandal* (1853) and Shakespeare's Benedick, Orlando, and Mercutio; he appeared briefly in Britain in 1856.

Murphy, Arthur (1727–1805) British playwright, born in Ireland, who was the author of numerous successful comedies based on works by Molière and others, including *The Way to Keep Him* (1760) and *Three Weeks after Marriage* (1764). Of his tragedies the best were *Zenobia* (1768), *The Grecian Daughter* (1772), and *Alzuma* (1773).

Murray, Alma (1854–1945) British actress, who was much admired by Browning for her performances in some of his dramas in the 1880s and by G B Shaw, for whom she played Raina in *Arms and the Man* at the Avenue Theatre in 1894. She was also highly praised for a single performance as Beatrice in Shelley's banned play *The Cenci*, given in 1888.

Murray, (George) Gilbert (Aimé) (1866–1957) British classical scholar, poet, and philosopher, who translated numerous works of ancient Greek drama. He was particularly noted for his translations of Euripides, whose plays *Hippolytus*, *Trojan Women*, *Electra*, the *Bacchae*, and *Iphigenia in Tauris* were successfully staged by Harley Granville-Barker in versions by Murray. He also provided translations of Sophocles, Aeschylus, Aristophanes, and Menander.

Murray, Thomas Cornelius (1873–1959) Irish playwright, who wrote several plays reflecting Irish rural life for the Abbey Theatre. *Birthright* (1910) established him as a leading Irish writer; in 1912 he followed it with *Maurice Harte*, his best-known play. His other works include *The Briery Gap* (1917) and *Autumn Fire* (1924).

Muses A group of nine Greek goddesses, of whom three were associated with the theatre. **Melpomene**, often depicted holding a tragic mask, was the Muse connected with tragedy, **Terpsichore** with dancing and lyric poetry, and **Thalia**, usually holding a comic mask, with comedy.

musical comedy A form of theatrical production in which songs and dances – usually of a lighthearted nature – are combined with the dialogue and action. The modern musical has its roots in the late 19th-century operetta (to which it is closely related) and, in the early days at least, placed the emphasis upon the musical content rather then the storyline, which was frequently implausible and sentimental.

The US musical play *The Black Crook* (1866) is usually considered the first production to have combined elements of ballet, melodrama, opera, and burlesque to create a distinct genre; perhaps more influential, however, were the light operettas of Gilbert and Sullivan and others in England (beginning with *HMS Pinafore* in 1878), which had the merit of applying music and dance to a libretto of some literary worth. The British approach was transported to the US by George Edwardes in the late 1890s when he presented his 'Gaiety Girls' in New York, stirring up further interest in musical drama and linking its transatlantic development.

The success of the early musical comedies, which included Lionel Monckton's *A Country Girl* (1902), Gustave Kerkev's *The Belle of New York* (1897), and Leslie Stuart's *Floradora* (1899), lured such European composers as Victor Herbert, Rudolf Friml, and Sigmund Romberg, who were familiar with the Viennese operetta tradition of Franz Lehár and others. These immigrants created numerous romantic and melodious musicals for both the stage and the cinema (of which the most popular included Romberg's *The Student Prince* (1924), *The Desert Song* (1926), and Friml's *Rose-Marie*, composed in 1924). Eventually, however, their romantic mid-European style gave way to a wave of energetic and sophisticated pieces staged after World War I by such composers as George Gershwin, Rodgers and Hart, Cole Porter, and Irving Berlin, who swept the popular theatre with such slick lightweight productions as *No, No, Nanette* (1925) and *The Girl Friend* (1926).

Jerome Kern's *Show Boat* signalled the next development as early as 1928, sounding a more serious note and heralding an increasing interest in plot, a transformation that was confirmed by Rodgers and Hammerstein's *Oklahoma!* in 1943. Thenceforth the musical showed itself capable of addressing all the subjects previously reserved for legitimate drama, the previously disparate elements of singing, dancing, and dialogue being increasingly integrated in such huge successes as *West Side Story* (1957). Although the occasional oldfashioned romantic production (most notably *My Fair Lady* in 1956) defied modern trends, the musical – after a flirtation with rock music in the 1970s – has continued to run more closely parallel with straight drama, successes of recent years having included musicals based on Shakespeare, Victor Hugo, Dickens, and T S Eliot.

Music Box A theatre on West 45th Street, New York, which opened in 1921 with a revue by Irving Berlin. Since then the theatre has housed a number of successful productions, including Kaufman and Ryskind's *Of Thee I Sing* (1932), Van Druten's *I Remember Mama* (1944), Inge's *Picnic* (1953), Rattigan's *Separate Tables* (1956), and Anthony Shaffer's *Sleuth* (1970). More recent successes have been the musical *Side by Side by Sondheim* (1977) and Ira Levin's *Deathtrap* (1978).

music hall A British theatrical entertainment, which flourished in the late 19th and early 20th centuries. A type of variety show, in which the programme comprised a series of 'turns' presented by singers, comedians, acrobats, eccentric dancers, and other performers and presided over by an avuncular chairman, the music hall tradition had its roots in the *song-and-supper rooms and taproom concerts held in London and other cities in the 18th century. The audience originally sat at tables and were encouraged to consume large amounts of alcohol; eventually, however, to avoid the restrictions imposed by the licensing act of 1751, such taverns opened their own music clubs, often housed in specially built halls, complete with a stage and conventional theatre equipment.

The Theatres Regulation Act of 1843 allowed both smoking and drinking in music halls, although they were banned from the legitimate theatre, and stimulated the growth of the phenomenon, which attracted all classes of customer from workmen to members of the royal family. Some of the most celebrated of these early venues in London included Charles Morton's Canterbury Music Hall (1852), the Holborn Empire (1857), Sam Collins's Hall in Islington Green (1863), the Alhambra (1860), the London Pavilion (1861), the Bedford (1861), Morton's Oxford Music Hall (1861) and those run by the Gattis; noted successors numbered amongst them the Trocadero (1882), the Palace Theatre (1892), and the Tivoli (1893).

As well as presenting familiar figures from the straight theatre, the halls also threw up stars of their own making, of whom the greatest included Marie Lloyd, Dan Leno, Vesta Tilley (one of the many successful impersonators of the aristocratic male), Little Tich, Harry Lauder, Will Fyffe, George Robey, Nellie Wallace, and Harry Champion. Performers from the legitimate theatre who also built up a strong reputation in the halls included Sarah Bernhardt, Beerbohm-Tree, and Albert Chevalier, who developed the popular cockney costermonger of the halls.

Many other performers appeared in speciality acts, some of the most popular being those featuring *lion comiques, balladeers, graduates of the *minstrel show, and clowns. Others again owed their success entirely to a single song or other item, as in the case of James Henry Stead's dance 'The Perfect Cure'.

In 1902 drink was banned from the music hall, a move that contributed to the eventual decline of the tradition, although at the time it was at its height with new and bigger venues being built throughout the country to house increasingly spectacular shows (see variety). The introduction of the cinema in the 1920s finally sounded the death knell of the halls; by the end of World War II only a few venues remained open. Since then the tradition has resurfaced from time to time with popular television programmes and revivals in both the amateur and professional theatre (notably by the Players' Theatre Club).

Mussato, Albertino (1261–1329) Italian statesman, poet, and playwright, who was the author of *Ecerinis*, a tragedy criticizing the tyrant Ezzelino da Romano that was modelled upon the work of Seneca. He was originally Paduan ambassador to Pope Boniface VIII but was exiled in 1325 when he fell from political favour.

Musset, (Louis-Charles-)Alfred de (1810–57) French poet and playwright, who was a major figure of the Romantic movement. In 1830 his first play, *La Nuit vénitienne*, opened at the Théâtre National de l'Odéon: its failure discouraged him from producing further works for public performance. Subsequently, however, he had lasting success with a series of light comedies, short plays illustrating proverbs, and the historical drama *Lorenzaccio*, written after his affair with the writer George Sand. His plays were especially significant for their restraint and use of poetic diction; *Lorenzaccio* provided Bernhardt with one of her most celebrated roles.

Principal works:

Les Caprices de Marianne: 1851 (written 1833).

Fantasio: 1866 (written 1833).

On ne badine pas avec l'amour: 1861 (written 1834); translated as *There's No Trifling With Love*.

Lorenzaccio: 1896 (written 1834).

Le Chandelier: 1848 (written 1835); translated as *The Decoy*.

Il ne faut jurer de rien: 1848 (written 1836); translated as *One Can Never Be Sure of Anything*.

Un caprice: 1847 (written 1837).

Il faut qu'une porte soit ouverte ou fermée: 1848 (written 1845); translated as *A Door Should Be Either Open or Shut*.

My Fair Lady See Pygmalion.

mystery play A dramatic entertainment based on a religious subject, which was the most important form of drama in Europe in medieval times. Also known as a **miracle play** in England, the mystery play was derived from the tradition of the *liturgical drama but was performed, originally during the feast of Corpus Christi (hence the alternative name **Corpus Christi play**), in the vernacular and included episodes featuring coarse humour and grotesque detail that may have been borrowed from folk theatre.

As the mystery play developed it gradually became the responsibility of trade or craft guilds, each of which would undertake the performance of a particular scene from the Creation to the Day of Judgement, as part of an entertainment that could last all day. These processional **bible-histories** were often acted on temporary mobile stages, usually converted wagons; they eventually made use of quite sophisticated stage production techniques and paid actors. Important surviving mystery-play cycles in England are those performed at Chester, Coventry, Lincoln, Wakefield, and York. Equivalent traditions in other countries included the *auto sacramental* in Spain and the *sacra rappresentazione* in Italy.

N

Naevius, Gnaeus (c. 270 BC–c. 203 BC) Roman playwright, who invented both the historical play known as the *praetexta* and the *palliata*. His plays in the *praetexta* form include *Romulus* and *Clastidium*, of which no more than the titles are extant; his other works included both tragedies and comedies (notably *Tarentilla*) written for contests against Livius Andronicus. He was imprisoned and possibly exiled as a result of his satirical writings.

Naharro, Bartolomé de Torres See Torres Naharro, Bartolomé de.

Naogeorg See Kirchmayer, Thomas.

Nares, Owen (1888–1943) British actor, who became a popular 'matinée idol'. After first walking on at the Haymarket in 1908, he soon attracted a large following in such parts as Julian Beauclerc in Sardou's *Diplomacy* (1913) and Thomas Armstrong in Edward Sheldon's *Romance* (1915). His later, more substantial, roles included the Reverend Robert Carson in St John Ervine's *Robert's Wife* (1937) and Maxim de Winter in Daphne Du Maurier's *Rebecca* (1940).

Narr The traditional Fool of the German medieval theatre, who became the central comic character of the *Fastnachtsspiel* during the 16th century. Not initially a comic character, he was later developed as a clown; many of his traits were later passed on to such comic figures as Jan Bouschet, Hans Stockfisch, Pickelhering, Hanswurst, and Kasperl.

Nashe, Thomas (1567–1601) English playwright and pamphleteer, who collaborated with Christopher Marlowe on *Dido, Queen of Carthage* (1587–88) and with Ben Jonson on the lost play *The *Isle of Dogs*. *Summer's Last Will and Testament* (1592), which blends comedy and masque elements, is the only surviving play wholly by him.

Nassau Street Theatre A theatre in Nassau Street, New York, which opened as the **New Theatre** in 1732 and was one of the first New York theatres. Its early history is unknown until 1750, when a Philadelphian company under Walter Murray and Thomas Kean opened a successful season with Cibber's adaptation of *Richard III*. In 1753, after extensive renovation by the elder Hallam, the theatre briefly prospered – opening with Steele's *The Conscious Lovers* – but closed later that same year.

Nathan, George Jean (1882–1958) US theatre critic, who did much to promote the drama of Ibsen, Shaw, Strindberg, and other European writers in the US. He also championed Eugene O'Neill, Sean O'Casey, and William Saroyan at the start of their careers and wrote over 30 books on the theatre.

Nathan the Wise (*Nathan der Weise*) A tragedy by Gotthold *Lessing. First performance: Berlin, 1783. Lessing's last play, it argues for religious freedom and was written in blank verse; it was subsequently acclaimed in a production by Goethe at Weimar (1801).

Nation, Théâtre de la *See* Comédie-Française.

National Concert Hall *See* Chatham Theatre.

Nationale Scene, Den A theatre in Bergen, Norway, which was founded in 1850 at the instigation of Ole *Bull. As Det Norske Teatret, it became a focus of native Norwegian drama, Ibsen becoming its first resident playwright in 1851. Bjørnson was director there from 1857 to 1859 and, after a brief closure from 1863 to 1876, subsequent notable managers included Gunnar Heiberg (1884–88) and Hans Jacob Nilsen (1934–39). It includes a small studio theatre, the Lille Scene, for experimental drama.

National Music Hall *See* Chatham Theatre.

National Operatic and Dramatic Association (NODA) A British theatre organization, which was founded in 1899. It aims to coordinate the activities of amateur theatre groups throughout Britain.

National Theatre *See* Nederlander Theatre; Royal National Theatre.

National Theatre Conference An honorary professional association consisting of 120 members of academic, community, and non-profit-making theatres in the US. The Conference seeks to share experience and ideas in the noncommercial theatre.

National Theatre of the Deaf (NTD) *See* O'Neill, Eugene.

Nationaltheatret A theatre in Oslo, which was founded in 1899 and is now regarded as the most important theatrical venue in Norway. Bjørn Bjørnson was the theatre's first director, leading a brilliant company including Johanne Dybwad and Sofie Reimers; subsequent celebrated performers who acted there include Alfred Maurstad and Tore Segelcke who appeared during the 1930s. The theatre now includes a flourishing experimental studio, the Amfiscenen, and in recent years has enjoyed new success under Toralv *Maurstad.

National Youth Theatre (NYT) A British theatre organization, which was founded in 1955 by the director **Michael Croft** (1924–86) to promote amateur productions featuring child actors from all over Britain. Initially the company presented plays by Shakespeare, winning critical acclaim in the West End, but later diversified with such works as *Zigger-Zagger* by Peter Terson (1967). The company moved into the **Shaw Theatre** in London in 1971 and set up an additional professional company – the Shaw Theatre Company – to produce plays suitable for young audiences; these have included works by Shaw, Wesker, and Barrie

Keeffe. Actors with the Shaw Theatre Company have included Derek Jacobi and Helen Mirren. The NYT itself continues to present regular productions and tours widely.

Nativity play *See* liturgical drama.

naturalism A movement in the theatre and the arts in general that developed in the late 19th century in response to a new desire to present an authentic version of real life. The first drama to aim towards a more naturalistic approach was Zola's *Thérèse Raquin* (1873), in which the *Realism of Ibsen was extended. Other early dramas written in the naturalistic style included works by Henri Becque and Strindberg's *Miss Julie* (1888), while André Antoine applied its principles in direction at the Théâtre Libre. Elsewhere it was adopted by the Freie Bühne in Germany, by Stanislavsky in Russia, and by O'Neill in the US. Ultimately it gave way to Symbolism and other movements.

Naughton, Charlie *See* Crazy Gang.

nautical drama A form of melodrama, popular in the early 19th century, in which the central character was a 'Jolly Jack Tar' or similar nautical hero. Distantly related to aquatic drama, the nautical drama was, however, enacted on an ordinary stage. Celebrated examples of the genre, many of which were performed at the Surrey Theatre, included Jerrold's *Black-Ey'd Susan* (1829) as well as parodies of the form.

Nazimova, Alla (1879–1945) Russian actress, who began her career with the Moscow Art Theatre and in St Petersburg before first appearing in the US in 1906. After success in an English-speaking version of Ibsen's *Hedda Gabler* at the Princess Theatre in New York in 1906 she became highly popular, notably in performances at her own Nazimova Theatre (later the 39th Street Theatre). After 1918 she concentrated upon films but later enjoyed further stage successes with Eva Le Gallienne's Civic Repertory Company and the Theatre Guild in plays ranging from Ibsen to Chekhov and O'Neill in the early 1930s.

Nazimova Theatre *See* 39th Street Theatre.

Nederlander Theatre A theatre on West 41st Street, between Seventh and Eighth avenues in New York, which opened as the **National Theatre** in 1921 with Sydney Howard's *Swords*. After success with such plays as John Willard's *The Cat and the Canary* (1922) and Clemence Dane's *Will Shakespeare* (1923), the theatre presented works by such major modern writers as O'Casey, Hellman, and Emlyn Williams with such stars as Ethel Barrymore. In 1959 the theatre was bought by **Billy Rose** (William Samuel Rosenberg; 1899–1966) and reopened – as the **Billy Rose Theatre** – with a revival of Shaw's *Heartbreak House*. Productions subsequently staged there included *Who's Afraid of Virginia Woolf?* (1962), Coward's *Private Lives* (1969), and Stoppard's *Jumpers* (1974). In 1978 the theatre was purchased by an English company and renamed the **Trafalgar Theatre**, staging works by Pinter and Brian Clark; this company left in 1980, when the theatre acquired its present name.

Neher, Caspar (1897–1962) German stage designer, who designed influential sets for early productions of Brecht's plays, including *Eduard II* (1924) and *Baal* (1926). He subsequently worked at the Deutsches Theater (1934–44) and later with the Berliner Ensemble, being particularly admired for his use of lighting.

Neidhart von Reuental (c. 1180–c. 1240) Austrian playwright and poet, who developed a new form of dramatic entertainment known as the *höfische Dorfpoesie*. Essentially a form of dance-song, the best known examples include the *Neidhartspiel,* which revolves around the central figure of a knight who, after humiliating his coarse peasant rivals, wins the love of a village girl.

Neighborhood Playhouse A theatre on Grand Street, New York, which was built in 1915. It housed a respected professional theatre company, which produced major works by such authors as Chekhov, O'Neill, Shaw, and Yeats before closing down in 1927; other productions included dance-dramas and ballets.

Neilson, (Lilian) Adelaide (1846–80) British actress, who was a millhand and barmaid before making her stage debut at Margate in 1865. She became famous as a Shakespearean actress; her Juliet, Rosalind, and Isabella were highly acclaimed at the Haymarket in 1876. She was equally popular in the US, which she visited on five occasions.

Neilson, Julia (Emilie) (1868–1957) British actress, who joined Tree's company in 1888 and married Fred *Terry in 1891. In management together from 1900 onwards, they established a popular reputation in such comedy melodramas as Paul Kester's *Sweet Nell of Old Drury* and Baroness Orczy's *The Scarlet Pimpernel*. After his death she appeared in Seymour Hicks's *Vintage Wine* (1934) and made a final comeback as Lady Rutven in Heron Carvic's *The Widow of Forty* (1944).

Nekrassov A play by Jean-Paul *Sartre. First performance: Paris, 1955. The central character of this political satire is the confidence trickster Georges de Valera, who assumes the identity of the Soviet minister Nekrassov. The play was first produced on the English stage in 1956.

Nemirovich-Danchenko, Vladimir Ivanovich (1859–1943) Russian director and playwright, who cofounded the *Moscow Art Theatre with Stanislavsky in 1898. He pioneered the development of *naturalism in the Russian theatre after being appointed head of the Moscow Philharmonic Society's Drama Course in 1891. Subsequently working alongside Stanislavsky, he helped to select plays for production – notably Chekhov's *The Seagull* in 1898 – and directed such plays as Pogodin's *Kremlin Chimes* (1942) himself. He also founded the Moscow Musical Studio, at which he applied his ideas to musical comedy and operetta.

neoclassical drama A form of drama that flourished in several countries in the 17th and 18th centuries. The genre reflected contemporary interest in the classical world and borrowed heavily from Greek and Roman theatrical traditions. Specific borrowings included the development of the rules of the three *unities, which were observed most rigidly in France by Corneille, Racine, and others, although early English imitators included Ben Jonson. Later, Dryden and Addison were among those who briefly responded to a new interest in neoclassical theories before the genre was swept away by the arrival of Romanticism. In terms of theatre architecture the movement stimulated the rejection of baroque and rococo styles and inspired attempts to invoke the grandeur of Greek and Roman temples.

Nero (37 AD–68 AD) Roman emperor (54 AD–68 AD), who prided himself upon his prowess as an actor. He appeared both as a *pantomimus* and in tragic roles and undertook a notorious acting tour of Greece, which contributed to the growing unrest that led ultimately to his downfall and suicide.

Nervo, Jimmie *See* Crazy Gang.

Nesbitt, Cathleen (1888–1982) British actress, who made her professional debut in 1910 and then went with the Irish Players to New York, where she was acclaimed in Synge's *The Well of the Saints*. Subsequently she played at the Abbey Theatre in Dublin and in London as well as returning frequently to the US. Her London credits included varied roles in plays by Webster, Dryden, Lonsdale, Zola, T S Eliot, Flecker, and Shakespeare, playing Goneril to Gielgud's Lear in 1940. Her last West End appearance was as the Dowager Lady Headleigh in Robin Maugham's *The Claimant* (1964), and she played Mrs Higgins in a revival of *My Fair Lady* in the US when she was over 90.

Nestroy, Johann Nepomuk (Eduard Ambrosius) (1801–62) Austrian playwright and actor, who became a leading writer of comedy for the Viennese stage in the mid-19th century. Having begun as an opera singer, he became popular as a character actor and was the author of more than 80 plays satirizing contemporary bourgeois society. His plays, in which he often played the central role himself, were largely adaptations of other works and included lively parodies of Wagner and other contemporaries (of which *Judith und Holofernes* is the best known). His adaptation *Einen Jux will er sich machen* was later rewritten as *The Matchmaker* (1954) by Thornton Wilder and provided the basis of the musical *Hello Dolly!* (1965). In 1854 he succeeded Karl Carl as director of the Leopoldstädter.

Principal works:

Der Zettelträger: 1827; translated as *The Billposter*.

Der böse Geist Lumpazivagabundus: 1833.

Das Haus der Temperamente: 1837.

Die verhängnisvolle Faschingsnacht: 1839.

Der Talisman: 1840.

Das Mädl aus der Vorstadt: 1841; translated as *The Girl from the Suburbs*.

Einen Jux will er sich machen: 1842; translated as *The Merchant of Yonkers* (or *On the Razzle*).

Der Zerrissene: 1844.

Der Unbedeutende: 1846.

Judith und Holofernes: 1849.

Nethersole, Olga Isabel (1870–1951) British actress and manager, who made her debut at Brighton in 1887. After her first London success, as Janet Preece in Pinero's *The Profligate* (1889), she formed her own management and built a reputation on both sides of the Atlantic in such challenging parts as Fanny Legrand in Clyde Fitch's *Sapho* (1900), which led to her arrest in New York for indecency, and the title roles in Sudermann's *Magda* (1904) and Maeterlinck's *Mary Magdalene* (1910).

Neuber, (Frederika) Carolina (Carolina Weissenborn; 1697–1760) German actress and manager, known as Die Neuberin, whose collaboration with the critic Gottsched transformed the German theatre. Having established her reputation in breeches parts, she set up her own company and – with Gottsched – presented a largely classical repertory as opposed to the conventional farces and harlequinades. In 1739 her influential partnership with Gottsched broke up; subsequently they indulged in a series of vitriolic exchanges and Neuber's company lost popularity. In 1748 she founded a new touring troupe to present the plays of the young Lessing; this met with only limited success and she died in poverty. Her insistence on discipline and careful rehearsal are now recognized, however, as having laid the foundations of the modern German theatre.

neume A melody based on vowel sounds sung as harmony in early church services; gradually this accompaniment developed into the *trope as an explanatory illustration of the meaning of the service itself.

Neville, John (1925–) British actor and director, who worked at Birmingham and Bristol before proving himself a fine classical actor with the Old Vic company in the 1950s, his parts including Hamlet, Romeo, Othello, and Richard II. As director of the Nottingham Playhouse (1963–68), he was responsible for many interesting productions, appearing himself in such roles as Willy Loman in Arthur Miller's *Death of a Salesman* (1967). He appeared as Macheath in *The Beggar's Opera* at the Chichester Festival Theatre in 1972, then went to Canada and became director of the Citadel Theatre, Edmonton. He was again in London in 1977 when he played at the National Theatre in Samuel Beckett's *Happy Days*, but returned to Canada as director of the Neptune Theatre, Halifax, Nova Scotia and in 1986 was appointed director of the *Stratford (Ontario) Festival.

New American Museum *See* American Museum.

New Amsterdam Theatre A theatre on West 42nd Street, New York, which opened in 1903 with a production of *A Midsummer Night's Dream*. It housed Ziegfeld's *Follies* from 1914 to 1924 and was then used for musicals and straight plays until 1937, when it became a cinema. A studio theatre on the roof was known as the **Aerial Gardens Theatre**.

New Bowery Theatre *See* Bowery Theatre.

Newcastle Playhouse A theatre in Newcastle-upon-Tyne, which was built in 1970 on the site of a previous theatre named after Flora Robson. Owned by the University of Newcastle, it became a venue for touring companies for a time. In 1978 the company was revived, since when it has staged a varied programme from Brecht to university productions in the small Gulbenkian Studio.

New Chelsea Theatre *See* Royal Court Theatre.

New Comedy A style of ancient Greek comedy that evolved from *Middle Comedy during the mid-4th century BC. An early manifestation of the *comedy of manners,

the New Comedy, in which the role of the chorus was reduced to an absolute minimum, reached its apotheosis in the plays of Menander and exerted a strong influence upon later Roman playwrights, including Terence and Plautus.

New Drama British drama from the period 1890 to 1914, during which the influence of such writers as Ibsen, Strindberg, Maeterlinck, and Hauptmann was first felt in the UK. G B Shaw's first play, *Widowers' Houses* (1892), effectively inaugurated the New Drama and led eventually to Harley Granville-Barker's seasons at the Royal Court (1904–07), which incidentally promoted the development of new repertory theatres at Manchester, Glasgow, Liverpool, and Birmingham specifically for the performance of such works. The movement was most important, however, for its introduction of socially relevant subject matter and assertion of the function of the theatre as a forum for debate and a force for change.

New English Opera House *See* Royalty Theatre.

Newes, Tilly *See* Wedekind, Frank.

Newington Butts Theatre A theatre at Newington Butts, London, which was built around 1576. The existence of the theatre was subsequently threatened by fear of the plague but is known from the writings of Henslowe to have been used for some years for performances of Marlowe, Shakespeare, and others. The site is now occupied by the Elephant and Castle traffic junction.

New London Theatre The most modern of London's West End theatres, which is equipped with a revolving stage and seats, walls, and lights that can be repositioned electrically. Designed by Sean Kenny and built on the site of the *Winter Garden Theatre in Drury Lane, the New London opened in 1973 with Peter Ustinov's *The*

Unknown Soldier and his Wife, followed by the rock-and-roll musical *Grease*. Used as a television studio in 1977–80, the theatre's original seating capacity of 907 was increased to 1102 for the Andrew Lloyd Webber musical *Cats*, which began a long run in 1981.

Newman Theatre *See* Public Theatre.

New National Theatre *See* Chatham Theatre.

New Olympic Theatre *See* Olympic Theatre.

New Park Theatre A theatre on Broadway, New York, which opened in 1874 with Fechter in his own adaptation of a French play. In the same year John T Raymond starred in a dramatization of Mark Twain's *The Gilded Age*. Success continued with the Florences appearing in Woolf's *The Mighty Dollar* (1875) and G F Rowe in his own drama *Brass* (1876). Under Henry E Abbey from 1876, it prospered until 1882 when, on the day set for Lillie Langtry's New York debut there, the theatre was burnt down.

Mainly furnished with materials left over after the demolition of Booth's Theatre, the second **New Park Theatre** was opened in 1883 with a programme of musical drama. Subsequently Belasco became manager, presenting melodramas starring the young Minnie Maddern and others. Afterwards it became a museum.

New Royalty Theatre *See* Royalty Theatre.

New Theatre *See* Albery Theatre; Century Theatre; Nassau Street Theatre; Park Theatre.

New Theatre Comique *See* New York Theatre.

New Victoria Palace *See* Old Vic Theatre.

New Victoria Theatre *See* Victoria Theatre.

New Way to Pay Old Debts, A A comedy by Philip *Massinger, written in 1625. First performance: London, c. 1632. The play is notable chiefly for the character of the scheming Sir Giles Overreach, based on the extortioner Sir Giles Mompesson, in which role Edmund Kean excelled.

New York City Centre *See* City Centre of Music and Drama.

New Yorker Theatre A theatre on West 54th Street, New York, which opened as the **Gallo Theatre** in 1927. The theatre reopened as the New Yorker in 1930 with Ibsen's *The Vikings* and was subsequently visited by leading foreign troupes. In the late 1930s the theatre was used for musical comedy and has since been converted into a broadcasting studio.

New York Shakespeare Festival A festival of Shakespearean drama founded in New York in 1954 by Joseph Papp. The Festival's first productions were staged at the Emanuel Presbyterian Church, the actors performing for nothing; in 1957 the Festival moved to Central Park where, in 1962, the *Delacorte Theatre was built as the Festival's permanent home.

New York Theatre A theatre on Broadway, New York, which was opened as **Lucy Rushton's Theatre** in 1865 and was used initially for the staging of popular classics. Renamed the New York Theatre in 1866, it became the home of Augustin Daly's company in 1873. Subsequently it was known as Fox's Broadway and then the **Globe Theatre**, hosting variety shows. As the **New Theatre Comique**, it was taken over by Harrigan and Hart for vaudeville in 1881. It was destroyed by fire in 1884.

Another **New York Theatre** on Broadway opened as the Olympia Music Hall in 1895 and housed primarily vaudeville until 1899, when it was renamed the New York Theatre. Both straight plays and musical comedies could be seen there until 1912, when the theatre reverted to vaudeville as the **Moulin-Rouge**. The theatre was demolished in 1935.

New Zealand Players A theatre company founded in Wellington, New Zealand, in 1953. It toured almost continuously with plays by such foreign authors as Anouilh, Shaw, and Fry as well as works by native writers, notably Bruce Mason's *The Pohutukawa Tree*. The company broke up in 1960.

Niblo's Garden A small theatre, originally called the **Sans Souci**, on Broadway, New York, which was opened in 1827 by William Niblo. Housing a successful season by the Bowery Theatre in 1828, it was renamed Niblo's Garden the following year. A fire in 1846 destroyed it but it was replaced in 1849. Enlarged in 1853, it was the venue for Rachel's last New York appearance; other notable players included Chanfrau and Charlotte Crabtree. It presented a mixed programme of drama and spectacle until 1868 the success of Boucicault's *After Dark; or, London by Night* changed the emphasis to melodrama. Burnt down in 1872 and reopened the same year, it never re-established its popularity and was finally demolished in 1895.

Niccolini, Giambattista (1782–1861) Italian playwright, author of several openly propagandist dramas on the themes of patriotism, despotism, and political freedom. His plays include *Nabucco* (1815), based on the life of Napoleon, and the poetic *Arnaldo da Brescia* (1843), in which he criticized the papal establishment.

Nichols, Mike (Michael Igor Peschowsky; 1931-) US actor, director, and producer, born in Berlin, who began his career in cabaret with Elaine May. He directed his first production, Neil Simon's *Barefoot in the Park*, in 1961 and later directed the same author's *The Odd Couple* (1965), *Plaza Suite* (1968), and *The Prisoner of Second Avenue* (1971) to great acclaim. He has also directed Murray Schisgal's *Luv* (1964), Lillian Hellman's *The Little Foxes* (1967), and Chekhov's *Uncle Vanya* (1973) with similar success.

Nichols, Peter Richard (1927-) British playwright, whose work has been successful both on television and on the stage. Several of his plays deal poignantly with the impact of physical suffering, the most famous being *A Day in the Death of Joe Egg* (1967), which depicts a couple's struggle to care for their handicapped daughter. His comedy *The National Health* (1969) contrasts hospital soap-operas on television with the reality of life on the wards, while *Forget-me-not Lane* (1971) is strongly autobiographical and *Passion Play* (1980) is a marital tragi-comedy. Other works include the musical *Privates on Parade* (1977), the comedy *Born in the Gardens* (1980), *Poppy* (1982), which depicts the Chinese Opium Wars, and *A Piece of My Mind* (1986).

Nickinson, John (1808–64) Canadian theatre manager and actor, born in London. Originally a soldier, he first appeared with the Garrison Amateurs at Montreal. In 1836 he joined the Theatre Royal, Montreal and then moved to the US. At Burton's Theatre in New York, he was the original Dombey in John Brougham's dramatization of the novel by Dickens. He also appeared regularly as Haversack in Boucicault's *The Old Guard*. He formed his own company in 1852 and managed theatres in Toronto, Quebec, and Cincinatti.

Nicolet, Jean-Baptiste (c. 1728–96) French acrobat and actor, who became popular at the Paris fairs during the 1760s. Subsequently he played young lovers and the role of Harlequin in his own theatre on the Boulevard du Temple and appeared before Louis XV, renaming his theatre the Spectacle des Grands Danseurs du Roi (later the Théâtre de la Gaîté).

Nicoll, Allardyce (1894–1976) Scottish theatre historian and academic, author of numerous books on both British and world drama. He also established an important collection of theatre material at Yale University, served as Director of the Shakespeare Institute for many years, and was President of the Society for Theatre Research from 1958. His books include the six-volume *History of English Drama 1600–1900*.

Nic Shiubhlaigh, Maire (Maire Price; 1888–1958) Irish actress, one of the pioneer players of the *Irish National Dramatic Society. She appeared in the first production of Yeats's *Cathleen ni Houlihan* (1902) and, at the opening of the Abbey Theatre, played Nora Burke in Synge's *In the Shadow of the Glen*. She left the company in 1905, returning for occasional guest appearances.

night scenes *See* Italian night scenes.

Nilsen, Hans Jacob (1897–1957) Norwegian actor-manager and director, who became famous for his realistic productions of plays by Holberg and Ibsen. He worked initially at the Nationaltheatret and later in Bergen and Oslo; his most notable productions included Ibsen's *Peer Gynt* (1948).

Nina Vance Alley Theatre A theatre in Houston, Texas, which was founded as the **Alley Theatre** in 1947. The name was changed in 1980 on the death of its founder. The resident company's first production was Lillian Hellman's *The Children's Hour*;

in 1968, it moved into a new home housing two auditoriums, the Large Stage and the Arena Stage. Productions there have included a variety of classics, children's plays, and new works.

Nō (or *Noh*) A form of Japanese theatre, which was created by the performers Kanami (1333–84) and his son *Zeami and has since become the most important element in the classical drama of Japan. Incorporating stately dances, music, and much noble language and based upon stories taken from novels, poems, and other sources, the Nō play was derived originally from the ritualistic code of honour of the Samurai warriors and is performed entirely by male actors; it dates in its present form from the early 17th century. The plays are performed on a square roofed stage, with the audience seated on two sides; little use is made of scenery. Most of the action revolves around two actors, the *shite* and the *waki*, both of whom are masked and dressed in magnificent costumes. In conjunction with the complementary *Kyōgen* interludes, a Nō performance might last seven hours in all. European writers who have been profoundly influenced by the Nō tradition have included W B Yeats.

NODA *See* National Operatic and Dramatic Association.

Nokes, James (d. 1696) English actor, who began as a boy actor playing female roles for John Rhodes at the Cockpit before joining Davenant's company. He developed into an excellent comedian, appearing in a wide variety of parts, most notably in the title role of *Sir Martin Mar-all*, which Dryden wrote for him.

Nora Bayes Theatre *See* 44th Street Theatre.

Norske Theatret, Det A theatre in Christiana (now Oslo), Norway, which was founded in 1913 as a venue for native Norwegian drama. The theatre has had a limited impact with productions of plays written in Nynorsk, the official Norwegian language.

Northcott Theatre A repertory theatre in Exeter, which was founded in 1967 with the support of the University of Exeter and the businessman G V Northcott. The theatre, equipped with a flexible stage and seating for up to 580, presents a wide variety of drama, including modern plays, musicals, and amateur productions.

Norton, Thomas (1532–84) English lawyer and playwright, who (with Thomas Sackville) wrote *Gorboduc, the first native tragedy written entirely in blank verse and heavily influenced by Seneca.

Norwid, Cyprian Kamil (1821–83) Polish poet and playwright, who contributed to the Polish Romantic movement whilst in penniless exile in Paris. Ignored in his own time, he wrote a number of poetic dramas on religious and historical themes, including *Zwolon*, and several comedies tackling social issues. His sophisticated plays were first recognized as significant in the early 20th century.

Norworth, Jack (1879–1959) US comedian, who became a major star of vaudeville in both New York and London alongside his wife, the singer Nora Bayes. After their divorce in 1913 he enjoyed success in revue in London and opened a theatre (later the Belmont Theatre) in New York; he was also the composer of the popular song 'Shine on, Harvest Moon'.

Nottingham Playhouse A large theatre in Nottingham, which was opened in 1963 to replace a theatre of the same name converted from a cinema in 1948. Seating 750, it has been used for major plays by Brecht, Shaw, Fry, and Brenton among others, many productions subsequently transferring to London. Notable Shakespearean successes have included *King Lear* with Sir Michael Hordern and *Hamlet* with Alan Bates.

Nouveau Monde, Théâtre du A French-Canadian theatre company established in Montreal in 1951. Led by Jean Gascon it enjoyed early acclaim with productions of plays by Molière, repeating its success in Paris in 1955 and subsequently in the US at the Stratford (Ontario) Festival. It consolidated its reputation with a wide range of Canadian and foreign plays, especially those of Marcel Dubé, presented at a succession of venues but suffered badly from a fire in 1963. In 1972 the company settled permanently at the Théâtre de la Comédie-Canadienne, where it presented lunchtime theatre and numerous original works. Its controversial production of *Les Fées ont soif* (The Fairies are Thirsty) by Denise Boucher in 1978 resulted in the withdrawal of its state grant.

Nouveautés, Théâtre des A theatre on the Boulevard Poissonnière in Paris, founded in 1920 as a venue for light comedy and musicals. The earliest Parisian theatre of the name was opened in 1827 close to the Bourse but was damaged in the revolution of 1830 and finally closed after incurring official disfavour. A second Théâtre des Nouveautés opened on the Boulevard St Martin in 1866 but was destroyed by fire almost immediately; a third theatre opened in 1878 on the Boulevard des Italiens and saw the establishment of Feydeau's reputation.

Novelli, Ermete (1851–1919) Italian actor, who became a leading performer of tragic roles upon the Italian stage. Although he began in comedy, he later won great acclaim – despite his large size – in such Shakespearean roles as Othello, Lear, Macbeth, and Hamlet, all of which he delivered with great passion; other successes included

Aicard's *Le Père Lebonnard*. He also ran his own theatre, La Casa di Goldoni in Rome, for a brief time in 1900 but was soon forced to close.

Novello, Ivor (David Ivor Davies; 1893–1951) British composer, actor-manager, and playwright, who first established his reputation as a composer with such songs as 'Keep the Home Fires Burning' and musical comedies during World War I. In 1921 he made his debut as an actor in Sacha Guitry's *Deburau*, after which he enjoyed success as a playwright with his drama *The Rat* (1924), in which he also acted. Subsequent successes included a series of plays and the romantic musicals *Glamorous Night* (1935), *Careless Rapture* (1936), *Crest of the Wave* (1937), and *The Dancing Years* (1939) – all performed at Drury Lane; later musicals included *King's Rhapsody* (1949) and *Gay's the Word* (1951).

Novelty Theatre *See* Kingsway Theatre.

Nunn, Trevor Robert (1940-) British director, who joined the Royal Shakespeare Company as director in 1965, becoming artistic director in 1968 and chief executive and joint artistic director with Terry Hands in 1978, stepping down in 1986. He directed his first production with the Marlowe Society in Cambridge and later worked at Coventry's Belgrade Theatre before joining the RSC. Among his most important productions have been the first modern presentation of Tourneur's *The Revenger's Tragedy* (1966), Vanbrugh's *The Relapse* (1967), *Much Ado About Nothing* (1968), *King Lear* (1968), *The Romans* cycle (1972) of Shakespearean plays, Ibsen's *Hedda Gabler* (1975), David Edgar's adaptation of *The Life and Adventures of Nicholas Nickleby* (1980), based on Dickens, and the popular musicals *Cats* (1981), from T S Eliot's poems, and *Starlight Express* (1984). He married the actress Janet Suzman in 1969.

nurseries The acting schools of the Restoration theatre in London. The three main nurseries were the **Hatton Garden Nursery**, founded by Killigrew around 1662 and later installed at the Vere Street Theatre, the **Barbican Nursery**, opened by Davenant's widow in 1671, and the **Bun Hill Nursery**, founded in 1671. Actors trained in the nurseries included Joseph Haines.

Nušič, Branislav (1864–1938) Serbian playwright, who was the author of several comedies still popular on the Yugoslavian stage. The most successful of his satires include *The Suspicious Person* (1887), *The Lady Minister* (1929), and *Power* (1938).

Nye Teater *See* Oslo Nye Teater.

O

Oakley, Annie *See* Cody, William Frederick.

Obaldia, René de (1918-) French novelist, poet, and playwright, born in Hong Kong. His witty avant-garde plays include *Génousie* (1960), *Le Satyre de La Villette* (1963), *Du Vent dans les branches de Sassafras* (1965), and *Le Cosmonaute agricole* (1965).

Oberammergau A town in Bavaria, scene of the most famous surviving Passion play. The play was first performed in 1634; since than it has been presented every ten years in gratitude for the town's survival during the plague.

Obey, André (1892–1975) French playwright and director of the Comédie-Française. In the early 1930s he became involved with the Compagnie des Quinze, for whom he wrote *Noé* (Noah; 1931), *Le Viol de Lucrèce* (1931), and *La bataille de la Marne*

(1931). His later plays include *Le Trompeur de Séville* (1937), *L'Homme de cendres* (1949), and *Lazare* (1951).

Obraztsov, Sergei Vladimirovich (1901-) Soviet puppeteer, who became director of the State Puppet Theatre. A specialist in rod-puppets, he is known for his elaborate productions featuring numerous lively puppet characters.

O'Casey, Sean (1880–1964) Irish playwright, author of several major plays on the themes of Irish nationalism and life in the tenements of Dublin. His first three plays, *The *Shadow of a Gunman* (originally called *On the Run*), **Juno and the Paycock*, and *The *Plough and the Stars* were all produced at the Abbey Theatre; for many people these tragi-comedies are his greatest and most lasting achievement. *The Plough and the Stars* provoked nationalist outrage and a riot in the theatre at its first performance; when the Abbey refused to stage his next play, *The *Silver Tassie*, O'Casey quarrelled with W B Yeats and moved to England, rarely returning to his native country. Subsequent plays, several of which were set in England and were influenced by Expressionism, were less successful despite their echoes of the superb characterization and use of comic devices in his earlier writing. At the heart of his most successful work is the concept of sacrifice for an idea and the contrast between the attitudes of men and women.
Principal works:
The Shadow of Gunman: 1923.
Juno and the Paycock: 1924.
The Plough and the Stars: 1926.
The Silver Tassie: 1929.
Within the Gates: 1934.
The Star Turns Red: 1940.
*Red Roses for Me: 1943.
Purple Dust: 1943.
Oak Leaves and Lavender: 1947.
Cock-a-Doodle-Dandy: 1949.
The Bishop's Bonfire: 1961.
The Drums of Father Ned: 1958.

Behind the Green Curtains: 1961.

Octagon Theatre A theatre in Bolton, which was founded in 1967 with financial support from the public. A flexible octagonal auditorium seating up to 420, it is used for a wide variety of productions, including regular presentations of Shakespeare and modern dramas, and also caters for children's theatre.

O'Dea, Jimmy (James Augustine O'Dea; 1899–1965) Irish actor, whose popular appearances in pantomime and revue included appearances as the rascally Biddy Mulligan. He toured England and Ireland many times and occasionally ventured into straight theatre, playing Bottom with the Gate Theatre company in 1940.

Odell's Theatre *See* Goodman's Fields Theatre.

Odéon, Théâtre National de l' A theatre in Paris, which began as the home of the Comédie-Française in 1781. Renamed the Odéon in 1795, the theatre was reconstructed in 1816, burnt down in 1818, and was again rebuilt as a venue for light comedy and operetta. Subsequently it established itself as a home for serious drama, a reputation which was further enhanced by André Antoine and Gémier in the early 20th century. In 1959 the Odéon became independent of the Comédie-Française and was renamed the **Théâtre de France**; notable directors included Jean-Louis Barrault, whose production of Genet's *Les Paravents* caused riots in 1966. The *Théâtre des Nations was based there under Barrault, but after the student riots of 1968 (with which the theatre was identified) the Odéon reverted to its original name and again housed the Comédie-Française (1971).

Odets, Clifford (1906–63) US playwright, whose first success came with the one-act play **Waiting for Lefty*, which was produced by the Group Theatre, of which he was a founder-member. Odets joined the Communist party in 1934 and built a reputation as a theatrical radical, although towards the end of his career he turned to script writing for Hollywood. His early works are enlivened with a sense of realism, excellent characterization, and political energy; later works, including the commercially successful *The Big Knife*, suffer from an element of self-pity.

Principal works:

Waiting for Lefty: 1935.

*Awake and Sing!: 1935.

*Golden Boy: 1937.

Night Music: 1940.

Clash by Night: 1941.

The Big Knife: 1949.

The *Country Girl: 1950.

The Flowering Peach: 1954.

odeum An early roofed theatre, used by the Greeks and Romans for musical and poetical contests.

Oedipus at Colonus A tragedy by *Sophocles. First performance: Athens, 406 BC. The sequel to *Oedipus Rex, the play was produced after the playwright's death and depicts the redemption through suffering of the central character, now old, blind, and in exile.

Oedipus Rex A tragedy by *Sophocles, often considered his masterpiece. First performance: 429 BC. Central to the play is the incest of Oedipus when he marries his mother Jocasta, after unwittingly murdering his father; the theme was later developed by many subsequent playwrights and, as an instance of a pyschological phenomenon, by Freud. It was memorably revived in 1945 in London with Olivier in the leading role.

Oehlenschläger, Adam Gottlob (1779–1850) Danish poet and playwright, who was a prominent figure of the Romantic move-

ment in Denmark. He drew heavily on Norse mythology for several of his plays and was much influenced by Kotzebue, Shakespeare, and Ewald. His most admired plays were written early in his career and include *Sanct-Hans Aften Spil* (1802), *Aladdin* (1804), and the tragedies *Hakon Jarl hin Rige* (1807) and *Baldur hin Gode* (1807), which reflected his meeting with Goethe at Weimar.

Oeuvre, Théâtre de l' *See* Art, Théâtre d'; Lugné-Poë, Aurélien-François.

off-Broadway US theatre that developed as an alternative to the commercial theatre of Broadway during the 1950s and 1960s. The production of Tennessee Williams's *Summer and Smoke* at the Circle-in-the-Square in 1952 heralded the emergence of a new artistically valid theatre that rapidly spread throughout the US, drawing on native talent and tackling challenging contemporary issues. Notable highlights included the Living Theatre's production of Jack Gelber's *The Connection* in 1959, Albee's *The Zoo Story* (1960), and Kenneth H Brown's *The Brig* (1963). Subsequently many of the leading off-Broadway venues in New York were absorbed into the conventional Broadway tradition and the genre was displaced by the *off-off-Broadway movement.

off-off-Broadway US theatre that succeeded the *off-Broadway movements as a focus of serious new drama, as opposed to the commercial Broadway tradition. This new wave of challenging alternative drama began in the late 1960s and has thrown up such significant companies as the San Francisco Mime Troupe and the Open Theatre; venues range from small theatres to halls and cellars. A group of eight venues was established near Times Square in New York in 1978 specifically for such productions.

O'Flaherty, Mrs *See* Winstanley, Eliza.

Ohel Theatre A Jewish theatre company, which was founded in Palestine in 1925. Under **Moshe Halevy** (1895–1974), the group was linked to the Jewish Labour Federation and began with dramatizations of stories by Peretz and biblical tales, mostly given to kibbutz audiences. Members of the group, who initially also held jobs in factories and on the fields, subsequently toured Israel and Europe but the company gradually declined after 1958, disbanding in 1969.

Ohio Roscius See Aldrich, Louis.

Oh, What a Lovely War! A documentary drama with music about World War I, created by Joan *Littlewood and her Theatre Workshop company. First production: Theatre Royal, Stratford East, 1963. A scathing yet entertaining indictment of the follies of generals and a moving celebration of the common humanity of the soldiers on both sides, the play transferred to the West End (and Paris) later the same year, and was filmed by Richard Attenborough in 1969.

O'Keeffe, John (1747–1833) British playwright, who began as an actor in his native Dublin but later settled in London, where he wrote a series of comic operas, farces, burlesques, and pantomimes. His plays include the farce *Tony Lumpkin in Town* (1778), *The Poor Soldier* (1783), *Peeping Tom* (1784), and *Wild Oats; or, the Strolling Gentleman* (1791).

O'Kelly, Seumas (c. 1875–1918) Irish playwright, novelist, short-story writer, and journalist. A prolific writer, he drew repeatedly upon the countryside of his youth in his work. Several of his plays on Irish rural life were favourably received, notably *The Shuiler's Child* (1909), which deals with the unusual theme of child desertion. *The Bribe* (1913) is also worthy of note.

Okhlopov, Nikolai Pavlovich (1900–67) Soviet actor and director, who became a leading figure of the experimental Soviet theatre during the 1930s. After spending four years under Meyerhold (1923–27) be became artistic director of the Realistic Theatre; there he presented innovative productions of contemporary works by such authors as Gorky and Pogodin before moving to the Vakhtangov Theatre, where his successes included Rostand's *Cyrano de Bergerac*. Later he worked at the Theatre of the Revolution (later renamed the Mayakovsky Theatre), notably upon plays by Ostrovsky and Shakespeare as well as modern playwrights.

Oklahoma! A musical, based on the play *Green Grow the Rushes* by Lynn Riggs, combining music by Richard *Rodgers, lyrics by Oscar *Hammerstein II, and choreography by Agnes De Mille. First performance: New York, 1943. The plot concerns a cowboy, Curly, who is determined to win the heart of the young girl, Laurie, despite the problems caused by Jud, the hired hand, who will stop at nothing to make Laurie his own.

Old Bachelor, The A comedy by William *Congreve. First performance: Drury Lane, 1693. The first of Congreve's dramatic works, the play explores sexual relationships through the various marriages of Heartwell, Sylvia, Vainlove, Bellamour, Tribulation Spintext, Fondlewife, Sir Joseph Wittol, Araminta, Laetitia, and Bellinda. Betterton, Mrs Mountfort, and Mrs Bracegirdle headed the original cast.

Old Bowery Theatre See Bowery Theatre.

Old Comedy The earliest comic theatrical tradition of ancient Greece, which evolved during the 4th and 5th centuries BC. The Greek comic drama developed later than the tragic form (the first contest for comedy not being held until 486 BC) and was descended from primitive mime and ritual performances, especially those connected with fertility rites (as reflected by the wearing of the phallus).

Early writers of Old Comedy included Magnes and Crates; the most important figure, however, was that of *Aristophanes, whose works observe a complex set structure, incorporating satire, fantasy, poetry, obscenity, speeches on unrelated topics delivered directly to the audience, and the use of masks and a large chorus. Other contemporary masters of the genre included Ameipsas, Cratinus, and Eupolis. By the time of Aristophanes's death the tradition had given way to *Middle Comedy.

Old Drury *See* Chestnut Theatre; Park Theatre.

Oldfield, Anne (1683–1730) English actress, whom Farquhar discovered while she was working as a barmaid. For a time she was the playwright's mistress, but it was Sir John Vanbrugh's interest that led to an engagement at Drury Lane in 1699. She was admirably suited to the plays of Colley Cibber, and established her reputation playing Lady Betty Modish in *The Careless Husband* in 1704. In 1706 she succeeded Anne Bracegirdle as Millamant in *The Way of the World* and in 1707 she created the part of Silvia in *The Recruiting Officer*. She died at the height of her fame and was the first actress to be buried in Westminster Abbey.

Old Globe Theatre An open-air theatre in Balboa Park, San Diego, California, which was designed for the 1935–36 California Pacific International Exposition. An annual Shakespeare festival began there in 1960 under Ben Payne. In 1978 the theatre was damaged by fire.

Old Man *See* stock company.

Oldmixon, Mrs (Georgina Sidus; c. 1763–1836) British actress, daughter of an Oxford clergyman, who made an impressive debut at the Haymarket in 1783 and acted in London for 10 years before going to the US. She appeared with Wignell's company in Philadelphia, in ballad operas, and later at New York's Park Theatre, where she played a range of parts, including Ophelia, Mrs Candour, and the Nurse.

Old Mo *See* Middlesex Music Hall.

Old Tote Theatre A theatrical company established at a racecourse in Sydney, Australia, in 1963. It soon acquired a formidable reputation with productions of Chekhov and various classical works; directors with the company included Tyrone Guthrie, who directed a version of *Oedipus the King* by Sophocles in 1970. It also presented a number of Australian dramas before being succeeded by the Sydney Theatre Company in 1978.

Old Vic Theatre One of London's oldest surviving theatres, built in 1816–18 on a site to the south of Waterloo Bridge. Originally named the **Royal Coburg Theatre** in honour of Prince Leopold and Princess Charlotte, it quickly became established not only as the home of melodrama but as one of the sights of London on account of its looking-glass curtain. Edmund Kean gave six performances at the theatre in 1831; in 1833 the theatre was renamed the **Royal Victoria Theatre** in honour of the young Princess Victoria. In 1858 a number of people were trampled to death in a stampede in the gallery caused by a false alarm of fire and the theatre's reputation declined.

In 1871 there was a change of ownership, the interior was reconstructed, and it reopened as the **New Victoria Palace**. The name was changed again in 1880, when the theatre was taken over by the social reformer Emma Cons; after further reconstruction it reopened as the **Royal Victoria Hall and Coffee Tavern**, providing entertainment for the working classes on strict temperance lines. When Miss Cons died in 1912 her niece Lilian *Baylis took over the management, subsequently experimenting with productions of Shakespeare at popular prices and making the Old Vic famous as the first theatre in the world to produce all the plays contained in the First Folio. The year 1931 saw the first performance of ballet, with Anton Dolin as guest artist, and the formation of the Vic-Wells Ballet Company under the direction of Ninette da Valois. In 1933 opera and ballet were transferred to the Sadler's Wells Theatre, while drama remained at the Old Vic, where the company included Gielgud, Olivier, and Richardson. Badly damaged by bombs in 1941, the theatre remained closed until 1950.

The Old Vic company was disbanded in 1963 when the National Theatre company, directed first by Olivier and later by Peter Hall, took over the theatre. The work of these two companies built up a great reputation for the old Vic throughout the world in the post-war years. After the National Theatre company's departure in 1976, however, a less successful period ensued under the management of the Prospect Theatre company and the theatre was put up for sale. In 1982 the Old Vic was purchased by the Canadian businessman Ed Mirvish; after extensive renovation it reopened with the Tim Rice musical *Blondel*. Subscription seasons were initiated and Shakespeare plays were reintroduced along with other drama and musical productions. The Royal Shakespeare Company's production of *Kiss Me Kate* transferred to the Old Vic from Stratford in 1987. Jonathan Miller's productions at the Old Vic since 1986 have included N F Simpson's *One-Way Pendulum* and Racine's *Andromache* (both 1988).

Old Woman *See* stock company.

Olimpico Teatro A theatre in Vicenza, Italy, which opened in 1585 with a performance of *Oedipus Rex* by Sophocles. Famous for its neoclassical architectural features, it was designed by Palladio and completed by Scamozzi but had little effect upon subsequent Italian theatres. It is the oldest surviving theatre in Europe.

Olivier, Laurence (Kerr), Baron (1907-) British actor, director, and manager, generally considered the foremost actor of the English-speaking theatre in recent times. He made his first appearance in 1922 at Stratford-upon-Avon as Katharina in an all-male production of *The Taming of the Shrew* and subsequently spent some years in repertory at Birmingham, as well as playing in a number of modern plays in the West End (including Coward's *Private Lives* in 1930).

In 1935 he alternated Romeo and Mercutio with John Gielgud at the New Theatre and went on to consolidate his reputation as an exceptional interpeter of major roles with performances with the Old Vic company, among them a full-length *Hamlet* in 1937. After World War II he became a codirector of the Old Vic company at the New Theatre, where once again he confirmed his standing as a great actor, playing among other parts Richard III, Hotspur, Oedipus, and Mr Puff in Sheridan's *The Critic*.

As an actor-manager in the early 1950s his appearances included the Duke of Altair in Christopher Fry's *Venus Observed* (1950), Antony in *Antony and Cleopatra*, and Caesar in Shaw's *Caesar and Cleopatra* (1951) opposite Vivien Leigh, to whom he was at that time married. After leading a brilliant Stratford-upon-Avon season in 1955 he had further spectacular West End triumphs as Archie Rice in John Osborne's *The Entertainer* (1957) and as Fred Midway in David Turner's *Semi-Detached* (1962).

He was director of the Chichester Festival Theatre from 1961 to 1963 and then became the first director of the National Theatre (1963–73), where he gave unique performances in many famous parts, including Astrov in Chekhov's *Uncle Vanya* (1963), Tattle in Congreve's *Love for Love* (1965), Othello (1965), and Shylock (1970). His many film appearances include those in *Henry V*, *Richard III*, and *Hamlet*, all of which he also produced and directed. He received a knighthood in 1947 and was created Baron Olivier of Brighton in 1970; his third wife is the actress Joan *Plowright. The Laurence Olivier Awards are presented annually in his honour for the best West End productions, under the auspices of the Society of West End Theatre.

Olivier Theatre One of the three theatres comprising the *National Theatre in London. Opened in 1976 with a performance of *Tamburlaine the Great* by Marlowe, it was named in honour of Lord Olivier and, seating 1160, is used primarily for spectacular large-scale productions. Plays presented on its open stage have included works by O'Casey, Congreve, Ibsen, Bond, Shaffer, and Brenton.

Olmo, Jacob (1690–1755) Jewish playwright. His play *Eden Aruch* (c. 1720) was much influenced by *Tofteh Aruch* by Moses Zacuto.

Olympia An entertainment complex on Broadway, New York, which was opened by Oscar Hammerstein in 1895. Containing a concert hall, a music hall (which became the New York Theatre), and the Lyric Theatre, it was sold in 1898. The Lyric reopened separately as the Criterion that same year.

Olympia Music Hall *See* Standard Theatre.

Olympia Theatre A theatre off Dame Street, Dublin, which opened as a music hall in 1855. Leading English performers appeared there until 1897 when the building was reconstructed, being renamed the Empire Palace of Varieties and then the Olympia in 1922. Subsequently serious drama was presented there, including works by native Irish playwrights. After World War II the theatre housed its own resident compa-

ny for several years until, in 1964, the theatre was sold; it was reorganized in 1974 as a venue for both serious dramas and variety acts. However, defects in the building itself led to the closure of the theatre until 1977, when it reopened with the musical *John, Paul, George, Ringo . . . and Bert*.

Olympic Theatre A theatre in the Strand, London, which was opened by Philip Astley in 1806. It was constructed largely from timber from a French sailing ship and was built in the form of a tent. Astley staged circus acts and other miscellaneous entertainments there until 1813 when R W Elliston took it over, renaming it the **Little Drury Lane Theatre** and presenting plays until being deprived of his licence as a result of the intervention of the Drury Lane management. As the Olympic Theatre it was then used for burletta and other forms of dramatic production and enjoyed considerable prosperity before being taken over by Madame Vestris in 1831. After opening with Maria Foote in *Mary Queen of Scots*, she established the theatre's reputation with a series of light entertainments and introduced Charles Mathews among others. The building was destroyed by fire in 1849 and rebuilt to seat 1750; performers who subsequently appeared there in romantic dramas included Kate Terry and Charles Wyndham. The theatre was again rebuilt in 1890 but was unsuccessful and was demolished in 1904.

The first **Olympic Theatre** on Broadway, New York, opened in 1837 and had many changes of management before, in 1839, William Mitchell made it successful – as **Mitchell's Olympic** – as a venue for burlesque and spectacle. It was the first New York theatre to present a weekly matinée; notable productions included John Poole's *Hamlet Travestie*, burlesques of *Richard III*, Boucicault's *London Assurance*, and the opera *The Bohemian Girl*. After an outstanding season in 1847–48 with Planché's *The Pride of the Market* and Benjamin Baker's *A*

Glance at New York in 1848, starring Frank Chanfrau, it eventually closed in 1850, reopening briefly to stage plays in German. The theatre was burnt down in 1854.

A second **Olympic Theatre** on Broadway opened in 1856 as **Laura Keene's Varieties** and was the first US theatre to have a female manager. In 1863 she left and, under Mrs John Wood, the theatre was renamed the Olympic. She presented the New York debuts of Mrs G H Gilbert and G F Rowe, while in 1867 G L Fox starred in *A Midsummer Night's Dream* (with scenery by Telbin), and in his pantomime *Humpty-Dumpty*, which had 483 performances. It was a home of variety from 1872 to 1880, when it was finally closed and demolished.

A **New Olympic Theatre** was opened on Broadway in 1856 by Chanfrau but failed as a venue for drama and subsequently housed minstrel shows and was renamed **Buckley's Olympic**.

Other theatres to have used the name, albeit briefly, include the Anthony Street Theatre (1812) and Wallack's Theatre (1862).

ombres chinoises See shadow play.

O'Neal, Frederick (1905-) US Black actor, who made his first appearance on the professional stage as Silvius in *As You Like It* (1927). He helped found the *American Negro Theatre in 1940 and made his first Broadway appearance four years later playing Frank in *Anna Lucasta* (1944), for which he won several awards.

O'Neil, Nance See Rankin, Arthur McKee.

O'Neill, Eliza (1791–1872) Irish actress, who first appeared in her father's company at Drogheda. In 1815 she was immensely successful as Juliet at Covent Garden, where she remained for five years until her final appearance in Kotzebue's *The Stranger*. She

retired on her marriage to William Becher, MP for Mallow.

O'Neill, Eugene Gladstone (1883–1953) US playwright, who was the son of the actor James O'Neill and wrote his first plays while recovering from tuberculosis in a sanatorium. From 1914 to 1915 he studied under George Pierce Baker at Harvard and became associated with the Provincetown Players, who produced several of his early dramas. *Beyond the Horizon*, his first full-length play, reached Broadway and won him a Pulitzer Prize. Of his many subsequent successes, several treated such themes as racism, human resilience, exploitation, sexual passion, the conflict between reality and spirituality, and faith in humanity itself, establishing him as major philosophical dramatist of the 20th century, despite his somewhat uneasy command of language.

After the enormous success of *Mourning Becomes Electra*, a treatment of Aeschylus's *Oresteia*, O'Neill retired from the theatre but continued to write in a more autobiographical vein. From this period came some of his finest works, notably The *Iceman Cometh*, A *Moon for the Misbegotten*, and *Long Day's Journey into Night*, which most closely mirrored his own disappointment, dogged by Parkinson's disease and alcoholism. He was also involved with the foundation of various theatres, while the **Eugene O'Neill Theatre Centre** in Waterford, Connecticut, where numerous conferences are held and the **National Theatre of the Deaf** and the **Little Theatre of the Deaf** have their home, was founded and named in his honour in 1963. He was awarded a Nobel Prize in 1936.

Principal works:

Beyond the Horizon: 1920.

The *Emperor Jones*: 1920.

Anna Christie: 1921.

All God's Chillun Got Wings: 1924.

Desire Under the Elms: 1924.

The Great God Brown: 1926.

Marco Millions: 1928.

Strange Interlude: 1928.
Lazarus Laughed: 1928.
The Dynamo: 1929.
Mourning Becomes Electra: 1931.
Ah, Wilderness!: 1933.
The Iceman Cometh: 1946.
A Moon for the Misbegotten: 1947.
Long Day's Journey into Night: 1956.
A *Touch of the Poet: 1957.
More Stately Mansions: 1963.

O'Neill, James (1847–1920) US actor, born in Ireland, who became a popular performer of strong romantic roles. Highly acclaimed in such adventures as *The Count of Monte Cristo* (1883) by Dumas *père*, in which he performed for over 30 years, he rivalled the success of Edwin Booth until his alcoholism and frustration as an artist led to his decline.

His second son was the celebrated playwright Eugene Gladstone *O'Neill.

O'Neill, Maire (Mollie Allgood; 1887–1952) Irish actress, who was in all the Abbey Theatre's productions until 1913, coming to London in 1907 in Synge's *The Playboy of the Western World*. Later she was with the Liverpool Repertory Theatre and played a Shakespearean season at His Majesty's; subsequent triumphs included leading roles in several of O'Casey's plays.

Open Air Theatre A permanent open-air theatre in Regent's Park, London, where performances of Shakespeare were first given by Ben Greet in 1900. The idea was revived by Sydney Carroll in 1933 with a production of *Twelfth Night*. The theatre was reconstructed in 1961 and again in 1972; it has a seating capacity of 1187 and continues to present an annual summer season of Shakespeare.

Open Space Theatre *See* Marowitz, Charles.

open stage *See* thrust stage.

Open Theatre A US theatre company, which was founded in New York in 1963 by Joseph Chaikin. The group seeks to explore the power of live theatre through abstraction and illusion. The first full-length play created and produced by the group was *Viet Rock* (1966); other productions included *The Serpent* (1968), *Terminal* (1969), *Mutation Show* (1971), and *Nightwalk* (1973). The group was disbanded in 1973.

Opera Comique A theatre built in the Aldwych, London, in 1870 and known as one of the Rickety Twins (together with the Globe Theatre, Newcastle Street). The Comédie Française and other foreign visiting companies played there, while in 1877 Richard D'Oyly Carte produced the first of several Gilbert and Sullivan operas at the theatre. Marie Tempest appeared in *The Fay o' Fire* in 1885. The theatre was closed in 1899 and demolished in 1902.

Opéra-Comique *See* Comédie-Italienne.

opposite prompt side *See* prompt side.

OP Riots *See* Covent Garden.

Orange Moll *See* Meggs, Mary.

Orange Street Theatre *See* Smock Alley Theatre.

orchestra A circular or semicircular area in front of the proscenium in the Greek theatre, on which the chorus performed. Subsequently the term has been applied to the area in front of the stage where the musicians sit (*see* auditorium).

Oregon Shakespearean Festival A festival of Shakespearean drama, which was founded in 1935 at Ashland, Oregon. The oldest such festival in the US, it was staged in a new theatre from 1947, professional actors replacing the amateurs who presented the earlier performances.

Oresteia, The A trilogy of plays by *Aeschylus, which constitutes the most complete surviving example of his work. First performance: Athens, 458 BC. Consisting of the plays *Agamemnon*, the *Choephori*, and the *Eumenides*, the *Oresteia* follows the pattern of thesis, antithesis, and resolution, culminating in the gods' judgement upon the murder of Clytemnestra by Orestes.

oriental drama See *Bugaku*; *Bunraku*; *Gigaku*; *Jōruri*; *Kabuki*; *Kagura*; *Kyōgen*; *Nō*; Peking Opera; *Shimpa*; *Shingeki*.

Orjasæter, Tore (1886–1968) Norwegian poet and playwright, who is best known for the drama *Den lange bryllaupsreisa* (The Long Honeymoon; 1949), which considers the position of collaborators at the end of World War II. Other works include *Anne på torp* (Anne on the Farm; 1930) and the Expressionist play *Christophoros* (St Christopher; 1947).

Orlenev, Pavel Nikolayevich (1869–1932) Russian actor, who encouraged the adoption of naturalism outside Russia during a wide-ranging tour. Leading his own company from 1904 in conjunction with Alla Nazimova, he presented the first production in the US of Chekhov's *The Seagull* (1905) and later toured the USSR; his finest parts included the title role of Ibsen's *Brand* and Raskolnikov in Dostoevsky's *Crime and Punishment*.

Orlov, Dmitri Nikolayevich (1892–1955) Soviet actor, who became highly popular in comic roles in the years following the Revolution of 1917. Influential upon the theories of Meyerhold, he also enjoyed success in works by Pogodin and Simonov.

Orrery, Lord (Roger Boyle, First Earl of Orrery, 1621–79) English playwright, credited by Dryden with being the first to write heroic drama. His more successful surviving plays, which contain detailed stage directions, include *Mustapha* (1665) and *The Black Prince* (1667).

Orton, Joe (Joe Kingsley Orton; 1933–67) British playwright, whose black comedies shocked audiences by combining scandalous action with bland everyday language. Sexual perversion and official corruption are common elements throughout his plays, which began with *Entertaining Mr Sloane* in 1964. Subsequent successes included *Loot* (1966), *The Erpingham Camp* (1967), *The Ruffian on the Stair* (1967), and *What the Butler Saw* (1969). He was eventually murdered by his homosexual lover, who committed suicide.

Osborne, John (James) (1929-) British playwright and actor, whose extraordinarily successful play *Look Back in Anger* triggered a new era in British drama. An actor in post-war repertory, Osborne in his early work drew heavily upon the conventional three-act naturalistic drama of the day, but soon began to experiment with a wide range of dramatic styles, from The *Entertainer* onwards. Throughout his work there runs a central preoccupation with the rebel at odds both with society and with those closest to him, expressing itself frequently in dramatic monologues of great power. Nurtured by George *Devine at the Royal Court Theatre, he has also written for the National Theatre and for television. Since *West of Suez* he has never repeated the success of his earlier work.

His second wife, the actress **Mary Ure** (1933–75), appeared in the premiere of *Look Back in Anger* and equally successfully in plays by Arthur Miller, Pinter, and Shakespeare.

Principal works:

Look Back in Anger: 1956.

The Entertainer: 1957.

Epitaph for George Dillon: 1958 (written with Anthony Creighton, 1955).

The World of Paul Slickey: 1959.

Luther: 1961.

Plays for England: The Blood of the Bambergs and *Under Plain Cover*: 1962.
**Inadmissible Evidence*: 1964.
*A *Patriot for Me*: 1969 (written 1966).
A Bond Honoured: 1966.
Time Present: 1968.
Hotel in Amsterdam: 1968.
West of Suez: 1971.
A Sense of Detachment: 1973.
Watch it Come Down: 1976.

Oscarsson, Per (1927-) Swedish actor, who has won acclaim for his interpretation of intense roles in both classics and modern plays. At the Kungliga Dramatiska Teatern from 1947 to 1952 and subsequently based at Gothenburg, he has been praised as Hamlet and in the plays of Strindberg and O'Neill among others.

Oslo Nye Teater A theatre in Oslo, which opened in 1929 (called Det Nye Teater) as a venue for native Norwegian drama. The theatre was soon obliged, however, to stage a more varied programme until 1947, when a new emphasis was placed upon serious drama under Axel Otto Normann. The theatre amalgamated with the Folketeatret in 1959 and, renamed the Oslo Nye Teater, eventually came under civic control; in recent years it has enjoyed considerable success with a reduced company under the directorship of Toralv Maurstad.

Ostler, William (d. 1614) English actor, who began as a boy actor at the Blackfriars Theatre. Acclaimed in female roles, he appeared in plays by Jonson and Beaumont and Fletcher and created Antonio in *The Duchess of Malfi*. He married the daughter of John Heminge and owned shares in the Globe and Blackfriars theatres.

Ostrovsky, Alexander Nikolayevich (1823–86) Russian playwright, whose plays in the Realist tradition linked the drama of Gogol and Chekhov. His best-known plays depict the world of the merchant class; his play *The *Bankrupt* was banned for 13 years after it offended the traders of Moscow. Of those that have also been acclaimed in translation, the best known include *The Forest* and the domestic tragedy *The *Storm*. *The Poor Bride* was praised for its depiction of Russian women, while *The Snow Maiden* became an opera by Rimsky-Korsakov. Most of his works were first presented at the Maly Theatre, also known as the House of Ostrovsky.

Principal works:
Bankrot: 1849; translated as *The Bankrupt* (or *It's All in the Family*).
Bednaya nevesta: 1852.
Bednost' ne porok: 1854.
Dokhodnoye mesto: 1856.
Groza: 1859; translated as *The Storm*.
Dmitry Samozvanets: 1867.
Na vsyakogo mudretsa dovol'no prostoty: 1868.
Les: 1871; translated as *The Forest*.
Snegurochka: 1873; translated as *The Snow Maiden*.

Othello, The Moor of Venice A tragedy by William *Shakespeare, written c. 1602. First performance: 1604. A study of racial prejudice and sexual jealousy, the play depicts the decline of the respected Othello, a Moor, as a result of his love for Desdemona and the machinations of the malignant Iago. Based upon an Italian model, the play has been much discussed for its use of the 'double time scheme', by which events lasting several weeks are compressed into two days; it has been greatly admired for its richly poetical language.

Other Place A studio theatre established in 1974 at Stratford-upon-Avon by the Royal Shakespeare Company for small-scale productions of classic and new plays as well as works of dramatists not often seen today, such as Ford's *Perkin Warbeck* (1975). A production of *Hamlet* starring Ben Kingsley was particularly acclaimed in 1975. It has also staged premieres of plays by many leading contemporary authors, including Christopher Hampton's *Les Liaisons Dangereuses* (1985).

Other Stage *See* Public Theatre.

O'Toole, Peter (1932-) British actor, born in Ireland, who began his career at the Bristol Old Vic in 1955. During the 1960 Stratford-upon-Avon season his roles included Petruchio and a celebrated Shylock, while in 1963 he played Hamlet in the National Theatre's inaugural production at the Old Vic. After establishing a new reputation in major film roles, he returned to the London stage as Macbeth in a notorious production at the Haymarket Theatre in 1980. Subsequently he played in two Shaw revivals, as Tanner in *Man and Superman* (1983) and as Professor Higgins in *Pygmalion* (1984).

Otto, Teo (1904–68) German stage designer, who attracted attention for his designs for the plays of Brecht. He worked on the premieres of both *Mutter Courage and ihre Kinder* (1941) and *Der gute Mensch von Sezuan* (1943) in Zurich; other successes included his designs for plays by Frisch and Goethe's *Faust* (1957).

Otway, Thomas (1652–85) English playwright and poet, who is best known for the blank verse tragedy *Venice Preserv'd* (1682). The most successful of his plays in his own lifetime, however, was the farce *The Cheats of Scapin*, which was based on Molière. Several of his finest plays were written for Mrs Barry, with whom Otway was hopelessly in love; they included *Alcibiades* (1675) – a rhyming tragedy, and *The Orphan; or, the Unhappy Marriage* (1680), which was a blank verse domestic tragedy. Other works included *Don Carlos* (1676), *The Soldier's Fortune* (1680), and a sequel – *The Atheist; or, the Second Part of the Soldier's Fortune* (1683); he also adapted plays by Racine.

OUDS *See* Oxford University Dramatic Society.

Ouest, Comédie de l' *See Décentralisation Dramatique.*

Our Town An Expressionist drama by Thorton *Wilder. First performance: New York, 1938. Set in New England, the play revolves around Emily Webb and George Gibbs, and follows the course of their lives from childhood, through their marriage, and up to Emily's early death, offering various comments upon the significance of their lives. The play won a Pulitzer Prize.

Ouville, Antoine Le Metel d' (c. 1590–1657) French playwright, elder brother of Boisrobert. Having established his reputation with *L'Esprit follet* (1638–39), based on a play by Calderón, he went on to adapt other Spanish works for the French stage.

Owens, John Edmond (1823–86) US actor, born in London, who excelled in comic and Yankee roles in both New York and London. He appeared widely as Sholon Shingle in Joseph S Jones's *The People's Lawyer*, while other successes included eccentric characters in plays by H J Byron, Colman the Younger, and Dion Boucicault.

Oxberry, William (1784–1824) British actor, who broke his indentures with a printer to work in the theatre. After work in the provinces he appeared unsuccessfully at Covent Garden, then toured Scotland before returning to London to appear in minor roles at the Lyceum, Drury Lane, and the Haymarket. He wrote the farce *The Actress of All Work* (1819) and founded the *Dramatic Mirror*.

His son was the actor **William Henry Oxberry** (1808–52), whose theatrical publications included *Oxberry's Weekly Budget* (1843–44). A popular actor in burlesque, he was also the author of several plays, notably

Matteo Falcone; or, the Brigand and His Son (1836).

Oxford Music Hall A music hall opened by Charles Morton in 1861 in an old galleried tavern at the corner of Oxford Street and Tottenham Court Road, London. It was a leading venue during the heyday of the music hall, was twice destroyed by fire and rebuilt, and was replaced by a new building in 1893. Charles Cochran produced Bruce Bairnsfather's *The Better 'Ole* there in 1918; three years later it became the New Oxford Theatre. Sacha Guitry, Yvonne Printemps, Duse, and the Old Vic company all appeared there before the theatre closed in 1926.

Oxford Playhouse A repertory theatre in Beaumont Street, Oxford, which was opened in 1938 by Eric Dance to replace an earlier theatre adapted by J B Fagan as a home for his famous Oxford company. In 1956 the theatre won financial support from the Arts Council and from the actor Richard Burton. The **Meadow Players**, under Frank Hauser's direction, reopened the theatre with Giraudoux's *Electra* and remained for 17 years. In 1961 Oxford University acquired the lease and, in 1966, Richard Burton and his wife, Elizabeth Taylor, starred in an OUDS production of Marlowe's *Dr Faustus* to raise funds for an extension. The new Oxford Playhouse Company (known as **Anvil Productions**) was installed in 1974, their regular work being interspersed with university productions and visits from outside companies, despite continuing financial crises.

Oxford's Men An English theatre company formed from the household of the Earl of Oxford around 1492. Based in the provinces, the company caused controversy in 1547 when it performed during public mourning for Henry VIII; reformed in 1580 it later performed at the Theatre until a scandal provoked by a brawl resulted in its return to the provinces. In 1584 young members of the group appeared at Blackfriars and at Court. The company disbanded in 1602.

Oxford University Dramatic Society (OUDS) A theatre club founded at Oxford University in 1885 by Arthur Bourchier and other undergraduates. The society has built up a strong reputation over the years for its performances of Shakespeare and the classics; its productions, some of which have been presented outdoors, are often directed by professionals. Until 1939, professional actresses played all the female roles. A subsidiary society, Friends of the OUDS, staged successful productions from 1940 to 1946. The OUDS now has its base at the Oxford Playhouse, from which it also organizes tours and a festival of drama.

Oyono-Mbia, Guillaume (c. 1940-) African playwright, who was born in French Cameroon. His popular comedies on African themes, which make use of the conventions of classical European comedy, include *Trois Prétendants, un mari* (Three Suitors, One Husband; 1964) and *Notre Fille ne se mariera pas* (Our Daughter Will Never Get Married; 1971).

P

Pace-Egg Play *See* mummers' play.

Pacuvius, Marcus (220 BC–c. 130 BC) Roman artist and playwright, one of the first great writers of Latin tragedies. The nephew of Quintus Ennius, he is known to have written one play in the *praetexta* tradition, *Paullus*, and about 12 plays based on Greek originals; only the titles of these works survive. He was noted in his own time for the elegance of his style and his free treatment of Greek models.

Page, Geraldine (1924–87) US actress, who made her New York debut in 1945. Her performance as Alma Winemiller in Tennessee Williams's *Summer and Smoke* (1954) was her first big success; later the same year she excelled as Marcelline in *The Immoralist* (based on Gide's novel) and Lizzie Curry in N Richard Nash's *The Rainmaker*. Subsequent triumphs included performances in Williams's *Sweet Bird of Youth* (1959), Chekhov's *Three Sisters* (1964), Hellman's *The Little Foxes* (1974), Ayckbourn's *Absurd Person Singular* (1974), and Williams's *Clothes for a Summer Hotel* (1980). Her last role was in Coward's *Blithe Spirit* on Broadway.

pageant A medieval festivity, which originally consisted of a procession of decorated carts, each organized by a different town guild. Later the term was also used of the speeches or short dramatic entertainments given in the open-air in honour of a visiting dignitary, such performances being repeated at various sites throughout the town during the course of the celebration. Most liturgical drama was presented in this way.

Later still, the term was used of masques of the Tudor period, specifically of the stages themselves, which were made of canvas and wood; these were sometimes still capable of movement.

A third application of the word was made in the early 20th century with the popularity of processional open-air entertainments celebrating the history of a local town or some historical anniversary. Such productions combine amateur and professional talent and are often staged in conjunction with numerous other attractions. Similar pageants focusing on the history of a particular theatre have also been staged at professional venues.

pageant lantern A unit of lighting, producing a narrow beam, which is capable of being used as either a spotlight or a foot-light. In the US it is usually referred to as a **projector unit**.

Paige, Elaine (1952–) British actress and singer, whose first adult successes included the rock musical *Hair* (1969), *Jesus Christ Superstar* (1972), and the leading role in *Grease* (1973). Her performance as Eva Peron in Lloyd-Webber's *Evita* (1978) won her several awards and she has since starred in the musicals *Cats* (1981) and *Chess* (1986).

Palace Theatre A theatre in Shaftesbury Avenue, London, which was originally intended as a home for English opera. It opened, as the **Royal English Opera House**, in 1891 with Sullivan's *Ivanhoe*; later in the year Sarah Bernhardt appeared there. The theatre was subsequently sold and reopened as the Palace Theatre of Varieties in 1892. Marie Tempest made her first appearance in variety there in 1906 and in 1910 the great Russian ballerina Anna Pavlova also made her debut there. Renamed the Palace Theatre in 1911 it staged the first Royal Command Variety Performance. In 1925 *No, No, Nanette* starring Binnie Hale ran for 655 performances and during World War II Jack Hulbert and Cicely Courtneidge starred in a succession of musical comedies. Postwar successes have included *The Song of Norway* (1946), Novello's *King's Rhapsody* (1949), *The Sound of Music* (1961–67), and *Jesus Christ Superstar* (1972–80). The Royal Shakespeare Company's musical *Les Misérables* transferred from the Barbican Theatre to the Palace in 1985. Subsequently it became the home of Andrew Lloyd Webber's Really Useful Theatre Company.

Another **Palace Theatre** was opened in Manchester in 1891 as a venue for touring companies. Specializing initially in music hall and variety, it was reconstructed in 1913 and in recent years has been used for more varied productions following the closure of the Manchester Opera House. It was extensively renovated in 1978–80, since when notable performances there have included *Jesus Christ Superstar* (1981) and operas staged by the Royal Opera and other touring companies as well as pantomime and straight drama.

A third **Palace Theatre** opened in Watford in 1908 as a music hall and became a repertory theatre in 1932. Seating 667, it is used for productions by touring companies and for pre-West End runs; notable productions under the management of Michael Attenborough have included plays by Tennessee Williams, Pinter, Osborne, and Simon Gray. The auditorium was renovated in 1981.

The **Palace Theatre** on Broadway, New York, seats 1358 and opened in 1913. Sarah Bernhardt and numerous vaudeville stars were seen there before the theatre was eventually transformed into a cinema. After 1965 it reverted to live theatre, housing mainly musicals, of which the most successful have included *Sweet Charity* (1966), *Applause* (1970), a revival of *Oklahoma!* (1979), and *Woman of the Year* (1981).

Palais-Royal, Théâtre du A theatre in Paris, which was originally the private theatre of Cardinal Richelieu. Rebuilt and re-equipped, the theatre opened in 1641; after Richelieu's death a year later the theatre was used for Court productions until 1660, when it was handed over to Molière. Again rebuilt in 1670, it was the scene of Molière's death in 1673, after which it was taken over by Lully as a concert hall. It burnt down in 1781 and underwent several reconstructions, eventually becoming the home of the Comédie-Française. Another Palais-Royal, opened in 1831, housed productions of notable farces by Labiche, Bernard, and others during the 19th century; in 1958 Barrault installed his company there. It is now used chiefly for the presentation of comedies and *Boulevard* plays.

Palaprat, Jean de Bigot (1650–1721) French playwright, born in Toulouse. He wrote a number of comedies in collaboration with David-Augustin de Brueys, notably *Le Grondeur* (1691) and *Le Muet* (1691). Palaprat's own plays were less successful.

Palitzsch, Peter (1918–) German director, who became one of the leading directors with the Berliner Ensemble in the 1950s. He directed the first production of Brecht's *Der aufhaltsame Aufstieg des Arturo Ui* (1959) while subsequent productions have included a version of the Royal Shakespeare Company's cycle *The Wars of the Roses* (1967).

Palladio, Andrea (Andrea di Pietro; 1508–80) Italian architect, whose designs had a major influence upon subsequent architects of all types of public buildings throughout Europe. His use of classical styles, in such buildings as the Teatro Olimpico, and his discussion of them in his *Quattro libri dell'architettura* (1570) had a particularly profound effect in England, where his followers included Inigo Jones.

Palladium *See* London Palladium.

Pallenberg, Max (1877–1934) Austrian actor, who was closely associated with Reinhardt's productions. He was particularly popular in comic roles, which included the Barker in Molnár's *Liliom* and Shweik in Piscator's adaptation of Hašek's famous novel.

palliata (*or crepidata*) A form of Roman *fabula*, denoting comedies translated from or written in imitation of Greek New Comedy. Initially the *palliata*, named after the *pallium* (a Greek cloak), was faithful to the original Greek model in terms of both plot and characters; under Plautus, however, it became a lively and distinct Roman form. Other writers of the *palliata* included Terence, Naevius, and Sextus Turpilius; it was eventually superseded by the **togata*.

Palmer, John (1742–98) British actor, who began as a strolling player. Subsequently he was employed by Foote at the Haymarket, after which Garrick engaged him at Drury Lane. In 1777 he created Joseph Surface in *The School for Scandal*; other roles included comic characters in Shakespeare. Palmer opened the Royalty Theatre in 1787, but failed to get a licence and was forced to close. He died suddenly on stage in Liverpool.

Palmer, Lilli *See* Harrison, Rex (Carey).

Palmer's Theatre *See* Wallack's Theatre.

Palsgrave's Men *See* Admiral's Men.

Pandora's Box (*Die Büchse der Pandora*) A play by Frank *Wedekind, written in 1894. First performance: 1905. A sequel to *Earth Spirit*, the play follows Lulu's decline and her violent death at the hands of Jack the Ripper as an inevitable consequence of her repressed sexuality; the two plays were later made into an opera by Alban Berg as *Lulu*.

Panopticon of Science and Art, Royal *See* Alhambra.

panorama A length of painted canvas, depicting a distant landscape or other view, which is unfurled across the back of the stage between two cylinders so as to present a continually changing scene.

Pantalone A character of the *commedia dell'arte*, an elderly, cunning, but frequently deceived Venetian merchant. Bearded and distinguished by his large nose, he was conventionally dressed in red and black and gradually evolved into the Pantaloon of the English harlequinade. He is traditionally the father and guardian of Columbine and is implacably opposed to her association with Harlequin.

pantomime An English theatrical form, derived from the *harlequinade. Traditionally a Christmas entertainment with a special appeal for younger audiences, the pantomime inherited its fairytale and comic elements from the harlequinade, which was gradually absorbed by the new form and disappeared altogether in the 20th century, having been reduced to a mere epilogue. The modern pantomime is distantly related to the *ballets-pantomimes* staged in France during the 18th century, which were themselves a somewhat inaccurate imitation of a Roman tradition, also called pantomime, that comprised a popular dumb show performed by a single masked dancer (*see pantomimus*).

Pantomime as it is now understood first emerged as a distinctive English form under John Rich and others. Together with music, trickwork, audience participation, topical references, dancing, and transformation scenes, features of the genre conventionally include the playing of the *principal boy by a woman and the casting of a man as the *dame, while the productions themselves are often exceedingly lavish and may run for several weeks. The advent of the music hall provided a further supply of popular singers and comedians for the pantomime, which in recent times has also recruited performers familiar from television appearances.

The most popular traditional pantomimes include *Cinderella, Aladdin, Red Riding Hood, Babes in the Wood, The Sleeping Beauty, Mother Goose, Jack and the Beanstalk*, and *Dick Whittington*. The term pantomime has also been used of mime and of melodrama (when performed as a dumb show).

pantomimus A dancer in dumb shows of the ancient Roman tradition (*see* pantomime), in which he played all the roles. He wore a number of different masks and performed his dance to musical accompaniment; noted *pantomimi*, who remained popular with audiences throughout the history of the Roman Empire, included Bathyllus, Paris, and Pylades.

Paper Boys' Play *See* mummers' play.

Papp, Joseph (Joseph Papirofsky; 1921-) US director and producer, who founded the New York Shakespeare Festival in 1954. He presented several Shakespearean works in Central Park until, in 1962, the Delacorte Theatre opened there as a permanent home for the festival. His productions of a musical version of *Two Gentlemen of Verona* (1971) and other plays have attracted many leading US performers, including Julie Harris and James Earl Jones. In 1967 he founded the *Public Theatre and, in 1973, he became the director of the *Vivian Beaumont and *Mitzi E Newhouse theatres at the Lincoln Centre. In 1980 his production of *Pirates of Penzance* was a huge success and transferred to the Uris Theatre, helping to relieve his financial pressures. In 1988 he launched a series of Shakespearean plays featuring popular stars of television and cinema.

Pappus A stock character of the Roman *atellana*. Probably depicted as a gullible old man, he was the central character of several plays, which exploited the comic possibilities presented by his incompetence.

parade A short dramatic entertainment that developed in France during the 18th century. *Parades* were performed outside booths at fairgrounds in order to entice passers-by into paying to see a play; they incorporated features of the *commedia dell'arte* and were later revived by Beaumarchais and other writers in the late 18th century.

paradiso A piece of stage machinery, by means of which a group of actors representing various angels or other supernatural characters might be lowered to or raised from the stage in a copper dome. The device was originally designed by **Filippo Bru-**

nelleschi (1377–1446) and remained in use until the 18th century. *See also* Glory.

parallel *See* rostrum.

Parigi, Giulio (1590–1636) Italian scene designer, a pupil of Buontalenti. Together with his son **Alfonso Parigi** (d. 1656) he did much to disseminate Italian concepts of scenery throughout Europe, having a particular influence upon the masques of Inigo Jones.

Paris (d. 67 AD) A noted *pantomimus* of ancient Rome, whose popularity eventually provoked the jealousy of Nero, who had him executed. Another celebrated performer of the same name was executed by Domitian in 83 AD.

Paris, Théâtre de A theatre in Paris, which opened in 1891 as the Nouveau Théâtre. Under Réjane and subsequently Léon Volterra it acquired a reputation for performances of plays by Verneuil, Sacha Guitry, and Marcel Pagnol, among others. A smaller auditorium, the Théâtre Moderne, was added in 1958.

Parker, Louis Napoleon (1852–1944) British playwright and pageant organizer, who produced and directed a number of civic pageants during the Edwardian period and in London during World War I. His most successful plays were *Rosemary* (1896), upon which he collaborated with Murray Carson, *Pomander Walk* (1911), and *Disraeli* (1911).

Park Lane Theatre *See* Daly's 63rd Street Theatre.

Park Theatre A theatre in Park Row, New York, which was nicknamed the **Old Drury** of the US in recognition of its importance as the earliest significant venue there. , It opened in 1798 under Hallam and Hodgkinson, initially as the **New Theatre,**

with *As You Like It*. At first it enjoyed only limited success despite its good company, but subsequently its reputation grew under Stephen Price's management (from 1808). In 1809, he produced the first American play, *The Indian Princess; or, La Belle Sauvage* by J N Barker; in this year he also added John Howard Payne to the company. Barker's use of foreign actors, however, caused the decline of the stock company and after 1818 its members simply provided support for such touring stars as Edmund Kean.

Burnt down in 1820 and rebuilt in 1821 the theatre then emerged as the most important venue in the US, with appearances by almost every leading contemporary actor. Closed between 1829 and 1834, Jean Davenport Lander, the child prodigy, made her debut there in 1837. Her later roles there included Sir Peter Teazle in *The School for Scandal*, Shylock in *The Merchant of Venice*, and Richard III. After Price's death in 1840 the company left and the theatre was sold (1841). Apart from such notable productions as Boucicault's *London Assurance* in 1841 and an appearance by Macready in 1843, the theatre's fortunes never recovered; Hamblin took over in 1848 but that same year the theatre was burnt down and was not rebuilt.

Another **Park Theatre** was erected in 1863 in Brooklyn, New York, and was successfully managed by F B Conway until 1871. When Conway left it became a venue for touring companies and was the last New York theatre to support visiting stars with its own stock company. Burnt down in 1908, it was never rebuilt.

See also Curtain Theatre; Herald Square Theatre; Majestic Theatre; Pitlochry Festival Theatre.

Pasadena Playhouse A theatre in Pasadena, California, which was one of the first community theatres in the US. It was founded in 1918 by the Pasadena Community Playhouse Association and opened in its 820-seat home in 1925. In 1928 a College of Theatre Arts was founded there. The playhouse, which was highly regarded for its productions of Shakespeare and of new plays, closed in 1970.

Pasco, Richard (Edward) (1926-) British actor, who first appeared at the Q Theatre in Goldsmith's *She Stoops to Conquer*. Subsequently he developed into a fine classical actor and worked with most of the principal companies, including the English Stage Company and the Royal Shakespeare Company. His many performances have included Thomas à Becket in T S Eliot's *Murder in the Cathedral* (1972) and alternation with Ian Richardson as Richard II and Bolingbroke in *Richard II* (1973). More recent successes have included Turgenev's *Fathers and Sons* (1987) at the National Theatre.

Pashennaya, Vera Nikolayevna (1887– 1962) Soviet actress, who became a leading performer first at the Maly Theatre (1905– 22) and then with the Moscow Art Theatre. She was noted for her intelligent and forceful interpretation of roles in the plays of Gorky, Schiller, Shakespeare, Sofronov, and Tolstoy among others.

paso A brief comic interlude common to drama in Spain during the 16th century. Originated by Lope de Rueda, such pieces were based on events from daily life and anticipated the development of the **entremé*; written in simple language, they usually featured popular characters from the *commedia dell'arte*.

Paso, Alfonso (1926-) Spanish playwright, who has become the most successful contemporary writer for the Spanish commercial theatre. He began writing in collaboration with his father and was briefly associated with the more controversial writer Alfonso Sastre; his plays include many unsophisticated comedies and thrillers.

Pasquati, Giulio (16th century) Italian actor of the *commedia dell'arte*, who was famous as Pantalone. He appeared with the Gelosi and was instrumental in causing the company to be invited to France in 1577.

Pasquino A character of the *commedia dell'arte*, one of the *zanni*. As a satirical valet he also featured in the Comédie-Italienne, called Pasquin.

pass door A door linking the backstage areas and the auditorium, for the use of theatre staff.

Passion play A genre of medieval liturgical drama, based on the events surrounding the Crucifixion. Traditionally performed on Good Friday, the Passion play was popular throughout Europe from the 14th century until the Reformation and was often presented in the open air. The most famous surviving example is that given every ten years at *Oberammergau.

Pastor, Tony (Antonio Pastor; 1837–1908) US actor, who made his first appearance as a child with Barnum, travelling in circuses and minstrel shows as a clown and singer. In 1861 he made his variety debut and, in 1865, opened Tony Pastor's Opera House, where he suppressed the more vulgar acts. In 1881 he presented early vaudeville performances at his 14th Street Theatre on Broadway.

pastoral A genre of drama, popular from the 15th to the 17th centuries, that evoked an idealized world of rustic shepherds and nymphs free from the corruption of contemporary urban existence. It evolved in Italy from an older poetical tradition and was typified by Tasso's *Aminta* (1573). This and the works of Guarini, Poliziano, Epicuro, Cinthio, and Beccari were subsequently much imitated in France and, to a lesser extent, in England, where writers of pastorals included Fletcher, Lyly, Daniel, and composers of masques; the genre also had a marked influence upon Shakespeare's *As You Like It*. In France, Mairet's *Silvie* (1626) was the supreme example, although the allegorical depiction of rural pleasures later also became an element of the comedies of Corneille and many others. The genre finally came to an end with the development of Romanticism.

'Pataphysics *See* Jarry, Alfred.

patent theatres The Theatres Royal, Drury Lane and Covent Garden, which were granted Letters Patent by Charles II in 1662, thus acquiring a monopoly of the theatre within the city of Westminster. The privileges were given specifically to Thomas Killigrew, who managed Drury Lane, and William Davenant, who ran Lincoln's Inn Fields (the patent eventually being inherited by the Dorset Garden company before reaching Covent Garden). The restrictions placed upon other theatres for the next 180 years were gradually eroded and reinterpreted as referring only to straight drama; they were ultimately lifted in 1843 although both Drury Lane and Covent Garden still operate under the terms of the original charters.

Patriot for Me, A A play by John *Osborne about the political intrigue and scandal that surrounded the career of Alfred Redl, an officer in the Austro-Hungarian Army at the turn of the century. First performance: Royal Court Theatre, 1965. It was heavily censored by the Lord Chamberlain and given its first performance as a club production, with Maximilian Schell as Redl. A successful revival took place in 1983, with Alan Bates in the leading role.

Pavilion *See* Anthony Street Theatre; Chatham Theatre.

Pavilion Music Hall *See* London Pavilion.

Pavilion Theatre A theatre in the White-chapel area of London, which was built in 1828 and known as the 'Drury Lane of the East'. It was rebuilt after a fire in 1856, and again in 1874. Morris Abrahams, who became manager in 1871, and then Isaac Cohen successfully attracted a large Jewish audience; after bomb damage in World War II the theatre was demolished in 1961.

Pavy, Salathiel (1590–1603) English child-actor, who appeared frequently at the Blackfriars Theatre, where he became famous. He acted in Jonson's *Cynthia's Revels* and *The Poetaster* and was praised by the author for his playing of old men; he died at the age of 13.

Paxinou, Katina (Katina Konstanto-poulou; 1900–73) Greek actress, who was closely associated with the productions of her husband Alexis Minotis. She made her first stage appearance in 1924 and was seen in the US (1930) before joining the Greek National Theatre in 1932. There she excelled in such roles as Clytemnestra in the plays of Sophocles and Aeschylus, as well as in modern works by O'Neill and Ibsen, notably as Mrs Alving in *Ghosts* (1934–40). She also triumphed in Shakespearean roles opposite her husband and in plays by García Lorca, Christopher Fry, and Euripides.

Payne, Ben Iden (1881–1976) British actor and director, who was first associated with Benson's company (1899) and later with Miss Horniman's theatre in Manchester. He then moved to the US (1913–34), where he was active both as an actor and as a lecturer in drama. Subsequently he became director of the Shakespeare Memorial Theatre, a post which he occupied until 1943 when he returned to the US. In 1950 he established a summer Shakespeare Festival at Balboa Park, San Diego.

Payne, John Howard (1791–1852) US actor and playwright, who had his first play successfully presented in New York at the age of 14. Subsequently he toured to great acclaim in such roles as Hamlet and Romeo, appearing in Britain in 1813 and then in Paris, where he became friendly with Talma and began a long association with the Comédie-Française. Of his many plays the most successful was the tragedy *Brutus; or, the Fall of Tarquin* (1818) starring Edmund Kean; others included adaptations of Pixérécourt's melodramas and collaborations with Washington Irving. He was briefly manager of Sadler's Wells, consequently spending a year in prison for debt, and from 1842 was US consul in Tunis. His libretto for the opera *Clari, the Maid of Milan* (1823) included the popular song 'Home Sweet Home'.

Peace, The A comedy by *Aristophanes. First performance: Athens, 421 BC. The plot revolves around a farmer who travels to heaven on the back of a dung-beetle and discovers that the gods have forsaken mankind; it was intended as an appeal for peace between Athens and Sparta.

Peacock Theatre *See* Abbey Theatre.

Pedrolino A character of the *commedia dell'arte*, one of the *zanni*. Pellesini excelled in the role, which gradually evolved from being that of a simple honest servant, conventionally dressed in white, to the pathetic lover *Pierrot of the Comédie-Italienne. He was usually played without a mask, but with his face whitened.

Peele, George (c. 1558–97) English playwright, one of the University Wits. His *The Arraignment of Paris* (1581) contributed to the development of romantic comedy, whilst *The Old Wives' Tale* (1590) elevated farce to a new more sophisticated level. His other works include the patriotic *Edward I* (1591) and the biblical drama *The Love of King*

David and Fair Bathsabe (1587). Peele may also have written the first act of Shakespeare's *Titus Andronicus* and collaborated with Greene.

Peer Gynt A poetic drama by Henrik *Ibsen, published in 1867. First performance: Oslo, 1876. Consolidating the success of *Brand*, which preceded it, the play is a critical examination of traits of the Norwegian character and draws heavily upon folklore and legend; incidental music for the first production was composed by Grieg.

Peking Opera A genre of popular drama, which has ancient roots but became established as the main theatrical tradition of China in the 19th century. Combining elements of music, dialogue, and acrobatics, it revolves around a virtuous central protagonist who, communicating in both dialogue and song, experiences numerous melodramatic adventures before finally triumphing over evil.

The plot is usually involved and derived from a variety of mythological and literary sources; plays of the genre are divided into *weu* (civil) and *wu* (military) forms. Productions are presented on a bare square stage with minimal use of props, the choice of which has been long established by convention.

The actors themselves are trained to achieve the greatest effect with economy of movement, each usually specializing in one of four main roles – the male characters (*sheng*), female characters (*dan*), large males with painted faces (*jing*), and comedians (*chou*) – or subdivisions of them. Female roles were traditionally played by men, of whom the greatest interpreter was Mei Lanfang, although women have been permitted in these roles since 1911. Lines are generally delivered in a falsetto voice with orchestral accompaniment and performers are expected to develop the basic storyline themselves, the script being normally little more than an outline, as in the European *commedia dell'arte*. Costumes, like most other aspects of the Peking Opera, obey convention in terms of colour, ornamentation, and headwear; make-up is similarly dictated by tradition with certain colours suggesting specific temperaments.

Along with *hua ju*, a form of modern spoken drama influenced by Western models, the Peking Opera remains China's best known and most popular form of theatre, despite a period during the Cultural Revolution (1967–72) when all such productions were prohibited in favour of a small repertory of officially-sanctioned revolutionary dramas and ballets.

Pelléas et Mélisande A play by Maurice *Maeterlinck. First performance: Paris, 1893. Drawing on legendary sources, the play was a big success in both New York and London with Mrs Patrick Campbell as Mélisande and with incidental music by Fauré. In 1904 Sarah Bernhardt partnered her, playing Pelléas. It later became an opera by Debussy.

Pellesini, Giovanni (c. 1526–1612) Italian actor of the *commedia dell'arte*, who played the role of Pedrolino. He led his own company for a time before joining the Confidenti, of which he subsequently became the director.

Pellico, Silvio (1789–1854) Italian patriot and playwright, usually remembered for his memoirs based on his imprisonment for political offences. His plays include several classical tragedies, notably *Francesca da Rimini* (1815), which were much influenced by Alfieri and Foscolo; the part of Francesca herself later provided a favourite role for Adelaide Ristori.

Pellio, Titus Publilius (2nd century BC) Roman actor, who became famous for his performances in the plays of Plautus. He is known to have appeared in the *Menaechmi*, the *Stichus*, the *Bacchides*, and the *Epidecus*.

Pemán y Pemartín, José Mariá (1898–1981) Spanish poet and playwright, whose best-known play was *El divino impaciente* (A Saint in a Hurry; 1935). A staunch Catholic and royalist, he also enjoyed success with such plays as *La santa vivreina* (1939) and *Callados como muertos* (Silent as the Dead; 1952).

Pembroke's Men An English theatre company formed from the household of the Earl of Pembroke around 1592. The company was closely associated with the plays of Shakespeare, especially *Titus Andronicus* and the later parts of *Henry VI*, until 1594 when he joined the Chamberlain's Men. In 1597 Pembroke's Men moved into the Swan Theatre, where their production of the controversial *The Isle of Dogs* by Jonson and Nashe precipitated their dissolution, actors from the company joining the Admiral's Men and other troupes.

Penço de la Vega, Joseph (1650–1703) Jewish playwright, author of the first printed Hebrew play. Printed in Amsterdam in 1673 and later reprinted in Leghorn in 1770, *Asiré Hatiqva* is a morality play probably written for a religious festival.

Penkethman, William (d. 1725) British actor, who at one time travelled the provinces with a peepshow and ran fairground booths. He appeared in comedy at Drury Lane under Christopher Rich and specialized in playing masked harlequins. Colley Cibber wrote for him the characters of Don Lewis in *Love Makes a Man* (1701) and Trappanti in *She Would and She Would Not* (1702).

Penley, William Sydney (1852–1912) British actor-manager, who made his stage debut at the Royal Court Theatre in 1871. He became an accomplished farceur and light opera singer, achieving outstanding success in such parts as the title role in Hawtrey's *The Private Secretary* (1884) and, most notably, Lord Fancourt Babberley in *Charley's Aunt* (1892), which he played for 1466 consecutive performances.

Penny for a Song, A A comedy by John *Whiting. First performance: London, 1951. A study of eccentricity and a satire upon the nature of war, it is set during the Napoleonic Wars and was successfully presented by the Royal Shakespeare Company in a revised version in 1962.

penny plain, twopence coloured *See* toy theatre.

Penthouse Theatre A theatre-in-the-round at the University of Washington, Seattle. Built in 1940 by Glenn Hughes, it was the first theatre-in-the-round in the world.

People Show A British theatre company founded in London in 1966 to present experimental drama. Relying upon the techniques of collective creation, the company aims for an effect of spontaneity and has dispensed with the use of a director or writer; it has toured successfully throughout Europe and the US.

People's National Theatre *See* Price, (Lilian) Nancy (Bache).

Pepper's ghost A stage effect by means of which a transparent ghost can be presented alongside real actors. Developed by John Henry Pepper (1821–1900), the effect is achieved by reflecting the image of a live actor walking in the pit onto an inclined sheet of glass positioned on the stage.

Pepys, Samuel (1633–1703) English administrator, diarist, and playgoer. His famous *Diary* provides a vivid picture of the Restoration theatre. A friend of many actors and actresses, notably Mary Knepp, he recorded invaluable comments on the theatre during the 1660s, as well as much backstage gossip.

perch A small raised platform behind the proscenium arch, used for the manipulation of additional lighting units.

Percival, Susanna (1667–1703) English actress, wife of William *Mountfort. She was very popular as a performer of breeches parts and was admired by Colley Cibber, among others, in such plays as Buckingham's *The Rehearsal* and Dryden's *Marriage à la Mode*.

Percy, Esmé (Saville) (1887–1957) British actor and director, who worked in Benson's company and with Miss Horniman at Manchester. In 1913 he formed his own touring company, producing plays by Shaw and Wilde – including the first staging of *Man and Superman* in its entirety. After World War I he became general producer and a leading performer with Macdona's Shaw Repertory Company; his roles included Dobelle in Denis Johnston's *The Moon in the Yellow River* (1934) and Matthew Skipps in Fry's *The Lady's Not for Burning* (1949). His last months were spent with the English Stage Company at the Royal Court Theatre.

Peretz, Isaac Leib (1852–1915) Jewish poet and playwright, living in Poland, who is regarded as one of the fathers of Yiddish literature. He tried to combine the elements of traditional Judaism with modern secular trends in such plays as *The Golden Chain* and *Bei Nacht oifn alten Mark* (Night in the Old Market; 1925).

Peréz, Cosmé (c. 1585–1673) Spanish actor, whose comic roles included several *Gracioso* characters. He was especially popular in *entreméses* by Cervantes and Quiñones de Benavente as Juan Rana and is known to have appeared before the Spanish court in 1665.

Pérez Galdós, Benito (1843–1920) Spanish novelist and playwright, whose quest for realism and an honest portrayal of contemporary society is reflected in such plays as *Realidad* (Reality; 1892) and *Electra* (1901), which aroused much controversy with its discussion of hypocrisy within the Church. Many of his plays and dramatizations of his own travels revealed the influence of Ibsen and Zola.

Performance Group A US theatre company founded in New York in 1967 by Richard Schechner. The group experimented with environmental theatre, training techniques, and the relationships between actor and audience, presenting innovative productions of Brecht and Shakespeare among others. In 1970 the group reformed as the Wooster Group under the direction of Spalding Gray and Elizabeth LeCompte.

periaktoi The earliest known examples of the use of scenery, as used in the ancient Greek and Roman theatre. They probably consisted of painted prisms, which revolved to suggest a change in setting and also helped to project sound from the stage into the auditorium. Subsequently they were further developed on the Renaissance stage and renamed **telari**.

Pericles, Prince of Tyre A romance by William *Shakespeare, written c. 1608. First performance: c. 1608. Possibly containing passages by another playwright, the play was based on a Greek original and depicts the separation and ultimate reunion of Pericles with his wife Thaisa and his daughter Marina. Marina survives an attempt to kill her and a stay in a brothel in Mytilene, where she remains untouched on account of her beauty and virtue, before the joyful meeting with her long-lost parents. The uneven quality of the first half of the play has led to suggestions that it has been reconstructed from memory.

Perkins, Osgood (1892–1937) US actor, who won acclaim in both comic and serious roles in a wide range of productions. He established his reputation in Hecht and MacArthur's *The Front Page* in 1928, while subsequent successes included roles in plays by Chekhov and Molière; he also appeared alongside the Lunts in Coward's *Point Valentine* (1935) and briefly in Rachel Crothers's *Susan and God* (1937).

Persians, The A tragedy by *Aeschylus, regarded as the earliest surviving drama of the Western theatre. First performance: Athens, c. 472 BC. The play depicts the defeat of the Persians at Salamis in 480 BC and was, unlike much of his other surviving work, probably not part of a tetralogy.

Peruzzi, Baldassare (1481–1536) Italian architect and artist, who executed early perspective scenes for the theatre. He was the first artist to employ perspective in such designs for the stage; his pupils included Serlio.

Peter Pan A play by J M *Barrie, adapted from his novel *The Little White Bird*. First performance: 1904. With Nina Boucicault as the first Peter Pan, the boy who never grows up, the play – a children's fantasy adventure – has remained a popular item in the theatrical repertory, especially at Christmas. Copyright fees on the play pass automatically to the Great Ormond Street Children's Hospital in London, as stipulated by the author.

Petit-Bourbon, Salle du A theatre in Paris, which was first used as a venue for professional performances in 1577. The Gelosi and other noted Italian companies appeared there, later being joined by Molière's company, which performed some of the great playwright's early works there. When the theatre was threatened with demolition in 1668 Molière's troupe moved to the Palais-Royal, taking much of the scenery designed by Torelli and others as well as much of the equipment with them.

Petri, Olaus (1493–1552) Swedish humanist and churchman, who was the author of the first Swedish vernacular play, *Tobiae Comedia* (1550). Chancellor to Gustavus Vasa and a leading figure of the Reformation in Sweden, he was the subject of Strindberg's play *Mäster Olof* (1872).

Petrified Forest, The A play by Robert *Sherwood. First performance: New York, 1935. The play examines the destructive force of Fascism in a world where good men are helpless and power remains with the criminals.

Phantom of the Opera, The A musical by Andrew *Lloyd Webber. First performance: London, 1986. Based upon a story by Gaston Leroux, this version of the story of a demented composer haunting the nether regions of the Paris Opéra was highly popular despite its lack of suspense or mystery, largely due to the acting of Michael Crawford.

Phèdre A tragedy by Jean *Racine. First performance: Paris, 1677. Based on Euripides's *Hippolytus*, the play is generally considered to be Racine's greatest work. The plot concerns Phèdre's passion for Hippolyte, son of her husband Thésée, and culminates in Hippolyte's death and Phèdre's suicide.

Phelps, Samuel (1804–78) British actor and manager, who became an actor in 1826 and played in the provinces for 11 years, establishing himself as a fine tragedian. In 1837 Ben Webster engaged him at the Haymarket, where he opened successfully as Shylock. Subsequently he joined Macready's Covent Garden company, appearing as Othello to Macready's Iago. In 1843 he took over Sadler's Wells; during the next 18 years he produced numerous Shakespeare plays, restoring many of the texts to their original versions and appearing in such roles as Lear and Bottom. He continued to act in the provinces and other London theatres after he gave up management, usually in Shakespeare or dramatizations of Scott's novels.

Pherecrates (5th century BC) Greek playwright, author of several examples of Old Comedy. He won his first victory around 437 BC; many fragments of his plays survive.

Philanderer, The A play by G B *Shaw, written in 1893. First performance: London, 1905. The play examines love and marriage through the relationships of the three central characters, Charteris, Julia, and Grace. Through his satirization in the play of Ibsenism and feminism – two causes that he supported – Shaw demonstrated his capacity for self-criticism; the play failed to find a producer for many years.

Philemon (c. 368 BC – c. 264 BC) Greek playwright, who was regarded in his own time as the equal of Menander. He was the author of 97 moralistic comedies, of which only fragments survive; Plautus was amongst the Roman playwrights much influenced by his writing.

Philipe, Gérard (1922–59) French actor, who became highly popular in romantic roles following his first major success, in the title role of *Caligula* (1945) by Camus. He then embarked upon a successful film career before returning to the stage in 1951 when he joined Jean Vilar's Théâtre National Populaire. He was particularly admired there and elsewhere in Corneille's *Le Cid*, Musset's *Lorenzaccio*, Hugo's *Ruy Blas*, and Shakespeare's *Richard II* among other plays; following his early death he was buried in the costume he wore in *Le Cid*.

Philippides (c. 4th–3rd century BC) Greek playwright, author of several examples of New Comedy. His excitement at winning a

dramatic competition as an old man is reputed to have precipitated his own death.

Philips, Ambrose (1674–1749) English poet and playwright, for whom the nickname 'Namby-Pamby' was coined with reference to his insipid verses. His translation of Racine's *Andromaque*, entitled *The Distrest Mother*, was received with great acclaim at Drury Lane in 1712; two other tragedies, *The Briton* (1722) and *Humfrey, Duke of Gloucester* (1723), were less successful.

Philips, Katherine (1632–64) English poet and playwright, dubbed 'the matchless Orinda'. Her *Pompey* (1663) was the first play by a woman to be professionally produced on the London stage.

Phillipin *See* Villiers, Claude de.

Phillips, Augustine (d. 1605) English actor, who appeared in Tarleton's *Seven Deadly Sins* in about 1590 and later joined the Chamberlain's Men (1594). He acted in Jonson's early plays and is in the First Folio list of Shakespearean players; he was also an original shareholder in the Globe Theatre.

Phillips, Robin (1942–) British director and actor, who began his career at the Bristol Old Vic in 1959 and was subsequently praised for his work as artistic director (1974–80) of the Stratford (Ontario) Festival. He has also worked at the Chichester Festival Theatre (1962–64 and 1971–72), the Oxford Playhouse (1964–65), with the Royal Shakespeare Company (1965–67 and 1970), at Exeter's Northcott Theatre (1967–68), and at the Greenwich Theatre (1973). His most celebrated productions have included plays by Congreve, Coward, Shakespeare, O'Neill, and Shaw, starring such leading performers as Maggie Smith and Peter Ustinov.

Phillips, Stephen (1864–1915) British playwright, poet, and actor, whose *Herod* (1900), staged by Tree, was widely believed to signify the dawn of a new era of poetic drama. *Paolo and Francesca* (1902) and *Ulysses* (1902) were similarly acclaimed, but the failure of *Nero* (1906) effectively ruined his reputation.

Phillip Street Theatre A theatre in Sydney, Australia, which was used for a series of successful revues beginning in 1954. Relying heavily upon Australian writers and performers, a more varied programme was staged at a new venue, the Phillip Theatre, from 1961 until 1974, when the series finally came to an end.

Phillpotts, Eden (1862–1960) British novelist and playwright, whose most successful work was the rustic comedy *The Farmer's Wife* (1916). His other plays include *Devonshire Cream* (1924), *Jane's Legacy* (1925), and *Yellow Sands* (1926), which was written in collaboration with his daughter, **(Mary) Adelaide Eden** (1896-).

Philocles (5th century BC) Greek playwright, nephew of Aeschylus. No fragments of his tragedies survive, although he is believed to have defeated Sophocles in one dramatic contest.

Philoctetes A tragedy by *Sophocles. First performance: Athens, 409 BC. The plot revolves around the central character, who has been cast away on a desert island and fears he may never escape.

phlyax A form of mime play or farce popular in ancient Greece. It developed from Middle Comedy and was much performed in southern Italy during the 3rd and 4th centuries BC. Writers of the form, which usually comprised various burlesques, included **Rhinthon of Tarentum** (4th century BC); eventually the form was absorbed into the *atellana. It is now known mainly from vase paintings of the period.

Phoenix Arts Centre A theatre in Leicester (originally the Phoenix Theatre) that opened in 1963 with Thornton Wilder's *The Matchmaker*. It was erected on a short-term basis pending building of a larger theatre but proved so popular, particularly with young people, that it continued in use; its range of activities has since been extended to concerts, dance, art exhibitions, and films.

Phoenix Society A British theatre group founded in London in 1919 under the aegis of the Stage Society. Dedicated to the performance of early English drama, the society presented 26 influential productions of major plays from the period between 1919 and 1925, enthusiastically supported by such notable theatre figures as Edith Craig, Allan Wade, and Norman Wilkinson, while Sir Thomas Beecham arranged the music for Fletcher's *The Faithful Sherpherdess* in 1923.

Phoenix Theatre A theatre in Charing Cross Road, London, which was built on the site of a former music hall, the Alcazar. The opening production, in 1930, was *Private Lives* by Noël Coward with the author, Gertrude Lawrence, and Laurence Olivier in the cast. Coward scored another hit in 1936 with a programme of one-act plays under the title *Tonight at 8.30*. During World War II John Gielgud successfully revived William Congreve's *Love for Love* (1943) there and in 1945 Cicely Courtneidge enjoyed a long run in *Under the Counter*. Subsequent productions have included plays by Thornton Wilder, Rattigan, John Osborne, Brecht, and Chekhov, while in 1968 a musical drama based on Geoffrey Chaucer's *Canterbury Tales* ran for over 2000 performances. More recent successes have been Tom Stoppard's *Night and Day* (1978) and Simon Gray's *The Common Pursuit* (1988).

The **Phoenix Theatre** on East 74th Street, New York, was founded as Maurice Schwartz's **Yiddish Art Theatre** on 12th Street and was reopened as the Phoenix in 1953 with Sidney Howard's *Madam, Will You Walk?*. The theatre concentrated on plays by such notable European authors as Chekhov, Shaw, and Strindberg before switching to Yiddish revue in 1961, when the company moved to its current Lower East Side location, which was initially called the **East 74th Street Theatre**. Productions there included Kopit's acclaimed *Oh Dad, Poor Dad, Momma's Hung You in the Closet and I'm Feelin' So Sad* (1962) before the company moved again to the Lyceum Theatre and onto Broadway. A New Phoenix Repertory Company was established in 1972 and eventually settled at a new Phoenix Theatre. The original Phoenix Theatre on 12th Street presented burlesque from 1961 to 1965 and was then renamed the **Eden Theatre**, enjoying success with *Oh, Calcutta!* (1969) and the musical *Grease* (1972). It 1977 it was renamed the Entermedia and enlarged to house a variety of events. The Phoenix Theatre on East 47th Street became the **Eastside Playhouse** in 1968 and housed both plays and musicals before concentrating on light opera.

See also Cockpit.

Phrynichus (c. 6th-5th century BC) Greek playwright, a contemporary of Aeschylus. His tragedies included a controversial account of the capture of Miletus and *Phoenissae*, which was based on events following the battle of Salamis; he won drama contests in 512 BC and 476 BC. Another Greek writer of the same name flourished in Athens in the 5th century BC, winning two victories for his plays, which were examples of Old Comedy; many fragments of his writings survive.

Piaf, Edith (Giovanna Gassion; 1915–63) French singer, who became a celebrated star of French cabaret and music hall. Adopting the name *piaf* (French slang for sparrow) on account of her diminutive stature, she became famous for her distinctive raw singing voice and resilient personality. She appeared throughout France and in the US, being much admired by Cocteau and other influential figures. Her life, which was marred by an unhappy childhood, failed marriages, alcoholism, and addiction to drugs, provided the basis for the play *Piaf* (1980) by Pam Gems, in which Jane Lapotaire won great acclaim.

Picard, Louis-Benoît (1769–1828) French playwright, actor, and manager, who was born in Paris. His comedies of manners, which gently satirized bourgeois society, were immensely popular during the Napoleonic era. *La Petite Ville* (1801; adapted as *The Merry Widow*), is probably his best-known and most popular play; others include *Médiocre et rampant* (1797), *Les Provinciaux à Paris* (1802), *La Vieille Tante* (1811), and *Les Deux Philibert* (1816).

Piccadilly Theatre A theatre close to Piccadilly Circus that was the first in London to be fully air-conditioned. It was built in 1928 on the site of derelict stables and opened with *Blue Eyes*, a romantic musical starring Evelyn Laye. The Piccadilly's early history was not one of spectuacular success; in 1960 the theatre was acquired and improved by the Albery family, who installed the air-conditioning. Since then successful runs have included Edward Albee's *Who's Afraid of Virginia Woolf?* (1964), Robert Bolt's *Vivat! Vivat Regina!*, transferred from Chichester in 1970, and Willy Russell's very popular *Educating Rita* (1980), one of several Royal Shakespeare Company transfers.

Piccolo Teatro della Città di Milano An Italian theatre company, the earliest permanent troupe of its kind to be established in Italy, which was founded in 1947. Organized by the director **Giorgio Strehler** (1921-) and the actor-director **Paolo**

Grassi (1919–81), the company established a reputation for high artistic standards with productions of Gorky, Goldoni, Brecht, and others and quickly built up a large audience in Milan, its leading performers including Marcello Moretti (1910–61). The model for many other similar Italian companies, the group has toured internationally in a wide range of productions. It has been run solely by Strehler since 1973.

Pickelhering See Reynolds, Robert.

Pierrot A character of the French Comédie-Italienne and the English harlequinade, derived from that of *Pedrolino in the Italian *commedia dell'arte*. Traditionally dressed in a loose white suit with a large hat and whitened face, Pierrot owed his later development to Deburau and others, who exaggerated the melancholic side of his nature and made him an increasingly pathetic figure. After disappearing from the harlequinade, he was reintroduced into the English theatre through the dumb play *L'Enfant Prodigue* in 1891, his costume subsequently being adopted by numerous concert parties at British holiday resorts (*see* pierrot troupes). In France he was further developed by Marcel Marceau in his creation of the mime character Bip.

pierrot troupes Theatrical companies established in Britain in the late 19th and early 20th centuries in which a group of performers assumed collectively the white costume of the traditional *Pierrot character. Such troupes were inspired by the success of the mime play *L'Enfant prodigue* (1891), which was based on a Pierrot figure, and included singers, dancers, and comedians, performing at various seaside holiday resorts and elsewhere. The most successful groups included the **Co-Optimists**, who played in London under **Davy Burnaby** (1881–1949) in the 1920s.

Pigott-Smith, Tim (1946-) British actor, who worked in repertory before joining the Royal Shakespeare Company in 1972 and becoming established as a television star. He played Colin in Michael Frayn's *Benefactors* (1984) at the Vaudeville Theatre and portrayed many characters in a one-man show, *Bengal Lancer* (1985), at the Lyric, Hammersmith. At the National Theatre in 1987 he was Octavius Caesar in *Antony and Cleopatra* and, in 1988, Iachimo in *Cymbeline*, Leontes in *The Winter's Tale*, and Trinculo in *The Tempest*.

Pike's Opera House See Grand Opera House.

Pike Theatre A small experimental theatre in Dublin, which was opened by Alan Simpson in 1953. Among his productions there were the premieres of Brendan Behan's *The Quare Fellow* (1954) and Beckett's English version of *Waiting for Godot* (1955), and many contemporary plays by international authors, including Tennessee Williams's *The Rose Tattoo* (1957), which led to Simpson's arrest on obscenity charges. The size of the theatre made it inviable and after Simpson's last production, J B McGowan's *God's Child* (1959), the theatre was eventually sold.

Pilgrim Players See Browne, E Martin; Jackson, Sir Barry Vincent.

Pillars of Society (*Samfundets Støtter*) A play by Henrik *Ibsen. First performance: Copenhagen, 1877. The first of Ibsen's acclaimed series of social dramas, it depicts the guilt suffered by a public figure whose reputation is founded on a lie.

Pinero, Sir A(rthur) W(ing) (1855–1934) British playwright, who began his career as an actor in 1874. He was encouraged to write by Sir Henry Irving; his earliest play to be staged was *£200 a Year* (1877), but it was not until his series of farces written for the Royal Court Theatre in the 1880s that he achieved real popularity. Pinero was especially influenced by the realism of T W Robertson, by the well-made plays of Eugene Scribe, and by the social dramas of Ibsen, as is apparent in his 'thesis' plays of the late 1880s and 1890s. The innovative The *Second Mrs Tanqueray* was particularly well received, with Mrs Patrick Campbell in the leading role; following *Trelawney of the 'Wells'* and The Gay Lord Quex, however, his work was progressively less successful.

Principal works:

The *Magistrate*: 1885.

The Schoolmistress: 1886.

Dandy Dick: 1887.

The Profligate: 1889.

The Cabinet Minister: 1890.

The Second Mrs Tanqueray: 1893.

The Notorious Mrs Ebbsmith: 1895.

Trelawney of the 'Wells': 1898.

The Gay Lord Quex: 1899.

pin spot A spotlight capable of throwing a very small, precise beam of light onto the stage.

Pinter, Harold (Harold Da Pinta; 1930-) British playwright, who began as an actor and whose brilliantly constructed plays are sometimes identified with the Theatre of the Absurd. His first play, the one-act The *Room*, established the atmosphere of menace that was to characterize most of his subsequent work, while The *Caretaker* marked him out as a leading contemporary writer. The action and the comedy of his plays frequently arise from a struggle for dominance in which language is more usually a weapon than a tool for communication; the term Pinteresque is now commonly used for dialogue that conceals as much as it reveals and is punctuated frequently by portentous pauses. More recent plays, including Betrayal (1978) and A Kind of Alaska (1982), have moved into rather different territory, the first more a comedy of manners than of menace, the second a

delicate portrayal of a woman waking after a long period of sleeping sickness. Pinter has written successfully for radio, television, and cinema and has also directed at the National Theatre and in the West End. His first wife was the actress Vivien *Merchant and he is now married to the writer Lady Antonia Fraser.

Principal works:

The Room: 1957.

The *Birthday Party*: 1958.

The *Dumb Waiter*: 1959.

A Slight Ache: 1959.

The Caretaker: 1960.

The Collection: 1961.

The Homecoming: 1965.

Tea Party: 1965.

Old Times: 1968.

The Basement: 1968.

Landscape: 1969.

Silence: 1969.

No Man's Land: 1975.

Betrayal: 1978.

Other Places: Family Voices, Victoria Station, A Kind of Alaska: 1982.

One for the Road: 1984.

pipe See batten.

pipe batten See batten.

Pip Simmons Theatre Group A British theatre company, which was founded in London in 1968 to present experimental drama. Named after its founder, the group employs the techniques of collective creation and has performed works based on such diverse sources as Chaucer, Lewis Carroll, Dostoevsky, and Edgar Allan Poe. The company broke up in 1973 but was reformed by Simmons in 1974.

Pirandello, Luigi (1867–1936) Italian playwright, actor, novelist, critic, and short-story writer, who first established his reputation on the stage with Right You Are (If You Think So), a dramatization of one of his early short stories. His most important dramas, which deal chiefly with the absurdity of human existence and the relativity of truth, include the tragedy *Henry IV*, which examines the uneasy relationship between sanity and madnes, and *Six Characters in Search of an Author*, which is the first part of a trilogy that also includes *Each in His Own Way* and *Tonight We Improvise*.

Regarded as one of the best interpreters of the period between the two world wars, he attempted to portray the degeneration of middle-class values and broke away from the conventional dramatic techniques that had stunted Italian theatre in the early 20th century. After his wife's confinement in a mental home in 1919 he founded his own company; for many years the leading lady in his plays was **Marta Abba** (1900–88). He was awarded a Nobel Prize in 1934.

Principal works:

Così è (se vi pare): 1917; translated as *Right You Are (If You Think So)*.

Il giuoco delle parti: 1918; translated as *The Rules of the Game*.

Sei personaggi in cerca d'autore: 1922; translated as *Six Characters in Search of an Author*.

Enrico IV: 1922; translated as *Henry IV*.

L'uomo dal fiore in bocca: 1923; translated as *The Man With a Flower in his Mouth*.

Ciascuno a suo modo: 1924; translated as *Each in His Own Way*.

Lazzaro: 1929; translated as *Lazarus*.

Questa sera si recita a soggetto: 1929; translated as *Tonight We Improvise*.

Come tu mi vuoi: 1930; translated as *As You Desire Me*.

Piron, Alexis (1689–1773) French playwright and poet, who made his name at the fairground theatres with monologues, comic operas, and farces, notably *Arlequin Deucalion* (1722). His first play written for the official stage was produced at the Comédie-Française in 1728. Piron's comedy *La Métromanie* (1738) enjoyed considerable success; *Gustave Wasa* (1734) was the best of his tragedies. A licentious poem penned in his youth prevented his election to the Académie Française in 1753.

Piscator, Erwin Friedrich Max (1893–1966) German director, who played a key role in the development of *epic theatre, being one of the first directors to use filmstrips and cartoons in conjunction with live actors. A pupil of Reinhardt, he was a close associate of Brecht, whom he greatly influenced, and a member of the Communist party, believing in the theatre as a tool for propaganda and social reform. His early Expressionist productions, notably Brecht's *The Good Soldier Schweik* (1927) and Elm Welk's *Gervitter über Gottland* (1927) provoked his dismissal from the Volksbühne. He then opened his own theatre (1927–29) where he staged revolutionary versions of Brecht, Tolstoy, and Toller; subsequently he moved to New York where he influenced such notable figures as Arthur Miller and Tennessee Williams. In 1962 he returned to Berlin to the Freie Volksbühne where he directed documentary dramas. His influence was also profound upon the Living Theatre in the US and the Theatre Workshop in Britain.

Pisistratus (d. 528 BC) Ruler of Athens, who did much to reorganize the early theatre in Greece. He made extensive changes to the *Dionysia and founded contests for dithyrambs and tragedies.

Pistoia, Il *See* Caminelli, Antonio.

pit *See* auditorium.

Pit *See* Barbican Centre.

Pitlochry Festival Theatre A theatre at Pitlochry on Tayside in Scotland, established by John Stewart (founder of Glasgow's **Park Theatre**) in 1951 for summer seasons of plays in repertory. It was originally housed in a marquee but then transferred to a semi-permanent structure (1953–

80) and finally to the present theatre, specially built on a new riverside site. The annual festival itself, under **Kenneth Ireland**'s direction, includes the production of six plays as well as concerts and exhibitions.

Pitoëff, Georges (1887–1939) French actor, director, and playwright, born in Russia, who founded his own company in 1924. Having begun his career in Russia in association with such figures as Stanislavsky and Meyerhold, he joined Copeau's company in France in 1921 (after a period in Switzerland) and then presented his own productions at the Théâtre des Arts and then at the Mathurins. These included influential versions of plays by such foreign playwrights as Chekhov, Pirandello, Shakespeare, and Shaw as well as much contemporary French drama.

His wife, **Ludmilla Pitoëff** (1896–1951), took over the company upon her husband's death and led it on an acclaimed tour of the US and Canada. As an actress she was much acclaimed in plays by Ibsen and Shaw among others.

Their son, **Sacha Pitoëff** (1920-   ), began his career with Barsacq's Compagnie des Quatre Saisons and then worked in his parents' company. He founded his own troupe in 1949 and has produced numerous plays by foreign playwrights, including several from Japan, often appearing in them himself with great success.

Pitt, Charles Isaac Mungo (1768–1833) British playwright and manager, who was the illegitimate son of Charles Dibdin. He wrote several successful plays and pantomimes and became the manager of Sadler's Wells. He also wrote *History of the London Theatres* (1826).

Pitt, Thomas *See* Dibdin, Thomas John.

Pixérécourt, (René-Charles) Guilbert de (1773–1844) French playwright, who wrote the first melodramas for the Parisian

Boulevard theatres and introduced the genre to the English stage through translations of his early works. A prolific writer, he was known as 'the Corneille of the boulevards' and wrote over 100 plays. His melodramas are a successful blend of violence, spectacular effects, and sentimentality and culminate in the inevitable triumph of virtue over vice; they had a major influence on the Romantic drama that was to follow. He was also a director of the Théâtre de la Gaîté; when it burned down in 1835 he retired from the theatre.

Principal works:

Victor ou l'Enfant de la forêt: 1798.

Coelina ou l'Enfant du mystère: 1800; translated as *A Tale of Mystery*.

Marguerite d'Anjou: 1810.

Valentine ou la Séduction: 1821.

Le Château de Loch-Leven: 1822.

Latude ou Trente-cinq Ans de captivité: 1834.

Place, The *See* Royal Shakespeare Company.

Placide, Henry (1799–1870) US actor, who became one of the most admired performers in classic comedy in Colman the Younger's *The Heir at Law* (1823) at New York's Park Theatre and as Sir Peter Teazle in Sheridan's *The School for Scandal*. Several other members of his family were also well-known upon the US and Canadian stage.

Plain Dealer, The A comedy by Sir William *Wycherley. First performance: c. 1674. Manly, the misanthropic plain dealer, returns from war to find that his fiancée, to whom he entrusted money, has secretly married his best friend; he brings about her disgrace and finally marries the faithful Fidelia.

Planché, James Robinson (1796–1880) British playwright and theatrical designer of Huguenot descent, who wrote numerous burlesques, extravaganzas, melodramas, and pantomimes for the London stage. His most popular works included the melodrama *The Vampire; or, the Bride of the Isles* (1820), in which a *vamp trap was first used, and the burlesque *The Island of Jewels* (1849), which was produced at the Lyceum Theatre. As a designer he was responsible for the first authentically-costumed version of Shakespeare's *King John*, directed by Charles Kean in 1823. He was also active in arguing for copyright protection of theatrical works.

Planchon, Roger (1931-) French director, actor, and playwright, who has done much to transfer the focus of the French theatre from Paris to the provinces through his work in Villeurbanne, near Lyon. Much influenced by Artaud, Vilar, and – above all – Brecht, he opened a small theatre in Lyon itself in 1950 and moved to Villeurbanne in 1957, subsequently becoming head of the local *centre dramatique* (1959) and concentrating on attracting a popular audience. In general he rejected the French classical theatre in favour of such authors as Adamov and Brecht and built up a huge audience, although he also attracted much critical attention with his savage interpretations of such works as Marlowe's *Edward II*, Molière's *George Dandin*, and Shakespeare's *Henry IV, Parts I and II*.

In 1972 his company was renamed the *Théâtre National Populaire in recognition of his achievement; since then he has toured provincial France on a regular basis but has adopted a less prominent role with the group and has concentrated on writing his own dramas, which include *Bleus, blancs, rouges* (1967), *Le Cochon noir* (1974), and *Gilles de Rais* (1976).

platform stage *See* thrust stage.

Plato (427 BC–348 BC) Greek philosopher, who was the author of numerous major philosophical works in dialogue form and of critical studies on the nature of theatre in society. He burned his own early dramatic writings when he became convinced that drama and poetry could exercise a destructive influence upon the community through their appeal to the emotions rather than the intellect. Nonetheless, in such dialogues as the *Protagoras* and the *Phaedo* there is ample evidence of his mastery of dramatic technique and feeling for characterization as well as for poetic language. His views, which favoured strict censorship and the harnessing of drama for the good of the state, prompted important responses from Aristotle.

Plato Comicus (c. 5th–4th century BC) Greek playwright, a contemporary of Aristophanes. Few fragments of his plays, with which he won several contests, survive.

platt The plot or synopsis of a play as used by the stage crew in the Elizabethan theatre. Surviving examples include details of exits and entrances and lists of props.

Plautus, Titus Maccus (c. 254 BC–184 BC) Roman playwright, author of numerous major comedies that have had a profound influence upon subsequent comic drama. The most popular playwright of his day, his life remains obscure, little being known beyond the tradition that he spent his youth in the theatre and, after losing the fortune earned from his writing in business, was obliged to work in a grain mill. Most of his 150 plays, of which about 21 probably by him survive, were loosely based upon works of Greek Old Comedy and are characterized by complex plots, lively language, and much ribald and often outrageous farce. Among the more influential of his plays were the *Amphitruo*, which Dryden imitated in his *Amphitryon*, the *Aulularia*, upon which Molière based his *L'Avare*, and the *Menaechmi*, which provided the inspiration for Shakespeare's *The Comedy of Errors*; in the 20th century several of the plays were successfully combined in the musical *A Fun-*

ny Thing Happened on the Way to the Forum.
Principal works (some dates unknown):
Amphitruo.
Aulularia.
Bacchides.
Captivi.
Cistellaria: 204 BC.
Menaechmi.
*Miles Gloriosus: 204 BC.
Mostellaria.
Pseudolus: 191 BC.
Rudens.
Stichus: 200 BC.
Truculentus.

playbill A theatre programme, giving details of a particular performance, or a **poster** advertising the show in production or forthcoming attractions. The first such publications to appear in Britain were produced at Drury Lane and Covent Garden in 1737 and have since developed as a distinct art form in their own right.

Playboy of the Western World, The An ironic comedy by J M *Synge, which is generally regarded as his masterpiece. First performance: Abbey Theatre, Dublin, 1907. A young man, Christy Mahon, arrives fearfully in a Mayo village, claiming that he has killed his domineering father. Christy is welcomed as a hero by the local women until his supposedly dead father turns up in pursuit of him.

Players Club A gentleman's club founded in New York in 1888 by Edwin Booth, who was also its first president. Like his successors, Joseph Jefferson and John Drew, he died in office. Subsequent presidents have been Walter Hampden (1928–55), Howard Lindsay (1955–65), Dennis King (1965–70), Alfred Drake (1970–78), and currently Roland Winters (1978-). The club has a fine library and an extensive theatrical collection.

Players' Theatre A theatre club situated (until 1987) under the railway arches in Villiers Street, Charing Cross, London. It was opened as **Playroom Six** in New Compton Street in 1927 and was reopened (as the Players' Theatre) in 1936 in King Street, Covent Garden, in what was once Evans's song-and-supper rooms. Here began the nightly Victorian burlesque and music hall performances called *Late Joys* for which the theatre, having moved to Villiers Street in 1946, is now famous. In 1953 the theatre staged the premiere of Sandy Wilson's musical comedy *The Boy Friend*. During redevelopment of the area in 1987 the club went into temporary exile at the Duchess Theatre, Catherine Street.

Playfair, Sir Nigel (1874–1934) British actor-manager and director, who was noted for his management of the Lyric Theatre, Hammersmith, from 1918 to 1934. His greatest successes there included Drinkwater's *Abraham Lincoln* (1919), Gay's *The Beggar's Opera* (1920), Congreve's *The Way of the World* (1924), and Wilde's *The Importance of Being Earnest* (1930). As an actor he appeared in the first productions of plays by Shaw and in many productions at the Lyric. He also collaborated in the translation and production at the Regent Theatre of *The Insect Play* (1923) by the Čapek brothers.

Playhouse A theatre on the Embankment near Charing Cross, London, which was opened by Cyril Maude in 1907. It replaced the **Royal Avenue Theatre** (built 1882), which had housed the premiere of Shaw's *Arms and the Man* (1894). In 1905 six people died when the neighbouring Charing Cross station partially collapsed on it; after the theatre was rebuilt Maude and his wife, Winifred Emery, appeared in many distinguished productions until 1915. Frank Curzon took over in 1917, with Gladys Cooper as his leading lady; she later ran the theatre on her own, presenting several of Somerset

Maugham's plays, including *The Letter* (1927). Nancy Price ran her People's National Theatre company at the Playhouse prior to World War II but, in 1951, it became a BBC studio and was not reclaimed as a theatre until 1987, when it reopened with a new musical, *Girl Friends*.

Playhouse Theatre A theatre on West 48th Street, between Broadway and Sixth Avenue, New York, which opened in 1911. Both classical and modern plays were housed there, of which the most important included Broadhurst's *Bought and Paid For* (1911), the US premiere of Shaw's *Major Barbara* (1915), Robert Sherwood's *The Road to Rome* (1927), Rice's *Street Scene* (1929), Tennessee Williams's *The Glass Menagerie* (1945), and Gibson's *The Miracle Worker* (1959). The theatre was demolished in 1968.

Playroom Six *See* Players' Theatre.

Playwrights' Theatre *See* Provincetown Players.

Plenty A play by David *Hare. First performance: National Theatre Company, Lyttleton Theatre, 1978. The play explores the predicament of Susan Traherne who, following wartime active service, experiences profound disillusionment with prosperous but class-ridden and complacent British society; it was filmed in 1985.

Plinge, Walter A fictitious name used on British playbills to disguise the fact that the same actor is playing two roles. The name dates from about 1900 and was possibly that of the landlord of a public house near the Lyceum Theatre; the US equivalent is **George Spelvin**, which is also sometimes used for animals.

Plough and the Stars, The A play by Sean *O'Casey. First performance: Abbey Theatre, Dublin, 1926. Set during the 1916 Easter Rising, the play details the effects of the violence upon the inhabitants of Dublin's slums; its unromantic depiction of the struggle provoked riots at its first performance.

Plough Monday The first Monday after Twelfth Night, when in certain English villages an early example of *folk theatre is performed. Linked to ancient rural ritual, it involves the blessing of a plough and a collection; it may have inspired the development of the Wooing Ceremony (*see* mummers' play). The ritual is now usually carried out on the first Saturday after Plough Monday.

Plowright, Joan (Anne) (1929-) British actress, who made her first appearance at the Grand Theatre, Croydon, in 1951. Subsequently she was acclaimed for her work at the Royal Court Theatre with the English Stage Company, especially as Margery Pinchwife in the 1956 revival of Wycherley's *The Country Wife*. Contemporary roles have included Jean Rice in Osborne's *The Entertainer* (1957) opposite *Olivier, whom she married in 1961. She was the original Beatie in Wesker's *Roots* (1959) and has played many leading roles with the National Theatre Company. Other successes have included de Filippo's *Saturday, Sunday, Monday* (1973) and *Filumena* (1977), the Chichester Festival production of *The Way of the World* at the Haymarket (1984), and Lorca's *Yerma* (1986). In 1988 she made her debut as a director with the play *Married Love* for Kenneth Branagh's Renaissance Company.

Pluchek, Valentin Nikolayevich (1909-) Soviet director, who began his career under Meyerhold in the 1920s. He worked with Arbuzov during World War II, taking productions to the war front, and subsequently became artistic director of the Moscow Theatre of Satire (1957); his greatest successes have included plays by Beaumarchais, Gogol, and Shaw.

Plummer, (Arthur) Christopher (Orme) (1929-) Canadian actor, who has appeared in a wide variety of stage roles, ranging from comedy to Shakespearean tragedy, as well as in films. He began his career in the theatre in Ottawa and established his reputation in such Shakespearean roles as Henry V (1956), Hamlet (1957), Richard III (1961), Antony (1967), and Iago (1981); other successes have included Fry's *The Dark is Light Enough* (1955) and Shaffer's *The Royal Hunt of the Sun* (1965) as well as plays by Anouilh, Chekhov, and Neil Simon.

Plymouth Theatre A theatre on West 45th Street, New York, which opened in 1917. Among the productions seen there were the premiere in English of Ibsen's *The Wild Duck* (1918), Maxwell Anderson's *What Price Glory?* (1924), Sherwood's *Abe Lincoln in Illinois* (1938), Shaw's *Don Juan in Hell* (1952), Neil Simon's *Plaza Suite* (1969), Peter Shaffer's *Equus* (1974), and the Royal Shakespeare Company's *Nicholas Nickleby* (1981).

Pocock, Isaac (1782-1835) British playwright, who became popular for his many farces and melodramas. He followed *Yes or No*, staged at the Haymarket in 1808, with *Hit or Miss* (1810), in which the elder Mathews had great success. His most famous piece was the melodrama *The Miller and His Men* (1813); often revived, it became a toy theatre favourite. His dramatizations of Scott's novels included *Rob Roy* (1818).

Poel, William (William Pole; 1852-1934) British actor and director, who attracted much attention for his interest in recreating the theatre of Shakespeare's day. After training as an actor under Charles James Mathews, he founded the influential *Elizabethan Stage Society in 1894 and over the next 11 years presented works by most of the leading Elizabethan and Jacobean writers, ranging from *Twelfth Night* (1895) to the long-forgotten morality play *Everyman*, all of which were distinguished by their unfashionably austere settings and use of a stage approximating to that of the typical Elizabethan theatre.

Poelzig, Hans (1869-1936) German architect, who designed the Grosses Schauspielhaus in Berlin for Max Reinhardt. Seating 3000 on three sides of a flexible stage, it profoundly influenced subsequent theatre design and hastened the decline of the proscenium arch.

poetic drama Any play in which the dialogue is written in a highly poetic style. Although both early comedies and tragedies were customarily written in verse – Shakespeare being one of the masters of its use – the term poetic drama is more commonly applied to such works written since the Restoration, at which time it became usual for comedies to be written in prose and tragedies in verse. Subsequently the tradition veered towards closet drama with many writers of such works (including Byron, Keats, and Shelley) being better known as poets than as skilled dramatists; it was not until the early 20th century that attempts were made to restore a degree of practical theatricality.

Ibsen and writers of the Irish literary revival, influenced by the Japanese *Nō* drama, began to create such works specifically designed for stage production, although it was not until the adoption of free verse by T S Eliot and others in the 1930s that the genre became once more a significant feature of contemporary theatrical tradition. Auden and Maxwell Anderson were among those who fostered poetic drama after World War II, providing such works for the Mercury Theatre and other venues specializing in the genre; more recent writers who have contributed dramas with a high poetical content with some success have included Dylan Thomas, Christopher Fry, Beckett, and Ionesco. In the US impetus was also added by performances given under the aegis of the Federal Theatre Project and the Poets' Theatre of Cambridge, Massachusetts.

Pogodin, Nikolai Fedorovich (Nikolai Fedorovich Stukalov; 1902–62) Soviet playwright, who began to write for the stage during the 1930s. His early plays, which deal chiefly with the working man's struggle to overcome economic and personal difficulty, include *Ten'* (Tempo; 1930) and *Poem About an Axe* (1931). Other major works include *Aristokraty* (Aristocrats; 1934) and an historical trilogy on the life of Lenin – *Chelovek s ruzhiem* (The Man with the Gun; 1937), *Kremlevskiye kuranty* (Kremlin Chimes; 1942), and *Tret'aya paticheskaya* (The Third Pathétique; 1958).

Poisson, Paul (1658–1735) French actor, son of *Belleroche, who inherited several of his father's comic roles as well as his stutter. He joined the Comédie-Française in 1686 and was married to the actress **Marie-Angélique de L'École** (1657–1756), who was the stepdaughter of Du Croisy and the author of various pieces on Molière.

Their son **Philippe Poisson** (1682–1743) had a short career as an actor but later wrote several popular plays, as did their daughter **Madeleine-Angélique Poisson** (1684–1770), author of the tragedy *Habis* (1714). Their other son **François Arnould Poisson** (1696–1753) became an actor with the Comédie-Française, also inheriting his grandfather's stutter and excelling in comic roles.

Poliakoff, Stephen (1952–) British playwright, who has emerged as a leading writer for the contemporary stage since his first play – *Granny* – in 1969. Among his most successful works have been *Hitting Town* (1975), *City Sugar* (1975), *Strawberry Fields* (1977), about a neo-Nazi sect, *Breaking the Silence* (1984), and *Coming in to Land* (1987), which starred Maggie Smith as a Polish emigrant.

Polichinelle A character of the French Comédie-Italienne, derived from the character of *Pulcinella in the Italian *commedia dell'arte*. A hunchback similar to Pulcinella in appearance, he was cunning and witty in the French version and anticipated the subsequent development of the English character Punch (*see* Punch and Judy).

Polish State Jewish Theatre See Kamińska, Ida.

Politis, Fotos (1890–1934) Greek director, who did much to make the Greek National Theatre, founded in 1930, an important centre of European drama. He emphasized revivals of classical plays but also encouraged the application to them of modern experimental staging techniques.

Poliziano, Angelo (Angelo Ambrogini; 1454–94) Italian scholar, also known as Politian, who was the author of the first major play written in the vernacular. His *Favola d'Orfeo* (1472) shared features of the *sacra rappresentazione* but was based upon mythological rather than biblical material and anticipated the development of the pastoral.

Polotsky, Simeon (Samuil Yemelyanovich Petrovsky-Sitnianovich; 1629–80) Russian monk, poet, and playwright, whose plays initiated school drama in Russia. His two plays, the *Comedy-Parable of the Prodigal Son* and *Nebuchadnezzar the King, the Golden Calf, and the Three Youths Unconsumed in the Fiery Furnace*, were given elaborate productions at the royal court, where Polotsky was tutor to the tsar's children.

Polus (4th century BC) Greek tragic actor, traditionally believed to have taught Demosthenes elocution. Acting in *Electra* by Sophocles, he reputedly carried his own son's ashes in an urn in a particular scene in order to make his grief on stage seem more convincing.

Ponsard, François (1814–67) French playwright, who led a reaction against Romantic drama and advocated a return to the classical tradition. His first play, the tragedy *Lucrèce* (1843), enjoyed considerable success; it was followed by a number of other dramas and comedies, notably *Charlotte Corday* (1850), *Horace et Lydie* (1850), *L'Honneur et l'argent* (1853), and *Le Lion amoureux* (1866).

Ponti, Diana da (fl. 1582–1605) Italian actress of the *commedia dell'arte*, who appeared under the stagename **Lavinia**. She acted with the Confidenti and the Gelosi before forming her own troupe – possibly the Desiosi – and is known to have appeared in France in 1601.

Pope, Jane (1742–1818) British actress, who began her career at Drury Lane as Corinna in Vanbrugh's *The Confederacy* in 1759. She gradually took over the roles associated with Kitty Clive and, in 1765, played Beatrice to Garrick's Benedick in *Much Ado About Nothing*. She also appeared in the first production of *The Clandestine Marriage* (1766) and created Mrs Candour and Tilburina in Sheridan's plays.

Pope, Thomas (d. 1604) English actor, an original shareholder in the Globe and Curtain theatres, who is in the First Folio list of actors in Shakespeare's plays. He joined the Chamberlain's Men on their formation and probably inherited Kempe's roles as a clown.

Popov, Alexei Dmitrevich (1892–1961) Soviet director, who won acclaim for his work at the Red Army Theatre after having established his reputation at the Moscow Art Theatre (1912–18) and the Vakhtangov Theatre (from 1973). His most influential productions included Pogodin's *Poem About an Axe* (1931) at the Theatre of the Revolution (later the Mayakovsky Theatre), *Romeo and Juliet* (1936), *The Taming of the Shrew* (1938) at Moscow's Red Army Theatre, and *A Midsummer Night's Dream* (1940); later successes were Gogol's *The Government Inspector* (1951) and Pogodin's *Kremlin Chimes* (1956). He also helped to found the International Federation for Theatre Research in 1955.

His son, **Andrei Alexeyevich Popov** (1918–), became artistic director of the Red Army Theatre in 1963 after his father's death, continuing to present a programme of plays based on military themes. As an actor, he has been praised in plays by Gogol, Shakespeare, and Tolstoy among others.

Porgy and Bess An opera, based on a play by Du Bose *Heyward and Ira *Gershwin. First performance: New York, 1935. Featuring the music of George Gershwin, the action takes place on Catfish Row and concerns a Black slum girl who falls in love with a crippled beggar.

Porta, Giambattista Della *See* Della Porta, Giambattista.

portal opening *See* false proscenium.

Porter, Cole (1892–1964) US composer, who was the author of about 20 popular stage shows, for which he also usually wrote the lyrics. Beginning with *See America First* (1916), his best-known productions included *Wake Up and Dream* (1929), *The Gay Divorce* (1932), *Anything Goes* (1934), *Kiss Me Kate* (1948) – loosely based on *The Taming of the Shrew*, and *Silk Stockings* (1955). Performers who appeared in his shows numbered amongst them Fred Astaire, Mary Martin, Ethel Merman, and Alfred Drake.

Porter, Eric (Richard) (1928–) British actor, who made his professional debut at Stratford-upon-Avon in 1945. Subsequently he gained experience with Wolfit's company and at the Birmingham Repertory Theatre before triumphing as Bolingbroke in *Richard*

II and Fainall in Congreve's *The Way of the World* in Gielgud's 1952–53 season at the Lyric, Hammersmith. He subsequently appeared in numerous important parts at the Old Vic and Stratford-upon-Avon and elsewhere, being acclaimed in such roles as Shylock (1965), King Lear (1968), and Malvolio (1976). He also established a wide reputation as a television actor.

Porter, Hal (1911–) Australian novelist, whose most notable work for the theatre has been *Eden House* (1961). Other dramatic works include *The Tower* and *Toda-San*, which reached the Royal Court Theatre in 1965.

Porter, Mary Ann (d. 1765) British actress, who began acting as a child. She was taught by Betterton and made her first recorded appearance in 1699 at Lincoln's Inn Fields. Over the next 40 years she became a highly respected tragic actress, excelling as Belvidera in *Venice Preserv'd*.

Porter's Hall A theatre built near Blackfriars, London, by Philip Rosseter and Philip Kingman in 1615 to house the combined Queen's Revels and Lady Elizabeth's companies. However, their licence was revoked before the theatre (also called the **Puddle Wharf Theatre**) was complete, and although some early performances may have taken place, there is no evidence of use after 1618.

Porte-Saint-Martin, Théâtre de la A theatre in Paris, which was erected in 1782 as a new home for the company from the Paris Opéra. After a period of disuse (1794–1802), the theatre established itself as a venue for performances of the plays of Pixérécourt and prospered from appearances by Frédérick and Mlle Dorval in *Trente Ans, ou la vie d'un joueur* (1827) and other plays. During the 1830s the theatre consolidated its reputation with plays by Dumas *père* and Hugo before controversy surrounding Balzac's *Vautrin* (1840) caused the theatre's closure. Subsequently it was used for more sentimental pieces and occasional revivals, being destroyed during a riot in 1870 and then rebuilt on a smaller scale. Sarah Bernhardt ran the theatre during the 1880s with some success, after which Rostand's *Cyrano de Bergerac* restored it to its former glory. From 1936 to 1978 it concentrated on musical comedy, eventually being taken over by Marcel Marceau.

Portman, Eric (1903–69) British actor, who first came to London in 1923 playing Shakespearean roles. He joined the Old Vic company in 1927 and was acclaimed as Undershaft in Shaw's *Major Barbara* at Wyndham's (1929). Subsequently he played important parts in many plays and films, to all of which he brought remorseless energy and integrity, most notably in works by Terence Rattigan, J B Priestley, Graham Greene, O'Neill, and Robert Bolt.

Portman Theatre *See* West London Theatre.

Porto-Riche, Georges de (1849–1930) French playwright, whose psychological studies of the 'eternal triangle' of wife, husband, and lover established a genre known as the *théâtre d'amour*. *La Chance de Françoise*, produced at the Théâtre Libre in 1889, was followed by *Amoureuse* (1891), *Le Passé* (1897), and *Le Vieil Homme* (1911), which are generally considered to be his finest plays.

Posset, Jean *See* Sackville, Thomas.

poster *See* playbill.

Potier des Cailletières, Charles Gabriel (1774–1838) French actor, highly regarded in his own day as a performer of comic roles. He achieved fame after appearing at the Théâtre des Variétés in Paris in 1809, later enjoying further success at the Palais-Royal.

Pouget, Madeleine de See Beauchâteau.

Poulsen, Emil (1842–1911) Danish actor, who – with his brother **Olaf Poulsen** (1849–1923) – won acclaim in the plays of Shakespeare and in many native Scandinavian dramas. They both excelled in plays by Holberg and Ibsen, while Olaf was particularly admired as Falstaff and other comic characters in Shakespeare.

Emil's sons, **Adam Poulsen** (1879–1969) and **Johannes Poulsen** (1881–1938), were connected respectively with the Dagmarteatret and the Kongelige Teater.

Powell, George (1668–1714) British actor, who originated numerous leading roles at Drury Lane, including Bellamour in Congreve's *The Old Bachelor* and Lothario in Rowe's *The Fair Penitent*. Noted for his volatile temper, he left Drury Lane on the advent of Wilks. The most successful of his own plays was *The Imposture Defeated; or a Trick to Cheat the Devil* (1697).

Powell, Martin (fl. 1710–13) British puppeteer. He became famous for his puppet shows in Bath and in London's Covent Garden Piazza, satirizing Italian opera.

Power, Tyrone (David Powell; 1797–1841) Irish actor, who became successful in such 'Irish' parts as Sir Lucius O'Trigger in Sheridan's *The Rivals*. He also appeared in comedies and farces of his own, including *St Patrick's Eve* (1832) and *O'Flannigan and the Fairies* (1836). He left the Haymarket for a tour of the US in 1840 but was drowned on the way home.

He was the great-grandfather of the US actor **Tyrone Power** (1914–58), who made his first stage appearance, as a page in *Hamlet*, in 1931. Primarily famous as a film star, his successes on the US stage included such Shakespearean roles as Benvolio in *Romeo and Juliet* (1935), de Poulengy in Shaw's *Saint Joan* (1936), and Gettner in Fry's *The Dark Is Light Enough* (1955).

Pradon, Jacques (1644–98) French playwright, sometimes incorrectly referred to as Nicolas Pradon. Having enjoyed some success with his first play, *Pyrame et Thisbé* (1674), he wrote *Phèdre et Hippolyte* (1677), which was timed to coincide with Racine's *Phèdre*, a version of the same legend. The latter opened just two days before Pradon's inferior play and was undeservedly eclipsed by it.

praetexta A form of Roman *fabula*, comprising serious dramas based on mythological or contemporary themes. The genre was invented by Naevius, while noted writers included Accius, Ennius, Pacuvius, and possibly Seneca. Few examples survive.

Praga, Marco (1862–1929) Italian playwright and novelist, who was a leading writer in the *verismo* tradition. His plays satirize such targets as bourgeois complacency and were much influenced by contemporary French drama; the most successful of his works included *Mater dolorosa* (1888), based on a novel by Girolamo Rovetta, *La moglie ideale* (The Ideal Wife; 1890), in which Duse was highly acclaimed, and *La Porta chiusa* (The Closed Door; 1913). He was also a director of the Stabile Milanese company for a time and promoted the early career of Pirandello.

Pratinus of Phlius (c. 540–470 BC) Greek playwright, author of the earliest satyr-plays. He is believed to have written more than 30 such pieces, as well as 18 tragedies.

Pray, Malvina See Florence, William Jermyn.

Prehauser, Gottfried (1699–1769) Austrian actor, who inherited the part of *Hanswurst from Stranitsky in 1725. An experienced performer with travelling companies, Prehauser further developed the role, making him a more recognizably Viennese creation; after Prehauser's death Hanswurst fell from favour on the Viennese stage.

prelude A brief theatrical entertainment occasionally presented in British theatres in the late 18th century. Preludes usually consisted of a satirical sketch discussing current theatrical issues and were presented at the opening of a new theatre or at the start of a theatre season.

Present Laughter A comedy by Noël *Coward. First performance: London, 1943. The plot revolves around an actor (first played by Coward himself), who maintains an unconventional household with the help of his wife from whom he is separated but who remains more important to him than his casual flirtations.

Prestes, Antônio (d. 1587) Portuguese playwright, regarded in his own time as being of the same stature as Gil Vicente. His seven surviving plays comprise six comedies and a morality play, the *Auto de Ave Maria*.

Preston, Thomas (fl. 1570) English playwright, about whom little is known beyond the fact that he wrote *Cambyses King of Persia* (c. 1570). A popular early tragi-comedy written in a bombastic style, the play marks the transition of the morality play into the Elizabethan historical drama.

Préville (Pierre-Louis Dubus; 1721–99) French actor, who excelled as a player in comedy after joining the Comédie-Française in 1753. He inherited many of the roles of François Poisson and was particularly popular in the plays of Marivaux, Boursault, and as Beaumarchais's Figaro.

Price, Maire *See* Nic Shiubhlaigh, Maire.

Price, (Lilian) Nancy (Bache) (1880–1970) British actress and manager, who joined Benson's company in 1899 and first won attention as Calypso in Stephen Phil-

lips's *Ulysses* in 1902. Admired in a variety of roles, she also founded the **People's National Theatre** company (1930) and went on to produce numerous significant plays, among them the Čapeks's *The Insect Play* and Hsiung's *Lady Precious Stream* at the Little Theatre in London. She retired in 1952.

Priestley, J(ohn) B(oynton) (1894–1984) British novelist, journalist, and playwright, who wrote many successful plays in a wide variety of styles. The West Riding farce *When We Are Married* (1938), in which he originally played a leading role, and An *Inspector Calls* (1947) are possibly his best-known dramas. He also wrote a series of experimental Expressionist plays reflecting his preoccupation with the nature of Time: *I Have Been Here Before* (1937), *Time and the Conways* (1937), and *Johnson over Jordan* (1939). *Laburnum Grove* (1933) and *Eden End* were among his best comedies. Among his many adaptations was a dramatization of his first commercially successful novel, *The Good Companions* (1929) on which he collaborated with Edward Knoblock.

Principal works:

Dangerous Corner: 1932.

Laburnum Grove: 1933.

I Have Been Here Before: 1937.

Time and the Conways: 1937.

When We Are Married: 1938.

Johnson over Jordan: 1939.

An Inspector Calls: 1946.

*The *Linden Tree*: 1947.

Prime Minister of Mirth *See* Robey, George.

Prince, Hal (Harold Prince: 1928–) US director, whose first success was *The Pajama Game* (1954). Since then he has directed or produced *Damn Yankees* (1955), *West Side Story* (1957), *A Funny Thing Happened on the Way to the Forum* (1963), *Fiddler on the Roof* (1964), *Cabaret* (1966), and Stephen Sondheim's *Company* (1970), *Follies* (1971), *A Little Night Music* (1973), *Pacific Overtures* (1976), and *Sweeney Todd* (1979). Other recent successes include *The Phantom of the Opera* (1987).

Prince Charles's Men An English theatre company founded in 1616 by Alleyn. Usually referred to as the Prince's Men, the company enjoyed the patronage of the future Charles I and performed at the Porter's Hall, the Hope, the Cockpit, the Curtain, and the Red Bull theatres between 1616 and 1625. On Charles's coronation the company was broken up, several of the actors joining the King's Men; in 1631 the name was revived for a new company that came under the patronage of the future Charles II and performed regularly at the Salisbury Court and Fortune theatres until 1642.

Prince Edward Theatre A theatre in Old Compton Street, housing the third largest stage in London. It opened in 1930 but was reconstructed in 1936 as a cabaret-restaurant and renamed the **London Casino**. Closed in 1940, it later became the Queensbury All-Services Club. Post-war productions included Ivor Novello's *The Dancing Years* (1947) and an annual pantomime. In 1954 the theatre became a cinema, but in 1974 there followed a period of stage shows alternating with films. In 1978, on the opening of *Evita*, the theatre reverted to its original name. Another Tim Rice musical, *Chess*, opened in 1986.

Prince Henry's Men *See* Admiral's Men.

Prince of Wales' Theatre A theatre in Coventry Street, London, which has a long record of successful revues and musicals. The present building is the second theatre on the site. The first was financed by the profits made on a burlesque, *The Colonel*, at an earlier Prince of Wales' Theatre in Tottenham Street (later the Scala Theatre). Opening in 1884 as the **Prince's Theatre**, it enjoyed early success with Charles Hawtrey's farce *The Private Secretary*, with Beerbohm Tree in the title role. Lillie Langtry made several appearances at the theatre in 1885–86 and in 1886 the theatre's name was changed to the Prince of Wales' Theatre. Mrs Patrick Campbell, Sir Johnston Forbes-Robertson, and Marie Tempest all played here in ensuing years. From 1918 to 1926 André Charlot, then the lessee, presented a series of revues. For a short time in 1930 Edith Evans took over as manager. Later, under the control of Charles Clore, and then of Alfred Esdaile, the policy became one of revues only.

In 1937 the theatre was rebuilt and reopened with *Les Folies de Paris et Londres*. There was a short-lived return to mixed entertainment in the 1940s, which included Sid Field's success in *Harvey* (1949), but thereafter revue, musical comedy, and the occasional farce held sway. *The Danny La Rue Show* was presented from 1973 while the US musical *South Pacific* was revived there in 1988.

Princess's Theatre A theatre in Oxford Street, London, opened as a concert hall in 1840, remodelled as an opera house in 1842, and then used for drama. Macready, Fanny Kemble, the Cushman Sisters, and other leading players appeared there, but it was under the management of Charles Kean with his magnificent Shakespearean productions from 1851 to 1859 that the theatre, now called the **Royal Princess's Theatre**, achieved its highest distinction. In the 1860s, Augustus Harris presented Irving there while under George Vining's management the melodramas of Dion Boucicault, especially *The Streets of London* (1864), were highly successful, as was Charles Warner who caused a sensation as Coupeau in Charles Reade's *Drink* in 1879. In 1880 the old theatre was rebuilt, opening with Edwin Booth as Hamlet. From 1881 to 1886 Wilson Barrett attracted large audiences with such melodramas as *The Silver King*, but the theatre then declined. The theatre finally closed in 1902, becoming a warehouse and being demolished in 1931. *See also* Glasgow Citizens' Theatre.

Princess Theatre A theatre in Melbourne, Australia, opened in 1886 on the site of an older theatre. It was much admired for its decor and has since been used as a venue for a wide variety of entertainments, including opera.

The **Princess Theatre** on West 49th Street in New York opened in 1913 with a series of one-act plays. The Provincetown Players appeared there in 1920–21, while important premieres included Maxwell Anderson's *The White Desert* (1922). In 1928 the theatre was renamed the **Lucille La Verne Theatre**; a year later it became the **Assembly Theatre** and then a cinema. In 1937 it reopened briefly as a home for live drama as the **Labor Stage**. From 1944 to 1947 it was known as the **Theatre Workshop** but then reverted to use as a cinema, being demolished in 1955.

Prince's Theatre *See* Prince of Wales' Theatre; Shaftesbury Theatre.

principal boy The traditional hero of the English pantomime, conventionally played by a female. The playing of the principal boy – a role which was in part derived from that of Harlequin – by a woman may have its roots in ancient ritual and subsequently in the popularity of actresses playing *breeches parts. Famous principal boys include Nellie Stewart, Fay Compton, and more recently such popular singers as Lulu.

Printemps, Yvonne (1895–1977) French actress and singer, who became a leading star of musical theatre. She began her career in revue in Paris, performing at the Folies-Bergère and the Palais-Royal, and then married (1919) Sacha Guitry, in whose plays she frequently appeared. Later she married the actor Pierre Fresnay, acting with him in

such successes as *O Mistress Mine* (1936) by Ben Travers. Other notable performances included Guitry's *Mozart* (1926) and Coward's *Conversation Piece* (1934); from 1937 she also ran the Théâtre de la Michodière.

Pritchard, Hannah (Hannah Vaughan; 1711–68) British actress, who began her career as a strolling player. She first appeared at Drury Lane in 1732, after which she built a reputation as an excellent comic actress, being particularly admired as Rosalind in *As You Like It* and Beatrice in *Much Ado About Nothing*. In 1748 Garrick engaged her at Drury Lane once more and installed her husband as treasurer. Over the next 21 years she added leading tragic roles to her celebrated comedy parts, including a notable Lady Macbeth, which she performed many times between 1748 and her retirement in 1768, by which time she had put on a great deal of weight.

Private Lives A comedy by Noël *Coward. First performance: London, 1930. The play follows the fortunes of a divorced couple and their new partners who find they are all honeymooning in the same hotel; the eccentric original pair finally reunite, rejecting their conventional spouses. The original cast was led by Coward himself, with Gertrude Lawrence as Amanda.

producer The person who, until the term director was officially adopted in 1956, was responsible in Britain for the overall control of a production, including the direction of the cast and the interpretation of the play. In the US the producer organizes the financial and managerial aspects of a production and undertakes other tasks performed by the **manager** in Britain.

Professor Taranne (*Le Professeur Taranne*) A play by Arthur *Adamov. First performance: Lyons, 1953 (produced by Roger Planchon). The plot, based on a dream, deals with the problems of a university professor accused of obscene behaviour and reflected the writings of Kafka.

profile board A small section of wood and canvas attached to a flat in order to alter its shape for scenic purposes.

profile spot A spotlight capable of throwing a bright, clean-edged beam onto the stage; it is generally known in the US by the tradename **Leko**.

projector A projection unit, by means of which large glass slides can be used to create atmospheric lighting on stage. Special effects projectors, known in the US as **sciopticons**, are capable of producing complex mobile patterns of light suggesting such phenomena as stormy skies, snow, and fire.

projector unit *See* pageant lantern.

Proletkult Theatre *See* Trades Unions Theatre.

prologue A brief scene or speech given at the beginning of a performance, first used by Euripides. It usually announced the theme of the main drama and, during the Restoration, contained comments upon contemporary affairs. In Elizabethan times it was known as the Chorus.

promenade A development of theatre-in-the-round, in which the audience, which usually remains standing, is invited to accompany the actors from one area of an auditorium to another in order to follow the action.

Prometheus Bound A tragedy by *Aeschylus. First performance: c. 460 BC. The first part of a tetralogy, it condemns tyrannical rule and bears the influence of the ideas of Sophocles. It revolves around the central character of Prometheus, who has been bound to rocks for stealing fire from heaven but remains defiant.

prompt corner An area immediately behind the proscenium arch in which the prompter sits. In Britain the prompt corner is traditionally downstage left, whilst in the US it is usually downstage right. On the Continent and in most opera houses the prompter occupies a prompt box situated at the front of the stage and concealed by a hood.

prompter The person employed to provide an actor who forgets his words with the correct line; in his own copy of the play he may also keep a record of all the moves settled on during rehearsals. In Elizabethan times these duties were fulfilled by the *book-holder.

prompt side (PS) A term used in the British theatre to denote the side of the stage (stage left) where the prompter usually sits. The other side of the stage is conventionally referred to as the **opposite prompt side** (OP).

prop Any inanimate item that appears on the stage, with the exception of the scenery, furniture, costumes, and various pieces of technical equipment. More formally referred to as stage properties, these articles are ultimately the responsibility of the stage manager. Props that are carried onto the stage by the actors themselves are known as **hand-props**.

proscenium The long, narrow acting area of the ancient Greek theatre. Originally referred to as the *proskenion*, it denoted the space between the orchestra and the *skene. *See also* proscenium arch.

proscenium arch The wall and opening that divides the stage from the auditorium in most theatres built between the 17th and 20th centuries. Deriving its name from the *proscenium* of the classical stage, the earliest proscenium arch was that erected at the Teatro Farnese in 1618; by the 19th century most theatres had dispensed with the forestage altogether and the proscenium arch developed as an elaborate 'frame' for the scene presented on the stage. Many modern theatre designs have, however, dropped the proscenium arch in favour of a more open stage plan.

proscenium border A border situated immediately upstage of the proscenium arch, referred to in the US (together with other short masking cloths) as a **teaser**.

proscenium doors One (or more) pairs of doors set into the proscenium arch, providing actors with access to and from the apron in the Restoration theatre. By the 19th century they were only used for actors to take their bow at the end of a performance, becoming known as **call doors**.

Prospect Theatre Company A British theatre company, founded in Oxford in 1961. Originally called Prospect Productions, the company moved under **Toby Robertson** (Sholto David Maurice Robertson; 1928-) in 1964 to the Arts Theatre, Cambridge from where it toured successfully in classic plays until 1969. In 1977 it transferred to the Old Vic Theatre in London, being renamed the Old Vic company in 1979. Its most acclaimed productions included Shakespeare's *Richard II* (1968), Marlowe's *Edward II* (1969), Turgenev's *A Month in the Country* (1975), *Antony and Cleopatra* (1977), Shaw's *Saint Joan* (1977), and *Hamlet* (1978); actors with the company included Ian McKellen, Dorothy Tutin, Alec McCowen, Eileen Atkins, Derek Jacobi, Peter O'Toole (who was much criticized for his Macbeth in 1980), and **Timothy West** (1934-), who was artistic director when the company was disbanded in 1980 on the loss of its state grant.

protagonist The principal actor in ancient Greek drama, who began as the leader of the chorus during the performance of dithyrambs and gradually became one of the two or three central characters of the plays of Euripides, Sophocles, and other early writers (the others being the **deuteragonist** and the **tritagonist**). The earliest use of a protagonist in drama was probably as a result of an innovation by Thespis.

Provincetown Players An organization of US actors and playwrights founded in 1916. The group began at the **Wharf Theatre** in Providence, Rhode Island and later moved to the **Playwrights' Theatre** in Greenwich Village, New York before settling into their own Provincetown Playhouse in 1918. Among the playwrights they helped to launch was Eugene O'Neill, whose play *Desire Under the Elms* was first produced in Greenwich Village in 1924. The group disbanded in 1921, but the Playwrights' Theatre prospered under Kenneth MacGowan and others until demolition in 1930, being renamed the **Irish Theatre** in 1929. The Provincetown Playhouse has since played host to many companies, housing the US premieres of Albee's *The Zoo Story* and Beckett's *Krapp's Last Tape* in 1960.

Provoked Wife, The A comedy by Sir John *Vanburgh. First performance: Drury Lane, 1697. The play explores the predicament of Lady Brute in her unfortunate marriage and debates her obligation to remain faithful to her husband.

Pryce, Jonathan (1947-) British actor, who was with the Everyman Theatre Company at Liverpool (where he also directed on occasions) before achieving great success as Gethin Price in Trevor Griffiths's *Comedians* at Nottingham Playhouse and the Old Vic. His major roles since then have included Hamlet (1980) at the Royal Court, Macbeth (1986) at Stratford-upon-Avon and the Barbican, and Astrov in Michael Frayn's version of Chekhov's *Uncle Vanya* (1988) at the Vaudeville.

Public Theatre A theatre on Lafayette Street, New York, which houses four auditoriums and was converted from the Astor Library in 1967 by Joseph Papp. The four auditoriums opened at different times: the **Anspacher Theatre**, which seats 275, in 1967 with *Hair*; the 108-seat **Other Stage** in 1968 as a workshop for playwrights; the **Newman Theatre**, with 300 seats, in 1970 with Dennis J Reardon's *The Happiness Cage*; and the 191-seat **Martinson Hall** in 1971 with the musical *Blood*. The theatre operates on a permanent subsidy from the City of New York.

Publilius Syrus (1st century BC) Roman playwright, author of early mime dramas. Originally a slave, he was judged superior to Laberius, and was highly regarded as a performer in his own pieces; of his works only a number of aphorisms have survived.

Puddle Wharf Theatre *See* Porter's Hall.

Pulcinella A character of the *commedia dell'arte*, one of the *zanni*. Possibly first played by Fiorillo, Pulcinella was a hunchback with a hooked nose and little intellect and probably inherited many of his traits from the Roman *Maccus. In the French Comédie-Italienne he became *Polichinelle, while in England he evolved into the irascible Punch (*see* Punch and Judy).

Punch and Judy The central tradition of the English puppet theatre. Traditionally presented by a single puppeteer in a small booth made of striped cloth, the Punch and Judy show has Italian and French origins. The character of Punch, a crafty hunchback with a large nose, vicious temper, and high voice – achieved by means of a small diaphragm (a **swazzle**) placed in the operator's mouth – was derived from that of *Polichinelle, although his wife Judy (sometimes called Joan) first appeared around 1688. Other characters in the show include the Baby, *Toby, the Hangman, the Croco-dile, and the Devil. Originally the puppets were marionettes, but by the early 19th century almost all Punch and Judy puppeteers favoured the use of glove puppets. Equivalents of Punch and Judy in other countries include the puppet shows revolving around the Austrian character *Kasperl and the Russian Petrushka.

Punch and Judy Theatre A theatre on West 49th Street, New York, which opened in 1914 with Harold Chapin's *The Marriage of Columbine*. In 1926 the theatre was renamed the **Charles Hopkins Theatre**, reopening with Karel Čapek's *The Makropulos Secret*. In 1933 it was converted into a cinema.

Punch's Playhouse *See* Strand Theatre.

puppet theatre A form of dramatic entertainment in which the characters are represented by puppets. Traditionally made of wood and manipulated by hand (**glove puppets**) or by means of rods, string (in which case they are technically **marionettes**), or wires, puppets have been used since ancient times and are still widely seen in *Punch and Judy shows. Puppet theatre has a long history in many countries, notably in Europe, the Soviet Union, and in India, Japan, and elsewhere in the Far East. *See also* Jōruri, motion, shadow play.

Purim play A tradition of Jewish drama, performed during the festival of Purim in mid-March. With its roots in the 14th century, the genre reached its height in rural areas in the 17th century, consisting of performances of lively musical comedies with elements borrowed from Italian carnival. Such entertainments became popular throughout Europe and contributed to the development of a distinct Jewish dramatic genre. Later the tradition was also influenced by the *commedia dell'arte* and, in Germany, by the English Comedians. Most plays in the form were based on the Old

Testament story of Esther and Haman, upon which the festival of Purim was originally based. The Purim play declined in the 18th century after it grew too licentious for the Jewish religious authorities. It was cleaned up in Germany by the so-called Haskala groups before finally disappearing upon the establishment of a fresh Yiddish theatrical tradition.

Pushkin, Alexander Sergeivich (1799–1837) Russian poet and playwright, whose most significant work for the theatre was the historical drama *Boris Godunov*. Best known for his poetry, Pushkin began writing drama while still a boy and particularly admired the plays of Shakespeare, which exercized a strong influence upon his one great dramatic work. Intended as the first of a series of major dramas on Russian themes, *Boris Godunov* (completed in 1825) reflected the troubled political atmosphere of the time and is notable for its combination of poetic and conventional language; it was later turned into an opera by Mussorgsky. Pushkin's short play *Mozart and Salieri* was set to music by Rimsky-Korsakov.

Principal dramatic works:

Boris Godunov: 1870 (written 1825).

Don Juan: 1837.

Mozart and Salieri: 1837.

Pushkin Theatre A theatre in Leningrad, opened in 1824 as the **Alexandrinsky Theatre**. After enjoying early success with appearances by Karatygin, it presented a varied programme of ballet, opera, and melodrama for many years before achieving new acclaim with the Realist dramas of Strindberg and others. The conventional approach of the company led, however, to the failure of Chekhov's *The Seagull* in 1896 and it was not until the arrival of Meyerhold that the theatre's fortunes revived. Subsequent directors have included Lunacharsky and Radlov; the theatre (given its present name in 1937) has enjoyed success with plays by Chekhov, Lermontov,

Shakespeare, and others, while the company has established a strong reputation for the quality of its acting.

Another theatre of the same name was founded in Moscow in 1951 and achieved early success with Sukhovo-Kobylin's *Krechinsky's Wedding*. Since then it has won attention with productions of plays by Ostrovsky, Oscar Wilde, and others, notably under the direction of Tumanov (1953–61).

Pygmalion One of the most popular plays by G B *Shaw, written in 1912. First performance: Vienna, 1913. The plot, concerning the social transformation of the cockney flower-seller, Eliza Doolittle, by the professor of linguistics, Henry Higgins, provided the basis for the musical *My Fair Lady* and for a film starring Wendy Hiller and Leslie Howard. The musical version was first staged in New York in 1956 and provided a major success for Rex Harrison, with famous sets by Cecil Beaton.

Pylades (1st century BC) A noted *pantomimus* of ancient Rome, who was responsible for the introduction of the mime dance tradition from his native Greece. His success in tragic roles drew audiences away from straight tragedy.

Q

Q Theatre A theatre on the north side of the River Thames at Kew Bridge, London, which was converted from the former Prince's Hall by Jack de Leon. It opened in 1924 with a revival of Gertrude Jennings's *The Young Person in Pink*. For upwards of 30 years he produced revivals of West End hits and many new plays there, including Frederick Knott's *Dial M for Murder* and Philip King's *See How They Run*. Unable to meet the requirements of the licensing authority, the theatre closed in 1956.

Quaglio, Lorenzo (1730–1804) Italian artist, who was the eldest member of a notable family of scene designers for various European court theatres. Lorenzo and his brother, **Giuseppe Quaglio** (1747–1828), executed numerous influential neoclassical designs, eventually settling in Germany, where succeeding generations of the family were active in designing scenery until the late 19th century.

Quality Street A play by J M *Barrie. First performance: London, 1902. The play is a Regency period romance in which a young woman, disappointed in her lover after a long absence, woos him again in the disguise of an imaginary niece.

Quare Fellow, The A tragi-comedy by Brendan *Behan. First performance: Dublin, 1954. First seen in a Gaelic verison, the play was highly acclaimed when performed by Joan Littlewood's Theatre Workshop in 1958; it depicts events in an Irish prison on the eve of a hanging, with both bitterness and humour.

Quartermaine, Leon (1876–1967) British actor, who made his London debut in Forbes-Robertson's company in 1901. Throughout his long career he played a wide range of parts, from the Emperor in Shaw's *Androcles and the Lion* to Ishak in Flecker's *Hassan* and Osborne in R C Sherriff's *Journey's End*. He was also admired for performances during Gielgud's season at the Haymarket (1944) and as a member of the Stratford-upon-Avon company.

Quayle, Sir (John) Anthony (1913-) British actor, who made his professional debut in 1931 and spent the next eight years in supporting roles at the Old Vic and elsewhere. After World War II he reappeared as Jack Absolute in Sheridan's *The Rivals* (1945) and then went to Stratford-upon-Avon (1948) as actor and director. Over the following eight years he played several major roles, including Iago, Falstaff, and Othello. In New York in 1956 he starred in Marlowe's *Tamburlaine the Great*; since then he has made numerous film appearances, but also triumphed on stage in such parts as Eddie in Arthur Miller's *A View from the Bridge* (1956) and Andrew Wyke in Anthony Shaffer's *Sleuth* (1970). In 1984 he launched a touring company (Compass Productions), opening with his own production of Colman and Garrick's *The Clandestine Marriage*, in which he played Lord Ogleby.

Queen Anne's Men An English theatre company formed in 1603 from members of Oxford's and Worcester's Men. Usually referred to as the Queen's Men, the company included Christopher Beeston and Thomas Heywood; it performed at the Curtain and Red Bull theatres until 1616, when it moved to the Cockpit. It was disbanded in 1619.

Queen Elizabeth's Men An English theatre company founded in 1583. Usually known as the Queen's Men and performing at inns as well as at the Theatre, Curtain, and Rose theatres, it enjoyed considerable success through the popularity of such members as Richard Tarleton. It was disbanded in 1594.

Queen Henrietta's Men An English theatre company, founded in 1625 on the coronation of Charles I and Henrietta Maria. Usually referred to as the Queen's Men, the company was led by Christopher Beeston and performed numerous plays by James Shirley and others at the Cockpit from 1625 to 1636. Inigo Jones also designed scenery for their appearances at Court. An outbreak of the plague forced the company's dissolution in 1636, although a new company of the same name performed at Salisbury Court from 1637 to 1647.

Queen's Theatre A theatre in Long Acre, London, originally called **St Martin's Hall**. Converted into a theatre in 1867 and in its day the largest theatre in London next to Drury Lane and the opera houses, Queen's enjoyed a brief period of popularity. Actors there including Henry Irving and Ellen Terry. Renamed the National in 1877 it was finally closed in 1878 and later demolished.

In 1907 a new **Queen's Theatre** was opened in Shaftesbury Avenue as a twin to the Globe Theatre, but was not immediately successful. In 1913 the management introduced tango teas, for which patrons paid half a crown for dancing, a dress parade, and afternoon tea. The comedy *Potash and Perlmutter* (1914) was the Queen's Theatre's first real success; this was followed in 1916 by a sequel, *Potash and Perlmutter in Society*. Among subsequent notable productions were Bernard Shaw's *The Apple Cart* (1929), with Cedric Hardwicke and Edith Evans, *The Barretts of Wimpole Street* (1930), and, in 1937, a brilliant season of plays by Shakespeare and others featuring John Gielgud and Peggy Ashcroft. Bombed in 1940, the theatre remained derelict for nearly 20 years; it reopened in 1959 with a modern exterior but with the original style largely retained inside, seating 989. Currently under the management of Stoll Moss Theatres, it has a reputation for good drama and domestic comedy, as well as such musicals as *Stop the World, I Want to Get Off* (1961) and *Wonderful Town!* (1986). *See also* Her Majesty's Theatre.

Quem Quaeritis? The most famous example of the *trope tradition of the early medieval church. Consisting of a brief exchange concerning the events surrounding the Resurrection, the *Quem Quaeritis?* evolved during the 10th century and was gradually embellished with extra scenes and comic characters as an early development of *liturgical drama.

Questors Theatre A theatre at Ealing in West London that is the headquarters of a prominent group of amateurs, founded in 1929 by **Alfred Emmett**. The building itself,

financed through fund-raising appeals, opened in 1964. At one period the group staged annual festivals of new drama, introducing the plays of James Saunders (including *Next Time I'll Sing to You* in 1962), and became (in 1946) one of the founder-members of the Little Theatre Guild of Great Britain.

Quête See mummers' play.

Quick, John (1748–1831) British actor, who worked in the provinces before being engaged by Foote at the Haymarket. He then transferred to Covent Garden, where he remained for the rest of his career playing clowns, rustics, and comic servants, notably in plays by Shakespeare and Sheridan. He was much admired by George III.

quick-change room A dressing-room or convenient recess situated close to the stage, where actors may make rapid adjustments to their costume and make-up when so required.

Quilley, Denis (Clifford) (1927-) British actor, who began his career at the Birmingham Repertory Theatre and came to London to replace Richard Burton in Fry's *The Lady's Not for Burning* (1949). Subsequently he worked with the Old Vic and Young Vic companies; in 1955 he had his first leading West End role, in the musical *Wild Thyme*. From then on he combined musical and straight theatre, his roles including Jamie in O'Neill's *Long Day's Journey into Night* for the National Theatre (1971), Sidney Bruhl in Ira Levin's *Deathtrap* (1978) at the Garrick Theatre, and roles in the musicals *Sweeney Todd* (1980) and *La Cage aux Folles* (1986).

Quin, James (1693–1766) British actor, who first appeared on stage in Dublin in 1712 and made a success deputizing as Bajazet in Rowe's *Tamerlane* at Drury Lane in 1714. He then joined John Rich at Lincoln's Inn Fields, playing leading Shakespearean roles, including Falstaff, for which he was particularly renowned. Subsequently he went on to Covent Garden and thence to Drury Lane, where he was often at loggerheads with Macklin.

Quinault, Abraham-Alexis *See* Dufresne.

Quinault, Philippe (1635–88) French playwright, born in Paris. The son of a baker, he began writing for the theatre while in the service of Tristan L'Hermite. Quinault's sentimental comedies were his most successful works – *Le Comédie sans comédie* (1655) and *La Mère coquette* (1665) are notable examples. He also wrote tragedies, the most famous being *Astrate roi de Tyr* (1664), which was criticized by Boileau, libretti for Lully's operas, and lyrics in collaboration with Pierre Corneille and Molière.

Quiñones de Benavente, Luis (c. 1593–1651) Spanish playwright, a contemporary of Lope de Vega. His comedies, several of which revolved around the character of Juan (based on a character from Cervantes), influenced the development of the *loa* and the *entremé*.

Quintero, José Benjamin (1924–) US director, born in Panama, who cofounded the *Circle-in-the-Square, where his successes included O'Neill's *The Iceman Cometh* (1956), Behan's *The Hostage* (1958), and *Our Town* (1959). He directed the US premiere of O'Neill's *Long Day's Journey Into Night* at the Helen Hayes Theatre in 1956 and, in 1958, directed O'Neill's *A Moon for the Misbegotten* in Spoleto, Italy. Other productions have included O'Neill's *Desire Under the Elms* (1963), *Marco Millions* (1964), and *Anna Christie* (1977).

Quintero, Serafín Álvarez *See* Alvarez Quintero, Serafín.

R

Rabe, David (1940–) US playwright, whose first play to be produced in New York was *The Basic Training of Pavlo Hummel*, which was presented at the New York Shakespeare Festival in 1971. This play, together with *Sticks and Bones* (1971) and *Streamers* (1976), formed a trilogy on issues relating to the Vietnam War and earned several awards. His other works include *The Orphan* (1973), *In the Boom Boom Room* (1973), and *Hurlyburly* (1984).

Rabémananjara, Jacques (1913–) African playwright, living in Madagascar, who has established a strong reputation with a series of eloquent – though rarely acted – plays on historical themes. Written in French, his most admired works include *Agapes des Dieux* (Feasts of the Gods), published in 1962, and *Les Dieux Malgaches* (The Gods of Madagascar), published in 1964.

Racan, Honorat de Bueil, Seigneur de (1589–1670) French poet and playwright, whose play *Les Bergeries* (1620) is considered to be one of the finest pastoral comedies in the French theatre. A disciple of François de Malherbe, Racan served at the court of Henri IV and in the army before retiring to his château in Touraine.

Rachel (Élisa Félix; 1820–58) French actress, of poor Jewish parentage, who rose to become one of the most celebrated of all French tragic actresses. She sang in the streets of Lyons and Paris as a child and, after training at the Théâtre Molière and the Conservatoire, appeared for the first time at the Comédie-Française in 1838, encouraged by Joseph-Isidore Samson and the critic Jules Janin. Despite her slight figure, she gave performances of great energy and went on to triumph in the title roles of Racine's *Phèdre* (1843) and Scribe and Legouvé's *Adrienne Lecouvreur* (1848) as well as in other classical plays by Corneille and others. She came to dominate the Comédie-Française and toured widely, becoming notorious for her many love affairs; her early death was caused by consumption brought on by physical exhaustion.

Racine, Jean (1639–99) French playwright, who made an unequalled contribution to the development of French classical tragedy. Orphaned at an early age, he was educated by the Jansenists at Port-Royal, where he developed an interest in Greek and Latin literature and a talent for writing poetry. After studying at the University of Paris and a brief taste of ecclesiastical life in Languedoc, he eventually opted for a career in the theatre, contrary to the wishes of his relatives.

His first two plays were produced by Molière at the Palais-Royal, but Racine's decision to move *Alexandre le Grand* to the Hôtel de Bourgogne and his enticement of his mistress Mlle du Parc from Molière's company turned the friendship to hostility. *Andromaque* was the first of a series of great poetic tragedies, differing from those of his rival Pierre Corneille in that Racine's heroes and heroines are motivated by passion rather than duty: Corneille is said to have portrayed men as they should be, Racine to have shown them as they are. This period of Racine's career also saw the production of his only comedy, *Les Plaideurs*, which was inspired by Aristophanes's *Wasps*.

The success of **Phèdre*, the last of Racine's tragedies to be publicly performed in his lifetime, was marred by the popularity of an inferior play by **Pradon*, written deliberately in competition with Racine's masterpiece; he subsequently retired from the theatre, devoting himself to family life and to his new position as historiographer-royal. This break with the world of drama enabled him to renew his connections with the Jansenists of Port-Royal. His last two plays,

commissioned by Madame de Maintenon for the young ladies of her school at Saint-Cyr, were not staged in public until after his death: **Athalie* in 1716 and *Esther* in 1721. Racine's masterly characterizations and poetic powers have ensured constant revivals of his plays throughout modern times. Principal works:

La Thébaïde ou les Frères ennemies: 1664.
Alexandre le Grand: 1665.
Andromaque: 1667; translated as *Andromache*.
Les Plaideurs: 1668; translated as *The Litigants*.
Britannicus: 1669.
Bérénice: 1670.
*Bajazet: 1672.
Mithridate: 1673.
Iphigénie: 1674.
Phèdre: 1677; translated as *Phaedra*.
Esther: 1689.
Athalie: 1691; translated as *Athaliah*.

RADA *See* Royal Academy of Dramatic Art.

Radio City Music Hall An auditorium within the Rockefeller Centre in New York that seats 6200, making it the largest theatre in the world. It opened in 1932, presenting films and spectacular variety shows. Today it is the home of the Rockettes, who perform four shows daily.

Radius A British theatre organization, founded around 1929 to coordinate religious drama in Britain. Originally known as the Religious Drama Society of Great Britain, it promotes the use of drama by all denominations and encourages new writing on religious themes. A similar organization, **Sesame**, organizes drama involving the handicapped.

Radlov, Sergei Ernestovich (1892–1958) Soviet actor and director, who emerged as a leading Soviet director of the plays of Shakespeare. Having worked under

Meyerhold, he later developed Expressionist staging techniques and experimented with opera. His best-known success was the Moscow State Jewish Theatre production of *King Lear*; other notable productions were plays by Ibsen and Ostrovsky.

Raimund, Ferdinand (Jakob Raimann; 1790–1836) Austrian playwright and actor, who was the author of several popular Viennese comedies in which he usually appeared himself. Highly acclaimed as a comic actor, he enjoyed enormous success with such farces as *Der Barometermacher auf der Zauberinsel* (1823) and *Der Alpenkönig und der Menschenfeind* (1828). However, he allowed a note of bitterness to enter his writing (a result of his dissatisfaction with both his audience and his own private life) and later attempted less successfully to imitate the style of Shakespeare and Calderón. *Der Verschwender* (The Prodigal; 1834) restored his reputation but the rivalry of Nestroy eventually led to his suicide.

rain machine A mechanical device, by means of which the sound effect of falling rain, waves, or hail may be produced live. It usually consists of a large cylinder containing dried peas, beans, or marbles, which is revolved by hand.

Raisin, Jean-Baptiste (1655–93) French actor, who appeared as a child alongside his sister **Cathérine Raisin** (1649–1701) and brother **Jacques Raisin** (1653–1703). He excelled in comedy and later appeared with success at the Hôtel de Bourgogne, together with his wife **Françoise Pitel de Longchamp** (1661–1721); in 1680 they both joined the Comédie-Française.

Raisin in the Sun, A A play by Lorraine *Hansberry. First performance: New York, 1958. A drama about a Black Chicago family's struggles, it was made into a film in 1961 with Sidney Poitier and Ruby Dee. The plot revolves around Walter Lee, a Black chauffeur, and his wife Ruth who long to acquire middle-class status.

rake The slope of the auditorium or stage floor downwards towards the footlights. Stages in older theatres were frequently raked for reasons of perspective, but most modern theatres have level stages with raked seating for the audience.

Ralph Roister Doister A doggerel verse comedy in five acts, written by Nicholas *Udall c. 1534. First performance: Eton, c. 1534. The first true English comedy, it was modelled on the plays of Plautus and Terence and follows the central character's unsuccessful courtship of Dame Christian Custance.

Ramsay, Allan (1686–1758) Scottish poet, originally an Edinburgh wigmaker, whose pastoral *The Gentle Shepherd* won acclaim when adapted as a ballad opera with Scottish tunes. In 1730 it was successfully produced at Drury Lane as *Patie and Peggy; or, the Fair Foundling*. Subsequently Ramsay attempted to open a theatre in Edinburgh in 1736 but was thwarted by the licensing laws.

Ranch, Hieronymus Justesen (16th century) Danish playwright, author of an early example of Danish school drama. *Karrig Niding* (The Miser) is one of the few surviving plays of the period based on Danish sources.

Randall, Harry (1860–1932) British comic actor, who succeeded Dan Leno as dame in the annual Drury Lane pantomime in 1903. Previously he was associated for 10 years with the Grand Theatre, Islington, where he first played Mother Hubbard in 1893.

Rankin, Arthur McKee (1841–1914) Canadian actor-manager, who became a leading performer of melodrama and native Canadian plays. He began his career as an amateur and later made his reputation in Philadelphia, subsequently touring in melodrama with his wife, the actress **Kitty Blanchard** (1847–1911). His greatest successes included Joaquin Miller's *The Danites* (1877) and *The Canuck* (1890), his own adaptation of a French-Canadian novel. He was also seen in plays in London and elsewhere with the actress **Nance O'Neil** (Gertrude Lamson; 1874–1965), whose most acclaimed roles included Juliet and Marguerite Gautier in *Camille* by Dumas *fils*. He was the grandfather of Lionel *Barrymore.

Rapier Players See Little Theatre.

Rastell, John (d. 1536). English playwright, brother-in-law of Sir Thomas More and father-in-law of John Heywood. He was probably the author of *Calisto and Meliboea*, adapted from *La *Celestina* by de Rojas, and *The Dialogue of Gentleness and Nobility*; both were performed in about 1527. He may also have written the interlude *The Play of the Four Elements* (c. 1517).

Rattigan, Sir Terence (Mervyn) (1911–77) British playwright, whose well-constructed plays demonstrate the author's command of stagecraft. *French Without Tears* established his reputation as a writer of excellent middle-class comedies. Of the plays that followed, the most successful included the war drama *Flare Path*, but it was not until *The *Winslow Boy* in 1946 that Rattigan was recognized as a writer of serious drama. *The *Browning Version* consolidated this reputation; subsequent works tackling similarly intense themes included The *Deep Blue Sea*, about adultery and suicide, *Separate Tables*, and *Ross*. *Cause Célèbre* depicted events surrounding a real murder trial. He was also responsible for creating the fictional character 'Aunt Edna', who represents the conventional unadventurous theatregoer.
Principal works:
French Without Tears: 1936.
Flare Path: 1942.

While the Sun Shines: 1943.
The Winslow Boy: 1946.
The Browning Version: 1948.
The Deep Blue Sea: 1952.
Separate Tables: 1954.
Ross: 1960.
A Bequest to the Nation: 1970.
Cause Célèbre: 1977.

Räuber, Die The first play by Friedrich von *Schiller, written in 1781. First performance: Mannheim, 1782. Written when Schiller was only 22 years old, the play, a controversial attack upon tyranny, was a major development in the *Sturm und Drang* movement and established the author's reputation. It was highly influential in English translations.

Raucourt, Mlle (Françoise-Marie-Antoinette-Josèphe Saucerotte; 1756–1815) French actress, who was much admired in tragic roles at the Comédie-Française until her notorious private life obliged her to leave Paris for a time. Marie-Antoinette engineered her return but she later fell foul of Madame Vestris and during the Revolution was imprisoned.

Ravenscroft, Edward (fl. 1671–97) English playwright, whose most successful work, the farce *The London Cuckolds* (1681), was performed annually on Lord Mayor's Day at both Drury Lane and Covent Garden for 70 years. He wrote numerous other plays, drawing on various sources, including *The Careless Lovers* (1673), which was based on Molière, *The Wrangling Lovers* (1676), *The Anatomist; or, the Sham Doctor* (1696), also based on Molière, and a version of *Titus Andronicus* (1686).

Raymond, John T (John O'Brien; 1836–87) US actor, who became a highly successful performer of comic roles in numerous classic and contemporary plays. A member of Laura Keene's company from 1861, he excelled in such plays as Tom Taylor's *Our

American Cousin, Goldsmith's *She Stoops to Conquer*, and Sheridan's *The School for Scandal*. His most famous parts, however, were those of Colonel Mulberry Sellers in Mark Twain's *The Gilded Age* (1874) and Ichabod Crane in an adaptation of Washington Irving's *The Legend of Sleepy Hollow* (1879).

Raynal, Paul (1885–1971) French playwright, who made his name in 1920 with *Le Maître de son coeur*, a psychological drama. He went on to write plays modelled on classical tragedy, including *Le Tombeau sous l'Arc de Triomphe* (1924: translated as *The Unknown Warrior*, 1928), which contrasts the lives of soldiers and civilians during World War I and is his most famous work. Later plays include *La Francerie* (1933) and *Le Matériel humain* (1947).

Reade, Charles (1814–84) British novelist and playwright, whose first play, *Masks and Faces* (1852), was based on the relationship between Garrick and Peg Woffington and was written in collaboration with Tom Taylor. Subsequent successes included *Gold* (1853), *The Courier of Lyons* (1854), which was made famous by Irving as *The Lyons Mail*, and *Drink* (1879), in which Charles Warner collaborated with him. A number of Reade's novels were also successfully dramatized.

Realism A theatre movement of the late 19th century, in which the artificial style of the *well-made play was rejected in favour of a more naturalistic depiction of real life situations and characters. Key figures in the movement, which revolutionized the contemporary theatre, included Ibsen, Shaw, and Stanislavsky; ultimately it inspired the more extreme approach of *naturalism.

Realistic Theatre A small theatre in Moscow, founded in 1921 as part of the *Moscow Art Theatre. Also called the **Krasnya Presnya Theatre**, it enjoyed particular success with experimental productions under Okhlopkov from 1930, staging works by contemporary writers until it closed after failing to amalgamate with Taïrov's company at the Kamerny Theatre in 1938.

Reaney, James Crerar (1926–) Canadian poet and playwright, who is the author of a number of acclaimed plays depicting small-town life in Canada. *The Killdeer* (1959), set in Ontario, established his reputation; subsequent works have ranged from the melodramatic *The Sun and the Moon* (1965) and the children's play *One-Man Masque* (1959) to the puppet play *Apple Butter* (1965) and *Colours in the Dark* (1967), which combined autobiographical and historical detail. A trilogy of plays in the 1970s, beginning with *Sticks and Stones* (1973), followed the story of an immigrant Irish family and was written under the techniques of collective creation with members of a theatre company in Toronto.

Rebhun, Paul (c. 1500–46) German playwright, remembered for the biblical play *Suzanna* (1535). The play, the writing of which was much influenced by Luther, combined features of both medieval and Renaissance drama.

Recital Theatre See Daly's 63rd Street Theatre.

Recruiting Officer, The A comedy by George *Farquhar. First performance: 1706. Drawing upon Farquhar's own experience as a recruiting officer, the play revolves around the adventures of Captain Plume and Sergeant Kite, who trick recruits into signing up for the army.

Red Army Theatre A theatre in Moscow, founded in 1919 from troupes organized to entertain the armed forces. Properly called the **Central Theatre of the Soviet Army**, the company established a strong reputation under Zavadsky and then Alexei Popov, who directed it from 1937 to 1961, and moved into a specially built star-shaped theatre in 1940. As well as contemporary Soviet works, the company staged (and continues to present under Andrei Popov and others) plays by Shakespeare and other foreign playwrights.

Red Bull Theatre A theatre in Upper Street, Clerkenwell, in London, which began as an inn where plays were presented from time to time in the courtyard. In 1605 it became a permanent theatrical venue and the home of Queen Anne's Men; it was subsequently reconstructed in 1625 but declined in reputation, probably being used for the presentation of more sensational drama. During the Commonwealth the theatre staged occasional shows without permission; actors who appeared there included Killigrew and Mohun. It was demolished during the 1660s.

Rederykers *See* Chambers of Rhetoric.

Redgrave, Sir Michael (Scudamore) (1908–85) British actor, who began his career in repertory at the Liverpool Playhouse in 1934 and made his London debut as Ferdinand in *Love's Labour's Lost* at the Old Vic in 1936. The following year he played important parts in Gielgud's Queen's Theatre season, including Bolingbroke in *Richard II*. A subtle and intelligent actor, he reached the height of his career after World War II, playing such roles as Macbeth (1947), Crocker-Harris in Terence Rattigan's *The Browning Version* (1948), and Shylock, Antony, and Lear at Stratford-upon-Avon (1953). Subsequently he was much admired as H J in his own dramatization of Henry James's *The Aspern Papers* (1959), in the title role of Chekhov's *Uncle Vanya* (1961) at Chichester and the National Theatre, and as Hobson in *Hobson's Choice* (1963) before ill health limited his appearances. Later roles included the part of the Father in John

Mortimer's *A Voyage Round My Father* (1972), in which he toured overseas.

He was married to the actress **Rachel Kempson** (1910–) and their elder daughter, **Vanessa Redgrave** (1937–), also became a major star of stage and films, making her first London appearance in N C Hunter's *A Touch of the Sun* in 1958. Later she was acclaimed in performances over several seasons at Stratford-upon-Avon, notably as Rosalind, Katharina, and Imogen. Her other successes include the title role in Muriel Spark's *The Prime of Miss Jean Brodie* (1966), Gilda in Noël Coward's *Design for Living* (1973), Ellida in Ibsen's *The Lady from the Sea* (1976), Shakespeare's Cleopatra (1973 and 1986), and a revival of O'Neill's *A Touch of the Poet* (1988). She was married for a time to the director Tony Richardson and has aroused controversy with her involvement in Marxist political activity.

Sir Michael Redgrave's other children, **Corin Redgrave** (1939–) and **Lynn Redgrave** (1943–), are also known as performers on stage and screen.

Red Lion Inn A tavern in Stepney, London, where plays were staged in the late 16th century.

Red Roses for Me A play by Sean *O'Casey. First performance: Dublin, 1943. The play is largely based upon O'Casey's experiences during the 1913 General Strike in Dublin.

Rees, Roger (1944–) British actor, who attracted attention after joining the Royal Shakespeare Company in 1967. Among his parts have been Hamlet, Charles Courtley in Boucicault's *London Assurance*, and the title role in the much-acclaimed *Nicholas Nickleby* (1980). Other successes have included Terry Johnson's *Cries from the Mammal House* (1984) and Tom Stoppard's *Hapgood* (1988).

reflector A spotlight or floodlight in which the lamp and metal reflector exist as one unit.

Regency Theatre *See* Scala Theatre.

Regent Theatre A theatre in King's Cross, London, that opened as a music hall called the **Euston Palace** in 1900. Nigel Playfair took it over in 1924, renaming it the Regent Theatre and opening with Arnold Bennett's *Body and Soul*. Later that year Barry Jackson presented Rutland Boughton's musical drama *The Immortal Hour*; subsequent successes included John Gielgud and Gwen Ffrangcon-Davies in *Romeo and Juliet* (1974). Among other interesting productions were plays by Shaw, the Čapeks' *The Insect Play*, and John Drinkwater's *Robert E Lee*. The theatre was also used by the Phoenix Society for revivals of classic plays and by several other notable groups before it became a cinema in 1935.

Regnard, Jean-François (1655–1709) French playwright, whose witty comedies continued the tradition established by Molière. After an adventurous early life he settled down to write, collaborating with Dufresny on plays for the Comédie-Italienne. His best-known and most successful plays were produced by the Comédie-Française; these include *Attendez-moi sous l'orme* (1694), *La Sérénade* (1694), *Le Joueur* (1696), and *Le Légataire universel* (1708).

Rehan, Ada (Ada Crehan; 1860–1916) US actress, born in Ireland, who became a leading performer with Augustin Daly's company in both New York and London from 1879. Previously with Mrs John Drew's troupe in Philadelphia and other companies, she excelled in comic roles in many classic plays, among the most notable being Katharina in *The Taming of the Shrew* (1887) and Lady Teazle in Sheridan's *The School for Scandal*. She retired in 1905 after her style of acting fell from fashion.

rehearsal A meeting of director, cast, and others at which every aspect of a show can be worked upon in order to bring the production to performance standard. In medieval times there were few rehearsals and emphasis was placed upon an actor's skill at improvisation; in the 19th century, however, they became widely accepted practice.

Rehearsal, The A comedy by George Villiers, Duke of *Buckingham. First performance: Drury Lane, London, 1671. This burlesque of heroic drama – especially that of Dryden – effectively ended the genre and inspired numerous imitations, notably Sheridan's *The Critic*. The central character, Bayes, was intended to represent Dryden himself.

Reid, Beryl (1920–) British actress, who established herself as a highly talented comedienne in revue, pantomime, and variety before appearing in straight theatre, when she was cast with great success as Sister George in Frank Marcus's *The Killing of Sister George* in 1965. Among her subsequent appearances have been the Nurse in *Romeo and Juliet* (1974) for the National Theatre, Lady Wishfort in Congreve's *The Way of the World* (1978) for the Royal Shakespeare Company, and roles in *Born in the Gardens* (1979) by Peter Nichols and Sheridan's *The School for Scandal* (1983).

Reid, (Daphne) Kate (1930–) Canadian actress, born in England, who made her London debut as Lizzie in N Richard Nash's *The Rainmaker* in 1956. She has since appeared mainly in Canada and the US, often in leading Shakespearean parts. Her New York roles have included Caitlin Thomas in Sidney Michael's *Dylan* (1964) and Esther Franz in Arthur Miller's *The Price* (1968), in which part she also appeared in London in 1969. She has worked several times with the American Shakespeare Company and also appeared in plays by Albee, Tennessee Williams, and G B Shaw.

Reigen A play by Arthur *Schnitzler, written 1896–97 and subsequently filmed as *La Ronde*. First performance: Budapest, 1912. The play revolves around a succession of sexual liaisons involving the same characters and is notable for its sophisticated wit; it was greeted with riots on its first performance in German in 1921.

Reimers, Arnoldus (1844–99) Norwegian actor, husband of Johanne Juell-Reimers, who appeared for many years at the Kristiania Theater, being particularly admired in the plays of Ibsen.

His sister was the actress **Sofie Reimers** (1853–1932), who was especially popular in the comedies of Holberg and Wessel. She first appeared at the National Scene in Bergen, transferring later to the Kristiania Theater and then the Nationaltheatret in 1899.

Reinhardt, Max (Max Goldmann; 1873–1943) Austrian director, actor, and manager, who became the first leading international director, dominating the Berlin stage and profoundly influencing the theatre in Britain, the US, and many other countries. He began as an actor (1890–1900), specializing in playing older men and establishing himself as a leading performer under Otto Brahm at the Deutsches Theater in Berlin. He then ventured into direction, scoring his first major success in 1903 with Gorky's *The Lower Depths* and subsequently also directing at the Neues Theater am Schiffbauerdamm, where his productions in a variety of styles included works by Hofmannsthal, Lessing, Shakespeare, and Schiller.

His production in 1910 of *Oedipus Rex* by Sophocles inspired a revival of interest in Greek classical drama and was toured through 10 European capitals, while his series of Shakespearean productions (1913–14) also had a major impact. At the same time he demonstrated his versatility with successful versions of contemporary plays by Ibsen, Strindberg, and Wedekind among others and encouraged the performance of new drama at the Berlin Voksbühne (1915–20).

Although he was equally adept at using such restricted acting spaces as that at the Kammerspiele, he is usually remembered for his spectacular productions at such huge venues as London's Olympia and the Grosses Schauspielhaus, as well as for those at the Deutsches Theater (which he bought in 1906 and where he installed his own acting school), controlling massive casts with supreme skill. He also worked at a number of important festivals, founding the Salzburg Festival in 1920 and directing there regularly until 1934.

The Nazis deprived him of the ownership of his theatres in 1933 and from 1938 Reinhardt worked in the US, where his productions included a film of his famous version of *A Midsummer Night's Dream* (first given in 1905 and later reinterpreted by him many times).

Réjane (Gabrielle-Charlotte Réju; 1857–1920) French actress, who became one of the most popular performers of comedy in Paris during the 1890s and 1900s. She began her career in 1875 at the Théâtre du Vaudeville and specialized in comic roles in fairly inconsequential plays; her few performances in dramas of major significance included the title role in Sardou's *Madame Sans-Gêne* (1895).

Relapse, The A comedy by Sir John *Vanbrugh. First performance: Drury Lane, 1697. Colley Cibber's *Love's Last Shift* (1696) partly suggested the plot although Vanbrugh rejected Cibber's sentimentality in his frank exploration of marriage. The most memorable character in the play, Lord Foppington, was based on Cibber's fop Sir Novelty Fashion.

Renaissance, Théâtre de la A theatre in Paris, opened on the site of the Théâtre de la *Porte-Saint-Martin in 1873. After staging dramas by Zola and others it diversified with the farces of Feydeau and Labiche until Sarah Bernhardt took it over in the 1890s. Notable successes under her included plays by Rostand and Musset as well as earlier works by Racine and Dumas *fils*; subsequently Gémier and Lucien Guitry ensured the theatre's continued prosperity for some years before a long period of decline set in. After 1956 the theatre was restored and used for staging a new contemporary programme.

An earlier theatre of the same name opened in Paris in 1826 and was used for plays by Hugo and Dumas *père*, scoring its greatest success with Frédérick in Hugo's *Ruy Blas* (1838) before closing in 1841.

Renaissance drama European drama of the period roughly between the 14th and early 17th centuries, when the influence of classical drama combined with a revival of intellectual aspirations effectively laid the foundations of the modern theatre. Although the theatre was initially considered too vulgar for the attention of the serious scholar, the rediscovery of such classical playwrights as Plautus, Euripides, and Seneca (as well as such theorists as Aristotle) inspired imitators in Italy and later throughout Europe. The earliest Renaissance tragedy based on classical lines was Trissino's *Sophonisba*, written in 1515 and performed in 1562. Cinthio, Rucellai, Aretino, Speroni, Groto, and Tasso were among other early writers of tragedy in Italy, while those in other countries included Étienne Jodelle in France, Cristóbel de Virués, Juan de la Cueva, and Cervantes in Spain, and Marlowe, Kyd, and Shakespeare in England (*see* Elizabethan drama).

The development of a revived comic tradition during this era was more complicated, with elements from the classical theatre being combined with features of the mystery play, morality play, and liturgical drama of the Middle Ages. Ariosto was a key figure in the early emergence of the *commedia erudita*, which, together with the early *commedia dell'arte*, established the popularity of two very different types of Italian comedy. Elsewhere Grévin and Larivey were among those who revolutionized comedy in France, while in Spain Torres Naharro distinguished between two national comic styles, the *comedia a noticia* (later popularized by Lope de Vega) and the *comedia a fantasia*; in England Shakespeare and Jonson were unmatched.

The influence of Renaissance thought also extended to theatre design, with the period witnessing the building of the first permanent playhouses, much influenced by the theories of Vitruvius. Classical staging techniques, including the use of *periaktoi*, were also revived and led to the introduction of new scenic devices (as well as the study of perspective) in theatres designed by Sangallo, Serlio, Palladio, Scamozzi, and Aleotti among others. France saw the establishment of its first permanent theatre, the Théâtre de l'Hôtel de Bourgogne, in 1548, although stages in Britain and Spain remained generally uncovered until well into the 17th century and owed much of their design to their origins in inn yard performances. The period also witnessed early experiments with stage lighting. *See also* interlude; masque; pastoral; *sacra rappresentazione*.

Renaissance Theatre Company *See* Branagh, Kenneth.

Renaud, Madeleine-Lucie (1900-) French actress, who became a leading performer of French classical comedy, notably under the direction of her husband, Jean-Louis *Barrault. She began her career at the Comédie-Française, being particularly admired in the plays of Molière, Marivaux, and Musset, before marrying Barrault in 1940. Subsequently (1946) they founded their own Compagnie Renaud-Barrault, with which Renaud has appeared throughout France and abroad in plays by Anouilh, Beckett, Chekhov, Claudel, Kafka, and many others.

repertory A group of plays or other productions that are prepared by a company for presentation on different nights of the week or on a weekly basis. Formerly standard practice, it is now more common in both Britain and the US for companies to present *runs of a single play, thus avoiding the dangers of exhaustion and under-rehearsal. *See also* Repertory Theatre Movement.

Repertory Theatre Movement The development, during the 20th century, of a theatrical tradition whereby various British theatres offered a series of their own productions in quick succession, independent of touring companies. High standards of production, the promotion of new plays by British writers, and a responsiveness to the multiplicity of interests in the community around it are all now considered part of such a theatre's responsibility. Beginning as a campaign at the end of the 19th century in reaction to the dominance of the actor-manager and the long run, the movement flourished particularly in the provinces. In 1907 Miss Horniman established the first English repertory theatre company in Manchester; by 1914 similar companies had been established at Glasgow, Liverpool, Birmingham, and Bristol, some financed by wealthy entrepreneurs and others by shareholders. Such theatres generally presented new productions each week and provided an excellent training ground for young actors.

The opening of the Belgrade Theatre in Coventry (1958) signalled a revival of interest in the system and there are now some 60 regional repertory theatres operating in Britain.

Representative, The (*Der Stellvertreter*) A documentary drama by Rolf *Hochhuth.

First performance: Berlin, 1963. Seen in the US as *The Deputy*, this embittered criticism of papal inaction during the massacre of the Jewish population in Nazi-occupied Europe inspired a revival of German drama and effectively founded the documentary drama movement, despite its inordinate length and wealth of detail.

Republic Theatre A theatre on 42nd Street, between Seventh and Eighth avenues, New York, which opened in 1900 with James A Herne's *Sag Harbor*. In 1902 it was taken over by David Belasco and renamed the Belasco Theatre. It reverted, however, to its original name in 1910; from 1931 it was a burlesque house until, in 1942, it became a cinema.

République, Théâtre de la *See* Comédie-Française.

Restoration drama English drama from the coronation of Charles I in 1660 to around the end of the 17th century. The period saw the revival of the English theatrical tradition following its interruption by the *Interregnum. The theatre became once more the province of the Court and the upper classes and was reorganized under the *patent theatres system.

Initially plays dating to the period before the closure of the theatres in 1642 provided the basic fare, although gradually the early development of the *comedy of manners represented the beginning of a new and genuinely original phase in English drama. Aphra Behn, George Etherege, Thomas Shadwell, William Wycherley, Congreve, and Vanbrugh were among the leading playwrights for the Restoration stage and it is for comedy that the period is now usually celebrated, although other features of the period included the now largely forgotten *heroic drama of Dryden and others. The only significant Restoration writer of tragedy was Thomas Otway, whose *Venice*

Preserv'd, for instance, harked back to Jacobean times.

Popular performers of the day included Nell Gwynn, Mrs Barry, and Anne Bracegirdle – who were among the first females to be allowed upon the English stage – and Thomas Betterton.

return A flat or cloth used to mask off any backstage area not screened by a tormentor or other parts of the set.

Reumert, Poul (1883–1968) Danish actor, who became the most celebrated actor in Denmark of his day. Closely associated with the Kongelige Teater from 1911, he was particularly admired in the plays of Molière as well as in contemporary Scandinavian drama.

Reuter, Christian (1665–c. 1712) German playwright, noted for his attacks on bourgeois values. His early comedies include *L'Honnête Femme, oder Die ehrliche Frau zu Plissine* (1695) and *La maladie et la mort de l'honnête femme, das ist: Der ehrlichen Frau Schlampampe Krankheit und Tod* (1696), which satirized his landlady and resulted in his imprisonment. Later works include a further attack on his landlady and a satire upon the aristocracy.

Revels Office *See* Master of the Revels.

Revenger's Tragedy, The A tragedy in blank verse first published in 1607, possibly by Cyril *Tourneur although Thomas *Middleton is favoured as the author by some scholars. First performance: London, c. 1607. Vindice uses the skull of his beloved to poison the Duke who has murdered her, but then becomes involved in a wider conspiracy culminating in scenes of violent mayhem.

revenge tragedy A genre of English tragedy popular during Elizabethan and Jacobean times. The essentials of the revenge trag-edy were derived from classical models by Seneca and include ghosts, murder, madness, and intrigue as embellishments of a central theme of revenge, often of the bloodiest kind. Shakespeare's *Hamlet* is one of the supreme examples and is typical in its concluding carnage; other notable plays of the genre include Shakespeare's *Titus Andronicus*, Kyd's *The Spanish Tragedy* (c. 1585–89), Tourneur's *The Revenger's Tragedy* (1607), and Webster's *The Duchess of Malfi* (1614).

reverberator An early lighting unit, used to light the apron in the Restoration theatre. It was a forerunner of the modern floodlight.

Revolution, Theatre of the *See* Mayakovsky Theatre.

revolving stage A stage equipped with a turntable, allowing a large part of the acting area to revolve, thus revealing one or more new sets in succession. The first complete revolving stage was constructed at Osaka in Japan in 1758; the first British example was installed at the London Coliseum in 1904.

revue A musical entertainment in which a team of performers presents a programme of unrelated songs, dances, and sketches in quick succession (*compare* musical comedy). Such shows are usually enlivened with an element of satire or topicality and are distantly descended from the satirical tradition of French street performers in the Middle Ages.

Such shows were first presented at the Théâtre de la Porte-Saint-Martin in Paris in the late 19th century and later became highly popular at the Folies-Bergère and elsewhere. The first English revue was Seymour Hicks's *Under the Clock* (1893), while the first on Broadway was *The Passing Show* (1894). An emphasis upon large-scale spectacle was a feature of many subsequent revues, notably Ziegfeld's *Follies*, which became the longest-running annual revue (1907–57) and achieved wide fame for its fabulously-costumed chorus girls and celebrity acts.

In Britain C B Cochran and André Charlot had similar success in the 1920s with somewhat smaller-scale shows (known as 'intimate' revues) featuring such talents as Noël Coward, Gertrude Lawrence, and Jack Buchanan; many of these later transferred to the US where they won equal acclaim. Subsequent intimate revues, which created such stars as Jack Hulbert and Cicely Courtneidge, included *Sweet and Low* (1943) at the Ambassadors Theatre and a series of productions at the Gate Theatre. Back in the US George White also concentrated on a more intimate version of Ziegfeld's *Follies*, presenting his own successful annual *Scandals* revue, which concentrated more on comedy than upon spectacle; stars of such productions included Ed Wynn, Eddie Cantor, and W C Fields.

In the 1950s a surreal element was introduced by the choreographer John Cranko in *Cranks* (1955) and by such revues as *Pieces of Eight* (1959), which included contributions by such unlikely revue writers as Harold Pinter and N F Simpson; new stars of the genre that emerged included Joyce Grenfell, Kenneth Williams, and Flanders and Swann. The success of the highly satirical *Beyond the Fringe* (1961) by the Cambridge Footlights Club, however, signalled the end of the conventional spectacular revue (which had become hugely expensive to present) and its virtual desertion of the stage for television where greater topicality was possible. The same era also saw the end of a third variety of revue, the *Revuedeville* of the Windmill Theatre and elsewhere, the distinguishing feature of which was the frequent appearance of nudes on stage. *Compare* music hall; Pierrot show; vaudeville.

Rey de Artieda, Andrés (1549–1613) Spanish playwright, remembered for the tragedy *Los amantes* (The Lovers; 1581). Based upon tales from Boccaccio, this was one of the earliest treatments in Spain of the theme of tragic love.

Reynolds, Frederick (1764–1841) British playwright, whose first play, *Werter* (based on Goethe's novel), was presented at Covent Garden in 1786. Subsequently he wrote a number of comedies, notably *The Dramatist* (1789) and *How to Grow Rich* (1793). His dog drama *The Caravan; or, the Driver and his Dog* (1803) was immensely popular when staged at Drury Lane, chiefly for its scene featuring a dog saving a child from drowning.

Reynolds, Robert (fl. 1610–40) English actor, who became immensely popular in Germany as the clown **Pickelhering**, many of whose characteristics were later assimilated into the stock German comic figure of *Hanswurst. He appeared as one of the English Comedians with Robert Browne and John Green, succeeding the latter in 1627 as leader of the troupe.

Rhinoceros (*Rhinocéros*) A play by Eugène *Ionesco. First performance: Paris, 1960. The central character (played by Olivier in the first London production) watches with increasing concern as all his friends turn into rhinoceroses; he wonders whether to conform or make a stand in defence of mankind.

rhinthonica A form of Roman *fabula*, comprising burlesques of earlier Greek tragedies. Named after the Greek playwright **Rhinthon of Tarentum** (4th century BC), who also wrote plays in the *phlyax tradition, the form was especially popular among Greeks in southern Italy and scenes from it appear on numerous vases of the period.

Rhinthon of Tarentum See *phlyax*; *rhinthonica*.

Rhodes, John (b. 1606) English theatre manager and bookseller, who was appointed Keeper of the Cockpit in 1644 and re-opened it with a small company that included Betterton and Kynaston in 1660. However, his licence was withdrawn when the patent theatres opened.

Riccoboni, Luigi (1676–1753) Italian actor-manager and writer on the theatre, who ran his own *commedia dell'arte* company for many years. Popularly known as **Lélio**, he revived the Comédie-Italienne in Paris, using written scripts, as well as twice visiting London. His books on the theatre include his *Histoire du théâtre italien*.

Rice, Elmer (Elmer Reizenstein; 1892–1967) US playwright, whose first play, *On Trial* (1914), introduced the innovation of the flashback in US drama. Of his other works the most influential was *The *Adding Machine* (1923); others included **Street Scene* (1929), *Counsellor-at-Law* (1931), *We, The People* (1933), *Judgement Day* (1934), *Between Two Worlds* (1934), *American Landscape* (1938), *Flight to the West* (1940), *A New Life* (1942), the fantasy *Dream Girl* (1945), and *Cue for Passion* (1958). In 1936 he helped found the Playwright's Producing Company.

Rice, John (b. 1596) English actor, who, as a boy, played female roles and appeared in 1610 in a water-pageant with Richard Burbage. He later joined the King's Men and appeared in Shakespeare's plays. He is also known to have acted in *The Duchess of Malfi* but eventually probably retired to take Holy Orders.

Rice, Thomas Dartmouth (1808–60) US vaudeville performer, who was popularly known as **Jim Crow**, after the character he created in his most famous act. His adoption of blackface make-up in the 1820s inspired the development of the minstrel show, while the success of the Jim Crow character led to appearances throughout the US and in London (1836).

Rice, Tim(othy Miles Bindon) (1944-) British lyricist, who established his reputation with a number of successful musicals during the 1970s, mostly written in collaboration with Andrew *Lloyd Webber. They include *Joseph and the Amazing Technicolor Dreamcoat* (1968), **Jesus Christ Superstar* (1970), and **Evita* (1976).

Rich, Christopher (d. 1714) British theatre manager, who acquired control of Drury Lane in 1693. He cut salaries and reduced his expenses at every opportunity, causing Betterton and most of his company to withdraw. When the Lord Chamberlain forced Rich to close the theatre, he removed to Lincoln's Inn Fields, but died before he was able to reopen the theatre there.

His son, **John Rich** (1681–1761), was an actor and succeeded his father at Lincoln's Inn Fields. He was a successful Harlequin, appearing as **Lun**, and contributed greatly to the establishment of the English pantomime. As a manager his outstanding success was *The Beggar's Opera*, which provided him with the funds to build the first theatre at *Covent Garden.

Richard II, The Tragedy of King A history play by William *Shakespeare, written c. 1595. First performance: c. 1595. The play details the downfall of the ineffectual Richard II at the hands of the pragmatic Bolingbroke; the deposition scene was omitted in early performances for fear of offending Elizabeth I. The play is especially notable for its excellent characterization and for Richard's soliloquies in prison, in which he realizes his faults and thus meets his death with a new dignity.

Richard III, The Tragedy of King A history play by William *Shakespeare, written 1592–93. First performance: c. 1593. Drawing on Holinshed, Hall, and Sir

Thomas More, the plot traces the process by which the deformed but defiant Richard seizes the throne and is then himself killed in battle by Richmond, later Henry VII. One of the most celebrated roles in the theatre, Richard III – who is depicted as a savage, brilliant, and highly complex character – has provided such actors as Kean, Garrick, Olivier, and most recently Anthony Sher with one of their greatest successes.

Richards, Elizabeth Rebecca *See* Edwin, John.

Richardson, Ian (1934-) British actor, born in Edinburgh, who was one of the founder members of the Royal Shakespeare Company in 1961. His roles with the company have included Edmund in Peter Brook's production of *King Lear* (1964), Ford in *The Merry Wives of Windsor* (1964), Coriolanus (1967), and Richard II (1973). On Broadway he appeared as Higgins in a revival of *My Fair Lady* (1976) and in a dramatic version of *Lolita* (1981); other roles have included Marat in Weiss's *Marat / Sade* (1964) and Vindice in Tourneur's *The Revenger's Tragedy* (1966).

Richardson, Sir Ralph (David) (1902– 83) British actor, who made his debut as Lorenzo in *The Merchant of Venice* in 1921, worked with the Birmingham Repertory Theatre, and came to London in Eden Phillpotts's *Yellow Sands* in 1926. After success in Barry Jackson's modern-dress production of classic plays at the Royal Court seasons at the Old Vic and Malvern he became a leading West End actor, establishing his reputation especially in the plays of Priestley and Shakespeare. As joint-director of the Old Vic Company during the legendary seasons (1944–47) at the New Theatre his stature as a great actor was confirmed with performances of such parts as Falstaff, Vanya, Peer Gynt, Cyrano, and Inspector Goole in *An Inspector Calls*. In his many subsequent appearances his unique ability to

blend pathos with eccentric good humour ensured his continued popularity in roles as varied as Dr Sloper in *The Heiress* (from a novel by Henry James) in 1949, Prospero (1951), Timon of Athens (1956), Jim Cherry in Bolt's *Flowering Cherry* (1957), Bottom (1964), Shylock (1967), Dr Rance in Orton's *What the Butler Saw* (1968), Jack in David Storey's *Home* (1970), Hirst in Pinter's *No Man's Land* (1975), and Cecil in William Douglas Home's *The Kingfisher* (1977). Also distinguished as an actor in films, he gave his final stage performance at the National Theatre as Alberto in Eduardo de Filippo's *Inner Voices* in the year he died.

Richardson, Tony (Cecil Antonio Richardson; 1928-) British director, who established his reputation during the 1950s at the Royal Court Theatre with his direction of such epoch-making plays as Osborne's *Look Back in Anger* (1956) and *The Entertainer* (1958). Similarly successful were Ionesco's *The Chairs* (1957) and initial forays into Shakespeare – notably *Othello* with Paul Robeson – at Stratford-upon-Avon (1958). His acclaimed production of Osborne's *Luther* (1961) was (like several of his other productions by such authors as Brecht and Ibsen) subsequently seen on Broadway. Vanessa Redgrave, to whom he was then married, appeared succesfully in his version of Chekhov's *The Seagull* (1964), while Nicol Williamson won great acclaim in his *Hamlet* (1969); more recent productions have included a number of Shakespearean productions and several notable films. He now lives in the US.

Richelieu, Armand-Jean du Plessis de, Cardinal (1585–1642) French statesman, who was the chief minister of Louis XIII and a patron of the arts. His private theatre, which housed Montdory's company, became one of the first professional public playhouses in France (*see* Palais-Royal, Théâtre du). He also encouraged several notable playwrights, including Corneille, Boisrobert, and Rotrou.

Richepin, Jean (1849–1926) French poet and playwright, born in Algeria. His first collection of poetry, *La chanson des gueux* (1876), brought him a month's imprisonment for its vulgar language. He wrote several successful plays, notably *Nana Sahib* (1883), written for Sarah Bernhardt, *Par le glaive* (1892), and *Le Chemineau* (1897).

Richmond Hill Theatre A theatre in Charlton Street, New York, which staged its first play in 1831. Headed by Mrs Duff, the resident company gave two successful seasons until a plague outbreak forced its closure. Productions included revivals and Sheridan Knowles's *The Hunchback*, which boldly opened on the same night as the Park Theatre's first performance of it in 1832. The theatre reopened with a season of Italian opera; subsequently it was managed by Mrs Hamblin and staged the New York debut of James E Murdoch. Between 1845 and 1848 it presented circus and variety shows, being briefly known as the **Tivoli Gardens**. It was demolished in 1849.

Richmond Theatre A theatre in Richmond, Virginia, which was built in the 1700s but burned down in 1811, claiming 72 lives. Rebuilt and opened as the **Marshall Theatre** in 1818, it staged the first US appearance of the elder Booth in 1821 and Edwin Forrest in 1841. Joseph Jefferson III was manager between 1854 and 1856. Again destroyed by fire in 1862, a very grand theatre, called the New Richmond, replaced it in 1863. It became the leading theatre of the Southern states before demolition in 1896.

riciniata A form of early Roman *fabula*, comprising a mime play. It was named after the *ricinium*, the hood worn by the actors during the performance.

Rickman, Alan (1946-) British actor, who first attracted attention during the 1978 season at Stratford-upon-Avon, his roles including Angelo in *Measure for Measure*. Subsequently he appeared at the Royal Court Theatre in Chekhov's *The Seagull* and, in 1985, enjoyed success as Le Vicomte de Valmont in Christopher Hampton's *Les Liaisons Dangereuses*.

Riders to the Sea A tragedy by J M *Synge. First performance: Abbey Theatre, Dublin, 1904. The play revolves about an old woman, Maurya, and her fatalistic acceptance of the implacable force of nature after losing all her menfolk at sea; it was adapted as an opera by Vaughan Williams in 1937.

Rifbjerg, Klaus (1931-) Danish poet, novelist, and playwright, who is the author of several plays tackling such themes as identity and the nature of theatre. His works include *Hva skal vi lave?* (What Shall We Make?; 1963), *Voks* (Wax; 1968), and *Âr* (A Year; 1970), which is set during the German occupation of Denmark.

Rigg, Diana (1938-) British actress, whose parts with the Royal Shakespeare Company, which she joined after working in repertory, have included Philipe Trincante in John Whiting's *The Devils* (1961), Cordelia in *King Lear* (1962), and Viola in *Twelfth Night* (1966). For the National Theatre Company she was Dottie in Tom Stoppard's *Jumpers*, Lady Macbeth in 1972, and Célimène in Molière's *Le Misanthrope* (1973). Among her many leading West End roles have been Hesione Hushabye in Shaw's *Heartbreak House* (1983) and, in 1987, Phyllis Stone in Sondheim's musical *Follies*; she is also well known for her television and film appearances.

Ring An octagonal building in Blackfriars Road, London, built in 1783 as the Surrey Chapel and later used as a boxing ring.

Robert Atkins brought the Bankside Players to the venue in *Henry V* in 1936, subsequently presenting *Much Ado about Nothing* and *The Merry Wives of Windsor* in celebrated theatre-in-the-round productions in 1937. The building was demolished after the World War II.

Ring Round the Moon (*L'Invitation au château*) A *pièce brillante* by Jean *Anouilh. First performance: Théâtre de l'Atelier, Paris, 1947; Christopher Fry's English translation appeared in 1950. The central characters of the play are identical twins – one cunning and cynical, the other sincere and romantic – and their matchmaking aristocratic aunt.

rise-and-sink A former method of changing an entire set, by means of which the upper half of the scenery on the stage rises into the flies and the lower half sinks into the cellar, revealing a new set behind.

Ristori, Adelaide (1822–1906) Italian actress, who became famous as a performer of tragic roles and was regarded by some as ranking with Sarah Bernhardt. She first appeared on stage as a child and was subsequently highly acclaimed in the title role of Schiller's *Maria Stuart* at the age of 18. She became leading lady with the Campagnia Reale Sarda and in 1855 her performances in Paris rivalled those of Rachel – Dumas *père* was amongst those deeply impressed by her passionate delivery in such plays as Goldoni's *La Locandiera* and Alfieri's *Mirra*. She also acted in Britain and the US, sometimes performing in romantic melodrama.

Ritchard, Cyril (1898–1977) British actor, director, and comedian, born in Australia, who became a leading star in the revues of Herbert Farjeon. He also appeared with success in Coward's revue *Sigh No More* (1945) and in plays by Congreve, Vanbrugh, and Shakespeare; he spent the last 20 years of his career in the US.

Ritterdrama A theatrical genre linked to the *Sturm und Drang* movement of the late 18th century in Germany. It was distinguished by its passion for all things medieval and plays of the genre typically depicted jousting, battles, and various other displays of chivalry and romance. Productions of such plays, which were initially inspired by the historical dramas of Goethe and Klinger, were enacted with authentic historical settings and costume. The genre fell from favour by the end of the century.

Ritz Theatre A theatre on 48th Street, New York, which opened in 1921 with Drinkwater's *Mary Stuart*. Plays by such authors as Sutton Vane and Ashley Dukes followed and in 1937 the theatre was taken over by the Federal Theatre Project. It was then used for broadcasting and reopened briefly as a theatre in the 1970s.

Rivals, The A classic comedy by *Sheridan. First performance: 1775. Captain Absolute, in love with Mrs Malaprop's niece, Lydia Languish, assumes the character of an ensign to appeal to her romantic notion of marrying a penniless young officer, rather than an heir to a baronetcy. Set in fashionable Bath, the play is best known for Mrs Malaprop herself and her linguistic foibles.

Rivas, Duke of *See* Saavedra Remírez de Baquedano, Ángel.

Riverside Studios An arts centre in Hammersmith, London, where both classic and contemporary plays are performed by resident and visiting companies. Originally a foundry, then film studios and a television centre, the arts centre opened in 1976; successes have included the Joint Stock Company's *The Ragged Trousered Philanthropists* (1978), Chekhov's *The Cherry Orchard* (1978), and *Julius Caesar* (1980), which was directed by the resident director Peter Gill. In the 1980s the theatre was taken over by United British Actors, a company organized by Albert Finney, Glenda Jackson, Harold Pinter, Diana Rigg, and Maggie Smith.

Rix, Sir Brian (Norman Roger) (1924-) British actor, who began his career with Wolfit's company in 1942. He then joined the White Rose Players at Harrogate and played in farce for the first time. After World War II he toured in Colin Morris's army farce *Reluctant Heroes*, bringing it to the Whitehall Theatre in 1950. It ran for four years and was the first of a series of long-running farces at that theatre and at the Garrick that established him as a leading comic actor. He retired in 1980 to become general secretary of MENCAP, a charity for the mentally handicapped.

Robards, Jason (1922-) US actor, who made his stage debut in 1947. In 1956 he was praised in O'Neill's *The Iceman Cometh* and as James in O'Neill's *Long Day's Journey Into Night*. His successes since then have included Manley Halliday in Budd Schulberg's *The Disenchanted* (1958), Julian Berniers in Lillian Hellman's *Toys in the Attic* (1960), Murray Burns in Herb Gardner's *A Thousand Clowns* (1962), and O'Neill's *Hughie* (1964), *A Moon for the Misbegotten* (1973), and *A Touch of the Poet* (1977).

Robbins, Jerome (1918-) US director and choreographer, who began as a dancer in London. Successful works he has choreographed have included *On the Town* (1944), *Call Me Madam* (1950), *The King and I* (1951), *The Pajama Game* (1954), *Peter Pan* (1954), *West Side Story* (1957), *Gypsy* (1959), and *Fiddler on the Roof* (1964). Since then he has concentrated on ballet.

Roberts, Rachel See Harrison, Rex (Carey).

Robert S Marx Theatre See Cincinnati Playhouse in the Park.

Robertson, Agnes Kelly (1833–1916) British actress, born in Scotland, where she first appeared as a child. She made her London debut at the Princess's Theatre with Charles Kean's company in 1851. Accompanying her lover Dion *Boucicault to the US, she became very popular as the heroine in a succession of his plays. She eventually retired in 1896. Her four children included 'Dot' and Nina Boucicault.

Robertson, T(homas) W(illiam) (1829–71) British playwright, brother of Madge *Kendal. After training with his father as an actor, he scored his first success as a playwright with *David Garrick*, which was produced at the Haymarket in 1864. *Society*, produced by the Bancrofts at the Prince of Wales' Theatre in 1865, introduced the naturalistic kind of playwriting, sometimes referred to as *cup-and-saucer drama, with which his name is associated. Subsequent triumphs, which were often staged under his own direction, paved the way for the realistic settings of much 20th-century drama; *Caste is the most frequently revived of his plays.
Principal works:
David Garrick: 1864.
Society: 1865.
Ours: 1866.
Caste: 1867.
Play: 1868.
School: 1869.

Robertson, Toby See Prospect Theatre Company.

Robeson, Paul (Bustill) (1898–1976) US Black actor, who made his first stage appearance in 1921. He established his reputation with the Provincetown Players in 1924 when he played Jim Harris in O'Neill's *All God's Chillun Got Wings*. He went on to triumph as Brutus Jones in O'Neill's *The Emperor Jones* (1930), while subsequent successes included *Show Boat* (1928), in which he sang 'Ole Man River', *Othello* (1930, 1943,

1959), and O'Neill's *The Hairy Ape* (1931). His career was blighted by hostility aroused by his Communist sympathies and his support for Black causes.

Robey, Sir George (Edward) (George Edward Wade; 1869–1954) British music hall comedian and actor, known as the **Prime Minister of Mirth**. He made his West End debut at the Oxford Music Hall in 1891 and was subsequently acclaimed for such comic characters as The Mayor of Mudcumdyke and Daisy Dilwater and as dames in pantomimes. In 1916 he was in the first of many successful revues, *The Bing Boys Are Here*, at the Alhambra. In 1932 he extended his range, playing Menelaus in A P Herbert's *Helen* at the Adelphi, and in 1935 scored a remarkable triumph as Falstaff in *Henry IV* at His Majesty's.

Robin Hood play A tradition of rural English *folk theatre, in which the adventures of the legendary outlaw and his followers were celebrated at various country festivals. The figure of Robin Hood himself may have been in part derived from the character of **Jack-in-the-Green**, who appeared in pre-Christian ritual, or else from a French tradition. Such pieces were the work of various minstrels and were presented on May Day and other key dates in the agricultural calendar together with morris dances and other simple entertainments. The genre was also a feature of court festivities in Tudor times and was eventually absorbed into pantomime.

Robins, Elizabeth (1862–1952) US actress, who became a leading interpreter of the plays of Ibsen upon the London stage, having made her first appearance there in 1889. As well as winning acclaim in such roles as Hedda Gabler (1891) and Hilda in *The Master Builder*, she promoted the British premieres of many of Ibsen's works by such troupes as Grein's Independent Theatre.

Robinson, (Esmé Stuart) Lennox (1886–1958) Irish playwright, whose first play, *The Clancy Name*, was successfully staged in 1908 at the Abbey Theatre, of which he became manager in 1910. His plays range in theme from politics to social comedy. He experimented with Symbolism and Expressionism and the influence of Pirandello is evident in the innovative form of *Church Street* (1934).

Robinson, Mary (1758–1800) British actress, who was imprisoned with her husband for debt before being engaged by Garrick at Drury Lane in 1776. In 1778 she played Perdita in *The Winter's Tale* and captivated the Prince of Wales (later George IV), eventually becoming his mistress. In 1782, however, she was crippled by rheumatic fever.

Robinson, Richard (d. 1648) English actor, who probably began as a boy actor in female roles at the Blackfriars Theatre and later joined the King's Men. He appeared in plays by Webster, Jonson, and Shakespeare, and was included in the dedicatory list prefacing the Beaumont and Fletcher Folio of 1647.

Robson, Dame Flora (1902–84) British actress, who made her debut in Clemence Dane's *Will Shakespeare* on leaving the Royal Academy of Dramatic Art in 1921. She then appeared in repertory at Oxford but failed to attract any attention until 1931, when she won great acclaim as Abbie Putnam in O'Neill's *Desire Under the Elms* and Mary Paterson in Bridie's *The Anatomist*. She consolidated her reputation in numerous classical parts – including comedy – at the Old Vic as well as in films and later went to New York as Ellen Creed in Reginald Denham and Edward Percy's *Ladies in Retirement* (1940). Among her other outstanding successes were Gwendolen Fairfax (and later Miss Prism) in *The Importance of Being Earnest* (1933), Lady Macbeth (1948), Lady Cicely Wayneflete in *Cap-*

tain Brassbound's Conversion (1948), Lesley Storm's *Black Chiffon* (1949), Miss Giddens in *The Innocents* (1952), and Miss Tina in *The Aspern Papers* (1959), the latter two being adaptations from Henry James.

Robson, Frederick (1821–64) British actor, who toured the provinces before achieving fame at the Grecian Theatre, where he sang and appeared in farces. He had three years as principal comedian at the Queen's Theatre, Dublin, but returned to London to the Olympic Theatre in 1853, becoming joint-manager there in 1857.

Rodgers, Richard *See* Hammerstein II, Oscar.

Rodríguez Buded, Ricardo (1926-) Spanish playwright, who is the author of several influential and realistic dramas on social themes. His best-known works include *La madriguera* (The Warren; 1960) and *El Charlatán* (1962).

Rogers, Paul (1917-) British actor, who worked with the Bristol Old Vic company after World War II before appearing at the Old Vic in London, where he played many leading Shakespearean roles, including Henry VIII (1953) and King Lear (1958). He also played Sir Claude Mulhammer in *The Confidential Clerk* (1953) and Lord Claverton in *The Elder Statesman* (1958), both by T S Eliot, and later Max in Pinter's *The Homecoming* (1965) for the Royal Shakespeare Company. More recent successes have included *The Importance of Being Earnest* (1982) at the National Theatre and *The Apple Cart* (1986) at the Haymarket.

Rojas, Fernando de (c. 1465–1541) Spanish writer, author of the dialogue novel *La *Celestina* (1499). His authorship of the work was uncertain for many years, partly as a result of the writer's own efforts – possibly because of the probable similarities between the situation of the heroine Me-

libea and de Rojas himself as the offspring of unwilling Jewish converts to Christianity.

Rojas Villandrando, Agustín de (1572–c. 1635) Spanish actor and playwright, best known for the dialogue novel *El viaje entretenido* (The Pleasant Voyage; 1603) in which he depicts the Spanish theatre of the period. A member of a touring company of actors, he was also the author of several of the best examples of the Spanish *loa*.

Rojas Zorrilla, Francisco de (1607–48) Spanish playwright, a contemporary of Calderón, who developed the *comedia de figurón*, in which the action revolves around an eccentric central character. His best-known play is *Del rey abajo, ninguno* (Below the King, No One; 1650), which concerns the dilemma of a country nobleman who suspects that he has been cuckolded by the king but dares not complain.

Rolland, Romain (1866–1944) French novelist, playwright, and essayist, born in Burgundy. His works for the theatre included three tragedies, notably *Aërt* (1898), a series of plays on the French Revolution, and the treatise *Le Théâtre du peuple* (1903). Rolland is chiefly remembered, however, for the novel cycle *Jean-Christophe* (1904–12). He was awarded a Nobel Prize in 1915.

Rollenhagen, Georg (1542–1609) German churchman and playwright, who was the author of three plays dealing with biblical subjects, intended for performance in schools.

His son **Gabriel Rollenhagen** (1583–1619) was a lawyer and playwright, who adapted the tale of Euryalus and Lucretia in *Amantes amentes* (1609).

Roller, Andrei Adamovich (Andreas Leongard; 1805–91) Russian scene designer, who trained in various European countries before moving to St Petersburg in 1834. There he worked in several theatres, designing numerous influential Romantic sets with atmospheric lighting effects. Later in his career he helped to restore the Winter Palace after a fire.

roll-out A loose flap of canvas cut into a piece of scenery through which a performer can roll onto the stage, thus effecting an unexpected entrance. *See also* trickwork.

Romains, Jules (Louis-Henri-Jean Farigoule; 1885–1972) Fench poet, novelist, and playwright. His best-known plays are his three satirical farces of the mid-1920s – the two *Monsieur Le Trouhadec* comedies, which follow the adventures of a geography teacher, and the internationally successful *Knock* – in which Louis Jouvet participated as actor and producer. *Knock*, which revolves around the character of a cunning quack doctor, was successfully staged in Britain in a translation by Granville-Barker. Outside the theatre, Romains is remembered from the novel cycle *Les Hommes de bonne volonté* (1932–47; translated as *Men of Good Will*).
Principal works:
L'Armée dans la ville: 1911.
Cromedeyre-le-Vieil: 1920.
Monsieur Le Trouhadec saisi par la débauche: 1923.
Knock, ou le Triomphe de la médecine: 1923; translated as *Dr Knock*, 1925; filmed 1932.
Le Mariage de Monsieur Le Trouhadec: 1925.
Le Dictateur: 1926.
Donogoo: 1930.

Roman drama The theatrical tradition of ancient Rome, which first developed in the 3rd century BC from the older Greek theatre. Most early Roman drama consisted of translations of Greek plays; notable exponents included Plautus and Terence. The theatres themselves were initially temporary, but later venues were specially built in stone and echoed Greek designs. The Greek chorus largely disappeared during Roman times and masks and costumes were extensively employed. In the later stages of the Roman era drama became more spectacular and bawdy in content and comedy was the dominant form. Eventually audiences declined and serious drama became an intellectual preoccupation for the few, of whom Seneca was one of the most significant. Christian opposition finally resulted in the closure of the theatres in the 6th century AD. *See also fabula*.

Romanoff and Juliet A comedy by Peter *Ustinov. First performance: London, 1956. A parallel to Shakespeare's *Romeo and Juliet*, it concerns a love affair between the son of a Soviet diplomat and the daughter of a US diplomat; Ustinov himself appeared in the first production.

Romans in Britain, The A play by Howard *Brenton. First performance: National Theatre, London, 1980. An allegorical examination of the Roman conquest of Britain, the play aroused considerable controversy with its linking of the Roman occupation to the presence of British forces in Northern Ireland; its scene featuring the homosexual rape of druids led to a widely-publicized (and eventually abandoned) court case.

Romantic comedy A comedy in which the high ideals of Romanticism were applied to humorous material. Sharing much in common with the Comedy of Intrigue, it began its early development in Spain and achieved its apotheosis in France, where noted practitioners included Victor Hugo and Dumas *père*. It was characterized by its weakness for extremes in both character and plot and lavish settings and costume; the language of Romantic comedy was often intensely poetic but the genre frequently tended towards melodrama.

Romashov, Boris Sergeivich (1895–1958) Soviet playwright, who was the author of several popular dramas depicting events during and after the Russian Civil War.

These included *The Fiery Bridge* (1929) and *Fighters* (1934); other works were *Meringue Pie* (1925), which attacked bourgeois values, and *Shine, Stars!* (1942), which was based on the battle for Moscow in World War II.

Romeo and Juliet A tragedy by William *Shakespeare, written c. 1595. First performance: c. 1596. The plot traces the inevitable destruction of the young lovers Romeo and Juliet as a result of the prejudice and animosity between their two families, the Montagues and the Capulets. The play was based on an old story, which in Shakespeare's hands becomes a means to expose a whole society, contrasting the innocent love of the two central characters with the earthly preoccupations of such figures as Mercutio and the Nurse. The balcony scene, in which the two lovers secretly meet, remains one of the most well-known in world theatre.

Rondiris, Dimitrios (1899–1981) Greek director, who became well known for his work with the Greek National Theatre, which he joined in the 1930s after studying with Max Reinhardt in Vienna. His modern production of *Electra* by Sophocles in 1936 heralded a long series of celebrated festivals of classic plays, while other important productions included *Hamlet* (1939); in 1957 he founded a theatre in Piraeus.

Rookery Nook A farce by Ben *Travers. First performance: Aldwych Theatre, London, 1926. The second of the Aldwych farces, it consolidated the author's reputation and has been much revived; it originally ran for 409 performances.

Room, The A one-act play by Harold *Pinter. First performance: 1957. This, Pinter's first play, set the style he was to follow with increasing mastery in subsequent works; the room itself becomes a sanctum, a retreat from the world beyond.

Roots The second and most optimistic play in a trilogy by Arnold *Wesker. First performance: Belgrade Theatre, Coventry, 1959, directed by John Dexter. Joan Plowright played Beatie Bryant, the girl who returns to her family in rural Norfolk determined to pass on what she has learnt from Ronnie (one of the characters in *Chicken Soup with Barley*) and who in the process finds a voice of her own.

rope-house *See* hand-worked house.

Roscius Gallus, Quintus (c. 120 BC–62 BC) Roman actor, considered the foremost comic actor of his time. He was praised by Cicero, being defended by him in a lawsuit, and was given honours by the dictator Sulla. He excelled in the plays of Plautus, Terence, and others and did much to enhance the social status of actors. His name later became identified with any acting of quality.

Rose, Billy *See* Nederlander Theatre.

Rosencrantz and Guildenstern are Dead A play by Tom *Stoppard. First performance: National Theatre, London, 1967. Based upon two minor characters in Shakespeare's *Hamlet*, the play is an ingenious and witty exploration of the theme of fate in the tradition of the Theatre of the Absurd.

Rosenplüt, Hans (c. 1400–c. 1470) German playwright and poet, popularly known as *der Schnepperer* (the chatterbox). A native of Nuremberg, he was the first important author of the *Fastnachtsspiel* tradition; his satirical writings include *Des Türken Vasnachtspil* (1456).

Rose Tattoo, The A play by Tennessee *Williams. First performance: New York, 1950. The play concerns a Sicilian woman who is troubled by her dead husband's infidelity until she meets a rugged truck driver.

It was filmed in 1955 with Anna Magnani and Burt Lancaster.

Rose Theatre An Elizabethan theatre built by Philip Henslowe on Bankside, London in 1587. In 1592 Strange's Men, with Edward Alleyn as the leading actor, appeared there. In between closures on account of outbreaks of plague various other companies used the theatre, including the Admiral's Men, until they removed to the Fortune in 1600. The Rose, an octagonal partly-thatched building, remained open until the lease expired in 1605 and was then pulled down.

Rosimond (Claude la Roze; c. 1640–86) French actor and playwright. After appearances at the Théâtre du Marais he worked at the Palais-Royal and was briefly considered a possible successor to Molière. He wrote only one more play, however, after joining the company.

Ross A play by Terence *Rattigan. First performance: London, 1960. It revolves around the last years of T E Lawrence, who – in a bid to escape the demands of public attention – joined the RAF at a junior rank under the name of Ross; Alec Guinness was highly acclaimed in the title role in the original production.

Ross, W G (d. 1876) British music hall performer, born in Scotland, who became an overnight success at the Cyder Cellars in the 1840s with 'Sam Hall', a grisly ballad of a condemned murderer. When, however, the novelty of 'Sam Hall' wore off, Ross fell from favour and died in obscurity.

Rosseter, Philip (c. 1575–1623) English musician and manager, under whose direction children from several disbanded companies appeared together before royalty and at the Whitefriars Theatre (1609–14). In 1615 he began the building of Porter's Hall, presenting several plays there before it was suppressed.

Rossi, Ernesto Fortunato Giovanni Maria (1827–96) Italian actor, who was highly regarded in tragic roles, especially those of Shakespeare. He appeared in Italy opposite Adelaide Ristori with success and later moved with her to Paris (1855), where he was acclaimed in such roles as Othello, Hamlet, and King Lear; he was less popular, however, with English-speaking audiences.

Rosso di San Secondo, Pier Maria (1887–1956) Italian novelist and playwright, who wrote several plays in the *grottesco* tradition. Such plays as *Marionette, che passione!* (1917), in which the actors play puppets, reflect the influence of Chiarelli and Pirandello and tackle such themes as the contrast between fantasy and reality. Others include a series based on the myth of Persephone, notably *La Scala* (The Ladder; 1926) and *Il ratto di Proserpina* (The Rape of Persephone; 1954).

Rostand, Edmond Eugène Alexis (1868–1918) French Romantic playwright and poet, who rejected the naturalist and Symbolist movements of the late 19th century. Born in Marseilles, he made his name with the comedy *Les Romanesques* (1894). This was followed by *La Princesse lointaine* (1895), *La Samaritaine* (1897), the immensely successful heroic comedy *Cyrano de Bergerac*, and the tragedy *L'Aiglon* (1900), in which Sarah Bernhardt played the central role of Napoleon's son. The allegory *Chantecler* (1910) was Rostand's last complete play, *La Dernière Nuit de Don Juan* being left unfinished at his death.

rostrum A platform of varying dimensions, used to provide different levels of staging, or a complete temporary stage. Known in the US as **parallels**, rostra are usually collapsible, thus facilitating transport and storage.

Roswitha *See* Hroswitha.

433

Rotimi, Ola (Emmanuel Gladstone Olawole; 1938-) Nigerian playwright, who is the author of several plays based upon African history. His first plays, *To Stir the God of Iron* (1963) and *Our Husband Has Gone Mad Again* (1965), were written in the US; later works include an adaptation of *Oedipus Rex* by Sophocles and *If* (1973), which was set against the background of the recent Nigerian Civil War.

Rotrou, Jean de (1609–50) French playwright, who was a friend and rival of Pierre Corneille. Rotrou's early plays, the first of which was produced at the Hôtel de Bourgogne in 1628, brought him to the attention of Cardinal de Richelieu. Inspired by classical and Spanish literature, he wrote prolifically during his short career, producing comedies, tragi-comedies, and tragedies, notably *Le Véritable Saint-Genest* (1646), *Venceslas* (1647), and *Cosroès* (1649). He spent his latter years in his native Dreux, where he held an administrative post; he died there during a plague in 1650.

Rotunda A building that once stood in Albion Place, off Blackfriars Road, London, erected to house a collection of stuffed animals and curios in 1790. It degenerated into a penny waxwork show, but by 1829 some form of entertainment was being given there, perhaps an early form of music hall. An attempt to run it as the Globe Theatre in 1833 was a failure and it resorted to music hall and boxing, being renamed the **Britannia Music Hall**. It was closed down in about 1882 after an illegal cockfight.

Round House A circular 19th-century railway building in Chalk Farm Road, Camden Town, London, which was converted into a theatre in 1968, opening with Peter Brook's experimental in-the-round production *Themes on The Tempest*. Its foundation was largely the work of Arnold Wesker, who occupied it with his **Centre 42** arts group (founded in 1960) until it was licensed as a

theatre. It became the venue for many unusual and interesting productions, varying from the nude revue *Oh, Calcutta!* (1970) to Howard Brenton's *Epsom Downs* (1977). There were also seasons by leading provincial companies, particularly the Royal Exchange Theatre, Manchester, which presented Vanessa Redgrave in Ibsen's *Lady from the Sea* (1979) and Helen Mirren in Webster's *The Duchess of Malfi* (1981). Financial pressures forced the theatre, which was reconstructed in 1979, to close in 1983. It was subsequently turned into a centre for arts of the worldwide Black community.

Rousseau, Jean-Jacques (1712–78) French philosopher and writer, born in Geneva. His contribution to the theatre is of minor importance, consisting of the opera *Le Devin du village* (1752) and the comedy *Narcisse* (1753). In his *Lettre à d'Alembert contre les spectacles* (1758), however, Rousseau attacked the proposed establishment of a theatre in Geneva, condemning the potentially dangerous influences of drama and criticizing the plays of Molière.

Rover, The A play by Aphra *Behn. First performance: 1678. Dealing with the adventures of a band of exiled English cavaliers, the play's central character, the dissolute Willmore, was probably based on the Earl of Rochester.

Rovetta, Gerolamo (1851–1910) Italian novelist and playwright, author of many plays in the *verismo tradition. His plays, which are somewhat marred by a profusion of irrelevant detail, include *La trilogia di Dorina* (1889), *I dishonesti* (1892), and the historical drama *Romanticismo* (1901), which is generally considered his finest work.

Rowe, George Fawcett (1834–89) US actor, who was highly successful in leading roles in romantic dramas during the 1860s and 1870s in both New York and London. His most famous part was Digby Grant in

James Albery's *Two Roses* (1872); later in life he was also admired in an adaptation of Dickens's *David Copperfield* and in his own version for the stage of James Fenimore Cooper's *The Last of the Mohicans*.

Rowe, Nicholas (1674–1718) English playwright and poet laureate, who wrote several much-admired tragedies. Such early works as *The Ambitious Stepmother* (1700) and *Tamerlane* (1702) were written along conventional neoclassical lines. Powerful later works, including *The Fair Penitent* (1703), *The Tragedy of Jane Shore* (1714), and *The Tragedy of Lady Jane Grey* (1715), provided fine roles for Mrs Siddons among others.

Rowley, Samuel (c. 1517–1624) English playwright and actor, whose dramatic works included two biblical plays and one concerning Richard III, none of which have survived. His one surviving play is *When You See Me, You Know Me* (1603-05), which was based on Henry VIII's reign.

Rowley, William (c. 1585–c. 1637) English actor and playwright, who specialized in clown parts. Although he wrote several plays himself, he is usually remembered for his collaboration with such writers as Dekker, Ford, Fletcher, Webster, and Middleton, with whom he wrote *The *Changeling* among others.

Royal Academy of Dramatic Art (RADA) A leading British stage school, founded in 1904 at His Majesty's Theatre by Beerbohm Tree. Later the same year RADA moved to Gower Street, where it has its own Vanbrugh Theatre. **Sir Kenneth Barnes** (1878–1957) was its principal from 1909 to 1955 and, supported by G B Shaw and others, the school has trained such leading actors as Sir John Gielgud.

Royal Adelphi Theatre *See* Adelphi Theatre.

Royal Alfred Theatre *See* West London Theatre.

Royal Amphitheatre of Arts *See* Astley's Amphitheatre.

Royal Aquarium Theatre *See* Imperial Theatre.

Royal Arctic Theatre A tradition of theatre that flourished aboard ships of the British Royal Navy in Canada during the 19th century. Performed either on board the icebound vessels themselves or in temporary buildings erected nearby, the first plays were presented around 1819 and are known to have included Garrick's *Miss in her Teens*. The tradition, in which officers and men played both male and female roles, was revived 30 years later with comedies, harlequinades, and even Shakespeare's *Hamlet* (1852). The last such performances, which often involved quite elaborate staging, were seen in 1875–76.

Royal Artillery Theatre A theatre in Woolwich, London, converted from the Barracks Chapel in 1863 to house amateur shows by members of the Royal Artillery. After a fire it reopened in 1905 as a professional theatre and became a useful venue for first class touring companies. It was damaged in World War II and finally closed in 1954.

Royal Avenue Theatre *See* Playhouse.

Royal Brunswick Theatre *See* Royalty Theatre.

Royal Circus *See* Surrey Theatre.

Royal Coburg Theatre *See* Old Vic Theatre.

Royal Court Theatre A small theatre in Sloane Square, London, which first became famous for its adventurous productions in the early 20th century. The first theatre of this name, a converted Dissenters' Chapel on the south side of the square, opened in 1870, originally called the **New Chelsea** and then the **Belgravia**, but was closed in 1887 and demolished as part of improvements to the square. The present building, designed by Walter Emden and W R Crewe, was constructed nearby on the east side of the square and opened as the Royal Court Theatre in 1888 under the joint management of Mrs John Wood and Arthur Chudleigh.

The partnership of J S Leigh, J E Vedrenne, and Granville-Barker in the years 1904–07 saw the production of 32 plays by 17 authors, including the first performances of many by G B Shaw, and established the theatre's avant-garde reputation. Subsequently, under Barry Jackson's managership (1924–28), Eden Phillpotts's *The Farmer's Wife* ran for almost three years. In the early 1930s the theatre was closed and became a cinema for a short time; it was bombed in 1940. Reopened in 1952, its next major success was Laurier Lister's revue *Airs on a Shoestring* (1954), which ran for 772 performances. In 1956 the theatre was taken over by the English Stage Company, whose artistic director George Devine introduced a number of epoch-making plays by new writers, of which John Osborne's *Look Back in Anger* (1956) and Arnold Wesker's *Chips with Everything* (1962) were among the most important. Since then the theatre has enjoyed further success with plays by such authors as Ionesco, David Storey, Edward Bond, David Hare, and Caryl Churchill and productions by visiting companies. A small experimental theatre, the **Theatre Upstairs** was added in 1969.

Royal English Opera House *See* Palace Theatre.

Royale Theatre A theatre on West 45th Street, New York, which opened in 1927. A number of musicals and straight plays were staged there before it became a broadcasting studio in 1936; it was renamed the **John Golden Theatre** from 1934 to 1940. After 1940 it reverted to live drama, successes including plays by Christopher Fry, Wilder, and Tennessee Williams. Its greatest success to date was the musical *Grease*, which ran from 1972 to 1980.

Royal Exchange Theatre A theatre in Manchester, constructed inside the Victorian Royal Exchange in 1976. The impetus for the building of the theatre came from the success of Michael Elliott's **69 Theatre Company** (founded in 1959 as the 59 Theatre Company) and its need for a permanent base in Manchester. Initially the company occupied a temporary theatre within the Exchange before the new structure – a suspended seven-sided theatre-in-the-round – opened in 1976 with Sheridan's *The Rivals*. The prestige of the company grew rapidly with a range of classic and contemporary plays, major successes including works by Chekhov, Ibsen, Webster, and Ronald Harwood. In 1984 the company made its first national tour, culminating in roof-top performances of *Hamlet* at London's Barbican Centre.

Royal Holborn *See* Holborn Empire.

Royal Hunt of the Sun, The A play by Peter *Shaffer. First performance: Chichester Festival, 1964. Set in the time of the Aztecs, the play depicts the clash of cultures resulting from the arrival of the Spanish conquistadors and culminates in the murder of the Aztec King Atahualpa on the orders of the Spanish leader, Pizarro.

Royal National Theatre A theatre complex on the South Bank of the Thames in London, containing the *Olivier Theatre, the *Lyttelton Theatre, and the *Cottesloe Theatre. The idea of a National Theatre was first aired in 1848 but the project was not taken up seriously until 1907, when the Shakespeare Memorial National Theatre

Committee was established. In 1944 a site was offered on the South Bank and Denys Lasdun was appointed to design the complex. A National Theatre Board was set up in 1962, Sir Laurence Olivier being appointed artistic director of the newly created National Theatre Company; he was succeeded by Peter Hall in 1975. In 1976 the company moved to the South Bank from its temporary home at the Old Vic Theatre, the National Theatre itself opening later that year. The three theatres opened as each in turn was completed: the Lyttelton in March 1976, the Olivier in October 1976, and the Cottesloe in March 1977. There is a small experimental National Theatre Studio at the Old Vic Annexe, from which plays are transferred periodically to the Cottlesloe. The Royal National Theatre complex includes foyer space for live music and exhibitions, bookshops, restaurant and buffet facilities, and a car park. Plays are presented in repertory and range from Shakespeare and the classics to new (and sometimes controversial) drama. The prefix Royal was added in 1988 at about the time that Hall was succeeded by Richard Eyre and David Aukin.

Royal Opera House *See* Covent Garden.

Royal Princess's Theatre *See* Glasgow Citizens' Theatre; Princess's Theatre.

Royal Shakespeare Company (RSC) A British theatre company, founded in 1960 when the company at the *Shakespeare Memorial Theatre in Stratford-upon-Avon was reorganized. Under Peter Hall, the RSC quickly established itself with its *Wars of the Roses* cycle of Shakespeare's plays in 1963 and other productions performed at Stratford and also at the Aldwych Theatre (and briefly the Arts Theatre in 1962) in London. As well as Shakespeare, the company has presented modern plays and other classics and toured internationally, its members including many of Britain's leading theatrical figures.

From 1965 to 1971 the company also included **Theatregoround**, a subsidiary touring group that presented plays at various smaller venues. In 1968 Hall was succeeded by Trevor Nunn, who opened **The Place** in London as a venue for smaller-scale productions in 1971 (later transferred to the *Other Place in Stratford). During the 1970s the company also staged acclaimed productions in London at the Warehouse (opened in 1977) and annually at the Theatre Royal in Newcastle-upon-Tyne; in 1978 Terry Hands joined as joint artistic director. In 1982 the RSC transferred its London operations to the Barbican and continued through the 1980s to win much praise despite severe financial pressures. Recent years have also seen the company's conquest of Broadway with such musical shows as *Nicholas Nickleby* and *Les Misérables*, although Stephen King's *Carrie* (1988) was less successful. The company also used the Mermaid Theatre as a London base from 1987 to 1988 and presents plays by Shakespeare's contemporaries at the Swan Theatre in Stratford.

Royal Shakespeare Theatre The Stratford-upon-Avon home of the Royal Shakespeare Company, formerly called the *Shakespeare Memorial Theatre. The present name of the theatre dates from 1961, when the newly-constituted RSC gave its inaugural season under the direction of Peter Hall. Plays from the Shakespearean repertory are performed annually from March through to the following January; highlights in an outstanding record of interesting productions have been John Barton's adaptation in 1963 of the *Henry VI* trilogy and *Richard III* as *The Wars of the Roses* and Peter Brook's startling *A Midsummer Night's Dream* in 1970. A new cycle of Shakespeare's histories was first presented in 1988. *See also* Swan Theatre.

ROYAL SOHO THEATRE

Royal Soho Theatre *See* Royalty Theatre.

Royal Standard Music Hall *See* Victoria Palace.

royalty *See* copyright.

Royalty Theatre A theatre in Well Street, London, which was opened by John Palmer and John Bannister in 1787 with *As You Like It* and Garrick's *Miss in her Teens*. It was almost immediately forced to close by the intervention of the patent theatres; later it was used for burlesque and pantomime. As the **East London Theatre** from 1813, it had limited success but burned down in 1826. Reopening as the **Royal Brunswick Theatre** in 1828, it collapsed three days later during a rehearsal, killing 15 people.

Another **Royalty Theatre** was opened in Dean Street, London, in 1840. A small theatre, designed for Fanny Kelly and her acting school, it had to have the original stage machinery removed since it proved too noisy. After closing in 1849, it was successively renamed the **Royal Soho Theatre**, the **New English Opera House**, and the **New Royalty Theatre**. Thereafter it flourished with melodrama and (in 1875) the debut of the Gilbert and Sullivan partnership with *Trial by Jury*. Subsequently it established a reputation for modern drama with plays by Ibsen, Shaw, and Brandon Thomas. Other notable productions included William Poel's version of *Measure for Measure* (1893), revivals of Maeterlinck's *Pelléas and Mélisande* and Sudermann's *Magda* (both 1900), Galsworthy's *The Pigeon* (1912), the premiere of Maugham's *Caesar's Wife* (1919) with Fay Compton, and Sean O'Casey's *Juno and the Paycock* (1925). Long runs were also enjoyed by John Drinkwater's *Bird in Hand* (1928) and Priestley's *I Have Been Here Before* (1938), which was the last great success before, damaged by bombs in World War II, the theatre was demolished (1955).

A third **Royalty Theatre** was opened in Portugal Street, London, on the site of the *Stoll Theatre in 1960. It opened with Dürrenmatt's *The Visit*, starring Alfred Lunt and Lynn Fontanne but less than a year later became a cinema and did not reopen as a theatre until 1970, when the all-male revue *Birds of a Feather* was staged. The erotic revue *Oh, Calcutta!* (1970) ran for four years, while another success was the US musical *Bubbling Brown Sugar* (1977). In 1981 the Royalty became a television studio but was later acquired by Stoll Moss Theatres Ltd as a venue for plays, concerts, and business conferences. In 1987 the newly-formed Royalty Theatre Company launched a programme of revivals of late 19th and 20th century plays. It also enjoyed success with a stage version of *Winnie-the-Pooh* (1987).

Royal Victoria Hall and Coffee Tavern *See* Old Vic Theatre.

Royal Victoria Theatre *See* Old Vic Theatre.

Rozewicz, Tadeusz (1921-) Polish poet and playwright, who has emerged as one of Poland's leading contemporary writers for the theatre. His plays include *Card Index* (1960), *Laocoon Group* (1962), and the tragicomedy *White Wedding* (1975).

Rozov, Victor Sergeyevich (1913-) Soviet playwright, actor, and director, who originally trained as an actor at Moscow's Theatre of the Revolution (1934–38). Many of his plays deal with issues facing the younger generation; the best known outside the USSR is *Vecho Zhivye* (1957), which was filmed as *The Cranes are Flying*. During World War II he set up a children's theatre in Alma-Ata, Kazakhstan, and later returned to Moscow where he became director of the Theatre of the Central House of Culture for Railwaymen.

RSC *See* Royal Shakespeare Company.

Rucellai, Giovanni (1475–1525) Italian playwright, who wrote tragedies based on classical models. A friend of Trissino, by whom he was influenced, he was the author of *Oreste* (1514) – an unfinished tragedy borrowing from Euripides, and *Rosmunda* (1516), which took a medieval story as its subject.

Rueda, Lope de (c. 1505–65) Spanish actor-manager and playwright, who was one of the most prominent figures in the early Spanish theatre. His plays, written for his own company, were noted for their natural dialogue and influenced Cervantes. He was also the author of the first examples of the brief interludes known as *pasos; longer works influenced by Italian models included *Eufemia*, *Los enganados*, and *Prendas de amor*.

Ruggeri, Ruggero (1871–1953) Italian actor, who became famous in strong romantic roles. A noted member (1891–99) of Novelli's company and later of Pirandello's troupe, he gave passionate performances in such roles as Hamlet, Iago, Aligi in D'Annunzio's *La figlia di Jorio* (1904) as well as in the plays of Pirandello, but resisted any attempts to modernize his old-fashioned acting style.

Ruggle, George (1575–1622) English playwright, who is thought to have been the author of the comedy *Ignoramus* (1615), a popular satire on the law profession written in Latin and English. Based upon Della Porta's *La Trappolaria* (1596), it was subsequently translated fully into English as *Ignoramus; or, the Academical Lawyer* (1662).

Ruis de Alarcón y Mendoza, Juan (c. 1581–1639) Spanish playwright, born in Mexico, whose well-constructed plays are notable for their strong characterization and concern with moral issues. A hunchback, who suffered much ridicule in the plays of Lope de Vega and others, he wrote a number of comedies set in Madrid, of which *La verdad Sospechosa* discussed impulsive lying, *Las paredes oyen* took as its hero a much-slandered hunchback, and *La prueba* criticized ingratitude.

run A series of performances of a single play on successive nights, the length of which is commonly regarded as an indication of a play's success. The record for the world's longest run is held by Agatha Christie's *The Mousetrap*, which ran for 21 years at the Ambassadors Theatre before transferring to St Martin's Theatre in 1974. The world's longest-running comedy was *No Sex Please We're British*, which opened in 1971 and closed in 1987.

Rundhorizont *See* cyclorama.

runway A narrow extension of the stage over the pit or into the auditorium, along which a performer can walk.

RUR A play by Karel Čapek. First performance: Prague, 1921. A study of the dangers inherent in a society dominated by technology, which is then used as a weapon to control the population, *RUR* – short for Rossum's Universal Robots – was much influenced by German Expressionism and incorporated elements of revue; it also introduced the word 'robot' into the language.

Rural Dionysia Religious festivals held annually (in December) in ancient Greece in honour of *Dionysus, shortly before the Lenaea and the City Dionysia. These local festivals probably included drama contests featuring both new plays and revivals of better-known older works.

Russell, Fred (Thomas Frederick Parnell; 1862–1957) British ventriloquist, who made his first music hall appearance in 1896. With his cheeky doll, Coster Joe, he toured the world for 40 years and was a founder of the Variety Artists' Federation.

Russell, George William *See* AE.

Russell, Willy (1947-) British playwright, whose plays draw heavily upon his Liverpool background. They include a musical about the Beatles, *John, Paul, George, Ringo... and Bert* (1974), *Breezeblock Park*, *One for the Road*, *Stags and Hens*, and – most successful of all – *Educating Rita* (1980), which depicts the relationship between a tired university tutor and a young girl from whom he manages to learn far more than he is able to teach. In 1983 his acclaimed musical *Blood Brothers*, highlighting the gulf between rich and poor in contemporary Britain, transferred from the Liverpool Playhouse to the West End. Plays since then include *Shirley Valentine* (1986).

Russell Street Theatre *See* Melbourne Theatre Company.

Rutebeuf (c. 1245 – c. 1285) French poet and jongleur, who wrote comic monologues and witty poems characterized by biting satire. Little is known of his life and it is possible that the name Rutebeuf was a pseudonym. He was the author of one of the earliest miracle plays, *Le Miracle de Théophile*, in which the Virgin Mary intervenes to save a priest who has sold his soul to the devil.

Rutherford, Dame Margaret (1892– 1972) British actress, who began her career at the Old Vic in 1925. 15 years later, with much provincial repertory experience behind her, she enjoyed success as Bijou Furze in M J Farrell and John Perry's *Spring Meeting* (1938). The following year she excelled as Miss Prism in Gielgud's production of *The Importance of Being Earnest* and from then on specialized in playing quirky yet shrewd middle-aged ladies. Among her other roles were Madame Arcati in Coward's *Blithe Spirit* (1941), the headmistress in John Dighton's *The Happiest Days of Your Life* (1948), Lady Wishfort in Congreve's *The*

Way of the World (1953), and Mrs Candour in Sheridan's *The School for Scandal* (1962). She appeared in many films, notably as Agatha Christie's Miss Marple.

Ruy Blas A verse drama by Victor *Hugo. First performance: Paris, 1838. The valet Ruy Blas enters the Spanish court in the guise of his master's cousin; he wins the love of the queen and is appointed prime minister, but commits suicide when his true identity is revealed.

Ruzzante, Il *See* Beolco, Angelo.

Ryga, George (1932-) Canadian playwright, who is best known for *The Ecstacy of Rita Joe* (1967), which depicts the tragic death of a Red Indian girl and, like most of his other plays, includes folksongs and dances. His other works have ranged from *Nothing But a Man* (1966), which recounts the life of García Lorca, to the controversial *Captives of the Faceless Drummer* (1971), which explores the theme of urban violence.

S

Saavedra Remírez de Baquedano, Ángel, Duke of Rivas (1791–1865) Spanish poet, playwright, and statesman, who was one of the founders of the Romantic movement in Spain. Influenced by Victor Hugo, he was the author of *Don Álvaro, o la fuerza del sino* (1835), which was the first great Romantic drama of the Spanish theatre. Other plays included several unremarkable costume dramas.

Sabbattini, Nicola (1574–1654) Italian stage designer, who wrote the influential theatrical treatise *Pratica di fabricar scene e machine ne'teatri* (1638), which included details of contemporary stage lighting. He was also the designer of a theatre at Pesaro.

Sacchi, Antonio (1708–88) Italian actor of the *commedia dell'arte*, who appeared in the role of Truffaldino. He led his own touring company, performing in Venice and throughout Europe, and presented plays by both Gozzi and Goldoni, who wrote *Il servitore di due padrone* (The Servant of Two Masters; 1746) especially for him.

Sachs, Hans (1494–1576) German playwright, a leading figure among the *meistersängers* and subsequently the central figure of Wagner's opera *Die Meistersinger von Nürnberg*. A cobbler by trade, he wrote numerous rustic comic plays of the *Fastnachtsspiel* tradition as well as many moralistic tragedies and comedies. He is known to have directed the actors himself and to have installed them in what was effectively the country's first theatre.

Sackville, Thomas (fl. 1590–1613) English actor, who toured Europe with the English Comedians before forming his own group, which enjoyed the patronage of the Duke of Brunswick from 1596 to 1613. Speaking a mixture of English, German, and Dutch, he created the popular clown **Jan Bouschet** (or **Jean Posset**).

Sackville, Thomas, First Earl of Dorset (1536–1608) English poet and playwright, who collaborated with Thomas Norton in writing *Gorboduc, the first English tragedy in blank verse. He is generally assumed to have written the last two acts; his other writings included poems for *A Mirror for Magistrates* (1563).

sacra rappresentazione A form of early Italian religious drama, equivalent to the mystery play in England and France and the *auto sacramental* in Spain. Incorporating the *lauda and derived from the earlier liturgical drama, the *sacra rappresentazione* developed chiefly in Florence and consisted of dramatic re-enactments of biblical stories. Writers of such pieces included Feo Belcari,

Savonarola, and Lorenzo de' Medici. Eventually it became increasingly secular in form and was absorbed into the more classically-orientated drama of the 15th century.

saddle-iron A flat metal strip, known in the US as a **sill-iron**, which is fastened across the bottom of any flat with a large opening in it to give it greater rigidity.

Sá de Miranda, Francisco de See Miranda, Francisco de Sá de.

Sadler's Wells Theatre A theatre in Finsbury, North-East London, built in 1927–31 on a site that in the 17th century was a popular spa. The original Sadler's Wells was the wooden Musick House erected in 1683 by Thomas Sadler, in whose grounds a medicinal well had been discovered; under subsequent ownership, however, the place was badly neglected. In 1746 a local builder, Thomas Rosoman, built a new stone theatre and restored its popularity. For 10 years from 1772, it was managed by Thomas King, who had been associated with the Drury Lane Theatre and brought with him a fashionable audience. Joseph Grimaldi played at the Wells between 1781 and 1828, while in 1804 Edmund Kean appeared as a young boy in one of the nautical spectacles that caused the theatre to be renamed the **Aquatic Theatre** for a time. A false alarm of fire in 1807 resulted in the deaths of 20 people.

In 1844 Sadler's Wells was let to Samuel Phelps and Mary Warner, who presented no less than 34 of Shakespeare's plays there. After 1871, however, the theatre degenerated into a skating rink, a pickle factory, and then a boxing arena; it was closed in 1878. Revived briefly by Mrs Bateman and her daughter Kate, it later became a house of melodrama and a music hall, before closing again in 1906. Lilian Baylis opened the current building in 1931 in co-ordination with the Old Vic Theatre, but from 1934 onwards the Wells became devoted solely to opera and ballet. Its ballet company transferred to Covent Garden in 1946, as did the later Sadler's Wells Theatre Ballet, combining to form the Royal Ballet in 1957; in 1968 the resident Sadler's Wells Opera Company moved to the **Coliseum**. The theatre is now used by touring and foreign companies. The original well is concealed under a trap door at the rear of the stalls.

Sadovsky, Prov Mikhailovich (Prov Mikhailovich Yermilov; 1818–72) Russian actor, who began his career in Tula as a child and later appeared at the Maly Theatre in Moscow. He was particularly successful giving realistic performances in the plays of Ostrovsky.

safety curtain A fireproof curtain, also known as an **iron**, designed to reduce the risk of a fire in the stage area spreading to the auditorium. The first safety curtain in Britain was installed at Drury Lane in 1794.

sainete A short comic entertainment given during performances of full-length dramas in Spain chiefly during the 17th century. Such interludes featured music, urban themes, and some satirical content; notable authors included Ramón de la Cruz in the 18th century. The tradition has been revived periodically in modern Spanish drama and foreshadowed the *género chico*.

Saint-Denis, Michel Jacques (1897–1971) French director and actor, who founded the celebrated Compagnie des Quinze in 1930. The nephew of Jacques Copeau, he trained under him at the Vieux-Colombier before founding the Compagnie des Quinze and working with it as both director and actor in notable productions of plays by such authors as André Obey. After the company was broken up in 1936 he worked in London with such actors as Olivier and Gielgud on major plays by Shakespeare, Chekhov, Lorca, and others and founded the **London Theatre Studio** (1936–

39) to further drama study. After World War II he taught drama and directed at the Old Vic, founded the Centre Dramatique de l'Est in Strasbourg, and worked with the Vivian Beaumont Theatre Project in New York. Subsequently he collaborated (from 1962) with the Royal Shakespeare Company on plays by Brecht and others and also worked in Canada.

Sainte-Beuve, Charles-Augustin (1804–69) French theatre critic, who was famous for his 'Monday articles', written for several leading French journals. He championed the plays of Victor Hugo (becoming the lover of Hugo's wife) and much admired the actor Molé.

Saint-Étienne, Comédie de *See Décentralisation Dramatique.*

St George *See* mummers' play.

St George's Theatre A London theatre modelled on Elizabethan lines, complete with balconied stage, in a former church in Tufnell Park. It was founded by the actor George Murcell in 1976 with the aim of presenting Shakespearean plays in a form resembling their original productions. There is a strong emphasis on educational work and schools make up a large part of the audiences.

Saint-Germain fairground *See* fair.

Sainthill, Loudon (1919–69) Australian stage designer, born in Tasmania, who became famous for his romantic settings for the plays of both Shakespeare and modern playwrights. He worked at the Shakespeare Memorial Theatre and the Old Vic, his most acclaimed designs including those for *The Tempest* (1951), *Pericles* (1958), *Othello* (1959), Tennessee Williams's *Orpheus Descending* (1959), and Wilde's *A Woman of No Importance* (1953).

St James's Theatre A London theatre in King Street, St James's. It was built by the famous tenor, John Braham (1777–1856) to designs by Samuel Beazley and opened in 1835 with the burletta *Agnes Sorel*. In spite of attempts by succeeding managements that presented opera, French companies, burlesques, dramas, and magic shows, as well as appearances by such stars as Rachel, Fanny Kemble, and Ristori, and the triumph of Louisa Herbert in *Lady Audley's Secret* (1862), the theatre did not achieve stability until the joint management of Hare and the Kendals in 1879. In 1891 George Alexander began a celebrated period of management that established the St James's as the criterion of distinguished elegant theatre until his death in 1918. His productions included Wilde's *Lady Windermere's Fan* (1892) and *The Importance of Being Earnest* (1895); Pinero's *The Second Mrs Tanqueray* (1893) and *His House in Order* (1906); Anthony Hope's *The Prisoner of Zenda* (1896); and Stephen Phillips's *Paolo and Francesca* (1902). Gilbert Miller took over the lease in 1918 and subsequent notable productions included Lonsdale's *The Last of Mrs Cheyney* (1925), Emlyn Williams's *The Late Christopher Bean* (1933), and Turgenev's *A Month in the Country* (1943). After World War II, first John Clements then Laurence Olivier staged highly acclaimed seasons, while in 1954 Terence Rattigan's *Separate Tables* began a two year run. In spite of a vigorous campaign to save it, the theatre was, however, sold to a building speculator in 1957 and eventually replaced by an office block.

St James Theatre A theatre on West 44th Street between Broadway and Eighth Avenue in New York, which opened as **Erlanger's Theatre** in 1927. In 1932 it was renamed the St James. Productions staged there have included Goldsmith's *She Stoops to Conquer* (1928), Feuchtwanger's *Jew Süss* (1930), *Oklahoma!* (1943), *The King and I* (1951), Osborne's *Luther* (1963), *Hello,*

Dolly! (1964), Molière's *The Misanthrope* (1975), and *Barnum* (1980). Notable Shakespearean productions have numbered amongst them Margaret Webster's *Richard II* (1937), *Hamlet* (1938), and *Twelfth Night* (1940), all with Maurice Evans. For a brief period in the 1930s the theatre housed light opera.

Saint Joan A play by G B *Shaw, regarded as one of his finest. First performance: New York, 1923. Based on the story of the trial and death of Joan of Arc, the play discusses nationalism, protestantism, and the aristocracy. Joan's death is depicted as being the inevitable conclusion of her rebellion against the feudal state and threats against the spiritual authority of the church. In the epilogue Shaw sets out the arguments for Joan's canonization.

Saint-Laurent fairground *See* fair.

St Martin's Hall *See* Queen's Theatre.

St Martin's Theatre One of the smaller London theatres, planned as a twin to the Ambassadors Theatre but not completed until 1916. C B Cochran was the theatre's first lessee and manager (1916–20); subsequently the theatre experimented with matinée performances, known as 'The Playbox Theatre' (1923–24). In the 1920s plays by Clemence Dane and John Galsworthy were presented, while another major success was Arnold Ridley's *The Ghost Train* (1925). Thereafter a mixed selection of plays was staged and over the years St Martin's has acquired a history of short runs and transfers. A recent major success was Anthony Shaffer's *Sleuth* (1970) with Anthony Quayle, which ran for three years before being transferred to the Garrick Theatre. Agatha Christie's *The Mousetrap* was transferred from the Ambassadors Theatre in March 1974 to continue its record-breaking run.

St Martin's Theatre in Melbourne, Australia was founded in 1931 as the Melbourne Little Theatre and run on an amateur basis. It acquired its present name in 1962 and was noted for productions of Australian plays, especially works by Hal Porter. The theatre failed to prosper commercially and since 1973 it has been leased to the Melbourne Theatre Company.

saint play A type of play derived from the medieval liturgical drama. Focusing on various episodes in the lives of such saints as Nicholas and Paul, the plays were performed in England and France by laymen and clergy alike, despite the fact that they were not directly connected with the liturgy.

Saint's Day A drama by John *Whiting. First performance: London, 1951. Characterized by dark humour and violence, this controversial discussion of religious conversion anticipated the challenging drama of the late 1950s at the Royal Court Theatre and elsewhere.

Salacrou, Armand (1899-) French playwright and journalist, born in Rouen. After a number of unsuccessful Surrealist plays he found favour with the public and critics with the comedy *Atlas-Hôtel*, produced at the Théâtre de l'Atelier. His subsequent works include the farcical *Histoire de rire*, the historical drama *La Terre est ronde*, and *Les Nuits de la colère*, which centres on the activities of the Resistance in German-occupied Chartres.
Principal works:
Atlas-Hôtel: 1931.
L'Inconnue d'Arras: 1935; translated as *The Unknown Woman of Arras*.
Un homme comme les autres: 1936.
La Terre est ronde: 1938.
Histoire de rire: 1939; translated as *No Laughing Matter*.
Les Nuits de la colère: 1946; translated as *Nights of Wrath*.
L'Archipel Lenoir: 1947; translated as *The Honour of the Family*.
Une femme trop honnête: 1956.

Salisbury Court Theatre The last London theatre to be built before the Civil War, erected south of Fleet Street. It was used by the King's Men (1629–31), Princes Charles's Men (1631–35), and Queen Henrietta's Men (1637–42). Players attempted clandestine performances there during the Commonwealth, but the theatre was wrecked by soldiers in 1649. Refurbished by Beeston after the Restoration, various companies, including Rhodes's and Davenant's, performed there until its destruction in the Great Fire of 1666.

Salle des Machines A large theatre in the Tuileries, Paris, built in 1660 as a venue for entertainments celebrating the marriage of Louis XIV. Designed by Vigarani, it was subsequently used for elaborate stage productions, notably under the influence of Servandony, and was briefly the home of the Comédie-Française in the 1770s.

Salles, Aurélia de (16th century) French actress, the first woman known by name to appear on the French stage. She is recorded as having appeared on stage with a company in Mâcon in 1581.

Salmacida Spolia A masque by Sir William *Davenant. First performance: 1640. Designed by Inigo Jones and celebrating the reign of Charles I, this was the last court masque to be staged in England and included Charles himself and Queen Henrietta Maria amongst its participants.

Salom, Jaime (1925-) Spanish playwright, who established a reputation initially as a writer of comedies but has since won acclaim for serious dramas. *La casa de las Chivas* (1968) recalls the Spanish Civil War, while *Los delfines* (The Dauphins; 1969) examines contemporary society; more recent works include *El corto vuello del gallo* (1980).

Salomé A tragedy by Oscar *Wilde. First performance: Paris, 1896. A version of the story of the beheading of John the Baptist at the request of Salomé, who is portrayed as a dissipated neurotic, it was banned in England until 1931.

saltica A form of Roman *fabula*. It consisted of a play in which the chorus sang the text and the *pantomimus* mimed the action.

Saltikov-Shchedrin, Mikhail Evgrapovich (1826–89) Russian novelist and playwright, noted for his satirical writings on Tsarist Russia. His play *The Death of Pazukhin*, not performed until 1901, was a typical attack on official corruption; it was later revived by the Moscow Art Theatre (1914).

Salvini, Tommaso (1829–1915) Italian actor, who became famous for his playing of Othello in Italian. Having first appeared on stage at the age of 14 he was trained by Gustavo Modena and went on to establish his reputation opposite Adelaide Ristori in Alfieri's *Oreste* (1848). He was also fairly successful as Hamlet (in which role he appeared many times) but enjoyed his greatest success as a particularly forceful Othello in 1856, later repeating the role in many countries (in 1886 to the Iago of Edwin Booth). Other Shakespearean roles included Macbeth (1876) and Lear (1884). His habit of long study of the parts he was to play was referred to with approval by Stanislavsky in his influential book *My Life in Art*.

Sam H Harris Theatre A theatre on Broadway, New York, which originally opened as a cinema in 1914 and, as the **Candler Theatre**, also presented such plays as Elmer Rice's *On Trial* (1914) and Galsworthy's *Justice* (1916). It was renamed the **Cohan and Harris Theatre** in 1916, and the Sam H Harris Theatre in 1921. John Barrymore made theatrical history there in 1922 when he played Hamlet a record 101 times. After 1932 it became a cinema.

Samson, Joseph-Isidore (1793–1871) French actor, who – as a teacher at the Conservatoire – trained Rachel in the French classical tradition. He was himself highly popular as an actor at the Odéon (1819–26) and subsequently at the Comédie-Française and the Palais-Royal and influenced the revival of French tragedy.

Sam S Shubert Theatre A theatre on West 44th Street, New York, which opened in 1918 with *Hamlet*, starring Forbes-Robertson. The theatre was initially intended for musicals but a number of successful straight plays were staged there, including several produced by the Theatre Guild. Among the musicals were *Bloomer Girl* (1944), *Paint Your Wagon* (1951), *Stop the World – I Want to Get Off* (1962), *Promises, Promises* (1968), *A Little Night Music* (1973), and *A Chorus Line* (1975).

San Diego National Shakespeare Festival A festival of Shakespearean drama, founded in 1950 in San Diego, California at the Old Globe Theatre, which was constructed on the lines of the Elizabethan stage. Ben Greet presided over the first festival; recent years have seen the building of a new theatre to house the festival and the use of professional rather than amateur performers.

San Francisco Mime Theatre A US theatre company founded in 1959 to present political dramas and adaptations of *commedia dell'arte* sketches in San Francisco parks. The group wrote their own sketches after 1970, drawing on such varied sources as minstrel shows, vaudeville, melodrama, spy films, and television detective series.

Sanger's Grand National Amphitheatre *See* Astley's Amphitheatre.

Sans Pareil *See* Adelphi Theatre.

Sans Souci A theatre established by Charles Dibdin in the Strand, London in 1791. Five years later he moved to new premises off Leicester Square, opening with a topical show, *The General Election*. He gave three performances a week there during the winter months until 1804. The theatre then continued to be used for a variety of theatrical entertainments before becoming a warehouse and a hotel; it was demolished in 1898. *See also* Niblo's Garden.

Saracen's Head Inn A tavern in Islington in London, where plays were staged in the 16th century. One of the earliest such theatrical venues, it was much altered in the early 17th century.

Sarat, Agnan (d. 1613) French actor, who won fame when an old man as the leading comedian with Valleran-Lecomte's company. Earlier in his career he brought his own company to Paris in 1578 and installed it at the Hôtel de Bourgogne for a time before returning to the provinces.

Sardou, Victorien (1831–1908) French playwright, whose *well-made plays are characterized by complicated plots and spectacular theatrical effects. His first play was a failure, but after the success of *Les Pattes de Mouche* in 1860 he wrote prolifically, producing 20 plays during the next six years and some 50 more before his death. Sardou's works were very popular in their time but were subsequently attacked by critics, notably George Bernard Shaw, who categorized them under the disparaging label 'sardoodledom'. His most popular dramas included *Fédora* (1882), *La Tosca* (1887), and *Madame Sans-Gêne* (1893).

Sarment, Jean (Jean Bellemère; 1897–1976) French playwright and actor, whose melancholy comedies, which have been likened to those of Alfred de Musset, discuss the conflict between illusion and reality. They include *Le Pêcheur d'ombres* (The Fisher of Shadows; 1921), *Le Mariage d'Hamlet* (1922), *Je suis trop grand pour moi* (1924), *Léopold le Bien-Aimé* (1927), *Bobard* (1930), and *Le Discours des prix* (1934).

Saroyan, William (1908–81) US playwright and novelist, who began his theatrical career in management at the Lyceum Theatre (1941). After the Theatre Guild staged his one-act play *My Heart's in the Highlands* (1939), he went on to enjoy success with such plays as *The *Time of Your Life* (1939), *Love's Old Sweet Song* (1940), *Hello, Out There* (1942), *Get Away, Old Man* (1943), *The Cave Dwellers* (1957), and *Sam, The Highest Jumper of Them All* (1960), several of which were notable for their innovative structure and elements of fantasy.

Sarrazin, Maurice (1925–72) French director, who founded one of the most important companies established under the *Décentralisation Dramatique* policy. Le Grenier de Toulouse, founded in 1945, began as an amateur organization and established its reputation with its production of Shakespeare's *The Taming of the Shrew*; subsequently it also presented much new drama.

Sarthou, Jacques (1920–) French actor and director, who founded his own company in 1952 to present drama to working-class audiences throughout France. He established his reputation as an actor in Vilar's production of T S Eliot's *Murder in the Cathedral* in 1945; plays presented by his own company have included works by Giraudoux, Hugo, Molière, and Musset.

Sartre, Jean-Paul(-Charles-Aymard) (1905–80) French novelist, playwright, and philosopher, who began writing for the theatre during World War II. His plays, which are characterized by moral conflict and pessimism, exploit the theatrical devices of melodrama and suspense while expounding existentialist principles. *Les Mouches* was a reworking of the story of Orestes, *Le Diable et le Bon Dieu* was based on Goethe, and *Kean* was an adaptation of Dumas *père's* play. Sartre also wrote a number of film scenarios, notably *L'Engrenage*, which was adapted for the theatre in 1969. In 1964 he refused a Nobel Prize.

Principal dramatic works:

Les Mouches: 1953.

*Huis-Clos: 1944; translated as *In Camera*.

Morts sans sépulture: 1946; translated as **Men Without Shadows*.

La Putain respectueuse: 1946.

Les Mains sales: 1948.

Le Diable et le Bon Dieu: 1951.

Kean: 1953.

*Nekrassov: 1955.

Les Séquestrés d'Altona: 1959; translated as **Altona*.

Sastre, Alfonso (1926-) Spanish playwright and novelist, whose first play *Escuadra hacia la muerte* (The Condemned Squad; 1953) was banned by the authorities for its anti-militarist content. Later works, although seldom performed in his native country because of his political stance, include *La mordaza* (1954), *Muerte en el barrio* (Death in the Neighbourhood; 1955), *El cuervo* (The Raven; 1957), *La cornada* (The Death Thrust; 1960), and *En la red* (1960), which concerns Algeria's struggle for independence.

Satin Slipper, The (*Le Soulier de satin*) A play by Paul *Claudel, written in 1924 and regarded as his best. First performance: Comédie-Française, Paris, 1943. Set in the late 16th century, the play centres on two lovers who resist their earthly love in order to attain Christian salvation.

satire A form of comedy in which the humour is directed at a particular target with the aim of ridiculing it. A satirical element was, according to Aristotle, an aspect of the earliest classical tradition through the inclu-

sion of songs making fun of unpopular public figures; indeed, it has been suggested that the use of masks in comedy was a means of allowing an actor to make such criticism without being identified.

Aristophanes was the first great writer of satirical comedy, his targets including the army, national leaders, contemporary thinkers, and fellow playwrights; subsequent victims of satire have ranged from the petty and mean to the vainglorious and idealistic. Satire, which has traditionally been perceived by various authorities as a particularly subversive form of drama, began its development in the Middle Ages with the emergence of the mystery play; by the time of Jonson it had become an essential feature of the main comic tradition in European drama. Subsequently it added extra piquancy to the comedies of Molière, whose targets included greed, snobbery, and quack doctors.

The Restoration saw the resurgence of satire in England, after which it became increasingly political in nature. One of the most notorious uses of satire to lampoon politicians occurred in Gay's *The Beggar's Opera* (1728), which attacked Sir Robert Walpole's government so virulently that parliament was persuaded to tighten controls on the theatre in general in 1737.

The 20th century has witnessed the gradual freeing of comedy from such bonds and consequently a new role for satirical drama. Whereas the Victorians restrained the disguised satires of Oscar Wilde and punished the author himself, modern society has – with the exception of some authoritarian states – learnt to absorb satire and to regard it as a creative force, highlighting faults and challenging complacency.

Satire, Theatre of A theatre in Moscow, founded in 1924 as a home of revue. It soon developed a programme of satire and comedy, notably under Gorchakov and subsequently Pluchek, who diversified with productions of plays by Shaw, Gogol, and others. In the 1960s the resident company was rehoused in a larger theatre nearby.

satyr-play A farcical dramatic entertainment of the ancient Greek theatre, comprising an obscene burlesque of the adventures of various legendary heroes, notably Hercules. Usually the work of the same author who wrote the trilogy of tragedies with which it was performed at the Dionysia, the satyr-play always included a chorus of satyrs, borrowed from the cult of *Dionysus, who appeared as half human and half beast. The first writer of the satyr-play in Athens was, by tradition, Pratinus of Phlius; subsequent practitioners of the form numbered amongst them Euripides (author of *Cyclops*, the only intact surviving satyr-play), Aeschylus, and Sophocles. Aristotle claimed that Greek tragedy was directly descended from the satyr-play.

Saunders, James (1925-) British playwright, who established his reputation with *Next Time I'll Sing to You* (1962), a one-act play about the hermit Alexander James Mason. Other well-received one-act plays have included *Alas, Poor Fred* (1959), the Absurdist *Who Was Hilary Maconochie?* (1963), *After Liverpool* (1970), *Games* (1971), *Savoury Meringue* (1971), *Bye Bye Blues* (1973), and *Birdsong* (1979), many being first performed by the Questors Theatre.

Among his full-length plays have been *A Scent of Flowers* (1964), depicting events following a suicide, the children's play *The Travails of Sancho Panza (1969), The Island* (1975), *Bodies* (1977) – a very successful drama in which couples meet again after changing partners years previously, *The Girl in Melanie Klein* (1980), based upon Ronald Harwood's novel about a mental asylum, and *Fall* (1984). Saunders has also, together with the author, successfully dramatized Iris Murdoch's novel *The Italian Girl* (1967).

Saunderson, Mary (d. 1712) English actress, wife of Thomas Betterton. One of the first women to appear on the English stage, she excelled as Ianthe in *The Siege of Rhodes* by Davenant and was admired by Pepys and many others.

Saurin, Bernard-Joseph (1706–81) French playwright and lawyer, son of the mathematician Joseph Saurin. His dramatic works include the comedy *Les Moeurs du temps* (1759), the tragedies *Spartacus* (1760) and *Blanche et Guiscard* (1763) – inspired by James Thomson's *Tancred and Sigismunda* – and *Beverley* (1768), a *drame bourgeois* based on Edward Moore's *The Gamester*.

Saved A play by Edward *Bond. First performance: Royal Court Theatre, 1965. The Lord Chamberlain's refusal to grant the play a licence helped to accelerate the abolition of theatre censorship. The original controversy centred on the stoning of a baby in a pram, one of the more violent images deployed by Bond to express his view of contemporary British society.

Saville Theatre A theatre in Shaftesbury Avenue, London, built in 1931; the front elevation is distinguished by a frieze in bas-relief entitled *Drama through the Ages* by the sculptor Gilbert Bayes. It opened with H F Maltby and Clifford Grey's musical play *For the Love of Mike* and for the next few years pursued a successful policy of musical comedy and revue. Among interesting plays staged there later were Shaw's *Geneva* (1938) and Priestley's *Johnson over Jordan* (1939). John Clements staged a two-year season of classical plays from 1955, while subsequent productions included Ustinov's *Photo Finish* (1962) and the musical *Pickwick* (1963); actors who have appeared there include Emlyn Williams, the Redgraves, Paul Scofield, and Laurence Olivier. The theatre was converted into twin cinemas in 1970.

Savoy Theatre A theatre in the Strand in London, built specifically for the production of Gilbert and Sullivan comic operas. It was financed by Richard D'Oyly Carte and was the first theatre in the world to be lit by electricity. It opened in 1881 with *Patience*, which was followed by *Iolanthe* (1882), *Princess Ida*, *The Sorcerer*, and *Trial by Jury* (all 1884), *The Mikado* (1885), *Ruddigore* (1887), *The Yeomen of the Guard* (1888), *The Gondoliers* (1889), and *Utopia Limited* (1893). After a row over the expenses incurred for *The Gondoliers*, Gilbert and Sullivan became estranged and their last joint production, *The Grand Duke* (1896), was a failure. Subsequently the theatre was run by J E Vedrenne and Harley Granville-Barker, who presented a series of Shakespeare plays. Henry Brodribb Irving was lessee for nine years from 1910, playing Hamlet there in 1917. Later successes included Sherriff's *Journey's End* (1929) and, after the theatre was converted into a two-tier auditorium, revivals of Gilbert and Sullivan. A wartime success was *The Man Who Came to Dinner* (1941), with Robert Morley; more recent triumphs have been William Douglas-Home's *The Secretary Bird*, Michael Frayn's *Noises Off*, and the Royal Shakespeare Company's *Kiss Me Kate*.

Scala, Flamineo (fl. 1600–21) Italian actor-manager, popularly known as **Flavio**. He was an important member of the Confidenti *commedia dell'arte* group and was the author of a collection of scenarios entitled *Il teatro delle favole rappresentative* (1611).

Scala Theatre A theatre in Tottenham Street, London, which opened as the **King's Concert Rooms** in 1772. Converted into a theatre in 1802, it underwent several changes of management and name during the first half of the 19th century, becoming in turn the **Tottenham Street Theatre**, the **Regency**, the **West London**, and the **Fitzroy Theatre**. A rival of the patent theatres, its reputation had sunk so low by 1885 that it was widely referred to as the **Dust Hole**, until Marie Wilton (later, Lady Bancroft) took it over. She renamed it the Prince of Wales's and transformed it into one of the most respected theatres in town, introducing the new cup-and-saucer dramas of T W Robertson. The theatre did not long survive the Bancrofts' departure in 1880 after 14 successful years. It was ultimately demolished and replaced by a new Scala Theatre which opened in 1905 with J R Fyffe's *The Conquerors*. In spite of one or two respectable runs, including W G Wills's *A Royal Divorce* (1906) and Matheson Lang in *The Purple Mask* (1918), the theatre had little success. It was often given over to amateur shows, dance exhibitions, and films. After World War II, occasional seasons were staged by the D'Oyly Carte opera company and it was used for Christmas revivals of *Peter Pan*. It was demolished in 1972.

Scammacca, Ortensio (1562–1648) Italian playwright, one of the leading writers of Jesuit drama in Italy. He was the author of about 50 plays in the tradition, in all of which the religious content is paramount.

Scamozzi, Vincenzo (1552–1616) Italian architect, whose numerous influential buildings included several theatres. He was a pupil of Andrea Palladio and completed work on the Teatro Olimpico in Vicenza following Palladio's death in 1580; other important theatres included the court theatre at Sabbioneta (1588–90) with its horseshoe-shaped auditorium.

Scapino A character of the *commedia dell'arte*, one of the *zanni*. A cowardly rogue, Scapino (conventionally dressed in green and white) was first played by Gabrielli and ultimately evolved into the cunning and unprincipled Scapin of the Comédie-Italienne, as portrayed in Molière's *Les Fourberies de Scapin* (1671).

Scaramuccia A character of the *commedia dell'arte*, one of the *zanni*. Initially similar to Il *Capitano in character, Scaramuccia was transformed by Fiorillo (who played the role without a mask and dressed in black) into the comic valet Scaramouche of the Comédie-Italienne.

Scarron, Paul (1610–60) French playwright, poet, and novelist, born in Paris. Partially paralysed by rheumatism, he began writing for the theatre in 1643, producing two farces for Jodelet and other plays inspired by Spanish works. In 1652 he married Françoise d'Aubigné (Madame de *Maintenon), the future wife of Louis XIV. Scarron is also remembered for his burlesques, notably *Virgile travesti* (1648), and for the unfinished *Le Roman comique*, a novel based on the adventures of a company of strolling players.

scenario A synopsis of a dramatic work, first used of the loose plots of the *commedia dell'arte*. It is now more commonly used of musical entertainments or films.

scene A subdivision of an act, usually encompassing a distinct episode in a plot.

scene dock A part of the backstage area of a theatre used for the storage of scenery. Sometimes known in Britain as a scene bay, it is usually situated close to the stage itself.

scene of releave (*or* scene of relief) A scenic view, usually suggesting three dimensions, revealed by the opening of a pair of shutters. A feature of the Restoration stage, the illusion was achieved by extensive use of cut-out scenery.

scenery Any of the various flats, cloths, and other scenic pieces used to suggest a particular location or context on stage. Although there were a few isolated examples of the use of scenery in classical drama (*see periaktoi*) and during the Middle Ages (with the elaborate 'mansions' constructed to represent the entrance to hell, for instance), it was not until the Renaissance that it became an essential element in dramatic production. Such distinguished theatrical designers as Peruzzi, Serlio, and Scamozzi in this period introduced wings, the use of perspective designs, and the distinction between sets suitable for different types of drama.

The 18th century saw a preference for neoclassical designs as well as a growing taste for naturalistic and historically accurate scenery; this culminated in the 19th century in elaborately realistic sets and props and the use of the *box set. Scenery designs in the 20th century, often favouring economical and intimate sets rather than spectacular ones, have ranged from the completely naturalistic to the entirely abstract. Notable designers over the years have included Inigo Jones, Giacomo Torelli, the Bibiena family, David Garrick, Philippe James de Loutherbourg, William Capon, André Antoine, Paul Fort, Lugné-Poë, Stanislavsky, Adolphe Appia, Gordon Craig, Max Reinhardt, Beerbohm Tree, Cecil Beaton, Sean Kenny, and Ralph Koltai.

Schechner, Richard (1934-) US director and critic, who worked with the East End Players in Provincetown, Massachusetts and the Free Southern Theatre, a troupe that toured the southern US before founding the *Performance Group in 1967. For them he produced and directed such plays as *Dionysus in '69* (1968), adapted from Euripides, *Macbeth* (1969), and Brecht's *Mother Courage and Her Children* (1975). He resigned as head of the group in 1970, since when he has written much on drama theory.

Schelandre, Jean de (c. 1584–1635) French playwright and poet, born into a noble Protestant family of German origin. He is remembered for the tragedy *Tyre et Sidon*, which first appeared in 1608 and was remodelled 20 years later as a tragi-comedy, with a celebrated preface by François Ogier.

Schicksaltragödie A German theatrical genre, also known as **fate drama**, which became popular in the early 19th century. Its distinguishing feature was the inevitability of the central character's downfall at the hands of destiny, conventionally through his killing his own father or committing some other similar crime. Writers of the genre included Zacharias Werner and Franz Grillparzer.

Schiller, (Johann Christoph) Friedrich von (1759–1805) German playwright and poet, author of several highly influential Romantic dramas on classical lines. After the success of the anonymously published play *Die *Räuber* (The Robbers), which was a major contribution to the development of the *Sturm und Drang* movement, he deserted from the army and became resident playwright at the theatre in Mannheim. He then concentrated for a time on historical and academic writing but was persuaded by his friend Goethe (who first met him in Weimar in 1787) to embark upon a series of historical tragedies, notably the *Wallenstein* trilogy. Goethe produced several of these last plays, written before Schiller's early death from tuberculosis; all his works were translated into English at an early stage. His plays were remarkable for their lyrical beauty, while his last works anticipated the development of Expressionism.
Principal works:
Die Räuber: 1782.
Kabale und Liebe: 1784.
Don Carlos, Infant von Spanien: 1787.
Wallenstein: 1800.
Maria Stuart: 1801.
Die Jungfrau von Orleans: 1801.
Die Braut von Messina: 1803.
Wilhelm Tell: 1804.

Schiller, Leon (Leon de Schildenfeld; 1887–1954) Polish director and designer, who became a leading figure in the Polish theatre after World War I. Influenced by both Gordon Craig and Stanislavsky, he founded the celebrated left-wing Boguslawski Theatre in 1924, directing there such plays as Krasiński's *The Undivine Comedy* (1926) and Brecht's *Die Dreigroschenoper* (1930), which led to the closing down of his theatre. Subsequently he worked in Lwów and in Sofia, survived Auschwitz, and revived liturgical dramas from the Middle Ages. After World War II he took over at Łódź, where his productions included *The Tempest*.

Schlegel, Johann Elias von (1719–49) German playwright and diplomat, who played an important role in the development of a German national theatre. His early comedies were based on the French tradition, while such tragedies as *Hermann* (1743) reflected the influence of his teacher Gottsched; later, however, he revealed his admiration for Shakespeare in such essays as *Vergleichung Shakespeares und Andreas Gryphius* (1741).

His nephew, **August Wilhelm von Schlegel** (1767–1845), was a critic and the author of several plays, an early history of the stage, and still-performed adaptations of Shakespeare, Dante, Cervantes, and Calderón. With Tieck he established a model for subsequent Romantic criticism.

Schmeltzl, Wolfgang (c. 1505–c. 1557) Viennese playwright and schoolteacher, author of several plays on biblical themes. Such works as *Der verlorene Sohn* (The Prodigal Son; 1540), *Judith* (1542), and *David and Goliath* (1545), were influenced by Paul Rebhun and were all written in the vernacular.

Schnitzler, Arthur (1862–1931) Austrian playwright and novelist, whose plays analyse the growing decadence of contemporary Viennese society from a deeply psychological viewpoint. Under the fashionable influence of Freud, Schnitzler explored the problems connected with anti-Semitism, honour, marriage, love, and ultimately sex. The flirtatious young man and the sweet naïve girl are recurrent figures throughout his drama, being introduced in his first work, *Anatol* (1893) – a series of seven dramatic sketches – and reappearing in *Liebelei* (1896). *Reigen* caused a sensation with its depiction of ten casual sexual exchanges and was unperformed from 1921 to 1982. Of his historical plays, *Der grüne Kakadu* is set during the French Revolution and *Der Schleier der Beatrice* describes an Italian Renaissance city on the night before its downfall.

Principal works:

Anatol: 1893.

Liebelei: 1895.

Freiwild: 1896.

Das Vermächtnis: 1897.

Der grüne Kakadu: 1899; translated as *The Green Cockatoo*.

Der Schleier der Beatrice: 1899.

Reigen: 1900; translated as *The Round Dance*; filmed as *La Ronde*.

Der einsame Weg: 1903; translated as *The Lonely Way*.

Zurischenspiel: 1904.

Das Weite Land: 1911; translated as *Undiscovered Country*.

Professor Bernhardi: 1912.

Schönemann, Johann Friedrich (1704–82) German actor and director, in whose company, formed in 1740, several major German theatrical figures appeared. He established his own troupe after performing in Carolina Neuber's company and was at his best in comedy; members of his celebrated company included Ackermann, Ekhof (who took control after Schönemann ruined himself in horsedealing), and Sophia Schröder.

Schönherr, Karl (1867–1943) Austrian playwright, poet, and short-story writer, whose plays depict the problems faced by the peasant classes. His best-known naturalistic plays, written in dialect, are *Erde* (Earth; 1907), *Glaube and Heimat* (Faith and Homeland; 1910), and *Der Kampf*

(1920). Many of his works were first performed at the Burgtheater and Deutsches Volkstheater in Vienna.

school drama Plays written for performance by pupils at colleges and schools throughout Europe during the Renaissance. A feature of Jesuit drama, in which context such plays were usually written in Latin, the tradition also encompassed plays in the vernacular. English examples included *Ralph Roister Doister*, presented at Eton or Winchester, and *Gammer Gurton's Needle*, given at Christ's College, Cambridge. *See also* Westminster Play.

School for Scandal, The A classic comedy by *Sheridan. First performance: 1777. Joseph Surface, abetted by Lady Sneerwell, circulates malign rumours about his brother, while himself attempting to seduce the young wife of Sir Peter Teazle. Their uncle, returning from abroad, disguises himself to test the characters of his nephews.

School for Wives, The (*L'École des Femmes*) A comedy by *Molière. First performance: Paris, 1662. Agnès is raised by Arnolphe, who hopes to marry her but fears a clever wife. Horace falls in love with Agnès and confides in Arnolphe; the latter's subsequent attempts to prevent the union of the young lovers end in failure. *See also Critique de l'École des Femmes, La; Impromptu de Versailles, L'*.

school of drama *See* drama school.

Schouwburg *See* Campen, Jacob van.

Schreyvogel, Josef (1768–1832) Austrian director, who became the leading theatrical figure in Vienna in 1814. As director of the Burgtheater, the Kärntnertor, and the Theater an der Wien, he staged a wide variety of plays and championed the works of Grillparzer.

Schröder, Sophia Carlotta (Sophia Carlotta Biereichel; 1714–92) German actress, who became a leading actress with Ackermann's company, the finances of which she subsequently came to control, after achieving fame with Schönemann's troupe. Ackermann himself became her husband after the death of her first husband.

By her first marriage she was the mother of the actor **Friedrich Ludwig Schröder** (1744–1816), who began his career as a child in Ackermann's company but later worked as an acrobat and ropedancer. On rejoining the company he was inspired by Ekhof, whose roles he inherited, and excelled in comedy at the National Theatre in Hamburg. Although he was constantly at loggerheads with his mother over the financial control of the company, he went on to present influential productions of Goethe, Lessing, and Shakespeare as well as more traditional works before moving to the Burgtheater in Vienna, where he continued to renovate conventional German acting practices. Later he took over Ackermann's old company once more, producing minor works by Iffland and Kotzebue.

Schröder, Sophie (1781–1868) Austrian actress, who became a leading performer noted for the grace and restraint of her acting at the Burgtheater in Vienna. Directed by Schreyvogel, she excelled in plays by Goethe, Kleist, Schiller, Shakespeare, and Grillparzer, most notably in the title role of his *Sappho* (1818).

Schuch, Franz (c. 1716–64) Austrian actor, who was much admired for his refined comic interpretations. He led his own company of travelling players; members of his troupe included Johann Brandes, Ekhof, and Döbbelin, who settled the company in Berlin after Schuch's death.

Schuster, Ignaz (1779–1835) Austrian actor, who became a highly popular comic performer with the Leopoldstädter company

in Vienna, first appearing with it in 1801. He established his reputation in 1813 as Staberl in *Die Bürger in Wien* by Bäuerle; subsequently he was especially successful as the same character in pieces written by Karl Carl.

Schwartz, Evgenyi Lvovich *See* Shwartz, Evgenyi Lvovich.

Schwartz, Maurice (1889–1960) Jewish actor and director, born in Russia, who began his professional career in New York. Following success with the plays of Peretz Hirschbein and Sholom Aleichem, he toured Europe and later opened a shortlived theatre specifically for Jewish plays in New York. In 1926 he opened the more successful Yiddish Art Theatre, which became a national focus for Jewish drama, subsequently also visiting South America and Palestine and eventually working (1959) in Israel.

Science Fiction Theatre of Liverpool *See* Campbell, Ken.

sciopticon *See* projector.

scissor cross *See* stage direction.

Scofield, Paul (1922–) British actor, who made his debut at the Westminster Theatre in 1940. Subsequently he played leading roles in repertory at Birmingham before joining Barry Jackson's Stratford-upon-Avon company in 1946. In 1955 he led the company on a tour of the USSR, playing Hamlet himself; later successes at Stratford included Peter Brook's *King Lear* (1962) and *The Government Inspector* (1965). At the Globe Theatre in 1950 he scored an outstanding success in Anouilh's *Ring Round the Moon*; since then he has been highly praised in a variety of parts from the seedy agent in the musical *Expresso Bongo* (1958) to Chekhov's Vanya (1970), Prospero (1974), and Salieri in Shaffer's *Amadeus* at the National Theatre (1979). In 1986 he gave a memorably witty performance in Herb Gardner's *I'm Not Rappaport* at the Apollo Theatre.

Scott, Clement William (1841–1904) British theatre critic, who, as drama critic for the *Daily Telegraph* (1872–97) and editor of *The Theatre* (1877–97), tried to prevent the development of the new drama of Ibsen and others. His own attempts at playwriting were of little account, with the exception of *Diplomacy* (1878), which he adapted from Sardou in collaboration with B C Stephenson.

Scott, Sir Walter (1771–1832) Scottish novelist, poet, and playwright, whose novels inspired numerous stage adaptations. His own dramatic works, none of which were especially remarkable, included *The House of Aspen*, produced at the Surrey Theatre in 1829, and *Auchindrane*, produced at Edinburgh in 1830. Of the many stage interpretations of his novels and narrative poems, some of the more important were those of *Rob Roy* (of which there were several versions), *The Heart of Midlothian* (used by Dion Boucicault for *The Trial of Effie Deans*), *Montrose* (adapted by Thomas Dibdin), *Ivanhoe, Kenilworth*, and *Quentin Durward*. Scott himself collaborated on a Covent Garden production of *Guy Mannering* in 1816; other works, notably *The Bride of Lammermoor*, were turned into grand operas.

Scottish National Players A Scottish theatre company founded in Glasgow in 1921. The company toured during the summer to areas of Scotland where drama was rarely presented and encouraged native Scottish writing; writers whose plays were performed by the group before it was broken up in 1947 included John Brandane, James Bridie, and Robert Kemp. In 1926 and 1927 it was directed by Tyrone Guthrie.

Scottish Roscius *See* Johnston, Henry Erskine.

Scribe, (Augustin-)Eugène (1791–1861) French playwright, whose skilfully constructed plays were characteristic of the *well-made play. His output consists of some 350 works, including vaudevilles, comedies, historical dramas, and opera libretti, many of which were written in collaboration. Scribe began writing for the theatre in 1810 and made his name with the vaudeville *Encore une nuit de la Garde Nationale*. The popularity of his works was immense but short-lived, their superficial characterization and contrived plots being widely disparaged by the latter half of the 19th century. *Adrienne Lecouvreur* was his most successful play and provided Rachel, Bernhardt, and others with their most-acclaimed role.
Principal works:
Encore une nuit de la Garde Nationale: 1815.
L'Ours et le pacha: 1820.
Le Mariage de raison: 1826.
Bertrand et Raton: 1833.
Le Verre d'eau: 1840; translated as *A Glass of Water; or, Great Events from Trifling Causes Spring* (or *The Queen's Favourite*).
Une chaîne: 1841.
Adrienne Lecouvreur: 1849.

scrim *See* gauze.

scruto Thin strips of wood attached to a piece of canvas and used to conceal a trap or an opening in the scenery through which an actor may make an unexpected entrance.

Scudéry, Georges de (1601–67) French playwright, who was the brother of the writer Madeleine de Scudéry, many of whose novels were published in his name. Having abandoned a military career, he produced numerous tragedies, tragi-comedies, and comedies characterized by high rhetoric and inventive plots. They include *La Mort de César* (1635), *Le Trompeur puni* (1631), *La Comédie des comédiens* (1635), which depicted Montdory's company, and *L'Amour tyrannique* (1638). Scudéry was also one of Pierre Corneille's adversaries in the *'querelle du Cid'*.

Seagull, The A play by Anton *Chekhov. First performance: Alexandrinsky Theatre, St Petersburg, 1896. The first performance was a disaster, the actors failing to come to terms with the play's revolutionary naturalistic depiction of ordinary people; when, however, this story of disappointed love, aspiring artists, and suicide was revived at the Moscow Art Theatre in 1898 it created a sensation and established Chekhov's reputation.

sea row *See* groundrow.

Seattle Repertory Theatre A theatre in Seattle, built in 1963 to house a celebrated repertory company. The theatre opened with *King Lear* and presented numerous classics until financial constraints resulted in a more commercial programme in the 1970s. It works in close association with **A Contemporary Theatre** nearby.

Sebastian, Mihail (1907–45) Romanian playwright and novelist, whose promising career was cut short by his death in a road accident. His best play was the brilliant comedy *Ultima oră* (Stop Press; 1948); others include *Jocul-de-a-vacanţa* (Holiday Games; 1938), and *Steaua fără nume* (The Nameless Star; 1944).

Second Mrs Tanqueray, The A play by *Pinero. First performance: 1893. Mrs Tanqueray reveals that she has had an affair with the man whom her stepdaughter is intending to marry, thus sacrificing her own good name in order to protect the girl. Mrs Patrick Campbell was the first to play the central role.

Sedaine, Michel-Jean (1719–97) French playwright, who is remembered for his mas-

terpiece *Le Philosophe sans le savoir* (1765; translated as *The Duel*, 1772), an excellent example of the *drame bourgeois*. Sedaine began writing in 1750, having previously worked as a stonemason. His other works consist of libretti for comic operas, notably *Le Roi et le fermier* (1762), *Rose et Colas* (1764), and *Richard Coeur de Lion* (1784), and the comedy *La Gageure imprévue* (1768).

Sedley, Sir Charles (c. 1639–1701) English playwright and man of letters, whose comedy of manners *The Mulberry Garden* (1668) was influenced by both Molière and Etherege. His *Bellamira; or, the Mistress* (1687), based on Terence's *Eunuchus*, is also worthy of note.

Sedley-Smith, William Henry (1806–72) US actor, manager, and playwright, born in Wales, who became a leading performer in light comedy on the US stage. He began his career in the British provinces, but later established his reputation with his melodrama *The Drunkard; or, the Fallen Sword*, which was first presented at the Boston Museum (where he was stage manager from 1843 to 1860) in 1844. A tract against the evils of drink, it was frequently revived, enjoying long runs in both the 1850s and again in Los Angeles from 1933 to 1959.

Segelcke, Tore (1901–79) Norwegian actress, who became a leading performer in the plays of Ibsen at the Nationaltheatret, where she first appeared in 1928. Earlier in her career she was seen at the Norske Theatret in Oslo (1921) and in Bergen (1924–28); her finest roles included Nora in *A Doll's House* as well as parts in the plays of Shakespeare and contemporary playwrights.

segment stage A method of staging based on the use of one or more large wedge-shaped rostra pivoted on castor wheels at the upstage apex.

Selwyn Theatre A theatre on West 42nd Street, New York, which opened in 1918. Successful productions there included Ferber and Kaufman's *The Royal Family* (1927), Cole Porter's *Wake Up and Dream* (1929), and *Electra* (1932) by Sophocles. It became a cinema in the 1930s.

Semenova, Ekaterina Semenovna (1786–1849) Russian actress, who was noted for her beautiful voice and was regarded as the finest Russian actress of her day. She was trained by Dmitrevsky and excelled in the tragedies of Ozerov, Racine, Shakespeare, and Schiller.

Semper, Gottfried *See* Bayreuth.

Seneca, Lucius Annaeus (c. 4 BC–65 AD) Roman playwright, statesman, and philosopher, whose nine extant tragedies are the only surviving drama of the period of the Roman Empire. His plays were written to be read and present certain difficulties when they are staged; unlike earlier works, however, they were original plays and not adaptations of Greek plots, despite their indebtedness to Euripides and Aeschylus. Notable for the brutality of some scenes – significantly Seneca was Nero's tutor for a time – and usually based upon the Stoic concept of the conflict between passion and reason, the tragedies were much admired during the Renaissance and had a profound influence on early revenge tragedy, finding echoes in the plays of Shakespeare, Jonson, Webster, and others. Typical features include the use of stereotyped characters, supernatural elements, and melodramatic plots. Other writings included the political satire *The Pumpkinification of the Divine Claudius*. After Seneca's suicide under pressure from Nero little of any worth was written for the Roman stage.
Principal dramatic works (dates unknown):
Agamemnon.
Hercules Furens.
Hercules Oetaeus.
Medea.
Oedipus.
Phaedra.
Phoenissae.
Thyestes.
Troades.

sentimental comedy A form of moralizing comedy in which there is a strong element of pathos. Especially popular with audiences of the 17th and 18th centuries, the genre was epitomized in England by the plays of Steele and in France by the *comédie larmoyante.*

Separate Tables A play by Terence *Rattigan. First performance: London, 1954. Subdivided as *Table by the Window* and *Table Number Seven*, it is set in a hotel dining-room and explores the problems faced by individual guests in terms of their emotional inadequacy and the isolation sometimes caused by social conventions.

Serban, Andrei (1943-) Romanian director, who began his career working under Peter Brook and subsequently at La Mama in New York. He has won particular acclaim for such productions as the musical *The Umbrellas of Cherbourg* (1979) and plays by Chekhov.

Serjeant Musgrave's Dance A play by John *Arden. First performance: Royal Court Theatre, London, 1959. Set in a northern mining town in the late 19th century, the play follows an army deserter's attempts to exact revenge for the death of a fellow-soldier; the language of the play is remarkable for its combination of prose and ballad forms.

Serlio, Sebastiano (1475–1554) Italian architect and artist, who designed much influential perspective scenery. A pupil of Peruzzi and an admirer of Vitruvius, he detailed his theories concerning scenery and lighting in his treatise *The Second Book of Architec-*

ture (1545), in which he distinguished between sets suitable for tragedy, comedy, and fantasy.

Serrau, Jean-Marie (1915–73) French actor and director, who became famous for his productions of important new works for the stage in the 1950s and 1960s. As well as the plays of Brecht, he championed the Theatre of the Absurd and the avant-garde movement, presenting many experimental works at his own Théâtre de Babylone and Théâtre de la Tempête and elsewhere; other productions included several notable works by little-known African playwrights.

Servandony, Jean-Nicolas (1695–1766) French architect, noted for his early neoclassical theatre designs. He was trained in Rome but later worked on theatres and designed scenery throughout Europe.

Sesame *See* Radius.

set A collective term for the scenery, props, and lighting presented on stage to suggest the location or context of a play. Specific variations in settings include box sets and curtain sets.

set piece A flat shaped to represent a particular object on stage, usually standing by itself; the term is also used of built stuff.

Settle, Elkanah (1648–1724) English playwright, whose early works were drolls staged at various London fairs. When his tragedy *Cambyses, King of Persia* was successfully produced by Betterton at Lincoln's Inn Fields in 1666, he went on to write further bombastic heroic dramas, notably *The Empress of Morocco* (1671), which threatened to overshadow Dryden. It was also notable for being the first playtext to be published with scenic engravings. His later plays, however, failed to attract the same success.

Seven Against Thebes A tragedy by *Aeschylus. First performance: Athens, 469 BC. Set in Thebes during an attack by a neighbouring state, it is thought to be the third part of a tetralogy, the other parts of which have not survived.

7:84 Theatre Company A British theatre group founded in 1971 by the playwright John McGrath to present politically-orientated drama. The name of the group was derived from the statistic that 84 per cent of Britain's wealth is reputedly owned by seven per cent of the population and reflects the company's socially-committed stance on such issues as ownership and repression. Plays presented by the company have included several by McGrath himself as well as works by John Arden and David Edgar.

Seyler, Abel (1730–1801) German theatre manager, who inherited the leadership of Ackermann's company in Hamburg and later ran his own travelling company. He was married to the actress Sophie *Hensel and his career suffered greatly from the effects her evil temper had upon various hosts and patrons; he did, however, enjoy periods of success when Ekhof joined his troupe and when working under Iffland at Gotha.

Seyler, Athene (1889–) British actress, who won the Bancroft Gold Medal at RADA in 1908 and made her first professional appearance a year later. Her sharp sense of comedy and style suited her perfectly to such parts as Cynthia in Congreve's *The Double Dealer* (1916), Lady Fidget in Wycherley's *The Country Wife* (1924), and roles in other Restoration and contemporary comedies as well as those of Shakespeare and Wilde. In 1937 she played Prossy in Shaw's *Candida* and took part in Gielgud's Queen's Theatre season, playing Mrs Candour in Sheridan's *The School for Scandal*. Subsequent successes included Vita Louise in Mary Chase's *Harvey* (1949) and Martha Brewster in Joseph Kesselring's *Ar-*

senic and Old Lace (1966), after which she retired from the stage. Her husband was the actor Nicholas Thomas Hannen.

Seymour, William Gorman (1855–1933) US actor, son of theatrical parents, who made his debut as a child of two and subsequently appeared alongside most of the leading performers of the day, including Edwin Booth and Joseph Jefferson. In 1871 he joined the Globe Theatre in Boston, where he appeared with Edwin Forrest; subsequently he also managed several theatres and worked under Charles Frohman. His personal library eventually formed the basis of a theatre collection at Princeton University.

Seyrig, Delphine (1932–) French actress, born in Lebanon, who is recognized as one of the leading performers on the Paris stage. Acclaimed for her subtle use of movement as well as for her distinctive voice, she first attracted attention in the theatre as Nina in Chekhov's *The Seagull*; since then she has triumphed in plays by Pinter, Pirandello, Stoppard, and Turgenev among many others.

Shadow of a Gunman, The The first play by Sean *O'Casey. First performance: Abbey Theatre, Dublin, 1923. The central character, Donal Davoreen, is involved in the conflict between the Irish nationalists and the British army; the play challenges the concepts of patriotism, deception, and self-knowledge.

shadow play A form of puppet theatre (usually silent) in which the audience watch the shadows cast on a screen by two-dimensional puppets. Associated chiefly with the oriental theatre (especially that of Java and Bali), the tradition also played a part in early Greek drama, featuring the comic character Karaghiozis, and later in 18th-century France (known as *ombres chinoises*). In England a form of shadow play called the

galanty show was popular for a time in the late 19th century in conjunction with *Punch and Judy shows; other countries with a stronger tradition include Turkey and India. Figures are mounted on rods or manoeuvred by wires.

Shadwell, Thomas (c. 1642–92) English playwright, who became a rival of John Dryden whom he succeeded as poet laureate in 1689. His plays include the comedies *The Sullen Lovers* (1668), which was based upon Molière's *Les Fâcheux*, *Epsom Wells* (1672), which was influenced by Jonson, *The Virtuoso* (1676), which satirized the Royal Society, *The Squire of Alsatia* (1688), and *Bury Fair* (1689). He also adapted Shakespeare's drama *The Tempest* as the opera *The Enchanted Island* (1674) and *Timon of Athens* as *The Man-Hater* (1678).

Shaffer, Peter Levin (1926–) British playwright, who has won acclaim for dramas ranging from traditional farce to experimental psychological studies. He established his reputation with *Five Finger Exercise* (1958), which was followed by *The Private Ear* and *The Public Eye* – staged as a double bill in 1962. The *Royal Hunt of the Sun* was equally well-received in 1964, as was the popular farce *Black Comedy* in 1965, in which the actors behave as if they are on an unlit stage. His other works have included the one-act play *White Lies* (1967), the psychological drama *Equus* (1973), *Amadeus* (1979), and the comedy *Lettice and Lovage* (1988).

His brother, **Anthony Shaffer** (1926–), also enjoyed considerable success with the ingenious thriller *Sleuth* (1970), although such later plays as *Murderer* (1975) have attracted less attention.

Shaftesbury Theatre The first theatre to be built on London's Shaftesbury Avenue. It opened in 1888 with *As You Like It*, Johnston Forbes-Robertson playing Orlando. None of the early productions, which included Italian operas, were successful, but the theatre's fortunes were restored with the introduction to England of the first US musical comedy, *The Belle of New York*, which opened in 1898. Other musical comedies followed, including the all-Black cast play *In Dahomey* (1903). In 1909 Cicely Courtneidge appeared in *The Arcadians*, a musical play which ran for over two years. Subsequently musical comedy alternated with opera, farce, and light comedy until the theatre was destroyed by bombs in 1941.

A second **Shaftesbury Theatre** opened as the New Prince's Theatre (later simply the **Prince's Theatre**) at the northern end of Shaftesbury Avenue in 1911. In 1916 Seymour Hicks took over and presented musicals and light opera, a policy that was continued from 1919 by C B Cochran, who forged an association between the theatre and the D'Oyly Carte Opera Company that was to last for over 40 years. Plays were interspersed with ballet and opera through the 1920s and 1930s and included a notable performance by Sarah Bernhardt in Louis Verneuil's *Daniel* (1921), Sybil Thorndike and Henry Ainley in *Macbeth* (1926), and Gershwin's *Funny Face* (1928), starring the Astaires and Leslie Henson. Less frequent successes after World War II included appearances by Maurice Chevalier (1952) and *Antony and Cleopatra* (1953), starring Michael Redgrave and Peggy Ashcroft. In 1962 the theatre was refurbished, reopening as the Shaftesbury Theatre with the musical *How to Succeed in Business Without Really Trying*. This success was later consolidated by *Hair*, which ran for nearly 2000 performances until part of the ceiling collapsed in 1973. Public outcry saved the theatre from redevelopment and in 1983 the producer Ray Cooney's Theatre of Comedy company purchased it. The company occasionally plays host to outside companies, the most recent of such productions being the Sondheim musical *Follies*, which opened in 1987.

Shakespeare, William (1564–1616) English playwright and actor, author of several long narrative poems, the most famous of all sonnet sequences, and 36 plays, considered among the finest in the English language – or indeed, any other language. Little is known about his life, which has consequently been the subject of much conjecture. He was born in Stratford-upon-Avon and married Anne Hathaway in 1582; a daughter, Susanna, was born in 1583 and twins, Hamnet (d. 1596) and Judith, in 1585. In 1588 Shakespeare moved to London and became well-known as an actor; by 1592 he had begun to write for the stage, although the dating of his early plays is notoriously imprecise. By 1595 he was a shareholder in the Chamberlain's Men, who later became the King's Men; he finally retired to Stratford in 1610.

The success of his first historical tetralogy (written 1589–92) quickly established his reputation and encouraged him to diversify into other types of drama. His initial experiments with comedy (1593–95), which ranged from the broad farce of *The *Comedy of Errors* to the courtly **Love's Labour's Lost*, culminated in such masterpieces as *A *Midsummer's Night's Dream* and **Twelfth Night*, whilst his growing interest in characterization finally found expression in the first of his major tragedies, **Romeo and Juliet* (1595). The series (1600–06) of tragedies that followed, notably **Hamlet*, **Othello*, **King Lear*, and **Macbeth*, are (together with the Roman plays) among his best-known works, having remained in performance all over the world ever since; they provide many of the most challenging and rewarding roles in the theatre.

The *Merchant of Venice, with its emphasis upon the darker side of human nature, heralded the final phase in Shakespeare's writing – the complex and mystical 'problem plays'. These sophisticated dramas, culminating in the author's farewell to the stage in *The *Tempest*, reflect a more serene view of life and unite many of the disparate elements of the plays that preceded them.

The first comprehensive collection of Shakespeare's plays was published in 1623 and is known as the First Folio; it also includes an invaluable list of contemporary performers who appeared in them.

Principal dramatic works:

Henry VI: 1591–92 (in three parts).
Richard III: 1592–93.
The Comedy of Errors: c. 1592.
Titus Andronicus: c. 1592.
The Taming of the Shrew: c. 1593.
All's Well That Ends Well: c. 1593–1604.
Love's Labour's Lost: c. 1594–95.
The Two Gentlemen of Verona: c. 1594.
Romeo and Juliet: c. 1595.
Richard II: c. 1595.
A Midsummer Night's Dream: c. 1595.
King John: c. 1596.
The Merchant of Venice: c. 1596.
Henry IV: c. 1597 (in two parts).
The Merry Wives of Windsor: c. 1598.
Much Ado About Nothing: c. 1598.
Henry V: c. 1599.
Julius Caesar: c. 1599.
As You Like It: c. 1599.
Twelfth Night: c. 1599.
Hamlet: c. 1600.
Troilus and Cressida: c. 1602.
Othello: c. 1602.
Measure for Measure: c. 1604.
Timon of Athens: c. 1604.
King Lear: c. 1605.
Macbeth: c. 1605.
Antony and Cleopatra: 1607.
Coriolanus: 1607–08.
Pericles: c. 1608.
Cymbeline: c.1610.
The Winter's Tale: c. 1610.
The Tempest: c. 1611.
The Two Noble Kinsmen: c. 1613 (with Fletcher).
Henry VIII: c. 1613 (with Fletcher).

Shakespeare Memorial Theatre A theatre at Stratford-upon-Avon built by public subscription in 1879 on land beside the river given by Charles Edward Flower, member of a local brewing family. A controversial Gothic-style redbrick building criticized for its unsympathetic bleak interior, it was the home of the annual festival of Shakespeare's plays from 1886 to 1926. It was then destroyed by fire and the current theatre, designed by Elizabeth Scott, was opened on the same site in 1932 (again with help from the Flower family). Despite fresh criticism of its design, the theatre grew in prominence under successive directors, including W Bridges-Adams (who increased the month-long season to five months), Ben Iden Payne, Barry Jackson (who encouraged the use of a large team of directors and brought new young actors of the calibre of Paul Scofield and Peter Brook to Stratford), and Anthony Quayle, whose productions featured such stars as John Gielgud and Peggy Ashcroft. Glen Byam Shaw succeeded Quayle in 1956, overseeing further successful international tours and consolidating the theatre's reputation. In 1961 Peter Hall took over, forming the Royal Shakespeare Company and renaming the theatre itself the *Royal Shakespeare Theatre.

Shakhovsky, Alexander Alexandrovich (1777–1846) Russian playwright, who is credited with having founded the vaudeville tradition in Russia. The first of his witty entertainments of the type was presented at the Hermitage Theatre in 1795 and influenced many notable contemporary writers.

Shank, John (d. 1636) English actor, listed in the First Folio as an actor in Shakespeare's plays. He is thought to have succeeded Armin as chief clown with the King's Men. He played in several of Beaumont and Fletcher's works and was Hilario in Massinger's *The Picture*. Latterly, he bought shares in the Globe and Blackfriars theatres and was possibly concerned with the training of boy-apprentices.

sharer Any member of an Elizabethan theatre company who shared in the ownership of scripts and costumes. The sharer had a claim to any profits made; those who also had an interest in the building itself were *housekeepers.

sharing system A financial arrangement commonly agreed in English theatres in the early 18th century. The system involved the sharing of a night's profits equally among the company, the manager receiving up to five shares in all. It was, however, vulnerable to the activities of corrupt managements and was eventually superseded by the payment of set salaries. *See also* benefit.

Shaw, Fiona (Fiona Wilson; 1958-) British actress, born in Ireland, who made her debut at the Octagon Theatre, Bolton in 1982. Since then she has played Julia in *The Rivals* (1983) at the National Theatre and leading roles for the Royal Shakespeare Company, including Mme de Volanges in *Les Liaisons Dangereuses* (1985) and Katharina in *The Taming of the Shrew* (1987).

Shaw, George Bernard (1856–1950) Irish playwright, director and critic, born in Dublin, who won a Nobel Prize in 1925 and is considered one of the great theatrical figures of the 20th century. Shaw moved to London in 1876, where he became a founder member of the Fabian Society and worked for a time as a music critic and novelist. He then became drama critic for the *Saturday Review* (1895–98). His admiration for Ibsen and his own interest in seeing a new relevant social drama led him to write plays himself.

His first play, *Widowers' Houses* (1892), was a well-received comedy expressing his socialist views; thereafter he attempted a broader human comedy whose enduring qualities established his reputation. A series of 10 plays was presented by Harley Granville *Barker and John *Vedrenne at the *Royal Court Theatre (1904–07); they also staged later Shavian works at the Savoy Theatre, supporting his treatment of subjects previously banned by the censor, including prostitution, religion, and sexual politics. Occassionally Shaw's preoccupation with the intellectual content of his drama hampers its theatrical effectiveness, but in his best plays his eloquence and wit carry the action; many of his works have been revived time and time again. Of his 50 plays, Shaw considered *Back to Methuselah* (1922) his best, although other critics have singled out *Heartbreak House* and *Saint Joan* (1923). He was also noted for the lengthy prefaces to his plays, in which he further expounded his views on a wide variety of topics. Several of his early plays were first published in 1898 under the title 'Plays Pleasant and Unpleasant'.

Principal dramatic works:
Widowers' Houses: 1892.
*The *Devil's Disciple*: 1897.
Mrs Warren's Profession: 1902 (written 1893).
*The *Philanderer*: 1905 (written 1893).
Arms and the Man: 1894.
Candida: 1895.
You Never Can Tell: 1900.
Captain Brassbound's Conversion: 1900.
Man and Superman: 1901–03.
John Bull's Other Island: 1904.
Major Barbara: 1905.
*The *Doctor's Dilemma*: 1906.
Caesar and Cleopatra: 1906.
Misalliance: 1910.
Fanny's First Play: 1911.
Pygmalion: 1913.
Androcles and the Lion: 1913.
Heartbreak House: 1920.
Back to Methuselah: 1922.
Saint Joan: 1923.
*The *Apple Cart*: 1929.
Too True to Be Good: 1932.
Geneva: 1938.
In Good King Charles's Golden Days: 1939.

Shaw, Glen Alexander Byam *See* Byam Shaw, Glen Alexander.

Shaw Festival A major theatre festival founded at Niagara-on-the-Lake in Canada in 1962 by the playwright **Brian Doherty** (1906–74). Initially it was devoted exclusively to the plays of G B Shaw, but it now includes productions of plays by other European and Canadian writers. The season lasts from May to October.

Shaw Theatre *See* National Youth Theatre.

Shchepkin, Mikhail Semenovich (1788–1863) Russian actor, who began as an amateur in comic roles in Kursk and was later released from serfdom and became a leading theatrical figure in Moscow. He first appeared at the Maly Theatre in Moscow in 1822, subsequently winning much praise for his interpretation of roles in the plays of Gogol and Griboyedov, as well as in comic parts in Molière and Shakespeare. He was also highly influential in fostering interest in realism in the Russian theatre, anticipating the reforms of Stanislavsky.

Shchukin, Boris Vasilievich (1894–1939) Soviet actor, who became a leading performer at the Vakhtangov Theatre. Before his early death, he was particularly admired in Russian plays by such authors as Afinogenov, Gorky, and Pogodin, whose Lenin he was the first to portray.

Sheldon, Edward Brewster (1886–1946) US playwright, who was recognized as a leading exponent of Realism in the US with his first play, *Salvation Nell*, in 1908. Of the plays that followed, the most successful included *The Nigger* (1909), which tackled the problem of race, and *Romance* (1913), in which **Doris Keane** (1881–1945) was highly acclaimed as an Italian opera singer. He was also the author of several noted collaborations and translations.

Shelley, Percy Bysshe (1792–1822) British poet, author of several verse plays. His lyrical drama *Prometheus Unbound* and his burlesque *Oedipus Tyrannus; or, Swellfoot the Tyrant* were published in 1820. His tragedy *The Cenci* (1819) was first performed in 1886 but won acclaim for its poetry rather than for its theatrical effectiveness.

Shepard, Sam (Samuel Shepard Rogers; 1943-) US playwright, whose early works – many about the impact of technology – included the one-act plays *Cowboys* (1964), *Chicago* (1965), *Icarus's Mother* (1965), and *Rock Garden* (1964), which was incorporated into the musical *Oh, Calcutta!*. His first full-length play was *La Turista*, which appeared in 1966; his plays since then have included *Operation Sidewinder* (1970), *The Tooth of Crime* (1972), *The Curse of the Starving Class* (1977), *Buried Child* (1978), which received a Pulitzer Prize, *Seduced* (1979), which was based on the life of Howard Hughes, *True West* (1980), *Fool for Love* (1983), and *A Lie of the Mind* (1986).

Sher, Antony (1951-) British actor, born in South Africa, who made his London debut in Willy Russell's musical *John, Paul, Ringo… and Bert* (1974). In 1975 he attracted much attention at Edinburgh in Gogol's *The Government Inspector*. Joining the Royal Shakespeare Company in 1982, his roles have included the Fool in *King Lear*, Molière's Tartuffe, and an acclaimed Richard III, in which he was compared to Olivier and toured to Australia. He played Arnold Beckoff in Harvey Fierstein's *Torch Song Trilogy* (1985) and – at Stratford-upon-Avon in 1987 – Shylock, Malvolio, and Vendice in Tourneur's *The Revenger's Tragedy*.

Sheridan, Mark (Fred Shaw; 1867–1918) British comic singer, who became famous in music hall for such songs as 'I Do Like to be Beside the Seaside' and 'Who Were You With Last Night?', conducting the audience in chorus songs with his baggy umbrella. He toured his own burlesque company during

World War I but eventually shot himself while depressed.

Sheridan, Richard Brinsley (1751–1861) British playwright, theatre manager, and politician, born in Dublin, son of an actor and the writer Frances Chamberlaine (1724–66). The success of his early plays, notably The *Rivals, enabled him to buy Garrick's share in *Drury Lane and to take over the management there in 1776. After *A Trip to Scarborough*, his adaptation of *The *Relapse*, he presented his brilliant comedy of manners *The *School for Scandal* to universal acclaim. After staging the burlesque *The Critic* in 1779 he entered parliament and gained a reputation as a fine orator. The destruction of Drury Lane in 1809, however, compounded his financial difficulties and ended his career in the theatre. He was buried in Westminster Abbey.
Principal works:
The Rivals: 1775.
St Patrick's Day; or, The Scheming Lieutenant: 1775.
The Duenna: 1775.
A Trip to Scarborough: 1777.
The School for Scandal: 1777.
Robinson Crusoe; or, Harlequin Friday: 1781.
The Critic; or, a Tragedy Rehears'd: 1799.
Pizarro: 1799.

Sheridan Square Playhouse *See* Circle Repertory Company.

Sherlock Holmes A play by William *Gillette. First performance: Buffalo, 1899. Loosely based on three of Conan Doyle's popular stories, it introduced the detective play to the US stage; Gillette himself appeared for many years in the role of the fictional hero.

Sherman Theatre A university theatre in Cardiff, South Wales, which opened in 1973. It presents a mixed programme in each of its two theatres, one of which is the *Arena Theatre, based on productions by its resident company. It is the headquarters of the Welsh Drama Company and the Welsh Dance Company.

Sherriff, R(obert) C(edric) (1896–1975) British playwright and novelist, best known for his play *Journey's End* (1928), which realistically portrayed events in a World War I dugout and established his reputation. His other plays include *Badger's Green* (1930), which was a rustic comedy about cricket, *Home at Seven* (1950), a psychological drama about amnesia, *The White Carnation* (1953), *The Long Sunset* (1955), and *The Telescope* (1957).

Sherwood, Robert Emmet (1896–1955) US playwright, whose first successful play was *The Road to Rome* (1927), based on Hannibal's crossing of the Alps. Subsequently he was praised for such plays as *The Love Nest* (1927), *The Queen's Husband* (1928), *Reunion in Vienna* (1931), which starred the Lunts, *The *Petrified Forest*, the pessimistic *Idiot's Delight* (1936), which won a Pulitzer Prize, *Abe Lincoln in Illinois* (1938), *There Shall Be No Night* (1940), and *Small War on Murray Hill* (1957).

She Stoops to Conquer A comedy by Oliver *Goldsmith. First performance: 1773. Tony Lumpkin directs Young Marlow and his friend to the Hardcastles' house, having them believe it to be an inn; there they treat Hardcastle as the landlord and his daughter as one of the servants.

She Would if She Could A comedy by George *Etherege. First performance: 1668. When Sir Oliver and Sir Joshua, seeking opportunity for dissipation, bring their families to London, both Sir Oliver's wife and Sir Joshua's two nieces embark on intrigues; finally all parties come together at the Bear Tavern.

Shields, Arthur (1900–70) Irish actor, who was with the Abbey Theatre company for

23 years. His roles there included Denis in Lennox Robinson's *The White-Headed Boy* (1916) and leading parts in Synge's *The Playboy of the Western World* and O'Casey's *The Plough and the Stars*. After 1941 he concentrated on films.

Shields, Ella (1879–1952) British music hall singer, born in the US, who became famous as a male impersonator. Best known of all her songs was 'Burlington Bertie', which was written by her husband.

Shiels, George (1886–1949) Irish playwright, who from 1921 onwards had plays regularly staged at the Abbey Theatre. Having established his reputation with such satirical comedies as *Paul Twyning* (1922), he had success with his more serious plays, which included *The Passing Day* (1936), *The Rugged Path* (1940), and *The Summit* (1941).

Shifrin, Nisson Ambramovich (1892–1959) Soviet stage designer, who was particularly noted for his designs for the plays of Shakespeare. Some of his most admired designs, which made use of lavish tapestries, were executed for Popov at the Red Army Theatre, the most successful including *A Midsummer Night's Dream* (1940). He also designed productions of several modern Soviet plays.

Shilling Theatre *See* Grand Theatre.

Shimpa A Japanese theatre movement, which developed from the **Kabuki* tradition in the early 20th century. Known as the 'new school', *Shimpa* challenged many of the conventions associated with *Kabuki* productions and allowed women to appear on stage. Most *Shimpa* plays were sentimental melodramas.

Shingeki A Japanese theatre movement that flourished in the early 20th century. Known as the 'new drama', the *Sh-ingeki* repertory included works by noted European and US writers; the movement revived after World War II, providing an outlet for new Japanese writers as well as major contemporary foreign works.

Shirley, James (1596–1666) English playwright, who was a prolific writer of comedy. His 40 plays reflect the influence of both Jonson and Fletcher and were revived after the Restoration. His comedies of manners included *The Witty Fair One* (1628), *Hyde Park* (1632), *The Gamester* (1633), and *The Lady of Pleasure* (1635); among his other plays was the revenge tragedy *The Traitor* (1631). He wrote for the King's Men and many of his plays were performed in private theatres.

Shoemaker's Holiday, The A comedy by Thomas *Dekker. First performance: London, 1599. The play presents a romantic picture of harmony among London tradesmen and tells of the rise of Simon Eyre from master shoemaker to Lord Mayor.

showboat A floating theatre of the type once common on the Mississippi, Ohio, and other major US rivers. The first showboat, the *Floating Palace*, was built for William Chapman in 1831 and was typical in providing a variety of melodramas and sentimental plays; other floating companies also offered nautical dramas, vaudeville, and even equestrian dramas. The Civil War caused an interruption in the tradition but the showboats reappeared in 1878 when Captain A B French launched his *New Sensation*. The last showboat, the *Dixie Queen*, was launched in 1939.

Show Boat A musical, by Oscar *Hammerstein II, with music by Jerome *Kern, based on a novel by Edna *Ferber. First performance: New York, 1927. A saga about life on a Mississippi show boat, it includes such songs as 'Ol' Man River' and 'Only Make Believe'. It was filmed in 1929, again in 1936 with Paul Robeson, Helen Morgan, and Irene Dunn, and again in 1951 with Kathryn Grayson.

Shtraukh, Maxim Maximovich (1900–74) Soviet actor and director, who became famous for his portrayal of character roles at the Proletkult Theatre (later the Trades Unions Theatre). He also appeared under Meyerhold at the Mayakovsky Theatre and at the Maly Theatre; his successes included impersonations of Lenin in Korneichuk's *Truth* (1937) and in films and Vishnevsky's *The Unforgettable 1919* (1949).

Shubert Theatre *See* Sam S Shubert Theatre.

Shumsky, Yakov Danilovich (d. 1812) Russian actor, who was a founding member of the first professional acting company in Russia. He was highly popular playing old women, most notably in *The Minor* (1782) by Fonvizin, and in comic roles in the plays of Holberg and Molière.

Shusherin, Yakov Emelyanovich (1753–1813) Russian actor, who was highly regarded in a variety of roles, ranging from the neoclassical dramas of Sumarokov and Lessing to plays in the *comédie-larmoyante* style. He appeared with the companies of Meddocks and Dmitrevsky and won royal approval in plays written by Catherine the Great herself.

Shuter, Ned (Edward Shuter; 1728–76) British actor, praised by Garrick as the greatest comic genius he had known. After making his debut at Richmond in 1744 he moved to Drury Lane, where he created, among other characters, Old Hardcastle, Sir Anthony Absolute, and Justice Woodcock in Bickerstaffe's *Love in a Village*.

Shwartz, Evgenyi Lvovich (1896–1958) Soviet actor and playwright, who was the author of several popular plays for young

people. *The Dragon* (1944), a lively and provocative political satire, was his most successful work; others included several based on fairytales, among them *Red Riding Hood* (1937) and *The Snow Queen* (1938).

Siddons, Sarah (Sarah Kemble; 1755–1831) British actress, the eldest child of Roger Kemble (1722–1802) and Sarah Ward (d. 1807), whose touring company was well-known. She disappointed her parents by marrying William Siddons (1744–1808), an actor in their company, when she was 18. In 1745 she was invited by Garrick to Drury Lane but her debut in *The Merchant of Venice* was unsuccessful and she returned to the provinces. Sheridan recalled her to Drury Lane in 1782 and her performance in Garrick's *Isabella* established her as the leading tragic actress of her day, winning acclaim for her beauty and her noble manner. Other memorable parts included the title role in Rowe's *Jane Shore* and Belvidera in *Venice Preserv'd*; later in her career she excelled in Shakespearean roles, notably as Lady Macbeth, although she never attempted comedy. In 1802 she and her brother, John Philip *Kemble, took over Covent Garden, where she appeared regularly until 1812.

Sierra, Gregorio Martínez *See* Martínez Sierra, Gregorio.

sightline An imaginary line extending from any particular seat in the auditorium to the stage, used to determine what the audience can see of the set and the wings.

Sigurjónsson, Jóhan (1880–1919) Icelandic playwright, who wrote in Icelandic and Danish. His play *Fjalla-Eyvindur* (Eyvind of the Hills; 1911), a tragedy based upon an Icelandic love story, was an outstanding success in Scandinavia, Germany, England, and the US; subsequent plays included *Galdra-Loftur* (Loftur the Sorceror; 1915).

Silence, Theatre of A theatrical theory developed in the 1920s, which emphasized the conveyance of meaning or emotion through means other than dialogue alone, chiefly through the use of long significant pauses. Major works employing the technique (also called the **Théâtre de l'Inexprimé**) include plays by Maeterlinck and Jean-Jacques Bernard.

sill-iron *See* saddle-iron.

Silva, António José da (1705–39) Portuguese playwright, born in Brazil, who wrote several lively comedies, notably *As Guerras Do Alecrim e da Mangerona* (1737). Others written before his death at the hands of the Inquisition on account of the fact that he was a Jew include the puppet play *A Vida do Grande D Quixote* (1733).

Silver Box, The A play by John *Galsworthy. First performance: Royal Court Theatre, 1906. The play deals with the contrasting treatment given by the law to two men, one rich and one poor, who are both accused of theft.

Silver King, The A melodrama by Henry Arthur *Jones and Henry Herman. First performance: 1882. A young Englishman, wrongfully accused of murder, flees the country; having made a fortune in the US, he returns to avenge himself.

Silver Tassie, The A play by Sean *O'Casey. First performance: London, 1929. Through the experiences of the soldier Harry Heegan, O'Casey discusses the corruption of human nature by war; when the Abbey Theatre refused to put it on, the author left Ireland altogether.

Silvia (Zanetta-Rosa-Giovanna Benozzi; c. 1701–58) Italian actress, who became the leading lady at the Comédie-Italienne after arriving in Paris in 1716. She was especially admired as heroines in the plays of Marivaux.

Sim, Alastair (1900–76) Scottish actor, who began a theatrical career when almost 30 years of age. He was soon recognized as a superbly idiosyncratic comedian, both on stage and in films, after appearing as Ponsonby in Hubert Griffith's *Youth at the Helm* (1934). Subsequently he starred in and directed many plays by James Bridie, including *Mr Bolfry* (1943 and 1956) and *Dr Angelus* (1947). He also played Captain Hook in *Peter Pan* on five occasions, excelled as Lord Ogleby in Colman the Elder's *The Clandestine Marriage* (1966), and was highly praised in revivals of Pinero's farces, notably as Mr Posket in *The Magistrate* (1969) and as the Dean in *Dandy Dick* (1973).

Simon, (Marvin) Neil (1927-) US playwright, who began by writing sketches for revue. His first full-length Broadway show, *Come Blow Your Horn* (1961), was written in collaboration with his brother, Daniel; since then he has won great popularity for his witty studies of modern US relationships, most notably with *Barefoot in the Park* and the collections of short plays in *Plaza Suite* and *California Suite*. His other works include the book for several musicals and several more serious, though less successful, plays written in the 1970s.
Principal works:
Come Blow Your Horn: 1961.
Barefoot in the Park: 1963.
The Odd Couple: 1965 (revised 1985).
The Star-Spangled Girl: 1966.
Plaza Suite: 1968.
The Last of the Red Hot Lovers: 1969.
The Gingerbread Lady: 1970.
The Prisoner of Second Avenue: 1971.
The Sunshine Boys: 1972.
California Suite: 1976.
They're Playing Our Song: 1978.
I Ought to Be In Pictures: 1980.
Brighton Beach Memoirs: 1983.

Biloxi Blues: 1985.

Broadway Bound: 1986.

Jake's Women: 1988.

Simonov, Konstantin Mikhailovich
(1915–79) Soviet journalist, novelist, poet,
and playwright, whose plays have been
widely translated and performed in the
West. War and the need for peace are pre-
dominant themes. *Russkiye Lyndi* (1942) was
highly acclaimed when seen as *The Russians*
at the Old Vic in 1943; subsequent works
included *A Fellow from Our Town* (1942),
Wait for Me (1943), *The Russian Question*
(1947), and the comedy *A Good Name*
(1953).

Simonov, Reuben Nikolaivich (1899–
1968) Soviet actor and director, who established his reputation as an actor with the
Moscow Art Theatre, which he joined in
1920. Particularly acclaimed as Rostand's
Cyrano de Bergerac, he later won acclaim as
a director with his production of
Sholokhov's *Virgin Soil Upturned* (1931) and
subsequently became the foremost director
at the Vakhtangov Theatre. His greatest successes included plays by Gorky and
Pogodin.

Simonson, Lee (1888–1967) US stage designer, who became famous for his designs
for modern plays produced by the Theatre
Guild, of which he was a founding member.
His most celebrated contributions included
his designs for O'Neill's *Dynamo* (1929) and
for plays by Masefield, Shaw, and Strindberg.

Simov, Victor Andreyevich (1858–1935)
Russian stage designer, who spent most of
his career with the Moscow Art Theatre. He
dominated the designs of all the organization's early productions, attracting much
praise for his work on the plays of Chekhov, Gorky, Shakespeare, and Tolstoy; later designs included those for Ivanov's *Armoured Train 14–69* (1927).

Simpson, Edmund Shaw (1784–1848) US
actor and manager, who became a leading
performer at the Park Theatre in New York
from 1809 to 1848. He became highly popular alongside such stars as Cooke, Kean,
and the elder Booth in such plays as
Richard III but from 1833 was forced by
injury to turn to fulltime management of
the theatre, relinquishing it only a short
time before his death.

Simpson, N(orman) F(rederick)
(1919–) British playwright, whose popular
surreal comedies are characterized by brilliant verbal humour. His first success, *A Resounding Tinkle* (1957), was followed by the
highly praised *One-Way Pendulum* (1959),
which concerns a man who builds a model
of the Old Bailey in his living-room and
finds himself in the dock. More recent plays
have been *The Cresta Run* (1965) and *Was
He Anyone?* (1972).

simultaneous-scene setting *See* composite
setting.

Sinclair, Arthur (Francis Quinton McDon-
nell; 1883–1951) Irish actor, who began at
the Abbey Theatre in 1904 in Yeats's *On
Baile's Strand* and made his London debut
in Lady Gregory's *Spreading the News*
(1905). He appeared in numerous comic
Irish roles on both sides of the Atlantic, notably in plays by Shaw, Synge, O'Casey,
and Lennox Robinson.

Sinden, Donald (Alfred) (1923–) British actor, who began his career entertaining
the troops during World War II and then
spent two seasons at Stratford-upon-Avon
before making his London debut in *Richard
II* in 1947. He came to prominence in Ruth
and Augustus Goetz's *The Heiress* (1949)
and then went into films, before returning
to Stratford in 1963, where he was outstanding as Richard Plantagenet in a Shakespeare trilogy, *The Wars of the Roses*. A virtuoso performer with a sonorous and

unmistakable voice, he has alternated between classics and modern comedies, his parts including Lord Foppington in Vanbrugh's *The Relapse* (1967), Gilbert in Ray Cooney and John Chapman's *Not Now, Darling* (1968), the title role in *Henry VIII* (1969), Lear (1977), and Sir Percy Blakeney in *The Scarlet Pimpernel* (1985). He is also well-known for his many television appearances.

Singspiele See ballad opera.

siparium See curtain.

Six Characters in Search of an Author (*Sei personaggi in cerca d'autore*) A drama by Luigi *Pirandello. First performance: Rome, 1921. The most celebrated of Pirandello's plays, it challenges the whole illusion of the theatre by introducing characters already rejected by the author, who attempt to take control of their own fate despite their confusion over their own identity and the presence of 'real' actors.

69 Theatre Company See Royal Exchange Theatre.

Sjöberg, Alf (1903–80) Swedish director, actor, and manager, who did much work in the theatre before winning acclaim as a director in cinema. As well as the plays of Shakespeare, he directed notable productions of works by Brecht, Ibsen, García Lorca, and Arthur Miller; his most famous film productions included Strindberg's *Miss Julie* (1959) and *The Father* (1969).

Skelton, John (c. 1460–1529) English poet and playwright, whose *Magnyfycence* (c. 1515–18) is a morality play offering moral instruction to the young Henry VIII. None of his other works survive.

skene A building behind the *proscenium* in the ancient Greek theatre, which was used as a dressing-room. Actors portraying gods probably appeared on the roof of this building and were lowered from it to the stage below.

Skin Game, The A play by John *Galsworthy. First performance: London, 1920. The play explores the conflict of interests between a genteel aristocratic family and their newly prosperous neighbours (over a piece of land); both parties are morally compromised by events.

Skinner, Otis (1858–1942) US actor, who first appeared on stage in 1877. He made his New York debut two years later and then worked with Augustin Daly and Modjeska. Acclaimed in plays by Sheridan, he won further praise in *Your Humble Servant* (1910) and *Mr Antonio* (1916), which were both written for him by Booth Tarkington. His greatest success, however, was as Hajj in Knoblock's *Kismet* (1911). From 1926 to 1933 he appeared in various Shakespearean roles, including Shylock and Falstaff.

His daughter, **Cornelia Otis Skinner** (1902–79), appeared with her father and was known as a singer and writer.

Skin of Our Teeth, The A play by Thornton *Wilder. First performance: New York, 1942. In it a family recreates the history of the world, concluding that mankind has survived thus far by the skin of its teeth; it was the most experimental and Expressionistic of Wilder's plays.

Skuszanka, Krystyna (1924–) Polish director, who attracted international attention while director at the People's Theatre in Nowa Huta. Such productions as Gozzi's *Turandot* (1956) and *The Tempest* (1959) were well-received when seen in Paris; subsequently she has worked at the Polski Theatre in Warsaw, the Wrocław Theatre, and Cracow's Słowacki Theatre, frequently alongside her husband and the director Jósef Szajna.

sky border *See* border.

sky cloth *See* cloth.

Slade, Julian (Penkivil) (1930-) British composer and playwright, who was the author (with Dorothy Reynolds) of the book, music, and lyrics for the popular musical *Salad Days* (1954). Other successes have included a musical version of *The Comedy of Errors* (1954), *Vanity Fair* (1963), and *Trelawny* (1972).

slapstick The bat traditionally wielded by Harlequin. It consists of two strips of wood bound together, which when struck against another object – usually one of the other characters on the stage – produces a convincing slapping noise. Slapsticks have also been employed in music hall, vaudeville, and by clowns. Slapstick comedy is any boisterous comedy.

Sleeping Clergyman, A A play by James *Bridie. First performance: Malvern Festival, 1933. The play explores the conflict between good and evil through three generations of one family.

Sleuth A thriller by Antony *Shaffer. First performance: London, 1970. The play revolves around its two central characters, both writers of murder stories, who act out their plots with one another until reality and fiction merge and the audience can no longer tell them apart.

slips A British term used in the early 19th century to denote those seats at the ends of the upper tiers of an auditorium. Its use has been retained at Covent Garden.

slip stage *See* wagon stage.

Sloman, Charles (1808–70) British music hall performer, whose reputation was made in the song-and-supper rooms. He specialized in the improvisation of verses on subjects suggested by the audience. He also wrote songs for Sam Cowell and served as chairman at the Middlesex Music Hall; he died in the workhouse.

slote A mechanical device, comprising an arrangement of metal rails and weights, by means of which actors or scenery can be raised to or lowered from the stage, often through traps. The slote was developed in the early 19th century; in the US it is usually referred to as a **hoist**.

Słowacki, Juliusz (1809–49) Polish poet and playwright, who was a leading figure of the Polish Romantic movement. Writing in exile mostly in Paris, where he was a rival of Mickiewicz, he saw Edmund Kean in *Richard III* in London in 1831 and was subsequently much influenced by Shakespeare in such plays as *Horsztyński* and his masterpiece *Kordian* (written in 1833 and first performed in 1899). He also executed adaptations of Calderón, notably *Il principe constante*, further tragedies – including *The Silver Dream of Salomé* and *Samuel Zborowski*, the comedy *Fantazy*, and *Lilla Weneda*, which drew on mythological material. His poetic dramas were rediscovered by Leon Schiller in the early 20th century.

Sly, William (d. 1608) English actor, who is known to have appeared in Tarleton's *Seven Deadly Sins* in about 1590, with Strange's Men. He is in the First Folio list of actors of Shakespeare's plays and may have been the first Osric. He joined the Chamberlain's Men in 1594, eventually becoming a shareholder in the Globe and Blackfriars theatres.

SM *See* stage manager.

Smirnov, Boris Alexandrovich (1908-) Soviet actor, who became an admired performer of classical roles at the Moscow Art Theatre. Having previously appeared in Leningrad, he was particularly successful as

Lenin in Pogodin's *Kremlin Chimes* (1956) and *The Third Pathétique* (1959).

Smith, Albert (1816–60) British playwright and performer, noted for his one-man entertainments. After having a drama produced at the Surrey Theatre in 1842, he embarked upon a series of extravaganzas and adaptations, mainly for the Keeleys at the Lyceum. In 1850, following an Indian tour, he wrote and performed *The Overland Mail*, with scenery by William Roxby Beverley. It proved highly popular and was followed by the similar *The Ascent of Mont Blanc* and *China*.

Smith, Dodie Gladys (Dorothy Gladys Smith; 1896-) British playwright and novelist, who used the pseudonym C L Anthony until 1935. She established her reputation with the play *Autumn Crocus* (1931); her other plays include *Service* (1932), *Touch Wood* (1934), *Call It A Day* (1935), and *Dear Octopus* (1938), her most successful work, in which the family is depicted as "that dear Octopus from whose tentacles we never quite escape". The play ran until the theatres were closed in 1939 and re-opened in 1940.

Smith, Edward Tyrrell (1804–77) British theatre manager, noted for his often reckless support for a variety of theatrical ventures. He rented Drury Lane in 1852 and ran it for seven years, opening successfully with *Uncle Tom's Cabin*; his involvement with less remunerative productions, however, eventually ruined him. His introduction of 'morning performances' anticipated the modern matinée.

Smith, Maggie (Natalie) (1934-) British actress, who appeared at Oxford before making her professional debut in New York in the revue *New Faces of '56*. She then joined the Old Vic company, being much admired in Shaffer's *The Private Ear* and *The Public Eye* at the Globe, before trans-

ferring in 1963 to the National Theatre company, in which she played Desdemona to Olivier's Othello and Silvia in Farquhar's *The Recruiting Officer* among many leading parts. Since then she has demonstrated the diversity of her talent in such roles as Amanda in *Private Lives* (1972), Cleopatra, Millamant, Virginia Woolf in Edna O'Brien's *Virginia* (1981), Lady Macbeth, and Nadia in Ronald Harwood's *Interpreters* (1985). Her most recent successes have included Stephen Poliakoff's *Coming in to Land* (1986) and Peter Shaffer's *Lettice and Lovage* (1987). She has also appeared in many films and television productions.

Smith, Oliver (1918-) US stage designer and producer, noted for his works on both ballets and straight drama. His designs for musicals have won much praise, particularly those for *On the Town* (1944), *Brigadoon* (1947), *Paint Your Wagon* (1951), *Pal Joey* (1942), *My Fair Lady* (1956), *West Side Story* (1957), *Flower Drum Song* (1958), *The Sound of Music* (1959), and *Camelot* (1960).

Smith, Sol(omon) Franklin (1801–69) US actor and manager, who became a powerful figure in the early development of US drama in the South and West in collaboration with Noah Ludlow. Their **American Theatrical Commonwealth Company** was highly successful and inspired the building of permanent theatres. Smith also appeared in comic roles at the Park Theatre and elsewhere as did his son, **Marc(us) Smith** (1829–74).

Smith, William (d. 1696) English actor in Betterton's company at Dorset Garden, where he appeared as the original Sir Fopling Flutter in *The Man of Mode* and created Otway's Pierre in *Venice Preserv'd* and Chamont in *The Orphan*. He then retired in the face of his unpopularity with some young nobles, but later returned to the theatre and died on stage.

Smith, William (1730–1819) British actor, known as Gentleman Smith. Through the influence of Spranger Barry he was engaged for the 1753 season at Covent Garden, where he stayed for 20 years. He joined Garrick at Drury Lane in 1774, first appearing as Richard III and later creating the role of Charles Surface in *The School for Scandal* (1777). He retired in 1788 to live the life of a sporting country gentleman at Bury St Edmunds.

Smith, William Henry Sedley- *See* Sedley-Smith, William Henry.

Smithson, Harriet Constance (1800–54) British actress, daughter of the manager of the Waterford and Kilkenny theatre circuit. She began her stage career at the Crow Street Theatre, Dublin, and arrived at Drury Lane in 1818. Subsequently she played many Shakespearean roles alongside Edmund Kean; in 1828 she was well received with Macready in Paris. She married Berlioz, the composer, in 1833 but they separated in 1840.

Smock Alley Theatre A theatre in Dublin opened by John Ogilby in 1662 with Fletcher's *Wit Without Money*. Also known as the **Orange Street Theatre**, it survived collapses in 1671 and again in 1701 to become the only public theatre in the capital from 1701 to 1733. Appearances by David Garrick and Peg Woffington were highly popular, while R B Sheridan's father, Thomas Sheridan (1719–88), ran the theatre from 1744 to 1758. The theatre was wrecked during his production of Voltaire's *Mahomet* (1754) and later saw a succession of managers before being closed by Richard Daly; it was demolished in 1815.

Smoktunovsky, Innokenti Mikhailovich (1925–) Soviet actor, who is recognized as one of the leading contemporary performers in the Soviet theatre. He began his career with the Gorky Theatre company in Lenin-grad, later appearing in London (1966) and at the Maly Theatre; his most successful roles have included Prince Myshkin in a version of Dostoevsky's *The Idiot* (1957) and a filmed Hamlet.

Snow, Sophia (1745–86) British actress, daughter of the trumpeter Valentine Snow. She appeared at Drury Lane on her marriage to Robert *Baddeley and excelled as Shakespearean heroines. Famed for her beauty, she was also a popular singer until her extravagance and addiction to laudanum ruined her career.

soccus A soft low-heeled shoe worn by the comic actor in the classical Greek or Roman theatre. It was later more commonly referred to as a sock. *See also cothurnus*.

Socialist Realism A school of Soviet theatre and art criticism of the 1930s. Developed by Lunacharsky, Socialist Realism reflected the ideals of the Revolution of 1917, advocating the treatment of themes relevant to the common people. As well as new works, classics were also reinterpreted to achieve the same end; soon, however, the movement became almost totally subservient to the Soviet government's propagandist aims. Notable early figures closely associated with the ideals of Socialist Realism included Gorky and Mayakovsky.

sociétés joyeuses Amateur theatre companies that flourished in France during medieval times. Such groups consisted largely of young men who presented ribald tales in their own locality following the decline of the comic theatrical tradition of religious houses; they represented the earliest origins of secular drama in France.

Society The first of T W *Robertson's important realistic comedies. First performance: 1865. A father and son attempt to buy their introduction into society; when Sydney Daryl – the gentleman approached

– declines to cooperate, the son attempts in vain to ruin him.

Society for Theatre Research A British theatre organization founded in 1948 at the Old Vic Theatre to coordinate research in the theatre in Britain. As well as publishing a journal, the society arranges lectures, conservation of theatre artefacts and records, and contributed to the foundation of the national Theatre Museum. It also helped to found the International Federation for Theatre Research and has a US counterpart, the American Society for Theatre Research.

Society of West End Theatre *See* West End.

Sofronov, Anatol Vladimirovich (1911-) Soviet playwright and songwriter, whose works are immensely popular in the USSR. He wrote his first play, *In One Town*, in 1945; subsequent successes have included *Beketov's Career* (1949), *A Man in Retirement* (1957), and *Honesty* (1962), in which Vera Pashennaya was highly praised.

soggetto, commedia a *See commedia dell'arte.*

Soleil, Théâtre du A French theatre company founded in Paris in 1964 as a workers' cooperative under Ariane Mnouchkine (1938-). The society experimented with the techniques of collective creation and established its reputation with performances of Wesker as well as its own original works. In 1972 it moved into dilapidated premises in a former military base, the **Cartoucherie de Vincennes**, which became a popular venue and home for several other experimental companies.

Somi, Leone Ebreo di (1527–92) Jewish playwright and writer on stage techniques. His *Dialogues on Stage Affairs* (c. 1565) describes in detail contemporary lighting prac-

tices, including the positioning of lights and the achievement of atmospheric effects.

Sønderby, Knut (1909–66) Danish novelist, essayist, and playwright, whose plays exposed the underlying insecurity of fashionable society in the 1920s. He dramatized his novel *En Kvinde er overflødig* (A Woman is Superfluous; 1936) very successfully; other triumphs included *Krista* (1947) and *Kvindernes Oprør* (The Woman's Uprising; 1955).

Sondheim, Stephen (Joshua) (1930-) US composer and lyricist, whose first music for the theatre was the incidental music for *Girls of Summer* (1956). He went on to write the lyrics for **West Side Story* (1957), *Gypsy* (1959), the music and lyrics for *A Funny Thing Happened on the Way to the Forum* (1962), the lyrics for *Do I Hear a Waltz?* (1965), and the music and lyrics for *Company* (1970), *Follies* (1971), and *A Little Night Music* (1973). He used oriental instruments in the score to *Pacific Overtures* (1976). Among his more recent work is the score to *Sweeney Todd* (1979).

son et lumière A theatrical entertainment in which productions are usually presented outdoors, with considerable use of floodlighting and recorded sound effects. Staged in castles or similar spectacular sites, such productions conventionally consist of re-enactments of episodes of local history. The earliest *son et lumière* performances were staged in France in the 1950s.

song-and-supper rooms Venues for musical entertainment that became popular in London and elsewhere in the early 19th century and preceded the development of the *music hall. Customers sat at tables and were served with food and drink while varied programmes of comic songs and monologues were presented free. The most famous of these venues, Evans's, was typical, being based initially in the cellar of a tavern; it was eventually enlarged as a music hall proper. Such venues were themselves descended from earlier clubs of a similar type, of which the most celebrated included the **Coal Hole** and the **Cyder Cellars**.

Sonnenfels, Josef von (1733–1817) Austrian director, who oversaw the reformation of the Viennese stage after becoming director of the Burgtheater (1776). A disciple of Gottsched, he supported the suppression of Hanswurst and popular farce and introduced a programme of serious drama; after his death his reforms were continued by Schreyvogel.

Sophocles (496 BC–406 BC) Greek playwright and administrator, born at Colonus near Athens, who was the author of over 100 plays, of which seven tragedies and fragments of a satyr-play survive. Known for his dancing while still a boy, he defeated Aeschylus in the Dionysia in 468 BC and went on to win a further 18 drama contests. His intricate tragedies, of which *Oedipus Rex* has proved the most lasting, dwell upon the conquest of suffering and are especially notable for their development of character.

Sophocles enlarged many of Aeschylus's ideas about drama, introducing a third actor and limiting the role of the chorus, numbering 15, to one of commentary upon the main action. His theories about drama, which also led to the evolution of the *periaktoi* as an early scenic device, had a profound influence upon Aristotle and other subsequent playwrights, including Seneca, Corneille, Dryden, and T S Eliot.

Principal works:

Ajax: 450 BC.

Antigone: c. 442 BC.

Oedipus Rex: 429 BC.

Trachiniae: c. 425 BC.

Electra: 409 BC.

Philoctetes: 409 BC.

Oedipus at Colonus: 401 BC.

Sophron of Syracuse (5th century BC) Greek playwright, author of several mime plays. Although none of his works survive, he is believed to have influenced the writings of Plato, Theocritus, and Herodas.

Sorano, Daniel (1920–62) French actor, who was much admired in both classical French comedy and in the plays of Shakespeare and his contemporaries. He began his career with Sarrazin's Grenier de Toulouse (which occupied a theatre named in his memory in 1965) and was subsequently highly acclaimed in Paris in leading roles in the plays of Molière. He then joined the Théâtre National Populaire and excelled in further Molière classics as well as in plays by Beaumarchais, Brecht, Hugo, and Marivaux, and as Shakespeare's Richard III and Shylock.

Sorge, Reinhard Johannes (1892–1916) German poet and playwright, who pioneered Expressionism in his first play *Der Bettler* (The Beggar; 1912), which utilized symbolic sets and a series of tableaux on its first production (1917) under Reinhardt. His later mystical and religious dramas included *König David* and *Der Sieg des Christos*. He died in the Battle of the Somme.

Sorma, Agnes (Agnes Zaremba; 1865–1927) German actress, who established her reputation as a player of young girls at the Deutsches Theater in Berlin in the 1880s. Subsequently she excelled as Juliet, Ophelia, and Desdemona and in plays by Grillparzer, Goldoni, Hauptmann, Sudermann, and Ibsen, notably as Nora in *A Doll's House*, in which role she appeared in several countries.

Sosnitsky, Ivan Ivanovich (1794–1871) Russian actor, who was admired for his refined interpretations of young men in plays by Griboyedov and others. A pupil of Dmitrevsky, he later successfully introduced a note of realism and satire to his performances.

Sothern, Edward Askew (1826–81) British actor, born in Liverpool. After appearances in the provinces, he joined Lester Wallack's company in New York but did not meet with success until he played Lord Dundreary in Tom Taylor's *Our American Cousin* at Laura Keene's Theatre in 1858. He repeated the role at the Haymarket in 1861 and continued to appear as Dundreary in sketches and monologues throughout his career. Other roles included the lead in T W Robertson's *David Garrick.*

Of his three sons on the stage, **Edward Hugh Sothern** (1859–1933) was the most successful, playing similar comic roles to those of his father and also some romantic parts. In 1904 he joined Frohman at the Lyceum Theatre in New York; later he formed his own company, presenting plays by Shakespeare and by his second wife, Julia *Marlowe, with whom he often appeared. He donated most of his company's property to the Shakespeare Memorial Theatre in 1924.

sotie A theatrical tradition of France in the Middle Ages. Performers, called *sots*, of such pieces dressed in the full costume of the medieval fool and presented light and amusing satirical entertainments loosely based on political or religious themes, they could be amateurs or belong to permanent troupes. Several written examples of the form survive, notably those of Pierre Gringore. The *sotie* was eventually prohibited in the 16th century due to its strong satirical element.

soubrette A class of minor female roles in comedy, typically those of flirtatious lady's maids.

Soul-Cakers Play *See* mummers' play.

sound effects Any special effect dictated by a script that requires the production of a specific noise, usually engineered offstage. Typical sound effects include various weather effects, the sound of animals, warfare, doors, traffic, and bells. In recent years extensive use has been made of recorded sound effects, although many are still produced live. *See also* glasscrash, rain machine, thunder run, thundersheet, wind machine.

Sound of Music, The A musical, written by Howard *Lindsay and Russel Crouse, with music by Richard *Rodgers and lyrics by Oscar *Hammerstein II. First performance: New York, 1959. Set in Austria in 1938, the plot concerns a young nun who becomes governess to the children of an Austrian captain, with whom she falls in love. She later helps the family to flee the country after the Nazi takeover. It was filmed in 1965 with Julie Andrews and Christopher Plummer.

Southerne, Thomas (1660–1746) English playwright of Irish parentage, who provided prologues and epilogues for some of Dryden's plays. He wrote several moderately successful comedies of manners but his two best plays were tragedies based on the novels of Aphra Behn, *The Fatal Marriage; or, the Innocent Adultery* (1694) and *Oroonoko* (1696). His other tragedies include *The Loyal Brother; or, the Persian Prince* (1682) and *The Spartan Dame* (1719).

South London Music Hall The third music hall to be built in London, opened in 1856. Connie Gilchrist and Florrie Forde appeared here early in their careers and the chairman, Bob Courtney, was one of the most famous in London. The theatre remained in use (as the Shoreditch Empire) until it was bombed in World War II.

South Pacific A musical, with music by Richard *Rodgers and lyrics by Oscar *Hammerstein II and Joshua *Logan. First performance: New York, 1949. The story takes place during World War II and revolves around a navy nurse who falls in love with a French planter. Both the Broadway and London productions starred Mary Martin.

South Street Theatre *See* Southwark Theatre.

Southwark Theatre The first permanent theatre in Philadelphia, which was built by David Douglass for his American Company in 1766. Made of timber and brick and painted red, it opened with Vanbrugh's *The Provoked Wife*. In 1767 the theatre (sometimes called the **South Street Theatre**) staged the first professional production of an American play, Godfrey's *The Prince of Parthia*. Closed during the War of Independence, it reopened briefly in 1778 and was temporarily used again by the American Company in 1784. Plays were performed there until it was damaged by fire in 1821. It was demolished in 1912.

Soviet Army, Central Theatre of the *See* Red Army Theatre.

Sovremennik Theatre A theatre founded in Moscow in 1958 by a troupe of young performers assembled by Yefremov from various venues in the city. Encouraged by the Moscow Art Theatre, the group established a strong reputation with productions of plays by John Osborne and Edward Albee as well as contemporary Soviet writers, placing an emphasis upon humanist themes. In 1975 it presented Shakespeare for the first time.

Soya (Carl Erik Soya-Jensen; 1896-) Danish short-story writer and playwright, whose plays include the naturalistic *Parasitterne* (The Parasites; 1929) and *Hvem er jeg?* (Who Am I?; 1931), which is considered his finest. He also wrote a tetralogy (1940–48): *Brudstykker af et Mønster* (Fragments of a Pattern), *To Traade* (Two Threads), *30 Aars Henstand* (30 Years' Res-

pite), and *Frit Valg* (Free Choice), which explore themes of justice and retribution.

Soyinka, Wole (Akinwande Oluwole; 1934-) Nigerian poet, novelist, literary critic, and playwright, who won a Nobel Prize in 1986. He studied in Britain as a young man and began his association with the theatre when he became one of the writers at the Royal Court Theatre in 1958. His verse play *The Dance of the Forests* was performed at the Nigerian Independence celebrations (1960), since when he has become Africa's leading dramatist.

His plays reflect the experiences of modern West African society (in particular his own Yoruba tribal history) and adopt a deeply satirical perspective. His interest in politics led to his imprisonment from 1967 to 1969 – an experience he recounted in the novel *The Man Died* (1973). He also adapted the National Theatre production of Euripides's *Bacchae* (1973) and is important for his foundation (1960) of a national Nigerian theatre, The Masks, which later became the Orisun Theatre; he is also head of the Nigerian branch of the International Theatre Institute.

Principal dramatic works:

The House of Banegeg: 1956.

The Swamp Dwellers: 1957.

The Lion and the Jewel: 1957.

The Invention: 1959.

The Dance of the Forests: 1960.

The Republican: 1964.

Before the Blackout: 1965.

The Road: 1965.

Kongi's Harvest: 1966.

Madmen and Specialists: 1971.

Death and the King's Horseman: 1975.

Spanish Tragedy, The A tragedy in blank verse by Thomas *Kyd. First performance: London, c. 1585–89. Set in Spain, the play focuses on the plight of Hieronimo, who, following the murder of his son and his failure to secure legal justice, becomes drawn into a bloody revenge dispute.

Speaight, Robert William (1904–76) British actor, who made his professional debut at Liverpool in 1926, coming to the Arts Theatre, London, in 1927 in Avery Hopwood's adaptation of *The Duchess of Elba*. He then had a long run in R C Sherriff's *Journey's End* (1929) and joined the Old Vic company (1931), where he played King John, Malvolio, and Cassius among other roles. In 1935 he played Becket in T S Eliot's *Murder in the Cathedral*, a part with which he became identified and repeated in numerous revivals. Other successes included appearances in Wilder's *A Life in the Sun* (1955) and Bolt's *A Man for All Seasons* (1962).

spectacle theatres The earliest playhouse built in Europe after the Middle Ages. Distinguished by their elaborate ornamentation, these included the Teatro Olimpico and Teatro Farnese in Italy, the only surviving examples.

spectatory *See* auditorium.

Speed the Plough A play by Thomas *Morton. First performance: 1798. A drama concerning the return of Sir Philip Blandford, who mistakenly believes he has killed his own brother, the play is remembered chiefly for the character of Mrs Grundy, who does not appear but became a symbol of middle-class propriety.

Spelvin, George *See* Plinge, Walter.

Speroni, Sperone (1500–88) Italian playwright, remembered as the author of the bloodthirsty tragedy *Canace* (1543). The violence of this play provoked considerable unrest when it was first presented in Padua.

Sperr, Martin (1944–) German playwright and director, who has written several plays depicting life in rural Bavaria. His most successful works include *Landshuter Erzählungen* (Tales from Landshut; 1967)

and *Koralle Meier* (1970), which concerns the relationship between a small town and a nearby concentration camp.

spieltreppe *See* Jessner, Leopold.

spot bar *See* batten.

spotlight A lighting unit, capable of producing a bright, narrow, beam. Spotlights are often equipped with such devices as barn door shutters and colour-wheels; these are one of the standard lighting units of the modern stage.

Spring Awakening (*Frühlings Erwachen*) The first play by Frank *Wedekind, written in 1891. First performance: Berlin, 1906. Revolving around a tragic love affair between two 14 year-olds, which results in an abortion and their deaths as a result of their parents' disapproval, the play was considered too outrageous to be seen publicly in Britain until 1963.

Spring '71 (*Le Printemps '71*) A play by Arthur *Adamov. First performance: 1961. Influenced by the epic theatre of Brecht, the play centres on the Paris Commune of 1871.

Staberl A character of the Viennese comic theatrical tradition, related to the clowns Hanswurst and Kasperl. Usually depicted as a jovial but scheming umbrella-maker, Chrysostomos Staberl was first played by Ignaz Schuster in Bäuerle's *Bürger von Wien* (1813) and was then seen in a lengthy series of popular comedies.

stabile, teatro *See* teatro stabile.

Stadt Theatre *See* Bowery Theatre.

stage cloth Any painted canvas or other floor covering laid over the stage-floor.

stage crew Theatre staff who undertake duties backstage, including the building and setting of scenery, the supply of props, and the control of the lighting and sound effects. They are under the direction of the stage manager.

stage direction An instruction, given in the script or by the director, to an actor telling him to move to a particular area of the stage or to the stage manager to call for a particular stage effect. Traditionally such directions are given in relation to the actor's view from the stage as he looks into the auditorium, so that what appears to the audience to be on the left hand side, for example, is conventionally expressed as stage right. Any movement towards the audience is labelled **downstage**, while those away from the audience are **upstage**; the area in the middle of the stage is called **centrestage**. Stage directions that an actor should move **above** an object on the stage indicate that the actor should be upstage of it; **below** denotes that he should be downstage of it. **Exit** indicates that an actor should leave the stage, while **enter** denotes that he should come onto it; **manet**, now little used, indicates that he should remain on the stage. The direction **cross** indicates that an actor should move from one side of the stage to the other, while **scissor cross** requires two actors to exchange positions on opposite sides of the stage.

stage door An entrance at the back of a theatre, through which actors and other theatre staff have access to the backstage area from outside the building. It is also traditionally the place where admirers of particular performers await the reappearance of the cast as they leave the theatre after a show.

stage door-keeper An employee of a theatre, who is responsible for ensuring that no unauthorized person obtains access to the theatre via the stage door.

stage-keeper The person responsible in the Elizabethan theatre for ensuring that the stage itself was kept in a reasonable condition for performances.

stage lighting *See* lighting.

stage manager (SM) The person in charge of the stage crew and responsible for ensuring that all goes smoothly both on the stage and backstage during a performance. Before the position of the director was developed in the 20th century the stage manager was also often in charge of rehearsals. He is usually helped by an **assistant stage manager** (ASM), who sometimes also acts as prompter.

Stage Society, Incorporated A British theatre organization founded in London in 1899 to present rarely performed experimental dramas. The society played at West End venues at times when they were not being used for more commercial productions, usually on Sunday nights. The first production was Shaw's *You Never Can Tell* (1899), while later successes included Shaw's *Mrs Warren's Profession* (1902), which had previously been refused a licence for public performance. Plays by Gorky, Wedekind, Tolstoy, Pirandello, James Joyce, Cocteau, and others, were also performed. Many of these transferred to the commercial stage. Later in its life the society presented classic plays and encouraged the foundation of the Phoenix Society, despite the fact that it faced mounting financial pressures itself.

In 1926 it amalgamated with the **Three Hundred Club**, founded in 1923, after which its productions included works by D H Lawrence and García Lorca. Notable theatrical figures associated with the Stage Society included the directors Granville-Barker, Michel Saint-Denis, and Allan Wade as well as such performers as Peggy Ashcroft, Edith Evans, and Laurence Olivier; Theodore Komisarjevsky made influential innovations in scenery in connection with the society's productions. The society was disbanded during World War II.

Stagnelius, Erik Johan (1793–1823) Swedish poet and playwright, author of several notable Romantic dramas. His highly poetic plays, several of which tackle the relationship between eroticism and religious feeling, include *Martyrerna* (1821) and *Bacchanterna* (1822), which were his only dramatic works published during his lifetime.

stalls *See* auditorium.

Standard Theatre A theatre in Shoreditch, London, which originated as part of the Royal Standard Public House and Pleasure Garden, where entertainment was offered in the early 1830s. It housed a circus ring, which was also used for plays and concerts, and was rebuilt in 1866 after a fire. It reopened as the New Standard Theatre, managed by John Douglass, who retained a first class company, staged fine pantomimes, and attracted visiting stars. The Melville brothers took over in 1888 and continued a similar policy until 1907, when the theatre became the **Olympia Music Hall**. It changed to a cinema in 1926 and was demolished following bomb damage in 1940.

The **Standard Theatre** on Broadway, New York, opened as the **Eagle Theatre** in 1875 as a variety house. Renamed the Standard, it was the venue in 1879 for the New York debut of Gilbert and Sullivan's *HMS Pinafore*; other productions were Bret Harte's *M'liss; An Idyll of Red Mountain, Patience*, which ran for the whole 1881 season, and *Iolanthe* (1882). Burnt down in 1883, it reopened the following year as a home of light opera. However in 1896, under William A Brady (who renamed it the Manhattan Theatre), the bill switched to straight drama. The theatre subsequently housed a successful company led by Mrs Fiske from 1901 to 1906. In 1909 the building was demolished.

Standing, John (Sir John Ronald Leon; 1934–) British actor, son of the actress Kay Hammond, who, after his first London appearance as Mr Charlton in *The Darling Buds of May* (1959), emerged as a fine comedy actor in such elegant roles as Algernon in Wilde's *The Importance of Being Earnest* (1968) and Elyot in Coward's *Private Lives* (1973). His appearances at the National Theatre have included Freddy Malone in Ben Travers's *Plunder* (1978) and Turai in Tom Stoppard's *Rough Crossing* (1984).

Stanfield, Clarkson (1793–1867) British marine painter and scenic designer, the son of an actor. He worked as a scene painter in Edinburgh and the Coburg Theatre (*see* Old Vic) before moving to Drury Lane. His theatre work diminished as he became increasingly successful as an easel-painter, although he did later paint at Covent Garden for Macready.

Stanislavsky, Konstantin (Konstantin Sergeyevich Alekseyev; 1863–1938) Russian director and actor, who founded the Moscow Art Theatre and first developed the principles that were later exaggerated as the basis of the *Method theory of acting. Having begun his career as an amateur actor, he subsequently trained under the Komisarjevskys and directed major plays by Leo Tolstoy and Dostoevsky before establishing the Moscow Art Theatre with Nemirovich-Danchenko in 1898.

That same year he produced his innovative version of Chekhov's *The Seagull*, in which conventional interpretations were rejected in favour of an intense psychological approach and a new naturalism in terms of acting, setting, and costume. A celebrated series of Chekhov's works followed, all characterized by subtle control of atmosphere and simplicity of delivery; most including Stanislavsky himself in the cast. Other productions included plays by Shakespeare, Ostrovsky, and, in 1902, Gorky's *The Lower Depths*.

Later he experimented with Formalism and Symbolism, notably through the plays of Maeterlinck and Andreyev, before concentrating upon teaching. His revolutionary theories concerning the psychology of acting, which have had a fundamental effect upon 20th-century drama, were summed up in 1936 in An *Actor Prepares and other essays.

Stapleton, (Lois) Maureen (1925-) US actress, who made her New York debut in Synge's *The Playboy of the Western World* (1946). She established her reputation as Serafina in Tennessee Williams's *The Rose Tattoo* (1951); subsequent successes have included Ann in *Richard III*, Elisabeth Proctor in Miller's *The Crucible* (1953), Masha in Chekhov's *The Seagull* (1954), Lady Torrence in Williams's *Orpheus Descending* (1957), Carrie in Lillian Hellman's *Toys in the Attic* (1960), Amanda Wingfield in Williams's *The Glass Menagerie* (1965), Evy Meara in Simon's *The Gingerbread Lady* (1970), and Birdie Hubbard in Hellman's *The Little Foxes* (1981).

Star Theatre A theatre on Broadway, New York, which was opened in 1861 as Wallack's Theatre by the elder James Wallack and was later run by his son Lester Wallack (1864-81). The theatre then staged plays in German until it was reopened as the Star in 1882. In 1883 this was the venue for Irving's New York debut with Ellen Terry and his Lyceum company. Managed by H E Abbey, the theatre won acclaim for modern plays; distinguished players who appeared there included Edwin Booth, Mary Anderson, Modjeska, Bernhardt, and Wilson Barrett. The building was demolished in 1901.

star trap A circular trap consisting of wooden segments divided into the shape of a star that spring open to allow an actor to make a sudden entrance onto the stage.

Staunton, Imelda (1956-) British actress, who made her debut in 1976 as Goldoni's *Mistress of the Inn* at the Swan Theatre, Worcester. In 1982 she joined the National Theatre where her parts included Lucy Lockit in *The Beggar's Opera* and Miss Adelaide in *Guys and Dolls*. In 1985 she won awards as Hannah in Ayckbourn's *A Chorus of Disapproval* at the National and as Bessie in Emlyn Williams's *The Corn is Green* at the Old Vic. She has also played leading roles with the Royal Shakespeare Company (1986-87) and, in 1988, appeared in *Uncle Vanya* at the Vaudeville Theatre.

Stead, James Henry (d. 1886) British music hall performer, who delivered songs at breathtaking speed, accompanied by frenzied acrobatic dancing. His most famous song was 'The Perfect Cure', which he first performed in 1861. He died in poverty after the novelty of his act had worn off.

Steaming A play by Nell Dunn. First performance: 1981. Set in a Turkish bath and having an all-female cast, the play caused a considerable stir at first with its nudity, but was soon recognized as a sympathetic examination of issues relating to women's rights.

Steele, Sir Richard (1672-1729) English essayist and playwright, of Anglo-Irish parentage. His first comedy, *The Funeral; or, Grief à la Mode* (1701), was followed by *The Lying Lover* (1703) and *The Tender Husband* (1705), all of which attempted to curb the excesses of earlier Restoration drama. A co-patentee of Drury Lane, he devoted most of his time to writing and editing *The Spectator*, *The Tatler*, and *The Theatre* (1719-20), which was the first English theatre paper. His final comedy, *The Conscious Lovers*, was adapted from Terence and successfully produced at Drury Lane in 1722.

Steele, Tommy (Thomas Hicks; 1936-) British singer and actor, who began as a pop idol of the 1950s but later became a star of variety and musical comedy. As well as such shows as *Half-a-Sixpence* (1963) and *Singin' in the Rain* (1983), he has also ventured into straight theatre, playing Tony Lumpkin in *She Stoops to Conquer* in 1960 and Truffaldino in Goldoni's *The Servant of Two Masters* in 1968.

Stein, Peter (1937-) German director, who has attracted much attention for his work at the Schaubühne Theatre, founded in 1962 in West Berlin. His most widely-acclaimed (and much-rehearsed) productions have included Bond's *Saved* (1967) and plays by Aeschylus, Gorky, Ibsen, and Shakespeare, several of which have been seen in other countries. In 1982 he supervised the Schaubühne's transfer to a larger building.

Steinbeck, John (Ernst) (1902–68) US novelist, who adapted his own novels *Of Mice and Men* (1937) and *The Moon Is Down* (1942) for the stage. The Rodgers and Hammerstein musical *Pipe Dream* (1955) was based on his novel *Sweet Thursday*. Among his other works to be dramatized were *Tortilla Flats* (1938) and *Burning Bright* (1950). He won a Nobel Prize in 1962.

Stephen Joseph Theatre in the Round A theatre in Scarborough, North Yorkshire, that was established by Stephen Joseph in the Public Library in 1955. The theatre moved to new premises overlooking Valley Bridge in 1976, adhering to its original policy of producing new plays in the round. Alan Ayckbourn, who became artistic director in 1970, has had most of his plays premiered there since 1959.

stereopticon *See* projector.

Stern, Ernst (1876–1954) German stage designer, born in Bucharest, who became famous for his designs for many of Reinhardt's productions. He was much admired for his work on the plays of Aeschylus, Goethe, and Shakespeare as well as more recent plays by such authors as Ibsen and Noël Coward; he also executed several designs for Shakespearean productions by Donald Wolfit's company.

Sternheim, Carl (1878–1942) German playwright, who satirized German bourgeois society in a number of grotesque comedies. His best-known play is *Die Hose* (The Knickers; 1911), which is the first in a series of plays that follows a bourgeois family's decline and was banned after its first production by Reinhardt. Other plays include *Bürger Schippel* (Citizen Schippel; 1913), *Der Snob* (1914), and *Die Marquise von Arcis* (1919), which was highly successful in its English translation as *The Mask of Virtue* (1935), starring Vivien Leigh.

Stevenson, Juliet (1956-) British actress, who made her debut with the Royal Shakespeare Company in *The Tempest* (1978) at Stratford-upon-Avon. Within a few years she graduated to such leading roles as Isabella in *Measure for Measure* (1983) and Rosalind in *As You Like It* (1985). With the National Theatre in 1987 she was highly acclaimed in the title role of Lorca's *Yerma*.

Stevenson, William (1521–75) English playwright. He is generally assumed to have written *Gammer Gurton's Needle* during his time as a fellow of Christ's College, Cambridge, thereby helping to establish the basis of native comedy within the formal framework of Plautus and Terence.

Stewart, Douglas (1911-) New Zealand-born poet, playwright, and critic, living in Australia, who wrote several poetic dramas based upon folk stories and legends. Much of his work was originally written for the radio; his plays include *Fire on the Snow* (1941), *The Golden Lover* (1943), *Ned Kelly* (1945), *Shipwreck* (1947), and *Fisher's Ghost* (1961).

Stewart, Nellie (1858–1931) Australian actress, who became a leading performer of comic opera in the late 19th century. Having made her acting debut as a child she enjoyed her greatest success after a long singing career when, in 1902, she acted in Kester's *Sweet Nell of Drury Lane*. Subsequent successes included Sheldon's *Romance* and Romeo to the Juliet of her daughter **Nancy Stewart** (1892–1973).

stichomythia A form of dialogue in which actors exchange a series of rapid single lines, usually for emotional or comic effect. The device was first developed in classical Greek verse drama.

Stiernhielm, Georg Olofson (1598–1672) Swedish poet and playwright, often referred to as 'the father of Swedish poetry'. His dramatic writing comprises a number of masques written for the royal court, notably *Then Fåoangne Cupido* (Cupid Captured; 1649).

Stirling, Fanny (Mary Anne Kehl; 1815–95) British actress, who first appeared under the name Fanny Clifton at the Coburg Theatre (now the Old Vic) in 1832. Subsequent London appearances included two seasons with Macready. She was particularly successful in such parts as Mrs Candour in *The School for Scandal*, Mrs Malaprop in *The Rivals*, and the Nurse in *Romeo and Juliet*.

stock company A number of actors organized into a company, which performed a limited repertory at a particular theatre or group of theatres in the 18th and 19th centuries. Usually led by the **Tragedian** and the **Low Comedian**, actors in the company were recruited to fulfil the roles of **Juvenile Lead**, **Old Man**, **Old Woman**, **Heavy Father**, **Heavy Woman**, **General Utility**, **Walking Lady**, **Walking Gentleman**, **Supernumerary**, and other lesser characters. The system ended with the advent of professional touring companies in the late 19th century.

Stoll Theatre A theatre in Kingsway, London, which was opened as the London Opera House by the elder Oscar Hammerstein in a bid to rival Covent Garden. Early productions were failures and in 1917 Oswald Stoll turned it into a cinema. It became a theatre again in 1941 and for 10 years housed revivals of such musicals as *Rose Marie* and *The Student Prince*, as well as spectacular ice shows. Subsequently it presented ballet and opera seasons as well as the long-running musical *Kismet* (1955). Its final show was a five-week season of the Stratford-upon-Avon *Titus Andronicus*, starring Laurence Olivier and Vivien Leigh. It closed in 1957 and was replaced by an office block and the *Royalty Theatre, which opened in 1960.

Stoppard, Tom (Tom Straussler; 1937–) British playwright, born in Czechoslovakia, whose distinctive combination of satire, verbal dexterity, and brilliant plot structure has produced many award-winning plays. His first play, *Rosencrantz and Guildenstern are Dead*, brought him instant recognition as a writer in the tradition of the Theatre of the Absurd. *The Real Inspector Hound* and *After Magritte* were among the successful one-act plays that followed, the former revolving around two drama critics who become fatally linked to the murder mystery they are reviewing. *Jumpers* and *Travesties* consolidated his reputation for inventive dialogue and intelligent discussion of complex intellectual issues, while *Dirty Linen* and the musical play *Every Good Boy Deserves Favour* tackled contentious political issues, the latter depicting a political dissident in a Soviet psychiatric hospital. *The Real Thing* was a marital tragi-comedy, while *Hapgood* was modelled upon the conventional spy-thriller. Other works have included adaptations of Schnitzler's *Das Weite Land* as *Undiscovered*

Country (1979) and of Nestroy's *Einen Jux will er sich machen* as *On the Razzle* (1981). Principal works:

Enter a Free Man: 1964.

Rosencrantz and Guildenstern are Dead: 1966.

The Real Inspector Hound: 1968.

After Magritte: 1970.

Jumpers: 1972.

Travesties: 1974.

Dirty Linen: 1976.

New Found Land: 1976.

Every Good Boy Deserves Favour: 1977.

Night and Day: 1978.

Dogg's Hamlet: 1979.

Cahoot's Macbeth: 1979.

The Real Thing: 1982.

Hapgood: 1988.

Storey, David Malcolm (1933-) British novelist and playwright, whose first play, *The Restoration of Arnold Middleton*, was staged at the Royal Court Theatre, London, in 1967 to immediate acclaim. This was followed by *In Celebration* (1969), which depicted a 40th wedding anniversary party, *The Contractor* (1970), the action of which centres on the erection of a marquee for a wedding reception, and *Home* (1970), an examination of life in a mental institution. Other plays have included *The Changing Room* (1971), *Cromwell* (1973), *The Farm* (1973), *Life Class* (1974), *Mother's Day* (1976), *Sisters* (1978), *Early Days* (1980), and *Phoenix* (1984).

Storm, The (*Groza*) A play by Alexander *Ostrovsky, regarded as his masterpiece. First performance: 1859. Set in a small town on the Volga, the play depicts the tragic love and suicide of the young wife of a merciless trader.

Storm and Stress *See Sturm und Drang.*

Strand Musick Hall *See Gaiety Theatre.*

Strand Theatre A theatre in the Strand in London, which opened in 1832 after several years' use without a licence. It staged burlesque and melodrama before reopening in 1833 under Fanny Kelly and housing a theatre school. It was again reopened in 1836 by Douglas Jerrold, who presented popular adaptations of the novels of Dickens; subsequent successes under William Farren included a version of Goldsmith's *The Vicar of Wakefield* (1848). In 1850 the theatre was renamed **Punch's Playhouse** but failed to prosper until 1858, when burlesques by H J Byron were successfully staged. The theatre was altered in 1865, closed in 1882, and then reopened with classical comedies and revivals of H J Byron. The theatre closed for good in 1905 and was demolished to make way for the Aldwych underground station.

Another **Strand Theatre** was opened in 1905 as a companion to the Aldwych Theatre on the opposite corner of Catherine Street and the Aldwych, and was originally called the Waldorf Theatre. It was leased to the US impresarios the Shubert brothers and began with a season of Italian opera, which alternated with plays performed by Eleanora Duse and her company. Beerbohm Tree, H B Irving, and Cyril Maude all played at the theatre in its early years. In 1909 the name was changed to the Strand; two years later it became the **Whitney Theatre**, after the US manager F C Whitney (who purchased the building); however, in 1913 it reverted to the Strand. Under Louis Mayer's directorship (1913–16) the theatre scored its first major success, Vernon and Owen's *Mr Wu*, with Matheson Lang. José Levy, who took over in 1916, was followed in 1919 by Arthur Bourchier. Among a number of popular Bourchier productions was R L Stevenson's *Treasure Island* (1922), which was revived each Christmas until 1926, and again in 1929. Fred Terry and Julia Neilson presented a season of plays from 1928, including *The Scarlet Pimpernel*. During the 1930s the Strand presented several musical farces as well as *1066 and All That* (1935). Donald Wolfit gave lunchtime performances of Shakespeare throughout the London blitz (1940–41); in 1942 *Arsenic and Old Lace* began its run of 1337 performances, a record only surpassed by the more recent *No Sex Please – We're British* (1971–82). Notable productions in the intervening years were *Sailor Beware* (1955) and *A Funny Thing Happened on the Way to the Forum* (1963), starring Frankie Howerd. The theatre was completely refurbished in the early 1970s. In 1987 a revival of *Cabaret* had to be cancelled because of a trade union dispute.

Strange's Men An English theatre company, first recorded performing at Court in 1582. Closely associated for some years with the Admiral's Men, the company appeared at the Theatre (1590–91) and included Shakespeare among its members; subsequently it performed at the Rose Theatre (1592–93) in several of Shakespeare's plays as well as in works by Greene, Marlowe, and others. After 1594 the company moved to the provinces, although several members left to join the Chamberlain's Men.

Stranitsky, Joseph Anton (1676–1726) Austrian actor, who played a key role in the creation of the stock comic character *Hanswurst. He developed the role while performing with his own troupe at their home in the Kärntnertortheater in Vienna and made him the central figure in numerous comic plays.

Strasberg, Lee (1901–82) US director and producer, born in Austria-Hungary, who began as an assistant stage manager at the Garrick Theatre in 1924. He went on to direct plays for the *Group Theatre, which he cofounded in 1931, before becoming director for the *Actors' Studio in 1950. There he directed such successes as Chekhov's *Three Sisters* (1965), the premiere of Odets's *The Silent Partner* (1972), Paul Zindel's *The Ef-*

fect of Gamma Rays on Man-In-the-Moon Marigolds (1973), and O'Neill's *Long Day's Journey into Night* (1973).

Stratford (Ontario) Festival A major theatre festival founded in Stratford, Ontario, in Canada in 1953, specifically for the production of the plays of Shakespeare. Under Tyrone Guthrie and Tanya Moiseiwitsch the festival rapidly acquired a strong reputation and a permanent theatre was erected in 1957, arousing great interest with its semicircular auditorium and intimate atmosphere.

Michael Langham succeeded Guthrie in 1956 and, like his predecessor, presented notable foreign stars alongside a well-respected resident Canadian company; actors associated with the festival have included Alec Guinness, Gratien Gélinas, Christopher Plummer, William Hutt, Paul Scofield, Jessica Tandy, and Maggie Smith. As well as Shakespeare, the company has presented plays by such authors as Marlowe, Molière, and Shaw; contemporary works have also been presented and the company has also travelled widely. A second theatre, the **Avon Theatre**, was opened in 1963 and an experimental venue, the **Third Stage**, was added in 1971.

Jean Gascon and John Hirsch succeeded Langham in 1967 and Gascon was sole director from 1969 to 1974, encouraging the performance of European classics; the company had presented all of Shakespeare's plays by 1978. Robin Phillips took over in 1975, emphasizing the native Canadian aspects of the festival and making many reforms; John Hirsch replaced him in 1980.

Strattis (4th century BC) Greek playwright, author of examples of Old Comedy. Fragments of his satirical writings on contemporary figures survive.

Stratton, Eugene (Eugene Augustus Ruhlmann; 1861–1918) British music hall singer, born in the US, who came to

London in 1881 and had a brilliant career as a coon singer. He performed such sentimental songs as 'Lily of Laguna' and 'Little Dolly Day Dream'.

Streater, Robert (1624–80) English artist, one of the earliest known English scene painters. Several times praised by John Evelyn, 'His Majesty's Sergeant Painter' worked at the Court theatre in Whitehall and was particularly praised for the sumptuous scenes for Dryden's *The Conquest of Granada* (1670–71).

Streetcar Named Desire, A A Pulitzer Prize-winning play by Tennessee *Williams. First performance: Broadway, 1947, directed by Elia Kazan, with Jessica Tandy as the precocious but neurotic Blanche DuBois. Blanche's mental disintegration in the face of her brother-in-law Stanley's brutality is the central theme of the play. Stanley was played by the young Marlon Brando.

Street Scene A play by Elmer *Rice. First performance: New York, 1929. The play takes place on a slum street on a hot summer night, when an adulterous wife is shot by her husband. The film, made in 1931, starred Silvia Sidney. A musical version by Kurt *Weill was staged in 1947.

Strehler, Giorgio *See* Piccolo Teatro della Città di Milano.

Streisand, Barbra (1942-) US actress and singer, who made her first appearance in cabaret. She went on to play Miss Marmelstein in *I Can Get It For You Wholesale* (1962) and Fanny Brice in Styne's *Funny Girl* in 1964, taking the part to London in 1966; subsequently she has concentrated on acting in and directing films.

Strife A play by John *Galsworthy. First performance: London, 1909. The play vividly dramatizes the struggle between industrial management and working men during a prolonged strike, depicting with sympathy the suffering it causes.

strike To remove an item of scenery or other object from the stage, or the entire set itself.

Strindberg, (Johann) August (1849–1912) Swedish playwright and novelist, whose best-known plays are characterized by his compulsive interest in the conflict between the sexes. Strindberg's unsettled childhood influenced much of his writing, which frequently demonstrates his emotional instability. After early experiments with historical dramas and farces influenced by his reading of Ibsen he adopted an increasingly embittered tone culminating in the mysogenistic drama *The *Father*, which he wrote during the first (1877–91) of his three unhappy marriages (to the actress Siri von Essen).

**Miss Julie* and *The *Creditors* were equally savage and pessimistic in their indictment of sexual relationships and constitute a landmark in the Scandinavian theatre with their naturalistic dialogue. After the failure of his second marriage (1893–94), to the Austrian journalist Frida Uhl, however, Strindberg underwent a complete mental breakdown; subsequently (as well as becoming interested in alchemy) he exchanged his naturalistic approach for a more Realist tone and widened the scope of his drama. Works of this prolific period include the lengthy mystical play *To Damascus* and explorations of a range of topics, from historical subjects to the more sombre symbolism of such plays as *The Dance of Death* and *A *Dream Play*, which anticipated the development of Expressionism.

In 1904 his third marriage, to the Norwegian actress Harriet Bosse, whom he had married in 1901, ended in divorce; at the same time Strindberg became more closely involved with the Intima Teatern in Stockholm, where such late dramas (sometimes called the Chamber Plays) as *The *Ghost

Sonata, The *Storm, and The Burnt House were first performed. Several of his many dramatic works are regularly revived on the international stage and remain influential for their sexual subject matter, as well as for their technical virtuosity.
Principal works:
Mäster Olof: 1890 (written 1872).
Lycko-Pers Resa: 1883.
Fadren: 1887; translated as *The Father*.
Fröken Julie: 1889; translated as *Miss Julie*.
Fordringsägare: 1890; translated as *The Creditors*.
Advent: 1898.
Folksungagen: 1899; translated as *The Saga of the Folkungs*.
Gustaf Vasa: 1899.
Erik XIV: 1899.
Gustaf Adolph: 1899.
Brott och Brott: 1899; translated as *Crimes and Crimes*.
Påsk: 1900; translated as *Easter*.
Till Damaskus: 1900.
Dödsdansen I–II: 1905 (written 1901); translated as *The Dance of Death*.
Kronbruden: 1901; translated as *The Crown Bride*.
Ett drömspel: 1905 (written 1902); translated as *A Dream Play*.
Spöksonaten: 1908 (written 1907); translated as *The Ghost Sonata*.
Oväder: 1907; translated as *The Storm*.
Brända tomten: 1907; translated as *The Burnt House*.
Pelikanen: 1907; translated as *The Pelican*.

strip light *See* batten.

strip-tease *See* burlesque.

Stritch, Elaine (1926-) US actress, who made her first stage appearance in 1944. Her successes since then have included Regina Giddens in Lillian Hellman's *The Little Foxes* (1947), Sally Adams in *Call Me Madam* (1953), Grace in Inge's *Bus Stop* (1955), Martha in Albee's *Who's Afraid of Virginia Woolf?* (1963), and a starring role in Sondheim's *Company* (1970).

stroboscope A unit of lighting, capable of producing rapid flashes of light that create the illusion of slow motion on the stage.

Strømsted, Liv (1922-) Norwegian actress, who became a leading performer at the Nationaltheatret in Oslo. She has won acclaim in a wide range of plays, from the tragedies of Shakespeare to dramas by Brecht and Ibsen, notably *The Master Builder*, *Peer Gynt*, and *A Doll's House*.

Student Prince, The An operetta by Sigmund Romberg, based on the play *Old Heidelberg* by Wilhelm Meyer-Foerster. First performance: New York, 1924. The plot revolves around a prince studying in Heidelberg and his romance with a barmaid.

Studio Arena Theatre A US theatre company originally called the Buffalo Community Theatre, which was founded in 1927. By 1965 they were a completely professional theatre company specializing in contemporary US drama. Among the many premieres given by the group have been Albee's *Box Mao Box* (1968), Truman Capote's *Other Voices, Other Rooms* (1973), and Paul Giovanni's *The Crucifer of Blood* (1978).

Sturdza-Bulandra, Lucia (1873–1961) Romanian actress, who – with her husband – founded a noted company in 1914. Highly acclaimed in a wide range of parts, she and her husband led the company until 1943, noted successes including Zamfirescu's *Miss Anastasia* (1928). Upon her husband's death she became manager of the Municipal Theatre, which was subsequently renamed the Bulandra Theatre in her honour.

Sturm und Drang (Storm and Stress) A theatrical movement of 18th-century Germany based upon the principles of Romanticism. Taking Shakespeare as their model, writers of the genre – of whom Goethe and Schiller were the most important – tackled such themes as injustice and passion in highly emotional terms. The movement's philosophy was largely derived from Rousseau's writings, and took its name from the title of a play by Klinger (1776). The form was highly influential upon the development of *melodrama and spawned a subsidiary genre, the *Ritterdrama.

Stuyvesant Theatre See Belasco Theatre.

Sudakov, Ilya Kayovleivich (1890–1969) Soviet actor and director, who began his career at the Moscow Art Theatre. After success with such plays as Ivanov's *Armoured Train 14–69* (1927) and Afinogenov's *Fear* (1935), he moved to the Maly Theatre (1937) and finally to the Gogol Theatre in Moscow. Notable productions after World War II included Chekhov's *Uncle Vanya* (1947) and Alexei Tolstoy's *The Road to Calvary* (1957).

Suddenly Last Summer A play by Tennessee *Williams. First performance: New York, 1958. The plot concerns the rape and beating of a homosexual poet; his young cousin, witnessing the crime, goes mad. The play was filmed in 1959 with Katherine Hepburn, Elizabeth Taylor, and Montgomery Clift.

Sudermann, Hermann (1857–1928) German novelist, playwright, and pioneer of Realism in Germany. His brilliant dramatic technique transformed otherwise superficial treatments of the problems facing contemporary Berlin society; his most famous play – *Heimat* (Magda; 1893) – was performed worldwide with such leading ladies as Sarah Bernhardt, Eleonora Duse, Mrs Patrick Campbell, and Minnie Maddern Fiske. He also wrote historical and biblical plays but was better known for such dramas of intrigue as *Es lebe das Leben!* (The Joy of Living; 1902) and *Der gute Ruf* (A Good Reputation; 1913).

Sud-Est, Centre Dramatique du See *Décentralisation Dramatique.*

Suett, Richard (1755–1805) British actor, known as Dicky Suett. An actor from the age of 14, as a member of Foote's company at the Haymarket, he was eminently successful playing Shakespearean clowns. Admired by George III, he was noted for his practical jokes and collection of wigs.

Sukhovo-Kobylin, Alexander Vasilievich (1817–1903) Russian playwright, who wrote three dramas depicting the changing nature of contemporary Russian society. A nobleman, he was imprisoned while writing his first play, the comedy *Svad'ba Krechinskogo* (Krechinsky's Wedding; 1855), after being implicated in the death of his mistress and thereafter suffered from the attentions of the censor. Together with his other two plays, the satires *Delo* (The Case; 1881) and *Smert' Tarel'kina* (Tarelkin's Death; 1900), this play was much influenced by Gogol and Saltikov-Shchedrin.

Sullivan, Sir Arthur See Gilbert, Sir William Schwenk.

Sullivan, (Thomas) Barry (1821–91) British actor, who gained a reputation in Ireland before touring the provinces and managing a theatre in Aberdeen for three years. In 1852 he played Hamlet at the Haymarket, subsequently joining Phelps at Sadler's Wells and touring the US and Australia. In 1879 he played opposite Helen Faucit at the inaugural performance in the Memorial Theatre, Stratford-upon-Avon.

Sumarokov, Alexei Petrovich (1718–77) Russian playwright and poet, known as 'Racine of the North'. His neoclassical dramas drew heavily on Russian history and include several comedies and nine tragedies as well as an adaptation of *Hamlet*. He encouraged the foundation of the first professional acting company in Russia and was director of the Russian Theatre in St Petersburg from 1756 to 1761.

Summer and Smoke A play by Tennessee *Williams. First performance: New York, 1948. The plot concerns a spinster, Alma, and the local rebel, John; at the beginning of the play John pursues Alma, who will have nothing to do with him, but by the end of the play Alma pursues John, who has since become the town doctor and turns her down.

Sumner, John (1924-) British director, who has become recognized as a leading figure in Australian theatre. He was closely associated with the Melbourne Theatre Company from 1959, having previously directed the premiere of Ray Lawler's *Summer of the Seventeenth Doll* (1955) for the Union Theatre Repertory Company. Other significant productions have included several other plays by Lawler.

Supernumerary *See* stock company.

Suppliant Women, The A tragedy by *Aeschylus. First performance: Athens, c. 460 BC. The first part of a tetralogy, it depicts the adventures of Danaus and reflects the threat to contemporary Athens presented by various neighbours. Another tragedy of the same name was written by *Euripides (date unknown) but was based on a different plot.

Surrey Music Hall *See* Winchester Music Hall.

Surrey Theatre A theatre in Blackfriars Road, London, which was converted by Elliston in 1809 from an amphitheatre known as the **Royal Circus**, originally opened in 1782. He incorporated ballets in all his productions to overcome the Patent Act, but

without much success and he relinquished the theatre to Thomas Dibdin after five years. However, Elliston returned as manager in 1827 and had an outstanding success with Douglas Jerrold's *Black-Ey'd Susan* (1829); later managements established the theatre as a home of popular melodrama. It was burned down in 1865, but was rapidly rebuilt and after George Conquest took over in 1880 it became famous for sensational dramas and pantomime. When he died the theatre suffered a decline and was demolished in 1934.

Susie *See* Toby.

Sussex's Men An English theatre company formed by the Earl of Sussex in 1569. The company played at Court, in the provinces, and at the Rose Theatre under Henslowe, performing Shakespeare's *Titus Andronicus* and other works before the Earl's death in 1593 and its subsequent dissolution.

Sutherland, Efua (1924-) Ghanaian playwright, who has done much to popularize theatre in Ghana. She founded the Experimental Theatre Players in 1958 and the Ghana Drama Studio in Accra in 1960, since when she has also been very active as a teacher of drama. Her own plays include *Edufa* (1957), which is an adaptation of *Alcestis* by Euripides, *Foriwa* (1967), *The Marriage of Anansewa* (1975), and plays for children.

Suzman, Janet (1939-) British actress, born in South Africa, who has established a strong reputation in both Shakespearean and modern drama. Married to Trevor *Nunn, she joined the Royal Shakespeare Company in 1962; early successes included performances as Portia, Ophelia, and Rosalind as well as roles in plays by Willis Hall and Pinter. In 1972 she was acclaimed as Shakespeare's Cleopatra, while more recent successes have included Athol Fugard's *Hel-*

lo and Goodbye (1973), Masha in Chekhov's *Three Sisters* (1976), Ibsen's *Hedda Gabler* (1977), and Clytemnestra and Helen in *The Greeks* (1980).

Svoboda, Josef (1920-) Czech stage designer, who has attracted much attention for his work as head designer since 1948 of the National Theatre in Prague. His innovative and highly influential designs for theatres in other countries have included his abstract set for Ostrovsky's *The Storm* (1966) and Chekhov's *Three Sisters* (1967), both seen at London's National Theatre. Other notable productions have included Gogol's *The Government Inspector* (1948), *Hamlet* (1959), and Dostoevsky's *The Idiot* (1970). He is also widely known for his development of the **Laterna Magica**, a method by which cinematic projections and live performances are combined. In 1973 he founded a group specifically to present such productions.

Swann, Donald (Ibrahim) (1923-) British composer and performer in revue, who became highly popular working in collaboration with Michael *Flanders. From 1956 he and Flanders toured the world in their revue *At the Drop of a Hat* and subsequently *At the Drop of Another Hat*. Swann's solo shows have included *Between the Bars* and *Swann con Moto*.

Swanston, Eliard (d. 1651) English actor, who became well known as a member of the King's Men from 1624. His roles ranged from Othello to Chapman's Bussy d'Ambois. He was also involved in the business management of the company; during the Civil War he worked as a jeweller and supported the Parliamentarians.

Swan Theatre The fourth Elizabethan playhouse to be built in London, erected on Bankside by Francis Langley in about 1595. The theatre is known from a sketch made by a Dutch visitor, Johanne de Witt. The theatre was first let to Pembroke's Men but their controversial production of the satirical play *The Isle of Dogs* caused the suspension of dramatic performances there for some months. Various contests and exhibitions also took place while Lady Elizabeth's Men, led by Henslowe, performed for two years there before moving to the Hope. Middleton's *A Chaste Maid in Cheapside* was produced in 1611 and it is possible that Prince Charles's Men appeared there a few years later; after 1621 it seems to have been used for prize fights and, by 1632, was derelict.

The **Swan Theatre** at Stratford-upon-Avon was designed by Michael Reardon, who was not uninfluenced by de Witt's drawing, and built in the shell of the old *Shakespeare Memorial Theatre, a space used for years as a rehearsal room. Here the Royal Shakespeare Company produces plays from the apocryphal Shakespearean canon or works that he might have influenced, or been influenced by. The theatre opened in 1986 with *The Two Noble Kinsmen*; subsequent productions have included Thomas Heywood's *The Fair Maid of the West*, Aphra Behn's *The Rover*, and Ben Jonson's *The New Inn*. Edward Bond's *Restoration* was the first contemporary play to be staged there (1988).

swazzle *See* Punch and Judy.

Sweet Bird of Youth A play by Tennessee *Williams. First performance: New York, 1959. Chance, a Hollywood drifter, brings the Princess Kosmonopolous back to his hometown, only to meet with trouble from the father of a girl he had once seduced.

Świnarski, Konrad (1930-75) Polish director, who had attracted a wide reputation before his early death in an air crash. After training with the Berliner Ensemble he presented the premiere of Weiss's *Marat/Sade* (1963) and subsequently worked in Cracow, where he took over the Stary Theatre in 1969. His innovative productions included such works as Krasiński's *The Undivine*

Comedy (1965) and plays by Shakespeare, while his production of Mickiewicz's *Forefathers' Eve* was seen in London in 1975; among his last works was Mayakovsky's *The Bed Bug*.

Swinbourne, Charlotte Elizabeth *See* Vandenhoff, George.

Swiney, Owen (1675–1754) British actor and manager, born in Wexford, Ireland, who appeared with the Drury Lane company in 1700 and also acted as Christopher Rich's manager. He leased the Haymarket in 1705, where he was forced to stage opera due to the licensing laws, and managed Drury Lane for a brief period before returning to the Haymarket. He left the country to escape creditors in 1710 and did not return for 20 years, when he called himself **MacSwiney**. He was the constant companion of Peg Woffington.

Sword Play *See* mummers' play.

Sydney Opera House A distinctive theatre and operatic complex on the harbour front in Sydney, Australia, designed by Jorn Utzon and opened in 1973. It houses four separate auditoriums, of which one (seating 500) is used for straight dramatic productions. The Old Tote Theatre company was resident there for a time until the formation of the Sydney Theatre Company, which was installed there in 1980.

Symbolism A philosophical movement in the theatre and the arts in general, which constituted a reaction against Realism. It emphasized the deliberate use of artificial representation in order to convey the inner significance of life as opposed to superficial realities. The first Symbolist dramas were created by Paul Fort and subsequently Lugné-Poë at the Théâtre d'Art in the late 1890s; noted writers of such plays included Maeterlinck, Yeats, and O'Neill. In a wider sense the same philosophy has been applied in practical terms in the theatre since early times with, for example, the highly developed use of symbolic props in the Japanese and medieval drama.

symphonic drama *See* Green, Paul.

Syndicate *See* Theatrical Syndicate.

Synge, John Millington (1871–1909) Irish playwright, born in Dublin, whose plays reflect his understanding of character and his poetic use of language. Educated at Trinity College, Dublin, he spent some years travelling in Europe before settling in Paris. In 1896 he met W B Yeats, who persuaded him into visiting the Aran Islands off Galway, where he spent every summer between 1898 and 1902. He recounted his experiences in *The Aran Islands*; his work as a dramatist began after 1902, when he joined the Irish National Dramatic Society. All of his six plays explore life in remote rural communities with irreverence and ironic humour; however, they angered nationalists, who felt that they misrepresented the Irish people and Catholicism and offended decency. Synge's early death deprived the Abbey Theatre of its first great dramatist; such masterpieces as The **Playboy of the Western World* are constantly revived.
Principal works:
In the Shadow of the Glen: 1903.
*Riders to the Sea: 1904.
The Well of the Saints: 1905.
The Playboy of the Western World: 1907.
The Tinker's Wedding: 1908.
*Deirdre of the Sorrows: 1910.

Syrus, Publilius *See* Publilius Syrus.

Szajna, Józef (1922-) Polish director and set designer, who became famous for his work at the People's Theatre in Nowa Huta (of which he was director from 1963 to 1966) and subsequently at the Studio Theatre in Warsaw. As well as classic plays by Dante, Goethe, and Shakespeare, he has also staged numerous contemporary Polish dramas, many of which have been influenced by his experiences in Auschwitz. Productions seen in the UK have included *Macbeth* (1970).

Szigligeti, Ede (1814–78) Hungarian playwright, who became the first professional Hungarian writer for the stage. Closely associated with the National Theatre of Hungary, as both secretary and then director, he contributed over 100 plays, including such histories as *The Captivity of Ferenc Rákóczi II* (1848), comedies, and folk dramas.

T

Tabarin (Antoine Girard; d. 1626) French actor, who was highly popular in booths on the Pont Neuf and the Place Dauphine in Paris, where he gave performances designed to attract customers for his brother Mondor, a quack doctor. He performed farcical pieces much influenced by the Italian *commedia dell'arte* and was famous for his wide-brimmed hat, which he manipulated into numerous forms.

tabernaria See togata.

tableau A grouping of motionless actors assembled to achieve a particular visual effect. The practice was especially popular in the 19th century, notably in imitation of famous paintings, and was also used in the nude *tableaux vivants* of the 20th century.

taboos Many of the various superstitions associated with the theatre are common throughout the world. Most have a sound basis in commonsense, particularly those surrounding the use of unreliable props (real flowers, for instance, should never appear on stage) and the conduct of rehearsals (a good dress rehearsal is considered unlucky

because it can create a false sense of security). Others that are more enigmatic include the taboos prohibiting the presence in the theatre of peacock feathers, whistling in the dressing-room, the wishing of good luck to an actor before he goes on, and the many superstitions linked to *Macbeth* – probably a consequence of the element of black magic involved in the play and the long history of mishaps in its production. The tradition that no actor should wear green on stage dates from the time when limelight, which itself cast a greenish hue, was in use, making performers in that colour seem to disappear.

tabs *See* curtain.

Tadema, Sir Lawrence Alma- *See* Alma-Tadema, Sir Lawrence.

Taganka Theatre A theatre in Moscow, properly called the **Theatre of Drama and Comedy**, which was established in 1946. Seating 600 people, it began with a lengthy programme of Soviet works but diversified from the 1960s with avant-garde productions of Brecht, Weiss, Gorky, Molière, and Shakespeare.

Tagore, Rabindranath (1861–1941) Indian poet, philosopher, and playwright, who wrote in Bengali and has been widely translated into English. His sympathy for the rural poor together with his love of the Bengali countryside are common themes throughout his work. Among his best-known plays are *Visarjana* (Sacrifice; 1890), *Dakaghan* (The Post Office; 1913), and *Rakta-Karabi* (Red Oleanders; 1924); later works include the dance play *Chitrangada* (1936).

tail *See* leg.

Taïrov, Alexander Yakovlevich (Aleksandr Kornblit; 1885–1950) Soviet director, who founded the celebrated *Kamerny

Theatre in Moscow in 1914 and was the leading director there until his death. His productions were remarkable for his combination of various forms of performance, including ballet and music hall, and reflected his opposition to the theories of Stanislavsky. Although influenced by Meyerhold in his preference for highly theatrical drama, he nonetheless upheld Stanislavsky's ideas about the importance of the actor, emphasizing the physical aspects of the actors' presence and employing heavy make-up and long rehearsals; he used strongly symbolic – often Cubist – sets and insisted upon the director's overall control. He presented both classics and plays by contemporary playwrights, including Shaw and O'Neill; after the Revolution of 1917 he gradually adapted to official pressure to take up the aims of Socialist Realism. Successes from this later period included Vishnevsky's *An Optimistic Tragedy* (1935) and *Madame Bovary* (1939). His wife was Alisa Koonen, the leading actress at the Kamerny Theatre.

Tale of Mystery, A A melodrama by Thomas *Holcroft, adapted from Pixérécourt's *Coelina, ou l'Enfant de mystère*. First performance: 1802. The play revolves around the wicked Count Romaldo, who plots a murder in order to marry a wealthy heiress; it effectively inaugurated melodrama in Britain.

Talfourd, Sir Thomas Noon (1795–1854) British playwright, theatre critic, and lawyer, who was also the author of several verse tragedies in the French style. *Ion* (1836) was a personal success for Macready when produced at Covent Garden; *The Athenian Captive* (1838) and *Glencoe* (1840) were less popular. As a member of parliament he became identified with the Copyright Act of 1833.

Talk of the Town *See* Hippodrome.

Talma, François-Joseph (1763–1826) French actor-manager, who spent his childhood in England before training as an actor in Paris under Molé and others. He made his first appearance as a professional actor at the Comédie-Française in 1787 in Voltaire's *Mahomet*. In 1789 his passionate interpretation of Chénier's antimonarchical *Charles IX* caused an uproar and the closure of the theatre. His reputation established, he went on to form his own company at the Théâtre de la Révolution and to produce realistically staged and costumed versions of plays by Corneille, Shakespeare, and others. In 1799 the companies were reunited at Talma's theatre and, with Napoleon's approval, he set about reforming the national theatre and establishing himself as the foremost player of tragedy in his day.

Tamayo y Baus, Manuel (1829–98) Spanish playwright, who wrote numerous plays in both the Romantic and Realist traditions. Early in his career he wrote such popular dramas as the patriotic *La ricahembra* (1854), which was influenced by Schiller, and the historical drama *La locura de amor* (The Insanity of Love; 1855). Later he turned to social issues in such works as *Lances de honor* (1863) and *Los hombres de bien* (1870); other plays include *Lo positivo* (Materialism; 1862) and a tragedy set in Elizabethan England, *Un drama nuevo* (A New Play; 1867), which he published under the name **Joaquín Estebánez** and which is considered his finest play.

Tamburlaine the Great A drama in blank verse by Christopher *Marlowe, written in two parts. First performance: London, 1587–88. The play's poetic language influenced many contemporaries; the theme of Tamburlaine's rise from shepherd to imperial ruler typified the confidence of the Renaissance period but his subsequent fall reveals Marlowe's interest in characterization. Notable scenes include the deaths of the Turkish ruler Bajazet and his wife in a cage and Tamburlaine's own demise after his beloved Zenocrate has died.

Taming of the Shrew, The A comedy by William *Shakespeare, written c. 1593. First performance: date unknown. Ostensibly a comedy of love and marriage, the play comments, through the enforced subservience of Katherina (the 'Shrew') by Petruchio, upon the role of women in society. Features of the play include the device of a play within a play and Katherina's final speech on the subject of marital obedience.

Tandy, Jessica (1909-) US actress, born in Britain, who first appeared on stage in London in 1927. She made her New York debut in G B Stern's *The Matriarch* (1930) and then returned to London to appear in such plays as Dodie Smith's *Autumn Crocus* (1931), *Hamlet* (1934), and Rattigan's *French Without Tears* (1936). She played for a season with the Old Vic company, mainly in Shakespearean roles, and then returned to New York to play Kay in Priestley's *Time and the Conways*. She went on to triumph as Blanche Dubois in Tennessee Williams's *A Streetcar Named Desire* (1947); subsequently she has been acclaimed alongside her second husband, Hume *Cronyn, in such plays as N C Hunter's *A Day By the Sea* (1955), Chekhov's *Three Sisters* (1963), and Miller's *Death of a Salesman* (1963). They have also appeared with great success in plays by Dürrenmatt, Albee, and Beckett, among others. Her first husband was the film actor Jack Hawkins.

Tapping, Florence (Florence Cowell; 1852–1926) British actress, daughter of the music hall star Sam *Cowell. As a child she toured with the Wyndhams in the US, then worked in the companies of Kate Vaughan, Ben Greet, and the Kendals, and was in Miss Horniman's company at Manchester. She rejoined this company in 1916 for a revival of Houghton's *Hindle Wakes*.

Tardieu, Jean (1903-) French poet and playwright. Many of his short dramatic works, such as *Conversation-Sinfonietta* (1951) and *La Sonate et les trois messieurs* (1955), explore the themes of music and language. He also wrote burlesque sketches and experimental plays, notably *Les Amants du métro* (1952), *La Serrure* (1955), and *Le Guichet* (1955).

Tarkington, (Newton) Booth (1869–1946) US novelist and playwright, whose most famous play was *Monsieur Beaucaire*, which he adapted from his own novel in 1901. His other plays include *Your Humble Servant* (1910), *Mr Antonio* (1916), *Clarence* (1919), and *Tweedles* (1923).

Tarleton, Richard (d. 1588) English actor, who was considered the finest player of rustic clowns of his day. Short in stature and described as "flat-nosed" and having a squint, he inspired the characters of Bottom in Shakespeare's *A Midsummer Night's Dream* and Yorick in *Hamlet*. He joined Queen Elizabeth's Men in 1583 and became a great favourite of Elizabeth I until jokes about Sir Walter Raleigh and the Earl of Leicester provoked his dismissal from the Court. None of his own roles are known for certain and it is thought that much of his clowning was composed on an extemporaneous basis. He popularized the *jig – of which he was the finest interpreter – and composed ballads; he was also credited with several lost plays and numerous jestbooks (including many certainly by later writers).

Tartuffe; ou, l'Imposteur A comedy by *Molière. First performance: Versailles, 1664. A satirical attack on religious hypocrisy, the play was banned in Paris until 1669. Tartuffe gains entrance to the household of Orgon through exaggerated displays of false piety and takes advantage of his host's gullibility: he is finally unmasked when he attempts to seduce Orgon's wife.

Tasso, Torquato (1544–95) Italian poet and playwright, usually remembered for the epic poem *Gerusalemme liberata* (1581). His play *L'Aminta* (1573) was one of the earliest of all pastoral dramas and inspired numerous imitations, including passages in *Love's Labour's Lost*. His other dramatic works include the early romantic tragedy *Torrismondo* (1587) and the comedy *Intrighi d'amore*.

Taste of Honey, A A play by Shelagh Delaney. First performance: Theatre Workshop, 1958. The plot, which revolves around the pregnant and rebellious Jo, celebrates working-class values and female independence.

Tate, Harry (Ronald Macdonald Hutchison; 1872–1940) British comedian, born in Scotland, who began as a mimic at the Camberwell Empire in 1895. He developed his sketch 'Motoring' into one of the most famous comic acts on the halls and followed it with a series of similar sporting sketches.

Tate, Nahum (1652–1715) English poet and playwright, born in Ireland, usually remembered for his eccentric versions of the plays of Shakespeare. His most notorious adaptation was that of *King Lear* (1681), in which he omitted the Fool altogether and allowed Cordelia to marry Edgar; it remained the most performed version of the play until 1838. His other Shakespearean adaptations included *The Sicilian Usurper* (1681), from *Richard II*, and *The Ingratitude of a Common-Wealth* (1681), from *Coriolanus*. He became poet laureate in 1692.

Tavistock House Theatre A private theatre created by Charles Dickens at his house in Tavistock Square, London. Albert Smith's burletta *Guy Fawkes* was the inaugural performance; subsequently the first productions of *The Lighthouse* (1855) – in which Dickens played the lighthouse-keeper – and *The Frozen Deep* (1857), both by Dickens's friend Wilkie Collins, were given there.

Tavistock Repertory Company A British amateur theatre company founded in London in 1932. In 1952 it was revived in Islington in new premises and established a strong reputation with the London premieres of plays by Tennessee Williams, Arrabal, and John Whiting among others. Their home venue was opened as the **Tower Theatre** in 1953; the company continues to present about 20 productions there annually.

Taylor, C(ecil) P(hilip) (1929–81) Scottish playwright, whose many successful plays were mainly performed in regional theatres, notably the Traverse Theatre, Edinburgh. Although his plays were often political the dominant theme throughout his work is the value of simple honesty. This is apparent in *Allergy*, a comic one-act play attributing political failure to the human weaknesses of its proponents, and in his most highly acclaimed play, *Good*. First staged in 1981 by the Royal Shakespeare Company at the Warehouse, it examines the psychology behind a progressive German professor's decision to work at Auschwitz.

Despite Taylor's strong reputation, relatively few of his plays appeared in West End theatres. Among those that did were *Good, Schippel*, as *The Plumber's Progress*, (1975) and *And a Nightingale Sang...* (1979).

Principal works:

Happy Days Are Here Again: 1965.
Of Hope and Glory: 1965.
Allergy: 1966.
Bread and Butter: 1966.
Lies About Vietnam: 1969.
Truth About Sarajevo: 1969.
Passion Play: 1971.
The Black and White Minstrels: 1972.
Next Year in Tel Aviv: 1973.
Columba: 1973.
Schippel: 1974.
Gynt!: 1975.

TAYLOR, JOSEPH

Walter: 1977.
And A Nightingale Sang . . . : 1979.
Good: 1981.
Bring Me Sunshine, Bring Me Smiles: 1982.

Taylor, Joseph (c. 1585–1652) English actor, who was a shareholder in the Blackfriars Theatre and was named in the First Folio list of Shakespearean players. He joined the King's Men in 1619, later becoming (with John Lowin) the company's business manager. He appeared as Hamlet, Ferdinand in *The Duchess of Malfi*, and in other parts created by Richard Burbage; he also acted in plays by Jonson, Massinger, and Beaumont and Fletcher.

Taylor, Laurette (Laurette Cooney; 1884–1946) US actress, who made her stage debut as a child. She was subsequently acclaimed in the title role of her second husband John Manners's play *Peg o' My Heart* (1912). In 1938 she returned to the stage as Miss Midget in Sutton Vane's *Outward Bound* and won further praise in Tennessee Williams's *The Glass Menagerie* (1945–46).

Taylor, Tom (1817–80) British playwright, journalist, and amateur actor, who was the author of around 100 dramatic pieces. His best-known works include *Masks and Faces* (1852), which was based on the life of Peg Woffington and was written with Charles Reade, *Still Waters Run Deep* (1855), *Our American Cousin* (1858), in which Sothern triumphed as Lord Dundreary, and *The Ticket-of-Leave Man* (1863). As an actor he often took part in the amateur productions presented by Dickens.

Tchehov or **Tchekhov** *See* Chekhov, Anton.

Tearle, (George) Osmund (1852–1901) British actor, who made his first appearance in Liverpool in 1869. Two years later he performed Hamlet for the first time at Warrington. He made his London debut at the Gaiety Theatre in 1875. Later he spent five years in the US at Wallack's Theatre and in 1888, on his return to Britain, formed a Shakespearean company that toured the country.

His son was the actor **Sir Godfrey Seymour Tearle** (1884–1953), who made his stage debut in his father's company at the age of nine. After initial success in romantic dramas, he played Othello (1921) and Hamlet (1931) without distinction; later, having been acclaimed in Charles Morgan's *The Flashing Stream* (1938) and Emlyn Williams's *The Light of Heart* (1940), he was praised in numerous Shakespearean roles at the Shakespeare Memorial Theatre.

teaser *See* proscenium border.

Teatro Campesino *See* Chicano Theatre.

Teatro Chicano *See* Chicano Theatre.

Teatro de la Esperanza *See* Chicano Theatre.

Teatro de la Gente *See* Chicano Theatre.

Teatro de los Barrios *See* Chicano Theatre.

Teatro del Piojo *See* Chicano Theatre.

Teatro Eslava *See* Martínez Sierra, Gregorio.

Teatro Farnese An elaborate theatre in Parma, Italy, designed by Giovanni Aleotti. Begun in 1619 and opened in 1628, the theatre was one of the first to have a stage framed by a proscenium arch; in front of this there was a further open space, which could also be used by the actors. The building has survived but is now rarely used for dramatic performances.

Teatro Intím *See* Gual, Adriá.

Teatro Popolare Italiano *See* Gassman, Vittorio.

teatro por horas See zarzuela.

Teatro sperimentale degli Indipendenti *See* Indipendenti, Teatro sperimentale degli.

teatro stabile Any one of the professional companies founded in Italy in the later half of the 20th century. The establishment of *teatri stabili* throughout the country marked the first attempt to form permanent troupes in the Italian theatrical tradition; leading companies that have emerged in this phase have included the *Piccolo teatro della Città di Milano.

technical rehearsal A rehearsal, usually shortly before the first actual performance, at which all the technical aspects of a production are run through.

Teirlinck, Herman (1879–1967) Belgian playwright, who became one of the leading writers associated with the Vlaamse Volkstoneel in Antwerp, writing in Flemish. *The Slow-Motion Film* (1922) inaugurated Flemish Expressionism; other significant works included a revived miracle play, the experimental *Man Without a Body* (1925), and *De Oresteia* (1946). He also imported the ideas of Appia and Gordon Craig and published much theoretical work on the theatre as well as teaching drama and founding the Flemish National Theatre.

telari See periaktoi.

Telbin, William (1813–73) British scene painter, who worked extensively in the provinces before joining Macready at Drury Lane. Later he painted sets at Covent Garden and the Lyceum.

His son, **William Lewis Telbin** (1846–1931), was for many years scene designer at the Theatre Royal, Manchester and collaborated with Hawes Craven on sets for Henry Irving at the Lyceum.

Téllez, Fray Gabriel *See* Tirso de Molina.

Tempest, Dame Marie (Mary Susan Etherington; 1864–1942) British actress, who made her stage debut in 1885 in Suppé's comic opera *Boccaccio*. She enjoyed great success as Kitty Carol in *The Red Hussar* (1889) and subsequently starred in operetta in the US before returning to London in 1895 to appear in musicals and, after 1900, in straight comedy. She triumphed as Kitty in *The Marriage of Kitty* (1902), adapted from Thackeray by her second husband **Cosmo Gordon-Lennox** (1869–1921), and as Judith Bliss in *Hay Fever* (1925), specially written for her by Noël Coward. She was also admired in St John Ervine's *The First Mrs Fraser* (1929), Kaufman and Ferber's *Theatre Royal* (1934), and Dodie Smith's *Dear Octopus* (1938).

Tempest, The The last play of William *Shakespeare. First performance: Whitehall, c. 1611. It revolves around Prospero, an old man with supernatural powers, who – aided by Ariel (a spirit) and the brutish Caliban – presides over the first meeting of his daughter Miranda with other mortals who are shipwrecked on the island where they live; Prospero's final speech has been frequently interpreted as Shakespeare's own farewell to the stage. Ostensibly concerned with the world of Naples and Milan, the island itself has been interpreted as a reflection of the contemporary interest in the recently-discovered but largely unknown New World.

Tennyson, Alfred, Lord (1809–92) British poet laureate and playwright, author of several undistinguished poetic dramas. Of those produced by Irving – *Queen Mary* (1876), *The Cup* (1881), *The Foresters* (1892), and *Becket* (1893) – only the last enjoyed any success. *The Falcon* (1879), produced by the

Kendals at the St James's Theatre, and *The Promise of May* (1882) were both failures. Another play, *Harold*, remained unacted until 1928.

Terence (Publius Terentius Afer; c. 190 BC–159 BC) Roman playwright, six of whose plays – examples of the *pallatia* – survive. His verse comedies were based upon those of Menander and other writers of Greek New Comedy and are notable for their attention to structure and characterization. His early plays have a strong farcical element, which is less marked in his later, more thoughtful and sentimental, work; all his writing is, however, distinguished by his pure and elegant style. Born a slave and probably of African descent, Terence was overshadowed during his lifetime by Plautus but was much admired during medieval times and after as a model for contemporary playwrights, influencing Udall, Shakespeare, Molière, and Steele among many others. *See also* Terence-stage.
Principal works:
Andria: 166 BC.
Hecyra: 165 BC.
Heauton Timorumenos: 163 BC.
Eunuchus: 161 BC.
Phormio: 161 BC.
Adelphi: 160 BC.

Terence-stage A form of staging used for performances of the plays of Terence during the Renaissance. Woodcuts from the period indicate that the plays were presented in a two-storey building with tiered seating and a large apron; entrances were made through arches on the lower level. Eventually the Terence-stage contributed to the development of the proscenium arch and the adoption of the horseshoe-shaped auditorium.

Terpsichore See Muses.

Terriss, William (William Charles James Lewin; 1847–97) British actor, who began in minor roles in Birmingham. In 1873 he achieved fame in Hannah Cowley's *The Belle's Stratagem* at the Strand Theatre. His biggest triumph, however, came in 1878 at the Royal Court Theatre when he appeared opposite Ellen Terry in W G Wills's *Olivia*. He joined Irving at the Lyceum in 1880 and later became famous in melodrama at the Adelphi Theatre. It was outside the stagedoor of this theatre that he was stabbed to death by a deranged actor.

His daughter was the actress **Ellaline Terriss** (1871–1971), who was born in the Falkland Islands. She made her stage debut at the Haymarket in 1888 and later appeared at the Criterion Theatre with Wyndham. She was acclaimed in several plays by her husband, Seymour *Hicks, and in J M Barrie's *Quality Street* (1902). She also appeared in music hall and entertained the troops in World War I.

Terry, Benjamin (1818–96) British actor and manager, who married the actress **Sarah Ballard** (1817–92) and became the progenitor of a great theatrical family. With their 11 children they toured the provinces for some years before joining Charles *Kean's company at the Princess's Theatre in London.

Their eldest daughter was **Kate Terry** (1844–1924), who began her career as an actress at the age of eight, playing Prince Arthur in Charles Kean's production of *King John*. She was highly acclaimed when she played Cordelia at the age of 14 and, in 1861, as Ophelia at the Lyceum. She caused a further sensation at the Adelphi when she appeared in Charles Reade's dramatization of Tennyson's poem *Dora*, but left the stage in 1867 on her marriage to Arthur Lewis and became, in due course, grandmother of Sir John *Gielgud. Her youngest daughter was the actress Mabel *Terry-Lewis.

Benjamin Terry's second daughter, **Ellen (Alice) Terry** (1847–1928), also began her acting career with Charles Kean's company at the Princess's Theatre, appearing as Mamillius in *The Winter's Tale* and then touring for several seasons and joining the company at the Haymarket (1861). The first of her three marriages, to the painter G F Watts in 1864, was shortlived and she returned to the stage to appear with Irving in *The Taming of the Shrew*. She then retired for a time, living with the designer E W Godwin and having two children, Edith and Edward Gordon *Craig. She returned to the theatre as a lively Portia in the Bancrofts' production of *The Merchant of Venice* at the Prince of Wales' Theatre in 1875, and three years later became Irving's leading lady at the Lyceum. A legendary partnership lasting 25 years ensued and she won great fame playing Shakespearean heroines and major roles in contemporary dramas. She took over the management of the Imperial Theatre in 1903 and in 1906 was the original Lady Cicely Wayneflete – which Shaw wrote for her – in *Captain Brassbound's Conversion*. The following year, however, she virtually retired from the stage to travel in the US and Australia, lecturing on Shakespeare. Her autobiography was published in 1908.

Benjamin Terry's third daughter, **Marion Terry** (1856–1930), first appeared on stage at the age of 16 and soon established a reputation in such plays as *Much Ado about Nothing*, Bulwer-Lytton's *Money*, and W S Gilbert's *Engaged*. She went on to work in the companies of Tree, the Bancrofts, Irving, Forbes-Robertson, and Alexander, creating the role of Mrs Erlynne in Wilde's *Lady Windermere's Fan* in 1892. Other successes included Barrie's *Quality Street* (1902) and Maugham's *Our Betters* (1923).

Florence Terry (1855–96), Benjamin Terry's fourth daughter, also appeared on stage at an early age and later acted at the Lyceum alongside other members of her family. She inherited several of Ellen Terry's roles, notably Olivia in an adaptation of *The Vicar of Wakefield*, but retired on her marriage to a lawyer in 1882.

Fred Terry (1863–1933), was the youngest of Benjamin Terry's children and made his debut with the Bancrofts in 1880. He became a popular romantic actor in such parts as Sir Percy Blakeney in Baroness Orczy's *The Scarlet Pimpernel* (1905) and Sir John Manners in Paul Kester's *Dorothy o' the Hall* (1906), often appearing in partnership with his wife, Julia *Neilson.

Terry, Daniel (1789–1829) British actor, who toured the provinces in Stephen Kemble's company and became friends with Sir Walter Scott before making his London debut at the Haymarket in 1812. After appearances at Covent Garden and Drury Lane, he purchased the Adelphi Theatre in partnership with Frederick Yates, but retired within two years.

Terry, Edward (O'Connor) (1844–1912) British actor and manager. After establishing a reputation in the provinces in eccentric comedy roles he came to the Surrey Theatre in London in 1867 in Thomas J Williams's *A Cure for the Fidgets*. He soon became one of the leading actors in burlesque, first at the Strand Theatre, then at the Gaiety, where he remained until 1884. He opened his own theatre, Terry's, in 1887, and had an enormous success there the following year as Richard Phenyl in Pinero's *Sweet Lavender*, which he frequently revived in tours at home and abroad.

Terry,   Megan (Marguerite Duffy; 1932-) US playwright, who was a founding member of the *Open Theatre (1963). Her first play to be produced was *Beach Grass* (1933), which was followed by *Ex-Miss Copper Queen on a Set of Pills* (1963), her first play to be produced in New York. Since then her plays (mostly critical of modern US society) have included *Keep Tightly Closed In a Cool Dry Place* (1965), the musical *Viet Rock* (1966), *Approaching Simone* (1970), *Nightwalk* (1973), which was written in collaboration with Sam Shepard, *Hothouse* (1974), and *Goona Goona* (1979).

Terry-Lewis, Mabel (Gwynedd) (1872–1957) British actress, daughter of Kate *Terry. She began her career with Hare's company in 1895 and eventually established her reputation in such plays as Pinero's *The Gay Lord Quex* (1899) and, the following year, Shaw's *You Never Can Tell*. She left the stage on her marriage in 1904, but made a comeback in 1920, playing such ladies of quality as Dona Filomena in the Álvarez Quinteros' *A Hundred Years Old* (1928) and Lady Bracknell in Wilde's *The Importance of Being Earnest* (1930).

Terson, Peter (1932-) British playwright, who became closely associated with the National Youth Theatre after it staged his best-known play, *Zigger-Zagger*, about a young football fan, in 1967. His first play, *Make the Angels Weep*, and his popular dramatization of Arnold Bennett's *Clayhanger* were produced at the Victoria Theatre, Stoke-on-Trent, where he was briefly resident dramatist (1964).

Following the success of *Zigger-Zagger* his plays have concentrated on the problems of youth and on examinations of modern British society. Of his other works the most successful include the semi-documentary *The 1861 Whitby Lifeboat Disaster* and his dramatization of Herman Melville's *Moby Dick*.
Principal works:
A Night to Make Angels Weep: 1964.
The Mighty Reservoy: 1964.
Mooney and his Caravans: 1967.
Clayhanger: 1967.
Zigger-Zagger: 1967.
The Apprentices: 1968.
Fuzz!: 1969.
The 1861 Whitby Lifeboat Disaster: 1970.
Good Lads at Heart: 1971.
Family Ties: 1977.
England My Own: 1978.
The Ticket: 1980.
The Pied Piper: 1980.
Strippers: 1984.

tetralogy A series of dramatic entertainments, comprising a **trilogy** of tragedies followed by a satyr-play, all written by the same playwright for performance in drama contests in ancient Greece. Initially the satyr-play shared the same theme as the preceding trilogy; the only surviving such trilogy is *The *Oresteia* by Aeschylus.

Thaddädl A stock character of Viennese comedy, descended from the *commedia dell'arte*. A high-voiced foolish youth, Thaddädl was the creation of Anton *Hasenhut but was too ridiculous to enjoy more than temporary popularity.

Thalia *See* Muses.

Thalia Theatre *See* Bowery Theatre.

Theater an der Wien A theatre in Vienna, which opened as a venue for the old-fashioned folk comedy of Kasperl and Thaddädl after such entertainment was banished from the Burgtheater. Noted managers of the theatre included Mozart's librettist Emanuel Schikaneder (1751–1812). In more recent years it has become a home of operetta and musicals.

Theatr Clwyd A civic theatre at Mold in North Wales, housing three auditoria and a resident company, that opened in 1976 with a production of *Macbeth*. At the same time David Cregan's *Arthur* was staged in its studio theatre, called the Emlyn Williams, after the playwright. There is also a film theatre and a very large exhibition concourse.

Theatre The first purpose-built public playhouse in England, designed and constructed by James Burbage in 1576. Situated in Shoreditch, just outside the limits of the City of London, the Theatre was used by such companies as Leicester's Men and the Queen's Men as well as the Chamberlain's Men, with whom Richard Burbage was the leading actor. Together with premieres of

Hamlet and other great plays, there were also exhibitions and competitions at swordplay and athletics. In 1598, being unable to agree terms with Giles Alleyn, the landlord, for renewal of the lease, the Burbages dismantled the circular wooden structure and used the materials in the construction of a new playhouse, the Globe, on Bankside.

Théâtre Antoine A theatre in the Boulevard de Strasbourg, Paris, which opened in 1866. Existing under various names until renamed the Théâtre Antoine in 1896, it flourished under Antoine himself until 1906 when Gémier took over with similar success. It became a centre of existentialist drama after World War II.

Theatre Behind the Gate A theatre in Prague, Czechoslovakia, founded by Otomar Krejča in 1965. It opened with the resident playwright Josef Topol's *Cat on the Rails* and became the home of a famous company, which toured internationally in 1969. Krejča lost his post there in 1971 and the theatre closed a year later.

Théâtre d'Art *See* Art, Théâtre d'.

Théâtre de l'Atelier *See* Atelier, Théâtre de l'.

Théâtre de l'Hôtel d'Argent *See* Argent, Théâtre de l'Hôtel d'.

Théâtre de l'Hôtel de Bourgogne *See* Bourgogne, Théâtre de l'Hôtel de.

Théâtre de l'Inexprimé *See* Silence, Theatre of.

Theatre de Lys A theatre on Christopher Street in Greenwich Village, New York, which opened in 1952. From 1954 to 1961 Brecht's *The Threepenny Opera* was housed there; subsequent productions have included *Brecht on Brecht* (1962), Arden's *Serjeant Musgrave's Dance* (1966), David Mamet's *A*

Life in the Theatre (1977), and Sam Shepard's *Buried Child* (1978). The theatre was also known for its matinée series, which was discontinued after 1975.

Théâtre des Nations A major theatre festival first organized by UNESCO in 1954 at the Théâtre Sarah-Bernhardt (now the **Théâtre de la Ville**). Companies from 50 countries appeared at the festival between 1955 and 1965, after which Barrault took over its management until the riots of 1968 disrupted its organization. Since then it has been revived on an irregular basis in various countries.

Théâtre du Vieux-Columbier *See* Vieux-Columbier, Théâtre du.

Théâtre Français *See* 14th Street Theatre.

Théâtre-Français *See* Comédie-Française.

Theatregoround *See* Royal Shakespeare Company.

Theatre Guild A US production company founded in New York in 1919. Initially based at the Garrick Theatre, it soon attracted attention with its productions of noncommercial US and foreign drama and eventually moved into its own Guild Theatre in 1925. Among its most influential early productions were G B Shaw's *Heartbreak House* (1920), Molnár's *Liliom* (1921), Andreyev's *He Who Gets Slapped* (1922), Ibsen's *Peer Gynt* (1923), and Rice's *The Adding Machine* (1923); subsequent triumphs ranged from further plays by Shaw to Chekhov, Marlowe, O'Neill, and the musical *Oklahoma!* (1943). Notable performers with the group included Helen Hayes, the Lunts, and Alla Nazimova. The Guild came under the aegis of the American National Theatre and Academy in 1950.

Theatre in Education A pioneering form of educational theatre that originated in

Britain in 1965 at the Belgrade Theatre, Coventry, and has since become widespread in Britain, Australia, and in parts of Canada and the US. A distinguishing feature has been its innovative use of audience participation. Programmes range from 'full participation' (in which children make decisions alongside the actor-teachers, who remain in role throughout) to 'semi-participation' (in which children may quiz characters about their behaviour). Subject matter ranges from social history to racism and drug dependency. Many teams are based permanently in one locality and receive funding from their education authority.

theatre-in-the-round A form of staging in which the audience is seated on all sides of a central acting space. Although many early theatrical traditions necessarily involved such an arrangement, it was not until the 20th century that it was deliberately developed in favour of more conventional layouts based upon a proscenium arch. Theatre-in-the-round encourages a sense of intimacy and symbolic intensity as it is impossible to use elaborate artificial sets, the emphasis is thrown upon the performers themselves. It was first employed in the 1930s by Okhlopkov in the USSR and by Robert Atkins at the Ring in Britain, but it was only fully realized in the 1950s, initially through experimental productions in the US. The first permanent venue of the kind was the Penthouse Theatre in Seattle, built in 1940; later noted venues adapted for theatre-in-the-round have included the Circle-in-the-Square in New York, the Arena Stage in Washington DC, the Stephen Joseph Theatre in Stoke-on-Trent, the Royal Exchange Theatre in Manchester, and André Villiers's Théâtre en Rond de Paris. *See also* promenade.

Théâtre-Italien *See* Comédie-Italienne.

Théâtre Libre A theatre club in Paris, founded in 1887 by André Antoine to present contemporary drama. Early productions included influential naturalistic performances of adaptations of Zola and works by Hauptmann, Ibsen, Strindberg, and others. The society was dissolved in 1896 chiefly as a result of financial pressures.

Theatre Masque *See* John Golden Theatre.

Theatre Museum A museum housing material relating to the British theatre, opened in 1987 in Covent Garden, London. A branch of the Victoria and Albert Museum, whose Gabrielle Enthoven Collection became a major component of the new venture, the museum covers drama, opera, ballet, music hall, and pop music. Prompt scripts, costumes, posters, props, stage designs, engravings, paintings, photographs, and a variety of ephemera all have their place; the main galleries trace the history of the theatre, while short-term exhibitions focus on special topics.

Théâtre National Populaire (TNP) A French theatre institution, founded by Jean Vilar in 1951. An earlier organization of the same type was established by Gémier in 1920 and staged performances by visiting companies for working-class audiences at the Palais de Chaillot with government support until 1934. Under Vilar, and subsequently (1963–72) Georges Wilson, the TNP was revived at the Palais de Chaillot, complete with its own company, which undertook tours from 1956. As well as introducing innovations in the handling of bookings and publicity, it built up a strong reputation for its economical interpretations of classic plays as well as works by such contemporaries as Jarry and Brecht before audiences of up to 1800. The TNP declined in popularity somewhat after the implementation of the *Décentralisation Dramatique* policy and finally closed in 1972, its name passing to a group based in Lyon under Planchon.

Theatre of Cruelty *See* Cruelty, Theatre of.

Theatre of Drama and Comedy *See* Taganka Theatre.

Theatre of Fact *See* Fact, Theatre of.

Theatre of Satire *See* Satire, Theatre of.

Theatre of Silence *See* Silence, Theatre of.

Theatre of the Absurd *See* Absurd, Theatre of the.

Theatre of the Baltic Fleet A theatre founded in Leningrad in 1934 utilizing actors serving with the Soviet navy. Performances, which are given on board ship and in various home ports, have included such patriotic dramas as Vishnevsky's *At the Walls of Leningrad* (1943) and other pieces chiefly on military and naval themes.

Theatre of the Revolution *See* Mayakovsky Theatre.

Theatre Royal A title granted to the theatres in *Covent Garden and *Drury Lane under Letters Patent in 1662. Since then the title has also been adopted by notable theatres at Bath, Brighton, Bury St Edmunds, Exeter, Lincoln, Manchester, Newcastle-upon-Tyne, Norwich, Nottingham, and York.
See also Adelphi Theatre; Astley's Amphitheatre; Bristol Old Vic; Haymarket Theatre; John Street Theatre.

Theatre Royal (Stratford East) A theatre in Stratford East, London, which was opened by W Charles Dillon with Bulwer Lytton's *Richelieu* in 1884. For two years he produced revivals of famous plays there, but when he left the theatre concentrated on pantomime and touring melodramas. Twice-nightly variety was established in 1927, followed by an unsuccessful return to melodra-ma. From 1946 to 1949 David Horne presented seasons of plays with only modest success and for a brief spell in 1952 the theatre became the Palace of Varieties. The advent of Joan Littlewood's *Theatre Workshop company in 1953 brought a change of fortune to the Theatre Royal and such productions as Shelagh Delaney's *A Taste of Honey*, Brendan Behan's *The Hostage*, and Frank Norman and Lionel Bart's musical *Fings Ain't Wot They Used T'Be*, went on to successful West End runs. The Stage Sixty Company occupied the theatre from 1964, but Joan Littlewood returned for another six years in 1967. Since 1980 the theatre has continued a lively policy of new plays and occasional classic revivals, achieving a major success with Nell Dunn's *Steaming* (1981). More recent productions have included Barry Keeffe's *King of England* (1988).

Theatres Act *See* licence.

Théâtres Nationaux *See* Décentralisation Dramatique.

théâtre total A theory of drama that advocates the absolute control of the director over all aspects of a production, including the text itself. Jean-Louis Barrault is the best-known director to have worked within the technique.

Theatre Union *See* Littlewood, Joan.

Theatre Upstairs *See* Royal Court Theatre.

Theatre Workshop A theatre company founded in Kendal in 1945. Under the leadership of Joan *Littlewood, the company toured Britain and Europe before settling at the Theatre Royal, Stratford East, in London (1952). There it rapidly established a strong reputation with productions ranging from *Twelfth Night* (1953) to Hašek's *The Good Soldier Schweik* (1956), many of which were also seen at leading foreign venues – including the Théâtre des Nations in Paris and the Moscow Art Theatre. The company concentrated particularly on plays with a strong left-wing bias but nonetheless enjoyed lengthy West End runs with such works as *The Hostage* (1958) by Brendan Behan and *A Taste of Honey* (1958) by Shelagh Delaney. In 1963 the company's own documentary drama **Oh, What a Lovely War!* provided another major success, after which the company dispersed for a time before regrouping in 1967 and finally disbanding in 1973. *See also* Princess Theatre.

Theatr Gwynedd A theatre in Bangor, owned by the University College of North Wales and opened in 1974. It presents a mixed programme of drama, dance, opera, concerts, films, and pantomime in both English and Welsh. The resident company, **Cwmni Theatr Cymru**, stages and tours Welsh language productions with financial support from the Welsh Arts Council.

Theatrical Commonwealth A troupe of actors who, under Thomas Twaits, left the Park Theatre, New York, in 1813 after falling out with the management and took over a converted circus on Broadway. They disbanded upon the death of Mrs Twaits (a member of the company) one season later, having staged excellent productions of *As You Like It*, Sheridan's *The School for Scandal*, and Frederick Reynolds's *The Virgin of the Sun*.

Theatrical Syndicate An association of US businessmen, which was formed in 1896 to rationalize theatre organization and became a suppressive influence upon competition and artistic standards. Its members included Klaw and Erlanger, Al Hayman, and Charles Frohman. They controlled most municipal theatres in the US until opposition from Mrs Fiske, Sarah Bernhardt, and Belasco, among others, broke their monopoly.

Theatr y Werin A theatre in Aberystwyth, Dyfed, in Wales. Belonging to the University of Wales, it is located in the arts centre and, since opening in 1973, has pursued a mixed programme policy, playing host to touring companies and local amateurs.

Theocritus (c. 310 BC–250 BC) Greek playwright, one of the leading writers of Hellenistic drama. A native of Syracuse, he probably spent much of his life in Egypt where he wrote several pastoral *Idylls* and the mime play *Adoniazusae*, translated into English by Matthew Arnold.

Theognis (5th century BC) Greek poet and playwright, usually remembered for his love poems addressed to one Cyrnus. His plays, however, were so frosty in tone that – according to Aristophanes – they caused the rivers to freeze in Thrace when they were performed in Athens.

Théophile de Viau (1590–1626) French poet and playwright, born in Clairac. A Huguenot and free-thinker, Théophile was imprisoned for his suspected collaboration in *Le Parnasse satirique*, a collection of licentious verse, and died soon after his release. His single contribution to the theatre was the tragedy *Pyrame et Thisbé* (published 1623), which was unjustly criticized by Boileau and is now acknowledged as a fine example of baroque tragedy.

Theoric Fund A grant organized by the state in ancient Athens to enable the poorest citizens to afford a visit to the theatre during the festival of Dionysus. The practice was eventually discontinued in 338 BC.

Thérèse Raquin A play by Émile *Zola, based on his novel of the same name (1867). First performance: 1873. The eponymous heroine has an adulterous affair with Laurent, the friend of her husband Camille, whom the lovers conspire to drown. Haunted by guilt and fear, Thérèse and Laurent ultimately commit suicide in front of Camille's mother.

Thesiger, Ernest (1879–1961) British actor, who started with George Alexander's company in 1909. Subsequently he worked with Hawtrey and Tree before appearing in Walter Ellis's farce *A Little Bit of Fluff* (1915), which ran for three years. In 1920 he had an unexpected success in Barrie's *Mary Rose* and went on to establish himself as an excellent actor of high comedy. He played the Dauphin in *Saint Joan* – the first of many Shavian parts which delighted the author – in 1924 and was also acclaimed in supporting roles in the plays of Shakespeare.

Thespis (6th century BC) Greek poet, usually credited with being the founder of the acting profession. A native of Attica, he was the first to introduce an actor alongside the chorus and to give him a distinct narrative role. He was the winner of the very first drama contest held during the Dionysia (534 BC) and led his own travelling company; the word Thespian, taken from his name, now denotes anything theatrical.

Thieves' Carnival (*Le Bal des voleurs*) A *pièce rose* by Jean *Anouilh. First performance: Paris, 1938. Lady Hurf knowingly admits into her home three confidence tricksters posing as Spanish grandees; the plot centres on the romantic involvement of two of the men with Lady Hurf's nieces.

Third Stage *See* Stratford (Ontario) Festival.

39th Street Theatre A theatre on West 39th Street, New York, which opened as the **Nazimova Theatre** in 1910 with the New York premiere of Ibsen's *Little Eyolf*. It reopened as the 39th Street Theatre in 1911 with *Green Stockings* and saw appearances

by John Barrymore and Walter Hampden among others. It was demolished in 1925.

This Happy Breed A play by Noël *Coward. First performance: London, 1943. The play is an episodic and sentimental history of a suburban family between the wars and extols British middle-class values.

Thomas, Augustus (1857–1934) US playwright and manager, whose plays were among the first to be based solely upon US material. His best known work is *The Copperhead* (1918); other plays include *Alabama* (1891), *A Man of the World* (1883), *The Burglar* (1889), and *In Mizzoura* (1893).

Thomas, (Walter) Brandon (1857–1914) British playwright, actor, and composer of music hall songs, who is usually remembered for his farce *Charley's Aunt*, first performed in London in 1892 and revived many times since. It was made into a musical, *Where's Charley?* (1948), and has also been filmed; Thomas himself sometimes appeared in the transvestite leading role.

Thomassin *See* Vicentini, Tommaso Antonio.

Thompson Shelterhouse *See* Cincinnati Playhouse in the Park.

Thorndike, Dame (Agnes) Sybil (1882–1976) British actress, who began her career in the theatre with Ben Greet's Pastoral Players in 1904. In repertory with Miss Horniman's company at Manchester from 1908, she met and married Lewis Casson, with whom she later appeared in various jointly-managed productions, including the plays of J B Priestley. During World War I she was in Lilian Baylis's Old Vic company and afterwards consolidated her reputation in Gilbert Murray's versions of Euripides, playing such roles as Hecuba in *The Trojan Women* (1919) and the title role in *Medea* (1920). Probably her most famous part was the heroine of Shaw's *St Joan*, which she first played in 1924; subsequent successes included Volumnia in *Coriolanus* at the Old Vic (1938) and Miss Moffat in Emlyn Williams's *The Corn is Green* (1938). She toured mining towns and villages with a mainly Shakespearean repertoire during World War II and gave her last performance in London as Abby in Joseph Kesselring's *Arsenic and Old Lace* (1966). She returned to the stage for the last time in 1969 for the opening of a theatre named after her in Leatherhead.

Thorne, Charles Robert (1840–83) US actor, son of theatrical parents, who began his career as a child and later became very popular in leading romantic roles. As a member of the Union Square Theatre company from 1871, he appeared successfully in numerous melodramas, also performing in London in 1874; his last appearance was in Boucicault's *The Corsican Brothers* (1883).

Thorne, Thomas (1841–1918) British actor-manager, who came from a large family with theatre connections. He first appeared at his father's theatre in Margate but later moved to London where he played at the Strand Theatre (1864–70). Subsequently he opened the Vaudeville Theatre with Henry Montague and David James, serving as sole manager from 1882 to 1892.

Three Hundred Club *See* Stage Society.

Threepenny Opera, The (*Die Dreigroschenoper*) A musical play by Bertolt *Brecht with music by Kurt *Weill. First performance: Berlin, 1928. Derived from Gay's *The Beggar's Opera*, it has as its central theme the corruption of good men by evil values and provided Brecht with his first major success in the theatre. The central story of the marriage, imprisonment, and eventual pardon of the robber Macheath was used by the author to satirize European society before World War II.

Three Sisters (*Tri sestry*) A play by Anton *Chekhov. First performance: Moscow Art Theatre, 1901. Regarded as one of Chekhov's finest plays, it realistically and sympathetically depicts the various longings of three women – Irina, Masha, and Olga – living in the country. Instead of realizing their dream of returning to Moscow they face disappointment in love and work and the destruction of their illusions.

throwline Any rope used to secure flats or other pieces of scenery by tying them together; also referred to in the US as a **lashline**.

thrust stage A stage that projects into the auditorium, with seating arranged on three sides of it. Such stages, also called **open stages**, echo the **platform stage** of the Elizabethan and Restoration theatre and thus facilitate revivals of plays from that period.

Thunder Rock A play by Robert *Ardrey. First performance: New York, 1939. Set in a lighthouse, the play centres on a young intellectual's attempt to face up to the approaching World War through the challenges presented by the ghosts of shipwrecked travellers.

thunder run A series of wooden channels mounted on a wall in the backstage area of some 18th-century theatres; a cannon ball rolling down them created a noise resembling that of thunder. Such runs were eventually superseded by thundersheets.

thundersheet A large sheet of iron or thin wood suspended from the flies; when shaken it produces a noise resembling thunder. In the modern theatre such sheets have often been replaced by tape recordings.

Ticket-of-Leave Man, The A melodrama by Tom *Taylor, adapted from *Léonard* by Edouard Brisbarre and Eugène Nus. First performance: 1863. A young man falls in with bad company and is imprisoned for a crime of which he is innocent; the play had a strong influence upon subsequent writers of melodrama.

Tidings Brought to Mary, The (*L'Annonce faite à Marie*) A medieval mystery by Paul *Claudel. First performance: Paris, 1912. Based on an earlier work, *La Jeune Fille Violaine* (written 1892), the play centres on the innocent young Violaine, who miraculously cures a leper but contracts the disease herself, and her evil sister Mara.

Tieck, (Johann) Ludwig (1773–1853) German poet, novelist, and playwright, who was a leading figure of the German Romantic movement. His writings for the stage include such Romantic tragedies as *Karl von Berneck* (1797) and several influential plays based on fairytales, including *Ritter Blaubart* (Bluebeard; 1796), *Der gestiefelte Kater* (Puss-in-Boots; 1797), and *Die verkehrte Welt* (The World Upside-Down; 1798). As director of the Court Theatre in Dresden, he attempted to produce historically authentic versions of Shakespeare and also assisted in Schlegel's translations of Shakespeare's plays.

Tiger at the Gates (*La Guerre de Troie n'aura pas lieu*) A play by Jean *Giraudoux. First performance: Paris, 1935. Christopher Fry's translation, with Michael Redgrave as Hector, opened in London in 1955. A retelling of the events preceding the Trojan War, the plot centres on the conflict between patriotism and pacifism.

Tilley, Vesta (Matilda Alice Powles; 1864–1952) British music hall singer, who first appeared at St George's Hall, Nottingham (where her father was chairman) in 1868. She established a reputation as a fine male impersonator, coming to the Royal Holborn, London, in 1878 as 'The Great Little Tilley'. By 1880 she was billed as 'The London Idol' and so she remained for another 40 years, singing such songs as 'Burlington Bertie' and 'After the Ball'. She visited the US several times and appeared at Daly's, New York, in a musical comedy, *My Lady Molly*, as well as touring in a comedy, *Algy*, which was based on one of her numbers. She was also popular in pantomime at Drury Lane.

Tilney, Sir Edmund (d. 1610) English public official, *Master of the Revels from 1579. Despite the fact that his tenure of office saw the greatest period of Elizabethan and Jacobean drama, Tilney did little in pursuit of his duties beyond the basic censorship of plays.

Time and the Conways A play by J B *Priestley. First performance: London, 1937. The first and third acts present a family party in 1919 while the second act, set in 1937, contrasts reality with the aspirations expressed 20 years before.

Time of Your Life, The A play by William *Saroyan. First performance: New York, 1939. A group of eccentrics meet to talk about life and philosophy in a bar in San Francisco. The play was filmed in 1948 with James Cagney and William Bendix. As a play it won a Pulitzer Prize.

Times Square Theatre A theatre on West 42nd Street, New York, which opened in 1920 with *The Mirage*. Successful productions there included *Charlot's Revue of 1924*, Anita Loos's *Gentlemen Prefer Blondes* (1926), and Coward's *Private Lives* (1931). The theatre was converted into a cinema after *Forsaking All Others*, with Tallulah Bankhead, transferred to Broadway in 1933.

Timoneda, Joan (c. 1520–c. 1583) Spanish playwright, poet, and novelist, who published plays by Alonso de la Vega, Lope de Vega, and many others. His own dramatic works include imitations of Plautus, comedies, and five *autos sacramentales*.

Timon of Athens A tragedy by William
*Shakespeare, written c. 1604. First performance: 1678 (adapted by Thomas
Shadwell). The play revolves around Timon,
a generous Greek statesman who becomes
disillusioned after his friends refuse to help
him when his own wealth is gone: he eventually dies alone in self-imposed exile. The
play represents an experiment by Shakespeare with the tragic form, with little character development except for Timon himself
and a loose plot; some argue that the play
as it survives is still in a draft stage.

Tipteerers' Play *See* mummers' play.

tireman An official of the Elizabethan
theatre, who organized all matters relating
to the wardrobe. He also arranged seating
for the audience on the stage and in some
theatres had responsibility for the lights.

Tirso de Molina (Fray Gabriel Téllez;
c. 1571 – 1648) Spanish playwright, who was
much influenced by the plays of Lope de
Vega and wrote numerous secular works as
well as four *autos sacramentales* and religious
pieces. His 80 surviving plays include the
tragedies *El condenado por desconfiado*
(c. 1624) and *El Burlador de Sevilla y Convidado de Piedra* (1630), which introduced
the character of *Don Juan; other works
are notable for his interest in psychology as
well as his understanding of female characters and his clever handling of clowns.

'Tis Pity She's a Whore A tragedy by
John *Ford. First performance: c. 1627. The
play concerns the incestuous relationship between Giovanni and Annabella, which so
deranges him that he murders her and stabs
her husband, only to be killed himself.

Titinius (2nd century BC) Roman playwright, noted for his plays in the *togata* tradition. Fragments of his work and 15 titles
survive; he was probably much influenced
by the works of Menander.

Titus Andronicus A tragedy by William
*Shakespeare, derived from Seneca. First
performance: c. 1593. Sometimes attributed
to other authors, this bloody tale of revenge
and madness revolves around a victorious
Roman general whose daughter Lavinia is
raped and mutilated. He exacts his own
vengeance when he tricks Tamora – in
whose name Lavinia was assaulted – into
eating a pie in which her two sons have
been baked. The play is cruder than Shakespeare's later Roman tragedies but was popular for many years, largely as a result of
the violence of many of the scenes.

Tivoli A music hall in the Strand, London,
opened in 1890. From 1891 until 1914 it
was a thriving centre of the London music
hall, presenting such great stars as Marie
Lloyd under the management of Charles
Morton. The Tivoli Cinema was erected on
the site in 1923.

Tivoli Gardens *See* Richmond Hill Theatre.

Toby The name of the live dog that traditionally accompanies performers of the British *Punch and Judy show. Usually a terrier, Toby wears a ruff and sits on the ledge
of the booth whilst the entertainment takes
place; after the show the dog collects money
from the audience in a small bag.

In the US theatre **Toby** was a stock character of the travelling tent-shows and showboats of the early 20th century. The character typically portrayed was the simple
country bumpkin who triumphs over the
evil 'city slicker'; the role called for an excellent gymnast and spawned a female
counterpart called **Susie**. The last Toby appeared in 1962.

togata (*or* **tabernaria**) A form of Roman
fabula, that evolved from the *palliata* in the
2nd century BC. More satirical than its
predecessor, the *togata* consisted of bawdy
lampoons of the lower classes. Writers of

the form included Afranius, Atta, and Titinius; none of their plays survive intact.

Toller, Ernst (1893–1939) German Expressionist poet and playwright. His communist sympathies were reflected in such plays as *Die Wandlung* (The Inner Change; 1919) and *Masse-Mensch* (Masses and Man; 1920) and led to his imprisonment in 1919. His early dramas, noted for their symbolic characters and elements of unreality, deal chiefly with the recurring themes of martyrdom and revolt, as in *Die Maschinenstürmer* (The Machine Wreckers; 1922) and *Feuer aus den Kesseln* (Draw the Fires!; 1930), which deals with the Kiel mutiny in 1917. Other major works include *Hinkemann* (1923), *Hoppla, wir leben* (Hoppla!; 1927) and *Die blinde Göttin* (The Blind Goddess; 1932). He committed suicide in New York on the outbreak of World War II.

Tolstoy, Count Alexei Konstantinovich (1817–75) Russian poet, playwright, and diplomat, who was distantly related to Leo Tolstoy and was the author of a celebrated historical trilogy, first performed in St Petersburg in 1898. Consisting of *Smert' Ioanna Groznogo* (The Death of Ivan the Terrible), *Tsar Fedor Ivanovich*, and *Tsar Boris*, the trilogy has been much revived since censorship of it was lifted.

Tolstoy, Alexsei Nikolaivich (1882–1945) Soviet poet, novelist, and playwright, who was the author of several plays in support of the new regime following the Revolution of 1917. As well as several historical dramas, his plays include *The Road to Victory* (1939), which numbers both Lenin and Stalin amongst the characters.

Tolstoy, Count Leo Nikolaivich (1828–1910) Russian writer, author of novels successful in stage adaptations and several plays. His early dramatic writings consisted of a number of unfinished comedies written in the 1850s; later, however, he broke new ground with such plays as *The First Distiller* and the tragedy *The Power of Darkness*, in which he made peasant characters the centre of the action. *The Fruits of Enlightenment* was a satirical comedy on social issues, attacking the rural gentry, while *The Living Corpse* or *Redemption* and *Light Shining in the Darkness*, which were both left unfinished, criticized the contemporary marriage laws and class differences respectively. Of his novels, *Anna Karenina* and *War and Peace* have been the most successful in the theatre.

Principal works:

Pervy vinokur: 1887; translated as *The First Distiller*.

Vlast tmi: 1888; translated as *The Power of Darkness*.

Plodi prosveshcheniya: 1891; translated as *The Fruits of Enlightenment*.

Zhivoi trup: 1911 (written 1900); translated as *The Living Corpse* (or *Redemption*).

I svet vo tme tsvetit: never performed; translated as *Light Shining in the Darkness*.

Tomelty, Joseph (1911–) British playwright, actor, and novelist, born in Northern Ireland. He was closely involved in the founding of the *Ulster Group Theatre, for which he both wrote and acted. His best plays deal with Northern Irish life and include *The End House* (1944), *All Souls' Night* (1948), and *Is There a Priest at Home?* (1954).

Tom Thumb the Great A satirical burlesque by Henry *Fielding. First performance: 1730. Tom Thumb, whose diminutive stature represents a mockery of the grandiose central character of contemporary heroic tragedy, is betrothed to Princess Huncamunca; although he overcomes an infamous rival, Lord Grizzle, he himself gets eaten by a cow.

Tony Award The Antoinette Perry Award, which was named after the Chairman of the Board and Secretary of the American Theatre Wing and was first bestowed in 1947. The award is given for 'distinguished achievement' in the US theatre, reflecting Perry's own dedication to perfection and the highest standards of quality.

Toole, John Laurence (1830–1906) British actor, who made his first professional appearances in the provinces under the name John Lavers. In 1856 he appeared at the Lyceum; over the next nine years he was seen in a variety of parts at the Adelphi Theatre, notably in plays by Dickens. He appeared frequently at the Gaiety Theatre, toured in the US, and managed the Folly Theatre (later the Charing Cross Theatre), renaming it Toole's Theatre in 1879.

Too True to be Good A play by G B *Shaw. First performance: Boston, 1932. Through the play's 10 characters Shaw analyses the workings of capitalism and a wide range of other topics with varying degrees of success. The play's basic theme is the moral bankruptcy of mankind.

top drop *See* border.

Topol, Chaim (1934-) Israeli actor, who is best known for his performance both on stage and in the cinema as Tevye in the musical *Fiddler on the Roof* (1967). Earlier in his career he founded a highly popular satirical theatre in Tel-Aviv and appeared in various countries in plays by Brecht, Brendan Behan, Ionesco, and Shakespeare among others. He has appeared frequently at the Cameri Theatre in Tel-Aviv since 1965. In 1988 he reappeared in London's West End in *Ziegfeld*.

Torch Theatre A small repertory theatre at Milford Haven in Wales, which houses a resident company. It is also equipped for film shows and exhibitions and sometimes presents visiting companies in opera and dance.

Torelli, Achille (1841–1922) Italian playwright, who pioneered drama on social themes in the Italian theatre. *I mariti* (1867) established his reputation, exploring the relationship of two married couples; subsequent equally influential plays included *La moglie* (1868) and *L'ultima convegno* (1898).

Torelli, Giacomo (1608–78) Italian stage designer, known as 'the great magician' for his many inventions of stage devices. A pupil of Giambattista Aleotti (at whose Teatro Farnese he installed what was probably the first set of wings ever used), he did his most important work at the Teatro Novissimo in Venice (1641–45) and at Molière's Théâtre du Petit-Bourbon, most notably for Corneille's *Andromède* (1650). His innovations included the *carriage-and-frame system and an early revolving stage.

tormentor A narrow flat or curtain used to mask the wings; it is usually black or grey in colour.

Torres Naharro, Bartolomé de (c. 1485–c. 1524) Spanish playwright, regarded as the founder of the comic theatrical tradition in Spain. His plays, which were mostly written in Rome, were collected in the *Propalladia* (1517) and foreshadowed the development of the *comedia* of the Golden Age, notably in the case of *Himenea*, which was based on *La Celestina*. As a drama theorist, he also distinguished between the *comedia a noticia* and the *comedia a fantasía* as separate genres, the former relating to realistic dramas and the latter to those based on fantasy.

Tortoriti, Giuseppe (fl. late 17th century) Italian actor of the *commedia dell'arte*, who began in the role of Pasquariello but later became famous as Scaramuccia. He appeared with the Duke of Modena's company in London (1678–79) and with the Comédie-Italienne before unsuccessfully attempting to lead his own touring company.

Totaltheater A theatre designed by **Walter Gropius** for Piscator in 1926. Although it was never built, the theatre would have seated an audience of 2000 and have included a proscenium arch with a rotating forestage and various ambitious adaptations to facilitate the use of film projection and other special effects. It foreshadowed the development of the flexible stages of the modern era.

Tottenham Street Theatre *See* Scala Theatre.

Touch of the Poet, A A play by Eugene *O'Neill, written c. 1940. First performance: Stockholm, 1957. The play examines the conflict between an immigrant father and his American-born son. It was part of an intended cycle of 11 plays about a single family, examining the mercenary and self-destructive aspects of the national psyche.

Toulouse, Grenier de *See* Grenier de Toulouse.

touring company A theatre company that presents plays at a series of different venues, often part of a set circuit based on a particular city or theatre. Touring companies in Britain have burgeoned since the disappearance of the stock companies and the demise of the repertory system. Typical companies travel by road and present a wide variety of works – some politically-orientated or in the tradition of fringe theatre – at both large and small venues. Surviving on slender government subsidies, they comprise a significant part of many professional theatre programmes. Formerly many West End hits were also extensively toured before expense brought the practice to an end.

Tourneur, Cyril (1575–1626) English playwright, whose life is largely shrouded in obscurity. He is usually credited with writing *The *Revenger's Tragedy* (1607), which con-

veys a deeply pessimistic view of human nature, although some recent scholarship attributes it to Thomas Middleton. He was also the author of *The Nobleman* (1607), now lost, and *The Atheist's Tragedy* (1611).

Tovstonogov, Georgyi Alexandrovich (1915-) Soviet director, who has established a strong reputation for his innovative interpretation of many classic plays. He began his career in Tbilisi in Georgia in 1931, and since then has worked at the Lenkom Theatre, the Gorky Theatre, and the Pushkin Theatre, while other productions have been seen internationally. Among his most controversial works have been Dostoevsky's *The Idiot* (1957), Arbuzov's *It Happened in Irkutz* (1959), Shteyn's *The Ocean* (1961), Chekhov's *Three Sisters* (1964), Shakespeare's *Henry IV* (1969), and Gogol's *The Government Inspector* (1972).

Tower Theatre *See* Tavistock Repertory Company.

Toys in the Attic A play by Lillian *Hellman. First performance: New York, 1950. The plot concerns two elderly spinsters living in New Orleans and their struggle to take care of their brother. The play was filmed in 1963 with Geraldine Page and Dean Martin.

toy theatre A miniature theatre, made of cardboard, complete with actors and scenery imitating that used in contemporary theatre productions. Popular in several European countries during the 19th century, toy theatres are now a valuable source of information about the sets of the period. In Britain sheets of figures and scenery from about 300 plays for use in the toy theatre (or **juvenile drama**) were available in both **penny plain** and **twopence coloured** forms.

trabeata A form of Roman *fabula, closely related to the *togata. It was named after the *trabea, a robe worn by Roman knights, who were apparently the main characters in the play. Originated by Melissus, no examples of the form have survived.

Trachiniae A tragedy by *Sophocles. First performance: Athens, c. 425 BC. As in several other works by Sophocles, the play studies the impact of suffering and culminates in the death of Deianeira, the central character.

Trades Unions Theatre A theatre in Moscow, originally called the **Proletkult Theatre**, founded shortly after the Revolution of 1917 to present plays on proletarian themes. Sergei Eisenstein worked there from 1921 to 1923, directing plays by Ostrovsky and Tretyakov before switching to films; later it enjoyed acclaim under Alexei Dikie before finally closing in 1936.

Trafalgar Square Theatre See Duke of York's Theatre.

Trafalgar Theatre See Nederlander Theatre.

Tragedian See stock company.

tragédie-Bourgeoise See drame.

tragedy A form of drama characterized by its serious tone and unhappy ending. The concept of the tragedy, meaning 'goat-song' after the prize probably given to the winning playwright at the *Dionysia, was first developed in ancient Greece from the earlier tradition of the *dithyramb. The theories of Aeschylus, Euripides, Sophocles, and others – subsequently codified by *Aristotle – established a number of basic groundrules, stipulating for instance that the central characters should come from the upper echelons of society and that their downfall, usually culminating in their death, should be essentially a consequence of the workings of fate. The closet plays of Seneca helped to transmit Greek ideas about tragedy to the Elizabethan theatre of Marlowe and Shakespeare, in which the poetic possibilities of the form were fully realized. Subsequently the theories of Aristotle were developed into the concept of the *unities (notably by Racine and Corneille) and the downfall of the central figure was presented not only as a result of the influence of destiny, but also of a crucial flaw in his personality. During the 18th century the requirement for characters to come from the upper classes was relaxed and the form subsequently splintered into various subdivisions, including – via the plays of Goethe and Schiller amongst others – melodrama, domestic and social drama, and tragi-comedy.

Tragical History of Dr Faustus, The See *Dr Faustus, The Tragical History of.*

tragi-comedy A form of drama combining elements of both comedy and tragedy. Initially experimented with by Plautus, the form had its roots in the Renaissance when it first emerged as a distinct genre. It ignored the unities but capitalized upon the more sensational aspects of tragedy and borrowed the happy ending typical of comedy; the central characters were conventionally of noble but not royal status. By the 18th century it was already becoming increasingly confused with other forms of drama. Writers of the form in its early stages of development included Giraldi, Dolce, Garnier, Alexandre Hardy, and Corneille. It has re-emerged in the 20th century in the plays of such authors as Ibsen, Beckett, and Pinter.

transformation scene A convention of the English *pantomime, in which a rapid and spectacular change of scenery is effected by means of falling flaps and other devices. Use of a *rise-and-sink or of *scruto could facilitate the effect, whilst other methods of achieving it included the **fan effect**, which involved the removal of scenery by collapsing it sideways in the manner of a folding fan. In the modern theatre transformation scenes are often effected by means of transparencies.

transparency An expanse of gauze or other thin fabric, which when painted with transparent dyes and lit from the front appears to be a normally painted cloth; when lit from behind, however, the gauze becomes transparent, revealing whatever lies behind it.

Transpontine melodrama Popular melodrama that was performed south of the Thames in mid-19th century London. Played at such theatres as the Old Vic and the Surrey, the term was originally intended to be insulting but was later used as a generic description of any crude melodrama.

trap Any of the various trapdoors cut into the stage floor and scenery, through which performers can make entrances and stage machinery can be operated. *See also* bristle trap, cauldron trap, corner trap, footlights trap, ghost glide, grave trap, slote, star trap, vamp trap.

Traveller Without Luggage, The (*Le Voyageur sans bagage*) A *pièce noire* by Jean *Anouilh. First performance: Paris, 1937. The central character is an ex-soldier suffering from amnesia. On learning with disgust of his dishonourable youth, he contrives to adopt a new identity.

Travers, Ben (1886–1980) British playwright, whose particular genius was for farce. Beginning with *A *Cuckoo in the Nest* (1925), he wrote a series of plays that became known as the 'Aldwych farces' because they were first performed in the Aldwych Theatre. *Rookery Nook* (1926), *Thark* (1927), and *Plunder* (1928) are among the most famous, while later farces include *Banana Ridge* (1939) and *The Bed Before Yesterday* (1975). He also wrote two volumes of autobiography.

Traverse Theatre A studio theatre in Edinburgh, the first of its kind in Britain, that developed out of the International Festival of 1963. Originally situated in the Lawnmarket, the stage lay between two opposite banks of seats; in 1969 it was moved to a larger and more flexible space in the Grassmarket. Committed to the production of new and experimental work, it has premiered many modern plays, including Berkoff's *East* and John Byrne's *The Slab Boys*. It achieved the status of a public (as opposed to a club) theatre in 1988 after structural work had been carried out on the building.

Tree, Ellen *See* Kean, Charles.

Tree, Sir Herbert (Draper) Beerbohm (1853–1917) British actor-manager of mixed European descent. He made his professional debut in 1878 and nine years later took over the Comedy Theatre. After a number of successes, he moved to the more prestigious Haymarket, where he remained for 10 years, scoring a personal triumph as Svengali in an adaptation of George Du Maurier's *Trilby*. The success of these years enabled him to build *Her Majesty's, which opened in 1897 with a series of magnificent Shakespearean productions. He was also acclaimed for his interpretations of Professor Higgins in *Pygmalion* opposite Mrs Patrick Campbell, and as Nero, Herod, Beethoven, and Fagin. Tree also founded (1904) the Royal Academy of Dramatic Art. He was knighted in 1909. His wife **Helen Maud Holt** (1863–1937) was his leading lady in many productions. *See also* Beerbohm, Sir Max.

tree border *See* border.

Trelawny of the 'Wells' A comedy by *Pinero. First performance: 1898. Rose Trelawny breaks off her engagement to Arthur Gower to return to the stage but finds it impossible to deliver unnatural stage dialogue. A sentimental comedy, the play ends with her triumph in a realistic play and her reunion with Arthur.

Tremblay, Michel (1942-) French-Canadian playwright, who established a controversial reputation with his use in his first play, *Les Belles-soeurs* (1968), of mixed English and French, as spoken in Quebec. Later plays, which have similarly highlighted Quebec's mixed culture, include *En pièces détachées* (1969), *La Duchesse de Langeais* (1970), *Hosanna* (1973), which depicts a transvestite's suffering as a result of his confused sexual identity, *Bonjour, Bonjour* (1974), *Carmen of the Boulevards* (1976), *Albertine in Five Times* (1984), and *Le Vrai Monde?* (1986).

Trenev, Konstantin Andreievich (1884–1945) Soviet playwright and short-story writer, whose works remain popular in the USSR. His best-known play is *Lyubov Yarovaya* (1926), which depicts the conflict of loyalties facing a young teacher and was performed with great success by the Moscow Art Theatre at the 1937 World Exhibition in Paris. Other plays included *Pugachevshchina* (1924), which depicts a peasant revolt in the 18th century, *On the Banks of the Neva* (1937), and *Anna Luchinina* (1941).

Tretyakov, Sergei Mikhailovich (1892–1939) Soviet poet and playwright, who is best known for the play *Roar, China!* (1926), which recounts the clashes that took place between British imperialists and the Chinese in 1924. His other propagandist plays include *Are You Listening, Moscow?* and *Gas Masks*, on both of which he collaborated with Sergei Eisenstein. Later he helped to popularize the plays of Brecht in the USSR.

Trevelyan, Hilda (Hilda Tucker; 1880–1959) British actress. She made her stage debut as a child but her first serious en-

gagement was in 1898 at the Royal Court Theatre, understudying the part of Avonia Bunn – a part she later played many times – in Pinero's *Trelawny of the 'Wells'*. She came to be associated particularly with the plays of J M Barrie, creating the role of Wendy in *Peter Pan* in 1904.

trickwork The use of traps and other mechanical devices in creating illusions on stage, as practised particularly throughout the British theatre in the 19th century. A popular feature of pantomime, the success of such displays of technical virtuosity depend upon the acrobatic skills of the performers as well as upon the meticulous preparation of machinery to render such tricks as the roll-out and the leap effective.

trilogy *See* tetralogy.

Trinity Square Repertory Company A US theatre company founded in 1964 in Providence, Rhode Island. The company soon established a reputation for its productions of contemporary US drama and moved into a permanent home in the **Lederer Theatre Complex** in 1973. It also runs training courses and produces a summer repertory programme.

Trissino, Giangiorgio (1478–1550) Italian writer, author of the influential tragedy *Sofonisba* (1562), written c. 1514. His use of classical Greek models in this play, observing the unities of time and action, and his employment of blank verse set the pattern for much subsequent Italian tragedy. His other plays include the verse comedy *I simillimi*, based on Plautus.

Tristan l'Hermite (François l'Hermite; c. 1601–55) French playwright, poet, and gambler, who was a pioneer of French classical drama. Tristan's first play was the tragedy *La Mariane* (1636), based on Herod's jealousy for his wife, which enjoyed considerable success, rivalling that of Pierre

Corneille's *Le Cid*. His other works include the tragedies *La Mort de Sénèque* (1644) and *La Mort de Crispe* (1645) and the comedy *Le Parasite* (1654).

tritagonist *See* protagonist.

Triumph of Horus, The A play written in Egypt around 1200 BC. Thought to be the oldest-known written drama in the world, the script of the play – which recounts a ritual battle between an heroic king and a hippopotamus-demon called Seth – was recorded on the walls of the Temple of Edfu in 110 BC. It was revived in translation in Britain in 1971.

Trivellino *See* Locatelli, Domenico.

Trocadero Palace of Varieties A music hall in Windmill (now Great Windmill) Street, London, which occupied the site of a tennis court built in 1744. Opened by Robert Bignell in 1851 as the **Argyll Rooms** for various kinds of entertainment, it met with scant success and was closed in 1878. Bignell reopened it in 1882 as the Trocadero Palace, and in 1886 Charles Coburn drew large audiences for 14 months singing 'Two Lovely Black Eyes'. Music hall continued until 1894, when the property was reopened as a restaurant (1896). In the 1920s C B Cochran staged a celebrated nightly cabaret in the Grill Room, remaining there until 1946. The property subsequently became a shopping centre.

Troepolskaya, Tatiana Mikhailovna (d. 1774) Russian actress, one of the first women to join a professional company in Russia. She excelled as heroines in the tragedies of Sumarokov.

Troilus and Cressida A tragi-comedy by William *Shakespeare, written c. 1602. First performance: date unknown. Against a background of the Trojan wars, the play is a sardonic examination of the ideals of ro-mance and chivalry and was little performed before the 20th century. Based on Homer and on Chaucer's *Troilus and Criseyde*, the play is notable for its frank discussion of sexual desire and its rejection, through Thersites, of the concepts of love and honour.

Trojan Women, The A tragedy by *Euripides. First performance: Athens, 415 BC. Of all Euripides' works, this play, relating the fate of both armies after the fall of Troy, was his fiercest condemnation of war but failed to end the prolonged conflict then being continued between Sicily and Athens.

trope A brief sentence or short passage inserted into the early Mass as an illustration of the meaning of a religious service. The first recorded trope, a natural development of the *neume, was a feature of the 10th-century Easter service at the Monastery of St Martial at Limoges; subsequently such tropes gradually evolved into rudimentary plays as an early form of *liturgical drama.

Troupes Permanentes *See Décentralisation Dramatique.*

trouvère *See* jongleur.

truck *See* boat truck.

Tuccio, Stefano (1540–97) Italian playwright, born in Sicily, who was a major writer of Jesuit drama. His plays, written for the Jesuit college at Messina, include *Juditha* (1564) and a trilogy, consisting of *Christus Natus*, *Christus Patiens*, and *Christus Judex*, which was one of the earliest such works written in the vernacular.

Tuke, Sir Samuel (d. 1674) English courtier, who (at the prompting of Charles II) wrote the tragi-comedy *The Adventures of Five Hours*, based on a play by Calderón. It was performed at Lincoln's Inn Fields in 1663 and was praised by Samuel Pepys.

Tumanov, Joseph Mikhailovich (Joseph Mikhailovich Tumanishvili; 1905-) Soviet director, who established his reputation as one of Stanislavsky's leading successors. A pupil of Stanislavsky himself from 1928 to 1932, he has won acclaim for such productions as Dickens's *Little Dorrit* (1953) at the Pushkin Theatre and other major venues in Moscow.

tumbler A batten used in rolling up canvas scenery, specifically to prevent it from becoming creased.

Turgenev, Ivan Sergeivich (1818–83) Russian novelist and playwright, best known as a dramatist for *Mesiats v derevne* (A *Month in the Country*; written in 1850 and staged in 1872). This play, which anticipated Chekhov, was the first Russian psychological drama and his final work for the stage, which he abandoned in the face of opposition from the censor. His earlier plays include the satirical comedies *Bezdenezhe* (Insolvency), *Gde tonko, tam i rvyotsa* (Where It's Thin It Breaks), *Kholostiak* (The Bachelor), and *Privubtsialka* (A Provincial Lady).

Turkish Knight *See* mummers' play.

Turlupin (Henri Legrand; c. 1587–1637) French actor, who was highly popular in farce at the Hôtel de Bourgogne alongside Gaultier-Garguille and Gros-Guillaume. He also appeared in tragedy, using the stagename **Belleville**.

Turnham's Grand Concert Hall *See* Metropolitan Music Hall.

Turpio, Ambivius (2nd century BC) Roman actor, who created numerous roles in the plays of Terence. He also appeared in works by Caecilius Statius.

Tutin, Dorothy (1930-) British actress, who, after working at Bristol and at the Old Vic, came to prominence as Rose in Graham Greene's *The Living Room* (1953) and as Sally Bowles in *I Am a Camera* (1934). She has since been acclaimed in many parts with the Royal Shakespeare and National Theatre companies, being especially admired as Hedvig in *The Wild Duck*, Portia, Viola, Cressida, Juliet, Sister Jeanne in Whiting's *The Devils*, Desdemona, Rosalind, Kate in Pinter's *Old Times* (1971), and Peter Pan (1971–72). More recent roles have included Madame Ranevskaya in *The Cherry Orchard*, Cleopatra, Lady Macbeth, and Lady Fanciful in *The Provoked Wife*.

Twaits, William (d. 1814) US actor, born in Britain, who excelled in farce and comedy first in Britain and then in the US. His most successful roles included Shakespeare's Polonius, Dogberry, Launcelot Gobbo, and the First Gravedigger, in which parts he was highly popular at such venues as the Chestnut Street Theatre in Philadelphia and the Park Theatre in New York.

Twelfth Night; or, What You Will A comedy by William *Shakespeare, written in 1599. First performance: c. 1602. Probably written as a Christmas entertainment, the play is the last and finest of Shakespeare's romantic comedies, revolving about the figures of the disguised Viola and the scheming Sir Toby Belch. Its use of the imagery of war, storms, and madness and the anguish of the yellow-stockinged Malvolio are often interpreted as anticipating the series of great tragedies that was to follow.

Twentieth Century Theatre *See* Bijou Theatre.

two-fold *See* book flat.

Two Gentlemen of Verona, The A comedy by William *Shakespeare, written c. 1594. First performance: 1672. The first and least successful of Shakespeare's romantic comedies, the play was derived from Jorge de

Montemayor's prose romance *Diana* and focuses on the conflicting demands of love and friendship through the relationship of Valentine and Proteus.

Two Noble Kinsmen, The A tragi-comedy by John *Fletcher and William *Shakespeare, written c. 1613. First performance: c. 1619. Probably Shakespeare's last play, it is based on Chaucer's *Knight's Tale* and follows the contest by tournament between Palamon and Arcite for the hand of Emilia, the whole event being presided over by Theseus. It has been suggested that Shakespeare wrote the first and fifth acts and Fletcher the remainder.

Tyl, Josef Kajetán (1808–50) Czech playwright and actor, who is commonly regarded as the father of the modern Czech theatre. He led his own theatrical company, for which he wrote his first play – the folk comedy *The Fair* (from which came the Czech national anthem) – in 1834. He was famous for his patriotic plays arguing for Czech independence, notably *The Bagpiper of Strakonice* (1847), *The Bloody Trial, or the Miners of Kutná Hora* (1848), and *Jan Hus* (1848).

Tyler, Royall (1757–1826) US playwright, who wrote the first US comedy – *The Contrast* – in 1787. Influenced by the works of such English writers as Goldsmith and Sheridan, it introduced the stock rural Yankee character, whose simple native honesty triumphs over foreign affectation. His later plays were less successful.

Tynan, Kenneth Peacock (1927–80) British theatre critic, who wrote for *The Observer* (1954–58 and 1960–63) and the *New Yorker* (1958–60) and was closely associated with the National Theatre (1963–69). He was noted for his support for the radical socially-motivated drama of such authors as Anouilh and was in constant conflict with the censors; he was also the main force behind the popular nude revue *Oh, Calcutta!* (1969).

Tyrone Guthrie Theatre *See* Guthrie Theatre.

U

Ubu roi A satirical farce by Alfred *Jarry. First performance: Paris, 1896. Ubu, a caricature of one of Jarry's schoolmasters, is the embodiment of bourgeois stupidity and greed and human savagery; this ferocious attack on society proved a major source of inspiration for Jarry's successors.

Udall, Nicholas (1505–56) English playwright, chiefly remembered for *Ralph Roister Doister*, the earliest known native comedy, written for the boys of Eton school, of which he was headmaster. None of his other dramatic pieces have survived intact.

Ulster Group Theatre A small repertory theatre established in Ulster Hall, Bedford Street, Belfast, in 1932. Known as the Little Theatre and then the Playhouse, it was renamed in 1940 when an organization of amateur groups took it over. Eventually this organization acquired professional status and built a reputation for productions of plays by such writers as James Bridie, St John Ervine, George Shiels, and Joseph Tomelty; actors at the theatre have included Colin Blakely and J G Devlin. After surviving a period in decline in the late 1950s it concentrated on comedy until 1972, when it was closed for four years due to the sectarian conflict in Northern Ireland. Re-equipped in 1976, it reopened in 1978 as a venue for amateur groups.

Unamuno y Jugo, Miguel de (1864–1936) Spanish writer and philosopher of

Basque descent. As a playwright he was best known for *Sombras de sueño* (Dream Shadows; 1930); his other works for the theatre included *Abel Sánchez* (1917), based on his own novel, and *El hermano Juan* (Brother Juan; 1929), an adaptation of the Don Juan legend. One of his short stories was later dramatized by Julio de Hoyos as *Nada menos que todo un hombre* (Nothing Less Than a Total Man).

Uncle Vanya A play by Anton *Chekhov. First performance: Moscow Art Theatre, 1899. A reworking of his earlier unsuccessful play *The Wood Demon* (1899), it depicts the sense of purposelessness in the lives of the inhabitants of a large house in the countryside. The roles of Uncle Vanya, his niece Sonya, and their companions – an elderly professor and his wife – have provided many leading performers with rewarding roles.

Underhill, Cave (c. 1634 – c. 1710) British actor, noted as a comedian. His most famous parts included Codpate in Shadwell's *Epsom Wells* and Sir Sampson Legend in *Love for Love*. In 1681 he created the role of Blunt in Aphra Behn's *The Rover*.

Under Milk Wood A poetic drama by Dylan Thomas. First performance: London, 1956. Written originally as a radio play, this depiction of life in the Welsh town of Llaregub became extremely popular both for its humour and human sympathy as well as for its sonorous language.

understudy An actor who learns the part of another, so that he is able to replace the latter in the case of an emergency.

Underwood, John (c. 1590 – 1624) English actor, who appeared as a boy in Jonson's *Cynthia's Revels* and *The Poetaster* at the Blackfriars Theatre. He was with the King's Men from 1608 and is in the First Folio list of Shakespearean actors. He held shares in the Blackfriars, Globe, and Curtain theatres.

Union Square Theatre A theatre in Union Square, New York, which opened in 1871. It was managed by A M Palmer and had one of the best stock companies in the US, presenting such plays as John Oxenford's *The Two Orphans* (1874) and *La Dame aux Camélias* by Dumas *fils*; after 1885, when Palmer and the company left, it housed travelling companies. In 1888 it was burned down and rebuilt as a vaudeville house. In 1936, after it had been used as a cinema, it was demolished.

Union Theatre *See* Chatham Theatre.

Uniti An Italian *commedia dell'arte* company, which drew on actors from a number of other companies to present special performances. In its various forms its directors included Drusiano *Martinelli, whilst Silvio *Fiorillo numbered amongst its actors.

unities The conventions that a play should observe consistency of time, place, and action, as developed in Italy in the 17th century and formulated by Jean Mairet. According to its proponents, a play should represent a single action taking place in a single day in the same setting. A strong influence upon classical French tragedy, the concept of the unities was derived, somewhat inaccurately, from the theories of Aristotle but had little influence in England.

Unity Theatre A communist theatre in London, founded by a left-wing amateur group in a hall near King's Cross in 1936. It moved to permanent premises in Goldington Street, St Pancras, in 1937, and introduced the Living Newspaper technique of presenting current issues in documentary style. Among other productions were the first Brecht play to be staged in London, O'Casey's *The Star Turns Red* (1940), and

Adamov's *Spring '71* (1962). Fire destroyed the theatre in 1975.

The Unity Theatre in Glasgow was a similarly motivated amateur company formed in 1941. Having won acclaim for its production of Gorky's *The Lower Depths*, which was seen at London's Unity Theatre in 1945, it became a professional company. It continued to play in Glasgow as well as touring Scotland, achieving an outstanding success with Robert MacLeish's *The Gorbals Story* (1948). Financial insecurity led to the company's disbandment in the early 1950s.

university drama departments The study of the history, theory, and practice of drama as the basis of a degree course was first undertaken in the US, specifically at the Carnegie Institute of Technology in Pittsburgh (1914). In Britain the first such department was established at Bristol University in 1946; Manchester, Hull, and Birmingham followed during the early 1960s and expansion continued into the mid-1970s. Most departments have their own studio theatres or access to larger campus theatres, which in their turn have made important contributions to the cultural life of their surrounding communities. Vocational training is rarely provided (that being the province of the drama schools) but extensive practical work is usually undertaken and many graduates at universities throughout the world go on to become successful actors, directors, designers, and administrators both in the theatre and in the media.

University Wits A group of Elizabethan playwrights, who were notorious for their wild behaviour and rejection of the high ideals of Shakespeare and others. They included Greene, Nashe, Marlowe, and Peele among other graduates of Oxford and Cambridge.

Unreason, Abbot of *See* Misrule, Lord of.

Unruh, Fritz von (1885–1970) German playwright and poet, who resigned his commission in the cavalry following Reinhardt's successful production of his patriotic play *Offiziere* in 1911. Throughout World War I he served in the army, but soon after he became known for his strongly pacifist views, as expressed in the Expressionist plays *Ein Geschlecht* (One Generation; 1917) and *Platz* (1920).

upper circle *See* auditorium.

upstage *See* stage direction.

Urban, Joseph (1872–1933) US theatre architect and stage designer, born in Austria, who became famous for his sets for Ziegfeld's *Follies*. Other designs included sets for opera in Boston and for Shakespearean productions in New York. As an architect, he designed the innovative Ziegfeld Theatre in New York.

Ure, Mary *See* Osborne, John.

Uris Theatre A theatre on 51st Street and Broadway, New York, which opened in 1972 with the musical *Via Galactica*. Other productions seen there have included Sondheim's *Sweeney Todd* (1979) and Gilbert and Sullivan's *The Pirates of Penzance* (1981).

Ustinov, Peter (Alexander) (1921–) British actor, playwright, and director of Russian descent, who trained under Saint-Denis and made early appearances at the Players' Theatre, London, in his own sketches. After serving in World War II, during which five of his plays – including *House of Regrets* (1942) and *The Banbury Nose* (1944) – were produced, he returned to the stage as Petrovich in Rodney Ackland's adaptation of Dostoevsky's *Crime and Punishment* (1946). After directing and appearing as Sergeant Dohda in Eric Linklater's *Love in Albania* in 1949, he embarked upon a successful film career, being seen in the theatre for 30 years only in his own plays; the most successful of these included *The *Love of Four Colonels* (1951) and *Romanoff and Juliet* (1956). He played Lear at Stratford, Ontario, in 1979 and in 1983 appeared as Ludwig in his own play *Beethoven's Tenth*. As well as being a highly versatile man of the theatre, he has also acquired a reputation as a brilliant raconteur and mimic.

V

Vadstena Theatre A private theatre in Vadstena, Sweden, established in 1826. Although the last professional performance was in 1878, it survives as a venue for amateurs.

Vakhtangov, Eugene V (1883–1922) Soviet actor and director, who became a leading director of the Moscow Art Theatre, initially as a pupil of Stanislavsky. With his own splinter group, the Third Workshop (renamed the Vakhtangov Theatre after Vakhtangov's death) he won acclaim with his production of *Macbeth* in 1921, with Vakhtangov himself in the leading role. The group thrived on a combination of the naturalism of Stanislavsky and the experimentalism of Meyerhold; Vakhtangov's energetic leadership culminated in a highly praised version of Gozzi's *Turandot*, presented after Vakhtangov's early death at the height of his fame. In 1918 he also founded the Habimah Theatre, famous for its production of Ansky's *The Dybbuk* (1922).

Vakhtangov Theatre A studio theatre in Moscow, established in 1921 as part of the *Moscow Art Theatre. Founded by Eugene V Vakhtangov, who did some of his best work there, it was later used for productions directed by such notable figures as Akimov, Meyerhold, Popov, and Zavadsky, of which *Hamlet* (1932) and plays by Gorky attracted the most attention. Okhlopkov and Shchukin staged plays by Pogodin with success, while after World War II a series of both modern and – under Reuben and Yevgenyi Simonov – Shakespearean works were presented.

Valle-Inclán, Ramón María del (1866–1936) Spanish novelist, poet, and playwright, who was the author of a number of avant-garde dramas. These ranged from the children's play *La cabeza del dragón* (The Dragon's Head; 1918) and the Carlist poetic drama *Voces de gesta* (Epic Voices; 1912) to the highly satirical *La marquese Rosalinda* (1913) and *Divinas palabras* (Divine Words; 1920). His targets included the oppression of the poor, the extravagance of the rich, and the decadence of high society; several of his plays anticipated the Theatre of the Absurd.

Valleran-Lecomte (fl. 1590–c. 1615) French actor-manager, who presented various plays in Bordeaux, Strasbourg, Frankfurt, and elsewhere before establishing his own company. Acting plays by Alexandre Hardy and others, his company appeared at the Hôtel de Bourgogne and undertook several tours. Performers with the company included Marie Venier and Agnan Sarat; Valleran-Lecomte himself appeared in farce and in *commedia dell'arte* roles. He also ran a training school for young actors.

Valli, Romolo (1925–80) Italian actor and manager, who became highly popular in character parts. He first attracted attention while at the Piccolo Teatro della Città di Milano, excelling in such plays as Goldoni's *La locandiera* and as Malvolio in *Twelfth Night*. In 1954 he founded his own Compagnia dei Giovani (later I Giovani del Teatro Elisio), with whom he won acclaim in plays by Fabbri and Pirandello. He died in a car accident.

vamp trap A trap, more formally called a vampire trap, by means of which an actor, passing through two spring flaps, can appear to walk through a solid piece of scenery. It acquired its name from Planché's play *The Vampire*, in which it was first used in 1820.

Vanbrugh, Sir John (1664–1726) English playwright and architect, whose first successful comedy, *The *Relapse; or, Virtue in Danger*, was produced in 1696. The **Provoked Wife* followed in 1697 at Lincoln's Inn Fields; other plays and translations were less successful, although *The Confederacy* (1705) enjoyed many revivals. It was originally produced by Betterton at the Queen's Theatre (on the site of Her Majesty's), which Vanbrugh himself had designed. His unfinished play *A Journey to London* was completed by Cibber as *The Provoked Husband* (1728).

Vanbrugh, Violet (Augusta Mary) (Violet Augusta Barnes; 1867–1942) British actress, who began her career at Margate and subsequently worked in the Kendals' company and with Irving. She had particular success as Queen Katharine in *Henry V* (1910) opposite her husband, Arthur *Bourchier, and often appeared as a leading lady under his management. Other acclaimed roles included Lady Macbeth and several modern parts.

Her sister was the actress **Dame Irene Vanbrugh** (Irene Barnes; 1872–1949), who made her London debut in *Alice in Wonderland* in 1888. She became a leading lady in the companies of Tree, Alexander, and Hare, and, during a 13 year connection with Charles Frohman at the Duke of York's Theatre under the direction of her husband, the younger Dion *Boucicault, proved herself a superb exponent of the plays of Pinero and Barrie. Her most celebrated roles included the very first Gwendolen Fairfax in *The Importance of Being Earnest* (1895) and Sophie Fullgarney in *The Gay*

Lord Quex (1899). The Vanbrugh Theatre of the Royal Academy of Dramatic Art was named in honour of the two sisters by their brother, Sir Kenneth Barnes.

Vance, Alfred (Alfred Peck Stevens; 1839–88) British music hall performer, known as **The Great Vance**. After appearing at the St James's Theatre, London, he went on the halls in a blackfaced double act with his brother. In 1864 he switched to singing broad cockney songs; later he became a popular *lion comique*. He died on stage at the Sun Music Hall in Knightsbridge.

Vance, Nina *See* Nina Vance Alley Theatre.

Vančura, Antonín (1882–1939) Czech playwright, who – with his brother, the novelist **Vladislav Vančura** (1891–1942) – was associated with the Free Theatre. Antonín, writing as **Jiří Mahen**, wrote *Heaven, Hell, Paradise* (1919), *Progeny* (1921), and *The Deserter* (1924), all depicting contemporary turmoil in Central Europe. He committed suicide in 1939. Vladislav's best-known plays were *Teacher and Pupil* (1927) and *The Sick Girl* (1928). He died in a concentration camp.

Vandenhoff, George (1813–85) US actor, born in Britain, who settled in the US after appearing successfully as Hamlet at the Park Theatre in New York in 1842 and became a popular leading man. Previously at Covent Garden in London, he acted under Madame Vestris and subsequently returned in 1853 to appear as Hamlet once more and then to retire. Overcoming his own dislike for the theatre, he came out of retirement briefly in 1878 to appear as Wolsey in *Henry VIII* opposite Geneviève Ward.

His sister, **Charlotte Elizabeth Vandenhoff** (Mrs Swinbourne; 1818–60), was much admired playing such roles as Juliet, Cordelia, and Antigone. She also created the parts of Lydia in Sheridan Knowles's *The Love*

Chase (1837) and Parthenia in Mrs Lovell's *Ingomar* (1851).

Vanderbilt Theatre A theatre on 48th Street, New York, which opened in 1921 with O'Neill's *Anna Christie*. Infrequent subsequent triumphs included a revival of Wilde's *The Importance of Being Earnest* (1939); it was then converted into a broadcasting studio and was demolished in 1954.

Van Druten, John (1901–57) London-born playwright and novelist, who became a US citizen in 1944 after emigrating to the US when his first play, *Young Woodley* (1925) – a study of adolescence – was banned in Britain. His later plays include such popular light comedies as *The Voice of the Turtle* (1943) and *Bell, Book and Candle* (1950). He is perhaps best known for his *I am a Camera* (1951), which is based on *Goodbye to Berlin*, Christopher Isherwood's portrait of Berlin between the wars; it was later turned into the musical *Cabaret* (1966).

Van Itallie, Jean-Claude (1936-) US playwright, born in Belgium, whose first play to be produced, *War*, was written in 1963. Since then he has written a number of plays for such avant-garde theatres as the Café La Mama and the Open Theatre, including *American Hurrah!* (1966), *The Serpent* (1968), *Mystery Play* (1973), and adaptations of plays by Chekhov. He was writer-in-residence at the McCarter Theatre in Princeton from 1972 to 1976. More recent works include *The Traveller* (1987).

Variétés, Théâtre des A theatre in Paris, opened in 1807 and still surviving in substantially its original condition. Partially altered in 1823, it was used for a wide range of productions, including revues, the plays of Dumas *père*, and vaudeville.

An earlier theatre of the same name was founded in the Boulevard du Temple in 1779, its company eventually spending a short period in residence at the Palais-Royal.

variety A tradition of musical entertainment that developed from *music hall in the late 19th century. Variety represented the later, less spontaneous, period of the halls, with the audience being seated as in an ordinary theatre and with bills often consisting of twice-nightly programmes; these often included elaborately staged extracts from ballets and plays. *See also* vaudeville.

Variety Artists' Federation *See* British Actors' Equity Association.

Varius Rufus, Lucius (c. 74 BC–14 BC) Roman playwright, a friend of both Virgil and Horace. His tragedy *Thyestes* (29 BC), now lost, was considered the equal of any Greek tragedy.

Varro, Marcus Terentius (116 BC–27 BC) Roman scholar, poet, and satirist, author of several theatrical pieces, all of which are lost. His works are thought to have included examples of closet drama and *didascaliae* as well as histories of the theatre.

Vasconcelos, Jorge Ferreira de (1515–85) Portuguese writer, author of several dialogue novels. These included *Eufrósina*, *Ulissipo*, and *Aulegrafia*, which were all intended for reading aloud rather than for actual performance.

vaudeville A tradition of satirical musical drama that developed originally in Normandy, as the *vaux-de-vire* or *voix des villes*, during the 15th century. Subsequently the term was applied by Boileau to certain forms of satirical ballads in the 17th century and then to dumb shows in the booth theatres of Paris. These dramas were presented as musical entertainments in order to circumvent the Comédie-Française's monopoly of straight drama. The most famous writers of these dramas included Lesage and

Favart, whose works foreshadowed the development of popular farce and light opera in the 19th century, notably those of Scribe and Labiche.

In the mid-19th century the word vaudeville came to be used for variety entertainments for the first time, particularly in the US. Roughly equivalent to the *music hall in Britain, the US tradition shared similar roots in beer halls throughout the country; typical programmes comprised a mixture of songs, comic sketches, and various dance, magic, and acrobatic acts, usually about a dozen in number (although the US tradition sometimes included more diverse elements than was customary on the other side of the Atlantic). Following the opening of a vaudeville theatre in New York by Tony Pastor in 1881 the tradition became steadily more respectable, attracting family audiences and taking over from variety. Successful chains of vaudeville theatres were subsequently set up, the most celebrated venue being the Palace Theatre on Broadway. As well as performers from the straight theatre and Europe, US vaudeville stars numbered amongst them Lew Dockstader, Jimmy Durante, W C Fields, Bert Lahr, Bert Williams, Weber and Fields, Jack Norworth, Lillian Russell, Ed Wynn, and many others.

By 1932, when the Palace Theatre finally closed, vaudeville had gone into decline with the arrival of radio and the cinema, although for a time films were presented as part of vaudeville programmes with some success. Many of its most popular stars subsequently deserted the medium for the screen.

Vaudeville, Théâtre du A theatre in the rue de Chartres, Paris, opened in 1792 as a home for actors formerly with the Comédie-Italienne. The company initially provoked official hostility for its satirical comments but later concentrated on less contentious historical pieces. In 1838 the company moved to the Place de la Bourse, then (in 1869) to the Chaussée d'Autin, which became a cinema in 1927.

Vaudeville Theatre An elegant theatre in London's Strand where Sir Henry Irving once played, now known for its musical and comedy productions. The Vaudeville was built in 1870 by C J Phipps but has been reconstructed twice since, in 1891 and again in 1925. Sir Seymour Hicks, his wife Ellaline Terris, and Sir Charles Hawtrey all acted here in the early 1900s; its first big success was H J Byron's *Our Boys* (1875), which ran for 1362 performances. From 1915 André Charlot presented a long series of revues here, while in the post-World War II years its most outstanding success was the record-breaking Julian Slade musical *Salad Days*, which opened in 1954 and ran until 1960. In 1969 Peter Saunders purchased the theatre from the Gatti family, who had owned it since 1892. Recent long runs have included John Chapman and Ray Cooney's popular farce *Move Over Mrs Markham* (1970), Agatha Christie's *A Murder is Announced* (1977), and a revival of Chekhov's *Uncle Vanya* (1988).

Vaughan, Hannah See Pritchard, Hannah.

Vaughan, Kate (Catherine Candelon; c. 1852–1903) British actress and dancer. She made her debut as a dancer on the music hall stage in 1870 and played a prominent part in burlesque at the Gaiety Theatre (1876–83); in 1886 she gave up dancing to organize a comedy company and appeared in plays by Sheridan and others.

Vauthier, Jean (1910-) Belgian playwright, whose best-known plays revolve around the character Captain Bada, who is constantly struggling with his own idealism. He first appeared in *Capitaine Bada* (1952), while Barrault was acclaimed in the role in *Le Personnage Combattant* (1956); he is also the central figure in *Le Sang* (1970). Other works include an adaptation of Machiavelli's *La Mandragora* (1952).

Vauxhall An area in London on the south side of the river where, in 1660, a complex of pleasure gardens was opened. They reached a peak of popularity in the 18th century, being renowned as a venue for concerts, fireworks, dances, and occasional spectacular dramas and operettas. They were closed in 1859, having acquired a reputation for low behaviour and disorder.

Vauxhall Garden and Theatre An open-air theatre opened in 1808 in the grounds of Vauxhall Garden on 4th Avenue, New York. It was destroyed in a fire a short time after opening and was not replaced until 1838. The new theatre had several successful seasons in the 1840s and was demolished in 1855.

Vazov, Ivan Minchev (1850–1921) Bulgarian poet, novelist, and playwright, whose works on strong patriotic themes remain extremely popular in Bulgaria. His most successful play *Khushove* (1894) depicts Romania's struggle for liberation; other plays included *Kam Propast* (Towards the Abyss; 1907), *Borislav* (1909), and a series of dramas set in medieval Bulgaria.

Vedrenne, John Eugene (1867–1930) British theatre manager, whose most important work was done in conjunction with Harley Granville-Barker at the Royal Court Theatre (1904–07) and the Savoy Theatre (1907). Together they presented many major new works by G B Shaw and others.

Vega, Ventura de la (Buenaventura José Mariá Vega y Cárdenas; 1807–65) Spanish playwright, author of plays in a variety of styles, of which the most successful was the drama *El hombre del mundo* (A Man of the World; 1845). Less successful works include a tragedy, a history, comedies, and translations of French plays.

His son, **Ricardo de la Vega** (1841–1910), wrote several notable examples of the *género chico*, notably *La canción de la Lola* (Lola's Song; 1880).

Vega Carpio, Lope Félix de (1562–1635) Spanish playwright and poet, considered the most influential (as well as the most prolific) writer of the Golden Age of Spanish literature. He sailed with the Armada in 1588 and was famed for his many passionate love affairs, which continued after his ordination as a priest in 1614; he claimed to be the author of 1500 plays, although only 470 or so now survive.

His drama, which established the groundrules for the Spanish *comedia* for many years to come, reflects both his Catholicism and his belief in codes of honour and in the divine right of kings and ranges from tragicomedy to farce and accounts of the lives of the saints. His earlier works were written for the open-air theatres of Madrid; subsequently, however, he also wrote plays, generally pastorals and mythological dramas, for performance at the royal court, thus influencing the development of the *zarzuela*. He was also the author of notable *autos sacramentales* and of the treatise *Arte neuvo de hacer comedias* (New Art of Writing Plays; c. 1609), in which he analysed the nature of drama.

Principal works:

Castelvines y Monteses: c. 1608.

Fuenteovejuna: c. 1612; translated as *The Sheep-Well*.

Peribáñez y el comedador de Ocaña: 1614.

El perro del hortelano: c. 1615.

La dama boba: 1617.

El villano en su rincón: 1617.

La selva sin amor: 1629; translated as *The Loveless Forest*.

El mejor alcalde, el rey: 1635; translated as *The King the Best Magistrate*.

Por la puente, Juana: 1635.

El caballero de Olmedo: 1641.

Veigel, Eva Maria *See* Garrick, David.

Vélez de Guevara, Luis (1579–1644) Spanish playwright, poet, and novelist, who was a distinguished follower of Lope de Vega. His 400 lively plays include examples of the *comedia* and the *entremé*, *autos sacramentales*, and versions of Lope de Vega's works; his novel *El diablo cojuelo* (The Crippled Devil; 1641) was highly influential in an adaptation by Alain Lesage as *Le Diable boileux* (1707).

Velten, Johannes (1640–92) German actor, whose touring company was eventually inherited by Carolina Neuber, Schönemann, Koch, Ackermann, and Schröder. Under Velten the company became well known for its high theatrical standards, performing plays by Molière and Shakespeare and avoiding improvisation.

Venice Preserv'd; or, a Plot Discovered A tragedy by Thomas *Otway. First performance: 1682. It tells of the secret marriage of Jaffier to a senator's daughter, Belvedira, and of his subsequent downfall; in the original production the leading roles were played by Betterton and Mrs Barry.

Venice Theatre *See* Century Theatre.

Venier, Marie (Marie Vernier; fl. 1590–1627) French actress, one of the first women to appear on the Parisian stage. The daughter of an actor-manager, she became the leading lady with Valleran-Lecomte's company at the Hôtel de Bourgogne; subsequently she and her actor-husband **Laporte** (Mathieu de Febvre; 1572–c. 1626) were criticized for appearing without permission at the Hôtel d'Argent.

Venne, Lottie (1852–1928) British actress, who first made a name for herself in burlesque. She was a clever mimic and a popular performer in George Edwardes's musical comedies, but in her later years specialized in playing older ladies in straight comedy,

being especially admired as Mrs Malaprop in *The Rivals* (1910).

Vere Street Theatre A theatre converted from a tennis court – **Gibbon's Tennis Court** – built in 1634 in Clare Market, London, close to Lincoln's Inn Fields, where actors attempted to perform after the closure of theatres in 1642. Davenant used it to stage "music and instruction", thus evading the law. Killigrew, in 1660, reopened it with *Henry IV, Part I* and remained there until moving to Drury Lane in 1663. Vere Street was then used as an acting school until 1671; it burnt down in 1809.

Verfremdungseffekt *See* alienation effect.

Verga, Giovanni (1840–1922) Italian novelist and playwright, born in Sicily, who became a notable writer in the *verismo* tradition with his tragedies of Sicilian life. His most important works were all produced from the 1880s following his return to Sicily; these include *Cavalleria rusticana* (Rustic Chivalry; 1884), later an opera by Mascagni, *La Lupa* (The She-Wolf; 1896), about sexual psychology, *La caccia al lupo* (The Wolf-Hunt; 1901), and *In portieria* (In the Porter's Lodge; 1885).

Vergerio, Pier Paolo (1370–1445) Italian playwright, remembered as the author of the Latin comedy *Paulus* (c. 1390). The play, influenced by Terence, depicts the moral dilemma of the central character when faced with a choice between leading a studious or degenerate life.

verismo A movement in the theatre and the arts in general that developed in Italy in the late 19th century. Advocating the principles of *naturalism, as popularized by Zola and Balzac, the movement inspired many plays based on political and social themes and set in working-class surroundings; writers associated with the *verismo* tradition included the Sicilian novelists Luigi Capuana and Giovanni Verga and the playwrights D'Annunzio, Giacosa, and Pirandello. The movement was suppressed by the Fascists in the 1920s but was revived after World War II.

Verneuil, Louis (Louis-Collin Barbie de Bocage; 1893–1952) French actor and playwright, who became a leading writer of plays in the *Boulevard* tradition. His best-known play was *Ma Cousine de Varsovie*, while Sarah Bernhardt herself made her last appearance in his *Daniel* (1921). He subsequently spent some years in films, before eventually committing suicide.

Versailles The principal residence of the French royal family until the Revolution and the scene of numerous theatrical entertainments. Although many performances were presented during the time of Louis XIV, a purpose-built stage was not installed there until 1768, when Louis XV had a well-equipped, oval-shaped theatre built in the north wing. The theatre was then used for banquets as well as for plays by Racine, Voltaire, and others; during the Revolution it became a meeting place for the Jacobins. Since then it has hosted further banquets, plays, and concerts, being restored to its original condition in the 1950s. Another theatre at Versailles, built in 1777 by Mlle Montansier, was abandoned in 1886.

Verulamium A Roman town in southern England (now St Albans), which was the site of a 2nd-century theatre. It is believed that it was used for sporting events as well as for mime and dancing before being rebuilt in the 3rd century. It was not used after 400 AD and was rediscovered in 1847.

Vestris, Françoise (Françoise Gourgaud; 1743–1804) French actress, who was a noted member of the Comédie-Française, where she appeared with her brother Dugazon. She

was acclaimed as tragic heroines in the plays of Belloy, Chénier, and Voltaire.

Vestris, Madame (Lucy Elizabeth Bartolozzi; 1797–1856) British actress and manager, whose first husband, the French ballet dancer Armand Vestris, left her in 1820. She established herself as an actress in 1817 in burlesque at Drury Lane. After several seasons in Paris, she became a popular performer at both Drury Lane and Covent Garden. In 1830 she took over the Olympic Theatre, where she remained until 1839, and introduced numerous reforms. In 1838 she married Charles James Mathews; together they managed Covent Garden and the Lyceum for a short period.

Vezin, Herman (1829–1910) British actor, born in Philadelphia. After appearances at York, he played Pembroke in *King John* at the Princess's Theatre in London. He became manager of the Surrey Theatre in 1859 and came to the fore playing the major tragic parts. He was subsequently engaged by Phelps at Sadler's Wells and by Irving at the Lyceum; his last appearance was under Tree in 1909.

His wife was the Australian actress **Jane Elizabeth Vezin** (Jane Elizabeth Thomson; 1827–1902), who came to England in 1857 and was immediately acclaimed at Sadler's Wells; she later excelled in numerous Shakespearean roles.

Vian, Boris (1920–59) French novelist and playwright, whose works (influenced by Alfred Jarry) blend satire and poetic fantasy with nightmare and violence. *Les Bâtisseurs d'empire, ou le Schmürz* (1959; translated as *The Empire Builders*, 1962), Vian's most successful play, depicts the decline of bourgeois values. War and militarism are the targets of *L'Équarrissage pour tous* (1950) and *Le Goûter des généraux* (1963; translated as *The Generals' Tea-Party*, 1967).

Viau, Théophile de *See* Théophile de Viau.

Vice A character of the English morality play, notable as an early clown figure. In his original form he was portrayed as the cynical servant of the Devil.

Vicente, Gil (c. 1465–c. 1536) Portuguese playwright and poet, regarded as the most distinguished writer of drama in the Portuguese tradition. His 44 surviving plays – some written in Spanish – include *autos sacramentales*, tragi-comedies, comedies, and farces, many of which were intended for performance at the royal court, where he occupied the post of Court poet from 1502 to 1536. His earliest plays were chiefly eclogues written in imitation of Encina; these gradually developed into a distinctive type of morality play, the best examples of which – tackling both religious and social issues – were contained in the *Barcas* trilogy and had a profound effect upon subsequent Spanish religious drama.

As well as his many farces, his romantic comedies – written after 1520 and modelled upon the plays of Bartolomé de Torres Naharro – were highly influential, as were the allegorical fantasies of his last years, which are notable for their satirical content and use of the sophisticated stage devices familiar from the mummers' tradition.

Principal works:
Auto da Alma: c. 1517.
Barca do Inferno: 1517.
Barca do Purgatório: 1518.
Barca do Glória: 1519.
Farsa de Inês Pereira: 1523.

Vicentini, Tommaso Antonio (1682–1739) Italian actor, who began in tragedy but later became famous as Arlecchino in the *commedia dell'arte* under the stagename **Thomassin**. In 1716 he moved to Paris with the younger Riccoboni, appearing at the Palais-Royal and the Hôtel de Bourgogne with great success, being noted for his acrobatic skills. He was much acclaimed in the plays of Marivaux, some of which may have been written specifically for him as well as for Silvia.

Victoria Palace Theatre A theatre opposite Victoria station, London, which was once the capital's most popular music hall. It began as a venue for entertainment attached to the Royal Standard tavern in the mid-19th century, being known successively as Moy's Music-Hall and (from 1863) the **Royal Standard Music Hall**. Following the construction of the railway station, the Standard was rebuilt in 1886 and finally demolished in 1910. The Victoria Palace opened in 1911 with a variety bill and over the next decade all the leading music hall stars appeared there. Revues were presented in 1929–34 and in 1934 (renamed the Victoria Palace Theatre) it staged Walter Reynolds's infamous patriotic play **Young England*, which quickly acquired cult status. Seymour Hicks took over the management for a season in 1935, reviving some of his earlier productions, while later successes included revues and the musical comedy *Me and My Girl* (1937–39). The home of the Crazy Gang from 1947 to 1962 and then of the Black and White Minstrels, the Victoria Palace next played host to a stage version of the popular 'Carry On' films. Since then its musical tradition has continued with *Annie*, *High Society*, and *Winnie* (1988), a musical based upon the life of Winston Churchill.

Victoria Regina A group of one-act plays by Laurence *Housman depicting the court of Queen Victoria. First performance: Gate Theatre, London, 1935. Banned by the censor, they were originally presented privately and only received a public performance after the intervention of Edward VIII.

Victoria Theatre A theatre-in-the-round at Stoke-on-Trent, established by Stephen Joseph in a converted cinema in 1962. Under its artistic director, Peter Cheeseman, the resident company has maintained close links with the neighbourhood, producing plays and musicals concerned with local history, including *The Jolly Potters* (1964), *The Knotty* (1966), and *Plain Jos* (1980). At one time Peter Terson was the theatre's playwright-in-residence. The theatre closed when a new purpose-built theatre-in-the-round was constructed for the company at adjacent Newcastle-under-Lyme and opened in 1986 as the **New Victoria Theatre**. *See also* Gaiety Theatre; Old Vic Theatre.

Victor ou l'Enfant de la forêt A melodrama by Guilbert de *Pixérécourt, based on a novel by François-Guillaume Ducray-Duminil. First performance: Paris, 1798. The hero, Victor, is faced with a moral dilemma – in order to protect his adopted father he must kill his real father, a bandit.

Viertel, Berthold (1885–1955) Austrian poet, actor, and director, who established his reputation under Reinhardt after joining the Deutsches Theater in Berlin in 1922. After success with Hebbel's *Judith* he won acclaim with Bronnen's *Vatermord* and founded his own company, Die Truppe. Subsequently he worked in London and the US before returning to Germany to direct the Berliner Ensemble (1949) and then transferring to the Vienna Burgtheater.

Vieux-Colombier *See* Garrick Theatre.

Vieux-Colombier, Théâtre du A theatre erected near the Abbey of St Germain, Paris, in the early 19th century and used as a venue for touring companies. In 1913 Jacques Copeau and Louis Jouvet established its reputation with a series of experimental and austere productions of serious contemporary dramas, altering the interior to place the audience on three sides of the stage. Notable productions included the plays of Molière, Shakespeare (especially *Twelfth Night*), and other 17th-century writers as

well as works by Gide, Musset, and Romains. After four years as a cinema (1926–30) the theatre became the home of the Compagnie des Quinze, who staged the plays of Obey there; subsequently it housed productions of Eliot, García Lorca, Sartre, and Vilar before finally closing in 1972.

View from the Bridge, A A drama (originally a one-act play but later rewritten in three acts) by Arthur *Miller. First performance: New York, 1955. The plot revolves around a longshoreman who desires his wife's niece; these feelings erupt when the niece announces her engagement.

Vigarani, Gaspare (1586–1663) Italian architect and stage designer, who built and equipped the Salle des Machines in Paris in 1660. Previously he had worked in Modena before being given charge of the entertainments at the marriage of Louis XIV. Jealous of Torelli, he destroyed many of the devices invented by his rival for the Petit-Bourbon after Torelli's death.

His son, **Carlo Vigarani** (d. 1693), was also a stage designer, who contributed to the building of the Salle des Machines. He also developed machinery for Louis XIV's entertainment *Les Plaisirs de l'île enchantée* in 1664 and worked on operatic productions.

Vigny, Alfred de (1797–1863) French poet, novelist, and playwright, a major figure of the Romantic movement. His first dramatic works, adaptations of Shakespeare, were followed by the historical drama *La Maréchale* (1831), *Quitte pour la peur* (1833), and the immensely successful *Chatterton* (1835), which was his final contribution to the theatre and is generally considered to be his masterpiece.

Vilar, Jean (1912–71) French actor, director, and manager, who was the founder of the Théâtre National Populaire. Having trained as manager to Charles Dullin, he established his reputation as a director in Paris and elsewhere during World War II (founding the Compagnie des Sept in 1943) and subsequently won acclaim for his long association with the Avignon Festival, which he founded in 1947. In his characteristically large-scale productions he favoured the use of sparse settings and strong movement, paying great attention to costume and lighting; he also helped to promote the theatre in remote areas of France as well as presenting productions elsewhere in Europe. He was appointed director of the Théâtre National Populaire in 1951 and remained in the post for 12 years. As an actor he appeared in his own version of Eliot's *Murder in the Cathedral* in 1945; other successes included plays by Aristophanes, Brecht, Büchner, and Molière. In his later years he also directed a number of notable operas.

Vildrac, Charles (Charles Messager; 1882–1971) French poet and playwright, whose plays include *Le Paquebot Tenacity* (The SS Tenacity; 1920), *Michel Auclair* (1922), *Madame Béliard* (1925), and *La Brouille* (1930). The first and last of these, both of which deal with rivalry and conflict between friends of very different characters, are regarded as Vildrac's finest dramatic works.

Ville, Théâtre de la *See* Théâtre des Nations.

Villiers, Claude Deschamps de (1600–81) French actor and playwright, who became highly successful in farce under the stagename **Philippin**. He appeared with Lenoir and Montdory at the Théâtre du Marais and subsequently at the Hôtel de Bourgogne with his wife; his plays had some influence on Molière, who satirized him in *L'Impromptu de Versailles*.

Villiers, George *See* Buckingham, Duke of.

Villiers, Jean de (1648–1701) French actor, who appeared as a child with the Rai-

sin family before joining Molière at the Palais-Royal in 1672. Subsequently he moved to the Hôtel de Bourgogne and ultimately to the Comédie-Française, where he continued to excel in comedy. His wife was the actress Cathérine Raisin.

Vilna Troupe Russian theatre company, founded in 1916 by **David Hermann** (1876–1930) as the Union of Yiddish Dramatic Artists to perform contemporary Yiddish dramas. After early success with *Landsleute* by Sholom Asch the company transferred to Warsaw in 1917 from where it toured internationally with its best-known work, Ansky's *The Dybbuk*. In 1924 the company moved to Vienna then split into two groups, one moving to the US and the other to Romania before returning to Warsaw in 1927.

Vincennes, Cartoucherie de *See* Soleil, Théâtre du.

Violetta, Mlle *See* Garrick, David.

Virginia Company of Comedians *See* Kean, Thomas.

Virginia Museum Theatre A theatre in Richmond, Virginia, which was founded in 1955 under the auspices of the Virginia Museum. It later became one of Virginia's state theatres and has a conservatory with a training programme.

Virués, Cristóbal de (c. 1550–c. 1614) Spanish playwright. He was the author of the five neoclassical tragedies *Elisa Dido*, *Atila furioso*, *Le gran Semíramis*, *La cruel Casandra*, and *La infeliz Marcela*.

Visconti, Luchino (1906–76) Italian director and stage designer, who won equal acclaim as a director for the theatre and the cinema. He began his career in Paris and established his reputation in the theatre when he presented various European classics at the Teatro Eliseo in Rome after World War II. Subsequent productions (many of which were presented by the Paolo Stoppa-Rina Morelli company) included plays by such writers as Anouilh, Chekhov, Jean Cocteau, Ford, Arthur Miller, and Tennessee Williams, on several of which he worked alongside Franco Zeffirelli. Among his later works were notable versions of *A Streetcar Named Desire* and Pinter's *Old Times* and several acclaimed operas.

Visé, Jean Donneau de (1638–1710) French playwright and theatre critic, who cofounded the periodical *Le Mercure galant* in 1672. His views of Molière's *L'École des femmes* (1662) precipitated a heated pamphlet war; de Visé's play *Zélinde* (1663) was subsequently written in response to Molière's own *Critique de l'École des femmes*, while he also wrote a malicious play in reply to the latter's *L'Impromptu de Versailles* in the same year. Later, however, de Visé's play *La Mère coquette* (1665) was performed by Molière's company and de Visé published admiring reviews of Molière's *Le Misanthrope*.

Vishnevsky, Vsevolod Vitalevich (1900–51) Soviet playwright, whose dramas – noted for their social and political content – have been widely performed throughout Europe. His most successful plays include *Optimisticheskaya Tragediya* (The Optimistic Tragedy; 1932), which was first presented by Taïrov at the Kamerny Theatre. During the siege of Leningrad he wrote *Raskinulos' morye shirokoye* (At the Walls of Leningrad; 1942) with Kron and Azarov; he is also remembered for the pro-Stalinist play *Nezabyvaemyy 1919* (The Unforgettable 1919; 1949).

visor *See* mask.

Vitez, Antoine (1930-) French actor and director, who became recognized as a leading Marxist director during the 1960s.

His early work in Marseilles and Caen was much influenced by Brecht and was later seen at a variety of venues in and around Paris; some of his most successful productions have included Sophocles's *Electra* and plays by Brecht. Following the upheaval of 1968 he was attached to the Conservatoire, later taking control of the Théâtre National de Chaillot in 1981.

Vitrac, Roger (1899–1952) French poet and playwright, who was involved with Dadaism and the Surrealist movement. His first two plays, *Les Mystères de l'amour* (1927) and *Victor ou les Enfants au pouvoir* (1928), were produced at the Théâtre Alfred Jarry. *Victor* enjoyed two successful revivals, the second of which was directed by Jean Anouilh in 1962. Among Vitrac's other plays are *Le Coup de Trafalgar* (1934), *Le Camelot* (1936), *Les Demoiselles du large* (1938), and *Le Sabre de mon père* (1951).

Vitruvius Pollio, Marcus (1st century BC) Roman architect and engineer, author of the treatise *De Architectura*. The fifth book of this treatise discusses the building of theatres and had a profound effect upon theatre architecture of the Renaissance.

Vivian Beaumont Theatre A theatre on West 65th Street in the Lincoln Centre complex, which opened in 1965 with Büchner's *Danton's Death*. The theatre houses the Lincoln Centre Repertory Company and presented plays by such authors as Brecht, Sartre, Tennessee Williams, and Strindberg under such directors as Joseph Papp before closing for a period between 1977 and 1980. It reopened with Philip Barry's *The Philadelphia Story* in 1980; recent productions have included *Macbeth* and Woody Allen's *The Floating Light Bulb*. A smaller auditorium, opened in 1966 as the Forum, was known as the **Mitzi E Newhouse Theatre** from 1973, being used for plays by David Rabe and Shakespeare, among others.

Vlaamse Volkstoneel A Belgian theatre company, founded after World War I to present Expressionist drama. During the 1920s it established a strong reputation with productions of plays by Herman Tierlinck (1879–1967) and others.

Vokes, Frederick Mortimer (1846–88) British actor, the eldest of the pantomime act known as The Vokes Children, formed in 1861 and later called The Vokes Family. His sister, **Jessie Catherine Biddulph Vokes** (1851–84), looked after the troupe's business. **Victoria Vokes** (1853–94) made her stage debut at the age of two, whilst **Rosina Vokes** (1854–94) was carried on as a baby. From 1869 the family monopolized the Drury Lane pantomimes for 10 years.

Volkov, Feodor Grigoryevich (1729–63) Russian actor, who was a leading member of the first professional acting company in Russia, which he joined in 1756. He studied under Dmitrevsky after appearing before the Tsar in 1752 and later became Sumarokov's leading actor; his involvement in the overthrow of Peter III subsequently won him the honour of arranging the celebrations for Catherine the Great's coronation. A chill contracted while he was doing this, however, caused his death.

Volksbühne A German theatre organization founded in Berlin in 1890 as the **Freie Volksbühne** to present drama for working-class audiences. In 1914 the organization opened a theatre in the Bülowplatz; subsequently over 300 subsidiary organizations were founded throughout Germany by 1930. The movement languished under the Nazis but resurfaced in 1948 in both East and West Germany, complete with a new theatre in West Berlin (relocated under Piscator in 1963) and reorganized in East Berlin by Benno Besson between 1969 and 1979.

Volpone; or, The Fox A satirical comedy by Ben *Jonson. First performance: 1606.

The play depicts Volpone's exploitation of the gullibility of those around him and his ultimate downfall at the hands of his servant, Mosca, in consequence of his own greed.

Voltaire (François-Marie Arouet; 1694–1778) French philosopher, novelist, playwright, poet, and historian, who was one of the most influential writers of the 18th century. Born in Paris and educated by the Jesuits, he soon established his reputation as a wit. He wrote his first play, the tragedy *Oedipe*, during a spell of imprisonment in the Bastille (1717–18); its success brought him fame and fortune. From 1726 to 1729 he lived in exile in England, where he was impressed by English literature in general and the works of Shakespeare in particular: on his return to France he produced a number of plays based on Shakespearean themes, notably *Zaïre*.

The scandal that followed the publication of Voltaire's *Lettres philosophiques* (1734), in which French institutions were unfavourably compared with the intellectual, philosophical, and political life of England, caused their author to take refuge at Cirey in Champagne, where he lived with Madame du Châtelet and continued to write successful tragedies, notably *Alzire*, *Mahomet*, and *Mérope*, and historical and scientific works. His contributions to the genres of sentimental comedy and the *drame bourgeois*, such as *L'Enfant prodigue* and *Nanine*, were less popular. After the death of Madame du Châtelet in 1749 Voltaire moved to Berlin and ultimately settled in Switzerland, where he wrote the comedy *L'Écossaise* and the spectacular tragedy *Tancrède*. He returned to Paris in 1778 for the first performance of *Irène* and died two months later.

Principal dramatic works:

Oedipe: 1718.

Brutus: 1730.

Eriphyle: 1732.

Zaïre: 1732.

Le Mort de César: 1735.

Alzire: 1736.
L'Enfant prodigue: 1736.
Mahomet ou le Fanatisme: 1741.
Mérope: 1743.
Nanine: 1749.
L'Orphelin de la Chine: 1755.
Tancrède: 1760.
L'Écossaise: 1760.
Irène: 1778.

Vondel, Joost van den (1587–1679) Dutch playwright and poet, whose best plays were written after he was 60 years old. His early work, notably *Het Pascha* (The Passover; 1612), combined the influence of such Roman authors as Seneca and Virgil with his own intense religious faith; later, however, he wrote plays based on Old Testament stories and modelled on classical Greek lines. The most important examples of these later works include *Jeptha* (1659) and the trilogy *Lucifer* (1654), *Adam in ballingschap* (1664), and *Noah* (1667). Through adaptations by Gryphius he also influenced German baroque drama.

Vortex, The A play by Noël *Coward. First performance: London, 1924. In the original production, which established the author's reputation, Coward himself played the drug-addicted son who compels his adulterous mother to confront reality.

Vos, Jan (c. 1620–67) Dutch playwright, author of several popular neoclassical tragedies. He was particularly important for his innovatory use of scenery and stage machinery.

Voysey Inheritance, The A play by Harley *Granville-Barker. First performance: Royal Court Theatre, 1905. The play depicts the dilemma faced by the honest Edward Voysey on inheriting his father's business, which he discovers has prospered on trickery and malpractice.

VTO *See* All-Russian Theatrical Society.

W

Wade, Allan (1881–1954) British actor, manager, and director, who was a founder of the Phoenix Society and its principal director. In 1906 he became assistant to Harley Granville-Barker at the Royal Court; three years later he arranged the first English tour of the Abbey Theatre players. His dramatic writings include translations of Giradoux's *Intermezzo* and Cocteau's *The Infernal Machine*.

Wagner, (Wilhelm) Richard (1813–83) German composer, whose attempts to reform the conventional opera house had a major influence upon theatre design. His work on the Festspielhaus at Bayreuth, opened in 1876, renewed interest in sightlines and prompted the replacement of traditional box and gallery arrangements.

wagon stage A method of staging in which one or more boat trucks are employed to enable rapid changes of scene; it is referred to as a **slip stage** in the US.

wait The nightwatchman of medieval England, who gradually became a part of the national theatrical tradition. Originally sounding out the hours by playing upon a musical instrument, waits later joined into groups to provide the music for plays in the Elizabethan theatre or became attached to a household or town as resident musicians (unlike minstrels who travelled from one venue to another). The last waits disappeared in the early 19th century with the foundation of the police force, by which time their activities were largely confined to performing festive music in the streets at Christmas.

Waiting for Godot (*En attendant Godot*) A two-act play by Samuel *Beckett, written in French, 1949. First performance: Theatre de

Babylone, 1953. Despite the bewilderment it initially caused critics and audiences, the play rapidly gained the status of a modern classic on the absurdity of human existence. Two tramps wait in vain for the arrival of Godot, who they believe will give purpose to their lives. In their efforts to divert themselves from the prospect of total meaninglessness they devise various physical and verbal games and exploit the interruptions of a passing master and his slave.

Waiting for Lefty A play by Clifford *Odets. First performance: Group Theatre, New York, 1935. The plot depicts the poverty of a group of taxi drivers and culminates in a riot. The play was interpreted as an impassioned plea for the rejection of capitalist values and avarice. Lefty, a trade-union leader, never arrives.

Wakefield Master The unidentified author or reviser of the Towneley cycle of mystery plays, of which five complete dramas survive. Written in the early 15th century, his plays are considered the finest examples of this kind in terms of both wit and style.

Wakhevitch, Georges (1907-) French stage designer, born in Odessa, who began his career in the theatre under Lugné-Poë at the Théâtre de l'Oeuvre after working in the cinema. His much-acclaimed sets included those for *Macbeth* in Marseilles and for plays by Anouilh, Claudel, and others at such venues as the Théâtre de l'Atelier and the Comédie-Française.

Waldis, Burkard (c. 1490–c. 1556) German playwright, who wrote dramas attacking the Roman Catholic church during the Reformation. Formerly a Franciscan monk, he became widely known for his reworking of the parable of the prodigal son in his anti-Catholic play *Vom verlorenen Sohn* (1527).

Waldorf Theatre A theatre on West 50th Street, between Sixth and Seventh avenues,

New York, which opened in 1926. The theatre housed live drama – notably plays by Gorky, Chekhov, and J B Priestley – until 1933, when it was turned into a cinema and subsequently demolished. *See also* Strand Theatre.

Walking Gentleman *See* stock company.

Walking Lady *See* stock company.

Walkley, Alfred Bingham (1855–1926) British theatre critic, satirized by Shaw as Mr Trotter in *Fanny's First Play* (1911). He was theatre critic of *The Times* from 1900 to 1926; his writings were published in a number of volumes between 1892 and 1925.

walk-on A role in which an actor appears on stage but has no lines to deliver.

Wallace, (Richard) Edgar (Horatio) (1875–1932) British novelist, journalist, and playwright, who wrote several successful detective dramas, many of them adapted from his own fiction. Among his most popular plays are *The Ringer* (1936), *On the Spot* (1930), and *The Case of the Frightened Lady* (1931).

Wallace, Nellie (Eleanor Jane Wallace; 1870–1948) British music hall performer, who first appeared as a child clog dancer in 1882 and later as part of an act called the Three Sisters Wallace. She became highly popular singing such songs as 'My Mother Said Always Look Under the Bed' and 'Three Cheers for the Red, White, and Blue' and was one of the few successful female pantomime dames. At the London Palladium she starred in several revues.

Wallack, Henry John (1790–1870) US actor, born in London, who emigrated to the US in 1818 and subsequently appeared successfully on both sides of the Atlantic in leading roles. He took over the Chatham Theatre in 1826 and ran the Manchester

Theatre Royal for a time; his most popular roles included Sir Peter Teazle in Sheridan's *The School for Scandal* (1847) and Falstaff (1858).

His younger brother, **James William Wallack** (1791–1864), was an actor and manager, dividing his time between England and the US for 20 years and winning praise in romantic and tragic roles. *Wallack's Lyceum, New York, which he opened in 1852, became a leading US venue. Subsequently (1861) he also opened the Star Theatre on Broadway.

Henry John Wallack's son, also **James William Wallack** (1818–73), trained under his father before joining his uncle's company at New York's National Theatre, where he excelled in such leading roles as Macbeth and Richard III. Subsequent successes included the parts of Fagin in an adaptation of Dickens's *Oliver Twist* (1867) and Mathias in Lewis's *The Bells* (1872).

The elder James Wallack's son, **Lester Wallack** (1820–88), began his career in Britain but later moved to the US, where he triumphed in both romantic and comic roles. Acclaimed in the plays of Shakespeare and Sheridan in particular, he managed the Star Theatre from 1861 to 1881 and then transferred to a new Wallack's Theatre, his productions including plays by T W Robertson and Shakespeare.

Wallack's Lyceum A theatre on Broadway, New York, which opened in 1850 as Brougham's Lyceum, housing burlesque and farce. Subsequently the elder James Wallack became manager (1852) and renamed it Wallack's Lyceum. It prospered, with a good stock company producing both classic and modern material, until 1859 when Wallack retired. After reopening in 1861 as the **Broadway Music Hall**, it was renamed the Olympic and then the Broadway Theatre. It was the venue for Florence's pirated adaptation of Robertson's *Caste* in 1867 and was demolished in 1869.

Wallack's Theatre A theatre on Broadway, New York, which was built by the actors James Wallack (1795–1864) and his son Lester Wallack (1820–88) and opened in 1861. It saw appearances by Lillie Langtry but failed to prosper; it was taken over by Palmer in 1888 as **Palmer's Theatre** but soon returned to its original name and closed in 1915, despite giving the first US production of Shaw's *Androcles and the Lion*.

A second **Wallack's Theatre**, on West 42nd Street, between Seventh and Eighth avenues, New York, opened as the **Lew Fields Theatre** in 1904. The theatre changed names in 1906, when it became James Hackett's Theatre. In 1911 it became the **Harris Theatre**, in 1920 the **Frazee Theatre**, and in 1924, it finally became Wallack's Theatre. It became a cinema in 1931.

Wallenstein A major historical trilogy by Friedrich von *Schiller, completed in 1789. First performance: date unknown. Inspired by his study at Jena of the history of the Netherlands and of the Thirty Years' War, the trilogy, a study of the corrupting influence of power, constitutes Schiller's dramatic masterpiece and was translated into English by Coleridge in 1800.

Waller, Emma (1820–99) US actress, born in Britain, who became a leading performer of classic drama in the US after making her debut there in 1857 in the role of Ophelia. Subsequent successes included Lady Macbeth, Scott's *Guy Mannering*, and Sheridan Knowles's *The Hunchback*, as well as the roles of Hamlet and Iago.

Waller, Lewis (William Waller Lewis; 1860–1915) British actor-manager, who began his career in Tree's company and was subsequently idolized in picturesque romantic parts. He entered management at the Haymarket in 1895 and later ran the Comedy Theatre (1902), the Imperial (1903–06), and the Lyric (1906–10). As an actor he was acclaimed as Hotspur and Henry V as well as in the title roles of such plays as Conan Doyle's *Brigadier Gerard* and Booth Tarkington's *Monsieur Beaucaire*.

Walls, Tom (Kirby) (1883–1949) British actor and manager, who began in a pierrot troupe at Brighton, making his name in musical comedy. In 1922, with Leslie Henson, he produced the farce *Tons of Money* with great success, following it with the great series of 'Aldwych farces' by Ben Travers, in which he played such roles as Clive Popkiss in *Rookery Nook* (1926) and Freddy Malone in *Plunder* (1929). He starred in films in the 1930s and indulged his passion for horseracing, winning the Derby in 1932.

Walnut Street Theatre A theatre in Philadelphia, which was built in 1809 and is the oldest in the US. Initially the home of a circus, it has been used as a theatre since 1811. It was remodelled in 1970 to seat 1052 people; from 1971 to 1980 the Philadelphia Drama Guild was based there.

Walser, Karl (1877–1943) Swiss stage designer, who became famous for his work in Berlin before World War I. His successes there under Reinhardt included *A Midsummer Night's Dream* (1905), with its revolving stage, and Wedekind's *Frühlings Erwachen* (1906) at the Kammerspiele.

Walter, Eugene (1874–1941) US playwright, whose early plays anticipated the social subjects of modern US drama. His 16 plays ranged from the three melodramas *Paid in Full* (1908), *The Easiest Way* (1909), and *Fine Feathers* (1913), to a dramatization of John Fox's *The Trail of the Lonesome Pine* (1912).

Waltz of the Toreadors, The (*La Valse des toréadors*) A *pièce grinçante* by Jean *Anouilh. First performance: Paris, 1952. The play depicts a marriage in which love has died and the husband's unconsummated

passion for a young girl, with whom he once danced the Waltz of the Toreadors.

Wanamaker, Sam (1919-) US actor, director, and producer, who is best known for his work in Britain since 1952. His successes have included Odets's *Winter Journey* (1952) and *The Big Knife* (1954), N Richard Nash's *The Rainmaker* (1956), and the British premieres of Inge's *Bus Stop* and Tennessee Williams's *The Rose Tattoo* (both staged at Liverpool's New Shakespeare Theatre where he was manager from 1957 to 1959). He also excelled in performances with the Royal Shakespeare Company and has led the campaign to rebuild the Elizabethan *Globe Theatre near its original site on Bankside in London. Work upon the new **Globe Playhouse** began in earnest in 1988.

Warburton, John (1682–1759) British antiquarian, whose manuscript collection of some 60 unpublished Elizabethan and Jacobean plays was unique. All but three were mistakenly destroyed by his servant; according to Warburton himself the greatest losses were works by Massinger, Ford, and Dekker.

Ward, Fannie (Fannie Buchanan; 1872–1952) US actress, who became a leading performer of light comedy on the London stage, following her first appearance there in 1894. Subsequently she divided her time between London and New York, also appearing in variety during the late 1920s.

Ward, Dame (Lucy) Geneviève Teresa (1838–1922) US actress, who began her career as a singer but later won acclaim in such roles as Lady Macbeth and Portia. The first actress to be created DBE, she also appeared in plays by Sophocles, Sheridan Knowles, and Otway in Paris, New York, and London, where she managed the Lyceum Theatre for a time and scored a great success with *Forget-Me-Not* by Herman

Merivale and F C Grove. She also acted opposite Henry Irving and with Frank Benson's company with great success.

Warde, Frederick Barkham (1851–1935) US actor, born in Britain, who established his reputation after joining Booth's Theatre in New York in 1870. Acclaimed in Shakespeare and in a range of well-established plays, he remained there for three years and then toured widely, never attempting modern works.

wardrobe All the items of costume required for a particular production, often part of a larger collection permanently housed in a theatre. Many theatres have a full-time wardrobe master or mistress who supervises all matters relating to costume.

Warehouse *See* Donmar Warehouse Theatre.

Warfield, David (1866–1951) US actor, who established a reputation in musical comedy and burlesque before winning acclaim as an actor under Belasco in Klein's *The Auctioneer* in 1901. Subsequently he won even greater praise in Klein's *The Music Master* (1904), in which he appeared widely for three years. He also appeared in plays by Belasco and as Shakespeare's Shylock before retiring in 1924.

Warner, Charles (Charles John Lickfold; 1846–1909) British actor, whose father was in the Sadler's Wells company. After his London debut as Romeo in 1864, he became a supporting actor at Drury Lane and scored his first success in H J Byron's *Daisy Farm*. Later he was acclaimed in the same author's *Our Boys* (1875). He subsequently appeared at the Adelphi Theatre in melodrama. He committed suicide while on a tour of the US.

Warren, William (1767–1832) US actor, born in Britain, who emigrated to the US in 1796 to join Thomas Wignell in Philadelphia. Eventually he took over the Chestnut Street Theatre, presiding over the debut of Edwin Forrest in 1820 and attracting praise himself in such roles as Sir Toby Belch in *Twelfth Night* and Sir Peter Teazle in Sheridan's *The School for Scandal*. His three wives included the actress Mrs Merry and Joseph Jefferson's sister-in-law, by whom he had six children.

Of these, the most famous in the theatre was **William Warren** (1812–88), who became a leading performer at the Boston Museum, where he first appeared in 1847. He was especially admired in comic roles in Shakespeare and Sheridan as well as in contemporary plays by such authors as T W Robertson.

Washington Square Players A US theatre group founded in New York in 1914. The group produced its first full-length plays in 1916, of which the most influential included Chekhov's *The Seagull*, Ibsen's *Ghosts*, and Shaw's *Mrs Warren's Profession*. The group broke up in 1918 but not before it had inspired the foundation of the Theatre Guild; associates of the group included Lee Simonson and Katharine Cornell.

Washington Square Theatre A theatre on West 4th Street in Greenwich Village, New York, which was used by the Lincoln Centre Repertory Company before they moved to the Vivian Beaumont Theatre. It opened in 1964 with Miller's *After the Fall*. When the Lincoln Centre company moved to their permanent home in 1965, the musical *Man of La Mancha* was housed at the Washington Square. In 1968 the production closed and the theatre was demolished.

Waste A tragedy by Harley *Granville-Barker. First performance: London, 1907. The play deals with the topics of illicit love and suicide; the Lord Chamberlain refused to license it for public production because it contained an abortion.

Watch on the Rhine, The A play by Lillian *Hellman. First performance: New York, 1941. The plot concerns a fight between a German underground worker and a Nazi and foreshadowed US involvement in World War II.

Waterhouse, Keith (Spencer) *See* Hall, Willis.

water row *See* groundrow.

Waters, Ethel (1900–77) Black US actress, who first appeared in cabaret and vaudeville. She became a leading star of revue, her successes including Berlin's *As Thousands Cheer* (1933). Her straight roles included parts in Dubose Heyward's *Mamba's Daughters* (1939) and Carson McCullers's *The Member of the Wedding* (1950).

Watt, Joachim von (1484–1551) Austrian playwright, author of the early Viennese farce *Gallus pugnans* (1514). The play depicts a trial at which cocks and hens argue over the difference between the sexes and over cockfighting.

Way of the World, The A comedy by William *Congreve. First performance: 1700. A stylish comedy of sexual liaisons, the play revolves around the efforts of the gallant Mirabell and the witty Millamant to secure Lady Wishfort's consent to their union.

Weaver, John (1673–1760) British dancing master, who was actively associated with London theatres from 1702, when he produced a balletic mime at Drury Lane. He went on to produce a series of *Italian night scenes, which contributed to the development of pantomime.

Webb, John (1611–72) English architect and scene painter, who became a pupil of Inigo Jones in 1628. He painted scenery for plays staged by Davenant, beginning with *The Siege of Rhodes* (1656), for which his designs were based on contemporary engravings.

Weber and Fields A popular US comedy act, which was one of the best-loved turns in US vaudeville and burlesque. **Joseph Weber** (1867–1942) and **Lew Fields** (1867–1941) had such success with their slapstick act that eventually they formed their own company (1885), presenting their own burlesques at the former Broadway Music-Hall. Later in their careers Weber took up direction while Fields appeared in musical comedy; he was the father of the playwright Joseph Fields.

Webster, Benjamin Nottingham (1797–1882) British actor, manager, and playwright, who began by playing Harlequin and other small parts in the provinces. After appearing at Drury Lane and the Olympic Theatre, he established himself as a leading comedian, also playing at Covent Garden, the Haymarket, and Adelphi theatres and creating many roles in contemporary comedies. He became lessee of the Haymarket in 1837, of the Adelphi in 1844, and took over the Princess's Theatre in 1869. He was the author of numerous comedies and farces and as an actor was particularly acclaimed as Triplet in *Masks and Faces* by Tom Taylor and Charles Reade.

His great grand-daughter was the actress and director **Margaret Webster** (1905–72), who began with the Cassons' company in 1924 and later joined Gielgud's Old Vic company (1929). She acted with Gielgud again in Ronald Mackenzie's *Musical Chairs* (1932) and Gordon Daviot's *Richard of Bordeaux* (1933) and subsequently became a notable classical director, working chiefly in the US, where Paul Robeson's *Othello* (1943) was one of her major successes. She was a cofounder of the **American Repertory Company** and led her own Shakespearean touring company from 1948 to 1950. In England in the 1950s she directed *The Mer-*

chant of Venice at Stratford-upon-Avon, *Measure for Measure* at the Old Vic, and, in 1960, Noël Coward's *Waiting in the Wings* at the Duke of York's Theatre.

Webster, John (c. 1580–1634) English playwright, who collaborated with Thomas Dekker, John Ford, William Rowley, and John Heywood, as well as writing four extant plays known to be entirely his own. His two tragedies, The *White Devil* and The *Duchess of Malfi*, have been revived many times in recent years. Webster's plays are notable for their rich imagery, complex and violent plots, and their treatment of female characters.

Wedekind, Frank (1864–1918) German playwright and actor, whose bizarre and grotesque dramas, influenced by Strindberg, aroused both admiration and considerable controversy. His political poems led to his imprisonment in 1899, while his subjective rhetorical plays, peopled with clowns, harlots, and charlatans, contain violent attacks on bourgeois hypocrisy and warn of the dangers of sexual repression.

His preoccupation with sexual enlightenment and equal rights forms the basis of such plays as *Spring Awakening, which anticipated Expressionism, and the two 'Lulu Tragedies', *Earth Spirit and *Pandora's Box. Of his other works the most important include Der Marquis von Keith, first seen in an influential production by Jessner, and Such is Life. His wife, **Tilly Newes** (Mathilde Newes; 1886–1970), appeared in many of his plays.

Principal works:

Frühlings Erwachen: 1906 (written 1891); translated as *Spring Awakening.*

Erdgeist: 1902 (written 1893); translated as *Earth Spirit.*

Die Büchse der Pandora: 1905 (written 1894); translated as *Pandora's Box.*

Der Marquis von Keith: 1901.

König Nicolò, oder So ist das Leben: 1902; translated as *Such is Life.*

Schloss Wetterstein: 1917; translated as *Castle Wetterstein.*

Wehr Theatre *See* Milwaukee Repertory Theatre.

Weigel, Helene (1900–71) Austrian actress, who was closely associated with the plays of Bertolt Brecht, who became her husband in 1928. She began her career in intense dramas by Büchner and others before appearing under Jessner in Berlin from 1923, attracting attention with her compelling portrayal of impoverished women and her stark appearance. In 1928 she won acclaim in Brecht's *Mann ist Mann* and subsequently in his adaptation of Gorky's *The Mother* (1932), after which she and her husband left Germany for the US, not returning until 1948. They then founded the celebrated *Berliner Ensemble, with Weigel playing such roles as Mother Courage. After Brecht's death in 1956 she ran the company alone, consolidating her fame as the leading exponent of the *Verfremdungseffekt* theory of acting.

Weill, Kurt (1900–50) German composer, who became famous for his collaborations with Brecht on such plays as *The Threepenny Opera* and *The Rise and Fall of the City of Mahagonny* during the 1930s. Subsequently he worked in the US, his musicals including *Lady in the Dark* (1941) and *One Touch of Venus* (1943). His wife was Lotte *Lenya.

Weise, Christian (1642–1702) German playwright, author of a number of minor tragedies and more influential comedies. His later comedies were important for their depiction of bourgeois society for the first time in German drama and for their interest in characterization.

Weiss, Peter Ulrich (1916–82) German-born playwright and novelist, whose works – mainly documentary dramas – have been translated and performed worldwide (*See*

Living Newspaper). The *Marat/Sade*, his first play, was an instant international success; his reputation established, he went on to write *The Investigation*, based on the 1964 Frankfurt War Crimes Trial, which ran simultaneously in 14 German theatres. In 1966 a translated version was produced by Peter Brook in London and New York.

Recurrent themes are war and suffering, as in *Song of the Lusitanian Bogey*, which discusses the uprising in Angola, *Vietnam Discourse*, and *How Mr Mockingpott was Relieved of his Sufferings*, in which the principal protagonists are two clowns. Other notable works include the allegory *The Insurance*, with human and animal characters, and *Trotsky in Exile*, in which Trotsky is both physically and mentally exiled from his people.

Principal works:

Die Verfolgung und Ermordung Jean Paul Marats dargestellt durch die Schauspielgruppe des Hospizes zu Charenton unter Anleitung des Herrn de Sade: 1964.

Die Ermittlung: 1965; translated as *The Investigation*.

Der Turm: 1967; translated as *The Tower*.

Gesang vom lusitanischen Popanz: 1968; translated as *Song of the Lusitanian Bogey*.

Viet Nam Diskurs: 1968; translated as *Vietnam Discourse*.

Herrn Mackingpott das Leiden ausgetrieben wird: 1968; translated as *How Mr Mockingpott was Relieved of his Sufferings*.

Die Versicherung: 1969; translated as *The Insurance*.

Trotzki in Exil: 1970; translated as *Trotsky in Exile*.

Hölderlin: 1971.

Wekworth, Manfred (1929-) East German director, who established his reputation while with the Berliner Ensemble in the 1950s. He was involved in a series of successful collaborations with Brecht on the latter's adaptations of Gorky's *The Mother* and Shakespeare's *Coriolanus* among other plays but later resigned from the company

(1971) when he perceived that it was moving away from its founder's ideals. He then worked with the National Theatre in London and elsewhere before returning to the Berliner Ensemble as its manager in 1977.

Welfare State International A British theatre company, founded in 1968 to present experimental drama. The group employs the techniques of collective creation and is noted for its unconventional approach to the theatre, its productions including several theatrical events based on the adventures of the imaginary character Lancelot Quail.

Welles, Orson (1915–85) US director, actor, and writer, who began his career in Dublin in 1933 when he appeared in Feuchtwanger's *Jew Süss*. Over the next year he played such roles as Mercutio in *Romeo and Juliet*, Marchbanks in Shaw's *Candida*, and Octavius in Besier's *The Barretts of Wimpole St*; subsequently he collaborated with **John Houseman** (1902-) on the Federal Theatre Project, for whom he directed an acclaimed *Macbeth* (1936) with a coloured cast and *Dr Faustus* (1937), cofounded the *Mercury Theatre (1937), and established his reputation in the cinema. Later stage roles included an appearance in his own musical version of Verne's *Around the World in 80 Days* (1946), Othello (1951), Lear (1956), and Falstaff in *Chimes at Midnight* (1962) – his own adaptation of *Henry IV* and *Henry V*.

well-made play A play in which the central drama depends upon the complexity of the plot rather than upon characterization. Initially used in France in the early 19th century as a compliment to a playwright's skill, the term (in French *pièce bien faite*) was later applied to any play in which the use of artificial plots was interpreted as weakening the piece's effectiveness (notably by G B Shaw and Zola). Writers of such works included the prolific Sardou and Scribe in France and Wilkie Collins, Henry Arthur Jones, and Arthur Pinero in Britain. Ultimately the well-made play provoked the development of naturalism.

Werfel, Franz (1890–1945) Austrian novelist, poet and playwright, who became deeply antimilitarist after service in World War I. In the 1920s he emerged as a popular writer of the Expressionist movement with such plays as *Bocksgesang* (The Goat Song; 1921) and the historical tragedy *Juarez und Maximilian* (1924). *Der We der Verheissung* (1936) depicted the persecution of the Jews in reaction to the rise of Nazism and in 1938 he fled Austria, eventually settling in the US, where he died. His last play was the comedy *Jacobowsky und der Oberst* (Jacobowsky and the Colonel; 1940).

Wergeland, Henrik Arnold (1808–45) Norwegian poet and playwright, whose early works for the stage were such farces as *Ah!* (1827), *Phantasmer* (1829), and *Harlequin Virtuos* (1830). Subsequently he came under the influence of Shakespeare's plays, as reflected in the tragedy *Sinclars Død* (The Death of Sinclair; 1828) and the comedy *Opium* (1828). An ardent nationalist, he gave full rein to his exuberant imagination in such late plays as *Den indinske Cholera* (Indian Cholera; 1835) and *Barnemordersken* (The Child Murderess; 1835).

Werner, (Frederick Ludwig) Zacharias (1768–1823) German playwright and priest, who founded the German *Schicksalstragödie* with his one-act play *Der vierundzwanzigste Februar* (1810). Later poetic dramas, including *Das Kreuz an der Ostsee* (1806) and *Martin Luther* (1807), had a strong religious content.

Wesker, Arnold (1932–) British playwright, of Jewish parentage, whose East-End background provides a recurring theme in his plays. His first critical success was *Chicken Soup with Barley* (1958). This became the first part of a trilogy, including *Roots* and *I'm Talking About Jerusalem*, which charted the history of a family from 1936 to 1959. In subsequent plays he continued to develop the theme of beleaguered idealism (sometimes using historical settings – as in *The Merchant*, his version of *The Merchant of Venice*) and that of the exile, especially the Jew, within hostile societies. Wesker has only occasionally met with box office success in Britain. In 1961 he took a leading role in setting up Centre 42; he then acquired the Round House in London but steady financial backing never materialized and the Centre was formally wound up in 1970.

Principal works:

Chicken Soup with Barley: 1958.
Roots: 1959.
The Kitchen: 1959.
I'm Talking About Jerusalem: 1960.
Chips with Everything: 1962.
The Four Seasons: 1965.
Their Very Own and Golden City: 1966.
The Friends: 1970.
The Old Ones: 1972.
The Wedding Feast: 1974.
The Merchant: 1976.
Caritas: 1981.
One More Ride on the Merry Go Round: 1981.
Sullied Hands: 1981.
Mothers: 1982.
Annie Wobbler: 1983.
Whatever Happened to Betty Lemon: 1986.

Wessel, Johan Herman (1742–85) Danish poet and playwright, born in Norway, who is remembered for the play *Kierlighed uden Strømper* (Love Without Stockings; 1772). This parody of French neoclassicism curtailed the current popularity of such drama in Denmark.

West, Mae (1892–1980) US actress and singer, who enjoyed enormous notoriety both on stage – chiefly in musical comedy and revue – and in the cinema. After making her debut as a child, she cultivated a provocative and flamboyant stage persona. In constant conflict with the censors, she was confined in prison on one occasion (1926), only to emerge with her greatest success, *Diamond Lil*, in 1928. Other stage triumphs included *Catherine was Great* (1944) and a revival of *Diamond Lil* in London in 1948.

West, Timothy *See* Prospect Theatre Company.

Westcott, Sebastian (d. 1582) English theatre manager, Master of the Children of St Paul's. Under his direction the company performed regularly, not only at Court, but also in their own cathedral courtyard or school hall.

West End The chief commercial theatre district in London, corresponding to Broadway in the US. Situated west of the City of London and centred around Shaftesbury Avenue, Aldwych, St Martin's Lane, Charing Cross Road, and the Strand, it first developed in the late 17th century around the Lincoln's Inn Fields Theatre and Drury Lane. The **Society of West End Theatre** (SWET), founded in 1908, is a forum for the managers of the 45 or so theatres that are situated in central London.

West London Theatre A London theatre first opened in 1832 as the Royal Pavilion West, off the Edgware Road. Its name was changed to the **Portman Theatre** in 1835, the Royal West London in 1836, and the **Marylebone Theatre** in 1837. Melodramas, farces, and the occasional classic were staged there at low prices; noted performers included Macready and T W Robertson, who made his debut there. Rebuilt in 1868 it was called the **Royal Alfred Theatre**, reverting to its former name five years later, until becoming the West London Music Hall (1893–95) and then the Royal West London Theatre. Charles Warner played there in 1896, but it gradually declined, finally becoming a cinema. It was bombed in 1941 and burnt down in 1962. *See also* Scala Theatre.

Westminster Play A drama presented annually at Westminster School in London since 1560. The only surviving example of a largely unbroken tradition of *school drama in Britain, the Westminster Play is performed in Latin and is usually chosen from the plays of Plautus, Terence, or other classic authors. Until the 1920s it was presented in the ancient College Hall. There was a break in performances – which were frequently attended by members of the royal family – during the Civil War but the tradition was revived upon the Restoration, with such child actors as Barton Booth appearing in a set cycle of plays comprising the *Adelphi*, *Andria*, *Phormio*, and *Eunuchus* (which was replaced for a time by Plautus's *Trinummus* and then *Rudens* in 1926). After a break in World War II, the Westminster Play was revived on a biennial basis in 1954 in Little Dean's Yard in the open air, the performers appearing in contemporary dress and with few props. In recent years the cycle of plays has been varied to include other Roman classics.

Westminster Theatre A theatre in Palace Street, London, which opened in 1931 after several years' use as a cinema. It opened with James Bridie's *The Anatomist*, produced by Tyrone Guthrie; plays by Ibsen, Shaw, Eliot, and others followed. From 1938 to 1940 J B Priestley directed the Mask Theatre here; productions included his own play *Music at Night* (1939). From 1943 to 1945 the theatre was managed by Robert Donat, whose production of Oscar Wilde's *An Ideal Husband* (1943) ran for 266 performances. Subsequent successes included Lesley Storm's *Black Chiffon* (1949) and *Dial M for Murder* (1952). The Moral Re-Armament Movement controlled the theatre from 1960, its productions mostly written by Peter Howard and Alan Thornhill, with a regular Christmas play for children. In 1966 the Westminster was closed for rebuilding as part of an arts centre; since 1969 it has staged several revivals.

Weston, Thomas (1737–76) British actor, son of the head chef to George II, who joined some strolling players and eventually appeared at Bartholomew Fair. Foote spotted his talent as a comedian and engaged him at the Haymarket; from 1760 he appeared regularly there and at Drury Lane.

Weston's Music Hall *See* Holborn Empire.

Westray, Mrs Anthony (d. 1836) British actress, who went to the US in 1792 with her second husband, John Simpson, to play at the Park Theatre, New York. Her three daughters by her first husband – Ellen, Juliana, and Elizabeth – all became actresses in due course.

West Side Story A musical by Arthur Laurents, with music by Leonard *Bernstein, lyrics by Stephen *Sondheim, and choreography by Jerome *Robbins. First performance: New York, 1957. Set in the slums of New York, the plot applied the story of *Romeo and Juliet* to US gangland with vivid dancing that has since become the hallmark of American musicals.

Wharf Theatre *See* Cruger's Wharf Theatre; Provincetown Players.

What Every Woman Knows A play by J M *Barrie. First performance: London, 1908. A social comedy revolving around the resourceful wife of a promising politician, the play sympathizes with feminist views; it was highly successful.

What the Butler Saw A comedy by Joe *Orton. First performance: 1969. This paro-

dy of farce takes place in the surgery of Dr Prentice, a specialist in mental health. It shocked its first audiences with its unrestrained discussions of sexual perversions, the police, and parts of the anatomy of Sir Winston Churchill.

Whelan, Albert (Albert Waxman; 1875–1961) Australian singer, who became a leading performer in British music hall. He first appeared (at the Empire) in 1901 and – immaculately dressed – became the first performer to adopt his own signature tune (*'Lustige Brüder'*).

When We Are Married A play by J B *Priestley. First performance: London, 1938. Three well-respected Yorkshire couples, on the anniversary of their joint wedding day, discovering that they are not legally married face both public disgrace and new personal choices.

When We Dead Awaken The last play by Henrik *Ibsen. First performance: Oslo, 1900. In the central figure of Rubek, Ibsen makes his final analysis of the relationship between the creative artist and life itself.

White, George (George Weitz; 1890–1968) US dancer, producer, and director, who became famous for his series of revues, *George White's Scandals,* which lasted through 13 editions until 1939. His other shows included *Runnin' Wild* (1923), *Manhattan Mary* (1927), and *Flying High* (1930).

White, Patrick (Victor Martindale) (1912–) Australian novelist and playwright, born in Britain, who won a Nobel Prize in 1973. White first achieved international acclaim with the publication of his novel *Voss* (1957); of his plays the most significant are *The Ham Funeral* (1961), *The Season at Sarsaparilla* (1961), *A Cheery Soul* (1962), and *Night on Bald Mountain* (1964). Others include the comedy *Return to Abys-*

sinia (1946), *Big Toys* (1977), *Signal Driver* (1981), and *Netherwood* (1983).

White Devil, The A tragedy in blank verse by John *Webster. First performance: London, 1612. The play centres on Vittoria Corombona, whose courage, conscience, and intelligence during her trial and eventual death earn her sympathy in spite of her treachery and infidelity. None of the major characters in the play are noted for their virtue but are distinguished by their intense and self-destructive passions; the play is remembered for its rich poetry and use of ghosts, dumb shows, and bloodshed.

White-eyed Kaffir *See* Chirgwin, George H.

Whitefriars Theatre A theatre near Blackfriars, London, converted from the refectory of a dissolved monastery and leased in 1605 by Michael Drayton and Thomas Woodford. First used by the Children of His Majesty's Revels, it later became the home of an amalgamated company called the Children of the Queen's Revels (1610). At least one important play, Ben Jonson's *Epicoene*, was written for this company. The theatre, later used by Lady Elizabeth's Men, is thought to have declined after 1614 and been abandoned by 1629.

Whitehall Theatre A theatre situated at the Trafalgar Square end of Whitehall, London, built in 1930. Decorated internally in black and silver, it made its name as a home of modern comedy under Walter Hackett before switching to revue during World War II. Subsequently the success of R F Delderfield's *Worm's Eye View* (1945) heralded a new phase of farce, for which the Whitehall was to become famous under the management of Brian Rix (1950–67). Major successes of this period were *Reluctant Heroes* (1950) and *Uproar in the House* (1967). The impresario Paul Raymond then staged his long-running *risqué* comedy

Pyjama Tops (1969–74), London's first nude production, buying the lease in 1971. The theatre changed ownership in 1985, when it was acquired by the Maybox Group. It was then fully restored and reopened in 1986.

Whitelaw, Billie (1932–) British actress, who made her London debut as Victoire in Feydeau's *Hotel Paradiso* in 1956; she went on to play important parts with the National and Royal Shakespeare companies. Her biggest successes have included Maggie in Harold Brighouse's *Hobson's Choice* (1965), Clare in David Mercer's *After Haggerty* (1971), Eleanor in Peter Nichols's *Passion Play* (1981), and Nelly Mann in Christopher Hampton's *Tales from Hollywod* (1983). She has also appeared in many of Samuel Beckett's plays, including a trilogy of his works in New York (1984) and London (1986).

Whitemore, Hugh (1936–) British playwright, who first attracted attention with the play *Stevie* (1977), about the poet Stevie Smith. Successes since then have been *Pack of Lies* (1983), about a spy case, *Breaking the Code* (1986), and *The Best of Friends* (1988). He also wrote several television and film screenplays – notably *84 Charing Cross Road* and *Cider with Rosie*.

Whiting, John (1917–63) British playwright, who first achieved success with the comedy *A *Penny for a Song* (1951). In the same year his award-winning play **Saint's Day* was staged at the Arts Theatre. His other works include **Marching Song* (1954), *The Gates of Summer* (1956), and *The *Devils* (1961), which was produced very successfully by the Royal Shakespeare Company. Whiting also translated a play by Anouilh as *The Traveller Without Luggage* in 1959; his last work, presented posthumously, was *Conditions of Agreement* (1965). After his premature death an annual award scheme for promising young playwrights was set up in his memory. Winners have included Edward Bond and Tom Stoppard.

Whitley, James Augustus (c. 1724–81) British provincial actor-manager, born in Ireland. He began at the Smock Alley Theatre and later developed a strong Midlands circuit, appearing regularly at Manchester, Stamford, and Nottingham, where he built the first Theatre Royal.

Whitney Theatre *See* Strand Theatre.

Whittle, Charles (1874–1947) British music hall singer, who made his first London appearance in 1899. He was best known for the song 'Let's All Go Down the Strand'.

Who's Afraid of Virginia Woolf? A play by Edward *Albee. First performance: New York, 1962. The play revolves around the obsessive love-hate relationship of a history professor and his wife; it provided rewarding roles for Richard Burton and Elizabeth Taylor.

Widowers' Houses The first play by G B *Shaw, written 1885–87. First performance: London, 1892. A young doctor, Harry Trench, falls in love with Blanche Sartorius, whose wealth is derived from the ownership of slums; the play presents the conflict of conscience in a corrupt capitalist system. Originally a collaboration with the critic William Archer, the play caused a sensation with its rejection of conventional romantic drama, its echoes of Ibsen, and its presentation of Socialist arguments.

Wied, Gustav (1858–1914) Danish playwright, who became famous for the four humorous one-act plays collected as *Adel, Gejstlighed, Borger og Bonde* (Nobility, Clergy, Burgher, and Peasant; 1897). Longer plays included *Danesmus* (Dancing Mice; 1905) and Ranke Viljer (2 × 2 = 5; 1906); he committed suicide shortly after the outbreak of World War I.

Wieth, Mogens (1919–62) Danish actor, who became a leading performer of classical roles at the Kongelige Teater in Copenhagen, where he first appeared in 1939. As well as Shakespearean tragic heroes, he played leading roles in plays by Ibsen, Wilde, and many others and made guest appearances in London before his early death.

Wignell, Thomas (1753–1803) US actor, who founded a celebrated company, consisting largely of English performers, at the Chestnut Street Theatre in Philadelphia in the 1790s. Previously he had attracted much praise as leading man with the American Company, which he joined in 1774, and had also presented Royall Tyler's *The Contrast*, the first native US comedy, in 1879. His famous company included amongst its members James Fennell, Mrs Oldmixon, and Mrs Merry, to whom Wignell was briefly married.

Wild Duck, The A play by Henrik *Ibsen. First performance: 1884. The play revolves around the photographer Hjalmar Ekdal; when his sanity is threatened by the suggestion that his daughter Hedvig is not his she responds by shooting herself. The duck of the title is kept captive in the attic and symbolizes the various self-delusions surrounding the Ekdal family.

Wilde, Oscar (Fingal O'Flahertie Wills) (1854–1900) Irish playwright, whose first major success in the theatre came with George Alexander's production of *Lady Windermere's Fan* at the St James's Theatre in 1892. Lionized by society for his elegance and wit, he followed this success with two more sentimental drawing-room comedies, *A *Woman of No Importance* (1893) and *An *Ideal Husband* (1895), before reverting to the true comedy of manners in his masterpiece, *The *Importance of Being Earnest*, which remains one of the most frequently revived comedies in the English language. *Salomé*, banned in London, was performed by Sarah Bernhardt in Paris in 1896. In 1895 he was imprisoned for homosexuality;

the hardships he suffered over the next two years broke his health and culminated in his death in straitened circumstances in Paris.
Principal dramatic works:
Lady Windermere's Fan: 1892.
A Woman of No Importance: 1893.
An Ideal Husband: 1895.
The Importance of Being Earnest: 1895.
Salomé: 1896.

Wilder, Thornton (Niven) (1897–1975) US playwright, best known for his evocation of small-town society in the US in *Our Town*. Of his other plays, *The Long Christmas Dinner* was later made into an opera and *The *Matchmaker* provided the basis for the musical *Hello Dolly!*. Other dramatic works included translations of Obey's *Le Viol de Lucrèce* (as *Lucrece*; 1932), Ibsen's *A Doll's House* (1937), and an adaptation of Eurpides's *Alcestis* (as *A Life in the Sun*; 1955).
Principal works:
The Trumpet Shall Sound: 1927.
The Long Christmas Dinner: 1931.
Our Town: 1938.
*The *Skin of Our Teeth*: 1942.
The Matchmaker: 1954.
Three Plays for Bleeker Street: 1962.

Wildgans, Anton (1881–1932) Austrian poet, playwright, and director of the Burgtheater, Vienna (1921–22 and 1930–31). Wildgans first received acclaim with the production of such tragic plays as *Armut* (1914), *Liebe* (1916), and *Dies Irae* (1919), but is now probably best remembered for his poetry.

Wilhelm Tell The last complete play by Friedrich von *Schiller. First performance: 1804. Probably the most popular of all Schiller's plays, it explores the ethics of the use of violence against tyranny.

Wilkinson, Norman (1882–1934) British artist, who achieved particular success with his set and costume designs for Granville-Barker's productions at the Savoy Theatre, especially those for *Twelfth Night* (1912) and *A Midsummer Night's Dream* (1914). Later he worked for Nigel Playfair, C B Cochran, the Phoenix and Stage Societies, and for the Shakespeare Memorial Theatre.

Wilkinson, Tate (1739–1803) British actor-manager. He began his career with Garrick at Drury Lane, where his imitations of other actors were much admired. Foote then took him to Dublin where he was well received, although his subsequent appearances in London were not a success. Consequently, his major contribution to the theatre was his masterly control of York and the northern circuit, which lasted for some 30 years. Wilkinson grew rather eccentric in later life and was also satirized by Foote in *The Minor* (1760) and by Charles Mathews.

Wilks, Robert (1665–1732) British actor and manager, born in Ireland. After establishing his reputation in Dublin, he was engaged by Christopher Rich at Drury Lane in 1692 to replace William Mountfort. In 1709 Wilks became one of the famous triumvirate managing Drury Lane, with Colley Cibber and Thomas Doggett. As an actor he excelled in the plays of Cibber and Farquhar.

Willard, E(dward) S(mith) (1853–1915) British actor, who began his career at Weymouth in 1869, coming to London in 1875 in Thomas Morton's *A Roland for an Oliver*. From 1881–86 he was with Wilson Barrett's company, in which he was acclaimed in such melodramatic roles as Captain Skinner in Henry Arthur Jones and Henry Herman's *The Silver King* (1882). At the Haymarket in 1886 he played James Ralston in Charles Young's *Jim the Penman*, the play with which he launched his own management of the Shaftesbury Theatre in 1889.

Williams, Bert (Egbert Austin Williams; 1876–1922) Black US actor, born in the

Bahamas, who began his career in a minstrel show. Later he appeared in a double act with the comedian George Walker in New York and, in 1903, they produced an all-Black musical comedy there entitled *In Dahomey*, the first of a series of such shows. Williams formed an all Black actors' society in 1906 and – after Walker's death – appeared in Ziegfeld's *Follies*, performing his own songs.

Williams, Bransby (Bransby William Pharez; 1870–1961) British actor and music hall performer, who spent some years in stock companies before taking to the halls, becoming famous for his renderings of characters from Dickens. In the 1920s he acted in several plays, reviving, for instance, Irving's part in *The Lyons Mail*. His monologues included 'The Green Eye of the Little Yellow God'.

Williams, (George) Emlyn (1905–87) Welsh actor, director, and playwright, who made many successful appearances in his own plays. He established himself as a leading character actor in the 1930s and 1940s and was highly acclaimed as the maniacal Danny in *Night Must Fall*, his first great success as a playwright.

His plays often depict life in his native Wales, most memorably in his portrayal of childhood in *The *Corn is Green*, which remains his best-known work. Of his many subsequent plays, the most popular included *The Wind of Heaven*, in which Christ is reincarnated as a Welsh boy. He also adapted Ibsen and Turgenev as well as the works of Dylan Thomas and Charles Dickens for stage performance, being much acclaimed for his readings on world tours. Other successes as an actor included Angelo in *Measure for Measure* (1937), Rattigan's *The Winslow Boy* (1940), Shylock and Iago (1956), Robert Ardrey's *Shadow of Heroes* (1958), Robert Bolt's *A Man For All Seasons* (1962), and Alan Bennett's *Forty Years On* (1969).

Principal works:
A Murder Has Been Arranged: 1930.
Spring 1600: 1934.
Night Must Fall: 1935.
He Was Born Gay: 1937.
The Corn is Green: 1938.
The Light of Heart: 1940.
The Morning Star: 1941.
The Druid's Rest: 1944.
The Wind of Heaven: 1945.
Trespass: 1947.
Accolade: 1950.
Someone Waiting: 1953.
Beth: 1958.

Williams, (Ernest George) Harcourt (1880–1957) British actor and director, who appeared as a young man alongside such leading contemporary performers as Ellen Terry, George Alexander, and Henry Irving, with whom he toured the US. He excelled in the plays of Shakespeare and Shaw and developed the theories of Granville-Barker in his Shakespearean productions at the Old Vic Theatre, of which he became a director in 1929.

His wife was the actress **Jean Sterling Mackinlay** (1882–1958), who promoted children's theatre in Britain and became famous for her Christmas shows.

Williams, Kenneth (1926–88) British comic actor, who made his London debut in *Peter Pan* in 1952. Subsequently he appeared in plays, revues, and pantomime, his roles including Maxime in Feydeau's *Hotel Paradiso* (1956) and Julian in Peter Shaffer's *The Public Eye* (1962). His flamboyant style and mastery of comic voices was also exploited in numerous radio shows and films.

Williams, Michael (Leonard) (1935–) British actor, who came to London from the Nottingham Playhouse in Keith Waterhouse and Willis Hall's *Celebration* in 1961. In 1963 he began a long association with the Royal Shakespeare Company, his numerous parts including Petruchio (1967) and the title role in Brecht's *Schweyk in the Second World War*. Opposite his wife, Judi Dench, he played Bob in Hugh Whitemore's *Pack of Lies* (1983) and was George in Ray Cooney's *Two into One* (1984).

Williams, Peter Vladimirovich (1902–47) Soviet stage designer, who became famous before his early death for his work at the Moscow Art Theatre. His most admired designs included those for *The Pickwick Club* (1934), based on Dickens, and Alexei Tolstoy's *The Death of Ivan the Terrible* (1946).

Williams, Tennessee (Thomas Lanier Williams; 1911–83) US playwright, born in Columbus, Mississippi, and brought up in St Louis from the age of 12. After graduating in 1938 he won a Theatre Guild prize for four one-act plays (*American Blues*); six years later he established his reputation with *The *Glass Menagerie*, which was largely based upon the author's own experience of family life. Thereafter his reputation soared and a number of his plays, which often tackle the extremes of human behaviour, were successfully filmed. His plays typically depict the frustration of aspiring central characters in a society that suffocates ambition. His *Memoirs* (1975) disclosed his homosexuality and his breakdown in 1969.
Principal works:
Battle of Angels: 1940.
The Glass Menagerie: 1945; filmed 1950.
*A *Streetcar Named Desire*: 1947; filmed 1952.
Summer and Smoke: 1948; filmed 1961.
The Rose Tattoo: 1951; filmed 1956.
Camino Real: 1953.
**Cat on a Hot Tin Roof*: 1955; filmed 1958.
Orpheus Descending: 1957 (new version of *Battle of Angels*).
Suddenly Last Summer: 1958; filmed 1959.
Sweet Bird of Youth: 1959; filmed 1963.
Period of Adjustment: 1959.
The Night of the Iguana: 1962; filmed 1964.
The Milk Train Doesn't Stop Here Any More: 1962.

Slapstick Tragedy: 1966.
Two Character Play: 1967.
In the Bar of a Tokyo Hotel: 1969.
Clothes for a Summer Hotel: 1980.

Williamson, David (Keith) (1942-) Australian playwright, who established his reputation with the award-winning plays *The Removalists* (1972) and *Don's Party* (1973). Several of his scripts, including his first full-length drama, *The Coming of Stork*, have been made into films and Williamson has also written expressly for the cinema – notably with *Gallipoli*. His more recent works include *Travelling North* (1980), *The Perfectionist* (1981), and *Emerald City* (1987).

Williamson, Nicol (1938-) British actor, who began in repertory at Dundee before making his first London appearance in Henry Chapman's *That's Us* in 1961. He has since played in many productions at the Royal Court Theatre, including the part of Bill Maitland in John Osborne's *Inadmissible Evidence* (1964). He was highly praised as Hamlet at the Round House in 1969 and later played Coriolanus (1973) and Macbeth (1974) with the Royal Shakespeare Company.

William Street Theatre A theatre in New York, which was opened around 1790 for entertainments staged by amateurs. Productions presented there included Dodsley's *The King and the Miller of Mansfield*, Lillo's *The London Merchant*, Dunlop's farce *The Soldier's Return*, and a pantomime version of *Robinson Crusoe*. It was also used for shadow shows.

Will's Coffee House A meeting place of critics and members of theatre audiences in Covent Garden, London during and after the Restoration. Also known as the Rose Tavern, it was a favourite haunt of many notable wits and literary figures, including John Dryden.

Wilson, Georges (1921-) French actor, director, and manager, who succeeded Jean Vilar as manager of the Théâtre National Populaire in 1963. Earlier in his career he worked with the Grenier-Hussenot company before joining Vilar's group in 1952 and excelling in leading roles in plays by Jarry and Musset among others. As manager he promoted the plays of Brecht, Brendan Behan, and Edward Bond before the troupe broke up in 1972; since then he has worked at the Avignon Festival and elsewhere.

Wilson, Lanford See Circle Repertory Company.

Wilson, Robert (c. 1550–c. 1600) English actor and playwright, who in 1583 cofounded Queen Elizabeth's Men. His three surviving works are loosely constructed morality plays in which personified virtues and vices play the leading parts, as in his *Three Ladies of London* (1584).

Wilson, Sandy (Alexander Wilson; 1924-) British composer and playwright, who established his reputation writing songs for revues but whose major success was *The *Boy Friend* (1953). His later musicals include *The Buccaneer* (1956), *Valmouth* (1958), which is based on Ronald Firbank's novel, *Divorce Me, Darling* (1965), *The Clapham Wonder* (1978), and *Aladdin* (1979).

Wilton, Marie Effie See Bancroft, Squire.

Wilton's Music Hall A music hall in Whitechapel, London, which began in 1850 as the music room of a public house. A new music hall was built behind the pub and opened in 1858, remaining active until 1887. An official preservation order was later made, when it was recognized as the earliest surviving music hall building in London.

Winchester Music Hall The first concert room in a pub (opened in the 1830s in Southwark, London) to be called a music hall. It was known as the **Surrey Music Hall** from 1848 until 1856, when its name was changed to the Winchester. It was destroyed by fire in 1861, but the hall was rebuilt and later remodelled as a theatre (1872), being demolished in 1878.

wind machine A mechanical device consisting of a large drum, which rubs against a stretch of canvas when rotated, producing a sound effect resembling that of wind. In many modern theatres such machines have been superseded by tape recordings.

Windmill Theatre The only London theatre to remain open during the whole of World War II, its slogan being 'We never closed'. Originally a cinema built in 1910, it took its name from a windmill which stood on the site up to the late 18th century. After an unsuccessful opening as a theatre in 1931 films were reintroduced until the manager, Vivian Van Damm, inaugurated (1932) a programme of non-stop variety called *Revuedeville*. This proved extremely popular and the Windmill became celebrated for its tableaux of scantily clad girls. Subsequently many comedians, including Jimmy Edwards, Harry Secombe, and Tony Hancock, began their careers here. The Windmill was closed in 1964 and reconstructed as a cinema; in 1974 it was purchased by Paul Raymond, who revived the policy of nude revues. It was closed again in 1981 for futher conversion.

Windsor Theatre See 48th Street Theatre.

wings The offstage areas on either side of the main acting space. The term is also used of the flats used to screen these areas from the audience's view.

Winslow Boy, The A drama by Terence *Rattigan. First performance: 1946. Based on an actual case, the play depicts a father's attempts to clear the reputation of his son

– a cadet at a naval college – after he has been accused of petty theft.

Winstanley, Eliza (1818–82) Australian actress and writer, also known as **Mrs O'Flaherty**, who was born in England but made her debut in Australia in 1834. She was highly acclaimed in melodrama and also made successful appearances in Britain and the US, acting with Charles Kean's company for several years.

Winter, William (1836–1917) US theatre critic, who exercised enormous influence as critic with the *Albion* (1861–65) and then the *New York Times* (1865–1909). He followed the majority opinion in most matters but failed to appreciate the importance of such notable figures as Sarah Bernhardt, Ibsen, and Shaw.

Winter Garden Theatre A theatre on Broadway, between 50th and 51st streets, New York, which opened in 1911. It is used primarily for musicals, some of the more recent having included *West Side Story* (1957), *Funny Girl* (1964), *Mame* (1966), *Pacific Overtures* (1976), *42nd Street* (1980), and *Cats* (1985).

The **Winter Garden Theatre** in Drury Lane, London, opened as the New Middlesex Theatre of Varieties on the site of the *Middlesex Music Hall in 1911. Music hall and touring revues held the stage until 1919, when the theatre was acquired by George Grossmith and Edward Laurillard, refurbished, renamed the Winter Garden, and reopened with Guy Bolton and P G Wodehouse's musical *Kissing Time*. A series of successful musicals under various managements followed, ending with Gracie Fields in the revue *Walk This Way* (1932). Following World War II Joan Temple's *No Room at the Inn* (1946) and Agatha Christie's *Witness for the Prosecution* (1953) had long runs, while such plays as Shaw's *The Devil's Disciple* (1956), starring Tyrone Power, and O'Neill's *The Iceman Cometh* (1958) trans-

ferred there from the Arts Theatre. The Winter Garden was demolished in 1960 and in 1973 the *New London Theatre opened on the site.

Winter's Tale, The A romance by William *Shakespeare, written c. 1610. First performance: c. 1611. Based upon Robert Greene's *Pandosto*, the play is Shakespeare's last treatment of sexual jealousy and depicts the consequences of Leontes' mistaken belief that his wife Hermione has had a love affair with his friend, Polixenes, King of Bohemia. The play is remarkable for its combination of disjointed episodes, one break covering 16 years, and for the final scene, in which the statue of Hermione, long believed dead, comes to life. The play also contains an interesting stage direction indicating that the character Antigonus exits pursued by a bear. It was revived by Garrick as *Florizel and Perdita* during the Restoration.

Winthrop Ames Theatre *See* Little Theatre.

Withers, Googie (Georgette Lizette Withers; 1917-) British actress, who started her stage career as a child and signed her first film contract at the age of 17. Her roles have included such parts as Georgie in Clifford Odets's *Winter Journey* (1952) and Hester Collyer in Terence Rattigan's *The Deep Blue Sea* (1955) as well as characters in plays by Noël Coward, J B Priestley, Shakespeare, Chekhov, Wilde, and Ionesco. With her husband, the actor John McCallum, she has played often in Australia and New Zealand, returning to England at intervals, sometimes to appear at the Chichester Festival Theatre.

Witkiewicz, Stanisław Ignacy (1885– 1939) Polish writer, artist, and philosopher, who wrote over 40 pessimistic grotesque comedies, which remained virtually unknown and unperformed during his lifetime. It was not until the 1960s that he was rediscovered and came to be regarded as a major forerunner of the Theatre of the Absurd. Among his most important works are the plays *The Water Hen, The Crazy Locomotive, The Shoemakers,* and the tragedy *The Pragmatists,* written in 1918. Witkiewicz committed suicide when Poland was invaded by the Germans.

Woffington, Peg (Margaret Woffington; c. 1714–60) British actress, born in Dublin, of Irish parentage. She went on the stage originally with a children's company, making a brief appearance at the Haymarket. Subsequently she appeared at Dublin's Smock Alley Theatre, where she played Ophelia and was a notable Silvia in *The Recruiting Officer,* although it was as Sir Harry Wildair in Farquhar's *The Constant Couple* that she established her reputation as a performer of breeches parts. In 1740 she repeated the role with phenomenal success at Covent Garden. After a quarrel with John Rich she transferred to Drury Lane and lived with Garrick for a time. Famed for her beauty, she was particularly admired as Millamant in *The Way of the World* and Lady Betty Modish in Colley Cibber's *The Careless Husband.* Off the stage she was also celebrated for her tempestuous relations with other actresses.

Wolf, Friedrich (1888–1953) German playwright, who was the author of several notable Realist dramas exposing political and social injustice. *Kolonne Hund* (1926) espoused the cause of poverty-stricken coal miners while *Cyankali* (Potassium Cyanide; 1929) criticized the contemporary anti-abortion laws. His later Marxist plays were more politically outspoken, *Matrosen von Cattaro* (The Sailors of Cattaro; 1930) depicting a naval mutiny and *Tai Yang erwacht* (1931) being a stand against Fascism; *Professor Mamlock* (1935) decried the persecution of the Jews by the Nazis.

Wolff, Pius Alexander (1782–1828) German actor, who played many leading roles in the plays of Goethe at Weimar. He and his wife, also an actress in the company, eventually left and became established favourites in Berlin.

Wolfit, Sir Donald (Donald Woolfitt; 1902–68) British actor-manager, who began in Shakespearean roles, then joined Matheson Lang at the New Theatre (1924). He played seasons at the Old Vic and at Stratford-upon-Avon and, in 1937, formed his own Shakespearean company, occasionally visiting London in the course of lengthy tours. He twice visited the US after World War II, his outstanding parts being Shylock, Volpone, Richard III, a masterly King Lear, and Solness in Ibsen's *The Master Builder.* In 1951 he returned to the Old Vic as Marlowe's Tamburlaine.

Woman Killed with Kindness, A A domestic tragedy by Thomas *Heywood. First performance: London, 1603. The infidelity of Mrs Frankford is discovered by her husband, who refrains from killing her lover but cannot forgive her for dishonouring their marriage.

Woman of No Importance, A A comedy by Oscar *Wilde. First performance: 1893. Lord Illingworth dismisses Mrs Arbuthnot as "a woman of no importance" but seeks to employ Gerald as his secretary, unaware that he is their son. When he tries to seduce Gerald's fiancée, his former mistress reveals the truth.

Women Beware Women A tragedy by Thomas *Middleton. First performance: London, c. 1621. The play explores the sexual indiscretions and decaying standards of the central characters and is notable for its understanding of female psychology.

women's theatre Drama with particular relevance to feminist issues, as popularized in the US during the 1960s in tandem with the development of the Women's Liberation movement. A number of theatre groups were founded throughout the US to promote opportunities for women in all aspects of the theatre, presenting experimental drama treating such subjects as women's rights. Celebrated groups of the kind include the It's All Right To Be a Woman Theatre in New York, which specializes in improvisation; British counterparts include The Monstrous Regiment and Mrs Worthington's Daughters.

Wood, Charles Gerald (1932-) British playwright, whose first work, *Cockade* (1963) – a triple bill comprising *Prisoner and Escort, John Thomas*, and *Spare* – was the first of several reflecting his experiences in the army. Subsequent plays have included *Don't Make Me Laugh* (1965), the farce *Meals on Wheels* (1965), *Fill the Stage With Happy Hours* (1966), and the war plays *Dingo* (1967) and *H, or Monologues at Front of Burning Cities* (1969). More recent plays have been *A Bit of a Holiday* (1969), the triple bill *Welfare* (1970), *Jingo* (1975), *Veterans* (1972), *Has 'Washington' Legs?* (1978), *Red Star* (1984), and *Across From the Garden of Allah* (1986). He has also written screenplays for the cinema.

Wood, John (1930-) British actor, who was president of OUDS before joining the Old Vic company in 1954 and making his West End debut as Don Quixote in Tennessee Williams's *Camino Real* (1957). In 1967 he was admired as Guildenstern in Stoppard's *Rosencrantz and Guildenstern Are Dead* in New York (1967) and subsequently – after further acclaim in Joyce's *Exiles* (1970) – gave a series of highly praised performances with the Royal Shakespeare Company, his parts including Brutus, Sherlock Holmes, and Henry Carr in Stoppard's *Travesties*. After success in Ira Levin's *Deathtrap* (1978) he joined the National Theatre, for whom he excelled as Richard II

(1979) and Salieri in Peter Shaffer's *Amadeus* in 1981. In 1988 he returned to Stratford-upon-Avon to play Prospero in *The Tempest*.

Wood, William Burke (1779–1861) US actor, born in Montreal, who was the first native American to play a significant part in the development of the national theatre. He was manager with William Warren of the Chestnut Street Theatre in Philadelphia for many years and also wrote a diary giving valuable information about the theatre of his day. As an actor he was particularly admired in comedy, although he also appeared in tragedy and promoted the performance of new US drama.

Wood's Museum *See* Daly's Theatre.

Woodward, Harry (1717–77) British actor, who began acting as a child. In 1729 he joined John Rich at Lincoln's Inn Fields, where he later appeared in *The Beggar's Opera*. Subsequently he played comedy roles at Drury Lane and Covent Garden, appearing as **Lun** junior, and spent a year at the Smock Alley Theatre with Sheridan in 1747. He also wrote several pantomimes for Garrick. In 1777 he created the role of Captain Absolute in *The Rivals*.

Wooing Ceremony *See* mummers' play.

Woolcott, Alexander Humphreys (1887–1943) US theatre critic and playwright, who worked for the *New York Times*, the *New York Herald*, the *Sun*, and the *New York World*. Popular for his light and amusing style, his reviews nonetheless prompted several New York theatres to attempt to ban him in 1915; later in his career he entirely failed to perceive any merit in the plays of O'Neill. He also collaborated with Moss Hart and George S Kaufman on *The Channel Road* (1929) and *The Dark Tower* (1932).

Woolgar, Sarah Jane *See* Mellon, Mrs Alfred.

World Theatre Season A major theatre festival for foreign drama founded in London by Peter Daubeny in 1964. Taking place in the Aldwych Theatre, it played host to such celebrated foreign companies as the Comédie-Française, the Abbey Theatre company, and the Moscow Art Theatre, as well as famous companies from Austria, Belgium, Czechoslovakia, Germany, Greece, India, Israel, Italy, Japan, Poland, Spain, South Africa, Sweden, Turkey, Uganda, and the US. The last of these annual seasons was in 1973, with one revival in 1975.

Worms, Gustave-Hippolyte (1836–1910) French actor, who excelled as young lovers at both the Comédie-Française and in Russia, where he remained for several years. He was successful in both comedy and tragedy, most notably – as Don Carlos – with Sarah Bernhardt in Hugo's *Hernani* (1877) and in the plays of Dumas *fils* as well as in earlier works.

Worth, Irene (1916-) US actress, who made her stage debut in 1942 in Margaret Kennedy's *Escape Me Never*. She first appeared on the New York stage in 1943 and, in 1951, joined the Old Vic company, excelling as Desdemona and Portia and in *A Midsummer Night's Dream*. Remaining in Britain largely until 1959, she won further acclaim in plays by N C Hunter, Betti, Feydeau, Schiller, and Graham Greene; after success in the US in Lillian Hellman's *Toys in the Attic* (1960) she returned to Britain to join the Royal Shakespeare Company. Her roles with him included Lady Macbeth, Goneril in *King Lear*, and Dr Zahnd in Dürrenmatt's *The Physicists*. She has also played roles in works by Albee, Coward, Shaw, Sophocles, Ibsen, and Chekhov; more recent parts have included Winnie in Beckett's *Happy Days* (1979), Ella in Ibsen's *John Gabriel Borkman* (1980), and roles in

The Bay at Nice and *Wrecked Eggs* (both 1986) by David Hare.

Woyzeck A play by Georg *Büchner, unfinished at his death. First performance: Vienna, 1913. A pessimistic story of an illiterate soldier's descent into madness and suicide, it provided the basis of the opera *Wozzeck* (1925) by Alban Berg and has been successfully revived several times in the 20th century.

Wycherley, Sir William (1640–1716) English playwright, noted for his savage moralistic comedies, which are regarded as some of the finest examples of Restoration drama. His first play, *Love in a Wood; or, St James's Park* (1671), was followed by an adaptation from Calderón, *The *Gentleman Dancing-Master* (1672); his biggest success, however, came in 1675 with *The *Country Wife*, which was later revived at Drury Lane as *The Country Girl* by Garrick in 1766. His fourth play, *The *Plain Dealer*, was inspired by Molière's *Le Misanthrope*.

Wyndham, Sir Charles (Charles Culverwell; 1837–1919) British actor-manager, born in Liverpool, whose first appearance on the London stage was in 1862. Trained in medicine, Wyndham served as a surgeon during the US Civil War. From 1865 onwards he began to acquire a reputation in comedy roles on both sides of the Atlantic; he also had a shortlived spell in management at the Queen's Theatre (1868), after which he returned to the US. Following his success in Bronson Howard's *Saratoga* in 1870, he became manager of the Criterion Theatre in 1876, where he remained for 23 years. In 1886 he excelled in T W Robertson's *David Garrick*. In 1899 he opened *Wyndham's Theatre; subsequently he opened the New Theatre (*see* Albery Theatre) in 1903. Wyndham was knighted in 1902. Following the death of his first wife in 1916, he married his leading lady, **Mary**

Moore (1869–1931), widow of James Albery.

Wyndham's Theatre A theatre in the Charing Cross Road, London, which was opened in 1899 and named after the actor-manager Sir Charles Wyndham. The first production, a revival of T W Robertson's *David Garrick*, was followed by *Cyrano de Bergerac* and Henry Arthur Jones's *Mrs Dane's Defence*, which ran for over 200 performances. Gerald Du Maurier joined the management in 1910 and enjoyed considerable success as an actor there. In the period 1926–32 Wyndham's was widely known for its productions of the plays of Edgar Wallace. Post-war successes include *The Boy Friend*, which ran for a record-breaking 2078 performances in the 1950s, Ronald Millar's *Abelard and Heloise* (1970–72), *Godspell* (1972–74), and *Side by Side by Sondheim* (1976–77). Another recent success was Dario Fo's *Accidental Death of an Anarchist* (1980). Now one of a group of six West End theatres under the same management, Wyndham's has been managed since 1978 by Ian Albery, a great-grandson of the actress Mary Moore (Mrs James Albery, later Lady Wyndham).

Wynn, Ed (Edwin Leopold Wynn; 1886–1966) US comedian, who began in vaudeville when he was 15. He consolidated his reputation as a comic, appearing in a ridiculous costume, in the *Ed Wynn Carnival* revue of 1921; subsequently he starred in Ziegfeld's *Follies* and other revues and musical comedy.

Wynyard, Diana (Dorothy Isobel Cox; 1906–64) British actress, whose first big success was as Charlotte Brontë in Clemence Dane's *Wild Decembers* (1933). After further acclaim as Belinda Warren in Joyce Carey's *Sweet Aloes* (1934), she appeared in many West End comedies, at Stratford-upon-Avon, and starred opposite Gielgud in *The Winter's Tale* (1951) and

Much Ado About Nothing (1952). She appeared with the National Theatre company at the Old Vic until shortly before her death. She also excelled in plays by Coward, Lillian Hellman, and Tennessee Williams.

Wyspiański, Stanisław (1869–1907) Polish playwright, artist, poet, director, and stage designer, who studied art in France and Italy and wrote 16 plays. Four of these are poetic dramas with classical settings, notably *The Return of Ulysses* (1907); of the remaining 12, which deal largely – often in allegorical form – with the problems of Poland and its people, *The Legion* (1900), *The Wedding* (1901), *Akropolis* (1903), and *November Light* (1904) are the most important. As a director he aroused interest with his production of *Hamlet* (1901), in which the Ghost was the central character.

Y

Yablochkina, Alexandra Alexandrovna (1868–1964) Russian actress, who spent most of her career at the Maly Theatre, where she first performed in 1888. Between her first appearance at the age of six and her last at the age of 94, she played numerous celebrated roles from the plays of Shakespeare, Gorky, Korneichuk, and Wilde; from 1916 she was chairman of the All-Russian Theatrical Society.

Yakovlev, Alexei Semenovich (1773–1817) Russian actor, who established a reputation as a strong – if unpredictable – performer of leading roles with the St Petersburg Imperial Theatre company. A pupil of Dmitrevsky, he supported a more realistic approach to drama but suffered from his weakness for drink and his reliance on inspiration.

Yale Repertory Theatre A theatre at Yale University, which was founded by Robert Brustein in 1966. The company moved off-campus in 1968 to a church with a stage, which was renovated in 1975, providing the company with a 491-seat theatre. Plays produced there have included Aeschylus's *Prometheus Bound*, Eric Bentley's *Are You Now or Have You Ever Been...?*, Kopit's *Wings*, and works by Edward Bond.

Yanshin, Mikhail Mikhailovich (1902–76) Soviet actor and director, who established his reputation while with the Moscow Art Theatre, which he joined in 1924. Acclaimed in plays be Bulgakov, Chekhov, Ostrovosky, and Sheridan, he later became director of the Gypsy Theatre (1937–41) and subsequently (1950) producer of the Stanislavsky Theatre in Moscow.

Yates, Frederick Henry (1795–1842) British actor and manager, who was persuaded to begin his stage career by Charles Mathews. He played Shakespearean roles in Edinburgh, including Bolingbroke to Edmund Kean's Richard II, before making his Covent Garden debut as Iago in 1819. Subsequently he took over the Adelphi Theatre in partnership with Daniel Terry. His wife was the actress **Elizabeth Brunton** (1799–1860).

Yates, Richard (1706–96) British actor, noted for his performances of Shakespearean clowns. With Ned Shuter he set up a booth in Bartholomew Fair, playing Pantaloon to his partner's Harlequin. He later appeared at Covent Garden and Drury Lane, where he created the role of Sir Oliver Surface in *The Rivals* in 1777. His second wife was the actress Mary Ann *Graham.

Yavorov, Peio (Peyo Kracholov; 1877–1914) Bulgarian poet, playwright, and pioneer of Symbolism in Bulgarian poetry. His output as a dramatist included the tragedies *V Polite na Vitosha* (In the Foothills of Mount Vitosha; 1911) and *Kogato Gram Udari* (When the Thunder Rolls; 1912), which told the life-story of the Macedonian leader Gotse Delchev. He committed suicide on the death of his wife.

Yeats, William Butler (1865–1939) Irish poet and playwright, one of the founders of the *Abbey Theatre. Yeats wrote some 30 plays, beginning with such poetic dramas as *The *Land of Heart's Desire* (1894) and *The Countess Cathleen* (1899). Dedicated to the development of a distinct Irish drama, he drew extensively upon Irish legend and the aristocratic Japanese *Nō* theatre for his plays, upon which he often collaborated with Lady Gregory. In addition to his roles as playwright, director, and manager of the Abbey theatre, Yeats also championed his fellow Irishmen J M Synge and Sean O'Casey, although he subsequently fell out with the latter after rejecting *The Silver Tassie* for production. He was awarded a Nobel Prize in 1923.

Principal works:

Cathleen Ni Houlihan: 1902.

On Baile's Strand: 1904.

Deirdre: 1906.

At The Hawk's Well: 1917.

The Only Jealousy of Emer: 1919.

The Dreaming of the Bones: 1919.

The Player Queen: 1919.

Calvary: 1920.

The Words Upon the Window Pane: 1930.

Purgatory: 1938.

The Death of Cuchulain: 1949.

Yefremov, Oleg Nikolayevich (1927–) Soviet actor and director, who became famous for his work with young actors and audiences at the Sovremennik Theatre in Moscow. He installed a company of young performers there in 1958 and presented with them a variety of modern Soviet and European dramas; in 1971 he succeeded Livanov as head of the Moscow Art Theatre.

Yerma A tragedy by *García Lorca. First performance: Madrid, 1934. The second part of a famous trilogy of folk tragedies, the other parts being *Blood Wedding (1933) and The *House of Bernarda Alba (1945), the play depicts the suffering of a childless woman who finally murders her sterile husband.

Yermolova, Maria Nikolaievna (1853–1928) Russian actress, who became a leading performer of tragic roles at the Maly Theatre. Much admired by Stanislavsky, she excelled in such parts as Lady Macbeth, Joan of Arc, and Phèdre both before and after the Revolution of 1917. The Yermolova Theatre, founded in 1930, was named in her honour.

Yermolova Theatre A studio theatre in Moscow, founded in 1930 and named after the actress Maria Nikolaievna *Yermolova. In 1937 it amalgamated with the Khmelev Studio and enjoyed success with Khmelev's productions of Russian works and Shakespeare. Notable performances have included the premiere of Dostoevsky's *Crime and Punishment* (1956) and foreign plays.

Yevreinov, Nikolai See Evreinov, Nikolai Nikolaivich.

Yiddish Art Theatre See Phoenix Theatre.

York, Susannah (Susannah Fletcher; 1942-) British actress, who has appeared worldwide in parts ranging from Amanda in Coward's *Private Lives* in Australia to the title role in Ibsen's *Hedda Gabler* in the US and Ann Whitfield in Shaw's *Man and Superman* in Dublin, as well as appearing with Barrault's company in Paris. In spite of a busy film career, she has played regularly in London in productions as diverse as *Peter Pan* (1977) and Clare Boothe Luce's *The Women* (1986).

You Never Can Tell A play by G B *Shaw, written 1895–97. First performance: Strand Theatre, 1900. A cheerful domestic comedy, the play tackles the theme of love through the relationships of husband and wife, parents and children, and lovers it involves a hotel in an English seaside town, where a waiter plays a leading role; it was one of the '*Plays, Pleasant and Unpleasant*'.

Young, Charles Mayne (1777–1856) British actor, born in London. Having made his debut in 1798, in Liverpool, he played leading parts at Manchester, Edinburgh, and, again, at Liverpool. Invited to the Haymarket by Charles Mathews in 1820, he was much acclaimed as Hamlet and acknowledged as a leading tragedian. Later triumphs included his performances as Cassius to John Philip Kemble's Brutus at Covent Garden and appearances with Kean at Drury Lane.

Young American Roscius See Cowell, Samuel Houghton.

Young England A play by Walter Reynolds. First performance: London, 1934. Intended as a patriotic celebration, it was received as a riotous parody and gained ironic popularity as the butt of audience humour and mockery.

Young Roscius See Betty, William Henry West.

Young Vic Theatre A theatre opened in London in 1970 on a bombsite close to the Old Vic Theatre in Lambeth, specifically to offer good theatre to young audiences at low prices. It was founded by Frank Dunlop and officially opened by Dame Sybil Thorndike, the first production being *Scapino*, an adaptation from Molière. Initially under the management of the National Theatre, the Young Vic became independent in 1974. It has a seating capacity of 456 and a small studio theatre seating 100. Michael Bogdanov was its director from 1978 to 1980. Recent successes have included Ibsen's *Ghosts*, which transferred to Wyndham's in 1986.

Yovkov, Yordan Stefanovich (1880–1937) Bulgarian short-story writer, novelist, and playwright, whose plays are chiefly based upon Balkan peasant life. He wrote about the effects of war in *Albena* (1930) and *Boryana* (1932); his best-known play was the comedy about a poor vet's marriage into a rich family *Milionerut* (The Millionaire; 1930).

Yubani, Zef (1910–58) Albanian actor, who became a leading performer at the Üsküdar Migjeni Theatre. He was highly acclaimed in parts ranging from Molière's Harpagon to Ibsen's Stockman.

Yurka, Blanche (Blanche Jurka; 1893–1974) US actress, who first appeared in New York in 1907. She played Gertrude to John Barrymore's Hamlet in 1922 and later appeared in various plays by Ibsen, including *The Wild Duck* (1928), *Hedda Gabler* (1929), *The Lady from the Sea* (1929), and *The Vikings* (1930). She toured the US in a solo production from 1936 to 1938, performing scenes from great plays. She went on to play Mrs Antrobus in Wilder's *The Skin of Our Teeth* (1958) and Miss Moffat in a revival of Emlyn Williams's *The Corn Is Green* (1961).

Z

Zabłocki, Franciszek (1754–1821) Polish playwright, author of satirical comedies largely based on French models. Typical of his works was the verse comedy *Sarmatyzm* (1785), the plot of which was also explored by Fredro and Mickiewicz.

Zacconi, Ermete (1857–1948) Italian actor, who became a leading performer of plays of the *verismo* tradition. He formed his own company in 1894 and pioneered performances of the plays of Ibsen in Italian as well as translating major works by Hauptmann, Tolstoy, and Strindberg; he was also much admired in numerous Shakespearean roles, particularly as Hamlet.

Zacuto, Moses (1625–97) Jewish playwright, much influenced by Vondel. His plays include *Yesod Olam*, which was first presented in Italy, and *Tofteh Aruch*, performed in Ferrara in about 1700.

Zakhava, Boris Evgenevich (1898–1976) Soviet actor and director, who established his reputation as Timur in Vakhtangov's production of Gozzi's *Turandot* (1922). Subsequently he joined Meyerhold's company and directed plays by Dostoevsky, Gorky, Ostrovsky, and Shakespeare before taking charge of the Shchukin School of Acting in Moscow.

Zangwill, Israel (1864–1926) British novelist, playwright, and poet, who was regarded as the most important Anglo-Jewish writer of his day. He first came to notice with novels about Jewish ghetto life in London; his best-known play, *The Melting Pot* (1908), deals with the assimilation of the US immigrant population.

zanni The servant characters of the *commedia dell'arte*, several of which were later developed into major roles of the English harlequinade. Wearing masks and specializing in slapstick humour, the *zanni* include *Arlecchino, *Brighella, Columbina (*see* Columbine), *Mezzetino, *Pantalone, *Pasquino, *Pedrolino, *Pulcinella, *Scapino, and *Scaramuccia.

zarzuela A form of musical play first developed in Spain during the 17th century. Consisting of narrative passages combined with music and dances, the *zarzuela* (named after the royal palace of La Zarzuela near Madrid) usually took a mythological or heroic subject as its theme. Writers of notable examples included Lope de Vega and Calderón; the form was later revived in the 19th century by Ramón de la Cruz and others, who produced plots based on everyday life. Gradually it became divided into the **género chico** (or **teatro por horas**), a one-act comedy, and the **grande**, a serious musical play akin to opera.

Zavadsky, Yuri Alexeivich (1894–1977) Soviet director and actor, who trained under Vakhtangov before ultimately taking over the Gorky State Theatre in Rostov. His highly-acclaimed lyrical productions there included plays by Gorky and Shakespeare; later in his career he also worked at the Mossoviet Theatre. His pupils included Grotowski.

Zeami (1363–1443) Japanese playwright and actor, who played a key role in the development of the **Nō* play. The son of the actor Kanami, Zeami appeared in his father's company at the court of the shogun Yoshimitsu while still a child; after his father's death in 1384 he continued the transformation of the *Nō* drama into the complex and aristocratic tradition still performed in modern times. He wrote about 200 plays (of which 124 survive) for the form and was the author of immensely influential theatrical treatises setting out the nature and structure of the *Nō* play, delineating the role of the actor and discussing the symbolic and spiritual content. His most celebrated plays include *Matsukaze*, which is typical of the main body of his work.

Zeffirelli, Franco (1923–) Italian director and stage designer, who began his career working in collaboration with Visconti and subsequently became famous for his productions of both operas and the classics. His greatest successes have included *Romeo and Juliet* (1960) at the Old Vic, *Othello* (1961)

at Stratford-upon-Avon, and *Hamlet* (1964) at the Old Vic, as well as plays by Albee, Eduardo De Filippo, Dumas *fils*, and Arthur Miller presented by the National Theatre and other leading companies and several major films.

Ziegfeld, Florenz (1867–1932) US producer, who first staged the famous *Ziegfeld Follies* in 1907. Modelled on the shows at the Folies-Bergère in Paris, the *Follies* represented the height of revue, with lavish costumes, beautiful girls, and spectacular sets; it ran in a continuous series until 1932 and then periodically until 1957. Ziegfeld also produced such musicals as *Show Boat* (1927) at his own Ziegfeld Theatre, as well as a number of straight plays.

His first wife was the actress **Anna Held** (1873–1918), a star of musical comedy, and his second was **Billie Burke** (Ethelbert Appleton Burke; 1884–1970), who was also popular in light comedy.

Ziegfeld Theatre A theatre on Sixth Avenue and 54th Street, New York, which opened in 1927 with the musical *Rio Rita*. After successes with plays by Coward and Ziegfeld's *Follies* the theatre was used as a cinema from 1932, when Ziegfeld died, to 1944, when Billy Rose reopened it. It was used for broadcasting from 1955 to 1963 but returned to live theatre for four years before it was demolished in 1967.

Ziegler, Clara (1844–1909) German actress, who established herself as a popular performer of leading tragic roles in both Leipzig and Munich. Her finest performances included roles in the plays of Euripides, Grillparzer, and Schiller, as well as Shakespeare's Romeo. Her house and library later provided the basis of a theatre museum in Munich.

Zola, Émile(-Edouard-Charles-Antoine) (1840–1902) French novelist and playwright, leader of the naturalist movement in

19th-century literature. Remembered for his novels, Zola made a comparatively small, but not insignificant, contribution to the theatre. He wrote several plays, of which the most successful was *Thérèse Raquin* (1873), based on his novel, and his critical works *Le Naturalisme au théâtre* (1878) and *Nos auteurs dramatiques* (1881) had an important influence on the development of naturalistic drama in the plays of Henry Becque and André Antoine's Théâtre Libre.

Zorrilla, Francisco de Rojas *See* Rojas Zorrilla, Francisco de.

Zorrilla y Moral, José (1817–93) Spanish poet and playwright, who was the author of several dramas of the Romantic tradition. His plays include *Don Juan Tenorio* (1844), a popular version of the *Don Juan story, and the historical plays *El zapatero y el rey* (The Cobbler and the King; 1840) and *Traidor, inconfeso y mártir* (1849).

Zuckmayer, Carl (1896–1977) German playwright, poet, and novelist, whose first success in the theatre came with the play *Der fröhliche Weinberg* (The Merry Vineyard; 1925), a lively rustic comedy set in his native Rhineland. His finest drama was *Der Hauptmann von Köpenick* (The Captain of Kopernich; 1930), a satire on German militarism. Following the rise of Nazism, Zuckmayer left Germany to live variously in Austria, Switzerland, and the US; his other important works include *Das Teufels General* (The Devil's General; 1946) and such late works as *Das Kalte Licht* (The Cold Light; 1956) and *Der Rattenfänger* (The Pied Piper; 1974).

Zweig, Stefan (1881–1942) Austrian poet, novelist, and playwright, who came from a wealthy Jewish background and established his reputation in the theatre with *Jeremias* (Jeremiah; 1917), in which he expressed his pacifist beliefs. Later works included satires upon the hypocrisy of public figures and an adaptation of Jonson's *Volpone* (1926); after leaving Austria in the 1930s, he eventually settled in Brazil, where he committed suicide.